The Epic Histories:
Buzandaran Patmutʿiwnkʿ
Harvard Armenian Texts and Studies, 8

The Epic Histories Attributed to P⁣ᶜawstos Buzand

(*Buzandaran Patmutᶜiwnkᶜ*)

Translation and Commentary by

Nina G. Garsoïan

Distributed for the Department of Near Eastern
Languages and Civilizations, Harvard University
by
Harvard University Press
Cambridge, Massachusetts
1989

IN MEMORIAM

S.I.G.   G.I.G.

Lux perpetua luceat eis

Contents

Acknowledgments ix

Abbreviations xiii

Introduction 1

Translator's Preface 57

The Epic Histories—*Buzandaran Patmutᶜiwnkᶜ* 63

    Book III 67
    Book IV 101
    Book V 181
    Book VI 231

Commentary 243

Appendices and Indices 339

    I Prosopography 343
    II Toponymy 435
    III Technical Terms 505
    IV Scriptural Quotations and Allusions 577
    V Epic and Scriptural Formulae 586

Bibliography 597

    I Manuscripts, Editions and Translations of the Text 601
    II Sources 604
    III Literature 619

Maps 665

    I Armenia at the death of Trdat the Great (ca. A.D. 330)
    II Armenia after the partition of the Aršakuni kingdom
      (ca. A.D. 387)

Acknowledgments

Before I express my deep appreciation to the many friends who have kindly helped in the long task of translating and commenting on the present text, a special group of five colleagues and students, both past and present, should be singled out for particular thanks. Dr. (now Fr.) Krikor Maksoudian, over the years since he first became my student, has always put his inexhaustible knowledge of Armenian classical literature at my disposal. In this work, he has illuminated and corrected the translation of troublesome passages in the text and supplied religious references. I am indebted to the expertise of Professor James Russell of Columbia University for most of the suggestions on Iranian etymologies and for information on many Zoroastrian beliefs and customs. To Professor Peter Cowe of Columbia University I owe most of the Syriac references and a number of insights into early literary practices. Professor Robert Hewsen of Glassboro State College not only prepared the maps appended to this book but was ever ready to supply information on and discuss problems in his particular specialty, what was until recently the *terra incognita* of Armenian medieval geography and toponymy. My former graduate student Dr. Roberta Ervine, had the expertise and the patience to trace most of the Scriptural citations and allusions in the text to their sources. Without their help this book could not have been completed, and their names belong by right on the title page.

For their courtesy in granting me permission to consult repeatedly their manuscript collections and to obtain the necessary microfilms, as well as for their expertise and patience in giving me much helpful advice, I would first like to express my thanks to the directors of the State Manuscript Collection of the Armenian SSR (Matenadaran), the late Academician L. S. Xačʿikyan and his successor Dr. S. S. Arewšatyan, the deputy director B. L. Čʿukaszyan, and the successive academic secretaries, L. H. Ter Petrosyan and A. Ter Stepʿanyan. Likewise, his grace, Archbishop Norayr Bogharian, keeper of the manuscripts at the Patriarchal Library of St. James in Jerusalem, had the great kindness to take time from his own scholarship to assure me that no additional manuscripts of "Pʿaw-stos's" text were included in the still unpublished volume of his monumental Catalog. Also, Fr. Nersēs Der Nersessian, librarian of the Mekhitarist Congregation of San Lazzaro degli Armeni in Venice, graciously verified the manuscripts of the text in the collection of the congregation and sent me the necessary microfilms.

For sharing their own expertise in the many areas in which mine was insufficient, calling my attention to overlooked sources, giving me frequent valuable advice and criticism, and helping to clarify my own ideas, I am deeply grateful, now as ever, to Professor Emerita Sirarpie der Nersessian; to my Soviet colleagues—Dr. G. A. Abgaryan, the editor of the forthcoming critical edition of the text; Academician S. T. Eremyan, for the benefit of his vast geographical information on Arsacid Armenia; the archaeologists Academician B. N. Aṛakelyan and Dr. G. A. Tiracʿyan, for guiding me through the excavations of Artašat, Duin, and Armawir; the orientalist and patristic specialists Dr. G. X. Sargsyan, director of the Institute of Oriental Studies, Dr. P. M. Muradyan and Dr. K. M. Muradyan, Dr. L. H. Ter Petrosyan in Erevan, and Dr. A. G. Perikhanian in Leningrad—to my colleague and friend, Professor R. W. Thomson, director of the Dumbarton Oaks Research Library and Collection, on whose expertise in early Armenian and patristic literature I have always relied; to Dr. L. Avdoyan of the Library of Congress, for calling my attention to parallel material in the *History of Tarōn* and for constant help with elusive bibliography; to Dr. R. Edwards, for a number of geographical precisions, especially in the Armeno-Georgian Marchlands; to Dr. M.-J. Delage of Smith College, for acquainting me with the *Vita* of St. Honoratus of Lérins; and to my European friends and colleagues—Fr. A. Renoux, O.S.B., for pointing out the importance of the early Basilian Anaphora; Dr. J.-P. Mahé, editor of the *Revue des études arméniennes,* Dr. N. Thierry, and Dr. J.-M. Thierry, all of the University of Paris, for help with a series of Armenological, geographical, and art-historical problems; and Fr. M. van Esbroeck of the Bollandist Congregation, as well as Dr. E. Follieri of the University of Rome and Dr. H. W. J. Drijvers of the University of Groningen, for patristic and hagiographic suggestions.

Finally, for allowing me to test my hypotheses in their seminars, I am most grateful to Professor G. Dagron of the Collège de France, Professor H. Ahrweiler, rector and president of the University of Paris, and Professor E. Patlagean, of the University of Paris X; also to Dr. L. Rose, on whose historical and stylistic judgment I have always relied; and to my own graduate students who participated over the years in the doctoral seminar on Armenian historiography that I have taught at Columbia University.

This translation was undertaken with the support of a grant from the National Endowment for the Humanities, and the leisure for the complementary research was made possible by a John Simon Guggenheim Memorial Fellowship; to both of these institutions I would like to express my gratitude for making this work possible.

For the many flaws which such a work must perforce still contain, the responsibility remains, of course, mine alone.

NINA G. GARSOÏAN

Abbreviations

Aa	See Bibliography, II.A–Armenian texts
AAASH	*Acta Antiqua Academiae Scientiarum Hungaricae*
AASS	*Acta Sanctorum Bollandiana* (Brussels)
AAWG	*Abhandlungen der Akademie der Wissenshaften in Göttingen* (Phil.-hist. Klasse)
AaT	See Bibliography, II.A–Armenian texts
AB	*Analecta Bollandiana*
Ag	See Bibliography II.B–Classical texts
AG	H. Hübschmann, *Altarmenische Grammatik* I. *Etymologie* (Leipzig, 1895; repr. Hildesheim, 1962)
AI	*Acta Iranica*
AIPhO	*Annuaire de l'Institut de philologie et d'histoire orientales et slaves*
AIr Wb	*Altiranisches Wörterbuch*, ed. C. Bartholomae (Strassburg, 1904; repr. Berlin, 1961)
AJT	*American Journal of Theology*
AM	See Bibliography II.B–Classical texts
AMI	*Archäologische Mitteilungen aus Iran*
AMS	*Acta martyrum et sanctorum*, ed. P. Bedjan, 7 vols. (Paris, 1890–1897)
ANS	*American Numismatic Society*
AOASH	*Acta Orientalia Academiae Scientiarum Hungaricae*
AON	H. Hübschmann, *Die altarmenische Ortsnamen* (Strassburg, 1904; repr. Amsterdam, 1969)
ASMO	*Acta sanctorum martyrum orientalium et occidentalium*, ed. E. Assemani, I (Rome, 1748)
BARB	*Bulletin de l'Académie royale de Belgique* Classe des lettres
BF	*Byzantinische Forschungen*
BHG	*Bibliotheca hagiographica graeca*, ed. F. Halkin, 3d ed., 3 vols. (Brussels, 1957)
BHO	*Bibliotheca hagiographica orientalis*, ed. P. Peeters (Brussels, 1910)
BM	*Banber Matenadarani*
BMFB	*Bulletin of the Museum of Fine Arts* (Boston)

BP	*Buzandaran Patmut'iwnk'*
BSGW	*Berichte der königlichen sächsichen Gesellschaft der Wissenschaften*
BSL	*Bulletin de la Société de linguistique de Paris*
BSOAS	*Bulletin of the School of Oriental and African Studies*
Byz.	*Byzantion*
BZ	*Byzantinische Zeitschrift*
BzN	*Beitrage zur Namen–Forschung*
CATRS	*Classical Armenian Text Reprint Series*, ed. J. Greppin (Delmar, NY)
CD	See Bibliography II.B–Classical texts
CE	*The Catholic Encyclopedia*
CFHB	*Corpus Fontium Historiae Byzantinae*
CHAMA	*Collection des historiens anciens et modernes de l'Arménie*, ed. V. Langlois, 2 vols. (Paris, 1867–1869)
CHI	*Cambridge History of Iran*
CJ	See Bibliography II.B–Classical texts
CJC	See Bibliography II.B–Classical texts
CPD	*A Concise Pahlavi Dictionary*, ed. D. N. MacKenzie, (Oxford, 1971)
CSCO	*Corpus Scriptorum Christianorum Orientalium*
CSHB	*Corpus Scriptorum Historiae Byzantinae*
CTh	See Bibliography II.B–Classical texts
DACL	*Dictionnaire d'archéologie chrétienne et de liturgie*
DHGE	*Dictionnaire d'histoire et de géographie ecclésiastiques*
DMA	*Dictionary of the Middle Ages*
DOP	*Dumbarton Oaks Papers*
DS	*Dictionnaire de spiritualité*
DTC	*Dictionnaire de théologie catholique*
EI^2	*Encyclopaedia of Islam*, 2d ed.
EIr	*Encyclopedia Iranica*
EO	*Echos d'Orient*
GCS	*Griechischen christlischen Schriftsteller*
GLRB	*Greek Lexicon of the Roman and Byzantine Periods*, ed. E. A. Sophocles, rev. ed. (Cambridge, Mass., 1887; repr. New York, 2 vols., n.d.)
GT^c	See Bibliography II.A–Armenian texts
HA	*Handēs Amsorya*
HAnjB	*Hayoc^c anjnanunneri baŕaran*, ed. H. Ačaryan, 5 vols. (Erevan, 1942–1962; repr. Beirut, 1972)
HArmB	*Hayeren armatakan baŕaran*, ed. H. Ačaryan, 7 vols. (Erevan, 1926–1935; repr. in 4 vols., Erevan, 1971–1979)
HBB	*Hayeren bacatrakan baŕaran*, ed. St. Malxasyanc^c, 4 vols. (Erevan, 1944; repr. Beirut, 1955–1956; repr. Tehran, n.d.)
HE	*Historia ecclesiastica*
HH	*Haykakan hamabaŕbar* (Erevan)
HŽP	*Hay Žołovrdi Patmut'yun* (Erevan)
IA	*Iranica Antiqua*

IANA	*See Tełekagir*
ICMC	*Ecole des langues orientales anciennes de l'Institut Catholique de Paris, Mémorial du Cinquentenaire, 1914–1964* (Paris, 1964)
II	*Indo-Iranica: Mélanges présentés à Georg Morgenstiern . . .* (Wiesbaden, 1964)
IIJ	*Indo-Iranian Journal*
InL	*Incontri linguistici* (Turin, 1974)
IZ	*Istoricheskie Zapiski*
JA	*Journal asiatique*
JANES	*Journal of the Ancient Near Eastern Society*
JAOS	*Journal of the American Oriental Society*
JIN	F. Justi, *Iranisches Namenbuch* (Marburg, 1895; repr. Hildes-heim, 1963)
JPKS	*Jahrbuch der preussischen Kunstsammelungen*
JRAS	*Journal of the Royal Asiatic Society of Great Britain*
JRCAS	*Journal of the Royal Central Asiatic Society*
JRS	*Journal of Roman Studies*
JSAS	*Journal of the Society for Armenian Studies*
JTS	*Journal of Theological Studies*
KhV	*Khristianskiĭ vostok*
KSINA	*Kratkie soobshchenie Instituta Narodov Azii*
KV	*Kavkaz i Vizantiia*
KWCO	*Kleines Wörterbuch des Christlichen Orients*, ed. J. Assfalg and P. Krüger (Wiesbaden, 1975)
Lampe, *Lexicon*	*A Patristic Greek Lexicon*, ed. G. W. H. Lampe (Oxford, 1968)
LeM	*Le Muséon*
Liddell and Scott	*Greek English Lexicon*, ed. H. G. Liddell and R. A. Scott, revised and augmented by H. S. Jones (with the assistance of R. Mackenzie), with a supplement by E. A. Barker (Oxford, 1968)
Loeb	*Loeb Classical Library* (Cambridge, Mass.-London)
Lraber	*Lraber hasarakan gitutᶜyunneri*, Haykakan SSR Akademia; replaced *Tełekagir* in 1962
LVVS	See Bibliography, II.A–Armenian texts
Mansi	*Sacrorum conciliorum nova et amplissima collectio*, ed. G. D. Mansi, 30 vols. (Florence, 1759–1798; repr. Paris, 1901)
MD	See Bibliography, II.A–Armenian texts
MGH AA	*Monumenta germaniae historica, Antiquissimi auctores*
MHD	See Bibliography, II.C–Oriental texts
MK	See Bibliography, II.A–Armenian texts
MK/D	See Bibliography, II.A–Armenian texts
MSL	*Mémoires de la société de linguistique*
MSOS	*Mitteilungen des Seminars für orientalische Sprachen*
MX	See Bibliography, II.A–Armenian texts
NBHL	*Nor Bařgirkᶜ Haykazean Lezui*, ed. G. Awetikᶜean, X. Siwrmē-lean, and M. Awgerean, 2 vols. (Venice, 1836–1837)
NH	*Naturalis historia*
NTS	*New Testament Studies*
OA	*Oriens Antiquus*

OC	*Oriens Christianus*
OCA	*Orientalia Christiana Analecta*
OCD	*Oxford Classical Dictionary*
OCP	*Orientalia Christiana Periodica*
ODCC	*Oxford Dictionary of the Christian Church*, 2d ed. (Oxford, 1974)
OP	See Bibliography, II.C–Oriental texts
OS	*L'Orient syrien*
OSu	*Orientalia Suecana*
PBA	*Proceedings of the British Academy*
PBH	*Patma-banasirakan Handes*
PG	*Patrologiae cursus completus, Series graeca-latina*, ed. J.-P. Migne (Paris, 1857–1866)
PL	*Patrologiae cursus completus, Series latina*, ed. J.-P. Migne (Paris, 1844–1855)
PO	*Patrologia Orientalis*, ed. R. Graffin and F. Nau, (Paris, 1903–)
PS	Preliminary Statement
PSb	*Palestinskiĭ Sbornik*
PW	*Real-Encyclopädie der classischen Altertumswissenschaft*, ed. A. Pauly, G. Wissowa, and W. Kroll (Stuttgart, 1893)
REA	*Revue des études anciennes*
REArm	*Revue des études arméniennes*
RGG	*Die Religionen in Geschichte und Gegenwart. Handwörterbuch für Theologie und Religionswissenschaft*, ed. H. V. von Campenhausen *et al.*, (Tübingen)
RHE	*Revue d'histoire ecclésiastique*
RHR	*Revue de l'histoire des religions*
RL	*Ricerche linguistiche*
ROC	*Revue de l'Orient chrétien*
RR	*Revue des religions*
RSJB	*Revue de la société Jean Bodin*
RSO	*Rivista di studi orientali*
SC	*Sources chrétiennes*
SI	*Studia Iranica*
ŠKZ	See Bibliography, II.C–Oriental texts
SonoM	*Actes et mémoires du VIe Congrès international des sciences onomastiques* (Munich, 1961)
Sop'erk'	See Bibliography, II.A–Armenian texts
T'A	See Bibliography, II.A–Armenian texts
Tełakagir	*Tełakagir hasarakan gitut'yunneri*, Haykakan SSR Akademia; replaced by *Lraber*
Thom. Arts.	See Bibliography, II.A–Armenian texts
TPS	*Transactions of the Philological Society*
TU	*Texten und Untersuchungen*
USAFM	*United States Air Force Aeronautical Approach Charts* (St. Louis, 1956–1958)
Va	See Bibliography, II.C–Oriental texts
VDI	*Vestnik drevneĭ istorii*

Vg	See Bibliography, II.B–Classical texts
Vk	See Bibliography, II.C–Oriental texts
VV	*Vizantiĭski vremennik*
WZKM	*Wiener Zeitschrift für die Kunde des Morgenlandes*
ZAP	*Zeitschrift für armenische Philologie*
ZDMG	*Zeitschrift der deutschen morgenländischen Gesellschaft*
ZMNP	*Zhurnal Ministerstva Narodnogo Prosveshcheniia*
ZVO	*Zapiski vostochnogo otdeleniia Imperatorskago Russkago Arkheologicheskago Obshchestva*

Introduction

Introduction

The work that has come down to us under the name of the *History of Armenia* (*Patmut⁽iwn Hayoc⁽*), attributed to "a certain P⁽awstos Buzandac⁽i"[1] or "Buzand," consists of a more or less chronological account divided into four books or "registers" (*dprut⁽iwnk⁽*) of unequal length covering the period of the later Aršakuni/Arsacid dynasty in Greater Armenia from the accession of Xosrov Kotak, the son and successor of Trdat the Great, to the partition of the Armenian kingdom between Byzantium and Sasanian Iran (A.D. ca. 330–387). It is the most detailed account of the events in Greater Armenia during the major part of the fourth century most of which are merely summarized, as we shall see, in the better known *History of Armenia* of Movsēs Xorenac⁽i, the only other independent source covering this period.[2] The general setting of the work is provided by the endemic war between Byzantium and Persia and the critical situation of the Aršakuni kingdom, poised precariously between the two world powers. A situation that reached its climax in the devastating campaigns of the Sasanian king of kings Šāhpuhr II following the disastrous peace concluded by the Emperor Jovian with Persia in 363, the terms of which led to the destruction and depopulation of the main Armenian cities, the deportation and death of King Aršak II and his queen, P⁽aṙanjem of Siwnik⁽, and the stay of the crown prince, Pap, in

---

[1] ŁP⁽, I.i, p. 2 (= CHAMA II, p. 260), "*P⁽ostos omn Buzandac⁽i*," also iii, and below, pp. 11–16.

[2] For Movsēs Xorenac⁽i, *Patmut⁽iwn Hayoc⁽*, see Commentary, *passim*. All other Armenian sources referring to this period depend primarily on MX for their information (e.g. Yovhannēs Kat⁽oɫikos, pp. 15–69 = trans. p. 66–87, or the long and short versions of the *Vita of Aristakēs*, etc.), though some (e.g. T⁽ovma Arcruni, occasionally the *History of Tarōn*, and especially the *Vita* of St. Nersēs) derive at least in part from "P⁽awstos." See below, pp. 4–5 and nn. 9, 11–12.

Byzantium (IV.1–lix). Thereafter, despite the return of Pap supported by an imperial army and the temporary reconquest of most of the Armenian border territories lost during the Persian invasions, the history of the Aršakuni dynasty—marked by the unworthiness of its rulers and the growing tensions among the crown, the church, and the magnates led by their hereditary commanders, the Mamikonean *sparapets*—tended inexorably to its end, although the account stops short of the dynasty's disappearance, which is merely adumbrated in the mournful closing words of Book VI chapter i.

Three main parallel strands are clearly discernible in the work.

I) *The Royal History*, covering the reigns of the last Aršakuni kings:

Xosrov Kotak, the son and successor of Trdat the Great	III.iii–xi
Tiran, his son and successor	III.xii–xxi
Aršak II, his son and successor and the Persian conquest of Armenia	IV.i–lix
Pap, Aršak's son and successor	V.i–xxxii
Varazdat, Pap's nephew and successor	V.xxxiii–xxxvii
Aršak III and Vałaršak, Pap's sons under the regency of their mother Queen Zarmanduχt and the commander-in-chief Manuēl Mamikonean	V.xxxvii–xliv
The partition of Greater Armenia after the death of Manuēl Mamikonean with the installation of Aršak III in the western portion and another Aršakuni, Xosrov, in the eastern portion	VI.i

II) *The Ecclesiastical History* providing the only detailed account of the hereditary succession, with brief interruptions, of the patriarchs from the house of St. Gregory the Illuminator:

Aristakēs, St. Gregory's younger son and successor	III.ii
Vrtʿanēs, his elder brother and successor	III.iii–vi, xi
Yusik, Vrtʿanēs's son and successor	III.v, xii
The interruption in the Gregorid succession after Yusik's murder because of the unworthiness of his sons	III.xiii–xix
Nersēs I the Great, Yusik's grandson, whose figure dominates much of books IV and V	IV.iii–vii, xi–xv, li; V.i, iv–v, xxi–xxv, xxx–xxxi
The breach between Armenia and Caesarea of Cappadocia as a result of Nersēs's murder and the royal appointment of his successor	V.xxix

With this episode the ecclesiastical history comes to an abrupt halt, except

2

for the desultory and dubious series of biographies that make up the last part of the work (VI.ii–xvi).[3]

III) *The Mamikonean History* cataloguing the constant loyalty and unrewarded valor of the mighty Mamikonean house, hereditary "grand marshals" (*sparapet*s) of the realm and royal "tutors" (*dayeak*s), ultimately regents and kingmakers, whose unrestrained glorification throughout the work has led scholars to call "Pᶜawstos" the family historian of the Mamikoneans.[4] Appearing in successive generations, the leading figures among them—related by blood but not necessarily in direct line—are:

Vačᶜē, *sparapet* under Xosrov Kotak	III.vii–ix, xi
Vasak, *sparapet* under Tiran and Aršak II	
and Aršak's *dayeak*	III.xviii; IV.ii, xvi, xviii–xliii, xlv–l,liv
Mušeł, Vasak's son, *sparapet* under Pap	IV.lv; V.i–ii, iv–v, viii–xx, xxxiv, xxxiii–xxxvi
Manuēl, *sparapet* under Varazdat and regent for	
Pap's sons Aršak III and Vałaršak	V.xxxvii–xliv

In addition to the Persian war, the dominant themes of the work are the opposition between the Gregorid patriarchs and the Aršakuni kings, toward whom the author displays an almost invariable hostility, and the struggle of the crown to restrain the centrifugal tendencies of the great magnates (*naχarar*s) who resisted every attempt at centralization and any encroachment on their hereditary prerogatives and domains on the part of the king. All of these general lines are repeatedly interrupted, however, by various interpolations, the chief of which concern the fates of individual *naχarar* houses (III.iv, viii–ix, xviii; IV.xix) and the nefarious activities of the royal official known as the *Hayr-mardpet*[5] (III.xviii; IV.xiv, lv; V.iii, vi), or especially by hagiographic intrusions (III.x; IV.v–x, xvi–xvii, lvi–lvii; V.xxv–xxviii; VI.xvi).

Despite the evident importance of the material contained in the work attributed to Pᶜawstos, which is not only the best but often the only record of fourth-century Armenian history, it has never been included in the "received" tradition through which the Armenians have chosen to view their own past.[6] Writing presumably as a near contemporary, the late fifth-century historian Łazar Pᶜarpecᶜi, who first referred to "Pᶜawstos's" work as a history of Armenia, already complained that the work

---

[3] See below, p. 36.

[4] See below, p. 44.

[5] See Appendix III, s.v. *mardpet*.

[6] On the received account of Armenian history, see Thomson's introductions to Aa, p. xviii; MK, p. 1; Ełishē, p. 2. The neglect of "Pᶜawstos" in the Middle Ages may have helped preserve the authenticity of this text from the rewriting common among early Armenian sources. However, cf. below, pp. 4–5 and nn. 9, 11–12.

contained numerous "falsehoods" and "absurdities" unworthy of a "Byzantine scholar" such as "P'awstos" and attributed them to the unskilled interpolations of another ignorant author or to the errors of an incompetent scribe.[7] Thereafter, an almost unbroken silence descended on the work for the duration of the Middle Ages, though its information was clearly used though not acknowledged by Movsēs Xorenac'i, as has been shown by Robert Thomson,[8] as well as in the Xth-XIIth century *Vita* of St. Nersēs attributed to Mesrop the Priest, most of which derives from "P'awstos" with the addition of hagiographic embellishments and messianic prophecies.[9] Episodes occurring in the work of "P'awstos" (IV.liv; V.vii) are also to be found in the *History of the Persian War* by the sixth-century Byzantine historian Procopius, who attributed his information to an anonymous *History of Armenia*, though, as we shall see, this needs not have been the one ascribed to P'awstos.[10] Thus, the only explicit references to the work in the Middle Ages after that of Łazar P'arpec'i are to the episode of St. Thekla (IV.x) mentioned in passing by the

[7] ŁP', I.ii–iii, p. 3–4 (= CHAMA II, pp. 259–261). Łazar P'arpec'i's work is commonly dated to the fifth century, soon after "P'awstos." ŁP', I.xv p. 25 (= CHAMA II, p. 272) also refers to "P'awstos's" work, and to St. Nersēs's condemnation of King Aršak II (see below, p. 10). Likewise, the homily to the rebellious Armenian nobles attributed to St. Sahak I (ŁP', I.xiii, pp. 20–23 = CHAMA II, pp. 269–270) parallels the condemnation of the Armenian magnates in "P'awstos" (IV.li).

[8] See Thomson, MK, pp. 46–47; Malxasyanc', pp. 53–57.

[9] For the dependence of the *Vita* of St. Nersēs on "P'awstos," see the Commentary and the relevant entries in the Appendices. The date of the *Vita* is given as 910–975? by Połarean, *Hay grołner*; ca. 967 by Inglisian, "Literatur," p. 185; and twelfth century by van Esbroeck, "Témoignages littéraires," p. 392; see also Abelyan, *Grakanut'yun*, pp. 572–573. Unacknowledged material from "P'awstos's" work may also occur in the following subsequent works: the tenth-century *History of Tarōn* by the Ps. Yovhannēs Mamikonean, though some of the material that seems to indicate a familiarity with "P'awstos" (e.g. pp. 41, 43, 111, 198, etc.) may also have been drawn from Aa and MX; Gregory the Priest's continuation of MU, cclxv, pp. 513–514 (= trans. pp. 338–340), whose fanciful account of St. James of Nisibis's appearance to the Persians on the walls of his city garbed in imperial robes and carrying a plank from the Ark on his head may be a dim memory of "P'awstos," III.x, though no direct link can be found; Vardan Arewelc'i, some of whose material has been traced back to P'awstos by Ant'abyan, "Vardan," pp. 86–87, though in this case the filiation appears to be by way of MX; still more distantly, the insertion of a partiarch, Yusik, after Nersēs I in the list of primates attributed to Mixaēl Asori, YK' §15, p. 34 as well as in the "Greek List of Katholikoi," §8, p. 402, may perhaps point back to the order of Armenian patriarchs found exclusively in "P'awstos"; and finally, Melikset-bek, "Sledy," observed some traces of "P'awstos" in early Georgian literature.

[10] Procopius, *Bell. Pers.*, I.v.16–40. See below, pp. 10, 18, 20 and nn. 36–37; also the Commentary on IV.liv, nn. 8–9, 12, 15, 19; V.vii, n. 1. Cf., however, Abgaryan, *Sebēosi patmut'iwn*, pp. 100–107.

Continuator of T͑ovma Arcruni in the tenth century and to the punishment of Tiran in Asolik,[11] though occasional anachronistic listing of P͑awstos Buzand after Movsēs Xorenac͑i, Ełišē, and Łazar P͑arpec͑i in the initial portion of the thirteenth-century *History of Armenia* of Kirakos Ganzakec͑i as well as in similar listings of Armenian historians can also be found.[12] All other medieval Armenian historians preferred to follow the version of fourth-century events given by Movsēs Xorenac͑i.[13] The general neglect of "P͑awstos's" work began to abate, albeit slowly, only after its 1832 Venice edition, and its full value still remains to be appreciated.[14]

Whatever may have been the reasons that led to the exclusion of this text from the mainstream of Armenian historiography during the Middle Ages, the slow recognition of its outstanding value for the study of early Christian Armenia in modern times undoubtedly derives at least in part from a series of problems that have provoked heated controversies and contradictory theories among students of the work. Since M. Č͑amč͑ean's first attempt to compose a serious *History of Armenia* late in the eighteenth century,[15] scholars, repeating some of Łazar P͑arpec͑i's strictures, have noted irrelevancies, repetitions, contradictions, anachronisms, and a lack

---

[11] T͑A Cont., IV.xxxi, p. 275 (= *Thom. Arts.*, p. 338). T͑ovma Arcruni himself was evidently acquainted with the account of "P͑awstos," but he does not mention him by name. See T͑A, I.i.ix–x, pp. 19, 58–64 (= Thom. Arts., pp. 81, 123–129). Like T͑ovma's Continuator, Aсolik openly acknowledges his debt to "P͑awstos," II.i, p. 69, "*orpēs patmē Buzand.*"

[12] KG, pp. 6–7 (= Brosset tr., p. 3); also Mχit͑ar Ayrivanec͑i and a number of the late "Listings of Historians," pp. xlix–liv. Hakobyan, "Favst" also claims that some passages from MK/D, which he traces back to an earlier "Tale of Vačagan" are derived from "P͑awstos," though this borrowing is also unacknowledged. For the value of "P͑awstos's" evidence concerning the Armenian patriarchal succession in the second half of the fourth century (cf. above n. 9), see my study on "Šahak of Manazkert."

[13] See above n. 2.

[14] Praise for "P͑awstos" as a historian is to be found in both Gelzer, "Die Anfänge," p. 11 and Ananean, "La data," p. 356, but some twenty years ago, Dilleman, *Haute Mésopotamie*, p. 115 still qualified the work of early Armenian historians and particularly that of "P͑awstos" as "des fables ou des chansons de gestes, mais des romans à clé, ce qui n'améliore pas leur valeur historique." A number of studies have addressed particular problems found in "P͑awstos's" work, but no detailed analysis of the entire text and its content has been undertaken beyond EM's brief study and Malχasyanc͑'s introductory survey (see below nn. 16, 20). In the nineteenth and twentieth centuries, however, episodes drawn from "P͑awstos" have appealed to patriotic authors such as Raffi, *Samuēl*; St͑epan Zoryan, *T͑agawor Pap, Varazdat*, etc; and Perč Zeytuneanc͑, *Aršak II*, which served as the basis for Č͑uχajean's opera of the same name; see also Nalbandian, *Arshak Vtoroĭ*.

[15] Č͑amč͑ean, *Patmut͑iwn Hayoc͑*.

of chronological precision. Still more seriously, the language in which the original text was composed, its date, and its author have been disputed at length, and the question of whether the surviving text is complete or mutilated remains controversial to date. Many of the problems raised have found a solution in St. Malχasyancᶜ's incisive review of earlier studies,[16] but because of the inaccessibility of his work to most western scholars, the existence of more recent hypotheses, and the still open character of some of the problems, another brief survey does not seem unwarranted here.

The Language and Date of the Original Text

The first essential problems presented by the Armenian text that has come down to us are those of its original language and of its date of composition. The author speaks throughout as a contemporary or even an eyewitness of the fourth-century events he describes, yet the creation of the Armenian alphabet at the beginning of the fifth century makes a fourth-century Armenian original patently impossible. Moreover, a note inserted at the end of Book III states unequivocally that it marks the conclusion "of the third portion in twenty-one historical chapters of the chronography of the chronicler Pᶜawstos Biwzand the great historian who was a Greek chronicler."[17] Finally, the almost unrelieved antagonism of the author toward the Armenian Aršakuni rulers, especially Aršak II and his son Pap, struck later scholars as highly unsuitable for a native historian. Compounding the problem, external sources likewise seemed to suggest a non-Armenian original.[18] As already noted, Łazar Pᶜarpecᶜi insisted that "Pᶜawstos" or, as he calls him, "Pᶜostos," was a "Byzantine scholar" from the "most brilliant city . . . called Constantinople."[19] Consequently, most older scholars, beginning with Čᶜamčᶜean and followed by M. Awgerean, N. O. Emin, A. von Gutschmid, E. Matatᶜean, B. Sargisean, A. Garagašean, H. Gelzer, Ł. Ališan, N. Adontz, and more recently V. Inglisian and M. van Esbroeck have argued that the work had originally been composed in Greek by a Greek or a Hellenized Armenian

---

[16] Malχasyancᶜ, *Usumnasirutⁱyun*; essentially repeated in his "Introduction" and *idem*, "Nkatołutⁱiwn." Because Malχasyancᶜ incorporated most of the earlier scholarship into his "Introduction," no attempt has been made here to give an exhaustive account of the previous literature, which would have expanded the present survey beyond manageable size.

[17] "*Katarecᶜaw errord dartᶜ, kᶜsan ew mi patmutⁱeancᶜ dprutⁱiwnkᶜ, žamanakagir kanonkᶜ Pᶜawsteay* [var. *paχsteaykᶜ*, see below, p. 9] *Biwzandeay žamanakagir meci patmagri, or ēr žamanakagir Yunacᶜ*" (Venice ed. p. 68 = St. Petersburg ed., p. 50).

[18] Cf. pp. 4, 18, 20 and nn. 10, 80 for Procopius.

[19] ŁPᶜ, I.iii, p. 4 (= CHAMA II, p. 261), "*kᶜałakᶜ mecapaycaṙ, zor . . . Kostandnupōlis anuanēr.*"

writing in the fourth century and was only subsequently translated into Armenian.[20]

In contrast to this "Greek" thesis, but maintaining the fourth-century date of the original, K. Patkanean argued that references in the text to Armenia as the "realm" or "house of T⁣ᶜorgom" (for example, V.xxx) pointed rather toward a Semitic milieu, where such Biblical descriptions were familiar; he consequently opted for a Syriac original.[21] This thesis was subsequently supported by Fr. Peeters's identification of what he considered to be a series of Syriacisms in certain portions of the text.[22] Patkanean's Syriac thesis was also shared in some degree by G. Zarpᶜa-nalean, who oscillated between Greek and Syriac as the original language of composition,[23] and by Norayr Biwzandacᶜi, who distinguished two voices in the work, one of which, impudent and gay, belonged to the Greek author Pᶜawstos, while the other, pious and filled with invocations and miracles, was that of the subsequent Syrian ecclesiastic who gave the work its religious cast.[24]

More recent scholarship, however, has categorically rejected the translation theories in favor of an Armenian original. Following the analysis of A. Aytənean and Y. Tašean's demonstrations that "Pᶜawstos's" Scriptural citations were drawn from the Armenian version of the Bible rather than the Septuagint, M. Abełyan and Malχasyancᶜ concluded that "Pᶜaw-stos's" style, far from being formally correct and stilted as might be expected in a translation, is both rich and naïve, unhampered by grammatical strictures, filled with colloquialisms and *hapax legomena*.[25] In addition, the constant use by the author of Armenian forms for Greek names or of awkward and incorrect forms clearly filtered through Armeni-

---

[20] NHBL I, p. 10; J.-B. Emin, CHAMA I, pp. 204–205; Gutschmidt, "Glaub-würdigkeit"; M[atatᶜean], *Pᶜawstos*; B. Sargisean, *Agatᶜangełos*; Garagašcan, *Patmutᶜiwn*, II, pp. 67–68; Gelzer, "Die Anfänge," pp. 114–116; Ališan, *Hayapatum*; Adontz, "Nachal'naia istoriia." All of these theses are summarized by Malχasyancᶜ in "Introduction," pp. 8–17. See also Inglisian, "Literatur," p. 159; and van Esbroeck, "Le roi Sanatrouk," pp. 84–85.

[21] Patkanean, *Bibliograficheskij ocherk; idem, Vanskie nadpisi*, pp. 84–85.

[22] Peeters, "Persécution," pp. 61–64; *idem*, "Jacques de Nisibe," p. 313, n. 2; *idem*, "SS Serge et Théodore," pp. 70–73.

[23] Zarpᶜanalean, *Patmutᶜiwn*, pp. 242–250 ff.

[24] Norayr Biwzandacᶜi, *Koriwn*. This work has unfortunately not been available to me, but most of the author's conclusions are to be found in Malχasyancᶜ's "Introduction" and notes.

[25] A. Aytənean, *Kᶜnnakan kᶜerakanutᶜiwn*, pp. 58–59; Abełyan, *Grakanutᶜyun*, pp. 190–191; Garagašean, *Čašak*, pp. 43–51; Ačaryan, *Patmutᶜyun*, II, pp. 94–106; Malχasyancᶜ, pp. 40–43, 53–57. The originality of the Armenian text is also supported by Ter Mkrtčᶜyan, "Pᶜawstos," p. 286; and the liveliness of the style as well as its "popular" character was also noted by EM, *Pᶜawstos*, pp. iv, 12, 18. See also below, p. 23.

an, such as Barseł and Barsilios for Basilios (IV.vii–viii), and the inaccurate explanatory gloss on the word *enkomia* (IV.iv), cannot be the work of a native Greek speaker or even of one reasonably familiar with Greek.[26] The Armenian form of Greek toponyms such as *Gamirkʿ* for Cappadocia is used throughout, as opposed to the Greek calque *Kapadovk[ia]* used by the more learned Movsēs Xorenacʿi.[27] The author's language is not marked by Hellenic turns, nor can any latent cultural Hellenisms, such as are found in the *Life of St. Thekla*,[28] be detected in his work.

The Syriacisms observed by Patkanean and Peeters are likewise inconclusive. The "Semitic" phrase, "the realm of Tʿorgom," queried by Patkanean finds an obvious parallel in the equally "Semitic" form of Koriwn's characterization of Armenia as the "race of Askenaz [*Askʿanazean azg*]" in his *Life of Maštocʿ*, the Armenian origin of which has never been questioned,[29] and the two formulae are clearly Biblical in origin. The Syriacisms noted by Peeters occur in interpolated hagiographic chapters of Syriac origin (IV.x, xvii) or their passing recollection elsewhere (IV.xviii, liv). Consequently, they are poor evidence for the original language of the entire text. Other possible Syriacisms in the text seem merely idiosyncratic to the author and might perhaps be an additional indication of his origin in the southern district of Tarōn.[30]

---

26 See, IV.iv, vii–x. The same unskilled variations appear in the names of Ewsebios/Ewsebi, *idem*, and of Aršak II's Roman bride Olympias: Ołompi/Ołompinay (IV.xv). The incorrect form "Barsilios" seems to have been common in early Armenian writings since it also occurs in the Letter of the early VIth century Katʿołikos Babgēn I (GTʿ, p. 50; cf. also p. 69, "Barsełios").

27 "Pʿawstos's" invariable "*Gamirkʿ*" (III.xii, xvi–xvii; IV.iii–iv, vii, xi; is not to be found in MX's "*Kapadovkacʿwocʿ*," I.xiv, xxix; II.lxxv (= MK, pp. 94, 119, 221).

28 Dagron, *Ste. Thècle*, pp. 81, 110–112, 156–157, 290/1–296/7.

29 Koriwn, i, p. 22 (= trans., p. 21).

30 See the Commentary on IV.x, n. 3; xvii, n. 2. Traditionally, recourse has been made to "Syriacisms" to assist in determining the *Vorlage* of a particular text. The arguments adduced derive from the areas of etymology, phonology, and linguistic usage. (See, e.g., Cowe, *Daniel*, pp. 238–239, on the danger of the first argument in textual criticism; and Marr's examples in Ter Petrosyan, "Traduction"). As generally presented, however, these arguments fail to distinguish between the widespread and the particular (see Lehmann, *Some Questions*, pp. 57–82, esp. 59–60, 77–80). Several of the phenomena indicated are indeed common to both Syriac and Armenian, and in view of the former's longer history of writing and its influence on incipient Armenian literature, the Syriacisms may well be viewed as part of the larger pattern of cultural transfer. Yet in the particular, such a thesis may not be provable. The point overlooked, however, is that regardless of origin, these forms had become thoroughly acclimatized in the native Armenian idiom and consequently manifest themselves in the earliest original written examples of the language. As such, they are of but little use in demonstrating the source of a specific work. In the case of "Pʿawstos," three syntactic constructions often considered to be Syriacisms occur throughout the work, even

Despite its unequivocal tone, the note closing Book III of the text has proved equally unsatisfactory. Not only are the forms *"Pᶜawsteay"* and *"pᶜaχstiaykᶜ"* (in the plural) found in the manuscripts not necessarily variants of "Pᶜawstos's" name, but, as Malχasyancᶜ has observed, the note refers to the author in the third person singular of the past tense, and still more incongruously styles him "the great historian," a formula unsuitable for a reference to oneself. Consequently, Malχasyancᶜ has concluded that the note should properly be attributed to a later editor rather than to the author of the text, and that its information is unreliable.[31] This conclusion is all the more likely because this note bears a suspicious similarity to those following Books II and III of Movsēs Xorenacᶜi's *History of Armenia*.[32] Finally, Čᶜamčᶜean's observation of the curious antagonism of the author toward the Aršakuni kings of Armenia does not provide a reliable index of his foreign origin, for this hostility, as we shall see, categorically contradicts the favorable characterization of Aršak II and Pap in such contemporary classical sources as the *History* of Ammianus Marcellinus. It is rather a reflection of the opposition of the strictly Nicaean Armenian clergy to the Arianizing policy pursued by the Armenian court through most of the fourth century.[33]

If the internal evidence supporting a foreign original remains unsubstantial, the external sources are no more satisfactory. The authenticity of Łazar Pᶜarpecᶜi's initial section identifying "Pᶜostos" as a Greek has been called into question.[34] It rests on a misunderstanding of the term *Buzand*, which it identifies incorrectly with the city of Byzantium, to which it devotes an elaborate and irrelevant excursus while giving no evidence about "Pᶜostos" himself. The reference to an existing body of criticism of "Pᶜostos's" work, which had presumably already suffered extensive interpolations, according to Łazar, is equally curious if he wrote as "Pᶜaw-

---

where no *prima facie* case can be made for a Syriac origin. They may be adduced as illustrations:

1) The redundant subjective pronoun following a finite verb (IV.ii), *"gnayr na amenayn patuiranōkᶜn teaṙn."*

2) A redundant personal pronoun reinforcing a preceding relative pronoun (V.xxiv), *"zaynosik angam zors erbēkᶜ očᶜ čanačᶜēr znosa."*

3) Two finite verbs in asyndetic juxtaposition (IV.iv), *"ekin hasin noka mecaparc ereweli hogeworazgeacᶜ pᶜaṙōkᶜ."* They are part of the fabric of the work and may even cast some light on the spoken Armenian of southern district, and possibly on the hypothesis that the author of our text came from Tarōn. I am indebted to Dr. P. Cowe for the material of this note.

[31] Malχasyancᶜ, pp. 19, 44. See also, Abełyan, *Grakanutᶜyun*, p. 190.

[32] MX, pp. 250, 366 (= MK, pp. 253, 354).

[33] Garsoïan, "Politique"; see also Commentary, IV.v nn. 7, 17.

[34] Akinean, *Karmir Vardan*, pp. 9–10; Akinean and Tēr Pōłosean, "Łazar Pᶜarpecᶜi."

stos's" near contemporary.[35] Much has also been made of Procopius's presumed use of "P^cawstos's" history in the mid-sixth century. It is not impossible that the Byzantine historian was acquainted with it, though he never mentions the name of the author of the "History of Armenia" he claims as a source, and his tales do not match precisely the versions found in our text.[36] The stories themselves, relating the magic ordeal of Aršak II and his death in the "Castle of Oblivion" are, as we shall see, of epic character, and were probably current in Armenian and perhaps in Greek as well. As such they do not necessarily provide a direct link between "P^cawstos" and Procopius. Even if Abełyan's hypothesis that Procopius knew Armenian remains entirely unsupported,[37] the presence of these tales in a Greek work of the sixth century is proof neither of a Greek original for "P^cawstos's" work nor of its early date.

In conclusion, the objection to an Armenian original based on a pre-fifth century date of composition for the work likewise falls away in the light of a closer analysis of the text. "P^cawstos" is far too ignorant of fourth-century general history to have been a contemporary. He identifies only two Byzantine emperors: Constantine the Great (324–337) and Valens (364–378), whom he confuses with Constantius (337–361),[38] and he conflates battles fought in 297 and ca. 344.[39] In the Persian realm, he occasionally substitutes the king of kings Narseh (293–302) for his grandson Šāhpuhr II (309–379).[40] The historical events of the period have become legendary and filtered through the folk memory. Conversely, a number of anachronisms point to a knowledge of the fifth-century history of Armenia. The vision of the patriarch Yusik (III.v) referring to the "chief shepherds" (in the plural) descended from him must reach beyond St. Nersēs and the chronological terminus of "P^cawstos's" work to the patriarchate of Yusik's great-grandson, St. Sahak the Great, who died about 438. The curses of St. Daniēl against King Tiran (III.xiv) and of St. Nersēs against Aršak II (IV.xiii, xv) both foreshadow the end of the Aršakuni dynasty in 428. The consecration of Vač^cē Mamikonean and the Armenian dead in the homily of the patriarch Vrt^canēs (III.xi) recalls the commemoration of Vardan

---

[35] See below, p. 14, for the meaning of *buzand* and 11 for the date of composition of "P^cawstos's" work.

[36] See Commentary, IV.xvi n. 10; liv nn. 8–9, 12, 15, 17, 19; V.vii n. 1.

[37] Abełyan, *Grakanut*^c*yun*, p. 191. Abełyan's argument was based on Procopius's origin from Caesarea. But the Byzantine historian was a native of the Palestinian, not the Cappadocian, city of that name and consequently had no reason to know Armenian. Abełyan also notes, however, that the presence of the tales in Procopius's *Histories* is not a proof for a Greek original of "P^cawstos's" work.

[38] See Commentary, III.xxi n. 21; IV.v n. 5; etc..

[39] See below, pp. 30, 38–40, and Commentary, III.xxi n. 16.

[40] See Commentary, III.xx n. 9; xxi n. 16.

Mamikonean and his companions fallen at the battle of Awarayr in 451.[41] Finally, the quotations from the Armenian Bible and from Koriwn's *Vita* of Maštoc^c bring us once again to the second half of the fifth century.[42]

In the light of the patent weaknesses in the theses of foreign origin and the presence of textual anachronisms, there is no longer any reason to doubt that it was indeed composed from the first in Armenian, as supported by the stylistic and lexical evidence, and that it should be dated in the latter part of the fifth rather than in the fourth century. The *termini* for its composition are given by the quotations from Koriwn (ca. 443–451) found in the text and the presumed reference in Łazar P^carpec^ci, who places "P^costos" immediately after Agat^cangełos (ca. 460). Hence a date in the 470s seems most likely, and indeed it is difficult to imagine a time more suitable for a work glorifying the role of the Mamikonean family in Armenian history than the generation immediately following the *sparapet* Vardan Mamikonean's heroic defense of Armenian Christianity in 451.[43]

The Identity of the Author

The identity of the author of the "History of Armenia" has proved as enigmatic as its date. Another note in the text, this one found at the end of the Table of Contents of Book VI, has been interpreted by some as a promise that "At the end of all the histories there are for the readers of this book ten verses of counted meter with information concerning me."[44] Even if we disregard the difficulties involved in the ambiguous wording of

[41] See Commentary, III.v n. 5, xi n. 4, xiv nn. 35–36; IV.xiii n. 11, xv n. 26.

[42] See above, n. 25, and below, pp. 22–25. The date of Koriwn's *Vita* of Maštoc^c oscillates between 443 and 451 according to Abełyan, *Grakanut^cyun*, p. 171; cf. 190–191. For that of ŁP^c, see *ibid.*, pp. 343–376.

[43] LP^c I.ii–iii, pp. 2–3 (= CHAMA II, pp. 259–260). Thomson, Aa, p. xc gives a date of approximately 460 for the existing version of Aa, which presents no problems. However, he once places Aa after "P^cawstos," whom he dates in "the first half of the fifth century" (*ibid.*, pp. lxxv, but cf. xvi, xxv, lxxv–lxxvii). See also *ibid.*, pp. xxi–xxiii; Garitte, *Documents*, pp. 1–116, 407–420; van Esbroeck, "Nouveau témoin," pp. 14–20, 96, etc., for other versions. The quotations from Koriwn make such an early date impossible (see preceding note), but "P^cawstos" and Aa seem to have been nearly contemporary. "P^cawstos's" familiarity with the "received" version of St. Gregory's illumination of Armenia, enshrined in Aa suggests that his is the slightly later work, though this version was obviously current at the time (cf. pp. 25–26). "P^cawstos's" emphasis on the importance of St. Thaddeus in the Armenian ecclesiastical tradition as against Aa's silence on the subject, is part of his awareness of the Syrian current in southern Armenian Christianity, for which see below, pp. 46–47. Cf. also Malχasyanc^c trans., pp. 33, 37, despite the reservations of the editors of the 1968 edition.

[44] *Storot amenayn patmut^ceanc^c yałags im tełekut^cean, ork^c miangam zmateans ent^cernoyk^c, tunk^c tasn᷄ hamarakan t^cuōk^c.*" Cf. Commentary VI, Tables, n. 3.

this note, it has proved of singularly little help to scholars, for no trace of the promised colophon, if indeed it ever existed, has come down to us.[45] To supplement the missing information, early scholars noted within the work itself the presence of a bishop named P'awstos, associated with St. Nersēs the Great, and sought to attribute the composition of the *History* to this ecclesiastic, whom some went on to identify with the Armenian bishop named Faustus, who is known from the correspondence of St. Basil of Caesarea.[46] This identification was particularly suited to the thesis of a Greek author for the *History,* since Bishop P'awstos was explicitly identified in the text as being "of Roman [i.e., Greek] race" (VI.vi).[47] It soon proved inadequate, however. The Faustus known to St. Basil of Caesarea clearly seems to have been a resident of the imperial province of *Armenia Minor*, west of the Euphrates, with which the metropolitan of Caesarea was concerned, and not of the still-autonomous Aršakuni kingdom of *Armenia Maior*, east of the river.[48] As such, he cannot be associated with the bishop of Greater Armenia who wanders in and out of the *History*—already an "old man" when he conferred the diaconate on St. Nersēs, presumably ca. 353 (IV.iii),[49] still alive twenty years later to preside over the burial of the patriarch (V.xxiv),[50] and

---

[45] EM, *P'awstos*, pp. 6–7 argued that the first word of the note, *storot*, should be interpreted as a preposition meaning "after," and he rendered *tunk'* as "chapters," thus obtaining a somewhat different translation: "After all the information concerning me . . . there are ten chapters." This interpretation was shared by Garagašean, "P'awstos," but *storot* is a noun and not a preposition, and the use of *tunk'* for "chapters" is extremely unusual: see Malχasyanc', p. 13. The colophon was not known to "P'awstos's" near contemporary Łazar P'arpec'i, for he too had no information concerning this author's identity; and it probably never existed. Yet another hypothesis has *hamarakan* taken as meaning "counting," to obtain the translation: "the reader of this book seeking information about me [will do so] by counting ten chapters [back]," though there is no basis for this alteration of the text, which derives from the identification of the author of the work with the bishop P'awstos mentioned in VI.v–vi. Still another solution is proposed by Feydit, "Passage," and *idem* "Énigme." See below, pp. 13–16, and the following notes for the identity of the author. In any case it must be borne in mind that the note itself is not part of the original text, but an addition of the later editor, because it is part of a Table of Contents. See below, p. 35, and Commentary, VI, Tables, n. 3.

[46] See Malχasyanc', p. 12; cf. EM, *P'awstos*, pp. 7ff. and St. Basil, Ep. cxx–cxxii.

[47] VI.vi, "*azgaw Hoŗom.*" The use of Roman for Byzantine—i.e., Greek—is constant in the East throughout the Middle Ages; cf. Turk. "Rūm"; also below, n. 53.

[48] Garsoïan, "Nersēs le Grand," pp. 149–158.

[49] IV.iii, "*ceruni episkopos*"; cf. Appendix I, "Nersēs," for the dates of his pontificate.

[50] V.xxiv.

amazingly still active some twenty more years later after the partition of Armenia (VI.v–vi).[51]

We have already seen that the form of the presumed author's name is itself uncertain, since *Pᶜawsteay* is a later correction of the *pᶜaχsteaykᶜ* found in the manuscripts of the colophon closing Book III, while Łazar Pᶜarpecᶜi gives it as "Pᶜostos."[52] More seriously, with the abandonment of the Greek thesis for the original version of the work, both "Pᶜawstos's" non-Armenian name and the claim of "Roman" descent became unsuitable for its author.[53] Most categorically of all, the demonstration of the Armenian origin of the work placing it in the late fifth century ineluctably dissociated it from any mid-fourth-century bishop, no matter how long-lived.

The further attempt of Ł. Inčičean, followed by V. Langlois and H. Gelzer, to identify the author of the text as a member of the *naχarar* house of the Sahaṙuni on the basis of a presumed reference in a listing of Armenian magnates to the Sahaṙuni prince as being "of our house [and] race" (III.xii)[54] met with no greater success. Pointing out the unnecessary repetition "house" and "race," which does not occur elsewhere in the list; the fact that the given name of the Sahaṙuni prince is the only one omitted in the list; and finally the similarity of *m* and *T* in Armenian script, scholars soon argued for a *lapsus calami* whereby the words *meroy tohmi* "of our house" had replaced the prince's missing name, Tirocᶜ or perhaps Merohdazat. As a result, this hypothesis has found little favor in recent times,[55] and we consequently are left with no evidence whatsoever for the Christian or family name of the author.

---

[51] VI.v. Even if we are not dealing with a single individual throughout, chronology does not permit the identification of the author of this work composed late in the fifth century (see above, p. 11 and n. 43) with any of these fourth-century figures. This conclusion is shared by Thomson, Aa, p. xiv. Cf., however, Ter Mkrtčᶜyan, "Pᶜawstos" p. 286.

[52] See Commentary, III, Colophon, n. 2 for the correction; also ŁPᶜ, I.iii, p. 3 (= CHAMA II, p. 260, where the name is rendered "Faustus"). The *aw* of the name Pᶜawstos would normally be rendered as *ō* in the late manuscripts, but never as *o*.

[53] The name Pᶜawstos does not occur in Armenian mediaeval historiography outside of this work, and it is clearly derived from the Latin *Faustus* "fortunate, of good omen." See HAnjB V, pp. 196–198. EM, *Pᶜawstos*, p. 6, noted that Pᶜawstos's brother Aṙostom, named in the title but not in the text of VI.vi, did not have a "Roman name." It is, in fact, Iranian, See Appendix I, "Ṙastom," and above, n. 47.

[54] III.xii, "*zmeroy tohmi azgi išχann sahaṙuneacᶜ.*" See Inčičean, *Hnaχōsutᶜiwn* II, p. 185; Gatᶜrčean, "Pᶜawstos," pp. 40–43; Langlois, CHAMA I, p. 222; Gelzer, "Die Anfänge," pp. 112–113; Peeters, "Intervention," p. 227, with reservations.

[55] Ter Mkrtčᶜyan, "Pᶜawstos," pp. 273, 276–277; Zarpᶜanalean, *Patmutᶜiwn*, p. 249; EM, *Pᶜawstos*, p. 27; Malχasyancᶜ (1947 edition), pp. 317–318 n. 41. This note was omitted from the 1968 edition, but see the editors' note p. 88 suggesting the substitution of *Tirocᶜ* for *meroy*.

The second half of his presumed name, "Buzandacʿi" or "Buzand," proved equally problematic and troublesome. These forms, which are incorrect for the rendition of the locution "from Byzantium" in classical Armenian, were consequently altered at an early date to the more accurate "Biwzandacʿi," possibly also under the influence of Łazar Pʿarpecʿi's irrelevant excursus on the city of Constantinople, noted above.[56] The further attempts of K. Lehmann-Haupt and E. Stein to identify "Pʿawstos's" native city as Buzanta/Podandos, just north of the Cilician Gates, proved no more satisfactory and shed no light on the first half of the author's name.[57] Fortunately, a definitive solution to the entire problem, first tentatively suggested by Malχasyancʿ, has now been given by Anahit Perikhanian.[58] Through a detailed etymological analysis of the actual title of the work appended to the text, *Buzandaran Patmutʿiwnkʿ* as opposed to "History of Armenia" (*Patmutʿiwn Hayocʿ*), the title usually attributed to the work (perhaps as a result of its identification by Łazar Pʿarpecʿi)[59] Perikhanian divided the first term of the title into (1) *buzand*, derived not from a toponym as had formerly been attempted, but from Parth. *bozand, OP *bavant-zanda or **bavazanta/i*, "a reciter of epic poems, a bard"; and (2) *-aran*, the suffix denoting "place where, location" in both Iranian and Armenian. Taking this derivation in conjunction with the second term of the title, *patmutʿiwnkʿ* (in the plural, not the singular), "tales, histories," she concluded that the title of the work should correctly be rendered "Epic Tales" or "Epic Histories."

Suitable as this analysis is for the now-accepted Armenian origin of the work and satisfactory as it is for the solution of the enigmatic *Buzandaran*, it necessarily ends any further search for the name of the compiler or for that of his native city. The work hitherto incorrectly identified as a "History of Armenia" attributed to a Pʿawstos of Byzantium or Buzanta now emerges in reality as a late fifth-century compilation of tales known as the *Epic Histories*, composed by an anonymous author whose name is not to be found in the title of the work and concerning whom we have no

---

[56] See above, pp. 4, 9 and the discussion in Malχasyancʿ's 1947 edition, pp. 57ff. (= 1968 edition pp. 44ff.), and more particularly, 1947 edition pp. 309–310, n. 1. It is interesting to note in this connection that Asołik writing ca. A.D. 1000 still uses the form Buzand, see above n. 11.

[57] See Stein, *Excursus U*, p. 835 n. 2 for the bibliography of this thesis.

[58] Malχasyancʿ, "Neršapuh Řmbosean," pp. 91–93; *idem*, Introduction, pp. 44–46; Perikhanian, "Buzand." Cf., however, Abgaryan, "Mamikonyanneri zruycʿi ałbyurə," pp. 253–268, who distinguishes "Pʿawstos" from the *Buzandaran*.

[59] ŁPʿ I.ii–iii, pp. 2–4 (= CHAMA II, pp. 259–260) does not give the actual title of the work, but speaks of "historians of Armenia [*patmagracʿn Hayocʿ*]," among whom he lists "Pʿostos." See also Abgaryan, *Sebēosi Patmutʿyunə*, p. 106.

information.[60] It was later presumably attributed to a Bishop P⁽c⁾awstos to benefit from the prestige of St. Nersēs' putative collaborator named in the text, following an anachronistic pattern common in medieval sources.[61] There is, consequently, no further reason to speak of a *History of Armenia* by P⁽c⁾awstos Buzand, but rather of anonymous *Epic Histories*.

The most that can be deduced concerning the personality of the compiler on the basis of the internal evidence of the text is that he was obviously a cleric familiar with the Armenian version of the Basilian liturgy[62] and deeply concerned with ecclesiastical affairs, as evidenced by the continuous attention and emotion he devotes to this subject; the impassioned and moving tone of the numerous homilies he places in the mouths of the Armenian patriarchs bear witness to his skill as a preacher.[63] His dogmatic position set out in the great homily of St. Nersēs the Great before the emperor "Valens" (IV.v) was the rigorous Nicaean orthodoxy of the Armenian church.[64] This position necessarily dictated the open antagonism shown by him toward the Armenian crown, which sought to conform to the Arianizing policy of the successors of Constantine the Great through much of the fourth century.[65] In matters of ecclesiastical jurisdiction, he reflects the conservative aristocratic view that the patriarchate of Armenia was the hereditary office of the house of St. Gregory the Illuminator beyond any interference on the part of the king, repeatedly stressing that the descendants of St. Gregory were the legitimate holders of this office and displaying latent or open contempt or even hostility toward the non-Gregorid incumbents, for whom he often uses the term "head" or "chief" bishop (*glχawor episkopos*) rather than the customary "high-priest" or "patriarch" (*k⁽c⁾ahanayapet, hayrapet*) invariably used for the Gregorid primates. Another index of his "aristocratic" bent may also be the negative treatment of the royal official known as the *hayr-mardpet*, who is systematically depicted as the malignant opponent of the church and the magnates.[66] Finally, despite his solidarity with the Gregorid repre-

---

[60] Hereafter, the abbreviation BP (*Buzandaran Patmut⁽c⁾iwnk⁽c⁾*) will be used to designate the work formerly attributed to "P⁽c⁾awstos."

[61] Cf. Malχasyanc⁽c⁾ p. 44.

[62] See below, pp. 22–24 and n. 100.

[63] See below, p. 42, for the comparative amount of space devoted to religious matters by BP and MX.

[64] See, however, Commentary, IV.v n. 17.

[65] See above, p. 9 and n. 33; also Commentary, III.xiii n. 6; and IV.xliv n. 5.

[66] On the author's pro-Gregorid position, see III.xiii n. 25, xv n. 1; IV.iii n. 4. On his open or latent antagonism to the non-Gregorid primates, see III.xvi nn. 2, 5, xvii n. 3; IV.xv nn. 44, 46; V.xxix n. 8; VI.ii n. 3, iii n. 2. On the *hayr-mardpet*, see III.xviii; IV.xiv; V.iii, vi, and Appendix III, s.v. *mardpet*. The only favorable treatment of a *mardpet* is the episode of Drastamat, V.vii and n. 6, though neutral references to the *mardpet*'s presence can also be found, e.g., III.xvii; V.xxiv; etc.

sentatives of the northern Armenian church based on the religious center of Vałaršapat and his unquestionable adhesion to their dogmatic position, the author may have been a native of the southwestern district of Tarōn because of his unreserved devotion to the Mamikonean lords of the district and to its holy site of Aštišat, which he invariably presents as the original center of Armenian Christianity, as against the focus of the contemporary "Agatʿangełos Cycle" on the northern city of Vałaršapat.[67] This last hypothesis is not, however, passible of proof.

The Original Number of Dprutʿiwnkʿ

Troublesome as were the problems of language, date, and author of the *Epic Histories,* the question of the original text's length has presented still greater difficulties. The text as it has reached us consists of a "Preliminary Statement" followed by four "registers" (*dprutʿiwnkʿ*), numbered III (identified as the beginning), IV, V, and VI (marked the end) and divided into 21, 58 or 59, 44, and 16 chapters, respectively.[68] Each *dprutʿiwn* is preceded by its Table of Contents, and the chapters are given headings throughout the text. These headings and the Tables, the existence of which is recorded in the "Preliminary Statement," must belong to a date later than the text when this practice became common, probably in the Bagratid period,[69] and the two do not belong to the same hand because the wording of the corresponding headings almost invariably displays minor variations.[70] The obvious problems arising from the absence

[67] On the Mamikonean as lords of Tarōn, see Appendix II, s.v. "Tarōn," and III.xiv n. 11, for the author's glorification of the holy site of Aštišat (III.xiv; IV.iv) as against Aa's devotion to the northern holy city of Vałaršapat, also noted by Thomson in Aa, p. lxxvi. See also below, pp. 26, 46–47, for the author's interest in the Syrian current in Armenian Christianity especially apparent in Tarōn, and above, n. 30, for the possibility of Syriac influence on the Armenian speech of the region.

[68] Some manuscripts, though neither the Venice nor the St. Petersburg edition, unite the two chapters concerning Zuit's passion (IV.lvi–lvii) into one.

[69] The use of chapter headings does not seem to have been common before the Bagratuni period, and they seem to have been added at that time into some of the earlier sources, though not, for example, into ŁPʿ and Ełišē. The division of BP into *dprutʿiwnkʿ* and chapters must, however, be early, since they were known to ŁPʿ; see below, p. 35 and nn. 70, 74.

[70] The variations between the headings in the tables and those in the text itself do not affect their sense, but they are constant and consequently cannot be purely accidental. Of a total of 142 headings only 26 coincide verbatim, and a number of these are mere geographical indications, such as V.ix–xix, "*Yałags Noširakani*," "*Yałags Korduacʿew Kordeacʿew Tmoreacʿ*," etc. Some differences are minimal, but they are constant. Not a single heading coincides perfectly in the whole of Book IV, In general, the headings of the chapters in the text tend to be somewhat more accurate than those in the Tables, e.g., IV.viii, where the Tables refer to the Byzantine emperor improperly

of *dprut῾iwnk῾* I and II and the identification of III as "the beginning" of the text immediately led to a fundamental disagreement among scholars, who argued that either the missing *dprut῾iwnk῾* had once existed and been lost, leaving a mutilated text, or that they never existed at all, so that the original text has come down to us in its entirety. To date, a series of internal contradictions has impeded all attempts to find a solution to this difficulty.

Supporting the hypothesis of the integral survival of the text, the "Preliminary Statement" unequivocally identifies the first *dprut῾iwn* of the existing text as "Book III," but then goes on to assert with redundant clarity, "and [in addition] to it [there are] three [more] books. That is to say, there are altogether four books."[71] To drive home the fact that these four "books" indeed comprised the totality of the work, the heading *I skizbn* "beginning" was placed before Book III and *verĵ* "ending" at the end of the Table of Contents of Book VI, as was noted above.[72] These categorical statements did nothing, however, to explain why the work should "begin" with Book III.

A possible clarification was provided by the *History of Armenia* of Łazar P῾arpec῾i, who seems to have known the *Epic Histories* in the form in which they survive, for he mentions no earlier portion, and the division that he marks between them and the earlier work he identifies as that of Agat῾angełos—namely, the end of St. Gregory's mission—corresponds to the beginning of the present Book III.[73] Furthermore, in a separate allusion to St. Nersēs's curse of King Aršak II for the murder of his nephew Gnel, an episode found in Book IV, chapter xv of the present text of the *Epic Histories,* Łazar P῾arpec῾i locates it in "the fifteenth section of the second narrative."[74] On the basis of this evidence, and refuting Abełyan's tentative objections, Malχasyanc῾ came to the conclusion that in Łazar P῾arpec῾i's time, that is to say almost immediately after the original compilation of the *Epic Histories,* Book III had been known as Book I and that the books had been renumbered thereafter. As a consequence of this conclusion, the "Preliminary Statement" could not be taken as the

---

as *t῾agawor* "king" instead of the correct contemporary usage, *kaysr* "emperor." Consequently, the Tables are probably the work of the later second editor (see p. 35), though errors can also be found in the headings in the text, which would presumably be the work of the first editor.

[71] Preliminary Statement (p. 13 of the Venice 1933 ed.), "*Ays inč῾ ē i dprut῾iwns errord` . . . ew ar̄ nmin dprut῾iwnk῾ erek῾, ays ink῾n en sok῾a č῾ork῾ mateank῾.*"

[72] See p. 16. Cf. Malχasyanc῾ trans, pp. 19–20.

[73] ŁP῾ I.ii, pp. 2–3 (= CHAMA II, pp. 259–260).

[74] "*i patmut῾ean erkrordumn i čar̄in hngetasanerordi,*" ŁP῾ I.xv, p. 25 (= CHAMA II, p. 272 and n. 2), where the translator has inexplicably substitutes "thirteen" for "fifteen," though no such variant is indicated in the critical apparatus of the 1904 edition, p. 25.

work of the original author, but necessarily became an addition composed by a later editor.[75]

As an explanation for the renumbering of the books, Malχasyancʿ suggested that the *Epic Histories* had been included in a collection of texts such as were common in medieval Armenia and of which the so-called "Agatʿangełos Cycle" is the most familiar.[76] In such a collection the separate components would have been viewed as the successive *dprutʿiwnkʿ* of a single unit. In such a case, the present text might well have been preceded by the *Vitae* of Sts. Thaddeus and Gregory, which would have formed the first two *dprutʿiwnkʿ*, leaving III–VI for the *Epic Histories* themselves, which might in turn have been followed by other works.[77]

The main objection to this analysis derives from the opening chapter of the present text (III.i). In it, the author readily conceded that the period from the early preaching of St. Thaddeus to the completion of the mission of St. Gregory the Illuminator "has been written by others,"[78] but he then went on to add, "But we too have set something [of this] down here in the order of our narrative, nor, passing it over, did we omit it, so as to conform to the sequence of events. For there is in our narrative something of what came first and something of what came last, but what came in between, that has been written by others."[79] From this confused explanation it would appear that the original text had contained material, now lost, dealing with an earlier period of Armenian history than the one covered in the present text, and that two *dprutʿiwnkʿ* had therefore preceded the now initial third. For Matatʿean, this hypothesis found further external support in the statement of Procopius that, "at one time, one of the kings of the Parthians appointed his brother, Arsaces by name, king of the Armenians as the history of the Armenians declares."[80] Because

[75] Malχasyancʿ pp. 19–21 and notes, refuting the objections of Abełyan, *Grakanutʿiwn*, pp. 644–647. This is probably the second rather than the first editor, see below, p. 35.

[76] See e.g. Garsoïan, "Substratum," p. 151 and n. 6.

[77] Malχasyancʿ, pp. 20–21. On the basis of a single manuscript (Mat. #3079) which gives both *dprutʿiwn* III and *dprutʿiwn* IV as *dprutʿiwn* III, V. Aṙakʿelyan argues that every *dprutʿiwnkʿ* (or rather χostabanutʿiwn) was headed *skizbn*, "beginning" and that the entire work was Book III of a larger collection. See also V. Gevorgyan, *Pʿawstos Byuzand*, p. 8. This thesis resting on a single case which may easily be a *lapsus* seems insufficiently supported to be convincing.

[78] III.i, "*I kʿarozutenēn Tʿadēosi Aṙakeloy . . . minčʿew i katarumn vardapetutʿeann Grigori ew iwroy hangsteann . . . ayn amenayn i jeṙn aylocʿn grecʿan.*"

[79] III.i, "*Baycʿ ew mekʿ i merum ast edakʿ pʿokʿr i šatē i kargi patmutʿeans, očʿ zancʿ arareal tʿołakʿ vasn patšač iracʿ kargin. Vasn zi ē inčʿ mer patmutʿiwn` or aṙajin ē, ew ē inčʿ or verjin ē; isk or mijin inčʿ ełew, ayn i jeṙn ayocʿ grel grecʿaw.*"

[80] Procopius, *De aed.* III.i.6, "καὶ ποτέ τις τῶν ἐν Πάρθοις βασιλέων τὸν ἀδελφὸν τὸν αὐτοῦ Ἀρμενίοις βασιλέα καταστέσατο, Ἀρσάκην ὄνομα ὥσπερ ἡ τῶν Ἀρμενίων ἱστορία φησί." See above, n. 19.

this information does not occur in the existing text of the *Epic Histories* it must have come from one of its lost portions.[81]

The fundamental contradiction between the evidence of the "Preliminary Statement" and that of the initial chapter of Book III has continued to be reflected in the scholarship. For those who, like Malχasyancᶜ, tended to believe that the original text had survived intact and the renumbering of the *dprutᶜiwnkᶜ* derived from its inclusion in a collection of other works, the task has been to identify the texts grouped together with the *Epic Histories* and forming the first two *dprutᶜiwnkᶜ* of this collection. Langlois was of the opinion that "Pᶜawstos's History of Armenia" was the author's third work, the first two having been devoted to the histories of other nations.[82] For N. Ia. Marr, the first two *dprutᶜiwnkᶜ* contained the anonymous *Primary History* of Armenia subsequently attached to the *History* attributed to Bishop Sebēos.[83] For Norayr Biwzandacᶜi, the histories of several Byzantine authors had been gathered together and a "foreign hand" had then selected only Books III–VI from among them.[84] Adontz also linked the first portion of the *Epic Histories* with the *Primary History,* postulating that the original Greek text of the work had consisted of six books, of which the first two contained the *History* of Mar-Abas of Mcurn and the preaching of St. Thaddeus, but that these were dropped by the translator, who rendered only Books III–VI into Armenian.[85] In opposition to these theses of an integral text inserted into a collection, A. Matikean, Abełyan, and more recently G. V. Abgaryan, as well as A. A. Hakobyan have argued for an original work composed of six books, the first two of which are now lost.[86]

[81] EM, *Pᶜawstos*, pp. 25–26. See also below, n. 86. For Hakobyan, "Favst," pp. 74–81, the parallels between "Pᶜawstos" and the "Tale of Vačagan" (see above n. 12) also support the existence of the two lost *dprutᶜiwnkᶜ,* but the passages in the "Tale" may equally have been derived from a lost version of the "Agatᶜangełos Cycle," possibly the lost archtype of the so-called V Cycle, or from some oral account of the Christianization of Armenia and the rest of Transcaucasia.

[82] Langlois, in CHAMA I, pp. 205–206.

[83] Marr, "O nachal'noĭ istorii;" cf. Malχasyancᶜ p. 24, n. 1.

[84] Norayr Biwzandacᶜi, "Pᶜawstos"; see Malχasyancᶜ, p. 12.

[85] Adontz, "Nachal'naia istoriia"; cf. Matikean, *Ananunə*, who argued that fragments of *dprutᶜiwnkᶜ* I and II had survived in the *Primary History* linked to that of Sebēos, as does Abgaryan, "Mamikonyanneri zruycᶜi ałbyurə," pp. 254–268, who argues, however, that they had reached Sebēos by way of the lost eleventh-century history of John of Tarōn. See also Zarpᶜanalean, *Patmutᶜiwn*, pp. 251–252, who hesitates among the *Vitae* of Thaddeus and Gregory, Labubna, Agatᶜangełos, and even pseudo-Yovhannēs Mamikonean; Tašean, *Aršakuni dramner*, p. 163; Abgaryan, *Sebēosi Patmutᶜyunə*, p. 12; Neuman, *Geschichte*, pp. 25–27, who suggested Agatᶜangełos for I and II.

[86] Abełyan, *Grakanutᶜyun*, pp. 644–647; Abgaryan, *Sebēosi Patumtᶜyunə*, pp. 100–107; *idem.* "Mamikonyanneri zruycᶜi ałbyurə," pp. 253–268, who distinguished

In view of the contradictory evidence with which we are faced and the considerable ingenuity already expended by scholars to resolve this problem, a definitive solution is probably impossible in the absence of any new information, as Malχasyancᶜ was the first to admit. Nevertheless, his thesis of the integrity of the surviving text and of its subsequent inclusion into a collection fits the compilatory nature of the work itself and seems more plausible than the hypothesis of lost books, for which we have little tangible evidence and which fails to account for the fact that Łazar Pᶜarpecᶜi, writing within a generation of the composition of the *Epic Histories,* already knew the work in the form in which we now possess it.[87] Under these circumstances one more consideration of the scant evidence may perhaps be acceptable.

The only external evidence for the existence of the "lost books"—the already-cited passage of Procopius on the appointment of a king of Armenia by his brother the Parthian ruler—is remarkably inconclusive. As was noted earlier, the general character of the material drawn from the "History of Armenia" claimed by Procopius as a source did not identify it directly with the *Epic Histories.*[88] In the present case also, the information given by the Byzantine historian is imprecise and could easily go back to the common fund of Armenian history current in the sixth century. The story of the brother kings was known to the author of the *Primary History* as well as to Movsēs Xorenacᶜi,[89] and for that matter at a very much earlier date to the third-century Roman historian Cassius Dio.[90] It was, in consequence, readily available to Procopius without any need to resort to the *Epic Histories.*

Given the inconclusive nature of the external evidence, we must turn once again to the puzzling opening chapter of the work, the confusing nature of which had already been noted by Malχasyancᶜ and several other scholars, who had suggested the possibility of corruption in the text even though no satisfactory rectification could be offered.[91] As it stands, the text of III.i is clearly contradictory. It claims simultaneously that, 1) the period before the mission of St. Gregory had been "written by others. . . . But we too have set something [of this] down here . . . to conform to the sequence of events," and that, 2) "there is in our narrative

the longer *Buzandaran* from the four books of "Pᶜawstos" contained in it. Hakobyan, "Favst," pp. 80–81 who gives slightly different categories of scholarly opinions.

[87] But see below, pp. 36–37, for the problematic Book VI.

[88] See above, pp. 10, 18–19. The link between Procopius's information and the "lost" *dprutⁱwnkᶜ* is maintained by Abgaryan, "Mamikonyanneri zruycᶜi ałbyurə," pp. 252–254, 265–268; cf. Manandyan, "Nachal'naia istoriia," esp. p. 77.

[89] *Primary History,* ii, p. 54 (= MK, p. 366). MX, II.iii (= MK, p. 132).

[90] CD, LXII.v.2.

[91] Malχasyancᶜ p. 23 and nn. 1–2. For a conclusion similar to mine but on a different basis, see Feydit, "Histoire."

something of what came first and something of what came last, but what came in between that has been written by others," yet, "lest a gap appear in the midst of our narrative, we have noted [it] as a brick is set in the wall of a structure for the completion of the whole."[92] Malχasyanc[c] despaired of making sense out of this confusion, but the answer may perhaps lie in one of the most common scribal errors, which has garbled the sense of the text: the automatic repetition of a passage occurring a little earlier. Thus, the phrase ". . . that has been written by others. But . . ." (*ayn i jeṙn ayloc[c] grel grec[c]aw. Bayc[c]*), referring to the earlier history of Armenia, was repeated triggered by the word "that" (*ayn*) and continued to the *Bayc[c]* opening the next sentence, where the copyist returned to the proper place in his text. If we excise the parasitic repetition, the sense of the entire passage becomes suddenly clear: the period from the coming of St. Thaddeus through the mission of St. Gregory had been written by others, but it was alluded to in order to maintain the continuity of the narrative, and a similar link was provided at the end; but the actual focus of the work itself was on "what came in between, lest a gap appear in the midst of our narrative: we have noted [it], as a brick is set in the wall of a structure for the completion of the whole." Hence, the work seemed to be conceived as providing a chronological link between two already extant accounts.

If we now set this corrected text against the few known Armenian works of the fifth century to which it might have been joined to form a coherent collection and with which the author was admittedly acquainted on internal evidence, the picture becomes even clearer. The existing accounts of the evangelization of Armenia by St. Thaddeus and St. Gregory the Illuminator (namely, the Armenian version of the *Acts of Thaddeus* or Addai and a version of the *Vita* of St. Gregory, though perhaps not the recension of "Agat[c]angełos" that we possess), both known to the author of the *Epic Histories,* who refers to them in the body of the text, had indeed been "written by others" and focused on the period preceding the one covered by him, as Malχasyanc[c] had already noted.[93] But "something of

---

[92] See above, nn. 78–79, for the first part of this quotation, the text of which then continues: "*Bayc[c] zi mi i miǰi meroy patmut[c]eans əndhat erewesc[c]i hun mi, nšanakec[c]ak[c]; zor ōrinak ałiws mi kargac i mēǰ ormoyn šinuacoy i katarumn bovandakut[c]ean.*"

[93] For the translation of the *Doctrine of Addai* and its adaptation in Armenia, see Anasyan, *Matenagitut[c]yun,* I, cols. 255–258; Zarp[c]analean, *Matenadaran,* pp. 13–17; Akinean, *Dasakan hayerēn,* p. 48; van Esbroeck, "Le Roi Sanatrouk," pp. 266–269; Mescherskaia, "Apotrpeichiskie teksty"; *idem,* "Legenda." Despite the reservations of Menewišean, "Abgar," p. 174 and Kogean, *Hayoc[c] ekełec[c]in,* p. 31, who treats the references to St. Thaddeus in BP as interpolations, van Esbroeck, "Le Roi Sanatrouk," pp. 269–272 shows that some at least are part of the text. Malχasyanc[c] pp. 35, 37, dates the *Vkayabanut[c]iwn* of Thaddeus to 465–470. See pp. 11, 25–26 and n. 43 for Agat[c]angełos.

what came first"—namely, the linking chapter (III.ii) describing the burial of St. Gregory and of his successor St. Aristakēs, neither of which is recorded by "Agatʿangełos"[94]—was still required for the chronological continuity of Armenian events. Similarly at the end, "something of what came last"—the description of the partition of the Armenian kingdom ca. 387 (VI.i)[95]—might well have served as a bridge to the other main source of the fifth century known to the *Epic Histories,* Koriwn's account of Mesrop Maštocʿ's creation of the Armenian alphabet in the reign of King Vramšapuh (387/8–413/4), almost immediately following upon the division of the realm. The grouping of the four named sources into a single collection would come entirely naturally, as such a compilation would provide a continuous account of the Christianization of Armenia from its first reception of the faith to its final rooting in the land through the creation of its alphabet, with the resultant translation of the Scriptures and the formation of the native liturgy in the first half of the fifth century. Thus, the proposed correction would resolve the problem of the enigmatic opening chapter of the *Epic Histories* and might put an end to the controversy over the original number of *dprutʿiwnkʿ.* Moreover, it would insert the *Epic Histories* at the logical point in the existing fifth-century accounts of the Christianization of Armenia. Attractive as this solution may be, however, it cannot be demonstrated without the proposed emendation of the surviving text, and its unsatisfactory and very late manuscript history all but precludes the possibility of further evidence.

The Sources

In sharp distinction to the author of the parallel *History of Armenia,* Movsēs Xorenacʿi, the anonymous compiler of the *Epic Histories* was in no sense a learned man. At no point in his work does he cite specific sources, nor does he refer to a written text except in the troublesome first chapter of his work. As we shall see, much of his information could readily have been obtained by word of mouth, and even most of the quotations traced in his text may well derive from oral transmission instead of depending on written authority.

As might be expected, the main identifiable written source for most of the quotations found in the *Epic Histories* is the Armenian version of the Bible translated in the first half of the fifth century, which the author

[94] Aa, dccclviii, mentions St. Gregory's death but not his burial, though they are mentioned in Vk, xxi and xxii, nor the death and burial of his son and immediate successor St. Aristakēs. Cf. Peeters, "Calendrier," pp. 99–100; Akinean, *Grigor*; van Esbroeck, "*Témoignages littéraires,*" pp. 387–398, etc.

[95] See below pp. 36–37 on the problematic Book VI.

22

follows wherever it varies from the Septuagint.[96] Even in the case of Scriptural quotations, however, it soon becomes evident that the author is citing from memory and by ear rather than referring directly to a written text. Again and again, the citations show slight variations from the Scriptural text—an altered word, a syntactical transformation, an interpolation or omission, a transposed phrase—none of which, however, alters the sense of the passage.[97] Throughout, the author adapts these quotations to his purpose with the ease and fluency of an ecclesiastic thoroughly familiar with the Biblical text and accustomed to preaching. Tags with Biblical overtones, such as hosts numerous "as the sands of the seashore" or "the stars in the heavens" run like refrains through the narrative.[98] The author's ecclesiastical rather than scholarly background is particularly evident in two extensive quotations. One—repeating the doxology of the three Hebrew youths in the fiery furnace in the Book of Daniel (V.iv)—is taken from the liturgy of the *Book of Hours* (*Žamagirkᶜ*), which it follows verbatim, and not from the slightly different version of the Scriptural text.[99] The other—consisting of two passages from the Armenian version

[96] See Norayr Biwzandacᶜi, *Koriwn* and Malχasyancᶜ, p. 33. Almost the entire network of Biblical quotations and allusions in BP was traced by my student Roberta Ervine, to whom I am most beholden for her meticulous and most valuable work, which is soon to be published.

[97] See, among many others, the following examples (cf. Commentary III.xiii n. 14):

Amos 5:10	III.xiii
"Atēcᶜin i druns zyandimaničᶜs, ew zbans surbs piłcs ararin"	*"Atēin i druns zyandimaničᶜs ew zbans surb arhamarhēin"*

(cf. Commentary, III.xiii n. 17):

Ezekiel 2:3-4	III.xiii
"orkᶜ daŕnacᶜucᶜin zis, inkeᶜeankᶜ ew harkᶜ iwreancᶜ. . . . Ordikᶜ ełjerikkᶜ ew χstasirtkᶜ en aŕ ors aŕakemn zkᶜez."	*"Ordikᶜ ełjerikkᶜ, χstasirtkᶜ, χstašunčᶜkᶜ, oykᶜ daŕnacᶜucᶜin zis nokᶜa ew harkᶜ iwreancᶜ"*
Luke 11:29, etc.	IV.vi
"Azg aysˋ azg čᶜar ē, nšan χndrē."	*"Azg čᶜar, nšan χndrē."*

(cf. Commentary IV.iv n. 34):

Galat. 2:7,9-10	IV.iv
"ibrew tesin etᶜē hawataceal ē inj Awetarann antᶜlpᶜatutᶜeann . . . ibrew gitacᶜin zšnorhsn or tueal ēin inj, Yakobos ew Kepᶜas ew Yohannēs, or karceal siwnkᶜn ēin, jeŕn etun hawanutᶜean inj ew Baŕnabay, zi mekᶜ i hetᶜanoss, ew nokᶜa i tᶜlpᶜatutᶜeann . . ."	*"ibrew tesin zšnorhsn, or dueal ēin inj Yakobos ew Kepᶜas ew Yovhannēsˋ or bun siwnkn ēin, ibrew tesin tᶜē hawatarim em es yawetarann antᶜlpᶜatutᶜean, . . . jeŕn etun hawanutᶜean inj ew Baŕnabay, zi mekᶜ i hetᶜanoss, ew nokᶜa i tᶜlpᶜatutᶜiwnn,"*

[98] See Appendix V, b, i.

[99] See Commentary, V.iv n. 27.

23

of the *Liturgy of St. Basil* and indeed following the early version of the *Basilian Anaphora,* to which it is a valuable early witness—is incorporated at the proper liturgical point in the prayer that is part of the hagiographic chapter that relates the miracle at Mambrē (V.xxviii). In general, the theology of the *Epic Histories* is consonant with the relevant portions of the liturgy and with contemporary doctrinal treatises.[100]

Two other contemporary sources evidently familiar to the author of the *Epic Histories* were the already mentioned "received" tradition of the illumination of Armenia by St. Gregory, and the account of the Armenian alphabet's creation by St. Maštocʿ. The references to Koriwn's *Life of Maštocʿ* have long been observed by scholars, and attempts have even been made to identify Koriwn as either the translator of the *Epic Histories* into Armenian, or, more recently, as their author, though neither thesis has gained general acceptance.[101] Several passages from Koriwn have also been traced in the *Epic Histories.* The main ones are found in III.x, where the comparison of St. James of Nisibis's miraculous reception of the wood of the Ark to the descent from Sinai with the Tables of the Law seems to be taken from the description of Maštocʿ's triumphant return to Armenia, and the end of IV.iv, where the Biblical quotations in the admonitions of St. Nersēs follow the same order as those found at the end of the prefatory section of Koriwn.[102] Even so, the example of Moses

---

[100] See V.xxviii n. 7. The fact that this prayer contains both brief references (given, however, in their proper sequence) and more extensive citations from the underlying liturgical text points once more to an oral rather than textual transmission. The insertion of the Anaphora at its proper place in the canon of the Mass in the scene of the miracle related in V.xxviii is additional evidence of the compiler's familiarity with liturgical practices. In general, the liturgical formulation often lies behind the doctrinal passages of the *Epic Histories*; this is particularly noticeable in the long homily of St. Nersēs (IV.v) and in the prayer of the celebrant at Mambrē (V.xxviii), but this pattern can also be found in III.xiv; V.iv; and elsewhere. The doctrinal position of BP normally coincides with that of contemporary Armenian catechetical works such as the *Teaching of St. Gregory,* with which it displays a number of parallels (see IV.v, but cf. n. 17).

[101] See Norayr Biwzandacʿi, *Koriwn,* who gave an extensive comparison of the language of the *Epic Histories,* Aa, the Books of Maccabees, and Koriwn to support his thesis that the latter was the translator of both BP and Aa into Armenian. This work has unfortunately not been available to me, but most of its conclusions are to be found in Malχasyancʿ's "Introduction." More recently, Archbishop Norayr Połarean/ Bogharian/Covakan has argued, also on the basis of stylistic and lexical similarities, that Koriwn was the author of both of these works. See "Koriwn"; also Akinean, *Koriwn,* pp. 118–119.

[102] See Koriwn, pp. 50, 52, for the quotations in III.x, and pp. 32–34 for those in IV.iv. See also Malχasyancʿ, p. 33 n. 1 for the objection to the reverse thesis that Koriwn had used BP at this point, and p. 34 for an additional reference. For the order

within the heavily Mosaic context of III.x is so obvious that it may well have been a *topos*. Moreover, all the citations in this passage show the same variations from the original as those already observed in Scriptural ones, suggesting oral transmission here too.[103]

Even better known are the parallels between the *Epic Histories* and the "Agatᶜangełos Cycle."[104] These have been collected by Małxasyancᶜ, who effectively rejected the hypothesis that the information in the *Epic*

---

of Biblical citations, cf. Koriwn, ii, pp. 32 lines 16–34, line 11 with IV.iv nn. 37–46. After an allusion to Titus 2:14 or 3:8, the order of the Biblical quotations in Koriwn is: 1 Cor. 14:1, 2 Cor. 9:2 (alluded to but not quoted), Galat. 4:18, Hebr. 12:2, 13:7, Phil. 2:5, James 5:10–11. The only variations in this order in BP IV.iv are the brief interpolation of 1 Thess. 5:12 into the second quotation from Hebrews, and the quotation of the ubiquitous Acts 1:1 (referred to but not quoted by Koriwn, p. 34, lines 6–7) between Philippians and James. See also the next note.

[103] The closest parallel to Koriwn in III.x is to be found in the central quotation referring directly to Moses, which is also the longest (BP p. 34 lines 5–19 of the text, "*Ew očᶜ aynpēs mecn Movsēs . . . zčanaparhacᶜ awetaberacᶜ*, = Koriwn [ix], p. 52, lines 1–12). Even here, although the incipit and explicit are identical, internal differences, such as *čᶜasēakᶜ* for *čᶜasemkᶜ*, or *novin* for *znorin*, and "*zyōžarutᶜiwn yusov ditaworutᶜiwn*" for "*yōžarutᶜiwnn ew ənduneleacᶜn yusov uraχutᶜeanʼ dasaworutᶜiwn*" (or *dataworutᶜiwn*), do not seem altogether explicable in terms of variants or scribal errors. The differences are greater in the two shorter quotations on either side:

BP, p. 34 lines 3–5	Koriwn, p. 50 lines 17–19
"*Ew aṙeal daṙnayr anti, handerj šnorhatur pargewelovn ew orkᶜ ənd nmayn ertᶜealkᶜ iwrovkᶜn čanaparhord linēr.*"	"*ew aṙeal tᶜułtᶜs awetagirs, handerj šnorhatur pargewōkᶜn ew amenayn iwrayiwkᶜn, i šnorhacᶜn Astucoy čanaparhord linēr.*"
BP, p. 34 lines 19–21	Koriwn, p. 52 lines 16–19
"*Kᶜanzi yaytneōkᶜ ew cackelovkᶜ, kᶜanzi mioyn miayn yamenazorēn aṙ amenayn azgs erkracnacᶜ šnorhkᶜn matakararēin.*"	"*kᶜanzi ew čᶜkay inčᶜ i veray yaytneōkᶜ ew cackakanōkᶜ (or cackanōkᶜ) zastuacakann χotel, kᶜanzi mioyn Astucoy amenazōri šnorhkᶜ aṙ amenayn azgs erkracnacᶜ matakararin.*"

Moreover, although these three passages form a continuous unit in BP, that is not the case in Koriwn where they are plucked out of their immediate context. In the case of the parallel passages in the admonition of St. Nersēs (BP, p. 88 lines 17–37 = Koriwn p. 32:16–34:11, where the parallel occurs in the general preface and in no way relates to St. Nersēs), the presence of the closely woven pattern of almost the same Scriptural quotations reinforces the parallel. Even so, the two passages are not identical. Tenses or forms of verbs—*linēr* for *linel*, *hayecᶜarukᶜ* for *hayecᶜeal*, *lerukᶜ* for *ełerukᶜ*—vary; numbers—*oroy* for *orocᶜ*—and phrases—*zbann kenacᶜ* for *bann Astucᶜoy*—differ, even within Scriptural quotations, where the two works alternate in their closeness to the Armenian Biblical text. Finally, neither the interpolation of 1 Thess. 5:12 nor the quotation of Acts 1:1 included in BP can be found in Koriwn (see also the preceding note).

[104] See, e.g., Norayr Biwzandacᶜi, *Koriwn*; Tašean, *Agatᶜangełos*, pp. 84, 108, 111, 129, 137, 139, 145, 151–155; Sargisean, *Agatᶜangełos*; etc.; also next note.

Histories might have been drawn from some earlier, Greek version of the Gregorid Cycle by pointing out a series of verbal parallels to the Armenian.[105] Despite these similarities with the version of the "Agatᶜangełos Cycle" [Aa] that has come down to us, however, Thomson has shown dissimilarities between the two works that make a direct relationship unlikely. Whereas the author of the *Epic Histories* repeatedly stresses the role of St. Thaddeus and the importance of the southern ecclesiastical center of Aštišat of Tarōn, both are ignored by our version of "Agatᶜangełos," which focuses exclusively on the activities of St. Gregory and on the divinely designated northern city of Vałaršapat.[106] The *Epic Histories,* moreover, display no knowledge of a series of details in the life of St. Gregory that are included in the extant "Agatᶜangełos." Consequently, it is possible that the author of the *Epic Histories* was acquainted with a different—perhaps less complete and possibly oral—though evidently Armenian version of the Gregorid Cycle, than the one we possess.[107] He may also have been acquainted with the section known as the "Teaching of Saint Gregory" (*Vardapetutᶜiwn*), which was probably part of the "Agatᶜangełos Cycle" in the fifth century, since it is part of the Armenian version that has come down to us, but is missing from all other surviving versions.[108]

We have already seen in the preceding section that an Armenian version of the *Acts of St. Thaddeus* was already in existence in the fifth century,[109] and irrespective of the problems presented by the first allusion to it in the opening chapter of the *Epic Histories* (III.i), there is no reason to treat all the references to St. Thaddeus in the text as interpolations.[110] These *Acts* are by no means, however, the only hagiographic source traceable in the *Epic Histories,* which are replete with such material. From the beginning to the end, entire episodes from the lives of Armenian, Syrian,

[105] Malχasyancᶜ, *Usumnasirutᶜiwn*, p. 82, and *idem*, "Introduction" (1968 edition), pp. 34–35. These similarities were also noted by earlier scholars; also see above, n. 30.

[106] Thomson, Aa, pp. lxxv–lxxvii. Although Aa, dcccxiv–dcccxv concedes that St. Gregory "first made a beginning of building churches" at "the place of the temples" (Aštišat, which he names only once in dcccix), the focus of his attention remains fixed on Vałaršapat with its divinely designated shrines, dccxxxi–dcclxxvi. See above, n. 67.

[107] Thomson, Aa, pp. lxxvi–lxxvii, but BP III.ii knows details of the burial of St. Gregory and particularly its site, not mentioned by Aa (see p. 22 and n. 94). It is tempting to identify the version of the Gregorid cycle known to BP with the lost Armenian archetype of the *V* cycle, but that is mere wishful thinking.

[108] Thomson, AaT, pp. 2–4, cf. III.i, "*minčᶜew katarumn vardapetutᶜeann Grigori,*" but *vardapetutᶜiwn* may be taken here in its general sense of "mission."

[109] See above, p. 21 and n. 93.

[110] III.i, xii, xiv; IV.iii–iv. See above, n. 93.

and Greek saints—Yusik and his brother Grigoris, James of Nisibis, Daniēl the Syrian, Nersēs the Great, Basil of Caesarea, Thekla, Sergios of Resapha, Theodore of Euchaïta, the Persian martyrs of the fourth century, Zuit^c of Artašat, Hamazaspuhi Mamikonean, Šałitay, Epip^{c}an, and Gind—intrude into the narrative, interrupting its sequence;[111] and hagiographic *topoi* abound.[112] Many of these figures are well known, but the source of the *Epic Histories*'s information is less clear.

Peeters suggested a borrowing from a "Life of St. Grigoris" because of the pious clichés found in the corresponding chapter (III.vi), but such a work is not attested.[113] Neither the account of the life of St. James of Nisibis (III.x) nor those of St. Thekla (IV.x) and St. Šałitay (V.xxv–xxvi) or concerning the Persian martyr Mari (IV.xvi–xvii) follow exactly the texts that have survived,[114] though there is no doubt that St. James was held in such esteem in early Christian Armenia that the works of Aphraat were mistakenly attributed to him, or that a version of the *Acts of Paul and Thekla* was also available in Armenian.[115] Seeking further sources for the various hagiographic intrusions, Y. Gat^{c}rčean, N. Akinean, and H. H. Melk^{c}onyan have suggested unspecified *Vitae patrum,*[116] a *Vita* of St. Erasimos (Gerasimos),[117] and the Armenian version of the *Vita* of Mār Augēn[118] as sources for the life of St. James of Nisibis, the miracu-

---

[111] See III.v–vi, x, xii–xiv; IV.iii–iv, vi–x, xvi–xvii, lvi–lvii, lix; V.xxv–xxviii; VI.xvi. The rapid travel of the accounts of Persian martyrs to the West is evidenced by the presence of their Greek *Acts*, see Delehaye, *Versions*.

[112] See III.iii and n. 13 for the evildoers restrained by invisible bonds; III.v and n. 9; IV.viii, x for angelic and other supernatural visions; IV.iv and nn. 7, 9, and vii for the descent of the Holy Spirit in the form of a dove; III.xiv and n. 14 for the various miracles performed by St. Daniēl; IV.vi and n. 12 for the miraculous food provided by St. Nersēs on the desert island; V.xxv for the vision of angels carrying St. Nersēs's soul to heaven; V.xxvi and n. 3 for Šałitay's healing of the lion with the wounded paw, and n. 5 for the disappearance of his body; V.xxviii for the miraculous vision of the real presence in the Eucharist at Mambrē, to mention only the main episodes.

[113] See Commentary, III.vi n. 1.

[114] See Commentary, III.x nn. 1, 10, 20 for James of Nisibis and the statement that the account in BP was perhaps taken from a homily; IV.x nn. 1, 5–7 for Thekla, where there are close parallels to her fifth-century Greek *Vita*, but there is no reference to Thekla's association with St. Paul, her two miraculous rescues from martyrdom, or even her own miracles. See also IV.xvi and nn. 7, 13 and xvii n. 2, for Mari and the *Acts* of the Persian martyrs; V.xxv n. 1 and xxvi nn. 3–5, for Šałitay; also Appendix I, "Epip^{c}an," "Mari," "Šałitay," "T^{c}ekł," and "Yakob."

[115] See Commentary III.x n. 2, for James and Aphraat, also below, n. 119, the preceding note, and Appendix I, "Tekł," "Yakob."

[116] Gat^{c}rčean and Tašean, eds., *Srbazan patarag*, p. 94. See also below, n. 119.

[117] Akinean, "P^{c}awstos," cols. 97–102.

[118] Melkonyan, "Armianskiĭ perevod"; *idem, Haraberut^{c}yunner*, pp. 72ff.

lous vision at Mambrē (V.xxviii) and the favorite tale of the anchorite healing and taming the wounded lion by removing the splinter lodged in its paw, attributed by the *Epic Histories* to the *Acts* of St. Šaḷitay (V.xxvi). None of these hypotheses has, however, proved satisfactory. Gatᶜrčean never went on to identify his presumed source with any accuracy.[119] The *Vita* of Mār Augēn surviving in Armenia in a thirteenth-century manuscript has long since been identified as a later forgery probably dating from the tenth century and as such useless for a fifth-century text.[120] Similarly, the *Vita* of St. Erasimos attributed by Akinean to the fifth century, though the manuscript that he cites dates from 1403, must also be rejected. The parallel passage in the *Epic Histories* (V.xxvi) shows variations from the version in the *Vita,* in which the Armenian, moreover, shows traces of the later Hellenizing School. Gerasimos himself, a familiar figure in early hagiography, is reputed to have died in 475, too late for any *Life* dedicated to him to have influenced the *Epic Histories.* And, most important of all, the *Vita* cited by Akinean is identical with the account of St. Gerasimos's miracles in John Moschus's *Pratum Spirituale* dating from the turn of the seventh century.[121] The failure to find antecedents for the hagiographic episodes in the *Epic Histories* makes them all the more interesting, in that they may provide the earliest attestations to date of tales soon to become familiar to the entire Christian community: the story of the lion with the wounded paw healed by the anchorite Šaḷitay was attributed in the mid-sixth century to St. Sabas by Cyril of Skythopolis,[122] then to St. Gerasimos, before becoming the sole possession of St. Jerome;[123] the miraculous flight of the snakes from the island on which St. Epipᶜan had landed (V.xxvii) would reproduce itself far to the west for St. Honoratus at Lérins and St. Patrick in Ireland.[124]

Most enigmatic of all the hagiographic material is the information pertaining to St. Basil the Great and its contamination of the life of St. Nersēs, who is substituted for the bishop of Caesarea in the episode of the

---

[119] See above, n. 115. To be sure, *Apothegmata patrum* soon made their way into Armenian (see *Varkᶜ harancᶜ* and Leloir, *Paterica armeniaca*); and much of the Armenian translation of the *Apocryphal Acts*, though not those of Thekla, dates from the fifth century: see Ter Petrosyan, *Abraham Xostovanoḷ*, pp. 50–73, 155–162 *et passim*; but none of them serve here.

[120] See Commentary, III.x n. 1; also Labourt, *Christianisme*, pp. 300–315, especially, 308–311; Vööbus, *Asceticism*, I, p. 139.

[121] John Moschus, *Pratum* §107, pp.84–87; also Commentary, V.xxvi n. 3 and next two notes.

[122] Cyril of Skythopolis, *Vie de S. Sabas*, xlix, pp. 65ff.; also Commentary, V.xxvi n. 3 and next note.

[123] Rice, *Jerome*, pp. 37–45; also Commentary, V.xxvi n. 3.

[124] See Commmentary, V.xxvii n. 8.

saint's refusal to heal the emperor's dying son because of his father's heretical beliefs (IV.v).[125] The consecrations of both are marked by identical miraculous descents of the Holy Spirit (IV.iii, ix). These Basilian intrusions, intended to stress the close relations between the two saints, unattested by external evidence,[126] play havoc with the chronology of the *Epic Histories,* because some of the episodes from the life of St. Basil are attributed to the elder St. Nersēs, while in others St. Basil appears in person in his proper chronological context, namely the reign of Emperor Valens (364–378), a period anachronistic for a number of events in the life of St. Nersēs, such as his banishment in 359.[127] These multiple confusions, as well as some inaccuracies in the events of St. Basil's life,[128] suggest that the source of the *Epic Histories* was not so much Gregory Nazianzenos's *Panegyric on St. Basil,* although it contains much of this material and may have been available at the time, but rather a hagiographic source.[129] The tale of the emperor's sick child was to be repeated by all the Greek ecclesiastical historians and must consequently have been part of a common Basilian fund known far and wide.[130] Similarly, the sufferings of St. Nersēs and his companions on the island to which they had been banished (IV.vi) match the tribulations of orthodox confessors in times of Arian persecution, which were also part of the contemporary pious stock-in-trade.[131]

In short, then, given the numerous variations from extant texts and the absence of identifiable antecedents for a number of the episodes, precise sources for the hagiographic material in the *Epic Histories* cannot be given at present. It may very possibly be derived from some prototype of the *Synaxarion* (*Haysmawurk^c*) or a *Lectionary* (*Čašoc^c*) containing the lives of native and neighboring saints that was already current in fifth-century Armenia. Still more probably, it was transmitted through oral recitations attendant upon the liturgy, especially on commemorative occasions such as the feast of St. John the Precursor recorded in III.iii, or

---

[125] See Commmentary, IV.v. n. 6.

[126] See Garsoïan, "Nersēs le Grand," pp. 145–149.

[127] See Commmentary, IV.v nn. 5–6, 44, 49; vi nn. 2, 12; vii n. 1; also IV.viii–ix.

[128] See Commmentary, IV.viii n. 7; ix n. 7.

[129] Greg. Naz., *Oratio XLIII.* A number of St. Basil's works were translated into Armenian in the fifth century, and this panegyric probably among them: see K. Muradyan, *Barseł; idem, Grigor,* pp. 104–142, who dates the translation before Koriwn; but cf. Lafontaine, *Grégoire de Nazianze,* on the precise date. Some of the more hagiographic passages, however, such as the descent of the dove on St. Basil, are to be found in his *Vita* by the pseudo-Amphilochos, pp. 172–177; and others, such as the vision in IV.viii, may have been part of the lost *Life* by Helladios.

[130] See Commmentary, IV.v n. 6

[131] See Commmentary, IV.v n. 49, vi n. 12.

of the saint honored on a particular day. As such, they would be readily accessible and familiar to an ecclesiastical compiler of the period.[132]

As far as can be judged, the author of the *Epic Histories* was not acquainted with classical or other foreign authors. Occasionally, some of his information, such as some of the clauses of the disastrous Roman–Persian peace treaty of 363 (IV.xxi), corresponds to that of Ammianus Marcellinus's *History,* but only in general terms.[133] At other times, the *Epic Histories* differ radically from the Roman historian, as in the case of the ultimate fates of the Aršakuni kings Tiran and Aršak II.[134] Most importantly, as already noted, the author's attitude toward the Armenian rulers in general is diametrically opposed to that of Ammianus.[135] Faint echoes of Galerius's rout of the Persians leading to the Peace of Nisibis of 298, described in the works of Aurelius Victor, Festus, and Eutropius, can also be discerned in III.xxi, but Adontz and K. Melikʿ-Ōhanǰanyan have demonstrated their vagueness and gross anachronistic inaccuracy, since they confuse the Roman victory of 297 with the battle of Singara, half a century later.[136] The same inaccuracy marks the reference to the presumed deportation of Jews to Armenia in the days of the high-priest Hyrkanos (IV.lv), so that this episode too cannot be related directly to a portion of Josephus's *Antiquities.*[137] All of these confused and anachronistic tales had obviously been filtered through a long oral transmission and become part of a common popular fund before they found their way into the *Epic Histories.*

Oral transmission, then, is the fundamental key to the problem of the sources in the *Epic Histories,* whatever their ultimate origin. It has already been said at the beginning of this section that their author does not seem to have been in any sense a learned man or to have searched for written evidence on which to base his account. His main source of information, as indicated by the very title of the work, was the living, oral tradition of Armenia's immediate past and the tales and songs still related by bards [*gusans*] in his own time. As a result he is our main source for the evidently vast oral literature of Early Christian Armenia, to which we have almost no other access.[138]

---

132 Peeters, "Intervention," p. 241, has already suggested a semi-epic, semi-hagiographic collection.

133 See Commmentary, IV.xxi n. 5. Both identify the prince J̌on/Jovianus of Kordukʿ (III.ix = AM, XVIII.vi.20), but BP obviously needed no help from Roman authors to identify a local Armenian magnate.

134 See Commmentary, III.xx n. 17.

135 See above, pp. 6, 9 and n. 33.

136 See Commmentary, III.xxi nn. 1, 11, 16–17, 20–21.

137 See Commmentary, IV.lv n. 20.

138 See below, pp. 31–35, 39, 41, 51, 54–55. Specific passages of pre-Christian literature are know from the famous quotations of them in MX, I.xxx–xxxi; II.xlix–l,

The most extensive and elaborate analysis of the epic character based on an oral tradition of the *Epic Histories* was attempted by Abełyan in his *History of Ancient Armenian Literature,* in which he not only related the work to a continuous epic that he called the "Persian War," subdivided into a series of cycles—Xosrov and Trdat, Xosrov and Vačʿē, Tiran, Aršak, Pap, Vasak and Mušeł, Manuēl Mamikonean—but which he sought to recreate by setting out much of the text of the *Epic Histories* according to a poetic, metric pattern.[139] Abełyan's poetic reconstruction must still remain hypothetical in the light of our ignorance of early Armenian metrics, but his thesis of an essentially epic and oral background and character for the *Epic Histories,* already suggested earlier by Patkanean and Gelzer[140] and subsequently shared by Adontz, Melikʿ-Ōhanǰanyan, Malχasyancʿ, and most other scholars, seems indisputable.[141]

---

lxi, lxv (= MK, pp. 120–121, 123, 191–193, 203, 210), but they are brief fragments out of context and may even have been reworked, whereas the epic oral tradition was part of the fabric of BP. That such tales were current is repeately attested by MX, I.xxx–xxi; II.xlix, lxi (= MK, pp. 120–121, 123, 190, 203) and, interestingly, by their condemnation as pagan in BP (III.xiii and n. 11). See also, Appendix III, s.v. *gusan.*

Another example of oral technique may be observed in the recurrence (with appropriate variations) of the phrase "*χōsel sksaw . . . ew asē*" in BP. It appears to be the standard formula for the introduction of an important speech in early Armenian storytelling. Its idiomatic quality is strongly suggested by its presence in the earliest stratum of the Armenian Bible, where the *Vorlage* simply uses the verb "to say." Its currency in the fifth century is amply attested by some twenty occurrences in Aa (e.g., l–li (Trdat), dcclxxiii (St. Gregory), clxvi (St. Gayanē), ccxv (the populace), etc., as well as in ŁPʿ, where the phrase accounts for most of the instances of the verb *χōsel.* The formula runs rife throughout *Epic Histories,* both verbatim and in a series of variants, none of which alters its prefatory nature (See Appendix V, a). In view of the problems that have arisen over the dating of the works of Ełišē and Movsēs Xorenacʿi, it is interesting to note in this connection that this phrase appears only eight times in the former and is totally absent in MX. The ubiquity of this introductory formula probably points to its origin in oral tales, where as for example in the Homeric epics, the extemporizing bard would make use of it to alert his audience to the beginning of an important speech while giving himself the time to fashion his opening statement. The tradition was maintained in early Armenian literature by the use of the same stereotype, primarily though not invariably for the utterances of important personages such as saints, patriarchs, or kings, as opposed to ordinary conversations. I am most indebted to Professor Cowe for calling my attention to the survival of this technique in the *Epic Histories.* See also below, n. 145.

[139] Abełan, *Grakanutʿyun,* pp. 193–195, 197–275. The Russian translation of this work (most recent edition, Erevan, 1975, pp. 106–135) condenses the argument and, of necessity, leaves out most of the metric reconstructions.

[140] Gelzer, "Die Anfänge," p. 119; Patkanean, *Bibliografichiskiĭ ocherk.*

[141] Adontz, "Favst"; Melikʿ-Ōhanǰanyan, "Tiran-Trdati vepǝ"; Malχasyancʿ, pp. 44–53, *et al.*

Instead of attempting another reconstruction from the text of the *Epic Histories* of a continuous epic of the "Persian War"—which probably never existed as a single coherent entity, but rather as a series of loosely connected tales focused on a particular theme or individual in the fashion of most oral literature[142]—it seems at present more prudent and useful to attempt some identification of the material derived from the two main aggregations of secular oral sources of the *Epic Histories,* to which may be given the arbitrary titles of the "Geste of the Aršakuni" and the "Geste of the Mamikonean," on the basis of their contents.[143] The passages based on these "Gestes" are usually identifiable by their ahistorical and at times transcendental character, unconcerned with chronological accuracy; their exaltation of the heroic virtues of valor, good fortune, and supernatural glory in the sovereign as well as unwavering loyalty in their vassals; their frequent setting in scenes of hunting, horsemanship, and banquets;[144] the use of heroic epithets; and the recurrence of formulaic refrains such as the unexpected attack on the enemy camp "by night," the extirpation of the enemy host so that not a single one survived, "not a one," and the escape of its leader, "alone on a single horse."[145] Despite some attempts to identify these tales as folk literature, they are not "popular" in character, but rather reflect the manners and values of an aristocratic and military society.

From the "Aršakuni Geste" is drawn a cluster of historically imprecise episodes celebrating the "valor" (*k^cajut^ciwn*) and the "supernatural glory" (*p^caṙk^c*), or bewailing the tragic fate, of the Armenian kings. These episodes are worked into the more sober narrative of historical events, and much of the material found in them undoubtedly goes back to the fourth century. Within the text of the *Epic Histories* this "Geste" manifests itself in the following episodes:

[142] The most obvious parallel is the Armenian folk-epic *Sasna crer,* composed of a variety of episodes loosely grouped into four cycles around four generations of heroic figures and only recently "homogenized" into a single continuous narrative (see N. G. Garsoïan, "Review," *Speculum* [1966], pp. 175ff.), but this loose pattern is as visible in the *Šāhnāme* and most oral compositions.

[143] Malχasyanc^c (pp. 46–47) added an ecclesiastical cycle to those of the Aršakuni and the Mamikonean, but, insofar as it is not historical, the ecclesiastical material belongs to a hagiographic rather than a purely epic tradition.

[144] See below, pp. 53–55 and Commentary, III.xx nn. 1, 5–6, 11–13, 16; IV.xxiv nn. 12–13; V.ii nn. 1, 9, v nn. 4–5, 8, 12, 16, 18, vii nn. 6, 12, xxxv nn. 8, 10, etc., for the Iranian nature of most of these characteristics.

[145] See above, p. 23 and n. 138, as well as Appendix V, c–e. As noted there and the relevant Commentary, the precise wording of these refrains shows variations, but these do not alter their formulaic character. See also Appendix V, k, for the alliterative formulae.

The wars of Xosrov Kotak against the
Mazkꜥutꜥkꜥ III.vii
The war of Tiran against the Persians and his
punishment III.xx–xxi
Aršak II's retaliatory raid against Ankyra IV.xi
Aršak II's glorification in Persia and his first flight
at the instigation of Vasak Mamikonean[146] IV.xvi
Aršak II's second flight from Persia at the insti-
gation of Andovk Siwni and the beginning of
the "Thirty years' war" IV.xx
The three Armenian victories over Persia won
"in the same month, on the same day, at the
same hour" IV.xxii
The rescue of the royal remains of the Aršakuni
seized by the Persians IV.xxiv
Aršak II's magic ordeal IV.liv
Aršak II's supernatural protection of the Armenian host V.v
Aršak II's suicide in the "Castle of Oblivion"[147] V.vii

With this episode the "Aršakuni Geste" vanishes from the text, since with the exception of the banquet setting for Pap's murder (V.xxxii)[148] and perhaps the manifestations of his devotion from infancy to the forces of evil (V.xxii, cf. IV.xliv) the royal epic tradition is not invoked for his reign and that of his successors, Varazdat, or for Aršak III, and his brother Vałaršak, and the focus of the narrative shifts altogether to the Mamiko-nean house. The dominant figure of this "Geste"—though not necessarily of the *Epic Histories,* whose ecclesiastical author dwells on the contrary on the king's crimes and sins—was undoubtedly Aršak II, whose "glory" and "valor" protect his realm even in his absence, and whose tragic sui-cide, attended to the end by his faithful retainer, has all the hallmarks of the epic ethos. As parts of the "Aršakuni Geste," or perhaps as attendant occasional pieces and minstrel songs, come the tales of King Tiran and his incomparable horse (III.xx),[149] the romantic tale of Gnel, Pꜥaranjem,

[146] The second part of the chapter following the lacuna may be part of the next episode. See IV.xvi n. 10.

[147] See also Commentary, III.xi n. 8, xx nn. 1, 6; IV.xi n. 6, xxiv n. 12, liv nn. 1, 8.

[148] The banquet setting of Pap's murder may be historical, since it is also found in AM, XXX.i, 19–21; but see Commentary, V.xxxii n. 7.

[149] See Commmentary, III.xx nn. 1, 5–6.

and Tiritᶜ,[150] the paean to "Aršak the Brave,"[151] and perhaps threnodies over both Gnel and Aršak II.[152]

The "Mamikonean Geste," glorifying successive generations of the hereditary grand marshals of Armenia, first runs parallel to and eventually substitutes itself for the royal tradition, preempting its supernatural virtues of *pᶜarkᶜ* and especially *kᶜaǰutᶜiwn* despite the repeated vows of loyalty on the part of the Mamikonean *sparapet*s to their "true Aršakuni lords."[153] In the earlier part of the work, it appears intermingled with the "Aršakuni Geste" as part of one and the same episode, but increasingly it provides the material for individual tales:

Vačᶜē I's victory over the traitor Databē	III.viii
Vasak's avenging of the insult to Aršak II at the Persian court	IV.xvi
The catalog of Vasak's victories	IV.xxv–xliii, xliv–xlix
The defiance and death of Vasak	IV.liv
The *kᶜaǰutᶜiwn* of Mušeł	V.ii
The loyalty and royal descent of Mušeł	V.iv
The catalog of Mušeł's victories and his panegyric	V.viii–xx
Mušeł's murder and funeral rites	V.xxxv–xxxvi
Manuēl's and Koms's heroic aspect and royal descent; Manuēl's defiance of Varazdat and avenging of Mušeł	V.xxxvii
Manuēl's victories	V.xxxix–xli
Manuēl's victory over Meružan Arcruni	V.xliii
Manuēl's deathbed admonitions and the lament over his death	V.xliv[154]

The monotonous catalogs of Vasak's, Mušeł's, and eventually Manuēl's victories must obviously be summaries of more extensive accounts, though they too exhibit a clearly formulaic pattern, ending in all but identical refrains.[155] The tale of Vardan Mamikonean's murder with the simultane-

150 See Commentary, IV.xv n. 1.

151 See Commentary, V.v nn. 4, 6, 8, 16, 18.

152 See Commentary, IV.xv nn. 30, 33 for Gnel's murder and Pᶜaṙanjem's lament, and V.vii nn. 6, 12, for the tragic setting of Aršak II's death.

153 See Commentary, IV.ii n. 2, xvi n. 5; V.ii n. 9, iv–v, xx, xxxvii and below, pp. 44–45, 49–50, as against the repeated assertions of the Mamikonean's loyalty to their "true-lords" the Aršakuni kings, IV.xvi, liv; V.iv and nn. 14, 39, and xx, xxxv, xxxvii, xliv. It is possible that the Mamikonean were though to be entitled to the royal virtues of *pᶜarkᶜ* and *kᶜaǰutᶜiwn* because of their own traditionally royal descent: see V.iv, xxxvii.

154 See also Commentary, III.viii n. 7; IV.ii nn. 2, 11, liv n. 17; V.iv n. 38, xxxv nn. 8–10, xxxix n. 1, xliv nn. 6, 9.

155 See Appendix, V, d, variants i; f–g.

ous birth of his homonymous son (IV.xviii) and especially the glorification of the valor and chivalry of Mušeł, "the rider of the white steed" (V.ii), bear clear marks of the their epic origin, and the long-observed pro-Mamikonean bias of the *Epic Histories* stems directly from their reliance on the heroic traditions glorifying the leading figures of this house.

A closer identification of the oral material underlying the *Epic Histories* does not seem possible because of the subsequent reworking by the author, who seems to quote directly only in the cases of the invocation to "Aršak *k^{c}aj*" (V.v) and the praise of the "rider of the white steed" just mentioned. This material is, however, invaluable in giving the work its unmistakable character and setting. In the case of the royal tradition in particular, it also provides a second secular voice, extolling the Aršakuni dynasty and thus counterbalancing the strictures of the ecclesiastical compiler of the *Epic Histories*.

The Composition of the Work

As suggested in the previous survey of possible sources, the *Epic Histories* are not so much a systematic composition as a compilation of varied sources linked together by their relevance to the history of fourth-century Armenia. Under such circumstances it is hardly surprising that the intertwining of historical and epic material, the shifts in attention from royal history to ecclesiastical history or to that of the Mamikonean house, the intrusions from the careers of other magnates or from the hagiographic material should have prevented a systematic unfolding of the subject—a process further obscured by the single or double revision that the work probably underwent, if indeed such a systematic presentation had ever been the intent of the compiler.

On the external form of the work, there seems to be little reason to question Malχasyanc^c's conclusion that the "Preliminary Statement" introducing the first *dprut^{c}iwn* as Book III rather than as Book I, as Łazar P^{c}arpec^{c}i knew it, is the work of a later editor,[156] and the Tables of Contents are probably also the work of his hand, as he took special pains to call attention to them.[157] As we have already noted, the chapter headings throughout the text are presumably also of later date, but they cannot be the work of the author of the "Preliminary Statement" because they do not coincide with those of the Tables. Consequently, they suggest an earlier revision, though the actual division into chapters must belong to the original since it was already known to Łazar P^{c}arpec^{c}i.[158]

---

[156] Malχasyanc^c, p. 19. See above, p. 16 and n. 69.

[157] "Preliminary Statement," p. 13 of the Venice 1933 ed.: "*Ew č^{c}ors χostmuns č^{c}oric^c č^{c}orec^{c}unc^c dprut^{c}eanc^{c}s yiwrak^{c}anč^{c}iwr iwr gluχs patuastec^{c}i minč^{c}ew i katarac sorin, ar̀ i zōgutn žar̀angeł ork^c miangam kamin srti mtōk^c hasu linel smin zor aseloc^{c}s em.*"

[158] See above, p. 17 and n. 74.

The division of the work into *dprutᶜiwnkᶜ* has already been considered, but the brief and unsatisfactory ecclesiastical biographies that form almost the whole of the last book (VI.ii–xvi) and close the entire work present a number of additional problems and show signs of tampering. Once again there can be no doubt that the first chapter of Book VI, with its mournful closing sentence bewailing the fragmentation of the Armenian realm and its "decline from its greatness at that time and thereafter,"[159] marked the original ending of the entire work. Malχasyancᶜ, moreover, accepted the statement heading the book to the effect that its content was "a restitution at the end of the missing portions,"[160] which should consequently be reintegrated into the body of the work.[161] This conclusion seems acceptable for the greater part of the book. It is entirely possible that the biography of Gind (VI.xvi), together with that of Artitᶜ of Basean (VI.vii), originally belonged alongside those of their colleagues Epipᶜan and Šalitay (V.xxv–xxviii), for they are all said to have been disciples of St. Daniēl (III.xiv) and devotees of the same ascetic life.[162] The brothers Pᶜawstos and Aṙostom as well as Zortᶜ (VI.v–vi) should presumably have found their place in Book IV together with Xad of Marag (IV.xii) as familiars and collaborators of St. Nersēs the Great. The "chief bishops" Zawēn, Šahak Korčeay, and Aspurak (VI.ii–iv), who are also known from other sources albeit not in the same order, could also presumably belong somewhere in the patriarchal confusion following the murder of St. Nersēs (V.xxiv, xxix) and remedy the silence on ecclesiastical affairs that marks the end of Book V.[163] Other episcopal biographies (VI.xi–xiv) might, despite their perfunctory character, have once been accommodated within the body of the work. But the repetition of the biography of the patriarch Aspurak (VI.iv, xv) containing no additional material is suspect, as are the three curiously unedifying and anti-clerical episodes concerning Bishop Yohan (VI.viii–x). Despite the identification of this personage as the son of the patriarch Pᶜaṙēn (III.xvi), the section devoted to him is so jarringly unsuited both in content and tone to the rest of the *Epic Histories* that it provides the best argument for G. Tēr Pōłosean's thesis that all of Book VI after its initial chapter should be

159 VI.i, p. 266, "*nuazeacᶜ bažanecᶜaw cᶜruecᶜaw tᶜagaworutᶜiwnn Hayocᶜ, pakaseacᶜ yiwrmē mecutᶜenēn yayn žamanakn ew yapay.*"

160 VI., p. 265, "*Verǰ, aṙaǰabanutᶜean včarumn mnacᶜuackᶜ banicᶜ i cayrē.*"

161 See Commentary, VI.i, n. 1.

162 This possibility is reinforced by MX, III.xx (= MK, p. 275), who makes Gind the disciple of St. Nersēs along with Epipᶜan and Šalitay, presumably because they had been granted the miraculous vision of St. Nersēs's translation to heaven (V.xxv). Cf. also the list in Aa, dcccxlv.

163 See Commentary, V.xxix nn. 1–2, for the contradictory evidence on the successors of St. Nersēs.

rejected as extraneous to the work.[164] Without going so far, it seems altogether likely that the original text consisted of only three books, ending with the present VI.i, which is consequently identified as "the end." At a subsequent date—preceding, however, the composition of the "Preliminary Statement" listing four books—some of the ecclesiastical biographies were extracted from their original positions, extended by the addition of the dubious tales of Bishop Yohan and possible duplication, and added to the original closing chapter of the work to form the unhistorical and still abnormally brief sixth book.[165]

Signs of confusion and possible tampering are also visible in the first three books of the text. The account of the mission of St. Nersēs to the imperial court (IV.v–vi, xi) is interrupted by the episodes taken from the life of St. Basil (IV.vii–ix, end of x), which are interrupted in turn by the episode of St. Thekla and the sophist (IV.x). Repetitions such as the one just noted for the biography of Aspurak in Book VI also occur elsewhere. The unworthiness of Yusik's sons is stressed three times (III.xiii, xv, xix). The activities of St. Nersēs are described on numerous occasions (IV.iv–vi, xi, again in V.xxi, and especially in V.xxxi). The defeats of the Persian commanders Gumand Šapuh and Mřkan appear, suspectly, in the catalogs of victories of both Vasak (IV.xxxi, xlix) and Manuēl Mamikonean (V.xxxix, xli), though the fault here may lie with the "Mamikonean Geste" rather than with the compilation of the *Epic Histories* themselves. The same repetition is most glaringly obvious in the twin chapters setting forth the misdeeds of King Pap and his devotion to the *dew*s from infancy (IV.xliv; V.xxii), the first of which is furthermore clearly out of place as it intrudes into the middle of the catalog of Vasak's victories (IV.xxvi–xliii, xlv–xlix), while the second comes at its logical chronological place as a preface to the king's murder of St. Nersēs.[166]

This evidence of an occasionally chaotic pattern has cast some doubts on the skill of the original compiler of the *Epic Histories,* or perhaps more justly on that of his subsequent editors. Nevertheless, the work as a whole, excluding the dubious Book VI after its initial chapter, lacks neither balance nor form. It is in no sense a haphazard collection of information. The three main strands of the royal, ecclesiastical, and Mamikonean histories are maintained in proportion and interwoven with care through

[164] Tēr Połosean, "Pᶜawstos."

[165] If VI.ii–xvi were integrated into the preceding material or rejected altogether, it would be possible to suppose that VI.i "the end" was in fact the last chapter of Book V, linking it to "what came last," as III.ii linked BP to "what came first." We have only the word of the later editor of the "Preliminary Statement" for the existence of Book VI as a separate entity. See above, p. 35 and n. 157.

[166] See Commentary, IV.xliv nn. 1, 3, 7, for a possible contradiction within the chapter.

the work. The catalogs of victories balance each other in the successive generations of Mamikonean commanders. The capping panegyric of Mušeł (V.xx) finds its counterpart in the "seven years' peace" crowning the victories of his successor Manuēl (V.xlii), as do those of St. Yusik (III.xii) and his grandson, St. Nersēs (IV.iii). The dominant theme of the work—the defense unto death of the Christian faith, of the church, of the covenant, of the community of the faithful, and of the "true lords" (*bnak teark ᶜ*) of the realm—is passionately reiterated at intervals from beginning to end of the three main books: in St. Vrtᶜanēs's commemoration of the Armenian dead (III.xi), in the dedication of the army raised by the *sparapet* Vasak Mamikonean against the Persians (IV.xxiv), in St. Nersēs's reproof of the rebellious *naχarar*s abandoning King Aršak II (IV.li), in Mušeł Mamikonean's avowals of loyalty to King Pap (V.iv, xx), and in Manuēl Mamikonean's deathbed admonitions (V.xliv). The style and more importantly the ethos of the work shows no appreciable variations,[167] so that in spite of occasional awkwardness and distortions, possibly due to later revisions, the ultimate purpose of the work, the image of fourth-century Christian Armenia, emerges clearly from the text.[168]

As in the case of their composition, the *Epic Histories* have been criticized as a historical source for their chronological imprecision and anachronisms,[169] though Abełyan noted that the Aršakuni regnal sequence was correctly given.[170] Most particularly, their author has been taken to task for the absence of any date within the work, for the absence of any indication of regnal or patriarchal spans carefully noted in the parallel *History* of Movsēs Xorenacᶜi, for the failure to identify any of the foreign rulers contemporary with the Armenian Christian Aršakuni except for the Roman emperors Constantine (324–337) and Valens (364–378) and the Sasanian kings of kings Narseh (293–302) and Šāhpuhr II (309–379), and for his repeated reliance on such vague designations as "the king of the Greeks" and "the king of the Persians."[171] Still more seriously, the very precisions in giving royal names have been seen to play havoc with

---

167 A variation in style has been suggested for the epic passages, but there is no more variation in tone than is warranted by changes of subject except in the highly suspect section of Book VI (viii–x) dealing with bishop Yohan, and possibly in giving the patriarchal years of tenure, VI.ii–iii and ii n. 7, since this practice is not found elsewhere. See below, p. 39 and n. 173.

168 See below, pp. 45–55.

169 See e.g. Malχasyancᶜ, pp. 30–32, 53.

170 Abełan, *Grakanutᶜyun*, pp. 194, cf. 263, on the Persian war.

171 BP usually refers to the Byzantine emperor as the "king of the Greeks" rather than by his correct title of "emperor" (*kaysr*), thus providing additional proof of the author's ignorance of the correct imperial terminology at the time and consequently of his lack of familiarity with the classical world.

his chronology, as has already been noted.[172] At first glance these objections seem well founded, and an absence of chronological precisions unquestionably marks the *Epic Histories,* which prefer to rely on locutions such as "and so," "and after this," "and at that time," to indicate the sequence of events.[173] As a result, they are not to be used as an explicit source for the reconstruction of the problematic chronology of fourth-century Armenia.[174] Nevertheless, a consideration of the purpose of the work and a clearing of the confusion and anachronisms resultant from extraneous intrusions and the reliance of the author on oral tradition go far toward a mitigation of these difficulties.

Far from recurring regularly throughout the text, the anachronisms center on two foci: first, the naming of the defeated Persian ruler contemporary with Tiran of Armenia (330–338?) as "Narseh" (III.xx–xxi); and second, the identification of the emperor to whom St. Nersēs's ill-fated mission of 358 was addressed and who was the opponent of St. Basil of Caesarea as "Vałeš/Valens" (IV.v–xi). As Adontz (followed by Melikᶜ-Ōhanǰanyan) convincingly demonstrated, the anachronistic appearance of King "Narseh" of Persia during the reign of Tiran in Armenia derives from the reliance of the *Epic Histories* on oral tradition at this point. The overwhelming victory of the Caesar Galerius over the real Narseh in 297, resulting in the king's flight from the battlefield and the capture of his camp and entire household by the Romans, indelibly marked the folk memory, where it expunged or fused with the far less brilliant encounter at Singara under the emperor Constantius ca. 344 in which another Narseh, the son of Šāhpuhr II, had met his death. The conflation of the two events resultant from similar circumstances and the identical names of the Persian protagonists had firmly established itself in the oral tradition by the fifth century and provoked the intrusion of the earlier Narseh into the events of the mid-fourth century.[175] In other episodes of the Persian war related in the *Epic Histories,* however, the contemporary Persian

[172] See above pp. 5–6.

[173] See *inter alia*, III.ii, *Ard*; III.iii, *Apa yet*; III.iv, *Ew zayn žamanakaw*, etc. Cf. Abełyan, *Grakanutᶜyun*, p. 194, with the possible exception of VI.ii–iii. See above, n. 167.

[174] It may be worth noting in passing that no source has so far permitted the clarification of the formidable problems surrounding the chronology of fourth-century Armenia, despite persistent and increasingly tortuous efforts to resolve the difficulties. The sequences offered by BP are entirely coherent and acceptable in themselves. Cf. below, n. 186.

[175] See Commentary, III.xx n. 1 and xxi nn. 1, 11, 16–17. This conflation was also noted by Gelzer, "Die Anfänge," pp. 118–119 n.; E. Stein, *Histoire du Bas-Empire*, trans. J. R. Palanque (Paris and Brussels, 1949), I, p. 483 n. 209*; and Peeters, "Intervention," pp. 230–237.

king is correctly identified as Šāhpuhr II, whose seventy-year reign spanned most of the fourth century.[176]

Though somewhat more complicated, the anachronistic manifestations of the emperor "Valens" can also be explained by the Basilian episodes intruding into and contaminating the life of St. Nersēs. In the case of events actually relating to St. Basil himself (IV.vii–x), the references to Valens are entirely correct and appropriate, since the two men were indubitably contemporaries.[177] In the cases where the name of St. Nersēs has been substituted for that of St. Basil, however—as in the episode of the emperor's dying son with the subsequent persecution of the orthodox confessors (IV.v–vi, xi)—Valens's name was carried over from the original Basilian version of the story in which it belonged, instead of being replaced by that of St. Nersēs's contemporary at this point in his career, the emperor Constantius (337–361), to whom Nersēs's mission of 358 had been addressed, but whose name never appears in the *Epic Histories*.[178] Such an error would be all the more likely in that the memory of the two persecuting "Arian" emperors of the fourth century might readily be confused in the mind of an "orthodox" clerical compiler writing more than a century after the events.[179]

Despite these two anachronisms, the author of the *Epic Histories* seems to have made no further mistakes; neither do these errors, once understood, interfere with the correct sequence of events in contemporary Armenia, so that he cannot be properly accused of systematic distortion. He even successfully avoided two gross errors common to the Armenian sources covering the events of the fourth century: the intrusion of the emperor Theodosius (379–395) into the affairs of King Pap (ca. 369–374), found in both Movsēs Xorenacᶜi and the *Vita* of St. Nersēs,[180] and the all but unanimous inclusion of St. Nersēs among the bishops present at the Council of Constantinople in 381, some eight years after the patriarch's death.[181] Finally, it should be remembered that the epic and ecclesiastical

---

[176] The one exception is IV.lviii, where "Narseh" reappears, but this may well be a scribal error since Šāhpuhr is correctly identified in the episode (IV.xx) alluded to in the later passage.

[177] St. Basil's pontificate (370–379) coincided with Valens's passage through Caesarea of Cappadocia on his way to the East in 372, as is amply attested by the sources. See Fedwick, *Basil*, p. 144; etc. See also Commentary, IV.viii n. 2 and x n. 8.

[178] See Commentary, III.xxi n. 21; IV.v n. 5, vi n. 2, xi n. 2.

[179] See Commentary, IV.v n. 5. The tales of the persecuted orthodox confessors are also transferred to St. Nersēs and his companions (see Garsoïan, "*Quidam Narseus*," p. 154 n. 26). The same confusion between Constantius and Valens seems to have occurred in the account of Tiran's wars, even though Melikᶜ-Ōhanǰanyan proposed the reading Valerius for Vałēs/Valens. See Commentary, III.xxi n. 21.

[180] See Commentary, V.i n. 3.

[181] Garsoïan, "Nersēs le Grand," p. 169.

world of the *Epic Histories* was primarily concerned with constant social patterns and virtues and eternal verities; as such it neither required nor was bound to the rigorous chronological framework expected of a more strictly political and analytical history which was not their author's goal.

In recapitulation, then, the *Epic Histories* may at present be described as the compilation in four, or perhaps even three, books of an anonymous Armenian ecclesiastical author of the late fifth century, which has come down to us in its entirety but which formed a component part of a still larger collection of sources from the fifth century that covered the history of *Christian* Armenia from its conversion to the consolidation of the faith through the translation of the Scriptures and the Liturgy early in the fifth century. The original version of the *Histories* was probably modified by two later revisions. The first, presumably in the Bagratid period, added the chapter titles found within the text. The second, still later, was responsible for the "Preliminary Statement," the Tables of Contents, and the two puzzling notes at the end of Book III and of the Table of Contents of Book VI. The author of this original version, though unquestionably a Christian cleric, was thoroughly familiar with the still-current oral traditions with their pagan overtones, on which he relied extensively and which he reworked into a continuous narrative. His work does not seem to have been intended as a systematic survey of the political history of fourth-century Armenia, but even on these terms, his chronology, once cleared of its intrusive anachronisms and hagiographic interpolations, does in fact provide a reasonable sequence of the events of the period.

The Historical Value of the Epic Histories

Until recent times, the comparison of the only two independent sources covering the history of fourth-century Armenia—the *Epic Histories* and the *History of Armenia* of Movsēs Xorenacʿi—all but inevitably turned to the advantage of the latter.[182] Its scholarly "historicity," resting on written and acknowledged sources, and its preoccupation with chronological precision, marked by the careful indication of the lengths of reigns and pontificates, its "critical sense," all were compared favourably with the *Epic Histories'* failure to identify the authorities for their information, their disregard of specific chronology, and their predilection for supernatural manifestations. At best, the *Histories* were patronizingly accepted as "folk literature," even after Abełyan's elaborate reconstruction of their epic background[183] and the acknowledgment that Movsēs Xorenacʿi was indebted to them for much of his fourth-century material.[184] The most

[182] This is still the case even in Malχasyancʿ, "Introduction," pp. 53–57.

[183] See above, p. 31 and n. 138.

[184] Thomson, MK, p. 46 and, rather reluctantly, Malχasyancʿ pp. 53–57.

that even Malχasyanc‘ would say in his "Introduction" to the modern Armenian translation of the *Epic Histories* was that the two works should not be opposed to each other but that they reflected two different genres: Movsēs Xorenac‘i's *History of Armenia* being "purely" or "truly historical" (*zut patmakan*), whereas the author of the *Epic Histories* was to be taken as "a collector of historical traditions, tales, and stories replete with authentic historical elements" ("*patmakan awandut‘yunneri, zruyc‘neri ew verperi havak‘oł, oronc‘meǰ bun patmakan tarrerə čoχac‘vel en*").[185] This equivocal judgment is to some degree justifiable. We have already seen that the author of the *Epic Histories* was unquestionably less learned than his scholarly colleague, that he indeed seems to have made little effort to seek information in books and to have eschewed chronological calculations.[186] Consequently, he can be shown to have been guilty on occasion of confusions, anachronisms, and even contradictions. Nevertheless, such an appraisal falls far short of a realization of the true value of his work.

On the basis of the most elementary external criterion, it is immediately evident that the scope of the two works is not commensurate. The purpose of Movsēs Xorenac‘i was to relate the entire history of Armenia from its legendary founder, Hayk, to the death of St. Sahak the Great in the second quarter of the fifth century, while the author of the *Epic Histories* more modestly limited himself to a period of some fifty years in the mid-fourth century. As a result, the period covered by his entire text has been compressed into little more than half of Xorenac‘i's third book.[187] Superficial and unimportant as this aspect may seem, it necessarily forced a considerable condensation of events in Xorenac‘i's *History,* which distanced him from its material. The lists of Armenian *naχarar*s accompanying the patriarchal candidates to their consecration at Caesarea of Cappadocia or composing ambassadorial retinues, scrupulously given in the *Epic Histories,* are nowhere to be found in the work of Movsēs Xorenac‘i, who ignores the names of most of the magnates, hence reducing the

---

185 Malχasyanc‘, p. 57; cf. p. 55, "*mekə iskakan patmut‘yun ē, miwsə patmakan zruyc‘neri ew veperi žołovacu ē.*"

186 See above, pp. 38–39, 41. It may be noted in passing that Xorenac‘i's written sources and the use he made of them have now come under the perhaps harsh scrutiny of R. W. Thomson, MK, pp. 10–56, esp. the latter, "purpose," and that his vaunted precision have done little to clarify the chaotic and irreconcilable chronology of the fourth century; see above, n. 174.

187 The portion of MX covering the material of BP is comprised in his book III.i–xliii, or forty-four out of the sixty-eight chapters of the entire book, namely, 55 of 108 pages in the critical edition of the text as against the 276 pages of BP's text in the Venice edition (231 in the St. Petersburg edition). To be sure, prolixity is not a historical criterion, but the much greater length of BP is not mere rhetorical verbiage.

42

possibility of reconstructing the composition of the contemporary Armenian nobility.[188]

The ecclesiastical history of the period, so dear to the heart of the author of the *Epic Histories,* seems to have held little interest for Movsēs Xorenac'i. The lengthy account of the youth and patriarchate of St. Yusik, the lament over his murder, the equally passionate relation of the tragic fate of his successor St. Daniēl (III.v, xii–xiv) are dismissed in a few non-commital sentences.[189] No mention is made of the traditional consecration of the Armenian primates, P'aṙēn, Šahak, or even St. Nersēs, at Caesarea of Cappadocia (III.xvi–xvii; IV.iv).[190] The space devoted in general to the dominant figure of St. Nersēs the Great is similarly curtailed in Movsēs's *History,* where the saint's homilies—the defense of trinitarian orthodoxy before the Arian emperor Valens (IV.iv);[191] the prediction of the destruction of the city of Aršakawan (IV.xiii);[192] the curse on Aršak II for the murder of his nephew Gnel (IV.xv);[193] the invocation during the battle on Mount Npat (V.iv), an engagement incidentally fused by Xorenac'i with another Armenian victory[194]—have all been omitted, as are St. Vrt'anēs's panegyric of the Armenian dead (III.xi); the lament over the murder of St. Yusik (III.xiii); and the consequent curse of King Tiran by St. Daniēl (III.xiv).[195] Thus, not only do the *Epic Histories* provide far more detail concerning the patriarchal succession of the period, but the absence of the deeply emotional homiletic material repeatedly embodying the author's intense engagement in the events and doctrinal positions of the times underscores once again the detachment of Xorenac'i. The defense of trinitarian orthodoxy arouses no echo in his work, as though the controversy over it, settled once and for all, no longer provoked a passionate response.[196] The same absence of emotion marks Xorenac'i's attitude toward the Aršakuni kings, whom the author of the *Epic Histories* may condemn as sinners (IV.li), but whom he invariably

---

[188] See Commentary, III.xii n. 6; IV.iv n. 4, xi n. 4..

[189] MX, III.xi (last sentence), xiv (= MK, pp. 264, 267). He is especially curt concerning Daniēl. See Commentary, III.xiii n. 1, xiv n. 1.

[190] See Commentary, III.xvi n. 1, IV.iv n. 4.

[191] MX, III.xxx (= MK, p. 287).

[192] MX, III.xxvii (= MK, p. 283).

[193] MX, III.xxiv (= MK, p. 279), where one sentence is devoted to St. Nersēs.

[194] MX, III.xxxviii (= MK, p. 297 and n. 7), where one sentence is devoted to the invocation. See also, Commentary, V.iv n. 1.

[195] See above, n. 189.

[196] The omission of much of this homiletic material in the translations of BP has also served to distort the character of the work. See Commentary, IV.v n. 7; V.iv nn. 15, 27, xxviii n. 7.

acknowledges as the "true lords" (*bnak teark^c*) of the realm,[197] a term not to be found in Xorenac^{c}i's *History*.[198]

It has long been observed that Movsēs Xorenac^{c}i supported the claim of the Bagratuni family to a preeminent position in Armenian history, while the *Epic Histories* have always been characterized as the history of the Mamikonean house. There can be no doubt concerning these evident biases, or that both authors exaggerate the qualities and achievements of their respective houses, while denigrating the other.[199] The author of the *Epic Histories* gives short shrift to the Bagratuni, whom he reduces to mere "companions-in-arms" (*nizakakic^c*) of Vač^{c}ē I Mamikonean (III.vii), and whose hereditary titles of *aspet* and royal "coronant" (*t^{c}agakap*) are mentioned only once in connection with the marriage of King Pap's younger son Vałaršak to a daughter of this house (V.xliv).[200] As we have already seen, the dependence of the *Epic Histories* on a preexistent "Geste of the Mamikonean" simultaneously led their author to a systematic apotheosis of the leaders of the house as "chevaliers sans peur et sans reproche," with the transfer to them of the heroic epithet "valiant" (*k^{c}aǰ*) properly reserved for the ruling house alone; practices that provoked Abełyan's objection that all individuality had been obliterated in these images of unflawed perfection.[201] But the systematic obliteration of the role of the Mamikonean house by Xorenac^{c}i is far more extensive and ultimately damaging. Except for the repetition of the traditional account of the Mamikoneans' royal descent, also known to the *Primary History* (V.iv, xxxvii),[202] and passing, usually contemptuous, references to their *tanutēr* Vardan and his brother the *sparapet* Vasak (both of whom he reduces to the insignificant status of "royal squire" [*zinakir ark^{c}ayi*][203] and to the first of whom he attributes the actual murder of the king's nephew Gnel),[204] as well as to the traitor and apostate, Vahan,[205] Xore-

---

[197] See, e.g., III.xi, xx, xxi; IV.xxiv, li; V.iv, v, vii, xx, xliv. This does not, of course, preclude the condemnation of individuals: IV.xv, xliv; V.xxix, etc.

[198] Cf. *Hamabaṙbar*, "Xorenac^{c}i," I, pp. 388–389; III, pp. 482–483.

[199] This bias is ubiquitous. On MX see Thomson, MK, pp. 46, 49.

[200] For a possible reference in IV.iv, see Commentary IV.iv n. 5. BP's neglect of the Bagratuni may be due to their disgrace in the later fifth century after their support of Vasak Siwni against Vardan Mamikonean: see ŁP^c, xxxvi, pp. 36–37 (= Ełišē, p. 281); Ełišē, iii–iv, pp. 74, 98 (= *Ełišē*, pp. 125, 144).

[201] See Abełyan, *Grakanut^{c}yun*, p. 249; also Commentary, IV.xxiv nn. 12–13; Vv. nn. 8, 16, and Appendix III, s.v. *k^{c}aǰ* for the royal *k^{c}aǰut^{c}iwn* of the Aršakuni; and above, pp. 34–35 and n. 153 for its transfer to the Mamikonean. Cf., however, n. 215.

[202] See Commentary, V.xxxvii n. 1 and Appendix I, "Čenk^c," "Mamikonean."

[203] See Appendix I, "Vardan I" and "Vasak Mamikonean."

[204] See Commentary, IV.xv n. 12.

[205] MX, III.xxix, xxxv (= MK, pp. 286, 293–294).

nac^{c}i makes no reference whatsoever to the *sparapetut^{c}iwn* of Vač^{c}ē (III.iv, vii–ix, xi) or to the long catalogs of Vasak's, Mušeł's, and Manuēl's victories, [206] to Vasak's defense of Aršak II at the Persian court (IV.xvi),[207] to the martyrdom of Princess Hamazaspuhi (IV.lix),[208] to Mušeł's initiative in the reconquest of the throne by Pap (V.i),[209] or to the regency of Manuēl for Pap's young sons (V.xxxvii–xliv).[210] In this process, he alters the name of the *sparapet* Artawazd from Mamikonean to Mandakuni[211] and transfers the victories of Mušeł over the Persians (V.v) and of Manuēl over Meružan Arcruni (V.xxxviii, xliii) to the *aspet* Smbat Bagratuni,[212] thus introducing serious historical distortions by obscuring the hereditary character of the *sparapetut^{c}iwn* in fourth-century Armenia and the dominant position of the Mamikonean house following directly after the royal Aršakuni in this period.[213]

Far more important than these comparative aspects of the two *Histories* is the internal evidence of the *Epic Histories,* some of which naturally reflects the particular bias of the author, but which nonetheless presents a remarkably coherent and extensive picture of Early Christian Armenian society. It has already been noted here that the conservatively aristocratic and orthodox attitude of the author normally placed him on the side of the Gregorid patriarchs and of the magnates in opposition to the Aršakuni's religious policy and their attempts at centralization.[214] Even so, the complicated and at times chaotic character of the Armenian kingdom during this period is neither simplified nor disguised by him to

[206] IV.xxvi–xliii, xlv–xlix; V.viii–xx, xxxviii–xliii; and IV.xxvi n. 1; V.viii n. 1, xxxix n. 1.

[207] See Commentary, IV.xvi n. 5.

[208] See Commentary, IV.lix n. 4.

[209] See Commentary, V.i n. 4.

[210] See Commentary, V.xxxvii n. 22, xxxviii n. 1, xliv nn. 1–2.

[211] MX, II.lxxvi, lxxviii, lxxxii, lxxxv; III.vi (= MK, pp. 223–226 and 223 n. 10, 232, 237, 258). See also Aa (dccclx and p. 497 nn. 1–2 to this chapter); Appendix I "Mamikonean," and below, n. 213.

[212] MX, III.xxxvii (= MK, p. 298 and nn. 12–13). See also Commentary, V.v n. 19, xliii n. 1; and Appendix I "Meružan Arcruni."

[213] See Commentary, III.iv n. 2, xi n. 7; V.i n. 5, xxxvii n. 9, xliv n. 5. See also IV.ii; Appendix I, "Mamikonean"; Appendix III, *sparapet,* and below, pp. 49–50. MX, III xli, xliii (= MK, pp. 303, 305) also alters the marriage of King Aršak III to Manuēl Mamikonean's daughter Varazduχt (IV.xliv) and substitutes an anonymous daughter of Prince Babik Siwni as the royal bride.

[214] See above, p. 15 and n. 66. The presumption of an aristocratic inclination on the part of the author of BP does not refer to his social status, of which we know nothing, but to the point of view that emerges from his work.

fit a preconceived point of view; the presence of pro-Roman and pro-Iranian parties within Armenia is, at least tacitly, admitted.[215]

Taken in conjunction with the contradictory position of the Roman historian Ammianus Marcellinus as to the merits of the Aršakuni kings, the author's religious antagonism furnishes clear evidence of the Armenian church's opposition to the royal attempts to bend it to the Arianizing policy of Constantinople, a confrontation that led to the murder of the patriarchs Yusik (III.xii–xiii) and Nersēs (V.xxiv) and ultimately to that of King Pap (V.xxxii).[216] At the same time, his stress on the importance of St. Thaddeus, whom he equates with St. Gregory the Illuminator (III.i, xii, xiv; IV.iii–iv); his devotion to "the great and first church . . . the mother-church of all Armenia" ("*i mecn ew nax̌ zaṙaǰin ekełec^cin i mayr ekełec^ceac^cn amenayn hayastaneayc^c*"), Aštišat of Tarōn (III.xiv); and his familiarity with Syriac hagiography and Syrian ascetic practices, emphasized in the various hagiographic chapters (III.x, xiv; V.xxv–xxviii; VI.xvi) preserve the memory of the early southern current of Armenian Christianity, derived from Edessa and eventually Antioch and all but obliterated by the Hellenization of the Armenian church under the patriarchs of the northern Gregorid house dependent on Caesarea of Cappadocia. Occasional references to this double current in early Armenian Christianity can also be found in the mention of Syriac as well as Greek teaching in "Agat^cangełos," despite his extolling of the northern church of Vałaršapat,[217] and also in Xorenac^ci, who speaks of the "throne of the apostle Thaddeus."[218] Nevertheless, together with Koriwn's account of Maštoc^c's journey to Mesopotamia, the *Epic Histories* remain the chief source for the importance of the Syrian current in the formation of the

---

[215] The occasional presence of opposing trends, such as the superimposition of a Christian ethos over an Iranian one (see below pp. 51–55) may at times result from the compilatory nature of the work or from the compiler's lack of skill, but it reflects the complexities of the transitional Armenian society of the fourth century with far greater clarity than a smoother synthesis.

The equivocal allegiances of the Armenian nobility, along with those of its king, are not disguised. The presence of a pro-Persian party in Armenia is admitted not only in the case of the traitors, Meružan Arcruni, the *bdeašx* of Ałjnik^c (III.ix), and the *mardpet* Głak (V.vi), among others, but even in the author's favorite Mamikonean house. Not only is there no attempt to hide the apostasy of the traitor Vahan (IV.l, lviii, lix), or the Sasanian sympathies of the *tanutēr* Vardan I (IV.xv–xvi, xviii, l), but even the heroes Vasak (IV.xx) and Manuēl (V.xxxviii–xxxix) are shown accepting presents or alliance with the king of kings.

[216] See Garsoïan, "Politique."

[217] Aa, dcccxl.

[218] MX, III.liv (= MK, p. 312), cf. III.xxxvi (= MK, pp. 294–295) for the burning of Greek books by the Persians; and II.lxxiv (= MK, p. 221 and n. 8), for the Throne of Thaddeus, cf. II.xxxiv (= MK, pp. 174–175).

Armenian church,[219] as well as for the strength of the Syrian ascetic tradition in the country.[220] Consequently, they provide important clarification on Armenian fourth-century solitary practices, which appear to have been eremitic rather than truly monastic,[221] and evidence that Gregory the Illuminator was normally referred to as "great" or "first patriarch" but not yet as "saint" in this period.[222]

The opposition to the Armenian crown in the fourth century was not exclusively ecclesiastical. The arrogance of the "lords with contingents and banners" (*gndic͑ ew drōšuc͑ teark͑*, IV.iii) continuously manifests itself in the narrative of the *Epic Histories,* as they record both the attempts of the kings to keep the unruly magnates under their eye at court (III.viii) and the more violent retaliatory measures intended to extirpate entire clans (e.g. III.viii, xviii; IV.xix). The tug-of-war between the Aršakuni kings and the *naχarar*s, that is to say the opposition between the centrifugal "dynasticism" of the nobility and the centralizing "feudalism" of the crown, first identified by C. Toumanoff,[223] clearly emerges from the hatred of the magnates, shared by the author, for such royal officials as the *hayr-mardpet,* or for the royal foundation of Aršakawan (IV.xii–xiii),[224] and from the king's unsuccessful attempt to bestow dignities and

[219] For the Syrian element in Armenian Christianity, see Ter Minasyan, *Armenische Kirche,* pp. 5–8, *et passim* and more recently, Melk͑onyan, *Haraberut͑yunner,* also Garsoïan, *Paulician Heresy,* pp. 220–230, and Commentary, III.xiv, n. 11. It is also evident from the numerous translations from Syriac, for which see in particular the studies of L. H. Ter Petrosyan.

[220] See Vööbus, *Asceticism,* pp. 353–359, for the presence of Syrian eremetic practices in Armenia. The presence of this tradition in fourth-century Armenia is amply attested. See also next note.

[221] For the presence of an "eremetic" rather than truly "monastic" tradition in Armenia during the fourth century, see III.xiv; V.xxvii–xxviii; VI.xvi, and Commentary, III.xiv, nn. 15, 17; IV.iv, n. 19; V.xxvii, n. 4, xxviii n. 3, xxxi nn.2, 4, 5; VI.xvi, nn. 3, 4, etc., and my forthcoming article on early Armenian "monasticism."

[222] BP refers throughout to the Illuminator most often as *mec,* "great," *passim*; also as *k͑ahanayapet,* "chief priest" (III.iii, v), *sk͑anč͑eli,* "wondrous, marvelous, admirable" (III.x), *hayrapet,* "patriarch" (III.xiv etc.), and even on occasion without any qualification whatsoever (e.g., III.iii, xii, xiv, xv, xvii, xix, etc.). It refers to his grandson Grigoris as having imitated the first Grigor through his "illuminating renewal of the churches [*norogeac͑ and zekelec͑isn lusawor kargōk͑, ařajnoyn Grigori . . . nmaneal*]" (III.v). But it never speaks of him as *surb,* "saint," even though the term is used for both his sons, Aristakēs and Vrt͑anēs (III.v), his descendant Nersēs (V.xxiv), and the bones of Vrt͑anēs (III.xi), as well as Šaḷitay and Epip͑an (V.xxvi–xxvii). Cf. Peeters, "Calendrier," pp. 92–101; Marr *Kreshchenie,* pp. 150–155; and P. M. Muradyan, "Kul͑t Grigoriia," pp. 11–12.

[223] Toumanoff, *Studies,* pp. 34–40, 77–80, 108–117, *et passim.*

[224] On the *mardpet,* see above, n. 66. On Aršakawan, see Commentary, IV.xii n. 9, xiii n. 21; and Garsoïan, "Mediaeval Armenian City," p. 81–82.

offices on his favorites in defiance of the hereditary prerogatives of the magnates (V.xxxvii).[225]

The author's sympathies with the *naχarar*s do not, however, appear to have been indiscriminate. Side by side with them, he continually displays a sense of loyalty, not only to his "true lords," but even more to the integrity of the Armenian kingdom, a distinct entity that he identifies by the characterization *ašχarh Hayocꞌ*, "the realm of Armenia," as against the more general geographical definition *erkir Hayocꞌ*, "the land of Armenia."[226] This physical unit, limited by Satala in Armenia Minor to the northwest and Ganzak of Atrpatakan in the southeast (III.vii; IV.xxi; V.iv–vi, xxxiv) is similarly defined by "Agatꞌangełos."[227] But it is from the *Epic Histories* that we learn of the loss of its marchlands at the time of the Persian conquest in the 360s (IV.l) and the return of its northern boundary to the Kur River, dividing it from Iberia and Caspian Albania, as a result of Mušeł Mamikonean's temporary reconquest ca. 370 (V.xiii, xv), geographical precisions not to be found elsewhere.

Transcending the purely physical aspect, the concept of a single Armenian realm is already fully, if not necessarily explicitly, formulated in the *Epic Histories,* and its preservation at all costs one of its guiding principles overriding all other considerations.[228] The rebellious *naχarar*s threatening to abandon their king in the face of Persia are cursed by St. Nersēs (IV.li). No sympathy is shown for the aspirations of the *bdeašχ* Bakur of Ałjnikꞌ (III.ix) or the arch-villain Meružan Arcruni (IV.xxii–xxiv, xxxi–xxxvii, xxxix–xliii, xlv–l, lviii–lix, V.xxxviii, xliii), both of whom are depicted as rebels against their lord the Armenian king rather than as rulers of semi-independent principalities entitled to pursue an autonomous policy. No mention whatsoever can be found of the autonomous Satrapies of south-western Armenia, despite the indications of the classical sources that these *civitates foederatae liberae et immunes* were in existence during this period,[229] except for the fleeting reference to Meružan's domain as an *ašχarh* or "realm" and the hesitation as to the precise relationship of Ałjnikꞌ to the Armenian kingdom.[230] In critical

[225] See also, Commentary, III.ix n. 6; IV.ii n. 7 for other attempts of the Armenian king to interpose his authority into the normal pattern of dynastic succession, and V.xxxvii and n. 9 for his failure.

[226] See Appendix III, *ašχarh, erkir.*

[227] See Aa, dcccxlii.

[228] See above, p. 38, for the repeated theme of the defense of the "realm," the Christian faith, and the "true-lords" of Armenia.

[229] Procopius, *De aed.*, III.i.17–27; cf. Adontz, *Armenia*, pp. 84–93.

[230] See Commentary, III.ix nn. 2, 4 and Appendix II, "Ałjnikꞌ," for the "great *bdeašχ*"; also IV.xxiii n. 1 and Appendix I, "Meružan." The satrapy of Sophenē [Copꞌkꞌ Šahuni] is also called a "realm" (*ašχarh*) in III.xii.

circumstances, compromises with Byzantium (V.xxxiii) or even Persia (V.xxxvii–xxxviii) seem to have been acceptable to the author in order to preserve the integrity of the kingdom, whose greatness inexorably declined and vanished with its partition at the end of the fourth century (VI.i; cf. Daniēl's curse, III.xiv).

The familiarity of the author of the *Epic Histories* with the *naxarar* milieu of the period enabled him to transmit a particularly sharp and diversified image of Armenia's essentially aristocratic society and consequently made his work the *locus classicus* for all reconstructions of early medieval Armenian social structure.[231] It is here that we find the fullest and most varied range of the contemporary social and administrative vocabulary: *bdeašχ, mecamec, satrap, naχarar, awaganin, tanutēr, nahapet, išχan, tēr, pet, zōrawar, zōragluχ, sparapet, aspet, tꞔagakap, hazarapet, senekapet, mardpet, małχaz, marzpan, ostikan, sahmanapah, ašχarhakal, berdakal, kusakal, kołmnakal, gawaṙakal, gawaṙatēr, sepuh, azat, gorcakal, dasapet, ṙamik, šinakan, caṙay, struk, gah, barj, gaherēcꞔ, barjerēcꞔ, patiw, azg, tohm, tun, sepꞔakan, ostan, dastakert, kaluac,* etc.[232] Together with the social differentiations implicit in this wealth of titles, we also find extensive evidence for the presence of an otherwise unknown institution, the Armenian council, composed of the various ranks of the greater and lesser nobility, but also of some representatives from the lower classes, meeting to advise the king and to select new patriarchal candidates, together with the king, in the absence of the king, or even on occasion in opposition to him (e.g. III.xxi; IV.iii, li; V.xxxiii)[233]

Perhaps of greatest importance for the reconstruction of the fundamental principles of fourth-century Armenian society is the *Epic Histories'* insistence on the hereditary character of the great offices of the realm, despite all the royal attempts to alter this pattern in order to reduce the threatening power of the magnates. The clearest example of this principle, as might be expected from the author's allegiance to the Mamikonean house, is found in the hereditary transmission of the office of *sparapet* or "grand marshal" and commander-in-chief of the Armenian forces within this family. From generation to generation, though not necessarily in direct line, this office is shown to pass to a member of the Mamikonean house without reference to the royal will, as in the case of Mušeł's immediate assumption of the position of his father Vasak (V.i). The king's explicit grant of this office to his tutor and favorite Bat Saha-

---

[231] See, *inter alia*, Adontz, *Armenia*; Manandyan, *Feodalizm*; Toumanoff, *Studies*; Kherumian, *Une féodalité oubliée*.

[232] See Appendix III, svv, for this terminology.

[233] See Manandyan, *Feodalizm*, pp. 79–83; and Garsoïan, "Prolegomena," cols, 183, 187–188 n. 46; as well as below, p. 52 and n. 242, for the Parthian character of this institution.

r̄uni proves insufficient to withstand the thrust of tradition, as Manuēl Mamikonean returns to succeed automatically to his murdered kinsman, Mušeł, and the royal interference results only in tragedy (V.xxxvii). Not even patent inability to perform the duties of the office is sufficient cause to withhold it. Little Artawazd Mamikonean receives his father's dignity as the last surviving male representative of his house, even though his youth precludes the possibility of his commanding any army in the field, so that this function must temporarily be delegated to others (III.xi).[234] Similarly, the linking of the terms Aršakuni and "king" or "lord" as synonyms throughout the work points to the hereditary nature of the Armenian kingship and to its being perceived as the exclusive prerogative of the Aršakuni house.[235]

The ecclesiastical dynasty of the Gregorids shared in the same pattern, despite its evident violation of canon law. Here too, despite his presumable familiarity with normal ecclesiastical practices, the author stresses again and again that the legitimate patriarchs must be drawn exclusively from the house of St. Gregory the Illuminator, if any are available (III.xiii, xv, xvii, and especially IV.iii), and even applies to the spiritual primacy the secular dynastic term *nahapet* (IV.iii) customarily used for the head of a noble house, thus indicating that he conceived both spiritual and secular dignities as belonging to the same tight nexus of hereditary prerogatives.[236] The economic bases of the *naxarar* power are also shown as having the same hereditary character, linking them to a particular house rather than to a particular individual. The sole surviving heir of an otherwise annihilated family is accepted without question as the legitimate claimant of the domain of his house even after a long lapse of time, as is evident from the case of the *bdeašx* Bakur's son Xeša's recovery of his inheritance long after his father's disgrace and death and the massacre of the rest of his family (III.ix).[237] Finally, the *Epic Histories* provide some of our best information on the great "marcher-lords" (*bdeašx*s) of the Aršakuni kingdom and on the disappearance of earlier Armenian cities in the fourth century.[238] As a result of these multiple examples, a remarkably systematic and clear image of Early Christian Armenian society emerges from the text and distinguishes its hereditary, aristocratic system from the

[234] On the *sparapetut'iwn* see above, nn. 211, 213.

[235] See Garsoïan, "Prolegomena," cols. 180, 196–197 n. 22.

[236] See Commentary, IV.iii n. 4; also III.xiii and n. 24, for the use of the term *hramanatar* in an ecclesiastical context.

[237] See Commentary, III.ix n. 6. This point is by no means as clear in MX's parallel version of this episode, III.iv, vii (= MK, pp. 257, 259).

[238] Cf. Aa, dxxcxv, dccclxiii, on the marcher lords; also Appendix III, *bdeašx*. On the early Armenian cities, see below, p. 52 and Garsoïan, "Mediaeval Armenian City," and Appendix III, *k'ałak'*.

elective ideology and bureaucratic structure based on merit rather than blood ties that prevailed *de jure*, if not always *de facto*, in the contemporary classical world, as well as from its essentially urban character.

Outwardly, the *Epic Histories* understandably shared the deep anti-Iranism of all Armenian early medieval sources, a position inevitable for a work composed within a generation of Armenia's desperate stand in 451 against the Sasanian attempt to reimpose Zoroastrianism on the country. Any other attitude would have been impossible and incomprehensible under the circumstances. But beneath the unquestionably wholehearted Christian voice of the author, his constant reliance on oral literature simultaneously preserved the echo of earlier traditions and different ideologies surviving in his society.

The continued presence of pagan beliefs and customs is bewailed but recorded in the text. The existence of idol worship in the south-western district of Tarōn (III.iii, xiv), the secret devotion to pagan gods (III.xiii), the casting of lots for the purpose of divination (V.xliii), and most of all, the continuation among the upper classes and indeed even at court of barbaric funeral practices unbefitting the Christian "hope . . . [in] the renewal of the resurrection" (IV.iv, xv; V.xxxi) are repeatedly condemned by the author.[239] Most curious of all is the appeal to the mysterious *Aṙalezkᶜ* expected to resurrect the murdered Mušeł Mamikonean (V.xxxvi), which the author unexpectedly records without any particular outburst of indignation, such as accompany his other references to pagan practices, so that this passage may be a direct transmission of a non-Christian account.[240]

Interesting as are these occasional glimpses of pagan survivals, the main value of the latent evidence in the *Epic Histories* lies in their Iranian or Zoroastrian character, which permits constant comparison and at times reconstruction of Iranian society and testifies to the profound and insufficiently recognized Iranization of Early Christian Armenia.[241] The *naxarar* world so extensively and accurately depicted in the *Epic Histories* finds its exact counterpart in the aristocratic Parthian world, even more than in the Sasanian society contemporary with the text, thus attesting the survival in Armenia of the earlier stage of Iranian society whose memory had been all but obliterated in Persian literature. The hereditary basis of power for both the king and the *naxarar*s distancing

---

[239] See Commentary, V.xxxi n. 14, on idol worship; V.xliii n. 9, for the casting of lots; and IV.iv n. 24, xv n. 32; V.xxxi nn. 9–10, xxxvi, xliv, for funeral practices and the injunctions against them.

[240] See also Commentary, V.xxxvi n. 2.

[241] For a more detailed discussion of Iranian elements in early Christian Armenia, see Garsoïan, "Prolegomena," *passim*; and Russell, *Zor. Arm.*

Armenia from any classical political theory is probably the main criterion for placing the country east of the cultural watershed separating the Mediterranean and Iranian worlds. But more particularly, the strict protocol of the Persian court, with its rigorous observance of precedence on ceremonial occasions, is best set out in the description of Aršak II's reception by Šāhpuhr II (IV.xvi) and of the Armenian king's subsequent outrage at his visible disgrace in the lowering of his position at the king's feast (IV.liv). The Armenian council shows clear parallels to the Parthian one described by Justin, and the Iranian antecedents of much of the Armenian administrative terminology are evident.[242] The Persian custom of admitting minstrels or *gusan*s at official banquets to entertain the guests, a practice that incidentally furthered the transmission of oral literature, is attested at the Armenian court (V.vii, xxxii). The existence in Christian Armenia of the polygamous and particularly consanguinous marriages practiced at the Sasanian court, and in the latter case urged as a pious act in Zoroastrian doctrine, is unmistakably if indirectly admitted (IV.iv, xv; V.xvi).[243]

Far from following the normal urban pattern imported by the classical world into the Orient, as was noted earlier, the Armenian *naχarar*s in the *Epic Histories,* like their Persian counterparts, habitually resided in inaccessible fortresses protected by the rugged terrain of the country (III.xvii; IV.i, xviii; V.iii) and were more or less forcibly brought to court by the king's express order (III.viii). Such cities as were found in the country before the Persian invasion following the peace of 363 were of the typical Hellenistic plan and eponymous type. They are said to have had heavily non-Armenian populations (IV.lv), and no evidence whatever is given for their rebuilding after the restoration of peace in the land.[244] The sole urban foundation attested in Armenia during the fourth century, the city of Aršakawan, is characterized invariably as an asylum for evildoers, and its destruction through God's wrath called down upon it by the curse of the patriarch Nersēs is recorded by the author with evident satisfaction (IV.xii–xiii).[245] Even the heroic Mušeł Mamikonean saw himself slandered for allowing the introduction of "Greek" cities into Armenia (V.xxxiv–xxxv).[246] The king himself seems to have resided normally in

---

[242] On the similar characteristics of the Parthian council, see Justinus, *Epitome*, XLI.iv.2; XLII.iv.l; and Garsoïan, "Prolegomena," cols. 183, 214 n. 46, 232 n. 78; also Appendix III *passim*, for the Iranian etymologies and prototypes of much of BP's terminology.

[243] See Commentary, IV.iv n. 25, xv n. 40; V.xvi n. 3.

[244] On the contrary, Zarehawan is explicitly referred to as being still in ruins (IV.lviii). See above, p. 50 and n. 238.

[245] See above, n. 224.

[246] See Commentary, V.xxxiv n. 4, and xxxv.

semi-temporary encampments (*banak ark⁽uni*), of which the chief one (*bun banak*) was located near Šahapivan in the district of Całkotn (IV.xv), or in "forest palaces" (*tačar mayri*) erected in conjunction with the creation of vast hunting preserves or "paradises" of purely Iranian type (III.viii).[247] The central diversions of the Armenian court and nobility accompanying most ceremonial events—the hunt and the banquet, with their concomitant implications of exalted social status and moral virtue—mirror exactly the practices and beliefs of their Iranian counterparts.[248] The very armament of the armor-clad Armenian noble cavalry matches in every detail that depicted on Parthian and Sasanian monuments.[249]

Transcending a purely secular milieu, the Iranian coloration of Early Christian Armenian society penetrated even into ecclesiastical circles. The title of "defender of the destitute" (*ĵagadov amenayn zrkeloc⁽*) attributed to the patriarch Nersēs the Great at the very beginning of his pontificate and found exclusively in the *Epic Histories,* is otherwise attested only by Iranian sources in reference to Zoroastrian *magupats.*[250] The ambivalent attitude of the author toward the question of ecclesiastical chastity displayed in his automatic acceptance of the precedence of St. Gregory's celibate younger son Aristakēs over his married elder brother Vrt⁽anēs (III.v) and his simultaneous and equally approving account of the divine grant of children to the same Vrt⁽anēs, along with the angelic reassurance of Yusik's misgivings over his marriage, suggest the presence of both points of view in contemporary ecclesiastical circles. Similarly, the marriage of St. Nersēs himself before his consecration as patriarch, and far more surprisingly his early military career, do not seem to have offended the sensibilities of the author (IV.iii). This is equally true in the case of the two daughters born to the patriarch's favorite collaborator, Bishop Xad of Marag, and the eventual transmission of his episcopal dignity to his son-in-law (IV.xii). To be sure, married bishops were not a rarity in the fourth-century church, but these examples suggest that the Armenian hierarchy, possibly under the lingering influence of Zoroastrian antagonism to celibacy, showed little of the obsession with virginity characteristic of much early patristic literature, and far less ascetic propensity

---

[247] See Commentary, III.viii n. 5; IV.xv n. 8; also Appendix II, "Ałiorsk⁽," and Garsoïan, "Banak ark⁽uni."

[248] For a more detailed account of the themes of the hunt and the banquet, See Garsoïan, "Locus," pp. 46–64.

[249] See Appendix III, *zōrk⁽,* I.A.

[250] See Garsoïan, "Protecteur de pauvres." St. Nersēs's pious foundations may also have had partially Iranian antecedents—see Menasce, *Fondations pieuses,* and Boyce, "Pious Foundations"—but the Armenian examples were more probably derived from earlier Greek models, as suggested in Garsoïan, "Nersēs le Grand."

than is shown in the Syrian tradition reflected in the hagiographic interpolations in the *Epic Histories* themselves.[251]

Least explicit, but unquestionably most significant for an evaluation and understanding of Armenian Early Christian beliefs, is the Iranian ethos that unconsciously pervades much of the *Epic Histories* despite their author's overt and unquestionable devotion to the Christian faith. The invariable choice of the hunt and the banquet as settings for crucial moments in the life of the king (III.xx; IV.liv; V.vii, xxxii) or of the equally heroic Mušeł Mamikonean (V.ii, xxxv), raises the possibility that it was not purely fortuitous, but rather the result of a tacit memory that these were the settings par excellence of the royal apotheosis in the Iranian epic tradition.[252] The elegiac tone and heroic character of Aršak II's death in the "Castle of Oblivion" (V.vii), presumably deriving from the oral "Geste of the Aršakuni," override the expected ecclesiastical condemnation of suicide and reveal the simultaneous survival of a different ethos in this period.[253] The presumably deliberate restriction in the use of the heroic epithet $k^c a\check{j}$ to the royal Aršakuni house and its transfer to the Mamikoneans implies an understanding of its transcendental connotations and a knowledge of the Iranian tradition in which supernatural "valor" was granted to the legitimate king or hero by the god Vərəθraγna, the Armenian Vahagn. The same knowledge is implicit in the reference to the birth of Vahagn from a fiery reed in the paean "to Aršak $k^c a\check{j}$" (V.v).[254] Although he condemned it as a "heathen belief," the author of the *Epic Histories* still knew and understood the implications of the Iranian belief that "the glory $[p^c ark^c]$ of the kings and the fortune $[ba\chi t]$ and valor $[k^c a\check{j}ut^c iwn]$ of the realm" were inextricably bound to the person of the legitimate ruler even after death, and that their protection would consequently be lost to the land with the removal of the royal remains (IV.xxiv). This accurate understanding of the Iranian heroic ethos was still shared by the contemporary Armenian version of the "Agat‘angełos Cycle" but not by its Greek translator, nor by Movsēs Xorenac‘i, who cited but no longer grasped the implications of the Persian attempt to kidnap the remains of the Aršakuni kings.[255] The very reliance of the *Epic Histories* on oral "gestes" and tales for the presentation of the narrative places them unmistakably in the Iranian tradition of an epic approach to the retelling of

---

[251] See also, Commentary, III.v n. 1; IV.iii n. 7, xii n. 14. To be sure, celibacy was not a requirement for ecclesiastical office in the fourth-or fifth century church, but both military careers and the hereditary transmission of episcopal offices ran clearly counter to contemporary norms.

[252] See Garsoïan, "Locus," pp. 63–64, and above, n. 248.

[253] See Commentary, V.vii nn. 6, 12.

[254] See Commentary, V.v n. 16; and Appendix III, $k^c a\check{j}$.

[255] See Commentary, IV.xxiv n. 12.

history, as opposed to Movsēs Xorenac⁽i's deliberate choice of classical models.[256]

It is on their own terms, therefore, as the accurate reflection of a living society and not the presentation of a political chronicle, that the ultimate value of the *Epic Histories* is to be sought. They are not a systematic exposition of political events from which other considerations have been omitted as extraneous, but neither are they a haphazard collection of folktales. They are rather a compilation, admittedly chaotic at times, of varied materials bearing on the events, institutions, customs, and beliefs of fourth-century Armenia set out in the order of successive generations, through which the complexities and contradictions of a society in transition from a still surviving Iranian past to fervent Christianity, yet fully aware of itself as a distinct entity, have been transmitted more successfully than might have been possible through a narrower and more synthesized approach. No strands have been discarded, no voices effectively stilled. Without the work of their author we would know but little of the Armenian patriarchate in the fourth century or of the influence of early Syrian Christianity on Armenia and its depth; of the hereditary social structure of the country or of its composition, and of the importance of the Mamikonean *sparapet*s culminating in their effective control of the realm during the regency of Manuēl; or of the extensive body of oral literature existing at the time; and we would know almost nothing of the Iranian aspects of this Christian society. As a result, no valid or balanced image of the culture of the period can be recreated without his testimony, and therein lies his best claim to have indeed provided a "history of Armenia" in its broadest sense.

NINA G. GARSOÏAN

[256] See MX, II.ii–iii (= MK, pp. 67–70). See also, Boyce, "Parthian Literature," especially pp. 1115–1160, for the presence of the epic-historical tradition among the Parthians and in Armenia; and *idem*, "Persian Literature," pp. 55–60, for its survival in the Sasanian period.

Translator's Preface

No attempt has been made to provide a critical edition of the *Epic Histories* in conjunction with the present translation, since such a text is now being prepared in Erevan by G. V. Abgaryan. Moreover, the editor was kind enough to indicate to me in personal conversations (June 1983 and June 1986) that no major variants suggesting the existence of a separate family of manuscripts had been noted by him during his review of the surviving ones not already included in the previous editions. In view of the very late manuscript history of the text, such a conclusion cannot, regrettably, be surprising. Consequently, the present translation has followed in the main the 1832 Venice edition in its 1933 fourth revision, incorporating the evidence of the different set of manuscripts used in the 1883 St. Petersburg edition. Some additional corrections have duly been indicated in the Commentary, wherever they occur. Earlier translations have naturally been consulted, especially the modern Armenian one first published by St. Malχasyanc^c in 1947 and reprinted posthumously, with some modifications, in 1968. The very useful and incisive, but only partially published "Review" of M. A. Gevorgian's Russian translation by H. S. Anasyan (the complete typescript of which was kindly made available to me by colleagues during my stay in Erevan in 1983) has also been taken into consideration.

Some attempt has been made to render the Armenian text into readable English, but the first concern has been to preserve the sense of the original wherever possible, a task rendered more difficult by the fact that the syntax of classical Armenian and that of modern English by no means follow the same pattern. Awkwardnesses and repetitions in the text have not been smoothed out, and formulaic patterns have been maintained. Some variations in style have been allowed, to indicate epic or homiletic passages in the original. Since the Biblical citations show numerous, even if minor, variants from the version found in the Armenian Bible, they have invariably been treated as part of the text without any attempt at correction. All technical terms marked with an asterisk in the

57

text (such as *asχarh*, *realm, *gund*, *contingent, and the like) have been translated whenever possible in the same manner throughout to show their usage by the author, and they are discussed in further detail in Appendix III. The few exceptions to this rule have been indicated either by giving the Armenian term in brackets, or by means of a commentary on the particular usage.

With the exception of the names of the apostles and prophets, Peter, Paul, John, etc. primarily in Biblical quotations, as well as some classical toponyms outside Armenia (such as Alexandria, Athens, Caesarea), proper names have been given in their Armenian form, i.e. Vałeš, not Valens; Šapuh, not Šāhpuhr; Gamirk⁽, not Cappadocia; Mcbin, not Nisibis; with the more familiar form added in brackets where it might not otherwise be evident. Similarly, the variants of a given name have been maintained in the translation—for example, both Barsilios and Barseł for Basilios/Basil—since these inconsistencies are indicative of the author's essential reliance on the Armenian forms familiar to him and his ignorance of their correct classical versions (see IV.iv, n. 8). These variants also provide additional evidence for the refutation of the thesis of a Greek original of the work, discussed in the Introduction. To avoid undue periphrases or awkward locutions, some Armenian technical terms, such as *naχarar* or *sparapet*, have not been translated and their meanings are discussed at the apposite place in the Appendix of Technical Terms. The spellings used in the text have been maintained in the translation and in the Appendices even when they are open to doubt. Where several words in the translation are equivalent to a single Armenian title, they have been linked by dashes: e.g. *sparapet ew zōravar* = *sparapet* and commander-in-chief.

A Commentary and five Appendices have been added to the translation. The purpose of the Commentary has been to indicate or discuss allusions or difficulties found in the particular passage in the text to which it refers, wherever this has seemed desirable or possible. Similar or parallel passages have been indicated by cross-references.

The first three Appendices containing all proper names and every term marked by an asterisk in the text, are intended as complements to the Commentary. Their purpose is to supply information on I–the Onomasticon, II–the Toponymy, and III–the Technical Terms (both in Armenian and in the translation) found in the text in a more general historical or linguistic context, but one still relevant to their appearance in the *Epic Histories*. Thus, for instance, the mention of Alexandria in Egypt (III.x) has been noted in Appendix II, but no general account of this famous city has been attempted, since such a discussion would be totally incommensurate with the passing reference to it in connection with the heresiarch Arius. The multiple Iranian etymologies for proper names and particularly technical terms are intended to underscore the degree of Iranization of the work. The inclusion of every appearance of a proper name or technical term in the Appendices allows them to serve simultaneously as Indices to the text.

In addition to this first group, two further Appendices have been included: Appendix IV provides a list of Scriptural references, both direct and presumed, in the text, together with the Book and chapter in which they occur. All of these references are given according to the order and numbering of the Armenian Bible (Zōhrapean/Zōhrab edition). Appendix V offers a list of all the repetitions of oral-formulaic refrains to be found in the text in both their verbatim and variant forms, together with the Book and chapter in which they occur. The beginning of these formulae has been indicated in the text by means of a dagger. No further stylistic analysis has been attempted, however, since such an undertaking would be beyond the competence of the present writer's historical and archaeological training.

All references to the pagination of the text, as against that of the translation, are to that of the 4th revised (1933) Venice edition. This pagination has also been indicated in Arabic numbers at the apposite points in the left-hand margin of the translation in order to facilitate any reference to the Armenian text. References omitting the author's name but giving Book and chapter are to the text of *Buzandaran Patmutⁱwnkᶜ* (BP). References to an author by name but without indication of title are to the respective translations of the text.

For the sake of brevity, abbreviations and short titles have been used in every part of this book. Full bibliographical information has been given, however, in the list of Abbreviations for journals and standard reference works and in the Bibliography for all other works.

* As indicated above, an asterisk within the text identifies a technical term discussed in Appendix III.

† As indicated above, a dagger within the text marks the beginning of one of the stereotype formulae listed in Appendix V.

To my knowledge, no satisfactory system has been devised as yet for the rendering of the variant forms of the same Armenian author's name that would conciliate without arbitrariness or insufferable pedantry the accepted transcriptions of an author's name in the various languages employed for his publications (e.g. Patkanean/Patkanov, Sargsyan/Sarkisian); the irreconcilable pronunciations of modern Eastern and Western Armenian, as well as the author's indicated preferences (Tašean/Dashian, Awgerean/Aucher); and, finally, twentieth-century spelling reforms (Yovhannēsean/Hovhannisyan). Consequently, any attempt at unification or standardization has reluctantly been abandoned, and the divergent forms of an author's name used in particular publications has been maintained. To provide a minimal guide through this perpetual chaos, however, all variants have been grouped together in the Bibliographical entries under the transcription of the form currently used by the Armenian Academy of Sciences, except in the case of individuals who were never subject to recent reforms. In all cases, the variants have been cross-indexed in the Bibliography.

In keeping with standard international practice, the system of transliteration for Armenian used throughout is that of Hübschmann-Meillet-Benveniste:

ա	բ	գ	դ	ե	զ	է	ը	թ	ժ	ի	լ	խ	ծ	կ	հ	ձ	ղ
a	b	g	d	e	z	ē	ə	t῾	ž	i	l	χ	c	k	h	j	ł

ճ	մ	յ	ն	շ	ո	չ	պ	ջ	ռ	ս	վ	տ	ր	ց	ւ	փ	ք
č	m	y	n	š	o	č῾	p	ǰ	ṙ	s	v	t	r	c῾	w	p῾	k῾

օ	ու
ō	u

The Epic Histories:
Buzandaran Patmut'iwnk'

Preliminary Statement[1]

Chronological tables[2] are to be found in this third book of the narratives;[3] and [in addition] to it [there are] three [more] books. That is to say, there are altogether four books, and the four are the commemoration of the same events recalling the accounts of the *race of the sons of T᷎orgom[4] in the *realm of Armenia;[5] that is to say, the order of past events: the lives and deeds of the holy men of God—the *high-priests[6]—until the departure of each one from this *world; and of the Aršakuni [Arsacid] kings— the *lords of the *realm;[7] and of the *military commanders—famous men and *valiant *naχarars; also peace and war, prosperity and ruin, justice and unrighteousness, worship of God and impiety. This chronicle has been compiled from the reign of Xosrov son of Trdat to the decline of the Armenian kings, until these late times,[8] and from the *high-priesthood of Vrt᷎anēs son of the first *high-priest Grigor until these last ones who were the *principal-bishops[9] of Armenia. Setting these down one by one according to date and number, I have described them in each chapter. And, I have set down four Tables of Contents [each] at the beginning of the four Books to the end, to assist all those who will wish to penetrate earnestly into what I shall relate.[10]

Third Table*

Twenty-one [Chapters] of Chronography

i. Concerning that which took place in the *land of Armenia, the *realm of the son of T͑orgom, after the preaching of the apostle T͑addeos.

ii. Concerning the first great *high-priest Grigor and their [sic] tombs.

iii. Concerning the reign of Xosrov son of Trdat and the great priest Vrt͑anēs son of Grigor.

iv. Concerning the two *houses of the Manawazean and the Orduni, which were annihilated in the *realm of Armenia.

v. Concerning the sons of the *high-priest Vrt͑anēs, the elder of whom was named Grigoris and the second Yusik.

vi. Concerning Grigoris son of Vrt͑anēs, his death, and the place of his burial.

vii. Concerning the battle resulting from the incursion of the king of the Maz-k͑ut͑k͑ into the *realm under the *dominion of the king of Armenia and how he was killed, together with his army.

viii. Concerning the planting of forests, and the wars with the Persians, and the annihilation of the *naxarar *house of Bznuni.

ix. Concerning the *bdeašx Bakur, who revolted against the king of Armenia, and the way that he was killed by the Armenian army, and that Vałinak Siwni became *bdeašx in his stead.

x. Concerning Yakob [James], bishop of Mcbin [Nisibis].

xi. Concerning the great war between the Persians and the Armenians and the death in this war of the *commander-in-chief Vač͑ē; and the death of King Xosrov; and the passing from the *world of the *patriarch Vrt͑anēs.

xii. Concerning the reign of Tiran over the *realm of Armenia after his father. Also, how Yusik ascended the *patriarchal *throne after his father Vrt͑anēs; and how he was killed by King Tiran for his rebuke of the king.

xiii. Concerning the reason for which the *lands of Armenia remained without *spiritual-leadership after the death of Yusik, and the sons of Yusik were unworthy of their father's *throne.

xiv. Concerning [the life] and deeds of the great man of God Daniēl; how he rebuked King Tiran, and how he was put to death by him as punishment.

xv. Concerning the sons of Yusik and how they scorned and trampled under foot the *dignity of the great *high-priest of God.

16   xvi. Concerning P^carēn, who occupied the *patriarchal *throne.

    xvii. Concerning Šahak, who was descended from Bishop Ałbianos and who succeeded to the *patriarchal *throne; and how at that time the *land of Armenia abandoned the *Lord and His Commandments.

    xviii. Concerning the *hayr[father]-*mardpet, who gave evil advice to the king, [i.e.] to destroy the *clans of the Armenian *naχarars.

    xix. Concerning the sons of Yusik, Pap and At^canaginēs; how and why they were struck down for their unrighteousness in the holy place.

    xx. Concerning King Tiran and how he was betrayed by his *senekapet P^cisak Siwni; how he was suddenly taken prisoner by the Persian *official Varaz in time of peace and destroyed; and how the entire *land of Armenia was destroyed and lost with him.

    xxi. Concerning the way in which all the Armenian *naχarars unanimously *gathered together and went and brought the king of the Greeks to the *land of Armenia to help them; and how the king of Persia came with a large army, and the Persian forces were massacred by the Greek army and the surviving Armenians; and how Nerseh king of Persia escaped from the *land of Armenia on a single horse and fled to the *land of the Persians.

---

    * References in the Table of Contents will be commented upon in the corresponding chapters.

Book III
The Beginning[1]

Chapter i. Concerning that which took place in the *land of the *realm of Armenia after the preaching of the apostle T^cadēos: Chronological account.[2]

[That which took place] after the preaching of the apostle Thaddeus and his martyr's death[3] to the completion of the *teaching of Grigor[4] and his [eternal] rest,[5] and from the apostle-killer King Sanatruk to the unwilling submission of King Trdat to the faith and his eternal rest:[6] past events [and] the deeds of virtuous men of old and of their opponents; all that has been written by others. But we too have set something down here in the order of our narrative, nor, passing it over, did we omit it, so as to conform to the sequence of events. For there is in our narrative something of what came first and something of what came last, but what came in between ‹that has been written by others. But›[7], lest a gap appear in the midst of our narrative, we have noted [it], as a brick is set in the wall of a structure for the completion of the whole. That which occurred hereafter will be narrated in sequence.

    Chapter ii. Concerning the great *high-priest[s][1] Grigor [and Aristakēs] and their tombs.

And so, in the reign of Trdat son of Xosrov, [Armenia] was illuminated through the God-pleasing love and worshipful faith that the great priest Grigor son of Anak had made known to it.[2] And his younger son Aristakēs was his father's collaborator-in-the-episcopate during the entire course of his *spiritual-teaching [mission], †through all the days of his life until the day that Christ called him to his rest.[3] Abiding places and fitting tombs were prepared for them:[4] for the great Grigor in the *district of Daranałik^c, in the *village named T^cordan.[5] As for his son, St. Aristakēs, after his confessor's death,[6] they carried him from the *district of Cop^ck^c and laid him to rest in the *district of Ekełeac^c, in the *town of T^cil, which was the *domain [kaluac] of his father, Grigor.

*Chapter iii. Concerning the reign of Xosrov son of Trdat and the great *high-priest Vrt*anēs son of Grigor.*[1]

And after this reigned Xosrov Kotak [the Lesser], the grandson of Xosrov and the son of the *valiant and virtuous King Trdat.[2] In his time Vrt*anēs, the elder son of Grigor, became *high-priest on the *throne of his father, in place of his father and his *brother. In their days peace and prosperity, increase in population and well-being, fertility, serendipity and profit, and great God-loving service in pleasing, virtuous ways grew and multiplied. Like his father and his *brother, St. Vrt*anēs enlightened and *guided them spiritually, and righteousness and justice flourished at that time.

At about that time, the *chief-bishop Vrt*anēs went to the first and *mother-church of Armenia,[3] which was in the *land of Tarōn, where formerly, the *altars of the *[pagan]-temples were destroyed by the great *high-priest Grigor through the appearance of the [holy] portents.[4] Having come there, he performed, in accordance with perpetual custom, the eucharistic sacrifice of the *Lord's redeeming crucifixion,[5] the communion in commemoration of His passion that is the vivifying and liberating body and blood of the Son of God our *Lord Jesus Christ. For, in this very fashion the *chief-bishops of Armenia, together with the kings and *magnates, the *naχarars, and the multitude of the people, were wont to *honor those places which were formerly the sites of heathen idols and were subsequently purified in the name of the Divinity and became a house of prayer and a place of *congregation for all. They gathered especially in the church of this chief place to commemorate the saints who were there, every year on the seventh day of the month [of Sahmi?],[6] and those maintaining the same tradition [gathered] particularly at the great chapcl, *martyrium-of-the-prophet [margarēaran] John.[7] Assembling also every year at the martyria-of-the-apostles [aṙakʿelaran] and disciples of the *Lord and at the *shrines-of-the-martyrs [vkayaran], they celebrated with jubilation the feast commemorating the deeds of their *valorous lives.[8]

But a certain event occurred at the time that the great *high-priest Vrt*anēs had come alone with a few [attendants] to perform the sacrifice of praise.[9] Then, those who had secretly kept until then to the ancient heathen idol-worshiping customs[10]—up to two thousand in number—*gathered together and plotted to kill the *high-priest of God, Vrt*anēs. They had been partially emboldened to commit this [deed] by [the instigation] of the king's wife, for the holy man had rebuked her for her secret adultery and dissolute ways.[11] And so they came and surrounded the great fortified [kʿałakʿormn] church of Aštišat.[12] A large force without sought to surround and besiege it while he was performing the sacrifice within. [But] the arms of each one in the *group [gund] were miraculously turned backward and tied behind his shoulders without being bound by anything.[13]

Thus, all of them found themselves on the *ground, enveloped, tightly bound, twisted, constrained, speechless, and motionless. These [men] were from the *families and *races of the evil *pagan-priests,[14] the devourers and destroyers of the *world. So then, the band was piled up, bound in this fashion, in the *gawit^c of the church, [until] Vrt^canēs himself came out, drew near to them, and asked: "Who are you?" and "Where have you come from? Whom do you seek?" or "Whence have you come?[15] And they †began to speak the truth and confessed: "We have come to destroy these places and to kill you, emboldened by the order and instigation of the *queen of Greater Armenia. But the *Lord God manifested His might and showed us that He alone is God, and now we have understood and believed that He alone is God. Thus we are bound in such a way that we are unable to move from this place." And the blessed Vrt^canēs, citing the word of *spiritual-teaching, strengthened them in the faith in one *Lord Jesus Christ and spoke a great deal to them. Then he prayed and implored God; he healed and freed them from their invisible bonds and from the irresistible tormenting constriction. And when they had been released from it, they all fell down before him and begged for the healing of penitence, and he gave [them] a set time for penance.[16] And when they had learned the faith in the Consubstantial and Holy Trinity, he baptized some two thousand of them, besides their women and children. Thus he brought them to the faith and sent them forth purified and believing.

21   *Chapter iv. Concerning the two *houses of the Manawazean and the Orduni, which were annihilated in the *realm of Armenia.*[1]

And around that time a great disturbance arose in the *realm of Armenia because two great *naχarars and *princes, *keepers-of-districts and *lords-of-realms, quarreled with each other, raised up a most rancorous conflict, and waged unlawful war against each other. The *prince of the Manawazean *house and the *nahapet of the Orduni *house, on the opposite side, perturbed the great *realm of Armenia. They fought a great war against each other, and many men were destroyed in the slaughter. Then, King Xosrov and the great *chief-bishop Vrt^canēs sent the *honored and great bishop Ałbianos to [come] between them [and] speak of peaceful reconciliation. The blessed Ałbianos set out and came to them to direct and win them over to a mutual reconciliation, [but] they insulted him and would not listen to his intercession. They scorned the senders, drove the bishop away with great hostility, and seized and destroyed the *domain of the king. Increasingly enraged, they hastened to join battle together. Then the king, in great anger and wrath, sent against them Vač^cē, son of Artawazd, the *nahapet of the Mamikonean *house—who was from the *clan of the *sparapets of Armenia and the *commander-in-chief of his army[2]—in order to destroy and annihilate the two *clans.

69

The *commander Vačʿē consequently set forth against them. He attacked and vanquished the two *clans and †did not leave [alive] a single male child from the two *families, not a one;[3] and he himself returned to King Xosrov, the king of Armenia, and to the *chief-bishop Vrtʿanēs. And [the king] gave to the church of bishop Ałbianos the *town and *village that was the *seat [bun gahoyicʿ] of the Manawazean *nahapet—[that is to say] Manawazakert—together with the whole of its *territories and the
22   *district around them that lies *alongside the Epʿrat River. And they gave the *home *village [bun gewłn] of the Orduni[4]—the name of which was Orduru and from which came the bishop of Basean—together with its *territories [to this bishop], for it lay in the *land of Basean.

*Chapter v. Concerning the sons of the *high-priest Vrtʿanēs, the elder of whom was called Grigoris and the second Yusik.*

Vrtʿanēs and Aristakēs were the sons of the great *high-priest Grigor. Aristakēs remained celibate and holy from childhood and therefore he ascended his father's episcopal *throne first, though he was the younger son. Vrtʿanēs, however, was married, though childless, and for a long time he implored God that He should not deprive him of the blessing of children, but that one of his progeny should stand before him in the service of the *Lord.[1] And in his old age the *Lord heard his prayer. His wife conceived and bore twin sons, and he named the elder Grigoris after his father, and the second Yusik. They were nurtured in the presence of the king of Armenia, and care was taken to teach them the knowledge of the Scriptures.

Then, the elder, Grigoris, attained the episcopal dignity in the *regions of Ałuankʿ [Albania] and Virkʿ [Iberia], for he was of handsome stature, outstanding in spiritual merit, and filled with the knowledge of God. He did not marry, but at the age of fifteen he attained the episcopal dignity over the *realms of Virkʿ and Ałuankʿ, that is to say the *borderlands of the Mazkʿutʿkʿ. When he came there, he renewed the churches with illuminating regulations, imitating the actions of his grandfather,[2] the first Grigor.

As for Yusik,[3] he was *nurtured by Tiran, the son of King Xosrov, and Tiran, the king's son, gave his daughter[4] in marriage to Yusik, the son of Vrtʿanēs. And while he was [still] a youth he knew her once on the first night, and his wife conceived. Then he immediately saw in a vision that he would have two sons and they would not be fit for the ministry of the *Lord
23   God; and he repented his marriage. He wept and implored God, repenting with great anguish. He had been forced by the king into marriage as a youth, yet this [too] was done through the grace of God, so that thereafter there should come forth from him chief shepherds[5] to serve the precepts of the Gospels for the good of the *realm and the prosperity of the

church. Although he did not go near his wife except for that one night, yet the woman bore twins, as had seen in his earlier vision, and the first was called Pap and the second At͑anaginēs. And after his intercourse with his wife on that one night he did not know her again because of his youthful virtue.

[It was] not that he considered marriage polluting, but that he was in doubt from the vision he had seen as to the reason that such an unworthy child should ever be born from him;[6] for he longed not for *earthly children but for such as would stand in the *service and ministry of the *Lord God. And holding all *earthly things as naught, he held as good not that which is passing, but that which is above, [and] looked with longing towards the heavenly life. He held it good to *serve Christ alone, and considered it his *glory.[7] He gave no thought to the love of the king or to the *honors received from him, or to greatness, or to his family relationship of son-in-law to the king,[8] but he rejected all these [things] altogether, considering them alien and odious and delusions. And after the first time he was never again led astray like a youth, but achieved a fatherly mind and the wisdom of old age, [that is,] the prudent striving toward immortality.[9] He preferred opprobrium for Christ's [sake] to the greatness of kings.[10] He chose for himself the ways of mortification and led a virtuous life from the age of twelve. He imitated his father and took his *brother Grigoris as an example and unflinchingly bore the yoke of Christ until his death.[11]

24

The royal *house had, therefore, been hostile to him, but while his in-laws oppressed him on account of this, his wife died; and [so] Yusik was delivered from calumny.[12] And as he was concerned about his [orphaned] children and raised in anguish a prayer to the *Lord on account of this, an angel of the *Lord appeared to him in a vision and said: "Yusik son of Grigor, fear not![13] for the *Lord has heard thy prayer, and from these children of thine will be born other children.[14] And they will be illuminators of knowledge[15] and founts of spiritual wisdom for this *realm of Armenia, and the grace of God's Commandments shall gush from them. And great peace and prosperity, and the foundation of many churches shall be given to them by the *Lord, with many victories and great might. And through them, many who had gone astray shall return to the path of truth and shall *glorify Christ in many tongues.[16] They shall be the pillars of the church,[17] the dispensers of the Word of life and the foundations of the faith, the ministers of Christ and the servants of the Holy Spirit; for wherever a building receives its foundation there shall be its completion. And many fruitful and useful and helpful plants shall be planted by their industrious hand in the spiritual garden and receive God's blessing. But those who shall be unwilling to be planted with them and to drink the same spiritual dew of knowledge, they shall be castigated and cast forth, and their end shall be the burning fire.[18] They shall be hated and envied many times by the unworthy because of the *Lord, but they shall be steadfast in the faith like a rock, and they shall vanquish them through great endurance.[19] And after them falsehood shall reign through unbridled[20] self-loving, silver-loving, deceitful, abandoned, useless, lying, and slanderous men, and thereafter, hardly anyone shall be found who holds fast to the *covenant of the faith." And when young Yusik heard all of this from the angel, he gave thanks in great consolation to the *Lord God who had made him worthy of such a revelation in [His] answer. And †through all the days of his life he ceaselessly gave thanks at all times.

25

Chapter vi. Concerning Grigoris son of Vrtᶜanēs, his death and the place of his burial.[1]

As for Bishop Grigoris the son of Vrtᶜanēs and the *brother of Yusik who was *katᶜołikos[2] of the *regions of Virkᶜ and Ałuankᶜ, though he attained his ministry when only a youth, he built and restored all the churches in those *regions, reaching [all the way] to the *districts of Atrpatakan. He became the preacher of the true faith in Christ, and he was to all [men a source of] marvel and amazement [because of] his most strict and severe, countless and weighty practices of the ascetic way of life, [his] fasts, saintliness, sleepless vigils, and tireless burning prayers to the *Lord God, interceding for all mankind. Through the grace of God he unfailingly fulfilled the evangelical course and the supervision of the holy church. Still more, he strove to incite all through exhortation to persevere in good deeds; night and day, through fasts and prayers, and powerful entreaties, and the utmost perfection of faith he aroused both near and far to spiritual fervor. Like a combat-loving athlete he always held himself in practice and readiness for all trials and afflictions so as to defend with the utmost boldness and fight for the true faith that is Christ's.[3]

And when he had restored and renewed all the churches of those *regions, he came to the *camp of the Aršakuni king of the Mazkᶜutᶜkᶜ, whose name was Sanēsan. For their kings and the Armenian ones were of the same *race and *house.[4] And so he came before the king of the Mazkᶜutᶜkᶜ, the *prince of the numerous *host of the Honkᶜ, and standing before them †he began to preach and announce Christ to them. He said unto them: "Acknowledge God!" At first, they listened and accepted and submitted. Then, [however,] they began to examine the laws of Christ and learned from him that looting and pillage, killing, greed, the deprivation of others, the devouring of what belongs to others, the envy of the possessions of others are odious to God. Then, when they truly understood [that], they became enraged at his words and said: "If we do not pillage, if we do not loot, if we do not seize [the possessions] of others, how shall we who are such a large army subsist?" And although he sought to soothe

26

their heart with myriads of good words, they were in no way disposed to give ear, but [rather] said to one another: "He has come with these words wishing to deprive us of the *valor⁵ in the hunt that is our livelihood. For if we listen to him and turn to the Christian laws, how shall we survive if we do not ride our steeds as is our own native custom? Moreover," they said, "this is a plot of the Armenian king, to send this man to us so as to halt with his teaching our plundering raids on his *realm. But come, let us kill him, and let us raid into Armenia and fill our *realm with plunder."

Then the king changed his mind and listened to the words of his army. And they caught a wild horse, hanged and bound young Grigoris to the tail of the horse, and drove him over the plain along the shore of the great Northern Sea,⁶ the plain of Vatneay [which lay] outside their *camp. And in this way they slew the virtuous preacher of Christ, the youthful Grigoris. Then those who had come with him from the *district of Haband took him up and bore him to their *district of Haband in the *region of Ałuankᶜ *bordering on Armenia,⁷ to the *village called Amaraz. And they buried him by the church built by the grandfather of Grigoris, the first great Grigor, the great *high-priest of the *realm of the Armenian *land. And year after year the inhabitants of these *regions and these *districts of the *realms gather together in a general *assembly and celebrate the feast day commemorating his *valor.⁸

27   *Chapter vii. Concerning the battle resulting from the raid of the king of the Mazkᶜutᶜkᶜ into the *realm ruled by the king of Armenia and how he was killed, together with his army.*¹

At that time, Sanēsan, king of the Mazkᶜutᶜkᶜ, nourished an implacable hatred and rancor against his *kinsman Xosrov, king of Armenia. And so, he gathered and assembled all the forces of the Honkᶜ and the Pᶜoχkᶜ, of the Tᶜawasparkᶜ, the Hečmatakkᶜ, the Ižmaχkᶜ, the Gatᶜkᶜ, and Głuarkᶜ, the Gugarkᶜ, the Šičbkᶜ, and the Čiłbkᶜ and the Bałaščikᶜ, and the Egersuankᶜ,² and masses of other rabble. [It was] an innumerable nomadic *host [*banak*], whose entire large force he led himself. He crossed his own *border at the great Kur River and came flooding over the *land of the Armenian *realm. And no one could number the vastness of the *cavalry *contingents, or reckon the force of the *club-bearers on *foot, so that they themselves could not number their own army. But whenever they held a muster by *contingents, *banners,³ and detachments at designated places, every man was ordered to carry a stone so as to throw it down from these very visible places in order to form a mound, so that as many as there were would be an indication of the size [of the army]; a fearful sign [left] for the morrow to understand past events.⁴ And wherever they passed, they left such markers at every crossroad along their way. And so they came, filled, and covered the whole of the *land of

Armenia; ravaged, captured, and destroyed it completely. They scattered and spread altogether over its *territory, and stretched all the way to the small *city of Satał and to Ganjak, [which is] the *border of Atrpatakan.[5] [And] they pushed on and gathered at the appointed *region of the *district of Ayrarat, [where] there was a large *encampment.

Xosrov, king of Armenia, fled from his *brother,[6]—that is, from
28 Sanēsan, king of the Mazk'ut'k'—and threw himself into the *fortified *stronghold of Darewnk' in the *land of Kovg; and the elderly Vrt'anēs, *chief-bishop of Armenia, [went] together with him. Then they kept fasts and begged God to deliver them from this cruel slaughterer, and they began to implore the *Lord God. [Meanwhile, Sanēsan] overran and subjected the whole of the *land for about one year. Then Vač'ē, the son of Artawazd from the Mamikonean *house, the *commander-in-chief of all Greater Armenia, came [back], for at that time he had gone on a long journey in the *regions of the Greeks. He collected together all the most *valiant[7] *naχarars and formed a very large *contingent. †He fell upon the *camp [of the Mazk'ut'k'] at break of day during the dawn service, for they were *encamped on the mountain called C'lu Gluχ [Bull's Head]. He †put all of them to the *sword, †left not one of them alive,[8] and brought back the multitude of those [held] captive. Then, after this, he gathered up the booty, set forth, and marched down into the plain of the *district of Ayrarat. Upon arriving [there], he found Sanēsan, king of the Mazk'ut'k', with his own *contingent [*bun gund*], as well as an †innumerable [and] countless host, in the *city of Vałaršapat. Drawing up his *contingent, Vač'ē fell on the *city unexpectedly, and the *Lord gave them into his hand.[9] And when they saw him falling upon them, they fled from the *city to the craggy *region of the *fortress of Ōšakan, counting on those desert and rocky places as a refuge. And an extremely fierce battle took place. And the *companions-in-arms of the Armenian *commander— namely Bagrat Bagratuni, Mehundak and Garegin Řštuni, Vahan *nahapet* of the Amatuni *house, and Varaz Kaminakan[10]—fell upon and slaughtered the forces of the Alank', Mazk'ut'k', Honk', and other *tribes and filled the rocky plain with the bodies of the dead until blood swelled up and flowed overwhelmingly like a river, and the number of the dead was beyond count.

And they drove the surviving few before them all the way to the *country of the Bałasčik' and brought the head of the great king Sanēsan
29 before the king of Armenia. But when he saw it, he began to weep and said: "He was my *brother from the *clan of the Aršakuni."[11] Then the king came to the battlefield together with the great *chief-bishop of Armenia, and they saw the massacre of the slaughtered host, for the *earth was putrid with the stench of the dead. Then they commanded that *irregular-levies be raised from the *country and [the dead] be covered over with a mound of stones[12] lest the *land be polluted by the putrid

stench of the bones of the dead. And so the *land rested in peace for many years, and in this way the murder of St. Grigoris was avenged on King Sanēsan and his *host, for †none of them survived, not a one.[13]

*Chapter viii. Concerning the planting of forests, and of wars with the Persians, and of the annihilation of the *naχarar *house of Bznuni.*[1]

When the *land of Armenia had been at peace for a time, Xosrov king of Armenia commanded that rewards be given to the *valiant men who had toiled for him and had given their lives for the *realm of Greater Armenia in every battle of the war. And to the *commander Vačᶜē he gave the springs of Ĵanĵanak, Ĵrabašχkᶜ, and Cᶜlu Gluχ, together with all their *districts. And likewise [he gave] the *greatest rewards to the other *naχarars.[2]

And the king gave the order to his *commander to call up a large force from the *realm, to bring wild oak[s] from the woods and plant them in the *district of Ayrarat, from the *fortified royal *stronghold called Gaṙni to the hill in the plain of the Mecamōr called Duin,[4] which is on the northern side of the great *city of Artašat. And so, they planted the oak forest downstream as far as the *palace of Tiknuni and he called it *Tačar Mayri* ["the Forest Palace"]. Similarly, they planted another forest to the south along the reed bed, filling the plain with oaks, and called it Xosrovakert. They built a royal *palace [*aparank*ᶜ] there and enclosed both places with a wall, [but] they did not unite them, so as [to leave] a road for traveling. And [the forest] throve and grew tall, and the king then ordered the gathering of all sorts of game and wild animals and the filling of the enclosures [*kᶜaḷakoḷmn*] [with them], so that these should become places for the king's hunt, diversion, and pleasure.[5] And the *commander Vačᶜē swiftly carried out the commands of the king.

And while he was occupied with the task of planting the forests, an unexpected bearer of ill tidings came to Xosrov from the *districts of Hēr and Zarawand [announcing]: "The Persian army is ready for a warlike attack against you."[6] Then King Xosrov ordered Databay the *nahapet of the Bznuni, to raise *irregular-levies beyond measure from the *country and troops together with the *elite -contingent [*matenik gund*] and march forth against them to attack and impede the foe. And so Databē set out against the Persian host with a massive Armenian force. But when he reached them, Databē made an agreement with the *princes of the Persian host, intending to hand his *lord the king of Armenia over to them. He ordered the enemy to make an ambush for his own army, and there †he delivered his own troops to the *sword. They slaughtered forty thousand Armenian troops altogether with a sudden and unexpected [attack], and the other forces fled. And the malevolent Databē took the Persian host [with him] and intended to attack the king of Armenia. But the fleeing troops quickly reached the *camp of the Armenian king with the sad news of the dreadful slaughter that had taken place and of the evil betrayal of the iniquitous Databē.

Then Xosrov king of Armenia, together with the *high-priest Vrtᶜanēs, fell to the ground and implored God with numerous supplications and vehement tears. After this, he hastened to call up his army—up to thirty 31 thousand [men]—with the *commander Vačᶜē and marched forth against [the enemy], together with all his *azat-contingent of *greatest *naχarars. And they came together on the shore of the sea of Bznunikᶜ [Lake Van], at the *town of Aṙest, on a little stream by the royal fisheries. And they saw the Persian host, which was countless in size—for they were †like the stars in the heavens or †like grains of sand on the shore of the sea⁷—for they had come with innumerable elephants and immeasurable forces. Nevertheless, [the Armenians] †fell on the *camp, placing their hope in God; they attacked, slaughtered, and massacred [the foe] and †left none of them [alive], not a one.⁸ And they carried off much booty, and elephants, and all the strength of their might. The *sparapet Vačᶜē and *valiant Vahan Amatuni captured Databē and brought him before the great king Xosrov; and they stoned him as a man who was a traitor to the *realm, the *contingent, and the army of his *lord.⁹ And his *clan, his wife, and his children were in the *fortress of the *prince of Ṙštunikᶜ¹⁰ on the island called Ałtᶜamar. The *sparapet Vačᶜē took ship, reached the island, and left alive neither female nor male, and that noble *naχarar-*house [azgatohm naχararutⁱeann] was destroyed in this way and its possessions confiscated for the royal treasury.

But the Persians did not stop waging war against King Xosrov after this. And he laid down the law that the *greatest-magnates, the *naχarars, the *keepers-of-realms, the *lords-of-realms, those with [contingents] of a myriad or a thousand [men],¹¹ should stay with the king and accompany him and not a single one of them was to go out with the royal army.¹² For he feared their faithlessness and that they might act like Databē and revolt against him. But he put his trust in old Vačᶜē, in the true¹³ *sparapet [who was] the *commander-in-chief of Greater Armenia, and in *valiant¹⁴ Vahan Amatuni. He united the forces of the *noble *houses with the royal army and entrusted all those assembled to [the two of] them, and they constantly fought *valiantly on the Persian *borders and did not allow them to raid unchecked and to devastate the *land of Armenia, or [even] to lay eyes upon it.¹⁵ And †during all the days of their lives the king was at rest and the *realm enjoyed prosperity and peace.

32   *Chapter ix. Concerning the *bdeašχ Bakur, who revolted against the king of Armenia, and the way that he was killed by the Armenian army, and that Vałinak Siwni became bdeašχ in his stead.*¹

At about that time, one of the king's *servants, the great *prince of Ałjnikᶜ called *bdeašχ—who was one of the four [bdeašχs] and the *senior

76

one by *throne and *cushion in the royal *palace²—revolted against the king of Armenia. He supported the king of Persia and handed over to him the royal *domain that was entrusted to him. He brought in³ an army of support from the Persian king, seceded from the *land of the Armenian *dominion, and fought against the king of Armenia with the forces of the Persian kingdom.⁴ And so the war grew fiercer. Then the king of Armenia sent out his good *servants: J̌on, *prince of Korduk͗; Mar, *prince of Great Cop͗k͗; Nerseh, *prince of Cop͗k͗ Šahēi; Vaḷinak, *prince of Siwnik͗; Dat, *prince of Hašteank͗; and Manak, *prince of Basean, together with many troops. They marched forth and defeated the Persian forces, †put them all to the *sword, and killed the *bdeašχ together with his *brothers and his sons. But they brought to the king the head of the *bdeašχ Bakur and a young girl who was his daughter. And †since there was no one else left from that *clan, the king gave the girl in marriage to his favorite Vaḷinak Siwni as well as the *domain of Aljnik͗, and made him *bdeašχ and successor of that *house.⁵ His heirs multiplied and the *bdeašχ Vaḷinak, together with his *realm and his forces, constantly *served the king. But one boy among Bakur's sons had fled and come to the Armenian *commander Vač͗ē, and he survived there secretly, in his *house. [It was he] who later became the heir of his *house; and who, at another time, returned and took possession of his own *house. [And] his name was Xeša.⁶

33   *Chapter x. Concerning Yakob [James], bishop of Mcbin [Nisibis].*¹

At about that time the great bishop of Mcbin departed. [He was] a wondrous old man diligent in the works of truth whose name was Yakob, surnamed *Zgōn* ["The Wise"]² Persian; a man singled out by God to come from his *city to the mountains of Armenia, to Mount Sararad in the *district of Korduk͗ ³ on the *border of the Araratean *dominion. He was a man filled with the grace of Christ so that the power [to perform] miraculous signs⁴ lay in his hands. He came with great desire and longing, and fervently prayed to God to see the redeeming ark built by Noah that had come to rest on that mountain after the flood, for he had received from the *Lord all that he had asked. Then, as he ascended through the difficult, waterless, and desert slopes of Mount Sararat [sic], he and those who were with him wearied and thirsted. Then the great Yakob fell on his knees, [prostrating himself] to the *ground, and prayed to the *Lord, and a spring gushed up on the spot that his head had touched, and he and those with him drank, and to this day it is called Yakob's Spring.⁵ But he himself toiled and persevered, imploring the *Lord with prayers that he might see the desired sight without delay.

Then, as he was weary at a difficult place up near the summit and utterly spent, he fell asleep, and an angel of God came down and said to him, "Yakob, Yakob!" And he answered, "Here I am, *Lord."[6] And the angel said, "Behold, the *Lord has received thy prayer and fulfilled thy request. That which lies by thy head is a piece of wood from the ark. Behold, I have brought it to thee [and] it is from there, but thou must not persevere to see it, for the *Lord wills it so." And [Yakob] rose with great exultation and prostrated himself before the *Lord in profound gratitude, and he saw a board [seemingly] taken and sliced off with a hatchet from a large plank.[7] Taking it, he returned from there with the gift bestowed [on him] and went on his way together with his companions. And not even the great Moses on his descent from the Sinaitic mountain exulted with such utter joy—although we do not say that [what Moses brought] was inferior, for that God-seeing man descended from the mountain with the divinely written Commandments received from God in his hands. But, because that iniquitous people, turning their backs on the *Lord to their own destruction, faithlessly prostrated themselves in worship of that which they themselves had cast, and thereby wounded and afflicted the heart of the bearer of the Commandments—for the anguish of the bearer was evident in the smashing of the Tables [of the Law]. But as for the blessed one concerning whom his homily was composed,[8] he was not treated in the same fashion as was done there, since he and his companions were filled with spiritual consolation, believing in the goodwill and hopeful intent of those who awaited the journeying bearers of good tidings. For only from the Almighty is grace given, openly or secretly, to the *races of the *earth.

So, when the man of God came bearing the eternal warning of the divinely ordained salvific punishment to all the rational and spiritual *races [of men]—the eternal symbol of the vivifying wood, the ark of Noah, symbol of the works of our fathers—the entire *city[9] and the *districts around it came out to meet [him] with immense and immeasurable joy and exultation, seeing the holy man as an apostle of Christ, as an angel from heaven. They beheld their *valiant shepherd as a divine messenger and [so] they crowded around and kissed the traces of his labor-loving and help-bringing feet. And they eagerly received the gift brought down as a grace to them, the renowned wood of the ark of the *patriarch Noah, which is preserved by them to this day as a miraculous sign.

After this, the wondrous bishop Yakob received news from the *land of Armenia. He set out to go to the great *prince and *lord-of-a-*realm, the great *servant of the king of Armenia, to Manačihr Ṙštuni, and came to his *realm.[10] For he had heard that [Manačihr] was an evil and maleficent man who needlessly and unjustly slaughtered countless innocent men from the bitter rage in his heart. He came to teach and admonish him so that he should turn to tractable ways from fear of the *Lord and lay aside the animal-like bestiality of his ferocity. But when the lawless Manačihr saw Bishop Yakob, he scorned, mocked and jeered at the man of God. Following the savage habits that were natural to him and to spite him [Yakob], he had eight hundred men[11] who had been kept in bonds without any guilt brought before him [Yakob] and ordered them thrown into the sea from a height.[12] He destroyed so many innocent souls and ordered [Yakob] driven with mocking derision from his *realm. And he said: "Have you seen how much I honored you for your intercession? I had them relieved from their bonds, and even now they are swimming in the sea." But [Yakob] went from there in great grief, and he shook the dust from his feet upon them, according to the Commandment of the *Lord.[13] Together with his companions, he went to the mountain in Ṙštunik᷃, where there were iron and lead mines. This was a tall dividing mountain named Ǝnjak᷃isar,[14] whence all the *districts were visible. As he came close to the foot of that mountain he felt a great thirst, for many days had elapsed since he had tasted anything at all. He prayed to the *Lord, kneeling and bowing his head to the *ground, and up gushed a spring, from which he and his companions drank. And this happened in the same way as before: what he had done on Mount Sararad, this he performed at the foot of Mount Ǝnjak᷃isar, by the shore of the sea of Ṙštunik᷃,[15] [and] like the first, this one is called Yakob's Spring to this day.[16] And the *high-priest of God Yakob climbed to the summit of Mount Ǝnjak᷃isar 36 and cursed that *realm so that total confusion should never decrease there instead of the peace of the *Lord, to which they had not hearkened. And [then] the holy, evangelizing bishop returned to his own home. But in that *district Manačihr's wife with her seven sons died two days after his departure, and after that, he himself, pierced through [on all sides],[17] departed in great agony from the *world. And in accordance with the words [Yakob] had spoken, there was no peace in that *realm from that day forth.

But Yakob performed the *greatest miracles. And he was present at the great *synod [sic] of Nikia, which took place in the days of Constantine, the emperor[18] of the Romans, [and] at which three hundred and eighteen bishops gathered together to anathematize the heresy of Arianos of Alexandria, who was from the *province of Egypt. All the bishops took their seats there before Constantine; and Aristakēs, the son of the wondrous Grigor the first *kat᷃olikos of Greater Armenia, was present from Greater Armenia.[19] And the wondrous secret deeds of the king began to be revealed to the [same] Yakob through the miraculous signs of the Holy Spirit. He saw that King [sic] Constantine was clad in a hair shirt under his purple *robe, and that a guardian angel was serving him.[20] Bishop Yakob was amazed and told of the presence of the angel to the multitude of other *assembled bishops, who did not believe this. But he †argued insistently and said, "Because you know things that are hidden, reveal first what the emperor wears under his *robe." [Then], raising himself among them he revealed with the help of the Holy Spirit the humility that was the sign of

King Constantine's pious love of God. He disclosed before all of them what he had observed, that [the emperor] was clad in a hair shirt under the purple for the ardent love of the faith he had in Christ. Then King Constantine saw the angel who was serving the person of Yakob, he fell at his feet and †magnified him with great *honors and great gifts,[21] and he raised his [Yakob's] *throne above those of many who were at that *synod. But his bones were given to the *city of Amid, together with the other Mcbnacikʿ [Nisibenites] at the time of the move there from [Mcbin] during the war between the Greek king and the king of Persia.[22]

37   *Chapter xi. Concerning the great war between the Persians and the Armenians and the death in this war of the *commander-in-chief Vačʿē; and the death of King Xosrov; and the passing from the world of the *patriarch Vrtʿanēs.[1]*

And after this, there was again a bitter contest between the Persians and the Armenians, because [the former] had collected an army and come to seize the *realm of the *land of Armenia. Then, the *sparapet Vačʿē, the *commander-in-chief of Greater Armenia, assembled an *azat-detachment from the *naχarar *host [banak]. He marched forth and gave battle to the Persian army and there was an enormous massacre on both *sides, a heavy loss of slaughtered *magnates among the *nobility. Vačʿē, the great *sparapet of Armenia, fell in the same war, and the entire *realm was in extreme mourning, because the *Lord had often sent salvation to the Armenians through him. Then, the *chief-bishop Vrtʿanēs gathered together and consoled everyone, both king Xosrov himself and the entire army, which mourned with profound, burning sorrow, tearful wailing, and heavily afflicted spirits, with great lamentations and vehement tears, considering that affliction for the departed [behoved] the ones left behind. The great Vrtʿanēs †gave them consolation and said:[2]

"Be comforted in Christ. For those who died [did so] above all for the *realm and the churches and the divinely ordained faith: lest this *realm be enslaved and overthrown and the holy churches destroyed, or the martyrs dishonored, or the holy vessels fall into the hands of the unclean and infidel, and the holy *covenant be perverted, and the children of baptism fall through captivity into the various pollutions of infidel cults. For if the enemy had taken this *realm, they would have implanted here
38   the laws of their †lawless, impious, godless religion, which we implore 'may it not be!' Our pious martyrs strove in battle because of this, they averted, removed, and drove evil out of the *realm. They died so that iniquity should not enter into such a God-worshiping and God-loving *realm, force it to *serve the will of evil, and divide and ruin many souls bound to one another by ardent love. For while they lived they toiled for this with faithful labor. Preserving in their death the steadfastness of their

faith [and] surrendering themselves for the Divine truth, they sacrificed themselves for the churches, for the martyrs, for the holy *covenant of the laws, for the precepts of the faith, for the priestly *congregation, for the countless neophytes baptized in Christ, and for the *true-lord of this *realm.³ Those who did not spare themselves for the sake of all this [have] the same *honor as the martyrs of Christ. Therefore, do not weep over them, but let us truly *honor them. Let us set down in the *realm a law for ever and ever, that every one preserve continually the memory of their *valor as martyrs of Christ. And we shall establish a feast day and rejoice, for God shall be pleased with us because of them and hereafter grant us peace."⁴

And the great *high-priest Vrtᶜanēs laid down a law in the *realm that their memory should be commemorated from year to year. And he set down a canon concerning those who should die like them for the sake of the salvation of the *realm: to commemorate them before God's holy altar at that point of the liturgy when the names of the saints are enumerated, and after them. And [he ordered] that compassion and care be given to the survivors of the fallen. "For," he said, "they fell in battle like Judah and Mattathias Maccabaei, and like their *brothers."⁵

Moreover, they gave his father's *gah and *cushion to the son of the *commander-in-chief Vačᶜē, who was a small child named Artawazd after his [grand]father.⁶ They placed his father's *diadem on his head in front of the king, and [bestowed upon him] the office of *sparapet in his place, for indeed he was the son of a worthy man from a worthy *clan, and because no other adult could be found in that *clan, since they had all died in the great war. And the duties of the *command were assumed by Aršawir Kamsarakan, *prince of Širak and of the *district of Aršarunikᶜ, and by Andovk, *prince of Siwnikᶜ, because they were sons-in-law of the *house of the Mamikonean *family.⁷ And the great *chief-bishop Vrtᶜanēs, together with the king, commanded Aršawir and Andovk to *nurture little Artawazd so that he might take the place of his ancestors and of his father, that he might perform deeds of *valor for Christ the *Lord of all and before his own *true-earthly-*lords, the *valiant Aršakuni,⁸ [defending] their *house and their lives; that he might be the guardian of widows and orphans; and that he might be the successor to the *valiant task of the office of *sparapet and to the illustrious *command [of the army] †all the days of his life.

After this, the *most-valiant-of-men, the builder of the *realm, Xosrov king of Greater Armenia passed away. Assembling from all the *territories of the *realm and *districts of Greater Armenia, they mourned and carried him to his ancestors, to Ani in the ecclesiastical *district of Daranałikᶜ.⁹ And after him, the great *high-priest Vrtᶜanēs also went from [this] *world.¹⁰ The entire *realm of Armenia assembled and [they brought] St. Vrtᶜanēs in a royal carriage with great ceremony, psalms, and spiritual songs, lamps and candles, and the fragrance of incense. And in profound affliction, because they had been left orphaned by their own *true-lord and by their *spiritual-teacher, they accompanied [him] with deep [and] tearful sorrow to the *village of T'ordan in the *district of Daranalik'.[11] And there they laid his holy bones to rest next to the great *patriarch Grigor, and returned home after celebrating the [first] annual commemoration of his living memory.

40   *Chapter xii. Concerning the reign of Tiran over the *realm of Armenia after his father; and how Yusik ascended the *patriarchal *throne after his father Vrt'anēs; and how he was killed by King Tiran for his rebuke of the king.[1]*

And at the passing of King Xosrov from the *world, Tiran son of Xosrov took up the royal *authority over the *realms[2] of Greater Armenia. And likewise the holy and blessed youth Yusik succeeded to the position of the *patriarchs of Armenia.[3] Then, as was the custom, King Tiran convoked the *greatest *naχarars: the great *hazarapet Valarš—from the *house holding the office of *hazarapet[4] in Greater Armenia—who was *prince of Anjit, and with him Zareh who was the *nahapet of Cop'k', and Varaz *prince of the *realm of Cop'k' Šahuni, and Gnit' from the Kaminakan *house who was *prince of the *district of Hašteank', Vorot' *prince of the *district of Vanand, and Šahēn *prince of the *house of Anjewac'ik', and Atom *prince of Golt'n, and Manawaz *prince of Kolb, Gorut' *prince of the *realm of Jor, and Manasp *prince Xoṙχoṙuni from the *malχazunean *house, and [Tiroc'] *prince of the *clan of the Sahaṙuni *house,[5] and *prince Aba Gnuni.[6] He ordered all of them to go with the great *hazarapet Valarš, place the blessed Yusik in the royal carriage, and set out to neighboring Caesarea, the *metropolis of Gamirk' [Cappadocia], to have young Yusik elevated to the apostolic *patriarchal *throne. They set forth, came to the *city of Caesarea, and had Yusik son of Vrt'anēs consecrated to the *kat'olikate. And they placed him on the *throne of the apostle Thaddeus and on the *throne of his grandfather the great Grigor.[7] And they returned from there with great joy, came in

41   good health, and successfully reached the *realm of Ayrarat. And they sent ahead the two *princes of Cop'k' as messengers of good news to the king.

Then, when the king himself heard [this], he came to meet him with the entire multitude of his *forces in the plain on the other side of the river at the bridge of Tap'er. After greeting and wishing each other well, they crossed the bridge of Tap'er, entered the great *city of Artašat, went to the church, and installed the [much] desired youth, Yusik, on the *patriarchal *throne. He followed the apostolic [ways] of his father Vrt'anēs, and was a son like unto his father's measure. †Altogether, in all things and all ways he showed his angelic traits, and accomplished everything in accordance with the grace granted to him by God.[8] He pastured the rational Christian flock [and] admonished it with evangelical precepts. For he was young in years, vigorous, tall in stature, with a face of wondrous beauty and grace, so that no other one like him could be found anywhere on *earth.[9] Pure and resplendent in spirit, he in no way concerned himself with things [here] below, but from the days of his youth, like a *valiant *armored [soldier] of Christ, like a heroic champion, he defied and threatened with victory the invisible foe.[10] He had no knowledge of partiality or of the respect of persons, but bore the word of the Holy Spirit like a *sword at his side.[11] And the grace-giving Spirit which filled him, like a fountain, [watered] with knowledge the ears and hearts of all hearers.

But King Tiran and the other *noble *magnates among the *naχarars, as well as the whole of the *realm, did not behave at all according to God's will or follow any wisdom. Especially the king and the *princes killed, unrestrainedly shedding just blood in vain, and they committed many other sins. Nor did they attend to the Commandments from on high, unadmonished by their daily hearing of the reminder to keep hope in God.[12] Consequently, the blessed *patriarch Yusik perpetually opposed [them] with skillful, temperate words of Christian reproach. Castigating, admonishing, [and] blaming [them] with constant reproof, he set out [before them] the eternal torments of [divine] wrath, telling of the unquenchable fire of the judgment, [and] called them to account. For although he was young in years, he displayed in himself the counsel of advanced age[13] and *valiantly fulfilled and increased the admonitory work of his fathers. Resembling his fathers in his youthful wisdom,[14] like a flower he achieved the †*honorable *honor of the *dignity of old age, the vigilant acuteness of the mind. He fought until death for the truth, wishing first to save himself and then to do the same for the souls of others.[15] So great was his fear of the *Lord that he held for naught the love and fear of the king. He was filled with the knowledge of God and the learning of the science of the Holy Scriptures, which he took up to castigate and admonish. And he forbade and would not allow the king and the *magnates to enter into the church.[16] Thus, he firmly chastized them with rebukes [and] with the admonitory words of priestly *authority for their iniquity, adultery, sodomy, and shedding of blood, depredations, pillaging, cruelty to the poor, and many other similar sins. And because he threatened with fear of the Commandments of the *Lord, he was considered the foe of those who perpetually transgressed the precepts of Christ, and who were constantly smitten by him with the holy words of God. And he waged this war of admonition against everyone †through all the days of his life.

And so, King Tiran with others from the *nobility presented himself on a day of annual [celebration] to enter into the church, but [Yusik] †spoke out against him and said: "You are unworthy! Why have you come? Do not go inside!" For this, they dragged him at once into the

43 church. Beaten with rods and shattered, the holy *high-priest of God, the blessed youth Yusik was flung there battered and half dead. [Then] the ministers from the palatine church of the royal *fortress of Bnabel in the *district of Great Cop⁽k⁽ raised him up and bore him to the *district of Daranaɫik⁽, to the *village of T⁽ordan, and he died there after a few days, and was laid [to rest] near Grigor and his fathers.[17]

*Chapter xiii. Concerning the reason for which the *land of Armenia remained without *spiritual-leadership after the death of Yusik, and the sons of Yusik were unworthy of their father's *throne.*[1]

And after this, some time passed after the beating to death of the blessed Yusik. And the *land [speaking] the language of the *realm of T⁽orgom, left without *spiritual-leader, went astray like the blind.[2] For the spirit of error was bestowed upon them: eyes that they might not see, ears that they might not hear, and a heart that they might not know [how] to turn to repentance.[3] And in the darkness they reached the abyss of perdition [to which] they themselves had beaten a path, fell into [it], and were destroyed, for †there was no one to hold them back[4] from the confusion of unreason and the commission of sins, as they were shepherdless. Impudent in evil they followed the road of perdition of their own will, having become of their own will sons of wrath;[5] and the stubborn *race of the *house of the Armenian *land wandered without God through the *realm.[6] They were like a flock of sheep who had rejected the protection of guarding and protecting dogs and given themselves over as prey to their enemies the wolves,[7] just like the great *city of Athens.[8]

And at that time they took the king as their example of evil, began to model themselves on that example, and to do the same. For from antiquity
44 when they had taken on the name of Christians, it was merely as [though it were] some human religion; and they did not receive it with ardent faith, but as some human folly [and] under duress.[9] [They did not receive it] with understanding as is fitting, with hope and faith, but only those who were to some degree acquainted with Greek or Syriac learning [were able] to achieve some partial inkling of it.[10] As for those who were without skill in learning and who were the great mass of the people—the *naχarars as well as the *peasantry—even had *spiritual-teachers sat night and day pouring the abundance of their *teaching over [their heads] like a torrent of rain from the clouds, †not one of them could keep in mind a single thing of what he had heard: †not a word, not half a word, not a minimal record, not a trace! For they devoted their minds exclusively to vain and useless things, just like small boys who give themselves up to games in childhood and youth paying no attention to useful and important matters. So they too, having savage, barbarous minds, consumed themselves with vile thoughts in perverse practices, [and] in ancient pagan

customs. They cherished with assiduous care their songs, legends, and epics, believed in them[11] and persevered in the same way, in hatred and in malignant envy toward one another, in vengeful enmity; to revile one another, and to deceive [both] companion and *brother. Friend laid traps against friend, relation against relation, family against family, *kinsman against *kinsman, in-law against in-law.[12] Men were found there thirsting to drink the blood of their companions, willingly seeking to do harm because of their incorrigible ways and senseless minds. And they performed in darkness like obscene acts the rites of the old pagan gods[13] and some even fulfilled on themselves the desire of lustful pollution. Therefore, they did not listen to the counsel of wisdom, nor submit to the Commandments of God spoken by their *spiritual-leaders, but hated, persecuted,
45 and killed them because of their rebukes. As was said of them by the prophet: "They hated him that reproved in the gates and depised holy speech."[14] For they were not like other *nations,[15] believers and wise men to whom the preaching of the Divine word gave knowledge of the true faith, and who, receiving it with thanksgiving, believed and rejoiced in the grace of the true love of mankind. But rather, they [received] it like the Jews in blindness and with darkened mind limping in the truth. Perhaps the prescient word of the prophet was intended also for this *race: "They are foolish children and not children of wisdom. They are wise to do evil, but to do good they have no knowledge."[16] And again he said: "They are hard-faced children, hard of heart, hard in spirit, who have embittered me, they and their fathers."[17] Thus were these too rejected, for they did not understand, and they did not believe in the invisible God through visible things. They did not recognize the Creator in the created here and they did not comprehend their Creator, ruler, and protector.[18] He multiplied His visible signs and marvels until He changed human nature into animal form, [and] these were the cause of their salvation.[19]

And during this worthless and senseless reign when Tiran was king,[20] they surpassed in evil all the centuries as they looked to him. More than all else, they murdered their chief *spiritual-leader [by] beating him to death, and thereafter followed their [own] will. For †there was not one single one then whose rebuke they feared, who prevented them from following the path of iniquity. They were abandoned by the *Lord [and] followed the will of their own hearts,[21] for there was then no *spiritual-leader nor any *high-priest. Yet they were not diligent in truth to seek for themselves a *spiritual-leader or pastor who would be a chief-shepherd for the people, but rather they sought a confidant who would act according to their will.

46 At that time the king and the *princes and the whole of the *realm took counsel as to whom they might find worthy of the [dignity], because [Yusik's] twin surviving children—one of whom was named Pap and the other Atꞌanaginēs—were known to be insubordinate and incorrigible.

85

They [knew] nothing of the Divine Scriptures, nor were they versed in the discipline of virtue. They in no way resembled their ancestors, neither looking to their own father Yusik, nor giving any attention to the virtues of the great Grigor, nor yet reflecting on their own spiritual *dignity, on the *honor of the eternal life. But rather, following the example of their own time, they gloried in the passing vanity of their *house and *clan, and chose the military life.²² For this reason they were not chosen but rejected because of their arrogance, in keeping with their father's prophetic vision, and did not come to assume the yoke of divine ministry.²³ And †there was not a single one else from this same *house of the descendants of Grigor, for these were his only children according to the flesh, and they followed ways unworthy of their ancestors. †And there was no one else who might succeed to the ministry of *spiritual-leadership and *high-priestly supervision, who might fulfill the task of *law-giver²⁴ in the *house of the *Lord.²⁵

*Chapter xiv. Concerning the life and deeds of the great man of God Daniēl; how he rebuked King Tiran; and how he was put to death by him as punishment.*¹

At that time, however, the holy elder, the *chorepiskopos* Daniēl, [who was] an admirable man, was still alive. He had been a pupil of the great Grigor² and the supervisor and head of the churches³ in the *province of Tarōn the appanage of Grigor. He had the *authority of the *office of *supreme justice⁴ in this *region, and he held this *authority alone. Moreover, he was the overseer, *law-giver,⁵ supervisor and guardian of all the churches of Greater Armenia, in every locality, and he also preached in foreign parts—in the *regions of Persia—and turned innumerable [men] from error.⁶

He was of Syrian *race and held the dignity of the chief *throne of Tarōn, of the great and first church of the *mother-of-the-churches in all Armenia. That is to say of the first and foremost place of *honor, for [it was] there [that] the holy church was built for the first time and an altar raised in the name of the *Lord.⁷ Likewise, below it was the *martyrium-of-the-prophet John and also, near the *house of the *Lord, the *resting-place of the apostles [*hangist aṙakʿeloc*ʿ].⁸ These places, then, were *honored in the first rank in accordance with the canon of the *patriarchs and kings, as the church of Tʿordan in the *district of Daranaɫikʿ was *honored on account of the tombs of the *patriarch Grigor and of Aristakēs,⁹ and likewise of the memory of King Trdat, who—willingly or not—became worthy of being the first to acknowledge the Christian faith.¹⁰ Because of this, it was the wish of the *realm to *honor these places of their father bishops from ancient times, [the places] where they had been laid [to rest]. It was pleasing to the *realm to *honor their king Trdat who first devoted himself to Christ; likewise their first bishop, the first-laborer Grigoris; likewise the first martyrs of Christ—

Gayianē and Hṙip°simē with their companions—in the *district of Ayrarat; and likewise above all, the first church.[11]

These places were entrusted to [Daniēl] together with the *districts in which they were located. He was devoted to this chief altar, to the *authority of the *patriarchal *throne, to the firm *covenant of the *catholic church. And he had received the consecration to the rank of *chorepiskopos from the hands of the great Grigor[12] in the days that he destroyed the *shrines of the *temple of Heraklēs, that is to say of Vahagn, at the place called Aštišat where he first laid the foundations of the holy church.[13]

48

He was an amazing man who performed the *greatest prodigies and miracles in the name of our *Lord Jesus Christ. He walked with his shoes on over the water of rivers and neither wetted them nor took them off. And in wintertime, when a great thickness of snow was piled on the wintery mountains, and he wished to cross somewhere over such mountains at such a time because of the needs of a journey somewhere, the snow suddenly became black earth before him. And if he wished to go to some distant place, he sped effortlessly on like lightning as though he were flying, and immediately found himself where he wished to be. He raised the dead and healed the sick and performed even greater prodigies and miracles than these, which writing is inadequate to encompass or retrace.[14] And his dwelling was set in uninhabited mountains, though he was never unmindful of care for the needs of mankind. He [had] only a single garment of skins and wore sandals; his food was the roots of plants, and he had no occasion for a staff.[15] And he was so mighty in the word of God that whatever he asked from God, he received, and whatever he said was accomplished. And whenever he came down from the *desert to inhabited places in order to do the work of God, his overseer's residence was at the main churches. And he often [came] to the spring below the lofty site of the *temple of Heraklēs opposite the great mountain called C°ul, at a distance of about one stone's throw below the site of the *shrine, in an exiguous little valley in a small wood of ash trees, at the place named Hac°eac° Draχt ["Ash Grove"]. This was the very spring where in earlier times the great Grigor had performed the baptism of a great host.[16] And on this spot was the place of St. Daniēl's cell, the cave that he had made his dwelling, and from this spot he carried out the purpose of his visitation.[17]

49

Then, having assembled, the *greatest *naχarars came together and took counsel, and persuaded the king to summon the elder Daniēl to his *camp so that they might establish him as their chief *spiritual-leader and install him on the *patriarchal *throne. And they dispatched to him a *prince from the Sahaṙuni *house,[18] and Artawan *prince of Vanand, and Karēn *prince of the Amatuni *house, and Varaz *prince of the Dimak°sean *house. And the naχarars went and found him in the *district of Ekeɫeac^c,[19] in the *village of T^cil [belonging] to the church, for he was still carrying out the work of God's service. And they took and brought him to King Tiran, to the *town of Baraēj in the district of Aɫjnik^c. And when the great *chorepiskopos* Daniēl came before the king, he undertook to reprove and rebuke him. He came forward and †began to speak [and] said:[20]

"Why have you forgotten God your Creator [and] the mercy of the signs, admonitions, and miracles He performed for your fathers and for yourselves? For you have returned to the error of the *idol-worship of your ancestors, to hatred, avarice, depredation, and extortion of the poor, to fornication, betrayal, mutual injury, and murder.[21] You have been over-thrown and abandoned; limping, you have strayed from the paths of righteousness. You have forsaken God your benefactor who created you out of nothing[22] and strengthened you, and have not acknowledged Him in your folly. He came to seek you when you were betaking yourselves beyond recall to perdition. For, although He was the Only Begotten Son of God, He came down to make His Father known to His creatures.[23] And although they did not listen to Him and tortured Him to death, He endured, even though He hid His might from no one so that He might be the cause of life for all. And so, He chose those whom He perceived worthy and prepared for His resurrection [and] He taught and sent them forth as preachers, summoners, and convokers to call you to the light of salvation.

"But then also, you returned ingratitude for benefactions. Hence, first you killed him who was sent and came to you to preach and summon, who came to call you to the saving grace of the kingdom of our *Lord Jesus Christ. For in your folly you shared in the design of the God-killing *race of the Jews, for they believed that they killed the *Lord, and your fathers killed His apostles, and afterward tortured those like them, for the same reason.[24] And after these events came a multitude of holy martyrs of God, the companions-in-toil of the same apostles, who toiled until they were in peril of torments, unto their own deaths; remaining steadfast so as to show you the truth, that you might perhaps turn through them to an understanding of the knowledge of the Son of God. However, toward them also you accomplished and fully consummated the murderous custom of your iniquitous will. Yet, as I said, through their[25] blood and through many and various signs He admonished you and did not give you over to death because of His great mercy. And He brought you close to Himself and united you to the nature of His own living *spiritual-teaching, of the true faith, [and] of the transcendent greatness of His beloved Son.[26]

"And after this He forgave you all your trespasses and gave you His beloved ones as *spiritual-teachers. But you remembered not a single thing of [all] this, you did not keep it in your mind, you did not receive it in your heart. But you turned back, like the *race of the Jews and took on, yourselves, the example of their deeds. For it was fitting that you remember the mercies of your *Lord Jesus Christ, who neither remembered the sins of your fathers nor your own iniquity. And it was not fitting

51 that you forget the striving of the holy fathers, of your admonishers and *spiritual-teachers who instructed you [and] who perpetually watched for the salvation of your souls.[27] It would have been right for you to have affection for those who through *teaching you concerning the Word travailed spiritually and bore you anew, and who upon your turning back once more to your depravity bore you yet again a second time through their prayers for the repentance of evildoers, until they fashioned in you the likeness [*kerparan*] of Christ,[28] that you might be worthy to enter into the Kingdom of Heaven. It was also fitting for you to care for their children and disciples—your *spiritual-leaders and overseers in the *Lord—who were their children according to divine birth in accordance with the spiritual Word, as well as because they were their descendants according to the flesh,[29] and in no way inferior to their fathers in spiritual deeds.

"But now you have abandoned God and remembered the evil of your former ways and overfilled the measure of your fathers' sins.[30] For they killed with torments the holy fathers because they would not hear their beneficent admonitions, and you have killed their sons and successors and collaborators and those like them who would not acquiesce to your sinful deeds: the holy youth Yusik, the *patriarch and holder-of-the-*throne, the sharer-in-the-lot of the apostle Thaddeus, and of Grigor who was like him.[31] And you have taken on the ways and example of the Jews, their custom of murder and oppression, and just as they, being incorrigible, slaughtered the apostles and prophets, so you have done the same, following their model.

"And so, the *Lord shall take your kingdom from you on account of so many lies and abominations; likewise will He take away your priesthood. You shall be scattered and divided, your *borders shall dissolve, as it also befell Israel. You shall be masterless, unprotected, and unpitied, and you shall be like sheep for whom there is no shepherd. You shall be like a flock handed over to wild beasts.[32] You shall be cast down from your *glory.[33] You shall be given over into captivity to foreign foes and into the yoke of *bondage, nor shall this yoke of *bondage ever lighten or be lifted

52 from you. The evil yoke of the *servitude of *bondage shall never grow lighter on you necks[34] [and] you shall be exhausted and consumed in the midst of your longings. As Israel was torn asunder and not made whole, so shall you be scattered and overthrown.[35] And others shall enjoy [the fruit] of your labors and eat your substance. And no one shall be found to deliver you. And the *Lord shall not be pleased with you, and He shall not look upon you and save you again.[36]

"But since you have called me to come to you, did you wish to hear all this from me? Even had I not related all this to you, yet all of it would come to pass because of the murder of the just youth, the great Yusik your virtuous *spiritual-leader who was from the *house of the descendants of Grigor. For all this shall come to pass for you, for so has the *Lord shown it to me. But as for your sending to me [saying]: 'Come, and be our leader and *spiritual-guide!' How shall I be a *spiritual-leader for those who do not follow in the steps of the *Lord? And how shall I be the head of a *race whom the *Lord has abandoned? Or how shall I raise my hands in prayer to God for those whose hands are stained with the blood of the saints of the *Lord? Or how shall we bring forth prayers and supplications for those who have turned their backs and not their countenances to the *Lord? Or how shall I be an intercessor for those who were not stead-fast?[37] Or how shall I speak for the reconciliation of those who have fled and do not wish to return, for whom the *Lord himself has designed and prepared all evils because you have said: 'The *Lord does not see all this,' and similar words?"[38]

The holy elder, the *chorepiskopos* Daniēl spoke these words before King Tiran and before the *princes, the *chiefs, and the entire host. And while he said all this, the king paid attention, stupefied and amazed, and 53 was merely silent. But when he had heard all this, raging in the wrath of his iniquitous fury, he commanded them to strangle [Daniēl] to death on the spot. Hearing this, the servants present hastily fulfilled the order, but the *greatest among the *naχarar *nobility strongly urged the king not to carry out his evil design; but because of the bitter rage of his heart, through his burning wrath he would not listen to them. And so a rope was thrown around his neck and he was strangled to death. And in this way St. Daniēl came to his end.

And many men who were familiar with him and knew him took up his body and wished to venerate it with the bones of the holy martyrs of Christ. But he appeared in person to a holy man named Epip^can [Epiphanios] who was his disciple so that they should not *honor his bones like those of the others, but take them to the place he himself had ordered and bury them in the ground. For he appeared thus and spoke to them: "If," he said: "the body of the *Lord was hidden two days in the tomb until the third day when He rose to His Father, how much more fitting to bury our earthly bodies in the ground." Then his body was taken up by his beloved holy disciples, among whom the chief was named Šaḷita, who had been appointed by him *spiritual-teacher in the *realm of Korduk^c, and the second Epip^can, who had also been appointed by him as *spiritual-teacher[39] for the *district of Aḷjnik^c and of Great Cop^ck^c; together with the ministers of the *camp. And they went and took his body to the place where his cell had formerly been in the *land of Tarōn, which is the *mother church of Armenia, near the spring where Grigor had baptized a multitude of the forces of the *realm, at the place called *Hac^ceac^c Draχt*. And at that place they concealed the body of St. Daniēl in the ground in accordance with the command he had given in the earlier vision.

54   *Chapter xv. Concerning the sons of Yusik and how they scorned and trampled underfoot the dignity of great *high-priest of God.*

Then it was planned to bring to the priesthood a son of St. Yusik for the *spiritual-teaching of his ancestors. And so, they seized Pap and Atᶜanaginēs without their consent and with the unanimous agreement of the bishops forcibly compelled them to receive ordination as deacons, against their will.¹ But they trampled underfoot the grant of spiritual *dignity, of their own accord served as soldiers in the turbulent military profession, and were struck down. They chose the *earthly life, likewise took the king's sisters as wives,² and rejected the inheritance of God. As for the names of their wives: the wife of Pap was called Varazduχt, and they went childless from this *world; the name of Atᶜanaginēs' wife was Bambišn, and from her was born the admirable and amazing Nersēs, who later attained the *high-priesthood.³

At that time, however, †there was no one who could give them *spiritual-guidance as *high-priest. Then they took counsel as to whom they might find as their *spiritual-leader, and the unanimous common agreement was that they should find someone from the *princely *house of Grigor who might occupy the *throne of his fathers.⁴

55   *Chapter xvi. Concerning Pᶜaŕēn, who occupied the *patriarchal *throne.*

At that time they deemed worthy a certain priest named Pᶜaŕēn¹ from the *district of Tarōn,² from the great *martyrium-dedicated-to-the-prophet John, which was first built as a *house of prayers and supplications at the *resting place of the saints,³ because this place had been entrusted to him. And so they summoned him to the king, and the king sent him out with gifts and *letters-patent. Illustrious *princes, great and leading *nahapets, were also sent with him: the Armenian *commander-in-chief whose name was Vasak from the Mamikonean *house, and Mehendak Ŕštuni, and Andovk Siwni, and Aršawir Kamsarakan, as well as ten other *honorable men.⁴ They took the holy Pᶜaŕēn and went to Caesarea the *metropolis of Gamirkᶜ and there ordained him to the *katᶜołikate of Greater Armenia. And they returned peacefully to their own *realm.

And Pᶜaŕēn occupied the *patriarchal *throne a short time. He was not bold enough to admonish anyone or rebuke anyone's error or transgression, but kept only his own person holy. Of necessity he accompanied the unrighteous king and acted submissively according to his will.⁵ And after this he went to his [eternal] rest and was gathered to his fathers.⁶ The ministers of the *camp took his body and went to the *district of

Tarōn, to the *agarak of the great *martyrium-of-the-prophet John where he himself had formerly lived. And there they built a handsome tomb and buried his bones.[7]

56   *Chapter xvii. Concerning Šahak, who was descended from Bishop Ałbianos and who succeeded to the *patriarchal *throne; and how at that time the *land of Armenia abandoned the *Lord and His Commandments*[1]

Then, at that time, the *council-of-the-*realm deliberated as to who should hold the *patriarchal *kat͑olikate.[2] Then, †since there was no one worthy of this dignity from the *house of Grigor, they designated a certain Šahak from the *house of the descendants of Bishop Ałbianos.[3] They entrusted him to the hands of the *prince *mardpet who was surnamed *Hayr [Father], and with him they took from the *nobility, the *prince of the valley of Gardman and ten more *naxarars, and they sent them with splendid *honor to the *land of Gamirk͑, to the great *city of Caesarea. There, they ordained Šahak to the *kat͑olikate of Greater Armenia and returned with *honor to the king.

And Šahak succeeded to the place of the *patriarchs and he imitated the conduct of P͑arēn; he gave *spiritual-guidance to the *realm in the same fashion. But those whom he shepherded—the king, the *naxarars, and the *princes in general—gave no ear to the admonitions of the truth or to other rebukes.[4] They committed sins openly and insolently; [and] they turned to every evil deed without remorse, forsaking the *Lord and His Commandments. Still worse than they [were] those impious to mankind who returned to the ancient, former practices of their fathers, were addicted to them, from the lowly to the *greatest, and outstripped [them] in this.[5] And because of all this the *Lord God grew angry with them, He abandoned [them and] allowed them to be trampled underfoot by their enemies, who had risen against them. Because, from the time of the reign of Trdat, when they had acknowledged the *Lord, He had given them peace and silenced the enemies around them. For the *Lord had calmed the wars on their *borders, and until that [later] time there was no perturbation or trouble with anyone and they lived in great peace.[6] [But]

57   then, at that time, He roused and intensified the quarrels of their enemies on every side around their *borders.[7] And †not a single one of the other kings, not a one, was a friend to them, but all [of them] were enemies.

*Chapter xviii. Concerning the *hayr-mardpet, who had the *clans of the Armenian *naxarars destroyed.*[1]

But at the time of that senseless reign, enemies were not the only ones [who were] hostile, for within the *land of Armenia, friends began to stir up plots and treachery against companions, and they committed innumerable kinds of hostile [actions]. For dissention had fallen upon

them from the *Lord, such an abomination and spirit of error[2] that they
began to ruin and destroy one another because of their unrighteousness.

But more than [all of them], an iniquitous and demonic man, the one
who held the great *dignity of *mardpet, incited King Tiran exceedingly
against the *naχarar *clans. He was a eunuch called *hayr ["Father"], a
man of †evil heart and evil counsel and evil deeds. He had many guiltless
*naχarars slaughtered through [his] slander, and he perturbed the great
*power [tērut‛iwn] of the kingdom. In particular, he had two *senior
*houses †put to the *sword and totally exterminated by means of his
calumnies: the *house of the Řštuni and the *house of the Arcruni. They
were extirpated without any guilt or transgression to the point where even
the women of those *clans were slaughtered. [And] at that time, two
children who had escaped were found with their *tutors: Tačat, the son of
Mehǝndat Řštuni, and Šawasp, the son of Vač‛ē Arcruni; they were
suckling babes whom they brought before the king. When he saw them,
he ordered the children's throats cut, for they were the only surviving
58 descendants of these *clans. But Artawazd[3] and Vasak from the Mamikonean *house, who were the *commanders of all the forces of Armenia,[4]
happened to be present; arising, they threw themselves on the little boys—
each one taking one [of them] under his arm—and went out brandishing
their *weapons, ready for combat and to die on behalf of these children.
For, although they had *nurtured the king's son Aršak, they left their
foster-son Aršak and went out from the royal *camp, outraged by this
day's deed.[5] They went to their own *realm to the *strongholds of Tayk‛
and they stayed there many years with their householders, abandoning
their other *domain [tun].[6] There they *nurtured the children, Šawasp and
Tačat, and gave them their own daughters as wives; consequently [those]
*clans multiplied once more, and for many years they [themselves] did
not participate in the councils of the Armenians.

*Chapter xix. Concerning the sons of Yusik, Pap and At‛anaginēs;
how and why they were struck down in their unrighteousness.*[1]

But the sons of Yusik, Pap and At‛anaginēs, led a life odious to God,
for they acted unrighteously and impiously. They were most impudent
†all of the days of their lives, and the fear of God was not before their
eyes.[2] They behaved with great wantonness and impurity, scorned and
scoffed at the Commandments of God.

They were in the *land of Tarōn, in the ecclesiastical *town of Aštišat
where their great-grandfather Grigor had first built a church.[3] And the
two *brothers, Pap and At‛anaginēs, came to that *village. Having given
themselves totally over to drunkenness, they scoffed at God's *temple
[tačar] and, entering into the bishop's-residence [episkoposanoc‛] which
was there, the two *brothers drank wine in it together with harlots,

93

singing girls, *gusans,[4] and buffoons, scorning the holy and consecrated place and trampling it underfoot. Then, while they were enjoying themselves greatly, as they reclined on *couches in the bishop's-residence, eating and drinking, an angel of the *Lord suddenly appeared like a bolt of lightning,[5] striking and killing the two *brothers together on their *feasting-couch.[6] And all the others who were present there sharing the *feasting-couch and rejoicing, their boon companions, abandoned them and fled together outside the *palace. And in great terror not a single one of them returned there. Indeed, †not a single other man among them dared contemplate entering inside, nor coming close to the doors and shutting them, for they had remained open after their flight. Nor in subsequent days did anyone dare come near the doors.

The two *brothers, Pap and At'anginēs, were killed in this manner and lay inside the episcopal-residence stretched out on the *feasting-couch. The doors of the *palace remained open, and no one dared come near them until the corpses decayed and were putrefied; their bones separated, fell apart, and were scattered.[7] And many months went by after these events. Then [only], they dared to go inside in order to pick up their bones, collect and remove [them]. They found the bones completely dried out and horny and brought them to a vineyard [belonging] to the church called *Agarak*.[8]

A son of At'anginēs by the king's sister Bambišn[9] survived, however. His name was Nersēs, and he subsequently ascended the *patriarchal *throne of the entire *land of Armenia, whereas Pap left [no son] by his legitimate wife. But he had a concubine from the *karčazat *village of Hac'ekac' in the *district of Tarōn, and he left a son named Vrik by his concubine.[10]

60   *Chapter xx. Concerning King Tiran and how he was betrayed by his *senekapet P'isak Siwni; how he was destroyed and taken prisoner by the Persian *prince Varaz, and how the entire *land of Armenia was made captive with him.[1]*

[Now] there was still friendship between the two kings, the king of Armenia and the the king of Persia.[2] [And] a high official [*barjrgah*] named Šapuh-Varaz was residing in Atrpatakan.[3] Then, while complete peace still reigned between the two kings,[4] a dissension arose over nothing, by the will of the *Lord through a worthless man who was not inferior to the *devil [as a sower of] discord. His name was P'isak from the *clan of Siwni;[5] he was the *senekapet of King Tiran, and he had been an envoy to Varaz-Šapuh whom the king of Persia had installed as *warden-of-the-marches in the *realm of Atrpatakan.

Around that time King Tiran had a horse, a truly amazing steed. He was a dark chestnut [*čartuk*] horse dappled with gray, he was full of *valor, famous and splendid, larger and taller than all other horses and more beautiful to see than any of them. [He was] so unusual that no other one like him could be found.[6] When the royal *senekapet* P꞊isak went as ambassador, he told Varaz about the horse—since he had become friendly with him—and having received from him a letter [concerning it], he took it back and presented it to the king of Armenia. [The king] did not agree, being unwilling to hand over [the horse]. However, because he distrusted that man [P꞊isak] and [feared] that he would foment discord between the two kings, [Tiran] sought and found a horse of the same color, the same markings, and the same appearance, except for his size (for there was none like that to be found anywhere), one that was of similar color (that is, a similarly marked dark dappled chestnut), and sent it to Varaz, *prince of Atrpatakan, together with *official-letters and gifts, through the pernicious P꞊isak. Having thought this over, [Tiran] instructed him as follows: "Tell him that [the king] says, 'This is the very one you requested, he has not kept it back from you out of love [for you].'" But when [P꞊isak] came to Varaz, he revealed to him the fact of the withholding. Seeking to arouse him, he had no wish to remedy his own malice but rather [sought] to sharpen his own calumny still further [by] saying: "Tiran king of Armenia [is filled] to such a degree with rancor, jealousy, malignity, hostility, hatred, resentment, perfidy, and insolence toward the Persian king and the entire Persian army that he has even kept back one single hide and hidden it, ridiculing you and cheating you by [substituting] another [horse], which he gave me to take [and] send to you, for the other. Moreover, that is not all that he says, but relying on the *emperor and on his army he plans to take the Persian kingdom from the *race of Sasan,[7] for, he says, 'That *dominion belongs to us and to our fathers. Therefore,' he says, 'I shall not rest until I recover the *dignity of our ancestors, until I return once again their former kingdom to their sons and children: to my *clan, to my *house, and to me.'"[8] So much, and with such words the iniquitous P꞊isak incited him against his own *true-lord and contrived the death of his own king.

When Varaz-Šapuh, *marzpan of Atrpatakan, had heard all this from the furious words of that slanderous [lit. dog-mouthed] P꞊isak, he hastily wrote a letter of denunciation against the king of Armenia [and] sent it to Nerseh,[9] king of Persia. And he so aroused, irritated, disturbed, agitated, infuriated, and angered the king of Persia against the king of Armenia that he received from him the order to find some means, devise some way through stratagems to entrap and lay hold of the king of Armenia. And so, while peace still reigned between the two kings, the wrath of the *Lord aroused vengeance against the unrighteous Tiran in retaliation for the holy blood of the two murdered *high-priests and *spiritual-leaders.[10]

Then Varaz sent a messenger to the king of Armenia at that time to

61

62

speak to him deceitfully concerning conciliation and peace, [and] he boldly sought permission to come to him under the pretext of his love. When Tiran king of Armenia heard this, he hastily ordered with great joy to invite him to come. Before he arrived, the king took counsel with his eunuchs, the *servants of his bedchamber, and said: "It is fitting that we entertain and give pleasure to the man who is coming to us, with hunts and *feasts and every type of diversion.[11] However, because of the ill-will, envy, malignity, and deceit of the Persian *race, there is no need for him to see the places of extensive hunting here in our *land, but rather show him some places of sparse hunting to entertain him solely with them. And do not hunt in any places of abundant hunting nor make a large kill for display, but," he said, "do it rather for the sake of form on account of the perverse bitterness of that evil *race. The place where you should hunt is in the *land of Apahunik' at the foot of the great Mount Masis, [at] the place called the *enclosure [k'ałak'] of Ałiorsk'.[12]

Then, Šapuh-Varaz arrived with three thousand [men] and presented himself to the king in the *land of Apahunik', and was †greatly honored by him. And the words spoken by the king concerning the hunt quickly reached the ears of the Persian *commander from the mouth of that mad slanderous informer, †faithless-to-his-*lord, false-to-his-*lord, murderer-of-his-*lord, betrayer-of-his-*lord,[13] from that destroyer of his own *realm, P'isak. And for a few days the two enjoyed themselves together, but the Persian *prince artfully veiled and hid his enmity inside himself and waited for the opportunity to carry out his plot.

Now it so happened at that time that the *commanders-of-the-army were not present there at that time but had withdrawn [from court],[14] and the other *greatest *naχarars and *senior *tanutērs from among the *azat, as well as the royal troops, were resting each in his own *domain [tun], his own station [or] his own home. And so, †there was no one at all who remained with the king, neither his own *contingent nor the *cavalry, but only a few servants, hunting snarers and beaters, an inferior force of *tent-guards and the *ŕamik-spas,[15] together with the *queen and the king's young son, Aršak. So small was the [number] of those present at that time. But although [the king] had seen that the Persian *commander had come with a powerful *contingent (since there were up to three thousand *armor-clad men with him), he remained unsuspicious and untouched by caution because he saw [Varaz] coming as though for peaceful purposes with †great gifts and *distinguished presents and splendid reverence.

And when a few days had passed, [the Persians] invited the king to a feast to *honor him greatly.[16] Then, when they had indulged in wine [and] the king and his attendants had become *very [k'aj] drunk, a detachment in ambush suddenly fell unexpectedly on each one [as he lay] †unprepared, unsuspecting, and unwary on his *banqueting-couch; and *club-

63

bearers carrying *shields surrounded King Tiran. They took and bound him hand and foot with iron chains. They seized as booty the *camp with whatever they found there, and carried off from the *land of Apahunik^c the king's treasure and possessions, as well as his wife and son, whom they found in the *camp.

When they reached a certain *village called Dalarik^c, the Persian *commander entered into the *village of Dalarik^c and took the chained King Tiran with him. And Varaz said: "Now then! Bring [glowing] coals with which to heat iron to the glowing point so as to burn out the eyes of the king of Armenia. And they immediately brought coals with which they burned out the eyes of King Tiran.[17] Then Tiran himself †began to speak and said: "In exchange for the darkening of the light of my two eyes in this place, let its name be changed for eternity from *Dalarik^c* ["Green"] to *Acuł* ["Coals"],[18] and let this remain as a sign in remembrance of me. For I remember and I know that this is a retribution sought from me for my evil deeds and sins. Because I darkened this *realm which I ruled, [depriving it] of its two illuminating *spiritual-teachers, and because I presumed that I could extinguish the light of truth preached by those two faithful men, for this has the light of my own eyes been darkened."[19]

Then quickly and hurriedly marching from the *village of Acuł, the *prince of the Persian king went in haste to the *land of the Persians together with King Tiran and all the prisoners, and he went to Asorestan,[20] to his *lord the king of Persia. And the sad news were heard of this destruction and of the sudden calamity that had befallen [Armenia].[21]

Then the *naχarars and *princes, the *officials and army *commanders, the *chieftains together with the multitude of the *general council came and assembled.[22] [But], although they gathered and formed a *contingent prepared to follow after Varaz, they were not able to catch up [with him]. Nevertheless, they reached and took a *portion of the Persian *realm, slaughtered all the men and burned the *country, reducing it to ruin. Then, after their return home they assembled and mourned their own *true-lord, the king of Armenia, with lamentations and tears, as well as the destruction of the *realm. And they bewailed bitterly their own downfall [because they were left] without a *lord.[23]

*Chapter xxi. Concerning the way in which the Armenian *naχarars unanimously *gathered together and went and brought the king of the Greeks to the *land of Armenia to help them; and how the king of Persia came with a large army; and how Nerseh king of Persia escaped on a single horse and saved himself in flight to the *land of the Persians.*[1]

Then the men of the *realm of the *land of Armenia—the *naχarars, *magnates, *nobles, *kusakals, *ašχarhakals and *azats, the *army leaders, *judges, *chieftains, and *princes, not to mention the army *commanders and even [some] of the *ṙamik and *šinakan—*gathered together in a

*council of still greater accord.[2] Then they †began to speak to one another
65 and said: "How is it that we stay and lament? The enemy has been successful in this and after a little time the enemy will attack again. So
come!" they said, "let us console one another, let us protect our *realm
and ourselves, and let us avenge our own *true-lord." Then all the men of
the *realm joined together in one agreement and counsel in order to find
help and support for themselves.

At that time the Armenian *nobility sent some of the great *naχarars
with gifts to the king of the Greeks[3] [to say that] they gave him their hand
[and that] they would *serve him obediently were he to support them with
aid to obtain revenge from their enemies. And so they sent out Andovk,
*nahapet of Siwnik῾, and Aršawir Kamsarakan, *nahapet of Aršarunik῾,
who set forth and came to the *realm of the Greeks to the *imperial
palace [pałatn] of the kings.[4] They presented their *letters-patent, set out
the gifts they had brought, and laid before the king the message of united
supplication of the *realm. When the *emperor[5] heard about these events
he met with great eagerness and readiness their request to be of help and
assistance to the *realm of Armenia, all the more when he recalled the
*covenant and treaty of alliance reinforced by oaths that had been con-
cluded between the *Emperor Constantine and King Trdat.[6]

Now [even] before the envoys who had gone from the *land of Armenia to the *imperial palace [pałatn] had returned to their own *realm,
Nerseh, king of Persia,[7] set out in person from the *regions of the East in
order to come and †seize, burn, devastate, destroy, and appropriate altogether for himself the *territory of the Armenian *land. He collected
his entire army together with his own baggage, the entire large *karawan[8]
and a multitude of elephants; he came—with innumerable supplies, his own
*royal-pavilions,[9] all his women and with the *queen-of-*queens—to the
*confines of Armenia and swallowed the *land altogether. At this time
the *azat-forces of the Armenian *naχarars took each his own household
66 and fled into exile to the *region of the Greeks, and they brought the sad
news to the *naχarars of the *emperor's *host [composed of] multiple-
*contingents [bazmagund banak].

When he heard all this, the king of the Greeks also mustered his own
forces and marched forth to the *land of Armenia against the Persian
king. He left his own *army around the *city of Satał[10] and personally
selected two leading wise men from the Armenian *army, namely Aršawir
and Andovk, because these were the men who had formerly come to him
as envoys. And so, disguised as a *peasant selling cabbages, the *emperor
went in person together with them into the Persian *camp.[11] As the
*camp of the Persian king was pitched in the *district of Basean in the
*village called Osχay,[12] they went and entered into it, observed, examined,
and reckoned the size and strength of its forces and returned from it to
their own *camp, prepared and made ready. [Then] they marched forth

98

and found the *camp of the Persian king pitched in the very same place in idle, †unconcerned, and unwary tranquility. They †attacked the Persian king at daybreak,[13] †put the entire *camp to the *sword, and †left not a single man alive.[14] They sacked and pillaged the *camp and captured the king's wives, the [chief] *queen [*bambišn*], and the ladies[15] accompanying them, together with their furnishings and possessions, and took into captivity their women, treasures, provisions, and supplies.[16] †But the king alone managed to escape, fleeing with a single mounted courier before him,[17] and barely reached his own *realm, whereas the *emperor presented himself in the *camp in great pomp and with glorious renown. All the adult men were slain and the others taken as captives to the *land of the Greeks. Then the *emperor left the *princes Andovk and Aršawir as overseers of the *land, †*honoring them with many gifts and multiple *dignities and entrusting to them all the *princes and their *realms.[18]

67 And the *emperor himself set forth and went to his own *land, to the *land of the Greeks.

And the king of the Persians came as a fugitive to his own *land, and when he reached it he gathered together all those remaining under his *authority and turned to inquiries and investigations. He took counsel with them and inquired; he ordered yet again that they should seek and reveal the source of this conflict and war. Then the facts came out and became clear to him: that these events had arisen over nothing, over malicious words, that the senseless Šapuh-Varaz had seemingly created this tumultuous uproar over a single horse. Then [the king] ordered that the *diadem be torn from Varaz, that his *honorific *ceremonial-robe be stripped off, and that he be subjected to great tortures.[19] According to the Persian custom he ordered his skin flayed off and stuffed with straw and hung in the *public square as a sight for obloquy. And repenting what had *happened, he himself sent *distinguished *princes submissively and peacefully to [obtain] from the *emperor the release of the prisoners, in return. He then sent mediators to speak with the *emperor concerning peace negotiations so that he should at least free his wives from captivity and [so] release him from this infamous and oprobrious shame.[20]

Then Vałēs [Valens],[21] king of the Greeks, wrote[22] the following *official-letter to the king of Persia, saying: "You first should return the captives taken from the *land of Armenia, King Tiran himself and all the others taken from there. Then, when you have done this, I too shall return those I have captured. It is imperative that you first return their booty, and [only] then shall I return yours." As soon as the king of Persia heard this command he hastened to fulfill its conditions. He took King Tiran out of his prison and his chains and spoke gently to him to go [saying] that he would reestablish him at once as king and send him with *honor to his

68 own *realm. Then, Tiran answered [him]: "It is useless, unsuitable, and indeed impossible for me to hold the kingship because of my blindness,

but crown my son Aršak king in my place." And [the Persian king] made
his son Aršak king over the *realm of Armenia at that time.²³ And he
returned from captivity the king's women²⁴ and all the other prisoners,
together with their treasures, gifts, and possessions. As for Tiran himself,
the Persian king made every arrangement with great preparations, and
sent him back from his own *realm to the *land of Armenia, [thus]
faithfully fulfilling the commands of the king of the Greeks.

And when he had sent them off to Armenia, he also sent back the
ambassadors who had come to him from the king of the Greeks so that
they might go and tell the king of the Greeks how and in what fashion he
had fulfilled the commands of the king of the Greeks and that the king of
the Greeks might [then] likewise return the captives he had taken to the
king of Persia. When the king of the Greeks heard all this, [namely] that
the king of Persia had entirely fulfilled the command received from himself and released the Armenian prisoners as well as King Tiran from
captivity, he was satisfied. And at that time the king of the Greeks also
returned his prisoners to the king of Persia. With great preparations and
*honor, the king of the Greeks returned the wives of the king of Persia
from the *land of the Greeks to the *land of Persia, together with all the
captives, and sent them safe and sound to the king.²⁵

[Colophon]

The third portion¹ in twenty-one historical chapters—the chronography
of the chronicler P⁽awstos² Biwzand the great historian, who was a Greek
chronicler—is concluded.³

Fourth Book of Biwzand

Fourth Listing of What I Shall Present,
[i.e.,] the Arrangement of the Book

Chronology [and] Sequence of
Promised Tales[1]

i. Concerning the way in which, after the great troubles of wars with the Persian king Narseh, he crowned as king Aršak the son of Tiran and sent him to the *realm of Armenia together with his father Tiran and all the prisoners.

ii. Concerning the organization of the *realm of Armenia, the regulation of conduct and order, and the regulation and renewal of the kingdom.

iii. Concerning St. Nersēs and his origin; and how he was chosen to be bishop of Greater Armenia.

iv. Concerning the way in which Nersēs was taken and went to Caesarea, and the miracles wrought by God.

v. Concerning Nersēs *kat῾ołikos of Armenia and how he was sent together with *naχarars by King Aršak to Vałēs [Valens], king of the Greeks; and how he was exiled; but how the other *naχarars were sent to the *land of Armenia together with gifts and other hostages.[2]

vi. Concerning the way in which St. Nersēs was exiled and thrown on a desert island; and how he nourished himself; and how God wrought miracles for nine years.

vii. Concerning God's miracles manifested over Nersēs and Basilios and of the jealousy of Bishop Ewsebi toward Basilios.

viii. Concerning the way that the king of the Greeks persecuted all orthodox believers, and how he wished to hold a disputation between the true believers and the sinister sectarians of Arianism. And how through a miraculous divine vision Basilos was convoked to the fray by the *emperor, and through God's might was victorious against the foe alongside of Bishop Ewsebi. And how the *chief-bishop of Caesarea Ewsebios died in prison; and how Barsilios was set free.

70

ix. Concerning the way in which Barsilos was made chief-bishop of Caesarea and the manifestations of God's miracles. And how the king gave the order to collect all the possessions of the believers in Christ, and how they gladly brought them to court and gave them for the sake of their faith; and how and with what entreaties they prayed to God for their own bishops.

x. Concerning the way in which the *emperor Vałēs called a sophist to oppose the true faith, and how the sophist beheld a miraculous vision; and how the emperor Vałēs was killed through manifest signs, and profound peace came to the churches.

xi. Concerning the return from the *land of the Greeks to the *land of Armenia of the *princes who had gone with the *patriarch of Armenia Nersēs to King Vałēs and returned again to king Aršak; and how Aršak king of Armenia was outraged, [and] damaged the *domain of the king of the Greeks by [his] raid.

xii. Concerning Xad, bishop of Bagrawand, whom Nersēs, patriarch of Armenia, left in his place, the kind of man that he was, and the marvels and miracles he performed; and how he held to the truth and paid no heed to the great King Aršak of Armenia, but opposed him because of his iniquitous deeds; and how he loved the poor like Nersēs the *patriarch of Armenia.

xiii. Concerning the way in which the holy *katʿołikos of Armenia Nersēs returned from the *land of the Greeks, and how he rebuked the great king of Armenia Aršak; and how God's blows descended upon the *town of Aršakawan, and the entire multitude of people *assembled together in that place suddenly perished.

xiv. Concerning the *hayr ["father"] *mardpet who came down into the *district of Tarōn; how he came to the place of prayers of Aštišat; and how he went from there condemned by the words of his own mouth; and how, since he deserved death, he was killed by Šawasp Arcruni.

xv. Concerning King Aršak: how he killed his brother's son Gnel because of the slander of Tiritʿ, and how he was reproved and rebuked by the man of God, Nersēs; and how he killed the same Tiritʿ; and how King Aršak took the wife of the murdered Gnel as his own, and how King Aršak in addition to that wife took another one whom he brought from the *realm of the Greeks and whose name was Ołimbi; and how the *court-priest Mrȷ̌iwnik killed Ołimbi, at the perfidious instigation of Pᶜaṙanjem, by mixing a mortal poison into the Eucharist.

xvi. Concerning how and in what way Šapuh king of Persia invited Aršak king of Armenia and greatly honored him; and how the *sparapet* of Armenia Vasak Mamikonean killed the *head-of-the-stables of the king of Persia; and how Aršak king of Armenia made a *covenant with the king of Persia by swearing on the Gospels; how he then lied and fled, and how the king of Persia slaughtered seventy of God's ministers on account of this.

xvii. Concerning the way in which Šapuh king of Persia aroused³ a persecution against the Christian faith.

xviii. Concerning the death of Vardan at the hands of King Aršak through the deceit of his brother Vasak.

xix. Concerning the way in which Aršak king of Armenia senselessly and arrogantly, came to kill the *naχarars indiscriminately.

xx. Concerning the way in which the war between the Greeks and the Persians intensified, and how Aršak king of Armenia became an ally of the king of Persia and put the Greek forces to the *sword; and how Aršak fled from Šapuh king of Persia because of the treachery of Andovk Siwni.

xxi. Concerning the war between Šapuh, king of Persia, and Aršak, king of Armenia, and how Aršak king of Armenia was victorious.

xxii. Concerning the fact that after this three battles took place against the Persian generals in three localities of the *land of Armenia, in the same month, on the same day, at the same hour, and in all three the Armenians raised the standard of victory.

xxiii. Concerning Meružan Arcruni, who revolted against Aršak king of Armenia and turned to Šapuh king of Persia and intensified the war still further; and how he apostatized from God, and how he was from then on a thorn in the side of the *land of Armenia.

xxiv. Concerning Meružan [Arcruni]: how he rebelled, incited Šapuh king of Persia, and waged frequent wars; and how, having become the *guide of Šapuh king of Persia, he led a bandit-raid against the *realm of Armenia; and how he captured the bones of the Aršakuni kings; and how the Armenian *commander Vasak freed the captives and vanquished the foe.

xxv. Concerning the way in which Aršak king of Armenia raided the *land of Persia and ravaged the *land of Atrpatakan; and how he ruined, destroyed, and seized the *camp of King Šapuh in Tᶜawrēš.

71

xxvi. Concerning Vin the Persian and the four hundred thousand [men] who came to fight and were defeated by the Armenian army.

72   xxvii. Concerning the Persian *commander Andikan, who came with four hundred thousand [men] to loot the *land of Armenia; and how the Armenian *sparapet Vasak came forth against him with an Armenian force of one hundred and twenty thousand and destroyed the Persian army together with its leader.

xxviii. Concerning Hazarawuχt who was one of the Persian *naχarars, whom king Šapuh sent with eight hundred thousand [men] to attack the *land of Armenia; and how Vasak came out against him with eleven thousand [men], attacked and destroyed him and his army within the *borders of Ałjnikʿ.

xxix. Concerning Dmayund [sic] Vsemakan, whom [Šapuh] sent with nine hundred thousand axe-bearers against Aršak king of Armenia. Then, the Armenian *sparapet Vasak came out and destroyed him and his army.

xxx. Concerning Vahrič the son of Vahrič, who came with four million [men] to wage war against the king of Armenia; and how he was given over into the hands of the *sparapet Vasak, and both he and his army fell into the hands of the Armenian forces.

xxxi. Concerning Gumand Šapuh, who boasted greatly before Šapuh king of Persia and who reached Armenia with nine hundred thousand [men]; and how he was defeated and driven from the *land of Armenia.

xxxii. Concerning the *nahapet Dehkan, who was sent with a large army by Šapuh king of Persia against Aršak king of Armenia; and how the Armenian *commander Vasak attacked and slaughtered him and his army.

xxxiii. Concerning Surēn Pahlaw, who came against Armenia with a large army and who was also defeated like his predecessors.

xxxiv. Concerning Apakan Vsemakan, who came with an innumerable and immeasurable host to wage war against the *land of Armenia and who was then also ill-fated like his predecessors.

xxxv. Concerning the Persian *nuirapet Zik, who was sent by the Persian king Šapuh with a large army to wage war against Armenia, and who was destroyed like his predecessors.

xxxvi. Concerning the Persian Suren, who came to wage war after Zik, and how Vasak overwhelmed him together with his army, which was destroyed with him.

xxxvii. Concerning Hrewšołom, who was sent with nine hundred thousand [men] by the Persian king against Armenia; and how in this case too the Armenians won and raised the standard of victory.

xxxviii. Concerning Ałanozan, who came from the Persian king with four million [men] to wage war against the king of Armenia; and how he was defeated and conquered by Vasak.

xxxix. Concerning Boyakan and four hundred thousand [men], whom the Armenian *sparapet Vasak attacked and exterminated.

xl. Concerning the Persian Vačᶜakan, who came to Armenia with one hundred and eighty thousand [men] intending to raid and lay waste the *land; then also the Armenian *sparapet Vasak defeated [him] and put him and his army to the *sword.

xli. Concerning Mšakan and three hundred and fifty thousand [men], who invaded the *land of Armenia; and how he was destroyed by Vasak and his forces.

xlii. Concerning Maručan and six hundred thousand [men]: how they marched against King Aršak from the *land of Persia, and how the *commander Vasak attacked and slaughtered them.

xliii. Concerning the *zndkapet who marched against the *land of Armenia with nine hundred thousand [men]. Then Vasak with his forces attacked and slaughtered them.

xliv. Concerning the son of King Aršak, whose name was Pap; and how he was filled with *dews from birth; and how the *dews manifested themselves in him; and how he performed foul acts with them.

xlv. Concerning the *handerjapet of Sakstan, whom Šapuh king of Persia sent with four hundred thousand [men]; and the *commander Vasak, together with the Armenian army, also put him to flight.

xlvi. Concerning the Persian *takaṙapet Šapstan, who marched with five million [men] against the *realm of Armenia; then, the Armenian army attacked and slaughtered them.

xlvii. Concerning the *handarjapet of the Magi, who marched forth with one hundred and eighty thousand [men] to give battle to the king of Armenia; and he was destroyed like his predecessors.

xlviii. Concerning the Persian *hambarakapet, who marched forth with nine hundred thousand [men] to fight the forces of the Armenian kingdom and was destroyed at Sałmas by the Armenian army, by the *contingent of Vasak.

xlix. Concerning Mṙkan, who came from Persia with four hundred thousand [men] to fight against the Armenian king, and was slaughtered with his forces at Maχazan [sic] by the Armenian *contingent and the *commander Vasak.

73

105

l. Concerning the decline and fall of the Armenian kingdom: how many of the Armenian *naxarars revolted against the king of Armenia and went over to the Persian king, Šapuh; and how they soon scattered hither and yon, and the Armenian kingdom was greatly weakened.

li. Concerning the way in which those remaining in the *realm *assembled all together in complete agreement before their *patriarch Nersēs and complained to him; and how they left and abandoned their king, Aršak.

lii. Concerning the Persian king: how he ceased to wage war against Aršak king of Armenia at that time, and how he deceitfully invited him to a reconciliation.

liii. Concerning Šapuh king of Persia's second summons to Aršak king of Armenia; his going to him, and [his] utter destruction.

liv. Concerning the way in which Šapuh, having turned to magicians, sooth-sayers, and sorcerers, magically tested the intentions of Aršak, and had him imprisoned in the *fortress of Anuš [Oblivion]; and how he likewise ordered the *sparapet of Armenia cruelly put to death.

lv. Concerning the captivity and devastation of the *realm of Armenia, and the removal of *Queen P'aṙanjem as captive to Persia, and the destruction of the Armenian *cities, and the total ruin of the *realm.

74   lvi. Concerning the martyrdom of Zuit', priest of Artašat, in the *land of Persia.

lvii. Zuit''s prayer at the hour of his death.

lviii. Concerning the coming of Šapuh king of Persia to the *land of Armenia, and the total extermination of those remaining in the *land of Armenia.

lix. Concerning Vahan and Meružan; how they remained in the *realm of Armenia and how much harm they caused to the *realm; and how Vahan and his wife were killed by their own son.

Book IV
*Chronological Accounts of the *House of the Sons of T^corgom in the *Realm of Armenia*

Chapter i. Concerning the way in which, after great troubles and wars with the Persian king Nerseh, he crowned as king Aršak the son of Tiran and sent him to the *realm of Armenia together with his father Tiran and all the prisoners.[1]

And when concord and profound peace were established between the king of the Greeks and Nerseh, king of Persia,[2] they agreed with much love to do each other's will, and the Greek *emperor returned the captives to the king of Persia. Then too, Nerseh king of Persia crowned as king Aršak the son of Tiran[3] and sent him forth with great *glory together with his father and their wives[4] and all the captives, as well as their treasures and possessions. Having become king in the *land of Asorestan, Aršak King of Greater Armenia set forth with his father and his entire household. He came to the *land of Armenia, reassembled those who had scattered throughout the *land, and ruled over them.[5]

76   And profound peace reigned at that time. All those in the *land of Armenia who had hidden, fled, or been lost reassembled and lived undisturbed in great peace under the protection of King Aršak. Then between the two kings, the *realm of Armenia became peaceful,[6] organized, ordered, and stable, and after this each one of the inhabitants peacefully enjoyed his own possessions.

Chapter ii. Concerning the organization of the *realm, the regulation of conduct and order everywhere, and the renewal of the Armenian kingdom.[1]

At that time, King Aršak went to seek the *family of the *commanders-in-chief of the *valiant *clan of the Mamikonean,[2] especially as they were his *tutors and *foster-fathers.[3] Consequently, he went forth and found them in the *strongholds of the *realm of Tayk^c,[4] in their own *realm, and appeased[5] them, for they had broken away and withdrawn from all the affairs of Armenia at the time of the unreason[6] of Tiran. And

107

the king set the eldest *brother Vardan as *nahapet of his *clan, and the middle *brother Vasak, his own *tutor, as *sparapet and *commander-in-chief of military matters, and he likewise made the youngest an army *chief.[7] Similarly he reinstated the military forces of the *mightiest *nahapets according to each one's rank, as had been done by former kings.[8] And he brought the *magnates into submission, apportioning their troops in every *region, and made them the *wardens-of-the-Armenian *marches.

And so, the *sovereignty of the kingdom of the Armenian *land was renewed and invigorated as it had formerly been: every *magnate on his *throne, every *official in his station.[9] First, [he entrusted] the office of *hazarapet, of the overseeing care for the *land, of the *supervision [dehkanut'iwn] over the enrichment and welfare of the *realm, to the *clan of the Gnuni, who cared for the *peasants as *hazarapets of the
77 entire *land.[10] Likewise, [he bestowed] the office of *sparapet-*stratelat, of military *command in war, of military action in hand-to-hand *spear fighting to the fearless, intrepid champions †renowned for *valor, renowned for good-fame and good-deeds, outstanding in military affairs according to the original rules of our ancestors, to the illustrious and noble *clan of the Mamikonean, who bore †dove banners and eagle *standards,[11] to the continually and ever-victorious *clan gifted by heaven with renowned *valor in military leadership; and he gave it total *authority over all the forces of Greater Armenia. And similarly, [he designated] others, from such and lesser *clans, who as *officials *took-their-ease upon *cushions before the king with *diadems on their heads.[12] Not counting the *mightiest *nahapets and the *tanutērs, those who were only *officials, [the holders] of nine hundred *cushions, came to the *palace in time of *feasting [and were] disposed on *banqueting-couches, in addition to those who stood around to serve officially.[13]

*Chapter iii. Concerning St. Nersēs and his origin, and how and by what means he was chosen to be bishop of the Armenian *realm.*[1]

The *mightiest *nahapets of every *clan and *house—the *lords with *contingents and *banners[2]—all the *satraps, *naxarars, and *azats, the *chieftains and *princes, the *commanders and wardens-of-the-marches *assembled in council before King Aršak in one unanimous agreement: that they might come together, consider and take counsel about their *spiritual-leader: namely, who might be worthy to sit on the *patriarchal *throne and shepherd Christ's rational flock. Then, this counsel prevailed over all those present: that they should find a *spiritual-leader among the remaining descendants of the *house of Grigor.[3] "For," they all said to the king,
78 "since God has renewed your kingdom, so must the *spiritual-leadership [hogewor *nahapetut'iwn] also be renewed through one of his descendants.

For," they said, "with the renewal of this *throne the moral luster of this *realm of Armenia shall likewise be renewed."4

Then the mass of the *general-council-of-the-realm looked at, named and asked for the one who was called Nersēs, the son of Atᶜanagenēs [sic], the grandson of the *high-priest Yusik who was the son of Vrtᶜanēs, the son of the first great *high-priest Grigor. The name of his mother was Bambišn [and] she was the sister of the King Tiran.5 In his youth he had been married and had led a secular life. From his boyhood, [however], he had been nurtured and taught by faithful *spiritual-teachers in the *city of Caesarea of Gamirkᶜ and had earned the love of his companions.6 But at that particular time he was serving as an *official in the military, as the beloved *senekapet of King Aršak entrusted with all the affairs of the kingdom, both internal and external.7

He was a large man of tall and pleasing stature, with an agreeable appearance, so that no one equal to his beauty could be found on the face of the *earth.8 He was attractive, admirable, and awe-inspiring to all beholders, and enviable for his prowess in military exercises. he was fearful of the *Lord God and a strict keeper of His Commandments, benevolent, holy, prudent, most wise and impartial, just in his judgments, humble, gently, modest, a lover of the poor, observant of the sanctity of marriage, and perfect in the love of God. And toward his companions he [held] to the Commandment to love every companion like oneself,9 so that in military life he was thus perfect in virtuous deeds. Though still a youth, he walked according to the Commandments of the *Lord: [according to] justice, integrity, and every service to his companions. He was tireless and zealous toward God,10 and burned with the Holy Spirit. Thus, in all ways he was perfect in all things.11 And he loved the poor and miserable, and cared for them so much that he shared his garments and food with them. He was the helper and overseer of the oppressed and the anguished, and he became the *defender-of-the-dispossessed.12

79 And as he stood, still in military dress, adorned in a handsome *ceremonial-robe with fitting ornaments, with his desirable beauty, tall stature, and splendid hair—standing at the head of the royal couch in the service of the king [and] holding the *king's sword [zarkᶜunakan susern] with a gold scabbard on a girdle enriched with pearls and jewels [as was his office]—the entire assembly unanimously raised a shout and called out: "Let Nersēs be our pastor!" [But] when he heard the clamor he refused, thinking himself unworthy, and would not accept.13 Then, he saw that they all insisted in the same words—†for they clamored the same before the king—saying: "Let no one else but he be our pastor, and no one but he sit on that [patriarchal] *throne!" But since he did not consider himself worthy, because of his great humility, he stepped forth

and began to speak some untruths about his own unrighteousness, and to impute [to himself] sins that he had not committed.

Hearing him, and aware of his lies about himself, the entire multitude together with the king was overcome with laughter. Whereas the whole of the army clamored together: "Let the sins thou hast committed fall on us and on our heads, let those deeds fall upon ourselves and upon our children.[14] But do thou renew the deeds of thy ancestor Grigor and renew the same *spiritual-leadership for us." But he, †since he found no other words to answer them, he became hostile to the troops, said: "You are unrighteous and impure, I am unable to be your pastor, or to take your sins upon myself. I cannot condone [them], nor tolerate your evil deeds. Today you happen to love me for no reason but tomorrow, hating and hostile, you will bind me on your heads like a beating club. Leave me alone! Then perhaps I may spend my life undistracted, in accordance with my own unworthiness, in anguish and in sins, concentrating on the eternal judgment." Then the multitude of the host [again] †raised a shout, and said: "[Even] thus a sinner, be our pastor!" For such human persistence came through divine providence. Then King Aršak, in the ferocity of his heart and great wrath, pulled over to himself the *royal sword with its belt (that Nersēs bore in his service to the king according to his duties as *senekapet), tearing it away from him. And he ordered him bound in his own presence. He ordered the crowning glory of his admirable curly hair, the like of which could not be found anywhere, cut off and his becoming *official-robe stripped off. Then [the king] gave an order and ecclesiastical vestments were brought and put on [Nersēs], and he ordered the elderly Bishop Pᶜawstos[15] called in to ordain him as deacon. Now, when [Nersēs's] hair was shaved off, many wept when they heard and saw, regretting that beauty [destroyed] through his altered appearance. But, when they saw him adorned with the beauty of Christ, many rejoiced that he had been called to be the keeper of Christ's *house through bountiful grace.

Then it was, that the *Lord put into the minds of all to request as their pastor the one who could be their *spiritual-leader and show them the path of life. For [even] while he himself still bore the outward appearance of the military state, he had put on Christ through the inner man[16] and molded himself for noble deeds. And through the hope that he possessed, he had been crucified with Christ and had shared his tomb, through [his] love from faith he had died to sins and in righteousness awaited the hope of the resurrection.[17] For all of this he was indeed worthy of the *patriarchal *throne and of the position of his forefathers: of the *throne of the apostle Thaddeus and of the inheritance of his ancestor according to the flesh and in the spirit, Grigor.[18] For it was from the *Lord that he was called to this dignity and that the request for him as worthy of such a dignity was planted in the minds of all; whereas he,

81   through his fear [of the *Lord] and his great humility, held himself unworthy of the great dignity of God's [service] to which they had impelled
him. But all this [came about] by compulsion and the unanimous [desire
of the people], and through God's commandment, and, most of all, in
accordance with what had been foretold about him at the time of his
ancestors in the divine vision to Yusik: "There shall be a man from thy
children who shall be a light for the *world."[19]

*Chapter iv. Concerning the way in which Nersēs was taken and
brought to Caesarea; and the great miracles wrought by God; and the
apostolic way that he pastured his flock.*[1]

Then the *mightiest *princes gathered together so that they might
take the much desired Nersēs and go [to the place] where it was the
custom to consecrate the *patriarch. And many Armenian bishops also
*assembled before the king over this matter and to counsel[2] with the
unanimous consent of all that he be chosen; [for] it was pleasing to all
that he be placed on the leading *throne.[3] With the unanimous agreement
and consent of all—the bishops, the king, and the whole of the *realm—
[the following] set forth and went:[4] the great *prince *Hayr*, the *mardpet*;
and the great *prince Bagarat; the *asparapet*[5]; and the great *prince
Daniēl of Copᶜkᶜ; and Mehendak Řštuni; and Andovk, *prince of Siwnikᶜ;
and Aršawir, *prince of Širak and Aršarunikᶜ; and Noy, *prince of the
Other Copᶜkᶜ; and Pargew, *prince of the Amatuni *house. [All] of them
got ready and were sent forth with many presents and the *greatest gifts
and authenticated *letters-patent to the *katᶜołikos of katᶜołikoi Ewsebios,
to the *land of Gamirkᶜ and to its *metropolis Caesarea, so that they might
have St. Nersēs consecrated there as *katᶜołikos of Greater Armenia.

   They set out, came there cheerfully and joyfully, and saw the holy
82   *katᶜołikos of katᶜołikoi[6], the noble, blessed, glorious, and admirable
Ewsebios. And they presented to him the *letter-patent of King Aršak
and set out before him the gifts that they had brought. And he received
them lovingly and with great splendor. [Then] following the canonical
regulations, the great *chief-bishop Ewsebios *assembled many holy
bishops in accordance with the apostolic canons, so that they might
ordain St. Nersēs as *chief-bishop of Greater Armenia.

   And a great miracle occurred. For, as they were entering the church,
a white dove came down upon the altar before the clergy and in front
of all the *assembly.[7] And when the great *chief archbishop Ewsebios
entered together with his presbyters and a holy archpriest [ericᶜapet]
named Barsiłios,[8] the dove left the altar and came to rest over him, and
remained there a long time. But when the time was come at which they
intended to consecrate Nersēs, the dove rose from St. Barseł and settled

down over the head of Nersēs. And when this miracle and sign from God took place over this man, all the *assembly marvelled, as did the great *archbishop Ewsebi. All together they cried out to him: "Thou art pleasing to God and the Spirit of God has rested upon thee, for this was the likeness of the All-Holy Spirit that manifested Itself above the *Lord."⁹ Then they consecrated him, took and installed him on the episcopal *throne, and paid *honor to him, and many spoke *ēnkomia* [praises] to him (that is: "The Holy Spirit rested upon him").¹⁰ But he still, all the more, considered himself unworthy of what had taken place. And they sent him forth with the most splendid honors, and likewise the *mightiest *naχarar-*satraps of Armenia.

And [so] they reached the *land of Armenia proudly clad in manifest spiritual *glory,¹¹ and King Aršak came forward to meet them as far as the mountain called *Aṙewc* ["Lion"]. And they met together there with great rejoicing, exchanged greetings with blessings and returned thence to the *realm. And St. Nersēs sat on the *patriarchal *throne, and there was great peace in the *realm during his pastoral care. For he was like his [fore] father the great Grigor in his ways and conduct. He truly found fatherly perfection, revived the same apostolic grace of his fathers, and showed the same care to preserve [his flock] safe from visible and invisible foes.

He most resembled the first trees, [for] he bore fruit of *spiritual-teaching of the same kind and the same maturity; from the beginning of his supervision and pastoral care he dispensed abundantly [to his flock] all that was profitable, feeding [it] in spiritual pastures. For grace rested upon him to such a degree that he performed the *greatest miracles and the healing of the sick. Wherever an opportunity occurred, he brought back those who had gone astray. He also performed miracles such as these: he convinced those whom he found most obdurate by striking them with fear, but those who were docile—the ears of whose hearts were opened— he persuaded with words of exhortation.

He rebuilt churches and raised up overturned altars. He confirmed the repentance of those of little faith so that they might live believing in God. He consoled believers with the perpetual hope of eternal rewards. He filled once more the *throne of St. Thaddeus and was a son like unto his fathers.¹² He silenced slanderers with rebukes and stopped altogether the words and deeds of the unrighteous. He fought for the truth until death¹³ and encouraged and made joyful the champion of righteousness. He *nurtured and nourished the fruit of righteousness with the rain of his *spiritual-teaching to attain blessings. And every place within the *confines of Greater Armenia where first his fathers had sown the preaching of the Word of life, he too watered it with his rain. As the companion of the sowers, the laborer-reaper caused the plants to flourish; he multiplied the

84   abundant yield in the granaries of the kingdom, and as a collaborator he
became the successor of his laborer-forefathers.[14]

He bore a great ineffable strength within himself and he displayed
particular zeal in the regulation of charity: first assuming the doing of
good himself, then giving to others the example of good deeds,[15] and in
general, he opened the closed doors of the mind to the good through the
exhortation of his *spiritual-teaching. He taught as the greatest good
love, hope, faith, holiness, gentleness, meekness, forgiveness, solicitude to
furnish care for the poor, and the hope of reward in the promised tidings of
Christ, and also the inextinguishable fire of the Judgment,[16] threatening
with the remembrance of eternal torments through the unswayable coming
of the Son of God, Jesus Christ. And through this he instilled such fear
into all those who dwelt within the *borders of Armenia, that all the
believers distributed whatever they possessed equally and willingly to the
poor, and they did this of their own accord, with joy and vigilance.

And he himself went to the *region of the *district of Tarōn and
summoned together all the bishops of the Armenian *realm. They
*assembled in the *village of Aštišat, where the first church had been built,
for this was the *mother-of-all-the-churches and the site of the earlier
*synods.[17] They all came willingly to the *council and deliberated profit-
ably together so as to perfect there the secular regulations of the church
and the uniformity of beliefs.[18] At that time they elaborated and set down
canonical regulations and turned the entire population of the *land of
Armenia into the likeness of an universal order of *solitary-communities,
except for the laws of marriage.[19] But the holy *chief-bishop Nersēs set
only the Apostolic Canons over everyone. For everyone he became the
exhorter and *spiritual-leader, the inciter, zealous in good deeds.[20] He
85   performed them first himself and then taught the same to everyone else.[21]
He ordered the same thing done throughout the entire *realm—in every
*district and every *region, on every side and in every corner within the
*confines of Armenia: to indicate the most suitable places to be set aside
for the building of almshouses for the poor and to collect the sick, the
lepers, the paralytics, and all those who suffered; leper-houses were
designated for them, assistance and *maintenance, as well as shelters[22] for
the poor. For this was the order of the great *chief-bishop Nersēs and
likewise of the entire holy *council: that these people should remain exclusively in their own lodgings and should not go out as miserable beggars;
indeed, they should not set foot outside their door, but everyone should
owe them protection. "For," he said, "the order of the *realm must not be
destroyed, but it is proper that everyone without exception should bring
assistance mercifully and piously [fearfully], and supply their needs."[23]

Likewise he built, ordered, and consolidated; he taught many other charities to the *realm and regulated many canonical rules of his fathers. He taught [everyone] to look forward to the hope of the resurrection; not to believe human death irreversible [and] without return once again to life, nor to perform hopelessly over the departed the excessive weeping and lamentations of unbridled mourning,[24] but rather to look forward with hope toward the coming of the *Lord and the renewal of the Resurrection, to await the day of the coming of the *Lord in the hope that each one would receive the eternal reward of his deeds. He also [taught] that marriage should be lawful, and neithe to deceive nor betray one's spouse, and above all to refrain from incestuous marriages with close *family relations within the *clan, especially from intimacy with daughters-in-law or anything of the kind, as had once been [the custom].[25] And he [set down] the canon: to forbid altogether the eating of dead animal food and blood, and the holding of intercourse during menses, for he held all such things to be impure before the *Lord.[26]

86

He held equally [destined] altogether for the same pit of perdition deceit, slander, covetousness, malice, lust, deprivation [of others], sodomy and effeminacy, defamation, unbridled drunkenness and gluttony, pillage, adultery, revenge on one's enemies, falsehood, hostility, mercilessness and the bearing of false witness, blood-shedding, murders, and foul bestiality, those who had no expectation of the Resurrection, and those who wept without hope over the dead. He commanded the entire *realm beginning with the king, the *magnates in general, and all those who had *authority over their fellows, to show mercy to their *servants, and their inferiors, and their followers, to love them like members of their own families, and not to opress them unjustly with exhorbitant *taxes, reminding [them] that they too had a *Lord in heaven. He likewise ordered the *servants to be obediently faithful to their *masters so that they might receive a reward from the *Lord.[27]

And in his day peace and renewal came to all the churches, and deep reverence for all bishops grew in every part of Greater Armenia. And the illuminating order of the church shone forth to the full, and the ceremonies of the *cathedral churches were regulated with utmost splendor. The orders of holy service grew, and [the number of] their ministers increased. And so, he multiplied the number of churches in all inhabited and uninhabited places and did the same for the number of religious.[28] He also set up Greek and Syriac schools in various localities throughout the *districts of Armenia.[29]

He saved may captives [who were] opressed or afflicted and obtained their release from captivity—*freeing some through his preaching of the fear of Christ's *glory, and others with ransoms—and he sent each one [of them] back to his home. He gave relief and maintenance to widows,

87

orphans, and the indigent, and the poor daily rejoiced with him, for his *hall [tačar] and table were ever [open] to the poor, the alien, and the stranger. So greatly did he love the poor, that although he had built almshouses in all of the *districts and set up maintenance for them there, so that they should have no other concern but to rise from their beds, nevertheless he did not keep his *palace without them, but the halt and the blind and the crippled, the deaf, the paralytic, the needy, and the indigent sat down and *feasted together with him. He washed and anointed all with his own hands, and bound [their wounds]; he personally fed his nourishment to each one of them and spent everything for their needs. Thus, every stranger found repose and rest under his roof.

Whatever he did himself he taught [to others],[30] and as he was himself holy, prudent, and vigilant, he prepared every man to receive the Word of God. Just like the prophets and the apostles he taught compassion [saying]: "Your sins must be expiated through compassion and your iniquities through charity and gifts to the poor."[31] He also reminded them of the disciples who designated for ministry to the poor the great protomartyr and first deacon, Stephen, and his companions, who opened up the Heavens and was thereby worthy to see the Son at the right [hand] of God His Father.[32]

He likewise spoke of *Aycemnik* ["Gazelle"], of her great charity and the compassionate lamentations of the widows, and of her restoration to life by the great Peter after she had passed away and died.[33] And again, he said: "The great Paul relates that, 'when they perceived the grace that was given unto me, James, Kephas, and John, who were true pillars, when they saw that I am entrusted with the Gospel to the uncircumcised as they are to the circumcised, they were greatly encouraged and gave to me and to Barnabas their consent, that we [should go] unto the heathen and they unto the circumcision. But they ordered me only,' he said: 'that we should take care of the poor, that which,' he said, 'I myself have striven to do.'"[34]

Likewise, and still more, he set forth the words of the *Lord to the master who was a rich man who had fulfilled all the Commandments and then heard [this] from the *Lord. "Sell that thou hast and give to the poor and thou shalt find a treasure in Heaven," and further [He said] to him: "It is easier for a rope to pass through the eye of a needle than for an avaricious rich [man to enter] into the Kingdom of God,"[35] and again: "Make yourselves friends from the Mammon of unrighteousness, that they may receive you into their eternal homes."[36] Or yet, like Paul himself, he was zealous in good works[37] and constrained everyone with the saying: "Follow after love and desire spiritual things."[38] Telling of the diligence of the Achaeans to serve the saints in Macedonia,[39] he exhorted [all] to emulate [them] and urged them toward assiduous virtue in good deeds [saying]:

88

115

"It is good to be zealous at all times in good things."[40] And again he strove together with everyone to follow in the steps of Christ. "'Let us fix our eyes,'" he said, "'on the leader and perfector of our faith, Jesus,'"[41] and [yet] again: "'Remember your *spiritual-leaders, and your guardians in the *Lord,'[42] who have spoken to you and the Word of life, and behold the end of their careers and imitate their faith.'"[43] And [he said] at the same time: "'Let each one of you keep in mind that which was in Christ Jesus,'"[44] and again, "'Jesus began to do and to teach.'"[45] And James the beloved *brother of the *Lord, modeling himself in his epistle on the entire *host [gund] of the saints, and on the *Lord who loves holiness, says: "'Take, my *brethren, the prophets who have spoken in the name of the *Lord, as an example of suffering affliction and endurance. [. . .] You have heard of the patience of Job, and have seen the end of the *Lord.'"[46]

89   He constantly spoke these and similar words to them, ceaselessly instructing and admonishing by day and night. Through the wisdom of the Holy Spirit that dwelt in him †during all the days of his life, the blessed *chief-bishop Nersēs thus proffered the admonition of his *spiritual-teaching to everyone like a caring father, like a compassionate mother. He urged everyone to ardent spiritual love: [both] the *mightiest and the inferior, the *honored and the lowly, the rich and the poor, the *azat and the *peasant. And until his death he fulfilled with the utmost solicitude the supervision of the *realm without the least negligence or delay, and there never was anyone like him anywhere in the *land of Armenia.

    Chapter v. Concerning Nersēs, *kat῾olikos *of Armenia, and how he was sent by King Aršak to the* *emperor Valēs *together with* *naχarars *; and how he spoke a great deal about the faith concerning the son of the* *emperor; *and how he was bound and exiled, while the other* *naχarars *were released with gifts.*[1]

    Because of the existence of a *covenant of peace and alliance between the *realm of Armenia and the *emperor of the Greeks,[2] it then seemed good to the king of Armenia to send with great pomp the great *kat῾olikos* of Armenia, Nersēs in person, together with ten of the *greatest Armenian *satraps[3] to the *emperor in order to renew the *covenant of accord and peace. And so, they set out and came to the *imperial palace [palat] of the kings of the Greeks.[4]

    [Now] at about that time, the great king of the Greeks, Valēs, had strayed from the faith into the heretical sect of the Arians.[5] When the king first saw them, †he honored them with the most brilliant *glory and great splendor. But it so happened that the king's one son, his only child, fell gravely ill and the king pressed the holy *kat῾olikos* of Armenia,
90 Nersēs, to pray for the child.[6] But he stepped forth, †began to speak, and said:[7]

"If you will believe that our *Lord Jesus Christ is the Only-begotten Son and Offspring of God—of his individuality [ink ᶜnut ᶜiwn] and essence [iskut ᶜiwn]⁸—born from the loins of the Father and not created, emanation [cagumn] of the Father, light of the *glory of the Existing-one [ēakan] and image [nkaragir] of His being [ēut ᶜiwn]⁹—for He is both born from and Son of His nature [bnut ᶜiwn], for as is the Father so is the Son of His nature, born of the Father before all the ages, before the coming into being of the creatures. [If you believe that He], from the beginning, was born the Collaborator and Co-creator of all with the Father,¹⁰ for everything in heaven and on *earth came into existence from the Father through Him; [He] who, from the beginning, was always with the Father in the fashioning of all the creatures; Who, with Him by nature [i bnē] and from the beginning had a form [kerparan] equal to the likeness [nmanut ᶜiwn] of the type of Him who generated Him in [full] equality; Who from the beginning of the *world bears all things through the word of His power,¹¹ and through His natural [bnakan] *authority rules, directs, and *guides all the creatures; Who from the beginning created and consolidated the foundations of the *earth and 'spread the heavens like a *canopy';¹² Whose hands have created and consolidated all the expanse of the heavens; Who created man from dust and made him rational [gifted] with speech, wise and [endowed] with free will [anjnišχanut ᶜiwn].¹³ And at the time that mankind was corrupted through its own volition and did not acknowledge its Creator or His Commandments, the Son—by nature and from the beginning—sat at the right [hand] of the Father, on the same *throne as His Begetter. But when He saw the Father scorned by mankind, He arose and came down from the right hand of the *throne; He contracted and reduced Himself, took flesh from the Virgin, became man, and abased his person [anjn].¹⁴ [That] He became man, bore torments of His own will, died, rose, and bestowed life on all mankind. [That] He then rose and sat on His own natural [iwroy bnut ᶜeann] *throne at the right hand of the Father who begat Him.

"If then you believe this in this fashion: that Christ is the Son begotten of God, we can satisfy you through Scriptures and through many and 91 innumerable testimonies, and wash off from you the false and foul baptism of your heretical faith. And do you receive in grace the baptism of the holy faith in the name of the Father, the Creator, and in the confession of the generation of the Son from the Father before eternity and the ages Who is according to the nature [bnut ᶜiwn] of His own essence [goyacᶜut ᶜiwn]¹⁵ and Who came down to the Holy Virgin to be incarnate at the end of time and for our salvation and vivification¹⁶, and in the death and burial of His Son, Jesus Christ, and in the peace, union, and gifts of His Holy Spirit. Receive baptism in these wondrous mysteries of the release and renewal of life, and we shall make your child worthy of this holy blessing of the light and remission of baptism. And we shall implore Christ our *Lord to take away the sins of unbelieving heresy and have mercy, for it is from them that all suffering and torments have come from the beginning and [still] exist. And I guarantee [in the name] of the merciful *Lord that I shall set your child safe and sound before you if you accept the true faith and confess with us as [do] the other orthodox.

"But if you do not confess [that] Christ [is] the Only-begotten Son of God, Whom the Father first and before all else begat from His own nature [*bnutenē*] and equivalent to His paternal nature as a perfect Only-begotten Offspring, His identical co-equal, co-ruler, and co-creator; Who for the love of Him loved us; Who was sent forth by the Father through love of us into the Holy Virgin Mary and appeared from that woman as man; [Who] was of like nature [*nman . . . bnut'ean*][17] to His Begetter and had as His own the nature [*i bnut'enē . . . zbnut'iwn*] of His Father's form [*kerparank'*], [Who], through the flesh and of His own volition, took on for our sake the form of a *servant.[18] Because mankind had fallen of its own volition into *servitude, the *Lord Himself took on the form of a *servant to free us from *servitude. For when God in the beginning fashioned the creatures and at last made man, He gathered the visible and invisible of His hypostasis [*zōrut'iwn*][19] into one and the same. And 92 in the same way He firmly cast all the creatures whom He fashioned according to the likeness and image of His own form [*nmanut'ean patkeri kerparanac'*][20] and gave him [man] power over his own will. Because of this, [men] were corrupted and ruined by Satanic envy and grew old in false and deceitful slander. But the *Lord visiting the lost ones, came down and was born of the Virgin in the form of a man to create peace in heaven and on *earth, and to unite the Father who begat Him into reconciliation with His creatures, through his own human image, so that all the rejected creatures might be set face to face with the invisible God.[21]

"Thus He truly renewed all things again in the renewal of creatures, 'for if anyone be in Christ, [he is] a new creature'; for 'old things are passed away; behold, all things are become new.'[22] For He came and took the form of men[23] and renewed and confirmed again all things through Himself. He was Himself the model of our vivification. Through His death, [He was] the first born of all the dead,[24] and the first through His resurrection from the dead so that through Him everything should be revealed, so that He should fashion us unaltered as to the spirit and immortal as to the body, so that we might behold as men not only the immutability of the spirit, but also the immortality of the body, for all the invisible and rational forces shall await this immutability with us. 'Because all creatures shall be delivered from the *bondage of corruption into the *freedom of the *glory of the Son of God.'[25] For it is said that God was born as a man from a virgin from amongst us for this [reason]: that driven from this present consolidation and reaching to the excellence of the days to come, we might await, hope, and expect [Him who] was the Creator from the beginning and the *guide of the new creatures. For He is the Begotten and the form [*kerparank*ᶜ] of the invisible God, the Only-begotten of the Father, the Creator of all creatures. Therefore, the apostle interpreting these circumstances †summarizes, exposes and says: 'For by Him were all things established that are in heaven and that are in the *earth, whether they be visible or invisible, whether they be *thrones, or *dominions, or *principalities, or *authorities [*petut ᶜiwnk*ᶜ] or powers.' And he further fully clarifies these words: 'For He is the first born from the dead, that in all things He might be preeeminent; for it was pleasing that all the fullness of God dwell in him and fulfill all things through Him; that He make peace through the blood of His cross [reconciling] through it that which is on *earth and that which is in heaven.'²⁶ For everything that is is heaven and on *earth was *gathered together through the suffering of Christ our *Lord, the Only-begotten Son of God.

"For the greatness of God created all things, and He set man as the *lord of all; he ordered and they multiplied.²⁷ Then He designated *princes and established *spiritual-leaders. But when they had once transgressed, they fell from the position of *authority that they had previously held. And the second time He allowed some *authority, and others not, only from sheer necessity: so that we might thereafter at least acknowledge grace through ruling, and that through non-ruling we might know the *dominion of the *Lord of all. For who does not seek greatness and the well-being of the flesh or the fulfillment of the will—that which is fitting only for the Only-begotten Son of God? For men are not [destined] altogether for greatness, or for absolute poverty; they are not always great or utterly poor; they become great through their will, and through will, poor. Some are born but were not *nurtured, reached maturity, and were dishonored by enemies. Who is there who loves sickness and hates health? Who lacks all, but is not in need? Some are bound in [the fetters of] *idol-worship and murder, in adultery and varied evildoings; some, having gone astray with erring minds, bind everything together by chance, whether it be good or evil.

"Now those on whom the Sun of righteousness²⁸ spreads the light of the faith and chases away the dark clouds of unknowing constantly rebuke falsehood and error. First through their good deeds and their display of a good example, then by teaching the same to others;²⁹ first through their unswerving faith in the creative power of the Trinity, then through purity, prudence, and humility to protect themselves from the *world. And they live in absolute tranquility according to the will of Christ the Son of God, our Creator. Scorning and treading underfoot all that is transitory, and lifted up on the wings of the Holy Spirit, they fly over the dense forces that impede us here below. And they reject and avoid the unnecessary to such a degree that they even scorn the daily-*portion [*ṙočik*] of food, let alone the consumption of meat and wine that loosens the belly and wraps the kidneys in thick fat, whence arise myriads of varied and countless transgressions. Those who give themselves up to such things love them and act according to their own will.

"Now let us rather rejoice in the grace of man-loving good deeds through which every *race and nation confesses our *Lord Jesus Christ, Begotten of the Father, Begotten and not created, of the same identity [*iskakicʿ*] as the Father, of the same nature [*bnakicʿ*] with His Begetter, the emanation, the light of His Father's *glory, and of one form [*kerparanakicʿ*] with His Begetter. And to those who possess the eyes of the mind and are not blind to the truth of the faith, He shows things to be seen that are visible on all *sides. [For] all the heavens and the *earth and all the *worlds are full of His light.[30] And for all hearers He distinguishes all that is to be heard. And all that is hidden in the heart and in thoughts reach His hearing, and He observes every breath of the body. And of His own will He manifested Himself through the flesh, through stature, through form [*kerparankʿ*] and through image [*patker*]. His mercies were operative. And those who love Him form Him in their hearts through their love, and they prostrate themselves before Him in spirit and truth[31]—purifying their hearts and bodies they make a *temple [*tačar*] for the Holy Spirit.[32] And they become partakers, equals, and sharers of our blessings, which the *Lord bestowed and said: 'Blessed are they who have believed in the truth,'[33] or, 'He who seeth me hath seen my Father,' or [again] 'Blessed
95 are they that have not seen me, and [yet] have believed in me, for they shall see the Father.'[34] And minds that do not share in the faith of divine vision are unformed and are empty as vanities.[35]

"But those who are enlightened see with the invisible eyes of the heart, as the prophet says: 'My heart said unto Thee, and my face has sought Thy face,' and again he says: 'I set the *Lord at all times before me, for He is at my right hand, that I should not be moved,' and yet again; 'I shall be gladdened with the joy of Thy countenance.'[36] Those who according to His will, see Him now through the mysteries of hidden illumination shall see Him at the end face to face, as the blessed apostle Paul has said: 'For now we see in a glass, through images,'[37] but when He comes in the future, He shall bring us the immortality and incorruptibility of His *glory: when the Son of the Father shall come and manifest Himself with the Holy Spirit, without likenesses or parables,[38] when all shall be summoned to come, who see God through immortality, and especially those many made worthy through hope; willingly He will reveal His *glorious coming so that the revelation of Christ begotten of God the Father, who comes to reward all the righteous for their witness to the faith, might come to those who bear with patience and await in hope: 'to those who had not yet received the promise: God provided better things for us, that they without us should not be made perfect.'[39] For anyone who examines the Holy Scriptures shall find the same abundance of Divine and spiritual commandments in all the books of the Bible: [that] resplendent royal crowns are kept for eternity for the righteous and the believers, but [that] for the unbelievers, the turbulent and the disobedient the punishment of their insolence [shall be] to [to serve] as fuel for the inextinguishable fire of the Eternal Judgment in the name of the *Lord, to [undergo] the inexhaustible, unbounded, innumerable, and immeasurable time of the torments of Gehenna, of the dark Judgment that is to come.

96   "But as for your son, if you turn to the true faith of orthodoxy, we shall implore the *Lord and place our hand upon him and say: 'Christ, Offspring of God, heals him in accordance with your faith,'[40] and he will rise up before you in good spirit and a healthy body and make you worthy of eternal blessings together with the renewal of the Kingdom.[41] But if you do not believe, indeed, what remission or healing can there be? Indeed, how shall we dare arise or make so bold as to entreat or offer prayers for those who in no way acknowledge the *Lord? For the wrath of the *Lord strikes down those who do not rightly confess the *Lord. Nor are you able to implore Him, you who neither believe in the knowledge of His Commandments nor bear in mind His laws. For 'The laws of the *Lord are pure, they convert souls. The testimony of the *Lord is faithful, it instructs youths. The justice of the *Lord rejoices the hearts. The Commandments of the *Lord are light and enlighten the eyes. The fear of the *Lord is holy and endures forever. The judgments of the *Lord are true, and thereby just. He is to be desired more than gold and many *precious stones, and he is sweeter also than the honeycomb.'[42] But He keeps those who give themselves over to perdition as fuel for the fire: 'There are no words or speeches whose voices are not heard, but their voice is gone out into all the *earth, and their words to the end of the universe.'[43] For the *Lord keeps a reward for those who do not hear and for those who hear."

    St. Nersēs spoke all these words and others which were like them and the same before the *emperor, and he added this: "In His mercy and benevolence He will wait fifteen days forward from this day to forgive you; this is the term of days that He shall await you [to see] whether you will not come to the true faith. And let this be your sign: that if by that day you have not been confirmed in the faith, the child shall die after the coming
97 of the term, so that you shall know that all I have said before you is true."[44]

    While the king was listening to all that was said in front of him until then he remained silent, one leg crossed over the other, his elbow on his knee and his hand under his chin. He sat in this fashion until [Nersēs] had completely finished his speech, and the royal *notarial-*tachigraphers who were placed in front of the king wrote all of this down. Then the king waxed exceedingly wroth and he ordered the holy *chief-bishop of Armenia Nersēs bound fast with iron chains and thrown into prison that watch might be kept over the child until it was seen whether the child lived or not, and that [the emperor] might afterward see what it was proper to do. Then, after the passage of the fifteen days the young son of the *emperor, his only successor, died. When [the emperor] had wept and lamented as much as he would lament, he then ordered St. Nersēs brought before him. He summoned him close to himself and asked: "Was it through you Christians that the child died?" But [Nersēs] †answered him and said: "For fifteen days after my words Christ delayed [hoping] that you might perhaps convert, but when you did not convert, you died. But even now, if you should believe, Jesus Christ the Son of God can raise him [the child from the dead] and your entire household together with your son."

Then the king was enraged at these words and intended to put him cruelly to death, but the *nobles of his court and his counselors came to the king and said to the *emperor [sic][45]: "These men have been sent from a foreign and distant *land for [the affairs of] a powerful king, they are the envoys of a mighty *lord, let no harm come to them from us, for otherwise a great war will break out between us and the great king of Armenia and there will be much hostility between us; for it was not on account of his words that the child lived or died." But although they spoke a great deal in this manner, they were not able to calm the anger and wrath of the king.

Then, when the events had reached an extreme [point] and the multitude persisted in insisting that he should not kill the man, then his army
98 barely succeeded in persuading the king that he should at least not kill [Nersēs]. They were not, however, able [to persuade him] to let [Nersēs] go, but achieved only this much: that he merely exiled him. For after long disputations, the wise men decided that if the man were only exiled he would at least live and return by and by, and thus there would be no dissension or war between the two kingdoms. "For:" they said: "It has never happened anywhere, neither among enemies nor in the midst of war nor [even] been discussed[46] that even some lowly envoy should be seized and bound, let alone put to death; this has never happened from ancient times; moreover, this man is great and *noble and the head of the whole *realm. For it is said that the king of that *realm and this man are reckoned as one, and it is said that the *realm from which they have come loves this man and he is renowned there. And as we have been told by those who came with him, he is considered a *kinsman and relative of the king,[47] and their *realm truly loves that man."

But the king answered them: "O wise men, you would have spoken well had this been the case, for if his *lord had insulted and injured us through him it would not be right to put the blame on the messenger, nor punish, nor accuse him. But he has injured me of his own volition, and of his own will pledged the death of my son; he said: 'Indeed, it is I who killed him.' But if his king has sent him with love and he has come to destroy us, he is guilty for this before his own king. For since he assumed this himself of his own will, it is right that he [answer for it] to him, for I myself know that this has not come from the other [king] and so, he is worthy of death.[48]

After this, the king did not listen to them any more but ordered the blessed Nersēs exiled, [that he be] taken and left on an island in the great sea, [in] so deserted a place that there was not a man there, nor water to drink, nor food, but only empty desert, so that he might perish from hunger.[49] And he gathered all the orthodox bishops, presbyters, and deacons who followed the true faith from all the *cities under his *dominion, and they assembled from the entire *dominion into a great *council.[50] And he spoke to them so that they might all convert to the perverted faith of the Arian heresy and then—each of them returning thence to his own post—subvert his people to the Arian faith. But when none of them agreed to accept this, he exiled them into alien *realms so that not one of them should return to his own post. And in their place he installed unrighteous pastors. He sent Arian pseudo-bishops to all the *cities and great changes, turmoil, and schisms arose in all the churches of the world [*tiezerac*ᶜ].

And greater tribulations and oppression and harm disturbed all of the universe than under earlier kings, even more wicked than the wars and conflicts that arose formerly among the heathens, in the time of the idol-worshiping, *temple-loving[51] kings. All the true *spiritual-teachers of orthodox confession were driven from their people and satanic workers installed in their place. And heavy oppression weighted down all those who believed in Christ, and all the people sorrowed and mourned. For all the churches were seized by the ministers of Satan, the shepherds separated from their flocks, and the sheep scattered since they had no *spiritual-leader,[52] and no place of prayer was left to the believers. And lest they accept the emissaries of Satan, they went to pray outside of *cities and of inhabited localities, in remote places in the open air. And at the completion of their prayers they entreated God with *vows that He alter and take away this evil time, that He return their true overseers, each to his own people, and [return] the churches built with their own toil from which they had been driven, so that they might perhaps return from these places.

As for the *princes who had come with St. Nersēs from the *land of Armenia, [the emperor] sent them forth with great treasures in order to

corrupt with bribes those who were there. And through them he sent
great hoards of gold, silver, and *precious stones to the king in order to
100 mollify the mind of the king. For there was neither count nor measure to
the innumerable treasures that he sent to the king of Armenia.[53] And he
sent him a letter of accusation against St. Nersēs, [saying] that he had
killed his son. And he also sent [back] to the king of Armenia the Aršakuni
hostages who were in the *imperial-*palace, for they were the nephews of
King Aršak in the male line—the name of one being Gnel and of the
other Tiritʿ. He entrusted them to the Armenian *satraps and sent them
from there in this fashion.[54]

*Chapter vi. Concerning the way in which St. Nersēs was exiled and
thrown on a desert island; and how he nourished himself; and how God
wrought miracles for nine years.[1]*

Now when King Vałēs[2] grew angry—inflicting persecutions on the
holy churches throughout all the *regions of his *dominion, separating
and removing all bishops from their flocks and sending them into alien
*lands[2]—his wrath was especially aroused against St. Nersēs because he
had been the cause of the death of his only beloved son and he wished to
repay him with a most painful and bitter death. The *magnates and all
the royal counselors would not agree to accept this, but were barely able
to save him from death. [The emperor] ordered [Nersēs] thrown on an
island in the dreadful sea of the great ocean, a desert and waterless place,
where there was no green plant, nor any root, nor anything else necessary
for mankind, but only rock and stony sand; and there was no path to it
nor any calling of ships.[3]

They transported him to the designated spot, and with him seventy
other men, half of whom were bishops of other *cities and half clerics of
other churches. But he was glad and rejoiced that it had fallen to him to
bear suffering in the name of our *Lord Jesus Christ the Son of God. Two
101 of his own [clerics] were exiled with him: one was a deacon named Ṙastom,
and the other was called Tiranam; and they collected from everywhere
the other seventy who were with them into the ship and transported them
to the island. And so, the ship carrying them set sail and with a favorable
wind reached the designated spot in fifteen days. The ship then unloaded
them on the island and itself returned.

And there was neither drinking water nor the barest root on that
island, as it consisted merely of sand without vegetation, for that was the
reason that they had been brought there in accordance with the king's
strict injunction that they might be starved to death. And after the space
of about one month had passed, the weakest among them began to lan-
guish and thirst, to be weakened, debilitated, and consumed with hunger

and thirst. Then, Nersēs †began to console and encourage all of them, and said:[4] "Be strong and steadfast, and do not fear! For it was our *Lord Jesus Christ who ordered the Sabek tree to bear a ram as fruit and received Isaac as a living sacrifice; who blessed Jacob in his wandering; who saved Joseph from *bondage and made him a *ruler; who ordered the thorn bush to be covered with leaves of fire and bloom; who ordered the air to send down from above sweet food as a dew; who gave quails from among the birds to the rebellious and contumacious people. And Christ Himself, having become a stone, wandered with them in the waterless desert and brought forth sweet water for the thirsty. And He foretold the design of things to come thereafter—piercing the rock through the rod in the hand of Moses to make water flow from it and saving them for the first time in this fashion—whereas He Himself fed the people in the desert with a few [loaves] of bread.[5] Like the tree that bore a ram, He Himself was crucified, bound, and hung on the cross, and like His prototype He was pierced through the side and from it flowed for us the water of salvation for our cleansing, purification, and repentance.[6] For the sake of our lives, He became bread for us and gave us His blood to drink,[7] so that flesh might mingle [*χaṙnescʿē*] with flesh and blood with blood, to unite the Divinity with our souls and us with the Holy Spirit and to make us in the end consubstantial [*bnakicʿ*] with the Godhead.[8] How then, do you think that He, who bestowed on us such benefactions when we did not [even] render words of thanks in return for His grace, will allow to starve those who in some small degree have been found worthy to be persecuted in His name? Not so! Let us ask with faith[9] and He shall give us food. Do we ask for a sign? No! A sign is needed for those of little faith and to convert evil to truth. But for us, the *Lord knows our needs and what avails us, and He will prepare accordingly what we require. We are not such, God forbid! of whom, it is said that He says; 'An evil generation [*azg*] seeks for a sign.'[10] For what is necessary for us is not possible without the participation of mankind, yet the *Lord can keep us alive without food and He can give us food; He can justify us, He can make us worthy and prepare us to die in his name; He can grant us the acceptance of a familiar natural death from which there is no escape for mankind; He places His name over the invisible flesh, He saves [us][11] and makes us partakers and sharers of His Kingdom. He is also able to bestow a peaceful death and make us worthy of the ranks of the Kingdom."

When he had †spoken this and similar [words], he then said: "Kneel down all together that we may be worthy of Christ's love of mankind." And when they had knelt three times and prayed, a violent wind rose from the sea and began to throw out on the island an enormous mass of fish until a great mound was piled up on the dry land of the island, and likewise and enormous mass of wood. And when they had collected and piled up the wood, they realized that they needed fire to light the logs. Then suddenly the wood lit of its own accord and burned with fire. And having completed their prayers, they rose thankfully, roasted the fish, and *took-their-ease to eat. And when they had eaten and were sated, they needed water to drink. Then St. Nersēs rose up and dug a hole in the sand

103   of the island, and from it gushed a spring of sweet water from which those staying constantly on the island drank.[12]

In this fashion they were fed on the island from the sea, and St. Nersēs constantly †consoled them, and said: "Remember and keep in your mind the Word of the *Lord, who said: 'Seek ye [first] the Kingdom of God and his righteousness, and all these things will be given and added [unto you].'[13] Behold, my *brothers, see how the *Lord appears to us as a father to his sons: to admonish us and make us useful, to make us inherit a *valorous name[14] and to make us worthy of great rewards. In return for this He requires of us a little goodness, only this much—that we love Him. Then He grants His †innumerable, immeasurable, inestimable and unequaled blessings, the bounty of his miracles and reveals Himself the giver of blessings and the returner of rewards because of His love of mankind. For He did not spare His own self laid down for our sake but became our food and drink."

Thus then, together with the *brothers, he constantly thanked and blessed our *Lord Jesus Christ. Both night and day they ceaselessly served the *Lord. The *brothers awaited the setting of the sun and then rejoiced in the nourishment sent by the *Lord that was thrown forth by the waves for the preparation of food. But St. Nersēs awaited the seventh day, the day of the *Lord, and then only he ate. And thus, St. Nersēs always encouraged them during the nine months [sic][15] that they were on that island.

Chapter vii. Concerning God's miracles manifested over Nersēs and Barsilios and the jealousy of bishop Ewsebi toward Barsilios.[1]

When the bishop of Caesarea Ewsebios saw the amazing first descent of the dove that came down from heaven and rested in the first place on the archpriest of Caesarea St. Barsilios,[2] he became ill-disposed in his

104   mind toward him and saw him as his rival[3] and an enemy.[4] For his fame filled the entire *land, and it was told and related that when the holy *kat^cołikos Nersēs was ordained, [the Holy Spirit] came down in the form of a dove and rested first on the archpriest St. Barsilios and then, rising up, came to rest on the *high-priest Nersēs. And this fame about them spread forth particularly in the *realm of Gamirk^c. Men greatly prized all the miracles, and everyone *honored St. Barsilios all the more for the saintliness of his ways, the righteousness of his rules, and depth of his humility; also for the extreme, divinely inspired fervor of his prayers, for

the modesty of his conduct and regulations, for his love of the poor and afflicted, and for his constant and perpetual fulfillment of the Commandments; likewise for his great knowledge—because he was a fount of inexhaustible wisdom, a faithful teacher of *spiritual-learning; because he constantly closed and sealed the idly opened mouths of all heretics with his philosophical art, and confirmed to all the true faith in the all-holy Trinity. For all these reasons he was looked upon as an apostle of Christ, as an angel from heaven, and everyone bore witness that he was indeed worthy of the Holy Spirit. But he kept himself most humble and deemed himself unworthy, although everyone desired to go to him because of his knowledge, especially the masters of the heathen philosophers hastened to him for the sake of their art. And he converted many to the true faith from their various errors and made inumerable men adorers of Christ. And so the entire *land began to look at him as though he had descended from the heavens above, and this to such a degree that anyone wishing to tell of it would not be able [to do so].[5]

105   But when he saw the malevolent countenance of his bishop toward himself, St. Barsilios yielded to him, left the *city, and going away from it dwelt in some locality where it was fitting for him to be.[6]

*Chapter viii. Concerning the way that the *emperor Vałēs persecuted all true believers; and how the *emperor wished to hold a disputation between the true believers and the sinister heresy of the Arians; and how St. Barsilios was convoked to the fray through a miraculous vision, and through God's might was victorious as a champion in the presence of Bishop Ewsebi; and how Ewsebios died in prison; and how Barseł was set free.*[1]

At that time, the iniquitous *Emperor Vałēs[2] in [his] great wrath ruled against those who labored for the truth, that is to say those who believed altogether correctly in Christ, [namely] that He was truly the Son of God begotten of the nature [*bnutenēn*] of God the Father. Because of this he wished to raise up persecutions, torments, and tortures against all of them, and so with harsh *authority he set down and gave out and edict in all places.

Then the raving *teachers of the Arian sect deliberated together and said: "O king, allow us to encounter them in disputation, and let it be clearly evident which *side comes out victorious, so that this victory may not seem won under duress or through injustice." King Vałēs rejoiced upon hearing this. He chose for himself expert and ready orators whom he considered to be learned scholars, and these were distinguished falsebishops of the Arian sect. He also sent to the bishop of Caesarea Ewsebios and demanded that he [set] a time for the examination of their doctrine so

106 that he should present it to him for review and the truth should be revealed. Then, when the time had been set, Bishop Ewsebios summoned all his clergy and was greatly troubled as to the way that he might[3] prepare his answer, for he was not particularly powerful with words. Then, in consultation, they decided to send to the blessed Barsilios in order to persuade him to come. "Because," they said: "he is skilled with words. He is great," they said; "he has the grace to foil the deceit of satanic malice for he is concerned about [Christ's] holy church, which He bought with His blood."

Bishop Ewsebios wrote and entreating letter to the archpriest Barseł with whatever solicitations [were] due to the *honor of his ministry, that he should not keep anything in his mind concerning their former dissensions, but that he should hasten to come without delay because the discussions and examinations concerned the faith in God. All the clerics likewise sent a letter of entreaty [saying] that he should in no way delay but come in all haste. And they sent trusty and *distinguished men to hasten his coming.

The men set out to go and urge him to come, but while they were still on the way, St. Barsilios, while he was performing the ministry of the *Lord in the place where he was, fell into a deep sleep and saw in a vision[4] a large and splendid vineyard richly filled with fruit, and three hogs had penetrated and entered inside the vineyard and were ruining and rooting it up. They dug extensively around the base of the vine, tore up the roots, tore out branch and off-shoot, and wrought an the *greatest damage inside. The winegrowers came and struggled [with them], but they were not able to drive the destructive hogs from the vineyard. Then †they cried out to Barsilios, and said: "If you do not come, Barsilios, no one will be able to drive the swine from the vineyard, nor will the great destruction cease. Hurry, come! for they have already done the *greatest damage." Then Barsilios came, drove the destructive swine out of the vineyard and restored the wreckage.

107 Then the wondrous Barseł awoke and marveled at the vision. He thought and turned over in his mind what might be the [meaning] of such a vision. And at that point the messengers arrived and presented to him the letter sent from the *city of Caesarea by Bishop Ewsebi. As soon as he read it, he rejoiced and was glad, because he understood that it was through God's design that he was summoned as a *defender[5] of the truth to give a rebuttal [to the heretics]. Therefore, he hastened to rise up and accompany those who had brought the letter of invitation, and he went to Bishop Ewsebios.[6] And after they had consulted together as to what would be proper, Barsilios told Bishop Ewsebios that he should ask the *emperor for the *authority to bring one of his presbyters with him.

And so, Ewsebios went to the *emperor †requested and said: "You have brought in two champions against me, allow me to have one of my own priests." The *emperor inquired of the Arian bishops and they agreed that Ewsebi should bring some companions with him when he came to the court.

When the time of the meeting arrived, the *emperor assembled Bishop Ewsebios together with the blessed archpriest Barsilios and the two opposing champions who were from the *party [kołmn] of Satan (that is to say the Arian pseudo-bishops), and they fell into discussion and disputation concerning our *Lord Jesus Christ the Son of God, namely whether or not He was begotten and Son of the [same] nature [bnutenē] as God the Father. Then the blessed Barsilios, who was standing behind Bishop Ewsebi, was filled with the Holy Spirit, and he brought forth and cited written testimonies from the Book of Genesis, from the beginning of the laws and the prophets and the apostles, and the whole of the Holy Scripture, and he reduced to silence, entrapped and shamed the two champions of Satan together with the *emperor.

Then King Vałēs looked at the bishop, and seeing that he was perspiring, †began to speak and said: "What is the matter, why is sweat pouring so greatly off you, since you have won the disputation concerning 108 the truth by means of a hired clerk?" And Basilios †answered the king, and said: "I have been driving two hogs and an ass such a long way, and you ask: 'Why am I sweating so much?'" Then the king repented that he had allowed Barsilios to come in as an assistant to Ewsebi, but the shamed Arians got up and said to the king: "What need is there for these laborious disputations? Give an order as the *master that those who do not obey your will should be subjected to the anguish of oppression." And so, the assembly was dissolved and came to an end.

Then [the emperor] ordered Ewscbios thrown into prison together with many others, had the true, orthodox Christians oppressed, and subjected the churches to *taxes with heavy fines. Then Bishop Eusebios, condemned to heavy bonds, died in prison.[7] But as for St. Barseł, the people of Caesarea said: "If you do not release him from prison, we will burn the entire *city." When [they] all shouted this out together, the king relented and ordered that the blessed Barsilios be released.[8]

*Chapter ix. Concerning the way in which St. Barsilios was made bishop and the manifestation of God's miracles; and how [the king] gave the order to collect all the treasures of the people believing in Christ and they gladly brought them out and gave them for the sake of the great vivifying God; and how they prayed for their bishops with *vows and entreaties.*[1]

Then all the bishops from the *jurisdiction of Caesarea *gathered

together and chose St. Barsilios as *archbishop of Caesarea.² And when all the bishops were *assembled all together to ordain St. Barseł, a dove came down from heaven and came to rest over him, as it had done the first time for the *chief-bishop Nersēs.³ Great was the amazement of everyone, and they began to give thanks to the man-loving Christ who had mani-
109 fested in Himself the signs of divinity, and had not withheld them from His *servants and saints. And so Barseł ascended the *throne of the *kat‛olikate of Caesarea.

But King Vałēs⁴ [continued] to oppress the Christian people, for, he said: "Whoever bears the name of Christian within my *dominion shall possess neither silver nor gold, but shall surrender it to the royal treasury." And so, they began to collect [it] under oath from the army and every *commander and all the *cities, so that not a particle⁵ of gold or silver should be found among those who bore that name, and should any be found belonging to anyone [of them], he should be put to death. And everyone gladly brought forth and gave up [his wealth] in the name of Christ, willingly and joyfully bearing this punishment. And when the royal *officials began to force the collection of silver and gold from the people of the *city of Caesarea, the blessed Barsilios began to encourage them so that they should bring it with joyful heart. He began to speak to them in this fashion: "Bring it into my hands, and I shall guarantee that as our *Lord Jesus Christ himself the Only-begotten Son of God, has been defied [by the king] in combat, so He shall kill him. But as for you, accept gladly the spoliation of your wealth for the sake of your *Lord, for He keeps for you in heaven a treasure that shall not pass away.⁶ But as for this treasure, I shall return it to you, from hand to hand, in a short time." Then all the people of the *city of Caesarea brought and collected in one place whatever gold or silver each one possessed. They filled the church, found entrusted royal *officials [išχank‛] and sealed the doors of the church.

After this, King Vałēs ordered once again that the *chief-bishop Barseł be bound and thrown into prison and confinement and [that] the same [be done] to all the bishops from every *city. But all the people prayed [meanwhile] with *vows and implorations that his wrath should be appeased and that every true pastor should return to his post and his people.⁷

110   *Chapter x. Concerning the way in which the *emperor Vałēs called a sophist to oppose the truth; and how the *sophist beheld a miracle, seeing a multitude of martyrs inside the martyrium; and how the *emperor Vałēs was killed through manifestly divine signs; and how peace returned to the churches of God.¹*

Then King Vałēs² gave an order for an expert to be sought and found who would be able to confront the Christian faith in writing.³ And he was told that there was a skilled *sophist in a certain *city. And so, the *emperor sent his *magistrianoi* to him so that they might hasten to go and bring the man to him without delay, and they hurriedly fetched him.

When they had traveled for two stages, they happened to chance on another *city at the *martyrium of the holy *lady Tᶜekł [which lay] outside the *city.⁴ When they arrived there the *sophist got down and chose the inside of the *martyrium for his *lodging, [vankᶜ] while the *magistrianoi* *lodged in the *city. When the *sophist had eaten, he made his bed, locked the doors of the *martyrium, sat down on the bed, and intended to lie down [to sleep].⁵ [But], while he was still awake, he saw with open eyes that the doors of the *martyrium had suddenly opened and there was *assembled a great multitude of martyrs who appeared in great *glory. And the holy *lady Tᶜekł went to meet them⁶ adorned in such brilliance that radiance like light seemed to emanate from her. They greeted each other, and the *lady Tᶜekł said to them: "Welcome, dear friends and laborers of Christ." After mutual greetings, each brought himself a *seat and they sat down according to rank. Then the saints †began to converse and said: "The saints of the *Lord who have not yet departed from this *earth are still oppressed here: some are in bonds, some in prison, some in exile, and some suffer other violence through injust *exactions and excruciating torments. Therefore, we have hastened to *assemble together so that we should not be carelessly neglectful of seeking redress for those who believe in the *Lord, especially because many of the *Lord's workers are impeded, many fields left untended, and many vineyards deserted. We must restrain Vałēs, who impedes the workers, so that every laborer may be vigilant in his task. And the *valiant laborer Basilios is likewise impeded in his task. Therefore, come, let us arise and send two from amongst us who shall go and deprive the evil Vałēs of life." Then they sent out one from among them whose name was Sargis and another named Tᶜēodoros,⁷ and they †set a time limit for them, and said, "Come [back] at this same time, and so shall we." Then they rose up and separated.

The *sophist who was in the *martyrium heard all of this and saw this vision with open eyes, and he was amazed and remained sleepless until break of day. At early dawn, the *magistrianoi* came and said to the *sophist: "Come, let us be on our way!" But he feigned sickness and could not budge from the spot. And when they began to compel him, he grew weak, sighed, and panted, and was unable to answer them until the evening. When the evening came, the *magistrianoi* left him in the *martyrium and returned to their own *lodgings in the *city. Then the *sophist locked the doors of the *martyrium and lay down in his place. And suddenly he saw again the doors of the *martyrium open, and the same martyrs come and assemble so that the *martyrium was filled with them.

They met one another with great joy and greeted one another; then they set down individual *chairs, arranged them in order, and sat down. Then both St. Sargis and St. Tʿēodoros came back from the task for which they had been sent and entered the *assembly of the saints. And the multitude of *assembled martyrs asked of them: "How did you carry out the task for which you went?" And † answering they said: "As soon as we left you we killed the enemy of the truth Valēs; we have returned at the same hour, and here we are come to you." Then the whole of the *assembled multitude rose up and gave thanks to our *Lord Jesus Christ, and they separated each to his own place. And the *sophist remained terrified until break of day.

Then at dawn, the *magistrianoi came and said to the *sophist, "Come, let us go to the *emperor!" And †he answered and said: "The *emperor is dead, to whom shall we go?" And a great quarrel broke out among them over these words, and they made a pledge up to three days' duration over these words. "If," he said, "goods are not pillaged, *cities not devastated, and the *emperor still the same [by that time], let me be beheaded for daring to say this." Then the *magistrianoi granted him the three days, and after the term of three days, the news was confirmed that the *emperor had died.

After this, all those who had been subject to punishments or were in exile were released,[8] and whatever had been looted from each one was returned to him. Similarly in the case of Caesarea, the order was given to return each one his own, and St. Barsel summoned them so that each one might take [back his own], but they would not come near though Barsel said to them: "Here are [the things] that I guaranteed to you would be released and [about which] I said that I would return what was yours with my own hands into yours." But they would not listen at all and answered: "Let them be [put] in the treasury of the *Lord who judged our cause and avenged the holy *congregation of his church." And †not a single inhabitant of the *city of Caesarea came near his silver—not a one,[9] but they left it in the treasury of the church. Then the *archbishop took it and had it made into baptismal fonts. And the silver baptismal fonts still stand in the baptistry[10] until the present day.

113   *Chapter xi. Concerning the return to the *land of Armenia of the *princes who had gone to the *emperor Valēs and returned again to their own *lord Aršak; and how King Aršak was aroused against the *emperor, and how much damage he caused by making raids into the *regions of the *dominion of the Greek kingdom.[1]*

These are the *princes who went from the Armenian *realm, and from the great king Aršak to Valēs, *emperor of the Greeks:[2] the great *chief-bishop of Armenia Nersēs in person, the great *nahapet* of the Mamikonean *house whose name was Vardan, the *brother of the great *stratelat* of Armenia named Vasak,[3] the ones who were the *tutors and *foster-fathers of King Aršak; and together with them [went] Mehen, *nahapet* of the Ṙštuni; and Mehaṙ, *nahapet* of the Anjewacᶜi, and Garjoyl, *malχaz* *nahapet* of the Xoṙχoṙuni; and Mušk, *nahapet* of the Sahaṙuni; and Demet *nahapet* of the Gntᶜuni, and Kiškēn *nahapet* of the Bagēan, and Surik *nahapet* of Hrsijor, and Vrkēn *nahapet* of the Habužean.[4] These [all] went to the *emperor Vaḷēs as ambassadors of loving union, but King Vaḷēs held and exiled the great *high-priest Nersēs and released in exchange the nephews of King Aršak, Gnel and Tiritᶜ. In order to mollify the mind of King Aršak he [also] sent an immeasurable mass of treasure through Vardan and those who were with him. Returning from the *emperor, the envoys came to Aršak king of Greater Armenia and presented to him the *letter-patent of the *emperor. Together with this they also presented a letter of complaint and displeasure, for the *emperor had written about St. Nersēs to Aršak king of Armenia that he had killed his only son and that he had been held there for that reason, and that: "so that you should not accuse us, receive the two youths, Gnel and Tiritᶜ, the nephews of Aršak, who have been released." And [the envoys] also brought an immeasurable load of treasure to the king.

But when King Aršak heard and saw all of this, he expressed his displeasure at [both] the giver and the bearers of the treasure. He raged in great fury against the *emperor:[5] how dare he hold [prisoner] so great and so *honored a man, the head, the *spiritual-teacher and *leader of the entire *realm and kingdom? "A mass of stones," he said, "[shall fall] on the *emperor and upon you bringing this. We too have many stones to smash his teeth for the sending and yours for the bringing. How shall I suffer such an insult? I shall rcpay his favoı! He then ordered his *commander-in-chief Vasak to gather an army, to replenish his *contingents, and to strike and devastate the *regions of Gamirkᶜ. The *sparapet* and the *commander-in-chief Vasak then swiftly carried out the order he had received. He collected a large force of some two hundred and sixty thousand [men], attacked and devastated the *region of Gamirkᶜ as far as the *city of Ankyra.[6] For six years[7] one after the other he ravaged the *realm of the Greek territory. Striking with ferocious violence and great hostility, [the Armenians] seized much loot and all kinds of treasure from these *regions.

*Chapter xii. Concerning Xad, bishop of Bagrewand, who was ordained by Nersēs and left as *vicar in his place, and the kind of man that he was, and the marvels and might that were in him; and how he held to the truth and paid no heed to the great King Aršak, but opposed him*

because of his iniquitous deeds; and how he cared for the poor like the
*chief-bishop Nersēs.[1]

This man Xad was originally from the *district of Karin, from the
*village of Marag, and he was a pupil of the *chief-bishop Nersēs, *nurtured
in his presence, Since he was promising in mind, progressing in the faith,
found faithful in all his actions, and especially in the love he bore toward the
Church of God in his ministry. He was also entrusted by St. Nersēs with the
supervision of the poor, and in this, too, he showed particular solicitude.[2]

115

Therefore, when the *chief-bishop Nersēs was about to go on his
journey to the *land of the Greeks, he ordained Xad bishop of Bagrewand
and Aršarunikʿ, left him as *vicar in his place, and set out. Now the entire
*realm of the *Armenian-tongue, in every *district, every *region, every
*locality; all the *magnates, the *keepers-of-realms and *lords-of-districts,
the **nahapet*s, the *members-of-great-*clans, and the whole *community
of the clergy together with the *assembly of *solitaries people fell into the
deepest mourning over their chief pastor who had gone far away from
them.[3] But the holy bishop Xad gave the order to the entire *realm that it
should keep to fasting and prayers, imploring the return of St. Nersēs.
And [so], all of the time that he was detained there, the people continually prayed with fasting. And Xad gave them *spiritual-leadership in all
things[4]—no less than their own chief-pastor Nersēs—until his return,
until the *Lord fulfilled the prayers of the *realm and sent St. Nersēs
back to his post.

Now at about that time Aršak king of Armenia strayed severely from
God's path.[5] As much as he had followed the path of Divine wisdom in his
youth, so much did he fall into impudence and shamelessness in his
maturity.[6] The holy pastor Xad often reprimanded and rebuked him, but
he paid no heed. It was around that time that the king built himself a
*dastakert in the designated valley of the *district of Kog. And he ordered

116

a royal edict proclaimed in every *district of his *dominion and announced
on every *public square in his *realm, and he filled all the *regions and
*districts with the royal proclamation [stating] that: "Should anyone be
indebted to anyone, or should anyone anywhere have wronged anyone
else, or should anyone have been summoned to judgment, let every one of
them come and settle in this *dastakert. Should anyone have shed the
blood of anyone, or have harmed anyone, or have carried off anyone's
wife, or be in debt, or have taken anyone's possessions, or be in fear of
anyone, let him come to this place and he shall not be subject to judgment
and law. But should anyone be indebted to someone and the creditor
come there, let him be taken without judgment or justice and thrown out."

As soon as the royal edict was proclaimed, every thief and robber,
[every] shedder of blood, murderer, liar, and harmful seducer, [every]

cutpurse, despoiler, false witness, slanderer, destroyer, pillager, and miser immediately collected there.[7] Many did every kind of damage and took cover there: many wives left their husbands and hid there, many men left their wives and hid there taking another man's wife, many *servants fled after taking their *master's goods and hid there, many holders of deposits took the deposits that they had in safekeeping and hid there; and thus they spoiled and ruined the entire *land. For although complaints multiplied indeed, there was no judgment and no one's rights were taken up by the royal court. Consequently, all men †moaned, groaned, and said in unanimous agreement, everyone using these words in the same fashion and saying in common: "Justice is dead and we therefore cannot find it, for if it existed and were lost, we would have searched and found it wherever it was." However, the place turned into a *town, then into a *city; it grew and increased, and filled the entire valley. Then King Aršak ordered the *dastakert called Aršakawan after his own name, and a royal *palace [aparankᶜ] was also built there.[8] And after that there was absolutely no fear of the *Lord and every man was deprived of his possessions because of this, and the many groans of lamentation and complaint grew more frequent and multiplied.[9]

For this reason, the holy bishop Xad often opposed and rebuked [the king], especially when pressure was brought to bear on him that [he] "come and set up an altar in the church of the *town of Aršakawan!" But [Xad] often reproved and opposed King Aršak as well as all the *magnates and *princes, saying: "I am but a *vicar, and I have *no authority to do

117   anything except what my father allowed me." Then King Aršak wished to subvert the holy bishop Xad with *honors and the desire for wealth. He bestowed much gold and silver on him, as well as many steeds from among the royal horses, together with royal ornaments of silk woven with gold, so as to deceive and satisfy his mind and [thus] draw him over to himself.[10] But [Xad] distributed the gifts he had received from the king to the poor in his [very] presence, and in no way mitigated his reproofs, until [the king] ordered Bishop Xad thrown out of his *camp.[11]

Then [Xad] went about the *realm to organize and admonish, teach, and take care of the poor as it had been entrusted to him by St. Nersēs at his departure. Many prodigies and marvels were wrought by his hands, and [he had] the power to heal the sick, and indeed he performed many *very great miracles. For when he ministered to the poor, drained and emptied every jar, vessel, and wine cellar and distributed every jar from the cellars to the poor, he saw them filled when he came the following day, as though at God's command, and so day after day he distributed [their content] to the poor and they were incessantly refilled.[12] Such were the *very great miracles performed by this man, and he was amazing, renowned, and eminent among all the Armenians. He went about, admonished and

taught the churches of Armenia everywhere just like his *spiritual-teacher Nersēs. And on one occasion thieves came, stole and carried off oxen belonging to the church of the holy bishop Xad, but on the next day the eyes of the thieves were blinded so that they groped their way senselessly and themselves brought all the oxen to the door of St. Xad. Then St. Xad himself rose up and saw them and he gave thanks to the *Lord who was so watchful and protective over those who believed in Him. Bishop Xad prayed and healed the eyes of the thieves; he ordered them bathed, set food before them, and made them *very [kᶜaȷ̈] joyful. He then blessed
118   them, gave them, the oxen they had stolen, and sent them on their way. And so they went.¹³ Thus, he showed great patience in all his actions, and he performed many prodigies and marvels. He had two daughters, and he gave one in marriage to a certain Asurk, who ascended Xad's *throne after his father-in-law.¹⁴

Chapter xiii. Concerning that which took place after the return of the holy katᶜolikos *Nersēs from the *land of the Greeks; how he rebuked the king, and the fearful portents that appeared over the *town of Aršakawan; and how the entire multitude of people in that place perished suddenly.*¹

After the *emperor had perished, all the shepherding bishops who had been exiled returned and dwelt in their own *cities. Then the holy *katᶜolikos* Nersēs also returned from the desert island on which they had been held.² The universal prayers were answered and the *realm was again graced [with his presence]. From every *district, bishops with their flocks came to meet him when he came to the *realm of Armenia, as well as all the *naχarars and all the *keepers-of-districts. And they brought all their sick before him and he healed them, wherefore exceeding thanksgiving to the *glory of God multiplied. And because of the great compassion of their chief-shepherd, all men thought that they had returned from captivity like them.

And there was great joy with much spiritual gladness. Everyone throughout the *realm fulfilled the *vows given to the *Lord God for the sake of their spiritual treasure the *patriarch who had been set over them, for [the *Lord] had answered their prayers and again healed altogether the affliction of their orphaned state, and the heart-rending pain of their sorrow, through the loving compassion of the *teaching of their spiritual
119   father. All of them lifted out of their sorrowful mourning, turned to joy. And King Aršak came in person to meet him as far as the *region of Bakᶜaser, and they returned thence greatly heartened. And the ways of the *realm began to be renewed and brightened, as were the laws and regulations of the churches.

When the *patriarch Nersēs returned to Armenia and found that his *vicar St. Xad had held to truth and orthodoxy and that he had followed the path of the *Lord God and had not strayed to the right or left,[3] he gave great thanks to God that found his spiritual son Xad such as he wished him to be, and beheld him with [deep] emotion. But when he heard from Xad all the evil iniquities and transgressions of the king, he mourned and wept, moaning and lamenting with the *greatest sighs,[4] and all the more over the *city of Aršakawan, which had been built though unrighteousness, evil deeds, rapine, and a multitude of sins.

Then, the holy *patriarch Nersēs came to the king, †spoke to him, and said:[5] "Why hast thou forgotten the *Lord and abandoned His Commandments, He who created all things out of nothing, who is the father of orphans and the arbiter of widows,[6] who came down for our sake into poverty,[7] who does not abandon the poor but feeds them through his compassion? But 'God is a righteous *judge and strong and patient'[8] who watches over all the unfortunates but accepts contempt from no one. How and why hast thou disregarded His Commandments? Did not thy father fall into perdition for such iniquities?[9] But thou hast not remembered Him who did not recall the sins of thy father and gave thee his place: that is, the *throne [at‘oṙ] and crown of thy father. But thou hast begun to sin before the *Lord thy God with impiety, lawlessness, and iniquity in the very likeness of the Sodomites,[10] and to speak of it with evident vainglory. And the entire *land weeps and laments from the deprivation of the spoliations through which thou hast wished to aggrandize thyself, and [yet] the great abundance of the kingdom granted thee by the almighty *Lord Christ has not satiated thee.

120   Then listen to me and to that which I tell thee, and accomplish it in order to redeem thyself and save thyself from the wrath of God, and so that the unfortunate *realm of Armenia may not perish on account of thee! For I have seen a vision that perdition and destruction are advancing on this doomed *realm of Armenia.[11] Give the order to tear down this place and disperse the people that thou hast gathered, that they might go, disperse, and scatter each to his own place and that they might duly give back to each what is owed him. [Do this] lest thou fall into the evil pit of wrath and perish.[12] As for the sins thou hast committed, we shall command the entire *realm to fast and pray for thee, and we shall repent together with thee, for who knows, the *Lord may forgive these dreadful sins thou hast committed. If indeed this place is so dear to thee, I myself will rebuild it on my own with righteousness, and hold the place [šēn] before thee."[13]

But the king scoffed at the *kat‘olikos and derided his words. Then [Nersēs] said a second time in anger: "Know, O King! that all of this was foretold through the mouths of all the prophets: 'Woe to him who builds his *house, and not with justice; and his upper chambers not by right,'[14] and they shall raise lamentations and say, 'woe to him that covets as covetousness for himself[15] that which is not his, for though his houses be fair and *very large, they shall be turned to ruin, for no man shall dwell in them'[16] For they shall be pastures for flocks, lairs and dens for wild beasts and hyenas, burrows for hares and foxes, nests for cranes and ravens, and fields for their neighbors. Because of this the work of thy hands shall be destroyed and not rebuilt, and the unrighteous dwelling therein shall perish altogether. It shall be a resting place for oxen and a pasture for wild asses, and foxes shall dart in and out of their roof-trees. And they shall not be rebuilt, nor shall they be inhabited unto eternity!"[17]

The *patriarch Nersēs spoke all of this, then he left the king and went around all the *districts, teaching, directing, organizing, and strengthening the churches in all the *districts of Armenia.[18]But hardly had three days passed after those words had been spoken by the mouth of the blessed Nersēs, than the *Lord gave over the *komopolis of Aršakawan to destruction. What some call evil pustules and other plague began to strike, and they appeared on men and beasts.[19] This scourge lasted no more than three days, for [the place] was depopulated. More than twenty thousand human households were destroyed and †none of them survived, not a one,[20] for they perished altogether and were unexpectedly annihilated because the destruction struck all of them down all at once.[21]

After this, the king went in person to seek the *patriarch Nersēs and, upon finding him, begged him to offer up a prayer for him: that he might not perish, for he was completely terrified. Then the *chief-bishop Nersēs †began to speak to the king and said:[22] "Because now the righteous and the sinners are mingled together in this *world, the sinners are spared for a time for the sake of the righteous and survive, and their lives are lengthened in this *world because of [the righteous]. Like tares sown by the foe in pure sown wheat, they flourish together with it, and the foul tares are spared for the sake of the good wheat, lest the good wheat be pulled up when the tares are uprooted and pulled out. Therefore, the wheat and the tares together enjoy for a time the care of dew and rain and watering, and they are warmed by the heat and comfort of the sun. And this lasts until the time of the harvest, until the fruit of the wheat is harvested and gathered in the granaries of the Kingdom, whereas the tares are burned in the eternal fire. And that is indeed the harvest at the end of time, when the Son of God shall come and order the heavenly laborers who shall have come down with Him from above to gather in all the sleepers arisen from their graves. Then He shall make His choice, He shall receive the just like wheat into His own Kingdom, and He shall order the sinners thrown like tares into the inextinguishable eternal fire. But now, when the time of the harvest has not yet come, thou hast plucked out the premature tares from the wheat and prematurely collected the tares without the wheat. Therefore, premature fire mercilessly burned down all of the tares gathered and found together, and destroyed them altogether. And as for thee, look to thyself, lest thou too perish, and the *realm as well, on account of thee!"23 And the king fell on his knees and begged with great entreaties and prayers to be reconciled with him, and the king bound himself with an *oath that he would never again stray from his words.

Chapter xiv. Concerning the *hayr-*mardpet*: when he came down into the* *district of Tarōn and to the place of prayers of Aštišat; and how he went from there condemned by the words of his own mouth; and how, since he deserved death, he was killed by Šawasp Arcruni.*[1]

And the *hayr-mardpet* was an evil and malignant man, more unjust and unrighteous than the previous *mardpet*s named *hayr* ["father"]. It was he who had destroyed all the *naχarar *clans during the reign of King Tiran, and likewise in the reign of Aršak he did even more harm to all men than before.[2] Now he set out on a tour of his *mardpet*'s jurisdiction and so, the *hayr-*mardpet came down into the *district of Tarōn to look at his own *villages.

At about that time, St. Nersēs was touring his own *principalities, for he held as a *principality fifteen *districts, the original *hereditary-appanage, that had been destined [for his house] as their own particular [holding]. And the major ones among these *districts were the following: Ayrarat, Daranałē, Ekełeac^c, Tarōn, Bznunik^c Cop^ck^c, those in between, and those around them.[3] And so, the *hayr-*mardpet was touring his own *principality and the holy *kat^cołikos Nersēs also came to the first place where a church had been built earlier by Grigor and the *martyria-of-the-holy-martyrs, and he performed there the commemorations of the saints.[4] Now it so happened that the *hayr-*mardpet was passing through these places and wished to go up to the holy places of Aštišat to offer prayers and receive the greeting of the holy *chief-bishop Nersēs. When they had prayed and exchanged greetings, the holy *patriarch Nersēs ordered a meal prepared for those who had arrived. And while they were preparing a sufficiently noble repast for him, [the *mardpet] went out from the episcopal-*palace toward the *martyria-of-the-saints, and he took a walk and wandered around the large and beautiful *open square. When he saw the beauty of these places, the splendid, high setting of the sites, and the views downward, he grew envious, for the place was most fair.

He then went in and *reclined to eat and drink, and when he had drunk and become inebriated, the eunuch began to speak drunkenly arrogant and presumptuous words. He reviled King Trdat, and both the living and the dead of the *race, origin, and *house of the Aršakuni kings of Armenia. "How," said he: "have such places been given to men in women's clothing and not to real men?"[5] He †contemptuously scorned

139

the holy places, and said: "We will tear down these places, for it is proper to build a royal *palace [aparank'] here. And if I, the *hayr-*mardpet, remain alive and come to the king," he said: "I shall transform everything altogether, remove those who are here and build a royal residence [seneak] in this place."[6]

124   When the holy *chief-bishop heard this, he said: "Our *Lord Jesus Christ who first chose this place in order to give it His name, He whose name is *glorified everywhere in every place with the Father and the Holy Spirit, commanded never to cast an eye on the possession of another or envy it. But whoever casts a covetous eye on what has been dedicated to Him and desires it shall not achieve what he threatens [to do], for this very reason, for his plan will be impeded by the great mass of sins he has committed."

Then the *hayr-*mardpet left the holy places and went down to the bank of the Ep'rat River, to a heavily wooded valley, a thicket of reeds and buckthorn at the junction of two rivers. [This was] the place where a *city had been built in antiquity by King Sanatruk, and the name of the place was Mcurn. He had hardly reached the place when the judgment of the *Lord's wrath was visited on the iniquitous *hayr, on his deeds and words, for he was handed over to a man named Šawasp, a descendant of the Arcruni *clan.[7] And while the *mardpet pursued his way sitting in his chariot, Šawasp came up, †began to tell lies to the *mardpet* according to his fancy, and said: "I saw a bear as white as snow." Lured [by this], the *mardpet got down from his chariot and rode off on horseback. They entered into the woods and began to pursue [the hunt]. But when they had penetrated into the thickets, Šawasp, who was a little in the rear, held back, and shot an *arrow from behind, striking the eunuch *hayr in the middle [of the back], in such a way that the arrow ran him through and he fell dead on the *ground. And so, the words of the man of God were immediately fulfilled, for the words of the man of God had not been in vain.[8]

125   *Chapter xv. Concerning the unrighteousness of King Aršak: how he killed his brother's son Gnel because of the evil slander of Tirit', and how he was rebuked by the man of God Nersēs; and how he also [killed] his other nephew Tirit'; and how he took Gnel's wife as his own; and how he brought himself a wife from the Greeks [named] Ołimpi [Olympias]; and how the priest Mrjiwnik killed her with a mortal poison [mixed] in the Eucharist at the instigation of P'aranjem.[1]*

Around that time Andovk, one of of the *naχarars of the nahapet of Siwnik',[2] had a beautiful daughter named P'aranjem who was greatly re-nowned for her beauty and her modesty, and the young nephew of the king, Gnel, took her as his wife. The fame of the maiden's loveliness spread about, and the renown of her beauty grew, increased, and resounded.[3] And another cousin of Gnel named Tirit[c] quivered with desire toward his sister-in-law[4] because of this fame, and he therefore sought some secret way whereby he might see her. Once he had succeeded in seeing the one whom he desired, he sought means of destroying the woman's husband so that by these means he might perhaps be able to carry her off afterward.[5] Tirit[c] then laid out his deceitful plot and bribed for himself many assistants and accomplices through whom he would be able to spread his slander. And he deceitfully presented malicious lies about Gnel to King Aršak [telling him]: "Gnel wishes to reign and to kill you," and "all the *magnates, *naχarars, and *azats love Gnel," and "all the *naχarars of this *realm desire his *lordship over themselves rather than yours."[6] Then they said: "Know this, O king, and look to what you should do in order to be able to survive." They inflamed King Aršak with such words until they had instilled their assertions into the mind of the king.[7]

And so, the king was filled with anger against the youthful Gnel. He persecuted him on numerous occasions and plotted deceitfully for a long time. Then around the time of *Nawasard, King Aršak plotted to summon the young Gnel [to come] to him, and to kill him. He then sent the *nahapet of the *clan of the Mamikonean *house, Vardan—the *brother of the *sparapet—so that, with great oaths and deceit, he might succeed in inviting Gnel without revealing the plot, lest Gnel should flee and survive. He should rather bring him with deceptions and enticements to the place of his death. Now, there was a royal *encampment at Šahapivan, the place of the *home-camp [bun banak] of the Aršakuni[8] below the walled hunting preserve above the *horse-racing-courses.[9] And so, the great *nahapet Vardan set out, sent by King Aršak, and found the young Gnel in a nearby locality, that is to say in the *village named Aŕawiwtk[c]. With great *vows and many deceptions he persuaded the young Gnel to come with his wife and his retinue to the royal-*camp [banakn ark[c]uni], as though the king were summoning him for some honor.[10] With many blandishments he brought him around, [assuring him] that "King Aršak does not want to spend the feast of *Nawasard without you, for he has become well intentioned and affectionate toward you, for he has found no evil in you as had been asserted by slanderers. And he has realized that until now he hated you to no purpose, for you deserve great love from him."

Then Gnel set out with his entire retinue and arrived at the royal-*camp, having hurried the entire night in great haste, because the following day, which was dawning, was a Sunday. And on that day fell the commemoration of the great [prophet] John established by Grigor and [King] Trdat in the *town of Bagawan.[11] The inhabitants of the *realm assembled for that commemoration as well as many bishops from other *districts, and the great *chief-bishop Nersēs sent his *co-bishop Xad in

141

his place, together with his episcopal *archdeacon, whose name was Murik, so that they should go to the assembly and perform for it whatever was necessary. He himself remained at the royal-*camp to perform the same [sacrament] of communion there. And on that night a great night service was held in the *camp in the presence of the *kat‘olikos.

At the break of day Gnel's train reached the royal-*camp, and notice of his arrival was given to the king as Gnel entered the royal-*camp. An order then came from the court that he should be kept outside, taken away, and killed. And so, as he was riding on his charger through the royal-*camp close by the royal-*square, many servants armed with *longswords, *spears, *sabers, *axes, and *javelins, as well as *shield-bearing *foot-soldiers arrived from court, drew near to young Gnel, dragged him from his horse, tied his hands behind [his back], and took him to the place of execution.[12] Now since his wife had come with him in a litter,[13] she was in the same train as her husband. And when she saw her husband seized and bound, she ran in haste to the assembly in the *church-tent where the divine service was performed for the people of the *camp, as they were offering morning prayers and the great *chief-bishop Nersēs was [also] present. As she reached the *chief-archbishop, the woman brought to him the evil news of her husband's undeserved destruction. She screamed aloud: "Hurry, go! They are unjustly killing my husband who has done no harm or wrong!" [Nersēs] halted the service, rushed to the royal-*tent, and, entering the doors, hurled himself at the king. But when the king saw the great *high-priest, he understood that [he had come] as an intercessor to persuade him about the man who was about to die: so that he should not die. Therefore, the king pulled his sables over his head,[14] hastily hid the features of his face, [and] snoring pretended to be asleep so that he should not hear his words. But St. Nersēs came close, grasped the king, †spoke to him, and said:[15] "King! remember thy *Lord, who came down from His natural highness out of love for us and became a *brother in *servitude to our unworthiness for no other reason than to be a *teacher of love. So that we, having compassion for each other as we look at the Divine *teacher, might love each other in the fear [of the *Lord], and that we might not dare do harm to each other! But if thou dost not spare thy *brother, who is a *servant like thyself, thy companion, thy kinsman, our *Lord, who of his own will became a *brother to us, will not spare thee. For thus has He spoken to us: 'He that heareth thee heareth me,' 'He that receiveth thee receiveth me,' and 'he that despiseth thee despiseth me.'[16] Listen to Christ, who now speaks to thee through me so that thou shouldst not perish! For thou mayest perhaps fall from thy kingship, and still alive, wander about alone, and no one shall help thee! But now, listen to Christ and have mercy on thyself! Do not spill the blood of thy own *brother,[17] do not unjustly and mercilessly kill the righteous!"

128

But the king, turning to stone, heard nothing, with his face hidden in his cloak. He did not uncover it and would not answer, but he remained lying on his *throne, muffled up and hidden, for he would not even move. And while [Nersēs] was speaking these and similarly entreating words to the king, Erazmak the *chief-executioner came into the royal-*tent from outside, †began to report the completion [of his task] and said: "I have carried out the king's command to the full. I seized Gnel, took him to the wall of the horse-course, killed him, and buried him there."[18]

Then St. Nersēs †spoke out and said: "Truly thou art 'a deaf asp that stops her ears'; which will not hear the skillfull voice of the charmer nor take the remedy from the wise healer.[19] Likewise thou hast stopped thine ears and covered thy hearing that thou mightest not hear the healing words of God's admonishment, but having assumed the ways of wild beasts, thou hast begun to be a devourer of men. Therefore, what has been said of them shall come upon thee, for it is said: 'God will crush their teeth in their mouth and the *Lord has broken the cheek-teeth of the lions.'[20] And because thou hast turned against the command of Christ thy *Lord, thou shalt be worthless, 'like water that is poured out,' and when 'He shall bend His bow,' thou shalt grow weak.[21] And the destruction foretold by the mouth of the prophet shall come upon you: that your Aršakuni *race drink the last cup. Ye shall drink it; ye shall be drunk and be destroyed,[22] and ye shall not rise again. And at the coming of the *Lord, the threat of the unending fire shall come down upon you, and ye shall be hurled into the darkness, and ye shall see no more the sun of *glory of the Son of God![23] As for thee, Aršak, because thou hast committed the deed of Cain, thou shalt bear the curse of Cain.[24] Thou shalt be hurled living from thy kingdom,[25] thou shalt endure sufferings greater than those of thy father Tiran, and in great torments shalt thou end thy life on this *earth by a bitter death!"[26]

Having said all this to the king, the great *high-priest Nersēs left the king, and he did not return thereafter to that *camp.[27] But they took the young Gnel near the royal horse-wall[28] and they beheaded him on a hill in the mountains at the place called Lsin near the fence enclosing the hunting [ground] opposite the royal *feasting hall,[29] at the myrtle springs in front of the *home-camp.[30]

Then an order came from the king [to] all men who might be in the *camp—both great and lowly: let no one dare fail to come, but let everyone go, lament bitterly, and weep over Gnel the *great-*sepuh* of the Aršakuni, who had been killed. And the king himself went among the mourners and sat weeping over his nephew, whom he himself had killed. He went and sat near the body, wept himself, and commanded that great mourning and lamentations be performed around the body of the victim.[31] As for

P‘aṙanjem, the wife of the slain, rending her garments and loosening her
130   hair, she lamented with bosom bared among the mourners. She wailed
aloud [and] made all weep by the mournful tears of her grievous lament.[32]
But when King Aršak saw the wife of the murdered man among the
wailers he was stricken with passion, and desired to take her as his wife.

But the one who had deceitfully and slanderously plotted this and
treacherously brought death upon his kinsman, had done this for the sake
of the [dead man's] wife, for he was greatly enamored of her. I speak of
Tirit‘, who was extremely taken with that woman and had consequently
deceitfully contrived the murder, by means of the king. And so, while
lamentations for him grew most vehement, Tirit‘ became unable to
withstand his passion. †He sent a message to the wife of the murdered
man, saying: "Do not put on such mourning for I am a better man than
he. I loved you, and I made him perish so that I might take you as my
wife." So, while they were still passionately lamenting around the corpse,
Tirit‘ sent such a message. [But P‘aṙanjem] raised a clamor: "Hear ye all,
my husband's death was because of me, my husband was put to death
because someone desired me!" And she tore her hair, cried out aloud, in
lamentation.

Then, when these grave matters became altogether clear in everyone's
hearing and among the mourners she became the mother of lamentations
and all the mourners began to sing in a lamenting tone [about] the episodes
of Tirit‘'s passion: his desire, his deceit, the plotted means of death, the
killing. They sang with moaning voices in the midst of their laments,
quavering with compassion over the victim.[33] [And so], in the singing of
their voices,[34] the events were revealed and spread abroad. When King
Aršak heard this and understood the events, he was amazed, stunned,
and benumbed, and he repented as he grasped the matter. Then the king
†began to speak, striking one hand against the other in great contrition
over the deeds he had done [and] said: "Because Tirit‘ was smitten with
shameful passion for the wife of Gnel, he plotted this evil [deed], this
131   treachery, this violent death, groundless and unjust. And because of his
lust, he stained us also with innocent blood. He gave his own *brother[35]
over to slaughter, and he made us the heir of irremediable torments and
maledictions, that shall not pass awây."

Then, when the king had achieved confirmation of the events and
verified the facts, he brooded over the matter for a time and listened. But
when they had buried the dead in the very place where he had been killed,
and many days passed over the deeds, Tirit‘ sent a message to the king:
†"May it be," he said: "your royal will,[36] may you give the order allowing
me to take Gnel's wife P‘aṙanjem as my wife." When the king heard this,
he said: "Now I know with certainty that what I had heard was true.

Gnel's death was [indeed] over his wife." And the king then planned to put Tirit⁣ᶜ to death as well in retaliation for the death of Gnel.³⁷ When Tiritᶜ heard of this he fled by night in fear of the king. Then King Aršak was informed of Tiritᶜ's flight and he ordered a *noble-contingent from the *camp to follow Tiritᶜ and kill him on the spot, wherever they caught up with him. And many *valiant [men] pursued the fleeing Tiritᶜ, they caught up with him in the midst of a forest in the *district of Basean, and they killed Tiritᶜ in the [very] place that they overtook him.³⁸

And after this Aršak took the murdered man's wife, Pᶜaṙanjem, as his own. But as much as King Aršak loved the woman, so much did the woman hate the king, saying: "He is hairy of body and dark of color." Then, when he could in no way win over his wife, King Aršak sent a request to the *land of the Greeks and brought from there a wife of the *race of the *imperial *house, whose name was Ołompi [Olympias].³⁹ And he loved her greatly and thus aroused the jealousy of his first wife. And so Pᶜaṙanjem nursed her resentment against Ołompi and she planned to kill her. But then Pᶜaṙanjem bore a boy to the king and he was called Pap, and he was *nursed and raised to manhood. And when he reached puberty and became strong, he was sent as a hostage to the court of the *emperor in the *land of the Greeks.⁴⁰

But Pᶜaṙanjem nourished a great jealousy and resentment against Ołompinay, and she sought to kill her by poison. However, she was unable to find any means of contriving [this], because [Olympias] was most careful of herself, especially in food and drink, for she ate [only] food prepared by her maid-servants and wine presented by them. And so, when no way could be found to infect her with a deadly poison, the iniquitous Pᶜaṙanjem then persuaded a certain priest from the royal court named Mrǰiwnik from a locality in Aršamunikᶜ, from the *province of the *district of Tarōn, who was there at the time. And he performed an †unworthy, unprecedented, unatonable, evilly sinful and unforgettable deed [worthy of eternal] torments—[a deed that was] †unworthy, never seen, and unheard of: that is, to mix into the draught of life the draught of death.⁴¹ [It was] a deed such as had never been performed by anyone anywhere on *earth. A mortal poison was mixed into the holy and divine Body of the *Lord, into the bread of the Eucharist, and in the church the priest named Mrǰiwinik gave [this] death-dealing thing to *Queen Ołompi, and so killed her. Filled with evil, he carried out the will of the consummately evil Pᶜaṙanjem. And the false priest received as a gift from the iniquitous Pᶜaṙanjem the *village called Gomkunkᶜ, from which he came, in the *province and *district of Tarōn.⁴²

But the holy *katᶜołikos Nersēs never saw again the face of King Aršak up to the day of his destruction.⁴³ And instead of Nersēs, a certain

132

Č⊂unak by name was appointed in his place as the head of the Christians, and he was the *slave of the *slaves of the king.[44] Then the king gave the order to summon all the bishops of the *realm of Armenia so that they would come to ordain Č⊂unak to the *kat⊂oɫikate of Armenia. But †not a single one of them agreed to come[45] except only for the bishops of Aɫjnik⊂ and Korduk⊂, who came and ordained Č⊂unak in accordance with the command of the king. And Č⊂unak was a docile man, and he had no tongue whatever for rebuke or admonition, but he agreed with the king in whatsoever he did.[46]

133   *Chapter xvi. Concerning how and in what way Aršak king of Armenia was invited by Šapuh king of Persia, and how he was greatly honored by him; and how the *sparapet of Armenia Vasak Mamikonean killed the *head-of-the-stables of the king of Persia; and how king Aršak swore an *oath on the Gospels to the king of Persia, and how he then broke his oath and fled; and how the king of Persia slaughtered seventy of God's ministers on account of this.[1]*

At that time Šapuh king of Persia invited Aršak king of Armenia, whom he *honored with the greatest deference and *glory, with great hoards of gold and silver, and with full royal pomp. He treated him as a *brother, like a son and gave him the second domain[2] in the *realm of Atrpatakan. And they *reclined together on one and the same banqueting-*throne in the hour of festivity,[3] and they wore the same garments of the same color with the same insignia and ornaments. And day after day the Persian king prepared the same crown for himself and for him. Linked together like two indivisible blood-*brothers, they enjoyed themselves jointly at festivals and reveled in indescribable pleasures.[4]

It then happened that on one of those days Aršak king of Armenia went for a stroll around one of the stables of the king of Persia, while the *chief-stabler of the Persian king sat within the stable *house. When [this man] saw the king he in no way honored him or paid him any respect, but displayed contempt and even hostility, saying in the Persian language: You [there], king of Armenian goats, come sit on a bundle of grass. Hardly had the *sparapet-*commander-in-chief of Greater Armenia, whose name was Vasak from the *house of the Mamikonean, heard these words than he flared up with great fury and rage. He raised the *sword that hung by his side, and on the spot he struck off the head of the

134   *chief-stabler of the Persian king, right there within the stables. For he could not hear or suffer this affront to his king; he considered it far better to meet his own death, than to hear his *lord contemptuously insulted. [And] although they were in the Persian *realm, in an alien place, he was capable of performing such a deed *publicly before them, at once, fearlessly, and without hesitation. But when the king of Persia heard of this,

he showed particular graciousness to the *commander Vasak, and he marveled at his *valor and great fearlessness. He bestowed on him many *honors and gifts, praising his *valor and his love for his *lord. For this reason he loved him greatly and *honored him in accordance with his deserts and made much of him during the all days of peace and harmony between them.[5]

Then, while the king of Armenia was still there with the king of Persia and there was much love and great peace between them, Šapuh the king of Persia suspected and feared that Aršak king of Armenia might perhaps be false in his love and ally himself with the *emperor of the Greeks, or that he should become in anyway disaffected from him. And he did not believe that [Aršak] would preserve his faithful love or maintain the *covenant of union with himself.[6] Therefore, he demanded an oath from him and compelled him, exerting the utmost pressure and saying: "Agree and swear to me on your own faith that you will not be false to me!" When [Aršak] had been pressed to the utmost and in dire straits, the priests of the church of the *city of Tispon—the chief of whom was called Mari[7]—were ordered to come. They brought the Holy Gospels, and Šapuh king of Persia made Aršak king of Armenia take an *oath, swearing on the Divine Gospels that he would never again be false to him, but that he would keep his *oath and maintain his alliance with him. And because the intermediary in this matter had been the elder *brother of the *sparapet Vasak—the *nahapet-*tanutēr[8] of the Mamikonean *house named Vardan—King Šapuh greatly regarded and loved him. But his *brother, the *commander-in-chief of Armenia Vasak, was envious of his elder *brother Vardan.[9] He wished to sow dissension between Aršak king of Armenia and [. . .] to flee.[10] But Šapuh said: "If the oath had been given by you wholeheartedly, how was it possible to break this oath according to the agreement and flee? But I know," he said, "that you have deceived me with witchcraft. You love him because he belongs to your faith. You deceitfully plotted with him and made him escape from me. You desire the *dominion of the Aršakuni over yourselves and you seek it."[11] Then King Šapuh swore by the sun, by water, and by fire:[12] "I will not leave a single man alive who belongs to this Christian faith," and he ordered them all taken away and killed. And so, they took their chief priest Mari and the other presbyters and deacons—more than seventy men—and slaughtered them all in a pit.[13] And as for the Holy Gospel on which King Aršak had taken the oath, he chained and bound it with iron bands, sealed it with his own seal, and he ordered that it be kept with care in the treasury.

Chapter xvii. Concerning the way in which Šapuh king of Persia aroused a persecution against the Christians.[1]

At the time that the presbyter Mari was killed together with the [other] seventy, King Šapuh raised a great persecution against the Christian faith.[2] He oppressed them with *taxes and all sorts of vexations and many torments. And after this, he gave out an edict to every place within his *dominion [proclaiming]: "Every single man who bears the name of Christian within my *dominion shall be †put to the *sword altogether and slaughtered, so that not a single individual bearing the name of 136 Christian may be found within my *dominion." Then they killed myriads upon myriads and thousands upon thousands, for the king had ordered it, so that the name of Christians should not be found at all within his *borders.

*Chapter xviii. Concerning the death of Vardan at the hands of King Aršak through the deceit of his brother, the *sparapet Vasak.[1]*

Then Vardan, the *tanutēr* of the Mamikonean *house, came from the king of Persia as an ambassador to Aršak king of Armenia and presented him with [his] *letter-patent.[2] And he spoke to him words of peace and harmony on [Šapuh's] behalf and of the confirmation of the oaths. And he transmitted this message: "Whatever happened, let that injury be forgiven, but henceforth do you keep your [sworn] word of *covenant and do not break the oaths you swore on your own faith! If not, you know it and also your faith to which you are false." And Aršak received him lovingly, lovingly listened to the message, and agreed with what was said [in it]. He then peacefully dismissed the great *nahapet* to his own *home [*tun*], so that he might rest from the toil of his long journey; and so he went.

At the time that the *nahapet* Vardan had come to Aršak, his younger *brother Vasak was not present there with the king. But subsequently Vasak came and incited the king against his elder *brother by saying: "Vardan is betraying you to the Persian king and he wishes to destroy you. If you do not hasten to kill him first you will perish and the Armenian *realm [together with you]."[3] The king's wife also incited him with the same words, and she confirmed to him the words of the *commander-in-chief Vasak. [She did this] on account of the grudge she bore against Vardan, because Vardan had been the one who had invited her husband Gnel deceitfully, treacherously, and with great oaths at the time that King Aršak killed him. On account of this, his wife still nursed this grudge 137 within herself and incited the king all the more against [Vardan], until a large force was mustered against Vardan so as to go and kill him. And his own *brother Vasak also went forth against him.[4]

They set out and found [Vardan] in his own *district of Tayk', in his *impregnable-*castle called Ēraχani. When [those who were there] saw that this was Vasak's own *contingent they had no fear, took no precautions, and had no misgivings, because they thought that these were the forces of his *brother coming in peace. [And they remained so] until they came to the very doors of [Vardan's] *tent, for the *tent was pitched in the gorge beneath the *fortress. Now the men of Vasak's *contingent were secretly armed with ordinary garments [worn] on top. And as [Vardan] was naked while washing his head, many men came upon him with *swords and wounded him repeatedly as he was bending over to have water poured over himself. He had no time to straighten up for they [ran him] through the side and killed him on the spot.[5]

His wife was pregnant and the time had come for her to give birth. While she sat on her *throne in the *fortress up above, a terrible clamor arose, and when she heard the mournful clamor, she ran down from her *throne, and as she ran, she gave birth to a child. And this child was called Vardan after his father.[6]

*Chapter xix. Concerning the way in which Aršak king of Armenia senselessly and mercilessly came to kill the *naχarars.*[1]

And then at the time that the holy *chief-bishop Nersēs abandoned the royal-*camp and there was no one to rebuke the king or to give him reproving admonishment, he began to follow his own evil will.[2] He slaughtered many of the *naχarars, destroyed and annihilated many of them and seized many *domains for the royal treasury. He extirpated the *house of the Kamsarakan, who were the *lords of the *districts of Širak and Aršarunikᶜ, and took their *districts for the *ostan.[3] But the *commander-in-chief of Armenia, Vasak, hid and saved one little boy from that *clan named Spandarat,[4] who later inherited his *realm.[5] But King Aršak ordered an impregnable-*stronghold named Artagers built for him in the *district of Aršarunikᶜ.[6] And the *district was left as a storehouse to supply food for the *fortress, for that *stronghold was very heavily *fortified.

Chapter xx. Concerning the way in which the war between the Greeks and the Persians intensified; and how Aršak king of Armenia became an ally of the king of Persia and put the Greek forces to the sword; and how the king of Armenia fled because of the treachery of Andovk Siwni.[1]

When King Aršak first fled from King Šapuh and affronted him with his [broken] oaths, Šapuh king of Persia did not pursue him with great severity at the beginning, because a great war was still raging between him and the king of the Greeks. As the war gradually dragged on, Aršak king of Armenia held himself haughtily at first and watched to see which of them would call him as a supporter in the war. He hoped for and would have gone willingly to the assistance of the *emperor of the Greeks, but he did not call him and showed him neither distinction nor honor.[2]

On the other hand, Šapuh king of Persia sent him messengers of peace and reminded him of his previous oath, saying: "†If it were your will *brother, to assist [me] in this war, if you were to support [me] with your *contingent, if you should be on our side, we know that victory would be ours." When Aršak king of Armenia heard this, he was gladly willing to come to his support and assistance, and to be an ally of Šapuh king of Persia.[3] King Aršak then gave an order to his *sparapet Vasak to 139 muster a *contingent and make ready the army. And [Vasak] hastened to carry out the king's command. He raised four hundred thousand well-armed men[4] [who were] specially selected, warlike, and filled with martial heroic skills: *spearmen, *swordsmen, skilled infallible *archers, *short-swordsmen, *axe-men, none of whom knew fear before the foe; [finally] the entire *armor-clad and *helmeted [heavy] *cavalry with their *banners, standards, and resounding trumpets.[5]

King Aršak set out with a multitude of *naχarars, he journeyed across his *dominion, through Aljnikʿ, and broke into the *land of Aruacʿastan opposite the *city of Mcbin, which was [set as] the place for combat.[6] When they arrived [there], they saw that this was the place designated for combat by both sides. The Greeks had already reached it, and their multitude, massed together in an *encampment, was †as great as the sands on the seashore.[7] But the Persian army had not yet arrived at the appointed place for combat. As for the forces of the king of Armenia, because they had arrived at the battlefield before the Persians, they took [their position] and waited.[8]

Then the Armenian forces began to grow restive at sitting idle. They would not agree to await the coming of the Persian army, but wished to attack and strike at the king of the Greeks on their own without the Persian army, and to finish the war by themselves alone. Everyman in the entire Armenian army moved increasingly boldly forward of his own accord, and their *commander Vasak outstripped everyone else in the army. He strained at the leash and would not agree to remain [inactive] until the arrival of the Persian army, but [urged] that they should finish the war alone, and by themselves. Then the Armenian forces rushed forth in unison to their King Aršak and begged him not to keep them back until the arrival of the Persian king Šapuh, but to allow them [to carry out] that for which they had come, [namely] to bring the war into [open] conflict as soon as possible, to attack rather than wait in an alien *realm. They were particularly stricken because they considered it better to die 140 than to tarry in a foreign *realm. Then King Aršak gave them leave and directed them to [open] military operations. And so Vasak, the *commander-in-chief-*sparapet of Greater Armenia, organized, arranged, and made ready the entire Armenian host. Vasak made ready and armed himself, and †fell on the *camp [of the Greeks] at the appointed time, together with the entire warlike forces of the Ayraratean *contingent. They †put to the *sword and slaughtered everyone, so that †not one of them survived, not a one.[9] And they took so much loot from the Greek army that there was neither count nor measure to it, and they were filled with treasures and satiated with the enormous mass of booty.[10]

After this, the king of Armenia, together with his army, held the ground until the arrival of the Persian king Šapuh †with all the countless and immeasurable army of the Persians. When he arrived and saw the *valiant deeds of the Armenian army he was greatly amazed, for they had closed in combat, carried out the war, won the victory, and brought the [entire] matter to a close. And so he greatly *honored Aršak king of Armenia with all the Armenian *magnates, and likewise the *sparapet of Armenia, Vasak.

Then Šapuh king of Persia †began to address his army [and said]:[11] "With what grants of benefits, or with what rewards can we recompense Aršak king of Armenia, he who has performed such a deed and been so *valiant, who has overthrown such a foe and engaged in such a fray, who has been victorious in such a combat and won such a name for us? For if we had been together with the entire Aryan host,[12] we would hardly have achieved such a success, although we might have been able to accomplish this deed together [with the Armenians] had we been *firmly [k'aj] joined with each other.[13] But the king of Armenia with his own might has been our champion, and he has performed a deed of such *valor that no one else can by any means perform it. Therefore, what benefits can we give in reward to him?" And so, he began to consider what he might give him.

141   Then his *naxarars †answered Šapuh king of Persia and said to him: †"Whatever is your will, you can please him with whatever you will.[14] You have much gold and silver, silk and pearls, whatever you may wish to bestow on him, give it to him." Then Šapuh king of Persia †answered his *princes and said to them: "It is not love that you speak of; let us create an indissoluble love [between ourselves] and Aršak so that he may remain forever inseparable from us. I shall give my daughter in marriage to Aršak king of Armenia and I shall give him a great *domain [tun], such a *domain that whenever he comes to us from Armenia, [all the way] to us in Tizbon, he will stay within his own *domain until he comes to us.[15] This is what we shall do for the king. But to the *commander-in-chief Vasak and to the other *magnates and *commanders we shall give gold and silver, silks and pearls." And the *magnates and counselors of the Persian king were pleased with this plan, and they confirmed what had been said, namely that it was proper to do this.

Then Šapuh king of Persia strongly urged Aršak king of Armenia to come with him to Asorestan that he might *honor him with great *glory, and elevate him to [the dignity] of son-in-law. But Aršak and all his army were distressed to go on such a long journey, for every one of them longed for his own *house, his own place, in accordance with the inborn ways of Armenian men. And when Andovk, *nahapet* of the *district of Siwnikʿ, understood these things—that Šapuh king of Persia wished to give his daughter in marriage to Aršak king of Armenia—he was greatly frightened and his mind was struck with misgivings. For he realized that when Aršak took the daughter of the king of Persia as a wife, his own daughter would obviously be dishonored as a consequence [of this]. For Andovk's daughter Pʿaṙanjem, who had [formerly] been the wife of Gnel, was at that time the wife of Aršak king of Armenia. And Andovk suspected that whenever the king took another [wife], his [daughter] would be dishonored.[16]

142   From that time on [therefore], Andovk devised schemes and plotted to find pretexts through which he might perhaps be able to destroy the great love between the two kings. He first gave a great deal of gold to the *commander-in-chief of Armenia, Vasak, and likewise bribed all the *magnates so that he might contrive to break the great love between the two kings. And all the *magnates gave their assent, blinded by the gold they had received as bribes. Then Andovk won over one of the *nobles of the Persian king, one of his closest counselors, in order that he might sow discord by some means—deceit, treachery, or some [other] contrivance— between the Persian king Šapuh and Aršak.[17] And Andovk gave him an immeasurable amount of gold and put words into his mouth: that he should go in the guise of a soothsayer to King Aršak and say: "Save yourself, for the Persian king has made a definite plan to seize and kill you." And [Andovk] told him: "When you have said this, direct him to call us for advice and the *nobles will confirm your words."

The counselor of the Persian king then went to the king of Armenia and †began to speak to him the words that the malevolent Andovk had put into his mouth, and said: "Aršak king of Armenia, save yourself. For Šapuh king of Persia has made a plan to seize and kill you." King Aršak was stunned and amazed at these words, and he said: "Is this [to be] my reward from him for such great labors?" Then King Aršak summoned before himself all his *magnates and counselors: the *sparapet Vasak, Andovk his father-in-law, and whatever *naχarars were [present] there, and he told them all that he had heard from the Persian. Then with one voice they said to him: "We heard this long ago. We did not dare tell you, but these things are certain. So now, O king, know and see how you can save yourself and us." Then King Aršak gave a great treasure of gold and silver as a gift to the Persian who had spoken these words to him. And Aršak king of Armenia 143 himself conceived a plan: they organized themselves and made ready, and all the men in the Armenian *camp rose at once in the night, took to horse, and fled. They left in place their *tents and pavilions, their furnishings, and baggage, their equipment, and their *camp, and they went off secretly so that no one in the Persian *camp knew of it until break of day.

When the time of the morning greeting to the king of Persia had come, all the kings and *mightiest *princes went to greet the king of Persia, but the king of Armenia, together with his *magnates, alone was nowhere to be seen among them. Then Šapuh king of Persia ordered his men to go and see what was happening in the *camp of Aršak king of Armenia that he delayed so long in coming to greet Šapuh king of Persia. So they went and saw that the *camp was deserted and without men, for they had abandoned their *tents and pavilions, their canopies, hangings, and *thrones and couches, their baggage, furnishings and equipment, and even their treasures, but had taken only the *weapons that they carried on their own persons, and gone. And so, the men who had gone to the *camp returned and reported everything to the Persian king Šapuh. And because he was a wise man, as soon as Šapuh king of Persia heard of this, he understood in his wisdom what had taken place, and he immediately said: "This flight of the king of Armenia was brought about by my [men], for those who brought about the flight of that man, Aršak were from amongst us, from this court." He then sent many of his *nobles and *magnates on horseback after the king of Armenia as messengers with oaths of loving union and reproach, that he should return so that they might root out and punish the slanderers in their midst. But the Armenian king would not listen to the words of the envoys of Šapuh king of Persia, and he would not return to the Persian *land.[18] And from that day forth, war [filled with] the conflict of combats, and battles flared up between Aršak king of Armenia and Šapuh king of Persia for more than thirty years.[19]

144   *Chapter xxi. Concerning the first war between Šapuh king of Persia and Aršak king of Armenia; and how Aršak king of Armenia was victorious.*[1]

For eight years after the flight of the Armenian king Aršak from the Persian king Šapuh, the Persian king kept his hostility quiet, always spoke entreatingly, and begged Aršak king of Armenia to remain in loving peace and concord with him, in accordance with the peace *covenant he [had made] with him.[2] The Persian king [did this] because he found himself in great danger and trouble from the very frequent and unending wars waged by the kings of the Greeks. But Aršak king of Armenia was unwilling to pay any heed to him, nor would he come near him, nor send envoys, nor give any offerings or gifts, and he was altogether unwilling to be close to him in any way or to hear their [sic] name. But the Persian king sent him frequent gifts and ambassadors while he fought vigorously against the Greek kings.

153

But when peace came between the Greek king and Šapuh king of Persia, the Greek king wrote a letter of *covenant, sealed it, and sent it to the king of Persia. And this is what was written in the letter of *covenant: "I give you," he said: "the *city of Mcbin,[4] which is in Aruestan and Syrian Mesopotamia. And I am withdrawing from the Armenian Midlands. If you are able to attack and *subject them, I shall not support them." The king of the Greeks was then in a difficult situation, and in these straits he was compelled to seal such words and send them to the king of Persia and free himself from him [by these means].[5]

Now as soon as peace was concluded between the kings of Greece and Persia, the Persian king Šapuh called up his army and set out to make war against Aršak king of Armenia.[6] But the *wardens-of-the-border of the Armenian king who were stationed at Ganjak of Atrpatakan gave him early warning of these events [even] before he [Šapuh] reached the *borders of Atrpatakan. As soon as Aršak king of Armenia learned of this, he gave the order to his *sparapet Vasak that he should muster all his forces, go forth to encounter and attack the Persian king Šapuh. The *sparapet Vasak hurriedly collected all the forces of Armenia together and reviewed them. And there were to be found six hundred thousand *armor-clad *horsemen well equipped and bearing *lances, [faithful men] †with one heart, one accord, and one mind.[7] And Vasak, *sparapet of Armenia, marched forth together with them, he caught up with the king of Persia and fell upon [him]. And they †put to the *sword the entire [enemy] host. And †Šapuh king of Persia alone escaped on horseback and fled.[8] And they followed after [them], they subjected, ravaged and burned the entire *land of Persia, and they themselves remained masters of the battlefield, that is, †they kept guard over the Persian *borders.

*Chapter xxii. Concerning the fact that after this, combats against the Persian forces took place in three localities in the *land of Armenia; and how on this occasion too the Armenians raised the standard of victory.[1]*

At that time, Šapuh king of Persia collected his †innumerable and countless army, which was †like unto the sands on the seashore,[2] and a multitude of elephants that were beyond reckoning. He divided the army into three parts, he placed Andikan and Hazarawuχt[3] at the head of two [of them], and the king led the third in person. And the king gave the command to the army to break into the *realm of Armenia at three points and to devastate [it]. The news of this also reached King Aršak and his *commander-in-chief Vasak in good time, and they likewise collected from the *realm a large host whose multitude was beyond count. But although they made great haste, the Persian army nevertheless devastated the *land of Armenia in three expeditions.

Then King Aršak also divided his army into three [parts], and he
entrusted one *contingent to the *sparapet* Vasak, and the second *contingent to his *brother Bagas, who was incredibly brave in deeds of *valor
but was foolish in sensible matters, and King Aršak took the other *contingent in person. He then ordered [them] to prepare to advance directly
to meet the Persian forces. And so, the *sparapet* Vasak set out and found
the first and foremost Persian army, led by Hazarawuχt, which had reached
the *district of Vanand at the place called Ereweal, he engaged in combat
with the Persians and gave battle. And the Persian forces suffered defeat.
They turned to flight and scattered, [but] the *commander-in-chief Vasak
caught up [with them]. He attacked the fleeing Persians and †none of
them survived, not a one.⁴ And [the Armenians] seized a great deal of
booty as well as elephants.

†In the same month, in the same week on the same day,⁵ Bagos with
the troops accompanying him came and found the second Persian army
headed by Andikan, which had reached, assembled, and *encamped at the
fisheries of Aṙest.⁶ The Persian army soon learned of the arrival of Bagos
and prepared to give battle to the Armenian army. Then Bagos came up
with his entire *contingent. They attacked the Persian front, they struck at
and slaughtered the entire Persian army on the spot, and killed its *commander Andikan. Bagos then met the *contingent of elephants and
observed that one of the elephants was greatly adorned and bore the royal
insignia. Thinking that the king was [riding] on that elephant, he dismounted from his horse, drew his *sword, and threw himself on the
elephant. He raised his *weapon, crawled under the elephant, hamstrung
him, and brought the elephant down on himself so that they were both
killed, for he did not have time to escape from under the elephant.⁷ In this
battle the *commander Bagos was the only one to die, but †none of the
Persian host was left alive, not a one.⁸

†And in the same month, in the same week, on the same day, for the
three battles took place on the same day,⁹ King Aršak arrived with his
army. And he found King Šapuh in person, who had arrived, gathered
[his troops] together, and *camped in the *district of Basean, at the place
called Osχa.¹⁰ Then King Aršak †attacked the Persian *camp by night¹¹
and †put everyone there to the *sword, and †King Šapuh alone barely
escaped on horseback and fleeing reached the Persian *realm.¹² Then the
messengers of victory from the three *contingents met one another at
that time. With the exception of Bagos, who died in one combat, †not a
single one of [the Armenians] perished,¹³ for their great success and
victory came from God. And they invaded the Persian *lands and raided
as far as the *region called Xartizan. And they acquired great treasures,
*weapons, ornaments, much booty and immeasurable magnificence, and
so became rich beyond measure.

Chapter xxiii. Concerning Meružan Arcruni, who revolted against Aršak king of Armenia and turned to Šapuh king of Persia, and intensified the war still further; and how he apostatized from God; and how from then on he became an obstacle and a hinderance for the *land of Armenia.[1]

Then one of the *mightiest *naχarars, named Meružan Arcruni, revolted against the king of Armenia. He went to the king of Persia and swore an *oath to him that he would always be his *servant. And he denied his own life that he had in God, for he abandoned the Christian faith and confessed about his own self: "I am not a Christian." And he accepted the Mazdean faith, that is to say that of the Magians, prostrated himself before the sun and before fire and confessed that: "The gods are those whom the king of Persia reveres."[2] And after that he swore the following *oath to Šapuh king of Persia: "If Šapuh succeeds in vanquishing the Armenians and taking their *realm,[3]" said he, "and I return to my *realm and *house, I shall first build an *atrušan in my *hereditary *domain, that is to say, a *house for the worship of fire. And he swore to them by life and death to [carry this out] through words and deeds.[4] Then a Persian army even larger than before was made ready to raid the Armenian *realm, and it had that miscreant wretch Meružan as *guide.[5] They unexpectedly burned and devastated the *land of Armenia, under the *leadership of Meružan, had †the men trampled by elephants and the women impaled on pointed carriage-poles, and so they destroyed the entire population of the upper *districts of Armenia.[6]

[Thus], while King Aršak was foraging for supplies[7] in the *region of the lower *districts, in Angełtun, the Persian army was brutally devastating and spoiling the Midlands. Then the Armenian *commander-in-chief Vasak collected an army, and there was at that time under his command a *cavalry of ten thousand choice and *valiant horsemen well supplied with *weapons and fully prepared. He set out with them and gained on the Persian army. But when the *commanders of the Persian king realized that the Armenian *commander-in-chief, Vasak, had collected an army against them, they pillaged those who were left in the *realm, took prisoners, and fled to their own *realm as quickly as possible. But Vasak Mamikonean hastened after them and caught up with them as they were moving through the *territory of Atrpatakan. And so the Persian army abandoned its captives and fled together with Meružan. And [Vasak] released from bondage an †immeasurable and innumberable number of captives and the [Armenians] returned peacefully to King Aršak.

Chapter xxiv. Concerning Meružan: how he rebelled, incited Šapuh king of Persia, and waged war; and how he became the *guide of Šapuh king of Persia and led a bandit-raid against the *realm of Armenia;

*and how he captured the bones of the Aršakuni [kings]; and how the
commander-in-chief Vasak freed the captives and vanquished the foe.[1]

After this, the infamous Meružan roused Šapuh king of Persia to
great wrath against King Aršak. Then Šapuh king of Persia mustered his
forces and sent spies to watch Aršak king of Armenia. And while Aršak
king of Armenia, together with his army, was still watching over the
*borders of Atrpatakan, because he expected the Persians there, they
took Meružan as their *guide, swerved aside,[2] and invaded the Armenian
*realm. Through Aljnikᶜ, Great Copᶜkᶜ, Angeltun, the *district of Anjit,
Copᶜkᶜ Šahuni, the *district of Mzur, Daranale, and Ekeleacᶜ,[3] Šapuh
king of Persia together with his innumerable host, invaded the *regions of
these *districts, poured over them and spread vastly like a mighty flood.

They devastated [the land] and put †countless men to the *sword;
†they impaled women and children on pointed carriage-poles,[4] and part
of them which was thrown under flails was threshed [to death]. They had
a †multitude of men trampled by elephants and took countless small
children into captivity. They destroyed many *fortresses and *fortified-
*strongholds, and they took and destroyed the great *city of Tigranakert,
which was in the *district of Aljnikᶜ, the *principality of the *bdeašχ[5] They
immediately took forty thousand families captive there and themselves
raided into Great Copᶜkᶜ. They captured some *fortresses there, but
some they were not able to take. And they went to lay siege to the
impregnable *fortress of Angl in the *district of Ankel tun, for there lay
the tombs [and] sepulchers of many of the Armenian Aršakuni kings, and
great treasures had been collected by their ancestors and remained [there]
150   from ancient times.[6] They went and besieged the *fortress, but when they
were not able to take it because of the [heavy] *fortifications of the place,
they left it and went on, and they passed many [other] *fortresses because
they were not able to overcome their *fortifications.

Only the *fortified-*stronghold of Ani in the *district of Daranalikᶜ
fell into their hands because the malignant Meružan devised a way to take
that *fortified-*stronghold. They climbed to the top, destroyed its protective [outer] wall, and brought countless treasures out of the *fortress.
And they opened the tombs of the former kings of Armenia, of the most
*valiant Aršakuni, and they carried off into captivity the bones of the
kings.[7] The only tomb that they were unable to open was that of King
Sanatruk, because of the disproportionately gigantic [size], stability, and
skillfulness of the work.[8] Then, they went away and abandoned it. They
turned to raid elsewhere [and] advanced into the *region of Basean, [for]
they intended to attack and fall upon the troops of the Armenian king
from the rear.

While all of this was taking place, the bearers of ill-tidings reached

King Aršak and said to him: "You are sitting here in Atrpatakan expecting the enemy from the front, but the enemy has fallen upon the *realm from the rear and destroyed it, and now he has turned to come against you." When King Aršak of Armenia and his *commander-in-chief Vasak heard this, they reviewed their forces. And at that time Vasak had under his command some sixty-thousand active men. [They were] choice and warlike [men] †with one heart, one mind, and one accord for military operations,[9] [that is] to go and fight for their children and their wives, and to lay down their lives unto death for the sake of their *realm and their native *districts; to fight for their churches and for the *community of ministers of their holy churches, for the *covenant of the faith [and] the name of their God, and for their own *true Aršakuni *lords.[10] For the very bones of their dead kings and great mass of the population had been torn from their homes and carried off to an alien land.

Then the *sparapet* Vasak set out with the sixty-thousand men, leaving behind King Aršak with his servants in a place in the *inaccessible *land of the Mark'. And he went himself to the Armenian Midlands, to the *district of Ayrarat, and came upon the Persian host, [which was] †as numerous as the sands on the seashore, assembled and *encamped in the *district of Ayrarat. Then Vasak arrived with the *contingent accompanying him, and he †attacked unexpectedly the *camp of the Persian king by night. And there, he †put the entire Persian host to the *sword, and †the Persian king alone escaped on horseback and fled.[11] But [the Armenians] harried the remaining fugitives over their *borders and took from them great and immeasurable booty beyond reckoning. And they †put all of them to the *sword, and they took away from them the bones of their own kings that the Persians were carrying away into captivity to the Persian *realm. For they said, according to their heathen beliefs: "This is the reason that we are taking the bones of the Armenian kings to our *realm: that the *glory of the kings and the *fortune and *valor of this *realm might go from here with the bones of the kings and enter into our *realm."[12] Then Vasak freed all the captives of the *realm of Armenia; and the bones of the Armenian kings freed by Vasak were taken and buried in the *inaccessible village named Aļjk' in the *district of Ayrarat,[13] which was in the middle of a difficult and narrow gorge in the great mountain called Aragac. And they strove to pacify the *realm, to put in order, arrange, and rebuild all that had been captured, ruined, or burned.

†But on this occasion also the malignant Meružan survived and fled with the Persian king.[14] And from then on King Aršak, together with the *commander-in-chief Vasak, guarded their *realm and †watched over the two gates of the *borders through †all the days of their lives.[15]

151

152   *Chapter xxv. Concerning the way in which King Aršak raided the
*land of Persia; and how he ruined and destroyed the *camp of King
Šapuh at Tᶜawrēš.*[1]

Then Aršak king of Armenia mustered his army and assembled a
host †as numerous as the sands [of the seashore],[2] and he set out against
the Persian *realm. And then Vasak took the Armenian *contingent and
calling the Honkᶜ and the Alankᶜ to his assistance,[3] he turned to the
support of the king of Armenia against the Persians. At the same time the
king of Persia, together with his entire *army [*banak*] also set out against
them toward the *land of Armenia, while they hastily reached Atrpatakan
and came upon the army of the king of Persia *encamped at Tᶜawrēš.[4]

The *sparapet* Vasak arrived with two hundred thousand [men] and
†fell on the Persian *camp.[5] †The king alone fled on horseback,[6] and the
entire Persian *karawan* was looted.[7] They slaughtered the entire mass of
the Persian host and took from the *camp such enormous booty that it
could not be counted. They raided the entire *land of Atrpatakan; they
laid waste the *land and destroyed it to its very foundations, and they took
from the *land †more prisoners than there are stars.[6] They †put all the
men of the *land to the *sword,[8] and they themselves, †keeping watch
over the *borders of their own *land, guarded them with the greatest care.[9]

153   *Chapter xxvi. Concerning Vin the Persian and the four hundred
thousand [men] who set out against Armenia and were defeated by the
Armenian army.*[1]

Then Šapuh the king of Persia assembled against Aršak king of
Armenia Vin, together with four hundred thousand [men]. And so, Vin
marched forth and spread out his raid over the entire *borderland of
Armenia. When Aršak king of Armenia perceived this, they came against
the Persian army, cut it to pieces, and †put all the Persian troops to the
*sword;[2] and he compelled the survivors to flee to the *regions of the
Persian *territory. [The Armenians] slaughtered them and once more
†kept the mastery over the battlefield.

*Chapter xxvii. Concerning the Persian *commander Andikan, who
came with four hundred thousand [men] to loot the *land of Armenia; and
how the Armenian *sparapet Vasak came forth against him with one hundred and twenty thousand [men] and destroyed both him and his army.*

Then after this, the Persian king sent, collected and thoroughly prepared a *contingent of four hundred thousand and warlike men against
the king of Armenia, so as to go forth, seize, burn, and ravage the *land
of Armenia. And their *commander, Andikan,[1] raided against the *land
of Armenia. Then Vasak Mamikonean, the *sparapet* of Armenia, came
out against him with one hundred and twenty thousand [men]. He slaugh-

tered him and his army, seized their ornaments, and †did not leave anyone of them alive, not a one,[2] while †he himself, *valiantly remained master of the battlefield.[3]

154   *Chapter xxviii. Concerning Hazarawuχt who was one of the Persian naχarars whom King Šapuh sent with eight hundred thousand [men] to attack the *land of Armenia; and how Vasak came out against him with eleven thousand [men], attacked and destroyed him and his army within the *borders of Ałjnik⁽.*

Hazarawuχt[1] came with the Persian army to burn, ruin and destroy the *land of Armenia to its very foundations. He directed his advance toward the *land of Ałjnik⁽, wishing to spread out from there toward the *land of Armenia and all of its *territories. Then Vasak came out against him with eleven thousand [men], attacked and destroyed them. He drove the remaining forces in flight to the Persian *land and killed Hazarawuχt on the spot.

*Chapter xxix. Concerning Dmawund Vsemakan, whom Šapuh king of Persia sent with nine hundred thousand axe-bearers[1] against Aršak king of Armenia. Then the *commander-in-chief of Armenia, Vasak, came out and destroyed him and his army.*

Then Dmawund Vsemakan[2] from the Kawosakan *house came out with nine hundred thousand [men]. He had been sent by Šapuh king of Persia to make war on the *land of Armenia. Then the forces of the Armenian *land were mustered and made ready, [with] Vasak as their *commander-in-chief, and they came out to fight against [the Persians]. Then the Persian forces were defeated by them and turned to flight. Vasak caught up with them, attacked, destroyed, and slaughtered them so that †not one remained alive,[3] and Vsemakan was killed in the midst of his army and the [Armenians] drove the [remaining] rabble out of their *borders.

155   *Chapter xxx. Concerning Vahrič, who came with four million [men] to wage war against King Aršak; and how he was delivered into the hands of the *commander-in-chief Vasak, together with his entire army.*

Then came Vahrič the son of Vahrič, with a Persian army of four million [men]. He was sent by King Šapuh against the Armenian *realm, to loot and destroy the *land and forces of the kingdom of Armenia, and they reached the place called Maχazean. Then the *commander-in-chief Vasak came out against them with forty thousand [men]. He attacked and slaughtered their forces, killed Vahrič, destroyed the [Persian] host, and †did not leave any of them [alive], not a one.[1] And †he watched over the *borders with care.[2]

160

*Chapter xxxi. Concerning Gumand Šapuh who boasted greatly before Šapuh king of Persia, and marched out with nine hundred thousand [men] against the *realm of Armenia; and how he was defeated and driven out unmercifully from the Armenian *realm.*[1]

After that came Gumand Šapuh, who had boasted before the king, and who was sent by Šapuh king of Persia with nine hundred thousand [men]. He came to the Armenian *realm with the infamous Meružan of the Arcruni house from the Armenian *land as a *guide.[2] He came and found lax the *border-guards who watched over the Armenian *frontier. [And] they spread out and filled the entire *land of Armenia to loot, destroy, and ruin the *land of the entire Armenian *realm.[3] Then the Armenian *commander-in-chief Vasak made ready, came and attacked the royal *contingent, and first of all he killed Gumand Šapuh[4] Then [the Armenians] attacked the scattered foe; they slaughtered the entire Persian host and †annihilated it completely.[5] But the malignant Meružan †alone fled on a single horse and took refuge in the *land of Persia.[6]

156

*Chapter xxxii. Concerning the *nahapet Dehkan, who was sent with a large army by Šapuh king of Persia against Aršak king of Armenia; and how the Armenian *commander-in-chief Vasak then met and slaughtered them.*

After all this, the Persian king Šapuh collected an †immeasurable and innumerable host, †like unto the sands of the sea:[1] an enormous army of four million armored [men], *spears in hand. And Šapuh king of Persia sent to the *land of Armenia the *nahapet Dehkan, who was a kinsman by *race of the *house of the *commanders-in-chief of Armenia, that is, the Mamikonean,[2] against the king of Armenia Aršak. He arrived at the *border of the Armenian *land, and he did not find the Armenians lax or asleep, but rather fully prepared for combat. And the *commander-in-chief Vasak came out against them with seventy thousand [men]. He attacked and slaughtered the entire Persian host, killed his *kinsman the *nahapet Dehkan, put the survivors to flight, and pursued them on horseback. But Meružan Arcruni, who had *guided them,[3] †escaped and survived.[4]

157

Chapter xxxiii. Concerning Suren Pahlaw, who also came with a large army and was also defeated like his predecessors.[1]

Then Šapuh king of Persia again assembled his forces. He organized and made ready many military *contingents—a choice and warlike host—as well as innumerable elephants. And he sent them against [the Armenians] under Suren Pahlaw, who was a *kinsman of Aršak king of Armenia,[2] and with Meružan as *guide.[3] Then the Armenian *commander-in-

161

chief Vasak came out against them with thirty thousand [men]. He attacked the Surēn head on, killed him, and destroyed his army. †But Meru-žan escaped.[4]

Chapter xxxiv. Concerning Apakan Vsemakan, who also partici-pated in this war and was ill-fated like his predecessors.

After the Suren came Vsemakan[1] who arrived with an immeasurable multitude and innumerable host *guided[2] by Meružan. He had been sent by Šapuh king of Persia to wage war on the *land of Armenia. The *sparapet Vasak, *commander-in-chief of Armenia, was sent against him. he attacked and slaughtered Apakan Vsemakan together with his entire host and †left not a single one of them alive.[3] †But the malignant Meru-žan alone made his escape.[4]

158   *Chapter xxxv. Concerning the *nuirakapet Zik, who was sent by King Šapuh with a large army to wage war against Armenia, and who was destroyed like his predecessors.*

After that, Šapuh king of Persia sent his *nuirakapet to wage war against the Armenians, and he gave them Meružan as a *guide.[1] And he assembled an army †as numerous as the sands of the sea,[2] and they advanced to the *land of Armenia. Then the Armenian *commander-in-chief Vasak came out and attacked them. He killed the Zik, but as for his army, he destroyed half of it and they drove the other half in flight before themselves. †But this time also they were not able to capture Meružan.[3]

Chapter xxxvi. Concerning the Persian Suren, who came to wage war after the Zik; and how Vasak overwhelmed and slaughtered him together with his army.[1]

And it so happened that after the death of the Zik, the Persian Surēn was sent by Šapuh king of Persia. He came with six hundred thousand [men] to wage war against Aršak king of Armenia, and he had Meružan as a *guide.[2] then the Armenian *sparapet Vasak assembled all the forces of the *naχarars; he came with ten thousand choice *men-on-foot, *sword in hand, and †fell by night on the Persian *fortified-camp.[3] They attacked, destroyed, and slaughtered the entire Persian host and seized the Persian Surēn, whom they brought to King Aršak And [the king] then ordered him stoned to death. †But Meružan escaped and survived.[4]

159   *Chapter xxxvii. Concerning Hrewšułum who was sent with nine hun-dred thousand [men] by the Persian king against Armenia; and how in this case too the Armenians raised the standard of victory.*

And Hrewšołum [sic] was sent to wage war against the *realm of

Armenia. He too was a *kinsman of the same *race of the Armenian kings, but at the command of King Šapuh he went with a force of nine hundred thousand [men] to wage war against Armenia. Then the Armenian *commander-in-chief Vasak arrayed, ordered, and made ready all the *contingents of his army and came out to meet them in combat. [The Armenians] put them to flight and drove them before themselves. And †Hrewšołum and Meružan escaped.[1]

Chapter xxxviii. Concerning Ałanayozan, who came from the Persian king with four million [men] to wage war against the king of Armenia; and how he was checked and destroyed by Vasak.[1]

Then Ałanayozan, who was a Pahlaw of the Aršakuni *house, boasted before Šapuh king of Persia and went to the Armenian *borders. News of this reached Aršak king of Armenia very early, and he too arrayed his army under his *sparapet Vasak. Having assembled all the Armenian *naχarars under him, [Vasak] went out to meet the Persian army. He attacked and destroyed it altogether, and drove the survivors in flight to the *land of Persia, whereas the [Armenians] themselves †kept watch over their own *borders.[2]

160   *Chapter xxxix. Concerning the great Persian *naχarar Boyekan, who also came with four hundred thousand [men], and whom the Armenian *sparapet Vasak attacked and exterminated.*

After this the great Persian *naχarar Boyekan came to Atrpatakan with four hundred thousand [men] with the intention of raiding into the *land of Armenia. Then Vasak came out against him with his Armenian *contingent. He destroyed the entire Persian army and killed Boyekan at Tᶜawrēš. There he burned down the *palace [aparan] of the Persian king, and finding in it an image of the Persian king, he shot and riddled it with *arrows,[1] †And only Meružan, who had come with them, escaped.[2]

*Chapter xl. Concerning Vačᶜakan, who came to Armenia with hundred and eighty thousand [men] with the intention of capturing Armenia, and the Armenian *sparapet destroyed him and his army.*

A certain Persian *naχarar named Vačᶜakan invaded the *land of Armenia with one hundred and eighty thousand [men]. Then the Armenian *commander-in-chief Vasak assembled the entire Armenian army. He left King Aršak in the *fortified *stronghold of Dariwnkᶜ and the Armenian *commander-in-chief Vasak in person went out with the Armenian forces to attack Vačᶜakan's *army [banak]. He killed Vačᶜakan and destroyed the Persian *army. †And only Meružan, who had come as their *guide[1] survived through flight with a few others.[2]

163

161   *Chapter xli. Concerning Mškan, who invaded Armenia with three hundred and fifty thousand [men]; and how he was destroyed by Vasak and the Armenian forces.*

And a certain Mšakan, who was one of the Persian *naχarars, also came and directed an attack against King Aršak. Then the Armenian *commander-in-chief Vasak arrayed the Armenian army against them and they fell on each other head on with great violence.[1] And the Armenian *contingent overcame the Persian host. They slaughtered them and †left not a single one of them alive.[2] And they killed Mškan himself, †but Meružan escaped.[3]

       *Chapter xlii. Concerning Maručan[1] and six hundred thousand [men]; how they marched against King Aršak, and how the *sparapet Vasak attacked and slaughtered them.*

A certain great *naχarar named Maričan [sic] came out to fight against the *land of Armenia. He then came with six hundred thousand [men] and thrust himself into the *land of Armenia with Meružan Arcruni himself as a *guide.[2] Then Vasak entered into combat with the entire Armenian host. He attacked and destroyed the Persian army and killed Maručan. †But Meružan alone escaped.[3]

162   *Chapter xliii. Concerning the *zindakapet who marched against the king of Armenia with nine hundred thousand [men]. Then the *commander-in-chief Vasak came out against them; he struck a great blow and destroyed the Persian host.*

A certain *zindakapet, who was the *commander-in-chief of the forces of the Persian king, marched to the *borders of Atrpatakan with nine hundred thousand [men]. Then the Armenian *commander-in-chief Vasak hastened to come out and meet him. He †attacked the Persian *fortified-camp by night,[1] †put them all to the *sword,[2] and killed the *zndkapet [sic] in the midst of the *camp. †But the infamous Meružan alone escaped and survived.[3]

       *Chapter xliv. Concerning the king's son Pap; and how the *dews manifested themselves in him; and how he performed foul acts with them.*[1]

Pap, the son of Aršak, was born from Pꞌaṙanjem of Siwnikꞌ, who had been the wife of Gnel whom King Aršak had killed and taken his wife Pꞌaṙanjem as his own wife. And she bore him a son, who was named Pap.[2] And when his mother gave birth to him she consecrated him to the *dews since she was an unrighteous person[3] who had no fear of God. And many *dews dwelt in the child and governed him according to their will. He was nurtured, grew, and committed [many] sins:[4] fornication, foul acts, sodomy, bestiality, and abominable turpitude, but above all else, sodomy. He turned himself into a woman for other men, and wallowed in filth in this manner.[5]

And once when his mother learned about his sodomy and could not tolerate the outrage of this infamy, she told to her son's *senekapet: "Whenever he summons those men with whom he is accustomed to perform foul acts, call me in." And so, when young Pap had already gone to 163 bed and summoned the men to foul acts, his mother came in and seated herself in front of her son. Then the youth †began to scream and wail and said to his mother: "Get up, go away! For I shall die, I shall burn, I shall be consumed, I shall burst, if you do not get up and go from this *house!" But his mother said: "I shall not go out of this *house." But he screamed over and over again and intensified his wailing. And his mother looked and saw with her own eyes white serpents which were wrapped around the feet of the *couch [gahoyk᷄] and were twisting themselves over young Pap as he lay there.[6] He remained on the bed wailing and calling to the youths with whom he was accustomed to have intercourse, but his mother understood and remembered those to whom her son had been devoted at birth. She knew that they were the ones who were twisting themselves around her son in the shape of serpents. [And] bursting into tears, she said: "Woe is me, my son, for you are possessed and I knew it not!"[7] And she rose up and went out, leaving the place to the fulfillment of his desires. In this fashion he was governed by the *dews, and to such acts did Pap the son of Aršak abandon himself †all the days of his life until his [very] death.

*Chapter xlv. Concerning the *anderjapet [sic] of Sakstan,[1] whom Šapuh king of Persia sent with four hundred thousand [men], and whom Vasak the *commander-in-chief of Armenia also put to flight.*

Then after this, Šapuh king of Persia collected his army of four hundred thousand [men], and the *anderjapet of Sakstan was their *commander. Then they set out and marched to the *regions of Armenia, they came, deployed, and fought against the Armenian king Aršak. Then all the *greatest Armenian naχarars assembled together and took counsel, because they would never accept that King Aršak should go to war together with them. Then the *commander-in-chief Vasak, with all the *magnates 164 and *naχarars of all of Greater Armenia, attacked and destroyed the entire Persian host. And he killed the *anderjapet of Sakstan. †But Meružan Arcruni alone escaped and survived.[2]

*Chapter xlvi. Concerning the Šapstan *takaṫapet,[1] who marched with five million [men] against the *realm of Armenia; and the Armenian* *army also attacked and slaughtered them.*

The Šapstan *takaṙapet* came against the *realm of Armenia with five million [men] and intended to invade the *realm of Armenia. Then the *contingent of the forces of the Armenian king was arrayed and made ready, and the Armenian *commander-in-chief Vasak went forth to meet and attack the Persian host. They struck at and destroyed the Persian army and killed the Persian Šapstan *takaṙapet. †But Meružan alone escaped and survived.[2]

*Chapter xlvii. Concerning the *handerjapet of the Magi[1], who marched forth with one hundred and eighty thousand [men] to give battle to the king of Armenia; and he was destroyed like his predecessors.[2]*

Then the *anderjapet* [sic] of the Magi also marched forth with one hundred and eighty thousand [men] to give battle to Aršak king of Armenia. Then all of the forces of the Armenian *land came together, and also the *sparapet and *commander-in-chief Vasak, who was the *tutor of Aršak king of Armenia. However much they hurried to arrive, they only had time to reach as far as Malχazan. There the two *contingents clashed together, and the Persian army having suffered defeat, fled from the presence of the *commander-in-chief Vasak and of the entire Armenian army. And there they killed the *andarjapet of the Magi and †annihilated the host.[2] †But Meružan alone escaped seated on a Tačik horse.[3]

165
*Chapter xlviii. Concerning the *hambarakapet, who marched forth with nine hundred thousand [men] to fight the forces of the Armenian king; and who was destroyed at Salamas by the Armenian forces and by the *commander-in-chief Vasak.*

Then the *hambarakapet of the king of Persia marched forth with nine hundred thousand [men] and reached Salamas in the *district of Korčēkᶜ. And he pitched a *fortified camp in an *inaccessible position with the intention of fighting against Aršak king of Armenia. Then the Armenian *commander-in-chief came with then thousand choice warriors. He lay in ambush *beside the *camp and †attacked the *fortified-camp by night. They †put everyone to the *sword and †not a single one [of them] survived.[1] †But Meružan alone chanced to be outside the *contingent and so escaped.[2]

Chapter xlix. Concerning Mrikan, who marched forth with four hundred thousand [men] to give battle, and was destroyed by Vasak and the Armenian forces.[1]

Then a certain Mrikan, a great Persian *commander, marched forth with four hundred thousand men to give battle to Aršak king of Armenia.

Then the Armenian forces with their *commander-in-chief Vasak fero-
ciously attacked head on, like lions. They destroyed the Persian host on
the spot and killed Mŕikan. †But this time too, Meružan escaped.²

166   *Chapter l. Concerning the decline and fall of the Armenian king-
dom; how many of the Armenian* naχarars *revolted and went over to the
Persian king Šapuh; and how they soon scattered hither and yon, and the
Armenian kingdom was weakened.*¹

For thirty-four years² our *land of Armenia was at war with the king
of Persia, and after that both *sides were weary, defeated, disheartened,
[and] worn out. And [the nobles] began to disperse from the Armenian
royal-*camp, abandoning Aršak their king.³ The first to start departing
were the *greatest-*nobles: first the *bdeašχ* of Ałjnikᶜ and the *bdeašχ* of
Noširakan, and [those*] of Mahkertun, of Nihorakan, and of Dassəntrē,⁴
and the entire *naχarar*dom of Ałjnikᶜ. And the forces and the *family of
the *house of the *region of Ałjnikᶜ revolted against Aršak king of Armenia and went off to present themselves to Šapuh king of Persia. They
raised a wall on the *side of Armenia called the Joray *side, pierced gates
through it, and separated their *realm from Armenia.⁵

And after this [went] the *bdeašχ* of Gugarkᶜ, and after him the
*lord of the *district of Jor, and the *lord of the *district of Kołb, and
together with them the *lord of the Valley-of-Gardman. And all those
who were in that *region, near them or around them, rebelled together
against Aršak king of Armenia and went to present themselves to Šapuh
king of Persia. The *inaccessible *district of Arjaχ revolted against Aršak
king of Armenia, and also the *inaccessible *district of Tmorikᶜ, and the
*inaccessible *realm of Kordikᶜ. Then, the *lord of the *district of Kor-
dukᶜ [sic] also went to present himself to the Persian king.

After this, the *principality of the Armenian King, [his own] *domain,
which lay around the *realm of Atrpatakan also revolted against the king
of Armenia.⁶ The *inaccessible *realm of the Markᶜ fell away from the
167 Armenian king. The *realm of Kazbkᶜ [also] fell away from the Armenian king. Sałamut *lord of Anjit abandoned the king of Armenia and
with him the *prince of Great Copᶜkᶜ, and they went to the king of the
Greeks.⁷ Those who were left in the Midlands distrusted the king and
would not listen to their king †not in a single thing that he wished. And
the kingdom was greatly diminished.

And Vahan, the *brother of the *sparapet* Vasak, who was from the
Mamikonean *house, was seduced by the words of Meružan Arcruni,
who was his sister's son.⁸ He too rebelled against Aršak king of Armenia
and went to present himself to the Persian king Šapuh. And to please
him, Vahan first renounced his own life that he had in Christ and agreed

167

to serve the religion of the Magians, that is, to worship fire, water, and the sun, and to apostatize from the Christian faith in which he had been born.[9] He endeared himself to the Persian king, likewise, he brought forth inflammatory denunciations against the king of Armenia and [against] his own *tanutēr* Vasak. And he also reminded him of Vardan's death, saying: "He died on account of you."[10] And from then on, he became so dear to King Šapuh that he gave his sister Ormizduχt to Vahan in marriage.[11] He granted to him the *cushion and *diadem that had formerly belonged to his ancestors, and made him his trusted son-in-law.[12] And [the king] elevated him in the midst of the army and promised him the *greatest possessions. And so the number of Armenians diminished after this and thereafter.[13]

*Chapter li. Concerning the way in which those remaining in the *realm *assembled together in complete agreement and unanimity before Nersēs *katʿolikos of Armenia and complained to him; and how they left and abandoned their king, Aršak.*[1]

Then all the men of the *realm under the *dominion of the Armenian kingdom *assembled and came to the great *chief-bishop of Armenia Nersēs: the *magnates, the *naχarars, the *kusakals, *kolmakals, the *lords-of-districts, *officials, and *dasapets of the *peasants.[2] They *assembled together, †began to speak to Nersēs, and said: "You know yourself, my *lord, that this is the thirtieth year [of the reign] of our king, Aršak, and that there has not been a single year of rest from war for us,[3] and constantly we have wiped the sweat off our faces with our *swords, and with *arrows, and the blades of our *spears. But now we can no longer endure this, we cannot fight another battle. It is better for us to *serve the king of Persia as has been done by our companions, who abandoned [Aršak] and went to the Persian king.[4] And we shall do the same, for we too can fight no more. If King Aršak should fight against Šapuh, let him go to war with Vasak and with his own father-in-law Andovk,[5] but †not a man, not a one,[6] from this *realm of Armenia will go to his support. Whether he wishes to go to war or not, we have left him; it is no concern of ours!"

But St. Nersēs †spoke to them as was right, [saying]: "Behold, keep *well [kʿaj] in mind and remember the command of the *Lord concerning concord: how he ordered *servants to be obedient to their *lords.[7] For every one of you stands as a witness that all of you especially have become what you are because of the *race of the Aršakuni. Some of you have become *lords-of-districts through them, and some of you *magnates of *realms, some of you have become *masters of various *noble *towns, *villages, and treasures as well as numerous *dastakerts. And even though the foul *race of the Aršakuni is guilty before God its Creator, nevertheless it wrenched you out of filth and gave all of you life: to some through *office and some through *dignity, to some through *authority and some through *official position.[8] For even through King Aršak is a sinner before God and bound to repay his Creator with interest and endure His vengeance, nevertheless God in His great and boundless love of mankind has had mercy on him, and because of him, on you.[9]

169 "And yet, behold, you wish to fall into the *servitude of heathens and lose your lives in God, to forsake your own *true-lords given to you by God, and *serve alien *lords, and covet their godless religion. For God forbid that you should love, accept, and believe it and ‹not› forsake your king who worships his Creator.[10] For were Aršak ten thousand times more evil, yet he worships God; and were he still more a sinner, he is your king![11] As you have said yourselves before me: so many years have there been that you have fought for yourselves and your souls, for your *realm, for your wives and your children, and for what is greatest of all, for your churches and for the *covenant of faith that we have in our *Lord Jesus Christ. And the *Lord has always given you victory in His name![12] Yet now, instead of Christ your Creator, you wish to *serve the godless false religion of the Magians and its ministers, forsaking our Creator and His Commandments; He who commanded you to be faithful to your earthly *lords whom He created.[13] The *Lord God mayhap will grow angry with you and uproot you. And He shall give you over for eternity into the evil *servitude of heathens, so that the yoke of *bondage shall not be lifted from you.[14] And you will cry out unto the *Lord and He shall not hear you, for of your own volition, you are going into *servitude to heathen *lords, to godless and ignorant men, to heathen and hard-hearted *masters. And many evils will arise before you, and you shall not be able to escape from them."[15]

But all those who were *assembled together †raised up a clamor, shouting to one another, created disorder, stirred up confusion, and said: "Come, let us go! Let us disperse each to his own place. For we do not wish to hear any words like these!" [And so] they dispersed each to his own *house.[16]

170 *Chapter lii. Concerning King Šapuh and how he ceased to wage war against Aršak king of Armenia at that time; and how he deceitfully invited him to a reconciliation.[1]*

Then, Šapuh king of Persia lovingly invited Aršak to come to him, [urging him] with many entreaties, gifts, and *official-letters, so that love, peace, and great friendship should thereafter reign between them, And although King Aršak wished to wage war, the entire force of the Armenian *realm would not agree to this. And so, he accepted, willy-nilly, to send an *official-letter of submission to Šapuh king of Persia, as befitted a *vassal to his *lord. And he [in turn] also sent gifts [in token] of reconciliation.

Chapter liii. Concerning Šapuh king of Persia's second summons to Aršak king of Armenia; his going and [his] total destruction.[1]

After this, Šapuh king of Persia †sent another message to Aršak king of Armenia, and said: "If you and I are satisfied with each other, come, and let us see each other, and let us thereafter be to each other as father and son. But if you do not [come] to see me, you are asking for war between me and yourself." But Aršak requested from him a solemn oath with a *pledge, so that he might then go to him without misgivings. And in accordance with the usage for solemn oaths in the kingdom of Persia, [Šapuh] had salt brought in,[2] sealed it with his own seal ring bearing the effigy of a wild boar,[3] and sent it off, so that if he still did not come after this oath, he might then prepare for war between them.

171   Then, when all the people of the *land of Armenia also saw and heard this, they pressed, constrained, and hurried their king Aršak to go and present himself before Šapuh king of Persia. After this, Aršak king of Armenia arose, willy-nilly, took with him the Armenian *sparapet and *commander-in-chief who was his *tutor, and set out from the *land of Armenia to the Persian *land, to Šapuh king of Persia. He set out and came before the Persian king Šapuh. And when [the Persians] saw them, they seized[4] both of them, both King Aršak and the *sparapet Vasak ‹put them in chains›[5] and held them free in the middle of an *azat-contingent of *guardsmen. And King Šapuh summoned King Aršak and berated him like a *servant, and [Aršak] acknowledged himself guilty before him and deserving death. And they again returned King Aršak the same *contingent of *guardsmen, so that he would be watched.[6]

*Chapter liv. Concerning the way in which Šapuh made inquiries of soothsayers and magicians and tested the intentions of Aršak; and how he had him imprisoned in the *fortress of Anuš [Oblivion]; and how he ordered the Armenian *sparapet Vasak cruelly put to death.*[1]

Then Šapuh king of Persia summoned soothsayers, astrologers, and magicians [Chaldæans], †spoke to them, and said: "I have desired to love Aršak king of Armenia many times, but he has always offended me. I made a *covenant of peace with him and he swore to me on that chief [object] of the Christian faith which they call the Gospels, and he was the first to break this oath.[2] I wished to bestow upon him ten thousand benefits, as a father on his son, and he returned to me evil for good. So, I called the priests of the church of the *city of Tisp'on, and I believed that they had brought him to the oath through some deceit and led him to lie to me. And I condemned them as deserving death, but their chief presby-
172   ter Mari said to me: 'We brought him to the oath faithfully, but if he lied, this very Gospel will bring him to your feet.' I did not listen to them, and I

ordered seventy of them slaughtered in one pit and their coreligionists
†put to the *sword.³ I had the Gospel on which Aršak swore the oath—
which is the chief [object] of their Christian teaching—bound with chains
and it is [still] in my treasury. But the words of the presbyter Mari remain
in [my mind], and I remember that he said: 'Do not kill us, for I know
that this same Gospel shall bring King Aršak to your feet.' And behold,
the words he spoke have been truly fulfilled.⁴ For it has been thirty years⁵
that the Aryans have waged war against Aršak king of Armenia,⁶ †and
not a single year have we been able to vanquish him,⁷ yet [now] he has
come on his own feet. But were I to know whether he would keep his
*pledge to me hereafter, and submit according to a true *covenant, I
would send him in peace with the greatest honors to his own *realm."

But the magicians †answered him and said: "Give us this day and
tomorrow we shall give you an answer." And on the morrow all the
magicians and astrologers assembled there and said to the king:⁸ "Now
that Aršak king of Armenia is come to you, how does he speak to you?
With what voice? How does he bear himself?" And the king said: "He
holds himself to be one of my *servants, he seeks to be the dust of my
feet." And they said: "Do what we tell you to do. Keep them here, and as
for you, send envoys to the *land of Armenia to bring two loads' worth of
soil and a jar of water from the *territory of Armenia. Then order half of
the floor of your *tent covered with the soil brought from Armenia, and
taking the Armenian king Aršak by the hand lead him first to the spot
where there is [our] native soil and put questions to him. Then take him
173 by the hand and lead him to the [spot] where the Armenian soil is piled
and listen to his words, and then you will know whether or not he will
keep his *oath and preserve the pact with you after you send him back to
Armenia. For if he speaks harshly [when] on Armenian soil, the day he
reaches the *land of Armenia he will raise the same voice against you,
and he will revive and stir up the same war against you, the same combats, the same enmity."⁹

When the Persian king heard this from the magicians, he sent men
with Tačik camels to Armenia for soil and water, which they were to
bring to him for the divination. And after a few days they returned and
brought that for which they had been sent. Then, King Šapuh ordered
half of the floor of his *tent covered with the soil brought from Armenia
and water poured over it, and half of it left with the same soil from his
own *land. And he had Aršak king of Armenia brought in before him,
and ordered the other men to leave, and taking him by the hand, he
walked all about.

And while they were walking back and forth in the *tent, [Šapuh]
said to him as they walked on Persian soil: "Aršak king of Armenia, why
have you been my enemy? For I loved you as a son and wished to give you

my daughter for a wife and make you a son. But you hardened against me and of your own volition became my enemy against my will. And it is [now] full thirty years that you wage war against me."[10] King Aršak answered: "I have sinned and am guilty before you. For I came and slaughtered and vanquished your enemies and I expected from you the gift of life, but my enemies led me astray and made me fear and flee from you. And the oath that I swore to you has brought me to you, and behold, I am come before you.[11] Behold, I your *servant am in your hands. †Do with me whatever you must, whatever you will. Kill me, for I, your *servant, am guilty before you and worthy of death!"

But King Šapuh, taking him by the hand, moved about feigning innocence, and brought him to the *side where the Armenian soil had been piled on the floor. As soon as he reached that spot and stepped on Armenian soil, [Aršak] *most haughtily and insolently changed tone. He †began to speak, and said: "Away from me, malignant, *servant, *lording it over your *lords! I shall not spare you or your children from the vengence [due] to my ancestors, nor forgive the death of King Artewan. For you who are [but] *servants have now taken the *cushion from us, your *lords. But I shall not concede this until that place of ours shall return to us!"[12]

Then again [Šapuh] took him by the hand and again led him to the Persian soil, and [Aršak] bewailed what he had said, abased himself, and fell at his feet in deep repentance of the words he had spoken. But whenever he led him by the hand [back] to Armenian soil, he spoke even more harshly than before. And yet again, Šapuh drew him away from that soil, and he returned to words of penitence. From morning until evening he tried him many times. And whenever [Aršak] was led to the piled [Armenian] soil, he persisted in his arrogance, whereas standing on the native [Persian] soil, he turned back to repentance.

And when in the evening the time had come for the banquet of the Persian king, it was customary for the king of Armenia to be placed together with him [and] next to him, on the same *banqueting-couch [*bazmakan*]. It was the rule that the king of Persia and the king of Armenia should *feast on the same *banqueting-couch on the same *throne.[13] But on that day, they first set couches for the kings who were present and arranged them for everyone. And finally, at the very end, they set Aršak's *couch all the way below everyone, where the Armenian soil had been spread on the floor. And first everyone took his ease [*bazmec⁽an*] according to his rank, and then they brought in and *installed [*bazmac⁽uc⁽anēin*] King Aršak. He remained *reclining [*bazmeal*] there for a while swelling [with anger]; then †he rose to his feet and said to King Šapuh:"That is my place where you are reclining, get up from it and let me *take my ease

175 there, for that has been the place of our *clan. And when I shall reach my own *realm, I shall seek the *utmost vengeance from you!"[14] Then Šapuh king of Persia ordered that iron chains be brought and put on Aršak's neck, feet, and hands, that he be taken to the *fortress of Andmǝš, which is [also] called Anuš, and that he be kept there until his death.[15]

And on the next day King Šapuh ordered Vasak Mamikonean, the *sparapet* and *commander-in-chief of Greater Armenia, brought before him and started to upbraid him. And because Vasak was small in stature, Šapuh king of Persia said to him: "You have been a destructive fox who caused us so much trouble, you are the one who slaughtered Aryans,[16] for so many years. What will you do now? For I will kill you with a fox's death." But Vasak †answered and said "Seeing now my small stature, you do not grasp the measure of my greatness, for until now I was a lion for you, and now [I have become] a fox. But while I was Vasak, I was a giant. One of my feet rested on one mountain and my other foot on another mountain. And whenever I leaned on the right foot, I drove the mountain on the right to the ground; whenever I leaned on the left foot, I drove the mountain on the left to the ground." Then Šapuh king of Persia †questioned him and said: "Come, let me know what are those mountains that you leveled with your feet." And Vasak replied: "Of those two mountains you were one and one was the king of the Greeks. As long as God granted it to me, I felled you to the ground and likewise the king of the Greeks. As long as the blessing of our father Nersēs rested upon us and God did not abandon us.[17] As long as we obeyed his words and his counsel reached us,
176 we knew how to teach you a lesson, until we now fall with open eyes into the pit.[18] So †now do what you will." Then the Persian king ordered the Armenian *commander Vasak flayed alive, his skin stripped off, filled with straw, and taken to the same *fortress of Andmǝš, [which is also] called Anuš, where they were holding King Aršak.[19]

*Chapter lv. Concerning the captivity and devastation of the Armenian *realm; and the taking into Persian captivity; and the cruel death of *Queen Pᶜařanjem; and the destruction of the Armenian *cities; and the total ruin of the *realm.*[1]

Then Šapuh king of Persia sent two of his *princes, one of whom was called Zik and the other Karēn, with five million men against the *realm of Armenia, to go, capture and destroy the Armenian *realm.[2] And so they set out and came down upon the *land of Armenia. Then, when the *queen of the *realm of Armenia Pᶜařanjem, the wife of Aršak king of Armenia, saw that the army of the Persian king was coming and filling the *realm of Armenia, she took with her some eleven thousand select *armored, warlike *azats, and together with them she avoided the Persian forces, sought [refuge] and entered the *fortress of Artagers in the *land of Aršarunik'. Then the entire Persian army came up, disposed itself around the *fortress, kept watch, enclosed, and besieged it. Now those who were *fortified within it trusted in the *impregnability of the place, while the others pitched a *fortified-camp and settled themselves all around through the gorges outside. And they besieged the *fortress for thirteen months but were unable to take it because of the extreme *impregnability of the place. They ravaged and devastated the entire *land. They went out and plundered throughout the *land, and from the surrounding *districts they carried captive men and animals back to their *fortified camp. They brought in supplies from elsewhere consumed them and kept the *fortress under siege.[3]

177   Now Pap the son of Aršak was not in Armenia at that time, for he was with the king of the Greeks.[4] When the *azat-contingent of the Armenian *army [banak] heard about all this, they went to seek help for themselves with Mušeł, the son of the *sparapet Vasak as their comander. They went to the son of their king, and during their negotiations with the king of the Greeks, they induced them to come to their assistance.[5] And they sent frequent messengers to the *land of Armenia, to the *realm's *queen P'aŕanjem, so that she should hold out in the *fortress and not surrender it to the Persians. And frequent messengers who contrived to enter the *fortress through a secret door came every week from her son Pap and gave encouragaments to the *queen.[6] And the siege of the *fortress continued thirteen months. And those who constantly came and went [reiterated]:[7] "Hold fast, for your son Pap is coming with an *imperial contingent of support." And these encouragements that he was coming dragged on, for they [kept] saying: "One moment more, be patient just a little while longer, and behold, help will come."

     And after the fourteenth month divine blows fell upon the refugees within the *fortress. Death came down upon those who were in the *fortress as a punishment from the *Lord. Those who were in the presence of *Queen P'aŕanjem were eating, drinking and making merry in the *hall [tačar] when suddenly one hundred men [died] in a single hour, and two hundred men in another, It even so happened that five hundred men died on their *banqueting-couches as they were *feasting; and so they were killed, day after day. Not even a month had passed from the beginning [of this] when everyone had been killed: some eleven thousand men and six thousand women. Not even a month had passed, when all those in the *fortress had been killed.[8]

     *Queen P'aŕanjem remained [alone] in the *fortress with two serving-
178 women. Then the eunuch *hayr the *mardpet secretly entered the *fortress and he greatly insulted the *queen as though she were a harlot. And he began to revile the *clan of the Aršakuni for being men of †ill-counsel

and ill-repute, as well as destroyers of the *realm. "Justly," he said, "has all of this come upon you, and [also] that which shall come!" And he left secretly and fled.⁹ And when *Queen Pᶜaṛanjem saw that she remained alone, she opened the gates and allowed the Persian army to enter the *fortress. And they entered, seized the *queen, and brought her down from the *fortress. Then the Persian *commanders¹⁰ went up into the *fortress and seized the treasures of the king of Armenia, which were [kept] in that *fortress. And they began to take and carry down all the treasures that were in the *fortress. Nine days and nine nights they continually brought down what they found in the *fortress of Artaragers [sic], and they carried it off together with the *queen.¹¹

Then they came to the great *city of Artašat and took it. They destroyed its wall, carried off the hoarded treasures that were there, and captured the entire *city. And they carried off from the *city of Artašat nine thousand Jewish *households who had been taken prisoners by King Tigran Aršakuni out of the *land of Palestine, and forty thousand Armenian families, whom they took from the *city of Artašat.¹² They set fire to all the wooden buildings of the *city, tore down all the stone ones, did the same to the wall, and destroyed every building in the *city to its foundations; †they did not leave a single one,¹³ indeed they did not leave stone upon stone. They emptied it of all its population and left it deserted.

And it so happened that after they had collected all the captives from the *city and had taken them across the bridge of Tapᶜer, counted the prisoners, and surrounded them with *club-bearing troops, the Persian *commanders said to Zuitᶜ, the presbyter of the *city of Artašat: "Come out of the midst of the captives, and go where you will." But the presbyter Zuitᶜ †would not agree to this, but said: "Wherever ye take the flock, there shall ye take the shepherd. For it is not fitting that the shepherd abandon his flock, but it is proper that the shepherd lay down his life for his sheep."¹⁴ Having said this, he entered into the midst of the prisoners and was taken into captivity with his people, into the *land of Persia.

They also took the *city of Vałaršapat, ruined and destroyed it to its foundations; and they also took away from that *city nineteen thousand families.¹⁵ They did not leave a single building in the entire *city but †destroyed and demolished everything. They also raided through the entire *land, killing all the adult men and taking captive the women and children. And they seized all the *fortresses of the king of Armenia, filled them with many supplies, and left *garrisons in them.

They also took the great *city of Eruandašat, and took away from it twenty thousand Armenian families and thirty thousand Jewish families.¹⁶ They dismantled and demolished the *city to its foundations. Then they took the *city of Zarehawan in Bagrewand, and from it they took away five thousand Armenian families and eight thousand Jewish families.[17] They demolished and destroyed the *city to its foundations. And they took the great *city of Zarišat, which was in the *district of Aliovit. [From it they took away] fourteen thousand Jewish families and ten thousand Armenian families, and they demolished it to its foundations.[18] They also took the *inaccessible *city of Van, which is in the *district of Tozb. They set it on fire and destroyed it to its foundations. From it they took away five thousand Armenians and eighteen thousand Jewish families.[19]

All this multitude of Jews, who were taken into captivity from the *land of Armenia, had been taken in ancient times from the *land of Palestine by the great Armenian King Tigran, at the time that he also took and brought to Armenia the *high-priest of the Jews Hiwrakandos. And the great King Tigran brought all these Jews in his own days, and settled them in the Armenian *cities.[20] But at this time, [the Persians] destroyed the *cities and took the inhabitants captive, as well as the entire *land of Armenia and all its *districts. They also took away captives from every *district, *region, valley, and *realm, and collected them in the city of Naχčawan, for that was the gathering place for their army. They also took that *city, destroyed it, and took away from it two thousand Armenian families and sixteen thousand Jewish families, and made them go with all the [other] captives.[21] They also left *ostikans and *overseers in the *land of Armenia to bring the survivors of the *land into *bondage,[22] while they themselves took *Queen P^caranjem together with the treasures and the multitude of captives to the *land of Persia. And so, they went and brought them to the *land of Persia, to the Persian king Šapuh.

And it so happened that when they came to the Persian *land bringing [with them] *Queen P^caranjem, when they brought before the king all the other Armenian captives, and the treasures, and P^caranjem the *queen, the king of Persia was most grateful to his *commanders. And since Šapuh king of Persia wished to insult the *race of the *realm and kingdom of Armenia, he ordered all of his troops, *magnates, base-born, and all of the men of the *realm under his dominion assembled together, and he brought P^caranjem *queen of Armenia into this mob. And he ordered a device for debauchery erected in the *public-square and had the woman thrown into it. And he delivered *Queen P^caranjem to foul and beastly copulation. And in this fashion they killed P^caranjem the *queen. As for all the other captives, they were taken and settled, some in Asorestan and some in the *land of Xužastan.[23]

*Chapter lvi. Concerning the martyrdom of the presbyter Zuit^c in the *land of Persia.*[1]

Now when they carried all the Armenian captives to the *land of Persia, they also brought the presbyter of the *city of Artašat in bonds before Šapuh king of Persia. And the Persian king Šapuh looked and saw that the presbyter Zuit^c was a tall, personable man and still young in years; the hair on his head had whitened but his beard was still black. Then [the king] first †began to speak and said: "See you the evil of this man? It is evident and clear from his hair that he is a sorcerer, for his hair is white and his beard is black." But the presbyter †answered [and] said: "If you need speak, say and do whatever you want, but as for these, know that it is entirely proper that my hair should have whitened first, for it is many years older; it sprang up some fifteen years before my beard." But the king ordered him kept under guard until the next morning. And in the morning he ordered him brought in chains into the *public-square, and royal *ostikans came to ask whether he would not accept to serve the religion of the Magians so as not to die. But he would not agree to this, desiring to die joyfully for his God. When they came to the place of execution, he asked the supervisors of his death that they allow him to pray a little. And he stepped forth, knelt down, and said:[2]

Chapter lvii. Zuit^c's prayer at the time of his death.[1]

"Our Creator who didst create the heavens and *earth and sea out of nothing, and didst create us from dust, and thus made earthly beings alive, wise, and rational,[2] and who didst bestow upon us Thy wisdom, which Thou didst show to the *races of the sons of men through Thy holy prophets, Thy precursors. Then Thou didst come down Thyself, become man, manifest Thyself on *earth, and walk among men.[3] And Thou didst bestow upon Thy creatures Thy perfect wisdom, which Thou didst preach through Thy apostles to Thy creatures in this *world. And Thou madest all wise through Thy holy *teachers, whom Thou didst put as luminaries in Thy church. And me, a man unworthy, Thou didst make worthy of Thy *service. And Thou didst prepare me, a miserable creature, to be nurtured and taught by the great and holy *high-priest Nersēs,[4] Thy minister, to receive from him priestly ordination, and to be consecrated into the priesthood by his hand. And in this dignity, Thou didst prepare me to drink the martyr's 'cup of salvation,' which I will drink 'calling upon the name of the *Lord, I will pray to the *Lord in the presence of all His people.'[5] To Thee be *glory and power and *dominion, and to Thy Only-begotten beloved Son Jesus Christ, and to Thy vivifying Holy Spirit, before all eternity, and now, and ever and unto eternity of eternities, Amen."

And when he had said all this, the large crowd that had assembled replied: "Amen." Then the *supervisors of the execution grew angry that they had allowed him to speak so long and they hurriedly brought him to the place of death. And with great joy he stretched out his neck and died by the *sword.

177

Chapter lviii. Concerning the coming of Šapuh king of Persia to the *land of Armenia; and the total extermination of those remaining in the* *land of Armenia; and the multitude evils that they endured.*[1]

After this, Šapuh king of Persia set out with all the forces under his *authority and came to the *land of Armenia, and his *guides[2] were Vahan from the Mamikonean *house and Meružan from the Arcruni *house. They came and invaded the *land of Armenia, took all the prisoners and collected them together. And many of the Armenian *naχarars abandoned their wives, children, and households and fled hither and yon.[3] And the invaders collected together all the wives of the Armenian *naχarars, whom they had abandoned in their flight, and brought them to Šapuh king of Persia.

The *camp of Šapuh king of Persia was then in the *district of Bagrewand, on the ruins of the *city of Zarehawan, which the Persian army had destroyed in its previous coming.[4] And all the remaining captives of the Armenian *realm were brought and assembled before the king of Persia. Then Šapuh king of Persia ordered †all the adult men trampled by elephants, and all the women and children impaled on carriage-poles.[5] They killed thousands upon thousands and myriads upon myriads, so that there was no number or count to the slain. As for the wives of the *azats and *naχarars who had fled, he ordered them brought to the *racecourse of the *city of Zarehawan. And he ordered all these *noblewomen stripped naked and seated here and there on the *racecourse. And King Šapuh himself rode out on horseback, galloped among the women, and took for himself one by one whichever of them caught his eye for foul copulation. For his *tent had been erected near the *racecourse [and] he entered into it to perform his iniquitous acts. And he treated the women in this fashion for many days.[6] And as for the *race of the *house of Siwnik⁽, they slaughtered all the adult men and killed all the women, and he ordered all the young boys made into eunuchs and carried off to the *land of Persia. And he did all this to avenge himself on Andovk,[7] because of the war against Nerseh king of Persia.[8]

Šapuh king of Persia likewise ordered *fortresses built in the most *impregnable localities of Armenia and he also ordered *keepers installed there. And he apportioned the *noblewomen among these *fortresses and left there, so that if their husbands did not come to *serve him, the *keepers-of-the-fortresses should kill the wives left with them. And he left the Zik and Karēn with a large army as *rulers in the *realm. And he gave *authority over the survivors to Vahan and Meružan, and went himself to Atrpatyakan.[9]

178

84   *Chapter lix. Concerning the time that Vahan and Meružan remained, and the great harm they did to the *land of Armenia; and how Vahan and his wife were killed by their own son.*[1]

Then Vahan Mamikonean and Meružan Arcruni, those two foul and iniquitous men who had rebelled against the *covenant of God's service and accepted to serve the godless doctrine of the Mazdeans, then began to destroy the churches and the place of Christian worship in all the *regions of the *land of Armenia, in every *district and every *region. And they constrained many men fallen under their power to abandon the worship of God and turn to the service of the Mazdeans.[2] And after this, Vahan and Meružan gave out an order concerning the wives of the *naχarars whom they had left behind as they fled. They gave an order to the *fortresses to compel the women to turn to the religion of the Mazdeans, and if they did not accept, to put all of them cruelly to death. And when the *keepers-of-the-fortresses received this order they constrained whichever one was in their keeping, in accordance with the order given. But when †not a single one agreed to apostatize from Christianity, they cruelly killed every one of them in all the *fortresses where they were confined.[3]

Now Vahan had a half-sister from the Mamikonean *house named Hamazaspuhi, she was the sister of Vardan and wife of Garegin, *lord of the *district of Ṙštunikᶜ.[4] Her husband Garegin fled and left her at the time that Šapuh king of Persia came to the *land of Armenia, but the *lady of Ṙštunikᶜ [remained] in the *citadel of the *fortress of Van, which was a *city in the *district of Tosb. But the iniquitous Vahan and Meružan ordered the *keeper-of-the-fortress to bring pressure on this woman, and if she did not accept the religion of the Mazdeans, they ordered her

185   hanged from a high tower and killed. Since Hamazaspuhi would not agree to keep the Mazdean laws, they carried her to a lofty tower that stood on a rocky height and looked in the direction of the lake on the side of the river, stripped her naked as she had come from her mother's [womb], tied her feet with a rope, and hanged her head down from that high place. And thus she died on the gallows. But her body was white and luminous to see, so that it remained hanging like a marvellous apparition. Her body shone from on high with a whiteness like snow, and day after day many people gathered to see it as a miraculous manifestation in the *realm. Beholding the sight of the *lady Hamazaspuhi, a woman, her *nurse [*dayeak*] put on a tunic called *anakiwłos*[5] and tied a girdle around herself. And she stood at the rocky height, below the tower from which her nursling was hanging, until all the flesh was stripped from her body. And as the bones happened to fall down, she gathered up into her bosom all the bones of her nursling, and taking them she went to her own [kinsmen].

So evil were these two men that they did not even have compassion on anyone of their own, but mercilessly condemned strangers and their own families alike. They erected *atrušan*s in many localities and subjected men to the Mazdean religion. They also built *atrušan*s in many of their own *hereditary domains[6] and handed over their children and *kinsmen to the teachings of the Mazdeans. Then a son of Vahan, whose name was Samuēl, killed his father Vahan as well as his mother Ormizduχt, who was the sister of King Šapuh, and himself fled to the *land of Xałtek[c].[7]

Fifth Book of Biwzand

Fifth Listing of What I Shall Present, [i.e.,] the Arrangement of the Book

Chronological Tables

i. Concerning the enthronement of Pap in the *land of the Greeks; his coming to Armenia and taking possession of his *realm; and how he was altogether successful in all he did.

ii. Concerning the Armenian *commander-in-chief, Mušeł; how he fell on the *camp of Šapuh king of Persia and struck it a frightful blow, so that Šapuh alone escaped on horseback.

iii. Concerning the *hayr-*mardpet and the way that King Pap ordered him killed.

iv. Concerning the second battle that took place at the *town of Bagawan in the *district of Bagrawand between Pap king of Armenia and the Persian army.

v. Concerning another battle between the Armenians and the Persians at Ganjak of Atrpayakan [sic], and the warning of Uřnayr, so that the Armenians were victorious on that occasion as well.

vi. Concerning the *mardpet Głak, who was appointed *guardian-of-the-*border and who became a confidant of the Persian king; and how he plotted to betray the king of Armenia. And concerning Głak's death at [the order of] King Pap.

vii. Concerning the death of Aršak king of Armenia. How he died by his own hand in the *fortress of Andməš in the *land of Xužastan, and Drastamat was the cause of his death.

viii. Concerning the way in which war came to an end on the Persian side. Then the *sparapet* Mušeł began to wage war against those who had once rebelled against the king of Armenia. struck with mighty combats on many sides, and first of all over the *domain of the Armenian king in Atrpayakan [sic].

  ix. Concerning Noširakan.

  x. Concerning Korduk‘, Kordik‘, and Tmorik‘.

  xi. Concerning the Mark‘.

  xii. Concerning Arjaχ.

  xiii. Concerning Ałuank‘ [Albania].

  xiv. Concerning the Kazbk‘.

  xv. Concerning Virk‘ [Iberia].

  xvi. Concerning the *district of Ałjnik‘.

  xvii. Concerning Great Cop‘k‘.

  xviii. Concerning Angełtun.

  xix. Concerning the *district of Anjit.

  xx. Concerning Mušeł, *sparapet* of Armenia.

  xxi. Concerning Nersēs, *chief-bishop of Armenia, the kind of man that he was, and the great marvels he performed.

  xxii. Concerning King Pap, how he was filled with *dews and was unrighteous.

  xxiii. Concerning the rebukes of St. Nersēs, and how he was ever opposed to King Pap because of his sins.

  xxiv. Concerning the death of the great *chief-bishop Nersēs [at the hands] of King Pap, how and why he was killed by him.

  xxv. Concerning the vision revealed to the holy men Šałitay and Epip‘an while they dwelled on the mountain.

  xxvi. Concerning St. Šałitay.

  xxvii. Concerning St. Epip‘an.

  xxviii. Concerning the great prodigies and miracles manifested by God at Mambrē after the departure of Epip‘an.

188

xxix. Concerning Yusik, who was from the *house of Bishop Ałbianos; whom King Pap installed instead of Nersēs of his own will and without [the approval] of the great *chief-bishop of Caesarea; and how thereafter the *authority of the Armenian *patriarchs to consecrate bishops was taken away.

xxx. Concerning mourning. How they mourned for the *patriarch Nersēs and how they longed for him.

xxxi. Concerning the way in which, after the death of the *patriarch Nersēs, King Pap destroyed out of jealousy all the canonical regulations laid down by Nersēs during his lifetime.

xxxii. Concerning King Pap. How he turned away from the king of the Greeks and was killed by the Greek military *commanders.

xxxiii. Concerning the subsequent council of the Armenian *princes, and how they endured and kept silent.

xxxiv. Concerning the enthronement of Varazdat in the *land of Armenia after Pap.

xxxv. Concerning the way that the Armenian king Varazdat listened to the words of ill-intentioned and senseless men and killed the *sparapet and *commander-in-chief, Mušeł.

xxxvi. Concerning the senseless fantasies of Mušeł's household and of other men.

xxxvii. Concerning the return of Manuēl from Persian captivity and his avenging of Mušeł; and his expulsion of King Varazdat from the *land of Armenia.

xxxviii. Concerning the way in which the Armenian *sparapet Manuēl, together with the entire *realm, gave his hand to the king of Persia and brought the Surēn as first *marzpan and *ruler of the *land of Armenia from the king of Persia; and how he was honored by him with great gifts; and how a rebellion occurred as a result of the deceit of Meružan Arcruni and war broke out.

xxxix. Concerning Gumand Šapuh; how he was sent by the Persian king to wage war against the Armenians and was slaughtered by Manuēl together with his army.

xl. Concerning Varaz; how he was sent by the Persian king and was slaughtered by Manuēl like the first.

xli. Concerning Mřkan, whom the Persian king sent again with a large army against the Armenian *land and against Manuēl, and who was slaughtered by Manuēl like the first ones.

xlii. Concerning the seven years' peace.

189

xliii. Concerning Meružan Arcruni, who marched with an army against Manuēl and was slaughtered by him.

xliv. Concerning the way that the great *sparapet* Manuēl enthroned the young Aršak, and Manuēl himself then died.

Book V
Chronological Accounts of the
*House of T⁣⁣ᶜorgom, Prince¹ of Armenia

*Chapter i. Concerning the enthronement of Pap in the *land of the Greeks; his coming to Armenia to take possession of his *realm; and the way that he was altogether successful in all he did.²*

After all this Mušeł, the son of Vasak, collected all the remaining men of the *azat-contingents who still survived and went together with them to the king of the Greeks.³ He presented the supplication of the Armenian *realm, [set forth] all the tribulations they had endured, and requested the *emperor [to set] Aršak's son Pap over the Armenian *realm. The great king of the Greeks enthroned Pap the son of Aršak over the Armenian *realm as [Mušeł] had requested him, and the king of the Greeks gave them great support, sending to Armenia together with Pap a *stratelat named Tērent and a certain *count Adē with six million men.⁴

They set out and reached the *border of Armenia, and Mušeł became *sparapet and *commander-in-chief of Armenia in place of his father Vasak.⁵ And all those who had scattered, fled, and hidden in the *land of Armenia returned and gathered together. Then the king, together with all the men of the Armenian *realm—the *magnates, *keepers-of-districts and 192 the *district-lords—sought the great *patriarch Nersēs. All those assembled sought the great kat⁣ᶜołikos Nersēs because they knew that he could pray and implore God for the welfare of the entire *realm of Armenia and for its salvation from its enemies; because God granted him whatever he requested from God; furthermore, that he could give them profitable counsel because of his wisdom. Hence, it was no small matter [for them] to seek out such a man able to give them profitable and wise counsel and, depending on current circumstances, to direct [them] toward useful means through which they might be able to pursue the paths that lay before them.⁶

Then King Pap himself, together with the Armenian *nobility, went and found the *chief-bishop Nersēs; he implored [him] that as the father of all Armenia he should be their *spiritual-leader with good counsel, and that he should also pray for them. And so they barely persuaded him with great difficulty to come with them to the *royal-camp, for he had not come to the *royal-camp from the time of the death of Gnel to that of the enthronement of Pap. But at that time, through great entreaties they brought him with them to the *royal-camp.[7] And so he was their overseer and counselor, their director and *spiritual-leader, and he constantly implored God for their sake. And he was a *spiritual-leader with wisdom in [all] things, the perpetual sharer of cares, the reliever of suffering through his prayers; and he ever showed himself to all in every way a father.

Then the *sparapet* Mušeł organized, equipped, and regulated all the *contingents of the Armenian army, and he reviewed all the army *contingents under his command, [which numbered] ten thousand men. He led all of them forth with resplendent *banners and unfurled standards, arrayed, and prepared to wage war. And so, the Armenian *sparapet* Mušeł displayed the Armenian army in review before their King Pap and the great *high-priest Nersēs, and before the Greek *commanders Tērent and Adē. And Pap king of Armenia was most grateful to the *commander-in-chief Mušeł and bestowed the *greatest gifts upon him, and the Roman *commanders were likewise grateful to him. And the *chief-bishop Nersēs also †blessed the *commander-in-chief Mušeł, and said: "May Christ the *Lord bless thee and favor thee, and bestow upon thee the grace of victory †for all the days of thy life. May He save the *land of Armenia through thee and thy *clan forevermore."[8]

Then the Armenian *commander-in-chief Mušeł arrayed a *contingent and made it ready, and he went together with the Armenian *contingent as a vanguard ahead of King Pap and the *imperial *contingent of the Greek army. Then, Mušeł attacked boldly[9] in the *district of Daranałikᶜ. He came in the van to the Armenian Midlands, killed the Persian *commanders, the Karēn and the Zik,[10] †put all their forces to the *sword, and †left not a one of them alive.[11] And he reconquered his own *land all the way to the *borders at Ganjak of Atrpatakan, and held it.[12]

And so, King Pap entered the *land of Armenia and ruled over it. He seized the strongly *fortified-*strongholds taken by the Persians, and also the *fortress of Darōynkᶜ in the *land of Kog where the immense treasures of the Aršakuni were kept. For the *keepers-of-the-fortress had proved faithful. And although the Persians kept attacking this *fortress from the time that the Armenian king Aršak had been taken to Persia, they had not been able to capture it from that time until the coming of Pap to the *land of Armenia, so that the treasure was preserved and transmitted in its entirety to Pap on his return. And the Greek forces in Eṙand and Baχišn were distributed throughout the *districts of the *land of Armenia,[13] †but the malignant Meružan alone fled on a single horse.[14]

The Armenian *commander-in-chief Mušeł moved about the *land

and destroyed the Mazdean *atrušans. As for the Mazdeans, wherever they seized them, the *sparapet Mušeł ordered them taken and roasted with fire.[15] And they cruelly put to death many of the *keepers-of-fortresses. Many *distinguished *lords who had been *honored before by the Persian king were also taken by Mušeł;[16] he ordered their skins flayed off, stuffed with straw, and placed on top of the walls. He did this in many places to avenge his father Vasak.[17]

And so, everything that had been destroyed by the enemy was rebuilt and the churches restored. The kingdom was gradually renewed and current affairs gradually improved and prospered. And St. Nersēs [their] wise *patriarch gave *spiritual-guidance and illuminated them. He admonished and regulated and built refuges for the poor as had been his custom from the beginning,[18] and he instituted the best regulations for the conduct of the kingdom, such as he had seen under the ancient kings. And above all [else] he restored and put in order the service of the church, the offices of bishops, priests, and deacons, and he completely restored the buildings of the church and the *martyria [*vkayanoc*k*c] and so he [both] taught and embellished.

[As for] the Armenian *commander-in-chief, Mušeł, he put his *contingent in order, went to the *border, and took his stand there. And at the order of Pap his king, he †watched carefully over the *borders of his *land and guarded his *realm.[19]

*Chapter ii. Concerning the Armenian *commander-in-chief, Mušeł; how he fell on the *camp of Šapuh king of Persia and struck it a frightful blow, so that Šapuh alone escaped on horseback.[1]*

Then Mušeł son of Vasak, the *stratelat of Greater Armenia, selected from among the *azats and his *kinsmen forty thousand choice men †with one mind, one accord, and one will.[2] He equipped them with horses, *weapons, and provisions, and taking them with him, he went to the *border of Atrpačank*c [sic] to guard the Armenian *realm. At that time Šapuh king of Persia likewise made ready his own army with every preparation and came to the *land of Atrpayakan [sic]; Meružan *led[3] a *contingent of his *army [banak], whereas the *home-camp [bun anak] of the king was *disposed [banakeal] at T*cawrēš.[4]

Then Mušeł, the *sparapet and *commander-in-chief of Armenia, †attacked the *camp with his forty thousand [men], set to the task, and destroyed it. And Šapuh king of Persia then †barely escaped alone on horseback and fled, while Mušeł together with the Armenian forces †put to the *sword the entire *karawan of his *camp;[5] for they slaughtered many, took prisoner many of the Persian *nobles, and seized as booty the treasure of the Persian king. They also seized the *queen-of-queens, together with the other women.[6] And the *sparapet Mušeł captured the whole of the *royal-pavilion as well as all the *nobles, some six hundred men. The Armenian *commander-in-chief Mušeł ordered their skins flayed off, stuffed with straw, and taken to Pap king of Armenia. And he did this to avenge his father Vasak.[7]

But the Armenian *commander-in-chief Mušeł allowed no one to insult the wives of Šapuh king of Persia in any way. On the contrary, he had litters prepared for all of them and he sent them all back to their husband King Šapuh. And he sent off some of the Persians along with them so that they would come safe and sound to Šapuh king of Persia. And the Persian king was amazed at the benevolence of Mušeł, at his *valor and his *nobility [*azatut^ciwn*], because he had inflicted no offense on him on account of his wives.[8] Now in those days Mušeł possessed a charger, a white steed. And whenever Šapuh king of Persia took [a cup] of wine in his hand to drink in the hour of festivity, as he entertained his forces, he would say: "Let the rider of the white horse drink!" And he ordered a cup decorated with the portrait of Mušeł with his white steed, and in the hour of festivity he placed the cup in front of himself and constantly he remembered, repeating the same words: "Let the rider of the white horse drink!"[9]

But Mušeł and the whole Armenian army took boundless booty from the Persian *camp and became immeasurably rich with treasures and possessions. And they also reserved a large portion of the booty for
196   Pap their king and for the Armenian forces that had remained there with King Pap. They also gave part of the booty to the Greek *commanders who were with the king of Armenia, and they likewise gave a portion[10] of the great booty they had taken to all the troops. But when the Armenian army returned to its own *realm, many of the troops accused the *sparapet Mušeł before King Pap, saying: "Why did he let the wives of our enemy the king of Persia go free?" And for this reason Pap king of Armenia was quite hostile to Mušeł for a long time.[11]

Chapter iii. Concerning the *hayr-*mardpet *and the way that King Pap ordered him killed.*[1]

Then King Pap was told of the curses of the *hayr-*mardpet against King Pap's mother, *Queen P^caṙanjem; of his taunts during the siege of the *fortress, when he had berated her like a harlot at the time that he had secretly entered [into the *fortress], insulted the *queen, come out, and fled. They related all of this to the king.[2]

And so, while the *hayr-*mardpet was touring his *principality in the *land of Tarōn and the Armenian *sparapet Mušeł was in the same *district in his own *fortress named Ołakan, which stood above the Ep^crat River,[3] a messenger came from the king bearing an *official-letter to the *commander-in-chief, Mušeł. The letter contained a command to put the *hayr-*mardpet cruelly to death. As soon as he received

this command, he undertook it. He deceitfully sent to the *hayr-*mardpet,
197 inviting him to come to him so as to be *honored at the *fortress of
Ołakan. It was then winter time and the Ep‘rat River was frozen solid.
The *hayr-*mardpet came to the *fortress of Ołakan, since he had been
invited [there] to be greatly *honored. [Then] the *commander-in-chief
Mušeł ordered the guards to seize him, strip him naked as he had come
from his mother's [womb], tie his hands under his knees, lower him to the
river, and place him on the frozen river. And so he was killed there, for
when they came the next morning, they saw that his brain had flowed
down from his head because of the cold and emptied out through his
nose. And a certain Głak, who had once performed the same duties of
*mardpet under King Aršak or his father Tiran, [was appointed] to the
office of *hayr-*mardpet in his place.[4]

*Chapter iv. Concerning the second battle that took place at the
*town of Bagawan in the *district of Bagrawand between Pap king of
Armenia and the Persian army.*[1]

After this, the king of Persia once again gathered all his strength and
all his might, set forth with his entire army, and came to the *realm of
Atrpayakan [sic]. He himself remained there with a few men, but he sent
the entire mass of his forces to make war against King Pap. And so, the
Persian army came and raided into the Armenian Midlands. Then Pap
king of Armenia likewise ordered the army assembled at Bagawan. And
the Greek forces that were in Ełand and Baχišn[2] came to King Pap and
assembled together. And they dug a ditch around their *camp near Mount
Npat by the Ep‘rat River, arrayed themselves and made ready for battle.
Then the *sparapet and *commander-in-chief of Armenia, Mušeł,
collected the entire Armenian army, more than ninety thousand [men],
and made it ready. Now Uṙnayr, king of Ałuank‘, was with the Persian
198 king at the time that Šapuh king of Persia was disposing his forces against
the Armenian *realm and the Greek army.[3] And Uṙnayr came forth and
†asked a reward from Šapuh king of Persia, and said: †"May it please
you, *most-valiant-of-men![4] to order this reward [granted] to me: that I,
with my own *contingent, might go forward as a champion against the
*contingent of Pap king of Armenia; for it is proper that the Aryan[5]
*contingent face the Greek forces, whereas I will go against the Armenian
*princes with my own *contingent. King Šapuh was pleased, thanked
him, and gave the order. But Meružan Arcruni †answered Uṙnayr, [and]
said: "You are now grasping thorns in your arms, but if you are able to
gather them, that will be most surprising."[6] And Meružan sent a secret
warning to the Armenian *commander-in-chief Mušeł by means of a
courier, telling him: "Mušeł, be advised and ready! For with much boast-
ing, King Uṙnayr of Ałuank‘ has asked for you as a reward, now you
know what you should do."

Now at the time that the Persian army was marching[7] against Armenia together with Uṙnayr king of Ałuankᶜ and his contingent, the king of Ałuankᶜ †spoke to those who were with him, and said: "Bear in mind and remember when you take the Greek troops prisoner that you should leave many of them alive, for we will take them in fetters to Ałuankᶜ[8] to work as brickmakers, stonecutters, and masons for the needs of our *cities, *palaces, and other needs."[9]

When the two *contingents of the Greeks and the Persians drew near to each other and were preparing to engage each other, King Pap of Armenia in person equipped himself, armed and made ready, desiring to enter the fray. But the Greek *commander Terēnt †would not agree to his entering the contest and said: "The king of the Greeks sent us [here] on account of you [saying]: 'Go and protect him.' But now, should anything happen to you, how shall we face our king or answer him? Should it happen that we survive here without you and come before our king, we shall then answer our king with our heads. Therefore, O king, do what we say. Take the *chief-bishop of Armenia Nersēs and go up to sit in a safe and *inaccessible place on Mount Npat. And let the holy *chief-archbishop offer up prayers and implore the *Lord that the *Lord give us victory. And looking [down] from on high you will see our zealous efforts in the fray and the *valor or cowardice performed before you."

King Pap was convinced by these words, he took the great *high-priest Nersēs with him, went up, and took his stance on Mount Npat, while all the forces of the Greeks and the Armenians went down to the site of the combat. Then the *sparapet and *commander-in-chief Mušeł also came up, bringing his standards and *weapons[10] to the *chief-bishop Nersēs so that he should bless them, and [then] he [himself] would go down into the fray. And at that moment King Pap †remembered the old tales and said: "I have [now] remembered that Mušeł is a friend of the Persian king Šapuh. Is he not the Mušeł who sent off the wives of the Persian king Šapuh in litters and with attending guards? And I have also heard that he is talking to the Persians. Therefore, let him not enter into combat."[11]

Then the *commander-in-chief Mušeł made the great *high-priest Nersēs his intercessor before King Pap. But the king said to the *chief-bishop Nersēs: "Do not intercede for him! For as soon as he goes down he will fall in with the Persian army." But [Nersēs] intensified his mediation all the more.[12] And since at that time the king did not disregard any of his words, he said to Nersēs: †"Your will be done,[13] but first let him swear by your right hand that he shall not be false to us, then let him go into battle." Then Mušeł was called before the king; he came and prostrated himself in front of the king, grasped the right hand of the *chief-bishop Nersēs, and swore. Similarly, he also took the hand of King Pap, †swore, and said: "I shall live and die for thee like my ancestors for thy ancestors, like my father for thy father Aršak,[14] this also shall I do for thee, but only do not listen to slanderers."

Then the Armenian *high-priest Nersēs blessed him with many benedictions. And Pap king of Armenia ordered his own warhorse and *spear given to the *valiant *commander-in-chief Mušeł, but he did not take them, saying: "I shall fight with my own [arms], and then, O king, whatever you give, I am in your hands." And he proffered his own standard and *weapons to Nersēs for his blessing. Then he rode off with his *contingent, and drawing up the entire Armenian battle line to the right of the Greek army, he advanced forward on the right [flank].

King Pap and the *chief-bishop Nersēs remained on Mount Npat, and raising his ever-outstretched arms to heaven, St. Nersēs prayed to the *Lord:[15] "May the *Lord preserve His *covenant and His holy church bought with His *precious [*patuakan*] blood.[16] Let Him not give over His people into the hands of the godless heathens, so that it shall never be said among the heathen: 'Where is their God?'"[17] While he offered his prayers to God, the entire front of the Armenian forces charged forth like fire against the Persian army, and Mušeł's *contingent rushed forward impetuously ahead of the other *contingents until it disappeared from the sight of the watching king, until Mušeł's standards were no longer visible to the king.[18] And when his standards became invisible, King Pap †began to shout at Nersēs, and said: "You have deceived[19] me and burned me for I said to you: 'Do not send that man into battle.' [Now] behold, he has gone over to the Persians and will cause us the *greatest harm." But the *chief-bishop Nersēs replied: "No, king, do not believe it! For that many is not false to us, and you will see yourself the [deeds] of *valor that your *servant will perform before you."

And King Pap insistently urged the *chief-bishop Nersēs, saying [to 201 him]: "Pray assiduously and implore the *Lord while they are still in combat." But since he importuned him greatly, the *chief-bishop Nersēs said to King Pap: "If you were to turn your heart unto the *Lord, He would show compassion to you and to this *realm. And if you were to cleanse yourself of your foul deeds, He would receive you and would not let you go from [His] hand. He would not give you over to your enemies.[20] But who am I that you should entreat me, as though I, a miserable creature, in opposition to His will, to whatever God wishes to do, were able to address prayers to Him, prayers that would alter His will. For it is He who created all out of nothing and holds the universe in His hand,[21] 'and the inhabitants in it are as grasshoppers';[22] Who 'measured . . . the heaven with a span, and all the *earth in His palm; Who has placed the mountains on the scales and the fields in a balance; Who has known the wisdom of His Father; and was His counselor;'[23] and Who together with His Father renders all judgments. For even now He has put the East, the West, the North, and the South on the scales and holds high the scales. And, depending on the side to which the scales shall incline according to the weight of sins, so shall He judge His creatures. For He knows the measure of the deeds of His creatures and rewards them in accordance with the worth of their deeds. For now is the time of castigation and the time of rebuke[24] and the time of judgment. For at this time it is not men who contend with men in war, but the *Judge-of-judges who has risen to judge the *earth. For this hour is the time of judgment. Who is it who shall be able to open his mouth before Him at such a time? 'Who knows the mind of the *Lord that he may also be His instructor?'[25] For all is from Him and in Him and through Him, and *glory be to Him for evermore.[26] For if the *Lord reward us according to our sins, we cannot go against His will or ask anything of Him; but we must say,[27] 'Justly hast Thou brought all this upon us, for Thou art righteous, *Lord, and all Thy works are true. Thy ways are straight and all Thy judgments are right. For just are the judgments that Thou hast brought upon us in all that Thou hast brought upon 202 us . . . for justly and rightly hast Thou brought [all this] upon us because of our sins. For we have sinned and transgressed and rebelled against Thee. We have sinned altogether and not obeyed Thy Commandments. We have not kept them, neither have we done as Thou commanded us, that we might find good from Thee. Now all that Thou hast done and whatever Thou hast brought upon us, Thou has done through true judgment. For Thy judgments are sweet.[28] . . . Do not give us over altogether for Thy name's sake. . . . Deliver us according to Thy marvelous works . . . and give *glory to Thy name, O *Lord! . . . So that those who hope in Thee may never suffer shame. Let their violence be shamed and let all their might be crushed and let them know that Thou alone art the *Lord God, who art *glorified over the entire universe. Everywhere and in all ways let only Thy almighty will be done, Who art mighty and powerful and just in all things, and Who lovest to show mercy to the oppressed and the anguished. Thou knowest that which profiteth us, O *Lord, and to prepare for us what pleaseth Thee. For if affliction profit us, augment it. And if mercy be pleasing to Thee, grant it to us. For whatever shall be the will of the *Lord in heaven, so may it be fulfilled; and with whatever rod Thou shalt wish to chastise us, we are every hour in Thy hands. Have mercy, O *Lord, on the iniquities and sins and transgressions of Thy *servants. For who is the man who has not transgressed or sinned before Thee? For no one is just upon the *earth, †not a single one, [not] a one.[29] For Thou alone art without sin, and only Thou art just who hast created us out of nothing, and brought us to this life; and [thou] hast shown us the way of life and salvation,[30] and thus hast made us terrestial beings wise and rational, and who hast become our salvation, for Thou hast made us reach an immortal lot. Remember Thy church, which Thou didst buy with Thy holy blood, and do not hand over to dogs what has been consecrated to Thee.[31] But [because] Thy mercy is all-encompassing, may

it turn the fury of Thy wrath away from Thy *congregation and deliver
Thy church, O *Lord our God.'"

Thus he spoke such and similar words all the while that he was on
203 the mountain, and still more than these, while King Pap stood on the
mountain beside him. And he offered up numerous and varied prayers
until evening, until the setting of the sun, until the end of the combat.

And during the battle, God's help came down upon the Greeks, and
the Armenian *contingent became victorious, while the Persian *contingent was given over to defeat. They turned in flight, dispersed, and
scattered over the fields, the lofty mountains, and the deep gorges. The
Greek and Armenian forces followed, caught up with them, and slaughtered them both great and small. But †a few of the multitude who were well
mounted [kʿaǰajikʿ] escaped.³² Then the Armenian army pursued the fugitives; they harassed the Persian forces all the way to Ganjak of Atrpayakan
[sic] on the *borders of Armenia, and slaughtered many of the fugitives
along the way. And the Armenian *sparapet Mušeł struck frightful blows
at the Persian forces; he lay in wait for the *contingent of the Ałuankʿ,
encountered and annihilated their entire army. And he caught up with
Uṙnayr king of Ałuankʿ, who was fleeing, and struck him over the head
with many blows of the shaft of his *lance, saying, "Be grateful that you
are a king and wear a crown, for I will not kill a king, even though great
harm come to me."³³ And he allowed him to escape with eight horsemen
and go to the *realm of Ałuankʿ.

And when all the Armenian forces returned, the number of enemy
heads brought by the Armenian *commander-in-chief Mušeł before Pap
king of Armenia was beyond count. And the same [was done] by all the
*naxarars and *magnates, each according to his capacity, as well as the
whole of the army. And [so] there was a great victory in the *land of
Armenia and among the Greek troops. And they were satiated with
abundant booty—treasures, *weapons, ornaments, gold and silver, and
many supplies, as well as horses, mules, and camels that they captured—
for there was neither count nor measure to it, but it was exceedingly great.

Then, however, †slanderous reports concerning the *commander-in-
chief Mušeł [reached] the great King Pap and said: "Know, O king, that
204 he is deceiving you greatly and is plotting your death,³⁴ for he has always
allowed your foes to go free. He has seized enemies a great many times
and is accustomed to let them go free, for he released King Uṙnayr and
allowed your opponent whom he had seized to remain alive."³⁵ And
discord arose many times between King Pap and the *commander-in-
chief Mušeł on account of these things, and the king reproached him
many times for these things. But the *commander-in-chief Mušeł †an-
swered King Pap, and said: "I have killed all of my equals, but those who
wear the crown are not my equals but yours.³⁶ Go and kill yours, as I have
killed mine. But I have never raised my hand against a man [who is] king,

against one who wears a crown; nor do I raise it [now], nor will I ever. If you wish to kill me, kill me. But as for me, if ever a king falls into my hands, as has happened many times, I will not kill a king, one who wears a crown, even though anyone should kill me."[37]

When King Pap heard these words he shed tears, rose from his *throne, grasped Mušeł, embraced him, †wept on Mušeł's neck, and said: "Those who dare speak ill of a man as *valorous and *honorable as Mušeł deserve death. For he is a man of as *honorable a *race as ours, and his ancestors were like ours. For his ancestors abandoned their kingdom in the *realm of the Čenkʿ and came to our ancestors.[38] They lived and died for our ancestors, his father died for my father,[39] and he has faithfully toiled to the [very brink] of death. Many times God has granted us victory through the prayers and supplications of our wondrous father Nersēs, and he has granted us much peace by the hand of this [man]. How [can] they speak such words to me as: 'Mušeł is plotting your death'?[40] For he is a loyal man indeed. If he has spared foreign kings through friendship, how could he raise his hand against his *true lord?" And at that time King Pap granted many rewards and *honors and numerous *villages to the *commander-in-chief Mušeł.[41]

205   *Chapter v. Concerning another battle between the Armenians and the Persians at Ganjak of Atrpayakan, and the warning of Uṙnayr, so that the Armenian *contingent was victorious on that occasion as well.*[1]

Then Uṙnayr king of Ałuankʿ warned Mušeł. He sent him a messenger, †gave him information, [and] said: "I am deeply grateful that you did not slay me, for the *Lord delivered me into your hands and you spared [me]. I shall not forget this kindness of yours as long as I live.[2] But [now] let me forewarn you that Šapuh king of Persia is preparing to come with his entire army and fall unexpectedly upon you." Then, the Greek *stratelat[3] arrayed the forces that were under his command and led them forth to the *border of Armenia toward the *side of Ganjak in the *domain [tun] of Atrpayakan. In like manner, Mušeł also gathered together all the Armenian forces, which consisted of ninety thousand choice well-armed men [bearing] *spears in their hands, in addition to the *shield-bearers. And these too, in accordance with the forewarning, made haste and soon reached their own *borders. But the king alone remained where he was in the Armenian *realm. The *chief-bishop Nersēs also remained in the *realm and sent out a call ordering the entire *land to pray for the soldiers who were at war.

Šapuh king of Persia came with his entire army to the site of the battle and found the Greek army and the Armenian *contingent already drawn up and ready for military action.[4] They joined in battle, and the Persian forces suffered defeat. Above all the *contingent of the *spearmen attacked fiercely, *valiantly hurling their foes to the ground from their steeds directly before Šapuh king of Persia.[5] And at their fall the entire host of

206   Armenian warriors called out encouragingly, shouting out these words: "To[6] Aršak the *Brave!" Every foe whom they slew in this fray they dedicated to their *valiant king Aršak.[7] [To] every one whom they slew they said: "Be thou a sacrifice to Aršak our king." And whenever the heroic Armenian *azat *spearmen attacked and felled the host of Persian *spearmen, they shouted out inspiringly: "To Aršak the *Brave!" And whenever they slew their foes and struck off their heads, they said: "Be thou a sacrifice to Aršak!"[8]

And the multitude of the *legion,[9] that is to say the *shield-bearers of the Greek forces and likewise the *shield-bearers of Armenia, supported the Armenian host enclosed within their *shields, like a *fortified *city [standing] in the rear.[10] Whenever the Persian army began to crowd the Greek army or the *contingent of Armenian *spearmen, these [turned] to the Greek *shield-bearing *legion or to the *shield-bearers of Armenia as though entering into a *fortress, and sought respite. But when, barely having caught their breath, they sallied forth from there and attacked, they killed and struck off the heads of countless Persian warriors fallen before them. And calling out the same invocation to Aršak their king, they slew immeasurable and untold numbers of the Persian host. But when the Persian army again gained over them to some degree, they turned as to an *impregnable *fortress to the *shield-bearing forces of the *legion, and these, opening their *shields, let them in and held them enclosed. And on that day, the Greek army with its *stratelat, Terēnt, and the Armenian *contingent with its *sparapet, Mušeł, struck down and destroyed the Persian host. And †Šapuh king of Persia with a few men fled from the battlefield,[11] whereas they [the Armenians] set *border-guards and themselves returned to their own king Pap with great renown, fair booty, and magnificent splendor.

But when Šapuh king of Persia reached the *realm under his *dominion, †he wondered at the *valor of the fighting *contingent displayed before him, and said:[12] "I marvel at what I myself have seen. For
207   from my childhood I have constantly taken part in warfare and battles, and many years have passed since I became king, and not a single year have I lived without combat. Yet the most ardent contest that ever I saw was the one I witnessed on this occasion. For whenever the Armenian *spearmen advanced, they attacked like a lofty mountain or like a solid, powerful, and immovable tower, and whenever we pressed them a little, they found refuge in the *legion of the Romans,[13] and these, opening the protective wall of their *shields, received them as into a walled and *fortified *city. Then, barely having caught their breath, they sallied forth again and fought until they had annihilated the Aryan host.[14] And at this too do I marvel, at the †steadfast devotion of the Armenian *contingent in its love for its *lord.[15] For so many years have passed since Aršak their *lord has been lost to them, and yet, they were inspired by him in battle. And

whenever they struck down their foe, they ever called out: "To Aršak," and yet he was not among them. But because of the intense devotion they bore to their own *true-lord, they dedicated to him every foe that they slew. Or what of the raging *contingent of Mušeł? It seemed to me that fire and flames arose from that *contingent and from its standards. Like the blaze of a conflagration it coursed through the *host [*gund*] like flame through the reeds.[16] And so many years have passed since Aršak their *lord has been lost to them, for he lies in the *castle of Andməš in the *land of Xužastan,[17] yet they, in their piety, believed that he stood at their head as their king; that he stood with them in the midst of the *host [*gund*], at the head of the fray, and that they performed their service to him in his very presence.[18] "Lo," said he: "blessed be he who may be *lord of the Armenian *host, of such †faithful, and loyal warriors devoted to their *lord."[19]

208   *Chapter vi. Concerning the* *mardpet *Głak, who was appointed* *guardian-of-the-border, and who became a confidant of the Persian king; and how he plotted to betray the king of Armenia; and concerning Głak's death at [the order of] King Pap.*[1]

Then Terēnt the *commander of the Greek army and Mušeł the *commander-in-chief of the Armenian army left the *mardpet *Głak— who was called "Father of the king" because of his office—as *warden-of-the-border at Ganjak, which marked the *frontier between Persia and Armenia. And thirty thousand picked *spear-bearers in full array, well-armed, armored, and *mail-clad, remained with him; whereas Terēnt and Mušeł returned with all their forces to the *realm, to King Pap. But the *mardpet *Głak sent secret messengers to Šapuh king of Persia, promising to hand over to him Pap king of Armenia, and the Greek *commander Terēnt, and the Armenian *commander-in-chief Mušeł, and he received gifts of enormous treasures from him in recompense. But the other *mightiest *naχarars who were with him—Gnel *lord-of-the-district of Anjewac'ik' and others who had remained there—secretly informed King Pap.

Then King Pap sent an envoy to [tell] the *mardpet *Głak: "Collect the army that is under your command and hand it over to Gnel Anjewac'i, and come quickly, for I must send you to Šapuh king of Persia, for I shall make my *submission to him." The *mardpet *Głak was very pleased when he heard this and said to himself: "It will now be easy for me to carry out my plan, which I promised to the Persian king Šapuh. Now I have found the means to lull Pap with words into unwariness and carelessness, and then to bring the Persian king †suddenly and unexpectedly down on his head." And he was greatly encouraged to have been [chosen] as the spokesman between the two kings. He quickly dispatched a messenger on horseback to King Pap to the large *village named Ardeans, at the royal 209 [fortress][2] of the *district of Ayrarat, and he [then] presented himself in person before the king, and was †greatly honored by him. At feasting time, King Pap gave the order to garb the *mardpet in *robes [of honor],[3] and so they clad him in a tunic[4] and trousers. Now these garments were of disproportionately large size and hung down fold over fold, so that he could not adjust them on himself because the amplitude of the garment engulfed him.[5] And as he put on this wide *robe, he tied a girdle around himself from which hung a *short-sword [t ͤur] and he tied a *long-sword [ṣuser] to his side, and a fold of the tunic hung down from the girdle and covered the *short- and the *long-swords. And when he put on the trousers and slippers and strapped a *dagger [nran] to his thigh, the fold of the trousers hung over the *dagger,[6] covering him to the calf. But Głak did not realize that the amplitude of the garment might prove harmful for him.

Then at the ninth hour of the day, †they summoned Głak and said: "You are invited to a feast in the royal court." When they led him into a passageway of the *houses in which the king was residing—a passageway that was long and with many apertures in the ceiling to let through the light[7]—and as they were bringing him through it, *axe-men covered with *shields stood all around, and all the apertures of the ceiling were covered. Then the *shield-bearers closed in around him and pulled him to and fro. But although he grasped at a weapon, he was not able to reach a single one because it was caught in the multifold garment in which he was entangled. And so, although Głak was a tall and well-made man with large and *powerful [k ͤaǰ] bones, the *shield-bearers surrounded him, lifted him up, and carried him to the door of the royal *hall [tačarin ark ͤuni].

But when the king saw that they were bringing him there he said: "Not here, not here! Take him to the *house of the wardrobe." Consequently, the company of *shield-bearers tied his hands behind his back and took him into the passage to the *house of the wardrobe, that is to say to the place where the royal crown was kept. There Głak †began to speak and said: "Tell the king that I deserved this death, but that it was proper for you to kill me in the *public-square and not in the *house of the crown, so as to sully your crown with blood." He had only time to say this, when they cut his throat there in the *house [vank ͤ] of the wardrobe and struck off his head. They [then] fixed it on a *spear and set it up in the *royal-square.

*Chapter vii. Concerning the death of Aršak king of Armenia. How he died by his own hand in the *fortress of Andməš in the *land of Xužastan, and Drastamat was the cause of his death.*[1]

Now at that time Aršak king of Armenia was still alive in the *land under the *dominion of the king of Persia, in the *region of Xužastan, in the *fortress of Andməš, that is the one called the *castle of Anyuš.[2] And about that time, the war between the Persians and the Armenians calmed down because the Aršakuni king of the K ͤušan, who resided in the *city of

Balχ, had stirred up war against Šapuh, the Sasanian king of Persia.³ And so, King Šapuh mustered the entire Persian army and marched forth to wage war against him. He also collected the entire *cavalry taken prisoner from the *land of Armenia and took it along with him,⁴ and he likewise carried with himself to war the eunuch of Aršak king of Armenia. For the Armenian king Aršak had a eunuch, a favorite eunuch named Drastamat, a loyal *ostikan, much *honored and with great *authority.

Now when the war broke out between the king of the K^cušan and the king of Persia, the K^cušan army pressed the Persian forces exceedingly. It killed many of them, took many prisoners, and drove part of them into flight. As for the eunuch Drastamat, in the days of Tiran king of Armenia and of his son Aršak king of Armenia, he had been the *prince of the royal *district [*tan gawaṙin*]⁵ and had been entrusted with the treasures of
211 the *fortress of Angeł and with all the royal *fortresses in those *regions. The treasures of the *fortress of Bnabeł in the *land of Cop^ck^c were also under him, and his *cushion was above that of all the other *naχarars. And since the *office—and that of the *mardpet who was called "Father"— had been an *office held by an eunuch from the very beginning of the kingship of the Aršakuni, the eunuch Drastamat *prince of Angełtun was also carried as a captive into the *land of Persia when Aršak king of Armenia was taken there.

Now this Drastamat was [present] at the battle in which the K^cušan routed Šapuh king of Persia, and Drastamat performed incredible feats of *valor.⁶ He fought so bravely for King Šapuh that he saved him from death, and he slew many of the K^cušan there, and presented to [the king] many heads of his foes. And there he saved Šapuh king of Persia from the pressure of the enemy forces that had closed in on him in the tumult of the fray. And when Šapuh king of Persia returned to the *land of Asorestan, he expressed deep gratitude to the eunuch Drastamat for his services and said to him: "Ask anything from me, and whatever you ask, I shall give and not refuse." And Drastamat said to the king: "I need nothing more from you, but [only that] you give me the order to go and see my own *true-lord Aršak king of Armenia, for one day. And when I shall have come to him, order him released from his bonds. And that I be empowered to wash his head and anoint it, and garb him in a *robe-of-honor,⁷ and set up *banqueting-couches for him, and place roasted meat before him, and give him wine, and gladden him with musicians, for just one day." And King Šapuh replied: "Harsh are the requests you have made, for from the days when the kingdom of Persia was founded and that *fortress was called Anyuš, no one among mankind has dared remind
212 the kings of anyone confined by the kings in that *fortress, by remembering the man in that *fortress, all the more that he is a king and my colleague, my opponent; who has been held chained in that *fortress. Moreover, you have caused us trouble,⁸ and you have indeed destined

yourself for death by recalling Anyuš, [an action] that has never been lawful in the kingdom of the Aryans from its very beginning. But because your services to me have been great, [let] what you have requested be given to you. Go! Let it be given you! But it would have been more fitting for you to ask for *realms, or *districts, or treasures for your own benefit. But because you have requested this, you may transgress the laws of the Persian kingdom. Go! Let what you have asked of me be granted to you in return [for your services.]"

And he gave him a trusty *bodyguard and an *official-letter with the royal seal so that he might go to the *fortress of Anyuš and do what he wished, what he had asked, for the captive Aršak who had once ruled over Armenia. And Drastamat with his *bodyguard came to the *fortress of Anyuš with the *official-letter of the king, and saw his own *true-lord. And he freed Aršak from his iron chains—from the iron bonds on his hands and feet, and from the bonds of the iron yoke upon his neck. And he washed his head and bathed him, and garbed him in a precious *robe-of-honor. And he set out *banqueting-couches for him and made him *recline [on it].[9] And he set before him a meal suitable for kings, and placed before him wine such as was fit for kings. He heartened and comforted him, and gladdened him with *gusans.[10]

And at the time for the presentation of dessert, they placed fruit before [Aršak]—apples and cucumbers and amič,[11] that he might eat. And they gave him a knife that he might cut and eat what he wished. And standing [upright before him] on his feet, Drastamat greatly gladdened and consoled him. But when he had drunk and the wine had gone to his head, he became drunk, grew haughty, and said: "Woe is me, Aršak, and have I become this and come to such a state, and have these travails come over me?" Saying this, he thrust into his heart the knife that was in his hand and with which he had intended to eat the fruit or amič. And there he killed himself, and there he died at that very hour, as he lay on his *banqueting-couch. And when Drastamat saw this, he threw himself on [Aršak], drew the same knife from him, and thrust it into his own side. And there he died at the selfsame hour.[12]

*Chapter viii. Concerning the way in which war came to an end on the Persian *side. Then the *sparapet Mušeł began to wage war against those who had rebelled against the king of Armenia. He struck out with mighty combats on many side, and first of all over the *domain of the Armenian king in Atrpayakan.*[1]

Then, when the war had ceased in the *regions of Persia and military affairs were secured on that *side,[2] the Armenian *sparapet Mušeł began to strike against those who had rebelled against the Aršakuni kingdom.[3] First, he attacked the *domain of the Armenian king in Atrpayakan.[4] He destroyed all the *land of the *districts of Atrpačk[c5] and took a great many prisoners captive from there. He conquered the rest, †subjected [them] to *tribute, and took many hostages from them.[6]

Chapter ix. Concerning Noširakan.[1]

Mušeł attacked the rebellious *realm of Noširakan, which had revolted against the king of Armenia. He took it, destroyed it, took prisoners, and †took hostages from the survivors. And †he subjected the inhabitants of the *land to the imposition of a *tribute.[2]

214   *Chapter x. Concerning Kordukʿ, Kordikʿ, and Tmorikʿ.*[1]

The *sparapet* Mušeł also attacked the following *districts which had rebelled against the king of Armenia, Kordukʿ, Kordikʿ, and Tmorikʿ. He took them, destroyed them, took prisoners, †imposed *tribute on the survivors, and took hostages.[2]

Chapter xi. Concerning the Markʿ.[1]

And he also made a powerful attack on the *region of the Markʿ because they too had rebelled against the king of Armenia. He took many prisoners from them, †imposed *tribute on the survivors, and took hostages.[2]

Chapter xii. Concerning Arjaχ.[1]

He attacked the *land of Arjaχ in a great war and took many prisoners from it. †He took hostages from the survivors and imposed *tribute on the rest.[2]

Chapter xiii. Concerning Ałuankʿ.[1]

He made war on the *land of the Ałuankʿ and struck frightful blows at them. He took away from them many *districts that they had seized: Uti, Šakašēn, the Valley of Gardman, Kołtʿ, and other surrounding *dis-
215 tricts *bordering on them. They set the *border between the *land of Ałuankʿ and their own *land on the Kur River, as it had been before.[2] They killed many of their leaders, †imposed *tribute on the survivors, and took hostages from them.[3]

Chapter xiv. Concerning the Kazbkʿ.[1]

Then the *sparapet* Mušeł sought great vengeance from the *land of the Kazbkʿ[2] and from the *city of Pʿaytakaran in retaliation for their rebellion and betrayal of the king of Armenia. The *sparapet* and *commander-in-chief Mušeł came, beheaded many of them as punishment, took many of them prisoners, and †imposed *tribute on the survivors. He also †took hostages from them and left *ostikan*s there as overseers.[3]

Chapter xv. Concerning Virk^c.¹

Then the **sparapet* Mušeł marched against the king of Virk^c and pressed him hard. He attacked the *land, subjected the entire *realm of the Virk^c,² and †put to the *sword all the *azats and the *naxarar *clans that he found.³ As for the P^cařawazean, the **sparapet* Mušeł ordered them crucified in the *realm of the Virk^c.⁴ He seized and beheaded the **bdeašx* of Gugark^c, who had formerly *served the king of Armenia and subsequently revolted, killed the males of his *clan and took captive its wives and daughters.⁵ He likewise beheaded all the *naxarars of that *region who had rebelled against the king of Armenia. He ravaged the entire *district, †took hostages, and imposed *tribute on the survivors.⁶ Having reconquered the former *border that lay between the *land of Armenia and the *land of the Virk^c, that is, the great Kur River itself, he reinstated it.⁷

216

Chapter xvi. Concerning the king¹ of Ałjnik^c.

Then the *commander-in-chief Mušeł turned to the *land of Ałjnik^c and dealt it mighty blows, for they too had rebelled against the king of Armenia.² He captured the **bdeašx* of Ałjnik^c, killed his wives³ in front of him, and took their children prisoner. †He imposed *tribute on the survivors and left overseers and *ostikans in the *land of Ałjnik^c.⁴

Chapter xvii. Concerning Great Cop^ck^c.¹

Then he raided against Great Cop^ck^c, for it too had rebelled. Mušeł destroyed the *land and *district of Great Cop^ck^c, †put its [noble] *clans to the *sword,² †took hostages, and imposed *tribute on the *clans.³

Chapter xviii. Concerning Angełtun.¹

He greatly devastated Angełtun and †put it to the *sword.² But because it had been a royal *ostan from very ancient times, the population of the *district itself †was subject to *tribute.³

217

Chapter xix. Concerning the *district of Anjit.¹

Then Mušeł attacked and ravaged the *district of Anjit and the *regions of the *districts around it, for they too had rebelled against the Aršakuni kings. He †put to the *sword the *lords-of-the-district,² †took hostages, and conquered it. And he subjected every one of them to the [payment of] *tribute to Pap king of Armenia.³

Chapter xx. Concerning Mušeł, the *sparapet of Armenia.¹

The *valiant *commander-in-chief and **sparapet* of Armenia was filled with great zeal, [urge] for retaliation and much fervor †all the days of his life, and he constantly strove to serve the kingdom of the *realm of Armenia loyally and with faithful service.² Morning and night he was at work, striving and straining to go to war, and he did not allow any—not one handful—of *soil to be taken anywhere from the *confines of the *land of Armenia. He would ever give his life for his *realm and die for his *valorous name, for his own *true-lords, for the inhabitants of the *realm, for the Christian faith, for the people believing in God and baptized in Christ, for the churches, for [their] consecrated vessels, for the *martyria of Christ's [saints], for God's *covenant, for his sisters and his *brothers, for the close relatives of his *house, †for his good and faithful friends. The *commander-in-chief Mušeł fought heroically laying down his life for his *realm, not sparing himself from death. [Thus] he toiled before his own *true-Aršakuni-*lords †all the days of his life.

218   *Chapter xxi. Concerning the *chief-bishop Nersēs, the kind of man he was, and what he did.*¹

And Nersēs the *chief-bishop of Armenia rebuilt all that had been destroyed in the *land of Armenia. He provided for² and consoled, cared for and became the supervisor of all the poor.³ And he gave refuge to the lepers and the poor. He erected churches in every locality, restored all that had been destroyed, and renewed and corrected all the regulations that had been overturned. He built and strengthened, he admonished and reproved, he wrought many marvels of *greatest power and miraculous cures. He severely rebuked the unrighteous,⁴ and whomever he blessed, he blessed, and whomever he cursed became accursed.⁵ And he increased the ranks of the ministers [of the church] in every place within his *authority in the *territory of Armenia, and he placed bishops as overseers in every *district. And he always watched over his jurisdiction and *authority for as much time as was allotted to him.

*Chapter xxii. Concerning King Pap. How he was filled with *dews and how he conducted himself.*¹

But when King Pap was still an infant [newly] borne by his mother, his impious mother Pᶜaṙanjem then offered him up to the *dews, and so he was filled with *dews from childhood.² And because he always obeyed the will of the *dews, [he] would not seek a cure. For he constantly consorted with the *dews, and the *dews manifested themselves magically on him. And everyone could see with open eyes the *dews upon him.
219   For, whenever people entered every day to give him the morning greeting, they saw them in the guise of snakes rising from the bosom of King Pap and weaving themselves around his shoulders;³ and all those who saw him were afraid of him and of drawing close. But †he answered the people, saying: "Fear not, for they are mine." And every man at every hour saw

such shapes on him. For such a mass of **dew*s was accumulated on him; and this [sight] showed itself every hour to every man who came to see the king. But when the *patriarch Nersēs or the holy bishop Xad came before him, the **dew*s did not appear and became invisible.[4]

And King Pap wallowed in filth—sometimes, becoming a woman for others, he submitted to intercourse, and sometimes he turned others into females and foully copulated as a male, and sometimes he copulated with animals. And in this way he was ruled by **dew*s who dwelled in him †all the days of his life.[5]

Chapter xxiii. Concerning the rebukes of St. Nersēs, and how he was always opposed to King Pap because of his sins.[1]

But St. Nersēs, the *chief-bishop of Armenia, always rebuked King Pap; he admonished and reprimanded him with great admonitory testimonies. And Nersēs did not allow him to set foot on the threshold of the church, or to enter inside, because of his many evil deeds.[2] He constantly rebuked, reproved, and admonished him so that he might retrieve himself from his works of perdition. And he constantly spoke to him that he might bring him to repentance. He set before him the testimonies of the Scriptures, urging him through fear of the eternal torments of the Last Judgment to come to his senses, be amended, and to strive toward improvement in righteous precepts and purifying actions.

220 King Pap did not listen to him, however, but rather opposed him with hostility, plotted his death, and evidently wished to kill him. But because of the king of the Greeks,[3] he did not dare insult him openly even in words, or dare anything against him, or cause his death.[4] Indeed, neither the population of his *realm, nor the entire *army would have accepted such a thing being done to a man on whom everyone in the *realm of Armenia depended because of the righteousness of his actions, the holiness of his ways in the *world, and the peacefulness of his great *spiritual-leadership. And because of the manifest signs that he wrought, all men looked upon him as an angel from heaven. And so, the king nursed his hatred toward him and sought to kill him, but did not dare to speak of it openly lest his own army should kill him. For all men had recourse to his prayers, and everyone in general loved him—the *greatest and the least, those *honored and those of little worth, the **azat*s and the *peasants alike.

Chapter xxiv. Concerning the death of the great *high-priest Nersēs [at the hands] of King Pap; and how and why he was killed by him.[1]

But King Pap was continually hostile to the great *high-priest because of his rebukes of his sins and evil actions, for he was constantly reproved by the man of God Nersēs. He did not wish to repent or correct himself, neither could he endure the perpetual blame of his admonisher. And so, he plotted to kill God's great *high-priest, Nersēs. As it was not possible to do this openly, he falsely pretended to have corrected his ways, and implored God's *high-priest to grant him penance.[2] He invited him to his 221 *palace in the *town of Xax in the *district of Ekeleac⁽, had a banquet prepared, and invited the man of God to *recline on the royal *throne, as though he might cleanse himself thereby from his evil deeds, and thereupon come to repentance. When he had made him *recline in the leading place, the king in person standing on his feet, stripped off his robe and having come into the center offered unmixed [wine] to the man of God there at the feast. Having mixed a mortal poison into the *kotind*,[3] he presented it to him.

As soon as he had drunk the cup, [Nersēs] understood at once, †began to speak, and said: "Blessed is the *Lord our God who has made me worthy to drink this cup and attain a death for the sake of the *Lord, to which I have aspired from my childhood. Now, 'I will take the cup of salvation and call upon the name of the *Lord'[4] so that I too may equally come 'to be a partaker of the inheritance of the saints in light.'[5] As for you, O king, it befitted you as king to give the order openly to kill me. For who was there who hindered you or stayed your hand from the deed you wished to commit? But forgive them, O *Lord, this deed that they have done unto me, and receive the soul of this Thy *servant, Thou who art the refuge of those who toil and the Creator of all blessings."

He spoke these and many other similar words,[6] then he rose up and went to his *residence [*vank⁽*]. And all the *mightiest *naxarars of Armenia went together with him from the royal-*hall; both Mušeł the *sparapet* of Armenia and the *hayr-*mardpet*, and all those who were there together went into his *residence. And when they had entered into his *residence, he lifted up his tunic and showed them a spot the size of a small loaf above his heart, which had turned blue.[7] And the *magnates offered him *t⁽iwrakēs*[8] and antidotes that he might live. But he would not have it; he thrust it aside, but said: "It is my infinite benefit that it has fallen to my [lot] to die for my watchfulness over the Commandments of Christ. You yourselves know [full] well that whatever I said to you I said *publicly, and it would have been fitting that death come from you in 222 *public, as I desired it. But a blessed lot is mine together with the elect, and I am pleased with my inheritance.[9] I will bless the *Lord who preserved me to inherit this lot, and my joy is boundless that soon I shall be delivered from this iniquitous and impious *world." And he spoke much more to them, warning them and imploring them all to watch over themselves and keep the Commandments of the *Lord.[10]

Then blood began to flow from his mouth, *clot [*gund*] after *clot, and it flowed out for some two hours.[11] Then he arose and turned to prayers. Going down on his knees, he implored forgiveness for his murderer. Then he remembered all men in his prayers. He remembered in his prayers those close to him and those afar, the scorned and the *honored, even those whom he had never known. And when he had finished his prayers, he lifted up his hands and eyes to heaven and said: "*Lord Jesus Christ receive my spirit."[12] And having said this he yielded up the ghost.[13]

And the body of the holy man of God Nersēs was taken up by the ministers of the church, as well as Bishop Pᶜawstos[14] and the chief minister Trdac [sic], also the *sparapet Mušeł, the *hayr-*mardpet, and the entire *azat-contingent of the *royal-camp. They took him from the *town, from the *village of Xaχ[15] where the deed had been done, and carried him to the *town of Tᶜil, to his own *village.[16] They accompanied the saint [to his resting place] with psalms, benedictions and canticles, with lighted lamps and great pomp, and many commemorations. But before the body of the saint was buried, King Pap came in person and wrapped [his body] and buried him in the dwelling place of the martyrs. King Pap, as though he were sinless, pretended not to have heard, as though this deed were not his own.[17]

223   *Chapter xxv. Concerning the vision revealed to the holy anchorites Šałitay and Epipᶜan, while they dwelled in the mountains.*[1]

There were two *anchorite [*anapadawork*ᶜ] religious *living-in-the-mountains.[2] The name of one, who was a Syrian by *race and who lived on the mountain Aṙewc ["Lion"], was Šałita [sic]. The name of the other was Epipᶜan [Epiphanios]. He was a Greek by *race,[3] and he lived on the great mountain called the *Throne of Anahit, which was the home of the pagan gods. Both of them were the disciples of St. Daniēl, whom we mentioned earlier.[4] And as they sat, each on his mountain, at the time of the death of St. Nersēs, each saw from his mountain, with open eyes in [broad] daylight, as though Nersēs the man of God were lifted up into the clouds, for God's angels were carrying him upward, and *host [*gund*] upon *host went before him.[5] When they saw this vision the *anchorites marveled at this manifestation, but Šałitay, who was on Mt. Aṙewc, understood, as he was a learned man, that St. Nersēs had died and that his spirit had appeared to him, whereas Epipᶜan thought that he had been carried up bodily. Then they rose up, each from his mountain, and ran in haste to the *district of Ekełeacᶜ. And at their arrival they inquired and saw that the holy *patriarch Nersēs had died. They came to the *village of Tᶜil and saw the place where he had been laid to rest. Then the two faithful men met each other and related to each other what they had seen before the people. These were men of angelic life, nurtured and living in the desert, and they were able to perform the *greatest signs and their actions were known and familiar to all.

224   *Chapter xxvi. Concerning St. Šałitay.*[1]

This Šałitay was a holy man who had been a disciple of the great

205

Daniēl. From his childhood, he had been entirely nurtured in the desert and had eaten grass with the *anchorites-of-the-desert [*anapatawork ᶜ].[2] And after the death of St. Nersēs he went to the *district of Kordukᶜ, and he wrought signs and miracles and dwelt among lions; [indeed] more than twenty lions always accompanied him unceasingly. And whenever it happened that one of the wild beasts suffered an injury, they crowded around him, pulled at Šaḷitay, and begged with signs for healing. Once there was a large lion, and a reed had pierced the lion's paw, and so he came to St. Šaḷitay on the mountain where he dwelt, and lifting his paw in human fashion showing him the wound, indicated to him that he should heal him. St. Šaḷita pulled out the reed that had entered the wound, spat on the wound, wrapped a kerchief that he had taken from his head around the lion's paw, and so healed him.[3]

Thus he performed myriads of various miracles, and wild beasts were the companions of his life† through all the days of his life, as he wandered in the desert. And whenever he came to a river, he crossed shod over the water, and his shoes were not [even] dampened. And whenever he came down to some locality, he brought back [to the right path], through his portents and marvels, many who had gone astray. He wandered about alone. And whenever he came down to an [inhabited] locality, he healed many of the sick.[4]

He was very old, and everyone awaited and watched for his death in order to seize his body. But St. Šaḷita perceived this: that many men waited to seize his body, and so he implored God that no one should take his body. And it so happened, one day, that he was walking as was his
225 custom over the water of the river. And while he was crossing the river of Kordukᶜ, unexpectedly as he was standing in the middle of the river, St. Šaḷita suddenly entered into the water and was hidden from sight, as he had implored in his supplication. And there was much lamentation in the *district. A countless multitude of men assembled, cut off and moved the river to another bed, and searched for the body of St. Šaḷita, but they were unable to find it anywhere. For his earlier request to God that it should be so, had thus been fulfilled.[5]

Chapter xxvii. Concerning St. Epipᶜan.[1]

The blessed saint Epipᶜan had been a disciple of the great Daniēl together with Šaḷitay, and he had been nurtured from childhood in the desert.[2] And after the death of the great *high-priest Nersēs, he went and dwelt in the desert of Great Copᶜkᶜ at a place called Mambrē on the river named Mamušeḷ. And he dwelt in rocky caves, he was constantly with the wild beasts of the desert, and bears and pards gathered to him. And he was constantly in the desert and wrought the *greatest signs and miracles.[3] And he brought back many who had been led astray, from paganism to Christianity. He filled the *land of Copᶜkᶜ with *solitary-communities [vank ᶜ][4] and gave teachers to all of the *land of Cop^ck^c. And so, St. Epip^can became the light of the *land of Cop^ck^c and illuminated them greatly.

He also went to the *land of Aljnik^c and illuminated them too, and filled the *land of Aljnik^c with *solitary-communities. And he built a *martyrium [*vkayanoc^c*] in the *walled-town [*yawanin i k^całak^cin*] of Tigranakert, and on [their] day commemorated the saints for their intercession and their salvation of the *world.⁵ And he himself wrought marvelous signs, and then returned to his *solitary-community.

There was a spring near the Mamušeł River, and a great many fish rose out of that spring, and many people profited by catching the fish from it. Then, two †brothers quarreled over the fish and one killed the other. When St. Epip^can †learned of this, he said: "Henceforth, let no one eat the fish from here." And immediately, the fish in that place became bitter, and it has been bitter as gall up to the present day, and no one catches it to this very day. And he performed other powerful deeds and countless marvels.⁶

And so, St. Epip^can left many righteous regulations in these *districts, but he himself went forth to the *land of the Greeks, taking some five hundred of his disciples who were *hermits [*mianjunk^c*], dwellers-on-mountains [*leařnakank^c*], *dwellers-in-the-desert [*anapatakank^c*]. And as they were going, there chanced a woman on the way. And as they passed by the woman, Epip^can †began to try them and said: "How fair and attractive that woman was." And a youngster among his disciples replied: "The woman whom you have praised was one-eyed." And St. Epip^can said: "Why, indeed, did you look to see her face? Did you look because you have evil thoughts?" And he immediately separated the youth from himself and drove him away.⁷ And he himself came to a great sea, and they crossed by boat to a desert island. Now there was a multitude of snakes on that island—adders, asps and basilisks had been living on the island—as well as many ferocious and venomous beasts. But it so happened that as soon as St. Epip^can arrived on that island, the beasts withdrew, left the island and went away. And after that, there was no harm for them on that island but they lived there in peace.⁸ Then St. Epip^can came there, and there, on the same island, he died.

227   *Chapter xxviii. Concerning the great prodigies and miracles manifested by God at Mambrē after the departure of Epip^can.*¹

Now when St. Epip^can had gone from his *hermitage [*mianjnanoc^c*] called Mambrē in the *district of Cop^ck^c, he left there many *brothers² †of one mind and of one faith,³ believing, religious Christians—*dwellers-in-mountains [*leařnakank^c*], *ascetics [*čgnawork^c*], *hermits [*mianjunk^c*]— and he left there an elder at their head. And there were some among them who from their childhood had never eaten any food except for herbs and water, and as far as the taste of wine, they knew not what it might be.⁴

And there was there a [most] austere *brother, [yet] one who dwelt in darkness, for he would absolutely not drink from the vivifying cup of salvation in the hope of the Resurrection, that is to say of the blood of our *Lord Jesus Christ.[5] For he could not believe that it was truly the blood of the Son of God when it was raised on God's altar,[6] but rather he thought that it was merely wine. And he constantly disputed with many on this account.

Now it so happened one day that when they were performing the mystery of thanksgiving of the liturgy in the very *martyrium built there by St. Epip'an, and as they brought in the holy bread and wine so that it should become the blood of sacrifice on the altar, the incredulous brother was present in the *martyrium. And the priest rose and stood before the holy table. Then, before offering the sacrifice, the priest raised his hands above the altar, and said:[7]

"Lord God of Hosts, who hast created all out of nothing[8] and created man living and incorruptible from the dust of the ground.[9] And they transgressed Thy Commandments and fell into death because of their
228   transgression. By Thy just judgments Thou didst drive them out of the Garden of delight[10] into this *world, from which Thou didst create [them], and they became subject to the sentence of death.[11] But Thou didst not let them go from Thy hand, O beneficent God, but through the providence and grace of Thy Only-begotten Son, Thou didst renew Thy creatures by a second birth.[12] And in many forms didst Thou visit Thy creatures: Thou didst send the prophets. Thou didst perform deeds of might and various signs through Thy saints who, in each *generation, were greatly pleasing before Thee. Thou didst give laws for assistance and send angels as protectors. But when arrived the end of time, Thou didst speak to us through Thy Only-begotten Son through whom Thou didst create this *world. He who is the image [*patker*] of Thy *glory and the form [*kerparan*] of Thy essence [*ēut'iwn*],[13] who bears all things through the word of His power.[14] Who by no means snatched away the essential nature [*ēakan bnut'iwn*] of the Father to [bring] equal *honor to His person.[15] But the eternal God manifested Himself on *earth, walked among men, and was incarnate of the Holy Virgin.[16] He 'took upon himself the form of a *servant'[17] and was made in the likeness' of our helplessness so that he might make us in the likeness of His *glory.[18] For Thou didst deliver us from all scandal and error and lift from the entire *earth the hopelessness of disbelief. Thou didst give hope and faith in the Resurrection to all Thy creatures, to whom Thou didst grant the likeness of the image of Thy forms [*nman-ut'iwn patkeri kerparanac'*].[19] And through the faith given by Thee to strengthen mankind, Thou didst altogether grant life to all alike.[20] Not because of any righteousness of our own, for we have done nothing that is good upon the *earth, but because of Thy mercy and compassion that Thou hast spread over us we dare to implore Thee the knower of hearts, 'that

searchest the hearts and reins' of the sons of men.[21] Thou, O *Lord, who knowest the hearts of all,[22] Thou who knowest the true zeal of this man who leads most rigorously his diligent life yet does not have faith. Increase his faith 'as a grain of mustard seed'[23] so that his soul might not be lost. O *valiant shepherd, who hast gone forth to seek the lost sheep and 'gavest Thy life for Thy sheep,'[24] deliver him too from the lack of faith in which he is held fast, that the foe may not ravish his soul, and Thy creature, in the likeness of Thy forms, be given over to the eternal corruption of perdition."

29

The priest offered this prayer before the offering of the sacrifice, and after this he completed the offering of the entire sacrifice of the liturgy. And as he said: 'Our Father, who art in Heaven,'[25] he knelt down and prayed for a long time. And while he knelt and was at prayer, the *brother of little faith was standing and looking at the altar from the bema below. And with open eyes he beheld the *greatest miracle. For he saw Christ Who had come down, standing on the altar and the wound in his *side where it had been pierced by the lance was open. And blood spurted forth from the wound in his side and flowed into the cup of offering, which had been placed on the altar.[26] And when the religious [but] incredulous *brother beheld this, terrified, trembling, distraught, and anguished, he fell to the ground with writhing features, overwhelmed and fainting [as] his spirit drained from him.

The priest then rose up and completed the holy liturgy, and as he was taking the holy species down from the bema, he saw the *brother fallen in a faint on the ground. When he had given communion to those to whom it was proper to give it, he brought what remained back to the altar. [Then] coming close to the *brother, he grasped him and saw that he was lying senseless on the *ground. He poured water into his mouth, and when he had at last come to his senses and recollected, he rose up and recounted the great miracle which he had seen. Then the priest wished to give him communion from the holy species, but the *brother of little faith refused and would not accept it, considering himself unworthy. He then dug a pit for himself, went down into it, and for seven years repented his *very great sin of disbelief. And after seven years, he considered that he was worthy of repentance and went up to participate in the Eucharist. But then, he lowered himself into the same pit †for all the days of his life, until the *brother died in this very pit. Then the priest also died, and they were laid both together in the *martyrium in the *brotherhood [*ełbayranoc'*]²⁷ of Epip^can, where the miracle had occurred.

230

*Chapter xxix. Concerning Yusik, who was a descendant of Bishop Ałbianos; whom King Pap installed instead of Nersēs of his own will and without [the approval] of the great *chief-bishop of Caesarea; and how thereafter the *authority of the Armenian *patriarchs to consecrate bishops was taken away.*[1]

After the death of the *patriarch Nersēs, King Pap installed Bishop Yusik, who was a decendant of Bishop Ałbianos of Manazkert.[2] [The king] ordered him to assume the position of *patriarch and to rule in the place of the one whom he had killed, and so he replaced him.

But the *chief-bishop of Caesarea[3] heard that the great *patriarch Nersēs had been killed and Yusik installed in his place without his own order. This was not according to the custom that he [the Armenian candidate] be brought to the *patriarch of Caesarea for ordination.[4] Greatly amazed by this, the *patriarch [sic] of Caesarea grew angry because of this, and a *synodal-*council of the bishops of the *province of Caesarea took place[5] without the *patriarch,[6] and they wrote [him] a letter in great anger. And they likewise wrote a letter to King Pap, and they dissolved the *authority of the *katʿołikate, so that whoever became *patriarch of Armenia would have the *authority to bless the bread at the royal court but would not have the *authority to ordain Armenian bishops, as had originally been the custom. And after this, the *authority to ordain Armenian bishops was taken away, and all those who became bishops in all the *districts and *regions of Armenia — every one of the bishops found *within the *borders of Armenia — went after this to the *city of Caesarea and became bishops there. Hence after this, *authority was taken from the *land of Armenia, and consequently they did not dare ordain bishops, but whoever was the *senior-among-the-bishops merely sat higher and blessed the king's bread.[7]

231

Now [Yusik] was a Christian, but he did not dare to speak boldly or reprovingly to anyone, for he was timid and complaisant, and held his *dignity from the king's will alone. And so he kept himself silent and quiet †through all the days of his life.[8]

*Chapter xxx. Concerning mourning. How they mourned for the *patriarch Nersēs and longed for him.[1]*

And after Pap's murder of the holy *patriarch Nersēs, all men mourned deeply and everyone in the *land of Armenia †spoke with one accord, and said: "The *glory of Armenia has been taken away, since the just man of God was taken from this *land." The *princes and the *naxarars †spoke up and said: 'Now we know that our *land is destroyed, since innocent blood has been shed unwarrantedly and all the more because he was killed for God's sake." And Mušeł, the *sparapet of Armenia, †spoke up and said: The blood of God's saint has been shed unjustly. And after this I shall not be able to go forth against the enemy or direct my *spear against anyone. For I know that God has let us fall from His hand[2] and that we are abandoned, and we shall not be able to lift up our heads. I know that there will be no more victories over the foes of the *land of Armenia, for victory came from the prayers of him who is dead and from those of his *clan."[3] And all the *azats and *peasants from one

210

*border to the other of the entire *territory of the *land of Armenia mourned—the *azats and the *peasants and all the dwellers in the *house of Tᶜorgom alike [all the *speakers]-of-the-Armenian-tongue.⁴

.32   *Chapter xxxi. Concerning the way in which, after the death of the *patriarch Nersēs, King Pap destroyed out of jealousy all the canonical regulations laid down by Nersēs during his lifetime.*¹

Even though Pap king of Armenia had killed the Armenian *patriarch Nersēs, he was not satisfied with his death, but sought to obliterate and destroy whatever righteous regulation Nersēs had given to the church. And so, he began to manifest his hatred toward his earlier canons, and he began to order openly to the *realm the destruction of the asylums-for-widows and for-orphans that Nersēs had built in the various *districts, and also the destruction of the walled and *fortified *dwellings-of-virgins [kusastankᶜ]² in various *districts and *towns that the same Nersēs had built for them, for the care over their well-kept vows.³ For the blessed Nersēs had built these *dwellings in every *district during his lifetime so that all those who were consecrated virgins⁴ might assemble there in fasting and in prayers, and receive their food from the *world and their own families.⁵ King Pap ordered to destroy them and ordered the consecrated virgins handed over to foul intercourse.

And the same Nersēs had built hospitals in every *town and every *region, establishing *maintenance [ṙočik] and care for them. And he left trusted men as overseers for the sick and the poor. He also entrusted them to such men as were God-fearing and who awaited the eternal Judgment and the coming of Christ. But the king drove each overseer from his position of supervision and razed the places to the ground. He drove out
233   everyone who had been placed as overseer for the indigent and the poor, and he promulgated an order to the entire *realm under his *dominion: "Let the poor go out and beg, and let no one dare give them anything at that place, for if they do not, [the poor] will go out, entreat, beg, and find what they can." And as for the regulations of *ptuł and tasanords,⁶ that had been laid down as a custom from ancient times to give to the church, he gave the following order to the *realm concerning them: "Let no one give them."⁷

And in the days of the *patriarch Nersēs, no one in all of the *land of Armenia dared from [fear] of him repudiate or abandon his own wife whom he had taken with blessing under the veil and bridal wreath, or be so bold as to take another at another time.⁸ And if anyone suddenly died no one dared weep hopelessly over the dead beyond the canonical regulations of the church, no one dared wail or lament over the dead, and no one raised his voice over the dead in the days of Nersēs. But they accompanied the dead only with tears and fitting psalms and hymns, with lighted lamps and candles.⁹

But after his death, every man impudently received from the king the permission to leave his wife, and there was a man who exchanged ten wives, and everyone fell altogether into lewdness. And after Nersēs's death, whenever they mourned over the dead, men and women with slashed arms and lacerated faces accompanied the dead dancing mourning dances, with trumpets, *p'andur̄s, and *vins, and with foul and monstrous dances, which they performed face to face, striking their palms against each other.[10]

And in the days of Nersēs there were absolutely no poor to be seen begging anywhere within the entire *territory of Armenia. But everyone brought what they needed right there to their asylums, that is to say the leper-houses, so that they lacked for nothing there and were satisfied. But after the death of the *high-priest, if anyone gave solace to the poor, he received a severe punishment from the king.[11]

234 And in the days of Nersēs, the order of the ceremonies of the church were most splendid and the multitude of the holy minister regulated in all of the *land of Armenia. And in his days, the commemoration of the holy martyrs was always resplendent, with large *gatherings everywhere in Armenia. And the *honor of the father-bishops grew according to their deserts in all the *districts of Armenia. And the order of *solitaries [vanakanac']¹² flourished in inhabited and uninhabited places. But everything was obliterated, ruined, and destroyed after his death.

And in the days of the *high-priesthood of Nersēs, rest houses for strangers, hospitals, and hostelries were built by order of the *high-priest in all inhabited places, and in every *village, and in all the *regions of Armenia in general. And everyone in the *land of Armenia was generous and compassionate in remembering the poor and oppressed, the afflicted and the strangers, the mistreated, wanderers, pilgrims, visitors, and wayfarers. And St. Nersēs had set supervisors and care for them everywhere.

But after his death, King Pap destroyed all this. He was contemptuous of the *honor of the church. Many regulations and beneficial laws and canons set down by the *patriarch Nersēs were relegated to oblivion and the regulations overturned.[13] And after his departure from this *world, many *districts of Armenia, and many people turned back to the ancient worship-of-*demons [diwapaštut'iwn], and they erected idols in many places in Armenia with the permission of King Pap. For there was no one to oppose this, no one whom they need fear. They did whatever they wished to do with impudence, and so they erected many images and prostrated themselves before them.[14]

Moreover, King Pap took for the royal treasury the church land that King Trdat had given in the days of the great *high-priest Grigor to support the service of the church in all of the *land of Armenia. For out of seven plots [hoł] he took away five for the royal treasury and left only two plots [to the church].[15] And in accordance with the plots, he left in

235 each *village two [clerics], a priest and a deacon, and he subjected the *brothers and sons of the priests and deacons to his own *service. And he thought that he would fulfill his spiteful ill-will toward Nersēs—against the dead through the living—because of the enmity he bore him; and it did not occur to him that he was destroying himself. And at that time, all the regulations for the service of the church were weakened in the whole of the *land of Armenia.

Chapter xxxii. Concerning King Pap: how he turned away from the king of the Greeks and was killed by the Greek forces.[1]

King Pap changed his mind and turned his heart away from the king of the Greeks, and he wished to unite in love and alliance with the king of Persia. And so he began to rely on the king of Persia and he then sent him envoys concerning an alliance.[2] He also sent envoys to the king of the Greeks [to say]: "Ten *cities together with Caesarea belong to me, therefore return them [to me]. The *city of Uṙhay [Edessa] was also built by my ancestors; consequently, if you do not wish to initiate a conflict, give it back, otherwise we will fight a great war."[3] But Mušeł and all the Armenian *princes urgently sought to persuade the king not to break the *covenant with the kingdom of the Greeks. He, however, would not listen to them and openly manifested his hostility to the king of the Greeks.

But the Greek *officials [išχank^c]—the one named Tērēnt and the other Adē—were still in the *land of Armenia with their forces.[4] And the king of the Greeks secretly sent a messenger to the *officials of his army who were in the *land of Armenia with the order to kill the Armenian king Pap.[5] Consequently, as soon as the command of the king of the Greeks had been received by his *officials in the *land of Armenia, they awaited an occasion to kill Pap king of Armenia. And such an occasion came when the *commanders of the Greek army—Tērēnt [sic] and Adē—

236 learned that Pap king of Armenia was alone, because all the *magnates and *forces of Armenia were away. King Pap was [then] *encamped in the plain at a place called Xu in the *district of Bagrawand, and the Greek army was also *encamped there near the *camp of the Armenian king. The Greek *commander[6] prepared a great banquet and invited the great king of Armenia, Pap, to the feast with the great [honor] befitting him, as it was proper to invite a king to a banquet; and they made their preparations.[7]

King Pap came to the banquet, *reclined on the *banqueting-couch, to eat, and drink. And as the king entered into the *tent of the Greek *commander Tērēnd, the *legion of *infantry *shield-bearers [sparakirk^c], *shields in hand, *axes at their belts, stood inside on the watch all around the walls of the *tent, and they were likewise drawn up outside. They were armor-clad underneath and with [ordinary] garments above. But King Pap believed that they did this in his *honor. And while he was feasting, the force of *axe-men stood behind him and surrounded him on all sides.[8] And when they came to the wine, they offered the first festive cup to King Pap, and all the drummers, flutists, lyre-players, and trumpeters together skillfully sounded in the various voices [of their instruments].[9] The command was then given to the *legion of *shield-bearers [vahanaworkᶜ]. And while King Pap held the festive cup of wine in his hand and gazed upon the varied troop of *gusans, as he reclined to the left, leaning on his elbow and holding the golden cup in his hand, while his right hand rested on the hilt of the *dagger strapped to his right thigh;[10] at the very moment that he put the cup to his mouth to drink and fixed [his eyes] on the varied troop of *gusans, the command was given by a glance to the Greek soldiers. Then, two of the *axe-bearing *legionnaires with gold-embossed *shields, who were standing behind him to serve, suddenly lifted up their *axes and simultaneously struck King Pap. One struck straight at the neck with his *axe, while the other *axe-man struck at his right hand placed on the hilt of the *dagger, cut it off, and struck it aside. King Pap fell prone on the spot; the wine of the cup mingled with the blood from his throat fell together with his body over the salver of the cup. And King Pap was killed on the spot.

Gnel, *lord-of-the-district of Anjewacᶜikᶜ leapt to his feet from his *banqueting-couch at the uproar and tumult of the banqueting-*hall [tačar]. He drew his *sword, struck at one of the *legionnaires who had attacked the king, and killed him. But then, the Greek *commander Tērēnt drew his own *sword and from a distance struck off Gnel's skull above the eyes.[11] And †no one was so bold as to say anything else to them, not a thing.[12]

*Chapter xxxiii. Concerning the way that the Armenian *princes subsequently took counsel, and how they then endured and kept silent.[1]*

And all the *greatest Armenian *princes *assembled together, and the *sparapet Mušeł and the *hayr-*mardpet as well as all the other *princes said: "What shall we do? How shall we act? Shall we avenge our king's death or not?" †Then the following decision was taken at the council and they said: "We cannot become *servants of the heathen Persians or be hostile to the king of the Greeks. Neither can we carry on hostilities with both of them. Nor can we maintain ourselves without the support of one of them."[2] Consequently, this decision was taken at the council: "What has been, has been. Let us *serve the king of the Greeks. Let us make our *submission to the *authority of the kingdom of the Greeks, and let the kingdom of the Greeks treat us as it wills." And so, they no longer had any thought of either seeking vengeance or of doing anything else. But they endured and kept silent.[3]

238   *Chapter xxxiv. Concerning the enthronement of Varazdat in the*
land of Armenia after Pap.[1]

And after the death of Pap king of Armenia, the king of the Greeks
made a certain Varazdat from the same Aršakuni *house king over the
*realm of Armenia. He came with great pomp to the *land of Armenia
and ruled over the *land of Armenia. He was young in years, full of vigor,
with powerful hands and a *valiant heart, but he was light-minded, youth-
fully puerile of mind, and childish.[2] Nevertheless, when they saw him, all
of the *clans of the *greatest Armenian *naχarars came to him and
rejoiced at his willingness to rule over them.

Now the Armenian *sparapet Mušel led the Armenians, †he watched
carefully over the *borders of Armenia, and, as was his custom, kept the
*realm in excellent order; and he gave good counsel to the young King
Varazdat. He constantly took care of the kingship of the *realm of Armenia, seeking the way and means that it might prosper, and he constantly
strove prudently to consolidate the kingdom. He also took counsel with
the Greek *officials and through them with the *emperor,[3] on the necessity for them to build *cities in every *district of the *land of Armenia:
where there should be one-one, and where two-two,[4] to strengthen them
with strong *fortifications and garrisons throughout the *land of Armenia
as far as the *border of the *land at Ganjak, which was on the Persian
side and marked the Armenian *frontier. [They also decided] to arm all
the Armenian *azats with an *imperial stipend, and likewise the Armenian
army, so that all precautions should thus be taken against their enemy, the
Persian forces. And the king of the Greeks gladly agreed to do this,
that the *realm might thus be strengthened in every way and remain
unalterably on his side, and that the king of Persia might not be able to
seize the *realm of Armenia.[5]

239   *Chapter xxxv. Concerning the way that the Armenian king Varazdat*
listened to the words of ill-intentioned and senseless men and killed the
*sparapet and *commander-in-chief of Armenia, Mušel.*[1]

Now when the great *naχarars of Armenia saw that Varazdat king of
Armenia was a credulous child who did not know how to distinguish
good from evil, they then began to lead the king according to their own
will, and they guided and directed him with their words as they wished.
He [preferred] to listen to young men who were his equals in age rather
than to wise old men who were able to give him profitable counsel.

Now Bat, the *nahapet of the *clan of the Saharuni *house, who was
the *tutor and *foster-father of King Varazdat, intended to snatch from
Mušel the duties of the office of *sparapet and *commander-in-chief.[2]
Consequently he †began to whisper about him to King Varazdat his
foster-son, and say: "The Mamikonean *house has been pernicious to you

215

Aršakuni from the very earliest times, for they have been your rivals by nature. They have swallowed the entire *land of Armenia, especially Mušeł, for he is an evil and deceitful man. For he has loved your enemies and hated those who love you, and he has always acted falsely, equivocally, and insolently toward you. Is he not the Mušeł who during Pap's reign had so many times the opportunity to kill Šapuh king of Persia in the Persian war, yet did not kill him and let the enemy go free?[3] Or [who], when he captured the wives of King Šapuh, sent them off carefully and solicitously, in litters back to Šapuh?[4] Is he not the Mušeł who captured Uŕnayr king of Ałuank^c, but did not wish to kill him and let the enemy go?[5] Is he not the Mušeł at whose order and on whose advice the Greek *commanders killed King Pap? For he incited and 240 roused to anger the king of the Greeks against King Pap until he had him killed.[6] Thus, it is proper that he die by your hand. He has no right to live. For if you do not hurry, O king, he has now planned to fill the Armenian *land with *cities and make them garrisons for the settlement of Greek troops.[7] And after that, either the king of the Greeks will take the kingdom of Armenia from you, or this Mušeł will kill you and reign himself." He constantly incited the king in secret with such words, until he agreed to kill the *sparapet* and *commander-in-chief of Armenia in accordance with their wish.

They then planned how they might be able to lay hold of him, for they feared him greatly. "For," they said: "if he realizes this, he will provoke a great war, and no one is able to withstand his *valor [and so] some means must be contrived." And so, they lay in wait for him. Then, it so happened that one day, King Varazdat of Armenia gave the order to prepare a banquet and make great preparations, and he ordered to invite all the *nobles, *dignitaries, and *magnates, as well as the *commander-in-chief Mušeł.[8] Varazdat got ready select strong and powerful men prepared for action to attack Mušeł †suddenly and unexpectedly at an unforeseen time. He arranged great festivities and gave them much wine to drink and many joyous diversions. Before this, King Varazdat gave a preliminary sign to the prepared killers: "When you see that the *sparapet* Mušeł has drunk a great deal [k^caǰ] and that his mind is overcome with drink, I shall leave on the pretext of relieving myself, and you surround him. And it so happened that they were overcome with wine, having gone beyond measure, while King Varazdat kept away from the wine. Then, when Varazdat saw that they were senseless from drink, he rose as though on the pretext of relieving himself, and all the *nobles rose up together from their *banqueting-couches to do him *honor. And the twelve men to whom he had given the order suddenly seized Mušeł all at once from 241 behind, six men on one arm and six on the other. The king was standing on his feet and [Mušeł] looked at him as though [saying]: "What is this for?" †And the king answered: "Go to King Pap, ask him, and see what this is for." Then the king turned to the door and went out. And Mušeł said: "Is this my reward for so many of my services, and blood and sweat, for the sweat wiped off with *arrow [heads]?⁹ But since my death has overtaken me, would it had been met on horseback . . . "¹⁰ He had time to speak †only these words and not a thing more. Bat Saharuni, the *tutor of King Varazdat, at once drew the *dagger on his thigh, drove it into the throat of the *commander-in-chief Mušeł, and instantly struck off his head.¹¹ And they lifted him up and took his body [back] to his own *village.¹²

*Chapter xxxvi. Concerning the senseless fantasies of Mušeł's household and of other men.*¹

And when they brought the body of the *sparapet* Mušeł *home to his family, his household did not believe him dead, though they saw his head severed from his body. "For," they said: "he has been in countless battles and never received a wound, not a single *arrow ever reached him, nor did any other *weapon pierce him." But others expected his resurrection, consequently they joined his head to the trunk, took him up, and placed him on the roof of a tower, saying: "Because he was a *valiant man, the *Arlezkᶜ* will come down and revive him." They stood guard and awaited his resurrection until the body was decomposed.² Then, they brought it down from the tower, wept [over it], and buried it as was fitting.

242   *Chapter xxxvii. Concerning the return of Manuēl from Persian captivity and his avenging of Mušeł, his expulsion of King Varazdat from the *land of Armenia, and his taking over of the *land of Armenia.*¹

Then King Varazdat installed in the *office of *sparapet* and *commander-in-chief Bat, the *nahapet* of the Saharuni *house who was his *tutor and the slanderous killer of Mušeł. And so, he was *sparapet* in his place and *commander-in-chief of all Armenia.² And as *tanutēr* and *nahapet* of the *clan of the Mamikonean *house, the king installed the one called Vačᶜē, who was from the same *house.³

At that time, two *brothers from the Mamikonean *house, who had been taken by King Šapuh, returned from Persian captivity. The name of one was Manuēl and that of the other one Koms.⁴

For at that time, the Sasanian king of Persia had been waging war against the great Aršakuni king of the Kᶜušan, who held the *city of Bałh. And when the Persians went to war against the Kᶜušan, the king of Persia sent forth these men whom he had brought captive from Armenia together with his own forces.⁵ And so, this Manuēl went with his *brother Koms. And when the two *contingents clashed together in combat, the Persian army suffered defeat at the hands of the forces of the Kᶜušan and turned to fllight under frightful blows. [The Kᶜušan] caught up with the Persian army and †did not leave a single one from the Persian forces alive;⁶ no one survived to bring the news. But Manuēl son of Artašēn from the Mami-konean *house, together with his *brother Koms,[7] performed many deeds of *valor in this battle, though they survived [only] *on foot. And of all the Persian army only these two reached the Persian king, having survived safe and sound and performed many deeds of *valor.

243   But the king of Persia was greatly afflicted on account of the annihi-lation of his army. He became all the more enraged and furious because he saw that only these two had come out safe from his entire army. He raged against them, heaped insults on them, threw them out of his *borders, [and] dispatched them to their own *land. And so they set out, turning their faces toward their own *land. Now the two *brothers were *on foot, and both of them were of enormous size, both of them were as strongly built as giants. And when they were on their way, Manuēl [became] unable to walk because his feet hurt. Then his *brother Koms lifted him up on his back, and carrying this man of enormous size ten *χrasaχs a day, he came bearing him to the *land of Armenia.[8] Now when Manuēl reached the *land of Armenia, together with his *brother Koms, and when Vač⁽ᶜ⁾ē, who had previously been *nahapet before his return, saw him, he handed over to him the *princely *diadem that he had received from King Varazdat, because [Manuēl] was the senior member of the *clan. And so, Manuēl held the *dignity of *nahapet-*tanutēr of the *clan, and Vač⁽ᶜ⁾ē was in second place. And when Manuēl had attained the *glory of his *lordship, he first seized the office of *sparapet and *commander-in-chief without an order from King Varazdat. Manuēl took back for himself the *authority that his ancestors had naturally [i bnēn] wielded from the very beginning and which King Varazdat had granted to his *tutor, Bat.[9]

    Then after this, the Armenian *sparapet Manuēl †sent a message to King Varazdat, and said: "In return for all the services that our *clan faithfully rendered to you Aršakuni from the earliest times, sacrificing our lives for you, living and dying for you; for all our ancestors who first died in war for you; for Mušeł's father Vasak who perished for King Aršak;[10] for ourselves who perpetually served and toiled for the kingship of your *clan—instead of receiving life for our services, they died at the

244 hands of the foe, and you, Aršakuni, have slaughtered the ones who survived. Behold that *valiant man Mušeł my *brother,[11] who from his youth wore out his life for your sake, who routed and slaughtered your foes and whom the foe could not kill, you seized and strangled him on a *banqueting-couch.[12] You, then, are no true Aršakuni but a bastard child, that is why you have not acknowledged the faithful *servants of the Aršakuni. Indeed, we are not even your *vassals but your equals and [even] greater than you,[13] for our ancestors were kings in the *realm of the Čenk⁽ᶜ⁾. And on account of quarrels [between] *brothers, and because much blood flowed, we set out to seek a haven and settled [here].[14] The

first Aršakuni kings knew who we were and whence [we came], but you, since you are no Aršakuni, go from this *realm, lest you die by my hand!"

But King Varazdat †sent an answering message to the *commander-in-chief Manuēl, and said: "If I am not an Aršakuni, how have I assumed the crown of my Aršakuni ancestors, and taken the *realm of my predecessors, and avenged my father's *brother Pap[15] on your evil *brother Mušeł? But you are not from this *realm, for you yourself have said, 'Indeed we are from the *land of the *realm of the Čenk^c [where] we were kings by nature [*i bnut^cenē*], and we have come here as strangers.' Then do not die like your *brother, for out of my beneficence I let you go free. Go to the *land of the Čenk^c, live there and rule there in your own *land! But should you be unwilling to go, you shall die by my hand as Mušeł died.[16]

Then, when messengers had gone back and forth many times and they had sent each other harsher and harsher taunting words, they set a time to face each other in combat. And they met in combat when the fixed time arrived. King Varazdat took the forces of his *camp and came to the [appointed] place of combat, well armed and prepared for battle, and the other also [came] even better prepared. And so, the *sparapet* Manuēl reached the same place with his own *contingent, and the *contingents of both met in combat to attack each other on the plain of Karin.

King Varazdat and the *sparapet* Manuēl, carrying *lances, came forward against each other as champions. [Now] when King Varazdat lifted up his eyes as he came forward, looked, and beheld the *sparapet* Manuēl in the greatness of his stature, the splendor of his person, the extremely strong and impenetrable iron *armor [*zēn*] [that covered him] from head to foot, also the robustness of his person and the solidity of his *armor-clad charger, also bearing indestructible trappings,[17] he compared him in his mind to a tall and inaccessible mountain. He charged, even though he saw death in his mind, for there was no further hope of escape. But King Varazdat, when he saw [Manuēl] in this fashion, because he was a young man and still inexpert in combat, thought that his *lance would be unable to do anything against the *armor, [therefore] he drove his *lance with all the strength of his arm into the mouth of the *commander-in-chief Manuēl. But Manuēl seized the *lance, tore off its point, dragged it through his cheek, pulling out many teeth, and wrenched the *lance itself from the king.

King Varazdat then turned to flee from the *commander-in-chief Manuēl, while Manuēl, holding the spearhead in his hand, beat King Varazdat over the head with the [shaft] of the *lance, and he did this for some four *asparēz*. Manuēl's sons, Hmayeak and Artašēs, each with *lance in hand, immediately rushed out to kill the king. But Manuēl himself †called out from behind his sons and said: "Ho! Do not be murderers of your *lord!" And hearing their father's voice, they hastily turned away from him.[18] And on that day, the royal *contingent suffered

246 defeat at the hands of Manuēl's *contingent. And after it many dead lay prone on the field, many were injured, maimed, and wounded; many *naxarars were slaughtered, many were driven into flight.[19]

While Manuēl's *contingent was pursuing the fugitives, a *sepuh of the Mamikonean *house named Hamazaspean was passing by the corpses of the fallen and of the wounded [who had been] injured in the fray. Among them lay Garegin, *lord-of-the-district of Ṙštunikʿ, who was, however, [still] alive, neither injured nor harmed. This Garegin had formerly been the son-in-law [sic] of the same Hamazaspean, for he had married his sister Hamazaspuhi. When King Šapuh had come to the *land of Armenia, he had abandoned his wife and fled. Then the Persians took Hamazaspuhi to the *land of Tosp, to the *city of Van, and hanged her from a high tower which stood above a rocky cave, and [thus] killed her on the gallows.[20] But on that day, as Garegin lay among the fallen, his father-in-law Hamazasp [sic] passed by them. And Garegin †called out and said: "*Lord Hamazaspean, look after me, order a fresh horse brought [to me], and let me ride [away]." And Hamazaspean said to him: "Who are you?" And he answered: "I am Garegin Ṙštuni." Then Hamazaspean †gave an order to the *shield-bearers [vahanaworkʿ] who were with him, [and] said: "Get down, put your *shields over him, and guard him." He himself moved on, but the *shield-bearers dismounted, laid their *shields over him, and stood guard in accordance with the order given [to them].

After this came a certain Danun, a *gumapet of the *contingent of *shield-bearers [sparakirkʿ] in Manuēl's army. He saw that the *shield-bearers [vahanaworkʿ] had dismounted and were guarding Garegin, [and] he asked them: "Who is that? And why have you dismounted and are standing there?" And they said: "This is Garegin, *lord of Ṙštunikʿ, and Hamazaspean ordered us to dismount and guard him." And Danun, greatly angered and burning with rage, flared up and said: "So, Hamazaspean wishes to make him once more his son-in-law and give him his sister Hamazaspuhi as a wife, and for this he has spared him and ordered 247 him guarded." He then immediately got down from his horse, drew his *short-sword [tʿur], approached him, and cut him to pieces, killing him and scattering the pieces on the spot.

Meanwhile, all the other troops were still coming from the battle, bringing along many captives. And they brought before the *sparapet Manuēl Bat, the slanderer to King Varazdat, the killer of Mušeł, together with his son. And they also seized all the others who had been accomplices in the deed and brought them to him. And the *sparapet Manuēl laid a heavy judgment on the iniquitous Bat. He ordered first that the throat of his son be cut in front of him, and then that his head be struck off. And he slaughtered the others in the same fashion. And they drove King Varazdat out of the *land and *confines of Armenia. And he went to the *land of the Greeks and remained there as long as he lived. And there he died.²¹

And the *sparapet and *commander-in-chief Manuēl conquered the *realm. He gathered around himself all the Armenian *magnates and *naχarars and made himself their *leader [aṙaǰnord] and head. He wielded *authority and gave orders to the *realm in the place of the king, and he kept the *realm prosperous. He kept the wife of King Pap, *Queen Zarmanduχt, with her two Aršakuni sons in place of the king and took them around with *honor. He *guided the *realm of Armenia with great wisdom and great success as long as he lived. As for the Aršakuni children, the elder of whom was named Aršak and the younger Vałaršak, the *sparapet Manuēl *nurtured them as his nurslings, and he *honored their mother Zarmanduχt with the great pomp of a *queen.²² But when Manuēl saw that whatever he did ran counter to the orders of the king of the Greeks, he judged it fitting to find one person at least to give him support. He then took counsel with the *queen and they decided to seek the support of the Persian king.²³

248   *Chapter xxxviii. Concerning the way in which the Armenian *spa-rapet Manuēl, together with the entire *realm of Armenia, gave his hand to the king of Persia and brought the Surēn as the first *marzpan and *ruler of the *land of Armenia from the king of Persia; and how he was honored by him with great gifts; and how a rebellion then occurred as a result of the deceit of Meružan Arcruni, and war broke out.¹*

After this, *Queen Zarmanduχt and the *sparapet Manuēl sent Garǰoyl malχaz with many Armenian *naχarars as well as *letters-patent, gifts, and presents to the king of Persia [to say] that they would give him their hand, submit to him, *serve him faithfully, and hand the Armenian *realm over to him.² Garǰoyl set out with his companions, arrived at the court of the Persian king, presented to him the *letters-patent from the *queen and the *sparapet of Armenia, and transmitted to him the message of submission. When the king of Persia saw them, he received them with great joy, †highly *honored them with great esteem, and bestowed great gifts on Garǰoyl.

And he sent with him to the *land of Armenia the Persian Surēn, one of his illustrious *naχarars, and with him ten thousand *armor-clad *horsemen, so that the Surēn might go to the support of the *com-mander-in-chief Manuēl in the *land of Armenia, and protect *Queen Zarmanduχt from [her] enemies.³ The king of Persia also sent a crown, a *robe-of-honor, and the royal standard to *Queen Zarmanduχt through the Surēn, as well as crowns for her two young sons, Aršak and Vał-aršak. He likewise sent royal *robes to the *sparapet Manuēl, sables, and a *gargmanak *diadem of gold and silver for the head with the knot over the crest of the *diadem behind the eagle tied in an *ašχara-wand knot, and an *apizak chest *ornament [patiw], as is the rule for kings; also a crimson *pavilion with the insignia of an eagle on top of it and *very large hangings, as well as a sky-blue canopy. And he sent 249 *palatial gold serving plates to the *sparapet Manuēl, and granted him from his own hand great *authority over the *realm of Armenia.[4]

And Garjoyl Xorχoṙuni returned to the *land of Armenia bringing the Persian Surēn with his ten thousand [men]. They came and brought the gifts for the *queen and her children, as well as for the *sparapet Manuēl. And everyone of the *nobility received gifts, every *tanutēr and Armenian *magnate. And when *Queen Zarmanduχt and the *sparapet and *commander-in-chief Manuēl saw the esteem and love [shown them] by the king of Persia, they honored the Surēn most joyfully. They handed the *realm of Armenia over to the Surēn and submitted to the commands of the king of Persia. And it was laid down that the king of Persia should be given *tribute, gifts, and offerings from the *realm of Armenia.[5] Likewise, [they granted] to the *marzpan Surēn *has and *košik,[6] as well as the necessary *maintenance, and supplies and food for the ten thousand [men] according to their needs. And they whole-heartedly accepted the king of Persia as their supporter and *lord, and *served him. And envoys of the Persian king went back and forth very frequently to the *land of Armenia. And it †greatly demonstrated its affection and loyalty to the king, and he frequently sent gifts to *Queen Zarmanduχt and to the Armenian *commander-in-chief Manuēl. And Manuēl became very close to and beloved by the Persian king, and he was greatly *glorified and exalted by him.[7]

When Meružan Arcruni saw all the *glory and distinction with which the Persian king adorned Manuēl[8]—for he *honored him like a *brother, or a son[9]—he was extremely jealous of Manuēl's *glory and sought to contrive some device whereby to remove him from the sight of the king so that he himself might become favored in his place. And because he could not devise any other deceitful scheme to find his way to the Persians, he then thought up an evil ruse and furthered his plot through his own 250 dissimulation, for he relied on the ingenuousness of the *commander-in-chief Manuēl. First he began to win him over with deference and soothe his mind with cordiality, then he displayed to him his own care and concern, and finally came and unfolded before him his own false inventions, [saying]: "O Manuēl, be informed that an envoy has come from the king of Persia bringing an order concerning you to the Surēn [whereby] you should be seized and bound and either killed here or be taken with every precaution, bound hand, foot, and neck, to the king of Persia? Now that you know, look to it and think what you should do." When Manuēl heard this he was surprised and amazed, and said: "I have never wronged the Persians, for what reason are they doing this to us?" And Meružan said to Manuēl: "I have checked and confirmed that these things are certain, and I have warned you out of my love and solicitude."

When Manuēl believed Meružan's words and concluded that the words he had heard were true, then the *commander-in-chief Manuēl gathered a *contingent and arrayed a large force. And while the Surēn with his army sat peacefully in his *camp †unconcerned, unwary, and in untroubled tranquility—for there was none of the perfidious duplicity among them rumored about by the malignant Meružan—the *commander-in-chief Manuēl †fell suddenly and unexpectedly on the Surēn's *camp and slaughtered all of the ten thousand Persians. He allowed only the *marzpan Surēn †to go free on a single horse, granting him his life.[10] And the Surēn was amazed at these events, [and] asked: "Why? What was the reason that he did this?" And Manuēl said to the Surēn: "I am releasing you because of my loving friendship, go on your way safe and sound, but I shall not fall into another Persian trap." And Manuēl in person collected the Armenian *contingent, because he knew that after this he had aroused the great hostility and wrath of the Persian king. And thereafter, the Armenian *commander-in-chief Manuēl together with his entire *contingent placed at their head *Queen Zarmanduχt the wife of King Pap, and they displayed her all around in place of the king. And they themselves waged war on every side for the welfare of the *realm of Armenia; [they fought] against the enemies and neighbors around them, and most of all against the Persian forces, †during all the days of his [Manuēl's] life. But Meružan went off to the king of Persia to denounce Manuēl.[11]

251

Chapter xxxix. Concerning Gumand Šapuh, who was sent by the Persian king to wage war against Armenia, and who was slaughtered by Manuēl together with his army.[1]

Then the Persian king sent Gumand Šapuh with forty-eight thousand [men] against Armenia, in order to seize and devastate the *land. They set out and reached the *borders of Armenia on the side of Atrpayakan. When the Armenian *commander-in-chief Manuēl heard of this, he mustered his forces of twenty thousand [men], as many as he could lay hands on because of the troubled times. Then Manuēl hastened to face the Persian *contingent, and he †put their army to the *sword.[2] He also killed Gumand Šapuh and returned [having won] a great victory.[3]

Chapter xl. Concerning Varaz; how he was sent by the Persian king and was slaughtered like the first.[1]

After this, a certain Varaz who was a *commander of the Persian king came to the *land of Armenia with one hundred and eighty thousand [men] to fight against the *sparapet Manuēl and the entire Armenian

*contingent. Then Manuēl the *sparapet* and *commander-in-chief of
Armenia put in order and arrayed ten thousand *armor-clad *cavalry-
252 men² and marched forth to fight Varaz. He attacked, slaughtered, and
annihilated them, killing Varaz as well. He took much loot, the insignia
and *weapons of the [Persian] army, and returned most peacefully home.

*Chapter xli. Concerning Mr̊kan, whom the Persian king sent against
the Armenian *land and against Manuēl with a large army and who was
slaughtered like the previous ones.*¹

And after all this it so happened that the Persian king sent Mr̊kan²
with four hundred thousand [men] against the *land of Armenia. He
came to the *land of Armenia with the entire multitude of his host, took a
*portion of the Armenian *land, and *camped in the plain of Artandan.
Manuēl †fell on the *camp by night and immediately †put all those in the
*fortified- camp to the *sword. He also killed Mr̊kan, took much booty,
†and did not leave a single one of them alive.³

*Chapter xlii. Concerning the seven years' peace.*¹

For seven years after that, the Persian army did not dare to enter yet
again into the Armenian *borders, and there was peace in the *land. And
all those who had scattered throughout the *land gathered around the
*commander-in-chief Manuēl. They came, fell in with one another, and
*settled down [*banakeal*] undisturbed, and the Armenian *commander-
in-chief *guided them. Then three remaining youths from the *house of
Siwnikᶜ who had survived the Persian massacre came to the Armenian
*commander-in-chief Manuēl;² the name of the first was Babik, of the
253 second Sam, and of the last, Val̊inak. The Armenian *commander-in-
chief Manuēl received them, assisted them, and sent them back to their
own *land. He set Babik as *lord over the *land and [established] the two
others as well, according to their rank; and Babik was his *companion-in-
arms †for all the days of his life. The Armenian *sparapet* Manuēl likewise installed *nahapet*s and *lords for every *district, and provided
peaceful *leadership for all.³ And the entire *land of Armenia lived in
peace under the protection of Manuēl †all the days of his life. All the
people of the *land of Armenia savored their days, they ate, drank, and
rejoiced⁴ for those seven years of Manuēl's *lordship, until the division of
the *land of Armenia and the dissolution of the kingdom.⁵

*Chapter xliii. Concerning Meružan Arcruni, who marched with an
army against Manuēl and was slaughtered by him.*¹

Now Meružan Arcruni had revolted against the king of Armenia
long ago, even in the days of King Aršak. He had given his hand to the
king of Persia of his own free will, accepted the Mazdean religion, and

apostatized from the Christian faith.[2] Many times he had been the *guide[3] of the Persian army, and brought the *greatest harm to the *land of Armenia; and he was still with the Persian king.[4] Then this Meružan incited the Persian king, took a large force from him, and came to the *land of Armenia. He had boasted with much vainglory that either he would seize, bind, and bring Manuēl to the Persian king, or he would cut off his head and carry it before the Persian king.

He set out and came to the *land of Armenia with the entire multitude of the Persian army. He left the *camp of the Persian army in the *district of Korčēk[c], while he himself, with his own *hereditary *contingent of collected bandits, separated himself from the Aryan[5] *contingent.[6] He
254 intended to fall on Manuēl while he was unprepared and win a name for himself alone. He sought to accomplish this all alone, so that he would carry out the military action by himself to his own glory. Consequently †he spoke these words to the *commanders of the Aryan *contingent and said: "I will go first to seek information, and then lead you against [them] so that it will be easy to strike and seize them in this manner."

And so, he took his *contingent, set out and reached the *land of the *district of Kog, occupied the place, and sent scouts to Manuēl's *camp. The scouts went and spied out Manuēl's *camp, which was in the *district of Bagrawand, in the *town of Bagawan, which is near the ruins of the *city of Zarehawand.[7] They came and spied out Manuēl's *camp and the place within the *camp where the herd of horses was to be found; and they went and brought back the information. [Meružan] planned to seize the horses in the *camp and concentrated on this, and rejoicing he said boastfully to his troops: "Tomorrow at this time Manuēl will be captured, chained, and thrown down by me, and his wife Vardanoyš will be dishonored in front of him." And he hastily set out to carry out the deed which he intended to accomplish.

Now in the region through which the *contingent was marching, there were mountains called *Ełǰerk[c]* ["Horns"] by the inhabitants. And while Meružan, together with his *contingent, was on the way, he encountered wayfarers whom †he questioned and said: "Which way does the road lie to Bagrawand?" And the wayfarers †answered saying: "The road is through the 'Horns.'" and Meružan was greatly confused and displeased by these words, nevertheless he gave the order to drag the travelers brutally away and to beat them.[8] He himself continued along the same road. He turned to Chaldaean spells and the casting of lots, but he did not receive from his witchcraft the propitious augury which he had sought.[9]

Then, in great anger, he sent his scouts ahead, and raided the place where the herd of horses was tethered so that he might contrive to seize it first. But they did not find the herd of horses when they reached the place, for the Armenian *contingent had [received] a God-given faculty for
255 being ready, because the *sparapet* Manuēl had designated that [very]

hour for the entire Armenian *contingent to go out hunting. Consequently, it so happened that the entire herd of horses had been brought to the hamlet. [The men] were already prepared to ride forth on the hunt, when a bearer of ill-tidings reached the *commander-in-chief Manuēl [and] reported: "Look out, for Meružan Arcruni is coming against you with a large *contingent."[10]

Then, the entire force of the Armenian *contingent, as well as the *sparapet* Manuēl, made ready, and went to invoke the holy bones of John [the Precursor], which were in that *village.[11] They bound themselves by a *covenant, invoked God, and called the righteous *Judge to their aid, to be their help-giving overseer. Then they came forth from there, and sent off the Aršakuni *queen with her children Aršak and Vałaršak, as well as their own wives, to a *stronghold on the lofty mountain named Varaz. Manuēl also ordered the young Artawazd, the son of Vačͨē, to go with the women, but he would not consent and accept this. He was [still] a boy in years and in accordance with the pattern set for boys by Armenian custom, the head of the young Artawazd had been shaven at that time in boyish fashion according to regulation, leaving only the forelock and a hanging braid.[12] When he would not agree to go with the women, Manuēl raised his whip and beat Artawazd over his bare head, forbidding him to go into battle because of his youthful age. And so, [Artawazd] [while] under his eyes went with them, but afterward he armed himself and prepared for battle.[13]

When they had sent the *queen and all her serving-women to an *impregnable place, they armed, prepared for battle, and assembled together. With open standards and unfurled *banners he set out from the *village-*town[14] toward the western *region and there they met Meružan, who had come against them with his *contingent. [Now] that malignant sinner Meružan had given to many his *arms, his military ornaments, and insignia similar to that on his *helmet and [so] he had given his own 256 appearance to many in his *contingent, whereas he himself did not wear his insignia. When Manuēl saw [Meružan's] *contingent, he attacked it like a lion, like a wild boar,[15] together with his own *contingent, and tangled with their *contingent. He gave [particular] attention to those who bore Meružan's insignia, thinking that he would kill Meružan. And so, they struck off the heads of many enemies bearing Meružan's insignia, and perceived that it was not he.

Then the *sparapet* Manuēl †began to speak with his *companion-in-arms Babik, and said: "Do you see how that sorcerer Meružan is tricking us? But he and I have often been together before, in time of peace, and I know one of his traits: whenever he rode on horseback, his legs were not [held] close and did not touch up to the knee, but stuck out from the horse. So, let us both watch for that sign and we will perhaps be able to recognize that magician and sorcerer by that sign." The two of them watched closely and recognized Meružan by that trait, even though they saw that his appearance had been altered because he did not carry his own insignia.

Then Manuēl †raised his voice, shouted to Meružan, and said: "Ho, sorcerer! How long will you deceive us and have others slaughtered on account of you? But we know you, for there you are, and you will find no trick today to escape from our hands, for the *Lord God has brought your sins down upon your head, and the *Lord has given you over to us." When Meružan heard this, he immediately grasped his *lance and rushed forward as a champion against Manuēl. But since they were both power- ful men, both were hurled from their horses to the ground when they struck [each other] with their *lances. Manuēl's *companion-in-arms, Babik, *lord-of-the-*district of Siwnikᶜ, immediately came up and [pierced Meružan] with his *lance through the side from top to bottom, pinning him to the ground so that he could no longer rise. Meanwhile, Manuēl's grooms lifted him onto his horse. They struck off Meružan's head, and all his troops turned to flight when they saw that Meružan was dead;[16] while Manuēl's *contingent, heartened by this, took off after Meružan's forces, fell on them, slaughtered them, †and did not leave a single one of them alive.[17]

257

Now the young Artawazd had come to the battle in secret from Manuēl. He armed himself, got ready, and came down to the bank of the Epᶜrat River separately from Manuēl's *contingent. And there he struck and slaughtered many from Meružan's *contingent and killed countless *armor-clad men. When one of those who bore Meružan's insignia saw Artawazd, he scoffed at him because he saw that he was an active, beard- less youth with a pretty face. Then, wrapping his standard around his *lance, he charged against him. But [Artawazd], drawing the bow to the utmost, struck the man with an *arrow, and the *arrow piercing [him] through and through fell to the ground. And young Artawazd, the son of Vačᶜē, raised his *lance, pursued the fugitives, and †put Meružan's forces to the *sword.[18] He killed more than everyone else, and [returned] with a great name and much booty taken from the army of the foe.[19]

But a dreadful disaster occurred on that day, for the horse of Vačᶜē who was second to Manuēl[20] fell headlong and killed him. Likewise, the horse of Garǰoyl *maɫχaz broke away and killed him, for both of them were riding inexperienced and unbroken horses.

Then Manuēl returned, came to the *queen's *camp, and presented to her the head of Meružan. But Vahan's son Samuēl was not with Manuēl because he had [already] returned to the *camp. Now when the women from Manuēl's *camp saw the head of Meružan, they raised a fearful outcry and clamor because they thought that this was the head of Vahan's son Samuēl, for the two—Meružan and Samuēl—were alike. Then, they saw the long braid hanging from Meružan's head and realized from it that this was not the head of Samuēl but that of Meružan Arcruni. Nevertheless, they said: "Even so, he was our *brother."[21]

258   Then they brought to the *camp the body of Artawazd's father Vač‘ē and the body of Garǰoyl *malxaz, they mourned exceedingly and lamented over them. They [also] brought in the man bearing Meružan's insignia whom Artawazd had struck down with his *arrow. And everyone marveled that the *arrow had pierced him through, and because they tended him, he was saved from death.[22] And when the Persian army left by Meružan in the *district of Korčēk‘ heard that Meružan had been killed and his *contingent destroyed, it fled to the Persian *land, and profound peace settled on the *land of Armenia.

*Chapter xliv. Concerning the way that the *sparapet Manuēl enthroned the young Aršak; and Manuēl himself then died.*[1]

After he had done all this, the *sparapet* and *commander-in-chief Manuēl went with the Aršakuni *queen and her two children, Aršak and Vałaršak, to the *district of Karin, together with the entire Armenian *army, the *highest *nobility and the *naxarars, and all the *tanutērs went with them. The *sparapet* Manuēl gave his daughter Vardanduxt in marriage to the young Aršak Aršakuni and thus made him his son-in-law.[2] He also arranged a marriage for his *brother Vałaršak, giving him the daughter of the Bagratuni *aspet from the *district of Sper, who had been the royal *coronants from the very origin of the Aršakuni royal *clan.[3] The marriages were celebrated with great splendor, and the entire *land of Armenia rejoiced, jubilated, and was transported with joy.

After this, all the men of the Armenian *realm *assembled once more together and [Manuēl] made the young Aršak king of the Armenian *land, and his *brother Vałaršak second to him.[4] And at this too, the entire *land of Armenia jubilated and rejoiced with great joy.

259   After this, the *sparapet* and *commander-in-chief of Armenia Manuēl grew sick with a mortal illness. He summoned his son Artašir and transmitted to him his *dominion as well as his office of *sparapet* and *commander-in-chief.[5] And he commanded him to serve king Aršak obediently and be faithful, to strive and toil, to fight and sacrifice yourself for the *realm of Armenia, to die willingly for the *realm, "like your *valiant ancestors. For," he said: "this is right and most pleasing to God, and He will not abandon you as long as you remain so. You will leave a *valorous name on *earth, and offer your righteousness to heaven. Do not fear death at all, but put your hope in Him who has created and fortified all. Keep yourself away from deceit, foulness, and evil, and serve the *Lord God with purity and loyalty. Die bravely for your God-serving *realm, since that is in itself a death for God, for His church, and His *covenant, and for the *true-lords of this *realm, the Aršakuni."[6] He

then wrote an *official-letter to the king of the Greeks and entrusted to him the Armenian *realm and King Aršak.[7]

And after this, when everyone had come and gathered around him as he lay sick on his bed—Aršak the king and Vardanduχt the king's wife, all the *nobles, the *magnates, and *naχarars of Armenia, both men and women, and all the notable persons in general, Manuēl stripped and bared all his limbs before them all and showed that there was not a space of sound skin as large as a coin on his [whole] body, which had been wounded in battle, for there were more than fifty scars of wounds,[8] even on the virile member, that he uncovered and displayed before everyone. [Then] he †began to weep, and to say: "From childhood I was nurtured in battle, and I *valiantly accepted every wound. Why has it not been my lot to die in battle, rather than have a death fit for a beast? For it were good for me to have died in battle for my *realm so that the churches and God's *covenant should not be trampled under foot! Would that it had been my lot to die for the *true-lords of this *realm, the Aršakuni, for our wives, for our children, for the people serving God, for *brothers, companions, and faithful friends. But although I bore myself most gallantly, it is my lot to die a vile death in my bed!"[9]

He spoke these and many more similar words before King Aršak and before everyone. †He also implored King Aršak, and said: "I have lived before God in fervent Christian faith. Do not offer excessive tears or lament hopelessly for me like the heathens, for it is not fitting to weep for those who hope for resurrection and a second life and the [second] coming of Christ. I have lived until now in the hope and fear [of the Lord]; do not, you, transgress the Commandments of God; strive all the more for righteousness and mercy. For our great *patriarch Nersēs always commanded this,[10] he put it in practice himself every hour of his life and taught it to others.[11] For he comforted the poor, the homeless, the captive, the abandoned, the stranger, [and] the wanderer. He said: 'There is nothing greater and more *honorable before the *Lord than mercy and alms-giving.'[12] And he considered weeping and lamentation for the dead a grievous sin and in his own time he uprooted it from the *land of Armenia, and no one dared weep or lament in his time, but after his death, senseless men dared to perform this [again]. But as for me, do not weep! And should anyone do this, let him be condemned.[13] For after my death I do not have the *authority to order that the things that are against my will not be done, but let those who love me do [what I ask] in remembrance of me. Do not fear to die in battle, where I have not died, for nothing comes without God."

He spoke these and similar words. He distributed with his own hands great and boundless treasures to the poor and needy. And he gave a great part of his possessions to the churches and *martyria; and gave great treasures to the *high-priests.[14] And so, he died.[15]

But when the great *sparapet* Manuēl was dead, the command he had given about lamentations was not kept. No one heeded it, but the entire people of the *land of Armenia, the *azats and the *peasants alike, wept with great lamentations over him. For every man mourned for the illustrious fosterer of the *realm Manuēl as for a father,[16] for his gentleness, his love of mankind, his mildness, his calm, his careful charity. With open mouths all sighed after him and ardently longed for their *valiant *commander, their savior, the victorious, illustrious, and zealous [leader] who had thus detached and separated himself [from them] and gone far away.

Sixth Book of Biwzand

Sixth Listing of the Tales.

Chronological Tables

i. Concerning the division of the realm of Armenia in two because half of the Armenian *race was ruled by Aršak at the order of the king of the Greeks, and half of the *race was ruled by Xosrov at the order of the king of Persia. And how, having divided the *realm of Armenia in two, they set a *boundary between them; and how other *realms and *districts were dispersed, and the *borders of both portions were diminished on every *side.

ii. Concerning the bishops who were notable at that time in the portion that was Xosrov's *realm in the *land of Armenia. First concerning the actions of Zawēn.

iii. Concerning Šahak Korčēkᶜ, who became *senior-bishop after Zawēn.

iv. Concerning Aspurak of Manazkert, who became *senior-bishop after Šahak

v. Concerning the bishops Pᶜawstos and Zortᶜ.

vi. Concerning Aṙawstom, the brother of Bishop Pᶜawstos.

vii. Concerning Artitᶜ, bishop of Basean.

viii. Concerning Bishop Yohan, his actions, greed, and senselessness, and [his] shameless words and deeds; and the signs that God manifested over him; and how he sinfully begged and received [satisfaction of his] greed from kings.[1]

ix. Concerning the same Yohan.

x. Concerning the same Yohan.

xi. Concerning Bishop Kiwrakos.

xii. Concerning Zortꜥuaz, bishop of the *district of Vanand.

xiii. Concerning Tirik and Movsēs, bishops of the *district of Basean.

xiv. Concerning the bishop of Aršarunikꜥ.[2]

264   xv. Concerning the *senior-bishop Aspurak.

xvi. Concerning the holy and virtuous Gind, who was at that time the head of all Armenian *solitaries, *anchorites, *hermits, and *solitary-communities.

This is the end of all the tales, according to my information, this very book, readers, [ten houses in counted numbers(?)].[3]

Book VI
The End—
Conclusion of the Preceeding;
Omitted Portions from the Previous[1]

Chapter i. Concerning the division of the *realm of Armenia in two and the ruling of[2] Aršak at the order of the king of the Greeks, and the ruling of [the other] half of the *race by Xosrov at the order of the king of Persia. And how, having divided the *realm in two, they set a *boundary between themselves, and how the *realm was cut down on each of its two sides.[3]

Then, after the death of the Armenian *commander-in-chief Manuēl, nothing could sustain Aršak's rule over the *realm.[4] Many of the Armenian *naχarars broke away from him, went to the king of Persia, handed the *realm of Armenia over to him, and asked him for an Aršakuni king. And he, on his side, accepted with great joy to give [them] by his order [a king] from the same Armenian royal *house of the Aršakuni, and thus secure through him the *realm of Armenia for himself. He then found a youth from this same *house named Xosrov, placed the crown on his head, gave him his [own] sister Zruanduχt as a wife, and gave him the entire army under his power.[5] He also gave his deputy the Zik as a mentor[6] to King Xosrov. After this, they set out and came to the *realm of Armenia. And when King Aršak saw them, he withdrew, abandoned the place, and went to the *territory of the Greeks. And so [the king of the Greeks][7] was the supporter of Aršak king of Armenia and the king of Persia, that of Xosrov.

Then the forces of the king of the Greeks came to the support of King Aršak, [who was] around the *district of Ekełeac[c], while the Persian army and King Xosrov were in the *district of Ayrarat. And envoys and messengers of the two kings—of the Greeks and of the Persians—went back and forth from one to the other. Then a joint consultation for union and agreement was held between the two kings of the Greeks and the Persians, and they determined that first it would be good to divide the *realm of Armenia in two between themselves.[8] "For:" they said, "this powerful and wealthy kingdom is set between us. It will be good if we are

266

able to perturb and ruin this kingdom. First [let us] divide it in two with the Aršakuni kings whom we have installed, then [let us] strive to impinge on and impoverish them [and] drive them into *subjection so that they should not be able to raise their head between us."[9]

They confirmed this plan and divided the *realm in two. The portion on the Persian *side belonged to King Xosrov, and the portion on the Greek side belonged to King Aršak. But many *districts were gnawed and cut off from them here and there, and only a small portion of the two kingdoms was left to the two kings.[10] But nevertheless, the two Armenian kings, Aršak and Xosrov, divided the core *districts[11] of the Armenian kingdom that were left to them on both *sides between them; and the two Aršakuni kings peacefully set a *boundary between these two portions.[12] And so the *land of Armenia [was] in two parts [and] obeyed two kings, [with] each part [subject] to its own king. The portion of Xosrov was larger than that of Aršak, however, and many *districts were cut off from both. And the kingdom of Armenia was diminished, divided, and scattered. And it declined from its greatness at that time and thereafter.[13]

267   *Chapter ii. Concerning the bishops who were notable at that time in the portion of Xosrov's *realm in the *land of Armenia, the one in the hands of the Persians. First concerning the actions of Zawēn.*[1]

This Zawēn was a descendant of the famed Bishop Ałbianos from the *village of Manazkert.[2] He was a man of evil life, harsh and envious. And he introduced a [new] regulation in his own time, that is, he taught all the priests to wear military dress.[3] And so they abandoned the regulation of the apostolic churches, and began to go each according to his own will. For the priests no longer wore the regular ankle-length vestment, as had been the original rule, but began to wear a bias-cut tunic above the knees.[4] They decorated their clothing with multicolored braiding, and strutted about unsuitably. And priests unheedingly wore the pelts of dead beasts, which was [likewise] unsuitable. As for Zawēn himself, he arrayed himself in garments decorated with varied braiding and spangles;[5] he wore sables, and ermine, and wolf skins. He draped fox pelts around himself, unabashedly ascended the bema, and sat there.[6] Thus, Zawēn passed †all the days of his life in gluttony, greed, and debauchery. And he occupied his see †all the days of his life, three years in all.[7]

*Chapter iii. Concerning Šahak Korčēk', who became *senior-bishop in the place of Zawēn*[1]

Then Šahak from Korčēk' became *senior-bishop in the place of Zawēn for two years following the death of the latter. He was a Christian man, but he was in no way offended by Zawēn's regulations [so as] to alter what he had laid down. He gave *spiritual-leadership for two years and left the *world.

268   *Chapter iv. Concerning Aspurak of Manazkert, who became *senior-bishop after Šahak[1]*

After the death of Bishop Šahak, a certain Aspurak from among the descendants of Bishop Ałbianos became *senior-bishop.[2] He was a Christian man, righteous and God-serving, and he gave *spiritual-leadership to the court of Xosrov. But in the matter of dress only, he followed the regulations of Zawēn.

Chapter v. Concerning the bishops Pᶜawstos[1] and Zortᶜ.[2]

Bishop Pᶜawstos [lived] at that time. At the time of the *chief-bishop Nersēs he had served as the administrator of his house.[3] Likewise Zortᶜ was one of his familiars.[4] For there were twelve bishops in the *house of the *patriarch under his authority; they were his co-bishops, collaborators, and joint-planners. [They were] in addition to all the bishops of the other *districts who were under him, these two [Pᶜawstos and Zortᶜ] were among the twelve.[5] They were entrusted with the supervision of the poor and were entirely loyal to him during his time.[6] And they were still alive in the years of Xosrov and Aršak, the two kings of the divided [realm].

Chapter vi. Concerning Ařostom, the brother of Bishop Pᶜawstos.[1]

And Bishop Pᶜawstos had a *brother who was a wondrous *mountain-
269   dweller [leařnakan] of the religious *solitary-*anchorites. They were of Roman *race, and this man led an exemplary life †through all of the days of his life.[2] He lived in the *district of Ayrarat and was guided by the Holy Spirit. He wandered in the desert and the mountains dressed in skins and eating grass until the day of his [eternal] rest. Then, when he died, they took up his body, carried it from the desert, and buried it in the *patriarch Nersēs' own *village called Amokᶜ,[3] and they commemorated him year after year.

Chapter vii. Concerning Artitᶜ, bishop of Basean.[1]

Artitᶜ bishop of Basean was outstanding in those days among the existing bishops, for he was a *venerable [patuakan] and excellent old man. He led a life of purity and truth and was worthy of the Holy Spirit. He went about with great power and performed the *greatest signs for many years. He had been a disciple of the great Daniēl who lived in the time of King Tiran,[2] and he was still alive in the days of Xosrov and Aršak, the two kings of Armenia.[3]

Chapter viii. Concerning Bishop Yohan and his actions, and his senseless and shameless words and deeds; and the signs that God manifested over him.[1]

Bishop Yohan, if it be fitting to call him a bishop, was the son of the former *patriarch P'aren.[2] He was a hypocrite and he presented himself to men as a faster and the wearer of a hair shirt; he did not even wear shoes, but wrapped [his feet] with woven bands [of grass] in summer and with straw in winter.[3] But he overflowed with boundless greed and would not give up his greed [even] from the fear of God—so much so that he even performed unworthy and unbelievable actions.

Now once, it so happened that he was on a journey riding on a pack horse, and he met a young foreign layman riding on horseback with a *long-sword at his side, a *short-sword on his belt, and an archer's *quiver [hung] around his hips. He had well-washed and anointed hair, a headband on his head, and a fur pelt[4] on his shoulders; and he was riding on his way, possibly from a pillaging [expedition]. Now the horse on which he was riding was of large size, lively and swift, and when Bishop Yohan saw this horse from afar he was amazed and set his eye upon it. When the rider had come close to him, Yohan, who was waiting, seized the horse's bridle and said: "Get down from your horse at once, because [I want] to have [some] words with you." The man answered: "You do not know me and I do not know you, what words can you have to speak to me?" The man was all the more [insistent] that he happened to be drunk and obstinate about getting down from his horse. But Yohan forced him to get off the horse and led him a little way from the road. He then †ordered the man to bow down and said: "I am ordaining you priest." But the other answered, [saying] about himself: "I have been a brigand, a murderer, and evildoer, and a fornicator from childhood. I am still doing these same things, I am in no way worthy of such a thing." And the man was very stubborn and argued, but [Yohan] was even worse than he. Yohan forced the man to the ground, laid his hands on [him], to make him a priest. Then, raising him up he bade him loosen the ties of his cloak and put on a gown. And he said: "Go to your *village and be the priest of the *village from which you come," because he did not even know from what village he came.[5] Yohan himself came up to the horse, seized it, and said: "Let this be my *reward for making you a priest." The man continued to be stubborn about the horse and would not agree to give it up, but [Yohan] forcibly seized the horse and sent the man on his way. And all these things occurred because of a [mere] horse.[6]

Then the man who had put on the gown against his will went on to his own *house, and he went into his own household. And he said to his wife and to the household: "Come, let us pray!" And they said [to him]: "Are you mad, has some *devil gotten into you?" But he repeated: "Come, let us pray, for I am a priest." But they were amazed, some blushed, some laughed, and they were obstinate for a long time until they finally consented to pray with him. Then his wife said to her husband: "Are you not a catechumen and not baptized?" And the man answered his wife: "He took me by surprise and did not give me [a chance] to recollect, and I too did not remember to tell it to him. He made me a priest, took the horse with its bridle and saddle, and went off." Then the household told the man: "Get up, go again to the bishop, and say: 'I had not [yet] been baptized, how did you make me a priest?'" So he got up, went to the bishop, and said to him: "I had not [yet] been baptized, how did you make me a priest?" And Yohan said: "Bring water in a pitcher." And taking the water, he poured it on his head and said: "Go, I have baptized you." And he sent the man quickly away.

Chapter ix. Concerning the same Yohan.[1]

Once this same Yohan was passing by a vineyard, and it was the time of the vintage. And one of the vintners †called out to him and said: "*Lord Bishop, bless us and this vintage." And Yohan said: "May it produce thistles and thorns!" And the man answered: "May your own body produce thistles and thorns in return for your cursing us unjustly." And signs appeared from God, for when the bishop came to his *residence, [van(k^c)], blows fell upon him [and] he began to be pricked all over his limbs as though pierced by thorns. And he was extremely afflicted [and] suffered excessive torments from the blows, and he was in great anguish for many days. Then he sent for the vintner and begged him to pray over him so that he might be delivered from these torments. And the vintner said: "Who am I to bless or curse anyone, let alone a bishop?" But Yohan then pressed him until the vintner †offered up this prayer and said: "*Lord God, You know that I am a sinful and unworthy man, I do not understand the troubles in which I am embroiled. Deliver me from this evil! For they are saying to me: 'You cursed a bishop,' and they say: 'This happened because of your words.' Death would be better for me, for I do not understand what they are saying about me." And as soon as he had said this, the bishop was healed, and thorns began to emerge from all over his body, and they were like the thorns of plants. And he rose up immediately, healed from his sickness, and was well.

272

Chapter x. Concerning the same Yohan.[1]

This same bishop Yohan, the son of P^{c}aṙēn, turned into a buffoon whenever he came to the king of Armenia. He exercised the greed for which he longed and thirsted through buffoonery, and these were his tricks.[2] He got down on all fours, hands and feet, crawled in front of the king, braying with the voice of a camel and fawning like a camel. And †he mixed a few words into his howls, saying in his braying voice: "I am a camel, I am a camel, I bear away the sins of the king, put the sins of the king on me, let me take them away!" And the kings wrote and sealed deeds for *villages and *estates [*agarak*] and put them on Yohan's back in exchange for their sins. And so, he received *villages and *estates and treasures from the kings of Armenia by turning into a camel and, as he said, taking away their sins.

This is the kind of man that Yohan was, bound by greed and covetousness †all the days of his life. He did such things because of avarice, and it was unworthy.

273   *Chapter xi. Concerning Bishop Kiwrakos.*[1]

Kiwrakos, the bishop of Tayk', was called by the name Šahap ["lord, ruler"]. He was a just man serving God according to God's will, and he gave upright *spiritual-leadership to his people in accordance with the truth. And he fulfilled his duties as bishop according to God's will †all the days of his life.

Chapter xii. Concerning Zort'uaz, bishop of Vanand.[1]

And Zort'uaz, bishop of the *district of Vanand, was a holy and virtuous man, worthy of God and drunk with the Holy Spirit.[2] He conducted himself and acted in Christian fashion, and gave *spiritual-leadership to his people according to God's will.

Chapter xiii. Concerning the bishops Tirik and Movsēs.[1]

There were also two bishops in the *district of Basean, Movsēs and Tirik. They were good men of angelic life, holy, believing, worthy of the call. And each gave *spiritual-leadership to his people along God's path †all the days of his life.

274   *Chapter xiv. Concerning Bishop Aharon.*[1]

About that time, there was a bishop [named] Aharon in the Armenian *realm. He was an outstanding and distinguished man of *great [*k'aj*] virtue. And he gave illuminating *spiritual-leadership to his people †all the days of his life.

*Chapter xv. Concerning the *senior-bishop Aspurak.*[1]

And the *senior-bishop of Armenia was Aspurak, a holy and pious man, fearing God and men. But he was unable to address a word of reproof to anyone. He kept himself silent, meek, prudent, and modest. He implored God with fasts and prayers every hour. But as to dress, he conformed to the regulations of Zawēn and wore ornamented and braided garments. But he was a gentle and humble man, charitable and compassionate during †all the days of his life.

*Chapter xvi. Concerning the holy and virtuous Gind, who was at that time the head of all Armenian religious *anchorites, *solitaries, and *solitary-communities.*[1]

This Gind was from the *district of Tarōn and had been a disciple of the great Daniēl.[2] And after him, he was the head of the religious [*abełayicᶜ*] and the *spiritual-teacher of-hermits [*mianjkᶜ*] the *spiritual-leader of *solitaries [*menakkᶜ*], the overseer of *solitary-communities [*vanerraykᶜ*], the teacher of all *anchorites-dwelling-in-the-desert [*anapataworkᶜ*], and the supervisor of all those who had renounced the *world for the love of God.[3] They lived in the desert, in inaccessible rock-hewn
275 caverns, or "in caves in the *ground," having but one garment [and] going barefoot; they were abstemious, eating [only] herbs, vegetables, and roots. "They wandered about" like wild beasts "in the mountains, covered with skins, hides, and goatskins, †bearing want, suffering, and anguish, straying through the desert" in cold and in heat, in hunger and in thirst, for the love of God.[4] They were willing to bear such things patiently †through all the days of their lives, for, as it is written: "the *world was not worthy of them." Like flocks of birds, they dwelled "in the clefts of the rocks,"[5] in stony caves, †with nothing, possessing nothing, sparing themselves nothing, and giving no care to their bodies. And St. Gind was their true leader, for all the people of the *land of Armenia alike called him their *spiritual-teacher. But there were among them other disciples who resembled their *spiritual-teacher and had been trained by him, and their names were Vačᶜak, Artoyt, and Maraχ.[6] And their colleague was Trdat, who had been the chief-deacon of the great *high-priest Nersēs[7] and who had been drawn after Nersēs's death to this band of *desert-dwellers [around] this same *spiritual-leader. And St. Gind also took in the young Mušē,[8] whom he had brought up [and] who shared in the great Gind's way of life. And he had many other disciples with angelic ways, whose lives no one would be capable of relating.[9]

And St. Gind was filled with the Holy Spirit, as were those who were with him. And, in the same manner, they performed the *greatest signs and had many prodigies, and healed the sick in the name of our *Lord Jesus Christ. And they wandered in many heathen places in distant *realms and turned back many strayers in "the dispersion of the heathen."[10] And they brought many men to the knowledge of life and the way of the truth. And St. Gind filled all the deserts [*anapat*] with *solitaries [*menakkᶜ*] and all the inhabited places with *communities [*vaner*], and in the *world he corrected and set down many regulations for mankind, according to the God-loving religion. But for his own, lot, he took as a dwelling place the desert from
276 which spring the sources of the Epᶜrat River. He lived there in "a cleft of

the rocks," where the earlier dwelling of the first Grigor had been [located]. And the name of the place was Oskikᶜ.[11] And the great *anchorite [*anapatawor*] Gind dwelled in the same cleft, and St. Mušē was continually with him. But the others wandered about over other *districts at the command of their leader Gind. And St. Trdat lived in the *district of Tarōn, where he had built his *brotherhoods [*ełbarcᶜ*].[12]

Commentary

Commentary

The Commentary contains information pertinent to the corresponding chapters of the text and cross-references to similar material to be found in other portions. The Appendices should be consulted for more systematic and extensive treatment of individual names and terms.

The following conventions have been observed throughout this section: all titles have been given in abbreviated form, the full reference being reserved for the Bibliography; references to Book and chapter numbers, without indication of author or title, are taken from the text of the BP; references to the various translations of BP are given under the translator's name without further particulars, which are provided in the section of the Bibliography devoted to these translations (section I); cross-references to notes without an indication of chapter are to notes within the same chapter.

Preliminary Statement

1. According to Malχasyanc⁽, p. 19 #1, this Preliminary Statement was not the work of the original compiler of the work but of a subsequent editor. See Intro., pp. 16–18, 35.

2. See Intro., p. 16–22, for the problem of the numbering of the "Books" (*dprut⁽iwnk⁽*).

3. According to Anasyan, *Review*, p. 10, the phrase "*žamanakakan kanonk⁽ matenic⁽*" should be taken to mean *žamanakagrut⁽iwn* "chronography" or *k⁽ronikon* "chronicle," because *žamanakakan kanonk⁽* is precisely the terminology used to render the title of Eusebius's *Chronicle*, as *žamanakagir aṙnem* is the translation of Greek χρονογραφέω. In BP the phrase is used in apposition to *patmut⁽iwn*, "narrative, history," and *kanonel drošmel* is an idiom for "to set [something] in the order of chronological events." Hence, the first sentence should be given the translation adopted here. Cf. NBHL, I, p. 828, s. v. *žamanakagir*.

4. For the tradition identifying the Armenians as "sons of T⁽orgom," see Appendix I, "T⁽orgom." The alternate tradition, identifying the Armenians as "sons of Askenaz" (Gen. 10:3), is given by Koriwn, i, p. 22 (= tr. p. 21), and repeated by MK/D, I, xiv, p. 32 (= MD, p. 19), who associates the "descendants of Askenaz" with the "realm of T⁽orgom."

5. See Intro., pp. 48–49, and Appendix III, *ašχarh*, for the differentiation between *ašχarh*, "realm," *erkir*, "land," and *erkir haykakan lezui*, "land of Armenian speech."

6. BP alternates interchangeably the terms *k⁽ahanayapet*, "high-priest," *episkoposapet*, "chief-bishop," and *hayrapet*, "patriarch" to designate the primates of the Armenian church. See below, n. 9, for the term *glχawor episkopos* and Appendix III, s.v., for the anachronistic use of the term *kat⁽ołikos*.

7. See Intro., pp. 2, 38, 50, 54, for BP's emphasis on the hereditary position of the Aršakuni (Arsacids) as the "true/native lords" of the Armenian realm. See also Appendix III, *bnak tēr*.

8. See VI.i for the partition and decline of Arsacid Armenia.

9. See Intro., pp. 2, 15, 20, and Appendix III, *glχawor episkopos*, for use of this term to designate the non-Gregorid primates who ruled after the murder of St. Nersēs the Great. See also above, n. 6.

10. See Intro., p. 16 and above n. 1, for the subsequent addition of these tables to the original text.

III.i

1. See Intro., pp. 16–22, for the problem of the identification of Book III as the "Beginning" of the *Epic Histories*.

2. The characterization of Armenia as "the realm of the sons of T⁽orgom" given in the corresponding title of this chapter in the Table of Contents is omitted here, while the introductory characterization "chronological account" given here is missing in the Table of Contents. The minor variations found throughout between the titles of chapters in the Tables of Contents and in the text underscore the fact that they are not the work of the same hand; see Intro., p. 16 and n. 70.

van Esbroeck, "Le Roi Sanatrouk," p. 270, presents the opinions that this entire chapter and all references to Thaddeus are suspect, but given the correction suggested in Intro., pp. 20–22, it is a perfectly normal introduction to the work.

3. On the tradition of the apostolic foundation of Armenian Christianity, see Appendix I, "T⁽adēos."

4. For the "Teaching of Saint Gregory" incorporated in Aa but not in the other versions of the "Agat⁽angełos Cycle," see Thomson, AaT.

5. See Appendix I, "Grigor," for the various versions of St. Gregory's death.

6. On the "received tradition" of Trdat's "unwilling" conversion, see Aa and the other versions of the "Agat͑angełos Cycle," Thomson, Aa, pp. xxi–xxiii. Cf. also III.xiv, p. 86.
7. See Intro., p. 21, for this emendation of the text.

III.ii

1. The title of this chapter both here and in the Table of Contents is evidently defective, for Aristakēs' name has been omitted even though the possessive pronoun is given in the plural and the chapter treats the burial of both saints.
2. The reference here is unmistakably to the "received tradition" of Grigor's mission found in Aa. See Appendix I, "Grigor," also "T͑adēos" for the alternate tradition.
3. BP uses the identical phrase used by Aa, dccclviii, "*minč͑ew yōr k͑ristosakoč͑ hangstean iwroy*" (until the day that Christ called him to his rest). Nonetheless, none of the details of St. Gregory's later life found in Aa, dccclxi–dccclxii, and repeated by MX, II.xci; III.xi (= MK, pp. 247–250, 264) is given here. See Appendix I, "Grigor," for the various versions of the saint's death.
4. Possibly an echo of John 14:2.
5. BP is the first text to identify St. Gregory's burial place as T͑ordan, which is not mentioned in Aa (but can be found in the V cycle), while MX, III.xi (= MK, p. 264 and 250 n. 14) speaks of a later transfer and of the discovery of St. Gregory's relics there. For a discussion of the problem, see van Esbroeck, "Nouveau Témoin," pp. 161–162, and *idem*, "Témoignages littéraires."
6. According to MX, II.xci (= MK, p. 249), Aristakēs did not die a "confessor's death," but was murdered in the southern district of Cop͑k͑ by one Archileus, whom MX identifies anachronistically as the governor of Armenia IV, an administrative division that did not exist before A.D. 536. See Adontz, *Armenia*, pp. 127–154, 34*–37*.

III.iii

1. MX, III.v–vi (= MK, pp. 257–258) interpolates here a letter from the patriarch Vrt͑anēs to the emperor Constantius, requesting his support of King Xosrov, and records the coming of a Byzantine army to assist Xosrov's accession.
2. This is the first use in BP of the heroic epithet *k͑aǰ*, also used by Aa, xiii, dcccxcii, as an attribute of the Armenian Aršakuni kings. See IV.xxiv n. 12; V.v nn. 8, 16, and Appendix III, *kaǰ*.
3. See III.xiv and n. 11 on Aštišat of Tarōn as the "mother-church" of Armenia; also Intro., pp. 16, 46.
4. See Aa, dcclxxviii–dcclxxxi, dcclxxxiv–dcclxxxvi, dccxc, for the destruction of the heathen temples by St. Gregory, especially dcccix–dcccxvi, for the miraculous destruction of the temple of Vahagn/Heraklēs at Aštišat by means of the holy "sign" of the cross, and for the building there of martyria to contain the relics of the saints John the Precursor and At͑anaginēs (Athanogenēs). A late and highly garbled version is also to be found in the tenth-century *History of Tarōn*, attributed to Ps. Yovhannēs Mamikonean, pp. 75–77, 94–116 who seems to distinguish an *apostoleion* from the *propheteion* of St. John. Koriwn, p. 88 xxiv, [= trans. p. 48] mentions the presence of a martyrium at Aštišat in connection with the burial there of St. Sahak I. This may have been a single structure serving as a shrine for all the relics, possibly a multistoried structure such as the one represented on a stele of the monument at Ojun (see S. X. Mnac͑akanyan, "Ob odnom," pp. 95–105 and Garsoïan, "Substratum," fig. 1a). But cf. also, for the gradual expansion of early sanctuaries such as that of St. Thekla at Seleucia in Cilicia, Dagron, *Ste. Thècle*, pp. 55–165, and below, n. 6; as well as III.xiv, where the *propheteion* and the martyria of the saints seem to be distinguished.

5. Anasyan, *Review*, pp. 11–12 prefers to take the phrase "as was the . . . custom" in a general sense instead of applying it specifically to Vrtᶜanēs alone. He correctly notes that the "sacrifice offered" was, of course, that of the Eucharist, as was also understood by Emin (CHAMA, I, p. 211 and Lauer, p. 4) and not the animal sacrifice, or *matał*, suggested by Gevorgian (p. 8). Finally, Anasyan prefers the "giving" of communion to the "partaking" of it.

6. The text reads "*katarel and ami ami ewtᶜn angam*" (to celebrate there seven times a year or each year)." Following the suggestion of Norayr Biwzandacᶜi, Malχasyancᶜ corrected this in his modern Armenian translation (p. 68 and 311 n. 6) to read "*ami ami eōtᶜn sahmi amsoy*" (on the seventh day of the month of Sahmi) which would bring this passage into complete agreement with the information given in Aa, dcccxv, "*katarel and am yamē. . . zyišatak srbocᶜn, or ōr eōtᶜn ēr amsoyn sahmi*" ([to] celebrate there from year to year . . . the commemoration of the saints, which was on the seventh day of the month Sahmi), and reflect the normal contemporary custom of commemorating the saints only once a year. Recently, however, Anasyan, *Review*, p. 14 has objected to this correction as unwarranted and has argued that seven celebrations per year were entirely possible because the holy site of Aštišat contained several martyria in addition to that of St. John. This argument does not seem convincing in view of the closeness of this passage to the account in Aa and especially the absence of evidence for the existence of such celebrations in fourth-century Anatolia, where the geographical setting and the climate hindering travel would make such a frequency all but impossible. Cf. St. Basil's *Letters*, xcv, c, clxxvi, for the similar practice of a single yearly celebration at Pergamos in Armenia Minor and Caesarea of Cappadocia; also Delehaye, *Origine*, pp. 24–49, esp. 34–35, and Leroy, "Redoublement," p. 65 for the distributive *ami ami*, "chaque année."

7. As observed by Anasyan, *Review*, p. 16, the adjective *mec*, "great" properly qualifies the noun *margarēaran*, "*propheteion*/martyrium," as is clearly the case in III.xiv, rather than St. John himself, as is done by Emin (CHAMA, I, p. 211), Malχasyancᶜ (p. 68), Gevorgian, (p. 9), but not Lauer (p. 5). See above, n. 4, and IV.xv, n. 11 for the other shrine of St. John at Bagawan.

8. As martyrs and champions of Christ, the saints share in his "valor" (*kᶜajutᶜiwn*). For the transfer of the Zoroastrian concepts of *kᶜajutᶜiwn* and *pᶜaṙkᶜ*, "glory" to the Christian God and his saints also found in Aa, see Garsoïan, "Substratum," and III.v n. 7.

9. This is a rendering of the θυσία αἰνέσεως of the Basilian Liturgy.

10. See III.xiii, xiv; IV.xv; and V.xxxi, xxxvi, for other survivals of pagan customs in Arsacid Armenia.

11. A highly condensed version of this episode is given by MX, III.ii (= MK, p. 255) where no reference is made to the role of the queen of Armenia, about whom nothing else is known, and where vague references occur to "inhabitants of that mountain" and to "nobles," as opposed to BP's precise identification of the pagan priestly clans. Cf. also MK/D, I.xiv, pp. 35–36 (= MD, p. 21), which is closer to BP; also below, nn. 13–14.

12. The reference to the fortification of the church at Aštišat indicates an isolated shrine rather than a structure included within an urban complex. See Garsoïan, "Mediaeval Armenian City," pp. 79–81.

13. MX, III.ii (= MK, p. 255) equates this miracle with that of Elisha, though Thomson (MK, p. 255 n. 3) rightly observes that the parallel is not exact. A far closer one can be found in the invisible bonds restraining the thieves of St. Spyridon of Cyprus, which Sozomenos (Soz., EH, I.xi) cites among the bishop's miracles—a story also found in Socrates (Soc. Schol., EH I.xii) who takes it from Rufinus (I.v). This miracle is a favorite *topos* of early hagiography. See Festugière, "Lieux-communs," pp. 146–148, and Intro., pp. 26–30, for BP's familiarity with contemporary hagiographic traditions.

14. This may be a reference to the priestly clan of the Vahuni, who are not mentioned in BP, but whom MX, II.ii (= MK, p. 148) links with Aštišat and the cult of Vahagn, from whom they claimed to be descended. In any case, this passage provides evidence that

religious office, be it pagan (Magi, Vahuni) or Christian (Gregorids, Ałbianids) was conceived as hereditary in certain clans during this period. Cf. III.xiii n. 25; Thomson, Aa, pp. 489–490 § 809 n. 2; Toumanoff, *Studies*, p. 215, and Intro., pp. 49–51, on hereditary offices.

15. Malχasyanc^c (p. 311 n. 7) suggests that this sentence should be corrected to "Why have you come?" Gevorgian (p. 9) follows him without any annotation, and Emin (CHAMA, I, p. 212) and Lauer (p. 5) omit the redundant sentence.

16. Cf. Thomson "Instruction," pp. 99–100 for the preliminary instruction and repentance required for baptism; also V.v; and Winkler, "Agat^{c}angełos," pp. 136–141.

III.iv

1. This is the main account of the destruction of these two *naχarar* families, which MX, III.ii (= MK, p. 255) summarizes in two sentences, omitting the role of Bishop Ałbianos and that of the *sparapet* Vač^{c}ē I Mamikonean, and to which he adds the Bznuni, who are treated separately and in greater detail in BP, III.viii.

2. BP is our main source for the information that the office of *sparapet* was hereditary in the Mamikonean house during this period. See below, III.xi and n. 7; V.i and n. 5, xxxvii, xliv. This fact is deliberately obscured by MX—see Intro., p. 45—but it is familiar to ŁP^c, xxv–xxvii, pp. 261–265 (= CHAMA, II, pp. 283–288), who calls his hero, Vardan, jointly and interchangeably "lord of the Mamikonean" and "*sparapet* of Armenia." See also Garsoïan, "Prolegomena," cols. 211–212 and n. 44b; Bedrosian, "*Sparapetut^{c}iwn*," pp. 6–46; and Appendix III, *sparapet*.

3. This formula: "*ew oč^c t^{c}ołoyr . . . ew oč zmi,*" with occasional minor variants, runs like a refrain throughout BP. See Appendix V, c; also Intro., p. 32.

4. Each clan seems to have possessed a center or "home village" (*bun gewł*), which functioned primarily as a necropolis but does not seem to have been a full-fledged *ostan*. See III.ii, xii; V.xxiv for the Gregorid localities of T^{c}il and T^{c}ordan; also IV.xix n. 6, for the Kamsarakan stronghold of Artagers, and Appendix III, *ostan*.

III.v

1. The equivocal attitude toward marriage and asceticism displayed in this chapter and elsewhere in BP may well be a reflection of the contradictory influences of extreme Syrian sexual asceticism and the continuing Zoroastrian tradition, in which procreation is one of the pious acts that hasten the eventual victory of good over evil at the end of time. This ambiguity is not paralleled in MX. See IV.iii n. 7, and Intro., pp. 53–54.

2. The text reads "father," which is clearly to be taken in the general sense of "ancestor," as is corrected by Malχasyanc^c (p. 312 n. 9). Cf. also III.vii n. 6.

3. MX, III.xi (= MK, p. 264) gives a mere sentence to Yusik's virtues and mentions neither his marriage nor the vision.

4. The assertion that Yusik had wed the "daughter" of King Tiran creates a genealogical difficulty, for we find in III.xv, xix and IV.iii the equally unequivocal statement that the patriarch's sons Pap and At^{c}anaginēs had married the same king's "sisters" (i.e. their own great-aunts). Moreover, Yusik is referred to below once more as the king's "son-in-law" (see n. 8). The gap in generations is probably due to a *lapsus calami*, but these consanguineous marriages may also indicate the continuing influence in Christian Armenia of the Zoroastrian tradition in which consanguineous marriage (Pahl. χwētūkdas ‹ OP χ^{v}aētvadaθa) was a pious act: see Garsoïan, "Prolegomena," cols. 220–221 and n. 60. If accurately recorded, the generational span would be far more likely to occur in the milieu of the Persian royal harem, where the king of kings normally wed vertically his mother and his

daughters as well as his sisters. See III.xv n. 2; IV.v n. 47; also IV.iv n. 25 for the condemnation of this practice by the Armenian church; and Toumanoff, *Manuel*, pp. 74/6 and note 224/4, who suggests that Yusik had married the daughter of Trdat the Great.

5. As noted by Malχasyanc^c (312 n. 11), the reference here to Yusik's descendants in the plural must allude not only to his grandson, St. Nersēs (IV.iii–iv), but also to the latter's son, St. Sahak I, the last Gregorid primate of Armenia, whose pontificate (ca. 387–439) lay beyond the chronological span of BP. This fact provides additional confirmation for the fifth- and not fourth-century date attributed to the work: see Intro., pp. 6–11.

6. See above, n. 1.

7. See III.iii n. 8 and Appendix III, *p^cark^c*, for the Christianization of the Iranian royal glory.

8. "*p^cesayut^cean t^cagaworin*": see above, n. 4, for the genealogical puzzle.

9. The juxtaposition of youth and old age (*puer senex*) is a favorite *topos* of early hagiography; see Festugière, "Lieux-communs," pp. 137–139.

10. Hebr. 11:26.

11. Cf. Mark 11:29–30.

12. The Venice ed. (p. 24 and n. 1) gives *i yaneroyn*, "from his father-in-law" instead of the reading *i baneloyn* or *banereroyn* of most mss. Malχasyanc^c (p. 312 n. 10) follows the Venice reading. Nevertheless, *baneroyn ‹ banear* "talk" can be found in NBHL, I, p. 432 col. 1, "*Ban kam banear,*" citing this passage, and is entirely acceptable in context. I am indebted for this correction to H. Markaryan of the Institute of Oriental Studies in Erevan, to whom I would like to express my thanks for his help.

13. This passage is a direct quotation, *mutatis mutandis*, of the angelic announcement to Joseph (Matt. 1:20). The slight transposition characteristic of BP points to a quotation from memory or by ear, rather than from a written text; see Intro., pp. 24–26.

14. See above, n. 5.

15. Perhaps a reminiscence of II Cor. 4:6.

16. Malχasyanc^c (p. 312 n. 11) saw a reference to the Armenian translation of the Scriptures in the phrase, "glorify Christ in many tongues," but this seems rather far-fetched.

17. Cf. Gal. 2:9–10; Apoc. 3:12, and below, IV.iv n. 34

18. Cf. Matt. 13:37–42; Hebr. 6:7–8.

19. Perhaps a reminiscence of II Cor. 6:4.

20. *aparasan ‹ apa*[neg.] = Phl. **rasan*, "bridle, cord" = "unbridled," according to Leroy, "Composés en -apa," p. 369, who sees this form as direct Iranian borrowing, as against the variant *ap-erasan* (cf. Arm. *erasan*, "bridle" with a prothetic *e*, which he considers to be, "en arménien une forme refaite."

III.vi

1. Peeters, "Les Débuts," p. 21, is of the opinion that this episode is taken from a "Life of St. Grigoris" since it contains many of the standard banalities of the hagiographic genre. This is entirely possible, see Intro., pp. 27ff. Both the similarities of this account with that of MX, III.iii (= MK, p. 255–257) and their problematic differences (see Appendix I, "Grigoris"), however, suggest the presence of a historical core.

2. See Appendix III, s.v., for the anachronistic use of this term.

3. See III.iii n. 8, Cf. I Tim. 6:1–2 and perhaps I Peter 3:15.

4. See Appendix I, "Mazk^cut^ck^c," and the next chapter for the indentification of Sanēsan as an Aršakuni. This identification is sustained by MX III.iii (= MK p. 256), but he gives the king's name as Sanatruk; see III.vii n. 1.

5. As a member of the Aršakuni royal house (see preceding note), Sanēsan presumably shared in the "supernatural valor" bestowed on legitimate rulers, even though he was an enemy; see Appendix III, *k^caj*.

6. See Appendix I, "Grigoris," for the disputed indentification of the "northern sea."

7. MX III.iii (= MK, p. 256) calls this district P^cok^cr Siwnik^c; see Appendix II, "Haband."

8. See above, III.iii and n. 6.

III.vii

1. MX, III.ix (= MK, pp. 261–262) gives a different version of this war, in which he involves King Šāhpuhr II of Persia. He ignores Sanēsan and makes an Arsacid companion of St. Grigoris, named Sanatruk, the villain responsible for the saint's death and the war (cf. III.iii, vii = MK, pp. 256, 259). His heroes here are the *aspet* Bagrat Bagratuni and Vahan Amatuni, while BP's hero, the *sparapet* Vač^cē I Mamikonean, is not mentioned in keeping with MX's customary anti-Mamikonean bias. See Intro., pp. 44–45, and below, n. 10.

2. None of these tribes is mentioned in MX, III.ix (= MK, p. 261), which refers to "the inhabitants of the northern Caucasus" at this point. In III.liv (= MK, p. 322), however, he refers to the Garagac^cik^c by name. Malχasyanc^c (p. 312 n. 13) considers all of them to nomadic Scythian tribes, but Eremyan, "Narody," and *idem, Ašχarh.*, p. 102, notes similarities to modern toponymn and attempts to determine their geographical areas. See Appendix I, "Mazk^cut^ck^c," also "Egersuank^c, Gugark^c, T^cawaspark^c."

3. See IV.iii for the "lords with contingents and banners."

4. The numbering of the army by means of a cairn of stones is not mentioned by MX at this point, but he notes this device in connection with a presumed campaign of Artašēs of Armenia against the Lydian king Croesus; III.xii (= MK, p. 148). Cf. Herodotus, IV.81 and Procopius, *Bell. Pers.*, I.xviii. 52–53 for the Scythian and Persian custom of throwing arrows into a basket to keep count of the survivors of a battle; also Josh. 4:3–9 for a possible Biblical parallel, and Leroy, "Redoublement," p. 65 for the distributive, *gndi gndi*, "troupe par troupe."

5. Satala in Armenia Minor and Ganjak of Atrpatakan/Atropatenē marked the borders of Greater Armenia in this period. See Aa, dcccxlii, and Appendix II, "Satał," "Ganjak."

6. As noted by Malχasyanc^c, (p. 312–313 n. 14), BP uses the term *ełbayr*, "brother" as a general term for "kinsman." See below, IV.xv for Gnel Aršakuni and V.xliii for Meružan Arcruni; also Appendix III, *ełbayr.*

7 See Leroy, "Redoublement," p. 65 for the intensive *k^cajs k^cajs.* "très braves."

8. The surprise attack on the enemy camp by night or at daybreak also seems to be a *topos* of the epic victory. See Appendix V, b, c, e.

9. This phrase, with minor variants, is ubiquitous in Scriptures, consequently no direct reference can be identified.

10. BP refers to Bagrat Bagratuni and Vahan Amatuni among others as mere *nizakakic^c*, "companions-in-arms," lit. "fellow-spearmen" of his hero Vač^cē I Mamikonean. Cf. above n. 1 and Intro., p. 44, for BP's glorification of the Mamikonean house. According to Toumanoff, *Studies*, p. 320, this is the earliest mention of the Bagratuni by their gentilitial name rather than by their title of *aspet*, used by Aa, dccxcv, dccclxxiii.

11. See III.vi n. 4, and above, n. 6.

12. Cf. Josh. 7:26 and 8:29.

13. See Appendix V, c, for variants of this formula.

III.viii

1. MX, III.ii (= MK, p. 255) reduces this chapter to a single sentence in which he adds the destruction of the Bznuni house to that of the Manawazean and Orduni (see

above, III.iv). The planting of the forest preserve is described by MX in far less detail elsewhere, III.viii (= MK, p. 261). Finally, a different account is given for the rescue of the Bznuni heir: see below, nn. 5, 10.

2. MX, III.ix (= MK, p. 262) mentions none of these districts but only the grant of Ošakan to Vahan Amatuni.

3. The term *χašar* is a *hapax* of unknown etymology and meaning. Following Marr, Malχasyanc⁽ᶜ⁾ (p. 313 n. 17) proposed in this context the translation "force of workers, laborers," a suggestion accepted by Ačaryan in HArmB, II, p. 333; cf. NBHL, I, p. 922.

4. For the etymology of Duin, i. e. Pahl. "hill," also given by MX, III.viii (= MK, p. 261), see Minorsky, "Dvin," and Appendix II, "Duin."

5. The creation of hunting preserves or paradises (‹ Ir. *partēz*, "garden") was one of the characteristic activities of the aristocratic Iranian society, in which hunting was not merely an economic or even a social act but the visible expression of the qualities, both human and superhuman, that characterized the true hero and ruler, whose apotheosis during the hunt was a major theme in Sasanian iconography. Conversely, the uprooting of a forest preserve was a symbol of mourning in the Iranian epic tradition. Hence, this chapter gives a particularly clear description of the Iranized tastes of Armenian court life, focused on "forest palaces" and hunts in paradises, such as are depicted in the Sasanian reliefs at Taq-i Bostan, rather than on urban centers. See also IV.xii n. 8; xv n. 8; V.ii n. 9; v n. 5; also Harper, *Hunter*; Garsoïan, "Prolegomena," cols. 183–184 and nn. 50–59; *idem*, "Locus," pp. 46–54 and n. 82; *idem*, "Mediaeval Armenian City," pp. 78–79; Dandamayev, "Paradeisoi," p. 114; Seyrig, "Jardins," pp. 1[24]–8[31]; and Ghirshman, *Persian Art*, pp. 194–198, figs. 236–237.

6. The account of the Persian war in this chapter cannot be reconciled with that of MX, III.vi, x (= MK, pp. 259, 263) who says nothing concerning Databē Bznuni and his treason or of the participation of the *sparapet* Vač⁽ᶜ⁾ē I Mamikonean; cf., however, III.xx n. 5. Adontz, "Favst," p. 246, suggests that this was a Persian attempt to overturn the unfavorable terms of the peace of Nisibis of 298. See III.ix n. 5 and xxi n. 16.

7. These tags with Biblical overtones run like refrains throughout BP: see Appendix V, i. This passage is probably the first extract from the "Geste of the Mamikonean," for which see Intro., pp. 32, 34–35.

8. See Appendix V, c, for variants of this formula.

9. Cf. III.xx and n. 13 for the same characterization of P⁽ᶜ⁾isak Siwni.

10. BP does not name the prince of the Řštuni in this chapter, though cf. III.vii, xvii. MX, III.xv (= MK, p. 267, 269) calls him Zoray, a name otherwise unattested, in a garbled passage that confuses the fates of the Řštuni and the Bznuni.

11. See Malχasyanc⁽ᶜ⁾ (p. 314 n. 22). The relative sizes of the *naχarar* contingents given in the *Zōrnamak*, "Military List," are highly questionable, as shown by Adontz, *Armenia*, pp. 193–195, 206–209, 68*–69*, and by Toumanoff, *Studies*, pp. 135, 234–241. BP's term *biwrawork⁽ᶜ⁾*, "myriaders," "with incalculable thousands" is likewise vague at best and his military figures often fantastic (see, e. g., IV.xxvi and n. 1; xxviii–xxxii; V.i n. 4). Nevertheless, there can be little doubt that the senior magnates could raise contingents of several thousands among their *azat* retainers.

12. This passage records one of the few attempts of the Armenian Aršakuni kings to control the turbulence and centrifugal tendencies of their magnates. It is not mentioned by other sources, and the remainder of BP illustrates all too clearly the failure of the Armenian rulers to transform the decentralized Parthian structure of their realm into the more controlled hierarchical pattern of their Sasanian neighbors. See, e.g. III.ix and n. 6; IV.iii for the "lords with contingents and banners"; IV.xix and nn. 4, 6 for Aršak II's seizure of the Kamsarakan stronghold of Artagers; IV.l for the abandonment of Aršak by the Armenian magnates. See also Toumanoff, *Studies*, pp. 34–40, 108–119 for the distinction between Armenian "dynasticism" and "feudalism"; Manandyan, *Feodalizm*, pp. 58–59; and Garsoïan, "Prolegomena," cols. 187–190. On the lords with hundreds and myriads of

retainers, cf. Aa, dccxcvi, "*hazaraworkᶜ*, *biwraworkᶜ*."

13. The use of the term *bun*, "true, authentic" in reference to the *sparapet* Vačᶜē undoubtedly suggests that he was loyal to his king, but it also carries the implication that the Mamikonean were the "authentic" *sparapet*s of the realm. See III.iv and n. 2; xi, n. 7, and Intro., pp. 49–50.

14. The use of the heroic epithet *kᶜaǰ*, "valiant" with a name outside the royal Aršakuni dynasty and the Mamikonean house occurs only one more time, in connection with Aršak II's faithful retainer Drastamat. See V.vii and Appendix III, *kᶜaǰ*.

15. Malχasyancᶜ (p. 314 n. 23) suggests the removal of the phrase, *ew očᶜ nayel*, "nor to look at [it]" from the end of the sentence as a dubious intrusion. There seems, however, to be no valid reason for this excision as the phrase fits cogently into the context.

III.ix

1. MX, III.iv–vi (= MK, pp. 257–259) gives a different version of Bakur's revolt, to which he adds an embassy to Constantinople and the sending of a Byzantine army, and where he shortens the list of the Armenian magnates involved. See also below nn. 5, 6.

2. As opposed to Malχasyancᶜ (p. 80) followed by Gevorgian (p. 19), Anasyan, *Review*, p. 21, notes correctly that the *bdeašχ* of Ałjnikᶜ was not merely one of the four senior magnates at the Armenian court, but the senior one among them, a position in keeping with Aa, dccxcv's characterization of him as "the great *bdeašχ*."

3. The form *ēacᶜ*, "he led, brought," which recurs in BP, is post-classical; see Thomson, *Introduction*, p. 39.

4. The ambiguous position of Ałjnikᶜ vis-à-vis the Armenian crown is noted throughout BP. See Appendix II, "Ałjnikᶜ."

5. MX, III.iv (= MK, p. 257) does not mention Vałinak Siwni in the corresponding passage. But he claims in III.xviii (= MK, p. 272) that the Persian king Šāhpuhr II appointed *his* favorite Vałinak Siwni "commander of the Armenian eastern army" at the time of the accession of Aršak II. The shift of Vałinak from the favorite of the Armenian king to that of the Persian king of kings is curious in itself. Moreover, we have no evidence that the Persians appointed the Armenian *sparapet* in the fourth century, for that office was hereditary in the Mamikonean house (see III.iv n. 2); nor is there evidence that the Armenian army was divided into eastern and western northern or southern branches, as MX repeatedly asserts, II.vii, viii; III.vi, ix (= MK, pp. 138, 144, 258–259, 261–262). See the discussion in Adontz, *Armenia*, pp. 193ff. esp. 222–224 of the fictitious *Zōrnamak*, "Military List" with its artificial fourfold division. Consequently, MX's version (III.xviii) seems to be an anachronistic elaboration of BP's reference to Vałinak in this chapter, perhaps colored by the memory of Siwnikᶜ's pro-Persian policy in the fifth century under the notorious Vasak and Varazvałan. See IV.ii n. 1 and ŁPᶜ and Ełišē's accounts of the fifth-century Armenian revolt. See also Adontz, "Favst," pp. 246, 251, who suggests that Bakur's revolt was instigated by Persia; and III.viii n. 6.

6. The account of Xeša's rescue and return to claim the domain of his family is found only in BP. Cf. MX, III.vii (= MK, p. 259), who has him sent as a captive to the king. To be sure, the story of the rescued and hidden heir is one of the favorite *topoi* in Armenian history and in the Iranian epic tradition; nevertheless, the integrity of a clan's possessions as long as a single claimant survived, irrespective of royal grants, is one of the most crucial aspects of Armenian "dynasticism" as opposed to "feudalism" in this period. See III.viii n. 12; IV.ii, n. 7, lviii n. 7; V.xxxvii and n. 9 and xlii; also Perikhanian, "Agnaticheskie gruppy," and Garsoïan, "Prolegomena," cols. 187–188 and nn. 47, 61.

III.x

1. For the *Vita* of James of Nisibis and its variants, especially in Theodoret of Cyr, *Hist. Phil.*, i, "Iakobos," see Peeters, "Jacques de Nisibe," who notes that classical and Syriac hagiography know nothing of James's Armenian adventures—neither the grant of the wood from the ark, nor the confrontation with Manačihr Ṙštuni—of which MX, III.vii (= MK, pp. 259–260) gives a variant version of the second but omits the first. BP's version cannot be derived from Theodoret's source because it omits the crucial episode of the Theodoret *Vita*: the saving of Nisibis from the Persian assault. Melkonyan's thesis in "Armianskiĭ perevod," pp. 121– 124, that BP's version was derived from an early Armenian translation of the "*Vita* of Mār Awgēn" preserved in a thirteenth-century ms (Matenadaran 1552, fol. 216) is no more acceptable, since the "*Vita* of Mār Awgēn" is itself a tenth-century forgery; see Labourt, *Christianisme*, pp. 300–315 and Vööbus, *Asceticism*, I, p. 139. See also Ps Yovhannēs Mamikonean, *History of Tarōn*, p. 70, who makes James the cousin of Gregory the Illuminator, and Appendix I, "*Yakob.*" Peeters based his thesis that BP had originally been written in Syriac and subsequently translated into Armenian of the syriacisms he found in this chapter, cf. IV.x n. 3 and especially Intro., pp. 7–8 and n. 30. There seems to be little doubt that the *Vita* of St. James went back to a Syriac original translated and elaborated in Armenia at an early date, as is evident from the confusion between James and Aphraat (see next note); but it had obviously acquired in Armenia the episodes noted above, and possibly that of the Council of Nicaea noted by Peeters (though see below, nn. 19, 20). The inclusion of this episode into BP's narrative is in keeping with the compilatory character of the Armenian work and its author's familiarity with contemporary hagiography. See Intro., pp. 26–30, and n. 9; also Appendix I, "Yakob."

2. The text is clearly corrupt at this point, although Lauer (p. 17) attempted to translate "*pʿohanak azgawn Parsik kočēr*" as "anstatt seiner Familie der Perser hiess." Norayr Biwzandacʿi corrected *azgawn* to *zgawn*, "the wise." While accepting this correction, Malχasyancʿ (p. 314 n. 31 of the 1947 edition, but dropped in the 1968 edition) also substituted *ordi Anaka* for *pʿohanak* to obtain the translation, "James son of Anak called the wise Persian." Ter Minasyan, "*Zgon*," returned to the preferable reading of Norayr Biwzandacʿi without the intrusive Anak, thus obtaining the translation adopted here. The phrase "*pʿohanak azgaw Parsik*" is missing in certain mss (Venice ed., p. 33 n. 1, and Matenadaran ms §3079), so that the Persian identification may not have seemed essential. Finally, in a private conversation (June 1986), G. V. Abgaryan suggested a return to the earlier version, "instead of a name, he was called the Persian." For the attribution to James of Nisibis of the work called "*Zgōn*" (which is in reality the Armenian translation of the homilies of Aphraat), and attribution evidently accepted by BP, see Peeters, "Jacques de Nisibe," and more recently Ter Minasyan, "*Zgōn*" as well as Avdoyan, *Ps. Yovhannēs*, note to p. 70, *Zgawn. This mistake is perpetuated by Langlois, CHAMA I, p. 218 n. 1.

3. As noted by Markwart, *Südarmenien*, pp. 214–223, 350; Peeters, "Jacques de Nisibe," pp. 322–327; and Malχasyancʿ (p. 315 n. 26), the name of Mt. Sararad or Sararat, "*i leaṙnn Sararaday*" (also found in other sources) is a *lapsus* for the name of the mountain on which Noah's ark came to rest in Gen. 8:4, "*i leṙins Araratay*" = Septuagint, "ἐπὶ τὰ ὄρη τὰ Ἀραράτ," where the final *s* of *leṙins* was mistakenly transferred to the name of the mountain. Malχasyancʿ argued for a misreading, which is possible, but such an error could occur even more easily in an oral citation. It is particularly interesting that BP does not identify the mountain of the ark with a modern Mt. Ararat, normally called Masis in Armenian, as was done by later authors, but locates it in the southern border district of Korduk, as was noted by Peeters and Malχasyancʿ. The recent evidence of the Qumran scrolls had shown that the correct form of the toponym in Is. 37:38, and consequently of the same one IV Kings 19:37 and Gen. 8:4, was *hwrrt*, "Urartu," and not the "Ararat" of the Septuagint; as such, it gives a location in the southern mountains of present-day Kurdistan. The date of the transfer of the ark story in Armenian sources from one moun-

tain to the other is not known, but BP evidently preserved the memory of the earlier and more accurate tradition. This early tradition is also familiar to the Syriac tradition which places the ark on Mt. Ǧudi in Kurdistan as observed by Fiey, *Assyrie*, II, pp. 249–253 and *Nisibe*, pp. 221–223, among others. It is recorded by Josephus (*Ant. Jud.* I.iii; cf. xx.ii.2) and Eusebius of Caesarea, *Chron.*, p. 37, and preserved as late as the tenth century by T^{c}A, p. 19 (= *Thom. Arts.*, p. 81).

    4. Cf. Rom. 15:19.

    5. See below for James's second spring. The parallel with Moses, both in the miraculous appearance of the water (Exod. 17:6; Num. 20:2–11) and the descent from Sinai (below) is part of the hagiographic tradition of James of Nisibis; cf. Theodoret of Cyr, *Hist. Phil.*, i, iv–v, and Drijvers, "Origins," pp. 28–30.

    6. Cf. Gen. 22:11–12 for the identical beginning of the angelic vision to Abraham.

    7. The series of parallels to Koriwn run from here to the end of the paragraph; see Intro., pp. 24–25 and nn. 102–103.

    8. This reference to a homily might be an allusion to a source, but the phrase is also found in Koriwn, ix, p. 52 lines 8–9, and consequently does not concern BP.

    9. I.e., Nisibis.

    10. The account of the confrontation between James and Manačihr R̆štuni follows the same general lines in MX, III.viii (= MK, pp. 259–260); see below nn. 14, 17 for variations of detail. According to Peeters, "Jacques de Nisibe," 336–337, the elaborations of MX are his own invention, as is his addition of a series of Scriptural quotations.

    11. MX, III.vii (= MK, pp. 259–260) substitutes eight of James's own deacons for the eight hundred innocent men of BP.

    12. The text reads "*i dahčē miojē*," which is awkward both semantically and syntactically. The correction proposed by Malχasyanc^c (p. 316 n. 29), "*i gahē miojē*," taking *gah* to mean "height" or "summit" in this context, seems far more satisfactory.

    13. This is the classical Scriptural injunction repeated in Matt. 10:14, Mark 6:11, and Luke 9:5; cf. Acts 13:51.

    14. The ms reads Ǝnjak^{c}iars and MX, III.viii (= MK, p. 260) does not give the name of the mountain. The correct form Ǝnjak^{c}isar, found in both John Kat^{c}ołikos and Vardan, has been replaced in the Venice edition (p. 35) but not in the St. Petersburg edition.

    15. This unusual identification of Lake Van, usually known to medieval Armenian sources as "the Sea of Bznunik^c," is evidently inspired by the context.

    16. See above, n. 5.

    17. According to MX, III.vii (= MK, p. 260), one of Manačihr's sons repented and consequently survived to heal his domain.

    18. References to Byzantine rulers in BP alternate constantly between the correct title, "emperor" (*kaysr*) of the Romans, and the more common "king" (*t^{c}agawor*)." Cf. *inter alia*, III.xxi; IV.v; etc. This lack of precision may again point to a fifth-century date for the work at a time when Armenia's ties with the empire were not as close as in the preceding century.

    19. The presence of James of Nisibis at the Council of Nicaea together with St. Aristakēs of Greater Armenia is confirmed by the conciliar lists: Gelzer *et al.*, eds., *Nomina*, pp. 20–21, 64, 72, 84, 102, 126, 160, 196, and mentioned by MX, II.lxxxix (= MK, p. 246), though not in this context.

    20. Cf. Aa, dccclxxi, for the angel serving Constantine. It is possible that this episode, which has no parallel in Theodoret of Cyr's *Hist. Phil.*, is a purely Armenian invention, as is suggested by Peeters "Jacques de Nisibe," pp. 338–339; but in such a case one might have expected that Aristakēs, who plays distinctly second fiddle in this episode, would also have been granted the same angelic vision as James, cf. MX, II.lxxxix (= MK, pp. 245–246).

    21. Possibly a reminiscence of II Macc. 3:35.

    22. The transfer of the relics of St. James at the time of the surrender of Nisibis to the Persians through Jovian's Peace of 363 forms the final episode of his *Vita*, xiv, in Theodoret of Cyr, *Hist. Phil.* Cf. Peeters, "Jacques de Nisibe," p. 316; Fiey, *Nisibe*, pp. 35–36.

III.xi

1. MX, III.x (= MK, pp. 263–264), alludes briefly to this war and to the death of Xosrov Kotak, but he does not mention the Armenian defeat except indirectly and has no reference to Vačʿē I Mamikonean.

2. Cf. IV.li and n. 12.

3. Malχasyancʿ (p. 316 n. 32) corrects the St. Petersburg edition, p. 24, which has *banaki tearn*, "of the army of the lord," instead of the *bnaki tearn*, "of the true lord" given in the Venice edition, p. 38 and n. 1. The reference here is unquestionably to the Aršakuni repeatedly invoked by BP as the "true-lords" of the Armenian realm. See, e.g. IV.xxiv; V.xliv; etc., and Intro., p. 34 and n. 153, for the stress laid on the loyalty of the Mamikonean to their "true-lords." Also Appendix III, *bnak tēr*.

4. This long invocation of the patriarch Vrtʿanēs, with its unmistakable if anachronistic evocation of the martyrdom of Vardan Mamikonean and his companions at the battle of Awarayr in 451, is not found in MX; see Intro., pp. 10–11, 38. The implicit parallel between Vačʿē I Mamikonean and his fallen companions and his kinsman Vardan one century later, less than a generation before the compilation of BP, is underscored by the establishment of perpetual commemorations in both cases, and even more by the themes of the profaned temple and the covenant of the believers, as well as the explicit parallel between Vačʿē and his companions and the Maccabees, all of which are the main threads of Ełišē's *History of Vardan*; see e.g. pp. 9–16, 47, *et passim*, and Thomson's Introduction, *Ełishē*, p. 10–16.

5. This reference is to no particular passage in the Books of the Maccabees, but as indicated in the previous note, this entire section is redolent with parallel themes to Ełišē's identification of the "martyrs of Awarayr" with the Maccabees, especially v, p. 105 (= *Ełishē*, p. 157.)

6. Malχasyancʿ (p. 316 n. 33) corrects the ms "father" to "grandfather" as given in the Venice edition p. 39. The editors of the 1968 modern Armenian edition take this as a reference to Vačʿē's father instead of Artawazd's. In either case the meaning is entirely clear: Artawazd II was named after his own grandfather i.e., Vačʿē's father, Artawazd I; cf. Aa, dccclx. In general, terms such as "father" and "brother" are used in BP in a loose rather than a strict sense; see III.v n. 2, vii n. 6.

7. Together with IV.ii and V.xxxvii and n. 9, this passage is the *locus classicus* for the existence of hereditary offices in Arsacid Armenia; see Intro., pp. 49–50. Artawazd II Mamikonean received the dignity of *sparapet* because it belonged to his family, not through the king's grant, and in spite of his inability to discharge the duties of his office because of his youth. See III.iv n. 2 and Garsoïan, "Prolegomena," cols. 182, 187–188 and nn. 44, 77; cf., however, IV.ii and n. 7 and li and n. 8 for royal attempts to interfere with this pattern, usually with disastrous results, V.xxxvii. Malχasyancʿ (p. 316 n. 31) argues for a subtle difference between the terms *sparapet*, which he takes to be the hereditary office irrespective of capacity, and *zōrawar*, the actual command. However, the two terms are repeatedly used together where such distinctions do not obtain. This is the case for Artawazd's own father Vačʿē I, who is styled *sparapet-zōrawar* at the beginning of this chapter, as well as for all his Mamikonean successors: Vasak (IV.ii), Mušeł (V.i), Manuēl (V.xxxvii), *et passim*. See also III.iv n. 2; V.i and n. 5; xxxvii, xliv, and Appendix III, *sparapet*.

8. The conjunction of the two epithets characterizing the Aršakuni dynasty in BP— *bnak tēr*, "true, native lord" and *kʿaǰ*, "valiant" (cf. *kʿaǰ arancʿ*, "most valiant of men" immediately below as well as in Aa, xvii, dcccxii)—is a particularly clear formulation of the hereditary and partially supernatural concept of the royal office characteristic of fourth-century Armenian society. See Intro., pp. 32–33, 54, and Appendix III, *kʿaǰ arancʿ*.

9. The reading *yekełecʿagawaṙn*, "in the ecclesiastical district," rather than *yEkełeacʿ gawaṙn*, "in the district of Ekełeacʿ" is clearly preferable; see Venice ed., p. 39 n. 3. Eke-

łeac^c was not really a part of Daranałik^c, where ecclesiastical estates were to be found, as indicated further in this chapter as well as in III.ii and IV.xiv. Cf. also III.xiv and n. 3, where Ekełeac^c has also been put in for *ekełec^cac^c*. This is presumably the result of a *lapsus calami*, or the confusion of two adjacent districts. See also IV.xxiv and n. 7 for the Arsacid royal necropolis at Ani in Daranałik^c.

10. MX, III.x–xi (= MK, p. 264) has Vrt^canēs survive to the third year of Tiran's reign and gives him an improbably long pontificate of fifteen years, while BP does not specify the length of his rule. See Ōrmanean, *Azgapatum*, I, cols. 123–142, xv, who gives a pontificate of eight years, 333–341.

11. Cf. V.xxiv for the parallel ritual of St. Nersēs burial at T^cil, and Koriwn, xxvi, p. 94 (trans., p. 50), for the burial of Maštoc^c at Ošakan.

III.xii

1. MX, III.x–xi (= MK, pp. 263–264) includes an embassy of the patriarch Vrt^canēs to bring King Tiran from Constantinople, but this is not recorded by BP. See, however, III.xxi nn. 4, 23; and Appendix I, "Tiran," for a possible Byzantine enthronement of Tiran.

2. The text reads "realms" in the plural, with no suggestion of variants. This might be a reference to the autonomous Satrapies of southern Armenia, to which BP never refers explicitly. See Intro., p. 48.

3. MX, III.xi (= MK, p. 264) places Yusik's accession in the fourth year of Tiran's reign and reduces his pontificate to a single sentence here; cf. III.xiv (= MK, p. 267).

4. See IV.ii and Appendix III, *hazarapet* for the office of the *hazarapetut^ciwn* and its transfer to the Gnuni.

5. See Intro., p. 13, for the question of "Tiroc^c" Sahaṙuni and the putative link between Ps. P^cawstos and the Sahaṙuni house.

6. None of these *naxarar*s is known to MX, III.xi (= MK, p. 264), who does not mention Yusik's journey to Caesarea.

7. The distinction between the two founders of Armenian Christianity, St. Thaddeus and St. Gregory the Illuminator, is clearly brought out in this passage; see also III.i and IV.iii. van Esbroeck, "Le roi Sanatrouk," p. 271 is of the opinion that there were two "thrones" joined temporarily in the persons of Yusik and subsequently his grandson Nersēs I (IV.iii); see also Appendix I, "T^cadēos." The consecration of Yusik at Caesarea of Cappadocia followed the pattern set by his grandfather Gregory the Illuminator, Aa (dccxci–dcccviii), seemingly omitted for his two predecessors: Aristakēs, consecrated by his own father and Vrt^canēs, but repeated for most of his successors until the death of St. Nersēs; see III.xvi–xvii; IV.iv; and V.xxix n. 1.

8. Cf. e.g. Koriwn, iv, p. 38 (= trans., pp. 27–28).

9. See IV.iii for the parallel description of St. Nersēs.

10. Cf. Grigoris, III.vi and III.iii n. 8.

11. Eph. 6:17.

12. This might perhaps be a pun on *yoys*, "hope" and the name of Yusik, "little hope."

13. See III.v n. 9 on this *topos*.

14. Malχasyanc^c (p. 87) prefers the alternate reading *aṙak^celut^ciwn*, "apostolic" for *zaṙawelut^ciwn*, and *i mankut^cenē*, "from his youth" for *i mankut^cean*. See Venice ed. (p. 42 nn. 2–3).

15. Cf. Acts 1:1, as well as IV.iv and nn. 13, 15; and Aa, dccclii. This quotation was a favorite *topos* of early hagiography; see Festugière, "Lieux-communs," pp. 140–142.

16. Cf. V.xxiii for St. Nersēs and King Pap.

17. The entire section on Yusik's virtues and his castigation of the king is not to be found in the corresponding section of MX, III.xiv–xv (= MK, pp. 266–267), who attributes Yusik's death to his destruction of the image of the emperor Julian placed by Tiran in the church. On this, see Thomson, MK, p. 266 n. 7 and Appendix I, "Yusik."

III.xiii

1. This long homily, replete with biblical quotations and allusions, is not found in the corresponding section of MX, III.xi, xiv (= MK, pp. 264, 267) who gives short shrift to both Yusik and his successor Daniēl. Instead, he places here an anachronistic collaboration between Tiran and the emperor Julian and interpolates a fictitious letter from Julian to Tiran (MX, III.xv = MK, p. 268) highly reminiscent in form and content if not in style to Julian's *Letter* lvii, "To Aršak," usually considered a forgery (see Julian, *Letter* lvii, cf. pp. xxxv–xxxvii.) A relationship between Julian and Tiran is chronologically impossible since the emperor's campaign took place in 363, long after Tiran's reign, and AM, XXIII.ii. 7; XXVII.xii, etc. explicitly identifies the Armenian king at that time as Aršak. Cf., however, Thomson's reservations, MK, p. 266 nn. 4–5, 268, n. 4.

2. Cf. II Cor. 4:3–4; Deut. 28:29.

3. Cf. Is. 6:9–10; Ezek. 12:2; Ps. 113 (115):5–6; Jer. 4:22, 5:21; Matt. 13:13–15; Mark 4:12; Luke 8:10; John 12:40; Acts 28:26–27; Rom. 11:8. The phrase runs throughout the Scriptures.

4. Cf. Matt. 7:13, 15:14; Luke 6:39.

5. Eph. 2:3, with possible reminiscences of Jer. 11:8, 13:10; and Matt. 7:13.

6. This may perhaps be an allusion to the Arianizing policy of the Aršakuni house that aroused the opposition of the Armenian patriarchs. See IV.xii; xliv nn. 5–6; and Garsoïan, "Politique."

7. The symbol of the sheep gone astray is ubiquitous in the Scriptures so that no particular reference is evident here. See also next chapter, n. 30.

8. If it is not a *lapsus*, this puzzling allusion may perhaps be a reference to II Macc. 9:15 or to the mocking of St. Paul, Acts 17:16ff.

9. Cf. III.i and n. 6 on the "unwilling" conversion of King Trdat.

10. Cf. Aa, dcccxl, for this double tradition.

11. This explicit reference to pagan "songs" (*erg*), "legends" (*aṙaspel*), and "epics" (*vipasanutꜥiwn*) is similar to those in MX (see listing in MK, pp. 10–12). BP does not quote directly from these sources, as does MX, e.g. I.xxx–xxxi (= MK, pp. 121, 123), II.l (= MK, pp. 191–192)—though see V.v—and their presence emerges repeatedly throughout the narrative; see Intro., pp. 30–35.

12. Cf. Is. 3:5, 19:2; and next chapter, n. 21.

13. See III.iii, xiv, xviii; IV.iv, xv; V.xxxi, xxxvi; and Intro., p. 51, for the persistence of pagan customs in fourth-century Armenia.

14. Amos 5:10, with a slight modification at the end, *arhamarhēin*, "abhorred" for *piłcs ararin*, "befouled," indicative of the use of a different recension or more likely oral rather than textual transmission, see Intro., p. 23, and n. 97.

15. Malχasyancꜥ's correction of the corrupted text (p. 317 p. 37) from "*Kꜥanzi očꜥ ēin tꜥē orpēs aylocꜥ azgakanacꜥn*" to "*Kꜥanzi očꜥ tꜥē orpēs aylocꜥ azgacꜥn*" has been adopted here.

16. Jer. 4:22 slightly modified.

17. Ezek. 2:3–4. The verses of the quotation have been reversed and slightly modified. The word *eťjerik*, "hard faced" is attested in Armenian only in these two passages; see NBHL, I, p. 656 and HArmB, II, p. 24.

18. Cf. Rom. 1:20 and Hebr. 11:3.

19. The reference here is to the transformation of King Trdat into a wild boar in punishment for the martyrdom of the saints and as a prelude to his conversion. See Aa (ccxi–ccxii), etc., and Garsoïan, "Substratum."

20. Note the antagonism of BP to King Tiran as well as his successors, cf. III.xx; IV.xv, xliv; V.xxii, and Garsoïan, "Politique."

21. Jer. 3:17, 11:8, 13:10, 16:12.

22. Cf. III.xv, xix for the punishment of Yusik's unworthy children.

23. See III.v for the prophecy to Yusik.

24. The use of the title *hramanatar*, "lawgiver" in a religious context is unusual, but see West, PT, I, p. 145; II, pp. 152, 276 for the Iranian parallel and III.xiv n. 4. Also, Appendix III, *hramanadar*.

25. This passage is the first explicit statement of the hereditary character of the partiarchal office in the Gregorid house, a practice running clearly counter to canonical regulations on episcopal elections. BP is the *locus classicus* for our knowledge of this uncommon practice, see also III.xv, xvii; IV.iii and Intro., p. 50. Aa, dccclxii mentions the ordination of Aristakēs in succession to his father Gregory, and MX, III.xvi (= MK, pp. 269–270) is familiar with the Gregorid claim, but neither stresses the hereditary character of the patriarchal office to the same degree. See also Garsoïan, "Prolegomena," cols. 182–183 and n. 45.

III.xiv

1. Daniēl is barely mentioned by MX, III.xiv (= MK, p. 267), which turns him into a mere priest. The "Nouvelle Liste" of Sanspeur, pp. 186–187 #4, has him die together with Yusik. The garbled but crucial account of BP is our main source for his career and may be drawn from a hagiographic source. See Intro., pp. 27, 29-30.

2. There is no evidence that Daniēl was ever a disciple of St. Gregory, though this assertion is echoed by MX, III.xiv. He is not mentioned among the bishops sent out by St. Gregory at the time of the Christianization of Armenia. Aa, dcccxlv = Va clxxii, etc. Hence, this statement seems nothing more than an awkward attempt to link southern Armenian Christianity and its autonomous hierarchs to the northern received tradition of St. Gregory's illumination of Armenia. See Intro., pp. 46-47 and below n. 11.

3. As noted by Norayr Biwzandac⁣ʿi and Malχasyancʿ (p. 317 n. 39), the *Ekełecʿeacʿ* of the text is again a probable copyist's mistake for *ekełecʿeacʿ*, "of the churches"; cf. III.xi n. 9. The district of Ekełeacʿ is even less connected with Tarōn than with Daranałikʿ. But see below, n. 19.

4. The use of the legal title *datawor*, "lawgiver" as one of the prerogatives of the "supervisor and head of the churches" is the exact counterpart of the contemporary Zoroastrian usage. See Garsoïan, "Protecteur des pauvres"; and III.xiii n. 24.

5. See III.xiii n. 24.

6. James 5:20.

7. See below, n. 12.

8. See III.iii and n. 4 for the martyria of St. John the Precursor and the apostles.

9. The name of Aristakēs has obviously been added here by mistake, since St. Gregory was indeed buried at Tʿordan (III.ii) as were his elder son Vrtʿanēs (III.xi) and his grandson Yusik (III.xii), but Aristakēs was buried at Tʿil in Ekełeacʿ (III.ii) as Nersēs I was later (V.xxiv).

10. See III.i and n. 6.

11. This confused passage is the *locus classicus* for the evidence of two currents of Christianity in early Armenia. The "unwilling" conversion of King Trdat the Great, the primacy of St. Gregory (note the Greek form "Grigoris" used here as opposed to the Armenian "Grigor," immediately above *et passim*, suggesting the use of a different source at this point), and the martyrdom of the virgin saints Hṙipʿsimē and Gayanē at Vałaršapat in the district of Ayrarat all form the core of the received tradition of northern Armenian Christianity presented by Aa and its versions; see III.i n. 6. The insistence of BP on Aštišat of Tarōn as the "mother-church" and "above all the first church" of Armenia (cf. IV.iv), along with its identification of Daniēl as a Syrian, form—together with the emphasis on the throne of Thaddeus (III.i, xii)—the record of the earlier and largely submerged

Syrian current in early Armenian Christianity. For Aa, followed by most Armenian sources, the focus was on the dominant northern center of Vałaršapat miraculously designated to St. Gregory as the site of the resting place of the virgin martyrs (Aa, dccxxxi– dcclxxi), though he conceded the building of the first church at Aštišat (dcccxiv). For BP, despite the attempt to link Daniēl to St. Gregory (see above, n. 2), Vałaršapat plays a negligible role and is mentioned only twice in passing (III.vii, IV.lv), while the primacy of Aštišat is reiterated (III.iii, IV.iv). See Ter Minasyan, *Armenische Kirche*, pp. 5–8, and Garsoïan, *Paulician Heresy*, pp. 220–230, though the autonomy of Daniēl may have been underestimated there; also Intro., pp. 16, 46–47.

12. See above, n. 2.

13. On the destruction of temple of Heraklēs / Vahagn at Aštišat, see Aa, dcccix–dcccxv and III.iii n. 4; and for its implications, Garsoïan, "Substratum."

14. This entire section is a catalog of early hagiographic clichés culminating in the author's claim of inadequacy. See Festugière, "Lieux-communs," pp. 129–137, 145–146, and V.xxvi–xxvii for parallel examples.

15. The single garment of skins and the ascetic food haphazardly gathered are part of the stock-in-trade of the description of wandering anchorites in the Syrian hagiographic tradition: see, e.g. Theodoret of Cyr, *Hist. Phil.*, pp. 162–165, 246–247, 345–346, etc.; Soz., EH, VI.xxxiii *et al.* Also Aa, dcccliii, dcccclviii, dcccclxxxviii; Koriwn, xxii, p. 80 (trans., pp. 45–46); and below, V.xxvi, xxviii; VI.xvi, for Daniēl's disciples Šałitay, Epipᶜan, and Gind. On Syrian asceticism in general and its preference for the eremitic rather than the communal life, see *inter alia*, Vööbus, *Asceticism*; Canivet, *Théodoret*, esp. pp. 263–265; Leloir, "Ephrem," pp. 108, 126; Baus, ed. *Imperial Church*, pp. 337–367, etc.

16. Cf. Aa, dcccxiv.

17. The dwelling in a cave or pit, or even a tomb also characterize early Syrian ascetics. See e.g. Theodoret of Cyr, *Hist. Phil.*, pp. 162/3, 196/7, 146/7, 346/7, 410/1, 462/3, 476/7, etc.; Peña *et al.*, *Les Reclus*, pp. 44–45; Baus, ed., *Imperial Church*, p. 337; etc.; also for Armenia, Aa, dcccxlviii, dcccliii.

18. None of these names is known to MX, see above n. 1; see also Intro., p. 13, for the name of the Saharuni prince and the problem connected with it.

19. See III.xi n. 9, and above, n. 3. In this case however, the village of Tᶜil was indeed to be found in the district of Ekełeacᶜ. See Appendix II, "Tᶜil."

20. As in the case of the lament over Yusik's death (III.xii and n. 1), this lengthy homily is missing from the account of MX. It presents some parallels with other doctrinal expositions found in BP (see IV.v n. 7; V.xxviii n. 7, and below nn. 22, 26). See also Intro., n. 138, for the introductory formula, and Appendix V, a, for its repetitions.

21. See III.iii, xiii and n. 13, as well as Intro., p. 51, on the survival of pagan practices in Armenia. Cf. also Jer. 11:10, 13:10.

22. Cf. II Macc. 7:28. This phrase appears repeatedly in other homiletic passages and is almost certainly alluded to in BP in its liturgical context. See Gatᶜrčean and Tašean, eds., *Srbazan patarag*, p. 120 lines 3–4; Renoux, "Anaphore," p. 88; also IV.xiii n. 6, lvii n. 2; V.iv n. 21, xxviii n. 8.

23. Cf. IV.v n. 21.

24. The reference here is presumably to St. Thaddeus's martyrdom shifted to Artaz by the Armenian tradition, cf. MX, II.xxiv, lxxiv (= MK, pp. 174–175, 220–221); and to the tortures of St. Gregory at the order of King Trdat, Aa, xlviii–cxxiv.

25. Because the text reads *norin areamb*, "through his [another one's] blood," instead of giving the correct reflexive form of the possessive pronoun, *iwroy*, "his own" which would be required if the blood were that of Christ, Malχasyancᶜ (p. 317 n. 41) corrected the pronoun to the plural *nocᶜin*, "their" referring to the martyrs, whom he takes to be St. Gregory's contemporaries, the Hṙipᶜsimian saints. See Aa, cxxxvii–ccx; AaT, dlxii–dlxiii.

26. Cf. the first extensive quotation of the early Basilian Anaphora, V.xxviii nn. 11–17.

27. Hebr. 13:17.

28. Cf. Gal. 4:19, which is also cited in the early Basilian Anaphora, see V.xxviii n. 12.

29. I.e., the successors and descendants of St. Gregory as patriarchs of Armenia: his sons, Aristakēs and Vrtⁱanēs, and his grandson, Yusik.

30. Cf. Matt. 23:31–32.

31. See III.xii, on the killing of Yusik; and III.xii n. 7, on the double tradition of St. Thaddeus and St. Gregory in Armenia.

32. The scattering of the Jews recurs a number of times in the Scriptures, as does the image of the shepherdless sheep (cf. III.xiii and n. 7 and IV.v, n. 52 and below, n. 35). The closest parallels to the present passage are III Kgs. 14:15; II Chron. 18:16; Ez. 6:8, 34:5–6, 8; and Matt. 9:36/ Mk. 6:34 for the lost sheep. See also, however, Gen. 11:8–9; Lev. 26:33; Deut. 4:27, 28:64, 30:3, 32:26; I Kgs. 22:17; Neh. 1:8; Jer. 50:6, for the scattering of Israel, and Num. 27:17; I Kgs. 22:17; Zech. 10:2, 13:7, Jer. 3:13, 50:6, 17; Matt. 26:31/ Mk. 14:27; possibly Ps. 118:176; Is. 53:6 for the sheep; as well as Ez. 29:12, 30:23, 26, for the scattering of the Egyptians. See also AaT, ccxcvii, dlxxviii; cf. Thomson, *ibid.*, pp. 5–7, 23, on the scattering of the builders of the tower of Babel.

33. Cf. Lam. 2:1.

34. Deut. 28:48; Lam. 1:14, and cf. III Kgs. 12:4, 9–11, 14 = II Chron. 10:4, 9–11, 14; Jer. 28:10–14.

35. James 4:3; see above n. 32. Despite the obvious Scriptural allusion to the dispersion of the Jews, this passage may also be referring indirectly to the partition of Armenia, ca. 387. See VI.i, and St. Nersēs's curse of Aršak II, IV.xv.

36. See the preceding notes. The implied knowledge of the end of the Arsacid kingdom in Armenia again suggests a fifth-century date for BP. See also III.v and n. 5, xi and n. 4, as well as Intro., p. 11.

37. The translation given for the puzzling reading *nuačecⁱinn*, "who subdued, conquered, enslaved" found in both the St. Petersburg (p. 36) and Venice (p. 52) editions is obviously derived from the general context rather than the immediate text. Neither Emin (p. 226) nor Lauer (p. 34) seems to have been disturbed by the incongruity of the *nuačecⁱinn* in context and they translate it as given. But the Venice edition (p. 52 n. 4) suggests the substitution of *nahanjecⁱinn*, "recanted, retracted, withdrew," which makes considerably more sense; while Malχasyancⁱ (p. 99), followed by Gevorgian (p. 35), translates "revolted, resisted, grew insolent or stubborn."

38. Ps. 63:6; cf. Is. 29:15.

39. One ms reads *vardapet kargeal* instead of the *vardapet ēr* of the text (see Venice edition, p. 53 n. 4); consequently, Malχasyancⁱ (pp. 317–318 n. 42) proposes the reading *vardapet tueal ēr* identical with the phrase used for the preceding case Šaḷitay. See also V.xxv–xxviii for Šaḷitay, Epipⁱan and their other vision.

III.xv

1. This account is slightly different from the version in III.xiii, which does not mention the forcible ordination of Yusik's sons. The present version reinforces still more clearly the imperative character of the hereditary pattern of the patriarchal succession reiterated at the end of this chapter (see below, n. 4), even if the candidates were unwilling or unworthy. See III.xi and n. 7 for the parallel case of the *sparapetutⁱiwn*, as well as III.xiii n. 25, and Intro., pp. 49-50.

2. See III.v n. 4, and IV.v n. 47. The *Vita* of St. Nersēs, ii, p. 15 (= CHAMA II, p. 22) calls Atⁱanagines's son, St. Nersēs, the son of King Aršak II's paternal aunt (*hōrakⁱeṙ ordi*).

3. The names of the royal princesses are not known to MX, III.xvi (= MK, pp. 269–270), who gives no information whatsoever about Pap's and Atⁱanaginēs's wives and who

condenses BP, III.xv, xix and the youth of Nersēs (IV.iii) into one brief chapter. Cf. Appendix I, "Bambišn" and "Varazduχt."

4. This sentence is probably no more than the reiteration of the proper locus of the patriarchal office in the Gregorid house; see above, n. 1. But Ačaryan, HAnjB, V, pp. 190–191, uses it for his hypothesis that the patriarch Pʿarēn was a member of the Gregorid house, though this thesis is otherwise unsupported; see next chapter, n. 3. BP is the main source for the information that the council of the realm assembled to designate a new patriarch; cf. III.xvii, IV.iii.

III.xvi

1. MX, III.xvi (= MK, p. 270) merely identifies Pʿarēn, whom he calls Pʿaṙnerseh, and gives him a pontificate of four years, beginning in the tenth year of the reign of Tiran, without any further information.

2. The condescending qualification of Pʿarēn, "*omn erēcʿ i gawaṙēn Tarōnoy*, (a certain priest from the district of Tarōn)," hardly fits in with the usual respect shown by BP toward members of the Gregorid house (cf. preceding chapter, n. 4, for Ačaryan's thesis and below, nn. 5, 7). Even when contemptuous of King Varazdat, whom he also calls *omn* (V.xxxiv), BP identifies him as a member of the Aršakuni royal house, whereas there is no indication anywhere that Pʿarēn may have been a Gregorid; cf., however, Appendix I, s.n.

3. See III.iii.

4. None of these magnates is mentioned in the corresponding passage of MX, III.xvi (= MK, p. 270), though Mehendak Ṙštuni and Andovk/Antiochus Siwni are mentioned by him in other contexts: III.xv, xxiv, xxvi (= MK, pp. 269, 280–281).

5. The latent antagonism of BP toward Pʿarēn by contrast to his praise of the Gregorids, again suggests that this patriarch did not belong to their house; see above, n. 2. The stress on Pʿarēn's submission to the king's will—cf. III.xvii (Šahak); IV.xv (Čʿunak)— suggests that the non-Gregorid patriarchs may have been more favorable or more flexible than the descendants of St. Gregory to the arianizing policy of Tiran and his successors; see Garsoïan, "Politique."

6. Cf. Gen. 49:29, 33; also 15:15, 25:8; I Macc. 2:69; etc. The phrase with its variants is too common in the Scriptures to be identified with precision.

7. Pʿarēn was buried at Aštišat, his former jurisdiction, and not with the Gregorids at Tʿil or Tʿordan; cf. III.ii, xii; IV.xxiv.

III.xvii

1. BP is the only source for the interpolation of Šahak of Manazkert's pontificate at this point. All other sources go directly from Pʿarēn to St. Nersēs I. See Appendix I, "Šahak."

2. This curiously pleonastic construction with the anachronistic use of the title *katʿolikos* was noted by Thomson, Aa, p. lxxix.

3. The disdainful qualification of Šahak as *omn*, "a certain," as was Pʿarēn (see III.xvi, n. 2), and the reiteration of the hereditary character of the patriarchate in the Gregorid house (cf. III.xii n. 25 and xv n. 1) set the stage for the rivalry between the Gregorids and the Ałbianids of Manazkert observed by Adontz, *Armenia*, pp. 269, 271–272, 275; cf. Markwart, *Entstehung*, pp. 145–146. Despite BP's contemptuous tone, however, Šahak seems to have been duly consecrated at Caesarea like Pʿarēn and the Gregorids (III.xii and n. 7, xvi; IV.iv), as opposed to the royal candidates, Čʿunak (IV.xv) and Yusik II (V.xxix).

4. See III.xvi n. 5.

5. See III.xiv n. 21.

6. The reference here is perhaps to the peace of Nisibis of 298, which marked the return of Greater Armenia to the Roman sphere of influence and established Trdat the Great on the Armenian throne. See Toumanoff, "Third-century Arsacids," pp. 263–265.

7. According to this passage the "thirty-years' war" between Armenia and Persia began in the reign of Tiran. This would fit satisfactorily into the chronology of the Classical sources, A.D. 338–368, as against the attribution of the entire war to the reign of Tiran's son and successor Aršak II. Cf. III.xxi n. 4 and IV.xx n. 19.

8. Malχasyanc^c (p. 318 n. 44) corrects the last phrase from the "*oč^c mi ok^c i t^{c}agaworac^{c}n Hayoc$^{c"}$* of the text to "*t^{c}agaworac^{c}n ayloc^c*," which is syntactically and semantically preferable.

III.xviii

1. MX, III.xv (= MK, pp. 267-269) gives a different account of the end of the Řštuni house that shows contamination from the account of the annihilation of the Bznuni (III.viii n. 10). In the opinion of Adontz (*Armenia*, p. 514 n. 43), this chapter and the killing of the *mardpet*s (IV.xiv and V.iii) are "purely didactic . . . intended as condemnations of crimes," and are not historical accounts. The episode of the saving of the last heir of an exterminated house is unquestionably a favorite *topos* (see III.ix n. 6); nevertheless, in view of Adontz's own admission of the *mardpet*s' antagonism to the Arcruni (*Armenia*, p. 250), and the subsequent reference in BP (IV.ii) to the return of the Mamikonean to court, a historical core seems to be present. The episode fits in as part of the perpetual tug of war between the crown with its officials and the *naχarar*s that is one of the main themes in BP; see Intro., pp. 3, 47-48 and Appendix III, *mardpet*.

2. Cf. Is. 37:7.

3. This is presumably Artawazd II son of Vač^{c}ē I; see III.xi.

4. The *sparapet*'s office seems to have been split between Artawazd and Vasak at this point, although such a division was abnormal. Alternately, one of them may have been an ordinary commander and not *sparapet*, as was the case of the youngest Mamikonean brother under Aršak II (IV.ii). Artawazd II was presumably old enough to have daughters even though he was only a child at the end of Xosrov Kotak's reign (III.xi). He is never mentioned again, while Vasak's brilliant and ultimately tragic career is one of the dominant themes of Book IV. The confusion about Artawazd suggests that he was not one of the dominant figures of the Mamikonean house as recorded in its "Geste." See Appendix I, "Hamazaspean" on the problems of Mamikonean genealogy.

5. BP is our main source for the prerogative of the Mamikonean to serve as "tutors" (*dayeak*) and "foster-fathers" (*snuc^{c}ič^c*) of the heir to the Armenian crown. See also IV.ii, xi, and Appendix III, s.v.; also Bedrosian, "*Dayeakut^{c}iwn*."

6. The reference is presumably to Tarōn, part of which belonged to the Mamikonean in the fourth century: see Toumanoff, *Studies*, p. 209; and Appendix II, "Tarōn."

III.xix

1. MX, III.xvi (= MK, pp. 269–270) reduces this chapter, together with III.xv, to a few sentences.

2. Ps. 35:2 = Rom. 3:18 with minimal alterations.

3. See III.iii, xiv and n. 11 on Aštišat as the "mother church" of Armenia.

4. See V.vii, xxxii and Intro., p. 52, on the presence of *gusan*s, "minstrels, bards" at feasts.

5. MX, III.xvi (= MK, p. 269) has the brothers killed by a bolt of lightning and omits the angelic agent.

6. See IV.liv and Appendix III, *bazmakan*, for the special banqueting couch used on ceremonial occasions.

7. Ps. 140:8.

8. This is presumably the property at Aštišat where the patriarch Pᶜarēn had been buried. See III.xvi and n. 7.

9. See III.v and n. 4; xv and nn. 2–3.

10. Because St. Maštocᶜ was born in the village of Hacᶜekacᶜ, Koriwn, iii, p. 36 (trans. p. 27), it has been suggested that this Vrik might have been his father, though there is no evidence to support this hypothesis: see Malχasyancᶜ (1947 ed., p. 320 n. 57). On the possibility that *karčazat* is a *lapsus calami* for *harčazat*, see Appendix III, s.v.

III.xx

1. The two chapters III.xx–xxi jointly dealing with the end of Tiran's reign are not to be found in this form in the corresponding section of MX, III.xvii (= MK, pp. 270–272), which, with its author's scholarly preference for written texts, substitutes here a letter from the Persian king Šāhpuhr II that decoys Tiran to his doom. Fragments from BP's tale can, however, be found in his account: see below, n. 5 and III.xxi nn. 4, 16, 18, 23. MX sets Tiran's reign at eleven years, a precision not to be found in BP.

As first noted by Gelzer, "Die Anfänge," pp. 118–119, note; and amply demonstrated by Adontz, "Favst," and Melikᶜ-Ōhanjanyan, "Tiran-Trdati vepə," these two chapters form episodes taken from the popular tradition of the historical events of this period transmuted into the multi-cycled epic elaborated by Abełyan, *Grakanutᶜyun*, pp. 197–275, and named by him "the Epic of the Persian War." See Intro., p. 31. The present chapter—centering on the dispute over the king's magnificent and magic horse and ending in the lament over the king's tragic fate, filled with anonymous or misidentified rulers, the curious absence of the *sparapet* who should normally play a leading in a military context, replete with suspiciously symbolic names and accumulated epithets—has all the hallmarks of the oral epic tradition and probably derives from the "Geste of the Aršakuni." Its themes of the hunt and the banquet as the *loci* of the crucial events in the king's career are central to the Iranian epic tradition: see below, nn. 7, 9, 11–13, 16; and Intro., p. 53 and n. 248.

2. See below nn. 7, 9 and xxi nn. 16, 21 for the incorrect identification of both rulers in this episode. MX, III.x, xvii (= MK, pp. 263, 270–271) correctly identifies the Persian king as Šāhpuhr II.

3. Adontz, "Favst," p. 248, Melikᶜ-Ōhanjanyan, "Tiran-Trdati vepə," II, p. 66, and Peeters, "Intervention," p. 235, etc., identify Varaz-Šapuh with Βαρσαβώρης = Βαρ‹ασ›-σαβώρ(σ)ης, one of the Persian ambassadors sent to negotiate with Diocletian in 298 according to Petr. Patric, *ad gent.*, iii, and whom they take to be a member of the great Iranian noble house of the Sūrēn. This identification is both possible and tempting. BP's constant hesitation over the form of the name, however—Šapuh-Varaz, Varaz-Šapuh, and Varaz—*tout-court*, suggests the alternate possibility of a typical rather than a real name for a Sasanian viceroy. Varaz ‹ Pahl. *warāz*, "wild-boar," symbolizing the incarnation in this form of the god Vərəθraγna, was the Sasanian name par excellence, and the wild boar was the insignia of the Sasanian dynasty; see IV.liii and Garsoïan, "Substratum," pp. 160–162. Similarly, Šapuh = Pahl. Šāhpuhr ‹ OP χšāyaθiyahyā-puθʳa, "king's son" was both the name of the reigning monarch Šāhpuhr II (309–379) and perhaps overly apt. Consequently, the name of the Persian magnate seems suspiciously felicitous, especially in the context of a chapter replete with symbolic names. See above, n. 1, and below nn. 5, 12, 18.

Adontz, "Favst," pp. 246–247 objects that Atrpatakan could not have had a Persian viceroy in this period under the terms of the peace of Nisibis of 298, but Atrpatakan is not mentioned in the terms of the peace (see Petr. Patric., *ad. gent.*, iii); and although BP repeatedly sets the Armenian–Persian border at Ganjak of Atrpatakan (see Appendix II, "Ganjak") and speaks of Armenian royal domains in or along the border of Atrpatakan (IV.xvi and n. 2) there is no claim that the Armenians ever occupied the entire region (V.viii n. 4).

4. Cf. III.xvii n. 7 for the beginning of the war in Tiran's reign.

5. As noted by Melikᶜ-Ōhanǰanyan, "Tiran-Trdati vepə," II, pp. 66–68, 72–75, "Pᶜisak" ‹ ? OP *pisak* by way of Gk. πισάγας, "leper" is probably not a proper name but a derogatory epithet with obvious moral overtones. This is all the more likely that in the parallel tale of another of Tiran's magic horses, MX, II.lxii (= MK, pp. 204–205) gives the name of the hostile protagonist as "Datakē, a prince of the Bznunikᶜ," who is obviously to be equated with the treacherous Databē Bznuni of BP, III. viii; see also Adontz, "Favst," p. 242. The two accounts presumably go back to a common tale of a stolen magic horse (see below, nn. 6, 11), the name of whose original protagonist had been forgotten and which was consequently associated with various traitors. The identification of "Pᶜisak" as a member of "the clan of Siwni" would derive in the same manner by contamination from the notorious reputation of this house in the fifth century, as a result of the career of the traitor par excellence, Vasak Siwni, as set out in the received tradition" of ŁPᶜ and Ełišē.

6. As suggested in the preceding note, the tale of the stolen magic horse and his substitution was a favorite one recorded in both the Iranian tradition of the Šāhnāme, with Rustam's favorite steed Rakhš (I, pp. 354–357; cf. V, pp. 417–419) and the Armenian popular epic, *Sasna Crer*, with the exploits of horses, especially the magic horse J̌alali, pp. 101–104, 132–134, 226–227, 231–232, 240, 317–320 (= tr. 117–120, 156, 158–159, 262, 267–269, 277, 367–371). The application of the transcendental quality of *kᶜaǰutᶜiwn*, "valor" (see Appendix III, *kᶜaǰ*) to Tiran's horse underscores its supernatural character. See also Malχasyancᶜ's derivation of *čartuk* ‹ Phl. *čartuk* (p. 318 n. 46).

7. The Persian king is now identified by his dynastic name, but the emperor remains anonymous. See above, n. 1 and below, 21.

8. Cf. Aršak II's threats against the Persian king, IV.liv and n. 12. These threats recall the blood feud between the Armenian Arsacids and the Sasanian usurpers of their kinsmen's throne in Iran, which opens the account of Aa, xviii–xxii; see also Garsoïan, "Prolegomena," cols. 177–179, 188–189.

9. As has long been observed (see Malχasyancᶜ, *Usumnasirutᶜiwn*, p. 103) et al., the appearance at this point of the Sasanian king of kings Narseh (293–303) instead of his grandson Šāhpuhr II (309–379), correctly identified by MX (see above, n. 1) hopelessly confuses the chronology of this account. See next chapter, n. 16 for the most likely thesis on Narseh's anachronistic intrusion.

10. See III.xiii–xiv.

11. On the hunt and the banquet as the only suitable diversions for a nobleman in the Iranian epic tradition and the symbolism of horsemanship, cf. ŁPᶜ, I.vii; also Intro., pp. 53–54 and V.ii; Gignoux, "Chasse"; *idem*, "Pour une évaluation," pp. 10–11; also Garsoïan, "Locus," pp. 46–64 and n. 104.

12. On the "city" of Ałiorskᶜ, see Appendix II, "Ałiorskᶜ." However, Melikᶜ-Ōhanǰanyan, "Tiran-Trdati vepə," II, p. 70 also argued for a symbolic etymology: *ałi*, "salt" + *ors*, "hunt" reflecting the "bitter hunt" in which King Tiran himself became the victim, a thesis that seems rather far fetched even in this epic context.

13. The accumulation of parallel epithets, *tiranenkn ew tiradružn, tiraspanun, tiramatničᶜn* is typical of the epic oral style. See III.viii for the similar condemnation of Databē Bznuni, and Appendix V, k.

14. See III.xviii.

15. This is one of the rare references to the non-noble (*ṙamikspas*) contingents as opposed to the normal "noble cavalry" (*azatagund*). See Appendix III, *azatagund, ṙamikspas, zōrkᶜ*, I. b.

16. For the banquet as the locus of the critical moment in the life of the king, cf. V.vii,

xxxii; see Intro., p. 54 and Garsoïan, "Locus," pp. 46– 64; also above n. 1, for MX's different version of Tiran's capture.

17. The blinding of the Armenian king by the Persians, attributed by both BP and MX, III.xvii (= MK, p. 272) to the punishment of Tiran, is assigned by AM, XXVII.xii.3 to his son Aršak II (cf. IV.liv and n. 15; V.vii). Both rulers may have suffered the same punishment, though the blinding of Aršak is unknown to Armenian sources. Alternately, the epic tradition may have attributed this punishment to Tiran as particularly suitable for his sins against the patriarchs (see below, n. 19), while reserving suicide, fulfilling the curse of St. Nersēs, for Aršak II (IV.xv, V.vii). Melikʿ-Ōhanǰanyan, "Tiran-Trdati vepə," I, pp. 66–67, argues for a still more complicated triple cycle involving the successive reigns of Tiran, Aršak II, and Pap.

18. Melikʿ-Ōhanǰanyan, "Tiran-Trdati vepə," II, p. 70, rightly treats these toponyms, which are not otherwise attested, as entirely too apt in their symbolism of the darkening of Tiran's sight to be historical.

19. The *lex talionis* invoked by BP in this didactic passage explicitly linking Tiran's "two eyes" to the murdered "two illuminating spiritual teachers," Yusik and Daniēl (III.xiii–xiv) seems far more apt in the epic context than MX's far fetched scriptural quotations, III.xvii (= MK, p. 272). This passage is explicitly recalled by Asołik, II.i, p. 69 (= Dulaurier tr. p. 103).

20. Malχasyancʿ (pp. 319 n. 49 and 326 n. 108) takes the reference here and in IV.xx as being to the Persian capital of Ctesiphon, which was in the region of Asorestan; see Appendix II, s.n.

21. The reappearance of an anonymous "prince of the Persian king" and his equally anonymous "lord the king of Persia" maintain the epic, unhistorical ethos of the entire chapter. See above, nn. 1, 3, 7.

22. BP furnishes the most detailed information for the Armenian council similar to that of the Parthians; see Justinus, *Epitome*, XLI.iv.2; XLII.iv.1, for the distinction between the dynastic *naχarar*s and the parafeudal-administrative *gorcakal*s, and for the participation of the non-noble classes in the council of the magnates, see Garsoïan, "Prolegomena," cols. 183, 187–188, and 214 n. 46, and Appendix III, *žołov*.

23. Cf. the lament over the partition of Armenia, VI.i, and a possible foreshadowing of the destruction of the Armenian kingdom in the early fifth century.

III.xxi

1. See preceding chapter, n. 1. As traced by Adontz, "Favst," and Melikʿ-Ōhanǰanyan, "Tiran-Trdati vepə," this chapter is most probably a conflation of events dating from the end of the third and the middle of the fourth centuries as preserved in the folk memory; see below, nn. 4, 11, 16–17, 20–21, 23–24. Its tone continues the partly historical and heavily epic ethos of the preceding chapter, and it is likewise based on the "Geste of the Aršakuni."

2. See III.xx n. 22.

3. See III.xx nn. 1, 7, and below.

4. There is no record of this embassy in the corresponding passage of MX, III.xvii (= MK, p. 272), which places it earlier at the beginning of Tiran's reign, III.x (= MK, pp. 263–264), where it also gives an important role to Aršawir Kamsarakan even though he is not listed as one of the ambassadors. An embassy at the beginning of Tiran's reign would be far more in keeping with the statement of Julian, *Panegyric*, xx–xxi, that a king had been "returned" to Armenia by Constantius in 338. See Adontz, "Favst," pp. 249–251, followed by Melikʿ-Ōhanǰanyan, "Tiran-Trdati vepə," I, pp. 70–73, although here too, the latter goes on to argue for a parallel and confusion with the enthronement of Pap (*ibid.*, pp. 61–63). Peeters, "Intervention," however, argued the difficultly tenable thesis that the king returned to Armenia in 338 was Aršak II. See below, nn. 16, 23 and IV.xvi n. 13; xx n. 19.

5. See III.xx n. 7.

6. See Aa, dccclxvii–dccclxxxii for the tradition of King Trdat's journey to the court of Constantine the Great and for the "alliance" between them (dccclxxvii). Cf., however, Honigmann, *Patristic Studies*, pp. 18-27, who argues for an actual treaty in 314. Note that Armenia without its king is an *erkir* and not an *ašχarh*; cf. IV.i before and after Aršak II's accession, and Appendix III, s.vv.

7. See III.xx n. 9 and below, n. 16.

8. See Appendix III, *karawan*.

9. See Appendix III, *maškapačēn*.

10. Satala in Armenia Minor marked the western border of Greater Armenia (III.vii n. 5) and was one of the headquarters of the imperial army in the East. See Appendix II, "Sataḷ."

11. As observed by Adontz, "Favst," pp. 239-241, the investigation of the Persian camp by the emperor accompanied by only two Armenian nobles finds its exact counterpart in Festus's account of the Caesar Galerius's similar reconnaissance in A.D. 297, "in Armenia Maiore ipse Imperator cum duobus equitibus exploravit hostes," *Breviarium*, xxv; see below, n. 16. The disguise of the emperor as a cabbage seller smacks more of the Thousand and One Nights than of classical models, but Melikꞌ-Ōhanǰanyan, "Tiran-Trdati vepə," II, p. 65 attempted to find in it an allusion to Diocletian's raising of vegetables during his retirement at Nicomedia.

12. MX, III.x (= MK, p. 263) locates the battle with the Persians "on the plain called Mṙuḷ"; see AON, p. 359. Melikꞌ-Ōhanǰanyan, "Tiran-Trdati vepə," II, pp. 70-71, 76, argues rather inconvincingly that Osχay/Oχsay, both here and in IV.xxii, is not an actual toponym but a symbolic reference to the "bitterness, vengeance" (*oχkꞌ*, acc. *oχs*) of the Armenians against the Persians. See Appendix II, "Osχay" for the difficulties in locating this toponym.

13. See Appendix V, e. Cf. NBHL, II, p. 891, *tunčēn* for unusual uses.

14. See Appendix V, b, c.

15. As has been repeatedly observed, AG, I, p. 117 #100; Malχasyancꞌ (p. 318 n. 52), the meaningless *bansakan* of the text should be corrected in accordance with the context into *banukan* ‹ Pahl. *bānūg*, "lady." See CPD, p. 17 and Benveniste, *Titres et noms propres*, pp. 28-29.

16. This description of the sacking of the Persian camp and the capture of the royal harem is the key passage used by Adontz, "Favst," pp. 235-236 and Melikꞌ-Ōhanǰanyan, "Tiran-Trdati vepə," to elucidate its historical background and indeed that of the two chapters III.xx-xxi. They related this description to the almost identical one of Galerius's sack in 297 of the camp of the king of kings Narseh in Armenia, described in almost the same terms and probably derived from a common source by Aur. Vict., xxxix; Festus, *Breviarium*, xxv; and Eutropius, *Breviarium*, IX.xxiv-xxv, "Galerius Maximus . . . rursus cum Narseo . . . in Armenia Majori pugnavit. . . . Pulso Narseo castra ejus diripuit. Uxores, sorores, liberos cepit, infinitam extrinsecus Persarum nobilitatem, gazam Persicam copiosissimam. Ipsum in ultimas regni solitudines egit," and recalled by Petr. Patric., *ad gent.* iii; *ad Rom.*, xii. This episode preceded the negotiations leading to the Peace of Nisibis of 298 whereby the Roman protectorate over the lands of Greater Armenia was reaffirmed; the rightful Aršakuni heir, Trdat the Great, returned to his throne; and the Persian royal household released unharmed. See Petr. Patric., *ad gent.*, iii for the peace terms, and Toumanoff, "Third-Century Arsacids," pp. 263-265 for the enthronement of Trdat. The explanation for this anachronistic intrusion into the mid-fourth century of the late third-century Persian king of kings Narseh (see III.xx n. 9 and above) comes from the confusion between him and another Narseh—the son of Šāhpuhr II according to the classical sources (his brother according to MX, III.x = MK, p. 263) and consequently a contemporary of Tiran of Armenia—who had been left in command of his father's army after Šāhpuhr II's flight from the field at the battle of Singara in Mesopotamia ca. 344/5 (see below, n. 23). This later Narseh had been captured and killed by the Romans accord-

ing to Julian, *Panegyric*, xxvii–xxx; cf. Eutropius, *Breviarium*, X.x; Festus, *Breviarium*, xxvii; and AM, XVIII.v.7. The parallels, matching in every detail, between BP's account and that of Galerius's overwhelming victory over the Persians in 297, followed by the peace negotiations of 298, the return of a rightful heir to the Armenian throne, and the release of the Persian harem are too close and circumstantial to be fortuitous (see below, nn. 17, 20, 23, 24, but cf. also V.ii). Taken together with the less successful campaign of Singara followed by Šāhpuhr II's failure to take Nisibis in 346—which was the probable setting for the accession of Aršak II (see Adontz, "Favst," pp. 254–255; below, n. 23; and IV.xvi n. 13)—the events of 297–298 undoubtedly provided the historical background for this chapter. By the second half of the fifth century, however, their distant memory—in which the brilliant victory of 297 had preempted the dubious engagement of 344/5 and the two Narsehs had become fused—had passed into the semi-legendary oral tradition that served as a source for BP. Cf. V.ii for the parallel to this account.

17. The memory of the Persian king's flight from the battlefield has been preserved by classical sources, both in the case of the defeat of Narseh in 297 (Eutropius, *Breviarium*, IX.xxv; Festus, *Breviarium*, xxv, "Rex persarum Narseus effugit") and in that of Šāhpuhr II at Singara (Julian, *Panegyric*, xxviii). Cf. however, Appendix V, d, for BP's use of this epic *topos*, and Intro., p. 32 and n. 145.

18. Cf. II Macc. 3:35. The governorship of Andovk and Aršawir is not mentioned by MX, III. xvii–xviii (= MK, p. 272). There may be, however, a reminiscence of it in III.x (= MK, p. 263) that preserves some anachronistic fragments of these events, among which may be the statement that "the land of Armenia [had been entrusted] to Aršawir Kamsarakan, as the preeminent and most honorable man after the king" during the succession of Tiran to Xosrov Kotak. See III.xx n. 1, and above, n. 4.

19. The stripping off of a magnate's or official's diadem (*patiw*) and honorific robe (*patmučan*) were the preliminary steps to a death sentence in the Iranian world. Cf. e.g. the disgrace of the traitor Vasak Siwni in both ŁPᶜ, II.xlvi p. 85 (= CHAMA, II, p. 305) and Ełišē, vi p. 137 (= *Ełishē*, p. 188) and below, V.vi.

20. These negotiations are probably an echo of those which led to the peace of Nisibis, in which the release of the Persian royal household played an important part. See Petr. Patric., *ad Rom.*, xii and above, n. 16.

21. The appearance of the emperor Valens (364–378) at this point compounds the chronological chaos of this section. Melikᶜ-Ōhanǰanyan, "Tiran-Trdati vepə," II, p. 65, suggests that this name—Vałēs in Armenian—should be taken as a contraction of that of the victorious Caesar at the battle of 297: Galerius Vale⟨riu⟩s Maximianus and should thus be part of the recollection of his exploits set out in this chapter; see above n. 16. This hypothesis is not beyond the realm of possibility in view of the epic character of this chapter; nonetheless, the classical sources dealing with the events of 297–298 do not refer to the Caesar by this name, but call him "Galerius Maximianus" (Eutropius, *Breviarium*, IX.xxiv) or "Maximianus Caesar" (Aur. Vict., xxxix; and Festus, *Breviarium*, xxv), reserving the name "Valerius" for the contemporary senior Augustus, Caius Aurelius Valerius Diocletianus: see, e.g., Aur. Vict., xxxix, "Valerius, cujus nutu omnia gerebantur." The name of Valens, one of only two imperial names known to BP, as was observed by Baynes, "Rome and Armenia," p. 187 and Melikᶜ-Ōhanǰanyan, "Tiran-Trdati vepə," p. 64, occurs elsewhere in BP—likewise anachronistically—either as a result of intrusive material from the *Life* of St. Basil or of the confusion with the other Arianizing emperor of the fourth century, Constantius, which may well be the case here, as Constantius (337–361) was reigning at the time of the battle of Singara. See below, IV.v n. 5, vi n. 2, viii n. 2, ix–x, xi n. 2 and Appendix I, "Vałes"; also Baynes, "Rome and Armenia," p. 187; and Garsoïan, "Politique," p. 308; *idem*, "*Quidam Narseus*," pp. 151–152 and n. 12.

22. Malxasyancᶜ (p. 319 n. 53) corrects the *gtanēr*, "found" of the text to the more suitable *grēr*, "wrote."

23. Cf. IV.i. The date of the accession of Aršak II is problematic, as is indeed all of the

highly disputed chronology of fourth-century Armenia. Adontz, "Favst," pp. 254–255 suggests 345 after the battle of Singara (see above, n. 16); and indeed a brief truce seems to have followed Šāhpuhr II's failure to take Nisibis in 346 (see Pigagnol, *Empire*, pp. 84–85). However, the date of the Singara campaign has been disputed between 344/5 (Bury, "Singara," pp. 302–305; also Adontz, "Favst") and 348/9, (Pigagnol, *Empire*, p. 85). Furthermore, this battle was not a Roman triumph, after which terms could be dictated to the Persians; see Julian, *Panegyric*, xxvii versus xxviii; Eutropius, *Breviarium*, X.x; AM, XVIII.v.7; and perhaps an anachronistic echo in MX, III.xii (= MK, p. 265), according to which, "both sides were defeated, for many fell from both sides." Moreover, Šāhpuhr II attacked again in 348, besieging Nisibis for the third time in 350. Manandyan, *Kʿnnakan tesutʿyun*, II.1, pp. 166, 441, proposes the commonly accepted accession date of 350 for Aršak II, after the failure of the third Persian siege of Nisibis. This date is supported by the much longer truce that intervened at this point (see IV.i, xxi), when both Constantius and Šāhpuhr II were drawn by other concerns to the opposite ends of their respective realms. It also fits more satisfactorily with the religious policy of the period; see Garsoïan, "Politique," pp. 303, 306–307 and nn. 26, 36–37. This date does not however agree with MX's assertion, III.xxxv (= MK, p. 294) that Aršak reigned for thirty years or with the thesis that his reign began in 338; see IV.xvi, n. 13.

24. The term used here in the text is *zkanays* (acc. pl. of *kanaykʿ*), which Gevorgian translated throughout this chapter as "wives." Such a translation seems entirely acceptable in the case of the Persian royal household, whose more important female members were all "wives" and only the "queen of queens" was set apart (see III.v n. 4 on consanguineous marriages and V.ii). In the Christian context of this particular passage, however, the translation is not as certain, and the term may mean nothing more than the "women" of the Armenian royal household in general, since the first meaning of *kin* (pl. *kanaykʿ*) is "woman." It is nevertheless interesting to compare the usages here with that in V.xv, where the *kanaykʿ* of the house of Gugarkʿ (which was presumably Christian in this period) are differentiated from the "daughters" (*dsterkʿ*), so that "wives" seems to be the meaning intended at this point; and especially with V.xvi, for the *kanaykʿ* of the *bdeašχ* of Aljnikʿ. Cf. also the citation by St. Basil of Caesarea (Ep., ccxxi #80) of the canon against polygamy and the strictures of the Persian council of 544 against this practice; see *Syn. Or.*, pp. 335–336. If indeed the Aršakuni kings were still polygamous after their conversion to Christianity, as may be implied here as well as in the strictures of St. Nersēs and the council of Šahapivan against incestuous marriages (see IV.iv n. 25), such a practice would not only provide another index of an Iranian survival in Christian Armenia, but also help shed some light on the problem of Aršak II's two marriages (see IV.xv n. 40). Such a hypothesis is undoubtedly attractive but is not yet provable, for the two basic meanings of *kin* can be distinguished only through an interpretation of the context in which the term is found.

25. The return of Nerseh's captive family as part of the terms of the peace of Nisibis of 298 are duly recorded by Petr. Patric., *ad gent.*, iii and Festus, *Breviarium*, xxv, who also notes the admiration of the Persians for the care given to the captive ladies, "cum maxima pudicitiae custodia reservata. Pro qua admiratione Persae non modo armis, sed etiam moribus, superiore esse Romanos confessi sunt." Cf., however, V.ii and n. 8.

III Colophon

1. Malχasyancʿ's translation of the *darkʿ* (corrected to *dark*) of the text as *masn*, "part, portion" (p. 319 n. 54) has been followed here.

2. The form *pʿaχsteaykʿ* of the manuscripts, given in the St. Petersburg edition (p. 50), was altered to read "Pʿawsteay Biwzandeay" by Norayr Biwzandacʿi (see Malχasyancʿ, p. 319 n. 54). This reading was followed by the Venice edition (p. 68, but cf. n. 2) and most scholars, but it is unattested.

3. See Intro., pp. 6, 9 for this problematic colophon, which is altogether omitted by Lauer (p. 48).

IV Tables

1. Malxasyancʿ (p. 320 n. 55) considers a precise translation of this redundant title impossible and notes Vardanyan's correction of *darkʿ ew darkʿ* to *darkkʿ ew darkkʿ*.

2. This title, which does not correspond to the heading of the chapter in the text, led to a disagreement between Malxasyancʿ (p. 320 n. 56) and the editors of his 1968 edition. Malxasyancʿ corrected the *pataragovkʿ* of the text to *patandovkʿ*, "hostages" and further suggested the reading, "*ziard zayl naxararsn handerj aylovkʿn patandovkʿ arjakēr yerkirn Hayocʿ handerj pataragōk*, which fits the content of the chapter more closely. The editors, however, preferred *handerj pataragōk* omitting *aylovkʿn* and the hostages.

3. Malxasyancʿ (p. 320 n. 57) suggests the correction of *yułarkeacʿ*, "sent" to *yuzeacʿ*, "aroused," which is found in the actual heading of the chapter in the text and is also suggested in the Venice edition, p. 71 n. 1. Malxasyancʿ (p. 326 n. 103) also noted that the title of the chapter in the text is defective because the word "persecution" is missing, and he corrects it accordingly. Both corrections have been adopted here as clearly warranted.

IV.i

1. This chapter, which provides a summary of III.xx–xxi, adds no information and follows their anachronisms. The historical and detailed account of Aršak II's early reign begins in the next chapter.

2. See III.xx nn. 1, 7, 9 and xxi n. 16.

3. See III.xxi n. 23.

4. See III.xxi n. 24. We do not know the date of Aršak II's first marriage; see IV.xv n. 40.

5. See III.xxi n. 23.

6. Cf. III.xxi n. 6 on Armenia as an *ašxarh* and an *erkir*.

IV.ii

1. The reorganization of the realm under Aršak II is not mentioned by MX, III.xviii–xx (= MK, pp. 272–275), who attributes all the changes to St. Nersēs (see below IV.iv), emphasizes the control of Armenia by Šāhpuhr II, and makes Vałinak Siwni, "commander of the Armenian eastern army," the effective master of the realm. Cf. III.ix n. 5

2. The exhaltation of the Mamikonean house with the transfer to it of the royal epithet, *kʿaǰ*, "valiant" is especially manifest in this chapter and from here on. This is a probable indication of increasing reliance on the "Geste of the Mamikonean." See Intro., pp. 34–35.

3. See III.xviii n. 5.

4. See III.xviii; and Appendix II, "Taykʿ."

5. *Yəndanutʿiwn darjucʿanēr* is to be taken here as an idiom meaning "appeased." See NBHL, I, p. 784, *əndanutʿiwn*, secondary meaning.

6. Malxasyancʿ (p. 320 n. 59) and the Venice edition, p. 76 n. 1, correct the corrupt reading *xulutʿean* of the text to *xawlutʿean*, "unreason, madness."

7. The indication here that the king "appointed" (*kacʿoycʿ*) the *nahapet* of a clan as well as the "commander-in-chief" (*sparapet*) of the realm runs counter to the traditionally

hereditary character of these dignities, see Intro., pp. 47–48 and III.xi n. 7. This action may be an attempt to reorganize the Armenian traditional *naχarar* structure in order to centralize authority in the hands of the king, as was the policy of contemporary Iran. Note, however, that Vasak was already entitled "commander-in-chief" (*mec zōravar*) in the reign of Tiran (III.xvi). This attempt may explain Aršak II's subsequent difficulties with his unruly magnates (see IV.xix, li and n. 8), even if it was merely the ratification of a fait accompli. The unusual attribution of the dynastic title of *nahapet* to one member of the Mamikonean family and the hereditary office of *sparapet* to another, instead of the normal practice in which the *nahapet* served as *sparapet*, likewise caused difficulties (IV.xvi, xviii). See below, V.xxxvii for the normal pattern, and for the failure of the centralizing policy of the Armenian crown, III.viii n. 12, ix n. 6, and Garsoïan, "Prolegomena," cols. 187–190.

8. This is a clear indication that the rank of a *naχarar* clan corresponded to the size of its military contingent and consequently for the original linking of the later *Gahnamak*, "Rank List" and *Zōrnamak*, "Military List." See Adontz, *Armenia*, pp. 191–234; and Toumanoff, *Studies*, pp. 187–190. To reestablish the sense of this phrase, Malχasyanc^c (p. 320 n. 60) replaced the word *aṙ*, "by" dropped from the text in front of "former kings."

9. This is the statement par excellence of the proper social structure of Arsacid Armenia, of which this entire chapter is one of the best- known descriptions.

10. This is the best description of the office of *hazarapet* in fourth-century Armenia in contrast to its transformation in the fifth. See Appendix III, *hazarapet* and III.xii for the previous attribution of this office to the prince of Anjit.

11. As rightly observed by Malχasyanc^c (p. 321 n. 62), this wordy panegyric of the Mamikonean is confused and obscure, as is its counterpart in the *Vita* of St. Nersēs, ii, pp. 16–18 (= CHAMA, II, pp. 22–23), which adds to it elements taken from V.v. Following HArmB, I, p. 120, *ałan*, Malχasyanc^c derives the *ałanazgik^c*, "illustrious" of the text from Syr. *ālānā*, "prince, chief" and corrects the next word, *ałanadrošk^c*, which he considers contaminated by the preceding one, to *aławnadroš*, "dove banner." These corrections seem plausible, but EM, p. 30, preferred the readings *ałełnagikk^c*, "archers" and *ałełnadrošk^c*, which correspond to the text of the *Vita* of St. Nersēs; cf. also Perikhanian, "Inscription," p. 23 n. 9. As for the term *irap^caṙn*, which appears in four mss as *irawap^caṙn* (see Venice edition p. 71 n. l), it is not recorded in the NBHL, I, though the *Aṙjern*, p. 348 interprets *irawap^car* as *ardiwnk^cov p^caṙaworuac^c*, "glorified by accomplishments." See also IV.iii n. 2 on the clan banners and insignia.

12. The order of precedence of the Armenian magnates, as of their Iranian counterparts, was indicated by the position of their "throne" (*gah*) or "cushion" (*barj*) at court functions. This rigorous hierarchy was maintained and eventually set down in a *Gahnamak*, "Rank" or "Throne List," of which late versions have survived. See Adontz, *Armenia*, pp. 183– 234; and Chaumont, *Ordre*. In Armenia as in Iran, the lowering of a noble's place at court was taken as an open degradation and insult. See IV.liv, and MK/D, II.i, p. 107 (= MD, pp. 61–62) for the humiliation of Andovk Siwni; MX, III.li, lxv (= MK, pp. 316, 344) and Garsoïan, "Prolegomena," n. 58; as well as Appendix III, *barj, gah*.

13. This problematic passage is given in a somewhat different translation by Adontz, *Armenia*, p. 185. In any case there seems to be little doubt that he is correct in his conclusion that the figure given for the number of nobles is exaggerated.

IV.iii

1. MX, III.xvi (= MK, p. 269–270), devotes only a few sentences to Nersēs's early career, without any mention of his military service and official postition as royal *senekapet*. He also gives no account of his selection as patriarch. The *Vita* of St. Nersēs, III, 18–24 (= CHAMA, II, pp. 23–24) follows BP, though it adds the name of Nersēs's wife. See below, n. 6; also IV.iv n. 4 for other variations.

2. Both in Iran and in Armenia, the magnates were entitled to display their own

coats of arms and banners, especially in Parthian times; see IV.ii and n. 11 and V.iv for the Mamikonean. These coats of arms are clearly visible on the victory relief of Ardašīr I over the last Parthian ruler Artawan V at Firuzabad. See Toumanoff, *Studies*, pp. 134–135 and nn. 233–235; Christensen, *L'Iran*, pp. 210–212; Garsoïan, "Prolegomena," col. 224 and n. 62; and Ghirshman, *Persian Art*, figs. 163–166.

3. See III.xv, n. 4.

4. See III.xiii n. 25, for the hereditary character of the patriarchate in the house of St. Gregory. The terminology used here clearly seems to indicate that the primacy of the patriarchal house was a *nahapetut'iwn* equivalent to that of any other *naχarar* house; see Intro., p. 50.

5. See III.v nn. 4, 8; and xv n. 3.

6. MX, III.xvi (= MK, pp. 269–270) also has Nersēs educated at Caesarea, but then sends him to Constantinople to marry "the daughter of the great noble Aspion," otherwise unknown. The *Vita* of St. Nersēs calls the wife of the future patriarch "Sanduχt" and makes her the daughter of Vardan I Mamikonean, a statement that is also unsupported.

7. This seems to be an exaggeration to enhance Nersēs's position, as there is no evidence that the *senekapet* or royal chamberlain had such broad responsibilites, and an Iranian official titled the "sword bearer" is attested in SKZ (see Appendix III, *senekapet*). It is, however, interesting that like all the Gregorids except Aristakēs, Nersēs before his consecration as patriarch led a secular and even a military life like his father At'anaginēs and his uncle Pap, instead of following the ascetic tradition of much of early Christianity, especially in Syria. This may again be a reflection of the Iranian aristocratic and anti-ascetic Zoroastrian ethos of contemporary Armenia: see III.v and n. 1, xiii, xv; cf. III.xiv; VI.xvi; also Gaudemet, *L' Église*, pp. 142–143, on the exclusion of the military from the priesthood.

8. Cf. III.xii for the parallel description of Yusik. In both cases the presence of the standard clichés of early Christian virtue suggest a hagiographic rather than an historical source.

9. Mark 12:31/Matt. 22:39.

10. I Cor. 11:2; Rom. 10:2.

11. Cf. Acts 18:25; Rom. 12:11; II Tim. 3:17.

12. For the unexpected use here of the Iranian title *ĵatagov amenayn zrkeloc'* = Pahl. *dlgwš'n y'tkgw/ĵādag-gōw*, "protector/defender of the destitute," which is recorded in the MHD = *Sasanian Lawbook* (93.4–9) but is a *hapax* not only in BP but in Armenian literature in general, see Garsoïan, "Protecteur des pauvres."

13. The claim of unworthiness is the traditional *topos* for episcopal elections.

14. Cf. Exod. 20:5; Matt. 27:25.

15. See Intro., pp. 12–13 and Appendix I, "P'awstos," for the problems surrounding this personage.

16. Cf. Rom. 7:22.

17. This passage is a tissue of Pauline allusions. Cf. Gal. 2:20, 3:27; Col. 2:12; Rom. 6:2–5, 10; Acts 23:6.

18. See III.xii and n. 7.

19. See III.v for Yusik's vision, though the precise quotation given here with its echo of John 1:9 is not found there.

IV.iv

1. See V.xxi for the summary of this chapter, and V.xxxi. MX, III.xx (= MK, pp. 273–274) mentions Nersēs return from Caesarea, where he had been educated (see IV.iii n. 6), but does not allude to his consecration and as usual is far terser than BP in his treatment of the patriarch's career (cf. III.xiii n. 1, xiv n. 1). However, MX gives the date of Nersēs's

enthronement as "the third year of the reign of Arshak," a precision not found in BP. For the dates of Nersēs's pontificate, 353–373, as against the hypothesis of Baynes, "Rome and Armenia," pp. 187–191, see Ōrmanean, *Azgapatum*, I, cols. 163–222, xvi and Garsoïan, "*Quidam Narseus*," p. 152 n. 13, as well as above, III.xxi n. 23 for the problem of the date of Aršak II's accession.

2. Malχasyancᶜ (p. 321 n. 64) corrects the χonarhel of the St. Petersburg edition, p. 60 to χorhel. See Venice edition, p. 81 and n. 1.

3. See III.xv n. 4.

4. With the exception of the anonymous *mardpet* and Mehendak Ṙštuni, a totally different and far more extensive list of magnates and bishops is given by the *Vita* of St. Nersēs, iii, pp. 24–26 (= CHAMA, II p. 24) which obviously does not depend on BP at this point. MX omits any mention of Nersēs's consecration and consequently this list; see above, n. 1.

5. Malχasyancᶜ (p. 321 n. 65), following Norayr Biwzandacᶜi, corrects the *mec išχan asparapetutᶜeann* of the text to *aspetutᶜeann*, in keeping with the gentilitial title of *aspet* of the Bagratuni house. The correction is entirely possible. But in view of the fact that the mss read *asparapetuteann*, and that the Mamikonean *sparapet*—whose presence among the magnates accompanying the patriarch might well be expected, is missing (cf. III.xvi), as is the gentilitial name of the Bagratuni (cf. III.vii and n. 10)—a crasis may have crept into the text and the title of *asparapet* refer to the missing Mamikonean commander-in-chief rather than to Bagarat (Bagratuni).

6. The redundant and anachronistic title, *katᶜołikos-of-katᶜołikoi*, points to a late fifth century date (see Appendix III, *katᶜołikos*). The anachronistic intrusion of Eusebios of Caesarea (362–370), who could not have consecrated Nersēs (353–373), must be attributed to the contamination of this and the following chapters of BP by elements drawn from a *Vita* of St. Basil of Caesarea, for which see next note and Intro., pp. 28–29, 37, 39–40. The titles of Eusebios: *katᶜołikos-of-katᶜołikoi, episkoposapet, mec arkᶜepiskopos*, and the amazing pleonastic hybrid, *arkᶜepiskoposapet*, as well as the variants of his name, Ewsebios/Ewsebi, found throughout this passage suggest an underlying Greek source filtered through the Armenian tradition. See below, nn. 8, 10.

7. The miraculous intervention of the Holy Spirit is unknown to MX (see above, n. 1), but it is repeated, IV.vii, and elaborated by the *Vita* of St. Nersēs, iii, vii, pp. 27–29, 54–55 (= CHAMA, II, pp. 24–25, 30), which adds a column of fire and a vision of the heavenly choir singing the Trisagion to the symbolic white dove. See also below, n. 9, and IV.ix n. 3 for the same miracle at the consecration of St. Basil. On the artificial and anachronistic linkage of St. Basil and St. Nersēs that begins explicitly here, see Baynes, "Rome and Armenia," pp. 187–188; Ōrmanean, *Azgapatum*, I, cols. 168–169; Peeters, "SS Serge et Théodore"; Garsoïan, "*Quidam Narseus*," p. 152 and *idem*, "Nersēs le Grand," p. 145–147 *et passim*.

8. As observed by Ōrmanean, *Azgapatum*, I, col. 169 and Garsoïan, "Nersēs le Grand" pp. 147–148, Basil of Caesarea—who was studying philosophy in Athens at that time and was as yet unordained—could not have been present as "archpriest" (*ericᶜapet*) at St. Nersēs's consecration at Caesarea (see preceding note). As in the case of Eusebios (see above n. 6), St. Basil's name is rendered alternately in the incorrect Greek form, Barsiłios [sic], and the correct Armenian one, Barseł, in this and the successive chapters, thus providing additional evidence for an underlying but distant Greek source although the form "Barsilios" is also found in the sixth century second letter of the katoᶜlikos Babgēn I "To the Orthodox in Persia," GTᶜ, p. 50. See also below, n. 10 and Intro., pp. 6–7 and n. 26.

9. The allusion to the descent of the Holy Spirit upon Jesus in the Jordan—Matt. 3:16, Mark 1:10, Luke 3:22, John 1:32; cf. Is. 61:1 and Luke 4:18—is sustained throughout this section; cf. IV.ix n. 3.

10. The Venice edition, p. 82 and n. 2, places these words in parentheses. The intru-

sion of the transliteration *ēnkomia* sustains the Greek ethos of the chapter; see above, nn. 6, 8. But see also Peeters' observation, in "SS Serge et Théodore," p. 66 n. 2, that such a gloss would hardly be necessary had the text of BP originally been in Greek. See also Intro., p. 8, on the inaccuracy of the gloss.

11. See III.iii n. 8 and v n. 7. From here on note the parallels to the description of Yusik (III.xii).

12. See III.xii n. 7.

13. See III.xii , for the same phrase applied to Yusik.

14. This passage is a medley of scriptural allusions, cf. John 4:36; I Cor.3:6–9; Is. 55:10–11.

15. Acts 1:1; cf. III.xii n. 15. This *topos* is repeatedly applied to St. Nersēs in this chapter; see below, nn. 21, 30, 45.

16. The Venice edition (p. 84 n. 1) corrects the *amenin* of the text to *amenewin*, following the other mss, but Malχasyanc^c (p. 321 n. 67) prefers *atenin*, "seat, tribunal," which is also suggested by the Venice edition. Either version is possible in context.

17. See III.xiv n. 11 on Aštišat as the "mother church" of Armenia.

18. The so-called Council of Aštišat, also mentioned by MX, III.xx (= MK, p. 274), cannot be dated with precision, although Ōrmanean, *Azgapatum*, I, col. 169 suggests A.D. 354. In any case, it was unquestionably held early in St. Nersēs's pontificate: see Garsoïan, "Nersēs le Grand," pp. 161–162.

19. The usual interpretation of *karg miabanut^cean vanakanac^c* as referring to "monastic communities" is anachronistic for the fourth century, and the term *van(k^c)*, "dwelling, abode" did not necessarily carry a monastic sense in this period. Vööbus, *Asceticism*, II, pp. 34–35, already noted the problem of rendering the Greek term μοναχός in Syriac and its variants. The evidence in BP points away from any coenobitic monasticism in Armenia and rather to the Syrian pattern observed by Dom Leloir, "Ephrem," pp. 108–109: 'Le monachisme syrien garde ses notes propres: faveur particulière pour l'anachorétisme, malgré la multiplication, vers la fin de la vie d'Ephrem et surtout après lui, des centres cénobitiques" and supported by Rufinus's characterization, "Sunt enim [monachi] alii in suburganis locis, alii per rura, plures autem et egregii per eremum dispersi" (*Historia*), pp. 389–390. See also Guillaumont, in the discussion of Leloir's thesis, "Ephrem," p. 132, who qualifies the earlier manifestations in Syria as "un monachisme première manière, un pré-monachisme," a definition also suited for fourth-century Armenia, if not later. See also Peña *et al.*, *Les Reclus*, pp. 25–35 *et passim*; V.xxvii n. 4; VI.xvi nn. 3–4, for the peripatetic life of the "brothers"; and Appendix III, *anapatawork^c*, *kusastan*, *mianjn*, and *van(k^c)*.

20. Galat. 4:18; cf. I Cor. 14:1; Titus 2:14, 13:8.

21. See above, n. 15, for the first application of this *topos* to St. Nersēs; and below, nn. 30, 45, for its repetition.

22. Both the Venice edition (p. 85 n. 3) and Malχasyanc^c (pp. 321–322 n. 69) observe that the term *patank^c*, "shrouds" found in the text is improbable in this context. Consequently, they correct it to some form of shelter or residence, *kayaran*, or preferably the *patsparan* proposed by Malχasyanc^c.

23. On St. Nersēs's charitable foundations, which BP stresses repeatedly, see below, and IV.xii; V.xxi, xxxi. MX, III.xx (= MK, p. 274) traces them back to Greek models. See also Garsoïan, "Protecteur des pauvres," pp. 29–32; *idem*, "Nersēs le Grand," pp. 158–169.

24. For the description of the pagan rituals surviving in fourth-century Armenia and especially their connection with mourning rituals, despite their repeated condemnation in this chapter and elsewhere in BP and their formal condemnation by the contemporary Council of Šahapivan, A.D. 444, canon xi (see below); also IV.xv for the mourning over Gnel, V.xxxvi for the rites over the body of Mušeł Mamikonean, and xliv for the disregard of the admonitions of his successor Manuēl. These rituals were also noted by MX, III.xx (= MK, p. 275). and their condemnation is reiterated in Canon iv of the Persian Council of 576, SO, p. 376. The Scriptural injunctions against unbridled mourning are found in both

Lev. 19:28 and Deut. 14:1; see also next note.

25. The insistent condemnation of consanguineous marriages, also noted by MX, III.xx (= MK, p. 275) and the *Vita* of St. Nersēs, vi, p. 42 (= CHAMA, II, p. 28) reveals the presence of this practice, held to be pious and praiseworthy in the Zoroastrian tradition and characteristic of the contemporary Sasanian court (see e.g. KKZ, line 14 = Sprengling, *Iran*, pp. 48–52) in Christian Armenia. This practice was also formally condemned at the Council of Šahapivan, canons xii, xiii. Cf. III.v n. 4; Garsoïan, "Prolegomena," col. 184 and n. 60; also the preceding note.

26. Cf. Acts 15:20. For the injunction against eating animal food practiced by the followers of Eustathius of Sebastē but condemned by the Council of Gangra, see Garsoïan, "Nersēs le Grand," pp. 165–166.

27. For both injunctions, see Eph. 6:5, 9; Col. 3:22; I Tim. 6:1–2. The obedience to one's earthly lords is reiterated in IV.li.

28. See above, n. 19.

29. See III.xiii n. 10.

30. See above, n. 15.

31. Cf. Dan. 4:24.

32. Acts 7:55–56; cf. AaT, dxliii.

33. Acts 9:36–41.

34. Galat. 2:9–10 with an interpolation of 2:7; cf. Apoc. 3:12. The modification and interpolation of this passage from St. Paul, which links St. Nersēs directly back to the vision of his grandfather Yusik (III.v and nn. 5, 14) indicates once again that the author is quoting from memory rather than following a text of the Scriptures. Malχasyancᶜ (p. 322 n. 71) identifies the quotation but comments only on the modification of the *karceal siwnkᶜn*, "who seemed to be pillars" of the Scriptural text to *bun siwnkᶜn*, "true pillars"; cf. AaT, dclxxxiv–dclxxxv.

35. Matt. 19:21–24 with slight variations; cf. Mark 10:24; Luke 12:33.

36. Luke 16:9 with a lacuna.

37. Tit. 2:14; cf. 3:18.

38. I Cor. 14:1 verbatim. From here to the end of the paragraph the text of BP parallels Koriwn, ii, pp. 32–34 (= trans. pp. 25–26), almost verbatim.

39. Cf. II Cor. 9:2; Koriwn, ii, p. 33 (=trans. p. 25).

40. Galat. 4:18 with a slight variation and an inversion.

41. Hebr. 12:2.

42. Cf. I Thess 5:12, interpolated into Hebr. 13:7 here, but not in Koriwn. See Intro., nn. 102–103.

43. Hebr. 13:7 with a slight variation and an inversion.

44. Philip. 2:5 almost verbatim.

45. Acts 1:1. See also III.xii n. 14, and above, nn. 15, 21, 30; and Intro., nn. 102–103, for the omission of this quotation in Koriwn.

46. James 5:10–11 nearly verbatim, with an omission. Cf. AaT, dclxxxvi, and Koriwn, ii, p. 34 (= trans. p. 26).

IV.v

1. MX, III.xxi (= MK, pp. 275–276) places this embassy under altogether different circumstances and addresses it to the emperor Valentinian; see below n. 5 for the name of the emperor. The mention of Nersēs's exile comes with a later embassy, now addressed to Valens: MX, III.xxix (= MK, n. 286). Cf. IV.xi, which repeats and elaborates the account of the embassy in this chapter, and below, n. 4.

2. See III.xxi n. 6, though the reference here may also be to the *rapprochement* between Rome and Armenia as a result of the Peace of Nisibis of 298; see III.xxi n. 16.

3. See IV.xi and n. 4 for the names of the magnates accompanying Nersēs.

273

4. On St. Nersēs's embassy to the emperor Constantius in 358, see Garsoïan, "*Quidam Narseus*," also above, n. 1 and below, nn. 5, 49.

5. See III.xxi n. 21 for the anachronistic appearances of the emperor Valens in BP, and above, n. 1 for similar chronological aberrations, since the reign of Aršak II ending in 363/4 (see IV.liv n. 15) could not coincide with that of Valens (364–378). The confusion arises as a result of the attribution to St. Nersēs of a number of episodes taken from a *Life* of St. Basil of Caesarea (see below, nn. 6, 41), who was indeed a contemporary of Valens. This confusion was all the easier that Valens and Constantius (337–361), to whom Nersēs's embassy had really been addressed (see preceding note) both followed an Arianizing religious policy and could therefore serve as models for a "heretical emperor" in the work of an "orthodox" Armenian ecclesiastic writing one century later and apparently familiar with the names of only two Roman emperors: the Arian "heretic" Valens, and the Christian emperor par excellence, Constantine the Great (see III.x, xxi). None of the Basilian intrusions appears in the corresponding section of MX.

6. The story of the emperor's sick child, whom the saint neither can nor will save because of his father's heretical beliefs, is one of the favorite *topoi* of Basilian hagiography. See Greg. Naz., *Orat. XLIII*, liv; Soc. Schol., E.H., IV.xxvi; Soz., E.H., VI.xvi; Theodoret of Cyr, *Hist Rel.*, IV.xix; also Garsoïan, "*Quidam Narseus*," pp. 151–155, and *idem*, "Nersēs le Grand," pp. 145–146.

7. Although it set in the middle of a familiar tale of the emperor's sick child (see preceding note), this lengthy homily is not part of the Basilian material that has come down to us, to the best of my knowledge. Both Soc. Schol., E.H., IV xxvi and Soz., E.H., VI.xvi note St. Basil's defense of the anti-Arian creed before the emperor Valens, but neither one gives a theological excursus at this point. It is not found in the *Vita* of Basil attributed to the Ps. Amphilochus, but might conceivably have been part of the lost *Vita* of Helladius. On the other hand, it might be a set piece inserted into the compilation of BP. With one interesting exception (see below, n. 17) this homily is a typical presentation of the "orthodox" Trinitarian theology current in the mid-fourth and fifth centuries, insisting on the creation of the Son before the ages and on his "essential" identity with the Father, against the Arian differentiation between the two. Its theological position reappears throughout BP, especially in the prayer of the officiating priest that precedes the miracle at Mambrē (V.xxviii); see below, nn. 8–20. Its parallels with the early Armenian version of the Basilian Anaphora, commonly known as the *Anaphora of St. Gregory the Illuminator*, actually quoted in the prayer at Mambrē though not in the present chapter are evident (see Renoux, "Anaphore"). Likewise, a number of parallels, both doctrinal and lexical, can be found between this homily and the *Teaching of St. Gregory*, as well as with the appendix following the main text in some manuscripts of Aa (pp. 426–435, and Thomson, p. 503). Consequently, it is consonant with the standard theological position of the early Armenian church as found in contemporary works. The largest cluster of Scriptural allusions and citations is also to be found here.

This homily does not occur in the corresponding section of MX, or elsewhere in that text. The majority or the whole of it has been omitted in all translations of BP, with the exception of the 1968 edition of Malxasyancʿ's modern Armenian version, where it has been inserted by the editors into the text of the 1947 edition (see p. 322 n. 73 of the 1968 edition). For the technical theological vocabulary, I have followed in the main the translations of the crucial doctrinal terms proposed by Thomson, AaT, pp. 11–23, and *idem*, "Philosophical Terms," as they seemed appropriate here as well. For the standard introductory formula of this passage, see Intro., n. 138, as well as Appendix V, a, for its multiple repetitions.

8. Cf. AaT, cdxxxix and n. 2; Thomson, AaT, p. 12. As indicated in the preceding note, I have generally followed Thomson's analysis and translation of the doctrinal terminology which is also suitable for most early Armenian theological authors.

9. Hebr. 1:3 (first part) with the duplication of the word *ēakan*; cf. V.xxviii and n. 13, which does not have this duplication but alters the third to the second person singular.

10. Cf. AaT, cclix–cclx, cclxxv and Thomson's AaT, p. 13, and "Instruction," p. 105, though BP does not allude here to the Holy Spirit and prefers the form *gorcakic^c* to the *hamagorc^c* of AaT to render the "co-laboration" of the Father and the Son. See also below "*zugakic^c ew at^c oṙakic^c ew araṙč^c akic^c*" as another phrase underscoring the equality and collaboration of the first two persons of the Trinity.

11. Hebr. 1:3 (second part) verbatim; cf. V.xxviii and n. 14.

12. Is. 40:21; Ps. 103:2.

13. Gen. 2:7; cf. IV.lvii n. 2; V.xxviii n. 9.

14. This may be reference to the first part of Phil. 2:7, in view of the continuation of the reference to this Scriptural passage below; see nn. 18, 23. Cf. AaT, ccclxxxii, cccxc, and Thomson, AaT, pp. 18–21; also V.xxviii and n. 16, and the next note.

15. Cf. AaT, cccxci, and Thomson, AaT, pp. 11–12, for the translation of *goyac^c ut^c iwn* as "essence" or "hypostasis," also *idem*, "Instruction," pp. 99–100, for the preliminaries to baptism; cf. III.iii, n. 16.

16. I Peter 1:20 with an interpolation; cf. AaT, ccclxiv.

17. Despite the affirmations elsewhere and in this homily, indeed in the sentence immediately preceding, that "the Father begat *of his own nature*" the only-begotten Son, the use of the phrase *nman . . . bnut^c ean*, "of *like* [or *similar*] nature" (if it is not merely a careless lapsus), at this point suggests the homoiousian position more suited to the orthodox position of the mid-fourth century than the categorical homoousia of Nicaea. See Baus, ed., *History of the Church*, iii, pp. 32–50. I have not been able to trace the origin of this homily, which seems to be an insertion at this point (see above, n. 7). Its presence in the context of the Basilian material and the slight homoiousian tinge just noted might suggest an original fourth-century date before the final triumph of Nicaean homoousian theology. On the other hand, the numerous parallels noted with the Armenian version of the early Basilian *Anaphora* (see V.xxviii n. 7) point rather to the fifth century, when the Basilian material in general was translated into Armenian. See K. M. Muradyan, *Barseł*.

18. Phil. 2:7 (second part), where the Armenian Bible gives the participial form *aṙeal*, while BP, following the Anaphora of the liturgy, gives the third person singular *ēaṙ*; Gat^c rčean, *Srbazan patarag*, p. 134 line 80. Cf. V.xxviii n. 17.

19. See Thomson, AaT, pp. 11–12 for the possible translations of *zōrut^c iwn*. In the passage of Hebrews 1:3 (see above, n. 11), however, the sense of "power" seems indicated.

20. Cf. Gen. 1:26. Cf. V.xxviii n. 19.

21. Cf. AaT, ccclxxxv, dxci–dxcv and Thomson, AaT, pp. 17–18; and above III.xiv n. 23.

22. II Cor. 5:17 with modifications.

23. Phil. 2:7 (end); cf. above, nn. 14, 18.

24. Col. 1:18; cf. Apoc. 1:15. See also Gat^c rčean, *Srbazan patarag*, p. 136 line 95; Renoux, "Anaphore," p. 98; and below, n. 26.

25. Rom. 8:21, with minor variations.

26. Col. 1:16, 18–20 with modifications, especially in 19 and the omission of 17 and the first portion of 18. See above, n. 24; also Gat^c rčean, *Srbazan patarag*, pp. 126 lines 37–38, 128 line 49; and Renoux, "Anaphore," pp. 90–91.

27. In view of the earlier reference to Gen. 1:26 (see n. 20 above), it is probable that this is an allusion to Gen. 1:28 with the alteration of the tense.

28. Mal. 4:2; cf. AaT, dlxv–dlxvi, dclxxxiv.

29. Tit. 2:7, with alterations. Cf. Acts 1:1 and III.xii n. 15.

30. This seems to be an evident echo of the Trisagion. Cf. Gat^c rčean, *Srbazan patarag*, p. 130 line 57; Renoux, "Anaphore," p. 92.

31. Cf. John 4:24.

32. Cf. I Cor. 6:19.

33. Despite the fact that this phrase is set off in quotation marks in both the Venice (p. 94) and the St. Petersburg (p. 72) editions, and its obvious echo of the Beatitudes, Matt. 5:3–11, as well as Luke 1:45, and elsewhere, it is not a Scriptural quotation.

34. These passages are clear reminiscences of John 12:44–45 and 14:9 followed by 20:29, but none of them is a direct quotation except 14:9. See also AaT, cdlxxii, p. 107.

35. One ms reads *awerak*, "ruins" for *aχerakkʿ*, "vanities"; see Venice ed., p. 95 n. 1, and Malχasyancʿ (p. 139).

36. Ps. 26:8 verbatim; Ps. 15:8, with some variations; Ps. 20:7, with considerable variations in wording, though not in meaning.

37. I Cor 13:12, with a partial inversion of the sentence.

38. Cf. perhaps John 16:25.

39. Hebr. 11:39–40 nearly verbatim.

40. Cf. Matt. 9:29.

41. Cf. the words of St. Basil to the emperor, Soc. Schol., E.H., IV.xxvi; Soz., E.H., VI.xvi.

42. Ps. 18:8–11, with slight variations; cf. 118:39 (V.iv n. 28).

43. Ps. 18:4–5 nearly verbatim.

44. The setting of a fifteen-day term for Valens's conversion and the child's life is not found in the Basilian material; see above, n. 6.

45. See III.x n. 18.

46. The phrase *ew očʿ* is ambiguous at this point. Malχasyancʿ (p. 142), followed by Gevorgian (p. 70), corrects *bankʿ* to *band*, "prison" and translates accordingly, but no variants are attested in the manuscripts.

47. St. Nersēs was related to the Aršakuni through his mother, Bambišn (III.xv, xix; IV.iii) and through his grandmother, the wife of Yusik (III.v). See above, III.xv n. 2.

48. For the cause of the opposition between Aršak I and St. Nersēs, suggested here, see Garsoïan, "Politique," p. 308. There is no trace of this dialogue in MX, who substitutes a letter from Aršak to Valens at this point: III.xxix (= MK, p. 286).

49. For the confusion in BP between Nersēs's embassy and his exile, both here and again in IV.xi, see Garsoïan, "*Quidam Narseus*," p. 157. The presence of Nersēs in Armenia at the time of Gnel's murder, ca. 359 (IV.xv), indicates that he had returned from the embassy of 358 (see above, n. 5). The details of the patriarch's banishment are taken from the traditional tribulations inflicted by the Arianizing authorities on "orthodox" confessors according to the Greek ecclesiastical sources, which link these accounts to the tale of the emperor's sick child; see Greg. Naz., *Orat. XLIII*, xlvi and Garsoïan, "*Quidam Narseus*," pp. 154–155. The account of these tribulations is repeated in the next chapter, and a confused version is also found in MX, III.xxix–xxx (= MK, pp. 286–287), who anachronistically links this to the patriarchate of the heretic Macedonius (A.D. 342, 352–360). A version is also given in the *Vita* of St. Nersēs, viii, pp. 53–62 (= CHAMA, II, pp. 30–31); see below, IV.vi n. 12.

50. The reference here is presumably to the Arianizing Council of Seleucia of 359 and the subsequent exile of "orthodox" clerics. See, e.g., Soc. Schol., E.H., II.xl–xliv; Hefele-Leclerq, *Histoire*, II, pp. 346–371. Baus, ed., *Imperial Church*, pp. 47–49; and Garsoïan, "*Quidam Narseus*," pp. 150, 155–156.

51. See Appendix III, *mehean*.

52. See III.xiv n. 32 for the shepherdless sheep.

53. The imperial favors toward Armenia are confirmed by the classical sources. See AM, XX.xi.3, "[Aršak] obligatus gratiarum multiplici nexu Constantio," and Garsoïan, "Politique," pp. 304–305.

54. The release of the Aršakuni hostages, Gnel and Tiritʿ, repeated in IV.xi, is also recorded by MX, III.xxi (= MK, p. 276), but omitted in the *Vita* of St. Nersēs, viii, pp. 51–52 (= CHAMA, II, p. 30), which anachronistically places the embassy after Gnel's death. See Garsoïan, "*Quidam Narseus*," p. 150.

IV.vi

1. MX, III.xxx (= MK, p. 287) gives a different setting and a much briefer version of St. Nersēs exile. See IV.v nn. 1, 49.

2. The "Valens" persecuting the "orthodox" confessors and St. Nersēs was of course Constantius, to whom the Armenian patriarch's mission of 358 had been addressed and who had called the Arianizing Council of Seleucia in 359 (see IV.v nn. 5, 49–50). But see below, n. 12 for the contamination of Basilian material.

3. See the preceding chapter for the parallel version of this account.

4. The references in St. Nersēs homily to the divine protection of the patriarchs: Gen. 22:1–13; 35:9–13; 41:14, 39–45; Exod. 3:2–4; 16:4–22; 17:5–6 are self-evident; cf. Thomson, AaT, pp. 5-6, 10. Emin omits the entire homily: CHAMA, I, p. 31.

5. Cf. Matt. 14:15–21; Mark 6:35–44; Luke 9:10–17; John 6:5–13, 26.

6. Cf. John 19:34.

7. Matt. 26:26–28; Mark 14:22–24; Luke 22:19–20.

8. Cf. AaT, ccclxxxv, dclxxxvii and Thomson's AaT., p. 18.

9. Cf. James 1:6.

10. Luke 11:29; cf. Matt. 12:39, Mark 8:12.

11. The text is evidently corrupt at this point. The Venice edition gives *pahē*, "he preserves" but notes that one ms reads *mahē*, "from death" (p. 102 n. 1). Malχasyanc^c (p. 322 n. 76) suggested the omission of the entire phrase as incomprehensible, but it has been reinstated by the editors of the 1968 edition (p. 146 and n. *) with the exception of the word *mahē*. As noted by Anasyan, *Review*, p. 25 n. 33, no satisfactory reading or translation of this passage has been proposed up to now.

12. Cf. MX, III.xxx (= MK, p. 287) and the *Vita* of St. Nersēs, viii, p. 58 (= CHAMA, II, p. 31) for variant versions of these miracles. These hardships visited on "orthodox" confessors show contamination from Basilian material and attendant Greek hagiographic tales; see Garsoïan, "*Quidam Narseus*," pp. 154–155 and n. 26; and above, IV.v n. 49.

13. Matt. 6:33 with variations.

14. Cf. II Macc. 15:17.

15. The Venice edition p. 103 gives *amiss*, "months" as does the *Vita* of St. Nersēs, viii, p. 58 (= CHAMA, II, p. 31). MX, III.xxx (= MK, p. 287) reduces the exile still further, to eight months. But the St. Petersburg edition (p. 80) reads *ams*, "years," the reading preferred by Malχasyanc^c (pp. 147 and 322 n. 77). The longer exile (359–368) fits better into the account of Nersēs's career, since he seems to have been absent from the Armenian court from the murder of Gnel (ca. 359) to the enthronement of Pap (ca. 368), and Greater Armenia was represented by Iosakes/Isokakis at the Council of Antioch in 363: See Garsoïan, "*Quidam Narseus*," pp. 155–156 and *idem*, "Nersēs le Grand," p. 149, and IV.v n. 49. It is however, possible that Nersēs had returned to Greater Armenia, though not to court before the end of Aršak's reign; see IV.li n. 2.

IV.vii

1. The opening sentence of this chapter links it to the circumstances attendant upon St. Nersēs's consecration (IV.iv), but the remainder of the chapter, as well as the subsequent ones, deal explicitly with St. Basil himself instead of attributing his miracles to St. Nersēs, as was done in IV.v (see nn. 6–7, 41, and Peeters, "SS Serge et Théodore," pp. 67–70). None of these episodes appears in MX or in the *Vita* of St. Nersēs as they are clearly extraneous to the narrative.

2. See IV.iv n. 8 for the pseudo-Greek forms of Basil's name, and IV.ix n. 3.

3. Both the Venice edition (p. 104 n. 1) and Malχasyanc^c (p. 322 n. 78) correct the incomprehensible *zor* of the text to *ziwr*, "his."

4. The growing antagonism of Bishop Eusebios of Caesarea toward his great subordinate St. Basil is attested by the Greek sources. See, e.g., Greg. Naz., *Orat. XLIII*, xxvii–xxxvii; Soz., E.H., IV.x.

5. The author's claim of inadequacy is one of the *topoi* of early hagiography. See Festugière, "Lieux-communs," pp. 129–131; and III.xiv n. 14.

6. The retirement of St. Basil to his hermitage at Annesi in Pontus after his estrangement from Bishop Eusebios in 364 is attested by the Greek sources. See Greg. Naz., *Orat. XLIII*, xxix–xxx, and Fedwick, *Basil*, p. 140.

IV.viii

1. This chapter continues the purely Basilian material begun in the preceding one (IV.vi and n. 1), as observed by Peeters, "SS Serge et Théodore," pp. 68–69. Although Basil's return to Caesarea in 365 is attested (see Greg. Naz., *Orat. XLIII*, xxx–xxxi and Fedwick, *Basil*, p. 141), the circumstances of his return bear no relation to those related here, the origin of which must be purely hagiographic. Valens's Arianizing policy, his persecution of the "orthodox" party, and Basil's opposition to him are amply attested in the Greek sources, but the account given here is far more elaborate. See below, n. 6.

2. The "Valens" referred to here is indeed the historical emperor of that name contemporary with St. Basil, and his appearance here is due entirely to the intrusion of the truly Basilian material. Cf. III.xxi n. 21; IV.v n. 5 and vi n. 2.

3. The Venice edition (p. 106 n. 1) corrects the *karicʿes* of the text to *karicʿē*, but Malχasyancʿ's reading, *karicʿē*, "he would be able/he might" (pp. 322–323 n. 79), seems preferable.

4. I have been unable to trace the source of St. Basil's vision; cf. ? Is. 5:5–7, 16:10. See Murray, *Symbols*, pp. 95–130 for the connotations of the vineyard, esp. p. 123 on the threat to the vineyard.

5. On the uses of the Iranian term *ǰatagov*, "defender/protector" in early Armenian literature, see Garsoïan, "Protecteur des pauvres," pp. 24–26; and IV.iii n. 12.

6. The episode described here is presumably the elaboration of the allusions to disputations between St. Basil and the Arians in Soc. Schol., E.H., IV.xxvi and especially Soz., E.H., VI.xv, xvii, but they did not link these disputations with St. Basil's return to Caesarea. See above, n. 1.

7. According to Greg. Naz., *Orat. XLIII*, xxxvii, Eusebios died peacefully in St. Basil's arms.

8. Cf. Peeters, "SS Serge et Théodore," p. 69 for the possibility of a link to another passage in Greg. Naz., *Orat. XLIII*.

IV.ix

1. See IV.vii n. 1.

2. St. Basil succeeded Eusebios as bishop of Caesarea in 370; see Fedwick, *Basil*, p. 142.

3. On this miracle paralleling the one at St. Nersēs's consecration in 353, see IV.iv nn. 7, 9 and Markwart, "Untersuchungen," p. 225. Peeters, "SS Serge et Théodore," p. 66 suggests a possible link to the tale that the Holy Spirit descended upon St. Basil at the time of his baptism in the Jordan, which is found in his *Vita* attributed to Ps. Amphilochus of Iconium, pp. 172–173.

4. See IV.viii n. 2.

5. Malχasyancʿ (p. 322 n. 80) noted that one of the mss reads *danak*, "knife," which is clearly impossible in context and suggested the correction *dank*, "mite/obol." Nonethe-

less, both the Venice (p. 109) and the St. Petersburg (p. 85) editions read *zanak*, "bit/piece," which is entirely acceptable and of which the corrupt *danak* is probably a mere *lapsus*.

6. Matt. 6:19–20, Luke 18:22; cf. 12:33 and Hebr. 10:34.

7. The only allusion to St. Basil's imprisonment in the Greek sources is his one-day detainment by the prefect according to Soc. Schol., E.H., IV.xxvi, which is not even borne out by Greg. Naz., *Orat. XLIII*, xlviii–li.

IV.x

1. As in the case of the extraneous material of the preceding chapters, this episode is not to be found in MX (see IV.vii n. 1). The *Vita* of St. Nersēs, viii, p. 61 (= CHAMA, II, p. 31) substitutes here a dream of Valens in which the emperor is killed by St. Nersēs himself. On this entire chapter and its possible antecedents, see Peeters, "SS Serge et Théodore," and the parallel tale of the death of Julian the Apostate in Soz., E.H., VI.ii. Peeters is of the opinion that the original form of this episode was derived from the Basilian material emanating from Hellenized Asia Minor and was linked with the legends surrounding the death of Julian ("SS Serge et Théodore," pp. 75–78). It should be noted, however, that there is no mention of St. Basil in the episode of the sophist, which is inserted as an integral unit into the Basilian material and shows considerable familiarity with the tradition of St. Thekla (see Appendix I, "Tᶜekł," for the various versions and problems of the Armenian translations of her *Acts*). Moreover, the presence of St. Sergios, whose cult was focused on Resapha in northern Syria, a region where the cult of Thekla was also widespread (see Dagron, *Ste. Thècle*, pp. 44, 46, 110, and her *Vita*, xxv, p. 276/7), as well as the syriacisms noted by Peeters (see Intro., pp. 7–8 and n. 30 and below, n. 3) all suggest a Syriac rather than an Anatolian source. See also below, nn. 4–7. The recall of this episode by TᶜA Cont., IV.ii, p. 275 (= *Thom. Arts.*, p. 238) constitutes one of the few explicit references to BP in medieval Armenian historiography; see Intro., pp. 4–5.

2. See IV.viii n. 2.

3. This is the first of the syriacisms detected by Peeters in this chapter ("SS Serge et Théodore," pp. 70–73). They do not, however, constitute evidence for an original Syriac version of BP as claimed by Peeters, since this episode is clearly an interpolation.

4. This anonymous city should be Seleucia Trachea (modern Selifke) in Isauria on the border of Cilicia, as the famous martyrium of St. Thekla was to be found just to the south at the site now known as Mariamlik or Ayatekla near the village of Becili. It was already known in the late fourth century to Greg. Naz., *Poemata*, "de seipso," verse 548 and to Etheria (*Journal*, p. 182/3) who places it 1,500 paces from the city. It is identified in the fifth century in the *Vita* of Thekla, xxvii. A church-martyrium existed at the site of the saint's disappearance since the fourth century (*Vita*, xxviii), but its ruins have not been identified and the focus of the cult was shifted slightly with the building of a great basilica by the emperor Zeno after 476. See Dagron, *Ste. Thècle*, pp. 52–79, 278/9–280/1, and above, n. 1.

5. The custom of sleeping in the church-martyrium of St. Thekla is attested in her *Miracles*, e.g. xvii, xlvi, and her cult at Seleucia included the rite of *incubatio*; see Dagron, *Ste. Thècle*, pp. 103–105, 302/3, 408/9, and above, n. 1.

6. According to the tradition repeatedly stated in the fifth century *Vita* and *Miracula* of the saint, Thekla was believed to live within the church: "à l'emplacement qui est celui de la martyre au saint-béma" (*Mir.* vii.26), and the chancel screen surrounded her chamber (*Mir.* xviii.41–42). Cf. *Mir.* xxxiii, xxxiv, xl, xlvi, and xxxvi for the shift of her residence to the nearby cave. See Dagron, *Ste. Thècle*, pp. 72–73, 103, 302/3, 334/5–336/7, 374/5–382/3, 388/9, 396/7, 408/9; and above, n. 1.

7. These were presumably St. Sergios of Resapha in northern Syria and St. Theodore of Euchaïta in Pontus, though Malχasyanᶜ (p. 323 n. 83) links St. Sergios with Cappado-

cia. See Peeters, "SS Serge et Théodore," pp. 77–78, though he suggests the substitution of Quirios for Sergios (*ibid.*, pp. 84–85). Both were warrior saints, and the parallels with the death of Julian the Apostate noted by Peeters are evident. But Thekla too had warlike attributes taken over from the earlier cult of Athena at Seleucia (*Vita*, xxvii; *Mir.*, ii), and could both predict the death of evildoers (*Mir.*, xxxv) and kill at a distance (*Mir.*, xxix). See Dagron, *Ste. Thècle*, pp. 99, 368/9, 384/5–386/7; and above, n. 1.

8. At this point the narrative returns to the Basilian material of IV.ix. The reference is presumably to the return of the "orthodox" confessors exiled by Valens: see Soc. Schol., E.H., V.ii, who places it after Valens's death in 378 and MX, III.xxxiii (= MK, pp. 290–291).

9. Cf. III.iv n. 3 for the original epic setting of this refrain, and Appendix V, c, for its variants.

10. On *lusarar* = Gk. φωτιστήριον, Lat. *baptisterium*, see NBHL, I, p. 900; Lampe, *Lexicon*, p. 1540; and Malχasyancᶜ (p. 323 n. 85).

IV.xi

1. This chapter is a repetition and elaboration of IV.v, possibly drawn from a different and more prolix source.

2. As in IV.vi, the "Valens" of this chapter is really Constantius as against the true Valens of the Basilian material: see IV.vi n. 2 and viii n. 2.

3. See III.xviii n. 4, for the division of the dignities of *nahapet* and *sparapet* in the Mamikonean house at this time.

4. None of these magnates is mentioned in IV.v or in MX's version of Nersēs's mission, III.xxi, xxix (= MK, pp. 276, 286). A longer and somewhat different list is given in the *Vita* of St. Nersēs, viii, pp. 52–53 (= CHAMA, II, p. 24) where several names have been modified: Mehen/Mehendak, Mehaṙ/Mehewan, etc. Vrkēn Hambužean has been omitted, whereas the *mardpet*, Bagrat Bagratuni, Meružan Arcruni, Gnel Gnuni and a number of others have been added. See Malχasyancᶜ (pp. 323–324 n. 86).

5. No antagonism between the emperor Constantius and Aršak II is recorded by the classical sources, especially in 358, the probable year of Aršak's marriage to Olympias and of the particular favors shown by the emperor to the king of Armenia (see IV.v n. 53). But MX, III.xxi (= MK, pp. 275–276) also records "Arshak's insult" to the emperor, which provoked the execution of Aršak's brother Trdat, who was a hostage at the imperial court—an episode likewise unattested elsewhere. See also next note.

6. As in the case of Aršak's anger mentioned above, there is no historical evidence for an Armenian attack reaching across Asia Minor to Ancyra, which is furthermore incorrectly located in Cappadocia rather than in Galatia; and the estimate of the Armenian army at 260,000 men is obviously fictitious. The parallel account in the *Vita* of St. Nersēs, viii, p. 60 (= CHAMA, II, p. 31) even more improbably pushes the Armenian advance to Chrysopolis and makes it the cause of Valens's retirement to Thrace! In view of MX's reference, III.xxix (= MK, p. 286), to a presumed letter of Aršak II to Valens disclaiming any rebellion or the sending of "a marauding band into your Greek empire," this fanciful account may not be pure invention, but rather a distorted memory preserved in a "Geste of Aršak" of the Armenian kings' occasionally equivocal policy and of his rapprochement with Persia: see IV.xvi nn. 4, 6, 10; and xx nn. 2–3, 8, 18; and MX, III.xxv, xxix (= MK, pp. 280, 286); as well as Julian's threatening, if presumably apocryphal *Letter* lvii to Aršak (III.xiii n. 1).

7. Malχasyancᶜ (p. 324 n. 87) noted that the *Vita* of St. Nersēs, viii, p. 61 (= CHAMA, II, p. 31) has eight months in the corresponding passage, so that EM corrected the length of the Armenian campaign to six months. See, however, the preceding note for the unhistorical character of this entire episode.

IV.xii

1. A somewhat different account of Xad's career is given by MX, III.xxxi–xxxi (= MK, pp. 287–290), who includes here the massacre of the Kamsarakan family, for which see below, IV.xix. There is no mention of Xad in the *Vita* of St. Nersēs, ix, p. 64 (= CHAMA, II, p. 32), which merely speaks of Armenia as left "without spiritual-leadership" (*anaṙajnord*) during St. Nersēs's absence.

2. See IV.iv and n. 23 on Nersēs's charitable foundations.

3. The mourning stressed by BP is evidently related to Nersēs's long exile and not to his successful embassy: see IV.v and n. 41; xi; and below, IV.xiii.

4. See above, n. 1 for the *Vita* of St. Nersēs's ignorance of Xad's vicariate despite its usual dependence on BP.

5. On Aršak II's Arianizing policy paralleling that of the Byzantine court under Constantius, see III.xiii n. 6.

6. The text is clearly corrupt at this point. One ms reads *lkutᶜean*, which must be corrected to *lknutᶜean*, as in the Venice edition (p. 115), or the equivalent *lktutᶜean*, as suggested by Norayr Biwzandacᶜi. Moreover, the Venice mss have the metastasis *hawat*, which must be restored to *hataw*, "he fell." See Venice edition, p. 115 nn. 1, 2 and Malχasyancᶜ p. 324 n. 88.

7. See Malχasyancᶜ (p. 324 n. 89) for a possible corruption of the text here.

8. The reference to a palace (*aparankᶜ*) built in the "city," (which may not have actually been built) suggests a royal residence. But despite the foundation of Aršakawan, the Aršakuni court does not seem to have resided in cities but rather in elaborate encampments (*banak arkᶜuni*), usually in the proximity of one of the royal hunting preserves. Cf., e.g., III.viii and n. 4; IV.xv and n. 8; also Garsoïan, "Mediaeval Armenian City;" *idem*, "Banak arkᶜuni"; and next note. Cf., however, V.vi and n. 7.

9. The hostility of BP to the royal foundation of Aršakawan, the only urban foundation of the fourth century in Armenia, is echoed by the *Vita* of St. Nersēs, ix, pp. 62–65 (= CHAMA, II, p. 32) and by MX, III.xxvii (= MK, pp. 282–283), where the hatred of the nobles who destroy the city is explicitly spelled out (see IV.xiii and n. 21, as well as the preceding note). On the city as an alien element in the essentially aristocratic Arsacid society, which shared the tastes of the Iranian nobility, see V.xxxiv n. 4, xxxv, and Garsoïan, "Mediaeval Armenian City."

10. In the parallel passage, MX, III.xxxi (= MK, p. 288) does not mention Aršak II's attempt to bribe Xad, but he notes the bishops' fondness for rich garments and fine horses.

11. MX, III.xxxii (= MK, pp. 289–290) claims that Aršak II ordered Xad stoned to death, but the bishop was saved by the armed intervention of his Apahuni relatives in an episode reminiscent of the Mamikonean rescue of the Ṙštuni and Arcruni heirs above, III.xviii.

12. The closest Biblical parallel to Xad's miraculous wine jars are the ever-full oil cruse and barrel of meal of the widow Zarephath, who received Elijah (III Kgs. 17:8–16), but the corresponding passage in MX, III.xxxi (= MK, p. 288), speaks of the "barns" or "storehouses" (*štemarankᶜ*) of Elijah and Elisha. Cf. IV Kgs. 4:1–7, which incidentally also speaks of a "pot of oil" and not of "barns."

13. The tale of the stolen oxen does not occur in the corresponding passage of MX. It is reminiscent of one of the miracles of St. Spiridon of Cyprus; see above, III.iii and n. 13.

14. The daughters of Xad are mentioned by MX, III.xxxii (= MK, pp. 289–290), but not his son-in-law and successor, Asurk. According to him Xad's sons-in-law belonged to the Apahuni family (see above, n. 11). This hereditary transmission of an ecclesiastical office parallels the Gregorid tradition: see III.v, xi, xiii and n. 25, xv and nn. 1, 4, xvii and n. 3; IV.iii and n. 4; and Intro., pp. 53–54.

IV.xiii

1. MX, III.xxvii (= MK, pp. 282–283) gives a slightly different version of the destruction of Aršakawan; see IV.xii n. 9 and below, nn. 4, 21. This is also the case in the *Vita* of St. Nersēs, ix, pp. 63–65 (= CHAMA, II, p. 32), for which see below, nn. 5, 13.

2. See above IV.iv, xi.

3. I Macc. 2:2; cf. also Gen. 24:49; Deut. 5:32, 17:11, 28:14; Josh. 1:7; etc. The phrase "to the right to the left" is ubiquitous in the Scriptures, so that it cannot be identified with precision. The verb *tʿiwrem*, however, occurs only in BP and I Macc. 2:2. I am indebted to R. Ervine for this last observation.

4. On the orthodoxy of Nersēs I and his vicar Xad, as well as the Arianizing policy of Aršak II, see above, IV.xii n. 5 and Appendix I, "Aršak II"; "Nersēs I"; "Xad."

5. This long homily of St. Nersēs immediately preceding the destruction has no counterpart in MX, III.xxvii (= MK, pp. 282–283), where the patriarch merely intervenes to save the infants of the destroyed city. It is greatly shortened and altered in the *Vita* of St. Nersēs, ix, pp. 63–65 (= CHAMA, II, p. 32).

6. Ps. 67:6; II Macc. 7:28 (see III.xiv n. 22).

7. Cf. II Cor. 8:9.

8. Ps. 7:12.

9. See III.xx, for the fate of Tiran.

10. Cf. Gen. 13:10, 13; 18:20–19:29; Is. 3:9.

11. For this anachronistic prophecy of the partition of the Armenian kingdom and the end of the Aršakuni dynasty, see VI.i and Intro., pp. 10–11.

12. Ps. 7:16 and Gen. 14:10 with its link to Sodom, etc.

13. Exaggerating as usual, the *Vita* of St. Nersēs, ix, p. 64 (= CHAMA, II, p. 32) has Nersēs offer to build other cities that would produce seven times more wealth.

14. Jer. 22:13, verbatim.

15. Habb. 2:9, modified.

16. Is. 5:9, with transposition and alterations.

17. The end of this dramatic passage is a tissue of Scriptural allusions but not a direct quotation. Cf., e.g., Job 37:8 for the dens of wild beasts; Jer. 10:22, 12:8–14; and Is. 13:21 for the wild beasts, birds, and evil neighbors; Lam. 5:18 for the dens of foxes; Is. 13:20–22, 32:13–14 for the forsaken palaces and cities and the wild asses; Jer. 10:25, 27:10, etc.

18. The *Vita* of St. Nersēs, vii, pp. 48–49 (= CHAMA, II, p. 29) transposes a confused version of this passage to Nersēs' withdrawal from court after Gnel's murder (see IV.xv n. 26), while x, p. 66 (= CHAMA, II, p. 33) claims that after the destruction of Aršakawan, the patriarch had withdrawn to Uṙha (Edessa) and was thereupon replaced by Čʿunak. Cf. IV.xv nn. 44, 46.

19. Cf. Ex. 9:9–11, and perhaps Deut. 28:27.

20. See Appendix V, c. The *topos* is interestingly used here in a nonmilitary context.

21. Aršakawan is more mundanely destroyed by an attack of the Armenian nobility in the corresponding passage of MX, III.xxvii (= MK, p. 283); cf. IV.xii n. 9 and MX, III.xxxi (= MK, p. 287). The *Vita* of St. Nersēs, ix, p. 65 (= CHAMA, II, p. 32) adds an earthquake to the plague and gives the dead as 18,000 households rather than BP's 20,000. MX merely records that all the inhabitants except for suckling babes were killed (III.xxvii). Markwart, *Entstehung*, pp. 90, 97, suggests that the city may have been destroyed by the great earthquake of 358, while Malχasyancʿ (p. 324 n. 92) takes this passage as the first recorded epidemic of plague in Armenia. Cf. IV.lv for the plague that forced the surrender of the fortress of Artagers; and Garsoïan, "Mediaeval Armenian City," pp. 81–82, for the hostility of the Armenian nobility against cities; also IV.xii n. 9.

22. This homily is omitted by Emin (CHAMA, I, p. 249). Like the preceding one, it is found in neither MX nor the *Vita* of St. Nersēs: see above, n. 5.

23. This entire passage is a paraphrase and commentary on Matt. 13:18–30:37–42.

IV.xiv

1. This episode does not occur in MX, and the *Vita* of St. Nersēs, vi, pp. 41–42 (= CHAMA, II, p. 27) gives only a brief and inadequate summary.

2. See above, III.xviii. The *hayr-mardpet* is anonymous in both passages, but the reference to Šawasp Arcruni makes it clear that both deal with the same personage. See also IV.lv n. 9.

3. As noted by Manandyan, *Feodalizm*, p. 77, the Gregorids possessed vast holdings in these districts, but there can be no question of their possessing them *in toto*.

4. See above, III.iii, xiv, xvi.

5. This passage seems to indicate that not all *mardpets* were eunuchs in this period: see Appendix III, *mardpet*; but cf. V.vi, and especially vii, on Drastamat.

6. The antagonism of BP to the *mardpets* may be derived from their position as royal rather than dynastic officials: see Intro., pp. 15, 47, and Appendix III, *mardpet*.

7. See III.xviii and above, n. 2, for the massacre of the Arcruni at the instigation of the *mardpet* and the rescue of Šawasp by the Mamikoneans.

8. Lit. "had not fallen into the river," which is an idiomatic expression. This seems to be a reference to I Kgs. 3:19 = IV Kgs. 10:10; Nersēs would then be the new Samuel rather than the new Moses. This allusion was brought to my attention by Professor P. Cowe.

IV.xv

1. The *Vita* of St. Nersēs, vii–viii, pp. 43–51 (= CHAMA, II, pp. 28– 29) follows BP in this episode, but MX III.xxi–xxv (= MK, pp. 276–281), who apparently depends here on another source, gives a very different version of these events without the romantic elements, which may well derive from the minstrel tradition. See Abełyan, *Grakanutʿyun*, p. 170; also below, nn. 3–7, 11–12, 18, 26, 33, 38, 42; and also Intro., pp. 33–34.

2. This is the only occasion on which Andovk is identified as one of the secondary *sepuh*s of the Siwni house rather than as its *nahapet*. Cf. III.xxi; IV.xv later in the chapter; IV.xx; and the *Vita* of St. Nersēs, vii, p. 43 (= CHAMA, II, p. 29. See Appendix I, "Andovk," "Vałinak," for the theory that Andovk was Vałinak's younger brother.

3. This description of Pʿaranjem obviously derives from the standard clichés for "fair maidens" in romantic tales and hardly suits the subsequent treatment of the queen: see, e.g., below, n. 42.

4. Małxasyancʿ (p. 324 n. 94), following Norayr Biwzandacʿi, substitutes *nuann*, "sister-in-law" for the inexplicable *anuann* of the text.

5. According to MX, III.xxi (= MK, p. 276), Tiritʿ was jealous of Gnel because of the honors bestowed upon him by the Byzantine court, and the intrigue with Pʿaranjem is left out altogether; see above, n. 1.

6. The accusation against Gnel as a political threat to King Aršak II is even more explicit in MX, III.xxii (= MK, p. 277), where Tiritʿ's slander is supported by Vardan Mamikonean (see next note and n. 10). Such an accusation would not have been idle in the contemporary Armenian *naxarar* society, where the *nahapet* was merely the administrator and representative of his house but no particular family controlled the leadership of the clan. As *sepuh*s of the Aršakuni house, both Gnel and Tiritʿ were consequently entirely acceptable as substitutes for Aršak II, especially since Gnel is referred to as *mec sepuh* below (cf. Appendix III, s.v.). Cf. also the repetition of this threat in the tale of Gnel's superiority to the king in the hunting field, MX, III.xxiii (= MK, p. 278), a superiority that carried the implication of lèse-majesté in the Iranian world. See Garsoïan, "Prolegomena," cols, 183–184 and n. 55. Nalbandyan, "Gnel," sees Gnel and Tiritʿ as the respective leaders of pro-Byzantine and pro-Persian factions opposing the authority of Aršak II.

7. If it is not merely a *lapsus calami*, the shift into the plural here suggests a second slanderer, for the magnates supporting Gnel could hardly be speaking. MX, III.xxii–xxiii, xxv (= MK, pp. 277–278, 280– 281) has Tirit῾ seconded throughout by Vardan Mamikonean. The *Vita* of St. Nersēs, vii, p. 43 (= CHAMA, II, p. 28) also speaks of multiple slanderers but does not name Vardan. In any case, BP would underplay this unfavorable action, given his devotion to the Mamikonean house. But cf. below, n. 10.

8. This chapter gives the best available description of the peripatetic life of the Armenian Aršakuni court, with its encampments containing church tents and hunting preserves rather than royal residences of a more permanent urban type. See III.viii and n. 4; IV.xii n. 8 and Garsoïan, "Banak ark῾uni"; and IV.xxv, xxxix; V.ii, for the Sasanian royal camp at Tabriz.

9. *Siwneac῾n* (var. *Siwseac῾n*, Venice edition p. 126 n. 3) was long taken as a proper name, but HArmB, IV, p. 222, s.v. *siws*, defines it as a walled hunting preserve. See also Malχasyanc῾ (p. 324 n. 95).

10. On the treachery of Vardan Mamikonean and the subsequent vengeance of Gnel's widow P῾aṙanjem, see below, IV.xviii and n. 4, and especially MX, III.xxii–xxiii (= MK, p. 277–278).

11. On the celebration of the feast of Nawasard or New Year at Bagawan and the foundation there of a martyrium of St. John by St. Gregory the Illuminator, see Aa, dcccxxxvi and n. 1; MX, II.lxvi (= MK, p. 213) and Appendix III, *navasard*. There is, however, no mention of these celebrations and of the presence of Aršak II at Bagawan in the corresponding passage of MX, III.xxiii (= MK, pp. 278–279), who places the king in the district of Kogovit and subsequently near Lake Van. See next note, also III.iii and nn. 4, 6–7, for the other martyrium of St. John at Aštišat of Tarōn.

12. In contrast to Gnel's execution at Šahapivan, thrice reiterated in this chapter, MX, III.xxiii (= MK, pp. 278–279 and n. 3) has him treacherously slain by Vardan Mamikonean while hunting in the Caḷik Mountains north of Lake Van.

13. Malχasyanc῾ (p. 325 n. 97) rightly corrects the *žanuaw* of the text (Venice edition, p. 127) to *žanuaraw*, "in a litter."

14. On the problematic intrusion of the phrase "*i p῾oyt῾ knǰann mteal*" at this point, see Malχasyanc῾ (p. 325 n. 98), but cf. NBHL, I, p. 1096, *kinǰ*. H. Markaryan suggested to me in a conversation (June 1986) that *kunǰ/kinǰ* might be related to *kangmeni*, "ermine" (VI.ii), but the 1968 editors of Malχasyanc῾ prefers to keep "hastily."

15. Both this homily and the next are missing from the account of MX, III.xxiv (= MK, p. 279), which merely says that St. Nersēs "cursed Arshak . . . and . . . went and sat in mourning for many days, like Samuel over Saul." See Intro., n. 138 and Appendix V, a, for the introductory formula.

16. These quotations are an alternation of Luke 10:16 and Matt. 10:40, with slight alterations.

17. See III.vii n. 6 and Appendix III, s.v., for the use of the term *eḷbayr* in BP.

18. According to MX, III.xxviii (= MK, p. 279), Gnel was buried at the "royal city" of Zarišat in Aḷiovit.

19. Ps. 57:5–6 with slight omission. The entire following section is composed of quotations and paraphrases of Psalm 57: see below, nn. 20–21, 23, 25.

20. Ps. 57:7 verbatim; cf. AaT, dxxxv.

21. A paraphrase of Ps. 57:8; cf. AaT, dxxxvi.

22. Jer. 25:15. Cf. AaT, dviii, dxi, dxxxix–dxl, etc.; and Thomson, AaT, p. 8.

23. A reminiscence of Ps. 57:9, "*Ankaw hur ew oč῾ tesin zarew*"; cf. IV.v n. 20.

24. Cf. Gen. 4:11–12.

25. A reminiscence of Ps. 57:10, "*barkut῾eamb kendanwoyn kizc῾ē znosa.*"

26. See V.vii and n. 11 for the fulfillment of this curse in Aršak's suicide. It is repeated in the *Vita* of St. Nersēs, vii, pp. 47–48 (= CHAMA, II, p. 29), but barely mentioned by MX, III.xxiv–xxv (= MK, pp. 279– 281).

27. For Nersēs's exile at this point, see IV.v n. 49, as well as above, n. 15, for MX's version of the patriarch's activities. The *Vita* of St. Nersēs, vii pp. 48–49 (= CHAMA, II, p. 29) perhaps remembering Nersēs's withdrawal from court after the destruction of Aršaka-wan, pointlessly and inaccurately relates that the patriarch first went south to regulate ecclesiastical affairs in Vaspurakan and subsequently went north to Iberia, "where he restored many churches." Cf. IV.xiii n. 18.

28. One ms has *siwnsn* instead of *Siws*, a reading better suited to the probable site of the execution. See Venice edition, p. 129 n. 1 and above, n. 9.

29. Gevorgian, p. 95 and n. 56 follows the suggestion of S. T. Eremyan and takes *bazmoc^ck^c* here to refer to a royal bathing establishment; but in view of BP's use of the verb *bazmem* to refer to feasting and of *bazmakan* as the special ceremonial feasting couch (see IV.xvi, liv, and Appendix III, *bazmakan*), a royal feasting hall seems more likely. See Garsoïan, "Banak ark^cuni."

30. The elaboration of each repetition of Gnel's execution suggests a threnody, as does the repetition of the poignant noun *pataneak*, "youth/adolescent" attached as an epithet to Gnel's name throughout this chapter. See above, n. 1 and P^caṙanjem's lament below, n. 33.

31. MX, III.xxiv (= MK, p. 279) says on the contrary that "Arshak showed no repentance or contrition but shamelessly rifled the treasures and inheritance of the dead man." Cf. V.xxiv for King Pap's hypocritical mourning over St. Nersēs. Throughout the chapter, BP stresses that Gnel was the one "killed" (*spanel*). Consequently, I have preferred the translation "murdered" or "victim" to the more neutral "dead."

32. The mourning rituals performed here and later in this chapter at the king's order are presumably the very pagan practices forbidden by St. Nersēs; see IV.iv and n. 24 and V.xxxi nn. 9–10, xliv. MX, III.xxiv (= MK, p. 279) gives no description of Gnel's funeral; neither does the *Vita* of St. Nersēs. Cf., however, MX, II.lx (= MK, p. 202), for the practices presumably connected with royal burials; also V.xxxvi.

33. See above, nn. 1, 3, 30, for the possibility of a threnody on Gnel, from which the romantic episodes of this chapter unknown to MX might have been taken. The Iranian tradition of improvising laments over the body of the dead is noted by Boyce, "Parthian literature," p. 1158.

34. This reading is questionable since the mss give *nuagel*, "sing," *nuazel* or *nuajel*, "weaken, diminish" (Venice ed. p. 130 and n. 3), and *nuačel*, "master, subdue" (St. Petersburg ed., p. 103). On the basis of the latter, Malχasyanc^c (p. 326 n. 100) tentatively suggested the translation, "when their voices stopped," an interpretation also found in Emin (CHAMA, I, p. 253), Lauer (p. 94), and Gevorgian (p. 96). The Venetian reading, which I have followed, seems equally reasonable in context.

35. As in many other cases in BP, *ełbayr* does not refer here to an actual "brother," since Gnel and Tirit^c were cousins; see III.vii n. 6, above n. 17, and Appendix III, s.v.

36. This phrase seems to reflect the opening formula for the request of a favor. Cf. IV.xx and n. 14 for the answer of the Persian nobles to Šāhpuhr II, and especially V.iv for the request of Uṙnayr. Similar formulas are also found in the Book of Esther, 1:19, 3:9, 5:4, 8:5, 8, "*et^cē kamk^c ic^cen . . ark^cayi hraman tasc^ces . . . ,*" etc. See Appendix V, j, iii.

37. On the obligation of the blood feud in Arsacid society, see V.xxxvii and n. 16.

38. MX, III.xxv (= MK, pp. 280–281) has Tirit^c killed together with Vardan Mamikonean by the *sparapet* Vasak Mamikonean under entirely different circumstances. Cf. IV.xviii for Vardan's murder by his brother Vasak.

39. As with other Greek names in BP, that of Olympias appears in a number of variants. See IV.iv nn. 6, 8. The *Vita* of St. Nersēs, viii, p. 50 (= CHAMA, II, p. 29) identifies her incorrectly as "the sister of the emperor Valens." See Appendix I, s.n.

40. The sequence of Aršak II's marriages remains highly problematic. Both BP and MX, III.xxiv (= MK, pp. 279–280) agree that P^caṙanjem had been married to Gnel before she wed Aršak and that she bore the king's son and successor, Pap. But BP clearly makes

Pᶜaṙanjem the king's "first wife" and has Olympias brought from the Roman empire only subsequently. Pᶜaṙanjem is repeatedly called the "queen" (*tikin*) of Armenia (IV.liv), and she fears for her rank only in the case of the marriage of Aršak to the daughter of the king of kings (IV.xx). On the contrary, MX, III.xxi, xxiv (= MK, pp. 276, 278) makes Olympias the king's first bride, Pᶜaṙanjem the second, and has the latter jealous of Olympias's "queenly rank." Moreover, it is clear from the accounts of the Byzantine sources that Aršak II's marriage to Olympias must have taken place in 358, and that she could not safely have been killed before the death of her protector Constantius in 361, while Gnel had presumably been killed in 359 (see Garsoïan, "Politique," pp. 304–305, and *idem, "Quidam Narseus,"* pp. 156–157). Yet, in spite of BP's suggestion that Pap had been born "after" the marriage of Aršak and Olympias, by its own account, Pᶜaṙanjem's son had reached puberty before Aršak's downfall in 364, had been sent as a hostage to the empire (IV.xv, liv), and was of age to become king in his own right ca. 368/9 (V.i). Consequently, he cannot reasonably have been born much later than 352.

The Aršakuni chronology of the fourth century is still inextricably confused, and the intrusion at this point of the probably unhistorical romance of Gnel, Tiritᶜ, and Pᶜaṙanjem only compounds this. Even preliminary conclusions are still clearly premature and only the most tentative hypotheses can be proposed in this maze of contradictions. Nevertheless, despite St. Nersēs's injunctions (IV.iv and n. 25), Aršak II may well have had more than one wife simultaneously, among whom the chief was the "queen of queens" in keeping with Iranian practice. After Aršak's marriage to Olympias, BP continues to refer to Pᶜaṙanjem as the *kin*, "wife" of the king, or at the very least as a "woman" living in his household. Moreover, such an interpretation would coincide with similar suggestions in the text (III.xxi and n. 24; V.xv, xvi) that fourth-century Christian Armenian courts might have been polygamous, as well as with the aforementioned presumption that Pᶜaṙanjem's position would be threatened by a marriage between Aršak and a Sasanian princess, who would outrank and consequently "dishonor" her, without any suggestion that she would be dismissed from the royal household. Alternately, though less probably, according to Zoroastrian practices, a man who had entered into a "full (*patiχšay*) marriage," could under certain circumstances, give her to one of his agnatic kinsmen, with whom she then contracted a valid but "incomplete" (*čakar*) marriage while still remaining legally the wife of her first husband (see Perikhanian, *Iran* pp. 84–98, esp. 88). In such a case, Pᶜaṙanjem might conceivably first have wed Aršak II and borne him Pap, then have been handed over to Gnel, been taken back by the king after his nephew's execution, been supplanted by Olympias, and finally have regained her preeminent rank through the murder of her rival. These complicated patterns would have been in keeping with the customs of an Iranian milieu, and parallels for them can be found in the rivalry of Xosrō II's wives, especially Širin and Maria, "Caesar's daughter," in the *Šāhnāme* (xliii, vol. VII, pp. 107–111, 148–49, 216, 224ff., 239–240, 247, 321–329, etc.), but they naturally would have confused Christian writers relying on oral sources at a time that such practices had become repugnant to Christian Armenia.

41. BP juxtaposes here the two meanings of term *deł*, "remedy" and "poison," a play on words not readily translatable.

42. MX, III.xxiv (= MK, p. 280) does not know the priest's name, his origin, or his reward, but he accuses Pᶜaṙanjem of murdering Vałinak Siwni in order to further the career of her father Andovk, whom MX calls Antiokᶜ/Antiochus; cf. III.ix n. 5. This horrendous accusation against the "iniquitous" Pᶜaṙanjem, "consumed with evil" is difficult to reconcile with the romantic description of her at the beginning of this chapter (see n. 3). In general, BP's treatment of the queen throughout is notably incoherent and contradictory. See below, IV.xviii, xliv nn. 3, 6, lv; V.xxii; and Garsoïan, "Politique," pp. 311–312.

43. On Nersēs's absence from the Armenian court from Gnel's execution to the enthronement of Pap, see above, n. 27 and IV.vi n. 15; also below, IV.li and n. 2; V.i.

44. BP significantly uses the term *struk*, "slave" here instead of the indefinite and

generally more honorific *caṙay*, "servant, vassal" to underscore Č°unak's insignificance. Likewise the phrase "head of the Christians" is used for the new primate instead of the normal title of "chief-bishop" or "patriarch" see Appendix III, s.vv. and below, n. 46.

45. See Appendix V, c, for the repetitions of this phrase.

46. The stress on the presence of the only two bishops at Č°unak's consecration rather than the three mandated at the Council of Nicaea underscores the illegitimate character of the king's appointment. The coming of the bishops of Aljnik, and Korduk°, when all the Armenian bishops had refused, may also indicate the equivocal position of these regions vis-à-vis the Armenian crown: see Appendix I, "Č°unak"; Appendix II, "Aljnik," "Korduk°," and above, n. 44, as well as IV.iv for the "canonic" ordination of St. Nersēs by the bishops assembled at Caesarea of Cappadocia.

IV.xvi

1. No part of this episode is recorded by MX. The *Vita* of St. Nersēs, x, pp. 66–68 (= CHAMA, II, p. 33) conflates this journey with the one described in IV.liii–liv.

2. For the position of the Armenian king as "second" in the Persian realm and the title of "second after the king," see Aa, xviii; Benveniste, *Titres et noms propres*, 51–58; Garsoïan, "Prolegomena," col. 182, nn. 28, 44c; and below, IV.liv. Malχasyanc° (p. 326 n. 101) takes this as indicating a grant of an estate to Aršak II. It is true that Aršakuni royal domains lay along the border of Atrpatakan (IV.l), but there is no evidence of such an action on the part of Šāhpuhr II, and the reference is more probably to the honorific rank than to any landed property. See also V.xxxviii and n. 9; cf., however V.viii, nn. 4–5.

3. On the Iranian reclining banqueting couch with cushions piled at one end, used on ceremonial occasions, see Appendix III, *bazmakan*.

4. This passage is one of our best descriptions of Iranian court ritual in this period and of the favored position of Armenia in the Iranian empire even in the Sasanian period. See Garsoïan, "Locus," pp. 35–39, 57–61, and nn. 96–103. This chapter may also reflect the *rapprochement* between Armenia and Iran noted above (IV.xi n. 6). See also Procopius, *Bell. Pers.*, I.v.14 and IV.xx n. 18. However, the epic instead of historical character of this chapter, with its patent anachronisms (see below, n. 13), leaves this open to doubt.

5. This questionable excursus, presumably derived from the "Mamikonean Geste," is intended as an illustration of the kingly "*k°ajut°iwn*" to which the Mamikonean were entitled because of their royal descent and which forms part of their apotheosis in BP. See Intro., pp. 34–35 and V.ii, iv, v for other cases of its manifestation; also Intro., pp. 44–45 and n. 153 for their devotion to their Aršakuni lords.

6. Aršak II's equivocal allegiance is emphasized throughout by BP (IV.xx and especially liv), as against his loyalty to the Romans asserted by AM, XXV.vii.12–13. See also Garsoïan, "Politique," pp. 297–298, and *idem*, "Prolegomena," col. 177.

7. As observed by Peeters, "Persécution," pp. 71–74, no bishop of Ctesiphon named Mari is attested in the fourth century, though the name was common and prestigious in the church of Persia, purportedly founded by one of that name. See Labourt, *Christianisme*, pp. 12–20, 133 n. 6, and 254–255; and Appendix I, "Mari." This chapter seems evidently contaminated by an account of the great persecution inaugurated by Šāhpuhr II in 338–339 (Labourt, *Christianisme*, pp. 43–82, below, n. 13, and IV.xvii n. 2), as well as by the epic "Gestes" of Aršak II and the Mamikonean.

8. This tautology occurs agains in V.xxxvii. See Appendix III, svv.

9. See above, IV.ii n. 7, for the unusual division between the offices of *nahapet* and *sparapet* in the Mamikonean house at this time, which probably lay at the base of these dissentions. MX, III.xxv (= MK, p. 280) gives a frivolous reason for the antagonism between the two brothers.

10. Most scholars have argued that the text is mutilated at this point and interrupted by a considerable lacuna; see Malχasyancᶜ (p. 326 n. 102) and Peeters, "Persécution," p. 60 n. 2), although neither edition of BP nor the translations indicate this, except for Gevorgian (p. 99 and n. 57), who as usual follows Malχasyancᶜ. The text is unquestionably corrupt at this point. The context of Aršak's flight from the Persian court is missing (cf. IV.xx and nn. 17–18). Moreover, the entire episode is suspect because of its parallel to Aršak's other unexpected flight from Persia at the instigation of Andovk Siwni (IV.xx) and the probable contamination by the *Acts* of the Persian martyrs noted in n. 7 above and in n. 11 below. A flight of the Armenian king at this point is all the less likely in that Procopius, *Bell. Pers.*, I.v.15 says that Šāhpuhr II "dismissed Arsaces to return to his own country" after the swearing of an oath. At most, it may be a harbinger of growing tension between Armenia and the Sasanians, leading to the possible about-face of Aršak II toward the Romans in 358: see IV.v n. 53, xi nn. 5–6, xx n. 18.

11. The dialogue at this point is a clear echo of the Aršakuni claims voiced by Aršak in IV.liv and n. 12, and of the typical dialogues found in the *Acts* of the Persian martyrs. See Labourt, *Christianisme*, n. 46; Garsoïan, *Armenia*, pp. 347–352, and *idem*, "Hiérarchie," pp. 129–136.

12. The normal formula for Zoroastrian oaths invoked the god Miθra as the guardian of contracts (cf. IV.liii n. 3) though the Sun, Moon, and Fire were also commonly invoked (cf. *Mēnōg ī Xrad*, as cited in Asmussen, *Xuāstvanist*, p. 57). Nonetheless, in view of the Zoroastrian worship of fire and water attested in the regions contiguous with Armenia (see Herodotus, I.131; Strabo, *Geogr.*, XV.iii.13–14), and of the fact that at the temple of Anaïtis/Anahita, the goddess associated with water, "also revered by the Armenians . . . all the people of Pontus make their oaths concerning their matters of greatest importance" (Strabo, *Geogr.*, XII.iii.37), the accuracy of this formula is entirely probable. A similar if more extensive one is also known to Sebēos, xi, pp. 77–78 (= Macler tr. p. 19); cf. also MX, III.xlii (= MK, p. 305) and Widengren, *Religionen*, p. 176; as well as IV.liii for another form of oath.

13. The first great Christian persecution by Šāhpuhr II, beginning in 338–339, is clearly referred to here, as was observed long since by Peeters, see above n. 7 and next chapter, n. 2. The conclusion that he drew from this fact, however, that the reign of Aršak II had begun in 338 ("Persécution" and "Intervention," esp. p. 243)—a conclusion shared by Seeck, *Untergang*, V, p. 448, and Baynes, "Armenia and Rome," p. 189, though not by Markwart, *Untersuchungen*, p. 223—is by no means incontrovertible and runs counter to the customarily accepted date of 350 (see III.xxi n. 23). An anachronistic intrusion from the *Acts* of the Persian martyrs, both here and in the next chapter, seems far more likely, especially in view of the numerous hagiographic intrusions found in the text: see Intro., p. 37; also IV.xx n. 2, and Manandyan, *Kᶜnnakan tesutᶜyun*, II/1, p. 170 for the epic and unhistorical character of this chapter. See also next chapter, n. 2.

IV.xvii

1. The title of this chapter is defective both here and in the Table of Contents; see Venice edition p. 71 n. 1 and Malχasyancᶜ (p. 326 n. 103).

2. As noted in the preceding chapter, nn. 7, 13, this episode together with the end of the preceding chapter form an intrusion from the *Acts* of the Persian martyrs relating to the first great Christian persecution in Persia under Šāhpuhr II, beginning in 338–339. See also Peeters's suggestion, "Persécution," pp. 74–77, that the Mari of Seleucia martyred with seven companions according to the Syrian Acts of 412 (AASS, Nov. II/1 lxv) may well be the prototype of BP's Mari and his seventy companions. Cf. Abbeloos, "Acta Maris"; see also Appendix I, "Mari." The Syriacisms detected here by Peeters are again not relevant for the totality of the text: cf. IV.x n. 3 and Intro., p. 8 and n. 30.

IV.xviii

1. This chapter picks up the narrative from the middle of chapter xvi before the interpolation of the Christian persecution in Persia, though there is an allusion to Aršak's oath in Šāhpuhr's message to the Armenian king.

2. This episode is unknown to the *Vita* of St. Nersēs, which leaps directly to the end of Aršak II's reign—see IV.xvi n. 1—or to MX which records no embassy from Šāhpuhr II to Aršak II but mentions a flight of the Armenian king to the Caucasus, III.xxvii (= MK, p. 282), which is totally unknown to BP and the other sources. Leo, *Hayocʿ patmutʿyun*, I, p. 460 makes Vardan one of the leaders of the pro-Persian party in Armenia and consequently a threat to the Aršakuni realm—hence his murder by his own brother Vasak, the *sparapet* entrusted with its defense.

3. See IV.xvi and n. 9.

4. See IV.xv and n. 10.

5. MX, III.xxv (= MK, p. 281) has Vardan killed together with Aršak II's nephew Tiritʿ as they fled southeastward into Persia, and not in the Mamikonean northwestern district of Taykʿ: see IV.xv n. 38.

6. The coincidence of the birth of Vardan's homonymous son at the very moment of his father's murder suggests a return to the epic "Mamikonean Geste" rather than a historical account, see Intro., p. 34.

IV.xix

1. MX includes the massacre of the Kamsarakan in his account of the career of Xad of Marag: see IV. xii n. 1 and below, n. 3.

2. See IV.xv n. 27.

3. MX, III.xxxi–xxxii (= MK, pp. 287–289) locates the massacre at Armawir.

4. See III.ix and xviii for parallel examples of infant heirs of *naxarar* houses saved by the Mamikonean. According to MX III.xxxi (= MK p. 288), Spandarat Kamsarakan was not an infant but an adult who fled to the Byzantine Empire, together with his sons Šawarš and Gazawon and his entire household. MX adds (III.xxxii = MK, p. 289) that the king forbade the burial of the Kamsarakan dead, a detail unknown to BP.

5. The text uses the term *ašxarh*, "realm" to describe the Kamsarakan domains regained by Spandarat, thus implying that the *naxarar* principalities had considerable autonomy.

6. According to MX, III.xxxi (= MK, p. 287) the fortress of Artagers was already in existence as a Kamsarakan stronghold. His version is probably more accurate than that of BP because the fortress was known to early classical sources: see Appendix II, "Artagers." Most likely the place was reconstructed and refortified by Aršak II when it became part of the royal domain and seemingly the anchor point of its defense: see IV.lv.

IV.xx

1. There is no reference to this episode in the parallel account of MX (see below, n. 8). Malxasyancʿ (p. 326 n. 105) argues for a possible restitution of a reference to the Persian king at this point.

2. As noted by Manandyan, *Kʿnnakan tesutʿyun*, II/1 p. 171, this chapter contains a mixture of epic elements whose historicity must be analyzed with care. This all the more the case, that the events described repeat several episodes already found in IV.xvi. The endemic warfare between Byzantium and the Sasanians is, of course, well documented, but the anonymous reference to the "king of the Greeks" points again to an oral eastern

tradition rather than to written western sources, which would have recorded the name of the ruler.

3. Manadyan, *ibid.*, places these events at the very beginning of Aršak II's reign before 351; but the allusion to Aršak's aloofness from both sides just preceding suggests rather the period of relative truce between the two great powers on either side of Armenia preceding the failure of the inconclusive Roman-Persian negotiations (A.D. 350–358; see AM, XVII.v.1–2), because the distraction of their kingdoms during this period would have allowed Aršak II to pursue a relatively autonomous policy. See Manandyan, *K{c}nnakan tesut{c}yun*, pp. 162–163; Garsoïan, "Politique," p. 308; *idem, "Quidam Narseus,"* pp. 157–164. This interval would furthermore coincide with the eight years indicated at the beginning of the next chapter; see below, n. 18.

Despite the insistence of AM, XXV.vii.12 that Aršak II had always remained loyal to the Romans, the indications in BP point rather to a *rapprochement* with Persia before 358. See the preceding note and below, n. 18, as well as IV.xvi, nn. 6, 10.

4. This figure is obviously exaggerated and must have originated in the epic tradition.

5. See also V.xxxvii n. 17, and Appendix III, *zēn.*

6. Aruastan, the district surrounding the city of Nisibis known in Syriac as Bet Arabāyē, is often confused with Aljnik{c} inside Armenia—see AON, p. 319; Toumanoff, *Studies*, pp. 179–182—but a distinction is indicated here. Malχasyanc{c} (p. 326 n. 106) identifies it with Asorestan, and it is clearly the district known to classical sources as Mygdonia. See Appendix II, "Aruestan."

7. See Appendix V, g, for this formula.

8. There is no record of any disturbance near Nisibis between the failure of the third Persian siege in 350 and the surrender of the city to Šāhphur II by Jovian in 363 (see next chapter); neither is there any mention of an Armenian victory over an imperial army in its vicinity although Stein, *Bas Empire*, I, p. 154, attributes the devastation of the area of Nisibis to Aršak II. This is unlikely, since the Christian king of Armenia would hardly destroy monasteries. Šāhphur deliberately bypassed the city in his campaign of 359, which took Amida (AM, XIX.i–ix; cf. Manandyan, *K{c}nnakan tesut{c}yun*, II/1, pp. 170–171). The corresponding section of MX, III.xxvi, xxviii (= MK, pp. 281–282, 283–284) gives an account of the capture of Tigranakert, but BP places that event in a different context (IV.xxiv). A number of scholars, such as Tournebize, *Histoire*, pp. 63–64 and Markwart, *Entstehung*, pp. 94–95, 97, suggest that Aršak II was the ally of the Persians in the campaign of 359; but this is highly improbable (see below, n. 18). Consequently, this battle, if it has any historical basis whatsoever, must be the distorted memory of an episode in the siege of Nisibis in 350, or even of the campaign of 297, worked into the "Geste of Aršak"; see III.xxi n. 16.

9. See Appendix V, b, c, for the repetitions of these epic refrains, which are in keeping with the general epic tone of this entire passage.

10. Procopius, *Bell. Pers.*, I.v.11–12 records the victory of the Armenians over "certain other barbarians." See above, n. 8, and below, n. 18.

11. See V.v and n. 12 for a similar speech of Šāhphur II praising the Armenians, but on that occasion after an Armenian victory over the Persians.

12. The use of the correct Iranian term *Arik{c},* "Aryans/Iranians" instead of the more common Armenian term *Parsk{c},* "Persians" usually occurs in BP within an epic setting: cf. IV.liv; V.iv, v, vii, xliii.

13. The text seems clearly corrupt at this point. Consequently, I have followed Malχasyanc{c}'s reasonable correction (p. 327 n. 107).

14. This phrase seems to be an echo of the formula for royal requests noted in IV.xv and n. 36; see also V.iv and Appendix V, j, iii.

15. See IV.liv for the magic effect of Aršak II's standing on "his own domain." There is, of course, no question of the Armenian border having reached Ctesiphon at any time, and this hyperbole must undoubtedly belong to the epic tradition. On the ancient custom of

marriage alliances between the Persian and Armenian courts, which went back to Achaemenid times, see Garsoïan, "Locus," pp. 35–36.

16. See IV.xv n. 40 for the problem of P⁽ařanjem's marriage to Aršak II and the threats to her status as queen of Armenia. See also III.xxi n. 24 on the possible existence of polygamy in the Armenian royal house in the fourth century.

17. The anonymous Persian counselor disguised as a soothsayer and the repetition of the dialogue belong, once again, in the world of romance rather than that of sober fact. The elaborate setting of the Armenian king's escape from the Persians probably supplies the missing context of Aršak II's first flight back to Armenia in the lacuna of the parallel account in IV.xvi and n. 10.

18. As indicated at the beginning of the present chapter and implied at the beginning of the next, Aršak II seems to have attempted to maintain a relatively neutral position between the Romans and the Persians during the early years of his reign; later he may have inclined toward the Iranian side, if the account in IV.xvi and this chapter have any historical basis (see IV.xi n. 6; xvi n. 4). This hypothesis is supported by the participation of St. Nersēs in the Roman–Persian negotiations of 358 as a representative of Persia, according to the classical sources (see Garsoïan, "*Quidam Narseus*," pp. 157–164). Nonetheless, the favors of Constantius to Aršak II and the Armenian king's imperial marriage to Olympias in that year seem to have turned his allegiance away from Persia, as is implied by the fictionalized account of this chapter and AM's assertion of Aršak's faithfulness to the Romans. In view of AM's participation in the campaigns of the Persian war and his admiration for Julian, his evaluation of the Armenian king's faithfulness seems impossible if Aršak II had supported the Persians in 359 or 363, especially because AM, XVIII.vi–vii specifies that in the campaign of 359 the Persian king was accompanied by the rulers of the Chionites and the Caspian Albanians but does not mention Armenia (see above, n. 8). Furthermore, the savage punishment of Armenia by Šāhphur II (IV.liv–lix) would be inexplicable if he had just been supported by Aršak. The most reasonable pattern consequently seems to be that of Armenian quasi-neutrality at the beginning of Aršak II's reign, then an inclination toward Persia (IV.xi n. 5), and finally an abrupt turn to the Romans, as a result of Constantius's favors and possibly maintained by the presence of Julian's army in the East, which led to the disaster of 363. See above, n. 3; IV.v and n. 53, xi nn. 5–6, xvi nn. 4, 6, 10, xxi nn. 5–6, liv–lix.

19. The "thirty-years' war" with Persia covers precisely the period 338-368, from the revival of war between Rome and the Sasanians after the death of Constantine the Great and the return of Tiran to Armenia (cf. III.xvii n. 7; xxi n. 4, etc.) to the conquest of Armenia and the deportation and imprisonment of Aršak II, as has been observed by Manandyan, *Kʿnnakan tesutʿyun*, II/1, p. 171; Peeters, "Persécution," pp. 63, 67–70; etc. The round number thirty, however, which reappears in another epic context (IV.liv), instead of the more precise thirty-four (IV.l) and thirty-two of Procopius, (*Bell. Pers.*, I.v.10) suggests a global rather than a precise chronology for the Armenian-Persian war, which in the tradition that clustered around Aršak II included not only his reign but that of his father Tiran.

IV.xxi

1. MX, III.xxxiv–xxxv (= MK, pp. 291–294) and even more the *Vita* of St. Nersēs, x, pp. 66–68 (= CHAMA, II, p. 33) give highly condensed versions of the end of Aršak II's reign, which do not seriously contradict the account of BP but give none of its crucial historical details: see e.g. below, n. 5.

2. In contrast to the epic character of the preceding chapter, the tone here is factual and precise and consequently seems to emanate from a different source. The eight years' hiatus referred to here corresponds to the period 350/1-358 between failure of the third

Persian siege of Nisibis followed by the presumed enthronement of Aršak II (see III.xxi n. 23)—rather than his flight from Persia described in the preceding chapter—and the end of the Roman-Persian negotiations followed by Šāhpuhr II's attack of Amida with the support of the Chionites and the Caspian Albanians (see AM, XVIII.v.15; XVIII.iv, vi.17, 19, vii–ix, and above, IV.xx n. 18).

3. The plural "kings" presumably covers the three emperors: Constantius (337–361), Julian (361–363), and Jovian (363–364), who ruled between the resumption of the Persian war in 359 and the peace treaty of 363 described in the next paragraph. BP never mentions the emperors by name, as opposed to MX III.xvii (= MK, p. 270, etc.), and his information on the names of Roman rulers is minimal and inaccurate (see e.g. III.xx n. 9, xxi nn. 16,21; IV.v n. 5, vi n. 2).

4. The hybrid form of the name of Nisibis found in the mss., "Ncbin" instead of the normal Armenian form "Mcbin" was attributed by Malχasyancʿ (p. 327 n. 110) to a copyist's error. In view of the historical accuracy of this chapter, however, it may suggest an underlying classical source: see above, n. 1.

5. The peace terms set out here in BP correspond to the more detailed account of the *ignobile decretum* that Jovian was compelled to conclude with Persia as a result of the disastrous end of Julian's campaign in Mesopotamia, to be found in AM, XXV.vii.9, 14. This is one of the rare points at which Armenian and classical sources explicitly confirm each other. All the main clauses of the treaty—the surrender of most of Greater Armenia, together with the retrocession of a portion of the southern Satrapies, as well as the surrender of the great Mesopotamian city of Nisibis (all of which had been gained by the Romans as a result of the peace of Nisibis in 298)—are included (see III.xxi n. 16, but cf. Chrysos, *Legal Relations*, p. 33).

6. The disastrous attack on Armenia by Šāhpuhr immediately following the treaty of 363 is also noted by AM, XXV.vii.12, who, however, summarizes in one sentence the remaining chapters of BP book IV.

7. From here to the end of Book IV, BP gives a semi-historical, semi-fictional account of the invasion of Armenia by Šāhpuhr II, beginning with the revival of the Persian war in 359 and ending with the deportation of Aršak II, the devastation of his realm, and the imposition of Persian sovereignty on Greater Armenia ca. 367/8. The figures given throughout for the Armenian and Persian forces are clearly fantastic (see e.g. IV.xxvi n. 1). The epic alliterative formula characterizing the Armenian army, *miasirtkʿ, miaban, miamitkʿ*, "with one heart, one mind" recurs with slight variations in similar circumstances (see Appendix V, k, and III.xx and n. 13 for the parallel pejorative formula). The obvious echo of this passage (IV.xxiv and n. 9) gives the Armenian cavalry less fantastically as composed of 60,000 men, even though this too must be an exaggeration.

8. See Appendix V, b, d, for the repetitions of the *topoi* of the Persian king escaping alone from the fray and the Biblical formula of the enemy "put to the sword."

IV.xxii

1. These events are not known to MX, and their epic character is evident from the improbable and formulaic information that the three battles were fought simultaneously, as well as from the accumulation of epic *topoi* in the chapter. Manandyan, *Kʿnnakan tesutʿyun*, II/1, p. 175, however, attributes these engagements to the campaign of 359: see IV.xx n. 1.

2. See Appendix V, i for the repetition of this formula.

3. See IV.xxvii–xxviii on Andikan and Hazarawuχt.

4. See Appendix V, c, for the repetitions of this formula.

5. See above, n. 1.

6. Cf. III.viii for Vačʿē Mamikonean's rout of the Persians at the same site.

7. Cf. I Macc. 6:43–46, for the similar fate of Awaran.

8. See above and Appendix V, c, for the repetitions of this formula.

9. See above and n. 1.

10. See III.xxi for the location of the Persian camp in the same place in an earlier campaign.

11. See Appendix V, e, for the repetitions of this formula.

12. See Appendix V, b, d, for the repetitions of these formulae.

13. See Appendix V, c, for the repetitions and variations of this formula.

IV.xxiii

1. Cf. MX, III.xxix, xxxv–xxxvii (= MK, pp. 286, 292–298) for another version of the revolt of Meružan Arcruni. BP invariably treats the "malignant" Meružan as a traitor to his lord, the king of Greater Armenia, but if he were the ruler of one of the all-but-independent Satrapies of southern Armenia, Meružan would not necessarily have been a vassal of the Armenian king and would consequently have been entitled to pursue an autonomous policy. See Intro., pp. 48–49, on BP's conception of the "realm" of Armenia, and Toumanoff, *Studies*, p. 200, who attributes to the Arcruni the dignity of *bdeašχs* of Adiabenē; also below, n. 3, and IV.xxxi n. 2.

2. Apostasy was necessarily linked with treachery in the political theory of the fourth century, both in the Byzantine and the Persian empires: see Garsoïan, *Armenia*, pp. 346–352.

3. Meružan's domain is also characterized as an *ašχarh*, "realm" and consequently may indicate the degree of political autonomy implied by this term. Moreover, although BP invariably and constantly condemns his actions and links the epithet *č̣ʿaragorc*, "malignant," lit. "evildoer" to his name, it does not use in reference to him the accumulation of epithets specifying treason rather than more generalized evil heaped on Databē and Pʿisak Siwni, whose domains lay undeniably within the boundaries of Greater Armenia and indeed of the Armenian Midlands: see III.viii and xx n. 13, as well as above, n. 1.

4. See IV.lix for the fulfillment of this promise.

5. The term *ařǰnord* is used here, and throughout, with reference to Meružan Arcruni in its fundamental sense of "leader/guide" without any of its common spiritual implications also found in BP: see Appendix III, s.v.

6. See the next chapter and IV.lviii for the similar treatment of Armenia by Šāhpuhr II, and Appendix V, j.ii, for its formulaic character.

7. I have followed Malχasyancʿ (p. 327 n. 112) and Lauer (p. 110) in the translation of *yutest* in the text as *utesti kerakuelu hamar*, "to forage for supplies." Aršak II had presumably moved south to border district of Angełtun, which contained the royal fortresses, when Meružan broke directly through to the Armenian Midlands.

IV.xxiv

1. MX, III.xxvi, xxviii (= MK, pp. 281–284) gives a different version of these events; see below, nn. 5, 7, 12.

2. Malχasyancʿ (pp. 327–328 n. 113) following Norayr Biwzandacʿi, rejects the usual interpretation of *kartʿel* in the text as *kołmn*, "side" and prefers *kartʿeal*, "swerving, deviating," which is indeed more suited to the context.

3. As observed by Adontz, *Armenia*, p. 35, the listing of the districts given here corresponds exactly to their geographical position from east to west.

4. See Appendix V, b for the repetitions of this formula; also the preceding chapter and Appendix V, j.ii for the devastation of Armenia and its formulaic character.

5. MX III.xxvi, xxviii (= MK, pp. 281, 284) gives a different version of the capture of Tigranakert by the Persians at an earlier date. According to his account, the city was defended by Antiochus/Andovk Siwni, Aršak II's father-in-law, and it was taken with the help of captive Greek forces. But see Thomson, MK pp. 281 n. 1, 282 n. 5, 284 n. 4, for the literary parallels of MX's account. Dilleman, *Haute Mésopotamie*, pp. 115, 259–260, however, rejects the entire account as, "un morceau de bravour."

6. On the royal fortresses see Appendix II, under the corresponding names and Appendix III, *mardpet*.

7. See III.xi for the burial of Xosrov Kotak at the necropolis of Ani in Daranałikᶜ. MX, III.xxvii (= MK, pp. 282–283) associates the capture of Ani with the destruction of Aršakawan. Cf. below, n. 12, on the removal of the royal remains and III.xi n. 8 on the royal epithet, *kᶜaǰ arancᶜ*.

8. See Appendix I, "Sanatruk," for this king, whom BP associates with the Armenian Arsacids since he places his tomb in the royal necropolis of Ani in Daranałikᶜ. Cf. MX II. xxxiv–xxxviii (= MK, pp. 174–180, etc.) on the Arsacid descent of Sanatruk.

9. See Appendix V, k.i for this formula. The earlier parallel of this passage (IV.xxi n. 7) gives the impossible figure of 600,000 men for the Armenian cavalry.

10. Cf. the parallels to this homily, Intro., p. 39. The epic epithets of this passage, *kᶜaǰ arancᶜ*, "most valiant of men," and *bnak tearkᶜ*, "true lords" are all part of the oral literary ethos, as is its symmetrical and formulaic pattern.

11. See Appendix V, b, d, e.i for these formulae.

12. Despite the author's disclaimer that these were "heathen beliefs," this passage provides particularly clear evidence that the Iranian Zoroastrian belief that the supernatural qualities of legitimate kings—their "glory" (*pᶜaṙkᶜ*), "fortune" (*baχt*), and "valor" (*kᶜaǰutᶜiwn*)—clung to them even after death and protected their realm were still current in early Christian Armenia. The same beliefs are found in Aa, cxxvii, where the protection of the "glory [*pᶜaṙkᶜ*] of [our] kings and brave [*kᶜaǰ*] ancestors" is invoked. It is noteworthy that the Greek version of this text (Ag, lvii) omits this passage, which it presumably could not understand. MX, III.xxvii (= MK, p. 282) likewise fails to grasp the implication of this episode and dismisses the Persian attempt to carry away the royal bones with the comment, "I do not know if this was to insult Arshak or for some pagan incantation." The late *Vita* of St. Nersēs ignores the entire episode. On the transcendental royal qualities, see Garsoïan, "Prolegomena," cols. 184–186 and nn. 64–72; *idem*, "Locus," pp. 41–52; and *idem*, "Substratum," pp. 157–160; also Russell, *Zor. Arm.*, pp. 339–340, and below, V.v and n. 17.

13. The heroic reliefs of the hunt that decorate the royal hypogeum at Ałcᶜkᶜ sustain the epic motif of this passage, since both the *pᶜaṙkᶜ* and the *kᶜaǰutᶜiwn* of the king manifest themselves in the apotheosis of the hunt. The same is true of the newly found plaques with animal motifs, especially the one of the bird on which the undulating ribbons symbolizing the *pᶜaṙkᶜ* are still visible. See Harper, *hunter*; Aṙakelyan, *Patkerakᶜandaknerə*, p. 60; Kᶜalantᶜaryan, "Glinianye plitki," pp. 228–229, esp. fig. 1 and pl. I.1a; and the preceding note.

14. This is the first application to Meružan Arcruni of the "escape" formula normally applied to the Persian king: see Appendix V, d.i–ii.

15. The "two gates of Armenia" were presumably Atrpatakan and Ałjnikᶜ, through which invading armies from Persia normally broke into Armenia: see Malχasyancᶜ (p. 328 n. 114). See also Appendix V, g, h, for these formulae.

IV.xxv

1. This expedition to Tabriz in Atrpatakan is unknown to MX or the classical sources and it bears the hallmarks of the epic tale. See below, and nn. 2, 5–6, 8, for the

presence of formulaic refrains.

2. See Appendix V, i, for the repetitions of this formula.

3. Cf. III.vii.

4. The Sasanian "home camp" (*bun banak*) was apparently located at Tabriz. See IV.xxix; V.ii and n. 4; also IV.xv for the home camp of the Armenian Aršakuni at Šahapivan.

5. The usual specification that the camp was attacked "by night" is missing here. See Appendix V, e, for this formula.

6. See Appendix V, d, for the repetitions of this formula.

7. According to Malχasyancᶜ (p. 328 n. 116), this term is used by both BP and Ełišē to designate the camp equipment; but see Appendix III, s.v.

8. See Appendix V, b.i, for the repetitions of these formulae.

9. See IV.xxx, xxxviii; V.ii and n. 4; and Appendix V, g, for the repetitions of this formula and its variants.

IV.xxvi

1. This is the first of twenty-three chapters (IV.xxvi–l, with the sole exception of the probably misplaced xliv), which monotonously and formulaically catalog the Armenian victories over successive Persian invasions. They may be confused recollections of some episodes in the protracted Armenian–Persian war (359–367/8), which ultimately led to the overthrow of Aršak II and the temporary overlordship of the Sasanians in Armenia (IV.lv–lix). Nevertheless, none of these episodes is otherwise attested and their similarity, fantastic army figures, and persistent refrains make them historically suspect. See IV.xx n. 2 and xxi n. 7; as well as Adontz, *Armenia*, p. 225, on the probable strength of the Armenian army in this period.

2. See Appendix V, b, for the repetitions of this formula.

IV.xxvii

1. This Andikan is presumably the same as the one mentioned in IV.xxii and n. 3.

2. See Appendix V, c, for the repetitions of this formula.

3. See Appendix V, g, for the variants of this formula.

IV.xxviii

1. For Hazarawuχt see also IV.xxii and n. 3.

IV.xxix

1. The title of this chapter both here and in the Table of Contents reads *taprik zōrōkᶜn*, a term that has led to considerable controversy. Malχasyancᶜ (p. 328 n. 117), followed by Gevorgian (p. 115), interpreted it to mean troops from "Tabaristan." But, as indicated in Anasyan, *Review*, p. 26 and corrected by the editors of Malχasyancᶜ's 1968 edition, the correct etymology is *taprik* < Pahl. *tapar*, "axe" + the suffix -*ik*, and translation should consequently be "axe-men/axe-bearers" as it was given by Lauer (p. 116), "*axt-bewaffneten*." The term does not appear in the body of the text, where the term *sakraworkᶜ* is invariably used for "axe-men." See Appendix III, *zēn*, i, *zōrkᶜ*, ii.c.

2. See Appendix III, *vsemakan*, since this is a title and not a proper name.

3. This constant refrain is slightly altered here; cf. Appendix V, c, for its repetitions.

IV.xxx

1. See Appendix V, c, for the repetitions of this formula.
2. See Appendix V, g, for the repetition of this formula.

IV.xxxi

1. See Intro., p. 37, V.xxxix, and below, n. 4 for the parallel chapter.
2. See IV.xxiii nn. 1, 3, 5, for the status of Meružan. It may be significant in this connection that he is said to have come from the "land" and not the "realm" of Armenia. See also next note.
3. Note the distinction made between the "land" and the "realm" of Armenia. See "Preliminary Statement" n. 5 and the preceding note.
4. Despite this categorical statement, see above, n. 1; V.xxxix, and V.xli for the parallel case of Mŕkan.
5. The phrase here reads *anmi arareal*, but in view of the clearly formulaic context, it may well be a variant of the usual formula found at this point in victorious accounts: see Appendix V, c for its frequency.
6. The *topos* of the Persian king escaping alone on horseback is now systematically transferred here to the traitor Meružan Arcruni, whose escape with some variations almost invariably closes each episode in the subsequent catalog of Armenian victories. See IV.xxiv and n. 14 for the first appearance of this transfer and Appendix V, d.ii for its repetitions.

IV.xxxii

1. See Appendix V, i for the repetitions of this formula.
2. This is the only reference to a Persian lineage for the Mamikonean house. Cf. V.iv, xxxvii; and Appendix I, "Mamikonean."
3. See IV.xxiii n. 5.
4. See IV.xxxi n. 6. From here on this *topos* is usually condensed; see Appendix V, d.ii.

IV.xxxiii

1. See Intro., p. 37, and IV.xxxvi for a possible parallel chapter.
2. As a member of the Parthian/Pahlaw house, Surēn Pahlaw would be a kinsman of the Armenian Aršakuni kings descended from the Parthian royal house, though the link of the Surēn with the Gregorid patriarchal house is more commonly stressed by the Armenian sources. See Appendix I, "Aršakuni"; "Gregorids"; and for a possible distiction, "Surēn Pahlaw" and "Surēn Parsik."
3. See IV.xxiii n. 5.
4. See IV.xxxi n. 6.

IV.xxxiv

1. See Appendix III, *vsemakan*, since this is a title and not a proper name.
2. See IV.xxiii n. 5.
3. See Appendix V, c, for this formula, which is simplified here.
4. See IV.xxxi n. 6.

IV.xxxv

1. See IV.xxiii n. 5.
2. See Appendix V, i, for the repetitions of this formula.
3. See IV.xxxi n. 6, with considerable modification here.

IV.xxxvi

1. See IV.xxxiii and nn. 1–2 for a possible parallel to this chapter.
2. See IV.xxiii n. 5.
3. See Appendix V, e for the repetitions of this formula.
4. See IV.xxxi n. 6, with considerable simplification and contraction here.

IV.xxxvii

1. See IV.xxxi n. 6, simplified.

IV.xxxviii

1. Ałanayozan Pahlaw is the only one of the Persian generals named in the catalog of Armenian victories (IV.xxvi–xliii, xlv–xlix) who is also known to MX, III.xxxiv–xxxv (= MK, pp. 291–292). In MX's account, however, Ałanayozan, a relative of Aršak II, was first supported by the disaffected Armenian magnates who subsequently turned against him, and he brought about the deportation and captivity of Aršak: cf. below, IV.liii–liv.
2. The usual formula concerning Meružan Arcruni's escape (see V.xxxi n. 6 and Appendix V, d.ii) is unexpectedly missing here, but see Appendix V, g, for the closing formula given.

IV.xxxix

1. There is no record of an Armenian raid on Tabriz in this period. Cf. IV.xxv and n. 1, where the Persian king's residence is referred to as a "camp" (*banak*) rather than a permanent "palace" (*aparan*); also V.ii for the evidence that Tabriz was the Sasanian "home camp."
2. See IV.xxxi n. 6.

IV.xl

1. See IV.xxiii n. 5.
2. See IV.xxxi n. 6.

IV.xli

1. The text reads *mecaw bnuteamb*, and in one ms *mecabanutᶜeamb*, but the reading *bṙnutᶜeamb*, "with . . . violence" of the St. Petersburg edition, p. 130—also proposed by the Venice edition, p. 161 n. 1—clearly seems to be correct.
2. See Appendix V, c, for the repetition of this formula.
3. See IV.xxxi n. 6.

IV.xlii

1. As observed by Malχasyancʿ (p. 328 n. 119) and the Venice edition (p. 161 n. 2), the name of this personage is uncertain. It appears as "Maričan" in the text, "Maručan" in the title, and "*Mari anun mec naχarar*" in one of the mss.
2. See IV.xxiii n. 5.
3. See IV.xxxi n. 6.

IV.xliii

1. See Appendix V, e for the repetitions of this formula.
2. See Appendix V, b for the repetitions of this formula.
3. See IV.xxxi n. 6.

IV.xliv

1. As rightly noted by Malχasyancʿ (p. 328 n. 121), followed more categorically by Gevorgian (p. 218 n. 67)—who, however, omits most of this chapter—it is clearly out of place in the catalog of Armenian victories (IV.xxvi–xlix) into which it has been inserted. Its proper place is in Book V, where we find the parallel chapter V.xxii at the logical point in the narrative where it coincides with the corresponding accounts of MX and the *Vita* of St. Nersēs (see V.xxii n. 1). This chapter contains contradictions, and the reduplication may be the result of later editing; see Intro., p. 37. There is, however, no reason to attribute it to a malevolent interpolation, as is suggested by both Malχasyancʿ and (especially) Gevorgian, because BP's hostility to Pap is not restricted to it but pervades the text and appears especially in V.xxii and xxiv. See also below, nn. 3–6.
2. See IV.xv.
3. As noted above (n. 1), the information on Pap's demonic possession in this chapter is incoherent. The traditional version of the accusation of the young prince was devoted to the *dew*s by his mother, which is repeated in the parallel chapter V.xxii, runs directly counter to the queen's horrified discovery of her son's demonic possession given below. MX, III.xxxviii (= MK, p. 299) has nothing to say about Pap's demonic possession at any point but merely comments on his debauchery. The *Vita* of St. Nersēs, xii, pp. 83–84 (= CHAMA, II, p. 36), which usually follows BP even where it embellishes or distorts the account, attributes the tormenting snakes to Nersēs's curse of the young king. This tale is evidently derived from the confused and contradictory oral traditions that had clustered around the enigmatic figures of Pʿaṛanjem and Pap, as well as around Aršak II's problematic marriages (see IV.xv nn. 40, 42). Markwart, *Südarmenien*, pp. 138–140 saw a reference to pagan practices in this accusation; but see below, n. 5.
4. Gevorgian (p. 121) omits the rest of this chapter, as he does in the case of the parallel one. See V.xxii and n. 4.
5. As noted above (n. 3), both MX and the *Vita* of St. Nersēs condemn Pap's dissolute morals without giving any details or explanations. In direct contradiction to the Armenian sources, AM, XXX.i.5–15 gives a radically different and favorable characterization of the young king. The accusaton of sodomy may well have been one of heresy, as is often the case in mediaeval sources. See Garsoïan "Politique," esp. pp. 311–313.
6. See the preceding note for the significance of the white snakes as a sign of heresy and V.xxii n. 3 for their Iranian parallel.
7. The queen's disclaimer seems categorical: "*Vay inj ordeak im zi kʿez tagnap ēr ew es očʿ gitei*"; see above, n. 3.

IV.xlv

1. See Appendix III, *(h)anderjapet.*
2. See IV.xxxi n. 6.

IV.xlvi

1. See Appendix III, *takaṙapet* for the derivation and meaning of this title.
2. See IV.xxxi n. 6.

IV.xlvii

1. See Appendix III, *(h)andarjapet* and Christensen, *L'Iran*, p. 135 on the *mōghān-andarzbadh.*
2. The phrase here is *"ew zzōrsn anmi arareal,"* but in view of the frequent occurence of the formula for total annihilation in this context, this may well be one of its more distant variants; see Appendix V, c.
1. See IV.xxxi n. 6. This is the only case where a precision is given concerning Meružan's mount.

IV.xlviii

1. See Appendix V, b, c, e, for the repetitions of these formulae.
2. See IV.xxxi n. 6. This is the only case in which precisions concerning Meružan's circumstances are given.

IV.xlix

1. See V.xli for the parallel account.
2. See IV.xxxi n. 6.

IV.l

1. The account of the disaffection of the Armenian nobles is much shorter in MX, III.xxxiv (= MK, pp. 291–292), who does not name them and introduces Alanoazan at this point. See IV.xxxviii n. 1 and below, nn. 3, 7, 8, 11, and IV.lii n. 1.
2. See IV.xx n. 19.
3. This is the most detailed account of the borderlands of Greater Armenia and of the territories ruled by the *bdeašχ*s (cf. Aa, dcccxlii and n. 12), as well as of their defection from Aršak II at the time of the Roman–Persian peace of 363, ceding the dominion over Armenia to the Sasanians (see IV.xxi n. 5). It has no real counterpart in the *Vita* of St. Nersēs, x, p. 66 (= CHAMA, II, p. 33), which follows the terse statement of MX, III.xxxiv (= MK, p. 291) that Aršak II was "deserted by many princes who . . . willingly went to Šapuh in their dislike of their own king," in which the princes are not identified nor the *bdeašχ*s mentioned. See also below, n. 7 and Appendix III, *bdeašχ.*
4. Malχasyancᶜ (p. 329 n. 125) prefers the reading of the one mss, *"ew dassǝntir ēin sokᶜa,"* (and they were ten choice ones), because he consideres this toponym to be a *hapax.* There is, however, no reason to distinguish it from the district of Dasn, which is attested in this area: see Appendix II, "Dassǝntrē," and "Noširakan" which may have contained these three districts."

5. The translation follows here Anasyan's correction, *Review*, p. 23, of both Malχasyancᶜ (pp. 206–207) and Gevorgian (p. 123). According to this rectification, the Joray Pass (not to be confused with the northern district of Jor mentioned immediately below) would have remained in Armenian and not in rebel hands. See Appendix II, "Jor/Joray."

6. III.xx n. 3 (end); IV.xvi n. 2; V.viii nn. 4–5.

7. Cf. MX, III.xxxv (= MK, p. 292), who does not identify the magnates who withdrew to the Byzantine Empire any more than those who turned to the Persians; see above, n. 3.

8. His brother-in-law, according to MX, III.xxix (= MK, p. 286).

9. See IV.xxiii and n. 2, for the apostasy of Meružan Arcruni.

10. See IV.xvi, xviii for the pro-Persian policy of Vardan Mamikonean and his murder by his brother the *sparapet* Vasak, who apparently replaced him as *tanutēr* of the Mamikonean house; see IV.ii and n. 7, xxi.

11. According to MX, III.xxxvi (= MK, p. 294), Ormizduχt was given in marriage to Meružan Arcruni.

12. This may be a reference to the Mamikonean claim of royal ancestry. See Appendix I, "Mamikonean," but cf. V.iv; V.xxxvii.

13. Cf. the similar closing of VI.i.

IV.li

1. There is no reference to this assembly of the Armenian nobility with the patriarch, but seemingly in the absence of the king, in the corresponding section of MX, III.xxxiv–xxxv (= MK, pp. 291–292).

2. See Garsoïan, "Prolegomena," col. 183 and n. 46, for the possibility of the meeting of the Armenian council in the absence of the king. The patriarch Nersēs had presumably returned from exile by then, but he continued to remain away from the Armenian court. See IV.vi n. 15 and xv nn. 27, 43.

3. See IV.xx n. 19 on the "thirty years' war."

4. See the preceding chapter and V.xxxv for the similar complaint of Mušeł Mamikonean.

5. See IV.xvi.xx.

6. See Appendix V, c for the repetitions of this formula.

7. Eph. 6:5; Col. 3:22; I Tim. 6:1–2. Cf. IV.iv and n. 27; and below, n. 13.

8. This passage gives the clearest statement of royal grants of benefices to the nobility, as opposed to the normal pattern of hereditary offices, as well as of the distinction between *gorc*, "office" and *patiw*, "honor, dignity." Cf. III.xi n. 7; IV.ii nn. 7, 9; and Appendix III, *gorcakal, patiw*.

9. Cf. probably Matt. 18:23–35, rather than the parable of the talents, Matt. 25 [not 27]:14–28 suggested by Malχasyancᶜ (p. 329 n. 127), which does not fit as well.

10. The text reads "*Baycᶜ law licᶜi*," which is patently contradictory at this point. Malχasyancᶜ (p. 329 n. 128) corrects *law*, "good" into *kᶜaw*, "God forbid," and the Venice edition (p. 169 n. 1) notes that one ms omits the contradictory "not," as does the St. Petersburg edition (p. 137).

11. This passage is the clearest affirmation in BP that only the Aršakuni were the "true lords" of Armenia whom not even their sins could deprive of their hereditary crown. See Garsoïan, "Prolegomena," col. 179 and nn. 22–24; Intro., pp. 48, 50, 54.

12. Cf. III.xi and n. 2 for the parallel passage in the homily of the patriarch Vrtᶜanēs over Vačᶜē I Mamikonean and his fallen companions, and Intro., p. 39, for the central role of this theme in BP.

13. See above, n. 7.

14. Lam. 1:14; Deut. 28:48; cf. III Kgs. 12:4, 9–11, 14 = II Chron. 10:4, 9–11, 14, Jer. 28:

10-14; AaT, cxxxiii. See also III.xiv and the beginning of this paragraph.

15. As in III.xi and nn. 4–5, this passage contains an obvious allusion to the Sasanian attempt to reimpose Zoroastrianism on Armenia in the mid-fifth century, and the pro-Persian policies of Vasak Siwni and his party. Cf. IV.liv n. 17 for the curse of St. Nersēs over the rebellious Armenian magnates; also V.xxx and n. 3.

16. Cf. IV.liv for the *sparapet* Vasak's repentance and V.i for the return of the magnates to St. Nersēs.

IV.lii

1. MX, III.xxxiv (= MK, p. 294) ties Aršak II's journey to Persia to Ałanayozan's expedition and consequently sets it earlier. Cf. IV.xxxviii n. 1, and 1 n. 1. MX's account of the end of Aršak's reign, however, is far more compressed than that of BP: see IV.xxi n. 1.

IV.liii

1. The summons of Šāhpuhr II to Aršak II are not recorded by MX. See preceding chapter, n. 1, and below, n. 6.

2. The Persian practice of sealing salt in conjunction with the swearing of an oath is confirmed by Sebēos, xi, p. 78 (= Macler tr. p. 20).

3. For the royal seal ring bearing the effigy of a *varaz*, "wild boar," see Malχasyancᶜ (pp. 329–330 n. 129). In addition to being the symbol of the Sasanian dynasty, the *varaz* was the most familiar incarnation of the god Vərəθrayna, the companion of Miθra, the god of contracts, in the Zoroastrian pantheon, whose duty was to enforce oaths and punish their breach (see Gershevitch, *Mithra*, I.ii–iii, IX.xxxv–xxxviii, XVIII.lxx, XXVIII.cix, etc.; also pp. 26–30, 34–35, 43–44; Russell, *Zor. Arm.*, pp. 189–229, 340). Consequently, the symbolic meaning of the royal seal ring guaranteeing the sanctity of Šāhpuhr's oath was apparently still familiar to the Armenians. See Garsoïan, "Substratum," pp. 160–162 and n. 116; and IV.xvi and n. 12 for another form of oath.

4. Malχasyancᶜ (p. 330 n. 130) argued that the text is corrupt at this point and contains a brief lacuna, but the sentence is comprehensible as it stands and requires no correction, as was noted by the editors of his 1968 edition. See also next note.

5. The Venice edition (p. 171 n. 3) notes that the words "in chains," which patently contradict the statement immediately following that the king and the *sparapet* were held "free" in the midst of guards, are missing in one ms, as they are in the St. Petersburg edition (p. 139). They are consequently suspect and probably to be excised.

6. MX, III.xxiv (= MK, p. 292) compresses this account into a single sentence, and as usual omits any reference to the Mamikoneans. See Intro., pp. 44–45; cf. also Procopius, *Bell. Pers.*, I.v.16–19 and the next chapter.

IV.liv

1. This clearly epic chapter with mythical overtones presumably drawn from the "Geste of Aršak" and perhaps partially from that of the Mamikoneans (see Intro., pp. 32–35), has no counterpart in the corresponding section of MX, see IV.xxi n. 1. A version of its was, however, known to the Byzantine historian Procopius in the mid-sixth century; see below, n. 8, 9, 12, 15, 19. The presence of astrologers and soothsayers at the Sasanian is confirmed by Agathias, II.xxvi.

2. See IV.xvi.

3. See Appendix V, b for the repetitions of this formula.

4. See IV.xvi–xvii. Mari's prophecy that the Gospels would magically bring Aršak II

to Persia, however, is not to be found there.

5. See IV.xx n. 19.

6. As noted in IV.xx n. 12, the Iranian term *Arik'*, "Aryans/Iranians" usually occurs in an epic rather than a historical setting.

Anasyan, *Review*, pp. 18–19 argues that the interpretation that makes Aršak II the subject of the sentence contradicts the context, which has the Persians and not the Armenians as the aggressors, and he notes that classical Armenian syntax allows the use of the nominative, "Aršak" in apposition with the phrase *ənd nma*, "against him" This interpretation is the one adopted by Emin (CHAMA, I, p. 270) and Lauer (p.131), as against Malχasyanc' (p. 212), followed as usual by Gevorgian (p. 128). It has been tentatively adopted here, but see below, n. 12.

7. See Appendix V, c, for variations of this formula.

8. The magic tale of Aršak II's alternate responses to his contact with Persian soil and his own native Armenian earth—with its ultimate link to the myth of Herakles and Antaios—must have been part of the early Armenian tradition, because a version of it was known to Procopius, *Bell. Pers.*, I.v.16–19. His version is, however, somewhat distorted, since the Persian king figuring in it is given the all-purpose name of Pakourious/Bakur < Ir. *bag* + *puhr*, "god's son." Nevertheless, Procopius (I.v.9) states explicitly that his source for the tale was a "History of the Armenians" (ἡ τῶν Ἀρμενίων ἱστορία); see Intro., pp. 10, 18–20.

9. Procopius, *Bell. Pers.*, I.v.23, adds that the Magi insisted on being present as eye-witnesses during the testing of Aršak.

10. See IV.xx n. 19.

11. See IV.xvi, xvii and above, n. 4.

12. The specific recall of the blood feud between the Armenian Arsacids and the Sasanians, "to seek vengeance for the blood of Artewan," with its direct reference to Aa, xviii–xix, does not occur in Procopius, *Bell. Pers.*, I.v.25–26, who merely says that the Armenian king defiantly threatened vengeance against the Persians out of "youthful folly." See also above III.xx and n. 8; IV.xvi and n. 11.

13. See IV.xvi nn. 2–3.

14. See IV.ii n. 12 and xvi n. 2, and above, n. 12.

15. The imprisonment of Aršak II in the Castle of Oblivion is recorded by MX, III.xxxv (= MK, pp. 292–293) and the *Vita* of St. Nersēs, x, p. 67 (= CHAMA, II, p. 33) as well as by the classical sources: AM, XXVII.xii.3; and Procopius, *Bell. Pers.*, I.v.29. AM, however, does not include the magic tale of the ordeal but merely has Aršak tricked by a deceitful invitation to a banquet, blinded, imprisoned, and ultimately executed. See III.xx, n. 17 for the possible confusion of Aršak with his father Tiran. Whatever the precise circumstances, it is clear from AM, XXV.vii.14 that the tragic end of Aršak's reign resulted from the surrender of Greater Armenia to the Persians by Jovian in 363. See IV.xxi nn. 5–6.

16. See IV.xx n. 12.

17. This epic section, presumably taken from the "Geste of the Mamikonean," is naturally missing from Procopius's version as it is from the corresponding passage of MX who as usual ignores the Mamikoneans; see Intro., pp. 34, 44–45 and IV.li for the curse of the rebellious *naχarars* by St. Nersēs.

18. Cf., e.g., Num. 16:30, 33; Prov. 28:10, 17–18; Ps. 54:16; Jer. 48:44, etc. The image of the pit is ubiquitous in the Scriptures. See V.xxx n. 3 for the parallel characterization of St. Nersēs as the only intercessor for the Armenian realm.

19. According to Procopius, *Bell. Pers.*, I.v.28, Vasak's flayed skin was "suspended . . . from a lofty tree." The *Vita* of St. Nersēs, x, p. 68 (= CHAMA, II, p. 33) merely says that Vasak was killed in prison. See V.i and n. 17, ii for Mušeł Mamikonean's subsequent vengeance for the death of his father Vasak; and V.iv and n. 14 for the assertion that Vasak had given his life for his king, Aršak II.

IV.lv

1. See AM, XXV.vii.14, XXVI.iv.5 and above, IV.xxi nn. 5–6, liv p. 15 for the seizure of Armenia by the Persians after the peace of 363.

2. MX, III.xxxv (= MK, pp. 292–294) says nothing of the coming of the Zik and the Karēn to Armenia. He gives a different version of the surrender of Artagers, does not mention the death of Queen Pᶜaṙanjem in Persia, and condenses BP, IV.lv–lvii and V.vii into a single chapter: see below, nn. 8, 23, as well as V.vii and the next note.

3. The account of the Persian capture of Artagers and the conquest of Armenia presents serious problems because of the disagreements between it and the report of these events given by the usually reliable AM, XXVII.xii.5–29 as well as by MX, III.xxxv (= MK, p. 293). The Roman historian does not mention the sending of the Zik and the Karēn from Persia, but speaks rather of two Armenian officials: Cylaces, a former "prefect," and Arrabannes, a former "magister," who deserted to the Persian side. They obtained entrance to the fortress through the blandishments of Cylaces, who was then won back to the Armenian side through pity for its queen. The two deserters led an attack against the Persian besiegers, sought to negotiate with the emperor Valens, and finally fled from Šāhpuhr's wrath to the northwestern Armenian mountains bordering of Lazica, while the Persians captured Artagers with the royal treasure and carried it away, together with the Armenian queen. At a later date, both Cylaces and Arrabannes were executed by Aršak II's son Pap in order to effect his reconciliation with Šāhpuhr II: AM, XXVIII.xii.14; XXX.i.3; see also below, V.i. In the notes to the French translation of BP (= CHAMA, I, p. 273 n. 2), Langlois suggests very tentatively the possibility of identifying AM's Cylaces with BP's Zik and of taking Arrabannes as the personal name of the Karēn. This suggestion, followed by Justi, JIN, p. 385 #2, was categorically rejected by Christensen, *L'Iran*, p. 105 n. 3 and Markwart, *Untersuchungen*, pp. 213–214, and it is indeed improbable. Both AM and BP were familiar with the great Iranian clans of the Zik and the Karēn and could not have confused them with Armenian deserters. Moreover, according to BP, entrance into Artagers was gained not by the Zik (Cylaces) but by a third personage, the Armenian *mardpet* (see below, n. 9). Finally, far from shifting sides, the Zik and the Karēn of the Armenian account were rewarded by Šāhpuhr II for their victory with the governorship of conquered Armenia (IV.lviii) and were eventually killed by the Armenian *sparapet* Mušeł Mamikonean at the time of his victorious restoration of Pap to the Armenian throne (V.i). MX (loc. cit), adds to the confusion by attributing the capture of Artagers, and of Queen Pᶜaṙanjem to the apostates Meružan Arcruni and his uncle Vahan Mamikonean, see V.lviii, lix.

4. See IV.xv. According to AM, XXVII.xii.9–11 whose account is again more complicated that the one found in BP, Pap had first taken refuge at Neocaesarea in Pontus and been sent back with an army commanded by Count Terentius (cf. V.i). He then fled again from the Persians to Lazica, together with Cylaces and Arrabannes, and returned to Armenia a second time. See Malχasyancᶜ (p. 331 n. 134) for the correction of the reading *aṙ tᶜagaworn* in the text to *aṙ tᶜagaworin*.

5. According to AM, XXVII.xii.19, these negotiations were carried on by Cylaces and Arrabannes and not by Mušeł; see below, n. 9. The *Vita* of St. Nersēs, x, p. 67 (= CHAMA, II, p. 33) claims that Mušeł had fled to join St. Nersēs in Edessa; see IV.xiii n. 18, and Adontz, *Armenia*, p. 513 n. 43 on Mušeł.

6. These secret messengers may perhaps be the source of AM's account (XXVII.xii.6–7, 9–10) of Cylaces and Arrabannes' admission to Artagers, their interview with Queen Pᶜaṙanjem, and their negotiations with the emperor Valens for Pap's return to Armenia.

7. See the Venice edition (p. 177 n. 2) for the more probable reading *asēin*, "they spoke" instead of the *gayin*, "they came" of the text, which is presumably a repetition of this word found earlier in the sentence.

8. Only BP attributes the fall of Artagers to a divinely caused plague, which forced the queen to surrender. (Cf. IV.xiii and n. 21 for the similar fate of Aršakawan.) AM, XXVII.vii.12 says that the Persians finally stormed the fortress, "after some battles . . . and the exhaustion of the defenders," while MX, III.xxv (= MK, p. 293) claims that the garrison "refused to wait for news of Pap and surrendered willingly, without compulsion." The entire episode of the siege of Artagers is omitted from the *Vita* of St. Nersēs.

9. Adontz, *Armenia*, p. 513 n. 43 and Markwart, *Untersuchungen*, p. 214, suggest the possibility of identifying AM's Cylaces and Arrabannes with BP's Armenian *hayr-mardpet*, Głak, and the *sparapet*, Mušeł Mamikonean (see above n. 3 and V.vi n. 1 for the *mardpet*'s name). This identification is tempting at first glance, not only because of the similarity of the names Cylaces/Głak; but (2) of AM's insistence that Cylaces was a eunuch, "spado" (XXVII.xii.5), "eunuchus" (xii.6), which would normally have been the case for the *hayr-mardpet* in this period (see Appendix III, *mardpet*, but cf. IV.xiv n. 5); (3) of the *mardpet*'s secret admission to Artagers (IV.lv; V.iii), as was the case of Cylaces (AM, XXVII.xii.6); (4) of Mušeł's association with a *mardpet* (V.xxxii); and (5) of Mušeł's negotiations with "the king of the Greeks," paralleling Cylaces and Arrabannes' overtures to Valens (see above, nn. 3, 5). Nevertheless, this identification is no more satisfactory than the one proposed by Langlois (see above, n. 3): (1) there is no indication anywhere in BP that Mušeł Mamikonean ever favored the Persians, a policy that would run counter to his family's usual pro-imperial inclinations and his entire career (see V.i–ii, iv–v, viii–xx, xxxiv–xxxv); (2) BP clearly distinguishes in this chapter the *hayr-mardpet* of Armenia from the Zik and the Karēn sent from Persia; (3) far from endearing himself to Queen Pʿaṙanjem, as was the case with Cylaces (AM, XXVII.xii.6), the *mardpet* grossly insulted her and was subsequently executed by her son Pap for this reason (V.iii); (4) the *mardpet* associated with Mušeł Mamikonean (V.xxxii) could not be Głak, who had been executed by Pap at an earlier date (V.vi); and finally (5) as noted by Toumanoff (*Studies*, p. 178 n. 118), the anonymous *mardpet* who had insulted the queen and been executed by Pap could under no circumstances be identified with Głak, because BP explicitly states that Głak replaced him as *mardpet* (V.iii).

10. The term *zōravarn*, "commander" found in the text, or preferably the plural, as corrected by Norayr Biwzandacʿi, seems entirely apt, despite the misgivings of Malxasyancʿ (p. 331 n. 135).

11. BP corresponds exactly to AM, XXVII.xii.12 at this point.

12. The destruction of Artašat and the deportation of its population are also recorded by MX, III.xxxv (= MK, p. 293), cf. II.xlix (= MK, pp. 190–191). See also below, n. 20.

13. See Appendix V, c for the variants of this formula.

14. Cf. John 10:14–15, cf. 11; see also V.xxviii n. 24; and IV.lvi–lvii for Zuitʿ's martyrdom.

15. MX, III.xxxv (= MK, p. 293), cf. II.lxv (= MK, p. 211) mentions the deportation of the Jewish population of Vałaršapat, which he derives from the period of Tigran II, while BP records only an unidentified population, (see Khalatiants, *Ēpos*, pp. 335–336). Because both groups are scrupulously mentioned in the cases of the other cities, a lacuna at this point has been suggested by Abełyan, "Aṙaspelner," pp. 559–560; cf. Manandyan, *Trade and Cities*, p. 64 and nn. 52, 53. The formulaic pattern of this account is particularly evident from this point on.

16. MX, III.xxxv (= MK, p. 293) does not mention the capture of Eruandašat or the deportation of its Jewish population, although he is aware of its presence in this city: II.xlix (= MK, pp. 190–191).

17. MX, III.xxxv (= MK, p. 293) does not mention the Persian capture of Zarehawan in Bagrewand: see below, n. 20.

18. MX, *ibid.*, does not mention the capture of Zarišat in Ałiovit: see below, n. 20.

19. The capture of Van-Tosb, "the city of Semiramis" and the deportation of its Jewish population to Persia is also noted by MX III.xxxv (= MK, p. 293), cf. II.xix (= MK,

p. 157). See also next note.

20. The tradition of the settlement of Jews from Palestine in Armenia by King Tigran the Great is also known to MX, II.xvi, xix, xlix, lxv (= MK, pp. 154, 157, 191, 211), although he does not mention their deportation from as many cities as does BP (see above, nn. 12, 15–19, and below, n. 21). Such settlements are entirely possible, given Tigran's campaigns in Syria and possibly Palestine and his practice of shifting conquered population into his urban foundations (see, e.g. the transportation of the Greeks from Mazaka to the new capital of Tigranakert, Strabo, *Georgr.*, XII.ii.9; Plutarch, "Lucullus," xxi.4; xxix.2–4). But as noted by Manandyan, *Trade and Cities*, pp. 64–65, the association of such settlements with the captivity of the high priest Hyrkanos, though traditional in Armenian literature, is both inaccurate and anachronistic, for according to Josephus, *Ant. Jud.*, XIV.xv.1–5, Hyrkanos was deported to Parthia (not Armenia) in 40 B.C., some fifteen years after Tigran's death (56/5 B.C.). See also Appendix I, "Hiwrkandos." For the implications of large foreign populations in the early Armenian cities, see Garsoïan, "Mediaeval Armenian City."

21. There is no mention of the Persian capture of Naxčawan in MX, III.xxxv (= MK, p. 293). See also preceding note.

22. See IV.lviii.

23. There is no mention of the queen's hideous death in either AM or MX, III.xxxv (= MK, p. 293), who records the killing of the other captives in Asorestan and does not mention Xužastan.

IV.lvi

1. MX, III.xxxv (= MK, pp. 293–294) gives a passing mention to the martyrdom of Zuitᶜ, which he attributes to the slander of Meružan Arcruni and Vahan Mamikonean.

2. Cf. IV.lv. None of these details is given by MX (see preceding note). The two chapters concerning Zuitᶜ's martyrdom (IV.lvi–lvii) are probably derived from a current hagiographic account: see Intro., pp. 26–30.

IV.lvii

1. See IV.lvi n. 2. Some mss include this chapter in the preceding one.

2. II Macc. 7:28, cf. III.xiv n. 22; Gen. 2:7, cf. IV.v n. 13.

3. This quotation is taken from the Armenian version, slightly modified, of the Basilian Anaphora. See Gatrčean and Tašean, eds., *Srbazan patarag*, p. 134 line 79; Renoux, "Anaphore," p. 96; and cf. IV.v; V.xxviii and n. 7.

4. MX, III.xxxv (= MK, pp. 293–294) does not mention that Zuitᶜ was a disciple of St. Nersēs, but identifies him as a descendant of the converted Jews of Artašat. See IV.lv n. 20.

5. Ps. 115:13–14, 18. Cf. V.xxiv, xxviii.

IV.lviii

1. There is no mention of Šāhpuhr II's own coming to Armenia in MX, III.xxxv–xxxvi (= MK, pp. 293–294), who speaks only of the sending of Meružan Arcruni and Vahan Mamikonean supported by a large Persian army.

2. See IV.xxiii n. 5.

3. According to MX, III.xxxv (= MK, p. 292), the Armenian magnates took their wives and children along with them when they "fled to the land of the Greeks."

4. See IV.lv.

5. MX.xxxv (= MK, p. 293) transposes this massacre to the extermination of the garrison of Artagers in Asorestan and does not mention the elephants. See IV.xxiii–xxiv and MK, p. 293 n. 6, as well as Appendix V, j.ii, for the similar treatment of Armenia in Meružan Arcruni's first campaign.

6. This episode does not occur in the corresponding section of MX.

7. See III.xxi and especially IV.xx for Andovk's enmity to Persia. Despite BP's categorical statement here, some of the Siwni princes obviously survived (see V.xlii). MX, III.xxviii (= MK, p. 284) links the devastation of Siwnikʿ to the capture of Tigranakert.

8. See IV.xx, where the Persian king is correctly identified as Šāhpuhr II; and III.xx n. 9 and xxi n. 16 for the anachronistic intrusion of Narseh into BP's narrative.

9. MX, III.xxxvi (= MK, p. 294) does not mention Šāhpuhr's installation of the Zik and the Karēn as "rulers" (*išxan*) of Armenia, but only of his entrusting the country to Meružan Arcruni alone, to whom he promised the crown of Armenia if he converted to Zoroastrianism.

IV.lix

1. MX, III.xxxvi (= MK, pp. 294–295) gives a greatly abbreviated and slightly different version of the persecution in Armenia during the governorship of Meružan Arcruni and mentions neither the presence of Vahan Mamikonean nor his death. See below, nn. 2–4, 6.

2. MX, III.xxxvi (= MK, pp. 294–295) adds the burning of Greek books and the prohibition against the use of the Greek language in Armenia to the religious persecution.

3. Note the presence of a pro-Persian party supporting Meružan Arcruni in Armenia and its extirpation by Mušel Mamikonean (V.i).

4. On the problem of Hamazaspuhi's exact relation to the other members of the Mamikonean family, see Malxasyancʿ (p. 322 n. 142) and Appendix I, "Hamazaspuhi." She is not mentioned by MX, III.xxxvi (= MK, pp. 294–295), but he expands the tale of her martyrdom to all the imprisoned wives of the Armenian magnates. The story was still known to TʿA, I.x, p. 63 (*Thom. Arts.*, pp. 127–128). As in the case of Zuitʿ (see IV.lvi n. 2), this tale was presumably derived from a current hagiographic account.

5. *Anakiwłs* ‹ Gk. ἀνάκωλος is a *hapax*. It was presumably a type of short tunic according to NBHL, I, p. 179 and Malxasyancʿ (p. 332 n. 143).

6. There is no mention of fire altars in MX, III.xxxvi (= MK, pp. 294–295), though they are noted by the *Vita* of St. Nersēs, xi, p. 68 (= CHAMA, II, p. 33). The one found under the high altar of the cathedral at Ejmiacin may date from this period—see *Treasures of Ejmiacin* ninth page of plates,—as is probably the case for the newly discovered one in the basilica at Kasaχ. See IV.xxiii for Meružan's apostasy and his promise to build fire temples (*atrušan*) in his domain.

7. There is no mention of Samuēl and his parricide in the corresponding section of MX, who furthermore identifies Ormizduχt as Meružan's wife (see IV.l n. 1). This brief mention in BP, however, is the source of Raffi's famous novel, *Samuēl*.

V.i

1. Malxasyancʿ (p. 332 n. 144) corrects *išxanin*, "prince" into *ašxarhin*, "realm" to conform with the heading in Book IV.

2. The editors of the 1968 Malxasyancʿ edition (p. 229 and note) correct this title in accordance with Matenadaran ms #3079, altering the second phrase to read, "to rule the land of his father Aršak." See below, nn. 3, 4, 7, 12 for the alternate version of Pap's enthronement in MX, III.xxxvi (= MK, p. 295) and the *Vita* of St. Nersēs, xi, p. 68 (= CHAMA, II, p. 33).

3. The Roman emperor contemporary with Pap (369/70–374) was Valens (364–378), but MX, III.xxxv (= MK, p. 295) followed here by the *Vita* of St. Nersēs, xi, p. 68 (= CHAMA, II, p. 33) anachronistically calls him Theodosius (379–395). Cf. V.xxiii n. 3, xxxii n. 1, xxxiv n. 1, xxxvii n. 1, xxxviii n. 2. BP, as is often its wont, leaves the ruler anonymous: cf., e.g., III.xx, etc.

4. The return of Pap to Armenia ca. 369/70 with the support of Count Terentius and an imperial army is known to both Armenian and classical sources. According to MX and the *Vita* of St. Nersēs (see above, nn. 2–3), it was the patriarch Nersēs who interceded with the emperor "Theodosius" and obtained the return of Pap accompanied by Terentius, but with no mention of the Armenian *sparapet* Mušeł Mamikonean, in keeping with MX's customary omission of the activites of this house (see Intro., pp. 44–45). AM, XXVII.xxi.10, 16 speaks of the counts Terentius seconded by Arintheus (*ibid.*, 13) but mentions neither St. Nersēs nor Mušeł Mamikonean. BP's figure of six million for the imperial army is clearly imaginary. AM (XXVII.xii.16) gives Terentius a force of twelve legions, which would result in a maximum of 72,000 men (1 legion = 4,200–6,000 men); see also V.xxxii.

5. As usual, BP underscores the hereditary nature of the great offices passing from generation to generation in the same house without the need of royal sanction through his use of the inchoative verb *linēr*, "he became" (cf. III.xi n. 7). The *Vita* of St. Nersēs, xi, p. 68 (= CHAMA, II, p. 33) confuses matters by making Mušeł's succession dependent on St. Nersēs's intercession with the emperor "Theodosius," which is both anachronistic and impossible in the contemporary Armenian society: see n. 3 and Intro., p. 40.

6. Cf. IV.li (end) for the magnate's disregard of St. Nersēs's injunctions and IV.liv for the repentance of the *sparapet* Vasak Mamikonean.

7. BP stresses the fact that St. Nersēs had been absent from the royal court since the murder of Aršak II's nephew Gnel (see IV.xv and n. 27, and li n. 2) and that he had to be persuaded to return, as against the leading role in the negotiations with the Romans attributed to him by MX and the *Vita* of St. Nersēs (see above, n. 4). MX, III.xxxviii (= MK, pp. 298–299) also attributes the covenant between King Pap and the magnates that restores peace to Armenia to the patriarch's intervention, but BP knows nothing of this.

8. BP stresses throughout the collaboration between the Mamikonean house and the patriarchal house of St. Gregory: Cf. V.iv, St. Nersēs's intercession for the *sparapet* Mušeł; xxiv, St. Nersēs's burial; xxx, Mušeł's lament over St. Nersēs's death.

9. See Malxasyanc^c (p. 322 n. 145), who suggests the translation "boldly" for *lkneal*, adopted here, instead of taking it as a tautology, as is done by the editors of his 1968 edition.

10. See IV.lv nn. 2–3, also lviii and n. 9.

11. See Appendix V, b, c for the repetitions of these formulae.

12. MX, III.xxxvi (= MK, p. 295) does not mention Mušeł's expedition to Daranałik^c or the reconquest of Armenia. He merely notes that Terentius, St. Nersēs and Spandarat Kamsarakan "brought Pap to Armenia."

13. According to Malxasyanc^c's interpretation (322 n. 146), the imperial troops were stationed only in Ełand and Baxišn, as recorded in V.iv, and not deployed throughout Armenia.

14. See IV.xxxi n. 6.

15. See IV.lix and n. 6.

16. See IV.lix and n. 3 for the imprisonment and execution of the magnates' wives by the wardens of the Armenian fortresses, who sided with Meružan Arcruni.

17. See IV.liv for Vasak's death; also next chapter and III.xx n. 8; IV.liv n. 12; V.xxxvii n. 16, for the obligation of the blood feud.

18. See IV.iv.

19. See Appendix III, *ašxarh* and *erkir*, for the different connotations of these terms; also Appendix V, g.

V.ii

1. This entire episode glorifying the Mamikonean is omitted by MX but is repeated by the *Vita* of St. Nersēs, xi, pp. 69–70 (= CHAMA, II, pp. 33–34). Its clearly epic quality indicates its derivation from an oral "Geste of the Mamikonean" in the Iranian tradition. See below nn. 8–9 and Intro, pp. 34–35, 40.

2. See Appendix V, k. i for this alliterative formula.

3. See IV.xxiii n. 5.

4. See also IV.xxv, xxxix for the Sasanian royal encampment at Tabriz, and IV.xv for the *bun banak* of the Armenian Aršakuni at Šahapivan.

5. See Appendix V, b, c for the repetitions of these formulae.

6. The *Vita* of St. Nersēs, xi, p. 69 (= CHAMA, II, p. 33) gives her name as Sit῾ilhořak ‹ ? Arab. *sitti*, "lady"; see HAnjB, IV, p. 491, *St῾i*. This is unlikely, but it was accepted by Patkanean, *Essai*, p. 153. Cf. III.xxi nn. 16, 24; and below, n. 11.

7. See IV.liv also V.i, and n. 17 for Mušeł's similar vengeance.

8. Cf. III.xxi and n. 16 on the similar capture of the Persian harem. Adontz, "Favst" and Melik῾-Ōhanjanyan, "Tiran-Trdati vepə," pp. 66–67, were of the opinion that this episode, like its parallel in III.xxi, was an echo of Galerius's victory of 297 over the king of kings, Narseh, and of the capture of his entire harem on that occasion. The hypothesis is possible, especially in the earlier passage. But the return of the royal harem unharmed was a heroic gesture going back to the chivalry of Alexander the Great vis-à-vis the wives of Darius III after the battle of Issos (Plutarch, "Alexander," xxi) and may well have become an epic cliché. See also below and V.iv, xxxv, for the slander of Mušeł on account of this action.

9. For the apotheosis on horseback of Mušeł according to the classic iconographic representation of the transcendental "glory" and "valor" of the king of kings on Sasanian silver plates, see Harper, *Hunter*; Trever, "Sasanidskoe bliudtse," fig. 3 for the drinking cup of the feasting king; Amiranashvili, "Serebrianaia chasha," figs. 1–4 for a cup on a shallow foot with the representation of a magnate on the inside; also Garsoïan, "Locus," pp. 52–53, 62–64; and V.v n. 5. The late *Vita* of St. Nersēs, xi, pp. 69–70 (= CHAMA, II, pp. 33–34) no longer understands the Iranian ethos of this tale or its significance; hence, it gives a garbled account in which Mušeł's likeness is depicted on a tablet or board instead of a cup, and Šāhpuhr II drinks to the white horse instead of to its heroic rider.

10. Following Norayr Biwzandac῾i, Malχasyanc῾ (p. 333 n. 147) interprets the noun *bašχiš* as › the verb *bašχem*, "apportion."

11. Cf. V.iv.

V.iii

1. This episode is not to be found in either MX or the *Vita* of St. Nersēs.

2. See IV.lv and n. 9.

3. See IV.xiv for the *mardpet*'s coveting of the ecclesiastical domains in Tarōn and Appendix I, "Mamikonean," for the Mamikonean control of this district.

4. See IV.liv n. 9 on the identity of the *mardpet*.

V.iv

1. Both MX, III.xxxvii (= MK, pp. 296–298) and the *Vita* of St. Nersēs, xi, pp. 70–82 (= CHAMA, II, pp. 34–36) confuse or conflate this battle with the one called Jiraw by MX which is described in the next chapter of BP: see V.v n. 1. Cf. also Koriwn, v, p. 40 (= trans., p. 28).

2. See V.i n. 13.

3. The *Vita* of St. Nersēs, xi, p. 71 (= CHAMA, II, p. 34) calls Uṙnayr king of the "Honkʿ"; see IV.xx n. 18 and xxi n. 2 for the earlier collaboration of the Caspian Albanians with the Persians.

4. See Appendix V, j.iii for this formula; also Appendix III, *kʿaǰ aṙancʿ*.

5. See IV.xx n. 12.

6. The *Vita* of St. Nersēs, xi, p. 71 (= CHAMA, II, p. 34) puts this speech into the mouth of Manuēl Mamikonean, who was at the Persian court according to this account: cf. *ibid.*, x, pp. 67–68 (= CHAMA, II, p. 33) and V.xxxvii. In view of the warning sent to Mušeł immediately thereafter, and of the unrelievedly negative portrayal of Meružan Arcruni in BP, a *lapsus* in the present text requiring the corresponding correction seems reasonable, though it has not been proposed as far as I know.

7. Malχasyancʿ (p. 333 n. 148) corrects the reading χosecʿeal found in some of the mss and in the St. Petersburg edition (p. 162) to the more reasonable χałacʿeal, "set out/advance/march," given by the Venice edition (p. 198 n. 2).

8. Malχasyancʿ (p. 333 n. 149) corrects the reading yałtʿans found in a number of mss and the St. Petersburg edition (p. 162) to the far more understandable Ałuankʿ, "Albanians" found in one ms (St. Petersburg edition, p. 162 n. 1) and noted in the Venice edition (p. 198 n. 3).

9. This use of Roman prisoners as workmen in palaces and cities parallels the Sasanian practice at Bišāhpuhr, Gundēšāhpuhr, and "Caesar's dam" at Šustar. See Christensen, *L'Iran*, pp. 127, 220–221; Pigulevskaia, *Villes*, pp. 127 *et al.*

10. See IV.iii and n. 2 for the "lords with contingents and banners."

11. See V.ii and n. 8.

12. See V.i n. 8 and below.

13. Cf. IV.xv and n. 36 and Appendix V, j, iii.

14. See IV.liv; below, n. 39; also Intro., pp. 34, 38 and n. 153 on the loyalty of the Mamikonean to their Aršakuni lords.

15. The stance of Nersēs is that of Moses at the battle of Raphidim (Exod. 17:8–13), as is explicitly noted by MX, III.xxxvii (= MK, p. 297), though he does not record the patriarch's prayer. A version of it is to be found in the *Vita* of St. Nersēs, xi, pp. 74–78, but it is omitted in the French translation (CHAMA, II, p. 35); cf. also Koriwn, v, p. 40, ll. 15–17 (= trans. p. 28).

16. Acts 20:28; cf. Gatrčean and Tašean, eds., *Srbazan patarag*, p. 144 lines 156–157; Renoux, "Anaphore," p. 101, and the repetitions below.

17. Ps. 41:11, 78:10; Joel 2:17. See also Eusebius of Caesarea, E.H., V.i.60 and Ełišē, vii, p. 149 (= *Ełishē*, p. 199).

18. See V.v and n. 16.

19. Malχasyancʿ (p. 333 n. 150, followed by the editors of his 1968 edition) suggested that the χlecʿer of some of the mss and the St. Petersburg edition (p. 164) should be translated "you have destroyed/uprooted," while the Venice edition (p. 200 and n. 1), following other mss has χabecʿir, "you have deceived," which seems preferable. Moreover, in the next phrase, Malχasyancʿ suggested that the asacʿi . . . bans of the text is a distortion of asacʿi . . . bam, "I said that," where the confusion between the erkatʿagir captials, M [*Ա*] and S [*Ս*] led to an incorrect bas, and subsequently bans.

20. Ps. 40:2, cf. 26:12. The French translaton omits the remainder of the homily to the end of the paragraph (CHAMA, I, p. 282).

21. II Macc. 7:28; cf. Ps. 94:4; and III.xiv n. 22.

22. Is. 40:22.

23. Is. 40:12–13 with modifications; cf. AaT, cclvii.

24. Cf. I Macc. 2:49, "ays isk ē žamanak kštambutʿean ew yandimanutʿean," which must underlie BP's "zi deṙ ayšmik žamanak ē kštambutʿean ew žamanak yandimanutʿean" (p. 201); cf. AaT, dxxxiii/17–18.

25. I Cor. 2:16, with minor alterations.

26. Rom. 11:36, with one transposition.

27. This entire quotation is taken from the doxology of the three Hebrew youths in the fiery furnace (Dan. 3:27–45), which is part of the canon of the Armenian Old Testament. Nonetheless, the quotation in BP does not follow precisely the wording in the book of Daniel, but rather the liturgical version of the order for morning hours in the *Horologion* (*Žamagirkˤ*) of the Armenian church (Jerusalem, 1955, pp. 212–216). Cf. Winkler, "Night Office II," pp. 500–505 and Renoux, "A Propos," pp. 593–598. Malχasyancˤ (p. 333 n. 152) identified the quotation from Daniel but omitted it from his translation, into which it was inserted by the editors of the 1968 edition. The quotation from the *Žamagirkˤ* rather than from the Scriptures was called to my attention by R. Ervine.

28. This phrase is an intrusion from Ps. 118:39, cf. 18:11, into the quotation from Daniel. See also IV.v and n. 42; AaT, dxxxvii.

29. Cf. Eccl. 7:21 and Appendix V, c.

30. This is a quotation from the Armenian version of the Basilian Anaphora, which includes II Macc. 7:28. See Gatrčean and Tašean, eds., *Srbazan patarag*, p. 120 lines 3–4; Renoux, "Anaphore," p. 88; cf. V.xxviii and n. 7.

31. Cf. Matt. 7:6, modified; cf. above, n. 16.

32. A distant recall of the formula in Appendix V, d.

33. See below, n. 35. The account of Mušeł's mercy, though not his exact words, is found in the *Vita* of St. Nersēs, xi, pp. 79–82 (= CHAMA, II, p. 35).

34. Anasyan, *Review*, p. 18 gives the correction "he is plotting [lit. lying in wait for] thy death," for the phrase "*ew kˤez mahu spasē*" as opposed to the "he is awaiting thy death," of Malχasyancˤ (p. 241) and Gevorgian (p. 153).

35. Cf. V.ii, xxxv.

36. Cf. Manuēl Mamikonean's claim of equality with King Varazdat (V.xxxvii and n. 13), which may rather belong in the epic world; but see below, n. 38.

37. This is the most emphatic assertion in BP of the sanctity of kingship. Cf. V.v and xxxvii for Manuēl Mamikonean's sparing of King Varazdat; also below n. 41 and Intro., pp. 34, 38 and n. 153 on the loyalty of the Mamikonean house.

38. Cf. V.xxxvii for the tradition of the Mamikonean descent from the kings of the Čenkˤ and Appendix I, "Čenkˤ" for their identity. The use of the epithet *kˤaj aṙancˤ* in this context may therefore suggest both the royal status and the apotheosis of the Mamikonean. See Appendix III, *kˤaj aṙancˤ* and Intro., p. 34; but cf. the two preceding notes.

39. See Mušeł's oath, above; also IV.liv for Vasak and V.xliv for the deathbed advice of Manuēl to his sons.

40. See above, n. 34.

41. See above, nn. 14, 37.

V.v

1. See the preceding chapter, n. 1, for the confusion of this battle with the one at the foot of Mt. Npat in both MX and the *Vita* of St. Nersēs. MX, III.xxxvii (= MK, p. 296 and nn. 2–5) is the only one to give the name Jiraw to the site of the battle, to shift the command of the Armenian forces from its normal commander-in-chief, Mušeł Mamikonean, whom he ignores entirely, to the *aspet* Smbat Bagratuni, and to introduce an otherwise unknown *magister peditum* as well as Spandarat Kamsarakan and the king of the Łek. See below, nn. 3–4.

2. See the preceding chapter.

3. According to BP, this *stratelates* or *magister militum* was Terentius (see below), but MX, III.xxxvii (= MK, p. 296) calls him Gorgonos. See above, n. 1.

4. From this point on the chapter clearly leaves its factual, historical setting to rely on an oral source with characteristic repetitions, refrains, and anachronisms; its imaginary

310

soliloquy attributed to Šāhpuhr II; and a familiarity with the ethos and traditions of Zoroastrian Iran and Pre-Christian Armenia (see below, nn. 5–8, 12, 16, 18). None of these aspects, with one exception (see below, n. 10), is to be found in the corresponding passage of MX, III.xxxvii (= MK, pp. 296–298 and nn. 6, 8), which relies on Biblical and Patristic rather than Iranian imagery for its description of the battle. A dim and confused memory of some of its elements lingers in the *Vita* of St. Nersēs, xv, p. 117 (= CHAMA, II, p. 43), which, however, places them after the death of both St. Nersēs and King Pap. See below, n. 6.

5. The Armenian spearmen's unhorsing of their Persian opponents before the very eyes of their king is all the more humiliating and portentous in that riding was the hallmark of the hero in the Iranian tradition. The iconography of the king in the fullness of his glory represented him on horseback, while the man on foot was disgraced not only socially but morally. Cf. Justinus, *Epitome*, XVI.iii.4, p. 224/5, "Hoc denique discrimen inter servos liberosque est, quod servi pedibus, liberi non nisi equis incedunt." One of the first apocalyptic signs in Zoroastrian eschatological literature was that "a horseman will become a man on foot and the man on foot a horseman," *Jāmasp Nāmag* #35. See also III.viii n. 5; IV.xxiv n. 13; and V.ii n. 9.

6. *Aṙ* may be translated as either the preposition "to" or the second person singular imperative of the verb *aṙnum*, "take." In view of the insistence of the context that the slain were offered as sacrifices *to* Aršak, the first reading has been preferred, but both versions are possible without any appreciable change in meaning. See above, n. 4, for the presence of this element in the *Vita* of St. Nersēs.

7. The substitution here of *aṙaǰi*, "former" for *kʻaǰi*, "valiant" found in some mss and the St. Petersburg edition (p. 168; cf. the Venice edition, p. 206 n. 1) obscures the epic ethos of this entire section and must be a later *lapsus*. See also the next note.

8. The insistence on Aršak's "valor" (*kʻaǰutʻiwn*), with its allusion to the god Vǝrǝ-θraγna/Vahagn (see Appendix III, *kʻaǰ*) reinforces the hypothesis that this part of the chapter is composed of a paraphrase and possibly even of quotations from an epic or paean to Aršak II that was still current in the oral literature of the period; see above, n. 4.

9. The rendition into Armenian of the Latin military term *legio* suggests the oral survival of an anachronistic or at best obsolescent term; see also below, n. 13. The sense of an infantry unit, as opposed to the more usual contemporary cavalry detachment, is always preserved: see V.xxxii and Appendix III, *zōrkʻ*.

10. The image of the "fortified city" is the only one that occurs in the account of MX, III.xxxvii, who probably borrowed it from BP: see Thomson, MK, p. 296 n. 4.

11. The usual *topos* of the flight of the Persian king alone on a single horse (see Appendix V, d) is unexpectedly missing here. The *Vita* of St. Nersēs, xi, p. 79 (= CHAMA, II, p. 35) has Šāhpuhr disguise himself and hide in a cave.

12. This improbable soliloquy, which is yet another repetition of the already twice-described battle, would occur normally in an oral recitation but not in a written text. It is found neither in MX nor in the *Vita* of St. Nersēs. Cf. IV.xx n. 11.

13. The use here of the more classically correct *Hoṙomkʻ*, "Romans" instead of the commonly used *Yoynkʻ*, "Greeks" elsewhere in the text, again suggests an anachronistic memory orally transmitted; see above, n. 9.

14. See IV.xx n. 12.

15. See Intro., pp. 34, 44 and n. 153, on the loyalty of the Mamikonean. The phrase "faithful devotion" (*mtermutʻiwn miamtutʻeann*) is probably an allusion to the alliterative characterization of the Armenian army. See Appendix V, k.i and below, n. 19, for a repetition.

16. The image of the fire coursing "in the reeds" is an evocation of the fiery epiphany of the god Vahagn from the scarlet reed in the sea, described in the fragment of a Pre-Christian poem preserved in MX, I.xxxi (= MK, p. 123). Even the wording of the poem (MX, I.xxxi, p. 86 line 2), ". . . *ǝnd ełegan pʻoł bocʻ elanēr*," is echoed in BP's description

of the Armenian contingent, "*hur bocʿ i gndēn elanicʿēr . . . orpēs bocʿ ǝnd ełēgn.*" As such, it is yet another recall of Armenia's Zoroastrian past and of the "valor" (*kʿajutʿiwn*) that Vahagn bestowed on its kings. See IV.xxiv n. 12 and Garsoïan, "Substratum," pp. 157–164. The image is preserved in the *Vita* of St. Nersēs, xi, p. 73 (= CHAMA, II, p. 33), but it no longer understands the symbolic meaning of Vahagn passing through the fiery reed at his birth and gives the more prosaic explanation of a blaze devouring reeds. A reminiscent image, but without symbolic implications, also occurs in Ełišē, v, pp. 116–117 (= *Ełishē*, p. 169), and in Sebēos, iii, pp. 79–80 (= Macler tr., p. 21).

17. See IV.liv and V.vii.

18. The "real" presence of Aršak II on the battlefield provides another link between this passage and the Iranian epic tradition, in which the royal glory (*pʿaṙkʿ*) of the legitimate ruler can manifest itself protectively even away from him (cf. IV.xxiv and n. 12). The "glory" invoked is that of Aršak, not only because of the source of this passage is a part of his "Geste," but because the evil nature of the reigning king, Pap, would deprive him of this blessing in the Zoroastrian tradition. Cf. IV.xliv; V.xxii; and Garsoïan, "Prolegomena," cols. 184–186; *idem*, "Locus," pp. 42–45.

19. *miaban miamit*; see above, n. 15, for another version of this formula and Appendix V, k.i. MX, III.xxxvii (= MK, p. 298) places Smbat Bagratuni's capture and execution of Meružan Arcruni at the end of this battle (cf. below, V.xliii), while the *Vita* of St. Nersēs, xi, pp. 80–81 (= CHAMA, II, p. 35) adds a miracle performed by St. Nersēs.

V.vi

1. This episode is known to neither MX nor the *Vita* of St. Nersēs. See IV.lv n. 9 for the identity of the *mardpet*s and V.iii on the appointment of Głak. The form Dłak for Głak seems to be a *lapsus*. See Appendix I, "Głak."

2. Epʿrikean, *Baṙaran*, p. 843 takes *ǝnǰin* as a proper name. Ačaryan in HArmB, III, pp. 604–605, *unǰ* equates it with *ganj*, "base/floor" and suggests that the word *berd*, "fortress" may be missing here, since all the villages in the district of Ayrarat would necessarily be royal, as it was the Aršakuni's own domain.

3. See III.xxi n. 19 on the granting and taking away of honorific robes; also below, V.vii, Garsoïan, "Prolegomena," col. 219 n. 62, and Appendix III, *patmučan*.

4. Malχasyancʿ (p. 334 n. 144) notes that the word of presumably unknown origin, given as *drats* in the Venice edition (p. 209) and *drasts* in the St. Petersburg edition (p. 171 n. 1), also occurs under the forms *drast*, *grat*, and *grast*. See HArmB, I, pp. 603–604, *grat*. It presumably referred to a voluminous upper garment.

5. The excessive size of the *mardpet*'s garments obviously serves the purpose of the story, but it also recalls the ample robes of the Sasanian king at Taq-i Bostān, of the Parthian figures from Palmyra and Matheira, and of those on the ivory plaques from Olbia. See Ghirshman, *Persian Art*, figs. 290, 349, 351–352, 361; also Seyrig, "Armes," pp. 47–54.

6. As observed by Malχasyancʿ (p. 334 n. 156), the origin of the word *nran* is not known. He presumes it to have been a short sword or dagger (see HArmB, III, p. 477). The latter hypothesis is correct because the *nran* seems to have been worn strapped to the right thigh. Cf. V.xxxii for the case of King Pap. See Tiracʿyan, "Utochnenie," pp. 485–486 and fig. 6; Garsoïan, "Armement" and Appendix III, *zēn*, f.

7. This the only description in BP of actual buildings, as opposed to the tents (IV.xv) or hunting pavilions (III.viii and n. 5) in which the king normally resided. There are, however, allusions to the palace built or merely planned in the ill-fated city of Aršakawan (IV.xii and n. 8) and the equally abortive plans of the *mardpet* at Aštišat (IV.xiv); cf. also V.xxiv. In the present case, the plan and permanence of the complex also remain highly problematic. The most that can be said of it is that it apparently consisted of a series of

separate units—the royal hall, royal residences, the house of the wardrobe—strung together by passageways, and that it was in no sense a unified structure.

V.vii

1. The accounts of Aršak II's death vary. MX, III.xxxv (= MK, p. 294), followed by the *Vita* of St. Nersēs, x, pp. 67–68 (= CHAMA, II, p. 33), says that the king killed himself with his own sword like Saul (I Kgs. 31:4; I Chron. 10:4), and both ignore the lengthy episode of Drastamat altogether. AM, XXVII.xii.3 merely says that Aršak was tortured at a fortress named Agabana after being blinded and was then executed "by the penal steel." Procopius, *Bell. Pers.*, I.v.30–40 repeats almost exactly the account of BP, though he gives the name of the Persian king incorrectly and ignores both the K⸜ušans and Drastamat: see IV.liv nn. 8, 15.

2. See IV.liv.

3. The attack of the K⸜ušan in the middle of the reign of Šāhpuhr II is historically accurate: see Markwart, *Ērānšahr*, p. 50. BP links them to the Arsacids, while the invaders were presumably Chionites: see Frye, *Heritage*, pp. 216–218; Bivar, "Eastern Iran," pp. 211–213; and Appendix I, "K⸜ušan."

4. For the mustering of the Armenian magnates and especially of the renowned cavalry for distant expeditions, a practice that continued even in Arab times, see also below, V.xxxvii, and for the cavalry clause in the treaty with the Arabs, see Sebēos, xlviii, p. 164 (= Macler tr. p. 133).

5. Malχasyanc⸜ (p. 334 n. 158) follows EM in proposing to correct the *išχan tan gawaṙin* of the text to *Angeɫtan gawaṙin*. But this correction is unnecessary, as was observed by the editors of the 1968 edition, for the fortress of Angeɫ was a royal domain and the word *tun* can reasonably be taken in that sense. On the reunion of the office of *hayr-mardpet* entrusted with the supervision of the royal fortresses and the treasures they contained with the princedom of Angeɫtun in the person of Drastamat, and the problems raised by Adontz and Markwart, see the solution proposed by Toumanoff, *Studies*, pp. 177–179 and nn. 118–120, and Appendix III, *mardpet*.

6. From here to the end of the chapter, BP's account, with its Iranian ethos and setting and its improbable dialogue, must rely on an oral source, possibly a threnody for Aršak reinforced by the *topos* of the faithful retainer. This is the only occasion in BP in which the *mardpet* is presented in a favorable light by contrast to the evil figures of III.xviii; IV.xiv, liv; and V.iii, vi. It is also, with the one exception of III.viii and n. 14, the only other time that the epic epithet *k⸜aǰ* is used for an individual outside the royal Aršakuni and Mamikonean houses, or with reference to the saints; cf., e.g., III.iii n. 8. In this period eunuchs were not characterized as effeminate; cf. Justinian's general Narses (Procopius, *Bell. Pers.*, I.xii. 21–22, xxv.24; II.xxv.11, 20–24, etc.), and above, IV.xiv and n. 5.

7. See III.xxi n. 19 and V.vi n. 3 for the grant or withdrawal of honorific robes.

8. Malχasyanc⸜ (p. 334 n. 160), followed by Gevorgian (p. 160), proposed to correct the *k⸜an* of the text to *or aynk⸜an* and to attach it to the preceding sentence, which then would close with the phrase, "who has caused us so much trouble." As rightly noted by the editors of the 1968 edition, however, these words cannot refer to Aršak II but must be addressed to Drastamat, because the verb is in the second person singular. This is also the sense in which the passage is taken by Emin (CHAMA, I, p. 286, approximately) and Lauer (p. 164).

9. See IV.xv n. 29, xvi n. 3, and Appendix III, *barj* and *bazmakan*.

10. For the presence of *gusan*s, "minstrels/bards" at banquests, see also V.xxxii and Appendix III, s.v.

11. As observed by Malχasyanc⸜ (p. 334 n. 161), following the NBHL, I, p. 70 and HArmB I, pp. 156–157, the precise meaning of the word *amič*, which also occurs in Eɫišē,

cannot be ascertained. It seems to have been a choice dish, perhaps of meat or game.

12. The original mood of the closing episode of Aršak's suicide, followed by that of Drastamat, seems to have been one of epic pride, compassion, and loyalty (see above, n. 6). But in view of the hostility of the Christian compiler to the king (see Intro., pp. 6, 9), Aršak's death through Judas's ultimate sin of suicide may be the fulfillment of the curse laid upon him by St. Nersēs for the murder of Gnel (IV.xv and n. 26). See also III.xx n. 17 and n. 16 for the critical setting of the banquet. MX, III.xxxv (= MK, p. 294) notes at this point that Aršak II "had reigned for thirty years," thus creating one of the major chronological problems of fourth-century Armenia. Cf. III.xxi n. 23; *et al.*; BP gives no specific length for his reign.

V.viii

1. The next twelve chapters (V.viii–xix), concerning the temporary reconquest by Mušeł Mamikonean of the Marchlands of Greater Armenia lost after the Roman–Persian peace of 363 (IV.l and n. 3) and forming a parallel to the victories of Mušeł's father Vasak (IV.xxvi–xliii, xlv–xlix), are understandably omitted by MX because they redound to the glory of the Mamikonean house (see Intro., pp. 44–45). He merely observes tersely, III.xxxviii (= MK, pp. 298–299), that at the urging of St. Nersēs the princes made a covenant with the king whereby "they would no more rebel . . . but would serve him sincerely." The *Vita* of St. Nersēs, xi, p. 82 (= CHAMA, II, p. 36) is even terser. For the composition of Greater Armenia between 363 and ca. 387, when the reconquered territories were again lost after the partition of the Armenian kingdom; see Eremyan, *Ašχarh.*, p. 118*; Hewsen "Armenia," VI.i n. 10, the next note, and the maps at the end of this volume.

2. For the northern borders of Greater Armenia see Aa, dcccxlii and n. 12; and Toumanoff, *Studies*, pp. 458–460 n. 98, as well as the preceding note, V.xiii, xv and map.

3. From here to the very end of his narrative, BP never mentions the name of the Persian king except in retrospect (e.g. V.xxxv, xxxvii). The phrase normally used hereafter is "the Persian king" (*tʿagawor Parsicʿ*) or the awkward form, "the Sasanian king of Persia" (*tʿagawor Parsicʿ sasanakanin*) (V.xxxvii). With the closing of the great reign of Šāhpuhr II in 379 and the rapid succession of Ardašīr II (379–383), Šāhpuhr III (383–388), and Bahrām IV (388–399), BP no longer seems to be certain of the identity of the Persian rulers. See Benveniste, *Titres et noms propres*, p. 14, for the form *sasanakan.*

4. Atrpatakan was part of the Persian empire and governed by a *marzpan* even though the Armenian Arsacids possessed domains along the border (IV.l). BP insists throughout that the Armeno-Persian frontier was at or near Ganjak of Atrpatakan (cf. III.vii n. 5; xx n. 3, end; IV.xvi n. 2). The lands referred to must have been the territories lost to Persia in 363; but see next note.

5. Malχasyancʿ (p. 334 n. 162) notes the variations in the region's name with the evolution k › č. The earlier variant t/y is also observable throughout. But Eremyan, *Map* D6–7, distinguishes the district of Atrpatičkʿ along the eastern shore of Lake Urmiah, which he considers to have been the Aršakuni royal domain in Atrpatakan. See Appendix II, "Atrpatakan."

6. This phrase, with minor variatons, becomes a refrain in the catalog of Mušeł's reconquests; see Appendix V, f.

V.ix

1. See IV.l and V.viii n. 1.
2. See V.viii n. 6.

V.x

1. See IV.l. and V.viii n. 1.
2. See V.viii n. 6.

V.xi

1. See IV.l.
2. See V.viii n. 6.

V.xii

1. See IV.l
2. See V.viii n. 6.

V.xiii

1. See V.iv and Appendix II, "Ałuankᶜ" for the antagonism between Albania and Armenia in this period and the struggle over the control of the Marchlands south of the Kur River. See also IV.xxi and n. 2; V.iv; and next note.
2. This chapter is our main source for the brief reconquest of the Armeno-Albanian Marchlands all the way to the Kur River by Mušeł Mamikonean ca. 370/1. These lands reverted to Albania with the Armenian partition of ca. 387.
3. See V.viii n. 6.

V.xiv

1. See IV.l.
2. Malχasyancᶜ (pp. 334–335 n. 163) follows EM in correcting the "Parsicᶜ" of the text to "Kaspicᶜ" on the basis of the information in IV.l, the title of this chapter, and the fact that the city and district of Pᶜaytakaran/Balasakan were known to classical authors as "Kaspianē"; see Strabo, *Geogr.* XI.iv.5. But Neuman, "Die Fahrt," p. 174, has suggested that the reference here is to the "Parsioi" of Strabo, *ibid.*, XI.vii.1, though this hypothesis seems less likely.
3. See V.viii n. 6.

V.xv

1. There is no previous explicit statement in BP of the antagonism between Iberia/ Virkᶜ and Armenia; cf, however, III.vi–vii and Appendix II, "Virkᶜ."
2. This statement is probably an exaggeration since AM, XXVII.xii.16, speaks rather of the division of Iberia under the emperor Valens ca. 371 between a Roman and a Persian candidate.
3. See Appendix V, b for the repetitions of this formula.
4. The reference to the Pᶜaṙnabazid dynasty of Iberia is anachronistic, since the last descendant of this family had vanished long since and had been replaced first by Arsacids and subsequently by Iranian Mihranids or Chosroids at the turn of the fourth-century; see Toumanoff, *Studies*, pp. 80–84 and n. 105; and Appendix II, "Virkᶜ."
5. The execution of the *bdeašχ* of Gugarkᶜ marked the extinction of the local Gušarid

315

dynasty ca. 371 and the subsequent succession in Gugark' of another branch of the Iranian Mihranid dynasty already ruling in Iberia: see Toumanoff, *Studies*, p. 187 and Appendix II, "Gugark'."

6. See V.viii n. 6.

7. See V.xiii for the parallel reconquest of the Albanian Marchlands to the Kur River. Both reconquests were lost after the Armenian partition, ca. 387: see Appendix II, "Virk'."

V.xvi

1. Malxasyanc' (p. 335 n. 164) corrects the reading *t'agaworin*, "king" of the text to *gawaṙin*, "district," which is found in the Table of Contents. This correction is possible but hardly necessary, for the semi-autonomous "great *bdeašx*" of Ałjnik is the subject of the chapter. Cf. III.ix n. 2.

2. See III.ix and IV.l.

3. Note the plural as a possible indication of the survival of polygamy in fourth-century Armenia; cf. III.xxi n. 24; IV.xv n. 40.

4. See V.viii n. 6, and xiv for Kazbk', where *ostikan*s were also installed by Mušeł Mamikonean.

V.xvii

1. See IV.l.

2. See Appendix V, b for the repetitions of this formula.

3. See V.viii n. 6.

V.xviii

1. Angełtun is not mentioned in IV.l as having rebelled ca. 363.

2. See Appendix V, b for the repetitions of this formula.

3. As a former royal domain (*ostan*) the fortresses of which were held by the *mardpet* (see V.vii n. 5 and Appendix III, *mardpet*), Angełtun presumably returned to the *status quo ante*, so that its tribute was normative rather than punitive, as it was in the rebellious districts ruled by local dynasts, e.g. V.vii–xvii, xix.

V.xix

1. See IV.l.

2. See Appendix V, b for the repetitions of this formula.

3. See V.viii n. 6.

V.xx

1. Cf. V.ii, iv–v for the rest of the panegyric of Mušeł Mamikonean, and the next note, as well as V.xlii for the parallel encomiun on Manuēl.

2. See Intro., pp. 34, 38 and n. 153 for the parallel catalogs of virtues usually associated with the Mamikonean house in BP.

316

V.xxi

1. This chapter, which is a summary of the second half of IV.iv, is not found in MX; neither is it repeated in the *Vita* of St. Nersēs.

2. Malχasyancᶜ (p. 335 n. 165), following Norayr Biwzandacᶜi, corrects the *yanjn arnēr* of the text to *yanjanjēr*, "he provided for/cared for." This reading has been adopted here, but the alternative, "he took it upon himself," is equally acceptable in context.

3. See IV.iii n. 12, for the title of "protector of the destitute," which is implied but not repeated here.

4. Following the reading of one of the Venice mss (see Venice ed. p. 218, n. 1), Malχasyancᶜ (p. 335 n. 166) corrects the difficulty understandable *yōrēnsn*, "lawful" of the text to *yanōrēnsn*, "unrighteous," which seems far more acceptable, although the editors of the 1968 edition have returned to the former reading of the text.

5. These blessings and anathemata are the one element not present in IV.iv; but cf. IV.xv and li for St. Nersēs's curse of Aršak II and of the rebellious *naχarars*, and V.vii and IV.liv for their fulfillment. The *Vita* of St. Nersēs, xii, p. 84 (= CHAMA, II, p. 36) adds to this catalog a cure with a sign of the cross of a plague such as destroyed Aršakawan.

V.xxii

1. This chapter is the counterpart of the misplaced one in Book IV.xliv. The description of Pap's iniquities here, and in the next two chapters leading up to his murder of St. Nersēs, is obviously in its proper place in the sequence of events. It occurs at the same point in MX, III.xxxviii (= MK, p. 299), although he reduces it to a single sentence, and in the *Vita* of St. Nersēs, xii, pp. 83–84 (= CHAMA, II, p. 36), which follows the account of BP.

2. See IV.xliv nn. 3, 7, for a possible contradiction; and IV.xv n. 42, for the incoherent treatment of Queen Pᶜaṙanjem in BP.

3. The representation of Pap with the two snakes rising around his shoulders is identical (except for their color) with the Iranian one of the bedeviled and evil Aždahak or Zohhak (*Šāhnāme*, iv, I, pp. 44–45). The story of the evil king with his familiars was obviously current in Armenia, since MX refers to it in the section interpolated between Books I and II (= MK, pp. 126–128), even though he calls it a "ridiculous fable." It was still remembered as late as the eleventh century, as evidenced in *Letter* xxxvi of Gregory Magistros. See Khalatiants, *Arshakidy*, pp. 118, 372; Čᶜugaszyan, "*Byuraspi, Aždahaki aṙaspelnerə*"; and *idem*, "Echos," pp. 323–324.

4. See IV.xliv nn. 5–6. Gevorgian (p. 165) omits the remainder of this chapter, as is also the case for IV.xliv (p. 121). This part is summarized only in Emin (CHAMA, I p. 290).

5. See IV.xliv n. 4.

V.xxiii

1. See V.xxii n. 1 for the condensation of this and the preceding chapter in MX and the *Vita* of St. Nersēs.

2. Cf. III.xii for the similar defiance of the king, which precipitated the murder of the patriarch Yusik.

3. MX, III.xxxviii (= MK, p. 299) names the emperor "Theodosius" (379–395), even though these events must date from 373 (see V.i n. 3 and xxiv n. 13). For the hypothesis that St. Nersēs's support against his king came from the imperial commanders in Armenia rather than from the emperor Valens himself, see Garsoïan, "Politique," pp. 313–320.

4. All the Armenian sources agree that King Pap hid his hostility toward St. Nersēs, cf. *Vita* of St. Nersēs, xii, p. 84 (= CHAMA, II, p. 36).

V.xxiv

1. MX, III.xxxviii (= MK, p. 299) reduces St. Nersēs's death and burial to three sentences. On the contrary, the *Vita* of St. Nersēs, xii–xiv, pp. 87–113 (= CHAMA, II, pp. 37–42) elaborates extensively on the version of BP, which it follows. See below, nn. 6, 10, 13, 14, 16.

2. Cf. V.xxiii and n. 4.

3. As noted by Malχasyanc' (p. 335 n. 167), the word *kotind* is a *hapax* of unknown origin and meaning. It has been interpreted as either a type of cup or, preferably, a form of drink into which the poison could be admixed. Cf. HArmB, II, pp. 640–641.

4. Ps. 115:13; cf. IV.lvii and V.xxviii.

5. Col. 1:12, with the alteration of one word.

6. The *Vita* of St. Nersēs, xii, pp. 85–86 (= CHAMA, II, p. 36) elaborates slightly, though it follows BP closely at this point.

7. Malχasyanc' (p. 335 n. 168), followed by Gevorgian (p. 220 n. 86), attempted to give a natural explanation of St. Nersēs's death attributing it to the rupture of a pulmonary artery, which might produce the symptoms described. According to them, Pap was falsely accused of murdering the patriarch because of his subsequent destruction of Nersēs's charitable foundations (V.xxxi).

8. *tiwrakēs* = Gk. θηρίακος was considered an antidote against animal poisons and snakebites. It was attributed to Mithridates of Pontus. See Pliny the Elder, NH, XXIX.iv.21 #70. See also the preceding note.

9. Ps. 15:6.

10. The *Vita* of St. Nersēs, xii–xiv, pp. 87–113 (= CHAMA, II, pp. 37–42) elaborated St. Nersēs's last speech into a messianic prophecy of the fall of the Aršakuni dynasty, the end of the Gregorid house, the capture of the relic of the Holy Cross by the Persians, the fall of Jerusalem to the "Ismaelites," the coming of the "nation of the archers," the salvation of Christendom by the "Roman forces," the reign of the Antichrist, and the Second Coming of Christ. This prophecy was to have great currency in medieval and even early modern Armenia; see Johanisyan, *Israel Ory*, pp. 11–24. The *Vita* of St. Nersēs, xiv, pp. 104–105 (= CHAMA, II, p. 40), also adds a blessing of the Mamikonean house by the patriarch that is not found in BP.

11. These details are not found in the other sources and serve as the basis for Malχasyanc''s hypothesis: see above, n. 7. This is also the only occasion in BP that the term *gund* is used in its basic sense of "mass, ball, globe" rather than its usual military connotation: see Appendix III, s.v.

12. Acts 7:58–59.

13. Cf. Matt. 27:50. The *Vita* of St. Nersēs, xiv, pp. 112–113, 115 (= CHAMA, II, pp. 41–42), specifies that the patriarch died on a Thursday in the month of Hrotic' and, together with MX, III.xxxviii (= MK, p. 299) attributes to him a patriarchate of thirty-four years. This figure agrees with that of most Armenian sources (see Garitte, *Narratio*, pp. 74, 417), but it cannot be reconciled with fourth-century chronology or the successive generations of the Gregorid house. A pontificate of twenty years is the most probable, between 353 and 373, despite Baynes's attempt to push its beginning back to 340, "Rome and Armenia," pp. 187–193. See Ōrmanean, *Azgapatum*, I, cols. 168–169, xvi and Garso-ïan, "*Quidam Narseus.*"

14. See IV.iii and n. 15. The *Vita* of St. Nersēs does not mention the presence of this personage at St. Nersēs's burial.

15. Xaχ is called a "village" (*gewł*) at this point, but it is also referred to as a "town" (*awan*) here and at the beginning of the chapter. Consequently, it is possible that Pap's palace (*aparan*) there was more in the nature of a hunting pavilion (III.viii) or a "royal encampment" (IV.xv) than a permanent urban structure. See also next note.

16. See III.ii for T⁣ʿil as the domain of the Gregorids and the burial place of St. Aristakēs. As in the case of Xaχ (see the preceding note) the exact status of Tʿil is not clear, since it is called an *awan* in III.ii but only a *gewł* here. The *Vita* of St. Nersēs, xiv, pp. 113–114 (= CHAMA, II, p. 42) places the burial of St. Nersēs after the coming of the hermits Epipʿan and Šałitay (see next chapter). It adds moreover a column of light visible for forty days above the grave, the earth of which effected miraculous cures from the plague: cf. V.xxi n. 5.

17. MX, III.xxviii (= MK, p. 299) also stresses that King Pap maintained a pretense of innocence to the end.

V.xxv

1. The next four chapters (V.xxv–xxviii) do not occur in MX, although he is acquainted with Epipʿan and Šałitay; see below, n. 3. The *Vita* of St. Nersēs, xiv, pp. 113–114 (= CHAMA, II, p. 42) gives a brief summary of V.xxv but not of the other chapters and brings the holy men to Xaχ rather than to Tʿil before the patriarch's burial; see V.xxiv n. 16. These chapters are presumably drawn from current hagiographic accounts, and Šałitay is known from Syrian sources (see Appendix I, s.n.), although the version of his life in BP does not coincide with that in the Syrian *Acts*. Cf. III.x for the case of James of Nisibis.

2. The *leaṙnakan*, "dwellers-on-mountains" seem to be identical with the similarly named *tūrāyē* of contemporary Syria: see Appendix III, *anapataworkʿ*.

3. The presumed presence of both Syrian and Greek anchorites in Armenia is an additional token of the existence of two currents of influence on early Armenian Christianity; see III.xiii n. 10, xiv n. 11, and Garsoïan, "Prolegomena," col. 192 n. 9 for some of the bibliography on this subject; also Intro., pp. 46–47.

4. MX, III.xx (= MK, p. 275) calls the hermits disciples of St. Nersēs and does not mention Daniēl (cf. III.xiv).

5. Cf. I Thess. 4:16. The vision of the saint's soul carried to heaven by angels is one of *topoi* of early hagiography. See, e.g., Athanasius, *Vita Antonii*, lx; Soc. Schol., E.H., xxiii; etc. See also III.xiv for Epipʿan's earlier vision of his murdered teacher, Daniēl.

V.xxvi

1. See V.xxv n. 1 and below, nn. 3,5, for the Syriac version.

2. See III.xiv; V.xxv n. 3; cf. xxvii n. 4 and VI.xvi.

3. The tale healing the wounded lion was a great favorite in Christian hagiography. Its most famous version comes from the life of St. Jerome, and its pagan prototypes go back to Aesop, Fable 231 and to the story of Androkles first attested in the second century of the Christian era in Aulus Gellius (*Noct. Att.*, X.xiv) and repeated in the third century by Aelian (*De nat. anim.*, VII.xlviii); see also Rice, *Jerome*, p. 212 n. 38, for the iconographic bibliography. Numerous variants also existed, such as the lioness who defended St. Thekla from the wild beasts of the arena at the cost of her own life (*Acts of Paul and Thekla*, viii p. 490), or the lions who buried both Paul and Thekla (*Apothegmata*, lviii), as well as St. Jerome, *Vita S. Pauli*, col. 28; see also Rice, *Jerome*, pp. 37–45. The version given here in BP may be the first attested one. There is no evidence that the author had any knowledge of the classical prototypes, and the earliest attested Christian example to my knowledge, Cyril of Skythopolis' *Life of St. Saba*, xlix p. 65, was composed after 555 and consequently postdates BP by nearly a century, while the version in the life of St. Gerasimos found in the *Pratum Spirituale*, cvii, pp. 85–87 of John Moschos belongs to the turn of the seventh century. See also Theodoret of Cyr, *Hist. Phil.*, V.ii.x and p. 150 n. 4. This episode is not found in the Syrian *Acts* of Šałitay, although the Nestorian Chronicle of Seert xxxv,

p. 247 attributes a similar tale to an anchorite named Yohanān from Anbar, nor in St. Jerome's *Vita S. Pauli*, see Intro., pp. 27–28 and nn. 112, 121–123.

4. See III.xiv and n. 14 for similar *topoi* in the life of Šalitay's teacher, St. Daniēl.

5. The disappearance of the saint's body at the moment of death, which is also found in the version of the Syrian *Acts*, is another hagiographic *topos*. Cf. the entrance of St. Thekla into the rock face, in the *Acts of Paul and Thekla*, pp. 491–492. See Dagron, *Ste. Thècle*, pp. 52 and nn. 2–3, 54, 165, 408/9, also Drijvers, "Origins," pp. 27–28 and n. 12.

V.xxvii

1. See V.xxv n. 1.
2. See III.xiv and V.xxv n. 3.
3. See III.xiv and n. 14, and xxvi n. 3 on the companionable wild beasts.
4. The term *vankᶜ* used here is commonly translated "monastery" in accordance with its later usage (cf. Lauer, p. 176, *Klöstern*; Emin, CHAMA, I, p. 292, *monastères*; and Gevorgian, p. 170, *monastyri*); see, however, NBHL, II, pp. 269–270, 793. It is quite clear from all three hagiographic chapters (V.xxv–xxvii) and from the beginning of V.xxviii, where the community at Mambrē is called *mianjnanocᶜ*, "solitude/hermitage," that it was at most a lavra inhabited by hermits guided by a *protos* and not a monastic coenobium. The existence of true monasticism of the Basilian type in fourth century Armenia remains to be demonstrated, and consequently the more general term "solitary-community" has been chosen here as preferable: see IV.iv, n. 19; V.xxviii n. 3, xxxi nn. 2, 5; VI.xvi nn. 4, 12; also Appendix III, *kusastan, mianjn, van(kᶜ)*.
5. The passage that attributes to Epipᶜan the collection of the martyrs' relics usually assigned to St. Marūtᶜā is one of the main sources for the recently questioned identification of Martyropolis/Miyāfarīkīn (modern Silvan) with the Armenian southern capital of Tigranakert. See Appendix II, "Tigranakert" for the various hypotheses, and Labourt, *Christianisme*, pp. 87–89 for the career of Marūtᶜā. Because the status of Aljnikᶜ *vis-à-vis* the Armenian crown tended to be ambiguous (see Appendix II, s.n.), it is not possible to determine from the context whether the intercession here was for the "realm" or for the "world" in general; see Appendix III, *ašχarh*.
6. Pliny the Elder, NH XXXI, xix, 25, cites a passage of Ktesias describing a fountain in Armenia which contained black fish whose flesh caused instant death. There is no reason to suppose that BP was acquainted with this passage. There is, however, a lake now named Gölē Masiēn, some 15 kilometers west of Zok on the left bank of the Harzan suyu whose fish are so bitter as to make them inedible according to Kalhōkecᶜi, ACH, p. 55, and which may be the source of a local tradition. I am indebted to Dr. J-M. Thierry for this information.
7. The origin of this didactic tale is unknown.
8. Cf. Luke 10:19 and perhaps the episode of St. Paul's sojourn on Malta, Acts 28:3–6. The tale had a number of variants. It was, of course, very familiar and reached the West, where we find it in Hilarius of Arles's, *Life of St. Honoratus* III.xv–xvi, pp. 106–111, in the fifth century, as well as in the *Life* of St. Patrick: see Hanson, *St. Patrick*. As in the case of the anchorite and the lion, it was a hagiographic *topos* (see Festugière, *Moines*, I, pp. 53–57), but the direct source of BP cannot be identified. See also V.xxvi n. 3 and above, nn. 6–7, as well as Intro., pp. 27–28 and n. 112.

V.xxviii

1. See V.xxv n. 1 and xxvii n. 4.
2. See V.xxvii n. 4. Malχasyancᶜ (p. 262), followed by Gevorgian (p. 171) as well as by Lauer (p. 177), turns the "brothers" (*ełbarkᶜ*) into monks. In view of this tendency, it

may be worth noting that Epip^{c}an's community at Mambrē, which included hermits dwelling-in-mountains, is alternately called a *vank^c* (see preceding chapter) and a *mianjnanoc^c*.

3. The alliterative formula usually characterizing the Armenian army is recalled here for the hermits insofar as they are "athletes, champions" (*čgnawork^c*) of Christ: see Appendix V, f.

4. See III.xiv n. 14.

5. Cf. Ps. 115:13 and also IV.lvii, V.xxiv.

6. Malχasyanc^c (p. 263) follows the variant given in the Venice edition (p. 227 n. 3), which substitutes the elaboration "*i sełann surb ew bašχeal jeṙamb k^{c}ahanayanin*" (on the holy altar and given out by the priest) for the simpler "*i sełann Astucoy*" (on the altar of God), which was preferred by both the Venice (p. 227) and the St. Petersburg (p. 188) editions, and which has been maintained here.

7. It was noted by Fr. Gat^{c}rčean that the text underlying much of this prayer was drawn from the Armenian version of the *Liturgy of St. Basil* (see Gat^{c}rčean, *Srbazan patarag*, pp. 96–98, 130–135). Only phrases from the underlying text are cited at the beginning of the prayer, but they are followed by two more extensive quotations separated by an interpolation not found in the liturgical text. These references to the liturgy end with the second quotation, which is followed in turn by a series of Scriptural citations (see below, nn. 11, 17, 18, 21). More recently, Fr. Renoux has gone still further to show that the underlying text corresponds to an early version of the Basilian Anaphora, known as the *Anaphora of St. Gregory the Illuminator*, preserved in a few Armenian manuscripts, and of which this passage of BP is an important early attestation—all the more so, in that the scene described at the point at which it is cited in BP is precisely the one at which the recitation of the Anaphora would occur in the canon of the Mass (see Renoux, "Anaphore"). None of the translations of BP has noted the origin of this prayer, although Malχasyanc^c observed that it contained "some" Scriptural passages (p. 336 n. 172). The entire prayer is omitted by Emin (CHAMA, I, p. 293). The invocation to the "Lord of Hosts" marks the reliance of the prayer from the beginning (Gat^{c}rčean, *Srbazan patarag*, pp. 130–131; Renoux, "Anaphore," p. 92), but as indicated above, the first continuous quotation begins a few lines later (see below, n. 11). Cf. IV.v and nn. 7–8 for parallels to the doctrinal exposition and the translation of its terminology. See also Intro., pp. 23–24 and n. 100, for other references to the liturgy in BP as well as for parallels to AaT.

8. II Macc. 7:28. This Scriptural reference does not occur in the underlying text at this point; cf. III.xiv n. 22.

9. Gen. 2:7; cf. Gat^{c}rčean, *Srbazan patarag*, p. 130 line 62; Renoux, "Anaphore," p. 93. Cf. IV.v n. 13.

10. Gen. 3:3; cf. Gat^{c}rčean, *Srbazan patarag*, p. 132 lines 67–68; Renoux, "Anaphore," p. 94.

11. Beginning of the first extensive continuous quotation from the Basilian Anaphora; cf. Gat^{c}rčean, *Srbazan patarag*, p. 132 line 69; Renoux, "Anaphore," p. 94.

12. Gat^{c}rčean, *Srbazan patarag*, p. 132 line 70; Renoux, "Anaphore," p. 94, renders *verstin cnndeamb* as "une naissance d'en haut." Cf. III.xiv n. 28, and Gal. 4:19.

13. Cf. IV.v n. 9, with the quotation from Hebrews; also Gat^{c}rčean, *Srbazan patarag*, p. 126 line 40; Renoux, "Anaphore," p. 91.

14. Cf. IV.v n. 11 with the continuation of the quotation from Hebrews.

15. See Thomson, "Philosophical Terms," pp. 45–46 for the translation of *anjn*. Renoux, "Anaphore," p. 95 prefers "pour lui-même," which is also possible.

16. See IV.v n.14.

17. See IV.v n. 18, with the quotation from Phil. 2:7.

18. End of the first extensive quotation from the Anaphora; Gat^{c}rčean, *Srbazan patarag*, p. 134 line 81; Renoux, "Anaphore," p. 96.

19. Cf. IV.v n. 20 with the allusion to Gen. 1:26.

20. Beginning of the second, longer quotation from the Anaphora; Gat^{c}rčean, *Srba-*

zan patarag, p. 140 line 128; Renoux, "Anaphore," p. 99.
    21. Ps. 7:10, cf. 43:22; Hebr. 4:12; AaT, cdxix. The second quotation ends.
    22. Acts 1:24
    23. Luke 17:6.
    24. John 10:11, 14–15; cf. IV.lv n. 14; also AaT, cdlxxi.
    25. Matt. 6:9. Cf. Gat'rčean, *Srbazan patarag*, p. 152 line 233; Renoux, "Anaphore," p. 104.
    26. Despite its obvious liturgical links, I have not been able to find the source of this tale. The subject of the vision became a favorite on Carolingian ivories, but that is hardly a reference for BP. See Schiller, *Iconography*, II, p. 107, figs. 364, 371–373.
    27. See NBHL, I, p. 653 and V.xxvii n. 4, xxviii n. 3; VI.xvi n. 12 for the contemporary communities.

V.xxix

    1. For the problem of the successor of St. Nersēs as patriarch of Greater Armenia— whom the *Vita* of St. Nersēs does not mention, while MX, III.xxix (= MK, p. 300) calls him Šahak—see the next notes and Appendix I, "Yusik II" and "Šahak." In general, this chapter shows signs of tampering: the title of "patriarch [*hayrapet*]" shifts back and forth between Armenia and Caesarea (where it is incorrect in this or any other period and does not occur elsewhere in the text, e.g., IV.iv, vii–ix), thus creating confusion, and its information on the prerogatives of the Armenian primate is open to question. See below nn. 3, 5 and especially 7.
    2. See III.iv; IV.xvii; and VI.ii for Ałbianos of Manazkert and his descendants. Most Armenian sources, but not the *Greek List of Katholikoi* #8 in Garitte, *Narratio*, pp. 402, 418, follow MX in calling St. Nersēs's succesor Šahak. See the preceding note.
    3. The bishop of Caesarea in 373 was unquestionably St. Basil himself (370–379). In view of the repeated intrusions of St. Basil into BP's account and the stress laid on his relationship with St. Nersēs, it is all the more curious that he should not be named here. See IV.iv–v and nn. 5–6; vii–x; and below, n. 7.
    4. See III.xii (Yusik); xvi (P'aṙēn); xvii (Šahak); IV.iv (Nersēs); also Aa, dccxci-dcccviii for the beginning of the tradition with St. Gregory the Illuminator.
    5. There is no record of a synod of the province of Cappadocia I held at Caesarea in 373–374. St. Basil himself was away from his metropolis part of the time, supervising the affairs of Armenia Minor (not Major), and there are no references in his correspondence to a synod held at this point. Neither is there any mention of a council in the parallel section of MX, III.xxix (= MK, p. 300), although he notes that St. Nersēs's successor was enthroned "without [the permission of] the great archbishop of Caesarea." See Fedwick, *Basil*, pp. 145–147 for the chronology of St. Basil's life; and Garsoïan, "Nersēs le Grand," pp. 150–154 for the locus of his mission.
    6. Malxasyanc' (p. 336 n. 174) suggests altering the text, which reads at this point "*ełew žołov . . . aṙanc' hayrapetin; ew grec'in tułt*" to "*ełew žołov . . . ew aṙ hayrapetn grec'in*" "a council took place . . . and they wrote to the patriarch." The correction may be unnecessary, since the point of the chapter is that the Armenian patriarchal candidate had not presented himself for approval and consecration at Caesarea, as was the custom: see above and n. 4, but also nn. 1, 3, 5, 7.
    7. Scholars have long discussed the significance of this repetitive and confused passage, which presumably marks the breach between Greater Armenia and Caesarea of Cappadocia and the Armenian patriarch's loss of the jurisdiction over his own suffragans. There seems to be no doubt that St. Nersēs was the last Armenian primate consecrated at Caesarea, and both the *Greek List of Katholikoi* #12 and the account of the Georgian *kat'ołikos* Arsēn #12 (Garitte, *Narratio*, pp. 403, 406, 419–420) support BP's account. Nevertheless, both BP's ignorance of the name of the contemporary bishop of Caesarea (see above, n. 3), and the absence of evidence for the holding of a synod there at that time

(see above, n. 5) cast doubt on the accuracy of his information. Moreover, both the *Greek List of Katholikoi* #13 and the account of Arsēn, *katᶜołikos* #13 (Garitte, *Narratio*, pp. 403, 407), contradict their own information that the Armenian primate no longer had the authority to consecrate bishops by stating unequivocally that St. Nersēs's son, St. Sahak I did have that authority, and there is no evidence that any Armenian bishop subsequently sought consecration at Caesarea. Furthermore, both the *Narratio* #31–32, #65–66 and Arsēn *katᶜołikos, ibid.*, pp. 30, 35, 100–102, state that the Persians ordered the Armenians to consecrate their own bishops at the time of the deposition of St. Sahak, thus delaying the jurisdictional break by one more generation, and the *Greek List of Katholikoi* #25–26, *ibid.*, pp. 404, 426, pushes this event as late as the patriarchate of Giwt (461–478). In the light of these contradictions and of the increasing intrusion of the Persian king into Armenian ecclesiastical affairs after the affirmation of his authority over the church of Persia by the Council of Ctesiphon of 410, as well as the extinction of the Gregorid line with St. Sahak in 439, two separate events may have been conflated here: the end of the consecration at Caesarea *de facto* in the late fourth century, and the subsequent local consecration of Armenian bishops under Persian supervision in the fifth century, a practice contemporary with and consequently familiar to BP. See also Garsoïan, "Secular Jurisdiction," pp. 210–211, 216–224.

8. See BP's similar criticism of other royal and non-Gregorid appointees to the patriarchate, III.xvi–xvii, IV.xv, and VI.ii n. 3; see also Appendix V, h for the repetitions of the closing formula.

V.xxx

1. This threnody on St. Nersēs is not found in the corresponding section of MX, III.xxxix (= MK, p. 300, but it is briefly alluded to in the *Vita* of St. Nersēs, xv, pp. 115–116 (= CHAMA, II, p. 42).

2. Cf. the beginning of the first extensive quotation from the Armenian version of the Basilian Anaphora (V.xxviii and n. 11).

3. See IV.liv for Vasak Mamikonean's attribution of the woes of Armenia to the magnates' disregard of St. Nersēs's admonitions, and V.i and n. 8 for the collaboration between the Mamikonean house and the Gregorid patriarchal house.

4. See Appendix III, *erkir haykakan lezuin.*

V.xxxi

1. This chapter, which lengthily and repeatedly underscores the destruction by King Pap of all of St. Nersēs's institutions described in IV.iv, repeated in V.i and summarized in V.xxi, is not found in the corresponding section of MX, III.xxxix (= MK, p. 300). It is given one sentence in the *Vita* of St. Nersēs, xv, p. 116 (= CHAMA, II, p. 42).

2. The term *kusastan* "[dwelling] place for virgins" occurs in the Armenian version of II Macc. 3:19 and III Macc. 1:10 for the description of "enclosed virgins," but obviously not for nunneries in the medieval sense, as is done by Emin, "monastères de filles," CHAMA, I, p. 294 and Lauer, "weiblichen Klöster," p. 182, as well as Gevorgian, "zhenskie monastyri," p. 175. See Dagron, *St. Thècle*, p. 74 for the monastic community of Hagia Thekla and below, nn. 3–5, for this problematic passage.

3. Malχasyancᶜ (p. 336 n. 175) and the Venice edition, p. 232 n. 1, both note that six mss give *awandocᶜn*, "place of deposit," or preferably the second meaning, "vows," for the *arangocᶜn* of the text. Malχasyancᶜ proposes the further correction *arewandocᶜn*, "from abduction," for which there is, however, no authority.

4. Malχasyancᶜ (p. 336 n. 176), following Norayr Biwzandacᶜi, corrects the *kusankᶜ ew hawatacᶜealkᶜ*, "virgins and believers" of the text to *kusankᶜ hawatacᶜealkᶜ*, "believing" or "consecrated virgins."

5. As noted above, IV.iv n. 17; V.xxvii n. 4, and below VI.xvi n. 3, the entire question of the existence of a real monastic structure in fourth-century Armenia is still open. This

passage is BP's only reference to a *kusastan* (see above, n. 2), which was apparently separate and specially protected and yet was apparently set in town where the inmates could be supported by their families. Hence the "consecrated virgins" of Armenian may have been closer in this period to the Syrian *benat qeyāmā* of Aphraat than to any conventual community: see, e.g., Vööbus, *Asceticism*, I, pp. 197–208 etc., and Appendix III, "*kusastan.*"

6. Malχasyanc‘ (p. 336 n. 177) argues that the *tasanord*, "tithe" was the obligatory contribution made by the peasants to their landlord or to the state, but not to the church, while the *ptuł* was a voluntary contribution to monasteries. He admits, however, that BP's usage of this terminology cannot be determined with precision, and it is not discussed in Manandyan's *Feodalizm.*

7. For all of these institutions see IV.iv; also Garsoïan, "Protecteur de pauvres," and *idem*, "Nersēs le Grand."

8. The injunction of St. Nersēs was against incestuous rather than multiple marriages (IV.iv and n. 25); cf., however, V.xvi and n. 3.

9. See IV.iv and n. 24 for St. Nersēs's injunction against excessive mourning and its repetition by Manuēl Mamikonean (V.xliv). Cf. III.xi and V.xxiv for the "proper" funerals of the patriarchs Vrt‘anēs and Nersēs, also the next note.

10. See IV.xv for the self-laceration and lamentations of P‘aṙanjem over Gnel; V.xxxvi for the rites over the body of Mušeł Mamikonean; and V.xliv for the disregard to Manuēl Mamikonean's injunctions. These practices go back to Armenian paganism rather than to Zoroastrian customs, which likewise forbid excessive mourning; see Widengren, *Religionen*, pp. 53–54, and preceding note.

11. See above and n. 7.

12. The text reads *vanakanac‘*, but see IV.xiv n. 17; V.xxvii n. 4; and above, n. 5.

13. BP takes particular pleasure in reiterating Pap's destructive activities in this chapter, thus displaying an animosity not found in the other sources. See above, n. 1, III.xiii n. 6.

14. For the presence of idol worship, see Aa, xlix, lviii–lix, lxvii, lxxi, lxxiii, lxxx–lxxxv, cx, cxvii, dcclxxxiv, dcclxxxvi, dccxcix, dcccix; MX, II.xii, xiv, xl, xlix (= MK, pp. 148–149, 152, 182, 190, etc.); above, III.iii, xiv; also Appendix III. *dew.*

15. See Aa, dcccxxxvii, and p. 494 n. 4 for this grant of Trdat the Great to the church; also Malχasyanc‘ (p. 337 n. 179).

V.xxxii

1. BP's version of the murder of King Pap is corroborated by AM, XXX.i, but not by MX, III.xxxix (= MK, pp. 300–301), who places it anachronistically in the reign of "Theodosius" (see V.i n. 3) and has Pap executed rather than murdered. The *Vita* of St. Nersēs, xv, pp. 116–117 (= CHAMA, II, p. 42) gives a confused version that combines a summary of BP's account with MX's identification of the emperor as "Theodosius." See below, nn. 2, 5–7, 11.

2. MX.III (= MK, pp. 300–301) supports BP's accusation that Pap betrayed his Roman supporters. The *Vita* of St. Nersēs, xv, pp. 116–117 (= CHAMA, II, p. 42) attributes both the discontent of the magnates who plot to kill their king and the intervention of "Theodosius" to Pap's murder of St. Nersēs. On the contrary, AM, XXX.i shows the Armenian king as the innocent victim of Roman plots.

3. The city of Caesarea/Mazaka was briefly captured by King Tiran the Great in the last century B.C. (see IV.lv n. 20 and MX, I.xiv; II.vi, xiv–xv, xviii = MK, pp. 94–95, 135, 151–153, 155). There is no evidence for Pap's claim to Edessa or the other cities, which is borne out by neither AM nor any of the other Armenian sources and may perhaps belong to the epic tradition. Cf. Aršak II's claim of his ancestral rights (IV.liv). Cf. however, the link between the Abgarids of Edessa and Armenia introduced by MX II.xxvi–xxxvi

(= MK, pp. 13, 163–179).

4. See V.i, iv–vi.

5. The "secret message" of the emperor is also known to the *Vita* of St. Nersēs, xv, p. 116 (= CHAMA, II, p. 42), but MX, III.xxxix (= MK, p. 300) merely says that "Theodosius" sent an order to the general Terentius, whom Pap had expelled from Armenia—an expulsion unknown to AM, XXX.i. On these secret letters see Garsoïan, "Politique," pp. 313–320.

6. AM, XXX.i.18 places only Trajanus in Armenia at the time of Pap's death, although he accuses Terentius of instigating the plot. See Garsoïan, "Politique," pp. 313–315, 319 and Appendix I, "Adē."

7. Both the *Vita* of St. Nersēs, xv, p. 117 (= CHAMA, II, p. 42) and AM, XXX.i.19–22, place Pap's murder at a banquet to which he had been treacherously invited by the Roman commander, and the Roman historian gives almost the same details as BP, though his outrage at the murder (XXX.i.21–22, cf. XXXI.i.3) is not echoed by Armenian sources. According to MX, III.xxxix (= MK, pp. 300–301), however, Pap was captured in battle by Terentius, who spared the king and sent him to "Theodosius," but the emperor had him executed. For the particular poignancy of the king's death at a banquet in the Iranian tradition, see III.xx n. 16. The detailed parallels to the circumstances of Tiran's capture suggest a conflation of the historical and epic settings at this point.

8. Malxasyancᶜ (p. 337 n. 180) objects to the reading *psakealk*ᶜ of the text, which he takes to be an error for *patealk*ᶜ, "surrounded." But the editors of his 1968 edition rightly note that the two words were synonymous in the classical period. See NBHL, II, p. 663, *psakel*, fourth meaning.

9. Cf. V.vii and n. 9 for the presence of *gusan*s at feasts. AM, XXX.i.20 gives the same setting.

10. The position of King Pap on his feasting couch is precisely that of the reclining figure on the funerary monument from Palmyra in the Louvre, Colledge, *Art of Palmyra*, pl. 61, and the one from tomb 173c reproduced in Seyrig, "Armes," p. 58 fig. 12. See also the iconography of the Sasanian silver plate in the Walters Gallery for the reclining position of the feasting king, Ghirshman, *Persian Art*, fig. 259 and IV.xvi n. 3; also Dentzer, "Iconographie," pp. 231, 242, 242–243; *idem*, "Banquet," esp. p. 17 for the reclining position as a royal prerogative; and V.vi n. 6 for carrying the dagger on the right thigh.

11. MX, III.xxxix (= MK, pp. 300–301) has Gnel Anjewacᶜi killed in battle by the Roman commander Terentius.

12. Cf. Appendix V, c for the variants of this formula.

V.xxxiii

1. There is no mention of this council in MX, III,xl (= MK, p. 301), or in the *Vita* of St. Nersēs.

2. This apocryphal statement is a clear expression of the precarious position of Armenia between the two contending world powers flanking it on either side, especially after the end of the Arsacid dynasty early in the fifth century.

3. For the obligation of the blood feud see IV.liv n. 12 and V.xxxvii n. 16.

V.xxxiv

1. Both MX, III.xl (= MK, p. 301) and the *Vita* of St. Nersēs, xv, pp. 117–118 (= CHAMA, II, p. 43) identify the "king of the Greeks" whom BP leaves anonymous with the emperor Theodosius. MX goes on to title him correctly "augustus" and dates the events in his "twentieth year" thus continuing the anachronism of the preceding chapters

(cf. V.i n. 3, etc.), since Theodosius, born ca. 346 and proclaimed Augustus on 19 January 379, could patently not have been in the twentieth year of either his life or his reign in 374. See Jones *et al.*, *Prosopography*, I, p. 904, "Flavius Theodosius" #4.

2. BP refers to Varazdat vaguely and disdainfully here as *omn*, "a certain Varazdat from the same Aršakuni house," although he subsequently identifies him as King Pap's nephew in the male line (V.xxxvii and n. 15), an identification accepted by the *Vita* of St. Nersēs, xv, p. 118 (= CHAMA, II, p. 43, where Emin gives the translation, "à la place de son cousin"). BP brief reference to Varazdat's vigor and "valiant heart" is elaborated by MX, III.xl (= MK, pp. 301–302) into an Olympic victory at Pisa and other unlikely epic feats.

3. This is one of the clearest statements of the traditionally pro-imperial policy of the Mamikonean house (see V.xliv and n. 7). There is no mention of this in the corresponding portion of MX who as usual ignores the Mamikonean; see Intro., pp. 44–45.

4. Malχasyancʿ (p. 337 n. 180) argues that the word kʿałakʿ need not be taken to mean "cities" here. There is no doubt that this word can refer to a fortified walled enclosure in classical Armenian. With the exception of the possible reference to Ałiorskʿ (III.xx and n. 12), however, BP uses the term throughout for sizable urban agglomerations, lying for the most part outside Armenia: see Appendix III, kʿałakʿ. These were cities of classical Hellenistic type, not walled enclosures. The same was true of the urban complexes destroyed by Šāhpuhr II ca. 364 (IV.lv), to which BP also refers as "cities" (kʿałakʿ), as is indicated by their eponymous names—Arta-šat/Artašēs, Eruanda-šat/Eruand, Vałarš-apat/Vałarš, Zari-šat/Zareh, etc.—and by the recent excavations of Artašat, Ařakelyan, *Artashat I*. The cities to be erected and garrisoned by the Greeks in the various districts of Armenia at Mušeł's request were presumably of the same type, as opposed to Armenian "royal encampments" (IV.xv) and "forest palaces" (III.viii). As such they were an intrusion into the normal decentralized Armenian pattern and awakened the hostility of the magnates. Cf. IV.xii and n. 9, and also V.xxxv for the related slander of Mušeł; also see Garsoïan, "Mediaeval Armenian City," and the next chapter.

5. This account of the garrisoning of Armenia by Valens ca. 377 coincides with the statement of AM, XXX.ii.2–4, that the emperor refused to withdraw and abandon Armenia and that he consequently presented an ultimatum to the Persians.

V.xxxv

1. This entire episode is ignored by MX, III.xl (= MK, pp. 301–303), in keeping with his omission of references to the Mamikoneans: see Intro., pp. 44–45. The *Vita* of St. Nersēs, xv, p. 119 (= CHAMA, II, p. 43) summarizes and confuses this account; see below, nn. 2, 11–12.

2. The *Vita* of St. Nersēs, xv, p. 119 (= CHAMA, II, p. 43) calls him Smbat. See III.xi n. 7, V.xxxvii and n. 9, and Appendix I, "Mamikonean" for this family's hereditary control of the office of *sparapet*.

3. See V.iv for King Pap's misgivings and Mušeł's oath.

4. See V.ii

5. See V.iv.

6. There is no suggestion in V.xxxii that Mušeł Mamikonean was implicated in Pap's murder, but see Varazdat's accusation below and V.xxxvii. The *Vita* of St. Nersēs, xv, p. 116 (= CHAMA, II, p. 42) claims that the Armenian magnates had plotted to make Mušeł king after Pap's death. Such a plot would have been impossible in the fourth century, for the kingship was the hereditary office of the Aršakuni (see Intro., pp. 2, 43–44, 50); but the accusation may be significant.

7. See the preceding chapter, n. 4, on the alien character of the city in Arsacid Armenia and the consequent use of this building activity as a basis for the slander of Mušeł at this point.

8. See III.xx n. 11 for the critical setting of the banquet.

9. See IV.li for the similar complaint of the Armenian magnates.

10. See V.ii and n. 9 for the heroic implications of death on horseback in the Iranian epic tradition and the iconography of Mušeł's apotheosis.

11. The *Vita* of St. Nersēs xv, p. 118 (= CHAMA, II, p. 43) has the king strike the first blow.

12. The *Vita* of St. Nersēs xv, p. 119 (= CHAMA, II, p. 43) has Mušeł buried at the monastery of Glak in Tarōn, but this is probably a result of the association of the Mamikoneans with this foundation in the tenth-century *History of Tarōn* erroneously attributed to Zenob Glak and John Mamikonean; see Levon Avdoyan, *Ps. Yovnannēs.*

V.xxxvi

1. This curious episode, reflecting the survival of pagan customs in early Christian Armenia, is found in none of the other sources; see the next note.

2. The practice of placing a dead body on the roof of a building in the expectation of his resurrection through the intermediary of the *aṙalezkᶜ* or *aṙlezkᶜ* has its exact counterpart in the tale of Queen Semiramis's attempt to revive Ara the Fair MX, I.xv (= MK, pp. 96–98). See Appendix I, "Aṙlezkᶜ," and Intro., p. 51, for the survival of pagan customs in Armenia.

V.xxxvii

1. This long episode with its epic overtones noted by Manandyan, *Kᶜnnakan texutᶜyun*, II/1, p. 235, and its glorification of the Mamikoneans is not to be found in MX, III.xl (= MK, p. 302), who merely has King Varazdat recalled by Emperor "Theodosius" for intrigues with Persia and exiled to the island of Thulē after a reign of four years. He does, however, give a similar account of the origin of the Mamikonean house in another context, II.lxxxi (= MK, pp. 229–231); see Appendix I, "Mamikonean." The *Vita* of St. Nersēs, xv, pp. 119–122 (= CHAMA, II, p. 43–44), follows closely BP's account of Manuēl Mamikonean's return to Armenia and his victory over King Varazdat but omits the second half of the chapter; see below, n. 19.

2. Cf. V.xxxv n. 2 and III.xviii n. 5 for the prerogative of the Mamikoneans as royal *dayeak*s.

3. See IV.ii n. 7 for Aršak II's attempt to interpose his authority into the dynastic pattern of succession and offices, and below n. 9.

4. The *Vita* of St. Nersēs, x, pp. 66–67 (= CHAMA, II, p. 33) says that the brothers were deported to Persia at the time of Aršak II's captivity, which is entirely possible, but see below, nn. 7, 12, for its inaccuracies. All mss have "Kon" at this point but "Koms" elsewhere: see Venice edition, p. 242 n. 2 and Appendix I, "Koms."

5. See V.vii and nn. 3–4 for a parallel account of the Kᶜušan war and the exploits of Drastamat; also V.viii n. 3 for the form, "Sasanian king of Persia."

6. See Appendix V, c for variants of this formula.

7. The *Vita* of St. Nersēs, x, xv, pp. 66–67, 119 (= CHAMA, II, p. 33, 43) calls him Kon.

8. For the giant size of heroes and their feats in the epic tradition, see Garsoïan, "Substratum," pp. 156–157 and *idem*, "Locus," pp. 41–42.

9. Together with III.xi and n. 7, this is one of the clearest surviving statements in Armenian literature that under the Aršakuni, dynastic seniority and hereditary offices remained beyond the jurisdiction of the king; cf. IV.ii and n. 7.

10. See IV.liv.

11. The *Vita* of St. Nersēs, x, xv, pp. 66–67, 119–120 (= CHAMA, II, p. 33, 43) takes Manuēl's statement here at face value and makes him the "brother" of Mušeł and consequently the "son" of Vasak (see above, n. 7). But BP clearly identifies Mušeł as Vasak's son (IV.liv, V.i) while stating equally clearly at the beginning of this chapter that Manuēl and Koms were the son of Artašēn Mamikonean, and it uses the term *ełbayr*, "brother" throughout as general term for kinsman; see Appendix III, s.v.

12. Cf. V.iv for Mušeł Mamikonean's oath of loyalty to King Pap, and also V.xxxv, where Mušeł is killed, however, by a dagger thrust in the throat and decapitation, not by strangulation.

13. See above, V.iv and n. 36 for the more sober assessment of his rank by Mušeł Mamikonean.

14. The text reads "*zi ariwn mec ankeal ē i veray*" (Venice ed., p. 244 = St. Petersburg ed., p. 203). Malχasyancᶜ (p. 279), followed by Gevorgian (p. 184), adds a negative in the sentence to make it read "that much blood might not flow." this correction is, however, unattested, and it is found neither in Emin (CHAMA, I p. 299), nor in Lauer (p. 193). Moreover, the *Primary History*'s account of the origin of the Mamikonean (Sebēos, p. 56 = MK, p. 367) does not suggest that the rebel brothers withdrew to avoid bloodshed, but rather that their army was slaughtered and defeated in a major battle. The version in MX, II.lxxxi (= MK, p. 230) says that Mamkon fled so as not to be murdered by his brother, but it does not suggest that this was to avoid a major conflict. Cf. V.iv n. 38 on this traditional descent of the Mamikonean, and Appendix I, "Čenkᶜ" for its accuracy.

15. Cf. V.xxxiv n. 2.

16. For the implications of this apocryphal dialogue, repeated in the *Vita* of St. Nersēs, xv, pp. 121–122, (= CHAMA, II, p. 43), and the obligation of the blood feud, see Garsoïan, "Prolegomena," cols. 177–178, 187–190 and n. 5 and above, IV.liv n. 12.

17. The heavily armed cavalry described here was well known to classical authors, who referred to the armored knights as *cataphracti* or *clibanarii*. See Bivar, "Cavalry Equipment"; and Gabba "Influenze," esp. p. 65 and n. 66 on the identity of the two terms. See also Appendix III, *azatagund, zōrkᶜ*, I.a.

18. Cf. V.iv and n. 33 for Mušeł Mamikonean's parallel sparing of king Uṙnayr of Ałuankᶜ.

19. Except for a mention of Varazdat's flight to the Byzantine empire, the *Vita* of St. Nersēs, xv, pp. 122 (= CHAMA, II, p. 44) stops the account of this episode at this point.

20. See IV.lix and Appendix I, "Hamazaspean," for the confused relationship of Garegin Ṙštuni and Hamazaspcan Mamikonean. Malχasyancᶜ (p. 338 n. 188), followed by Gevorgian (p. 186 n. 94), corrects the *aner*, "father-in-law" in the next line of the text to "son-in-law" and Hamazasp to Hamazaspean. The editors of the 1968 edition argue that *aner* could have either meaning, but cf. HArmB I, p. 192, "*aner.*"

21. The *Vita* of St. Nersēs, follows this version (see above, n. 19), but not MX, for which see above, n. 1. As usual, BP does not specify the length of the king's reign, but MX III.xl (= MK, p. 302), gives it as four years.

22. This is the only account of the regency of Queen Zarmanduχt under the *de facto* control of the *sparapet* Manuēl Mamikonean, except for its brief résumé in the *Vita* of St. Nersēs, xv, pp. 122–123 (= CHAMA, II, p. 44) which is derived from BP.

23. As observed by Malχasyancᶜ (p. 338 n. 190), following EM, *Pᶜawstos*, p. 31, the "Greek king" of the St. Petersburg edition (p. 206) contradicts the context and must be corrected to "Persian king" as it is give in the Venice edition (p. 247). See the next chapter, n. 3, for the historical support of this correction.

V.xxxviii

1. None of the episodes in this chapter, or indeed the entire regency of Queen Zar-

manduχt and Manuēl Mamikonean is mentioned in MX, III.xli–xlii (= MK, pp. 303–304), who claims that the queen was kept as a hostage in Constantinople and moves from the accession of Aršak III and Vałaršak to the partition of Armenia approximately a decade later; see below, n. 2. The *Vita* of St. Nersēs, xv, pp. 122–123 (= CHAMA, II, p. 44) dispatches the regency in two brief paragraphs.

2. MX, III.xli (= MK, p. 303) claims that "Theodosius the Great" sent the sons of Pap back to Armenia "with governors [appointed] by himself, faithful men," whom he does not name. See V.i n. 3 for the anachronistic appearances of "Theodosius."

3. The coming of the Sūrēn and the establishment of a Persian protectorate over Armenia is confirmed by AM, XXX.ii.7–8. This Sūrēn is probably the one mentioned in IV.xxxvi; but see Appendix I, "Sūrēn Parsik."

4. On the ornaments sent from Persia, several of which are *hapax legomena*, see Malχasyancᶜ (pp.338–339 n. 191) and Appendix III, *apizak, ašχarawand*, and *gargamanak*; also Toumanoff, *Studies*, pp. 134–135 nn. 233–235. See also MX, II.xlvii (= MK, pp. 187–188 and n. 3) for other Armenian honorific ornaments; Ełišē, vi., p. 136 (= *Ełishē*, p. 187), for those granted to Vasak Siwni; and Procopius, *Aed.*, III.i.21, for the regalia sent to the Armenian autonomous sataraps.

5. Malχasyancᶜ (p. 339 n. 12) argues that this passage could also be read to mean that "gifts and offerings" (*ənjaykᶜ ew patarags*) were given instead of, or in place of, "tribute" (*hark*) and not in addition to it. There seems to be little reason for this reading, although it is grammatically possible.

6. The term *kōšik*, which is also found in VI.viii, with the sense of "salary/reward," is problematic here. Malχasyancᶜ (p. 339 n. 193) proposes to take it as meaning *ṙočik*, "stipend/maintenance" and the subsequent *zpitoys zṙočkacᶜn* as "means of subsistence/provisions," but his hypothesis fails to explain the redundancy that it creates.

7. As noted above, V.xxxvii n. 22 and xxxviii nn. 1, 3, the shift of Armenia's allegiance to the Persians at this point is known to the classical sources but is not mentioned by the Armenian ones. This silence may be due to the brief span of this shift in policy or to the subsequent unpopularity of a pro-Persian policy, especially in the second half of the fifth century; see Intro., pp. 51, cf., however pp. 45–46, 54–55.

8. From this point on, the chapter takes on an epic character. For parallels of Meružan's deceit intended to sow trouble between Armenia and Persia, see III.xx (Pisak Siwni); IV.xvi (Vasak Mamikonean); and IV.xx (Andovk Siwni). It is interesting to note that the materials drawn from epic oral literature are the ones that stress the friendship between Armenia and Persia rather than their antagonism and attribute breaches between the two kingdoms to deceit and treachery.

9. See IV.xvi for the identical phrase used of the honors received by Aršak II at the Persian court.

10. *šnorhel zarewn*, "to grant [someone's] life." See MX, II.xix (= MK, p. 156 and n. 6) for the use of *arew*, "sun" in the sense of "life." See also Appendix V, d for the variants of the formula of "escape on a single horse."

11. Cf. IV.xxxi n. 6 for the pattern of Meružan's escape from retribution, and Appendix V, h, for the formula indicating time.

V.xxxix

1. None of the episodes of Manuēl Mamikonean's victorious campaigns (V.xxxix–xli) is to be found in any other source. These catalogs of victories, which occur in each generation of the *sparapetutᶜiwn*, may be a standard part of the glorification of the Mamikonean. See IV.xxvi–xliii, xlv–xlix for Vasak; and V.viii–xix for Mušeł, as well as Intro., pp. 38, 44–45. Cf., however, note 3.

2. See Appendix V, b for the repetitions of this formula.

3. See IV.xxxi for the counterpart chapter dealing with the invasion and death of Gumand Šapuh at the time of Vašak Mamikonean.

V.xl

1. See V.xxxix n. 1.
2. See V.xxxvii n. 17 on the armored Iranian cavalry.

V.xli

1. See V.xxxix n. 1.
2. See IV.xlix for the counterpart chapter dealing with the invasion and death of Mṙkan under Vasak Mamikonean.
3. See Appendix V, b, c, e for this accumulation of formulae.

V.xlii

1. This chapter detailing the benefits of Manuēl Mamikonean's government following after the catalog of his victories corresponds to V.xx, which comes at the same point to cap Mušeł Mamikonean's career. No part of this chapter occurs in the corresponding section of MX, because it is part of the glorification of the Mamikonean family; see Intro., pp. 38, 44–45. The *Vita* of St. Nersēs, xv, pp. 122–123, (= CHAMA, II, p. 44) merely records that Manuēl ruled many years together with his three sons.
2. Cf. IV.lviii and n. 7
3. Cf. IV.ii and n. 7; and V.xxxvii and n. 3 for the royal attempts to "make appointments" to hereditary offices.
4. III Kgs. 4:20.
5. See VI.i.

V.xliii

1. None of this semi-epic chapter is to be found in the other sources. MX, III.xxxvii (= MK, p. 298) has Meružan Arcruni die in completely different circumstances after the battle of Jiraw, which took place in the reign of King Pap; see V.v n. 19.
2. See IV.xxiii and nn. 1–2; lix.
3. See IV.xxiii n. 2.
4. See IV.xxiii–xxiv, xxxi–xxxvii, xxxix–xliii, xlv–xlix, lviii–lix; V.xxxviii for Meružan Arcruni's long and damaging career.
5. See IV.xx n. 12.
6. For the contingents brought by each *tanutēr* and listed in the late and fictional *Zornamak*, "Military List," see Adontz, *Armenia*, pp. 193–195, 68*–69*; also, for its date and accuracy, *ibid.*, pp. 214, 220–223; Toumanoff, *Studies*, pp. 229–230, 239–241.
7. See IV.lv for the destruction of this city by the Persians about 364, and Garsoïan, "Mediaeval Armenian City," pp. 73–75 on the failure of the Armenians to rebuild the devastated cities.
8. Both Awdalbegean, "Meružan" and Ačemean, "Čanaparh," attempted to turn the wayfarers' answer into a sneer or a threat, but neither was sufficiently supported to prove convincing.
9. Chaldean divination was a byword in all of antiquity. The casting of lots was as much a classical practice (cf., e.g., Cicero, *De divinatione*; Horace, *Odes*, I.xi; the *Argo-*

nautica; or for that matter Homer), as on found in the Scriptures (e.g. Prov. 16:33; Matt. 27:35; Mark 15:24; Luke 23:34; John 19:24; Acts 1:24–26; etc.), or in the Zoroastrian writings (*Ardā Wīrāz Nāmag*). But cf. Basil, St., *Letters*, ccxvii, canons 72, 83 against the practice of divination, Eznik's condemnation §216–230, pp. 617–621, and the fifth canon of the Persian Council of 410, S.O. p. 264; AaT, dclxxxv and n. 1, on the influence of these practices in Armenia; see also AG, pp. 318–319 §122; Riess, "Astrologie;" Lenormand, *Divination*; etc.

10. This episode provides indirect evidence for the importance of the cavalry in the Armenian army of the period. Cf. ŁP^c, lxviii, p. 121 (= CHAMA II, p. 328) on the capture of the Persian horses by the Armenians. See also Appendix III, *zork* ^{c} I.

11. See IV.xv and n. 10 on the shrine of St. John the Precursor at Bagawan, as opposed to the equally famous one at Aštišat (III.iii).

12. In antiquity this practice denoted initiation into a cult, and it also appears to have been a Zoroastrian custom. Its survival in the orthodox Mamikonean family, closely connected with the Gregorid patriarchal house (V.i n. 8), seems unlikely, but cf. V.xxxvi for the performance of clearly pagan rites over the body of Mušeł Mamikonean. This practice is also recorded in the *History of Tarōn*, pp. 109–110, which associates it with the cult of Gisanē. This passage was called to my attention by my former student and friend Dr. Levon Avdoyan, to whom I am most grateful for this information.

13. The same episode of the young boy banned from the battlefield because of his youth and returning secretly to distinguish himself occurs in the Iranian *Ayādgar ī Zarērān*, nos. 79–80, p. 25 (= trans. p. 48). See Russell, "Review," p. 808.

14. Most of the translators (Emin, CHAMA, I, p. 304; Lauer, p. 203) follow the printed editions, which capitalize *Gewł awan*, and consequently translate, "le bourg de Kēough" or "der Stadt Giughn." Malxasyanc^c (p. 290) reverses the position and speaks of *Avan gyułic*^{c}, "from the village of Avan." Only Gevorgian (p. 194), departing for once from Malxasyanc^c, identifies this *gewł-awan* as the holy site of Bagawan. In view of the fact that the locality named Awan, now in the suburbs of Erevan, does not fit the geographical context (cf. AON, p. 410), and especially that the exact status of Bagawan was altogether unclear in this period—since Aa, dcccxvii, applies to it the composite Greek calque *k^{c}ała-k^{c}ageōł*, "komopolis"; both BP (IV.xv) and MX, II.lv (= MK, p. 198), etc. call it an *awan*, "town"; and the seventh century *Ašxarhac^{c}oyc*^{c} calls it a mere *gewł*, "village"—it seems clear that the hybrid *gewł-awan* here must refer to Bagawan, where Manuēl Mamikonean had just visited the famous shrine of St. John the Precursor.

15. For the incarnation of the god Vərəθaγna, the giver of valor, in the form of a wild boar (*varaz*), see IV.lii n. 3; also Intro., pp. 34, 44, for the grant of valor, *k^{c}ajut^{c}iwn*, to the Aršakuni and its transfer to the Mamikonean.

16. Cf. V.v n. 19 for MX's version of Merużan's death.

17. See Appendix V, c for the more usual forms of this formula.

18. See Appendix V, b for the repetitions of this formula.

19. Lauer (p. 205) incomprehensibly transfers this encomium to Manuēl Mamikonean.

20. As noted by Anasyan, *Review*, p. 20, Gevorgian (p. 195) was mistaken in turning Vač^{c}ē II Mamikonean into Manuēl's second "brother." There is no indication in BP that Vač^{c}ē was Manuēl's brother, but only the reference to him as junior to Manuēl within the clan: see V.xxxvii.

21. See III.vii.6 and Appendix III, s.v. for the use of the word *ełbayr* in the sense of kinsman. Merużan Arcruni was related to the Mamikonean through his mother, the sister of the apostate Vahan. See IV.l and Malxasyane^c (p. 340 n. 197).

22. Malxasyanc^c (p. 340 n. 198) argues that Artawazd Mamikonean risked the death penalty for disobeying the order of his *sparapet*, although there is no such indication in the text. See above, n. 13, for the tale of the boy-hero in the Iranian tradition.

V.xliv

1. None of the material in this chapter occurs in the parallel section of MX, except for a different version of Aršak III's marriage. See the next note.

2. According to MX, III.xli, xliii (= MK, pp. 303, 305), Aršak III married an unnamed daughter of Babik Siwni and not Vardanduχt Mamikonean, an assertion that is probably derived from his systematic obliteration of the Mamikonean from his narrative; see Intro., pp. 44–45.

3. This is the only reference found in BP to the Bagratuni's hereditary office of royal "coronant" (*tʿagakap*). Cf. MX, II.vii (= MK, pp. 136–137), and the parody of this office in the account of Smbat Bagratuni's execution of Meružan Arcruni with a molten "crown," III.xxxvii (= MK, p. 298). See Perikhanian, "Inscription," pp. 18, 22 for the earliest attestation of this title.

4. See IV.xvi n. 2 for the title of "second after the king." The two brothers seem, however, to have been co-rulers, even though Vałaršak was the younger and the effective power was in the hands of Manuēl Mamikonean. MX, III.xli (= MK, p. 303) says that Vałaršak "died in the same year." BP does not mention this fact, but it is probable that the young king did not live long, since he is never mentioned after this. See IV.i.

5. See III.xi and n. 7 and V.xxxvii and n. 9 for the automatic transfer of the *sparapetutʿiwn* in the Mamikonean house.

6. Cf. V.iv, V.xx for Mušeł Mamikonean's similar expressions of loyalty, and III.xi for the patriarch Vrtʿanēs's encomium of Vačʿē I; also, the repetition below and Intro., p. 38.

7. See V.xxxiv n. 3 for another example of the Mamikonean's usual pro-imperial policy, but cf. V.xxxvii(end)–xxxviii.

8. One ms mentions only ten wounds instead of fifty (Venice ed., p. 259, n. 2), a number which Malχasyancʿ considers more probable (p. 340 n. 199). However, the epic hyperbole is entirely possible in the present context.

9. See above, n. 6; also V.ii n. 9 and xxxv, for the same complaint of Mušeł Mamikonean and the implications of death on horseback in battle. Malχasyancʿ (p. 293) adds a negative at this point to preserve the interrogative turn of the text, "why has it *not* been my lot . . . ?" In view of the interrogative/negative found a little earlier in the same paragraph, this addition does not seen unwarranted, but it is not attested to my knowledge.

10. See IV.iv and n. 24; V.xxxi nn. 9–10.

11. Cf. III.xii n. 15; IV.iv.

12. See IV.iii–iv; V.i, xxi, xxxi.

13. See above, n. 10.

14. Note the plural. One ms (Venice ed., p. 261 n. 1) adds "to the priests and ministers."

15. The *Vita* of St. Nersēs, xv, p. 123 (= CHAMA, II, p. 44) has Manuēl buried in the monastery of Głak like his predecessor Mušeł. See V.xxxv n. 12 on the probability of this statement.

16. Cf. II Macc. 4:35 and the Venice ed., p. 261 n. 2.

VI Tables

1. The entire last phrase is missing in the heading of this chapter in the text. According to Malχasyancʿ (p. 340 n. 200), all the misdeeds of Bishop Yohan were at first included in a single chapter that was subsequently divided into three. The entire title was kept for the first chapter, while the other two remained without headings. These three chapters may well be a dubious interpolation; see Intro., pp. 36–37.

2. Malχasyanc͓ (pp. 297, 340 n. 201) corrects this title by removing the toponym to conform with the heading of the chapter in the text as well as with the content of the chapter, which does not mention Aršarunik͓.

3. This gloss has always presented, and still continues to present, many problems. Among the hypothetical translations of this obviously corrupt text, the standard one has usually been, "After (or at the end of) all the histories there are for the readers of this book ten verses of counted meter with information concerning me." Soon, however, it was observed that the first word of the gloss, *storot*, a noun in the nominative case, could not be translated as "after" or "at the end," but merely "end." The next attempt suggested: "This is the end of the tales. The readers of this book seeking information about me [will do so] by counting [back] ten chapters." This attempt solved the problem of the initial *storot* and introduced an ingenious explanation, since "ten chapters [back]" from the gloss could indeed be found VI.v–vi, the chapters dealing with a Bishop "P͓awstos." The explanation was particularly felicitous when the Greek authorship of "P͓awstos" seemed possible, since the "P͓awstos" of VI.vi was explicitly said to have been of "Roman [i.e., Greek] race." Nevertheless, new problems were introduced; *hamarakan* could not be rendered by the verbal locution "by counting," as it is not a verb. Indeed, one of the main difficulties of the gloss is that it does not seem to contain a verb. Moreover, nothing legitimately interpretable as containing the direction "back" can be found in the text. Finally, the translation of *tunk͓* as "verses" or "chapters" could not have been demonstrated, and most of the proposed interpretations seemed to accept that the mysterious gloss was the work of the author himself, and consequently contemporary with the work.

In view of the fragmentary form of the gloss, no final solution can yet be proposed, even after numerous discussions and consultations with Armenian specialists. One point should, however, be stressed. The gloss in almost certainly the work of the second editor (see Intro., pp. 11–12, 35) and consequently belongs to a period much later than the text itself. The commentator is under no circumstances the original author speaking about himself, and fifth-century Armenian is consequently a poor guide for deciphering this text. The first phrase does not seem to present difficulties and can be rendered "End of all the tales." Because the commentator is far removed from the author of the work, the second phrase "information concerning me" becomes meaningless, or at best a dubious forgery, besides being unidiomatic. The interpretation "according to my information" or " insofar as I know" seems preferable. The third phrase, reiterating the direction of the first, specifies, "this [is] the [very] book, readers," or (if the *ǝnt͓eṙnoyk͓* of the text might be taken as a minor slip for *ǝnt͓eṙnouk͓*, "you are reading") the phrase could fall even better into place as, "this [very] book you are reading," and incidentally supply the missing verb. Unfortunately, the final phrase still defies solution. The most that can be noted at this point is that instead of seeking recondite translations for the word *tunk͓*, the entirely correct and regular plural of *tun* "house(s)" might well be considered, and that *hamarakan* is used from the time of Anania Širakac͓i in the seventh century for mathematical calculations, particularly those based on a sexagesimal system. Whether the hidden allusion in this phrase is to *naχarar* houses mentioned in the text, or to one of the elaborate numerical puzzles of which later medieval scholars were so fond, still remains beyond reach. See Intro., nn. 44 (for the actual text of the gloss) and 45; also Malχasyanc͓ (p. 297), Gevorgian (p. 199), and Emin (CHAMA I, p. 306). Together with all the Tables of Contents, this gloss is omitted by Lauer.

VI.i

1. As noted by Malχasyanc͓ (pp. 340–340 n. 202), the word *verĵ*, "end" refers to Book VI, which marks the "end" of BP's account, just as Book III was its "beginning" (III.i n. 1). The first chapter of Book VI is indeed the end of the whole work, while the "omitted

portions" refer to the subsequent chapters of miscellaneous biographies, at best loosely related to the actual *Histories.* See Intro., pp. 36–37, and below, n. 13.

2. Malχasyancʿ (p. 341 n. 203) adds the phrase, "one-half by . . . " which is missing here but included in the heading of the chapter in the Table of Contents.

3. MX, III.xlii (= MK, pp. 304–305) gives a different version of the enthronement of Xosrov and of the partition of Armenia; see below, nn. 5–8.

4. There is no mention in this chapter of Aršak III's younger brother and presumed co-ruler Vałaršak. Cf. V.xliv and n. 4.

5. MX, III.xlii (= MK, p. 304 and nn. 2–4) has Xosrov sent to Armenia by the Persians after the partition of the kingdom, for which see below.

6. The Zik was sent to Armenia as the *dastiarak,* "preceptor/tutor." of the young king, but he was not his *dayeak,* "tutor/foster-father," a prerogative normally reserved for the Mamikonean, see III.xviii n. 5. MX does not mention this detail not the king's marriage to Zruanduχt (see above, n. 3).

7. MX III, xlii–xliii (= MK, pp. 304–305), says that the Armenian magnates with domains in Persarmenia returned home after the partition of the kingdom and the enthronement of Xosrov in the eastern portion; see above, n. 3. Malχasyancʿ (p. 341 n. 204) rightly includes the phrase in brackets; this is required by the sense of the passage but is missing in both the Venice edition (p. 266) and the St. Petersburg edition (p. 222 and n. 1).

8. On the partition of Armenia and the problem of its precise date (probably 387), see Manandyan, *Kʿnnakan tesutʿyen* II/1, pp. 238–248; Garitte, *Narratio,* pp. 70–72; Ē. L. Danielyan, "Haykakan bažanman taretʿivə"; Doise, "Le partage"; and Toumanoff, *Studies,* p. 152 n. 6. A somewhat different version is given by MX who sets the partition under Arcadius (395–408), see above, n. 3, and yet another by Procopius, *De aed.,* III.i. 1–15.

9. Cf. Sebēos, xv, p. 86 (= Macler tr., pp. 30–31) for similar sentiments expressed in the apocryphal letter of Xusrō II to the emperor Maurice, as was noted by Patkanean, St. Petersburg edition, p. 222 n. 2.

10. On the loss of the border district of the Armenian kingdom briefly reconquered by Mušeł Mamikonean ca. 370 (V.viii–xx and viii nn. 1–2), see Adontz, *Armenia,* pp. 178–180; Toumanoff, *Studies,* pp. 131–132; Eremyan, *Ašχarh* p. 118* col. 2; Hewsen, "Armenia" pp. 336–337. See also map II.

11. See Malχasyancʿ (p. 341 n. 205) for the suggestion that the *Siwnkʿn/Orsiwnkʿn gawatkʿn* of the text—which are capitalized in the St. Petersburg edition (p. 222) but not in the Venice edition (p. 266) and which are both incomprehensible in context and grammatically awkward—be taken as a common rather than a proper name; i.e. *siwn,* "pillar/base," which he takes here as designating the "fundamental" or "core" district of Armenia as opposed to the border regions.

12. The boundary between the two Armenias is also mentioned by MX, III.xlii (= MK, p. 304). On the uneven division of Greater Armenia that left approximately four-fifths of the kingdom under Persian dominion, see Adontz, *Armenia,* pp. 8–24; Manandyan, *Kʿnnakan tesutʿyun* II/1, pp. 245–247.

13. As also observed by Malχasyancʿ (p. 341 n. 206), it is evident from these words that the account of BP was compiled a considerable time after the partition of Armenia at the end of the fourth century. Consequently, they provide additional evidence that this work is not a contemporary account of the fourth-century events described and subsequently translated into Armenian, but an Armenian original compiled in the second half of the fifth century; see Intro., pp. 6–10. The finality of the closing words of this chapter likewise make it clear that BP's account closed at this point, so that the subsequent biographies were "omitted portions" and not a continuation of the narrative; see above, n. 1, and the closing phrase of IV.1.

VI.ii

1. See VI.i n. 1. References to the patriarchs Zawēn and Aspurakēs as well as to St. Gind (VI.ii, iv, xv, xvi) are found in other Armenian sources, but the other biographies are not generally known, unless they are taken to be coincident with the list of bishops found in Aa (see VI.v n. 5).

2. See III.iv and Appendix I, "Ałbianos" for Ałbianos of Manazkert and his descendants. MX, III.xl (= MK, pp. 302–303) merely records that Zawēn, an Ałbianid descendant, became patriarch in the second year of the reign of Varazdat and that his pontificate lasted four years; see below, nn. 3, 6.

3. BP does not even mention Zawēn's position as primate of Armenia following upon Yusik/Šahak; see the preceding note and V.xxix n. 8. Cf. the encomia lavished on the "legitimate" Gregorid patriarchs throughout the text: III.iii, v–vi, xi–xx; IV.iii–iv, xiii; V.iv, xxi, xxxi; and Intro., p. 15, for BP's indifference or hostility to primates from other houses.

4. See NBHL, I, p. 970, HArmB, II, p. 403, χotor and Małχasyanc⟨ (p. 341 n. 207), on the χotorktur, "bias-cut tunic" as a military dress. It was presumably a garment cut off short at the knees in front so as not to impede movement.

5. The text reads "*Ew inkᶜn Zawēnn atᶜineals ew ztapakeals zžapawineals narotōkᶜ aganēr*" (Venice ed., p. 267). The origin and meaning of both *atᶜineals* (or rather *natᶜineals*, as the second *n* of Zawēn probably belongs to it) and *tapak* (both of which are *hapax legomena*) are not clear. In the opion of Małχasyancᶜ (p. 341 n. 208) the first would have the sense of "adorned/arrayed" and the second of "decorated with spangles." Cf. NBHL, I, p. 12; II, p. 843, *tapak*, second entry; HArmB, I, p. 88; IV, p. 373. See Seyrig, "Armes," pp. 55 [13]–64 [22], figs 10–12, 14–15 and Pls. IV–V, etc. for the ornamentation of Parthian tunics with galloons and jewelled borders.

6. Małχasyancᶜ (p. 300) takes this phrase in the singular to refer to Zawēn. This seems more reasonable than the plural suggesting the entire clergy of the text.

7. Cf. above, n. 2. This is the first occasion on which the length of a pontificate or reign is recorded by BP as against MX's common practice. This atypical precision might perhaps be an additional indication that some of chapters VI.ii–xvi did not belong to the original text; see Intro., pp. 36–37 and n. 164 and Appendix V, h for the repetitions of the formula of time.

VI.iii

1. See VI.ii n. 1 Šahak Korčeay is not known to the other sources except for Michael the Syrian, who follows BP; see Appendix I, "Šahak II Korčeay."

2. BP uses the term *gluχ episkoposacᶜ*, "head/chief bishop" both here an in the next chapter, seemingly to distinguish these primates from true "patriarchs" (*hayrapet/episkoposapet*); see Appendix III, "senior-bishop."

VI.iv

1. This chapter is repeated with very little elaboration below (VI.xv). See also VI.ii n. 1.

2. See the preceeding chapter, n. 2.

VI.v

1. See IV.iii; V.xxiv and Intro., pp. 12–13 for the problems surrounding this personage.

2. See VI.ii n. 1.
3. There is no reference to this, either earlier in BP or elsewhere.
4. See Malxasyanc' (p. 241 n. 209) for the translation of *nerk'ini* here as "familiar" rather than "eunuch," which would presumably be canonically impossible for a bishop; see Nicaea Canon I. Cf. NBHL, II, p. 422; HArmB, III, p. 447.
5. This elaborate and probably imaginary organization is not attested elsewhere. It may derive from the twelve bishops presumably sent out by St. Gregory according to Aa, dccCxlv. Indeed, as observed by Thomson, Aa, p. 496 n. 4, a number of the bishops named in the present book—Artit' (VI.vii), Yohan/Yovhannēs? (VI.viii–x), Kiwrakos (VI.xi), and Movēs and Tirik (VI.xiii)—bear names also found in Aa's list. The number may, however, derive merely from the obvious association with the twelve apostles. See Markwart, *Entstehung*, pp. 155 ff. and Adontz, *Armenia*, pp. 266–268, for the reliability of Aa's list.
6. Neither P'awstos nor Zort' is named among the supervisors whom St. Nersēs appointed to oversee his charitable foundations; cf. IV.iv, xii; V.xxi, xxxi.

VI.vi

1. See VI.ii n. 1 and VI, tables n. 3 on the possible reference to this chapter in the gloss at the end of the Table of Contents. The name of Aṙostom is given in the title but does not occur in the body of the chapter. Cf. Intro., n 53.
2. See III.xiv and n. 15 on standard ascetic practices; also V.xxv– xxviii; VI.xvi, and Appendix V, h for the repetitions of the formula of time..
3. St. Nersēs was buried at T'il which is called "his own village" (V.xxiv and n. 16). Amōk is otherwise unattested.

VI.vii

1. See VI.ii n. 1.
2. See III.xiv, V.xxv–xxvii, where Artit' is not named among the disciples of Daniēl.

VI.viii

1. See VI, Tables n. 1 and ii n. 2. The curious anticlerical stories concerning Yohan (VI.viii–x) contain no indication of time or place beyond the reference to his father the patriarch P'aṙen (III.xvi), and are highly suspect from a historical and stylistic point of view. See VI.v n. 5 and Intro., pp. 36–37.
2. See III.xvi. Malxasyanc' (p. 342 n. 212) corrects the *hinawurc'*, "elderly" of the text, which he takes as a *lapsus calami* for *hin awurc'*, "formerly/long ago/in ancient times" referring to P'aṙen, since an identification of Yohan as being "very old" does not suit the context of the tales.
3. See III.xiv n. 15 on ascetic practices.
4. *zmiǰov* is the instrumental of place indicating encirclement, "around, about." A number of Sasanian plates show that the heavy quiver containing both the bow and arrows was worn on the right attached around the hips and not on the back. See e.g. Garsoïan, "Locus," figs. 1–2 and *idem*, "Armement." The editors of the 1968 edition (see Malxasyanc' p. 342 n. 214) prefer the translation "fur pelt/pelisse" for *ōdik*, but it may be no more than a sheepskin. Cf. NBHL, II, p. 1023.
5. The source of this curious tale is not identifiable. Might it be a parody of the hagiographic *topos* of the converted brigand? Cf. Cyril of Skythopolis, *Vita Antonii*.
6. Cf. III.xxi for the similar phrase referring to the troubles arisen over "a single horse" through the malice of P'isak Siwni and the Persian *marzpan* Varaz-Šapuh.

VI.ix

1. See VI.viii n. 1. See also IV.viii and n. 4 for St. Basil's vineyard vision.

VI.x

1. See VI.viii n. 1.
2. The word *miahanēsk^c* (*mi hanesk^c* in on ms) is a *hapax* of unknown origin and meaning. NBHL, II, p. 266 suggests "game/jest/ trick/mime/duplicity"; HArmB, III, p. 319 prefers "trial/danger/misfortune/temptation." Malχasyanc^c (pp. 305 and 342 n. 215) gives an approximate translation.

VI.xi

1. See VI.ii n. 1 and v n. 5 for the similar name in Aa's list.

VI.xii

1. See VI.ii n. 1.
2. Cf. Eph. 5:18.

VI.xiii

1. See VI.ii n. 1 and v n. 5 for the similar name in Aa's list; and Appendix I, s.n.

VI.xiv

1. See VI, Tables n. 2 and ii n. 1.

VI.xv

1. Cf. VI.iv, of which this chapter is a slightly more prolix repetition.

VI.xvi

1. See III.xiv. MX, III.xx (= MK, p. 275) makes him a disciple of St. Nersēs along with Šałitay and Epip^can; cf. V.xxv–xxviii.
2. See III.xiv, V.xxv–xxviii, where Gind is not mentioned, and the preceding note.
3. The term *abełay* ‹Syr. *'abīlā*, "mourner" does not occur outside this chapter, not is it found in Aa or Koriwn. The reference to a group of solitaries is evident, but no further precision is possible from the context. See Appendix III, *mianjn*, and next note.
4. The tautological accumulation of this passage: "*gluχ abełayic^c vardapet mianjanc^c ałajnord menakec^cac^c verakac^cu vanerayic^c, usuc^cič^c amenayn anapataworac^c, tesuč^c amenec^cun ork^c miangam . . . yašχarhē ēin mekneal,*" is the most detailed description giving us the general outline of the two types of solitaries found in Armenia in this period: (1) anchorites, wandering-in-the-desert and dwelling-in-mountains, *anapatawork^c*, and *leařan-*

akank'; (2) hermits grouped together under a leader, teacher, or supervisor in a sort of lavra, *mianjunk'*, *menakk'*, *vanerayk'*, with the former type predominating, according to the description given here and in V.xxv–xxviii. No indication is given here or elsewhere for the existence of a coenobium of Basilian type. Cf. Koriwn, iv, p. 38 (= trans., p. 27) and see Appendix III, *anapatawork'*, *mianjn*, *van(k')*. But, see also the next note for the possibility that much of this passage is a Biblical paraphrase.

5. Cf. Hebr. 11:37–38, of which this passage is alternately a direct quotation and a paraphrase. See also the preceding note, and below n. 12.

6. These are not personal names, but merely nicknames; see Appendix I, "Artoyt"; "Maraχ,"; "Vač'ak."

7. See V.xxiv, where he is called Trdac.

8. The Syrian milieu of these anchorites is underscored by the Syriac form of Mušē's name, as opposed to the usual Armenian, Movsēs.

9. See Festugière, "Lieux-communs," pp. 129–121, for the hagiographic *topos* of the narrator's inadequacy; also III.xiv and n. 15.

10. Cf. John 7:35.

11. "*cags* [or *caks*] *vimac'*," cf. Jer. 49:16, "*cakanut vimac'*." The retreat of St. Gregory the Illuminator, according to the received tradition, was at the "Caves of Manē" (*Maneay Ayrk'*) which were in the district of Daranalik' according to Aa, dccclxi, and MX II.xci (= MK, p. 248); see AON, pp. 284, 250. Oskik', on the other hand was located in the district of Całkotn, AON, p. 361 and Eremyan, *Ašχarh.*, p. 74. The allusion to Jeremiah is found in neither Aa nor MX who says that Gregory retired, "*yayrs inč' k'aranc'.*"

12. The Venice edition, p. 276 n. 2, gives the variant *ełbayranoc's*, found in the St. Petersburg edition (p. 231). Neither version implies that these "brotherhoods" were coenobia, although they may well have been lavras of the second type mentioned above in n. 3.

Appendices
Indices

Appendices and Indices

These Appendices are intended merely as a complement, collecting the scattered notes of the Commentary, and as a brief introduction to the subject of a particular entry and its problems. No attempt has been made to provide complete bibliographies or an exhaustive coverage, for such an attempt would reach beyond the competence of the author and extend this portion of the book beyond any reasonable length. Consequently, as already indicated in the Introduction, major figures and toponyms outside Armenia—such as St. Basil of Caesarea (Appendix I), or Athens, Alexandria, Egypt, etc. (Appendix II)—have been treated here only insofar as they are pertinent to the text of BP without any attempt to give the balanced, let alone the extensive treatment to which they would be entitled in a work of more general character. Similarly, the Technical Terms (Appendix III) will inevitably contain some omissions. Nevertheless, an effort has been made in the three first Appendices to give at least an acknowledgement of all persons and places mentioned in the text (except for such obvious cases as e.g. Moses, Noah, Sinai) and of every term marked with an asterisk in the body of the translation (but not in the subsequently added headings, the Introduction or the Commentary).

Wherever possible, etymologies have been suggested for all entries as a partial index of the cultural influences on Armenia during the period under consideration. Where such information is missing, no determination is as yet possible.

As in the case of the Commentary, bibliographic references are given throughout this section in abbreviated form, the full citation being reserved for the entry in the Bibliography.

References to Parthian and Pahlavi onomasticon, toponymy, and titulature found in the trilingual victory inscription of Šāhpuhr I at Naqš-i Rustam (ŠKZ) and likewise attested in BP have been given to illustrate the parallels between the societies reflected in these documents, but no attempt has been made to cite other examples in Iranian epigraphy, sphragistics, and the like because this material is becoming increasingly accessible through the work of such specialists as P. Gignoux, R. Schmitt, M. Mayrhofer, H. Humbach, P. O. Skjærvø, and others. The Parthian and Pahlavi form in the ŠKZ have been given according the Gignoux's *Glossaire des inscriptions pehlevies et parthes* and his *Noms propres sassanides en moyen perse épigraphique*, with cross-references to M. Sprengling's *Third-Century Iran*. The Greek version of the same inscription (RGDS) is cited according to A. Maricq, *Res Gestae divi Saporis*.

Because the first three Appendices are expected to serve simultaneously as Indices, they have obviously been set out in alphabetical order. For this purpose, the various diacritical marks required for the transliteration of Armenian forms have been disregarded, although they have invariably been included.

Numbers listed in brackets indicate a direct reference but one where the apposite name or term does not occur.

The map references are given as follows: (a) Eremyan, *Map* = Eremyan's *Mec Hayk'i t'agavorut'yunə IV darum*; (b) Eremyan, *Ašχarh.* Map = Eremyan's map appended to his *Hayastanə əst Ašχarhac'oyc'"-i*; (c) map (without author) = one of the two maps appended to this volume, which were kindly prepared by Professor Hewsen.

Appendix I: Prosopography

The names of the prophets of the Old Testament, of the apostles and martyrs of the New Testament (e.g. Moses, Job, Peter, Paul, Stephen), and obviously that of Jesus Christ, which is constant throughout the text, have have been omitted. Except for Scriptural allusions, the Greeks, and the Romans, all names have been maintained in their Armenian form to avoid a speciously classical or "western" character that is totally absent from the text. The spelling given is the one found in the text, even when it is an uncommon or aberrant form (with the exception of Artawan/Artewan, and of Dłak, which is a later *lapsus* for Głak). In all cases requiring them, alternate forms have been noted.

The leading Armenian *naχarar* families have been included in this Appendix, and are also noted under their domains in Appendix II. Minor families, or those indentified only by the name of their district, have been subsumed under the toponym in Appendix II. In all such cases, cross-references have been given.

The listing of the *naχarar* families in the *Gahnamak*, "Rank (or Throne) List" (Adontz, *Armenia*, pp. 191-193, 67*-68*), the so-called *Pseudo-Gahnamak* included in the *Vita* of St. Nersēs (*ibid.*, pp. 200-203, 70*-72*), and the *Zōrnamak*, "Military List" (*ibid.*, pp. 193-195, 68*-69*) has been included because of the familiarity and accessibility of these documents. It must, however, be noted that these are late and semi-fictitious records, as argued by Adontz (*ibid.*, pp. 191-234), though B. H. Harut°yunyan, ("Gahnamak") has recently attempted to push the date of composition of the *Gahnamak* back to A.D. 388.

Aba Gnuni
Armenian *naχarar*, not otherwise attested.
See HAnjB, I, p. 1
III.xii
p. 82
See also "Gnuni house."

Addai, see Tᶜadēos."

Addē, see "Adē."

Adē/Addē, Count
Roman count sent together with Terentius by the Emperor Valens ca. 369 to reestablish Aršak II's son Pap on the throne of Armenia after the Persian occupation of the
country and responsible, together with Terentius, for the young king's murder, according to BP (V.xxxii), though MX III.xxxvii (= MK, p. 296) does not mention this and
has Addē appear only once in support of the Armenians' victory over the Persians.
No Roman commander of this name is known to the classical sources. Nonetheless,
he seems clearly identifiable with the count Traianus, *dux aegypti* ca. 367–368 and
comes rei militari in the East ca. 371–374. According to AM (XXIX.i.2; XXX.i.18;
XXXI.vii.1, 5; viii.3; xi.1; xii.1; xii.1; xiii.8, 18) he fought the Persians, brought about
Pap's murder, was subsequently shifted to Thrace as *magister peditum*, temporarily
disgraced, and was finally killed together with Valens at the battle of Andrinople (378).
Like Terentius, Traianus was disliked by AM who calls him an incompetent
(XXXI.vii.1), but he was praised by both Theodoret of Cyr (HE, IV.xxxiii) and St. Basil
of Caesarea (Ep. cxlviii). Consequently, like Terentius, he must have been part of the
anti-Arian party that opposed Valens's and Pap's religious policy. The name Adē is
perhaps derived from a confusion with that of Count Arintheus, likewise *magister
peditum* (AM, XXVII.v.4), a partisan of Terentius (Theodoret of Cyr, HE, IV.xxxiii)
who was also sent to support the Armenians against the Persians (AM, XXVII.v.4, 9;
xii.13). This is the identification chosen in Jones *et al.*'s *Prosopography*, but the career
of Traianus is better fitted to the Armenian account. Arintheus's service against the
Persians in 371 is not the campaign that reestablished Pap on the Armenian throne
some two years earlier, but the two may well have been confused.
See Seeck, "Traianus"; Jones, *et al.*, *Prosopography*, I, pp. 103, "Flavius Arintheus,"
921–922 "Traianus" 2; Markwart, "Untersuchungen," p. 215; and Garsoïan, "Politique," pp. 313–320 on the religious aspect.
V.i, xxxii
pp. 185–186, 213
See also "Pap"; "Tērent"; "Vaɫēs"; and Appendix III, *koms*.

Aharon ‹ Hebr. Aharon, Gk. ᾿Ααρών
Bishop during the reign of Xosrov III/IV. He is identified as bishop of Aršarunikᶜ
in the title of the chapter in the Table of Contents, but nowhere else (see VI, Tables,
n. 2). He is otherwise unattested.
See HAnjB, I, p. 90 no. 1, who gives 415 as the date of his death; AG, p. 291.
VI.xiv
p. 238

Aɫanayozan Pahlaw ‹ MP *āyōz*, pres. part. act -*an*, "stirring up/fighting"
Persian general related to the Armenian Aršakuni dynasty, according to both BP (see
IV.xxxviii n. 1) and MX, III.xxxiv (= MK, pp. 291–292), who calls him "Alanaozan
Pahlawik," though their versions of his campaign against Aršak II do not coincide. JIN

makes him a member of the Sūrēn family, which is possible considering his surname of Pahlaw but is not explicitly stated in the sources.

See Nyberg, *Manual*, II, p. 40, *āyōz* and cf. the form *Šahrālānyōzān* on a sealed document, D. Weber, "Papyri," p. 41; also AG, p. 17 no. 3 and 64 no. 140 "Pahlav"; JIN, p. 13; Perikhanian, "Papirusy," no. 3, pp. 88–89; *idem*, "Inscription," p. 23 n. 9.

IV.xxxviii

p. 163

See also "Aršakuni"; "Surēn Pahlaw."

Alank⁣ᶜ/Alans

Attested as the Alan's Gate in ŠKZ, Parth. 2; RGDS no. 3, pp. 48–49, reconstr., KKZ, 12.

Irano-Sarmatian tribe first attested in A.D. 35 by Josephus (*Bell. Jud.*, VII.vii.4). They made repeated attempts to force their way southward through the main chain of the Caucasus and consequently left their name to the main pass through this range: the *Dār-i Alan/Darial*, "Gate of the Alans," though Honigmann and Maricq prefer the "Gate of the Albanians," for ŠKZ. They have often been identified with the Massagetae, but BP (III.vii) distinguishes them from both the Mazkᶜutᶜkᶜ and the Honkᶜ. They are portrayed alternately as invaders (III.vii) and allies (IV.xxv) of Greater Armenia.

See Bachrach, *Alans*; Rostovtzeff, *Iranians and Greeks*, pp. 114–120; Kovalevskaia, *Alany*; also Gignoux, *Glossaire*, p. 15; Sprengling, *Third-Century Iran*, pp. 7, 14, 47, 52; Honigmann and Maricq, RGDS, no. 3, pp. 11, 40, 88–94.

III.vii; IV.xxv

pp. 74, 159

See also "Mazkᶜutᶜkᶜ."

Alans, see "Alankᶜ."

Ałbianids, see "Ałbianos."

Ałbianos, bishop of Manazkert/Ałbianids

The precise identity and career of Bishop Ałbianos are still problematic. Aa, dcccxlv–dcccxlvi, attributes his jurisdiction over the lands bordering on the Euphrates River to his designation by St. Gregory the Illuminator immediately after the Christianization of Armenia (A.D. 314), while BP (III.iv) records a later grant of the lands around Manazkert and of the lands along the Euphrates, as a reward for the bishop's mission to the Orduni and the Manawazean, a mission unknown to other sources. Moreover, Aa, dcccxlvi, identifies Ałbianos as having jurisdiction "as overseer of the royal court" in the absence of St. Gregory and makes him the companion of St. Aristakēs as "the other bishop" from Greater Armenia (Aa, dccclxxiii) at the Council of Nicaea, although the other versions of the Agatᶜangełos cycle do not mention his name, which is also unattested in the conciliar lists.

On the basis of his analysis of the various versions of "Agatᶜangełos," Garitte differentiated two persons: Ałbianos, bishop of Bagrewand and the Euphrates regions, and Albios, the ecclesiastical supervisor of the royal court. By contrast, Adontz attributed all of these functions to a single Ałbianos whom he opposed, perhaps simplistically, to the Gregorids as the head of the other leading ecclesiastical house in fourth-century Armenia. There seems to be no doubt that Ałbianos was one of the dominant ecclesiastical figures of the period. He is singled out by Aa, who calls him "*the* other [*zmiws*] bishop" of Armenia, dccclxxiii, though he lists others elsewhere; and BP likewise gives him a leading role, together with the king and the patriarch, in III.iv. His descendants—Šahak, Yusik II, Zawēn, and Aspurakēs—are invariably identified as such both in BP (III.xvii; V.xxix; VI.ii, iv) and by MX, III.xxxix, xl (= MK, pp. 300,

345

303), and they unquestionably alternated with the Gregorids as primates of Armenia, even if their order is not always certain. If they really were the overseers of the royal court (see also V.xxix), their support of the Armenian Arsacids' Arianizing policy in the fourth century would help explain their putative rivalry with the "orthodox" Gregorids.
> See HAnjB, II, p. 103; Garitte, *Documents*, pp. 196–198, 322, 329; Adontz, *Armenia*, pp. 245, 257, 266–267, 269, 271–272, 274–275, 282, 472 n. 50a, 75*, 87*–91*; Gelzer, "Die Anfänge," pp. 145–146; Garsoïan, "Politique," for the Arsacid ecclesiastical policy in the fourth century; Gelzer *et al.*, *Nomina*.
> III.iv, xvii; V.xxix; VI.ii, iv
> pp. 69–70, 92, 210, 234–235
> See also "Aršakuni"; "Aspurakēs"; "Girgor/Gregorids"; "Manawazean, house"; "Orduni, house"; "Pʿarēn"; "Šahak I–II"; "Yusik II"; "Zawēn"; and Appendix II, "Manazkert."

Ałjnikʿ, see Appendix II, "Ałjnikʿ."

Ałuankʿ, see Appendix II, "Ałuankʿ."

Amatuni, house
Senior *naχarar* family of presumed Iranian, Caspio-Median descent, though MX, II.lvii (= MK, pp. 199–200 and n. 6, cf. 187 n. 10) also suggests a questionable Jewish origin for them as for the Bagratuni, at the same time as he gives a punning etymology for their name (= Ir. *amat*, third pers. sing. aorist, "he came"). The domain of the Amatuni was in Artaz in the southeastern region of Armenia, subsequently known as Vaspurakan, but they also ruled in Aragacotn, where MX, III.ix (= MK, p. 262) but not BP says that they were granted the fortress of Ōšakan, by King Xosrov Kotak. Koriwn, xxvi, p. 94 (= trans. p. 50) and ŁPʿ, I.xvii, p. 35 (= CHAMA, II, p. 278) also link the Amatuni with Ōšakan, but less explicitly. The Amatuni were known to most Armenian medieval sources. They are listed in the *Gahnamak*, "Rank List" and presumably the *Zōrnamak*, "Military List," though their name is given incorrectly there as Amaskoni or Hamastunean, with 100 or 200 retainers. They are also included in the List of *naχarar*s in the *Vita* of St. Nersēs, v, p. 32 (= CHAMA, II, p. 25). According to Koriwn, xxvi, p. 92 (= trans. p. 50, which gives "commander-in-chief" for *hazarapet*), they held the position of *hazarapet* in the fifth century, and their bishops are included in the conciliar lists from that time on. According to MX, III.xliii (= MK, pp. 305–306) they were disgraced for their failure to return to Persarmenia at the time of the accession of Xosrov III/IV. Their estates were consequently confiscated by the Persians, they lost their hereditary rank and were compelled to hide. As a result of the intercession of the Armenian primate, St. Sahak, however, their domains were returned, but not their position, so that they were ranked thereafter among the lesser nobility (see MX, III.li, lxv = MK, pp. 316, 344). Ca. 772, the Amatuni lost their domains to the Arabs, and some of them fled to the Byzantine Empire according to Łewond, xxxiv, xlii (pp. 144, 168). The branch in Artaz survived, however, in the ninth century as vassals of the Arcruni, and another branch ruled during the thirteenth and fourteenth centuries under the name of Vačʿutids in the districts of Aragacotn, Širak, and Nig with the great fortress of Amberd.
> See Adontz, *Armenia*, pp. 188, 201, 205, 207, 210–212, 228, 231, 239, 250, 256, 258, 263, 323, 445 n. 32, 447, n. 39, 447–448 n. 42, 464 n. 74, 494 n. 63, 511 n. 33, 67*, 70*, 76*-77*, 79*–80*, 92*–96*, 98*–100*, 102*; Toumanoff, *Studies*, pp. 197–198 and n. 223, 226, 228, 231, 237 nn. 305–306, 238, 245, 247, 248, 250, 251, 252, 254, 271, 329–330 n. 110, 457 n. 85; *idem, Manuel*, pp. 55–56, only for the Vačʿutean branch; Tournebize, "Amatouniq"; Oskean, *Usumnasirutʿiwnner*, pp. 79–119.

III.vii, viii, xiv; IV.iv

pp. 74, 76, 87, 111

See also "Karēn"; "Pargew"; "Vahan"; "Xosrov II/III"; "Xosrov III/IV"; Appendix II, "Ōšakan"; and Appendix III, *hazarapet; naχarar.*

Anahit ‹ Pth. *Anāhīt, OP *anā-hiti-š; cf. Phl. Anāhīd, Nāhīd; Av. *Anāhitā-,* "immaculate, undefiled"; usually known as *bānūg,* "the lady"; Gk. Ἀναῖτις
  Name attested in KKZ, 8, etc.

  Daughter of Ahura-mazda and one of the leading deities (*yazata*) of the Zoroastrian pantheon, to whom the fifth *Yašt* was dedicated and whose chief shrine was located at Staχr in Pars. Together with the lesser divinity Nana/Nanē, she shared in the fertility attributes of the Great Mother of the East and also had warlike aspects, but her primary association was with the domination of waters. She is also shown as the granter of the crown to the Sasanian king of kings Xusrō II on the relief at Tāq-i Bostān.

  Under the name of Anaitis, she was well known to classical authors (e.g. Strabo, *Geogr.* XI.xiv.16; Plutarch, "Lucullus," xxiv; and Tacitus, *Ann.,* III.lxiii), who calls her the "Persian Diana," though she is also associated with the warlike Athena (Plutarch, "Artaxerxes," iv), and even Aphrodite. The northwestern portion of Greater Armenia, also known as Akilisēnē (Arm. Ekełeac^c), was also identified by some classical authors as "Anaetica" or "Anaïtis chora," presumably because of the spread of the goddess' cult in the region (see Pliny the Elder, NH, V.xx.83–84, and CD, XXXVI.xlviii.1 liii.5).

  The cult of Anahita was widespread in pre-Christian Armenia (Aa, xlviii–xlix, liii, lix, lxviii, etc.), where her assimilation to Artemis was sustained by MX, II.xii, xl (= MK, pp. 148–149, 153, 182) and Aa, who calls her the "mother of all virtues" (liii), even though her chief designations in Armenia were *tikin,* "the lady" Aa, lix, cxxvii, as in Iran and especially *oskemayr,* "golden mother" (Aa, dcccix). The chief temple of the goddess seems to have been located at Erēz in Ekełeac^c, though other shrines are mentioned at Armawir and Bagaran (Aa, dcclxxxvi; MX, II.xii, xiv, xl = MK, pp. 148–149, 152, 182) as well as Artašat and Aštišat, and she is represented on a number of clay plaques recently discovered at Artašat. Anahit was still invoked as the protectress of the Armenians early in the fourth century (Aa, lviii, cxxvii), on the eve of the Christianization of the country and of the destruction of her shrines at Artašat, Aštišat, and Erēz by St. Gregory the Illuminator (Aa, dcclxxviii–dcclxxix, dcclxxxvi, dcccix).

  See Gignoux, *Glossaire,* pp. 16–46; *idem,* NPS, no. 97 p. 42; Schmitt, IN, p. 321; Sprengling, *Third-Century Iran,* pp. 47, 51; Windischmann, *Anahitā;* Melik^c-P^cašayan, *Anahit;* Chaumont, "Le culte"; *idem,* "Anahita"; Trever, "Anahita"; Carrière, *Huit sanctuaires;* Adontz, *Armenia,* p. 43; Russell, *Zor. Arm.,* pp. 73, 80–81, 235–253, 523–524; Ter Martirosov, "Terrakoty."

  V.xxv

  p. 205

  See also Appendix II, "At^cor Anahtay," "Ekełeac^c"; and Appendix III, *tikin.*

Anak ‹ ?Pahl. *anāg,* "evil"; ‹ ?**an-aka-* "non-evil"

  According to the "received" Armenian tradition, but not Ełiše, iii, p. 72 (= *Ełishē,* p. 123), Anak the Parthian, the murderer of King Xosrov K^caǰ, was the father of St. Gregory the Illuminator (Aa, xxv–xxxiv, cxxi–cxxii). MX, II.xxviii, lxxiv, xci, cf. lxvii (= MK, pp. 166, 214, 220, 250) adds that he was descended from the Iranian house of the Sūrēn. The reference in BP (III.ii) to Anak as St. Gregory's father indicates that the author was familiar with this tradition, but he gives none of its details. Scholars have noted the over-aptness of the name and suggested that it is merely a derogatory epithet; Gignoux renders it "non-mal."

See JIN, p. 15; AG, pp. 17–18 no. 4; CPD, p. 8; Gignoux, *Glossaire*, p. 16; *idem*, NPS, no. 96, p. 42, for the possible etymology of the name; Toumanoff, *Manuel*, p. 223/1.

III.ii

p. 67

See also "Grigor Lusaworičʿ"; "Surēn Pahlaw"; "Xosrov I/II."

Andikan/Andkan ‹ Pahl. **Andīgān*; cf. NP *Andiyān*

Name attested in ŠKZ, Parth. 23; Phl. 29; RGDS no. 57, p. 65,ʹΙνδηγαν.

Persian general presumably sent by Šāhpuhr II against Aršak II. Despite the fact that he is said to have been killed in the first campaign (IV.xxii), he should probably be identified with the homonymous Persian general defeated and killed in IV.xxvii. See the parallel case of his companion Hazarawuχt, if these episodes have any historical foundation (IV.xxii n. 7). The Iranian name Andikan is known, but the personage himself is not otherwise attested.

See JIN, p. 16; AG, p. 18 no. 16; Gignoux, *Glossaire*, pp. 16, 45; Schmitt. IN, p. 331; Sprengling, *Third-Century Iran*, pp. 9, 11, 18; Honigmann and Maricq, RGDS, no. 57, p. 17.

IV.xxii, xxvii

pp. 154–155, 159

See also "Hazarawuχt."

Andkan, see "Andikan."

Andovk/Andoyk/Anduk/Antiokʿ Siwni

The lord of Siwnikʿ, father of Queen Pʿaṙanjem and consequently father-in-law of Aršak II, remains an enigmatic figure in Armenian historiography, and even the forms of his name vary considerably. Modern scholars have attempted to link the various accounts of his career into a coherent unit, but contradictory elements still remain. BP provides the main source of our information, but additional and problematic episodes are provided by MX, who calls him Antiokʿ/Antiochus, and in the *History of Caspian Albania* of Movēs Kałankatuacʿi/Dasχurancʿi.

The account of BP itself contains paradoxes. In all cases but one, Andovk is presented as a great magnate, *išχan* and *nahapet* of Siwnikʿ, and a kinsman of the Mamikonean (III.xi). He is part of the brilliant retinues accompanying the Armenian patriarchs Pʿaṙēn and Nersēs I to their consecrations at Caesarea of Cappadocia (III.xvi; IV.iv), is sent as ambassador to the Byzantine court, and is selected as governor of Armenia in the interregnum preceding the accession of Aršak II (III.xxi). On one occasion, however (IV.xv), he is downgraded to the level of a mere "*naχarar* of the *nahapet* of Siwnikʿ," though he is restored to his dignity before the end of the chapter. Ačaryan suggested that Andovk was raised to the dignity of *nahapet* of Siwnikʿ formerly held by Vałinak by Aršak II. This thesis, based on MX III.xviii, xxiv (= MK, pp. 272, 280), is unlikely because, by MX's own evidence, Vałinak Siwni was *sparapet* of the Armenian eastern army with no indication of his status within the ruling house of Siwnikʿ. Moreover, the dynastic position of *nahapet* of a clan was hereditary and not an office in the king's gift (despite IV.ii) and BP makes it amply clear that Andovk was *nahapet* long before the accession of Aršak II. Finally, the treatment of Andovk in all the Armenian sources, MX and MK/D as well as BP, suggest a leading magnate rather than an inferior nobleman, and MK/D's account of Andovk's indignant rejection of the fourteenth place assigned to him at the Persian court (II.i, pp. 107-109 = MD, pp. 61-63) as unworthy of him further supports this characterization. Consequently, the one negligent reference to Andovk at the beginning of IV.xv is more likely an aberration, perhaps due to the semifictional character of this chapter (see IV.xv nn. 1, 30, 33), especially because a relatively minor figure would have been in no position to resent any offense to his daughter through an intended marriage of Aršak II to a Persian royal princess, the reason adduced by BP (IV.xx) for Andovk's treachery.

The course of Andovk's career between Armenia and Persia is likewise presented ambiguously. Greatly honored in Armenia, the prince of Siwnikᶜ is shown as provoking the thirty years' war between the two realms (IV.xx) to the ultimate destruction of the Armenian kingdom (IV.lv) and especially of his own principality of Siwnikᶜ (IV.lviii). MX, III.xxvi (= MK, p. 281) adds an unattested and perhaps fictional account of Andovk's defense of Tigranakert against the Persians (see Thomson, MK, pp. 281–282 nn. 1, 5), and Movsēs Kałankatuacᶜi, a still more unlikely sack of the Persian capital of Ctesiphon. According to him, Andovk ultimately fled to Byzantium where he was honorably received and died, a report anachronistically amplified by Stepᶜannos Ōrbelean's claim that he has been raised to the rank of patrician by Emperor Theodosius I (I.viii). BP knows nothing of this final expatriation or of the end of Andovk's career, but the absence of any mention of him in the account of the Persian devastation of Siwnikᶜ ca. 367/8 suggests that he was absent or dead by this time, although Toumanoff gives the date of his death as 384/5.

The ambiguities in the portrayal of Andovk and his daughter Pᶜaṙanjem in Armenian historiography may be due in part to mere ignorance of the facts. They may, however, also be colored by implicit antagonism resulting from Siwnikᶜ's particularism, possible religious heterodoxy in the fourth century, and the betrayal of the Armenian nobility led by Vardan Mamikonean on the part of the treacherous Siwni princes Varazvałan and Vasak during the Armenian revolt of 450, which forms the central theme of the *Histories* of ŁPᶜ and Ełišē.

See HAnjB, I, pp. 157–158; Adontz, *Armenia*, pp. 215–218; Toumanoff, *Manuel*, p. 226/2, *Antiochus/Andovk II*; JIN, p. 426.

III.xi, xvi, xxi; IV.iv, xv, xx, li, lviii

pp. 81, 91, 98–99, 111, 140, 152, 168, 178

See also "Aršak II"; "Aršawir Kamsarakan"; "Babik Siwni"; "Mamikonean, house"; "Pᶜaṙanjem"; "Siwni, house"; "Vałinak I,"; and Appendix III, *išχan*; *nahapet*; *naχarar*.

Andoyk, see "Andovk."

Anduk, see "Andovk."

Angełtun, house, see Appendix II, "Angełtun."

Anjewacᶜikᶜ, house, see Appendix II, "Anjewacᶜikᶜ."

Anjit, house, see Appendix II, "Anjit."

Antiochus, see "Andovk."

Apahunikᶜ, house, see Appendix II, "Apahunikᶜ."

Apakan vsemakan

Persian commander, not otherwise attested.
See JIN, p. 18, *Apakan Wsemakan*.
IV.xxxiv
p. 162
See also Appendix III, *vsemakan*.

Aṙalezk⁽ᶜ⁾, see "Aṙlezk⁽ᶜ⁾."

Arcruni, house
 Great *naχarar* family traditionally descended from Sennecherib of Assyria (MX, I.xxiii; II.viii = MK, pp. 112, 138), but presumably of Orontid descent and dynasts of Sophenē. They ruled over the district of Ałbak in the upper valley of the Great Zab with their center at Hadamakert (mod. Başkalē). Despite the massacre of the family recorded by BP (III.xviii), the Arcruni, who are also known to Aa, dccxcv, may have ruled the Median March of Greater Armenia before 371 and gradually acquired the *mardpet*'s domain of Mardpetakan at the end of the Aršakuni period. The house, of which a cadet line is also recorded, is listed in all Lists of *naχarars* and in the *Zōrnamak*, "Military List," which attributes 1000 retainers to them. Their bishops are included in the Armenian conciliar lists (GT⁽ᶜ⁾, pp. 42, 73, 146, etc.). The early history of the Arcruni house is poorly known because of the confusion of the sources, including their family historian, T⁽ᶜ⁾ovma Arcruni, and becomes well documented only with their emergence as the dominant house of Vaspurakan in the mid-ninth century and as its royal house between 908 and 1021.
 The role of the Arcruni in BP is relatively negative after the survival and vengeance of Šawasp for the massacre of his kinsmen (III.xviii; IV.xiv), as it then centers on the career of the archtraitor Meružan.
 See Tournebize, "Ardzrouniq"; Adontz, *Armenia*, 188–189, 191–192, 195–196, 200, 205–207, 228, 230, 250–251, 256, 258, 261, 263, 265, 271, 321, 344, 370, 442 nn. 18–20, 444 n. 24, 445 n. 28, 446 n. 34, 451 n. 85, 463–464 n. 72, 492 n. 52, 516 n. 53, 67*, 69*-70*, 73*-*77, 80*-82*, 93*-98*; Toumanoff, *Studies*, pp. 110 n. 173, 132, 135, where he attributes 2000 retainers to the Arcruni, 160, 162–165, 170, 182, 197, 199–200 and n. 228, 206, 213, 219, 221, 222, 226, 228, 231, 240, 244, 245, 247–248, 251–252, 295, 298 and n. 83, 303, 305, 318, 320–321; *idem, Manuel*, pp. 87–95, of which only p. 87 pertains to the period covered by BP; Barkhudarian, "Urartskoe proiskhozhdenie"; JIN, p. 416.
 III.xviii; IV.xiv, xxiii, xxxi, xxxii, xlii, xlv, l, lviii, lix; V.iv, xxxviii, xliii
 pp. 93, 140, 156, 161, 164–165, 167, 178–179, 189, 222, 224, 226, 228
 See also "Meružan"; "Šawasp"; "Vač⁽ᶜ⁾ē"; Appendix II, "Cop⁽ᶜ⁾k⁽ᶜ⁾"; "Noširakan;" and Appendix III, *naχarar, mardpet*.

Ariank⁽ᶜ⁾/Arians ‹ Gk. Ἀρειανοί; Lat. Ariani
 The heretical followers of Arius of Alexandria are referred to in BP only in connection with the emperor Valens in the intrusive sections from the life of St. Basil of Caesarea.
 See Harnack, *Dogma*, pp. 59–107; Baus, ed., *Imperial Church*, pp. 16–77; LeBachelet, "Arianisme."
 IV.v, viii
 pp. 116, 123, 127, 129

Arianos/Arius ‹ Gk. Ἄρειος; Lat. Arius
 The great heresiarch condemned at the First Council of Nicaea in 325 is mentioned only in passing in connection with the attendance of St. James of Nisibis at this council.
 See Harnack, *Dogma*, pp. 1–59; Baus, ed., *Imperial Church*, pp. 16–32.
 III.x
 p. 79

Arians, see "Ariank⁽ᶜ⁾."

Arik⁽ᶜ⁾/Aryans ‹ Parth. *'ry/ari* "noble," *'ry'n/aryān*, "Iranians," rather than Pahl. *ērān*; cf. Gk. Ἀριανῶν
 Attested in ŠKZ, Parth. 1; RGDS no. 1, p. 47; etc.

BP alternates the correct Iranian term for themselves, *aryān/arik^c*, with the more common Armenian term *Parsk^c*, "Persians." The form Arik^c occurs usually in the more epic contexts presumably derived from oral literature. See IV.xx n. 12.

> See AG, pp. 25–26 no. 22; CPD, p. 30; Gignoux, *Glossaire*, pp. 18, 47; Sprengling, *Third-Century Iran*, pp. 7–14; Honigmann and Maricq, RGDS, p. 11; Meillet, "Elisée," pp. 2–3.
>
> IV.xx, liv; V.iv, v, vii, xliii
> pp. 151, 171, 173, 189, 195, 199, 225
> See also "Parsk^c."

Aristakēs/R̄stakēs ‹ ?Pahl. *rist-āxēz*, "resurrection of the dead"; ‹ ?Pahl. *ristak*, "peasant"; ‹ ?Gk. Ἀρίσταρχος, "best ruling," most likely given the Greek ending -*ēs*

Younger son and immediate successor of his father St. Gregory the Illuminator as primate of Greater Armenia. His career is primarily known from Aa, dccclx–dccclxii, dccclxvi, dccclxxiii, dccclxxxiv–dccclxxv. BP has very little to say about him, though it is clearly familiar with the tradition recorded in Aa to which it adds the account of Aristakēs' burial, which was probably at T^cil in Ekeleac^c (III.ii) although the alternate site of T^cordan in Daranalik^c is also given (III.xiv). MX, II.xci (= MK, p. 249) claims that Aristakēs was murdered in Cop^ck^c and did not die the "confessor's death" recorded by BP (III.ii). In view of the anachronistic reference to "Armenia IV" in MX, the version in BP is probably preferable (see III.ii n. 6). The attendance of Aristakēs at the Council of Nicaea of 325 is known to Aa, dccclxxxiv–dccclxxxv, and to MX, II.lxxxix–xci (= MK, pp. 245–249) as well as to BP (III.x) and is confirmed by the various conciliar lists (*Nomina*, pp. 28–29, 65, 72, 89, 105, 129, 171, 199). MX, II.xci (= MK, p. 249) gives Aristakēs a pontificate of "seven years, from the forty-seventh year of Trdat until the fifty-second," but BP neither dates his pontificate nor gives its length.

> For the Greek and Armenian variants of the name and its proposed etymologies, see HAnjB, I, pp. 277–278 no. 1, and Garitte, *Documents*, pp. 226–227. On the disputed chronology, see Thomson, MK, p. 249 n. 10; Ōrmanean, *Azgapatum*, I, cols. 117–124, xv, who gives the dates 325–333; Toumanoff, *Manuel*, p. 223/3, who gives 320–327. See also JIN, pp. 262, *Rostakes* no. 1, and 423; Honigmann, "Liste," p. 49; Sanspeur, "Nouvelle Liste," cols. 186–187, 195; Garitte, *Documents*, pp. 323–327, 331–332; *idem*, *Narratio*, 57–58, 415–416; Markwart, *Entstehung*, pp. 160–163, 197–199; Peeters, "Les Débuts," p. 20 and nn. 1, 3.
>
> III.ii, v, x, xiv
> pp. 67, 70, 79, 86
> See also "Grigor/Gregorids"; and Appendix II, "Cop^ck^c"; "T^cil"; "T^cordan."

Arius, see "Arianos."

Arjaχ, house, see Appendix II, "Arjaχ."

Aŕlezk^c/Aŕalezk^c/Yaŕalezk^c ‹ ?Akk. *aralu*, "underworld"; This etymology is disputed, and the folk etymology ‹ Ara + Arm. *lezk^c*, "lickers" is untenable.

Composite creatures, presumably winged dogs descending to resuscitate dead heroes exposed in high places by licking their wounds. They are also known to the *Primary History* (Sebēos, i, p. 51 = MK, p. 363) and MX, I.xv (= MK, pp. 97–98 and n. 7). Their existence is explicitly denied by Eznik §122, 124, pp. 454–455 (= trans. pp. 591–592) and Dawit^c Anyalt, pp. 68, 142. T^cA, III.xviii, p. 215 (= *Thom. Arts*, p. 279) associates them with the village of Lezu or Lezk^c in the region of Van. The origin of the belief in the Aŕlezk^c, which was was still evidently current in fifth-century Armenia, is still disputed. Dogs as denizens of the underworld are familiar in most mythologies, from the dog-headed Anubis of Egypt and the four dogs of Marduk, "God of the dogs" and Lord of the Underworld, to the classical Cerberus. Ajello associates the Aŕlezk^c with the eagle-hound of Zeus in Aeschylus (*Prom. vinc.*, vv. 1021–1022) and the Iranian *senmurv*. In Zoroastrian ritual, a dog with spots over his eyes was led around the corpse to ascertain that life was extinct (*Vend.* 8:16–18).

> See NHBL, I, p. 306, HArmB, I, pp. 260–261; HBB, I, p. 229; Matikean, "Aralēznerə"; Ajello, "Aïlez"; Boyce, "Mysteries of the Dog"; *idem, History*, I, pp. 116–117, 120, 163, 302–303; Russell, *Zor. Arm.*, pp. 40, 172, 400, 416.
> V.xxxvi
> p. 217
> See also "Mušeł Mamikonean."

Armenians, see "Haykʿ."

Aïostom, see "Řostom."

Aršak II (350?–367/8) ‹ OP *aršaka-*, "male"; Gk. Ἀρσάκης; Lat. Arsaces

King of Armenia in the mid-fourth century as the successor of his father Tiran, and one of the major protagonists of BP. According to MX, III.xiii (= MK, p. 266), he was Tiran's second son, though this is not specified in BP, and Melikʿ-Ōhanǰanyan suggested, but did not prove, that Aršak's real name must have been Xosrov like that of his grandfather, as names presumably alternated from generation to generation in the Aršakuni house.

Like most of the chronology of the fourth century, the dates of Aršak II's reign are open to dispute, and firm conclusions are still impossible. The traditional dating given by Manandean, 350–367/8 continues to be generally accepted, despite the recent attempts of Hewsen, following Baynes and Peeters, to push the beginning of the reign back to 338 and make him the immediate successor of Xosrov Kotak. This revision would fit the chronology given by MX, III.xxxv (= MK, p. 294), who attributes a thirty years' reign to Aršak, but would require either the excision of the two preceding reigns of Xosrov Kotak and Tiran, or their simultaneous reigns in a divided Armenia, as proposed by Peeters, despite the fact that such a division is not recorded anywhere (see III.xvii n. 7; xxi n. 23). At the opposite end of the reign, there seems to be little doubt, despite Chrysos's reservations, that Aršak II's downfall came in the years closely following Jovian's abandonment of Greater Armenia to the Persians in 363, as attested by both BP (IV.xx–xxi, liv–lv; V.vii) and AM (XXV.vii.12; XXVII.xxi.3).

Aršak II's precise career is equally uncertain, for the information and attitudes of classical and Armenian sources vary considerably. For AM (XXV.vii.12) he was "the constant and faithful friend" of the Romans, distinguished by numerous favors from the emperor Constantius (XX.xi.3; XXI.vi.8), who granted him an imperial bride and an exemption from taxation (CTh, XI.i.1). He seems to have collaborated with the emperor Julian in the campaign of 363 (AM, XXIII.iii.5; XXIV.vii.8; XXV.vii.12) since the threatening letter of Julian "to Arsaces" (*Ep.* lvii) has been shown to be spurious. A far more ambiguous relationship of Armenia toward both Persia and the Romans is presented in BP (IV.xi, xvi, xx, liv), followed by Procopius (*Bell. Pers.*, I.v.19–25). Consequently, there may have been shifts in policy, from neutrality in the early part of Aršak's reign, to a possible rapprochement with Persia, followed by a sudden shift to Rome in 358, as a result of Constantius's favors (see IV.xx n. 18). Similar contradictions mark the accounts of Aršak's life. AM, XXVII.xii.3 has Aršak captured, blinded, and executed by the Persians, while BP (III.xx) attributes the imprisonment and blinding to his father Tiran and has the captive Aršak commit suicide in the "Castle of Oblivion" in Persia (V.vii), as do MX,III.xxxv (= MK, p. 294) and Procopius (*Bell. Pers.* I.v.29, 39). BP's own attitude is ambivalent. It stresses Aršak's position as the "true lord" of Armenia and as a Christian king in opposition to the rebellious *naχarars* (IV.li) and invokes the protective power of his valor (*kʿaǰutʿiwn*) in the Persian war (V.v), at the same time as it condemns the king for the construction of the evil city of Aršakawan (V.xiii) and portrays him as accursed for the murder of his nephew Gnel (IV.xv).

The reasonably certain features of Aršak II's reigns are: (1) the king's attempt to maintain an equilibrium between Rome and Persia, ending in his overthrow and captivity after Jovian's peace of 363; (2) Aršak's parallel attempt to consolidate the royal power within his realm by curbing or even extirpating the turbulent *naxarar* clans (IV.ii, xix) and by the creation of the new urban center of Aršakawan (IV.xii) both of which alienated the magnates, who failed to support him against Persia in 363 (IV.l); (3) his marriages to both the Roman Olympias and Pʿaṙanjem of Siwnikʿ, who bore his son and successor Pap, although the order of these marriages remains uncertain (see IV.xv n. 40); (4) the king's growing disagreement with the Armenian church, culminating in the departure from court and exile of the patriarch Nersēs the Great (IV.v[end]-vi, xv). In BP, these facts have been interpreted and contaminated by two elements, representing opposing points of view: (1) the reflected antagonism of the Armenian ecclesiastical milieu to Aršak's attempt to coordinate his religious position with the prevailing Arianizing tendencies of the Constantinopolitan court; (2) BP's reliance on oral traditions embodied in epic paeans and threnodies glorifying and mourning Aršak (V.v and nn. 4, 8, 18; V.vii n. 6).

See Gignoux, *Glossaire*, p. 46; Schmitt, IN, pp. 321, 326, 330; JIN, pp. 29 no. 21 and 414 no. 35; Jones *et al.*, *Prosopography*, I, p. 109, *Arsaces III*; Toumanoff, *Manuel*, p. 75/8; Manandyan, *Kʿnnakan texutʿyun*, II.l, pp. 141–161, 441; Hewsen, "Successors"; *idem*, "Tiridates," p. 42–43; "Rome and Armenia"; Peeters, "Persécution"; *idem*, "Intervention"; Chrysos, *Legal Relations*, pp. 32–36; Garsoïan, "Politique."

III.xviii, xx, xxi; IV.i-v, xi-xvi, xviii-xxvi, xxxii-xxxiii, xxxvi, xxxviii, xl-xli, xliv, xlv, xlvii-lv; V.i, iii-v, vii, xxxvii, xliii.

pp. 93, 96, 99–100, 107–112, 124, 132–136, 139, 141, 143–159, 161–174, 185–186, 189, 191, 195–199, 218, 224

See also "Aršakuni"; "Ołompi"; "Nersēs I"; "Pap"; "Pʿaṙanjem"; "Tiran"; Appendix II, "Aljnikʿ"; "Anjit"; "Anyuš"; "Arjax" "Aršakawan"; "Artagers"; "Copʿkʿ Mec"; "Gardman"; "Gugarkʿ"; "Kazbkʿ"; "Kordukʿ"; "Maracʿ amur ašxarh"; "Mec Haykʿ"; "Noširakan"; and Appendix III, *bnak tēr; kʿaj, naxarar.*

Aršak III (378–390?) ‹ OP *Aršaka-*, "male"; Gk. Ἀρσάκης; Lat. Arsaces

Elder son King Pap and Queen Zarmanduxt. He was enthroned together with his brother Vałaršak under the regency of their mother by the *sparapet* Manuēl Mamikonean (V.xxxvii), who gave him his daughter Vardanduxt in marriage (V.xliv), although MX, III.xli, xliii (= MK, pp. 303, 305) claims the young queen was the daughter of Babik Siwni and that Aršak's accession was entirely due to the will of the emperor "Theodosius the Great" (379–395), which is chronologically impossible. After the death of Manuēl Mamikonean (ca. 384) soon followed by that of Vałaršak, the Persians attacked Armenia once more under Šāhpuhr III, who supported another Aršakuni candidate, Xosrov III/IV. Aršak III fled to the northwestern district of Ekełeacʿ (ca. 385), where he ruled after the partition of Armenia between Rome and the Persians (ca. 387), and where he died soon thereafter, probably ca. 390, bringing the rule of the Aršakuni on imperial territory to a close. The end of his reign lay beyond the chronological limits of BP's account, but see MX, III.xli-xliii, xlvi (= MK, pp. 303–306, 308–309), who says that Aršak reigned for five years over the whole of Armenia and for two and a half years over the western portion; cf. ŁPʿ, I, vi-viii, pp. 8–12 (= CHAMA, II, pp. 262–264).

See HAnjB, I, p. 293 no. 8; Gignoux, *Glossaire*, p. 46; Schmitt, IN, pp. 321, 326, 330; JIN, p. 29 no. 24, who gives him a reign of only one year at Duin, and 414 §38a, where he gives Aršak III successively both the wives mentioned in the

Armenian sources; Toumanoff, *Manuel*, p. 76/10; Jones *et al.*, *Prosopography*, I, p. 109, "Arsaces IV"; AG, p. 27 §24; Manandyan, *K*ʿ*nnakan tesut*ʿ*yun*, II.I, pp. 235–248.

V.xxxvii–xxxviii, xliii–xliv; VI.i, v, vii

pp. 221, 226, 228–229, 233–235

See also "Aršakuni"; "Manuēl Mamikonean"; "Vałaršak"; "Vardanduχt"; and Appendix II, "Ekełeacʿ."

Aršakuni ‹ OP *Aršaka-*, "male"; Gk. Ἀρσάκιδαι; Eng. Arsacids

Armenian ruling dynasty in the fourth century. The Armenian Aršakuni were a junior branch of the Parthian royal house of Iran, who made their first appearance in Armenia in A.D. 12 with the king of kings Vonones. The position of the dynasty on the throne of Armenia was confirmed by the coronation of Trdat I by Nero in A.D. 66, but the Aršakuni do not seem to have established themselves as a continuous dynasty in Greater Armenia before A.D. 180. Their hereditary domain was the central district of Ayrarat, in which were located the capitals of Artašat and Duin, but they possessed domains in a number of other districts as well. The royal necropolis was first at Ani in Daranałikʿ, then at Ałjkʿ.

The precise succession and especially the chronology of the dynasty remain riddled with problems and open to considerable controversy in all periods, despite the information of classical and Armenian sources, which are often contradictory. The genealogical table proposed by Justi is obsolete, and the succession given by Toumanoff still incompletely accepted, even though it is most probable. Consequently, final conclusions remain impossible at present.

The overthrow of the senior Arsacid branch in Iran, ca. 224, created a blood feud between their Armenian kinsmen and the new Sasanian dynasty (Aa, xviii–xx; BP, IV.liv), and the conversion of Greater Armenia to Christianity in 314 separated it still further from Iran. Nevertheless, the Armenian Aršakuni sought to maintain an uneasy balance between Rome and the Sasanians and to control the centrifugal tendencies of their unruly nobles for nearly two centuries thereafter. The dynasty was deeply Iranized in ethos and manners, as is indicated by the Iranian names of all of its members and the transcendental Iranian virtues of *p*ʿ*arkʿ*, *baχt*, and *kʿajutʿiwn*, together with the formulaic epithet, "*kʿaj arancʿ*, most-valiant-of-men" attributed to them by Aa, xvii, cxxvii, dcccxcii, and BP (IV.xxiv; V.v), as well as by their possession of the kingship as a hereditary office, which made them the *bnak tearkʿ*, "true/native/basic lords" of Armenia, an Iranian concept altogether foreign to the classical world (III.xi; IV.xxiv; V.xx, xliv). At the same time, the Armenian Aršakuni were dependent on Rome, which had reinstated Trdat the Great in 298, probably Tiran in 338, and Pap ca. 369 on their ancestral throne and showered gifts and tax immunities on Aršak II (AM, XX.xi.3; XI.i.l). Consequently, they often aligned their policy with Constantinople against Persia and also followed the Arianizing policies of the successors of Constantine the Great during the fourth century, thus coming into conflict with the Armenian church under the "orthodox" patriarchs of the house of St. Gregory the Illuminator, an alienation reflected in the antagonism displayed toward them by BP. Nevertheless, Aršakuni princesses often married into the patriarchal house (III.v, xv, xix; IV.iii).

The abandonment of Greater Armenia to the Persians by Jovian's peace of 363 (AM, XXV.vii; BP, IV.xxi and n. 5) spelled the downfall of the Aršakuni dynasty despite the brief reestablishment of Pap and his successors on the throne. Probably in 387, though the date is disputed, Aršakuni Armenia was divided in two unequal portions (VI.i; MX, III.xlii = MK, p. 304; ŁPʿ, I.vi–viii, pp. 8–12 = CHAMA, II, pp. 262–264; Procopius, *De aed.*, III.i.4–15, who sets the division under Theodosius II), with Pap's elder son Aršak III/IV ruling under Roman auspices at Karin/Theodosioupolis until ca. 390, while another Aršakuni candidate, Xosrov III/IV held Persarmenia. The death of Aršak III/IV marked the end of the Aršakuni on imperial territory, where they were replaced by a *comes Armeniae* (Procopius *De aed.* III.i.15), although members of this house continued to play important roles at the Byzantine court (see e.g. Procopius, *Bell. Pers*, II.iii; *Bell. Vand.*, II.xxiv–xxviii; *Bell. Goth.*, III.xxxii; Sebēos, xliv, pp. 140–143 = trans. pp. 103, 105–106). In Persarmenia, the dynasty lingered until the early fifth century when, according to MX, III.lxiv (= MK, pp. 340–341) the Sasanians replaced the last Aršakuni king by a governor or *marzpan* at the request of the Armenian magnates themselves. BP (III.vii; V.vii, xxxvii) claims perhaps mistakenly that both Sanesan, king of the Mask⁣ᶜut⁣ᶜk⁣ᶜ, and the kings of the Kᶜušans were members of the Aršakuni house, and branches of this family are known to have ruled in neighboring Ałuankᶜ and Iberia. In Armenia, the Kamsarakan were considered to be their kinsmen and MX, II.viii, xxii (= MK, p. 146, 159) identifies the Kaminakan as the Aršakuni branch settled in Hašteankᶜ although he does not name them. Finally the Persian generals, Ałanayozan, Hrewšołum, and Surēn Pahlaw are also given as their kinsmen in BP (IV. xxiii, xxxvii, xxxviii).

See JIN, p. 414; Toumanoff, *Studies*, pp. 192–196; *idem*, "Third-Century Arsacids"; *idem, Manuel*, 73–76, for the Armenian line, 78 for the Iberians, and 79–80 for the Albanians; Hewsen, "Successors"; Manandyan, *Kᶜnnakan tesutᶜyun*, II/1; Ananian, "La Data;" Garsoïan, "Politique" on the religious policy of the fourth century; Krkyašaryan, "Išχanutᶜyunə"; Kanayeancᶜ, *Kᶜajancᶜ tan*; and the additional bibliography under "Aršak II."

P.S.; III.vi, vii, xi; IV.v, xiv–xvi, xxiv, xxxviii, li, lv; V.i, vii–viii, xix–xx, xxxiv–xxxv, xxxvii, xliii–xliv; VI.i.

pp. 63, 72, 74, 81, 124, 139, 141, 143, 147, 157–158, 163, 168, 174–175, 186, 197–199, 201–202, 215–219, 221, 226, 228–229, 233–234

See also "Aršak II"; "Aršak III"; "Aršakuni, anonymous princess"; "Aršakuni, anonymous queens"; "Ałanayozan"; "Bambišn"; "Gnel"; "Hrewšołum"; "Kaminakan, house"; "Kamsakaran, house"; "Pap"; "Sanatruk"; "Sasanians"; "Sanēsan"; "Surēn Pahlaw"; "Tigran"; "Tiran"; "Tiritᶜ"; "Trdat"; "Vałaršak"; "Varazdat"; "Varazduχt"; "Xosrov Kᶜaĵ"; "Xosrov Kotak"; Xosrov III/IV"; Appendix II, "Ałiovit"; "Ałjkᶜ"; "Angełtun"; "Ani"; "Artašat"; "Atrpatakan"; "Ayrarat"; "Copᶜkᶜ"; "Darewnkᶜ"; "Gaṙni"; "Hašteankᶜ"; "Karin"; "Kogovit Korčēkᶜ"; "Mec Haykᶜ"; "Zarišat"; and Appendix III, *baχt; bnak tēr; kᶜaĵ; kᶜaĵ arancᶜ; pᶜaṙkᶜ*.

Aršakuni, anonymous princess

Wife of the patriarch Yusik I and mother of Pap and Atᶜanaginēs. Her name is not given, and BP calls her the "daughter" of King Tiran, which seems unlikely chronologically (see III.v n. 4). She is not otherwise attested, but according to Toumanoff she must have been the daughter of Trdat the Great and the sister of Xosrov Kotak, rather than the daughter of Tiran and consequently the sister of Aršak II.

See Toumanoff, *Manuel*, p. 74/6 and note; JIN, p. 414 makes her the daughter of Xosrov Kotak and the sister of Tiran.

III.v

p. 70

See also "Atᶜanaginēs"; "Grigor/Gregorids"; "Pap (2)"; "Tiran"; "Varazduχt," for Aršakuni-Gregorid intermarriages; "Yusik I."

Aršakuni, anonymous queen I

Wife of Xosrov Kotak who sought the murder of the patriarch Vrtᶜanēs. BP does not give her name, and she is otherwise unattested even in Toumanoff's genealogy of the Aršakuni house.

See Toumanoff, *Manuel*, p. 74/6, where there is no indication of Xosrov Kotak's marriage, though his children are duly listed.
III.iii
pp. 68–69
See also "Aršakuni"; "Vrtᶜanēs"; "Xosrov II/III"; and Appendix III, *tikin.*

Aršakuni, anonymous queen II
Wife of Tiran taken captive with him and presumably the mother of Aršak II. She is otherwise unattested even in Toumanoff's genealogy.
See Toumanoff, *Manuel*, p. 74/7
III.xx
pp. 96–97
See also "Aršak II"; "Aršakuni"; "Tiran"; and Appendix III, *tikin.*

Aršakuni, queen, see "Zarmanduχt."

Aršarunikᶜ, house, see "Kamsarakan."

Aršawir Kamsarakan
Nahapet of the Kamsarakan house and consequently lord of Širak and Aršarunikᶜ in the first half of the fourth century. According to MX, II.xc (= MK, p. 247), he was the eldest son of the Aršakuni Kamsar, and was granted Aršarunikᶜ by Trdat the Great after his father's death. Both BP and MX list him among the greatest magnates of the realm, but they do not agree on the details of his career. BP does not mention his father or his Aršakuni descent, but makes him a son-in-law of the Mamikonean (III.xi). Along with other leading nobles he is said to have accompanied the patriarchs Pᶜaṙen and Nersēs I to their consecration at Caesarea (III.xvi; IV.iv). After the imprisonment of King Tiran by the Persians, he was sent together with Andovk Siwni to seek the help of the Byzantine court and was installed as governor of Armenia by the emperor in the interregum preceding the return of the Aršakuni heir Aršak II (III.xxi). MX knows nothing of the journeys to Caesarea or Byzantium and transposes Aršawir's governorship—at the order of the patriarch Vrtᶜanēs and not of the emperor—to the end of the reign of Xosrov Kotak (MX, III.x = MK, p. 263). This second version seems less probable, for MX speaks of embassies before and after Xosrov's reign, and we have no case of the patriarch appointing a governor for Armenia. MX, III.xxxi (= MK, p. 288 and n. 2) further makes Aršawir's son Spandarat the only survivor of the Kamsarakan massacre ordered by Aršak II; but BP does not mention this relationship, nor does it specify whether Aršawir was still alive at the time (IV.xix).
See HAnjB, I, pp. 296–297, *Aršawir* no. 4; JIN, p. 30, *Aršavir* no. 5 and p. 425; Toumanoff, *Manuel*, p. 266/4, where he accepts the relationship between Aršawir and Spandarat given in MX; *idem, Studies*, p. 171 n. 90.
III.xi, xvi, xxi; IV.iv
pp. 81, 91, 98–99, 111
See also "Andovk Siwni"; "Aršak II"; "Kamsarakan, house"; "Mamikonean, house"; "Spandarat"; and Appendix III, *nahapet.*

Artabanos, see "Artawan."

Artašēn Mamikonean, see "Artašēs/Artašēn."

Artašēs/Artašēn Mamikonean ‹ OP *Artaχšasa-*, "ruling righteously"
Sepuh of the Mamikonean house, father of the *sparapet* Manuēl and of his brother Koms. He may have been a son of the *sparapet* Vačᶜē I rather than of Artawazd II, but he is otherwise unattested. The form Artašēn is taken by Ačaryan as a diminutive of Artašēs and is a *hapax.*

See HAnjB, I, p. 305, *Artašēs*; JIN, p. 37, *Artašin*, and 424, where he gives his father's names as Šahēn?; Toumanoff, *Manuel*, p. 331/4d, who makes him a probable son of Artawazd II, which seems unlikely given Artawazd's youth (see III.xi, and xviii n. 3); Markwart, *Untersuchungen* p. 219; and Schmitt, *Artaxerxes* on the forms of the name; *idem*, IN, pp. 320-321, 324, 330; Gignoux, "Noms propres," p. 67.

V.xxxvii

p. 218

See also "Artawazd II"; "Hamazaspean" for the Mamikonean genealogy; "Koms"; "Mamikonean, house"; "Manuēl"; Vač̔ē I"; and Appendix III, *sepuh*.

Artašēs/Artašir Mamikonean ‹ OP *Artaxšasa-*, "ruling righteously"
Form Ardaxšīr attested in ŠKZ, Parth. 1, 18, 20-28; Phl. 22, 28-35; RGDS no. 1, 46, 55-57, 60, 62, 66, 67, pp. 60-72; etc.

Sepuh of the Mamikonean house and son of Manuēl, whom he succeeded as *sparapet* (III.xliv). His name is given alternately as Artašēs (V.xxxvii) and Artašir (V.xliv), but it seems clear from the context that the references are to the same person, even though Justi dissociates the two. The proper form of the name was probably Artašēs, for he would traditionally have been named after his grandfather Artašēs/Artašēn (see the preceding entry). The *Vita* of St. Nersēs, xv, p. 123 (= CHAMA, II, p. 44) calls him Artawazd and makes Manuēl's second son. He is not attested elsewhere.

See Gignoux, *Glossaire*, pp. 17, 46; *idem*, NPS nos. 126-129, pp. 46-47; HAnjB, I, p. 308, *Artašēs* no. 11; Toumanoff, *Manuel*, p. 332/6d, who calls him Artaschir/Artavazde III; AG, pp. 28-29, 31; JIN, p. 35, *Artaxšaθra* no. 18, and 37, 'Αρταξίας, no. 8, and p. 424; Markwart, *Untersuchungen*, p. 219; Benveniste, *Titres et noms propres*, p. 102 for the dissociation of MP Artašīr and Arm. Artašēs; Schmitt, "Artaxerxes"; *idem*, IN, p. 330.

V.xxxvii, xliv

pp. 219, 228

See also "Mamikonean, house"; "Manuēl Mamikonean"; and Appendix III, *sepuh*; *sparapet*.

Artašir Mamikonean, see "Artašēs/Artašir."

Artawan V/Artewan ‹ Parth. *Ardavān*; Gk. 'Αρτάβανος; Lat. Artabanus
Names attested in ŠKZ, Parth., 26, 28; Phl. 32, 33; RGDS no. 63, 67, pp. 70-73; etc.

Last Parthian king of Iran from the Aršakuni senior line, defeated and killed by the Sasanian Ardašīr I ca. 224. The "vengeance for the blood of Artawan" is the opening theme of Aa, xviii-xix. The Greek version in Ag, ii-ixa; p. 9, though no other, even precedes it by an interpolated passage on the revolt of Ardašīr derived from the Iranian *Kārnāmag-i Ardašīr*. This tradition is also known to MX, II.lxx-lxxi (= MK, pp. 217-218) and the obligatory blood feud for a murdered kinsman assumed and maintained from generation to generation is explicitly alluded to in the threats attributed to Aršak II by BP (IV.liv). The form "Artewan" given here by BP occurs in neither Aa nor MX who use Artawan, and is probably a *lapsus*, since Artawan is found elsewhere; see, e.g., next entry.

See JIN, pp. 31-32, 'Αρτάβανος no. 13 and 413; Debevoise *Parthia*, pp. 263-269; Bivar, "Arsacids." pp. 94-99; Thomson, Aa, pp. xxvi-xxvii, on the tradition in Armenia; Garitte, *Documents*, pp. 272-279 and Akinean, "Artašir," on the interpolation in Ag; also Garsoïan, "Prolegomena," cols. 178, 188-189, on the obligation of the blood feud among the Armenian Aršakuni and its political implications. Gignoux, *Glossaire*, pp. 17, 46; *idem*, NPS no. 425, p. 46; Schmitt,

IN, p. 321; Sprengling, *Third-Century Iran*, pp. 9, 12, 19; Honigmann and Maricq, RGDS, p. 18 on the attestations of the name.

IV.liv

p. 172

See also "Aršakuni"; "Sasanians."

Artawan of Vanand ⟨ Parth. Ardavān; Gk. Ἀρτάβανος; Lat. Artabanus

Name "Artawan" attested in ŠKZ, Parth. 26, 28; Phl. 32, 33; RGDS, no. 63, 67, pp. 70–73; etc.

Prince of Vanand and presumed successor of Vorot' (III.xii). He is not otherwise attested and BP mentions no princes of Vanand after him.

See HAnjB, I, p. 317, *Artawan* no. 4; JIN, p. 32 Ἀρτάβανος no. 14, who mistakenly identifies him as a member of the Saharuni house through a confusion with the anonymous Saharuni prince who precedes him immediately in BP's list at this point. See Intro. p. 13 and also additional bibliography on the name in the preceding entry.

III.xiv

p. 87

See also Appendix II, "Vorot"; "Vanand."

Artawazd I Mamikonean ⟨ Av. *Ašavazdah-*, "one who furthers righteousness"; cf. ?Phl. *Ard-vast*

First attested *sparapet* of Greater Armenia. He is named by Aa, dccclx and identified by BP as the father of his successor Vač'ē I Mamikonean (III.iv). Consequently, he was evidently a member of the Mamikonean house and not a Mandakuni, as is claimed by MX, II.lxxvi, lxxxii, lxxxv; III.vi (= MK, pp. 223–224, 232, 237, 258). Most scholars have followed the identification of BP, for, as Thomson rightly observes, the office of *sparapet* was hereditary in the Mamikonean house and MX's alteration must be attributed to his notorious anti-Mamikonean bias (see Intro., pp. 44–45). This interpretation is reinforced by MX's observation that Artawazd was the "foster-father" and "foster-brother" of the Aršakuni kings (II.lxxxii; III.vi = MK, pp. 232, 258), a relationship that BP also attributes to the Mamikonean (III.xviii; IV.ii), and by the identification of the *sparapet* Artawazd as a Mamikonean in several of the versions of the Agat'angełos cycle (Ag cxxiv, Aar cxii). Artawazd I was presumably killed in the great northern war under Trdat the Great (MX, II.lxxxv = MK, p. 237).

See Gignous, NPS, no. 137, p. 48 on *Ard-vast*; Schmitt, IN, p. 329; HAnjB, I, p. 313, nos. 9–10; JIN, pp. 39 no. 14 and 424; Toumanoff, *Manuel*, p. 331/1; Thomson, Aa, pp. 497–498, §860 n. 2; *idem*, MK, p. 224 n. 10; Adontz, *Armenia*, pp. 22, 517 n. 54; Garitte, *Documents*, p. 223; Markwart, *Untersuchungen*, p. 219.

III.iv, vii

pp. 69, 74

See also "Aršakuni"; "Mamikonean, house"; "Vač'ē I"; and Appendix III, *dayeak*; *sparapet*.

Artawazd II Mamikonean ⟨ Av. *Ašavazdah-*, "one who furthers righteousness"; cf. ? Phl. *Ard-vast*

Sepuh of the Mamikonean house, son of the *sparapet* Vač'ē I, who inherited his father's office when only a child (see III.xi n. 7). He seems to have shared this office with his more famous kinsman Vasak, and probably reached maturity by the end of Tiran's reign, since his daughters are presumably referred to (III.xviii). The *Vita* of St. Nersēs ii, p. 17 (= CHAMA, II, p. 22) attributes four sons, including Vasak, to him, which seems unlikely on chronological grounds, though this information is accepted by both

Justi and Toumanoff. Artawazd is no longer mentioned in the reign of Aršak II and he is unknown to MX, a silence that seems to confirm a short-lived career. The two mentions in the later sources, the *Vita* of St. Nersēs and TᶜA, I.ix, seem both derived from BP.

> See HAnjB, I, p. 313 no. 11; JIN, pp. 39 no. 15 and 424; Toumanoff, *Manuel*, p. 331/3; Markwart, *Untersuchungen*, p. 219. The Venice edition, index, p. 290, confuses this Artawazd with his homonymous grandfather, Artawazd I. See also Gignoux, NPS no. 137, p. 48; Schmitt, IN, p. 329 on *Ard-vast*.
>
> III.xi, xviii
> pp. 81, 93
> See also "Hamazasp Mamikonean" for the Mamikonean genealogy; "Mamikonean, house"; "Vačᶜē I"; "Vasak" and Appendix III, *sepuh*.

Artawazd III Mamikonean ‹ Av. *Ašavazdah-*, "one who furthers righteousness"; cf. ?Phl. *Ard-vast*

Sepuh of the Mamikonean house, son of Vačᶜē II, who distinguished himself despite his extreme youth at the final defeat of Meružan Arcruni in which his father was killed. This episode may, however, be part of the child-hero tale known to the Iranian epic tradition (see V.xliii n. 13).

> See HAnjB, I, p. 213 no. 12; JIN, pp. 39 no. 17 and 424; Toumanoff, *Manuel*, p. 332/6e; Markwart, *Untersuchungen*, p. 219. See also Gignoux, NPS, no. 137 p. 48; Schmitt, IN, p. 329 on *Ard-vast*.
>
> V.xliii
> p. 226–228
> See also "Mamikonean, house"; "Vačᶜē II"; and Appendix III, *sepuh*.

Artewan, see "Artawan V."

Artitᶜ/Artitᶜēs ‹ ?OIr., *Arta-*, "righteousness" + *-it*; ‹ ?Gk. Ἀρτίτης/Ἄρτιος

Bishop of Basean according to BP (VI.vii). He may be identifiable with the Artitᶜēs listed as the eighth disciple of St. Gregory the Illuminator (Aa, dcccxlv and Thomson, *ibid.* p. 496 n. 4), who is presumably the one whose apocryphal letter about St. Gregory is mentioned in MX, II.lxxx (= MK, pp. 228–229). The identification is tempting, as the names of the bishops listed in BP VI bear a considerable ressemblance to the list of Gregorid bishops in Aa. Nonethless, other factors tend rather to dissociate the two: (1) BP calls Artitᶜ bishop of Basean; Aa, dcccxlv, does not mention the name of his see, but Vg, clxxii (= Va, clx) identifies it as Malχazan; (2) the bishops in Aa's list were former pagans consecrated by St. Gregory, while Artitᶜ in BP was a disciple of St. Daniēl consecrated under King Tiran and nothing is said about his antecedents; (3) the Artitᶜēs consecrated by St. Gregory would be very old indeed at the end of the fourth century, some three generation later. Ališan identifies him with Trdat, bishop of Basean.

> See HAnjB, I, p. 319 nos. 1–2, who differentiates the two personages, also V, p. 178, *Trdat*, nos. 9–10; JIN, p. 327, *Tiridates*, no. 18; Ališan, *Ayrarat*, p. 43.
>
> VI.vii
> p. 235
> See also "Daniēl"; and Appendix II, "Basean"; "Malχazan."

Artitᶜēs, see "Artitᶜ."

Artoyt, Arm. "sky-lark"

Hermit and disciple of St. Gind. Not otherwise attested, and his name appears to be a nickname.

> See HAnjB, I, p. 319; and HArmB, I, pp. 343–344 on the meaning of the name; JIN, p. 40.
>
> VI.xvi
> p. 239
> See also "Gind"; "Maraχ"; "Vačᶜak."

Aryans, see "Arik^c."

Asirk, see "Asurk."

Asori, "Syriac/Syrian"
Term normally used in BP for both the language and the people of Mesopotamia.
See NHBL I, p. 314
III.xiii, xiv; IV.iv; V.xxv
pp. 84, 86, 114, 205
See also Appendix II "Asorestan."

Aspahapet, see Appendix III, *aspet.*

Aspurak of Manazkert ‹ OP *Aspagāra*, "horse rider"
Patriarch of Armenia who preceded St. Sahak I, according to all the Armenian
sources except for the *List of Katholikoi* (Paris. Arm. 121). He was one of the descendants of Bishop Ałbianos of Manazkert (III.iv) and the *List* makes him the brother of
Zawēn and Šahak/Yusik, although BP and MX, III.xli (= MK, p. 303) merely say that
he was their kinsman. BP has nothing to say about the length of his pontificate and
entitles him "senior bishop" rather than "patriarch"; MX, III.xli, xlix (= MK, pp. 303,
313) merely records his accession in the second year of the reign of Aršak III and his
death under Xosrov III/IV. According to the various Armenian sources, the length of
his pontificate varied from the usual five or seven years to as much as twenty. Ōrmanean
gives the dates 381–386.
  See HAnjB, I, p. 231 no. 1; JIN, p. 47; Ōrmanean, *Azgapatum*, I, cols. 245–256, xvii;
    Garitte, *Narratio*, pp. 87–88, 419–420; Sanspeur, "Nouvelle Liste," cols. 187–188,
    196–198; Garsoïan, "Šahak of Manazkert" on the order of the kat^{c}ołikoi from
    P^{c}aṙēn to St. Sahak I.
  VI.iv, xv
  pp. 235, 238
  See also "Ałbianos of Manazkert"; "Šahak II"; "Zawēn"; and Appendix III, *senior
    bishop.*

Asurk/Asirk
Son-in-law and successor of Xad of Marag as bishop of Bagrewand and Aršarunik^c.
Not otherwise attested. The correct nominative form of this name cannot be recon-
structed from this *hapax* because of the drop of the interconsonantal vowel in inflected
cases. The form Asurk has generally been preferred by scholars.
  See HAnjB, I, pp. 250–251; JIN, p. 47
  IV.xii
  p. 136
  See also "Xad"; and Appendix II, "Bagrewand"; "Aršarunik^c."

Atam, see "Atom."

At^{c}anaginēs ‹ Gk. 'Αθενογένης
Son of the patriarch Yusik, great-grandson of St. Gregory the Illuminator, and
father of the patriarch Nersēs I. At^{c}anaginēs was named after the saint whose relics were
brought to Armenia by St. Gregory (Aa, dccx, dcccxxxvi). Thereafter the name almost
disappears from the Armenian onomasticon thereafter, possibly as a result of his unfortunate memory. Together with his twin brother Pap, At^{c}anaginēs was considered
unworthy to assume the patriarchal office of his family, which both rejected in favor of
military careers, perhaps fearing the danger of the inflexible theological position that
had opposed their father to the Aršakuni kings of Armenia and led to his martyrdom.
Their decision created the first temporary hiatus in the hereditary transmission of the

patriarchate in the Gregorid house and resulted in their unanimous condemnation in the sources. BP gives a far more circumstantial account of his career and death than the brief notice in MX, III.xvi (= MK, pp. 269–270), and is the only source to mention his marriage to the Aršakuni princess Bambišn, except for the *Vita* of St. Nersēs, i, p. 13 (= CHAMA, II, p. 22), which merely condenses the information in BP. At^canaginēs, together with his brother Pap, was buried at Aštišat, and not with their ancestors.

See HAnjB, I, pp. 66–67 no. 1; JIN, p. 423; Toumanoff, *Manuel*, p. 224/5; Ōrmanean, *Azgapatum*, I, cols. 152–153; AG, I, pp. 333–334

III.v, xiii, xv, xix; IV.iii

pp. 71, 85, 91, 93–94, 109

See also "Aršakuni"; "Bambišn"; "Grigor/Gregorids"; "Nersēs I"; "Pap (2)"; "Yusik I"; and Appendix II, "Agarak."

Atom/Atam of Gołt^cn
Armenian *naχarar* not otherwise attested.
See HAnjB, I, p. 254 no. 1; JIN, p. 48, *Atam* no. 2; Ališan, *Sisakan*, p. 310.

III.xii

p. 82

See also Appendix II, "Gołt^cn"; and Appendix III, *naχarar*.

Aycemnik; Hebr. *Ṭbītā*; Syr. *ṣebāim*; Gk. Δόρκας, "gazelle"
BP, following the Armenian Bible (Acts 9:36–39), gives the direct translation of the name into Armenian from Hebrew, without reference to the Greek form.
See HAnjB, I, p. 142.

IV.iv

p. 115

Babik Siwni ‹ hypocoristic MP *bab*, "father"; cf. *Pap*
Nahapet of the house of Siwnik^c who survived the Persian massacre (IV.lviii) and returned to regain his domain with the help of the *sparapet* Manuēl Mamikonean (V.xlii). According to BP, he became the *sparapet*'s companion-in-arms and helped him kill the traitor Meružan Arcruni (V.xliii). The precise identity and career of Babik are disputed because the name was common in the Siwni house. Dowsett identifies him with the fourth son of Andovk Siwni, who was reinstated by the Persian king and not by Manuēl Mamikonean, according to MK/D (II.i, pp. 109–111 = MD, pp. 63–64 and n. 3), but Ačaryan differentiates the two Babiks. Adontz identified the Babik of MK/D, whom he made a descendant rather than a son of Andovk (despite MK/D's explicit identification), with the supporter of Vahan Mamikonean in the later part of the fifth century known to ŁP^c, III.lxiii, p. 112 (= CHAMA, II, p. 332), though this seems rather farfetched. There seems to be little doubt that as *nahapet* of Siwnik^c Babik probably was Andovk's son. Moreover, MX, III.xli, xliii, xlvi (= MK, pp. 303, 305, 308–309) confirms his importance by making him, rather than Manuēl Mamikonean, the father-in-law of Aršak III (cf. V.xliv) and by identifying his son Dara as the *sparapet* of Aršak III. Babik also appears to have been the father of the archtraitor Vasak Siwni, though this fact is not specified in the sources and lies beyond the chronological limits of BP.

See Gignoux, NPS, no. 175 p. 53, *Bābīg*; *idem*, "Noms propres," pp. 62–64; Schmitt, IN, p. 330; HAnjB, I, p. 351, *Babik* nos. 1–2; JIN, pp. 55 no. 1 and 426 no. 2; Toumanoff, *Manuel*, p. 226/3, who makes him Andovk's eldest son and the father of Vasak as well as of Dara; Adontz, *Armenia*, pp. 216–217, 449, nn. 51a–52.

V.xlii–xliii

pp. 224, 226–227

See also "Andovk Siwni"; "Manuēl Mamikonean"; "Meružan Arcruni"; "Siwni"; and Appendix III, *nahapet; nizakakicᶜ*.

Bagas, see "Bagos."

Bagean, house

Naχarar family not attested elsewhere, except in the late *Vita* of St. Nersēs, viii, p. 52, (= CHAMA, II, p. 30, "Parné") unless they are to be identified with the Baguankᶜ, *ibid.*, p. 35 (= CHAMA, II, p. 26 "Pakovan").
See Toumanoff, *Studies*, pp. 216, 223–224, 226, 237 n. 306, 253 n. 343.
IV.xi
p. 133
See also "Kiškēn"; and Appendix III, *naχarar*.

Bagos/Bagas Mamikonean ⟨ OP *Baga-*, "god"

Sepuh of the Mamikonean house, brother of the *nahapet* Vardan and the *sparapet* Vasak. He is not otherwise attested, and the episode concerning his death bears a suspicious ressemblance to the fate of Awaran in I Macc. 6:43–46. He may, however, be the anonymous younger brother of Vardan and Vasak mentioned in IV.ii.
See HAnjB, I, p. 359; JIN, pp. 59, *Bagas* no. 1, 424; Toumanoff, *Manuel*, p. 331/4e.
IV.xxii
p. 155
See also "Mamikonean, house"; "Vardan I"; "Vasak"; and Appendix III, *sepuh*.

Bagrat Bagratuni ⟨ OIr. *Bagadāta-*, "god-given"; Cf. Phl. *Bay-dād*, ŠKZ, 35; RGDS, no. 67, pp. 72–73 in the reduced form Βαδ

Armenian commander and hereditary *aspet* of the realm from Trdat the Great to the beginning of that of Aršak II and presumably *nahapet* of the Bagratuni house during that period; cf. MX, II.lxxxv (= MK, p. 237). Markwart splits him into two homonymous *aspet*s, a thesis categorically rejected by Toumanoff. Bagarat is presumably also the same as the anonymous *aspet* known to Aa (dccxcv, dccclxxiii). He is the only member of the Bagratuni house named by BP, who diminishes his role in the Mazkᶜutᶜkᶜ war, by contrast to the more exalted treatment of his participation in the parallel episode in MX, III.ix (= MK, pp. 261–262). Still, BP acknowledges Bagrat's rank as "great prince" and perhaps *aspet* in the list of magnates accompanying St. Nersēs to his consecration at Caesarea in 353 (IV.iv, but cf. n. 5)—an episode omitted by MX—and his special position as *nizakakicᶜ* of the *sparapet* Vačᶜē I. He is named as the father of the *aspet* Smbat Bagratuni who killed the traitor Meružan Arcruni after the battle of Jiraw, according to MX, III.xxxvii (= MK, p. 296–298), but BP gives a different version of Meružan's death in which the Bagratuni are not involved (V.xliii). There is no mention of Bagrat in BP after 353, which is the date given by Toumanoff for his death.
See Gignoux, NPS, no. 198, p. 57, *Bay-dāδ*; *idem*, "Noms propres," pp. 88–90; HAnjB, I, p. 356 no. 5; JIN, pp. 58, *Bagarat* no. 3, 417; Toumanoff, *Manuel*, p. 96/4; *idem*, *Studies*, pp. 320, 338–339; Adontz, *Armenia*, p. 319; Markwart, *Genealogie*, p. 11; *idem*, *Streifzüge*, p. 437.
III.vii; IV.iv
p. 74, 111
See also "Aršak II"; "Bagratuni, house"; "Trdat"; "Vačᶜē I"; and Appendix III, *aspet; nahapet; nizakakicᶜ*.

Bagratuni, house ⟨ Bagrat + suff. *-uni*

Major *naχarar* and subsequently royal house of Armenia and Iberia. It was of presumed Iranian descent, though a later tradition, possibly based on MX, I.xxii

(= MK, p. 111) and known to the DAI, xlv.2–8, gave them a Jewish origin derived from the house of David. During the ninth through eleventh centuries, the Armenian branch of the house controlled much of the territory of north-western and central Greater Armenia and was recognized as overlord of most Armenian principalities.

In the fourth century, the future kings of Armenia were the hereditary royal coronants (*t'agakap*) of the Aršakuni and *aspet*s of the realm, holding the districts of Sper and possibly Bagrewand and Kogovit. As opposed to the continuous exaltation of the Bagratuni in MX, the other Armenian sources are far more reticent for this period. Their name is not mentioned in Aa, though an anonymous *aspet* is explicitly noted as one of the leading magnates of Greater Armenia (Aa, dccxcv, dccclxxiii) and identified as the royal coronant in both passages. BP is likewise silent on the subject of the Bagratuni. No information is given concerning their origin, and only one member of the house is named. Bagrat Bagratuni is reduced to the level of a companion-in-arms of the *sparapet* Vač'ē I Mamikonean (III.vii), though the hereditary prerogatives of the Bagratuni as *aspet*s and royal coronants holding the principality of Sper are correctly acknowledged at the time of their marriage alliance with the younger Aršakuni king, Vałaršak (V.xliv; see however, IV.iv n. 5; and cf. MX, III.xli = MK, p. 303). This silence may reflect nothing more than BP's well-known pro-Mamikonean bias (see Intro., p. 44), but it may also be an index of the disgrace of the Bagratuni in the second half of the fifth century as a result of Tiroc' Bagratuni's support of the archtraitor Vasak Siwni in the great Armenian revolt of 450 (See ŁP', II.xxxvi; and Ełišē, iv, p. 92 = *Ełishē*, pp. 144, 281). The Bagratuni are listed as *aspet*s, though not by name, in the *Gahnamak*, "Rank List," and included in both the List of *naxarar*s in the *Vita* of St. Nersēs, v, p. 32 (= CHAMA, II, p. 25) and the *Zōrnamak*, "Military List," in which 1000 retainers are attributed to them; but the great period of the house beginning with the eighth and ninth centuries lay well beyond the chronological limits of BP.

See JIN, p. 417; Toumanoff, *Manuel*, pp. 96–178, of which only the first page bears on the period of BP; *idem, Studies*, pp. 110 n. 173, 132, 137, 201–203, 207, 210, 223, 226, 233 n. 291, 240, 244, 247–249, 251–252, 254, 306–354, 329 n. 110; Adontz, *Armenia*, 189, 191, 193, 196, 200, 203, 205, 228, 230, 237, 241–242, 263, 319–321, 68*, 70*–71*, 78*–79*; Šahnazaryan, *Bagratuni*; and additional bibliography on the name under the preceding entry.

III.vii; V.xliv

p. 74, 228

See also "Bagrat"; "Bagratuni, anonymous princess"; "Sahak (?)"; "Vač'ē I"; "Vałaršak Aršakuni"; Appendix II, "Bagrewand"; "Kogovit"; "Sper"; and Appendix III, *aspet; naxarar; t'agakap*.

Bagratuni, anonymous princess

Queen of Armenia as the wife of the younger son of Pap, Vałaršak (V.xliv). According to MX, III.xli (= MK, p. 303), she was the daughter of the *aspet* Sahak Bagratuni, who is not named by BP; but neither MX nor any other source has recorded her name.

See Toumanoff, *Manuel*, p. 96/5; JIN, p. 417.

V.xliv

p. 228

See also "Bagratuni"; "Sahak(?)"; "Vałaršak Aršakuni."

Bakur ‹ MIr. *bag-puhr*, "son of a god"; Gk. Πάκορος; Lat. Pacorus

Bdeašx of Ałjnik' and consequently holder of the first rank at the Armenian Aršakuni court according to BP, which specifies that he was the senior in rank of the four *bdeašx*s (III.ix n. 2). Aa, dccxcv, likewise refers to the *bdeašx* of Ałjnik' as the "great *bdeašx*." As the ruler of one of the great southern principalities, he may in fact have been semi-independent vis-à-vis the Armenian crown, but this is never mentioned in BP which treats Bakur as a rebel to his lord Xosrov Kotak and has his domains granted to Vałinak Siwni after his defeat and death. MX, III.iv (= MK, p. 257) gives a different version of Bakur's rebellion and does not mention the continuation of Bakur's line in Ałjnikʿ with the eventual return of his son Xeša. Adontz suggested, probably on the basis of MX's account of Bakur's Persian alliance, that the revolt had been instigated by the Persians to recoup the unfavorable terms of the peace of Nisibis of 298.

See Gignoux, NPS no. 741, p. 144, *Pakur*; idem, *Glossaire*, p. 31, *Pakōr*; HAnjB, I, pp. 367–368 no. 4; JIN, p. 239, Πάκορος no. 13; Adontz, "Favst," pp. 246, 251; Toumanoff, *Studies*, p. 180.

III.ix

p. 77

See also "Vałinak"; "Xeša"; "Xosrov II/III"; Appendix II, "Ałjnikʿ"; and Appendix III, *bdeašχ*.

Bałaščikʿ

Northern invaders of Armenia associated with the Mazkʿutʿkʿ. Eremyan places them north of the mid-lower Kur in Ałuankʿ.

See Eremyan, *Map*, B/7.

III.vii

pp. 73–74

Maps, L-M/4-5

See also "Mazkʿutʿk"; and Appendix II, "Ałuankʿ"; "Kur."

Bambišn Aršakuni ‹ Phl. *bāmbišn*, "queen"

Aršakuni princess, wife of Atʿanaginēs and mother of the patriarch St. Nersēs the Great. BP insists repeatedly that she was the "sister" of King Tiran, but see III.v n. 4 for the chronological difficulty. Her name is probably unknown, since the one given in BP is merely the Iranian title of any royal lady in the Sasanian period, and it is unknown to any other source except the *Vita* of St. Nersēs, i. p. 13 (= CHAMA, II, p. 22), which merely repeats the information in BP.

See Schmitt, IN, pp. 321, 329; HAnjB, I, p. 378; Toumanoff, *Manuel*, p. 75/7, who accepts BP's identification of the princess as a "sister" of Tiran; JIN, p. 414, who makes her a "daughter" of Tiran; and for the title, AG, pp. 116–117 no. 98; Benveniste, *Titres et noms propres*, pp. 27–28; CPD, p. 17.

III.xv, xix; IV.iii

pp. 91, 94, 109

See also "Aršakuni"; "Atʿanaginēs"; "Grigor/Gregorids," for Aršakuni-Gregorid intermarriages; "Nersēs I"; "Tiran"; "Varazduxt"; and Appendix III, *bambišn*.

Barseł/Barsilios/ Basilios of Caesarea, St.

The great Cappadocian father and bishop of Caesarea in Cappadocia (370–379) appears in BP only through the anachronistic transposition of some episodes from his life, especially the refusal to cure the son of the emperor Valens, to that of St. Nersēs the Great (see IV.iv; v nn. 5–7, 49; vi nn. 2, 12; viii nn. 1–2), or through the interpolation of episodes from St. Basil's life into the narrative (IV.vii–x). In both cases these intrusions have resulted in considerable chronological confusion.

See Baynes, "Rome and Armenia"; Ōrmanean, *Azgapatum*, I, col. 169; Garsoïan, "*Quidam Narseus*," pp. 149–152, 154–156; idem, "Nersēs le Grand"; Bardy, "Basile"; Fedwick, *Basil*, pp. 133–155, for the chronology of St. Basil's life; and Intro., pp. 27–29, 37, 40.

IV.iv–[v], vii–x, [xi]

pp. 111, [116, 121–122], 126–132, [133]

See also "Nersēs I"; "Vałēs."

Barsilios, see "Barseł."

Basean, house, see "Orduni."

Bat Saharuni ‹ *Bāt*; cf. Phl. *Pādīg* ‹ hypocoristic *Pād* (‹ *pāta*), "protected"
    Nahapet of the Saharuni house and *dayeak* of King Varazdat, who attempted to transmit to him the office of *sparapet* hereditary in the Mamikonean house (V.xxxvii). He murdered the *sparapet* Mušeł Mamikonean with the connivance of the king (V.xxxv) but was himself killed, together with his son by Mušeł's kinsman, Manuēl Mamikonean, who returned to claim the prerogatives of his family. Bat is unknown to MX and is called Smbat in the *Vita* of St. Nersēs, xv, p. 119 (= CHAMA, II, p. 43).
    See, Gignoux, NPS, no. 728, p. 142, *Pādīg*; JIN, p. 65, Βᾶτις no. 2; AG, p. 32 no. 39.
    V.xxxv, xxxvii
    pp. 215, 217–218, 220
    See also "Manuēl Mamikonean"; "Mušeł Mamikonean"; "Saharuni, house"; "Varazdat"; and Appendix III, *dayeak, nahapet, sparapet*.

Boyekan ‹ Phl. **Bōyag*, "sweet-smelling"; cf. Phl. *Bōy*
    Persian *naxarar* defeated and killed by Vasak Mamikonean. He is not otherwise attested.
    See Gignous, NPS, no. 212, p. 59, *Bōy*; Schmitt, IN, p. 331; AG, p. 33 no. 43; JIN, p. 70.
    IV.xxxix
    p. 163
    See also Appendix III, *naxarar*.

Bznuni, house
    Naxarar family holding the district north and west of Lake Van, which bore its name. MX, I.xii; II.viii (= MK, pp. 89, 142) attributes a Haykid descent to them through their eponymous ancestor Baz, and Toumanoff takes this to be an index of Urartian origin. According to both BP and the bare mention in MX, III.ii (= MK, p. 255), the entire family was annihilated under Xosrov Kotak as a consequence of the treason of its *nahapet* Databē, and its possessions passed to the royal treasury. Thereafter, the family (as opposed to the district) is no longer known to Armenian sources, though anachronistic references to it can occasionally be found in MX, II.lxii (= MK, p. 205), who mentions them under the reign of Tiran, thus contradicting his own information; and especially in the *Gahnamak*, "Rank List" and the *Zōrnamak*, "Military List," which attributes simultaneously 3000 retainers to the "Bəznunakan" and a mere 200 to the "Bužuni"; as well as in the *Vita* of St. Nersēs, v, p. 33 (= CHAMA, II, p. 25). The name of the family continued to survive in that of its homonymous district, from which bishops are known to ŁPᶜ, I.xiv; II.xxiii; III.lviii, pp. 23, 44, 106 (= CHAMA, II, pp. 270, 282, 318), and are attested in the Armenian conciliar lists of the sixth to the eight centuries (GTᶜ, pp. 41, 223), *et al.*
    See Adontz, *Armenia*, pp. 191–193, 195, 198, 201, 205–206, 208, 258–260 cf. 263, 370, 68*–70*, 94*–95*, 100*–102*; Toumanoff, *Studies*, pp. 199, 213, 216, 223, 226, 240, 246; who is of the opinion that the possessions of the Bznuni passed to the Ŕštuni.
    III.viii
    pp. 75–[76]
    See also "Databē"; "Xosrov II/III"; Appendix II, "Bznuneacᶜ cov"; "Bznunikᶜ"; and Appendix III, *nahapet, naxarar*.

Čenkʿ

Country and people from which the Mamikonean house originated, according to the Armenian tradition, which equates it with China (see the *Primary History*, Sebēos, pp. 56–57 = MK, pp. 367–368 and MX, II.lxxxi = MK, pp. 230–231). This hypothesis was accepted by Hübschmann, but Markwart proposed a link with the Kʿušan, and more recently Svazyan has placed them between the Oxus and the Jaxartes in the vicinity of the Aral Sea. On the contrary, Adontz did not seek them in the East, but identified them with the Tzans living to the northwest of Armenia in the Parhal Mountains and known to Procopius (*Bell. Pers.*, II.xxx.14; *Bell. Goth.* IV.ii.2–8; *De aed.*, III.vi.18, 20–26; vii.1). These are the Čaniukʿ found in Pontus, according to MX, II.lxxvi (= MK, p. 224) and whom the thirteenth-century Armenian historian Vardan places in the Caucasus, albeit at the eastern end (p. 37). Toumanoff, likewise, prefers a link with Georgia to the Central Asian location. In either case, the Chinese origin is no longer tenable.

See AG, p. 49 no. 101; Markwart, *Südarmenien*, pp. 78*–79*; Mlaker, "Die Herkunft"; Scöld, "L'origine"; Svazyan, "Čenerə"; Adontz, *Armenia*, pp. 312–313, 487 nn. 29–29a; Toumanoff, *Studies*, pp. 210–211, n. 238; Avdoyan, in *Ps. Yovhannēs Mamikonean*, pp. 70–71, who corrects CHAMA, I, p. 343, where the relation of the Čenkʿ to Derbent is omitted.

V.iv, xxxvii

pp. 194, 218–219

See also "Mamikonean, house."

Čiłbkʿ

Northern invaders of Greater Armenia associated with the Mazkʿutʿkʿ. Eremyan locates them in the north-central Caucasus.

See Aa, xix; Eremyan, *Map*, A/6.

III.vii

p. 73

Maps, I/1-2

See also "Mazkʿutʿkʿ."

Constantine, see "Kostandianos."

Čʿunak ‹ Arm. *čʿ*, negative prefix + root of *unim*, "have" + diminutive suffix *-ak*, "who has nothing"

Armenian prelate illegitimately consecrated at the order of King Aršak II during the exile of St. Nersēs. The name is obviously a mere pejorative epithet, for BP underscores that he was a "man of nothing [*čʿunak*], the slave of slaves of the king." BP, moreover, goes on to stress that none of the bishops of Greater Armenia was willing to consecrate him, so that bishops from the semi-autonomous border principalities or Marches of Ałjnikʿ and Kordukʿ had to be called in. Furthermore, the ordination was invalid because only two bishops were present rather than the minimum of three required by the Council of Nicaea (canon iv), with which BP seems to have been acquainted, not only because of the reference to the council itself (III.x) but because the assembly of bishops summoned to consecrate Nersēs I (IV.iv) is said to have been called "in accordance with the apostolic canons." MX ignores him altogether, and the late *Vita* of St. Nersēs, ix, p. 66 (= CHAMA, II, p. 33) also repeats that the Armenian bishops refused to ordain Čʿunak, though it then goes on to name a canonical group of three bishops different from the two in BP who performed the consecration. Despite its contempt for and denigration of Čʿunak, BP unexpectedly concedes anachronistically that he was consecrated "to the Katʿołikate of Armenia," rather than to the title of "senior-bishop" normally used for non-Gregorid primates.

The identity of this personage is highly problematic and controversial. He does not seem to be identifiable with the earlier patriarch Šahak of Manazkert (III.xvii), for that primate had duly been consecrated at Caesarea of Cappadocia in the reign of Tiran. The later Šahak, whom MX, III.xxxix (= MK, p. 300) but not BP (V.xxix) gives as a successor to St. Nersēs in 373 is no more satisfactory, since that Šahak seemingly made his appearance and was rejected by Caesarea under Aršak II's son Pap. Ačaryan's hypothesis that Čᶜunak should be identified with the Iosakes or Isokakis who represented Greater Armenia at the council of Antioch of 363 called by the emperor Jovian (Soc. Schol., EH, III.xv), and is probably referred to in St. Basil of Caesarea's *Letter* xcii, is also highly unlikely. It is chronologically acceptable, but the irregularly ordained Čᶜunak, who was moreover the chosen candidate of the Arianizing Aršak II, would have been equally out of place at Jovian's "orthodox" council and in St. Basil's list of "orthodox" eastern bishops. Consequently, no satisfactory identification has yet been proposed, and the succession of the non-Gregorid patriarchs of Armenia in general still requires considerable clarification.

> See HAnjB, III, pp. 733–734 no. 5; IV, pp. 103–104 no. 3; 216; Ōrmanean, *Azgapatum*, I, cols. 185–187; Garitte, *Narratio*, pp. 87–88; 418–419; Sanspeur, "Nouvelle liste"; Garsoïan, "Nersēs le Grand," p. 149; *idem*, "Šahak of Manazkert"; Akinean, "Reihenfolge," p. 85 = Šahak of Manazkert and Yusik II.
>
> IV.xv
>
> p. 146
>
> See also "Aršak II"; "Nersēs I"; "Šahak I and II"; "Yusik II"; Appendix II, "Aljnikᶜ"; "Kordukᶜ"; and Appendix III, *katᶜołikos; senior-bishop; struk*.

Daniēl, St. ‹ Hebr. *Daniēl*, "God is my judge"
> Syrian bishop, supervisor of the shrine at Aštišat and missionary to Persia. BP claims that he had been installed as overseer of the churches of Tarōn by St. Gregory the Illuminator, whose disciple he is said to have been. This seems a later gloss, however, intended to link Daniēl's career with the northern "received tradition" centered on the figure of St. Gregory, and it is far more likely that Daniēl was an autonomous hierarch of the southern Armenian church influenced by Syria and centered on Aštišat of Tarōn (see III.xiv nn. 2, 11). MX, III.xiv (= MK, p. 267) barely mentions him in passing, but the hagiographic tradition recorded by BP holds most of the Armenian anchorites to have been his disciples (V.xxv–xxvii; VI.vii, xvi).
>
> See HAnjB, II, pp. 10–11 no. 4; Ōrmanean, *Azgapatum*, I, cols. 150–152; Ter Minassiantz, *Armenische Kirche*, pp. 5–8, 21.
>
> III.xiv; V.xxv–xxvii; VI.vii, xvi
>
> pp. 86–88, 90–91, 205–206, 235, 239
>
> See also "Artitᶜ"; "Epipᶜan"; "Gind"; "Grigor Lusaworičᶜ"; "Sałitay"; Appendix II, "Aštišat"; "Tarōn"; and Appendix III, *anapataworkᶜ*.

Daniēl of Copᶜkᶜ ‹ Hebr. *Daniēl*, "God is my judge"
> Armenian *naxarar* who accompanied St. Nersēs to his consecration at Caesarea. He is not otherwise attested, but he presumably succeeded Zareh (III.xii) as ruler of Copᶜkᶜ Mec.
>
> See HAnjB, II, p. 11 no. 5
>
> IV.iv
>
> p. 111
>
> See also "Zareh"; Appendix II, "Copᶜkᶜ Mec"; and Appendix III, *naxarar*.

Danun

Commander of the mounted shield-bearers in Manuēl Mamikonean's army in the battle against King Varazdat. BP makes him the killer of Garegin Ṙštuni, but he is otherwise unattested.

See HAnjB, II, p. 16; JIN, p. 77.

V.xxxvii

p. 220

See also "Garegin II"; Appendix III, *zork῾* (I.e).

Dat/Gag of Hašteank῾ ‹ ?Phl. *Dād*; Av. *dāta-*, "given, created by"

Armenian *naχarar* who supported King Xosrov Kotak during the revolt of the *bdeašχ* Bakur, according to BP. MX, III.iv (= MK, p. 257) mentions a Prince Gag of Hašteank῾, who is presumably the same personage. MX presents him as one of the ambassadors sent to Constantinople by the patriarch Vrt῾anēs to request the help of Byzantium in the war provoked by Bakur but does not mention his participation in the war, while there is no reference to an embassy in BP. Both forms of the name are known, but there is no indication of the correct one in this case, despite the probable Iranian derivation which makes the first form more probable. He was presumably succeeded by Gnit῾ (III.xii).

See HAnjB, I, p. 429, *Gag*; II, pp. 18–19, *Dat*; JIN, pp. 81, *Datis* no. 4; 107, *Gag* no. 2; also Gignoux, NPS, no. 270, p. 68, *Dād*; Schmitt, IN, p. 329, on the form of the name.

III.ix

p. 77

See also "Bakur"; "Gnit῾"; "Varaz Kaminakan"; Appendix II, "Hašteank῾"; and Appendix III, *naχarar*.

Databay, see "Databē."

Databē/Databay Bznuni ‹ ?MP *dādbay, "god-given"

Nahapet of the Bznuni house and commander of the Armenian army, whose betrayal of King Xosrov Kotak in the war against the Persians led to his execution and the extirpation of his entire family, according to BP. The correct form of the name is disputed, as it occurs only in this passage of BP. This episode is not known to MX, but it may be related to the reference to a Databē Bznuni in the reign of "Tiran," despite its anachronistic appearance in MX, II.lxii (= MK, p. 205). See III.xx n. 5.

Gignoux, NPS, no. 279, p. 69, *Dād-bay*; Schmitt, IN, p. 330, *Databên*; HAnjB, II, p. 19, *Databēn*; JIN, p. 81, *Databē*; AG, p. 36, *Dat* no. 52.

III.viii

p. 75–76

See also "Bznuni, house"; "P῾isak"; "Tiran"; "Xosrov II/III Kotak"; and Appendix III, *nahapet*.

Dehkan ‹ MP *dehgān, "countryman/farmer"; cf. Arab. *dihkān*, "landed nobleman"

Persian commander, presumably related to the Armenian Mamikonean house. He is not attested elsewhere, and the name with its implication of a head of village is probably a title rather than a name.

See NBHL, I, p. 608, *dehkanut῾iwn῾*; AG, p. 37 no. 55, and 139 nos. 185–186; Schmitt, IN, p. 330; CPD, p. 26, *deh*, and 24, *dahigān*; JIN, p. 82, *Dehkan* no. 1; Christensen, *L'Iran*, pp. 112–113, who identifies the *dēhkān* as part of the lower nobility.

IV.xxxii

p. 161

See also "Mamikonean, house"; and Appendix III, *dehkan*.

Demet Gnt⁽ᶜ⁾uni
Nahapet of the Gnt⁽ᶜ⁾uni house, listed among the magnates who accompanied St. Nersēs to the Byzantine court in BP, but not otherwise attested.
See HAnjB, II, p. 65, *Demetr* no. 4; JIN, p. 82.
IV.xi
p. 133
See also "Gnt⁽ᶜ⁾uni, house"; and Appendix III, *nahapet*.

Dgłak, see "Głak."

Dimak⁽ᶜ⁾sean, house
Naχarar family of unknown origin, since the etymology of its name from Nersēs Dimak⁽ᶜ⁾sean's half cut-away face (*dem*) proposed by MX, II.xlvii (= MK, p. 188) is obviously apocryphal. BP gives the family only a passing mention, but it was well known to early Armenian sources and to all the late semi-fictional Lists of *naχarars*. The *Gahnamak*, "Rank List," gives three branches of the family: the Dimak⁽ᶜ⁾sean of Buχa in the southern portion of Tayk⁽ᶜ⁾ near Vanand; the Dimak⁽ᶜ⁾sean of Širak, whom Toumanoff considers to be a cadet line; and "another" Dimak⁽ᶜ⁾sean. The *Zōrnamak*, "Military List," attributes 300 retainers to them. MX, III.xliii, xlv (= MK, pp. 306–308) mentions the shift of the family from the Greek to the Persian side of Armenia after the partition of the kingdom ca. 387. Its participation in the Armenian revolt of 450 is known to both ŁP⁽ᶜ⁾, II.xxiii, xxx, xxxix, xlvii, pp. 45, 58, 72, 86 and Ełišē, pp. 76, 119, 193 (= *Ełishē*, pp. 258, 272, 287, 302; 128, 172, 238). But the family seems to have disappeared by the seventh century.
See Oskean, *Usumnasirut⁽ᶜ⁾iwnner*, pp. 25–33; Adontz, *Armenia*, 189, 192, 194, 202, 205, 207–208, 237, 370, 442 n. 20, 444 n. 24, 446 n. 35a, 452 n. 89, 520 n. 66; 68*–70*, 79*–82*, 84*; Toumanoff, *Studies*, 110 n. 173, 204, 223–224, 226, 228, 230 n. 278, 231, 240, 245, 247, 251, 252, 252–253 n. 343.
III.xiv
p. 87
See also, Appendix II, "Širak"; "Tayk⁽ᶜ⁾"; and Appendix III, *naχarar*.

Dłak, see "Głak."

Dmawund Kawosakan
Persian commander (*vsemakan*), possibly from the Iranian Kavian house. He is not otherwise attested.
See JIN, p. 85, *Dmavūnd Wsemakan*; AG, p. 46 no. 90, *Kawosakan*; Christensen, *L'Iran*, p. 106.
IV.xxix
p. 160
See also Appendix III, *vsemakan*.

Drastamat/Drstamat ‹ Phl. *drust*, "right/well/healthy" + *āmad*, "came" = "welcome"
Armenian *naχarar*, eunuch, and *Hayr-mardpet* of the realm under Tiran and Aršak II, though Markwart denied that he held the office despite BP's evidence, and Adontz even went as far as to deny his existence on the basis of the unlikely felicity of his name in context. His existence is, however, attested by Procopius (*Bell. Pers.*, I.v.30) on the basis of a "History of Armenia," though he does not name him. Drastamat was granted the title of prince of Angełtun and of governor (*ostikan*) of the royal fortresses in this district, in particular of Angł and of Bnabeł in Cop⁽ᶜ⁾k⁽ᶜ⁾. After his deportation to Persia together with Aršak II, ca. 363, he served Šāhpuhr II in the K⁽ᶜ⁾ušan war, obtained the reward of visiting Aršak in the "Castle of Oblivion," and committed suicide together with the king, according to both BP and Procopius. But he is not known to any other

Armenian source, not even the *Vita* of St. Nersēs, which usually follows BP. Consequently, the felicity of Drastamat's name and the epic tone of the episode in which he
appears suggest that it may belong to the epic tradition as a tale of the faithful retainer.
He is not named, but the episode is retold in Mandelstam's *Armenia*.
See HAnjB, II, p. 86; JIN, p. 87 no. 2 who makes him a son of Mehendak R̄štuni and
notes the unlikeliness of his name; AG, p. 38 no. 60; CPD, pp. 7, 28; Markwart,
Genealogie, pp. 33–34; Adontz, *Armenia*, pp. 35, 512 n. 42, 513–514 n. 43; Toumanoff, *Studies*, pp. 177, 178 n. 118, 179 nn. 120–122; Harut'yunyan, B. H.
"Mardpetakan."
V.vii
pp. 198–199
See also "Aršak II"; "K'ušan"; Appendix II, "Angełtun"; "Angł"; "Anyuš"; "Bnabeł";
and Appendix III, *mardpet, naχarar, ostikan.*

Drstamat, see "Drastamat."

Egersuank'
Northern invaders of Greater Armenia associated with the Mazk'ut'k'. On the basis
of the obvious link between the name of this tribe and the two toponymns Eger (Col-
chis) + Suaneti, Eremyan located them in this area. They were apparently already
known under the same name, Σουανόκολχοι (Suan- + Kolkhoi) to Ptolemy (V.viii.13).
I am indebted to Professor R. Hewsen for this information.
See Eremyan, "Narody."
III.vii
p. 73
Maps, F-G/1
See also "Mazk'ut'k'."

Epip'an ‹ Gk. Ἐπιφάνιος; Lat. *Epiphanius*; "manifest, revealed"
Greek anchorite and disciple of St. Daniēl (III.xiv), who designated him as missionary to Ałjnik' and Cop'k' Mec. He is also known to MX III.xx (= MK, p. 275), who
identifies him, however, as a disciple of St. Nersēs rather than of Daniēl and as one of
the overseers of the patriarch's hermitages. The reference in the *Vita* of St. Nersēs, xiv,
pp. 113–114 (= CHAMA, II, p. 42) merely follows the account of BP (V.xxv), and he
is not otherwise attested. BP presents Epip'an as one of the witnesses of the miraculous
assumption of St. Nersēs (V.xxv), but the details of his ascetic life (V.xxvii) fit more
readily into the southern eremitic circle, associated in the hagiographic tradition of BP
with the figure of St. Daniēl of Tarōn, than into the more officially structured Hellenizing world of St. Nersēs. In view of Epip'an's Greek name, however, and the insistence
that he was of Greek descent, the accounts of his life may contain a distant memory of
the rigidly austere and orthodox career of St. Epiphanius, bishop of Salamis on Cyprus
(ca. 315–403). Cf. a possible echo in the *History of Tarōn*, pp. 42, 111, etc.
See HAnjB, II, p. 123 no. 3; ODCC, p. 464.
III.xiv; V.xxv, xxvii, xxviii
pp. 90, 205–209
See also "Daniēl, St."; "Nersēs I"; "Šałitay"; Appendix II, "Ałjnik'"; "Cop'k' Mec";
and Appendix III, *anapatawork'; van(k').*

Erazmak ‹ ?OIr. *razm-aka-*, "warrior"; cf. Phl. *razm.*, "battle" with prothetic e-
Chief executioner (*dahčapet*) of Aršak II. He is not otherwise attested.
See Schmitt, IN, p. 330; HAnjB, II, p. 133; JIN, p. 88; AG, p. 39 no. 62; CPD, p. 71,
razm; Benveniste, "Mots d'emprunt," for Armenian loanwords from Iranian with
prothetic e-.

IV.xv

p. 143

Ewsebi/Ewsebios, bishop of Caesarea ‹ Gk. Εὐσέβιος; Lat. *Eusebius*, "pious, holy"

Bishop of Caesarea in Cappadocia (362–370) who succeeded Dianios and preceded St. Basil, whom he ordained priest. His early disagreements with St. Basil led to the retirement of the latter from Caesarea in 358, but Eusebios recalled him in 365 in the face of Valens's Arianizing persecution of the orthodox party and eventually made him the coadjutor of his see. The chronology of Eusebios's pontificate makes it impossible for him to have ordained St. Nersēs in 353, as represented in BP (IV.iv), and indeed, Eusebios appears only in the passages of intrusive Basilian material that contaminate the beginning of Book IV. Stripped of hagiographic embellishments, the details of his career approximate what we know of him from accounts of the life of St. Basil, but the version of his death does not agree with the one given by Greg. Naz. (*Oratio XLIII*, xxxvii).

See Le Quien, *Oriens*, I, cols. 372–373; Aubert, "Eusèbe de Césarée"; Ōrmanean, *Azgapatum*, I, cols. 168–169; also IV.iv n. 6.

IV.iv, vii, viii

pp. 111–112, 126–129.

See also "Barseł"; "Nersēs I"; "Vałēs"; and Appendix III, *katᶜołikosacᶜ katᶜołikos*.

Ewsebios, see "Ewsebi."

Gag, see "Dat."

Gardman, see Appendix II, "Gardman,"

Garegin I Ṙštuni ‹ ?Phl. *Gar*; Av. *gari-*, "mountain"; Cf. *Gar-Ādhur*

Armenian commander and companion-in-arms of the *sparapet* Vačᶜē I Mamikonean. BP mentions him as a kinsman of Mehandak Ṙštuni, but he is otherwise unknown. Because BP (III.xviii) records the annihilation of all the members of the Ṙštuni house with the exception of one child, this Garegin should presumably not be identified with his namesake, the husband of Hamazaspuhi Mamikonean (see next entry).

See HAnjB, I, p. 449 no. 1; JIN, p. 110 no. 1; also Gignoux, NPS, no. 387, pp. 88, *Gar-Ādhur*.

III.vii

p. 74

See also "Mehandak I"; "Ṙštuni, house"; "Vačᶜē I"; and Appendix III, *nizakakicᶜ*.

Garegin II Ṙštuni ‹ ?Phl. *gar*; Av. *gari-*, "mountain"; cf. *Gar-Ādhur*

Nahapet of the Ṙštuni house, not to be confused with the preceding. Garegin II was the husband of Hamazaspuhi Mamikonean, the sister of Vardan Mamikonean whom he abandoned at the time of Šāhpuhr II's conquest of Armenia (363/4). He presumably returned during the reign of King Pap and was killed in the battle between King Varazdat and the *sparapet* Manuēl Mamikonean (V.xxxvii). He is also known to TᶜA, I.x.p. 63 (= *Thom. Arts.* p. 127) who is obviously following BP at this point.

See HAnjB, I, p. 449 no. 3; JIN, p. 110 no. 2; also Gignoux, NS, no. 387, p. 88, *Gar-Ādhur*.

IV.lix; V.xxxvii

pp. 179, 220

See also "Danun"; "Hamazaspuhi Mamikonean"; "Ṙštuni, house"; "Vardan I"; Appendix III, *nahapet*; and the preceding entry.

Gargaracʿikʿ, see "Gugarkʿ."

Garǰoyl Xoṙxoṙuni ‹ ?Phl. *gar*; Av. *gari-*, "mountain"; cf. *Gar-Ādhur*
   Nahapet of the Xoṙxoṙuni house under Aršak II in succession to Manasp and bearing the title of *malχaz* hereditary in his house. Garǰoyl accompanied St. Nersēs in his embassy to the Byzantine court in 358 (IV.xi). He was perhaps the one sent as ambassador to Persia by the regent Manuēl Mamikonean after the expulsion of King Varazdat (V.xxxviii) and accidentally killed in the decisive defeat of Meružan Arcruni (V.xliii). He is included in the retinue of St. Nersēs's embassy given by the *Vita* of St. Nersēs, viii, p. 52 (= CHAMA, II, p. 30), which depends on BP at this point, but it gives both Hmayeak Xoṙxoṙuni and Varēn of the Maχazean [sic] house among the princes accompanying St. Nersēs to Caesarea (iii, pp. 24–25 = CHAMA, II, p. 24). Garǰoyl may be the same as the one mentioned in an earlier context by MX, III.ix (= MK, p. 262), though the name Garǰoyl seems to have been repeated from generation to generation in the Xoṙxoṙuni house, and BP (III.xii) lists Manasp Xoṙxoṙuni as *malχaz* in the train accompanying St. Yusik I to his consecration at Caesarea in the reign of Tiran.
   See HAnjB, I, p. 450 no. 1–2; JIN, p. 111; also Gignoux, NPS, no. 387, p. 88, *Gar-Ādhur.*
   IV.xi; V.xxxviii, xliii
   pp. 133, 221–222, 227–228
   See also "Manasp"; "Manuēl"; "Nersēs I"; "Xoṙxoṙuni, house"; and Appendix III, *malχaz; nahapet.*

Gatkʿ
   Northern invaders of Greater Armenia associated with the Mazkʿutʿkʿ.
   III.vii
   p. 73
   See also "Mazkʿutʿk."

Gayianē, St.
   Virgin martyr and companion of St. Hṙipʿsimē according to the Armenian "received tradition" recorded in Aa, cxxxvii–ccx.
   See HAnjB, I, pp. 443–444
   III.xiv
   p. 87
   See also "Hṙipʿsimē."

Gind, St.
   Hermit and disciple of St. Daniēl (III.xiv). According to BP, he was originally from the southern district of Tarōn, and MX, III.xx (= MK, p. 275) claims that he was a member of the Sḷkuni house. Gind seems to have been the overseer of all the eremitic communities in Armenia (see VI.xvi, nn. 3–4), a position to which he had been appointed by St. Nersēs but shared with others, according to MX (*ibid.*). Despite his presumed administrative duties, Gind maintained the classic wandering life of early anchorites until he retired with his disciple Mušē to a cave at Oskikʿ in the district of Caḷkotn. Like St. Epipʿan, Gind's eremitical mode of life seems more suited to the southern milieu of St. Daniēl than to the official Hellenizing world of St. Nersēs.
   See HAnjB, I, pp. 471–472.
   VI.xvi
   pp. 239–240
   See also "Artoyt"; "Daniēl"; "Maraχ"; "Mušē"; "Nersēs I"; "Vačʿak"; Appendix II, "Oskikʿ"; "Tarōn"; and Appendix III, *anapatawork ʿ; van(k ʿ).*

Głak/Dgłak/Dłak
    Mardpet of Armenia probably on two occasions: (1) under Tiran or Aršak II (V.iii), and (2) under Pap, who had him executed for intrigues with Persia (V.iii, vi). BP gives his name as Dgłak or Dłak, which is probably a scribal error confusing the hard-to-distinguish Armenian ɳ [d] and ɳ [g], as the form Głak occurs elsewhere in Armenian literature. See IV.lv n. 9 for Adontz's and Markwart's attempts to assimilate Głak with the anonymous *mardpet* who insulted Queen Pᶜaṙanjem and with the Cylaces known to AM; also Toumanoff, on the succession of the *mardpet*s.
    See HAnjB, I, p. 476 and II, p. 72; JIN, p. 85, *Dḷak*; Adontz, *Armenia*, p. 513 n. 43; Markwart, *Untersuchungen*, p. 14; Toumanoff, *Studies*, p. 178 n. 118.
    V.iii, vi
    pp. 189, 196–197
    See also "Gnel Anjewacᶜi"; "Pap"; and Appendix III, *mardpet*.

Głuarkᶜ
    Northern invaders of Armenia associated with the Mazkᶜutᶜkᶜ.
    III.vii
    p. 73
    See "Mazkᶜutᶜkᶜ."

Gnel Anjewacᶜi
    Nahapet of the Anjewacᶜikᶜ in Vaspurakan, whose loyalty to King Pap led to his denunciation of the intrigues of the *mardpet* Głak (V.vi) and to his own death in defense of the king at the hands of the Roman commander Terentius (V.xxxii). MX, III.xxxix (= MK, pp. 300–301) calls him the *sparapet* of the Armenian eastern army. This is unlikely because the undivided *sparapetutᶜiwn* of Armenia was hereditary in the Mamikonean family (see III.iv, xi n. 7; V.i), and BP merely says that Głak was ordered by the king to transmit the troops under his command to Gnel. Moreover, the Armenian army is not known to have been divided in Aršakuni times.
    See HAnjB, I, p. 476 no. 6; JIN, p. 116 no. 4; Adontz, *Armenia*, pp. 222–224 on the absence of divisions in the army.
    V.vi, xxxii
    pp. 196, 214
    See also "Głak"; "Pap"; "Tērent"; Appendix II, "Anjewacᶜikᶜ"; and Appendix III, *nahapet, sparapet.*

Gnel Aršakuni
    Sepuh of the Aršakuni house and nephew of King Aršak II. BP says only that Gnel was a nephew of the king in the male line (*ełbōrordi*, IV.v), but MX, III.xxi, xxiii (= MK, pp. 275–276, 277–278) specifies that he was the son of Aršak II's brother Trdat, who had been executed while a hostage at the Byzantine court, and of a mother from the Gnuni house. Gnel himself was one of the hostages sent back to Armenia as a result of St. Nersēs's embassy (IV.v, xi). According to MX, III.xxi (= MK, p. 276), he had been honored with the consulate, but this fact is not recorded in the imperial *fasti* or in any classical source. BP claims that Gnel was treacherously murdered by Aršak because of the slander of the king's other nephew, Tiritᶜ, who was enamored of Gnel's wife, Pᶜaṙanjem of Siwnikᶜ. It is more likely, however, that he was killed because he presented a direct threat to Aršak II as a *sepuh* of the Aršakuni house eligible for the kingship, and consequently providing a focus for the gathering against the king of all the discontented elements within the Armenian nobility. This danger is alluded to in BP (IV.xv) which calls Gnel *mec sepuh Aršakuni*, "the great Aršakuni *sepuh*," and more clearly spelled out by MX, III.xxii (= MK, pp. 277–278). See IV.xv n. 6.

See HAnjB, I, p. 477 no. 4; JIN, pp. 116 no. 3, 414; Toumanoff, *Manuel*, p. 75/9; V. S. Nalbandyan, "Gnel."

IV.v, xi, xv, xviii, xx, xliv; V.i

pp. 124, 133, 140–145, 148, 152, 164, 186

See also "Aršak II"; "Aršakuni, house"; "Gnuni, house"; "Pᶜatanjem"; "Tiritᶜ"; Appendix II, "Šahapivan"; and Appendix III, *mec sepuh.*

Gnitᶜ of Hašteankᶜ

Prince of Hašteankᶜ and presumably the successor of Varaz (III.vii). He is probably the same personage as the one listed in the retinue of St. Nersēs in the *Vita* of St. Nersēs, iii, p. 25 (= CHAMA, II, p. 24), though this late reference, which depends on BP, may have confused the attendants of St. Nersēs with those of his grandfather Yusik.

See HAnjB, I, p. 478 no. 2.

III.xii

p. 82

See also "Dat"; "Varaz Kaminakan"; and Appendix II, "Hašteankᶜ."

Gntᶜuni, house

Naχarar house of uncertain origin, but traditionally descended from the Canaanites and holding the office of master of the wardrobe, according to MX, I.xix; II.vii (= MK, pp. 104, 137). The Gntᶜuni are included in all the lists of *naχarar*s and the *Zōrnamak*, "Military List," attributes 300 retainers to them. Their domain was apparently the district of Nig in Ayrarat, according to an inscription found at Zovuni near Aparan in 1908, but a branch may have had possessions in Širak as well. The Gntᶜuni do not seem to have outlived the Aršakuni period and they are omitted from the parallel List in the *Vita* of St. Nersēs, viii, p. 52 (= CHAMA, II, p. 30), which substitutes Gnel Gnuni in the place of Demet Gntᶜuni, even though it is dependent on BP in its initial portion.

See Adontz, *Armenia*, pp. 188, 192, 194, 201, 205, 207, 239–240, 369, 444 n. 24, 455 n. 8 67*, 69*–70*; 77*, 79*–81*; Toumanoff, *Studies*, 110 n. 173, 204–205, 223, 227–228, 240, 245, 247, 249, 252, 252–253 n. 343; also Ališan, *Ayrarat*, p. 248; and Trever, *Armenia*, pp. 271–283 and pl. 87 for the Aparan inscription, and Sahinian, "Nouveaux matériaux," p. 193.

IV.xi

p. 133

See also "Demet"; Appendix II, "Ayrarat"; "Širak"; and Appendix III, *naχarar.*

Gnuni, house

Naχarar family probably of Orontid origin, but traditionally said to have been descended from Sennecherib of Assyria together with the Arcruni, according to MX, II.vii (= MK, p. 138), who derived their name from *gini*, "wine," and attributed to them the office of royal butlers. BP knows nothing of these fanciful etymologies and ancestry, and identifies the Gnuni with the far more important office of *hazarapet*, which had presumably passed to them from the house of Anjit at the beginning of Aršak II's reign (IV.ii), though Toumanoff dates this transfer after 363. The Gnuni are included in all the lists of *naχarar*s, and the *Zōrnamak*, "Military List," attributes 500 retainers to them. Gnuni clan bishops are also attested in the Armenian conciliar list of 505 (GTᶜ, p. 42). The original domain of the Gnuni seems to have been found around the localities of Arčēš and Berkri immediately north and east of Lake Van in the district of western Aḷiovit and Aṙberani, which subsequently belonged to Turuberan and they held land in Ayrarat, but probably not Šahapivan in Caḷkotn. Records of them found at Mastara in Aragacotn and in Širak probably relate to their move westward and eventually out of Armenia into Byzantine territory under Arab pressure in the eighth century.

See Oskean, *Gnunik^c ew Řštunik^c*; Adontz, *Armenia*, pp. 188, 192–193, 202, 205, 207, 228, 240, 251, 256, 258–260, 263, 339–340, 370, 442 n. 20, 444, n. 24, 455 nn. 11–14a, 15, 464 n. 75a, 510 n. 29c, 511 n. 33, 67*–68*, 71*, 79*–82*, 93*–94*, 96*–97*, 100*, 102*; Toumanoff, *Studies*, pp. 110 n. 173, 132, 135, 171 n. 88, 205, 206 n. 234, 223, 227–228, 240, 245, 247, 249, 251, 252, 298, 299, 303, 318, 327, 453 n. 63; Ališan, *Ayrarat*, p. 135.

III.xii; IV.ii

pp. 82, 108

See also, "Aba"; "Gnel Aršakuni"; Appendix II, "Aɬiovit"; "Anjit"; "Arčēš"; "Ayrarat"; Šahapivan"; "Širak"; and Appendix III, *hazarapet; naχarar.*

Gorut^c of Jor ‹ ?Pahl. *gōr*, "onager/wild ass"

Nahapet of the house of Jor or Jorop^cor who accompanied Nersēs I to his consecration at Caesarea. He may have been succeeded by Manawaz, whom the *Vita* of St. Nersēs, iii, p. 25 (= CHAMA, II, p. 24). but not BP (IV.xi), includes in St. Nersēs's embassy to the emperor Valens. Gorut^c is not otherwise attested, unless he is to be identified with the anonymous "Lord of Jor" who abandoned Aršak II in 363 (IV.l) although he would have been quite elderly at the latter date.

See Gignoux, NPS, no. 395, p. 89, *Gōr*; cf. *idem*, "Noms propres," p. 87; JIN, p. 118; Toumanoff, *Studies*, p. 190 n. 198.

III.xii; IV.l (?)

p. 82 [187]

See also "Manawaz of Koɬb"; Appendix II, "Jor/Jorop^cor"; and Appendix III, *nahapet.*

Greeks/Hellēn/Yoynk^c ‹ MP Yayna-, "Ionians"

Name normally used for the Byzantine world throughout BP, as opposed to the more correct contemporary form *Hřomk^c*, "Romans," which occurs on only three occasions.

See AG, p. 56 no. 122

III.vii, x, xiii, xxi; IV.i, iv, v, xi, xii, xv, xvi, xx–xxi, l, liv, lv; V.i, ii, iv–vi, xxiii, xxv, xxvii, xxxii–xxxv, xxxvii, xliv; VI.i

pp. 74, 80, 84, 98–100, 107, 114, 116, 132–134, 145, 147, 149–151, 153–154, 167, 173–174, 185–186, 188–191, 193–196, 203, 205, 207, 213–216, 221, 229, 233, 234

See also *Romans.*

Gregorids, see "Grigor Lusaworič^c Part^cew."

Gregory the Illuminator, see "Grigor Lusaworič^c Part^cew."

Grigor Lusaworič^c Part^cew/Gregory the Illuminator, St. ‹ Gk. Γρηγόριος Lat. Gregorius/**Gregorids**

Founder of Armenian Christianity in the early fourth century, according to the "received tradition" set out in Aa by the 460s. According to this generally accepted version, St. Gregory, the infant son of Anak the Parthian, was rescued by his nurse from the massacre of his family following the murder of King Xosrov K^caĵ by his father. He was brought up as a Christian at Caesarea of Cappadocia, returned as an adult to serve King Trdat the Great, was tortured for refusing to sacrifice to the goddess Anahit, and was thrown into a deep pit (*Xor virap*) at Artašat. Miraculously saved from death and raised from the pit, he healed the king, preached the true faith, destroyed the temples of the pagan gods throughout Greater Armenia, was consecrated bishop at Caesarea, and baptized the king together with entire realm. Gregory subsequently withdrew to the cave of Manē in the wilderness after consecrating his younger son Aristakēs as his successor.

None of the above details is mentioned in BP, which merely alludes to this tradition, with which the author was evidently familiar (see III.ii and Intro., pp. 24–26). He does not mention Gregory's death in the cave of Manē, concerning which Aa is also silent, but which is recorded by MX, II.xci (= MK, pp. 249–250), nor does he know the tradition of Gregory's conception at the grave of St. Thaddeus in Artaz, found in MX, II.lxxiv (= MK, pp. 220–221) and Vk, viii, p. 24. BP is, however, the first text to identify T῾ordan as St. Gregory's place of burial (III.ii n. 5) and as part of the patriarchal domains in western Armenia together with T῾il in Ekełeac῾ (see e.g., II.ii, xi–xii; IV.xiv; V.xxiv), and to note the other patriarchal domains in Ayrarat, Bznunik῾, Cop῾k῾, Daranałik῾, Tarōn, etc. This is also the main text to set out the succession and deeds of the patriarchs of the "Gregorid" house from St. Gregory's sons, Aristakēs and Vrt῾anēs, through Yusik I and eventually Nersēs the Great, bypassing the generation of Yusik's sons, Pap and At῾anaginēs (III.xiii, xv, xix; IV.iii), unworthy of the patriarchal dignity of their house, on the hereditary character of which the author is particularly insistent (III.xv, xvii; IV.iii).

The chronology of St. Gregory's mission has varied over an entire generation from A.D. 284 to 314, but the recent study of Fr. Ananian has set the date of Gregory's consecration at Caesarea during the ecclesiastical council held there in 314, despite the recent objections of MacDermott. BP does not refer to Gregory as "saint," nor does it use his traditional title of *Lusaworič῾*, "Illuminator," since its account relates to the fourth century, when these titles were not in use. It does, however, speak of his "illuminating mission" (III.ii, v); see Intro., n. 222.

See HAnjB, I, pp. 520–526 no. 1; Ōrmanean, *Azgapatum*, I, cols. 71–118; Peeters, "Calendrier"; Ananian, "La Data"; van Esbroeck, "Tēmoignages littéraires"; Thomson, Intro. to Aa; Garitte, *Documents*, pp. 280–288, 420–422; *idem, Narratio*, pp. 55, 57–58; Adontz, *Armenia*, pp. 270–275; MacDermott, *Conversion*; Thomson, Intro. to AaT, for the traditional version of St. Gregory's doctrine; Sanspeur, "Nouvelle List"; Akinean, "Reihenfolge"; Markwart, *Die Entstehung*; Gelzer, "Die Anfänge"; Garsoïan, "Prolegomena," cols. 182–183 and n. 45 for the Gregorid succession and its hereditary nature: Muradyan, P. M., "Kul't Grigoriia"; Małχasyanc῾, "Xndirner," on the first mentions of Gregory.

P.S.; III.ii–iii, v–vi, x–xv, xvii, xix; IV.iii–iv, xiv–xv; V.xxxi; VI.xv
pp. 63, 67–68, 70–71, 73, 79, 82, 84, 86–87, 89–93, 108–110, 112, 139, 141, 212, 240
See also "Anahit"; "Anak"; "Aristakēs"; "Aršakuni"; "At῾anaginēs"; "Grigoris"; "Nersēs I"; "Pap (2)"; "P῾aṙēn (?)"; "T῾adēos"; "Trdat the Great"; "Vrt῾anēs"; "Yusik I"; and Appendix II, "Ayrarat"; "Bznunik῾"; "Caesarea"; "Cop῾k῾"; "Daranałik῾"; Ekełeac῾"; "Tarōn"; also "Aštišat"; "T῾il"; "T῾ordan," for the Gregorid domains.

Grigoris, St. ‹ Gk. Γρηγόριος, Lat. Gregorius
Grandson of St. Gregory the Illuminator and twin brother of the patriarch Yusik. He was sent as a missionary to the northern lands and became a bishop at such an early age that King Trdat was concerned, according to MX, III.iii (= MK, p. 256), though BP makes no reference to this. Grigoris was martyred by the barbarians and buried at Amaras, which became an important site of pilgrimage.

Because the accounts of Grigoris's career in MX, III.iii and BP III.vi differ on important points, the precise locus of his mission and martydom remains disputed. BP associates his mission with the Mazk῾ut῾k῾ and makes him bishop of both Virk῾ and Ałuank῾, while MX places it in the region of P῾aytakaran in Ałuank῾ and does not include Virk῾ within his jurisdiction. Moreover, the plain of Vatneay on which Grigoris was martyred is placed by BP along the shore of the "Northern Sea," which Peeters identifies with Lake Çildir northwest of the Armenian plateau, while MX places it near the Caspian Sea. Finally, the district of Amaras is called "The Other" (*Miws*) Haband by BP, while MX identifies it as Lesser Siwnik^c (*Pok^cr Siwnik^c*).

MX's version of the area of Grigoris's activity, namely Ałuank^c and the border of the Caspian, has generally been accepted by Markwart, Ačaryan, and Eremyan, but it was firmly rejected by Peeters, who preferred BP's location farther to the northwest and its inclusion of both Virk^c and Ałuank^c within the sphere of Grigoris's mission. The problem is obviously tied to the identification of the Mazk^cut^ck^c and to the identification of the "Northern Sea" and the plain of Vatneay. In this connection it should be noted that missions to the northern land of the Mazk^cut^ck^c were already known to Aa, dcccxlii; that Armenian tradition has followed BP in making St. Grigoris the evangelizer of the north par excellence, even though Markwart rightly noted that the title of "*kat^cołikos*" of Ałuank^c and Virk^c given to him (in III.vi but not v) is a patent anachronism; and that Peeters attributed BP's information to an earlier hagiographic tradition. Morever, the location of the plain of Vatneay north or south of the lower Araxes, according to Eremyan, is by no means certain, and a plain of some importance is to be found northeast of Lake Çildir despite its generally mountainous setting.

See HAnjB, I, p. 526 no.2; Markwart, *Entstehung*, pp. 209–221; Peeters, "Les débuts," pp. 21–24; Garitte, *Narratio* p. 58; Eremyan, *Ašχarh.*, p. 83, *Vardaneay dašt* and map G/7.

III.v–vii

pp. 70–73, 75

Map I, F/G 3-4, "Northern Sea"; F-G/4, or L/2-3, or L/5-6, "Vat^cnean Plain"

See also "Grigor/Gregorids"; "Mazk^cut^ck^c"; and Appendix II, "Ałuank^c"; "Amaraz"; "Haband"; "Northern Sea"; "Vatneay, plain"; "Virk^c."

Gugark^c

Northern invaders of Greater Armenia associated with the Mazk^cut^ck^c. Adontz, however, was of the opinion that the proper reading of this name was Gargark^c or Gargarac^cik^c, contaminated in the text of BP by the association with the northern pricipality of Gugark^c. This is all the more likely in that the Gargarac^cik^c are recorded in MX, III.liv (= MK, p. 322).

See Adontz, *Armenia*, pp. 325, 497 n. 75; Eremyan, "Narody"; A. H. Hakobyan, "Gargarac^cinerə," who does not refer to BP.

III.vii

p. 73

Maps G/3

See also "Mazk^cut^ck^c"; and Appendix II, "Gugark^c."

Gumand Šapuh ‹ MP *Šāhrpuhr*, "king's son"

Persian commander named twice in BP. The two references may be to the same person, despite the fact that a Persian leader of that name had presumably been killed in the Armeno-Persian war by Vasak Mamikonean (IV.xxxi), while his namesake was killed at a later date by Manuēl Mamikonean (see IV.xxxi n. 4).

See JIN, p. 120; AG, p. 35 no. 50; Christensen, *L'Iran*, p. 410.

IV.xxxi; V.xxxix

pp. 161, 223

See also "Mŕkan"; "Surēn Parsik."

Habužean, house

Naχarar house not otherwise attested, perhaps the same as the Hambuzean in the *Gahnamak*, "Rank List."

377

See Toumanoff, *Studies*, pp. 218, 227, 245, 252, 253 n. 343; Adontz, *Armenia*, p. 192 no. 41, 68*.
IV.xi
p. 133
See also "Vrkēn"; and Appendix III, *naχarar*.

Hamazasp Mamikonean ‹ MP **Hamazāsp*; cf. Av. **hamāza-*, "colliding/clashing" + *aspa-*, "horse" = "one who possesses war steeds"
Name attested in ŠKZ, Parth. 25, Phl. 30; RGDS, no. 60, p. 69, Ἀμάζασπος.
Presumably a *sepuh* of the Mamikonean house, and possibly the father of Hamazaspean and Hamazaspuhi.
See Gignoux, *Glossaire*, p. 15; *idem*, NPS, no. 428 p. 95; *idem*, "Noms propres," pp. 85–86; Schmitt, IN, p. 329; Back, SSI, p. 181; Sprengling, *Third-Century Iran*, pp. 9, 12, 19; Honigmann and Maricq, p. 17.
V.xxxvii
p. 220
See also Appendix III, *sepuh*; and the next two entries.

Hamazaspean Mamikonean ‹ MP **Hamazāsp*; cf. Av. **hamāza-*, "colliding/clashing" + *aspa-*, "horse" = "one who possesses war steeds"
Form Hamazasp attested in ŠKZ, Parth. 25, Phl. 30; RGDS, no. 60, p. 69.
Sepuh of the Mamikonean house, and presumably the brother of Hamazaspuhi. The confusion of V.xxxvii (which also calls him the *aner*, "father-in-law" of her husband Garegin Ṙštuni) makes it possible that Hamazaspean was her father and consequently to be identified with Hamazasp Mamikonean, who is also mentioned in the same chapter but is not included in Justi's stemma of the Mamikonean house (see V.xxxvii n. 20). Both Justi and Toumanoff give Hamazaspean (called Hamazasp by Toumanoff) as the son of Artawazd I Mamikonean and the brother of Vardan, Vasak, Vahan Bagos, Hamazaspuhi, and others, probably on the basis of the *Vita* of St. Nersēs, ii p. 17 (= CHAMA, II, p. 22), which attributes four sons to Artawazd. This is inaccurate in the case of the apostate and traitor Vahan, because Hamazaspuhi is explicitly called the "sister" of Vardan but his "step-sister" (*kʿoyratʿiw*, IV.xlix). Furthermore, it seems improbable that Artawazd II (the son of Vačʿe I) should have fathered so many children, considering the fact that he is described as still a small child at the end of the reign of Xosrov Kotak, ca. 338 (III.xi) and never mentioned after that of Tiran, ca. 350—so that he seems to have died too young to produce such a large family. A chronologically more acceptable genealogy would postulate another son of Vačʿe I and brother of Artawazd II, named Hamazasp. This Hamazasp would have been the father of: (1) the *nahapet* Vardan; (2) the *sparapet* Vasak, who presumably collaborated with and subsequently replaced his uncle Artawazd II in this office (III.xi, xviii; IV.ii); (3) Bagos (IV.xxii); (4) Hamazasp or Hamazaspean; and (5) Hamazaspuhi (the last two of whom bore their father's name), all from the same marriage; while the traitor Vahan, and possibly others, were the offspring of this same Hamazasp from another wife. Such a hypothesis would help explain the confusion between Hamazasp and Hamazaspean (V.xxxvii). The name Hamazasp was common in the Mamikonean house, and the repetition of a father's name for a daughter was equally customary in medieval Armenia. It is also possible, however, that the variant versions of the name Hamazasp/Hamazaspean are merely due to a scribal error, though such a hypothesis would not explain either the genealogical or the chronological confusion.
See HAnjB, III, pp. 16 no. 4, 22 no. 1; JIN, pp. 124, *Hamazasp* nos. 4–5, 424; Toumanoff, *Manuel*, p. 331/4, *Hamazasp*; AG, p. 47 no. 94; also additional bibliography on the name in the preceding entry.
V.xxxvii
p. 220

See also "Artawazd II"; "Bagos"; "Garegin II"; "Hamazasp"; "Hamazaspuhi"; "Mamikonean, house"; "Vačče I"; "Vahan"; "Vardan"; "Vasak"; and Appendix III, *sepuh.*

Hamazaspuhi Mamikonean ‹ MP *Hamazāsp; cf. Av. *hamāza-, "colliding/clashing" = aspa-, "horse" = "one who possesses war steeds"
Form Hamazasp attested in ŠKZ, Parth. 25, Phl. 30; RGDS, no. 60, p. 69.
Sister of the *nahapet* Vardan Mamikonean and stepsister of the traitor Vahan (IV.lix), wife of Garegin II, prince of Řštunikᶜ. She was martyred during the Persian occupation of Armenia post 363. Her passion is also recorded by TᶜA, I.x, p. 63 (= *Thom. Arts.*, pp. 127–128), who is obviously following BP's account at this point even though he does not mention the princess's name and goes on to record that her remains were buried in the Hřipᶜsimean martyrium at Joroy vankᶜ. Because of the confusion in BP (V.xxxvii), it is not clear whether she was the daughter of Hamazasp or Hamazaspean Mamikonean, and both Justi and Toumanoff make her the daughter of Artawazd II Mamikonean.

> See HAnjB, III, p. 22 no. 1; JIN, pp. 125, *Hamazasp*, 424; Toumanoff, *Manuel*, p. 331/4; AG, p. 47 no. 94; Schmitt, IN, p. 321; Malxareancᶜ p. 322 n.142; and additional bibliography on the name under Hamazasp.
> IV.lix; V.xxxvii
> pp. 179, 220
> See also "Artawazd II"; "Garegin II"; "Hamazasp"; "Hamazaspean"; "Mamikonean, house."

Haykᶜ ‹? The Armenian eponymous hero Hayk according to the "received tradition" but etymologically impossible.
"Armenians"
MX, I, x–xii (= MK, pp. 85–90); HAnjB, III, pp. 31–34.
P.S.; III.vi–ix, xi, xvii, xxi; IV.iv, v, xii, xvi, xx–xxv, xxxi–xxxiii, xxxv–xliii, xlv–l, liii–lvi, lviii; V.i–viii, xxix–xxxiv, xxxvii–xl, xlii–xliii; VI.i
pp. 63, 72–75, 77, 80, 91, 93, 98, 100, 111, 124, 134–135, 146, 150–168, 170, 173–176, 178, 185–191, 193–199, 210—211, 213–215, 218, 221–226
See also Appendix II, "Mec Haykᶜ."

Hayr, see Appendix III, *mardpet.*

Hazarawuχt ‹ MP *hazār*, "thousand"
Persian general presumably sent by Šāhpuhr II against Aršak II. The statement that the first expedition commanded by him was destroyed to the last man (IV.xxii) may be poetic license if he is to be identified with the homonymous general defeated in IV.xxviii; cf. the parallel case of his companion Andikan (IV.xxii, xxvii). It is possible, however, that this name is merely a title, "thousander/chiliarch/commander-of-one-thousand-men," for a Zarmihr Hazarawuχt is also known to ŁPᶜ, III.lxvi, lxxviii–lxxxi, lxxxv–lxxxviii, pp. 118, 144–146, 148, 156–159 (= CHAMA, II, pp. 326, 343–346, 351–353).

> See JIN, p. 128; AG, p. 174 no. 328.
> IV.xxii, xxviii
> pp. 154–155, 160
> see also "Andikan."

Hečmatakkᶜ
Northern invaders of Greater Armenia associated with the Mazkᶜutᶜkᶜ. They are listed in the *Ašχ.* (27/37), and Eremyan places them near the Caspian Sea just north of Derbent.

> See Ełišē, p. 94 (= *Ełishē*, p. 147); Eremyan, *Ašχarh.*, p. 102 and map A/7-8.
> III.vii
> p. 73
> Maps, J-K/2-3
> See also "Mazkᶜutᶜkᶜ."

379

Hellēn, see "Greeks."

Heraklēs, see "Vahagn."

Hešay, see "Xeša."

Hiwrkandos ⟨ Gk.ʿΥρκανος; the addition of the *d* is an Iranism
    Jewish high-priest (79–40 B.C.), son of Alexander Jannaeus. He was carried off to Babylonia by the Parthians in 40 B.C., but Armenian tradition anachronistically has him brought as a captive to Armenia under Tigran II the Great (95–55 B.C.). See IV.lv n. 20.
    See OCD, p. 428; *Jewish Encyclopedia*, VI, pp. 517–518; Manandyan, *Trade and Cities*, pp. 64–65; Neusner, "Armenia."
    IV.lv
    p. 176
    See also "Hreaykʿ"; "Tigran II."

Hmayeak Mamikonean ⟨ Phl. *Hu-*, "good"; Av. *Humāya-* "having good spells, having magic power"
    Sepuh of the Mamikonean house and son of the *sparapet* Manuēl, whom he supported against King Varazdat. The *Vita* of St. Nersēs, xv, p. 122 (= CHAMA, II, p. 44) calls him Manuēl's elder son, but it ignores the participation in this battle of Manuēl's other son (whom it calls Artawazd and not Artašēs), who was in fact to inherit his father's office according to BP (V.xliv). Neither son is mentioned by MX, but BP's account is probably more accurate, since Hmayeak was a common name in the Mamikonean house.
    See HAnjB, III, p. 90; JIN, pp. 130 no. 2, 424; Toumanoff, *Manuel*, p. 332/6; AG, p. 47 no. 96; also Gignoux, NPS, no. 459, p. 99 *Humāy*; Schmitt, IN, p. 330.
    V.xxxvii
    p. 219
    See also "Artašēs/Artašir"; "Manuel"; "Mamikonean, house"; and Appendix III, *sepuh*.

Honkʿ
    People whose kingdom is placed by the Ašχ. (27/37) north of the Mazkʿutʿkʿ. They are commonly identified with the Huns, and Eremyan takes them to be the Sabirs. See, however, the other hypotheses under the heading *Mazkʿutʿkʿ*.
    See, Eremyan, *Ašχarh.*, p. 80, *Sawirkʿ* and map A-7; Maenschen-Helfen, *Huns*; Melikset-Bek, "K istorii."
    III.vi, vii; IV.xxv
    pp. 72–74, 159
    Maps, I-K/1-2
    See also "Mazkʿutʿkʿ."

Horomkʿ, see "Romans."

Hreaykʿ ⟨ Aram. *Yehūdāyē*, "Jews"
    BP is the best source for the presence of large Jewish colonies in the early Armenian cities destroyed by the Persians during the campaign following the Roman–Sasanian peace of 363. As indicated in the text, their presence there probably dated from the last century B.C. and resulted from the campaigns of Tigran II in Syria and possibly Palestine, although the tradition of the deportation to Armenia of the high priest Hyrkanos at that time is unquestionably inaccurate (see IV.lv n. 20). The figures given in BP for the number of deported Jewish families, as for the Armenian ones, are patently fantastic; nevertheless, they show almost invariably that the Jews composed the majority

of the early Armenian urban population. Outside of this episode, the only mentions of the Jews in the text are of Scriptural origin.

See NBHL, II, p. 142; HArmB, p. 134; HBB, III. p. 152; Manandyan, *Trade and Cities*, pp. 64–65; Neusner, "Armenia"; Garsoïan, "Mediaeval Armenian City," p. 81.

III.xiii, xiv; IV.lv

pp. 85, 88, 89, 175–176

See also "Hiwrkandos"; "Tigran II"; and Appendix II, "Artašat"; "Eruandašat"; "Naχčawan"; "Van"; "Zarehawan"; "Zarišat."

Hrewšołom ‹ Harēw; OIr. Haraiva + ?*šnom*, "joy"

Persian general, not otherwise attested although BP claims that he was related to the Armenian Aršakuni.

IV.xxxvii

p. 162–163

See also "Aršakuni."

Hřipᶜsimē, St.

Virgin martyr who rejected the advances of King Trdat according to the "received tradition," Aa, cxxxvii–ccx, ccxxx, ccxxlii. She and her companions were buried at Vałaršapat by St. Gregory directed by a divine vision, Aa, dccxxxi–dcclxx.

See HAnjB III, pp. 100–102

III.xiv

p. 87

See also "Gayianē"; "Grigor Lusaworičᶜ"; "Trdat the Great"; and Appendix II, "Vałaršapat."

Huns (?), see "Honkᶜ."

Ižmaχkᶜ

Northern invaders of Greater Armenia associated with the Mazkᶜutᶜkᶜ. They are listed in the *Ašχ.* (27/37) immediately after the Hečmatakkᶜ.

III.vii

p. 73

See also "Hečmatakkᶜ"; "Mazkᶜutᶜkᶜ."

James of Nisibis, see "Yakob."

Jews, see "Hreaykᶜ."

John, see "Yohan."

John the Precursor, see Appendix II, "John the Precursor, shrines of."

Jon of Kordukᶜ

Prince of Kordukᶜ and consequently presumably *bdeašχ* of the Assyrian March of the Armenian kingdom. The name Jon appears nowhere else in Armenian literature, so that the correct form may have been Čon. He should probably be identified with the Jovianus, "satrap of Corduena," who favored the Romans in 369, according to AM, XVIII.vi.20–21.

See HAnjB, IV, p. 304; JIN, p. 117.

III.ix

p. 77

See also Appendix II, "Korduk̔"; and Appendix III, *bdeašχ.*

Kaminakan, house

    Naχarar family identified by Toumanoff with the branch of the Aršakuni settled in Hašteank̔/Asthianenē, according to MX, II.viii, xxii, lxii; III.xxii, xxxi (= MK, pp. 144, 159, 205, 277–278, 288). The only mention of the family's name is found in BP, and they are unknown to later Lists of *naχarar*s.

    See Toumanoff, *Studies*, pp. 172, 192, 193 n. 207, 216, 223, 226, 245; AON, p. 292.

III.vii, xii

pp. 74, 82

    See also "Aršakuni"; "Dat"; "Gnit̔"; "Varaz"; Appendix II, "Hašteank̔"; and Appendix III, *naχarar.*

Kamsarakan, house

    Leading *naχarar* family traditionally descended from the great Iranian clan of the Karēn (MX, II.xxix = MK, p. 166) and related to the royal Aršakuni (MX, II.xlii, lxxiii; III.xlviii = MK, pp. 183, 219, 312). BP knows them only as lords of Aršarunik̔ and Širak (III.xix), of which they were the rulers in the fourth century and through the early Middle Ages, as attested on inscriptions such as the one on the church of the Theotokos at T̔alin. MX, III.xxxi (= MK, pp. 287–288) gives Eruandašat as their capital. The great fortress of Artagers probably belonged originally to them (MX, III.xxxi = MK p. 287), though BP (IV.xix) claims that it was built by Aršak II (see IV.xix n. 6). According to both BP (IV.xix) and MX, III.xxxi (= MK, p. 288), the Kamsarakan family was massacred under Aršak II and their domains confiscated, though they were presumably returned under King Pap (MX, III.xxxviii = MK, p. 299), so that some members of the family must consequently have survived. A further disgrace is hinted at by MX, III.li, lxv (= MK, pp. 316, 344). Nevertheless, the Kamsarakans are known to all the later Lists of *naχarar*s, and the *Zōrnamak*, "Military List," attributes 600 retainers to them. The family maintained itself in its domains of Širak and Aršakunik̔ until the ninth century, when it was compelled to sell them to the Bagratuni.

    See Kogean, *Kamsarakannerə*; Adontz, *Armenia*, pp. 188, 192, 194, 201, 205, 207, 210–212, 228, 237–238, 344, 414 n. 66, 442 n. 20, 443 nn. 22–23, 446 nn. 34–35a, 447 n. 339, 447–448 n. 42, 455 n. 15, 458 n. 41, 498 n. 76, 511–512 n. 36, 516 n. 53, 67*, 69*–70*, 80*, 82*, 86*, 94*, 96*; Toumanoff, *Studies*, pp. 110 n. 173, 132, 135, 171 n. 90, 202, 206–208 and n. 236, 223, 227–228, 240, 245–250, 252, 324 n. 81; idem, *Manuel*, pp. 266–267ff.; JIN, p. 425; Ališan, *Ayrarat*, p. 138, for the T̔alin inscription.

III.xi, xvi, xxi; IV.xix

pp. 81, 91, 98, 149

    See also "Aršak II"; "Aršawir"; "Karēn"; "Spandarat"; Appendix II, "Aršarunik̔"; "Artagers"; "Eruandašat"; "Širak"; and Appendix III, *naχarar.*

Karēn ‹ Parth. *Kārin*

    Name attested in ŠKZ, Parth.23, 26; Phl. 29, 31; RGDS, no. 57, 62, pp. 64–65, 68–69; *Paikuli*, etc.

    The Kārin were one of the seven great houses of Parthian Iran, considered to be one of the collateral branches of the ruling house, whence their surname Pahlaw (MX, II.xxvii–xxviii, lxviii, lxxi–lxxiii, lxxxviii = MK, pp. 165–166, 215–216, 218–220, 241). They maintained their position under the Sasanians and were entrusted with major offices. The Kārin are known to classical sources, e.g. Tac. (*Ann.*, XII.12ff.), and are recorded in the victory inscription of Šāhpuhr I at Naqš-i Rustam (ŠKZ, 29, p. 11 = trans., IV.6b, p. 18). According to the Armenian sources, they were the ancestors of the

Kamsaraksan *naχarar*s, lords of Širak and of Aršarunik^c. Justi, following Langlois (= CHAMA, II, p. 273 n. 1), suggests the possibility that the Karēn left with the Zik to govern Armenia in the name of Šāhpuhr II (IV.lviii) might be identified with the Arrabannes of AM, XXVII.xii.5; but see IV.lv n. 3.

> See Gignoux, *Glossaire*, pp. 25, 55; *idem*, NPS, no. 491, p. 104; Schmitt, IN, p. 327; Sprengling, *Third-Century Iran*, pp. 9, 11, 12, 18, 19; Honigmann and Maricq, RGDS, p. 17; Humbach and Skærvø, *Paikuli*, 3.1, p. 41; HAnjB, II, p. 613; JIN, pp. 156–157 no. 7; Schmitt, "Sūrēn"; Christensen, *L'Iran*, pp. 18, 20, 103–105, 294, 362; Adontz, *Armenia*, pp. 507–508 n. 22; Toumanoff, *Studies*, pp. 206, 207–208 n. 326; Lukonin, "Institutions," p. 705; Bailey, "Review," p. 232.

> IV.lv, lviii; V.i
> pp. 173, 178, 186
> See also "Kamsarakan, house"; "Zik."

Karēn Amatuni, ‹ Parth. *Kārin*
> Name *Kārin* attested in ŠKZ, Parth. 23, 26; Phl. 29, 31; RGDS no. 57, 62 pp. 64–65, 68–69; *Paikuli*; etc.
> Presumably the *nahapet* of the Amatuni house between Vahan (III.vii–viii) and Pargew (IV.iv). He is not otherwise attested.

> See HAnjB, II, p. 614 no. 2; JIN, p. 57 no. 6; and the additional bibliography on the name in the preceding entry.

> III.xiv
> p. 87
> See also "Amatuni, house"; "Pargew"; "Vahan"; Appendix III, *nahapet*; and the preceding entry for the name "Karēn."

Kawosakan, see "Dmawund."

Kiškēn Bagean
> *Nahapet* of the Bagean family not attested elsewhere except for the *Vita* of St. Nersēs, viii, p. 52 (= CHAMA, II, p. 30), which depends on BP in this portion, but gives the name of Kēškēn Baṙnēic^c.

> See HAnjB, II, p. 618; JIN, p. 164.
> IV.xi
> p. 133
> See also "Bagean, house"; and Appendix III, *nahapet*.

Kiwrakos/Kirakos ‹ Gk. Κυρίακος ‹ κύριος, "lord"
> Bishop of Tayk^c. His alternate name, Šahap, is merely the Armenian translation of its Greek form. He otherwise unattested, unless he is to be identified with St. Gregory the Illuminator's twelfth disciple in Aa, dcccxlv (see VI.v n. 5).

> See HAnjB, II, p. 620 nos. 1–2, who dissociates the two; AG, p. 335; HArmB, III. p. 482, *šahap* = Liddell and Scott, p. 1013, κύριος; Lampe, *Lexicon*, pp. 787–788; Schmitt, IN, p. 327, *šahrab*; Kostanyan, "Termin ShAhAP."

> VI.xi
> p. 238
> See also Appendix II, "Tayk^c"; and Appendix III, *satrap*.

Koms/Kon Mamikonean
> *Sepuh* of the Mamikonean house and brother of the *sparapet* Manuēl, whose exile in Persia he shared and with whom he returned to Armenia. Both were the sons of Artašēs/Artašēn Mamikonean (V.xxxvii), though the *Vita* of St. Nersēs, x, pp. 66–67 (= CHAMA, II, p. 33), which gives his name in the form Kon, mistakenly makes the brothers sons of the *sparapet* Vasak, and consequently brothers of the *sparapet* Mušeł

(V.xxxvii nn. 4, 7). All the mss of BP also give the form Kon, which may have been a diminutive of Mamikon (Malχasyancᶜ, p. 338 n. 183), but the Venice ed. (p. 242 and n. 2) prefers the form Koms.

See HAnjB, II, p. 646 no. 1; JIN, p. 424; Toumanoff, *Manuel*, p. 332/54; Markwart, *Untersuchungen*, p. 219.

V.xxxvii

pp. 217–218

See also "Artašēs/Artašēn"; "Mamikonean, house"; "Manuēl"; and Appendix III, *sepuh*.

Kon, see "Koms."

Kostandianos/Constantine the Great ‹ Gk. Κωνσταντῖνος; Lat. Constantinus

The only references to the first Christian Roman emperor (306–337) in BP occur in passing: in connection with the Council of Nicaea (III.x) and in the recollection of the tradition of an alliance between him and King Trdat of Greater Armenia, according to the "received" tradition (Aa, dccclxxvii). In general, Constantine as usual provides the model of the "perfect, orthodox" emperor. He is one of the only two Roman emperors identified by name in BP (see IV.v n. 5).

See Jones *et al.*, *Prosopography*, I, pp. 223–224, *Fl. Val. Constantinus* no. 4; "Constantinus," PW, IV, pp. 1013–1026.

III.x, xxi

pp. 79–80, 98

See also "Trdat the Great."

Kᶜušan

Cf. *Kušānšāhr*, attested in ŠKZ, Parth. 2; RGDS no. 4, p. 49 (reconstructed)

Kingdom founded by the western migration of the Yüeh-chih confederation on both sides of the Hindu Kush in modern Afghanistan and in the Punjab. It was established in the first century A.D., and presumably recognized the overlordship of the Sasanians under Ardašīr I. Thereafter, it was considered part of the Iranian empire and ruled by a Sasanian prince who bore the title Kūšānšāh, and whose capital was apparently at Balkh/Baχlo. Ca. 360, however, this kingdom was invaded by the Chionites, who attacked Šāhpuhr II, as noted by ΛM, XIV.iii.1 and XVI.ix.4, and by BP (V.vii, xxxvii), which calls the Kušan king of this period an Aršakuni, an identification supported by MX, II. ii, lxvii–lxviii, lxxii, lxxiv (=MK, pp. 131 and nn. 3–4, 213–214 and n. 3, 219–220) and accepted by Lozinski. Thereafter an endemic war in which the Armenian cavalry was often involved began between the Kušans and the Sasanians (cf. V.vii, xxxvii).

See, Gignoux, *Glossaire*, p. 55; Bivar, "Eastern Iran," pp. 181–231; Zeimal, "Transoxiana," pp. 232–262; Bailey, "Kusanica"; Henning, "Notes," p. 49; Livshits, "Cusano-Indica"; Ghirshman, *Mémoires*; Brunner, "Kušānšāhi"; Enoki, "Ephthalites"; Fussman, "Chronique"; Lukonin, "Zavoevaniia"; Christensen, *L'Iran*, pp. 29–30, 89, 102, 137–138 and 137 n. 1, 209–210, 227–228, 239 and n. 2, 287; Markwart, *Ērānšahr*, pp. 49–50, 87; Trever, "Kᶜushany"; Ēlčᶜibekyan, "Kᶜušanneri masin"; Sprengling, *Third-Century Iran*, pp. 7, 14; Honigmann and Maricq, RGDS, pp. 11, 98–110; Lozinski, "Parthian Dynasty," pp. 125–129.

V.vii, xxxvii

pp. 197–198, 217

See also "Aršakuni"; "Drastamat"; "Manuēl Mamikonean"; "Šapuh"; "Sasanians."

Magi/Magians see "Mogkᶜ."

Małχazean/Małχazuni, see "Xoŕχoŕuni."

Mamikonean, house

The Mamikonean were the most distinguished *naχarar* family in fourth-century Armenia after the royal Aršakuni and possibly the Gregorid holders of the patriarchal throne. They were known to Aa, dccclx, though he does not mention them by name but only by title, as well as to the *Primary History* (Sebēos, p. 56 = MK, pp. 367–368); but BP is the main source for their history in the fourth century, complemented by ŁPᶜ and Ełišē for the fifth. Although they are mentioned by MX, his anti-Mamikonean bias led him to denigrate, disguise, and most commonly omit their role during this period (see Intro., p. 44–45 and nn. 202–213). By contrast, BP's panegyric, based on oral sources and attributing to this clan the transcendental quality of *kᶜajutᶜiwn* (possibly because of their traditional claim of royal descent), exaggerates their importance, and the history of this house is one of the main themes of the work (see Intro., pp. 3, 34–35, 44). The precise rank of the Mamikonean in the *naχarar* hierarchy of the fourth century and the size of their military contingent cannot be determined with any precision from the late and semi-fictional *Gahnamak*, "Rank List," their listing in the equally late *Vita* of St. Nersēs, or the biased evidence of MX, III.li (= MK, p. 316). The *Zōrnamak*, "Military List," records separately the Mamikonean and the princes of Taykᶜ, each with 1,000 retainers, though they were probably one and the same.

Rightly or wrongly, the Mamikonean were traditionally considered to have been of royal ancestry. BP gives their usual descent from the kings of the Čᶜenkᶜ (V.iv, xxxvii), as do also MX, II.lxxxi (= MK, pp. 229–230) and the *Primary History* (Sebēos, pp. 56–57 = MK, pp. 367–368), but does not make the mistake of tracing them to China, as has often been done (see MK, pp. 229–230 and nn. 2–4). The family may also have had Persian kinsmen (V.xxxi). In the fourth century, however, their office was that of hereditary *sparapet* or commander-in-chief of the Armenian army, as BP repeatedly spells out (see III.xi n. 7), giving the only account of their succession in this office through most of the fourth century from Artawazd I, presumably in the reign of Trdat the Great (III.iv; cf. Aa, dccclx) to the death of Manuēl, the succession of his son Artašēs/Artašir, and the partition of the Armenian kingdom (V.xliv–VI.i). At the same time, the Mamikoneans apparently also served as royal *dayeak*s, "tutors" (III.xviii and n. 5), a fact obscured by MX's (II.lxxvi, lxxxii, lxxxv = MK, pp. 223–224, 237) alteration of Artawazd I's family name from Mamikonean to Mandakuni. As such, they were in a position to play the role of regent or even kingmaker under Mušeł (V.i) and Manuēl (V.xxxvii–xliv) at the end of the fourth century.

The original domain of the Mamikonean clan appears to have been in northwestern Taykᶜ (III.xviii), but by the end of the fourth century they held at least part of the southern district of Tarōn. After 438, they acquired the vast patriarchal lands in that district as well as in Daranałikᶜ and Ekełeacᶜ through the marriage of Sahakanoyš, the daughter of the last Gregorid patriarch, Sahak I, to Hamazasp Mamikonean and thereby became the largest landholders in Greater Armenia.

The Mamikonean continued to dominate Armenian history in the fifth century under the leadership of the *sparapet* Vardan in the revolt of 450 and the governorship of his nephew Vahan. The names of the family's bishops recur commonly in the Armenian conciliar acts of the sixth century and beyond (GTᶜ, pp. 41, 71, 223, etc). With the failure of the second Armenian revolt against Persia under Vardan II and his flight to Byzantium in 572, however, the family's fortunes began a slow decline, leading to the disappearance of its senior branch in the ninth century, though a cadet branch survived in Tarōn, while other members of the family played important roles at the Byzantine court.

See HAnjB, III, p. 184, Mamikon no. 1, though there is no entry for the entire
family; JIN, p. 424 for the stemma, which needs corrections; Toumanoff, *Manuel*,
pp. 331–335; *idem, Studies*, pp. 209–210 and n. 238; 244–246; *idem*, "Mamikonids"; Adontz, *Armenia*, pp. 100–101, 152, 191–192, 194, 200, 202–203,
206–207, 210–212, 244, 256–258, 262–264, 312–313, 320–321, 339–340, 380 n. 30,
381 n. 33, 443 n. 23, 458 n. 44, 467 n. 16a, 487 nn. 29a–b, 492 n. 52, 67*–71*,
75*–77*, 81*–85*, 94*–97*; Abgaryan, "Mamikonyanneri zruyc͑i ałbyurə";
Scöld, "L'origine"; Mlaker, "Die Herkunft."
III.iv, vii, xi, xvi, xviii; IV.ii, xi, xv, xvi, xviii, xxiii, xxvii, xxxii, l, liv, lviii, lix; V.xxxv,
xxxvii
p. 69, 74, 81, 91, 93, 107–108, 133, 141, 146–148, 156, 159, 161, 167, 173, 178–179,
215, 217–218, 220
See also, "Artašēs/Artašēn"; "Artašēs/Artašir"; "Artawazd I–III"; "Bagos"; "Dehkan"; "Hamazaspean"; "Hamazaspuhi"; "Hmayeak"; "Koms"; "Manuēl";
"Mušeł"; "Vač͑ē I–II"; "Vahan"; "Vardan I–II"; "Vardanduχt"; "Vasak"; Appendix II, "Eraχani"; "Ołakan"; "Tarōn"; "Tayk͑"; and Appendix III, *dayeak; k͑aj;
naχarar; sparapet*.

Manačihr R̄štuni ‹ Pahl. Manuščihr; Av. *Manuš. či̇θra*," "*Manu*" (the lawgiver) +
či̇θra," "seed, progeny" = "who has the nature of *Manu*" and not the spurious
derivation from OIr. *manyu*, "spirit"; name attested on a pre-Sasanian coin of Pars
that reads: *mnčtry MLK' BRH mnčtry MLK'* = *Manačihr šāh pus [ī] Manačihr šāh*
Presumably the *nahapet* of the R̄štuni house, as he is called both "great prince" and
"lord of the realm," although neither BP nor MX, III.vi–vii (= MK, pp. 258–260) states
this explicitly and their accounts of his confrontation with St. James of Nisibis show
only minor variations. MX, III.vi (= MK, p. 258) calls him the general of the Armenian
southern army, but no such division is known to have existed in Armenia in this period
(see III.ix n. 5). MX, III.vii (= MK, p. 260) also claims that Manačihr was survived by
a son who inherited his domains and that he was replaced as commander by Zawray
(MX, III.xv = MK, pp. 267–268).
See Gignoux, NPS, no. 559, p. 115; Schmitt, IN, p. 329; HAnjB, III, p. 192 no. 1,
who follows MX; JIN, pp. 191–192 no. 8.
III.x
pp. 78–79
See also "R̄štuni, house"; "Yakob"; and Appendix III, *nahapet*.

Manak of Basean ‹ OIr. **mana-ka-*; cf. Av. *manah-*, "mind"
Prince of Basean and perhaps *nahapet* of the Orduni house. He is not otherwise
attested.
See Schmitt, IN, p. 330; HAnjB, III, p. 192; JIN, p. 189.
III.ix
p. 77
See also "Orduni, house"; Appendix II, "Basean"; and Appendix III, *nahapet*.

Manasp Xor̄χor̄uni ‹ MIr. **Manāsp*, OIr. *manaṭ. aspa*? "spiritual steed"
Presumably *nahapet* of the Xor̄χor̄uni house and *malχaz* as the predecessor of
Garĵoyl. He is not otherwise attested.
See Schmitt, IN, p. 329; HAnjB, III, p. 196; JIN, p. 189.
III.xii
p. 82
See also "Garĵoyl"; "Xor̄χor̄uni, house"; and Appendix III, *malχaz, nahapet*.

Manawaz of Kołb ‹ OIr. **mana-vāzā-*, "progressing through the spirit"; cf. Gk. Μονοβάζης

Presumably prince of Kołb/Kołbopᶜor in the Iberian March, though he is not otherwise attested. He may perhaps be identified with the anonymous "lord of Kołb" who abandoned Aršak II in 363 (IV.l). Ačaryan also suggests that he might perhaps be identified with Manawaz of Jor, who accompanied St. Nersēs to Caesarea according to the *Vita* of St. Nersēs, iii, p. 25 (= CHAMA, II, p. 24), but not BP (IV. iv).

    See HAnjB, III, p. 197 nos. 2–3; JIN, p. 189 no. 6; Toumanoff, *Studies*, p. 190 n. 198;
    AG, p. 50 nos. 105–106
    III.xii; IV.l (?)
    pp. 82, [167]
    See also Appendix II, "Kołb."

Manawazean, house ‹ OIr. **mana-vāzā-*, "progressing through the spirit"

Naχarar family traditionally descended from the Armenian eponymous hero Hayk. They are also known to MX, I.xii; II.viii; III.ii (= MK, pp. 89, 142, 255), who traces their ancestry to Hayk's son Manawaz. Because the family was annihilated in the reign of Xosrov Kotak (III.iv), it is not included in the *Gahnamak*, "Rank List," which is of later date, but it is anachronistically listed in the *Zōrnamak*, "Military List," which attributed 1,000 retainers to it. The possessions of the Manazaean lay north of Lake Van around their seat of Manazkert of Manawazakert, as indicated in BP which transferred them to the Ałbianid house.

    See HAnjB, III, pp. 196–197; JIN, p. 189; AG, pp. 50–51 no. 106; Adontz, *Armenia*,
    pp. 193, 198, 201, 205, 222, 245, 271–272, 370, 68*, 70*; Toumanoff, *Studies*,
    pp. 110 n. 173, 199, 216, 218 and n. 253, 219, 224, 227, 240.
    III.iv
    pp. 69–70
    See also "Ałbianos"; "Xosrov II/III"; Appendix II, "Manazkert"; and Appendix III,
    naχarar.

Manuēl Mamikonean ‹ Hebr. 'Imānûēl, "the Lord is with us," cf. Gk. Μανυήλ

Sepuh of the Mamikonean house, son of Artašēs/Artašēn and brother of Koms. He was deported to Persia probably at the same time as Aršak II, as recorded by the *Vita* of St. Nersēs, x, xv, pp. 66–67, 119–120 (= CHAMA, II, pp. 33, 43), which erroneously makes him the son of the *sparapet* Vasak. The circumstances of his deportation are not given by BP. The *Vita* likewise makes him a brother of the *sparapet* Mušeł, but this too is incorrect (see V.xxxvii n. 11). Manuēl's career is known almost exclusively from the account of BP, followed by *Vita* of St. Nersēs. He is not mentioned by MX.

After serving the Sasanians in the Kᶜušan war, Manuēl returned to Armenia with his brother Koms. On the basis of traditional dynastic seniority he reclaimed the dignity of *nahapet-tanutēr* of the Mamikonean house granted by King Varazdat to his kinsman Vačᶜē II and wrested his family's hereditary office of *sparapet* from Bat Saharuni, to whom it had been granted by the king. He defeated the king and drove him from Armenia, killed Bat Saharuni, and ruled the kingdom *de facto* through King Pap's widow Zarmanduχt, whom he installed as regent for her two minor sons (V.xxxvii). At first, he reversed the traditionally pro-Byzantine policy of the Mamikonean (see V.xxxiv n. 3) and turned to Persia, with the result that the Sūrēn was installed as *marzpan*, "governor" of Armenia (V.xxxviii). This last is confirmed by the account of AM (XXX.ii.7-8) for 377–378. Subsequently, however, Manuēl turned against the Sasanians, whom he drove out of Armenia. He successfully put an end to the long rebellion of Meružan Arcruni, detailed by BP, by defeating and killing him in battle (V.xliii). He gave his daughter Vardanduχt in marriage to King Aršak III and apparently kept the control of Armenia until his death ca. 386 (V.xliv), probably benefitting from the concern of the Byzantine Empire with the Gothic war after the disastrous defeat of Andrinople in 378 and from the weakening of Persia at the end of Šāhpuhr II's long reign in 379. In keeping with their respective biases, BP exhalts Manuēl's valor and virtues, while MX totally ignores his existence, as noted above (see also Intro., pp. 44–45).

> See HAnjB, III, p. 205 no. 1; JIN, p. 424; Toumanoff, *Manuel*, p. 332/54; Markwart, *Untersuchungen*, p. 219; AG, p. 335.
>
> V.xxxvii–xliv; VI.i
>
> pp. 217–230, 233
>
> See also "Aršak II"; "Aršak III"; "Artašēs/Artašen"; "Artašēs/Artašir"; "Bat Sahaṙuni"; "Hmayeak"; "Koms"; "Kʻušan"; "Mamikonean, house"; "Meružan Arcruni"; "Mušeł"; "Sasanians"; "Surēn Parsik"; "Vačʻē II"; "Vałaršak"; "Vardanduxt"; "Vardanoyš"; "Varazdat"; "Vasak"; "Zarmanduχt"; and Appendix III, *nahapet, sepuh, sparapet.*

Mar of Copʻkʻ Mec ‹ ?Arm. Mar, "Mede"

Prince of Copʻkʻ Mec who supported Xosrov Kotak against the revolt of the *bdeašχ* Bakur. MX, III.iv (= MK, p. 257) mentions Mar as an ambassador sent to request the assistance of Byzantium in the war against Bakur but does not mention his participation in military operations. On the contrary, BP has no record of such an embassy. Mar was presumably succeeded by Zareh (III.xii).

> See HAnjB, III, p. 231; JIN, p. 194.
>
> III.ix
>
> p. 77
>
> See also "Bakur"; "Zareh"; and Appendix II, "Copʻkʻ Mec."

Maraχ ‹ Av. *maδaχā*, "locust/grasshopper"

Hermit and disciple of St. Gind, not otherwise attested, and his name appears to be only a nickname; see VI.xvi, n. 6

> See HAnjB, III, p. 232 no. 2; HArmB, III, p. 274 for the meaning of the name; AG, p. 192 no. 399.
>
> VI.xvi
>
> p. 239
>
> See also "Artoyt"; "Gind"; "Vačʻak."

Mardpet, see Appendix III, *mardpet.*

Mari ‹ Syr. *mar-ī*, "my lord"

Presumably the chief priest of the Christians in the Persian capital of Ctesiphon. No bishop of that name is attested in the fourth-century lists of Seleucia-Ctesiphon, though Peeters suggests that he might have been a *locum tenens*. It is more likely that the name was merely familiar from the tradition of St. Thaddeus, whose disciple Mari is reputed to have participated in the evangelization of Edessa (see IV.xvi n. 7), or perhaps it should be associated here with the martyr Mari of Seleucia, martyred with seven companions, according to the Syrian Acts (see IV.xvii n. 2), or again it is a conflation of the two.

> See Peeters, "Persécution," pp. 71–77; Labourt, *Christianisme*, pp. 12–20, 133 n. 6, 254–255; Addai, *Liturgia* (trans.) Brightman, *Liturgies*, pp. 245–305); Abeloos, *Acta Maris.*
>
> IV.xvi–xvii, liv
>
> pp. 147, 170–171
>
> See also "Tʻadēos"; and Appendix II, "Tispon."

Marič, see "Maručan."

Maričan, see "Maručan."

Mark^c, NW MIr. *Mār, OP Māda-, "Mede/Media"
Common Armenian form for the name of the Medes. The presence of numerous Medes in Armenia is attested by the toponym *Marac^c amur erkir*, "the inaccesible/impregnable land of the Medes," within the Aršakuni kingdom. In BP this name appears only in its geographical context.
See AG, p. 52 no. 112; Adontz, *Armenia*, pp. 306–307, 323.
IV.xxiv; V.xi
pp. 158, 200
See Appendix II, "Marac^c amur erkir."

Maručan/Maričan/Marič; var. of Arm. Meružan; cf. Gk. Μερυζάνης
Persian general defeated by Vasak Mamikonean. He is not otherwise attested.
See JIN, p. 197, *Maružan* no. 1; AG, pp. 52–53 no. 111.
IV.xlii
p. 164
See also "Meružan," for the etymology of the name; "Vasak Mamikonean."

Mazdeans, see "Mazdezn."

Mazdezn/Mazdeans ‹ Parth. *mazdayazn, Phl. *Māzdēsn*, "Mazda-worshiping"
Attested as part of the Sasanian royal title in ŠKZ, Parth. 1; RGDS no. 1, pp. 46–47; etc.
"Mazdeans, Zoroastrians"
Name normally given by Armenian sources to the Zoroastrians, in keeping with Iranian usage; cf. MX, III.xvii, xxvi, xxxvi, lv (= MK, pp. 271, 282, 294, 324); Ełišē, ii. p. 24 (= *Ełishē*, p. 77 and n. 5).
See CPD, p. 55; AG, p. 190 no. 385; Benveniste, "Le Terme"; Malχasyanc^c, pp. 331–332 n. 141; also Gignoux, *Glossaire*, pp. 29, 59; *idem*, NPS, no. 602, p. 122 for use as a personal name; Sprengling, *Third-Century Iran*, pp. 7, 14; Honigmann and Maricq, RGDS, p. 11.
IV.xxiii, lix; V.i, xliii
pp. 156, 179–180, 187, 224
See also "Mogk^c."

Mazk^{c}ut^{c}k^c
Northern barbarian tribe whose ruler, Sanēsan, called Sanatruk by MX, III.iii (= MK, p. 256), is identified as an Aršakuni kinsman of the Armenian kings (III.vi-vii). According to BP, the evangelizing mission of St. Grigoris was directed to them, but MX, III.iii directs it to the Alans. Their invasion of Armenia and attack of Vałaršapat was routed by the *sparapet* Vač^{c}ē I Mamikonean.
The identity of the Mazk^{c}ut^{c}k^c has presented considerable problems, which also bear on the career of St. Grigoris. Most scholars first identified them with the Massagetae, (cf. Strabo, *Geogr.*, XI.vi, 2; viii, 2, 6, 8) whom they took to be the Alans, but the evidence of the sources is not clear. Aa, dcccxlii, dccclxxiii, refers to them by name only without further clarification, but the Greek version of the text (Ag, clvii, clxiv) adds the qualification "Huns" (Μασαχούτων Οὔνων) attested in the genitive only, as it is in the Armenian. BP links the Mazk^{c}ut^{c}k^c with the Honk^c as well as with the Alans (III.vi-vii). Malχasyanc^c (p. 312 n. 12) still accepts the identification of the Mazk^{c}ut^{c}k^c with the Massagetae, but most recent scholars, except for Toumanoff, have preferred the thesis of Peeters, who sees the name Mazk^{c}ut^{c}k^c, with its plural ending, as that of a people

already settled in a geographical habitat. Consequently, he takes them to be not the Massagetae but the Caucasian Μόσχοι or Meskheti of Iberia, a thesis supported by the seeming equivalence of Aa, dccclxxii, "the Mazkʿutʿkʿ March" and ŁPʿ xxv, p. 47 (= Ełishē, p. 261), "the Iberian March," as well as MX II.viii; III.vi (= MK, pp. 140, 258). Trever, however, prefers an identification with the Mazamacae known to Pliny the Elder (V.vii.21), and recently, Lozinski has returned to identification with the Massagetae and accepted BP's qualification of their King Sanesan as an Arsacid.

Similarly, The Oŭνοι or Honkʿ of the Armenian sources were identified by Orbeli with the 'Ηνιόχοι or Heniochoi, rather than with a Hunnic people, despite the recent objection of Melikset-Bek. Finally, Maenschen-Helfen noted that none of the eleven peoples associated with the Mazkʿutʿkʿ—the Pʿoχkʿ, Tʿawasparkʿ, Hečmatakkʿ, Ižmaχkʿ, Gatʿkʿ, Głuarkʿ, Gugarkʿ, Sičbkʿ, Čiłbkʿ, Bałaščikʿ, and Egersuankʿ—has a name "even remotely similar to a Hun tribal name." Malχasyancʿ identifies them as a group of nomadic tribes of Scythian origin living in the north Caucasian plain as far as the Caspian Sea (p. 312 n. 13). Indeed, some of them can be localized by their names: the Tʿawasparkʿ, Hečmatakkʿ, Ižmaχkʿ, and Ciłbkʿ are to be found in the Ašχ. (long, 27/37) under "Asiatic Sarmatia"; the Gugarkʿ and Egersuankʿ are readily associated with the northern Armenian district of Gugarkʿ (cf., however, above, "Gugarkʿ"), and Eger/Abkhazia + Suaneti in the western Caucasus and along the Black Sea coast, respectively. The other remain unidentifiable to date. Eremyan, Map B/8, gives the Mazkʿutʿkʿ and extensive territory west of the Caspian Sea and north of the Kur.

See Markwart, Ērānšahr, pp. 155–157, 167–169, but cf. idem, Genealogie, p. 33; idem, Entstehung, 214–218; Peeters, "Les Débuts," pp. 22–24; Orbeli, "Gorod bliznitsov"; Melikset-Bek, "K istorii," p. 712; Trever, Albania, pp. 188–197; Struve, "Review," p. 182; Maenschen-Helfen, Huns, pp. 5–6, 458; Thomson, Aa, p. 455 n. 5; Toumanoff, Studies, pp. 459–460 n. 98; Eremyan, Ašχarh., pp. 34, 42–43, 48, 50; idem, "Narody"; idem, Map B/8; Lozinski, "Parthian Dynasty," pp. 126–129.

III.v–vii
pp. 70, 72–74
Maps, K-L/2-4
See also "Alankʿ"; "Grigoris"; "Sanesan"; "Vačʿē I"; and Appendix II, "Gugarkʿ"; "Kur"; "Vałaršapat."

Mehandak/Mehendak/Mehəndak/Mehundak I Ṙštuni OP *Miθra-bandaka-*, "servant of Miθra"; the name is attested in multiple variants
Armenian commander and companion-in-arms of the *sparapet* Vačʿē I in the Mazkʿutʿkʿ war (III.vii), and kinsman of Garegin I Ṙštuni. MX, III.xvi (= MK, p. 269) makes him a brother of the Ṙštuni *nahapet* Zawray, but BP does not mention this personage. Mehandak also accompanied Pʿaṙen of Aštišat to his consecration at Caesarea. But because all the Ṙštuni house was annihilated under King Tiran except for Mehandak's son Tačat, Mehandak I should not be confused with his namesake living in the reign of Aršak II, as has often been done (see next entry). He is also confused with his son Tačat by TʿA I.x, p. 60 (= *Thom. Arts.*, p. 124) who calls him Mehēdak.
See HAnjB, III, pp. 311–312; JIN, p. 202; cf. Gignoux, NPS no. 613, p. 123, *Mihr.*
III.vii, xvi, xviii
pp. 74, 91, 93
See also "Garegin I"; Mazkʿutʿkʿ"; "Ṙštuni, house"; "Tačat"; "Vačʿē I"; and Appendix III, *nizakakicʿ*.

Mehandak/Mehendak/Mehundak/Mehen (?) II Ṙštuni ‹ *Miθra-bandaka-*, "servant of Miθra"
Nahapet of the Ṙštuni house who accompanied St. Nersēs to his consecration at Caesarea, according to BP (IV.iv), followed by the *Vita* of St. Nersēs, iii, p. 25

(= CHAMA, II, p. 24), which gives the name as Mehendak. On chronological grounds and because of his identification by BP as "great prince," he should probably be identified with Mehen, *nahapet* of the R̆štuni, who accompanied St. Nersēs on his embassy to Constantiople in 358 (IV.xi), especially since the *Vita* of St. Nersēs, viii, p. 52 (= CHAMA, II, p. 30) lists the R̆štuni *nahapet* at this point as Mehendak. Mehendak II should not, however, be confused with his earlier namesake (see preceding entry).
   See HAnjB, III, p. 311–312; JIN, p. 202; cf. Gignoux, NPS, no. 613, p. 123, *Mihr*.
   IV.iv, xi
   pp. 111, 133
   See also "R̆štuni, house"; and Appendix III, *nahapet*.

Mehar̆/Mehewan Anjewac͑i ‹ ?OP *Miθra-bandaka-*, "servant of Miθra"
   Nahapet of Anjewac͑ik͑ who accompanied St. Nersēs on his embassy to Constantinople in 358. He is otherwise attested only in the *Vita* of St. Nersēs, viii, p. 52 (= CHAMA, II, p. 30), which depends here on BP but gives the long form of the name, Mehewan.
   See HAnjB, III, p. 311, *Mehar̆*, p. 312, *Mehewan* no. 1; JIN, p. 202; cf. Gignoux, NPS, no. 123, *Mihr*.
   IV.xi
   p. 133
   See also Appendix II, "Anjewac͑ik͑"; and Appendix III, *nahapet*.

Mehen R̆štuni, see "Mehandak II R̆štuni."

Mehendak R̆štuni, see "Mehandak R̆štuni."

Mehəndak R̆štuni, see "Mehandak R̆štuni."

Mehundak R̆štuni, see "Mehandak R̆štuni."

Mehružan, see "Meružan Arcruni."

Meružan/Mehružan Arcruni ‹ Phl. Mihrōzan (*Miθr* + *bauǰana-*)," pleasure, enjoyment of Miθra"; cf. Gk. Μερυζάνης/Μιθροβουζάνης; cf. Parth. *mtrbwznkn*
   Attested in ŠKZ, Parth. 23; Phl. 28, RGDS, no. 55, pp. 64–65.
   Nahapet of the Arcruni house and leader of the pro-Persian rebellion against Aršak II and his successors. Meružan is the *bête-noire* of BP's account, the traitor and apostate par excellence, and as such, the fourth-century counterpart of the fifth-century archtraitor Vasak Siwni, although the *Vita* of St. Nersēs, viii, pp. 52–53 (= CHAMA II, p. 30) still includes him among the *naxarar*s sent with Nersēs I as ambassadors to the court of the emperor "Valens" [Constantius]. The accounts of Meružan's career vary considerably in BP and MX, III.xxxv–xxxvii (= MK, pp. 293–298). Both record his rebellion and his government of Armenia during the Persian occupation following Jovian's peace of 363 (IV. lviii–lix; MX, III. xxvi = MK, p. 294), but according to the latter, Meružan married Šāhpuhr II's sister Ormizduχt (MX, III.xxxvi = MK, p. 294), while according to BP (IV.l), this princess was married to Meružan's maternal uncle and collaborator Vahan Mamikonean. Moreover, according to BP (V.xliii), Meružan was finally defeated and killed in battle by prince Babik Siwni during the regency of the *sparapet* Manuēl Mamikonean, but MX, III.xxxvii (= MK, p. 298) places this event much earlier, in the reign of King Pap, and attributes Meružan's death to the *aspet* and coronant Smbat Bagratuni, in keeping with his usual pro Bagratid bias. BP's version seems more verisimilar, considering the contrived character of MX's episode, in which Smbat kills Meružan by crowning him with a molten crown in parody of the Bagratuni's hereditary office of royal coronants (*t͑agadir/t͑agakap*). Both Armenian sources treat Meružan as a traitor to his lord the Armenian king, but the Arcruni as dynasts

in Sophēnē were rulers of one of the autonomous Satrapies of southern Armenia, and Meružan may well have been pursuing an independent pro-Persian policy, which northern Armenian sources present as treason (see Intro., p. 48–49).

See Gignoux, *Glossaire*, p. 29; *idem*, NPS, no. 653, p. 130, *Mihrōzan*; Schmitt, IN, p. 329, *Me(h)rowžan*; Back, SSI, p. 232; Sprengling, *Third-Century Iran*, pp. 9, 11, 18; Honigmann and Maricq, RGDS, p. 17; HAnjB, III, pp. 326–327 no. 2; JIN, pp. 209, Μιθροβουζάνης no. 4, 416; Toumanoff, *Manuel*, p. 87/3, who makes Meružan the son of Šawasp; AG, pp. 52–53 no. 114.

IV.xxiii–xxiv, xxxi–xxxvii, xxxix–xliii, xlv–l, lviii–lix; V.i, ii, iv, xxxviii, xliii

pp. 156–158, 161–167, 178–179, 186–187, 189, 222–228

See also "Arcruni, house"; "Aršak II"; "Babik"; "Manuēl"; "Šapuh"; "Šawasp"; "Vahan"; Appendix II, "Copʿkʿ"; and Appendix III, *nahapet*.

Mogkʿ ‹ Sasanian MP *Mog*, OP *magū*, "Magi"

Term used by Armenian sources for both the priestly caste of the Magians and their religion, which is explicitly equated by BP with Mazdeism (IV.xxiii). The term *Mazdezkʿ* is used more commonly in the text, whereas Ełišē, e.g. p. 15 (= *Ełishē*, p. 69 and 77 n. 5) prefers *mogutʿiwn*.

See Nyberg, *Manual*, II, *magū*; Russell, *Zor. Arm.*, p. 299.

IV.xxiii, xlvii, l, li, lvi, lix

pp. 156, 166, 168–169, 177

See also "Mazdezn."

Movsēs bishop of Basean ‹ Hebr. Môšeh

One of the bishops of Basean, according to BP. He is otherwise unattested, and the identification with St. Gregory's second disciple, sent to Basean, in Aa, dcccxlv, is unlikely since the name given there is not Movsēs but Ewtʿałios/ Euthalios, and Movsēs is listed in fourth place. The toponym "Basean" is not found in the title of the chapter.

See HAnjB, III. p. 420 nos. 2, 4; AG, p. 335; Ališan, *Ayrarat*, p. 43.

VI.xiii

p. 238

See also "Tirik"; and Appendix II, "Basean."

Mrikan, see "Mṙkan."

Mrǰiwnik ‹ Arm. *mrǰiwn*, "ant" + diminutive *-ik*

Court priest (*dran erēcʿ*) whom Pʿaṙanjem persuaded to murder Aršak II's Roman wife Olympias with the Eucharist, and who was rewarded with the grant of his native village for the crime. This last detail is found only in BP. Mrǰiwnik's name is attested in the *Vita* of St. Nersēs, viii, p. 51 (= CHAMA, II, p. 29), but MX, III.xxiv (= MK, p. 280) speaks only of an anonymous "unworthy priest."

See HAnjB, III, pp. 477–478 no. 1; JIN, p. 217, who turns him into a monk.

IV.xv

p. 145

See also "Ołompi"; "Pʿaṙanjem"; and Appendix II, "Gomkunkʿ."

Mṙkan/Mrikan

Persian general sent against Aršak II (IV.xlix). As in the case of Gumand Šapuh, he is said to have been killed in this campaign, but a namesake reappears under parallel circumstances, only to be killed again, this time by Manuēl Mamikonean (V.xli). He is not otherwise attested.

See JIN, p. 217; AG, p. 54 no. 116, *Muškan*.

IV.xlix; V.xli

pp. 166–167, 224

See also "Gumand Šapuh."

Mšakan, see "Muškan."

Mškan, see "Muškan."

Murik ‹ Gk. Μαυρίκιος; Lat. Mauricius
Archdeacon of St. Nersēs. He is not otherwise attested, but may be referred to in
VI.xvi.
See HAnjB, III, p. 472 no. 1; Malχasyanc^c, p. 325 n. 96.
IVxv
p. 142
See also "Trdat/Trdac"; and Appendix III, *ark^cidiakonos*.

Mušē ‹ Syr. Mušē; Hebr. Môšeh
Anchorite and disciple of St. Gind. He is not otherwise attested. Like Gind's teacher
Daniēl, Mušē may well have been a Syrian since his name is given in the Syriac form
"Mušē" rather than in its Armenian derivation, "Movsēs."
See HAnjB, III, p. 463 no. 3; AG, p. 295.
VI.xvi
pp. 239–240
See also "Gind."

Mušeł Mamikonean
Sepuh of the Mamikonean house, and possibly its *nahapet*, though this is not specified anywhere. He succeeded his father Vasak as *sparapet* of Armenia and personally
commanded the *azat* contingent of the Armenian army, which distinguished itself particularly in battle against the Persians (V.iv–v). During Šāhpuhr II's invasion of Armenia (post 363), Mušeł went to the Byzantine court to seek support for Aršak II's son,
Pap (IV.lv), whom he reestablished on the Armenian throne with the help of an imperial
army (V.i). As commander in chief, he helped drive the Persians from Armenia (V.ii,
iv–v) and, ca. 370, succeeded in temporarily reconquering the border territories that had
fallen away from the Armenian kingdom after the Roman–Persian peace of 363
(V.viii–xx). In spite of his avowed loyalty to the Aršakuni house (V.iv, xx), he was
slandered to King Pap (V.iv) and to his successor, Varazdat, who had him murdered
(V.xxxv).
Mušeł is the hero of BP's account, where all virtues are attributed to him, including
the supernatural *k^caǰut^ciwn* belonging by right to the ruler alone (V.ii, v). This apo-
theosis, drawn from traditional Iranian beliefs and following in every detail the royal
Sasanian iconography, as well as the account of the pagan practices that attended
Mušeł's burial (V.xxxvi), are probably derived from oral epic accounts current in Ar-
menia at the time (see Intro., pp. 34–35). Mušeł is barely mentioned by MX, III.xxxvii
(= MK, p. 298).
See HAnjB, III, pp. 455–456 no. 4; JIN, p. 424; Toumanoff, *Manuel*, 322/5b; Gar-
soïan, "Locus," pp. 52–53, 62–63.
IV.lv; V.i–vi, viii–xxi, xxiv, xxx, xxxii–xxxvii
pp. 174, 185–191, 193–196, 199–202, 204–205, 210, 213–220
See also "Aršakuni"; "Bat"; "Mamikonean, house"; "Pap"; "Šapuh"; "Varazdat";
"Vasak"; Appendix II, "Ałjnik^c"; "Ałuank^c" "Angełtun"; "Anjit"; "Arjaχ"; "Cop^ck^c
Mec"; "Gardman"; "Gugark^c"; "Jor/Jorop^cor"; "Kazbk^c"; "Kolb"; "Kołt^cn";
"Korduk^c"; "Kur"; "Marac^c amur ašχarh"; "Mec Hayk^c"; "Noširakan";
"P^caytakaran"; "Šakašēn"; "Tmorik^c"; "Utik^c"; "Virk^c"; and Appendix III, *aza-
tagund*; *k^caǰut^ciwn*; *nahapet*; *sepuh*; *sparapet*.

Mušk/Muškan Sahaṙuni, cf. Pers. Muškan

Nahapet of the Sahaṙuni house and one of the magnates accompanying St. Nersēs on his embassy to the Byzantine court in 358. He is otherwise attested only in the *Vita* of St. Nersēs, viii, p. 52 (= CHAMA, II, p. 30), which depends here on BP, but gives the name in the form Muškan.

See HAnjB, III, p. 464; JIN, p. 218 no. 1; AG, p. 54 no. 116.

IV.xi

p. 133

See also "Sahaṙuni, house"; and Appendix III, *nahapet*.

Muškan/Mšakan/Mškan, cf. Pers. Muškan

Persian general defeated and killed by Vasak Mamikonean. He is not otherwise attested.

See Schmitt, IN, p. 331, *M(ow)škan*; JIN, p. 218 no. 1; AG, p. 54 no. 116.

IV.xli

p. 164

Muškan Sahaṙuni, see "Mušk Sahaṙuni."

Nerseh, king; Parth. Narsēs, Phl. Narsē ‹ Av. *Nairyō. saŋha-*, "of manly speech," divine messenger

Name attested in ŠKZ, Parth. 19–21, 25, 27; Phl. 24–26, 31, 33, 34; RGDS nos. 48–49, 61–62, 64–65, pp. 62–63, 68–69, 70–71; *Paikuli*.

King of kings of Persia (293–303), last reigning son of Šāhpuhr I. Nerseh ruled over eastern Iran and subsequently over Armenia, according to the Paikuli inscription, before his transfer to the royal throne of Iran. He was routed by the Caesar Galerius in 297 and constrained to sign the Peace of Nisibis in 298 whereby the southern Satrapies and probably the northern kingdom of Greater Armenia shifted to the Roman sphere of influence. For the anachronistic appearance of Nerseh in BP, his probable conflation with his namesake, the son of Šāhpuhr II who was defeated and killed by the Romans at the battle of Singara, and his confusion with Šāhpuhr II himself, see III.xx n. 9 and xxi n. 16.

See Gignoux, *Glossaire*, pp. 30, 59; *ibid.*, NPS, no. 678, p. 134; Schmitt, IN, pp. 321, 329; Sprengling, *Third-Century Iran*, pp. 8–9, 11–12, 17–19; Honigmann and Maricq, RGDS, pp. 16–18; Humbach and Skærvø, *Paikuli*, 3.1, p. 114; JIN, pp. 222, *Nariyaþaha* no. 12, and 419, where the stemma, however, needs correction; Jones *et al.*, *Prosopography*, I, p. 616, *Narses* no. 1, cf. *Narses* no. 2; Frye, "Sasanians," pp. 126–131; *idem, Heritage*, pp. 206, 208, 211, 215, 283; *Paikuli*, pp. 98–99, 118–119; Toumanoff, "Third-Century Arsacids," pp. 256–261, 263–265; Ananian, "La data," pp. 58–59, 69–72; Adontz, "Favst"; Melikʿ-Ōhanǰanyan, "Tiran-Trdati vepə."

III.xx–xxi; IV.i, lviii

pp. 95, 98, 107, 178

See also "Šapuh"; "Sasanians."

Nerseh of Copʿkʿ Šahēi ‹ Parth Narsēs, Phl. Narsēh ‹ Av. *Nairyō. saŋha*, "of manly speech," divine messenger

Name attested in ŠKZ, Parth. 19–21, 25, 27; Phl. 24–26, 31, 33, 34; RGDS nos. 48–49, 61–62, 64–65, pp. 62–63, 68–69; 70–71; *Paikuli*.

Nahapet of Copʿkʿ Šahēi who supported Xosrov Kotak against the revolt of the *bdeašχ* Bakur. He was presumably succeeded by Varaz (III.xii), but is not otherwise attested.

See HAnjB, IV, p. 31 no. 4; and the additional bibliography on the name Nerseh under the preceding entry.

III.ix

p. 77

See also "Bakur"; "Varaz"; Appendix II, "Cop^{c}k^c Šahēi"; and Appendix III, *nahapet*.

Nersēs I the Great, St. ‹ Parth. Narsēs, Phl. Narsē ‹ Av. *Nairyō. saŋha-*, "of manly speech," divine messenger

Name attested in ŠKZ, Parth. 19–21, 25, 27; Phl. 24–26, 31, 33, 34; RGDS nos. 48–49, 61–62, 64–65, pp. 62–63, 68–69; 70–71; *Paikuli.*

Patriarch of Greater Armenia probably between 353 and 373. Nersēs was the son of At^{c}anaginēs and the Aršakuni princess Bambišn, and the great-great-grandson of St. Gregory the Illuminator. He was the dominant ecclesiastical figure in fourth-century Armenia as well as in BP's account, which is the main source for Nersēs's career, many details of which remain uncertain, as are the dates of his patriarchate. The span 353–373 given by Ōrmanean, and generally accepted, does not agree with the thirty-four years attributed to him by MX, III.xxxviii (= MK, p. 299), but Baynes's attempt to push the beginning of Nersēs's pontificate to 340 is chronologically impossible, in view of the fact that Nersēs's great-grand-uncle Aristakēs represented Armenia at the Council of Nicaea in 325, so that four generations of the Gregorid family would have to be compressed into fifteen years to fit this hypothesis. The intrusion of material from the life of St. Basil of Caesarea into that of St. Nersēs (IV.v–vi) also increases the chronological confusion (see Intro., p. 40).

Nersēs was educated at Caesarea of Cappadocia and presumably married there, though MX, III.xvi (= MK, p. 270), claims that he went to Byzantium where he married the daughter of the "great noble Aspion," who is otherwise unknown. BP knows nothing of this journey and does not name Nersēs's wife, while the *Vita* of St. Nersēs, ii, p. 14 (= CHAMA, II, p. 23), gives yet another version in which the future patriarch married Sanduχt, the daughter of Vardan Mamikonean, at Caesarea, where she died after bearing the future St. Sahak I. Nersēs's military career and his office as royal *senekapet* (IV.iii) are confirmed by the *Vita* (*loc. cit.*), but not by MX who also ignores the patriarch's consecration at Caesarea (IV.iv). Nersēs's subsequent career, however, follows the same general lines in BP and MX's far shorter account. The patriarch went to Byzantium on one (IV.v, xi) or probably two (MX, III.xxi, xxix–xxx = MK, pp. 275–276, 286–287) embassies, which resulted in the release of the Armenian royal hostages, but also in his own exile (IV.v–vi, xi). Nersēs returned to the Armenian court only at the enthronement of King Pap (V.i), which MX, III.xxxvi (= MK, p. 295), attributed directly to the patriarch's intervention with the emperor. Even so, hostility soon envenomed the relations between Nersēs and Pap, leading to the patriarch's murder at the instigation of the king (V.xxiv; MX, III.xxxviii = MK, p. 299) and possibly a resultant break between Caesarea and the Armenian church (V.xxix and n. 1). Both sources also record Nersēs's reorganization of the Armenian church at the so-called Council of Aštišat (ca. 354) and his extensive charitable foundations (IV.iv; V.xxi, xxxi), though MX, III.xx (= MK, p. 274), gives them a Greek model unknown to BP, as well as his murder at Xaχ and burial at T^{c}il (V.xxiv; MX, III.xxxviii = MK, p. 299).

The core of BP's account of Nersēs's career seems clearly grounded on fact, for the patriarch's embassy of 358 is recorded by both AM (XII.v.1–2) and the Constantinopolitan records (MGH, AA, IX, p. 239). His exile coincides *pace* Baynes, with that of the anti-Arian bishops after the Council of Seleucia of 359. His Hellenizing ecclesiastical policy and his anti-Arian orthodoxy, seemingly confirmed by St. Basil's *Letter* xcii, were the probable cause of his opposition to the Arianizing Aršakuni kings, rather than the murder of Aršak II's nephew Gnel (IV.xv) or the depravity of Pap (V.xxii–xxiv) invoked by BP. The Basilian intrusions, however, present problems because they obscure not only the chronology of St. Nersēs's life, but the probable influence of Eustathios of Sebastē on the patriarch's charitable activity. Moreover, BP's entire account of its spiritual hero Nersēs is an uncritical panegyric, which provided the basis for the still more elaborately hagiographical *Vita*.

See HAnjB, IV, pp. 35–38; JIN, pp. 222–223, **Nariyapaha*,no. 19; Toumanoff, *Manuel*, p. 224/6; Sanspeur, "Nouvelle Liste," cols. 186–187, 196; Ōrmanean, *Azgapatum*, I, cols. 163–222, xvi–xvii; Garitte, *Narratio*, pp. 61–62, 417–418, etc.; Markwart, *Entstehung*, pp. 152–154, 169–181, 223–231; Baynes, "Rome and Armenia," pp. 186–193; Garsoïan, *Armenia*, iv–vii; *idem*, "Šahak of Manazkert"; also the additional bibliography under the name Narseh.

III.xv, xix; IV.iii–vii, ix, xi–xv, xix, li, liv, lvii; V.i, iv–v, xxi–xxvii, xxix–xxxi, xliv; VI.v–vi, xvi

pp. 91, 94, 109–113, 116, 121–126, 130, 133–139, 141–143, 145, 149, 168, 173, 177, 185–187, 190–191, 194, 202–206, 210–213, 229, 235, 239

See also "Aršak II"; "Atˤanaginēs"; "Bambišn"; "Barseł"; "Gnel Aršakuni"; "Grigor/Gregorids"; "Pap"; "Vałēs"; Appendix II, "Caesarea"; "Tˤil"; "Xaχ"; and Appendix III, *senekapet*.

Noy of Copˤkˤ Šahēi ‹ Hebr. Noaḥ

Nahapet of Copˤkˤ Šahēi, who accompanied St. Nersēs to his consecration at Caesarea. He is not otherwise attested, but was presumably the successor of Varaz (III.xii). BP refers to him as the "prince of the other Copˤkˤ," as opposed to the "great prince Daniēl of Copˤkˤ," who was presumably the ruler of Copˤkˤ Mec.

See HAnjB, IV, p. 83 no. 1.

IV.iv

p. 111

See also "Varaz"; Appendix II, "Copˤkˤ Šahēi"; and Appendix III, *nahapet*.

Ołimbi, see "Ołompi"

Ołompi/Ołimbi/Ołompinay ‹ Gk. Ὀλύμπιας; Lat. Olympias

Daughter of the pretorian prefect Ablabius and betrothed of the emperor Constans (AM XX.xi.3). After Constans's death, his brother Constantius gave her in marriage to Aršak II of Armenia, probably in 358. She was murdered, presumably at the instigation of Pˤaṙanjem of Siwnikˤ, Aršak's other wife, soon after Constantius's death in 361. Olympias is correctly identified by MX, III.xxi (= MK, p. 276) as a "maiden . . . from the imperial family," but the *Vita* of St. Nersēs, viii, p. 50 (= CHAMA, II, p. 29) anachronistically turns her into a "sister . . . of Valens." See also IV.xv, nn. 39, 40.

See HAnjB, IV, p. 186 no. 1; Jones *et al.*, *Prosopography*, I, p. 642, *Olympias* no. 1; Toumanoff, *Manuel*, p. 75/8; Garsoïan, "Politique," p. 305; *idem*, "*Quidam Narseus*," pp. 149–151, 153, 157, 163; also IV.xv n. 40

IV.xv

p. 145

See also "Aršak II"; "Mrǰiwnik"; "Pˤaṙanjem."

Ołompinay, see "Ołompi."

Olympias, see "Ołompi."

Orduni, house

Naχarar family traditionally descended from the Armenian eponymous hero Hayk like their rivals the Manawazean. They are known to MX, I.xii, II.viii, III.ii (= MK, pp. 89, 141, 255), who also confirms that their domain lay in Basean (II.viii = MK, p. 141). Because the family was anihilated in the reign of Xosrov Kotak and its seat, Orduru, granted to the bishop of Basean, it is not included in any of the late Lists of *naχarar*s, but the *Zōrnamak*, "Military List," gives both a Prince Orduni with 700 retainers at the "Northern gate" and a prince of Basean with 600 at the "western gate." There may have been two houses for Manak of Basean is still mentioned in III.ix, after the presumed extinction of the Orduni.

> See Adontz, *Armenia*, pp. 193–194, 198, 205, 222, 245, 376, 383 n. 39, 69*; Touma-
> noff, *Studies*, p. 110 n. 173, 199, 216, 218–219 and n. 254, 224, 227, 231 nn. 284–
> 285, 235, n. 301, 240.
> III.iv
> pp. 69–70
> See also "Artit^c"; "Manak"; "Manawazean"; "Tirik"; "Xosrov II/III"; Appendix II,
> "Basean"; "Orduru"; and Appendix III, *naχarar*.

Ormizduχt ‹ Phl. Ormizd + *duχt*, "daughter"
Name attested in ŠKZ, Parth. 22; Phl. 27; RGDS no. 51, pp. 62–63
Sister of the Persian king of kings Šāhpuhr II and wife of the apostate Vahan Mamikonean (IV.l), according to BP. MX, III.xxxvi (= MK, p. 294) makes her the wife of Vahan's nephew Meružan Arcruni. She was killed, together with her husband, by their son Samuēl.

> See Gignoux, *Glossaire*, p. 24; *idem*, NPS, nos. 710–711, p. 139; Schmitt, IN, p. 331;
> Sprengling, *Third-Century Iran*, pp. 9, 11, 18; Honigmann and Maricq, RGDS,
> p. 16; JIN, p. 10 *Ahura-mazdāh* no. 4; AG, p. 62 no. 139; Raffi, *Samuēl*.
> IV.l, lix
> pp. 168, 180
> See also "Samuēl"; "Šapuh"; "Sasanians"; "Vahan."

Pap ‹ Phl. *Pāp/Bāb*, "father"; Lat. *Papa*; the mss of Ammianus Marcellinus read *Para*
Son of Aršak II and P^{c}aṙanjem of Siwnik^c. King of Armenia as successor of Aršak II (ca. 368–ca. 374). According to BP (IV.xv), he was sent as a hostage to the Byzantine court and subsequently educated at Neocaesarea in Pontus (AM, XXVII.xii.9). He returned to Armenia ca. 368/70 with the support of the *sparapet* Mušeł Mamikonean and a Roman army commanded by the general Terentius (V.i = AM, XXVII.xii.10). According to AM (XXVII.xii.11) but not BP, this event took place before the fall of the fortress of Artagers/Artogerassa to the Persians, and Pap was forced to flee to Lazica before returning successfully a second time to ascend his father's throne. Pap's relations with the Romans soon worsened, perhaps as a result of his putative claims on Roman cities (V.xxxii) or more probably his continuation of his father's Arianizing ecclesias-tical policy, which led to the murder of the Gregorid patriarch Nersēs the Great (V.xxiv). It was followed almost at once by the king's summons to Tarsus in Cilicia, whence he fled back to Armenia (AM, XXX.i.14–17), and his murder at Xu by the Roman com-mander (V.xxxii = AM, XXX.i.18–23), or his execution at the order of the emperor "Theodosius," according to MX's anachronistic version, III.xxxix (= MK, pp. 300–301). After a brief hiatus, Pap was succeeded by his sons Aršak III and Vałaršak under the regency of their mother Zarmanduχt and that of the *sparapet* Manuēl Mamikonean (V.xxxvii).

The characterization of Pap in the Armenian sources, which depict him as devoted to the powers of evil from birth is invariably hostile (BP, IV.xliv, V.xxii; MX, III.xxxviii = MK, p. 299). This is probably a consequence of his religious policy, since their por-trayal of Pap is in direct contrast to that of AM (XXX.i.15), who describes the young king being joyfully welcomed by his people. Pap's unilateral designation of the Armenian primate after the murder of St. Nersēs may have led to a breach between Caesarea of Cappadocia and the Armenian church (V.xxix and n. 1), though the precise form and date of this breach are still open to question, and Duchesne's identification of King Pap with the Papa of St. Basil's *Letters*, cxx–cxxii, who has been linked with these events, should probably be rejected.

See Gignoux, NPS, no. 722, p. 141, cf. nos. 169–178, pp. 52–54, *Bāb*; Schmitt, IN, p. 321; HAnjB, IV, p. 222 no. 2; JIN, p. 241 no. 2; Toumanoff, *Manuel*, p. 75/9a; Jones et al., *Prosopography*, I, pp. 665–666, *Papa*; AG, pp. 65–66 no. 141; Garsoïan, "Politique," pp. 298, 303, 307–308, 313–320; idem, "Nersēs le Grand," pp. 154–158; idem, "Secular Jurisdiction," pp. 236–237.

IV.xv, xliv, lv; V.i–vi, xix, xxii–xxiv, xxix–xxxii, xxxiv–xxxv, xxxvii–xxxviii pp. 145, 164–165, 174, 185–191, 193–194, 196–197, 201–203, 205, 210–216, 219, 221, 223

See also "Aršak II"; "Aršak III"; "Aršakuni"; "Manuēl"; "Mušeł"; "Pʿaṙanjem"; "Terent"; "Vałēs"; "Yusik II"; "Zarmanduχt"; Appendix II, "Artagers"; "Caesarea"; "Uṙhay"; "Xu"; and Appendix III, *dew*.

Pap (2) ‹ Phl. *Pāp/Bāb*, "father"

Son of the patriarch Yusik and great-grandson of St. Gregory the Illuminator. Together with his twin brother Atʿanaginēs he was considered unworthy to assume the patriarchal office, which both had rejected in favor of a military career, perhaps in fear of the inflexibly orthodox theological position that had opposed their father to the king and led to his martyrdom. Their decision led to the first hiatus in the hereditary transmission of the Armenian patriarchate within the Gregorid house. The account of Pap's career and death in BP is more detailed than the brief notice in MX, III.xvi (= MK, pp. 269–270), and it is the only source to name his wife, the Aršakuni princess Varazduχt and his illegitimate son Vrik (III.xix). Together with his brother Atʿanaginēs, Pap was buried at Aštišat and not with their ancestors.

See HAnjB, IV, p. 222 no. 1; JIN, p. 241 no. 1; Toumanoff, *Manuel*, p. 224/5; AG, pp. 65–66 no. 1; Ōrmanean, *Azgapatum*, I cols. 152–153; see also additional bibliography on the name in the preceding entry.

III.v, xiii, xv, xix pp. 71, 85, 90–91, 93–94

See also "Atʿanaginēs"; "Grigor/Gregorids"; "Varazduχt"; "Vrik"; "Yusik I"; and Appendix II, "Agarak."

Pʿaṙanjem of Siwnikʿ ‹ MP Xōranzem

Name attested in ŠKZ, Parth. 20–21; Phl. 25–26; RGDS, no. 46, 50, pp. 60–63

Daughter of Andovk Siwni, queen of Armenia as wife of Aršak II, and mother of his son and successor, Pap. All Armenian sources also record her marriage to Aršak's nephew Gnel and her murder of Aršak's other wife, the Roman Olympias (IV.xv; MX, III.xxii, xxiv = MK, pp. 277, 279–280). The *Vita* of St. Nersēs, vii–viii, pp. 43–51 (= CHAMA, II, pp. 28–29) follows the version of BP with some embellishments and names a second son of Aršak and Pʿaṙanjem, Trdat. At the time of the Persian invasion of Armenia in 363, the queen held out for a considerable time in the royal fortress of Artagers until plague (IV.lv) or the surrender of the garrison (MX, III.xxxv = MK, p. 293; AM, XXVII.xii.12) yielded it to the Persians. Like her husband, Aršak II, Pʿaṙanjem was deported to Persia, where she was brutally put to death at the order of Šāhpuhr II.

The figure of Pʿaṙanjem remains enigmatic in Armenian literature. The problem of the order of her marriages is based on the disagreement of BP, IV.xv and MX, III.xxiv (= MK, pp. 279–280). Both agree that she married Aršak II after the murder of Gnel, but they contradict each other over the question of her being Aršak's first or second wife, and the account of BP is undoubtedly contaminated by romantic oral traditions (see IV.xv nn. 1, 3, 33, 40, 42). This contamination probably also contributed to the incoherent portrayal of the queen in Armenian historiography. BP presents her in the same chapter (IV.xv) as the disconsolate mourner of her murdered first husband and as the sacrilegious murderess of Aršak II's imperial bride (cf. MX, III.xxiv = MK, p. 280). BP further attributes Pap's demonic possession to his mother (V.xxii; cf. IV. xliv and nn. 3, 7); yet stresses her position as queen (*tikin*) of Armenia in both her defense of the royal fortress of Artagers and the account of her odious death in Persia (IV.lx). This incoherence may also be due in part to the queen's dubious orthodoxy.

    See Gignoux, *Glossaire*, p. 24; NPS, no. 1018, p. 185, *Xōrānzēm*; Back, SSI, p. 222; Sprengling, *Third-Century Iran*, pp. 11, 17, 18; Honigmann and Maricq, RGDS, p. 16; HAnjB, p. 190; JIN, p. 426, *Pharandzem*; Toumanoff, *Manuel*, p. 226/3; Garsoïan, "Politique," p. 312 n. 51.

    IV.xv [xviii], xx, xliv, lv; V.iii, xxii

    pp. 140, [142], 144–145 [148], 152, 164–[165], 173–176, 188–202

    See also "Andovk"; "Aršak II"; "Gnel Aršakuni"; "Mrjiwnik"; "Ołompi"; "Pap"; "Šapuh"; "Siwni, house"; Tiritᶜ"; "Vałinak I Siwni"; Appendix II, "Artagers"; and Appendix III, *tikin*.

Pᶜaṙawazean, see "Pᶜaṙnawazean."

Pᶜaṙēn/Pᶜaṙnerseh ‹ Arm. *pᶜaṙkᶜ*; Ir. *χwarrah*, "glory, light"

    Patriarch of Greater Armenia following the murders of Yusik and Daniēl (348–352?), duly consecrated at Caesarea. Most scholars, following MX, III.xvi (= MK, p. 270), give his name in the form Pᶜaṙnerseh, which is not found in BP. According to MX, he ascended the patriarchal throne in the tenth year of King Tiran and kept it for four years, an indication followed by most scholars. Other Armenian sources oscillate between three and five years, while BP merely attributes "a short time" to his pontificate (III.xvi). He does not seem to have been particularly distinguished, for BP refers to him disdainfully as *omn*, "a certain" priest, and he seems to have been the first non-Gregorid primate of Armenia. Attempts have, however, been made to provide him with a pedigree. Adontz linked him with the family of Ałbianos of Manazkert, while Ačaryan suggested that he was in fact a Gregorid, on the basis of the last sentence in III.xv (see III.xv n. 4). This seems unlikely in view of BP's condescending tone toward him, as opposed to his veneration of the Gregorid house. Nevertheless, the burial of Pᶜaṙēn in the *agarak* of the holy site of Aštišat—which seems to have been a Gregorid family plot because not only the unworthy sons of the patriarch Yusik (III.xix), but also St. Sahak I were to be buried there (Koriwn, xxiv, p. 88 = trans. p. 48; MX, III.lxvii = MK, p. 348; ŁPᶜ, I.xix, pp. 37–38 = CHAMA, II, p. 278)—suggests that he may possibly have been a collateral or minor member of the Gregorid family. It may also be a prerogative to which he was entitled as guardian of the shrine of Aštišat. Like all the early Armenian primates except Aristakēs, Pᶜaṙēn appears to have been married, but only BP mentions his regrettable son, Bishop Yohan (VI.xiii–x), if these chapters are not an extraneous addition to BP (see Intro., pp. 35–36).

    See Schmitt, IN, p. 330, cf. p. 331, *Pᶜaṙnerseh*; HAnjB, V, pp. 190–191; JIN, pp. 93–94, *Pᶜaṙnerseh*; AG, pp. 88–90 no. 213; Akinean, *Nkaragir*, pp. 529–532 n. 16, for the unlikely theory that the form Pᶜaṙnerseh was a misreading of BP's *Pᶜaṙēn erēcᶜ*, Sanspeur, "Nouvelle Liste," pp. 186–187; Ōrmanean, *Azgapatum*, I, cols. 155–162; Garitte, *Narratio*, pp. 59–61, 402, 417; Adontz, *Armenia*, pp. 274–275; Garsoïan, "Šahak of Manazkert."

    III.xvi, xvii; VI.viii, x

    pp. 91–92, 236–237

See also "Ałbianos"; "Grigor/Gregorids"; "Tiran"; "Yohan"; and Appendix II, "Agarak"; "Aštišat"; "Caesarea."

Pargew Amatuni ‹ Arm. *pargew*, "gift"

Presumably the *nahapet* of the Amatuni house following Karēn (III.xiv), he is not otherwise attested. Because he is said to have accompanied St. Nersēs to his consecration at Caesarea ca. 353, he should probably not be identified with his namesake who unsuccessfully attacked the Persians in defense of King Xosrov III/IV MX, III.1 (= MK, p. 315) at the very end of the century, after the partition of Armenia ca. 387, as is done by Justi.

See HAnjB, IV, p. 230 no. 2, cf. no. 3; JIN, p. 242 no. 1.
IV.iv
p. 111
See also "Amatuni, house"; "Karēn"; and Appendix III, *nahapet*.

Pʿaṙnawazean/Pʿaṙawazean

Name of the Iberian dynasty claiming descent from an eponymous Pʿaṙnawaz, rather than of an individual. The *Primary History* (Sebēos, p. 51 = MK, p. 362) and MX, I.xxii (= MK, p. 111), list him among the Armenian kings, but their genealogies do not coincide. Despite BP's claim that Mušeł Mamikonean killed the king of Iberia and overran the entire country, ca. 370, AM speaks of the division of Iberia between Rome and Persia (XXVII.xii.6) and subsequently of the reunion of the country ca. 377/8 under the Persian candidate Aspacures (XXX.ii.2).

See Toumanoff, *Studies*, pp. 80, 81, n. 103, 103 n. 159, 294–296, 445–452; Markwart, *Ērānšahr*, p. 115.
V.xv
p. 201
See also "Mušeł"; and Appendix II, "Virkʿ."

Pʿaṙnerseh, see "Pʿaṙēn."

Parskʿ ‹ Phl. Pārs; OP Pārsa-, Fars/Persia/Persians

Term most commonly used in the Armenian sources for both the Persian country and its inhabitants, though BP occasionally used Arikʿ for the latter.

See AG, p. 67 no. 145; Gignoux, *Glossaire*, p. 31.
III.vii–ix, xiv, xx–xxi; IV.i, xvi–xviii, xx–xliii, xlv–lix; V.i–ii, iv–viii, xxxii–xxxvi, xxxviii–xliii; VI.i
pp. 75–77, 80, 86, 94–100, 107, 146–179, 186–191, 193–199, 213–225, 233–234
See also "Arikʿ"; "Sasanians."

Pʿawstos; Gk. Φαῦστος; Lat. Faustus, "of good omen"

Bishop of Byzantine origin referred to on several occasions in BP, but unknown to MX and to other Armenian sources, except for the *Vita* of St. Nersēs, iii, p. 23 (= CHAMA, II, p. 24), derived from BP, which mentions him once under the name "Pʿestos," but on no other occasion.

As indicated by Ačaryan, who gives four entries under this name (all related either to the Pʿawstos or Pʿawstoses mentioned in BP, or to the presumed author of BP) scholars since Čʿamčʿean have repeatedly attempted to identify the bishop mentioned in the text with its compiler and with the "Bishop Faustus" referred to in *Letters* cxx–cxxii of St. Basil of Caesarea. But the anonymous compiler of BP should no longer be associated with any Pʿawstos (see Intro., pp. 11–15), nor should a Greater Armenian bishop, such as the Pʿawstos in BP's text, be identified with the candidate from Armenia Minor to whom St. Basil refused consecration in 372–374, as I have recently shown. Consequently, the attributions attempted hitherto remain unacceptable. Moreover, the time span attributed in BP to P^{c}awstos, who is elderly (*ceruni episkopos*) at St. Nersēs's consecration as deacon ca. 353 (IV.iii), still alive at the patriarch's burial ca. 373 (V.xxiv), and even at the end of the century after the partition of Armenia ca. 387 (VI.v), is unnaturally long, yet the text clearly treats this personage as a single individual. In view of these difficulties, the silence of all other early Armenian sources concerning such an individual, and the non-Armenian origin of the name P^{c}awstos/ Faustus, which occurs in Armenian historiography only in the context of BP or in references to its putative author, no identification of this personage or personages seems plausible at present.

See HAnjB, V, pp. 196–198; Č^{c}amč^{c}ean, *Patmut^{c}iwn Hayoc^c*, I, 447–448; Perikhanian, "Buzand"; Garsoïan, "Nersēs le Grand," pp. 150, 154–158.
IV.iii; V.xxiv; VI.v–vi
pp. 110, 205, 235
See also next entry.

P^{c}awstos Biwzand (?)
Presumed reference to the author of BP added in the Colophon following Book III.
See Introduction, pp. 9, 11–16 and the preceding entry.
III. Colophon
p. 100

Persians, see "Parsk^c."

P^{c}isak Siwni ‹ MIr. **pēsag*, "multicolored/adorned"; OP **Pisak*, attested? through Gk. πισάγας, "leper"
Presumably *nahapet* of the Siwni house and treacherous *senekapet* of King Tiran. In view of the sinister overtones of P^{c}isak's name in the context, the absence of this name in the normal onomasticon of the Siwni house, the abrupt disappearance of P^{c}isak from BP's account, and the parallel tale related by MX, II.lxii (= MK, pp. 204–205) with another protagonist Databē Bznuni, the name P^{c}isak may be merely symbolic and part of the epic element of the chapter in which it appears (see III.xx n. 5). As observed by Melik^c-Ōhanǰanyan, the association of P^{c}isak with Siwnik^c may also be due to the generally "treacherous" character of the princes of Siwnik^c—the archtraitors Vasak and Varazvałan—in the history of fifth-century Armenia (see ŁP^c and Ełišē).

See HAnjB, V, p. 206; JIN, p. 100, *Phisak*; Melik^c-Ōhanǰanyan, "Tiran-Trdati vepə," II. pp. 66–68, 72–75. P^{c}isak is not included in Toumanoff's stemma of the Siwni house, *Manuel*, pp. 226–227.
III.xx
p. 94–96
See also "Databē Bznuni"; "Siwni, house"; "Tiran"; and Appendix III, *nahapet*; *senekapet*.

P^{c}oχk^c
Northern invaders of Greater Armenia associated with the Mazk^{c}ut^{c}k^c, and probably to be identified with the P^{c}asχk^c or P^{c}usχk^c of the *Ašχ.* (long, 27/37).
III.vii
p. 73
Maps, I/1-2
See also "Mazk^{c}ut^{c}k^c."

Řastom/Aṙostom ‹ Phl. **Rōstam*
Deacon who shared St. Nersēs's exile. He may perhaps be identified with Aṙostom, the hermit brother of Bishop P^{c}awstos (named in the title though not in the body of the

chapter, VI.vi), since P^{c}awstos is identified as a member of St. Nersēs's household (VI.v). But this identification is not suggested by the context, which stresses Aṙostom's eremitical life, and the identity of P^{c}awstos is highly controversial. Neither Ṙastom nor Aṙostom is attested elsewhere.

> See HAnjB, IV, p. 325, *Ṙostom* no. 1; JIN, p. 27 no. 1 and 259, who distinguishes the two personages.
> IV.vi; VI.vi (?)
> pp. 124, [235]
> See also "Nersēs I"; "P^{c}awstos."

Romans/Hoṙomk^c

Term used very rarely by BP for the Byzantine world in contrast to the standard term "Greeks" (*Yoynk^c*), although "Romans" was the correct form in contemporary classical usage. Cf. Pahl. *hlwmy/Hrōm*.

> See Gignoux, *Glossaire*, p. 23; cf. p. 27; AG, p. 362 no. 244.
> III.x; V.i, v; VI.vi
> pp. 79, 186, 195, 235
> See also "Greeks."

Ṙstakēs, see "Aristakēs."

Ṙštuni, house

Naxarar family ruling the homonymous district on the southern shore of Lake Van. It was traditionally considered to have been descended from the Armenian eponymous hero Hayk by way of the house of Siwni, of which the Ṙštuni were presumably a branch (MX, II.viii = MK, p. 143) but Toumanoff attributes to them a royal Urartian ancestry. Their ancestral domain, Ṙštunik^c and probably Tosp, lay south and east of Lake Van, but they also acquired the lands of the exterminated Bznuni family on the northwestern side of the lake. The Ṙštuni themselves were decimated at the end of King Tiran's reign (III.xviii; MX, III.xv = MK, pp. 267-269) if not earlier (III,viii[?]). This extermination cannot have been total, however, not only because of the account of the saving of Tačat Ṙštuni from the massacre of his house and his marriage into the Mamikonean house (III.xviii cf. MX III.vii = MK, p. 260), but because of the presence of Mehandak/ Mehen Ṙštuni in the retinue of St. Nersēs in the reign of Aršak II. The link between the Ṙštuni and the Mamikoneans seems to have been maintained through the marriage of Garegin II Ṙštuni and Hamazaspuhi Mamikonean (IV.lix), though it broke down in the Persian war (V.xxxvii). The Ṙštuni are included in all the Lists of *naxarars*, and the *Zōrnamak*, "Military List," attributed 1,000 retainers to them. The family continued to flourish until the seventh century, when Prince Theodore Ṙštuni negotiated the first accord between the Armenians and the Arabs. Soon thereafter, however, they lost the Bznuni lands to the Mamikoneans and their own domain to the Arcruni. They became extinct in the period of Arab domination.

> See Oskean, *Gnunik^c ew Ṙštunik^c*; Adontz, *Armenia*, pp. 189, 191, 195, 201, 205, 207, 228, 230, 442 nn. 19-20, 444 n. 24, 446 n. 34, 67*, 69*-70*, 73*-77*, 79*, 81*, 96*; Toumanoff, *Studies*, pp. 132, 204, n. 230, 213 and n. 234, 224, 227-228, 240, 244-248, 250, 252.
> III.vii-viii, x, xvi, xviii; IV.iv, xi; V.xxxvii
> pp. 74, 76, 78, 91, 93, 111, 133, 220
> See also "Bznuni, house"; "Garegin"; "Mamikonean, house"; "Manačihr"; "Mehandak/Mehen"; "Siwni, house"; "Tačat"; "Tiran"; Appendix II, "Ṙštunik^c"; "Tosp"; and Appendix III, *naxarar*.

Šahak I, patriarch ‹ Syr. Išahaq; Hebr. Yiṣḥaq; Isaac

This patriarch should not be confused with St. Sahak I the Great (387?–439), the last patriarch of the Gregorid house, whose pontificate lay beyond the chronological limits of BP's account.

According to BP (III.xvii), Šahak was a descendant of Ałbianos of Manazkert and the successor of P‹arēn of Aštišat as patriarch of Greater Armenia. He was duly consecrated at Caesarea of Cappadocia, as required by early Armenian custom, but his pontificate was no more effective than that of his predecessor. There is no record of either its end or of Šahak's death in BP, nor is there any explicit mention of the name of the immediate predecessor of the next patriarch, St. Nersēs, but only the suggestion that with the accession of the Gregorid Nersēs, "the spiritual leadership [would] also be renewed" (IV.iii). BP is, however, the only Armenian source to give this patriarchal sequence, namely P‹arēn, Šahak of Manazkert, Nersēs I. All the others give the alternate sequence found in MX, III.xxxix (= MK, p. 300), who attributes to Šahak of Manazkert a pontificate of four years following the death of St. Nersēs (ca. 373–377)— where BP places the patriarchate of Yusik II (V.xxix)—and has Nersēs follow directly after P‹arēn. Morever, because Šahak's accession came after the murder of St. Nersēs and the presumed consequent ecclesiastical break between Armenia and Caesarea, MX notes that Šahak was enthroned "without [the permission] of the great archbishop of Caesarea" (III.xxxix = MK, p. 300).

Many scholars have followed MX and the Armenian tradition and placed the pontificate of Šahak of Manazkert after rather than before that of St. Nersēs, thus achieving the sequence P‹arēn, Nersēs, Šahak. Nevertheless, BP's account of Šahak's journey to Caesarea accompanied by the *mardpet* and a train of Armenian magnates, his return to Armenia "with honor," and St. Nersēs's later journey to the same city for his own consecration (IV.iv) seems too circumstantial to be arbitrarily rejected, especially because BP is our closest and most extensive source for the history of the Armenian patriarchate in the fourth century. Consequently, a *lectio difficilior* on the basis of BP, suggesting the simultaneous tenure of Šahak and Nersēs, should perhaps be attempted, especially in view of the fact that Greek sources record both the presence of an Isokakis representing Greater Armenia at the Antiochene Council of 363 (Soc. Schol. EH, III.xxv) and the simultaneous existence of two "orthodox" bishops, named Iosakes and Narses, in the East in this period (Basil, St. *Ep.* xcii).

See HAnjB, IV, pp. 103–104; JIN, p. 272 no. 3, who confuses him with the predecessor of Zawēn; Ōrmanean, *Azgapatum*, I, cols. 223–238, xvii; Garitte, *Narratio*, pp. 87–88; Sanspeur, "Nouvelle liste," cols. 186, 188, 196–197; Akinian, "Reihenfolge," pp. 85–86; Garsoïan, "Nersēs le Grand," pp. 148–149; *idem*, "Šahak of Manazkert"; cf. Gignoux, NPS, no. 866, p. 163, *Šāhag*; Schmitt, IN, p. 330.

III.xvii
p. 92

See also "Ałbianos"; "Nersēs I"; "P‹arēn"; "Yusik II"; Appendix II, "Caesarea"; and the next entry.

Šahak II ? patriarch ‹ Syr. Išahaq; Hebr. Yiṣḥaq; Isaac

Patriarch of Armenia from the southern district of Korčēk‹ / Korčayk‹ and consequently known as Šahak Korčeay. He was the successor of Zawēn for a period of two years, according to BP (VI.iii), which grants him only the title of "senior bishop." This succession is accepted at a much later date by Michael the Syrian (Miχaēl Asori, YK‹, p. 34 no. 18), but not by MX III.xl–xli (= MK, pp. 302–303) and the other Armenian sources, who places Zawēn's kinsman, Aspurak (VI.iv, xv), as his immediate successor and the predecessor of St. Sahak the Great. But the fourteenth-century *List of Katholikoi* (*Paris. Arm.* 121) gives the joint five-year patriarchate of Aspurak and Šahak following after that of their brother Zawēn. As observed by Garitte, the complicated succession of St. Nersēs I, with its multiplicity of Sahaks or Šahaks, still requires elucidation.

> See HAnjB, IV, p. 104 no. 5; JIN, p. 272 no. 3, who confuses him with Šahak of
> Manazkert; Ōrmanean, *Azgapatum*, I, cols. 223–238, xvii, who does the same;
> Sanspeur, "Nouvelle Liste," cols. 186–188, 198; Garitte, *Narratio*, p. 87; cf.
> Gignoux, NPS, no. 866, p. 163 *Šāhag*; Schmitt, IN, p. 330.
> VI.iii, iv
> pp. 234–235
> See also "Aspurak"; "Zawēn" Appendix II, "Korček⁽"; Appendix III, *senior bishop*
> and the preceding entry.

Sahak (?) Bagratuni

Aspet and royal coronant of Armenia, father-in-law of King Vałaršak. BP does not mention his given name but only his titles, while MX, III.xli, xliii (= MK, pp. 303, 306) calls him Sahak and claims that after the enthronement of King Xosrov III/IV in the Persian portion of Armenia, Sahak went over to him and was made commander in chief of his army, MX, III.xliv, li, lvi (= MK, pp. 306–307, 309, 314).

> See HAnjB, IV, p. 350 no. 8; JIN, p. 417; Toumanoff, *Manuel*, p. 96/4.
> V.xliv ?
> p. [228]
> See also "Bagratuni, anonymous princess"; "Vałaršak Aršakuni"; and Appendix III,
> *aspet, t⁽agakap*.

Šahap, see "Kiwrakos."

Saharuni, house

Naχarar house known to Armenian sources, though curiously not to MX. Their domain lay in Ayrarat on the border of Širak, and Toumanoff gives Mren as their seat, but only a village called Šaharunik⁽ is attested in an eleventh-century inscription. The Saharuni are recorded in all the Lists of *naχarars*, and the *Zōrnamak*, "Military List," attributes 1,000 retainers to them. They were powerful enough to serve as *dayeak*s for minor Aršakuni and to be granted the *sparapetut⁽iwn* for a brief time at the end of the Aršakuni period, though they did not keep it (V.xxxv, xxxvii). The family reached the height of its prestige under David, prince and *curopalates* of Armenia in the sixth century, but are not attested thereafter. See Intro., p. 13, for the hypothetical link between this house and the presumed author of BP, which is still accepted by Toumanoff.

> See Adontz, *Armenia*, pp. 189, 192, 194, 202, 206–207, 209, 222, 241, 442 nn. 19–20,
> 444 n. 24, 446 n. 34, 456 nn. 17–18, 67*, 69*, 71*, 80*, 175*; Toumanoff, *Studies*,
> pp. 214 and n. 243, 227, 228, 240, 245, 249, 252.
> III.xii, xiv; IV.xi; V.xxxv, xxxvii
> pp. 82, 87, 133, 215, 217
> See also "Bat"; "Mušk"; "Tiroc⁽"; Appendix II, "Ayrarat"; and Appendix III, *da-
> yeak; naχarar; sparapet*.

Šahēn Anjewac⁽i ‹ MP *šāh* + adj. suff. *-ēn*

Attested as Šāhēn on seals.

Nahapet of the house of Anjewac⁽ik⁽, who accompanied Yusik I to his consecration at Caesarea. He is not otherwise attested.

> See Gignoux, NPS no. 867, p. 163; Schmitt, IN, p. 330; HAnjB, IV, p. 118 no. 2;
> JIN, p. 274 no. 3; AG, p. 59 no. 128.
> III.xii
> p. 82

See also Appendix II, "Anjewacᶜikᶜ"; and Appendix III, *nahapet.*

Saɫamut of Anjit
  Prince of Anjit who abandoned Aršak II after the Roman–Persian peace of 363 and withdrew to Byzantine territory. According to MX, III.xv (= MK, p. 269) he, or perhaps a homonym; was appointed by King Tiran to the office of Zawray R̄štuni after the capture of Aɫtᶜamar and the massacre of the R̄štuni house (cf. III.viii).
  See HAnjB, IV, p. 377; JIN, p. 280.
  IV.1
  p. 167
  See also "Aršak II"; and Appendix II, "Anjit."

Šaɫitay, St. ‹ Syr. Šallīṭā, "ruler"
  Syrian anchorite and disciple of St. Daniēl (III.xiv) who designated him as missionary to Kordukᶜ and witness with St. Epipᶜan of St. Nersēs's miraculous assumption. He is also known to MX, III.xx (= MK, p. 275), who identifies him, however, as a disciple of St. Nersēs rather than of Daniēl and as one of the overseers of the patriarch's hermitages. The reference in the *Vita* of St. Nersēs, xiv, pp. 113–114 (= CHAMA, II, p. 42) follows the general lines of BP. A different and lengthier *Vita* of Šaɫitay, lacking the episode of the wounded lion (V.xxvi), is also found in the Syrian *Acts*, where he is sometimes identified as a disciple of Mār Awgēn (AMS I, pp. 424–465; "Chron. Seert," xli). Akinean identified him with the fourth-century saint attested in Beθ-Qardū (see V.xxvi n. 3)
  See HAnjB, IV, p. 135; AG, p. 296 no. 30; D'iakonov, "Mar Evgen"; Labourt, *Christianisme*, p. 306; Akinean and Tēr Pōlosean, "Łazar Pᶜarpecᶜi," p. 142; Fiey, "Awgen"; *idem; Assyrie*, I, p. 292; II, pp. 559–561; *idem, Nisibe*, pp. 23 n. 48, 24, 201–202.
  III.xiv; V.xxv–xxvi
  pp. 90, 205–206
  See also "Daniēl"; "Epipᶜan"; Appendix II, "Kordukᶜ"; and Appendix III, *anapataworkᶜ.*

Sam Siwni ‹ Phl. Sām; cf. Av. *sāma-,* "black"
  Sepuh of the Siwni house and younger brother of Babik.
  See Gignoux, NPS, no. 823, p. 156; HAnjB, IV, p. 379 no. 2; JIN, pp. 281 no. 7, 426 no. 3, who confuses him with Sam Gntᶜuni (cf. HAnjB, *loc. cit.* no. 3); Toumanoff, *Manuel*, 226/3.
  V.xlii
  p. 224
  See also "Babik"; "Siwni, house"; and Appendix III, *sepuh.*

Samuēl Mamikonean ‹ Hebr. Šamuēl
  Sepuh of the Mamikonean house, son of the apostate Vahan and the Sasanian princess Ormizduχt, according to BP (IV.lix), but cf. MX, III.xlviii (= MK, p. 312 and n. 9), who gives him different parents and claims that he fled to the Byzantine emperor Arcadius. According to BP, Samuēl killed his parents because of their support of Zoroastrianism in Armenia, and he participated in Manuēl Mamikonean's victory over his kinsman Meružan Arcruni. TᶜA, pp. 65, 68 (= *Thom. Arts.*, pp. 130, 133) gives a version of Samuēl's parricide that follows BP, but inserts MX's name Tačatuχi instead of Ormizduχt for Samuēl's mother.
  See HAnjB, IV, p. 381 no. 2; JIN, p. 424; Toumanoff, *Manuel*, p. 332/5c; Raffi, *Samuēl.*
  IV.lix; V.xliii
  pp. 180, 227–228

See also "Mamikonean, house"; "Manuēl"; "Ormizduχt"; "Vahan"; and Appendix III, *sepuh.*

Sanatruk; Gk. Σανατρύκης; name attested in a Parthian context
King of Armenia, whose chronological position and family background remain highly controversial. Both BP and MX, II.xxxiv (= MK, pp. 174–175), make him the killer of the apostle Thaddeus, and BP (IV.xxiv) stresses that Sanatruk was a member of the Aršakuni house buried in the royal necropolis of Ani in Daranałikʿ. It is the only source that does not identify Sanatruk as the nephew (in the maternal line) of King Abgar of Edessa, as is the generally accepted Armenian tradition; see, e.g., MX, II.xxxi, xxxvi (= MK, pp. 171, 177–178). BP's identification of Sanatruk as the founder of the city of Mcurn (IV.xiv) is supported by both the *Primary History* (Sebēos, p. 47, with n. 9 for the mistaken reading "Mcbin" in the text = MK, p. 357 and nn. 3, 5), and MX, II.xxxvi (= MK, p. 177).
> See JIN, p. 382 nos. 3–6; AG, p. 72 no. 164; van Esbroeck, "Le Roi Sanatrouk," pp. 241–283; Toumanoff, "Third-Century Arsacids," p. 143 n. 53, *idem, Studies*, p. 284; Chaumont, *L'Arménie*, pp. 128–130, 141–142; Asdourian, *Armenien und Rom*, pp. 100–103; Debevoise, *Parthia*, pp. 217–218.
> III.i; IV.xiv, xxiv
> pp. 67, 140, 157
> See also "Aršakuni"; "Tʿadēos; and Appendix II, "Ani"; "Mcurn," and the next entry.

Sanēsan
King of the Mazkʿutʿkʿ, identified by BP as an Aršakuni kinsman of the Armenian kings and killer of St. Grigoris. He is otherwise unattested, though MX, III.iii (= MK, p. 256), makes an otherwise unknown Arsacid named Sanatruk the killer of Grigoris. The name *snysrk(n)/ Sanēsarakān*, "son of Sanēsar" is attested in a II-III century A.D. Parthian fragment from Dura, and Benveniste has suggested the possibility of identifying it with the form "Sanatruk" found in MX. Recently, Lozinski has accepted BP's identification of him as a Parthian Arsacid.
> See JIN, p. 282, *Sanatruk* no. 8; Henning, "Fragments," p. 414 for the Parthian fragment; Benveniste, *Titres et noms propres*, p. 106; Lozinski, "Parthian Dynasty," pp. 126–128.
> III.vi–vii
> pp. 72–75
> See also "Aršakuni"; "Grigoris"; "Mazkʿutʿkʿ"; and the preceding entry.

Šapstan, see Appendix III, *šapstan*

Šapuh ‹ MP *Šāhpuhr/Šābuhr*, "king's son"; Gk. Σάπωρ; Lat. Sapor
Attested in ŠKZ, Parth. 1, 11, 18, 20, 21, 23, 25, 27, 28; Phl. 23, 25, 26, 31, 33, 34; RGDS, nos. 1, 39, 42, 46, 47, 49, 51, 54, 60, 65, pp. 46–47, 58–65, 68–71; KKZ, 1, 3, 6, 12, 17; *Paikuli*, etc.
Šāhpuhr II, king of kings of Persia (309–379), under whom the Sasanian dynasty reached its full extent and who is the major Persian protagonist of BP, as his long reign covered almost the entire chronological span of the work (cf. III.xx n. 9, xxi n. 16; and V.viii n. 3). Šāhpuhr's war with the Romans began ca. 336 and was waged primarily in Armenia and Mesopotamia to the end of his reign. The first campaigns were inconclusive. Three attempts to take the Mesopotamian city of Nisibis failed, and the attack of the Chionites in the east ca. 359 temporarily distracted Šāhpuhr's attention from his western front. The disastrous campaign of the emperor Julian, however, and the consequent peace of 363 abandoned most of Greater Armenia, which was deurbanized, devastated and depopulated (IV.lv–lix), part of the southern Satrapies, and the city of Nisibis to the Sasanians (IV.xxi and n. 5; AM, XXV.vii). It resulted in the deportation

of Aršak II and his queen to Persia, and the temporary rule of Armenia by the Persian governors, Karēn and Zik, supported by Meružan Arcruni and Vahan Mamikonean, although a partial reconquest was attempted by the emperor Valens (cf. V.i–ii, iv–v), and BP suggests (V.xxxviii) that the Persian war began anew at the end of Šāhpuhr II's reign or in that of his successor. Šāhpuhr II probably began the fortification of the Caucasian passes against invaders from the north, and he strengthened the centralizing power of the crown against the Iranian magnates. His consolidation of Zoroastrianism as the state religion of Iran, coinciding with the Christianization of the Roman Empire, resulted in the first great Christian persecution in Iran, recorded in the *Acts* of the Persian martyrs and reflected in BP (IV.xvi–xvii).

See Gignoux, *Glossaire*, pp. 33–34; *idem*, NPS, no. 858, pp. 161–162; Schmitt, IN, p. 320; Sprengling, *Third-Century Iran*, pp. 7–9, 11–12, 14, 17–19, 49–53; Honigmann and Maricq, RGDS, pp. 11, 15–18; Humbach and Skjærvø, *Paikuli*, 3.1, pp. 33, 41, 57, 59, 60; JIN, p. 285, *Sāpōr* no. 7; PW, IA, pp. 2334–2354; Jones *et al.*, *Prosopography* I, p. 803, *Sapor II*; AG, pp. 60–61 no. 134; Frye, "Sasanians," pp. 132–141; *idem*, *Heritage*, pp. 214–217, 283; Christensen, *L'Iran*, pp. 195–197, 234–253, etc.; Labourt, *Christianisme*, pp. 43–82; Peeters, "Persécution."

IV.xvi–xviii, xx–xxvii, xxix–xxxviii, xlv, l–lvi, lviii–lix; V.ii, iv–vii, xxxv, xxxvii
pp. 146–157, 159–163, 165, 167–173, 176–180, 187–190, 194–196, 198, 216–217, 220
See also "Aršak II"; "Karēn"; "Kᶜušan"; "Mari"; "Meružan"; "Nerseh"; "Ormizduχt"; "Pᶜaṙanjem"; "Sasanians"; "Vahan"; "Zik [2]"; "Zruanduχt"; and Appendix II, "Mcbin"; "Tᶜawrēš"; "Tispon."

Šapuh-varaz, see "Varaz-šapuh."

Sargis, St. ‹ Gk. Σέργιος; Lat. Sergius
Roman officer on the eastern border, traditionally martyred together with his companion, Bacchus, under Diocletian, ca. 303. He was buried at Resapha in northern Syria, which became a great center of pilgrimage and was renamed Sergiopolis by Justinian in his honor; cf. IV.x n. 7. Sergios is always represented in military dress, so that BP follows the standard warlike tradition. His popularity in Armenia was noted by Abełyan and Orbeli while Nau observed that his worship was especially fervent among Christian Arabs.

See Peeters, "SS Serge et Théodore"; *idem*, "S. Serge"; *idem*, *Tréfond*, pp. 68–70; Löffler, "Sergius,"; AASS Oct. III, 833–883; Delehaye, *Légendes*; Köllwitz, *Ausgrabungen*, pp. 45–70; Sauvaget, *Sergiopolis*, p. 124; Fiey, *Assyrie*, II, pp. 458–460; Abełyan, *Volksglaube*, ix; Orbeli, "Bytovye rel'efy," p. 202; Nau, *Arabes*, p. 12; M. MacKenzie, *Resafa*; Ulbert, *Resafa*.

IV.x
pp. 131–132
See also "Tᶜēodoros"; "Tᶜekł"; "Vałēs."

Sasan ‹ Phl. Sāsān
Name attested in ŠKZ, Parth. 20, 22, 23, 25, 28; Phl. 25, 28, 29, 31, 34, 35; RGDS nos. 46, 54, 57, 60, 61, 66, pp. 60–61, 64–65, 68–69, 72–73; *Paikuli*.
Eponymous ancestor of the Sasanian dynasty.
See Gignoux, *Glossaire*, pp. 33, 63, 64; *idem*, NPS no. 827, p. 156; *idem*, "Noms propres," pp. 73–74; Sprengling, *Third-Century Iran*, pp. 9, 11–12, 17–19; Honigmann and Maricq, RGDS, pp. 16–18; Humbach and Skjærvø, *Paikuli*, 3.1, pp. 32, 33, 41; JIN, p. 291 no. 1, and next entry.

III.xx
p. 95

Sasanians ‹ Phl. Sāsān

Iranian dynasty descended from an eponymous Sāsān. The Sasanians were originally dynasts of the province of Pars, who overthrew the reigning Parthian Aršakuni dynasty ca. 224. Their rule maintained itself over the Iranian empire until the Arab invasion of the mid-seventh century. The Sasanians' overthrow of the senior Aršakuni line in Iran and their killing of its last king, Artawan V, caused the Armenian kings, who belonged to a cadet Aršakuni line, to regard the Sasanians as usurpers against whom they were obliged to pursue the blood feud owed to a murdered kinsman (see IV.liv and n. 12). A constant state of tension consequently existed between Armenia and Iran during the fourth century although the Armenian cavalry served in the Persian army during the K'ušan wars. Because the long reign of Šāhpuhr II (309–379) covered almost the entire span of BP's narrative, he is the only Sasanian ruler mentioned by name in the text, except for the anachronistic intrusions of his grandfather, Nerseh (293–303); see III.xx n. 9.

> See Frye, "Sasanians"; *idem, Heritage*, pp. 198–223; Christensen, *L'Iran*; Garsoïan, "Prolegomena," cols. 178–179, 188–189, for the obligation of the blood feud; Lukonin, *Iran, idem, Kul'tura.*
>
> III.xx; V.vii, xxxvii
>
> pp. 95, 198, 217
>
> See also "Aršakuni"; "Artawan V"; "Nerseh"; "Ormizduχt"; "Šapuh"; "Xosrov I/II"; "Zruanduχt"; and the preceeding entry.

Šawasp Arcruni ‹ MIr. **Šāwasp*, "black horse"

Sepuh and perhaps *nahapet* of the Arcruni house, although his position is not specified. He was the son of Vač'ē Arcruni and was saved from the general massacre of his family instigated by an anonymous *mardpet* (III.xviii). Šawasp avenged his clan by murdering the *mardpet* (IV.xiv), presumably married into the Mamikonean family that had rescued him, and may have been the father of the traitor Meružan, according to Toumanoff and Malχasyanc' (p. 324 n. 93), though this is not stated in the sources. Šawasp's rescue and his vengeance are known to his house historian T'A, pp. 60–62 (= *Thom. Arts.*, pp. 124–126), who follows the version of BP, but he is not mentioned by MX, since the Šawasp Arcruni to whom he refers (III.lv = MK, p. 325) must be another personage on chronological grounds.

> See Schmitt, IN, p. 329; Gignoux, "Noms propres," pp. 85–86; HAnjB, IV, p. 154 no. 2; JIN, p. 300, *Syāwāspa* no. 4, and p. 416, where the stemma is insufficiently accurate; Toumanoff, *Manuel*, p. 87/2; AG, p. 61 no. 135.
>
> III.xviii; IV.xiv
>
> pp. 93, 140
>
> See also "Arcruni, house"; "Mamikonean, house"; "Meružan"; "Vač'ē Arcruni"; and Appendix III, *mardpet; nahapet; sepuh.*

Sergios, see "Sargis."

Šičbk'

Northern tribesmen associated with Mazk'ut'k'. They are listed in the *Ašχ.* (long, 27/37) as Šiłpk' or Šipk', and Eremyan places them north of the Alazan River.

> See Eremyan *Ašχarh.*, p. 73 and *Map* B/6 (Šiłpk').
>
> III.vii
>
> p. 73
>
> See also "Mazk'ut'k'."

Siwni, house

Great *naχarar* house ruling over the homonymous district. The princes of Siwnik' tended to guard their autonomy and act as semi-independent dynasts vis-à-vis the

Armenian Aršakuni kings, a stance usually interpreted as treason by the Armenian sources (see ŁPᶜ and Ełišē on Varazvałan and Vasak, the traitor par excellence of the fifth century). This ambiguous relationship probably also colored the portrayal of Andovk (III.xi, xxi; IV.xx) and of Queen Pᶜaṙanjem (IV.xv, xliv; V.xxii). Sahakyan, however, argues that the Siwni were allies of the Armenian king against Persia in the fourth century, a hypothesis that finds some support in BP, III.xxi; IV.xx, li, lviii.

The importance and power of the Siwni is reflected in the late and semi-fictitious *Gahnamak*, "Rank List," which ranks them in first place and in the *Zōrnamak*, "Military List," which not only includes a cadet Siwni line but attributes to Siwnikᶜ the exorbitant and obviously fantastic figure of 19,400 retainers, far outstripping that of any other princely house included in the List. The Siwni briefly held the office of *bdeašχ* of Ałjnikᶜ after the rebellion of Bakur (III.ix), and they subsequently served as Persian *marzpan*s and presiding princes of Armenia before assuming the royal title in 963. Despite the division of the principality in two during the ninth century, branches of the family survived until the later Middle Ages. Siwnikᶜ was traditionally evangelized in the period of St. Gregory the Illuminator (Vg, clxxi = Va, clix), or by St. Mesrop according to Koriwn, xiv, p. 60 (= trans. p. 36), and its bishops are included in the Armenian conciliar lists (ŁPᶜ, xxiii, p. 44; Ełišē, ii, p. 28 = *Ełishē*, pp. 81, 257; GTᶜ, pp. 73, 146, 149, 151).

> See JIN, pp. 426-427; Toumanoff, *Manuel*, pp. 226-227; *idem*, *Studies*, p. 110 n. 173, 214, 223-224, 227-228, 231, 236-238, 244, 252; Adontz, *Armenia*, pp. 191-192, 194-197, 200-201, 205-207, 223-224, 226, 228-230, 435 nn.13b-14, 452 n. 91, 70*, 73*-77*, 82*, 94*, 96*; Garitte, *Documents*, pp. 101-102, 235; Sahakyan, "Syunikᶜ."
>
> III.ix, xi, xvi, xx, xxi; IV.iv, xv, xliv, lviii; V.xlii
>
> pp. 77, 81, 91, 94, 98, 111, 140, 164, 178, 224
>
> See also, "Andovk"; "Babik"; "Pᶜaṙanjem"; "Pisak"(?); "Sam"; "Vałinak I-II"; Appendix II, "Siwnikᶜ"; and Appendix III, *bdeašχ*; *marzpan*; *naχarar*.

Spandarat Kamsarakan ‹ NW MIr. *Spandarāt*, Phl. *Spandiyād* ‹ Av. *Spəntōdāta-*, "created through holiness"

Sepuh of the Kamsarakan house and only survivor from the massacre of his family ordered by Aršak II. BP does not name his father and has him rescued as a child by the *sparapet* Vasak Mamikonean, but makes him the eventual heir of all the Kamsarakan domains. However, MX, III.xxxi (= MK, pp. 287-288) makes him the son of the Kamsarakan *nahapet* Aršawir and an adult who had withdrawn to Tarōn because of a family quarrel, and had fled thence to Byzantium together with his two sons at the time of the massacre.

> See Schmitt, IN, pp. 323, 329; Boyce, "Zariadris," pp. 472-473; HAnjB, IV, pp. 557-558 no. 2, who notes the discrepancy of the sources; JIN, pp. 307, 425, who follows MX's version; Toumanoff, *Manuel*, p. 266/5.
>
> IV.xix
>
> p. 149
>
> See also "Aršak II"; "Aršawir"; "Kamsarakan, house"; "Vasak"; and Appendix III, *sepuh*.

Surēn Pahlaw ‹ MP Sūrēn; Gk. Σουρήνας; Lat. Surena

Name Sūrēn attested in ŠKZ, Parth. 23, 25; Phl. 29, 31; RGDS, nos. 57, 61, pp. 64-65, 68-69; *Paikuli*; etc.

The Sūrēn were one of the seven great houses of Parthian Iran considered to be one of the collateral branches of the ruling dynasty, whence their surname Pahlaw (see, e.g., MX, II.xxvii-xxviii, lxviii = MK, pp. 165-166, 215-216). They held the office of royal coronant (Plutarch, "Crassus," xxi.6-7), but cf. Theoph. Sim. (III.viii) for the Sasanian period. They maintained their exalted status under the Sasanians, being ranked "second after the king" (AM, XXX.ii.5) and entrusted with the command of the army so frequently that their name was mistaken for a military title (Zosimus, III.xv, p. 31).

Members of the Sūrēn house were well known to classical authors, e.g. Plutarch ("Crassus," xxi, xxiv) and AM (XXIV.ii.4; iii.1, iv.7, etc.), who both identify them as holding "the highest rank after the king." Armenian sources normally link the Sūrēn with the patriarchal house of St. Gregory, e.g. MX, II.xxvii–xxviii, lxxi–lxxii, lxiv, xci. (= MK, pp. 165–166, 220, 250 for St. Gregory himself; III.li, lxiv, lxv = MK pp. 317, 340, 344 for his descendant St. Sahak), and ŁPᶜ I.xiv, pp. 23–24 (= CHAMA, II, pp. 270–271), cf. lxxi, p. 128 (= trans. p. 107). Aa (xxv–xxvi) does not explicitly link the two houses, but associates St. Gregory's father Anak with the rank of "second after the king." BP ignores the patriarchal tie with the Sūrēn Pahlaw, whom he merely relates to the royal Armenian house of the Aršakuni (IV.xxxiii). Most scholars differentiate the Sūrēn Pahlaw from the Sūrēn Parsik (see next entry), and Justi identifies him with the Surena of AM (XXIV.ii–iv, vi).

> See Gignoux, *Glossaire*, pp. 34, 64; *idem*, NPS, no. 853, p. 160; Schmitt, IN, p. 320, *Sôwrên*; *idem*, "Sūrēn"; Sprengling, *Third-Century Iran*, pp. 9, 11–12, 18–19; Honigmann and Maricq, RGDS, p. 17; Back, SSI, p. 260; Humbach and Skjærvø, *Paikuli*, 3.1, p. 41; HAnjB, IV, p. 588; JIN, pp. 316–317 no. 4; AG, pp. 63–65 no. 140 and 73 no. 168, *Sūrēn*; Christensen, *L'Iran*, pp. 18, 20, 25, 26, 103–109, 114, 131, 139 n. 2; Lukonin, "Institutions," p. 705; Benveniste, *Titres et noms propres*, pp. 51–64 for the title of "second after the king"; Nöldeke, *Tabari*, pp. 437–438 and n. 4.

> IV.xxxiii–xxxiv
> pp. 161–162
> See also "Anak"; "Aršakuni"; "Grigor/Gregorids"; and Appendix III, *tʿagakap*, and next entry.

Surēn Parsik ‹ MP Sūrēn; Gk. Σουρήνας; Lat. Surena
Name *Sūrēn* attested in ŠKZ, Parth. 23, 25; Phl. 29, 31; RGDS, nos. 57, 61, pp. 64–65, 68–69; *Paikuli*; etc.

Presumably not the same personage as the Sūrēn Pahlaw, according to Justi as well as Christensen, who suggests that this may be a junior branch of the Sūrēn Pahlaw family. The explicit statement that the Sūrēn commanding the Persian invasion of Armenia in the reign of Aršak II (IV.xxxvi), had been captured and stoned to death should indicate that another member of this family (presumably from the senior branch) was the *marzpan*, sent to Armenia during the regency of Manuēl Mamikonean (V.xxxviii). The latter was also known to AM (XXX.ii.7–8), but, as in the case of Gumand Šapuh, the account of the Persian commander in the first case is somewhat suspect.

> See JIN, pp. 316–317 nos. 6, 8; Christensen, *L'Iran*, p. 105 n. 2; and additional bibliography on the name in the preceding entry.

> IV.xxxvi; V.xxxviii (?)
> pp. 162, 221–223
> See also the preceding entry; "Aršak II"; "Gumand Šapuh"; "Manuēl"; "Parskᶜ"; and Appendix III, *marzpan*.

Surik of Hrsijor ‹ ?Parth. *Sūr*, "sword" + diminutive suff. *-ik*
Armenian *naχarar* not otherwise attested, though the *Vita* of St. Nersēs, viii, p. 52 (= CHAMA, II, p. 30) equates him with Surik, *nahapet* of the well-known Gabełean house. Toumanoff identifies him as prince of Hēr or Xoy, but this is not supported by the sources.

> See HAnjB, IV, p. 589; JIN, p. 317; Toumanoff, *Studies*, pp. 219.

IV.xi

p. 133

See also Appendix II, "Hrsijor"; and Appendix III, *nahapet*; *naχarar.*

Syriac/Syrian, see "Asori."

Tačat Řštuni

Sepuh and perhaps *nahapet* of the Řštuni house, though his position is not specified. He was the son of Mehandak I and was saved from the general massacre of his house instigated by an anonymous *mardpet.* Tačat presumably married into the Mamikonean family that had rescued him, but the names of his wife and offspring are not known. MX, III.xv (= MK, p. 269) also mentions the rescue of Mehandak's son, but does not give his name. TᶜA I.x, p. 60 (= *Thom. Arts.*, p. 124) confuses him with his father, whose name is given in the form of "Mehēdak."

See HAnjB, V, p. 137 no. 3; JIN, p. 320 no. 2.

III.xviii

p. 93

See also "Mamikonean, house"; "Mehandak I"; "Řštuni, house"; and Appendix III, *mardpet*; *nahapet*; *sepuh.*

Tačik ‹ Pahl. *tāčīk*, "Arab"

Term used by BP for Arabs, but subsequently used by Armenian authors for all Muslims and eventually Turks.

See NBHL, II, p. 842; HArmB, IV, pp. 365–367; Aa, xxiii, ccii.

IV.xlvii, liv

pp. 166, 171

Tᶜadēos, St. ‹ Gk. Θάδδεος; Lat. Thaddaeus; Syr. Addai; Eng. Thaddeus

One of the twelve apostles according to Matt. 10:3 = Mk. 3:18, also known as Jude (Lk. 6:16; Acts 1:13), but also identified as one of the seventy-two (seventy) disciples sent out in Lk. 10:1 (cf. AaT, dclxxxvi). The name "Thaddeus" is philologically identical with that of Addai, the traditional founder of the church of Edessa, with whom he is explicitly identified by Eusebius (EH, I.xii.13). Accounts of his mission to heal King Abgar of Edessa and convert the Edessene are found in Eusebius (EH, I.xii) and in the Syriac *Doctrine of Addai*, probably dating from ca. 400 but dependent on earlier documents. The purported correspondence of King Abgar with Jesus was translated into Armenian in the fifth century by Lerubna or Lebubnay, as were the *Acts* of Addai. The Armenian version altered the story by confusing Addai with Thaddeus's successor Aggai in the Syriac version and bringing the saint to Armenia to be martyred at Artaz instead of dying at Edessa as in the original (see Addē, St., *Acta*; Labubna; Tᶜułtᶜ) and MX, II.xxxiii–xxxiv (= MK, pp. 171–175 with additions). The linking of Thaddeus's martyrdom with the "Armenian king" Sanatruk is not found in Labubna, but is first mentioned in BP (III.i) and is also known to MX, II.xxxiv (= MK, p. 174). This alternate version of the Christianization of Armenia, as opposed to the "received tradition" of the mission of St. Gregory the Illuminator, is not known to Aa, but the attempt to link the two traditions by having St. Gregory conceived at the grave of St. Thaddeus in Artaz is found in one of the versions of the Gregorid cycle (Vk, viii, p. 24) as well as in MX, II.lxxiv (= MK, pp. 220–221) though there is no mention of this in BP. References to the Armenian patriarchate as the "throne of St. Thaddeus" are common in BP (e.g. III.xii, xiv; IV.iii) and suggest the memory of a division in Armenia between his ultimate authority, reflecting the early Syriac tradition of Armenian Christianity, and that of St. Gregory, based on the Hellenizing tradition deriving Armenian Christianity from Caesarea of Cappadocia (cf. III.xiv, n. 11).

See Anasyan, *Matenagitut'yun*, I, cols. 255–258; Akinean and Tēr Połosean, "T'adēi vkayabanut'iwn"; van Esbroeck, "Le Roi Sanatrouk," who mentions, however, theories that the references in BP may be interpolations, though this is unlikely; Ōrmanean, *Azgapatum* I, cols. 21–38; ODCC, p. 16, *Addai*; Adontz, *Armenia*, pp. 270–272; Thomson, AaT, diii, p. 117 n. 1 and dclxxxvi; Meshcherskaia, "Apotrpeichiskie teksty"; *idem*, "Legenda"; Addai, *Doctrina*; *idem*, *Liturgia*; Addē, St., *Acta*; Labubna, *T'ułt'*; Tēr Minassiantz, *Armenische Kirche*, pp. 1–3; Fiey, *Assyrie*, pp. 323–324, 414.

III.i, xii, xiv; IV.iii, iv

pp. 67, 82, 89, 110, 112

See also "Grigor"; "Sanatruk"; and Appendix III, "Caesarea"; "Uŕhay."

T'awaspark'

Northern tribesmen associated with the Mazk'ut'k'. They are listed in the *Ašχ.* (27/37) and Eremyan places them near the Caspian Sea, just south of the Hečmatakk'. See Eremyan, *Ašχarh.*, pp. 34, 53, 120, and *Map*, B/7; *idem*, "Narody."

III.vii

p. 73

Maps, J–L/2

See also "Hečmatakk'"; "Mazk'ut'k'."

T'ekł/T'eklē, St. ‹ Gk. Θέκλα; Lat. Thecla

Saint first attested in the second- or third-century *Acts of Paul and Thekla*. These were known and translated into Armenian, presumably from Syriac, according to Conybeare, as early as the fifth century, if the date of the reused stone representing the two saints (with their names in Greek) set into the north facade of the cathedral at Ējmiacin is correct (see IV.x, n. 1). According to these *Acts*, Thekla is said to have been converted by St. Paul at Iconium and to have followed him to Antioch of Pisidia. She was thrown to the wild beasts but was miraculously saved, and retired for the rest of her life to Seleucia of Isauria.

This account is amplified by the fifth-century Greek *Vita* and especially the *Miracles* of the saint (earliest ms. Vat. Gr. 1853, dated by Dagron after the tenth century). Here, Thekla is said not to have died, but to have disappeared bodily into the rock face or into the earth of the cave to which she had retired (*Vita*, xxviii). her shrine at Seleucia became a great center of pilgrimages, and the original martyrium was transformed into a major basilica by the emperor Zeno at the end of the fifth century. This more extensive version is not attested in Armenian, but it must have been known to the Armenians in that century, not merely because of the wide spread of Thekla's cult noted by Dagron, but because the rite of *incubatio* at her shrine, the belief that she resided within the chancel of her church, and her military aspect, all of which are to be found in this recension, are also reflected in BP (IV.x and nn. 4–7).

Finally, it should perhaps be noted that two versions of Syriac *Acts* of another Thekla, linked with the martyrs of Adiabenē, were included in the Armenian translation of the *Acts of Eastern Martyrs* attributed to Abraham Xostovanoł and dating also from the fifth century (Mat. 3777, A.D. 1185–1188). These *Acts* of Thekla are not pertinent to BP, however, since Tēr Petrosyan dates their Armenian as showing characteristics of the ninth through twelfth centuries and consequently concludes that they must have been inserted into Abraham's collection at later date, though one evidently preceding that of the earliest twelfth-century ms. Even before Tēr Petrosyan's rejection, these *Acts* of Thekla had been found doubtful by Tēr Mkrtč'ean, who removed them to an appendix in his edition of Abraham's collection.

For the apocryphal *Acts of Paul and Thekla*, the fifth-century *Life and Miracles* and the *Acts of Thekla* inserted into the collection of Abraham Xostovanoł, see Lipsius, *Apokryphen Apostolgeschichte*, II.1, pp. 424–467; Holzey, *Thekla-Akten*, Dagron, *Ste. Thècle*; Leclerq, "Thècle"; Radermacher, *Hippolytus und Thekla*; Ter Petrosyan, *Abraham Xostovanoł*, pp. 20, 37, 95, 155–163; Peeters, "Adiabène"; Akinean, *Dasakan hayerēn*, p. 47; Conybeare, *Apology*, pp. 49–60. See also Ališan, *Ayrarat*, p. 213 and fig. 82; Eprik^cean, *Baŕaran*, I, p. 813 and fig. 333 and Khatchatrian, *Architecture*, pp. 67–68, for the Ejmiacin relief of Paul and Thekla; Forsyth, "Cilicia"; Gough, "Cilician Churches"; Herzfeld and Guyer, *Meriamlik*, for the shrine of Meriamlik/Ayatekla; as well as Bibliography, II, "Paul and Thekla, T^cekł, and Thekla" for the various versions of these *Acts*.

IV.x

p. 131

See also "Sargis"; "T^cēodoros."

T^cekłē, see "T^cekł."

T^cēodoros, St. ‹ Gk. Θεόδορος, "God-given," Lat. Theodorus.

As suggested by Peeters, the St. Theodore invoked in the miraculous episode of the killing of Valens in BP must be St. Theodore of Euchaïta in Helenopontus because of his military attributes. According to the hagiographic tradition, St. Theodore was a soldier (hence his surname *Tēron*, "the recruit") who was martyred under the rule of Maximinianus at Amaseia in Pontus for having burned down the temple of Cybele. His *martyrium* at Euchaïta, to which his remains had been brought, became a great center of pilgrimage, and an elaborate church decorated with mosaics was erected in the sixth century. As in the case of St. Sergios, the military element is appropriate to the episode in BP.

See Peeters, "SS Serge et Théodore"; Janin, "Euchaïtes"; Irmscher, "Theodor"; AASS, Feb. II, 30, 37; Delehaye, *Légendes*; Fiey, *Assyrie*, II, pp. 435–437 for the spread of Theodore's cult in the East.

IV.x

pp. 131–132

See also "Sargis"; "Vałēs."

Terent/Tērēnt ‹ Gk. Τερέντιος; Lat. Terentius

Dux and *comes rei militaris* commanding the imperial army sent by the emperor Valens to reestablish Aršak II's son Pap on the Armenian throne (ca. 369), after the occupation of the country by Šāhpuhr II according to both Armenian (BP, V.i; MX, III.xxxvi–xxxvii = MK, pp. 295–296) and classical (AM, XXVII.xii.10, 16) sources. Terentius was a well-known figure at the court of Valens (not Theodosius as erroneously given by MX), though he opposed the emperor's Arianizing policy (Theodoret of Cyr, H.E., IV.xxxii), and he was a friend of St. Basil of Caesarea (*Ep.* xcix, cv, cxviii–cxix, ccxiv). The praise lavished on him as a valiant general by MX, III.xxxvi, xxxix (= MK, pp. 295, 301) is, however, countered by AM (XXX.i.2–4), who accuses him of being a hypocrite and of planning Pap's murder, an accusation supported by BP's account (V.xxxii). He is not given the title of count in BP, by contrast to his colleague, Adē, despite the classical evidence.

See Jones *et al. Prosopography* I, p. 881, *Terentius* no. 2; Garsoïan, "Politique," pp. 313–320.

V.i, iv, vi, xxxii

pp. 185–186, 190, 196, 213

See also "Adē"; "Pap"; "Šapuh"; "Vałēs"; and Appendix III, *koms*.

Terentius, see "Terent."

Thaddeus, see "T'adēos."

Thekla, see "T'ekł."

Theodoros, see "T'ēodoros."

Tigran II the Great ‹ OP *Tigrāna; Gk. Τιγράνης; Lat. Tigranes

King of Armenia (95–55 B.C.) and conqueror of much of eastern Anatolia, Upper Mesopotamia, Cilicia, and northern Syria during his wars against the Parthians and the Romans. Tigran took Caesarea-Mazaka in Cappadocia and probably Antioch on the Orontes, and founded the new Armenian capital of Tigranakert before his defeat by the Romans under Pompey (Strabo, XI.xiv, 15; XII.ii, 9; Plutarch, "Lucullus," xxi, xxii, xxvi, xxix; "Pompey" xxx; Appian, *Syr.*,viii; *Mithr.*, xii) reduced his kingdom to the former boundaries of Greater Armenia. His settlement of numerous Jewish colonies in the Armenian cities, and the anachronistic tradition of his capture of the Jewish high priest Hyrkanos found in BP (IV.lv) are also known to MX, II.xvi–xix, xlix, lxv (= MK, pp. 154–157 and nn. 8, 191, 211, cf. pp. 27–29), and both sources refer to Tigran as an Aršakuni even though he was a member of the earlier Artašēsid/Artaxiad dynasty.

See Schmitt, IN, pp. 328, 331; HAnjB, V, pp. 147–148 no. 6; JIN, p. 324 no. 1; AG, pp. 87–88 no. 208; Manandyan, *Tigrane II*; idem, *Trade and Cities*, pp. 53–66.
IV.lv
pp. 175–176
See also "Aršakuni"; "Hiwrkandos"; and Appendix II, "Caesarea"; "Tigranakert."

Tigranes, see "Tigran."

Tiran ‹ MP Tīr (‹ *tīra-), the god of scribal arts

King of Armenia, (338–350?) son of Xosrov Kotak and father of Aršak II. As in the case of most rulers of fourth-century Armenia, the chronology of Tiran's reign is open to considerable doubt. He is probably the anonymous king restored to the Armenian throne by Constantius in 338 according to Julian's *Panegyric* (see III.xxi n. 4), though BP gives no date for his accession and does not record his being brought to Constantinople by the patriarch Vrt'anēs in the seventeenth year of Constantius (= A.D. 354) as does MX, III.xi (= MK, p. 264), who further attributes eleven years to his reign (III.xvii = MK, p. 272). Hewsen has even suggested recently that no such king existed in the fourth century and that he should be identified with the third-century Armenian ruler Trdat III (287–298) or removed from the succession, though this is unlikely. The end of Tiran's reign is equally problematic. Both BP (III.xx) and MX, III.xvii (= MK, pp. 271–272) agree that Tiran was seized and blinded by the Persians and ultimately abdicated in favor of his son Aršak II, though their accounts vary in details and contain considerable epic elements. MX adds that Tiran was secretly murdered by Aršak (III.xxii = MK, p. 278), though there is no record of this crime in BP. In classical sources, however, Tiran's punishment is visited on his son Aršak II (AM, XXVII.xii.3), and the two kings may have been confused in the epic tradition, on which BP depends at this point (see III.xx n. 17; xxi n. 21). The tension between the Aršakuni kings and the Armenian church seems to have surfaced in Tiran's reign with the murder of the patriarch Yusik and of St. Daniēl (III.xii–xiv) at the king's order, and MX, III.xi–xvii (= MK, pp. 264–272) follows BP in his condemnation of Tiran.

See Gignoux, NPS, no. 896, cf. 900, *Tīrēn*, p. 167; Schmitt, IN, pp. 321, 331; HAnjB, V, p. 156 no. 4; JIN, p. 325 no. 6; Toumanoff, *Manuel*, p. 74/7; Jones *et al.*, *Prosopography*, I, p. 913, *Tigranes VII*; Manandyan, *K'nnakan tesut'yun* II.l, pp. 155–

162; Hewsen, "Successors"; *idem*, "Tiridates," pp. 40–44; Garsoïan, "Politique," on the religious tension; and Melik^c-Ōhanǰanyan, "Tiran-Trdati vepə," on the epic elements.

III.v, xii–xiv, xviii, xx–xxi; IV.i, iii, xiv, xv; V.iii, vii; VI.vii

pp. 70, 82, 83, 85, 88, 90, 93–97, 99–100, 107, 109, 139, 143, 189, 198, 235

See also "Aršak II"; "Aršakuni"; "Daniēl"; "Xosrov II/III"; "Yusik I"; and Appendix II, "Dalarik/Acuł."

Tiran, daughter of, see "Aršakuni, anonymous princess."

wife of, see "Aršakuni, anonymous queen, II."

Tiranam ‹ MP Tīr (‹ **tīra-*), the god of scribal arts.

Deacon who shared St. Nersēs's exile. He is not otherwise attested.

See Gignoux, NPS, no. 896, p. 167, *Tīr*; *idem*, "Noms propres," p. 94; HAnjB, V, p. 157; JIN, p. 326.

IV.vi

p. 124

Tiridates, see "Trdat."

Tirik ‹ MP Tīr (‹ **tīra-*) + diminutive suff. *ik*, the god of scribal arts.

Presumably bishop of Basean, according to BP. He is otherwise unattested, unless he is identifiable with St. Gregory the Illuminator's disciple in Aa, dccccxlv. This is, however, unlikely because the bishop of Basean listed there is explicitly called Ewt^całios/ Euthalios and listed in second place, while Tirikēs/Tirik is given the eleventh place in the list. The toponym Basean is not found in the title of the chapter.

See Gignoux, NPS, no. 902, p. 167, *Tīrīg*; Schmitt, IN, p. 326; HAnjB, V, p. 167 no. 1; JIN, p. 327; Ališan, *Ayrarat*, p. 43, who dates his episcopate 370–373, though Tirik was presumably a contemporary of King Xosrov III, who reigned post 387.

VI.xiii

p. 238

See also "Movsēs"; and Appendix II, "Basean."

Tirit^c Aršakuni ‹ MP Tīr (‹ **tīra-*), the god of scribal arts.

Sepuh of the Aršakuni house, nephew of Aršak II and cousin of Gnel. BP (IV.v) records that both Tirit^c and Gnel were related to the king in the male line but does not name their fathers, while MX, III.xiii (= MK, p. 266) specifies that Tirit^c was the son of Tiran's eldest son, Artašēs, who had predeceased his father. As such, he was a descendant of Tiran in the senior line and a possible threat to Aršak II (see IV.xv n. 6). Tirit^c was one of the Armenian royal hostages released by Byzantium as a result of St. Nersēs's embassy, and he plotted the death of his cousin Gnel, either out of jealousy for the honors the latter had received in the empire (MX, III.xxi = MK, p. 276), or because of his passion for Gnel's wife P^cařanjem of Siwnik^c (IV.xv). When his treachery was revealed to Aršak II, the king had Tirit^c pursued and killed in Basean according to BP or, under different circumstances, on the way to Persia, according to MX, III.xxv (= MK, pp. 280–281).

See Gignoux, NPS, no. 896, p. 167, *Tīr*; HAnjB, V, p. 167 no. 2; JIN, p. 327 no. 2; Toumanoff, *Manuel*, p. 75/9; V. S. Nalbandyan, "Gnel."

IV.v, xi, xv

pp. 124, 133, 141, 144–145

See also "Aršak II"; "Aršakuni"; "Gnel"; "P^cařanjem"; Appendix II, "Basean"; and Appendix III, *sepuh*.

Tiroc' (?) **Saharuni** ‹ MP Tīr (‹ **tīra-*), the god of scribal arts.

Presumably *nahapet* of the Saharuni house, who accompanied Yusik I to his consecration at Caesarea. He is not attested elsewhere, and the name of the Saharuni prince is missing from the list of magnates in the printed texts, though it is given as Tiroc' in two mss. See Intro., p. 13, for the problem of this name and the postulated link between the Saharuni prince and the presumed author of BP.

See Gignoux, NPS, no. 896, p. 167, *Tīr*; cf. perhaps no. 907, p. 168, *Tīrōs*; see also HAnjB, III, p. 323, *Meroy*.

III.xii

p. 82

See also "Saharuni, house"; and Appendix III, *nahapet*.

T'orgom ‹ Hebr. Togarmah

Youngest son of Gomer, the grandson of Noah, through his third son Yaphet (Gen. 10:1–3). According to the Armenian "received tradition," Aa, xvi; MX, I.v, ix–xii (= MK, pp. 74, 84–88, 92) Hayk, the traditionally eponymous ancestor of the Armenians (see MK, p. 88 n. 6), was the son of T'orgom. This tradition was also known to Hippolytus, An alternate tradition making the Armenians "sons of Aškenaz" is also found in Koriwn, i, p. 22 (= trans., p. 21) and in MK/D, I.xiv. See Preliminary Statement, n. 4.

See Hippolytus, *Chronicle*, p. 12.

P.S.; III.xiii; V.xxx

pp. 63, 84, 211

Trdac, see "Trdat/Trdac."

Trdat the Great, St. ‹ OP **Tīridāta-*, "given/created by Tīr"; Gk. Τιριδάτης; Lat. Tiridates

First Christian Aršakuni king of Greater Armenia, reinstated on the throne by Diocletian after the peace of Nisibis of 298 (298–330?), His rescue as an infant after the murder of his father Xosrov K'aj and his return to Armenia, his persecution of St. Gregory the Illuminator, his divine punishment, and his conversion to Christianity together with his entire realm form the core of the "received tradition" of the Armenian conversion as recorded in Aa. BP (III. xxi) is also familiar with the purported alliance between him and Constantine the Great (Aa, dccclxvii). Nevertheless, a variant version of his death is to be found in MX, II.xcii (= MK, pp. 250–253). The multiple debates on the date of Trdat's reign that are linked to that of the Christianization of Armenia seem now resolved as a result of the studies of Ananian and Toumanoff.

See Gignoux, *Glossaire*, pp. 35, 65; *idem*, NPS no. 899, p. 167; *idem*, "Noms propres," pp. 61, 69, 94; Schmitt, IN, pp. 321, 329;HAnjB, V, pp. 175–177 no. 4; JIN, pp. 327, *Tiridates* no. 16, and 414 no. 32; Jones *et al*, *Prosopography* I, pp. 915–916, *Tiridates III*; the latter two accept the date 287 for the king's accession, which is impossible in view of the evidence of the Paikuli inscription; Humbach and Skjærvø, *Paikuli*, 3.1 §3, p. 28, §18–19, p. 35, 3.2, pp. 10–13; Toumanoff, *Manuel*, p. 74/5; *idem*, "Third-Century Arsacids," pp. 217–239, 241, 246, 261, 263, 265–275; Ananean, "La Data"; Manandyan, *K'nnakan tesut'yun*, II/1, pp. 106–141, 441; Garitte, *Documents*, pp. 237–238; Hewsen, "Tiridates."

P.S.; III.i–iii, xiv, xvii, xxi; IV.xiv, xv; V.xxxi

pp. 63, 67–68, 86, 92, 98, 139, 141, 212

See also "Aršakuni"; "Grigor"; "Kostandianos"; "Xosrov I/II."

Trdat/Trdac ‹ OP **Tīridāta-*, "given by Tīr"; Gk. Τιριδάτης; Lat. Tiridates

Chief minister at the burial of St. Nersēs the Great (V.xxiv). He is not otherwise attested, but should presumably be the the same individual as the patriarch's chief deacon who subsequently joined the group of anchorites associated with St. Gind (VI.xvi), although Nersēs had another archdeacon, named Murik. BP gives both forms of the name, and Malχsyancᶜ argues (p. 355 n. 169) that Trdac may have been a popular form rather than a *lapsus calami.*

> See Gignoux, *Glossaire*, pp. 35, 62; *idem*, NPS, no. 899, p. 167; Schmitt, IN, pp. 321, 329 on Trdat; HAnjB, V, p. 178 no. 7, who does not mention the Trdat of VI.xvi; JIN, p. 327 no. 21, who does not mention the Trdac of V.xxiv.
> V.xxiv; VI.xvi
> pp. 205, 239–240
> See also "Gind"; "Murik"; "Nersēs I."

Uṙnayr ‹ Arm. *uṙn*, "hammer/battle-hammer" + *ayr*, "man"

King of Ałuankᶜ, according to both BP and MX, III.xxxvii (= MK, p. 298), though there is no mention of him in the *History of Ałuankᶜ* of MK/D. The *Vita* of St. Nersēs, confusing its source, calls him alternately "king of the Honkᶜ," xi, pp. 70, 79 (= CHAMA, II, pp. 34–35) and "king of the Alans," xi, p. 81 (= CHAMA, II, p. 35). AM (XVIII.vi.22, XIX.ii.3) mentions the support given by the king of Caucasian Albania to Šāhpuhr II at the time of the Persian campaign of 359 and the siege of Amida, but he does not mention the king's name. The wounding of Uṙnayr by Mušeł Mamikonean is recorded by both Armenian sources, but Mušeł's chivalrous behavior and the resultant slander (V.iv, xxxv) are probably derived from the epic rather than the historical tradition and are omitted by MX, III.xxxvii (= MK, p. 298), who says only that after his wounding, Uṙnayr was "removed from the field."

> See HAnjB, IV, p. 204 no. 2; JIN, p. 314; Toumanoff, *Manuel*, p. 79/4, who identifies him as an Aršakuni.
> V.iv, v, xxxv
> pp. 189–190, 193–194, 216
> See also "Mušeł"; "Šapuh"; and Appendix II, "Ałuankᶜ."

Vačᶜak Phl. *waččag*, "child, youth, fledgling, cub"

Hermit and disciple of St. Gind, He is not otherwise attested, and his name appears to be a nickname; see VI.xvi n. 6.

> See HAnjB, V, p. 309; JIN, p. 342; CPD, p. 85, *waččag*.
> VI.xvi
> pp. 239
> See also "Artoyt"; "Gind"; "Maraχ."

Vačᶜakan Phl. *waččag*, "child, youth, fledgling, cub"

Persian commander, defeated and killed by Vasak Mamikonean. He is not otherwise attested.

> See JIN, p. 342, *Waçakan* no. 1; CPD, p. 85, *waččag*.
> IV.xl
> p. 163

Vačᶜē Arcruni Phl. *waččag*, "child, youth, fledgling, cub"

Presumably *nahapet* of the Arcruni house, though his position is not mentioned. He was the father of Šawasp, the sole survivor of the massacre of the entire family under Xosrov Kotak. He is unknown to MX, but is mentioned by TᶜA, I.x, p. 60 (= *Thom. Arts.*, p. 124), who is following BP at this point, though without acknowledgement.

> See HAnjB, V, p. 40 no. 4; JIN, pp. 342, *Wačē* no. 4, and 416; Toumanoff, *Manuel*, p. 87/1; CPD, pp. 85, *waččag*.
> III.xviii

p. 93
See also "Arcruni, house"; "Šawasp"; and Appendix III, *nahapet.*

Vačʿē I Mamikonean Phl. *waččag*, "child, youth, fledgling, cub"

Second known hereditary *sparapet* of Armenia, following his father Artawazd I. BP is the only source to provide information on his career under King Xosrov Kotak, whom he served loyally against the Mazkʿutʿkʿ (III.vii), the rebellious Databē Bznuni (III.viii), and the Persians against whom he died fighting (III.xi); but seemingly less wholeheartedly against the *bdeašχ* Bakur, whose son he sheltered (III.ix). BP also records his territorial rewards from the king (III.viii) and the commemorative service instituted for him and his fallen companions, whom he likens to the Maccabees (III.xi and nn. 4–5). The only other source to mention Vačʿē is the late *Vita* of St. Nersēs, i, p. 11 (= CHAMA, II, p. 21), which depends on BP at this point. True to his systematic pattern of denigrating the Mamikoneans (see Intro., pp. 44–45), MX omits the name of Vačʿē altogether in the parallel episodes he relates (III.ii–ix = MK, pp. 255–262), and makes Bagarat Bagratuni and Vahan Amatuni the heroes of the northern war, while BP (III.viii) reduces them to companions in arms of the *sparapet* Vačʿē. Adontz suggested that the grant of territories to Vačʿē by King Xosrov Kotak marked the establishment of the Mamikonean house in the district of Tarōn, but he could not identify the place-names given in BP (III.viii), while Hübschmann located two of them, Cʿlu Gluχ and Jrabašχkʿ in the district of Aragacotn north of the Araxes River.

See HAnjB, V, p. 39 no. 3; JIN, pp. 342, *Wačē* no. 3, and 424; Toumanoff, *Manuel,* p. 331/2; AON, pp. 465, 476; Adontz, *Armenia,* pp. 244, 458 n. 38; CPD, p. 85, *waččag.*

III.iv, vii–ix, xi
pp. 69–70, 74–77, 80–81
See also "Artawazd I"; "Bagarat"; "Bakur"; "Databē"; "Mamikonean, house"; "Mazkʿutʿkʿ"; "Vahan Amatuni"; "Xeša"; "Xosrov II/III"; Appendix II, "Cʿlu Gluχ"; "Janjak"; "Jrabašχkʿ"; and Appendix III, *sparapet.*

Vačʿē II Mamikonean Phl. *waččag*, "child, youth, fledgling, cub"

Sepuh of the Mamikonean house, whom King Varazdat appointed its *nahapet-tanutēr* after the murder of Mušeł. On the return of Manuēl Mamikonean, however, Vačʿē recognized his seniority and ceded the office to him in accordance with dynastic custom (V.xxxvii). He was the father of Artawazd III and was killed at the final victory of Manuēl over Meružan Arcruni (V.xliii). Vačʿē's father is not mentioned, and Ge-vorgian (p. 195) makes Vačʿē a brother of Manuēl, but there is no evidence for this assumption, as observed by Anasyan, since the brothers Manuēl and Koms are expli-citly identified in the same context as the sons of Artašēs/Artašēn Mamikonean, with-out any mention of Vačʿē.

See HAnjB, V, p. 40 no. 7; JIN, pp. 343, *Wačē* no. 6, who mistakenly has Vačʿē die at the battle of Jiraw against the Persians, probably by association with Meružan Arcruni who was killed after that battle according to MX, III.xxxviii (= MK, p. 298), and 424; Toumanoff, *Manuel,* p. 332/5e, who suggests that Vačʿē was the son of Bagos or Hamazasp Mamikonean; Markwart, *Untersuchungen,* p. 219; Anasyan, *Review*; CPD, p. 85, *waččag.*

V.xxxvii, xliii
pp. 217–218, 226–228
See also "Artašēs/Artašēn"; "Koms"; "Mamikonean, house"; "Manuēl"; "Meružan"; and Appendix III, *nahapet; sepuh.*

Vahagn ‹ Parth. *Varhragn ‹ Av. Vərəθraγna; Gk. Ἡράκλης
The explicit identification of the great Zoroastrian *yazata* Vərəθraγna—celebrated in
both the *Bahrām* and the *Mihir Yašts* and known in pagan Armenia as Vahagn—with
the Greek Heraklēs, in accordance with the Hellenistic syncretic pattern followed in
Armenia, is given by BP (III.xiv) as well as MX, I.xxxi, II.xii (= MK, pp. 123 and n. 5,
148). This identification is not found in Aa, though Ag invariably renders the Vahagn
of the Armenian text as Heraklēs. The presence of the great shrine of Vahagn/Heraklēs
near Aštišat of Tarōn and its miraculous destruction by St. Gregory, likewise mentioned
by BP (*loc. cit.*) is part of the "received tradition" of the Christianization of Armenia
(Aa, dcccix–dcccxiii). Finally, the role of Vərəθraγna/Vahagn as the giver of supernatural "valor" (*kʿaǰutʿiwn*) and consequently of victory in the Iranian tradition, and
of Vahagn's miraculous birth from the fiery reed in the sea, according to Armenian
mythology (MX I.xxxi = MK, p. 123), seem unmistakably alluded to in the epic account of the Armenian victory over the Persians (V.v and nn. 8, 16). Consequently, all
the aspects of this pre-Christian cult were apparently still familiar in late fifth-century
Armenia.
    See Schmitt, IN, pp. 321, 323; NBHL, II, p. 771; HAnjB, V, pp. 8–9; AG, pp. 75–77
    no. 176; Dumézil, "Vahagn"; *idem*, "Vərəθraγna"; Scarcia, "*Herakles*"; *idem*,
    "Eracle iranico"; Carrière, *Huit sanctuaires*; Russell, "Zoroastrian problems";
    Garsoïan, "Substratum," pp. 157–164 and notes for further bibliography.
    III.xiv; cf. V.v
    pp. 87, [196]
    See also "Grigor Lusaworič"; Appendix II, "Aštišat"; and Appendix III, *kʿaǰ*.

Vahan Amatuni ‹ Arm. Vahagn ‹ Parth. *Varhragn ‹ Av. Vərəθraγna-, Zoroastrian
deity associated with Miθra and the Iranian royal "glory" and "valor"
    Probably *nahapet* of the Amatuni house, Armenian commander and companion-
in-arms of the *sparapet* Vačʿē I, according to BP (III.vii). MX, III.ix (= MK,
pp. 261–262), records the grant to him of the fortress of Ōšakan, claims that he was the
commander of the Armenian "Eastern force" (III.vi = MK, pp. 258–259), and attributes
to him a more exalted role in the northern war than does BP, though he does not
mention Vahan's participation in the capture of Databē Bznuni (III.viii). The claim of
the command of the "Eastern force" is impossible, since no such division existed in the
Armenian army in the fourth century, and this title, which is not attested elsewhere, may
be derived from the artificial division of the Armenian forces into four "Gates," according to the points of the compass, found in the *Zōrnamak*, "Military List." The
length of Vahan's career is not known, and TʿA, I.x–xi, pp. 59–60, 67 (= *Thom. Arts.*,
pp. 123, 125, 131), has him still active in the reign of Aršak II and at the burial of St.
Nersēs in 373. This is unlikely, since the representative of the Amatuni house under
King Tiran, and Vahan's presumable successor, is named Karēn (III.xiv). In any case,
Vahan should not be identified with his fifth-century namesake, the *hazarapet* who
brought the remains of St. Mesrop to Ōšakan according to MX, III.lxvii (= MK,
p. 349), ŁPʿ, I.xix p. 38 (= CHAMA, II, p. 278), Koriwn, xxvi, p. 92 = (trans. p. 50).
    See Schmitt, IN, pp. 323, 329; HAnjB, V, p. 10 no. 5; JIN, p. 339, *Wahan* no. 3, as
    distinct from no. 7.
    III.vii–viii
    pp. 74, 76
    See also "Amatuni, house"; "Karēn"; "Vačʿē I"; Appendix II, "Ōšakan"; and Ap-
    pendix III, *nahapet*; *nizakakicʿ*.

Vahan Mamikonean ‹ Arm. Vahagn ‹ Parth. *Varhragn ‹ Vərəθraγna-, "Zoroastrian
deity associated with Miθra" and the Iranian royal "glory" and "valor"
    Sepuh of the Mamikonean house and maternal uncle of Meružan Arcruni. Vahan
must have been a half-brother of the *nahapet* Vardan and the *sparapet* Vasak, as this

is explicitly stated in the case of their sister Hamazaspuhi (IV.lix), though he is given as their full brother in the stemmata of Justi and Toumanoff. It is also unlikely that he was the son of Artawazd II, who does not seem to have lived long enough to have fathered the large family attributed to him (see above, "Hamazaspean Mamikonean"). Vahan rebelled against Aršak II together with Meružan, accepted Zoroastrianism, and was given Šāhpuhr II's sister Ormizduχt as a wife, according to BP (IV.l), although MX, III.xxix, xxxv (= MK, pp. 286, 293–294), who confuses him with Vardan, makes him Meružan's brother-in-law and identifies Ormizduχt as Meružan's wife. After the Persian conquest of Armenia following the Roman-Persian peace of 363, Vahan and Meružan were left, together with the Persian governors, as the administrators of the country for the Sasanians (IV.lviii–lix). But Vahan's support of the imposition of Zoroastrianism in Armenia resulted in his own murder by his son Samuēl (IV.lix).

    See Schmitt, IN, pp. 323, 329; HAnjB, V, p. 10 no. 7; JIN, pp. 38, *Wahan* no. 5, 424; Toumanoff, *Manuel*, p. 331/4c; AG, pp. 75–77 nos. 176, 509; Raffi, *Samuēl*.

    IV.l, lviii–lix; V.xliii

    pp. 167–168, 178–180, 227

    See also "Aršak II"; "Hamazaspean," for the Mamikonean genealogy; "Hamazasp-uhi"; "Mamikonean, house" "Meružan"; "Ormizduχt"; "Samuēl"; "Šapuh"; "Vardan I"; "Vasak"; and Appendix III, *sepuh*.

Vahrič ‹ Phl. *Wahrīz*

    Persian commander, son of Vahrič. He is not otherwise attested, and is considered unhistorical by Justi.

    See JIN, p. 340, *Warič* no. 6; AG, p. 78 no. 177.

    IV.xxx

    p. 160

Vałarš of Anjit ‹ Phl. *Vālaχš*

    Name *Vālaχš* attested in ŠKZ, Parth. 25; Phl. 31; RGDS, no. 60, pp. 68–69.

    Nahapet of the house of Anjit and *hazarapet* of Armenia, though this office was subsequently transferred to the Gnuni (IV.ii). The *Vita* of St. Nersēs, iii, p. 25 (= CHAMA, II, p. 24) lists him in the retinue of St. Nersēs on his journey to Caesarea, but this may be a confusion with the earlier journey of Yusik I recorded in BP.

    See Gignoux, *Glossaire*, p. 36; *idem*, NPS, no. 934, p. 173; Schmitt, IN, p. 330; Sprengling, *Third-Century Iran*, pp. 9, 12, 19; Honigmann and Maricq, RGDS, p. 17; HAnjB, V, p. 31 no. 5; JIN, p. 346, *Wałarš* no. 2.

    III.xii

    p. 82

    See also "Gnuni"; Appendix II, "Anjit"; and Appendix III, *hazarapet; nahapet*.

Vałaršak Aršakuni Phl. *Vālaχš* + dim. suffix *-ak*; Lat. Vologases

    Form *Vālaχš* attested in ŠKZ, Parth. 25; Phl. 31; RGDS, no. 60, pp. 68–69.

    Younger son of King Pap and Queen Zarmanduχt, king of Greater Armenia ca. 378–379. Vałaršak was enthroned, together with his elder brother Aršak III under the regency of their mother by the *sparapet* Manuēl Mamikonean (V.xxxvii), though MX, III.xli (= MK, p. 303) claims that the brothers' accession was due entirely to the will of the emperor "Theodosius" (see V.xxxviii n. 2). Vałaršak, who seeems to have been in a secondary position to his brother, was married to the daughter of the Bagratuni *aspet*, whom BP does not name (V.xliv), but whom MX, III.xli, xliii (= MK, pp. 303, 306), calls Sahak. Nothing more is known of Vałaršak's career in BP, but MX, III.xli (= MK, p. 303), claims that he died the very year of his accession.

    See Gignoux, NPS no. 934, p. 173, *Vālaχš*; Schmitt IN, p. 330; Sprengling, *Third-Century Iran*, pp. 9, 12, 19; Honigmann and Maricq, RGDS, p. 17; HAnjB, V,

p. 32 no. 2; JIN pp. 346, *Waḷarš/ Waḷaršak* no. 2, who gives 383 as the year of his death and has him rule in Ekeḷeacᶜ, 414 no. 38b; Toumanoff, *Manuel*, p. 76/ 10; Jones *et al.*, *Prosopography*, I, p. 929, *Valarsaces*; AG, p. 79 no. 179; Manandyan, *Kᶜnnakan tesutᶜyun*, II/1, p. 236.

V.xxxvii–xxxviii, xliii–xliv

pp. 221, 226, 228

See also "Aršak III"; "Aršakuni"; "Bagratuni, anonymous princess"; "Manuēl"; "Pap"; "Sahak (?) Bagratuni"; "Zarmanduχt."

Waḷaršak, wife of, see "Bagratuni, anonymous princess."

Vaḷenak, see "Vaḷinak II.

Valens, see "Vaḷēs."

Vaḷēs ‹ Lat. Valens

Roman emperor (364–378) who shared the empire with his brother Valentinian the ruler of the West. He is one of the only two Roman emperors mentioned by name in BP. Valens initiated the reconquest of the eastern territories lost by the Romans at the peace of 363, placing Pap; and subsequently Varazdat, on the throne of Armenia (V.i, xxxiv; AM, XXVII.xii) and supporting a Roman candidate in western Iberia (AM, XXVII.xii.6). He was, however, recalled to Thrace by the advance of the Goths and was killed at the battle of Andrinople in 378, although BP (IV. x) has him miraculously slain by Sts. Sergius and Theodore. Valens's strongly Arianizing policy opposed by St. Basil of Caesarea is the probable reason for his substitution for Constantius (337–361), the other Arianizing emperor of the mid-fourth century, in BP, thus causing a constant chronological confusion (see Intro., pp. 10, 38–40; III.xxi n. 21; IV.v n. 5, vi n. 2, xi n. 2). This confusion is compounded by the material relating to the real Valens in his relations to St. Basil (but not to Armenia), interpolated into the life of St. Nersēs (see IV.v nn. 5–6, viii n. 1–2, x n. 8). Melikᶜ-Ōhanǰanian also suggested that the Vaḷēs in III.xxi should be identified not with the emperor Valens but with the caesar Valerius Galerius of the end of the third century. This identification, however, seems improbable (see III.xxi n. 21).

See Jones *et al.*, *Prosopography*, I, pp. 930–931, *Flavius Valens*; PW, VIIA, cols. 2097–2137; Baynes, "Rome and Armenia," for the confusions with Constantius; Baus, ed., *Imperial Church*, pp. 85–86; Melikᶜ-Ōhanǰanyan, "Tiran-Trdati vepə," II, pp. 64–65.

III.xxi; IV.v, vi, viii–xi

pp. 99, 116, 124, 127, 129–133

See also "Barseḷ"; "Pap"; "Sargis"; "Tᶜēodoros"; "Varazdat."

Vaḷinak I Siwni

Armenian *naχarar* and commander of the Armenian army from the house of Siwni, whom BP calls the "favorite" of King Xosrov Kotak, while MX, III.xviii (= MK, p. 272), makes him the favorite of the Persian king, Šāhpuhr II. The precise position of Vaḷinak as the *nahapet*, or one of the *sepuhs*, of the Siwni house and his relationship to the other members of the house are not specified by any of the Armenian sources. Nevertheless, Justi makes him the uncle of Andovk, while Toumanoff suggests the more probable relationship that they were brothers, and Ačaryan claims that Andovk became *nahapet* after Vaḷinak (see above, *Andovk*). BP mentions Vaḷinak only once in connection with the rebellion of the *bdeašχ* Bakur of Anjit, whose daughter and domains were given to him, together with the title of *bdeašχ*, though this inheritance eventually returned to Bakur's son, Xeša. A less credible version of his career in the reign of Aršak

II is given by MX, III.xviii, xxiv (= MK, pp. 272, 280), who has him murdered at the order of Queen Pᶜaṙanjem (see III.ix n. 5).

See HAnjB, V, p. 33 no. 1; JIN, p. 346, *Waḷinak* no. 1; Toumanoff, *Manuel*, p. 226/2.

III.ix

p. 77

See also "Andovk"; "Bakur"; "Siwni, house"; "Xosrov II/III"; Appendix II, "Aljnikᶜ"; and Appendix III, *bdeašχ*; *nahapet*; *naχarar*; *sepuh*.

Vaḷinak/Vaḷenak II Siwni

Sepuh of the house of Siwni, who survived the Persian massacre of his family (IV.lviii); he was the youngest brother of Babik. No further information concerning him is given by BP, but presumably he subsequently became the *nahapet* of the Siwni house, for both Koriwn, xiv, p. 60 (= trans. p. 36), and Eḷišē, vi, p. 137 (= *Eḷishē*, p. 187), identify him as such. MX, III.xlvi (= MK, p. 310), knows him as a supporter of St. Mesrop, and Eḷišē claims that he was killed by his nephew, the traitor Vasak, who succeeded him.

See HAnjB, V, p. 33 no. 2; JIN, pp. 346–347 no. 2, who mistakenly makes him the son of Sam Gntᶜuni, prince of Siwnikᶜ [sic]; Toumanoff, *Manuel*, p. 226/3.

V.xlii

p. 224

See also "Babik"; "Siwni, house"; and Appendix III, *nahapet*; *sepuh*.

Varaz ‹ Phl. *warāz*, Av. *varāza-*, "wild boar"; one of the incarnations of the Zorastrian god Vərəθraγna

Name *Varaz* attested in ŠKZ, Parth. 23, 25; Phl. 29, 31; RGDS nos. 57, 62, pp. 64–65, 68–69; *Paikuli*; etc.

Persian general defeated and killed by Manuēl Mamikonean. He is not otherwise attested.

See Gignoux, "Noms propres," p. 57; *idem*, NPS, no. 940, p. 173; Schmitt, IN, p. 330; Sprengling, *Third-Century Iran*, pp. 9, 11–12, 18–19; Honigmann and Maricq, RGDS, p. 17; Humbach and Skjærvø, *Paikuli*, 3.1 p. 41; JIN, p. 348, *Warāza* no. 6; CPD, p. 87, *warāz*; Garsoïan, "Substratum," pp. 161–162 and pls. 8–12.

V.xl

p. 223–224

Varaz of Copᶜkᶜ Šahuni/Šahēi ‹ Phl. *warāz*, Av. *varāza-*, "wild boar"; one of the incarnations of the Zorastrian god Vərəθraγna

Name *Varaz* attested in ŠKZ, Parth. 23, 25; Phl. 29, 31; RGDS, nos. 57, 62, pp. 64–65, 68–69; *Paikuli*; etc.

Prince of Copᶜkᶜ Šahēi and presumably successor of Nerseh, the *nahapet* of the house under Xosrov Kotak (III.vii). Varaz is listed in the retinue of St. Nersēs in the *Vita* of St. Nersēs, iii, p. 25 (= CHAMA, II, p. 24), which calls him Varaz Šahuni, prince of Copᶜkᶜ. This is probably a confusion with the retinue of St. Yusik I on the same journey to Caesarea, for BP gives Noy, who presumably succeeded Varaz, as attending St. Nersēs (IV.iv).

See HAnjB, V, p. 62 no. 2; JIN, p. 348, *Warāza* no. 5; CPD, p. 87, *warāz*; and additional bibliography under the entry *Varaz*.

III.xii

p. 82

See also "Nerseh of Copᶜkᶜ Šahēi"; "Noy"; Appendix II, "Copᶜkᶜ Šahēi"; and Appendix III, *nahapet*.

Varaz Dimak^csean ‹ Phl. *warāz*, Av. *varāza-*, "wild boar"; one of the incarnations of the Zorastrian god Vərəθraγna
Name *Varāz* attested in ŠKZ, Parth. 23, 25; Phl. 29, 31; RGDS nos. 57, 62, pp. 64–65, 68–69; *Paikuli*; etc.
Presumably *nahapet* of the Dimak^csean house. He is not otherwise attested, and this is the only mention of his family in BP.
See HAnjB, V, p. 62 no. 3; JIN, p. 348, *Warāza* no. 4; CPD, p. 87, *warāz*; and additional bibliography under the entry *Varaz*.
III.xiv
p. 87
See also "Dimak^csean, house"; and Appendix III, *nahapet*.

Varaz Kaminakan ‹ Phl. *warāz*; Av. *varāza-*, "wild boar"; one of the incarnations of the Zorastrian god Vərəθraγna
Name *Varāz* attested in ŠKZ, Parth. 23, 25; Phl. 29, 31; RGDS nos. 57, 62, pp. 64–65, 68–69; *Paikuli*; etc.
Armenian *naxarar* and commander, who is given as a companion in arms of the *sparapet* Vač^cē I Mamikonean in BP. He is not otherwise attested, but Toumanoff identifies the Kaminakan with the Aršakuni branch settled in Hašteank^c/Asthianēnē, according to MX (II.viii = MK, p. 144).
See HAnjB, V, p. 62 no. 1; JIN, p. 348, *Warāza* no. 3; Toumanoff, *Studies*, pp. 172, 192, 193 n. 207, 216, 223, 226, 245; CPD, p. 87, *warāz*; and additional bibliography under the entry *Varaz*.
III.vii
p. 74
See also "Kaminakan, house"; Appendix II, "Hašteank^c"; "Vač^cē I"; and Appendix III, *naxarar, nizakakic^c*.

Varaz-šapuh/Šapuh-varaz ‹ Phl. *warāz*, Av. *varāza*, "wild boar"; one of the incarnations of the Zorastrian god Vərəθraγna; MP *šāh-puhr*, "king's son"; the text alternates the two components of the name and even gives Varaz without the second component
Persian *marzpan* of Atrpatakan and commander in the war that ended the reign of King Tiran, according to BP. He is not otherwise attested in the Armenian sources, and the personage may be fictitious, although he has been identified by Adontz, Peeters, and Melik^c-Ōhanǰanyan with the Persian ambassador called Βαρσαβώρης/Βαρασσαβώρσ)ης by Petr. Patric. (see, however, III.xx n. 3).
See Gignoux, NPS, no. 940, p. 173, *Vāraz*, no. 858, p. 161, *Šābuhr*; Schmitt, IN, p. 331; JIN, p. 350, *Warāz-Šapuh* no. 1; Adontz, "Favst," p. 248; Peeters, "Intervention," p. 235; Melik^c-Ōhanǰanyan, "Tiran-Trdati vepə," II, p. 66; CPD, p. 87, *warāz*; and additional bibliography under the entries Varaz and Šāhpuhr.
III.xx–xxi
pp. 94–97, 99
See also "Tiran"; Appendix II, "Atrpatakan"; and Appendix III, *marzpan*.

Varazdat Aršakuni ‹ Phl. *warāz-dat*, "given by the wild boar," i.e., the Zoroastrian god Vərəθraγna, of whom the *warāz* was one of the visible forms
Name *Varāz* attested in ŠKZ, Parth. 23, 25; Phl. 29, 31; RGDS nos. 57, 62, pp. 64–65, 68–69; *Paikuli*; etc.
Aršakuni king of Armenia, named by the emperor Valens to succeed Pap (ca. 374–378). Both BP and MX, III.xl (= MK, p. 301), refer to him rather contemptuously as *omn*, "a certain" Aršakuni. Nonetheless, the allusion to his paternal uncle King Pap (V.xxxvii) suggests that he may have been the son of Pap's younger brother Trdat,

unknown to BP and MX, but mentioned by the *Vita* of St. Nersēs, vii, p. 50 (= CHAMA, II, p. 29). MX, III.xl (= MK, pp. 301–302), gives a highly fanciful account of Varazdat's Olympic victories and of his exploits against the Lombards and Syrian brigands. BP (V.xxxiv) protrays him less enthusiastically as a brave but foolish youth, who believed the slander against the *sparapet* Mušeł Mamikonean and had him killed (V.xxxv). The young king then attempted to transfer the hereditary *sparapetut῾iwn* of the Mamikonean house to his *dayeak*, Bat Saharuni, with the result that he was driven from Armenia by Mušeł's kinsman Manuēl Mamikonean and was constrained to take refuge in the Byzantine empire (V.xxxvii). MX, III.xl (= MK, p. 302), gives a less probable version, which omits all mention of the Mamikoneans, has Varazdat intrigue with the Persians, be recalled after four years by the emperor "Theodosius," and finally be exiled to the island of Thulē.

See Gignoux, NPS, no. 940, p. 173; Schmitt, IN, pp. 321, 329; HAnjB, V, p. 65 no. 1; JIN, pp. 349, *Warāzdat* no. 1, p. 414; Toumanoff, *Manuel*, p. 76/10b; AG, p. 81; Jones *et al.*, *Prosopography*, I, p. 945, where his father is called *Anop* [sic]; Manandyan, *K῾nnakan tesut῾yun* II.1, pp. 228–235; CPD, p. 87, *warāz*; and additional bibliography under the entry *Varaz.*
V.xxxiv–xxxv, xxxvii
pp. 215–220
See also "Aršakuni"; "Bat Saharuni"; "Manuēl"; "Mušeł"; "Pap"; "Vałes"; and Appendix III, *dayeak*; *sparapet.*

Varazduχt Aršakuni ‹ Phl *warāz* + *duχt*, "daughter of the wild boar," i.e., the Zoroastrian god Vərəθraɣna, of whom the *warāz* was one of the visible forms
Name Varāzduχt attested in ŠKZ, Parth. 21; Phl. 26; RGDS no. 50, pp. 62–63.
Aršakuni princess and wife of Pap, the son of the patriarch Yusik I. BP is the only source to give her name and claims that she was the sister of King Tiran; but see III.v, n. 4, xv nn. 2–3. The Iranian form of her name (with Phl. *duχt* as attested in ŠKZ instead of Arm. *dustr*) with its allusion to the wild-boar incarnation of the god Vərəθraɣna (*Bahram Yašt*, 2, 7, 9, etc.) is an index of the continuing Iranian tradition in the royal Aršakuni house even after the Christianization of Armenian.
See Gignoux, "Noms propres," p. 87; *idem*, NPS, no. 941, p. 174; Schmitt, IN, pp. 321, 331; Sprengling, *Third-Century Iran*, pp. 9, 11, 18; Honigmann and Maricq, RGDS, p. 16; HAnjB, V, p. 64 no. 1; JIN, pp. 350, *Warazduχt*, 414; Toumanoff, *Manuel*, p. 74/7; AG, pp. 81, 144 no. 204; CPD, pp. 29, 87, *duχt* and *warāz*; Garsoïan, "Substratum," pp. 160–164 and notes.
III.xv, xix
pp. 91, [94]
See also "Aršakuni"; "Aršakuni, anonymous princess"; "Bambišn"; "Grigor/Gregorids," for Aršakuni-Gregorid intermarriage; "Pap (2)"; "Tiran."

Vardan I Mamikonean ‹ ?Parth. *vard*, "rose"; ‹ ?OIr. *vard-*, "to turn," cf. ?OInd.
Cakrovartīn, "one who turns the wheel" = "controls the world"
Name *Vardan* attested in ŠKZ, Parth. 24, 29; Phl. 35; RGDS, nos. 58, 67, pp. 66–67, 72–73.
Nahapet of the Mamikonean house and elder brother of the *sparapet* Vasak. According to BP, he was the *dayeak* of King Aršak II and one of the magnates who accompanied St. Nersēs to the Byzantine court (IV.xi), though MX, III.xxii (= MK, p. 277) reduces him to the level of "royal squire" (*zinakir ark῾uni*). He appears to have sided with the pro-Persian party in Armenia, in opposition to his brother the *sparapet* Vasak (III.xvi), and he served as ambassador between Šāhpuhr II and Aršak II (IV.xviii). He is also said to have participated in the decoying of Aršak's nephew, Gnel, to his death (IV.xv), and MX, III.xxi–xxiii, xxv (= MK, pp. 277–278, 280–281), even

makes him a co-conspirator with Tirit^c and the actual murderer of Gnel. His participation in this conspiracy earned him the enmity of Queen P^{c}aṙanjem, Gnel's widow, and she supported the slander of his brother Vasak, by whom he was killed, according to BP (IV.xviii).

The precise relations of Vardan with other members of his family are difficult to ascertain with precision because of the discrepancies found in MX, who confuses him with his brother Vasak (both are called Aršak's squires, III.xxii, xxv = MK, pp. 277, 280) and with his half-brother Vahan, thus making Vardan the father of Samuēl (III.xlviii = MK, p. 312, cf. BP, IV.lix). The confusion is compounded by the *Vita* of St. Nersēs, ii, p. 14 (= CHAMA, II, p. 22), which makes Vardan the father of Nersēs's wife, Sanduχt. This version of Nersēs's marriage is accepted by Ačaryan (cf. BP, IV.iii; MX, III.xvi = MK, p. 270), but in view of the late date of the *Vita*, its considerable inaccuracy, and the confusion in the accounts of Nersēs's secular life, there seems to be little reason for linking Vardan to the patriarch. BP attributes one posthumous son, Vardan II, to him (IV.xviii); Vasak, Bagos, and the Princess Hamazapuhi are given as his brothers and sisters and Vahan as his half-brother, either explicitly or through references to each other (IV.ii, xxii, lix). Finally, Vardan is usually taken as the son of Artawazd II, but this is unlikely, considering the brevity of Artawazd's career (see "Hamazaspean Mamikonean").

> See Gignoux, *Glossaire*, pp. 33, 66; *idem*, NPS no. 947, p. 174; Schmitt, IN, p. 331; Sprengling, *Third-Century Iran*, pp. 9, 18, 19; Honigmann and Maricq, RGDS, pp. 17–18; HAnjB, V, pp. 74–75 no. 1; JIN, pp. 351, *Wardān* no. 7, who follows the version of MX rather than that of BP, and 424; Toumanoff, *Manuel*, p. 331/4a
>
> IV.ii, xi, xv, xvi, xviii, l, lix
>
> pp. 108, 133, 141, 147–149, 168, 179
>
> See also "Aršak II"; "Gnel Aršakuni"; "Hamazaspean," for the Mamikonean genealogy; "Mamikonean, house"; "Nersēs I"; "P^{c}aṙanjem"; "Samuēl"; "Šapuh"; "Tirit^c"; "Vahan"; "Vasak"; Appendix II, "Eraχani"; and Appendix III, *dayeak*; *nahapet*.

Vardan II Mamikonean ‹ ?Parth. *vard*, "rose"; ‹ ?OIr. *vard-*, "to turn," cf. ?OInd. *Cakrovartīn*, "one who turns the wheel" = "controls the world"

> Name *Vardan* attested in ŠKZ, Parth. 24, 29; Phl. 35; RGDS no. 58, 67, pp. 66–67, 72–73.

Sepuh of the Mamikonean house and posthumous son of Vardan I, according to BP. He is not otherwise attested, and his birth at the moment of his father's murder may belong to the epic rather than the historical tradition (see IV.xviii n. 6).

> See HAnjB, V, p. 75 no. 2; JIN, pp. 351–352, *Wardān* no. 8, who follows the *Vita* of St. Nersēs in making him the brother of Nersēs's wife Sanduχt, and further makes him the father of St. Mesrop; Toumanoff, *Manuel*, p. 332/5a; Gignoux, "Noms propres," pp. 57–58; and additional bibliography on the name in the preceding entry.
>
> IV.xviii
>
> p. 149
>
> See also "Mamikonean, house"; Appendix III, *sepuh*; and the preceding entry.

Vardanduχt ‹ Arm. Vardan + Phl. *duχt*, "daughter"

Queen of Armenia as the wife of Aršak III. BP identifies her as the daughter of the *sparapet* Manuēl Mamikonean, but MX, III.xli (= MK, p. 303), who does not name Aršak's wife, says that she was the daughter of Babik Siwni. Because Vardan was one of the traditional dynastic names in the Mamikonean house and MX systematically denigrates its importance (see Intro., pp. 44–45), BP's version is probably the correct one.

See HAnjB, V, p. 107; JIN, pp. 353, "*Wardānduχt,*" and 424; Toumanoff, *Manuel,* p. 332/6d; AG, p. 83; CPD, p. 29, *duχt*; also additional bibliography on the name Vardan under "Vardan I."

V.xliv

pp. 228–229

See also "Aršak III"; "Babik"; "Mamikonean, house"; "Manuēl."

Vardanoyš ‹ ?Phl. *Vard,* "rose," + *ānōš,* "immortal"

Wife of the *sparapet* Manuēl Mamikonean and presumably the mother of his children, Artašēs/Artašir, Hmayeak, and Vardanduχt, the wife of Aršak III. She is not otherwise attested.

See HAnjB V, p. 107 no. 1; JIN, p. 353, *Wardanoyš*; Toumanoff, *Manuel,* p. 332/5d, as wife of Manuēl; also additional bibliography on the name Vardan under "Vardan I."

V.xliii

p. 225

See also "Artašēs/Artašir"; "Hmayeak"; "Mamikonean, house"; "Manuēl"; and the preceding entry.

Vasak Mamikonean; Gk. Βασσάκης/Βασσάκιος. Lat Vasaces

Sepuh of the Mamikonean house and *sparapet* of Armenia from the latter part of the reign of King Tiran to the end of that of Aršak II, whom he served constantly as commander in chief until the king's imprisonment in Persia and his own death (IV.liv); also *tanuter* of the Mamikonean after the murder of his brother Vardan (IV.xviii; l). BP attributes his designation as *sparapet* to Aršak II at the beginning of his reign (IV.ii), but this can at best have been a confirmation, for Vasak is mentioned as commander in chief in the retinue accompanying Pᶜaŕēn of Aštišat to Caesarea (III.xvi and IV.ii n. 7) in the reign of Tiran. Vasak is explicitly identified by BP as the brother of the Mamikonean *nahapet* Vardan, to whom he was opposed and whom he eventually killed (IV.ii, xvi, xviii), and of the commander Bagos (IV.xxii). He must therefore, have been the brother of the princess Hamazaspuhi and the half-brother of the traitor Vahan (IV.lix). Both Justi and Toumanoff make Vasak the son of Artawazd II, presumably on the basis of the *Vita* of St. Nersēs, ii, p. 17 (= CHAMA, II, p. 22), but this seems impossible, considering the short span of Artawazd's life (see above "Hamazaspean"). The office of *sparapet* was hereditary in the Mamikonean house but not necessarily in direct line, as Manuēl in a later generation was not the son of Vasak or of his son and successor Mušeł, but of Artašēs/Artašēn. The information in III.xviii seems to suggest that Vasak was commander together with his kinsman Artawazd II and subsequently replaced him (IV.ii).

The portrayal of Vasak in BP is largely favorable, as is the case with all the Mamikoneans (see Intro., p. 44). He is the centerpiece of the long catalog of victories (IV.xxv–xliii, xlv–xlix), the loyal defender of his king's honor (IV.xvi), the haughty defier of Šāhpuhr II's wrath (IV.liv). The uglier aspects of his mortal quarrel with his brother and *tanutēr* Vardan are not stressed (IV.xvi, xviii), though they are not omitted. This portrayal is also found in the Greek sources, as Procopius (*Bell. Pers.,* I.v.17–18, 28) follows BP in making the general Βασσάκιος a friend of King Aršak, and in recording his tragic death under similar circumstances. On the contrary, MX, following his usual anti-Mamikonean bias (see Intro., pp. 44–45), barely records his presence, not even mentioning his role in the Persian war, which is summarily treated; refers to him denigratingly as Aršak II's squire; and treats his rivalry with Vardan as a vulgar quarrel over a concubine (III.xxv = MK, pp. 280–281).

See Schmitt, IN, p. 330; HAnjB, V, pp. 43–44 no. 4; JIN, pp. 337, *Wasaka* no. 3, and
424; Toumanoff, *Manuel*, p. 331/4b; AG, p. 80 no. 181; Adontz, *Armenia*,
pp. 222, 225, 517 n. 54, 521 n. 77.
III.xvi, xviii; IV.ii, xi, xvi, xviii–xxv, xxvii–xliii, xlv–li, liii–lv; V.i–ii, xxxvii
pp. 91, 93, 108, 133, 146–152, 154–156, 158–168, 173–174, 185, 187–188, 218
See also "Aršak II"; "Artawazd II"; "Bagos"; "Hamazaspean," for the genealogy of
the Mamikonean house; "Hamazaspuhi"; "Mamikonean, house"; "Manuēl";
"Tiran"; "Vahan"; "Vardan I"; and Appendix III, *sepuh*; *sparapet, tanutēr.*

Vin ‹ MP *vīn*, Sk. *vina*, "kithara"
Persian commander against Aršak II. He is not otherwise attested.
See JIN, p. 368, *Win.*
IV.xxvi
p. 159

Vorot^c of Vanand
Prince of Vanand, presumably succeeded by Artawan (III.xiv). He is not otherwise
attested.
See HAnjB, V, p. 125; JIN, p. 133, **Hurauda*, "of shapely form" no. 9.
III.xii
p. 82
See also "Artawan"; and Appendix II, "Vanand."

Vrik ‹ ?Av. *vīra*, "man" + diminutive suff. -*ik*
Illegitimate son of Pap, the son of the patriarch Yusik I. He is not otherwise attested,
but because his mother came from the village of Hac^cekac^c, the birthplace of St. Mesrop
Koriwn, iii, p. 36 (=trans. p. 27), it has been suggested without any foundation that Vrik
might have been Mesrop's father.
See Schmitt, IN, p. 330; HAnjB, V, p. 134; JIN, p. 376, *Wrik*; Toumanoff, *Manuel*,
p. 224/6.
III.xix
p. 94
See also "Pap (2)"; and Appendix II, "Hac^cekac^c."

Vrkēn Habužean ‹ OP **Wrkaina*-; Av. *vahrka*-, "wolf"; Gk. Ὑρκανος
Armenian *naχarar* otherwise unattested. The *Vita* of St. Nersēs, viii, p. 53
(= CHAMA, II, p. 30) lists a Vrēn, *nahapet* of Virk^c/Iberia, but there is no indication
that the otherwise unknown Habužean house had domains in Iberia, and the etymology
of his name points rather to the region of Hyrcania, south of the Caspian Sea.
See HAnjB, V, p. 134; JIN, p. 355, **Warkaina* no. 4; Toumanoff, *Studies*, p. 218;
Gignoux, NPS, no. 405, p. 91, *Gurgēn*; idem, "Noms propres," p. 87, Schmitt, IN,
p. 323, *Vrkên, Gowrgên.*
IV.xi
p. 133
See also "Habužean, house"; Appendix II, "Virk^c"; and Appendix III, *naχarar.*

Vrt^canēs, St.
Elder son and second successor of St. Gregory the Illuminator as patriarch of
Greater Armenia. BP sets the beginning of his pontificate in the reign of King Xosrov
Kotak (III.iii) and does not specify its length, while MX, II.xci, III.xi (= MK, pp. 249,
264), inaugurates it in the fifty-fourth year of Trdat the Great and ends it fifteen years
later in the reign of King Tiran. The dates of Vrt^canēs's pontificate are usually given as
333–341, though Toumanoff pushes the beginning of it back to 328 and Justi gives the
dates 314–330, which are patently impossible, because Vrt^canēs's brother and prede-

cessor Aristakēs is attested at the Council of Nicaea in 325 by the conciliar lists. The accounts of BP and MX differ in that BP restricts the patriarch's activities to Greater Armenia, while MX, III.x (= MK, p. 263), sends him on an embassy to the Byzantine court to obtain the enthronement of Xosrov Kotak's son, Tiran. Both sources, however, record his burial at the village of T'ordan in the patriarchal domain in Daranałik'.

    See HAnjB, V, pp. 128–129 no. 1; JIN, p. 366, *Wĕrthanes*; Toumanoff, *Manuel*, p. 223/3; Ōrmanean, *Azgapatum* I, cols. 132–142; Garitte, *Documents*, pp. 207–208; *idem, Narratio*, p. 416.

    P.S.; III.iii–viii, xi–xii; IV.iii

    pp. 63, 68–70, 72, 74, 76, 80–82, 109

    See also "Aristakēs"; "Grigor/Gregorids"; "Xosrov II/III"; and Appendix II, "T'ordan."

Vsemakan, see Appendix III, *vsemakan*.

Xad of Marag ‹ ?Syr. *ḥad*, "to take/grasp."

    Disciple and deacon of St. Nersēs I, who ordained him bishop of Bagrewand and Aršarunik' and whom he left as vicar during his exile (IV.xii). Xad was also the supervisor of the patriarch's numerous charitable foundations. His support of St. Nersēs's orthodox position brought him into conflict with the Arianizing Armenian court. Aršak II had him driven from the royal camp (IV.xii), or even ordered him stoned (according to MX, III.xxxii = MK, p. 289), although he was rescued by his relatives and not killed, as claimed by Justi. Like all early Armenian hierarchs, Xad was not a monk or an ascetic. BP refers to his two daughters (IV.xii), and MX, III.xxxi (= MK, 288), blames him for his fondness for fastidious clothes and fine horses, from which he repented. His relationship with the *naχarar* house of the Apahuni, MX, III.xxxii (= MK, pp. 289–290), is not mentioned by BP which, however, records that he was succeeded as bishop by his son-in-law Asurk, thus indicating that ecclesiastical office was hereditary in houses other than that of St. Gregory. Despite its usual reliance on BP, the *Vita* of St. Nersēs surprisingly ignores him altogether.

    See HAnjB, II, p. 42 no. 2; JIN, p. 169; Garsoïan, "Politique," pp. 307, 310–312; *idem*, "Protecteur des pauvres," pp. 29–31; *idem*, "Nersēs le Grand," p. 161.

    IV.xii–xiii, xv; V.xxii

    pp. 134–137, 141, 203

    See also "Aršak II"; "Asurk"; "Nersēs I"; "Pap"; Appendix II, "Aršarunik'"; "Bagrewand"; and Appendix III, *etełapah; naχarar*.

Xeša/Hešay of Ałjnik'; one ms gives the name as "Xela," which is clearly a scribal error

    Only surviving son of the *bdeašχ* Bakur, saved by Vač'ē I Mamikonean according to BP, though MX, III.vii (= MK, p. 259), claims that he was surrendered in chains to King Xosrov Kotak. The king temporarily granted Ałjnik' to Vałinak Siwni together with the title *bdeašχ*, in defiance of the hereditary nature of offices and possessions in fourth-century Armenia, but Xeša eventually regained his domain, as is noted by BP. He does not seem to have been ruling Ałjnik' when it seceded from Aršak II after the Roman–Persian peace of 363, since the name of the *bdeašχ* is not give at that point (IV.l).

    See HAnjB, III, p. 81, *Hešay*; Toumanoff, *Studies*, p. 180.

    III.ix

    p. 77

    See also "Bakur"; "Vač'ē I"; "Vałinak I"; Appendix II, "Ałjnik'"; and Appendix III, *bdeašχ*.

Xoṙxoṙuni/Malxazuni, house

Great *naxarar* house, also commonly known as Malxazuni from its hereditary title of *malxaz*, which was probably of tribal origin. According to MX, I.xii (= MK, p. 89), the Xoṙxoṙuni were descended from the Armenian eponymous hero Hayk through their ancestor Xoṙ and preserved their name despite the existence of a second putative eponymous ancestor, Malxaz (MX, II.vii = MK, p. 137). BP knows nothing of these etymologies or of the nature of the *malxaz*'s office, which MX (*loc. cit*) identifies as that of the commander of the royal bodyguard.

The Xoṙxoṙuni were dynasts of a principality northwest of Lake Van known to early Armenian sources, but the toponym Xoṙxoṙunik^c appears only in the short version of the *Ašx.*, where it may be a later addition. The bishops of the house seemingly went back to the period of St. Gregory (Vg, clxxii = Va, clx), and the Xoṙxoṙuni are included in all the *naxarar* Lists, although their awkward insertion at the top of the *Gahnamak*, "Rank List," is probably an interpolation, according to Adontz. The *Zōrnamak*, "Military List," attributed 1,000 retainers to them. The family is attested until the Arab period, when it disappeared, and its principality became a part of the kingdom of Vaspurakan by the tenth century.

> See Oskean, *Usumnasirut^ciwnner*; JIN, p. 188, *Malxaz*; Adontz, *Armenia*, pp. 188, 191, 195–196, 200, 203, 205, 206, 208, 230, 311, 321, 344, 369, 441 n. 16, 443 n. 24, 451 n. 85, 68*, 70*, 75*–81*, 90*, 93*, 96*–97*, 99*–100*, 102*, 124*; Toumanoff, *Studies*, pp. 110 n. 173, 132, 135, 160–161, 208–209, 223, 227, 228, 240, 247–248, 250–251, 252 n. 342. On the principality, see AON, pp. 330, 435; Eremyan, *Ašxarh.*, pp. 55, 116; *idem, Map* G/5, where he places it north of Bznunik^c; while Hakobyan, *Ašxarhagrut^cyun*, pp. 104, 107, 150, 156, 256, and map places it west of Bznunik^c; Hewsen, "Armenia," p. 328.
> III.xii; IV.xi; V.xxxviii; [xliii]
> pp. 82, 133, [221]–222, [227–228]
> See also "Garǰoyl"; "Manasp"; and Appendix III, *malxaz*; *naxarar*.

Xosrov I/II K^caǰ ‹ Phl. Xusrō/Husrav; Av. *husravah-* "famous/of good repute" + Arm. *k^caǰ*, "valiant"

Aršakuni king of Armenia and father of Trdat the Great (279/280–287?). The chronology of his reign remains problematic, though Toumanoff has argued persuasively that he ruled over only the western portion of Greater Armenia and not over the entire realm. The account of his blood feud with the Sasanian usurpers of the throne of his Aršakuni kinsmen in Iran and of his murder by Anak the Parthian forms the opening section of the Armenian received tradition of its Christianization transmitted in Aa (xvi–xxxii). An alternate tradition, found in Ełišē, iii, p. 72 (= *Ełishē*, p. 123), has Xosrov murdered by his own brothers.

> See Toumanoff "Third–Century Arsacids," pp. 259–262, 274; *idem, Manuel*, p. 74/4; the more traditional interpretation is given by HAnjB, II, pp. 530–551 no. 2; JIN, p. 134, *Husrawanh*, who pushes his reign back to 222–238; Chaumont, *L'Arménie*, pp. 159–171; also Gignoux, NPS, nos. 465ff.; pp. 100–101, *Husrav*; Schmitt, IN, pp. 321, 329 on the name itself.
> III.ii–iii
> pp. 67–68
> See also "Anak"; "Aršakuni"; "Sasanians"; "Trdat the Great"; and Appendix III, *k^caǰ*.

Xosrov II/III Kotak ‹ Phl. Xusrō/Husrav; Av. *husravah-*, "famous, of good repute" + Arm. *kotak* ‹ Phl. *kōdak*, "young/small baby"

Aršakuni king of Armenia, son of Trdat the Great and father of Tiran. According to the generally accepted chronology he reigned from 330 to 338/9, but these dates still present problems, and Hewsen has even suggested that his reign does not belong in the fourth century but should be identified with that of Xosrov Kʿaǰ (see preceding entry). The length of his reign is not mentioned in BP, but MX, III.x (= MK, p. 263), gives it as nine years. Both sources speak disparagingly of his reign which was marked by numerous *naχarar* rebellions, though both BP, III.viii; and MX, III.viii (= MK, pp. 260–261) also record his creation of the great hunting preserve named Xosrovakert in his honor, near the site of Duin. Only MX, however, dates the shift of the Armenian capital from Artašat to Duin at this time.

    See, HAnjB, II, pp. 531–532 no. 3; JIN, p. 135, *Husrawanh* no. 9; CPD, p. 51, *kōdak*; Toumanoff, *Manuel*, p. 74/6; Manandyan, *Kʿnnakan tesutʿyun*, II.l, pp. 141–157; Hewsen, "Successors"; and the additional bibliography on the name in the preceding entry.

P.S.; III.iii–v, vii–ix, xi, xii
pp. 63, 68–70, 73–76, 80–82
See also "Aršakuni"; "Bakur"; "Manawazean; house"; "Orduni, house"; "Trdat the Great"; and Appendix II, "Artašat"; "Duin"; "Tiknuni"; "Xosrovakert."

Xosrov Kotak, wife of, see "Aršakuni, anonymous queen, I."

Xosrov III/IV ‹ Phl. Xusrō/Husrav; Av. *husravah*-, "famous, of good repute"
    Sepuh of the Aršakuni house appointed king of Armenia, presumably after the death of Vałaršak, by the Persian king, who gave him his sister in marriage (384–389? and 414–415). According to BP (VI.i), this enthronement clearly occurred before the partition of Armenia ca. 387, but MX, III.xlii (= MK, p. 304), places it after this event. Most of Xosrov's career lay beyond the chronological limit of BP and is related by ŁPʿ and MX. ŁPʿ, I.vi, p. 8 (= CHAMA, II, pp. 262, 264), clearly states that Xosrov had been installed by the Persians in the eastern portion of Armenia, while Procopius records (*De aed.*, III.i.14–15) that the Romans appointed a *comes Armeniae* over their portion after the death of Aršak III. MX, however, contradicts himself, stating first correctly (III.xlvi = MK, p. 309) that after Aršak's death, "the Greeks appointed no more kings in their sector . . . [but] appointed counts as governors of their part of the country," but then going on to claim that Xosrov extended his rule over the whole of Armenia (III.xlix = MK, p. 313). After some five years of reign, the Armenian magnates denounced Xosrov for intrigues with Byzantium and he was deported to Persia (MX, III.l = MK, pp. 314–315); ŁPʿ, I.ix, pp. 12–13 (= CHAMA, II, pp. 264–265). MX also records that Xosrov's disgrace was caused by his unauthorized appointment of St. Sahak I as patriarch of Armenia and that the Armenian king was kept captive in the "Castle of Oblivion," but these details are not mentioned by ŁPʿ. Xosrov briefly returned to the throne after the death of his brother Vramšapuh, who had succeeded him for twenty-one years, but he died soon thereafter, eight months according to ŁPʿ (I.xii, p. 18 = CHAMA, p. 268); MX, III.lv (= MK, p. 323).

    See HAnjB, II, pp. 532–533 no. 5; JIN, p. 135, *Husrawanh* no. 10; Toumanoff, *Manuel*, p. 76/11, both of whom make Xosrov the son of Varazdat, though the relationship is not specified in the sources; Manandyan, *Kʿnnakan tesutʿyun*, II/1 pp. 238–248; Garitte, *Narratio*, pp. 64, 70–72; Adontz, *Armenia*, pp. 411 n. 33a, 412 nn. 41–42a; Toumanoff, *Studies*, p. 152 n. 6, for the bibliography of the partition and its date; and still more recently, Ē. L. Danielyan, "*Haykakan bažanman taretʿivə*"; also the additional bibliography on the name under "Xosrov I/II."

VI.i, iv–v, vii
pp. 233–235
See also "Aršakuni"; "Vałaršak"; "Zik [3]"; "Zruanduχt"; and Appendix III, *sepuh*.

Yakob of Mcbin/James of Nisibis, St.

First known bishop of Nisibis, who is said to have saved his city miraculously from the Persians. Little is known of his life besides this event, which is recorded in the main source, Theodoret of Cyr, *Hist. Phil.*, i, though the *History of Tarōn* p. 70–71 makes him the cousin of Gregory the Illuminator. His attendance at the Council of Nicaea is known to MX, II.lxxxix (= MK, pp. 245–246) and is corroborated by the conciliar lists, and he is known to have been an ardent opponent of Arianism. The finding of the wood of the ark on Mt. Sararad and the confrontation with Manačihr R̄štuni recorded in III.x and MX, III.vii (= MK, pp. 259–260) are not found in Theodoret's *Vita* and may belong to a local Armenian tradition (see III.x nn. 1 and 3). After the Persian occupation of Nisibis in 363, James's relics were moved to Amida and eventually brought to Constantinople (ca. 970). His reputation as a doctor of the faith was so widespread through the East that he is often referred to as *Zgōn*, "the wise" and that the works of Aphraat were soon mistakenly attributed to him under that name (see III.x n. 2). Several Armenian version of his *Vita* are known.

See BHO nos. 405–411; AASS, Jul. IV, 28–41; Peeters, "Jacques de Nisibe"; Krüger, "Jacob von Nisibis"; Ter Minasyan, "*Zgōn*"; Melk⁽ᶜ⁾onyan, "Armianskiĭ perevod"; Tisserant, "Jacques de Nisibe"; DS, VIII, col. 50; ODCC, p. 721; Canivet, *Théodoret*, no. 71 n. 7 for the Armenian versions; Fiey, *Nisibe*, pp. 23, n. 48, 24, 221–223; Gelzer *et al.*, eds., *Nomina*, pp. 20, 21, 64, 84, 102, 126, 160, 196, for Nicaea.

III.x

pp. 77–80

See also "Manačihr"; and Appendix II, "Amid"; "Mcbin"; "Sararad."

Yaṙalezkᶜ, see "Aṙlezkᶜ."

Yohan/John ‹ syr. Yohanan (short form)

Presumably an Armenian bishop and son of the patriarch Pᶜaṙen of Aštišat. He is not attested elsewhere and the entire account of his regrettable career is suspect. The name of his see is not given; neither is the name of the Armenian king before whom he played the fool (VI.x). His identification with St. Gregory's sixth disciple, Yovhannēs (see Aa, dcccxlc and p. 496 n. 4), is chronologically impossible if he was the son of Pᶜaṙēn (348–352?), and the curiously anticlerical and moralizing tone of the chapters relating to him is unsuited to the rest of BP (see Intro., pp. 36–37).

See HAnjB, III, p. 539 no. 4, *Yovhannēs*.

VI.viii–x

pp. 236–238

See also "Pᶜaṙēn."

Yoynkᶜ, see "Greeks."

Yusik I, St. ‹ ?Arm. *yoys*, "hope" + diminutive suff. *-ik*; ?Gk. Εὐσύχιος

Son of St. Vrtᶜanēs, grandson of St. Gregory the Illuminator, and hereditary patriarch of Armenia under King Tiran (341–347?). BP gives no length to his pontificate nor the date of his accession, which is set in the fourth year of King Tiran by MX, III.xi (= MK, p. 264), with a tenure of six years (III.xiv = MK, p. 267). The accepted dates, 341–347, are derived from MX, but a totally different and improbable dating is suggested by Akinean. Like his grandfather, Yusik was consecrated at Caesarea of Cappadocia, and BP stresses the closeness of the royal and patriarchal houses in the account of Yusik's education at court and his marriage to an Aršakuni princess, whose identity is, however, disputed (III.v and n. 4). Despite these relations, Yusik's opposition to Tiran, which ended in the patriarch's murder (III.xii), was probably due to his adherence to the orthodoxy of the Gregorid house as opposed to the Arianizing tendencies of the Armenian court, rather than to Tiran's unspecified sins alluded to in BP (III.xii) or to the improbable tale of the setting up of the image of Julian the Apostate in the church related by MX, III.xiii–xiv (= MK, pp. 266–267)—a story reminiscent of Caius Caligula's order to place his statue in the temple of Jerusalem (Josephus, *Bell. Jud.*, XVIII.xi). Like his father and grandfather, Yusik was buried at Tʿordan in Daranałikʿ, one of the domains of his house. The unworthiness of Yusik's sons, reiterated by BP (III.xiii, xv, xix), is also recorded by MX, III.xvi (= MK, pp. 269–270), who does not, however, mention Yusik's prophetic vision (III.v).

    See HAnjB, III, p. 733 no. 3; JIN, pp. 423–424; Toumanoff, *Manuel,* p. 224/5; Ōrmanean, *Azgapatum* I, cols. 141–150; Sanspeur, "Nouvelle Liste," cols. 186, 187, 195–196; Garitte, *Narratio,* pp. 58–59, 416; Akinean, "Reihenfolge," pp. 80–84; Garsoïan, "Politique," for the religious opposition of the Gregorids and the Aršakuni.

    III.v–vi, xii–xv, xix; IV.iii

    pp. 70–72, 81–84, 86, 89–90, 93, 109, 111

    See also "Aršakuni"; "Aršakuni, anonymous princess"; "Atʿanaginēs"; "Grigor/Gregorids"; "Pap (2)"; "Tiran"; "Vrtʿanēs"; and Appendix II, "Caesarea"; "Tʿordan."

Yusik II ‹ ?Arm. *yoys,* "hope" + diminutive suff. *-ik;* ?Gk. Εὐσύχιος

    Descendant of Ałbianos of Manazkert, presumably appointed patriarch of Armenia by King Pap after the murder of St. Nersēs I and refused recognition by Caesarea of Cappadocia, where the Armenian patriarchs had been consecrated up to that time. Yusik is mentioned only by BP and the *Greek List of Katʿołikoi.* All other Armenian sources place the pontificate of Šahak of Manazkert at this point, and most scholars have accepted this version, though Ačaryan and Akinean have argued that Yusik and Šahak were the same person. In view of the confusion in the patriarchal succession introduced by the multiplicity of Sahaks or Šahaks in the second half of the fourth century and the fact that BP is both chronologically closest and the most detailed source for our knowledge of the early Armenian patriarchate, its evidence should probably not be arbitrarily rejected.

    See HAnjB, III, pp. 733–734, *Yusik* no. 5; IV, pp. 103–104, *Šahak* no. 3; JIN, p. 272, *Sahak* no. 3; Ōrmanean, *Azgapatum* I, cols. 223–225; Sanspeur, "Nouvelle Liste," cols. 186–187, 196–198; Gelzer, "Die Anfänge." pp. 145–146; Akinean, "Reihenfolge," p. 85; Garsoïan, "Šahak of Manazkert."

    V.xxix

    p. 210

    See also "Ałbianos"; "Nersēs I"; "Pap"; "Šahak I"; and Appendix II, "Caesarea."

Zareh of Copʿkʿ Mec ‹ Arm. **Zarehr,* attested as ZRYTR in the Aramaic inscription of Artašēs I (second century B.C.) ‹ ?OP **Zari. āθra-* "with golden fire"; Gk. Ζαρίαδρις

    Prince of Copʿkʿ Mec, who presumably accompanied Yusik I to his consecration at Caesarea. He is not otherwise attested, but presumably followed Mar, prince of Copʿkʿ Mec under King Xosrov Kotak (III.vii) and was in turn succeeded by Daniēl, who accompanied St. Nersēs to his consecration (IV.iv).

    See HAnjB, II, pp. 171–172 no. 6; JIN, p. 281 no. 3; Perikhanian, "Inscription araméenne," pp. 18–21, for the early attestation of the name, Boyce, "Zariadris."

    III.xii

    p. 82

    See also "Daniēl"; "Mar"; and Appendix II, "Copʿkʿ Mec."

Zarmanduχt ‹ Phl. *zarmān*, "old age" + *duχt*, "daughter"
Queen of Armenia as wife of King Pap. After the expulsion of King Varazdat, the *sparapet* Manuēl Mamikonean maintained her on the throne as nominal regent for her minor sons Aršak III and Vałaršak, according to BP. The *Vita* of St. Nersēs, xv, p. 123 (= CHAMA, II, p. 44) follows the version of BP, but MX, III.xli (= MK, p. 303), claims that the queen, whose name he does not give, was kept at Constantinople by the emperor "Theodosius" (see V.xxxviii nn. 1–2 for the improbability and anachronism of this version).
See Schmitt, IN, p. 331; HAnjB, II, pp. 173–174 no. 2; JIN, p. 383 no. 2; Toumanoff, *Manuel*, p. 75/9; AG, p. 41 no. 69; CPD, p. 29, *duχt*.
V.xxxvii–xxxviii [xliii]
pp. 221–223, [226–227]
See also "Aršak III"; "Manuēl"; "Pap"; "Sasanians"; "Vałaršak"; and Appendix III, *tikin*.

Zawēn ‹ MIr. *zav-*, "to call upon"
Descendant of Ałbianos of Manazkert and patriarch of Armenia following after Yusik II or Šahak of Manazkert, who is called his brother in the *List of Katʿołikoi* (*Paris. arm.* #121). Zawēn's pontificate is attested in all the Armenian sources, but very little is known about it. According to MX, III.xl (= MK, pp. 302–303), he was appointed in the second year of King Varazdat, and the sources give him a pontificate of three years.
See Schmitt, IN, p. 330; HAnjB, II, p. 176 no. 3; JIN, p. 384 no. 2; Ōrmanean, *Azgapatum* I, cols. 237–243; Sanspeur, "Nouvelle Liste," cols. 186–187, 197–198; Garitte, *Narratio*, pp. 87–88, 418–420.
VI.ii–iv, xv
pp. 234–235, 238
See also "Ałbianos"; "Šahak I" and "II"; "Varazdat"; "Yusik II."

Zgōn, See "Yakob of Mcbin."

Zik ‹ MIr. *Zīk*; Gk. Ζηκᾶς, Ζιγ, Ζικ(?)
Attested (?) in ŠKZ, Parth 22, 24, 26; Phl. 28, 30, 32, *Zyk*; RGDS nos. 54, 63, pp. 64–65, 70–71, *Ζιγ, Ζικ*.
One of the great families of Iran, though Justi, following Men. Prot. (I, p. 374), derives the name from its office. Both Hübschmann and Christensen, however, see Menander's identification of Zik as a title as another case of the common confusion in classical sources between the name of an Iranian family and its office (see, e.g., Sūrēn). In Armenia, both the Greek version of Agatʿangełos (Ag, vi, viii) and BP treat the term as a proper name (cf. Theoph. Sim., III.xviii.7–10).
Presumably three members of the family, none of whose names is mentioned, are referred to in BP: (1) the Persian commander killed in the war against Aršak II (IV.xxxv–xxxvi). (2) Another Persian commander sent together with the Karēn by Šāhpuhr II to capture the Armenian royal fortress of Artagers. He was entrusted with the government of Armenia after the Persian occupation of the country and was eventually killed by the *sparapet* Mušeł Mamikonean after the return of King Pap to Armenia (IV.lv, lviii; V.i). This Zik has been identified with the Cylaces to whom AM (XXVII.xii.5–6, 9, 14) attributes the capture of Artogerassa/Artagers, and who was executed by Pap on his return to Armenia (XXX.i.3). This identification has, however, been rejected (see IV.lv n. 3). (3) The representative of the Persian king sent as an adviser to King Xosrov III/IV at the time of the partition of Armenia (IV.i).
See Gignoux, *Glossaire*, p. 39; *idem*, NPS, no. 1086, p. 195, *Ziyak*; Back, SSI, p. 227; Sprengling, *Third-Century Iran*, pp. 9, 11–12, 18–19; Honigmann and

Maricq, RGDS, pp. 16, 18; HAnjB, II, p. 208; JIN, p. 385 no. 2; AG, p. 41 no. 72; Markwart, *Untersuchungen*, pp. 213–214; Christensen, *L'Iran*, p. 105 n. 3; Adontz, *Armenia* pp. 507–509 n. 22.

IV.xxxv–xxxvi, lv, lviii; V.i; VI.i

pp. 162, 173, 178, 186, 233

See also "Aršak II"; "Karēn"; "Mušeł"; "Šapuh"; "Xosrov III/IV"; and Appendix II, "Artagers."

Zort‘

Presumably a bishop and collaborator of St. Nersēs. His see is not mentioned, since he is said to have been attached to the household of the patriarch. He is not otherwise attested.

See HAnjB, II, p. 215; JIN, p. 387.

VI.v

p. 235

See also "Nersēs I."

Zort‘uaz

Bishop of Vanand according to BP, who praises him highly. He is not otherwise attested.

See HAnjB, II, p. 215; JIN, p. 387, *Zorthovaz*.

VI.xii

p. 238

See also Appendix II, "Vanand."

Zruanduxt ‹ Phl. *Zurwān*, "time/the god of time" + *duxt* "daughter"

Name Zurvān-dād attested in ŠKZ, Parth. 28; Phl. 35; RGDS, no. 67, pp. 72–73.

Queen of eastern Armenia as wife of King Xosrov III/IV. According to BP, she was a Sasanian princess, probably the daughter of Šāhpuhr II and the sister of Šāhpuhr III. Toumanoff, however, makes her a member of the Zik house. She is not otherwise attested.

See Gignoux, NPS, nos. 1089–1092, pp. 195–196; Schmitt, IN, p. 331; Sprengling, *Third-Century Iran*, pp. 9, 12, 19; Honigmann and Maricq, RGDS, p. 18; HAnjB, II, p. 220; JIN, p. 337, *Zrovanduxt* no. 1; Toumanoff, *Manuel*, p. 76/11; AG, p. 42 no. 76; CPD, p. 29, *duxt*.

VI.i

p. 233

See also "Šapuh"; "Sasanians"; "Xosrov III/IV"; "Zik."

Zuit‘

Priest of Artašat and disciple of St. Nersēs. He was captured by the Persians at the time of the sack of the Armenian capital by the Sasanians (IV.lv) and subsequently martyred in Persia. MX, III.xxxv (= MK, pp. 293–294), attributes Zuit‘'s martyrdom to the calumnies of Meružan Arcruni and Vahan Mamikonean, but they are not mentioned in BP's account. T‘A I.x p. 64 (= *Thom. Arts.*, pp. 128–129) follows the version of MX and also calls the priest Zuit‘ay.

See HAnjB, II, p. 216.

IV.lv–lvi

pp. 175, 177

See also "Nersēs I"; and Appendix II, "Artašat."

Appendix II: Toponymy

Armenian medieval geography still presents considerable difficulties, so that numerous identifications and suggestions must of necessity remain tentative or even impossible at this point, despite the major work of H. Hübschmann, J. Markwart, and more recently S. T. Eremyan, Tᶜ. X. Hakobyan, and R. H. Hewsen, as well as a number of others.

The seventh-century *Ašχarhacᶜoycᶜ* has been consulted despite its semi-synthetic or even occasionally fictional character, and despite the fact that it is obviously anachronistic for fourth-century Armenia, because it is the most familiar and often the most accessible source for Armenian medieval geography. Similarly, two of its major divisions of medieval Armenia—Turuberan and Vaspurakan—are mentioned only for the sake of convenience, because of their familiarity, even though neither toponym was known to BP and indeed, these units did not exist in the fourth and fifth centuries. It goes without saying that the anachronisms of the *Ašχarhacᶜoycᶜ* and the required rectifications have been noted in the pertinent entries. In all references to the *Ašχarhacᶜoycᶜ*, the pagination has been given according to both the original text and the translation of the Soukry edition (e.g. 33/44).

On the highly problematic identification of the two southeastern Marches of the Armenian kingdom in the fourth century—(1) the Assyrian March or Greater Kordukᶜ, situated in the middle of Armenia's southern border and presumably composed of the districts of (Lesser) Kordukᶜ, Kord(r)ikᶜ, and Tmorikᶜ; (2) the Adiabenian or Median March, presumably called Noširakan in BP, lying east of the preceding one and composed of the districts of Dassəntrē/Dasn, Mahkertun, and Nihorakan—I have followed the recent, and soon to be published, research of Professor Robert Hewsen, "Vitaxates," which he kindly made available to me. Some conclusions must perforce remain tentative because of the confusion of the sources and the contradictions between the evidence of BP and that of the later *Ašχarhacᶜoycᶜ*. In view of the complicated nature of the evidence concerning these areas, all the entries on the districts composing either one of these Marches might perhaps benefit from being consulted as a unit.

In the case of toponyms containing a personal name listed in Appendix I, the etymology of the name has not been repeated here. On the typically Iranian endings of a large portion of Armenian toponyms (*-apat, -aran, -(a)šat, -(a)stan, -kert,* etc., see Schmitt, "Iranisches Lehngut," pp. 101, 107–108; Leroy, "Suffixes," pp. 517-521; Hübschmann, "Namen"; Nöldeke, "Ortsnamen." For the suffixes *-awan* and *-gewl, see* Appendix III.

As in all other cases, the spelling given for toponyms is the one found in the text. The Armenian forms of toponyms, i.e. Mcbin rather than Nisibis, have been adopted, with a few obvious exceptions, e.g. Athens, Caesarea, Egypt, and the like. All variants have duly been noted in both cases.

The forms Artagers and Ekełeacᶜ for the respective toponyms have been preferred, as the only ones attested, to the bookish reconstructions Artagerkᶜ and Ekełikᶜ.

Purely Scriptural (e.g. the church of "Macedonia") or literary ("Chaldaean" spells) references have been omitted here and are discussed in the pertinent notes in the Commentary.

Acuł, see "Dalarik'."

Adiabene, see "Noširakan."

Adiabenian March, see "Noširakan."

Ægyptos, see "Egypt."

Agarak

Vineyard in Aštišat where the sons of the patriarch Yusik, Pap and At'anaginēs, were buried, presumably as members of the Gregorid family, since Aštišat was a patriarcal property, but as unworthy to share the tombs of their ancestors at T'ordan or T'il because of their sins. This property may also be the one in which the patriarch P'aŕēn was buried (III.xvi). This toponym is not otherwise attested and may consequently be nothing more than a common noun.

III.xvi?, xix.

pp. [92], 94

See also "Aštišat"; "T'il"; "T'ordan"; Appendix I, "At'anaginēs"; "Pap (2)"; "P'aŕēn"; and Appendix III, *agarak*.

Akilisenē, see "Ekełeac'."

Albania, see "Ałuank'."

Ałck', see "Ałjk'."

Aleksandria, see "Alexandria."

Alexandria of Egypt/Aleksandria

The capital of Egypt and major city of the East is mentioned by BP only in passing to identify the heresiarch Arius.

See Stengel, "Alexandria"; Jones, *Cities*, pp. 299, 302–304, 306, 310–311, 330–331, etc.

III.x

p. 79

Ałiorsk' ‹ ?Arm. (or possibly pre- Arm.) *ał*, "salt" + *orsk'*, "hunt"

Hunting preserve presumably in the district of Apahunik' at the foot of Neχ Masis (mod. Sip'an daği). It is referred to as a *k'ałak'*, but as Malχasyanc' correctly observes (pp. 318–319 n. 47), the term is used in this context in its original meaning of a "walled enclosure." Melik'-Ōhanĵanyan argued that this toponym is purely symbolic, but see III.xx n. 12.

See AON, p. 396; Ep'rikean, *Baŕaran*, p. 101.

III.xx

p. 96

Map, F/7?

See also "Apahunik'"; "Masis"; and Appendix III, *k'ałak'*.

Ałiovit/Ałoyhovit ‹ ?Arm. *ał*, "salt" + *hovit*, "valley"

Thirteenth district of Turuberan according to the *Ašχarhac'oyc'* (31/42), and eighth district of Vaspurakan (*ibid.*, 32/43). It originally seems to have consisted of two contiguous districts of which the eastern one is considered by Eremyan to have been an Aršakuni royal domain, since MX, II.xxii (= MK, p. 159), claims that junior members of the royal family were settled there. The city of Zarišat must have been located in this portion, since MX calls it a "royal city" (III.xxiii = MK, p. 279), as well as the royal fisheries at Aṙest. This portion subsequently became a part of Vaspurakan under the name of Aṙberan (*Ašχarhac῾oyc῾*, 32/43). The western portion, lying NNE of Lake Van and including the city of Arčēš on the north shore of the lake apparently formed the domain of the Gnuni house. It was lost to the Muslims when the Gnuni moved to Taykʿ, and the territory was acquired by the Kʿaǰberuni house, which gave its name to it. BP (IV.lv) treats both parts as a single *gawaṙ*.

> See AON, pp. 329, 396; Eremyan, *Ašχarh., pp. 33, 116; idem, Map* G/5, where he puts Zarišat in the western portion; Hewsen, "Armenia," p. 328; Toumanoff, *Studies*, pp. 205–206; Adontz, *Armenia*, pp. 240, 243, 245–246, 358, 459 n. 54, 522 n. 79, 119*, 124*, 143*; Tʿ. X. Hakobyan, *Ašχarhagrutʿyun*, p. 156.
>
> IV.lv
> p. 176
> Maps, G/6-7
> See also "Aṙest"; "Zarišat"; Appendix I, "Aršakuni"; "Gnuni, house"; and Appendix III, *gawaṙ*.

Aljkʿ/Alckʿ

Village in the district of Aragacotn, to which the Aršakuni royal necropolis was transferred after the Persian sack of their earlier burial place at Ani in Daranalikʿ, according to both BP and MX, III.xxvii (= MK, pp. 282–283). Ruins of an early basilica and a hypogeum with arcosolia intended for sarcophagi are still found at the site. The latter are decorated with reliefs of hunting scenes symbolizing the king's "glory" (*pʿarkʿ*) and "valor" (*kʿaǰutʿiwn*).

> See AON, pp. 397–398; Eremyan, *Map* B/6; Gandolfo, "Martyrium," p. 117; B. N. Arákʿelyan, *Paterakʿandaknerə*, pp. 28–32, fig. 60; Mnatsakanian, "Usipal'nitsy," pp. 19–20; Kʿalantʿaryan, "Glinianye plitki."
>
> IV.xxiv
> p. 158
> Maps, G/5
> See also "Ani"; Appendix I, "Aršakuni"; and Appendix III, *pʿarkʿ*; *kʿaǰutʿiwn*.

Aljnikʿ; Gk. ᾿Αρζανηνή Lat. Arzanena; Syr. Arzōn; Arabian March

Third region of Greater Armenia, according to the *Ašχarhac῾oyc῾* (30–31/41), known to classical sources as Arzanēnē or Arzanena (see, e.g., AM, XXV.vii.9; Procopius, *Bell. Pers.*, I.viii.21, II.xv.7, etc.). Aljnikʿ lay in southern Armenia, forming the westernmost or Arabian March of the Aršakuni kingdom (cf. Aa, dccclxxiii, "*sahmanakaln . . . yAruastan kolmanēn*"), and was separated from Aruastan by the Tigris River, though Dilleman questioned its strategic importance in the defense of the Aršakuni kingdom. It passed to the Roman sphere of influence as a result of the Peace of Nisibis of 298 (Patr. Patric., *Ad. gent.*, iii, p. 135) and was retroceded to Persia by Jovian's peace of 363 (AM, XXV.vii.9). According to BP (V.xvi), it was briefly reconquered by Musēl Mamikonean but was lost again with the partition of Greater Armenia ca. 387.

Like all the four Marches of the Armenian kingdom in the fourth century, Aljnikʿ was ruled by a *bdeašχ*, who, however, had precedence over not only the other magnates of the realm but his other three colleagues as well, and was consequently known as the "great *bdeašχ*" (see III.ix n. 2). The late and semi-fictional *Zōrnamak*, "Military List," attributes to him the disproportionately large number of 4,000 retainers. His name is curiously absent from the *Gahnamak*, "Rank List," perhaps because Aljnikʿ had by then long since ceased to be considered part of Armenia, though its ruler is still referred to as *bdeašχ* in the fifth century by ŁP^c, xxxiii, p. 63 (= *Ełishē*, p. 277). The equivocal position of semi-autonomous Ałjnik^c vis-à-vis the Aršakuni kingdom is reflected in BP, which identifies it as a "district" (*gawaṙ*; III.xiv, IV.xxiv), a "land" (*erkir*; IV.xxviii, V.xvi, xxvii), a "region" (*kołmn*; IV.l), and a "border" (*sahman*; IV.xxviii), variations that probably also reflect the changing status of the area and its loss to the Persians. The *bdeašχ* Bakur is treated as a traitor to his lord the king of Armenia and his domain forfited, yet it returned to his son Xeša (III.ix). The same ambiguity seems to have applied to the bishop of Ałjnik^c, who obeyed the summons of King Aršak II yet seems to have lain outside the Armenian episcopate (IV.xv). The presence of the bishop of Arzōn or Beθ Arzōn is also recorded in the conciliar lists of the Nestorian church of Persia as early as 410.

See AON, pp. 248–251, 305–322; Eremyan, *Ašχarh.*, pp. 33–34 and *Map* G/4–D/4; Hewsen, "Vitaxates"; Baumgartner and Streck, "Arzanene"; T^c. X. Hakobyan, *Ašχarhagrut'yun*, pp. 218–227 and map; Honigmann, *Ostgrenze*, pp. 22–24, 32–34; Marquart, *Ērānšahr*, pp. 25, 114, 162–163, 165–166, 169, 178; *idem, Südarmenien*, pp. 89–90, 115–116, 119–122, 215–220, 352–354, 357, 373–374; Adontz, *Armenia*, pp. 10–13, 172–173, 175, 182, 224–226, 230, 257, 375 n. 4, 391 nn. 25–26, 143*; Toumanoff, *Studies*, pp. 129, 131–133, 149–150, 159–160, 162–163, 165, 166 n. 63, 179–182, 183 n. 147, 240, 244–245, 304–305, 318, 468 n. 138; Dilleman, *Haute-Mésopotamie*, pp. 121–128; *Syn. Or.*, pp. 272, 274, 285, 311, 617, 666–667, etc.

III.ix, xiv; IV.xvi, xx, xxiv, xxviii, l; V.xvi, xxvii
pp. 76–77, 88, 90, 146, 150, 157, 160, 167, 201, 207
Maps, D–E/8
See also "Aruestan"; "Baṙaeǰ"; "Miǰnašχarh Hayoc^c"; "Tigranakert"; Appendix I, "Aršak II"; "Bakur"; "Epip^can"; "Mušeł"; "Vałinak I"; "Xeša"; and Appendix III, *bdeašχ; erkir; gawar; kołmn; sahman.*

Ałoyhovit, see "Ałiovit."

Ałt^camar
Island off the southern shore of Lake Van. It is given as part of Vaspurakan by the *Ašχarhac^coyc^c* (32/43) but is included in the domain of the Ṙštuni in the fourth century by both BP and MX, III.xv (= MK, p. 269). In the tenth century it became the domain of the Arcruni kings of Vaspurakan under Gagik I (T^cA Cont., IV.vii, viii and for the later history of the site IV.xii, pp. 292–299, 308, 312–315 [Cont. II], 319–322, 325 = *Thom. Arts.*, pp. 354–361, 371, 375–379, 381–384, 385).

See AON, p. 339; Eremyan, *Ašχarh.*, p. 33; *idem, Map* G/5; Der Nersessian, *Ałt^camar*; T^c. X. Hakobyan, *Ašχarhagrut'yun*, pp. 166–167.
III.viii
p. 76
Maps F/7–8
See also Appendix I, "Ṙštuni, house."

Ałuank^c ‹ Parth. Ardān, Phl. Ar(r)ān?; Gk. 'Αλβανία; Lat. Albania; Caucasian Albania
Attested in ŠKZ, Parth, 2; RGDS, no. 3, pp. 48–49; KKZ, 12, though Ulubabyan has argued for a change in the content of the term.
Kingdom to the northeast of Armenia and east of Virk^c/Iberia, lying between the Kur River and the Caucasus range to the Caspian Sea, according to the *Ašχarac^coyc^c* (28–29/39), which also calls it Albania and Ṙan (40/53). The name of Albania, derived from the tribe of the Albanoi, was known to Strabo (*Geogr.*, XI.i.5; ii.15; iii.2, 5; iv),

Ptolemy (V.xi) and Pliny (NH VI.xi, 29; xv, 36, 38–39). The Iranian forms Ardān, Ařān, Řan are attested in MX, II.viii (= MK, pp. 139–140), and Zach. Rhet. (II.vii).

From the first to the fifth centuries Ałuankᶜ formed an independent Aršakuni kingdom with its own language and Kapałak as its capital; BP invariably recognizes this royal status and usually refers to Ałuankᶜ as an *ašχarh*, though it also uses the term *erkir* (V.xiv). Ałuankᶜ was evangelized by St. Gregory the Illuminator's grandson Grigoris, according to BP (III.v–vi), and remained within the orbit of the Armenian church. According to Koriwn, xvii, p. 70 (= trans. p. 41), it received its alphabet in the fifth century from St. Maštocᶜ, the creator of the Armenian alphabet. Aa, xix makes the Ałuankᶜ allies of Armenia, as does MX, I.xix, II.xxii, III.liv (= MK, pp. 119, 159, 321–322), the last taken from Koriwn, but cf. II.lxxxiv–lxxxv, III.iii, vi (= MK, pp. 236–237, 256, 259). In the fourth century, AM (XVIII.vi.22; XIX.ii.3) presents the Ałuankᶜ as allies of Šāhpuhr II against the Romans in 359, as does BP (V.iv) in 369–370. The eastern marchlands south of the Kur River were disputed between Armenia and Ałuankᶜ. The Armenian *sparapet* Mušeł Mamikonean successfully reconquered them ca. 370, thus pushing the Armenian border northward to the Kur River (V.xiii), but the marchlands reverted to Ałuankᶜ after the partition of Greater Armenia ca. 387. Around 510, the ruling dynasty of Ałuankᶜ was suppressed by the Sasanians, and the country was ruled by a Persian *marzpan* residing at Partaw. The dynasty of the Mihranids of Gardman was, however, reestablished as "presiding princes" with Byzantine support in 628 and continued to rule under Arab suzerainty until 821, when the principality of Ałuankᶜ ceased to exist as an autonomous unit.

See Eremyan, *Ašχarh.*, pp. 34, 120; *idem, Map* B/6–8; Trever, *Albania*; Muraviev, "Ptolemeeva Karta"; Anasyan, "Ałuankᶜ"; A. Š. Mnacᶜakanyan, *Ałvankᶜ*; Hewsen, "Arcᶜaχ," pp. 48ff.; *idem*, "Albania"; Ulubabyan, "Albania"; Tomaschek, "Albania"; Bartold, "Arrān"; Iushkov, "Albania"; Aliev, "Albania"; Novosel'tsev, "Politicheskaia granitsa"; Marquart, *Ērānšahr*, pp. 116–120; Adontz, *Armenia*, pp. 7–8, 167, 170–176, 229–230, 318, 324, 90*–91*, 109*–111*, 117*, 123*–125*, 142*; Toumanoff, *Manuel*, pp. 79–80; *idem, Studies*, pp. 58–59, 83, 101–102, 132, 153, 257–259; Dumézil, "Les Albaniens"; Garitte, *Documents*, pp. 195–196; Shanidze, "Novootkityĭ alfavit"; Gignoux, *Glossaire*, pp. 15, 45; Sprengling, *Third-Century Iran*, pp. 7, 14, 47, 52; Honigmann and Maricq, RGDS, pp. 11, 40, 88–94 on the Albanian gates.

III.v–vi; V.iv–v, xiii, xxxv
pp. 70, 72–73, 189–190, 193–194, 200, 216
Maps I, H–L/2–5; II, H–L/2–7
See also "Gardman"; "Kazbkᶜ"; "Kołtᶜn"; "Kur"; "Šakašēn"; "Utikᶜ"; "Virkᶜ"; Appendix I, "Aršakuni"; "Grigoris"; "Mušeł"; "Uřnayr"; and Appendix III, *ašχarh*; *erkir*.

Amaras, see "Amaraz."

Amaraz/Amaras

Locality and subsequently monastery at the site where St. Grigoris was buried after his martyrdom. MX, III.iii (= MK, p. 256), calls it a "town" (*awan*) and locates it in Lesser Siwnikᶜ (*Pᶜokᶜr Siwnikᶜ*), while BP refers to it as a mere "village" (*gewł*) and places it in the district of Haband, an identification subsequently repeated by MK/D, I.xiv, pp. 35, 39 (= MD, p. 23). By this time Amaraz, which had become a center for pilgrimages, had apparently grown to the size of a *komopolis* (*gewłakᶜałakᶜ*). The seventh-century *Ašχarhacᶜoycᶜ* (33/44) records two Habands, one in Siwnikᶜ and the other, *Miws*, "the Other" Haband in Arcᶜaχ, farther east on the border of Caucasian Albania, of which it became a part by the seventh century. It is in this second district that Amaraz, the complex of which is known north of the lower Araxes, should be located in the opinion of Eremyan, as earlier by Hübschmann.

See AON, pp. 348–350; Eremyan, *Ašχarh.*, p. 34; *idem, Map* G/7; Hewsen, "Armenia," p. 341; Tʿ. X. Hakobyan, *Ašχarhagrutʿyun*, P. 234; Hasratyan, "Amaras," for the remains of the shrine.

III.vi

p. 73

Maps, J–K/5–6

See also "Haband"; and Appendix I, "Grigoris."

Amid/kʿalakʿ Amdacʿwocʿ; Gk. Ἀμίδα; Lat. Amida; Ar. Diyārbakir

One of the main centers of Upper Mesopotamia. Amida stood on the west bank of the Tigris, near the border of the southern Armenian district of Ałjnikʿ. At the surrender of Nisibis to the Persians by the peace of 363, many of the Christian inhabitants of the city fled to Amida, taking with them the relics of St. James of Nisibis, as well as to Edessa, thus increasing these cities' importance. The city of Amida maintained its position until the settlement of the Arab Bakr tribe in the district toward the end of the seventh century altered its demographic configuration, and the name of both the city and its district was changed to Diyārbakr/ Diyārbākir, "the house of the Bakr." As in the case of all the important Greek *poleis* in the east, BP refers to Amida as a *kʿalakʿ*, "city."

See Eremyan, *Ašχarh.*, p. 35; *idem, Map* D/4; Ter Ghewondyan, *Arab Emirates*, pp. 25–27; EI², pp. 343–345.

III.x

p. 80

Maps, B–C/8

See also "Ałjnikʿ"; Appendix I, "Yakob of Mcbin"; and Appendix III, *kʿalakʿ*.

Amida, see "Amid."

Amōkʿ

Village in the district of Ayrarat presumably forming part of St. Nersēs's domain. It is not otherwise attested, and Inčičean merely cites the reference in BP without further identification.

See Inčičean, *Storagrutʿiwn*, p. 507

VI.vi

p. 235

See also "Ayrarat."

Andməš, see "Anyuš."

Angeł, see "Angł."

Angelenē, see "Angełtun."

Angełtun/Ankeł tun; ‹ Arm. *Angeł* + *tun*, "house"; Gk. Ἰγγιληνή Lat. Ingilena/Angelena

District of former Sophēnē, between Anjit/Anzitēnē and Copʿkʿ Mec/Sophanēnē, known as Ingilena in the legislation of Justinian (CJ I.xviiii.5). It is not known to the *Ašχaracʿoycʿ*, which probably subsumed it under Anjit, the homonymous princes of which apparently ruled Angełtun as well. Eremyan, however, makes the improbable suggestion that it was part of Ałjnikʿ. The center of the district was the great fortress of Angł (see next entry). Angełtun passed to the Roman sphere of influence as one of the autonomous Satrapies ceded by Persia under the terms of the Peace of Nisibis of 298 (Petr. Patric., *Ad gen.*, iii, p. 135; the text reads "Intēlēnē"). Its homonymous princes are not mentioned by BP, which refers only to princes of Anjit and uses Angełtun exclusively as a toponym. They are, however, known under the name of princes of

Angełtun to Aa, dccxcv, dccclxxiii, the *Primary History*, Sebēos p. 51 (= MK, p. 362), and MX, I.xxiii, II.viii (= MK, pp. 113, 141), who gives them a dubious Haykid ancestry, though they were of probable Orontid descent, according to Toumanoff. They are not included in the *Gahnamak,* "Rank List," but are attributed 3,400 retainers by the *Zōrnamak,* "Military List," which makes them the commanders of the "Western Gate." The late *Vita* of St. Nersēs, v, pp. 32–33 (= CHAMA, II, p. 25), lists both "Angełeank^(c)" and "Anjteayk^(c)." Bishops from the district are also recorded from the time of St. Gregory the Illuminator (Vg, clxxi = Va, clix).

Under Aršak II, the major fortresses of the district were governed by the *mardpet* as a royal official (V.vii), and BP refers to it as a "royal domain" (*tan gawar,* V.vii; *ostan ark^(c)uni,* V.xviii), probably for that reason. The position of the district after the peace of 363 is unclear. It may have defected to the Romans along with other border districts, or may have been Roman all along except for the Armenian royal fortresses, and Adontz has argued that it always remained loyal. In any case, it was reconquered by Mušeł Mamikonean ca. 370 (V.xviii), and the treatment it received differed from that of the other reconquered territories (see V.xviii n. 2). This reconquest did not prove permanent, and in 536 Angełtun together with Anjit/Anzetēnē became part of the new Byzantine province of Armenia IV created by Justinian (*Novellae,* xxxi).

See AON, 219, 227–228, 230, 302–305; Eremyan, *Ašχarh.,* pp. 35, 116; *idem, Map* G/3–4; Hewsen, "Armenia," p. 327; T^(c). X. Hakobyan, *Ašχarhagrut^(c)yun,* pp. 216–217 and map; Adontz, *Armenia,* pp. 27, 34–35, 193, 197–198, 201, 205, 223–225, 230, 232, 257, 320, 356, 370, 68*, 70*, 143*; Toumanoff, *Studies,* pp. 131, 137, 138 n. 240, 166–179 (where he follows Markwart in making the princes of Angełtun *bdeašχs* of the Arabian March instead of the princes of Ałjnik^(c)), 218, 223–224, 227, 236, 244–245, 297, 299–304; Marquart, *Ērānšahr,* pp. 165–167, 170–172, 177–178; Garitte, *Documents,* pp. 102–104, for the evangelization of the district.

IV.xxiii–xxiv; V.vii, xviii
pp. 156–157, 198, 201
Maps, B–C/7–8
See also "Ałjnik^(c)"; "Anjit"; "Cop^(c)k^(c)"; and the next entry; Appendix I, "Aršakuni"; "Drastamat"; "Grigor"; "Mušeł"; and Appendix III, *gawar; mardpet; ostan; tun.*

Angł/Angeł; Gk. Ἀρταγίγαρτα

Major royal fortress and center of the later district of Angełtun, to which it gave its name. It should probably be identified with the Artagigarta of Ptolemy (V.xii.10) but should not be confused with the Anglon of Procopius (*Bell. Pers.,* II.xxv.15), which was in the district of Całkotn. Angł stood at the site of the modern village of Eğil on the right bank of the western Tigris (Arghana-su), near its confluence with the Dibene-su. It is already attested in the Hittite records of the fourteenth century B.C. under the form Ingilawa and should probably be identified with the capital of the kingdom of Sophēnē Arkathiokerta/Karkathiokerta, known to Strabo (XI.xiv.2) and Pliny the Elder (NH, VI.x.26), although both Adontz and Lehmann-Haupt place it elsewhere. The necropolis located at Angł probably belonged to the earlier kings of Sophēnē according to Markwart, rather than to the Aršakuni, as claimed by BP (IV.xxiv), because on its own evidence, the Aršakuni necropolis had first been located at Ani in Daranałik^(c) and had subsequently been moved to Ałjk^(c) in the second half of the fourth century. In the period of Aršak II it was governed by the *mardpet* in the name of the king (V.vii).

See AON, p. 399; Eremyan, *Ašχarh.,* p. 35; *idem, Map* G/4; Hewsen, "Ptolemy," pp. 142–143; *idem,* "Orontid," pp. 358, 360; Adontz, *Armenia,* pp. 35, 271, 456 n. 21, 186*; Markwart, *Südarmenien,* pp. 33–38, 107–112; Dilleman, *Haute-Mésopotamie,* pp. 120–121; Manandyan, *Trade and Cities,* pp. 33–35, 205 n. 24;

Toumanoff, *Studies*, pp. 131, 167, 176–179, 297–299, 310; Sargsyan, *Hellenistakan Hayastanə*, p. 64; Yovhannēsean, HB, pp. 684–687.
IV.xxiv; V.vii
pp. 157, 198
Maps, C/7-8
See also "Ałjk^{cc}"; "Angełtun"; "Ani"; "Cop‘k‘"; and Appendix I, "Aršakuni"; "Drastamat."

Ani in Daranałik‘

Ani in Daranałik‘, which should not be confused with the homonymous Kamsarakan fortress and subsequent Bagratuni capital in Širak, stood on the site of the modern Kemah on the Upper Euphrates. It was an ancient fortress and holy city, identified by Eremyan as the main city of Armenia Minor (second and first centuries B.C.), and should probably be identified with the Athua (*Anua) of Ptolemy (V.xii.8). Ani was known to Aa, dcclxxxv, and to MX, II.xii, xiv, liii (= MK, pp. 149, 152, 196), who claimed that a shrine of Ahura Mazda, identified with Olympian Zeus, was located there and that he had used its temple histories (II.xlviii, lxvi = MK, pp. 189 and n. 5, 212). All three historians, Aa, dcclxxxv; BP (III.xi, IV.xxiv), and MX, III.x, xxvii (= MK, pp. 263, 282), are familiar with Ani as the Armenian royal necropolis until its destruction by the Persians.

See AON, pp. 284, 287; Eremyan, *Ašχarh.*, pp. 35–36; *idem, Map* G/3; Hewsen, "Ptolemy," pp. 126–127, 149; Adontz, *Armenia*, pp. 40, 47, 187*; Toumanoff, *Studies*, p. 105 and n. 160; Sargsyan, *Hellenistakan Hayastanə*, pp. 62–64; Yovhannēsean, HB, pp. 14–18; Markwart, "Parskahayk‘," pp. 285–286; Honigmann, *Ostgrenze*, pp. 56–57.
III.xi; IV.xxiv
pp. 81, 157
Maps, A–B/5-6
See also "Ałjk‘"; "Angł"; and Appendix I, "Aršakuni."

Anjewac‘ik‘

Eleventh district of Vaspurakan encompassing the sources of the Bohtan-su, according to the *Ašχarhac‘oyc‘* (32/43). The homonymous dynasts are recorded in all the Lists of *naχarars*, with the *Zōrnamak*, "Military List," attributing 500 retainers to them. The *Gahnamak*, "Rank List," also includes a secondary cadet line, and bishops from the district are included in the Armenian conciliar lists (ŁP‘, xxiii, p. 44; Ełišē p. 28 = *Ełishē*, pp. 82, 258; GT‘; pp. 42, 146, 149, 151, etc.).

See AON, pp. 343–344; Eremyan, *Ašχarh.*, pp. 36, 117; *idem, Map* D/5; Hewsen, "Armenia," p. 331; T‘. X. Hakobyan, *Ašχarhagrut‘yun*, p. 172 and map; Adontz, *Armenia*, pp. 175, 188, 192, 195, 200, 201, 205, 207, 228, 247–248, 250, 256, 258–259, 442 n. 20, 446 n. 34, 67*, 69*–70*, 72*, 76*, 77*, 80*, 82*, 93*–96*, 98*, 100*, 120*, 125*, 144*; Toumanoff, *Studies*, pp. 110 n. 73, 132, 135 (with an erratum on the number of retainers), 198–199, 200, 226, 228, 230 n. 278, 231, 240, 245, 247–248, 252; Oskean, *Usumnasirut‘iwnner*, pp. 41–75.
III.xii; IV.xi; V.vi, xxxii
pp. 82, 133, 196, 214
Maps F–G/8
See also Appendix I, "Gnel"; "Šahēn."

Anjit/Hanjit; Gk. Ἀνζιτηνή Lat. Anzitena; Ar. Hanjīt ‹ Assyr. Enzitu

Sixth district of Cop‘k‘ or Armenia IV, according to the *Ašχarhac‘oyc‘* (30/40). It occupied the plain of Xarberd (mod. Harput) and reached as far as the Euphrates.

Originally part of Cop^{c}k^c/Sophēnē, where it is first identified by classical sources, it separated from it, splitting it into Cop^{c}k^c Mec/Sophanēnē and Cop^{c}k^c Šahēi/Sophēnē.

Anjit passed into the Roman sphere of influence, probably together with the rest of Sophēnē, as a result of the Roman–Persian Peace of Nisibis in 298 (Petr. Patric., *Ad gen.*, iii, p. 135). The homonymous princes of Anjit, who seem to have ruled adjacent Angełtun as well, presumably maintained some independence vis-à-vis the Aršakuni crown. They originally held the hereditary office of *hazarapet*, which they lost to the Gnuni (III.xii, IV.ii), and BP (V.l) presents their siding with the Romans after the peace of 363 as an act of defection from their lord, King Aršak II. Anjit, along with Angełtun, was apparently reconquered temporarily by Mušeł Mamikonean ca. 370 (V. xviii–xix), but it presumably reverted to the empire after the partition of Greater Armenia ca. 387 and became part of the new Byzantine province of Armenia IV in 536 under the reorganization of Justinian (*Novella* xxxi). The princes of Anjit are still included in the List of *naχarars* found in the *Vita* of St. Nersēs, v, p. 33 (= CHAMA, II, p. 25) together with those of Angełtun, but they are missing from both the *Gahnamak*, "Rank List" and the *Zořnamak*, "Military List," though they may have been subsumed under Angeł-tun in the latter. BP (V.xix) refers to it as a *gawař*.

> See AON, pp. 300–302; Eremyan, *Ašχarh.*, pp. 36, 116; *idem*, *Map* G/3; Hewsen, "Armenia," p. 327; T^c. X. Hakobyan, *Ašχarhagrut^{c}yun*, pp. 214–215 and map; Adontz, *Armenia*, pp. 26–29, 31–33, 107, 134, 137, 201, 387 nn. 7–10, 2* 53*, 74*, 114*, 118*, 124*, 144*; Toumanoff, *Studies*, pp. 131, 137, 138 n. 240, 170–171 and n. 88, 176, 178–179, 205, 218, 223, 227, 236, 240–241, 244–245, 303–304.
> III.xii; IV.xxiv, l; V.xix
> pp. 82, 157, 167, 201
> Maps, B/7
> See also "Angełtun"; "Cop^{c}k^c"; Appendix I, "Aršak II"; "Aršakuni"; "Gnuni, house"; "Mušeł"; "Sałamut"; "Vałarš"; and Appendix III, *gawař, hazarapet*.

Ankeł tun, see "Angełtun."

Ankurac^{c}woc^c k^{c}ałak^c, see "Ankyra."

Ankyra/Ankurac^{c}woc^c k^{c}ałak^c; Gk.῎Ανκυρα; Lat. Ancyra; mod. Ankara

City in the province of Galatia in central Anatolia. It is referred to in BP only in connection with Aršak II's unattested raid on the Byzantine Empire. In keeping with the practice throughout the text for classical *poleis*, it is identified as a "city" (k^{c}ałak^c).

> See Tomaschek, "Ankyra"; Jones, *Cities*, pp. 110–111, 117–119; Garsoïan, "Medi-aeval Armenian City," p. 70.
> IV.xi
> p. 133
> See also Appendix I, "Aršak II"; and Appendix III, *k^{c}ałak^c*.

Anuš, see "Anyuš."

Anyuš/Anuš/Andməš/Əndməš, "Castle of Oblivion"

Fortress in the Iranian district of Xužastan north-west of the Persian Gulf, where persons threatening the safety of the Sasanian state were confined. Its name of "Castle of Oblivion" was derived from the fact that neither the name of the prisoners nor of the castle itself might ever be mentioned (V.vii). BP is the only source to give the form Andməš, while MX, III.xxxv, lv (= MK, pp. 292–293, 323), calls it Anuš or Anyišeli. The castle was also known to Procopius (*Bell. Pers.*, I.v.7–8, 29, 40), who also calls it the "Castle of Oblivion" (φρούριον . . . τῆς Λήθης) and gives the same reason for its name, and to AM (XXVII.xii.3), who gives its name in the form Agabana. Its site is unidentified.

See AG, p. 19 no. 8; Christensen, *L'Iran*, p. 307.
IV.liv; V.v, vii.
pp. 173, 196–199
See also "Xužastan"; and Appendix I, "Aršak II"; "Drastamat."

Apahunik‘
Fourteenth district of Turuberan lying in the upper valley of the Euphrates–Arsanias (mod. Murad-su), according to the *Ašχarhac‘oyc‘* (31/42). Its center was Manazkert, north of Lake Van. BP refers to it as an *erkir*, "land" rather than a "district" (*gawaṙ*). MX, II.vii (= MK, p. 142), gives a Haykid ancestry to the homonymous princes of Apahunik‘, but they were probably of Urartian origin, according to Toumanoff. They are included in all the Lists of *naχarars*, and the *Zōrnamak*, "Military List," attributes 1,000 retainers to them. A secondary cadet line is also recorded in the *Gahnamak*, "Rank List," and the bishops of the district are included in the Armenian conciliar lists (ŁP‘, xxiii, p. 44; Ełišē, ii, p. 28 = *Ełishē*, pp. 82, 258; GT‘, p. 73).

See AON, pp. 328, 329–330; Eremyan, *Ašχarh.*, pp. 36, 116; *idem, Map* G/5; Hewsen, "Armenia," p. 328; T‘. X. Hakobyan, *Ašχarhagrut‘yun*, p. 156 and map; Adontz, *Armenia*, pp. 188, 192–193, 200, 202, 205, 207, 228, 370, 67*–68*, 71*–72*, 76*–79*, 93*–99*, 101*–102*, 119*, 124*, 143*; Toumanoff, *Studies*, pp. 110 n. 173, 132, 199, 223, 226, 230–231 and n. 278, 236, 240, 247, 248, 250–252.
III.xx
pp. 96–97
Maps, F–G/6–7
See also "Ałiorsk‘"; "Manazkert"; "Masis"; and Appendix III, *erkir; gawaṙ.*

Arabian March, see "Ałjnik‘."

Aragac, Mt.; Turk. Alagöz
Mountain in the region of Ayrarat, west of mod. Erevan, which gave its name to the adjoining district of Aragacotn, "foot of Aragac."
See Eremyan, *Ašχarh.*, p. 38; *idem, Map* B/6; Hewsen, "Armenia," p. 335.
IV.xxiv
p. 158
Maps, G/4–5

Ararat, see "Ayrarat"; "Sararad."

Aṙawiwtac‘ gewł, see "Aṙawiwtk‘."

Aṙawiwtk‘/Aṙawiwtac‘ gewł
Village presumably near Šahapivan in Całkotn. It is not otherwise attested or identified, though Eremyan places it in the district of Bagrewand, NE of Bagawan and north of the Euphrates–Arsanias (Murad-su).
See Eremyan, *Map* G/5.
IV.xv
p. 141
Maps, F/5–6?
See also "Bagrewand"; "Šahapivan."

Arc‘aχ, see "Arjaχ."

Ardeank‘, see "Ardeans."

Ardeans/Ardeank‘
Locality of some importance in the district of Ayrarat, since BP calls it *mec gewł*, "great/large village" and places a royal residence there. It is, however, otherwise unat-

tested, though Ep^crikean identifies it with the *ənǰin* in the same passage, which he takes to be a proper name (see V.vi n. 2). Eremyan locates it directly south of Artašat across the Araxes River.

See Ep^crikean, *Baŕaran*, p. 843; Eremyan, *Map* G/6; Sellwood, "Adiabene," pp. 456–458.

V.vi

p. 196

Maps, G–H/5–6?

See also "Artagers," for toponyms ending in *s*; "Artašat"; "Ayrarat."

Aŕest/Aŕestawan

Town in the district of eastern Aliovit, which was apparently a part of the Aršakuni royal domain. It was located in the extreme northeastern corner of Lake Van at the mouth of the Bendiman-su. The royal fisheries mentioned in BP are also recorded in the *Ašχarhac^coyc^c* (32/43) but in no other source, although ŁP^c III.lxx (= CHAMA, II, p. 332) refers to the locality as being sizable, for he calls it a *komopolis* (*k^calak^cagewł*). The name of the locality was presumably Aŕest, but the qualifying suffix -*awan*, "town" seems to have been frequently incorporated into it.

See AON, pp. 341, 402; Eremyan, *Ašχarh.*, p. 37; *idem, Map* G/5.

III.viii; IV.xxii

pp. 76, 155

Maps, F–G/7

See also "Aliovit"; Appendix I, "Aršakuni"; and Appendix III, *gelak^calak^c*.

Aŕestawan, see "Aŕest."

Aŕewc/Aŕiwc, "Lion," Mt.

Mountain located in the neighborhood of the district of Ekeleac^c, according to BP (V.xxv). Its relationship to the far western district of Aŕewc/Aliwn is uncertain, but Oskean identifies it with the mountain south of the plain of Erzincan. My attention was called to this reference by Dr. J.-M. Thierry, to whom I am most grateful.

See AON, pp. 284–285, 402; Cf. Eremyan, *Ašχarh.*, p. 33, *Aliwn*; Hewsen, "Armenia," p. 326; Oskean, *Barjr Hayk^c*, p. 82.

IV.iv; V.xxv

pp. 112, 205

Map I, B–C/6?

See also "Ekeleac^c."

Aŕiwc, see "Aŕewc."

Arjaχ/Arc^caχ

Tenth region of Greater Armenia composed of twelve districts, according to the *Ašχarhac^coyc^c* (29/40, 33/44), and subsequently known as Xač^cēn. It was a "rugged [*amur*]" district lying NE of Siwnik^c and should be identified with the Orχistēnē of Strabo (*Geogr.*, XI.xiv.4). As indicated in BP, this border region, comprized in the marchlands south of the Kur River, was disputed between Greater Armenia and Aluank^c in the fourth century. Under Aršak II it shifted to Aluank^c after the Roman–Persian peace of 363 (IV.l), was briefly reconquered by the *sparapet* Mušeł Mamikonean ca. 370 (V.xii), and passed again to Aluank^c after the partition of Greater Armenia ca. 387, as recorded by the *Ašχarhac^coyc^c* (33/44). Arjaχ is known to Ełišē, iv, vi, pp. 94, 125, 127 (= *Ełishē*, pp. 146, 177, 180), and to MK/D, II.xxxiv, p. 224 (= MD, p. 144, etc.), but not to the other early Armenian sources. BP refers to it as both a *kolm* (IV.l) and an *erkir* (V.xii).

See AON, pp. 266–267; Eremyan, *Ašχarh.*, pp. 41, 117; *idem, Map* B–G/7; Hewsen, "Armenia," pp. 332, 341; *idem,* "Arc'aχ," pp. 42–68; *idem, Artaxiad*s, p. 70; T'. X. Hakobyan, *Ašχarhagrut'yun*, pp. 233–235 and map.

IV.l; V.xii

pp. 167, 200

Maps, J–K/5–6.

See also "Ałuank'"; "Kur"; "Miǰnašχarh Hayoc'"; "Siwnik'"; Appendix I, "Aršak II"; "Mušeł"; and Appendix III, *amur.; erkir; kołmn.*

Armenia/Armenian, see "Mec Hayk'."

Armenia Maior, see "Mec Hayk'."

Armenian Midlands, see "Miǰnašχarh Hayoc'."

Arrān, see "Ałuank'."

Aršakawan ‹ Aršak + Arm. *-awan*, "town"

Foundation of Aršak II in the district of Kogovit and the only "city" founded in fourth-century Armenia, according to BP, despite MX's record of the shift of the Armenian capital to Duin in this period (III.viii = MK, p. 261). The facts that the city was named after its founder Aršak II and that it was to have contained a royal palace suggest that it was a foundation of Hellenistic eponymous type on the model of the numerous Alexandrias and Seleucias, or of the Armenian Artašat/Artaxata, Tigranakert, Vałaršapat, Zarehawan, and the like. BP traces its growth from a royal *dastakert* to a "town" (*awan*) and to a "city" (*k'ałak'*), the last of which may refer to its fortification rather than to its size, as it is also referred to as a *komopolis* (*gewłak'ałak'*; IV.xiii). The satisfaction at its destruction by supernatural or human means expressed by both BP (IV.xiii) and MX, III.xxvii (= MK, pp. 282–283), reflects the implacable hostility of the Armenian *naχarar* society toward urban foundations (see IV.xii n. 9, xiii n. 21). No identification of this locality is given, but Eremyan places it SE of Artašat and almost due east of Zarehawan.

See Eremyan, *Map* G/6; T'. X. Hakobyan, *Ašχarhagrut'yun*, pp. 134–135; Garsoïan, "Mediaeval Armenian City."

IV.xii–xiii

pp. 135, 137–138

See also "Artašat"; "Duin"; Kogovit"; "Zarehawan"; Appendix I, "Aršak II"; and Appendix III, *awan; dastakert; gewłak'ałak'; k'ałak'; naχarar.*

Aršamunik'

Fourth district of Turuberan, according to the *Ašχarhac'oyc'* (31/41). It lay in the valley of the Bingöl-su and bordered in the west on Xorjayn and Hašteank'. BP still attributes it to the district of Tarōn, but it had already emerged as a separate district according to ŁP', III.lxxxii, p. 149, lines 22–23 (= CHAMA, II, p. 346, though *ibid.,* line 1 should be corrected to Aršarunik' because of the association with the Kamsarakan lords of that district, according to Adontz and Toumanoff as well as the translation). The local dynasts of Aršamunik' were the Mandakuni, who presumably died out by the end of the fifth century and are not mentioned by BP, though they are included in all the Lists of *naχarar*s, and bishops of Aršamunik' are recorded in later conciliar lists (GT', pp. 42, 73; Dvin, *Canons*, p. 214).

See AON, pp. 322, 327, 370; Eremyan, *Ašχarh.*, pp. 40, 116; *idem, Map* G/4; Hewsen, "Armenia," p. 328; T'. X. Hakobyan, *Ašχarhagrut'yun*, p. 151 and map; Adontz, *Armenia*, pp. 16–19, 190, 192–193, 202, 242, 244–245, 256–258, 260, 267, 381 n. 32a, 458 n. 41, 119*, 124*, 147*; Toumanoff, *Studies*, pp. 212, 233 n. 290.

IV.xv
p. 145
Maps, C–D/6–7.
See also "Hašteankᶜ"; "Tarōn."

Aršarunikᶜ

Fifth district of Ayrarat, lying north of the Araxes River according to the *Ašχar-hacᶜoycᶜ* (34/45). It was known in antiquity as the "Araxene plain" ('Αραξηνοῦ πεδίον; Strabo, *Geogr.*, XI.xiv.4, 6, 13). This name is also known to MX, II.xc (= MK, p. 247), who gives the original name of the district as *Erasχajor*, "the Valley of the Araxes" but adds that it was altered by Aršawir Kamsarakan, who gave it his own name when he received it from Trdat the Great. In the fourth century Aršarunikᶜ with the great fortress of Artagers, together with neighboring Širak, belonged to the Kamsarakan house and was their *ostan*, as is explicitly stated by BP (III.xi; IV.xix), who normally refers to Aršarunik as a *gawaṙ* (III.xi; IV.xix) but on one occasion identifies it as an *erkir* (IV.lv). These districts remained in the Kamsarakan house until it was constrained to sell them to the Bagratuni in the ninth century.

> See AON, pp. 363, 407; Eremyan, *Ašχarh.*, pp. 40, 118; *idem*, *Map* B/5; Hewsen, "Armenia," p. 335; Tᶜ. X. Hakobyan, *Ašχarhagrutᶜyun*, pp. 117–120 and map; Adontz, *Armenia*, pp. 236–238, 458 n. 41, 498 n. 76, 121*, 126*, 147*; Toumanoff, *Studies*, pp. 202, 206–208 and n. 236, 324 n. 81.

III.xi, xxi; IV.iv, xii, xix, lv
pp. 81, 98, 111, 134, 149, 174
Maps, E–F/5
See also "Artagers"; "Ayrarat"; "Eruandašat"; Appendix I, "Kamsarakan, house"; and Appendix III, *erkir*; *gawaṙ*; *ostan*.

Artagerkᶜ, see "Artagers."

Artagers/Artagerkᶜ; Gk. 'Αρταγήρας/'Αρταγείρα; Lat. Artagera/Artogerassa

The name is attested only in the accusative plural, Artagers. As was suggested by Dr. P. M. Muradyan, however, this form may in fact be the nominative singular of a class of toponyms ending in *s*. This hypothesis is made all the more attractive by the presence of the Latin form Artogerassa and its Greek counterpart, 'Αρταγήρασα.

Fortress in the district of Aršarunikᶜ known to both Greek and Latin sources. It should not be identified with the *Artagigarta* of Ptolemy (V.xii.10), which is probably Angł in SW Armenia, but see Strabo (*Geogr.* XI.xiv.6, 'Αρταγήρας/'Αρταγείρα), Velleius Paterculus (II.xii, Artagera) and AM (XXVII.xii.5, Artogerassa). Consequently, it must have been in existence long before the fourth century, when King Aršak II wrested it from the Kamsarakan lords of the district, as implied by MX, II.xxxi (= MK, p. 287), though BP claims that it was "built" by Aršak (IV.xix). Artagers, as a royal fortress, was famous for its impregnability, and Queen Pᶜaṙanjem sustained a siege of thirteen months before surrendering it to the Persians (IV.lv). Even then, the fortress was not taken by storm but surrendered, according to the Armenian sources (see IV.lv n. 8). Artagers apparently remained a Persian stronghold defended by a Sasanian garrison after its capture, for it is listed as one of the Persian "inaccessible fortresses" retaken by the Armenians at the time of the rebellion of Vardan Mamikonean in 450–451, according to Ełišē, iii, p. 68 (= *Ełishē*, p. 119). Ališan placed the fortress at Kers near Kağizman, Eremyan locates it on one of the western tributaries of the Aχurean, halfway between Mren and Tekor, but Thierry prefers the site of Kečᶜror, now Tunçkaya, on the north slope of the Ala daği, some fifty-five kilometers south of Kars.

> See AON, pp. 407, 409; Eremyan, *Ašχarh.*, p. 40; *idem*, *Map* B/5; Hewsen, "Ptolemy," pp. 142–143; Tᶜ. X. Hakobyan, *Ašχarhagrutᶜyun*, pp. 119–120 and map;

Ališan, *Ayrarat*, p. 57 map; Thierry and Thierry "Kars," pp. 196–197, 202–203; Yovhannēsean, HB, pp. 669–674; P. Muradyan, "Vinitil'nye formy."
IV.xix, lv
pp. 149, 174–175
Maps, F–G/5.
See also "Aršarunikʿ"; and Appendix I, "Aršak II"; "Kamsarakan, house"; "Pʿaṙanjem."

Artandan/Artangan

Plain, not otherwise attested or identified. One ms reads Artangan, which is probably a scribal error, considering the similarity of *d* and *g* in the Armenian script. See Malxasyancʿ (p. 340 n. 140).
V.xli
p. 224

Artangan see "Artandan."

Artašat/Artaxata ‹ MIr. *Artašišat ‹Artaši + *šād*, "joy," "Joy of Artašēs"; Gk. Ἀρταξάτα; Lat. Artaxata

Aršakuni capital of Greater Armenia located in the royal domain of Ayrarat at the junction of the Araxes and the Mecamōr rivers, according to MX.II.xlix (= MK, p. 190), who gives the legendary account of its foundation. The subsequent shift in the course of the Mecamōr contributed to the difficulty in identifying the site, so that its excavations were begun only in 1970. It was in fact founded by Artašēs/Artaxias I early in the second century B.C., presumably on the model of the typical Hellenistic eponymous cities such as the multiple Alexandrias. It was known to Ptolemy (V.xii.5) as well as Pliny (NH VI.x, 27), etc. and its plan was traditionally attributed to Hannibal (see Strabo, *Geogr.*, XI.xiv.6; Plutarch, "Lucullus," xxxi), though there is no evidence that the Carthaginian general ever came to Armenia. After the sack of the city by the Romans in A.D. 58, it was rebuilt by Trdat I with the permission of Nero and briefly renamed Nerōneia (CD, LXII.vii.2). It is also represented on a coin minted there in A.D. 183, bearing a *tychē* of Hellenistic type and the legend ARTAXISATŌN MĒTROPOLEŌS.

Artašat is attested as the Armenian capital by all the Armenian sources, and BP almost invariably characterizes it as a "great city" (*mec kʿałakʿ*), even though he gives no description of it, and there is little evidence that the Aršakuni kings resided there in the fourth century. Recent archaeological excavations have revealed an extensive urban center with a citadel, public buildings, baths, etc. After its sack by the Persians (post 363) and the deportation of its Armenian and Jewish population, Artašat remained a stronghold at least for a time, as ŁPᶜ, lxvii, lxviii, pp. 121, 144 (= CHAMA, II, pp. 328, 343), refers to it as both a *berd*, "fortress" and a *kʿałakʿagewł*, 'komopolis,' or "fortified village." Likewise, it continued to be an important commercial center on the transit route crossing Armenia and was designated as one of the three official customs posts for trade between Byzantium and the Sasanians in the fifth century (CJ, IV, lxiii.4). After the transfer of the capital to Duin, probably in the second half of the fifth century, despite the assertion of MX, III.viii (= MK, p. 261), that it was the work of King Xosrov Kotak early in the fourth, Artašat maintained for a time its commercial importance, but gradually declined to the level of a village, though it was still known to Arab geographers of the tenth century.

See AON, pp. 362, 408–409; Eremyan, *Ašxarh.*, p. 41; *idem, Map* G/6; Hewsen, "Ptolemy," pp. 126, 149; Tᶜ. X. Hakobyan, *Ašxarhagrutʿyun*, pp. 136–138 and map; Yovhannēsean, HB, pp. 869–878; Manandyan, *Trade and Cities*, pp. 44–46, 52, 58, 80; Baumgartner, "Artaxata"; Aṙakʿelyan, *Artašat I*; Xačʿatryan, *Artašat II*; Garsoïan, "Artašat"; *idem*, "Banak Arkʿuni"; Chaumont, "Ere," pls.xl, xli; Sanspeur, "Arménie," pp. 99, 152; CPD, p. 78, *šād*.

III.viii, xii; IV.lv–lvi
pp. 75, 82, 175–176
Maps, H/5–6.
See also "Ayrarat"; "Duin"; "Mecamōr"; Appendix I, "Aršakuni"; "Hreaykᶜ"; "Xosrov II/III"; and Appendix III, *banak*; *berd*; *gewłakᶜ ałakᶜ*.

Artaxata, see "Artašat."

Aruacᶜastan, see "Aruestan."

Aruestan/Aruacᶜastan; Gk. Μυγδόνια; Lat. Mygdonia; Syr. Arabistan?
Region of the city of Nisibis in Upper Mesopotamia, directly across the Tigris from Ałjnikᶜ. Its name is also recorded by Aa, dccclxxiii, and the *Primary History*, Sebēos, p. 53 (= MK, p. 365). It was known to classical sources as Mygdonia (see, e.g., Strabo, *Geogr.* XI.xiv.2, XVI.i.23; Pliny, NH, VI.xvi.42) and was faced by the Armenian March of Ałjnikᶜ.
See AON, pp. 319–320; Eremyan, *Ašχarh.*, pp. 40, 118; *idem, Map* D/4; Hewsen, "Armenia," p. 336; *idem*, "Vitaxates"; Marquart, *Ērānšahr*, pp. 165–166; *idem, Südarmenien*, p. 378; Tᶜ. X. Hakobyan, *Ašχarhagrutᶜyun*, map includes it within the borders of Armenia; Dilleman, *Haute-Mésopotamie*, pp. 75, 88.
IV.xx–xxi
pp. 150, 154
Maps, D–E/9–10.
See also "Ałjnikᶜ"; "Mcbin."

Arzanēnē, see "Ałjnikᶜ."

"Ash Grove," see "Hacᶜeacᶜ draχt."

Asorestan/Mijagetkᶜ Asorocᶜ; Parth., Pahl. Āsūrestān; Gk. Ἀσσυρία; Lat. Assyria, Babylonia; Syr. Bēθ Aramāyē
Attested in ŠKZ, Parth. 3, 16; RGDS nos. 2.7.8.35, pp. 46–49, 56–57.
Term normally used by early Armenian sources to designate Mesopotamia or more precisely Babylonia, though on one occasion (IV.xxi) BP uses the translation of the Greek form, "Mesopotamia" (*Mijagetkᶜ Asorocᶜ*); cf. *Ašχarhacᶜoycᶜ* (37–38/49–50). Małχasyancᶜ (pp. 319 n. 49 and 326 n. 108) takes references to Asorestan in BP (III.xx, IV.xx) as relating to Ctesiphōn, because the Sasanian capital lay within the district.
See Eremyan, *Ašχarh.*, p. 38 and map D/5–6; Hewsen, "Vitaxates"; Gignoux, *Glossaire*, pp. 17, 47; Sprengling, *Third-Century Iran*, pp. 7–8, 14–16; Maricq, RGDS, p. 91; Honigmann and Maricq, RGDS, pp. 10–11, 39, 41–63, 171, 377; Dilleman, *Haute-Mésopotamie*, pp. 287–289; Nöldeke, *Tabari*, p. 15 and n. 3.
III.xx; IV.i, xx, lv; V.vii
pp. 97, 107, 151, 176, 198
Maps, E–G/10.
See also "Tispon"; and Appendix I, "Asori."

Assyrian March, see "Kordukᶜ."

Asthianēnē, see "Hašteankᶜ."

Aštišat ‹ Phl. Ašti + *šat*, "Joy of Ašti/Aštarte"; the popular form *Yaštišat* is incorrectly derived by Aa, dcccix, from Ir. *yašt*, "sacrifice" + Arm. *šat*, "much/many"
Locality in the district of Tarōn situated north of the Meł, identified as the main river of Tarōn by the *Ašχarhacᶜoycᶜ* (31/41). In pagan times, it was the site of three temples to Astłik/Aphrodite, Anahit, the "Golden Mother" and especially Vahagn/Heraklēs, who was of particular importance to the pre-Christian Aršakuni kings. The last of these

was miraculously destroyed by St. Gregory the Illuminator, according to Aa, dcccix–dcccxv; cf. MX, II.xii, xiv (=MK, pp. 148, 152), a tradition also known to BP (III.xiv). After the Christianization of Greater Armenia, Aštišat became an important religious center containing the major shrine of St. John the Precursor (III.iii, xiv), and BP insistently stresses its status, as the first and mother church of Armenia (see III.xiv n. 11) and as a Gregorid domain, as does MX, III.lxvii (= MK, p. 348), who speaks of Aštišat as the Gregorids' "own village," in connection with the burial there of the last patriarch of the house, St. Sahak I. The earlier patriarch Pʿarēn, who had been the supervisor of the shrine, was likewise buried there as were the sons of the patriarch Yusik I. Despite its prestige, however, Aštišat seems to have been a "holy place" and a shrine rather than a center of population. Most sources refer to it as a site or locality [*teł*] (BP, III, xiv; IV, xiv; Aa, dcccix; MX, II, xiv = MK, p. 152), or at most a village [*gewł*] (BP, IV, iv; MX, II, xii (= MK, p. 148). Only on one occasion (III, xix), does BP speak of it as an ecclesiastical town [*awan*], and its description of the church of Aštišat as being "fortified" (III.iii) implies that it was not otherwise protected as part of a larger populated unit.

See AON, pp. 400–401; Eremyan, *Ašχarh.*, p. 36; *idem, Map* G/4; Tʿ. X. Hakobyan, *Ašχarhagrutʿyun*, pp. 152–153 and map; Adontz, AG, p. 212; *Armenia*, pp. 243–244, 189*; Toumanoff, *Studies*, p. 215 and n. 246; Markwart, *Südarmenien*, pp. 288–290; *idem*, "Parskahaykʿ," p. 283; CPD, p. 78, *šād*; and Benveniste, "Terminologie," pp. 48–53, on the etymology of the name; Carrière, *Huit Sanctuaires*, pp. 26–27; Garsoïan, "Substratum," p. 158, on the pagan temple; Garitte, *Documents*, p. 205, for additional references; *idem, Narratio*, pp. 60–61, although he does not appreciate sufficiently the reference to Aštišat as a χώρα rather than a locality; Garsoïan, "Mediaeval Armenian City," pp. 71–74, 77.
III.iii, xiv, xix; IV.iv, xiv
pp. 68, 87, 93, 113, 139
Maps, D/6–7.
See also "Agarak"; "Bagawan"; "John the Precursor, shrines of"; "Taron"; Appendix I, "Anahit"; "Atʿanaginēs"; "Grigor"; "Pap (2)"; "Pʿarēn"; "Vahagn"; and Appendix III, *awan; gewł; mayr ekełecʿeacʿ*.

Atʿenacʿwocʿ kʿałakʿ, see "Athens."

Athens/Atʿenacʿwocʿ kʿałakʿ
The only reference in BP to the great Attic city remains as yet unelucidated (see III.xiii n. 8). In keeping with the references to Greek centers in the text it is called a city (*kʿałakʿ*).
OCD, pp. 114–116; Hülser, "Athenai."
III.xiii
p. 84
See Appendix III, *kʿałakʿ*.

Atʿoṙ Anahtay, "Throne of Anahit"
Large mountain, the name of which indicates that it probably lay in the district of Ekełeacʿ/Akilisēnē, since the great temple of the goddess at Erēz lay within this district (Aa, dcclxxxvi; Strabo, *Geogr.*, XI.xiv.16). It is almost certainly to be identified with the Surb Grigor (mod. Sipikor) range and village north of Erzincan.
See AON, p. 286; AG, p. 18 no. 5; Eremyan, *Map* G/3.
V.xxv
p. 205
Maps, B–C/5–6.
See also "Ekełeacʿ"; and Appendix I, "Anahit."

Atropatēnē, see "Atrpatakan".

Atrpatakan/Atrpayakan/Atrpatičk^c(?) ‹ Ātūrpātakān ‹ *ādurpat*, Av. *ātarəpāta-*, "fire-defended"; Gk ᾿Ατροπατηνή Lat. Atropatene/Media Atropatene.
Attested as part of the Sasanian Empire in ŠKZ, Parth. 1; RGDS nos. 2–3, pp. 46–49, ᾿Αδουρβαδηνή; Tansar.
Region of northwestern Iran south of the Araxes River bordering on Armenia. The *Ašχarhac^coyc^c* (41/53) gives it as the first "realm" (*ašχarh*) or northern quarter of Persia (cf. Aa, cciii; Va, clx, p. 138). It was familiar as Atropatēnē to classical authors (e.g., Strabo, *Geogr.*, XI.xii, 4; xiii, 1, 3; xiv, 1, 15; Pliny, NH, VI.xvi, 42), and was governed by a *marzpan* as one of the marches of the Sasanian Empire. The immediate region of the city of Ganjak in Atrpatakan marked the border between Greater Armenia and the Sasanian Empire, according to BP, and Aršakuni domains were apparently located along the frontier. Eremyan locates the Aršakuni royal domain on the eastern shore of Lake Urmiah in a district (singular) of Atrpatičk^c, which he distinguishes from the rest of Atrpatakan. But the reference in BP (V.viii) is to the districts (plural) of Atrpatričk^c, and this name is probably merely an alternate form of Atrpatakan (see Malχasyanc^c, p. 334 n. 162). BP normally uses the term *sahmank^c*, "borders, territories" in reference to Atrpatakan, though "realm" (*ašχarh*) also occurs (III.xx; IV.l; V.iv), as well as the curious forms *gawaṙakołmk^c*, "district-regions" (III.vi) and *erkir gawaṙic^c*, "land of the districts" (V.viii).
> See AG, pp. 23–24 no. 20; Eremyan, *Ašχarh.*, p. 38; *idem, Map* D/6–8, where "Atrpatričk^c" D/6–7 is indicated as a separate unit; Marquart, *Ērānšahr*, pp. 108–114; Weissbach, "Atropatene"; Brau, "Azerbaijan"; Adontz, *Armenia*, pp. 167–172, 149*; Garitte, *Documents*, pp. 104, 194; Gignoux, *Glossaire*, pp. 17, 47; Sprengling, *Third-Century Iran*, pp. 7, 14; Honigmann and Maricq, RGDS, pp. 11, 39; Fiey, "Aḍarbāygān"; Tansar, p. 63.
> III.vi–vii, xx; IV.xvi, xxi, xxiii–xxv, xxxix, xliii, l, lviii; V.i, ii, iv–v, viii, xxxix pp. 72, 74, 94–95, 146, 154, 156–159, 163–164, 167, 178, 186–187, 189, 193, 194, 199, 223
> Maps, I, I–M/7–10; II, H–M/5–10.
> See also "Ganjak"; "T^cawrēš"; Appendix I, "Aršakuni"; "Sasanians"; and Appendix III, *ašχarh*; *erkir*; *gawaṙ*; *sahman*.

Atrpatričk^c, see "Atrpatakan."

Atrpayakan, see "Atrpatakan."

Awšakan, see "Ōšakan."

Aχani, see "Eraχani."

Ayrarat/Ararat; term unknown to classical authors, perhaps the same as ᾿Αραξηνῶν πεδίον, Strabo, XI.xiv.4; cf. Pliny, NH, VI.ix, 25 and Arm. Erasχajor
Central region of the Aršakuni realm in the valley of the Araxes River, containing the successive capitals of Vałaršapat, Artašat, and Duin, as well as the royal hunting preserves (III.viii), and considered to form the innermost core of the "Armenian Midlands." The *Ašχarhac^coyc^c* attributes sixteen districts to Ayrarat, though the two recensions of the work disagree (29/40, 33–34/45–46). The term it applies to this region is "realm" (*ašχarh*), which occurs in BP as well (III.xii), but the lesser qualification of "district" (*gawaṙ*)) is more common (III.vii–viii; IV.xiv; V.vi). Armenian sources normally treat the region as the royal domain of the Aršakuni—e.g. Aa, dcclxxvi, dccclxi, *et passim*, and BP (V.vi)—but the most insistent is MX, I.xv–xvi, xxii, lxi, lxv, lxxvii; II.xxii; III.xlviii (=MK, pp. 97–98, 159, 203, 210, 225, 277–278, 311), who claims that

the Armenian kings drove even their own kinsmen out of the area. In fact, a number of other families, among them the Gnuni, also possessed domains in Ayrarat, and BP records the presence of ecclesiastical domains in the region (IV.xiv), so that, as the Aršakuni kings were lords of Ayrarat, so was the Armenian patriarch bishop of the district. It should not be confused with Mt. Ararat.

See AON, pp. 278–283, which equates Ayrarat with the Armenian Midlands; Erem-yan, *Ašχarh.*, pp. 35, 118; *idem, Map*, B/5-6-G/6; Hewsen, "Armenia," p. 335; T⁽. X. Hakobyan, *Ašχarhagrut⁽yun*, pp. 108–144 and map; Adontz, *Armenia*, pp. 100, 179–180, 182, 230–231, 236–241, 258, 286–287, 307, 352, 361, 454 nn. 1, 4, 459–460 n. 54, 75*–76*, 95*–96*, 118*, 120*, 121*, 124*–126*, 149*.

III.vii–viii, x, xii, xiv; IV.xiv, xx, xxiv; V.vi; VI.i, vi

pp. 74–75, 77, 82, 87, 139, 151, 158, 196, 233, 235

Maps, G/5-6

See also "Amok;" "Aragac"; "Ardeans"; "Aršarunik⁽"; "Artašat"; "Duin"; "Mijnašχarh Hayoc⁽"; Tiknuni"; "Vałaršapat"; "Vanand"; "Xosrovakert"; Appen-dix I, "Aršakuni"; "Gnuni, house"; "Grigor/Gregorids"; and Appendix III, *ašχarh; gawař.*

Bagawan ‹ Ir. *bag*, "god" + Arm, *awan*, "town"; Gk. Βαγαύνα; Lat. Raugonia

Town in the district of Bagrewand at the northern foot of Mt. Npat, according to the *Ašχarhac⁽oyc⁽* (34/45), which refers to it as a "village" (*gewł*). It is probably to be identified with Ptolemy's Saguana (V.xii.7) and is listed in the *Tabula Peutingeriana* as "Raugonia." Bagawan was familiar as a religious site to Armenian sources, and the correct Armenian translation of its name, *dicawan*, "town of the [pagan] gods," is given by Aa, dcccxvii, though MX, II.lv, III.lxvii (= MK, pp. 198, 347) incorrectly calls it the "town of the altars" (*bagnac⁽n awan*). Before the Christianization of Armenia, Bagawan was the site of a fire temple dedicated to Ahura-Mazda, according to MX, II.lxxvii (= MK, p. 225). The subsequent establishment of a shrine of St. John the Precursor (IV.xv) is confirmed by Aa, dcccxxxvi, as is the celebration there of the feast of Nawasard (IV.xv and n. 10), which was instituted by King Vałarš, according to MX, II.lxvi (= MK, p. 213). As in the case of Aštišat of Tarōn, Bagawan, as a former temple estate, became part of the domain of the Gregorid patriarchal house.

See AON, p. 411; Eremyan, *Ašχarh.*, pp. 42, 72; *idem, Map* G/5; Hewsen, "Pto-lemy," pp. 134, 149; T⁽. X. Hakobyan, *Ašχarhagrut⁽yun*, p. 121 and map; Adontz, *Armenia*, pp. 241–242, 120*, 121*, 125*, 191*; Toumanoff, *Studies*, pp. 309, 319–320; Manandyan, *Trade and Cities*, pp. 83, 86, 92–97; Perikhanian, *Khramovye Obedineniia*, pp. 9, etc.; Miller, *Tabula Peutingeriana*, pp. 676–677; cf. D'iakonov and Livshits, "*Nisa*," pp. 329, 332; Gignoux, NPS, pp. 10–11 on the meaning of *bag* and the presence of toponyms with *bag-* in Nisa documents.

IV.xv; V.iv, xliii

pp. 141, 189, 225

Maps, F–G/6.

See also "Aštišat"; "Bagrewand"; "John the Precursor, Shrines of"; "Npat"; Appen-dix I, "Grigor/Gregorids"; and Appendix III, *nawasard.*

Bagrawand, see "Bagrewand."

Bagrewand/Bagrawand; Gk. Βαγραυανδηνή ‹ Ir. *bag*, "god" + Av. *raēva-*, "rich"

Sixth district of Ayrarat, according to the *Ašχarhac⁽oyc⁽* (34/45), and already known to Ptolemy under the name of Bagrauandēnē (V.xii.9). Bagrewand, which in-cluded the plain of Alaškert, lay along the right bank of the middle Araxes south of Aršarunik⁽, and its main center, according to BP (IV.lv, lviii), was the city of Zarehawan on the border of the district of Całkotn; the holy site of Bagawan was located there as well. No mention of a princely house of this district is to be found in BP or elsewhere. Adontz held it to be an allod of the Bagratuni, but Toumanoff considered it to be a Gregorid domain, which passed to the Mamikonean at the death of the last Gregorid patriarch, St. Sahak I, and was wrested from the Mamikonean by the Bagratuni only in the mid-ninth century. It is, however, not listed among the patriarchal lands in BP (IV.xiv) though bishops were presumably sent to the region by St. Gregory himself (Vg, clxxii = Va, clx). BP refers to it exclusively as a *gawaṙ*.

See AON, pp. 363, 411; Eremyan, *Ašχarh.*, pp. 42, 118; *idem, Map* G/5; Hewsen, "Armenia," p. 335; *idem*, "Ptolemy," p. 115; T^c. X. Hakobyan, *Ašχarhagrut^cyun*, p. 121 and map; Adontz, *Armenia*, pp. 231, 236–237, 241–242, 257, 260, 319, 121*, 126*, 150*; Toumanoff, *Studies*, pp. 132, 137, 138 n. 240, 201, 209–210, 218, 241, 321, 324; Garitte, *Documents*, pp. 102–104; Gignoux, NPS, pp. 10–11, nos. 193–203, pp. 56–58; Russell, "Armeno-Iranica."
IV.xii, lv, lviii; V.xxxii, xliii
pp. 134, 175, 178, 213, 225
Maps, F/6.
See also "Aršarunik^c"; "Bagawan"; "Xu"; "Zarehawan"; Appendix I, "Grigor/Gregorids"; and Appendix III, *gawaṙ*.

Bahl, see "Bałχ."

Bak^caser
Presumably a region of western Armenia lying on the way to the Byzantine Empire, but otherwise unattested. The form of the name may well be due to a *lapsus calami*.
See Ep^crikean, *Baṙaran*, p. 411; Malχasyanc^c (p. 324 n. 90).
IV.xiii
p. 136

Balasakan, see "P^caytakaran."

Balh, see "Bałχ."

Bałχ/Balh/Bahl; Phl. *Bahl-i bāmīg*, "brilliant/glorious Bahl," *Baχl Šahastan*, "royal Baχl"
K^cušan capital in the valley of the Oxus (Amu-Darya) already attested in the inscription of Darius the Great (as Bactria), DBI 1.16 (= OP, p. 119; DBIII, ll.13–14, etc.) and known to Pliny (NH VI.xvii, 45). The Armenian *Primary History*, Sebēos, pp. 52–57 (= MK, p. 367, etc.) calls it Baχl Šahastan and makes it the refuge of the ancestors of the Mamikonean fleeing from the land of the Čenk^c, and the *Ašχarhac^coyc^c* (41/55), inaccurately translating *Bahl-i bāmīg* as Bahl of the "East" or "morning," knows it as part of the Aryan realm. The modern homonymous city in Afghanistan is located close to, but not on, the site of the ancient city.
See Marquart, *Ērānšahr*, pp. 87–91; Malχasyanc^c (p. 334 n. 157) who follows the translation of the *Ašχarhac^coyc^c*; OP, pp. 117, 119, 125, 127, etc.
V.vii, xxxvii
pp. 198, 217
See also Appendix I, "Čenk^c"; "K^cušan"; "Mamikonean, house."

Baṙaēj/Gaweč; perhaps the same as Gk. Βαλαλείσων
Locality in Ałjnik^c presumably of some importance, since BP calls it a "town" (*awan*) rather than a village (*gewł*). It is, however, otherwise unattested and the alternate form, Gaweč, found in one ms suggests a corrupted form, possibly of Bałałeš/Bałeš, mod. Bitlis.

See Inčičean, *Storagrut'iwn*, p. 84; Ep'rikean, *Baŕaran*, p. 400, lists the locality but does not identify it; Eremyan, *Ašχarh.*, p. 44.

III.xiv

p. 88

Maps, E/7–8?

See also "Aljnik'."

Basean/Basēn; Gk. Φασιανή; mod. Pasin/Pasinler

First district of Ayrarat, according to the *Ašχarhac'oyc'* (33/45). It lay southeast of Karin in northwestern Armenia at the junction of the upper Araxes and the Murc' rivers, according to both the *Ašχarhac'oyc'* and MX, II.liv (= MK, p. 197), and coincided approximately with the modern Pasinler kazasi. Aa, dcccxlv, refers to it as a "wild region." BP usually refers to it as a *gawaŕ*, but on one occasion (IV.xxiv) identifies it as a *kołmn*. The correct form of the name is Basean, as observed by Anasyan, but the forms Basēn and even Basan also occur. The Greek version Phasianē was presumably derived from the Phasianoi mentioned by Xenophon (*Anab.*, IV.vi.5).

The identification of the original rulers of the district as the Orduni house rests on the evidence of BP (III.iv). They are also known to MX, III.ii (= MK, p. 255), who is presumably following BP at this point. After the extermination of the Orduni and the transfer of their seat to the bishop of Basean (III.iv), however, BP records a later prince of Basean (III.ix), who must be a local dynast belonging to another family, though Toumanoff postulates some survival. These later rulers are still recorded in the *Gahnamak*, "Rank List," under the title of "judge" (*datawor*) of Basean, and known to the *Vita* of St. Nersēs, v, p. 35 (= CHAMA, II, p. 26), and the *Zōrnamak*, "Military List," which attributes 600 retainers to them, but simultaneously lists the Orduni with 700. Basean was evangelized by Bishop Ewtałios at the order of St. Gregory, according to Aa, dcccxlv; bishops from this district are also known to BP (III.iv; VI.vii, xiii), and they continue to be included in the Armenian conciliar lists (GT', pp. 41, 73, 146, etc.)

See AON, pp. 208, 362–363; Eremyan, *Ašχarh.*, pp. 44, 118; *idem, Map* B/4-5–G/4; Hewsen, "Armenia," p. 3; T'. X. Hakobyan, *Ašχarhagrut'yun*, pp. 115–116 and map; Adontz, *Armenia*, pp. 21–22, 190, 192–193, 202, 206–208, 222, 236–238, 245, 255–258, 260, 262, 267, 269, 307, 444 n. 24, 119*, 121*, 126*, 151*; Toumanoff, *Studies*, pp. 218–219, 230 nn. 277, 281, 231 n. 285, 233 n. 291.

III.iv, ix, xxi; IV.xv, xxii, xxiv; VI.vii, xiii

pp. 70, 77, 98, 145, 155, 157, 235, 238

Maps, D–E/5-6

See also "Ayrarat"; "Karin"; "Orduru"; "Osχay"; Appendix I, "Artit'"; "Grigor/Gregorids"; "Manak"; "Orduni, house"; "Tirik"; and Appendix III, *datawor; gawaŕ; kołmn.*

Basēn, see "Basean."

Baχišn

Locality otherwise unattested.

See Malχasyanc' (pp. 332–333 n. 146).

V.i, iv

pp. 186, 189

Bnabeł

Fortress in Cop'k' Mec, which should probably be identified with the Babila of Ptolemy in southwestern Armenia (V.xii.7), but not confused with the *kastron Banabēlōn* of George of Cyprus (p. 47), which stood northwest of Mardin. In the Aršakuni period Bnabeł was one of the royal fortresses in which the treasures of the crown were secured under the guardianship of the *mardpet*.

See AON, pp. 296 n. 1, 297, 310; Eremyan, *Ašχarh.*, p. 45; *idem, Map* G/3; Adontz, *Armenia*, p. 27, where he confuses the two fortresses, as does Dilleman, *Haute-Mésopotamie*, pp. 123–124; T^c. X. Hakobyan, *Asχarhagrut^cyun*, p. 216, but not on the map, which shows its namesake; Hewsen, "Ptolemy," pp. 133–134, 149.

III.xii; V.vii

pp. 84, 198

Maps, B/7–8.

See also "Cop^ck^c Mec"; Appendix I, "Drastamat"; and Appendix III, *mardpet*.

Bznuneac^c cov, "Sea of Bznunik^c"; Gk. Θωσπῖτις, perhaps the same as Lake Van

Name habitually given to Lake Van by medieval Armenian sources and the *Ašχarhac^coyc^c* (31/42), which incorporates it into the district of Bznunik^c and gives its dimensions as 100 by 60 "miles" (*miłon*). The transfer of the Bznuni family's name to the lake is explicitly made by MX, I.xii (=MK, p. 89). On one occasion, however, BP (III.x) refers to this lake as the "Sea of Ṙštunik," probably under the influence of the context. Markwart and Minorsky rejected the common equation Van = Thospitis and identified the latter with Lake Covk^c (Gölcik). But see Hewsen on this point.

See Eremyan, *Asχarh.*, p. 45; *idem, Map* G/5; Markwart, *Südarmenien*, pp. 28, 32*; Minorsky, "L'Ouvrage," pp. 146–147; Hewsen, "Armenia," p. 330 and nn. 43–44; *idem*, "Ptolemy," p. 136.

III.viii

p. 76

Maps, F/6–7.

See also "Bznunik^c"; "Tosp."

Bznunik^c

Eleventh district of Turuberan, according to the *Ašχarhac^coyc^c* (31/42). It lay along the northwestern shore of Lake Van (to which it gave its name) and included this body of water with its islands, though both BP (III.viii) and the *Ašχarhac^coyc^c* (32/43) include the southern island of Ałt^camar among the possessions of the Ṙštuni. The district took its name from the homonymous princes, whose name it perpetuated, but it reverted to the fisc after their annihilation under King Xosrov Kotak, according to BP (III.viii). Toumanoff is, however, of the opinion that it passed to the Ṙštuni. Gregorid domains were also found in the district (IV.xiv).

See AON, pp. 328–329, 342; Eremyan, *Asχarh.*, pp. 45, 116; *idem, Map* G/5; Hewsen, "Armenia," p. 328; T^c. X. Hakobyan, *Ašχarhagrut^cyun*, pp. 157–158 and map; Adontz, *Armenia*, pp. 192, 195, 245–246, 68*, 69*, 70*, 94*–102*; Toumanoff, *Studies*, pp. 213, 216.

IV.xiv

p. 139

Maps, E–F/7–8.

See also "Ałt^camar"; Appendix I, "Bznuni, house"; "Grigor/Gregorids"; "Ṙštuni, house"; and the preceding entry.

Bznunik^c Sea, see "Bznuneac^c cov."

Caesarea/Kesaria; Gk. Καισάρεια/Μηιακαρίρη

Attested as Kaisareia in ŠKZ, Parth. 14; Phl 19 (reconstr.); KKZ, 12; but RGDS no. 32, pp. 56–57, Μηιακαρίρη.

Metropolis of the province of Cappadocia until 372 and of Cappadocia I after the division of Greater Cappadocia in two by the emperor Valens. The city was called Mazaka (Arm. Mažak) in antiquity, a name known to Aa, dccxcvi, and to MX, I.xiv (= MK, pp. 94–95), but not to BP, where Caesarea is referred to exclusively as the place of consecration of the Armenian patriarchs until the death of St. Nersēs I and the rejection of his successor (V.xxix), in the interpolations from the life of St. Basil, and in the claim attributed to King Pap that it was an Armenian city (V.xxxii), possibly on the basis of its former conquest by Tigran the Great. The metropolitan status of Caesarea is acknowledged in its qualifications as *mayr kʿalakʿacʿ* (III.xii; IV.iv) or *mayrakʿalakʿ* (III.xvi), "metropolis," and *mec kʿalakʿ* (III.xvii), "great city."

> See Jones, *Cities*, 179, 183–185, 187–190; Foss, "Caesarea," p. 9; Ruge, "Kaisareia"; Gignoux, *Glossaire*, pp. 25, 56; Sprengling, *Third-Century Iran*, pp. 8, 16, 47, 51; Honigmann and Maricq, RGDS, pp. 14, 149, 151.
> III.xii, xvi–xvii; IV.iii, iv, vii–x; V.xxix, xxxii
> pp. 82, 91–92, 109, 111, 126–130, 132, 210, 213
> See also Appendix I, "Barseł;"; "Grigor/Gregorids"; "Nersēs I"; "Pap"; "Pʿarēn"; "Šahak I"; "Tigran the Great"; "Yusik I and II"; and Appendix III, *kʿalakʿ*; *mayrakʿalakʿ*.

Cappadocia, see "Gamirkʿ."

Castle of Oblivion, see "Anyuš."

Cʿlu Gluχ, "Bull's Head," Mt.
Mountain in the district of Aragacotn granted with its district to Vačē I Mamikonean by King Xosrov Kotak after his defeat of the Mazkʿutʿkʿ at that site. Its precise location is not known, but it should not be confused with Cʿul, the "Taurus" mountains, since its location in Aragacotn indicates that it stood north of the Araxes River.

> See AON, p. 465.
> III.vii–viii
> pp. 74–75
> See also "Janjanak"; "Jrabašχkʿ"; and Appendix I, "Mazkʿutʿkʿ"; "Vačʿē I"; "Xosrov II/III."

Copʿacʿ kolmn, see "Copʿkʿ."

Copʿkʿ/Copʿacʿ kolmn; Gk. Σωφηνή Lat. Sophena
Large region in southwestern Armenia along the course of the Euphrates-Arsanias (mod. Murad-su). It had formed a separate kingdom in the third and second centuries B.C., under the Zariadrid branch of the Armenian Eruandid/Orontid dynasty with Karkathiokerta as capital; until it was conquered by Tigran the Great at the beginning of the last century B.C. As such, it was familiar to classical geographers (see, e.g., Strabo, *Geogr.*, XI.xii.3–4; xiv.2, 5, 12; XII.ii.1; Ptolemy, V.xii.6). The entire region, which was composed of a number of principalities, passed into the Roman sphere of influence under the terms of the Peace of Nisibis of 298 (Petr. Patric., *Ad gen.*, iii), but is treated as part of the Aršakuni kingdom by BP. It apparently contained ecclesiastical domains (IV.xiv) as well as Arcruni holdings, and its princes are included in all the later lists of Armenian *naχarar*s, with the *Zōrnamak*, "Military List," attributing 1,000 retainers to them. Both Aa, dccxcv, and MX, II.viii, lxxxiv (but not xci); III.ix, xlv (= MK, pp. 142, 236, [249], 261, 307) call Copʿkʿ a "realm" (*ašχarh*), possibly alluding to its autonomous status; but BP normally refers to it as a "district" (*gawar*), though on one occasion (V.vii) it uses the term *erkir*, "land." BP is also the only Armenian source to give the division of this region into Copʿkʿ Mec/Sophanēnē and Copʿkʿ Šahēi or Šahuni/Sophēnē recorded in the Justinianic legislation (see next two entries). At the time of the Roman-Persian peace of 363, most of Sophēnē seems to have remained Roman (IV.l), and it became the Byzantine province of Armenia IV in the Justinianic

reform of 536 (*Novella*, xxxi). The later name is anachronistically recorded by MX, I.xiv, II.viii, xci; III.xliv (MK, pp. 95, 142, 249, 307), and the *Ašχarhac̣oyc̣* equates Sophēnē and Armenia IV.

See AON, pp. 216–219, 227–228, 230, 245–248, 294–300; Eremyan, *Ašχarh.*, pp. 24, 57, 107, 116 and map G/3–4; but not the fourth-century map; Hewsen, "Armenia," p. 149; *idem*, "Orontid," pp. 349, 357–362; Tc. X. Hakobyan, *Ašχarhagrutʿyun*, pp. 211–218 and map; Weissbach, "Sophene"; Adontz, *Armenia*, pp. 26–35, 100, 191, 193, 201, 155*, 177*; Garitte, *Documents*, p. 234; but cf. Dilleman, *Haute-Mésopotamie*, pp. 116–123.

III.ii; IV.xiv; V.vii

pp. 67, 139, 198

Maps, B–D/6–9

See also Appendix I, "Arcruni, house"; "Aršakuni"; "Grigor/Gregorids"; Appendix II, "Mec Haykc"; Appendix III, *ašχarh; erkir; gawaṙ*; and the next two entries.

Copc̣kc̣ Mec; Gk. Τζοφανηνή Lat. Sophanena

Southeastern portion of the former *Copc̣ac̣ koɫmn* (see preceding entry), lying along the Tigris River south of Hašteankc̣/Asthianēnē, to which BP usually refers to as a mere *gawaṙ*. It was known to Byzantine sources as Sophanēnē. Copc̣kc̣ Mec passed to the Roman sphere of influence, probably still as part of the former larger Sophēnē, under the terms of the Peace of Nisibis of 298 (Petr. Patric., *Ad gen.*, iii), but it is distinguished from the later Sophēnē/Copc̣kc̣ Šahēi (see next entry) by BP, which gives two separate lists of ruling princes, and by the Justinianic legislation (CJ, I.29.5; *Novella*, xxxi), though not by other Armenian sources or the later Lists of *naχarar*s. Byzantine sources include Sophanēnē among the autonomous Satrapies, but BP lists the ruler of Copc̣kc̣ Mec among the "good servants" of King Xosrov (III.ix) and considers his siding with the Romans at the time of the Roman–Persian peace of 363 as a defection from his lord Aršak II (IV.l). The autonomy of Sophanēnē was apparently limited by the emperor Zeno at the end of the fifth century (Procopius, *De aed.*, III.i.17–29), and it was abolished by Justinian, who incorporated it together with the other Satrapies into the new Byzantine province of Armenia IV in 536 (*Novella* xxxi).

See AON, pp. 295–299, 309–310; Eremyan, *Ašχarh.*, pp. 57, 116 and map G/3–4, but it is given as the district of Tigranakert on his fourth-century *Map*; Hewsen, "Armenia," p. 336; *idem*, "Orontid," pp. 359–360; 362; Tc. X. Hakobyan, *Ašχarhagrutʿyun*, pp. 215–216, who extends it south of Amida; Honigmann, *Ostgrenze*, pp. 7 n. 5, 8–9, 16, 18, 23–24, 32–33; Adontz, *Armenia*, pp. 10, 13, 26–27, 32–35, 91–93, 107, 134, 137, 182, 191, 193, 201, 375 nn. 4–5, 378 n. 20, 386 n. 2, 390 n. 20a, 391 n. 23, 412 n. 40, 2*, 35*, 45*, 75*, 90*–91*, 178*; Toumanoff, *Studies*, pp. 131, 137, 166 n. 63, 167–168, 170 n. 88, 172 n. 99, 173 n. 103, 179, 180, 219, 224, 227, 237 n. 306, 240–241, 244–245, 304; Garitte, *Documents*, p. 234.

III.ix, xii, xiv; IV.iv, xxiv, xxx, l; V.xvii, xxvii–xxviii

pp. 77, 82, 84, 90, 111, 157, 167, 201, 206–207

Maps, B–D/8

See also "Bnabeɫ"; "Copc̣kc̣"; "Copc̣kc̣ Šahēi"; "Hašteankc̣"; "Mambrē"; Appendix I, "Aršak II"; "Daniēl"; "Epipc̣an"; "Mar"; "Xosrov II/III"; "Zareh"; and Appendix III, *gawaṙ*.

Copc̣kc̣ Šahēi/Šahuni; Gk. Τζοφηνή Lat. Sophena

Northwestern portion of the former *Copc̣ac̣ koɫmn* lying north of the Arsanias-Euphrates (mod. Murad-su), between it and the Muzuron River. It was also known as "the Other Copc̣kc̣" (*Miws Copc̣kc̣*; IV.iv) and as Sophēnē, as *pars pro toto* to the Byzantine sources. Along with Copc̣kc̣ Mec, Copc̣kc̣ Šahēi passed to the Roman sphere of influence (probably still as part of the former larger Sophēnē) under the terms of the

Peace of Nisibis of 298 (Petr. Patr., *Ad gen.*, iii), but it is distinguished from Copʿkʿ Mec/Sophanēnē (see preceding entry) by BP, who gives two separate lists of ruling princes, and by the Justinianic legislation (CJ I.29.5; *Novella* xxxi), though not by the other Armenian authors or the later Lists of *naxarars*. Byzantine sources include Sophēnē among the autonomous Satrapies, but BP lists the ruler of Copʿkʿ Šahēi, Nerseh, among the "good servants" of King Xosrov Kotak (III.ix), though it refers to Copʿkʿ Šahuni as a "realm" (*ašxarh*) in III.xii. There is no mention of the defection of Copʿkʿ Šahēi from Armenia in 363 or of its subsequent reconquest, but it presumably remained on the Roman side. The autonomy of Sophēnē as well as of Sophanēnē was apparently limited by the emperor Zeno at the end of the fifth century (Procopius, *De aed.*, III.i.17–29), and it was abolished by Justinian, who incorporated it together with the other Satrapies into the new Byzantine province of Armenia IV in 536 (*Novella* xxxi).

See AON, pp. 295, 297–299; Eremyan, *Ašxarh.*, pp. 57, 116; *idem, Map* G/3; Hewsen, "Orontid," pp. 357–358; Honigmann, *Ostgrenze*, pp. 4–5, 7 n. 1, 16, 32, 204 n. 3; Marquart, *Ērānšahr*, pp. 117–118; *idem, Südarmenien*, pp. 91–95; Adontz, *Armenia*, pp. 26–27, 32–35, 38, 100, 107, 134, 137, 182, 386 nn. 2, 5, 6, 390 nn. 20a, 21–22, 391 nn. 23–25b, 396 n. 17, 411 n. 33b, 483 n. 1, 492 nn. 51a–52, 2*, 35*, 52*, 90*–91*, 113*, 178*; Toumanoff, *Studies*, pp. 131, 137, 167, 170 n. 88, 172 n. 99, 176 n. 112, 180, 219, 224, 227, 230 n. 280, 237 n. 306, 241, 245, 252, 304; Garitte, *Documents*, p. 234.

III.ix, xii; IV.iv, xxiv
pp. 77, 82, 111, 157
Maps, B/6–7.
See also "Copʿkʿ"; "Copʿkʿ Mec"; and Appendix I, "Nerseh"; "Noy"; "Varaz"; "Xosrov II/III"; and Appendix III, *ašxarh*.

Copʿkʿ Šahuni, see "Copʿkʿ Šahēi."

Corduena, see "Kordukʿ."

Ctesiphon, see "Tispon."

Cʿul; Gk. Ταῦρος; Lat. Taurus, Mts.
Major mountain chain in southeastern Anatolia. Like Aa, dcccix, BP describes it as being opposite the former temple of Vahagn/Heraklēs at Aštišat of Tarōn, but Aa uses the transliteration of the Greek form, "*Tawros*," while BP gives the Armenian translation, *Cʿul*, "bull."
See AON, p. 476.
III.xiv
p. 87
Map I, C–E/7–8.
See also "Aštišat."

Cyrus, see "Kur."

Dabil, see "Duin."

Dalarikʿ/Acuł ‹ Arm. *dalar*, "green, youthful; and ‹ Arm. *acux*, "coal"
Locality identified only as a village, without BP's characteristic specification of its district, and otherwise unidentified. The symbolic meaning of its name and its shift to the equally symbolic Acuł/Acux, reflecting the passage of light to darkness, suggest in context a fictitious toponym, as suggested by Melikʿ-Ōhanǰanyan (see III.xx n. 18).
See HArmB, I, pp. 612–613; Eremyan, *Map* G/5 places it just south of Manazkert.

III.xx
p. 97
See Appendix I, "Tiran."

Daranałē, see "Daranałikᶜ."

Daranałi, see "Daranałikᶜ."

Daranałikᶜ/Daranałē/Daranałi
    First district of Upper Armenia (*Barjr Haykᶜ*), according to the *Ašχarhacᶜoycᶜ* (29/ 40) and not familiar to classical sources before the Byzantine period. It may consequently have been treated by them as part of Akilisēnē/Ekełeacᶜ (cf. Strabo, *Geogr.*, XI.xiv.2, 5, *Xerxēnē*), but BP clearly distinguishes the two adjacent districts. Daranałikᶜ was located in westernmost Greater Armenia, southwest of Ekełeacᶜ, and the cave of Manē to which St. Gregory the Illuminator withdrew in his old age was located there, according to Aa, dccclxi, and MX, II.xc–xci (= MK, pp. 247–250), though BP makes no reference to it. The earlier Aršakuni necropolis of Ani was located in this district as was the Gregorid village and necropolis of Tᶜordan, and BP stresses repeatedly (III.xi, xii; IV.xiv) that it was part of the hereditary domain of the Gregorid house. No princely house is attested in the district. Both the plural form of the name, Daranałikᶜ, and the singular, Daranałē, occur in the text, which invariably identifies this region as a "district" (*gawar̄*), though the Karšuni version of the *Life of St. Gregory* (Vk, 294, p. 93) incorrectly describes it as a town. Bishops from the district are recorded at the oecumenical council of 680 (Mansi, XI, p. 645), and were consequently under Byzantine jurisdiction at that time.
    See AON, pp. 283–284; Eremyan, *Ašχarh.*, pp. 49, 116; *idem, Map* G/3; Hewsen, "Armenia," p. 326; *idem*, "Orontid," pp. 350–351; Tᶜ. X. Hakobyan, *Ašχarhagrutᶜyun*, pp. 205–206 and map; Tomaschek, "Daranalis"; Adontz, *Armenia*, pp. 39–40, 100, 155*; van Esbroeck, "Nouveau témoin," pp. 93–94 and n. 306; also III.xi n. 9.
    III.ii, xi–xii, xiv; IV.xiv, xxiv; V.i
    pp. 67, 81, 82, 84, 86, 139, 157, 186
    Map I, A–B/5–6
    See also "Ani"; "Ekełeacᶜ"; "Tᶜordan"; and Appendix I, "Grigor/Gregorids"; and Appendix III, *gawar̄*.

Darewnkᶜ/Dariwnkᶜ/Daroynkᶜ; mod. Doğubeyazit; the name is attested in numerous variations
    Fortress located in the district of Kogovit SEE of Zarehawan and some 25 km. SW of Mt. Ararat. It is perhaps to be identified with the Terua of Ptolemy (V.xii.7), but should not be confused with the homonymous locality in Basean. BP identifies it exclusively as an Aršakuni stronghold and one of the fortresses guarding the royal treasures associated successively with the kings Xosrov Kotak, Aršak II, and Pap, and it successfully resisted the great campaign of Šāhpuhr II (post 363) (V.i). There is, however, no mention of it in MX. At some point, which cannot be dated, Darewnkᶜ passed to the Bagratuni house, and by the seventh century it had become their *ostan* and necropolis (Sebēos, pp. 104, 144 = trans. pp. 52, 108).
    See AON, pp. 365, 441; Eremyan, *Ašχarh.*, p. 59; *idem, Map* G/6; Hewsen, "Ptolemy," pp. 131, 149; Tᶜ. X. Hakobyan, *Ašχarhagrutᶜyun*, p. 135 and map; Edwards, "Doğubeyazit"; Honigmann, *Ostgrenze*, pp. 29, 147; Adontz, *Armenia*, pp. 241–242, 456 n. 25, 516 n. 53, 196*; Toumanoff, *Studies*, pp. 202, 321–322 and n. 77, 342–344 and n. 16; Yovhannēsean, HB, pp. 833–839; Thierry and Thierry, "Monuments," pp. 175–176.
    III.vii; IV.xl; V.i

pp. 74, 163, 186
Maps, G/6.
See also "Kogovit"; "Zarehawan"; Appendix I, "Aršakuni"; and Appendix III, *ostan.*

Dariwnk', see "Darewnk'."

Daroynk', see "Darewnk'."

Dasn, see "Dassəntrē."

Dassəntrē/Dasn; Syr. Bēθ Dāsen
District on the border of southern Armenia, lying in the vicinity of Amadia on the upper course of the Great Zab. It probably formed part of the Armenian Adiabenian or Median March until the Roman–Persian peace of 363 (IV.l), after which it became part of the Persian province of Hedayab/Adiabēnē, although briefly reconquered ca. 370. It is not mentioned by MX or Aa and is not recorded in the later Lists of Armenian *naχarars*, because it had become part of the Sasanian Empire; but it is included in the Persian eparchy of Arbela at the Council of 410. Malχayanc' (p. 329 n. 125) takes this toponym as a *hapax* and rejects it (see IV.l n. 4), but it is identifiable with the eparchy of Dasn or Bēθ Dāsen of the Syriac sources, which is located in the same area (cf. Dionysius of Tell-Mahrē [Ps], clxxvii, p. 146), and is also known to Ełišē, i–ii, pp. 10, 51 (= *Ełishē*, pp. 65, 103).
See AON, pp. 320–321; Eremyan, *Ašχarh.*, pp. 49, 65, 70, 118; *idem, Map* D/5; Hewsen, "Vitaxates"; Marquart, *Ērānšahr*, pp. 25, 109, 158, 169–170; *idem, Süd-armenien*, pp. 378–379; Adontz, *Armenia*, pp. 175, 177–178, 156*; Toumanoff, *Studies*, pp. 165 n. 64, 182 n. 146; *Syn. Or.*, pp. 272, 285, 310, 316–317, 617–618; Manandyan, "Mahkertun," p. 39; Fiey, *Assyrie*, pp. 48, 227, 255–256, 271, 304, 307–308, 318, 543, 787, 816.
IV.l
p. 167
Maps, F–G/9–10
See also "Mahkertun"; "Noširakan."

Doubios, see "Duin."

Duin ‹ MIr. *duwīn*, "hill"; Gk. Δούβιος; Ar. Dābil
Locality in the district of Ayrarat on the east bank of the Azat river, some 20 kms. SSE of mod. Erevan and 10 kms NE of Artašat. According to MX, III.viii (= MK, p. 261), King Xosrov Kotak transferred the Armenian capital from Artašat to Duin be-cause of its healthier climate, but BP does not mention this transfer, which probably took place only in the second half of the fifth century. There is no record of any settlement at Duin in BP, which refers to the site as a *blur*, "hill" without noting that this was the meaning of the name in Persian, by contrast to the commentary of MX (*loc. cit.*), and the archaeological evidence is still under discussion. From the fifth century on, Duin became the residence of the Persian *marzpan* of Armenia and of the Armenian *kat'ołikos*, and it flourished as a commercial center through most of the medieval period (see, e.g., Procopius, *Bell. Pers.*, II.xxv.1–3).
See AON, pp. 365, 422; Eremyan, *Ašχarh.*, p. 49; *idem, Map* G/6; T'. X. Hakobyan, *Ašχarhagrut'yun*, pp. 138–140 and map; Minorsky, "Dvin"; Jahukyan, "Stugaba-nut'yunner," pp. 96–97; Manandyan, *Trade and Cities*, pp. 81–82, 143–144; K'alant'aryan, "Dvin K'ałak'ə"; *idem, Dvini mšukuytə*; Mnac'akanyan, S. X., "Dvin"; Łafadaryan, *Dvin*; *idem*, "Mehyan"; *idem*, "Fouilles"; Onofrio, *Dvin*; Yovhannēsean, HB, pp. 879–893.
III.viii

p. 75
Map II, G–H/5.
See also "Artašat"; "Ayrarat"; Appendix I, "Xosrov II/III"; Appendix III, *kat⁽c⁾ołikos*; *marzpan*.

Edessa, see "Uṙhay."

Egypt/Egyptos
The only reference to the imperial province of Egypt in BP is to identify the location of Alexandria with reference to the heresiarch Arius.
See Pietschmann, "Aigyptos."
III.x
p. 79

Egyptos, see "Egypt."

Ekełeac⁽c⁾; Gk. Ἀκιλισηνή Lat. Acilisena; attested in Armenian only in the genitive plural
Fourth district of Upper Armenia (*Barjr Hayk⁽c⁾*), according to the *Ašχarhac⁽c⁾oyc⁽c⁾* (29/40). It lay along the Euphrates directly northeast of Daranałik⁽c⁾, which it may originally have included, and from which it was separated by the Gohanam or Sepuh mountains (mod. Kara daği). The region was known to both Strabo (*Geogr.*, XI.xii.3; xiv.2, 5, 12, 16) and Ptolemy (V.xii.6) as Akilisēnē. It was, however, also known as Anaetica (Pliny the Elder, NH, V.xx.83–84) and Anaïtis Xōra (CD, XXXVI.xlviii.l, liii.5), because of the great temple of Anahit at Erēz in this district. BP, like all the other Armenian sources, speaks of Ekełeac⁽c⁾ as a "district" (*gawaṙ*), and stresses that it formed part of the domain of the house of St. Gregory, like neighboring Daranałik⁽c⁾, because one of the necropoleis of the patriarchal house was located in it at T⁽c⁾il (III.ii; V.xxiv).
See AON, p. 286; Eremyan, *Ašχarh.*, pp. 50, 116; *idem, Map* G/3; Hewsen, "Armenia," p. 326; *idem*, "Ptolemy," p. 115; *idem*, "Orontid," pp. 349–351; T⁽c⁾. X. Hakobyan, *Ašχarhagrut⁽c⁾yun*, pp. 206–207 and map; Adontz, *Armenia*, pp. 39–42, 100, 142*, 157*; Baumgartner, "Akilisene"; Markwart, *Südarmenien*, pp. 50–53; Honigmann, *Ostgrenze*, pp. 198–202. See also III.xi n. 9 and xiv n. 3.
III.ii, xiv; IV.xiv, xxiv; V.xxiv, xxv; VI.i
pp. 67, 88, 139, 157, 204–205, 233
Maps, B–C/5–6
See also "Ałewc"; "At⁽c⁾oṙ Anahtay"; "Daranałik⁽c⁾"; "T⁽c⁾il"; "Xaχ"; Appendix I, "Anahit"; "Grigor/Gregorids"; and Appendix III, *gawaṙ*.

Ełjerk⁽c⁾, "the Horns"
Mountain pass between the districts of Kogovit and Bagrewand. It is not otherwise attested or identified.
See AON, p. 424; Ališan, *Ayrarat*, p. 490; Ačemean, "Čanaparh."
V.xliii
p. 225
See also "Bagrewand"; "Kogovit."

Ep⁽c⁾rat ‹ OP Ufratū; ?Assyr. Purratu; Gk. Εὐφράτης; Lat. Euphrates
Major river of eastern Anatolia, running from the Bingol Mountains to the Persian Gulf. In modern times it has merged with the Tigris to form the Shatt-ul Arab separating Iran and Iraq, but in antiquity it had a separate outlet to the gulf. The Euphrates marked the traditional eastern boundary of the Roman Empire set by the emperor Augustus, and it separated the Roman province of Armenia Minor from the Aršakuni

kingdom of Armenia Major in the fourth century (cf. Strabo, *Geogr.*, XII.iii, 28). The references in BP are usually to the eastern branch or Arsanias (mod. Murad-su) rather than to the northern one (mod. Firhat nehri).

> See AON, pp. 204, 369, 404, 426; Eremyan, *Map* B/4–G–D–E/3.
> III.iv; IV.xiv; V.iii–iv, xliii; VI.xvi
> pp. 70, 140, 188–189, 227, 239
> Maps, A–G/5–7.

Eṙand

The name of this locality is a *hapax*. Adontz, however, suggested an identification with the Roman fortress of Rhandeia on the north bank of the Euphrates-Arsanias (mod. Murad-su).

> See Adontz, *Armenia*, pp. 31, 389 n. 18b, 217*; Eremyan, *Map* G/3, *Ḥràndea*, which
> he places, however, south of the Arsanias; Malχasyancᶜ, pp. 332–333 n. 146.
> V.i, iv
> pp. 186, 189
> Maps, B/7.

Eraχani/Aχani

Fortified stronghold of Vardan Mamikonean on the Çoruh River in the district of Taykᶜ. It apparently stood in the immediate vicinity of the modern town of Erkinis on the east bank of the Çoruh north of its junction with the Oltu çayi. The form Aχani is found in one ms.

> See Edwards, "Artvin," n. 105, *Eraχačì*; Yovhannēsean, HB, opp. p. 609, *Eraχačì*;
> Eremyan, *Ašχarh.*, p. 53 and map B/4, but not on the fourth-century *Map*.
> IV.xviii
> p. 148
> Maps, E/4.
> See also "Taykᶜ"; and Appendix I, "Vardan I Mamikonean."

Ereweal/Erewel

Locality in the district of Vanand, which should probably be identified with the homonymous plain in the same district known to MX, III.xlvi (= MK, p. 308).

> See AON, p. 425.
> IV.xxii
> p. 155
> See also "Vanand."

Erewel, see "Ereweal."

Eruandašat ⟨ Eruand + MIr. *šād*, "joy, joyous"

City founded ca. 200 B.C. by Eruand/Orontes, last ruler of the Eruandid/Orontid Armenian dynasty, as his new capital, replacing the earlier center of Armawir, MX, II.xxxix (= MK, pp. 181–182), and subsequently renamed Marmēt, according to MX, II.xlvi (= MK, p. 187), though this name is not otherwise attested. The city stood at the junction of the Araxes and Aχurean rivers in the district of Aršarunikᶜ (*Ašχarhacᶜoycᶜ*, 34/45). It was probably a foundation of Hellenistic type, in view of its eponymous name, patterned on the multiple Alexandrias as were Artašat or Tigranakert in Armenia. It was an important trade center with a considerable Jewish population, which was deported to Persia after the sack of the city by Šāhpuhr II (post 363). MX, II.xlii, III.xxxi (= MK, pp. 183, 287–288), claims that the city was given to the Kamsarakan house by Trdat the Great and that it was their capital in the fourth century, but none of this information is to be found in BP. There is no evidence that the city survived its destruction by the Persians and the deportation of its population.

See AON, pp. 363, 426; Eremyan, *Ašχarh.*, p. 51; *idem, Map* B/5; T͑. X. Hakobyan, *Ašχarhagrut͑yun*, pp. 117–118 and map; Arak͑elyan, "Ervandašat"; Manandyan, *Trade and Cities*, pp. 37–38, 96, 155; Toumanoff, *Studies* pp. 206, 310, 319; Garsoïan, "Mediaeval Armenian City," pp. 69, 73, 77; Yovhannēsean, HB, pp. 655–660; CPD, p. 78, *šād*.

IV.lv
p. 175
Maps, G/5
See also "Aršarunik͑"; Appendix I, "Hreayk͑"; "Kamsarakan, house"; and Appendix III, *k͑ałak͑.*

Euphrates, see "Ep͑rat."

Əndmeš, see "Anyuš"

Ənjak͑iars see "Ənǰak͑isar."

Ənjak͑isar/Ənǰak͑iars (see III.x n. 14 for the correct reading), mod. Ak Kul.
Mountain on the border of the districts of Řštunik͑ and Ałjnik͑ southwest of Lake Van. The *Ašχarhac͑oyc͑* (32/43) places it in Řštunik͑.
See Hübschmann, AON, pp. 339, 429; Lynch, *Armenia*, II, pp. 117 n. 2, 137, who places it by association with the village of "Ēndzakh͑."
III.x
p. 79
Maps, E/7–8?
See also "Ałjnik͑"; "Řštunik."

Gamirk͑ ‹ Ak., Ass. Gimirri (Gk. Κιμμέριοι); Gk. Καππαδοκία; Lat. Cappadocia
Known as part of the Roman Empire to ŠKZ, Parth. 8, 10, 11; Phl. 13; RGDS nos. 18, 22, 26, pp. 52–55; KKZ, 12; etc.
Major province of eastern Anatolia lying directly west of Armenia Minor. Armenian primates were consecrated at its metropolitan see of Caesarea until the murder of St. Nersēs I, ca. 373. BP refers to it only in this connection or in the intrusive passages from the life of St. Basil of Caesarea, and makes no allusion to the division of the province by the emperor Valens in 372. Aa and MX (with one exception, II.lxxx = MK, p. 228) use the Greek form, Kapadovkia, for the name of the province, while BP invariably prefers the Armenian Gamirk͑, derived from the name of the Gimirri or Kimmerians.
See OCD, p. 164; Ruge, "Kappadokia"; Jones, *Cities*, pp. 174–190, map II; Gignoux, *Glossaire*, pp. 25, 55; Sprengling, *Third-Century Iran*, pp. 7, 8, 10, 16, 47, 52; Honigmann and Maricq, RGDS, pp. 13–14; Hild, *Kappadokien*; Restle, *Architektur*.
III.xii, xvi–xvii; IV.iii–iv, vii, xi
pp. 82, 91–92, 109, 111, 126, 133
Maps, A/6–7.
See also "Caesarea"; and Appendix I, "Barseł"; "Nersēs I"; "P͑arēn"; "Šahak I"; "Yusik I-II."

Ganjak ‹ Ir. *ganǰ*, "treasure"; Gk. Γαζάκα; Lat. Ganzaca
Ganjak, also known as Ganjak Šāhastan, was the capital of Atrpatakan and the site of the "Warrior fire" (*Ādur Gušnasp*), one of the main shrines of the Sasanian Empire as it was the particular fire of the king. It was also known to classical sources (e.g. Strabo, *Geogr.*, XI.xiii, 3; Pliny, NH, VI.xvi, 42). Ganjak was probably located at the

site of the ruins of Takht-i Suleiman (Shīz) and should not be confused with its namesake (mod. Kirovabad) in Soviet Azerbaijan, as is done by Langlois (CHAMA, I, p. 215 n. 1). The fire shrine was destroyed by the emperor Heraclius in 623 in retaliation for the Persian seizure of the relics of the True Cross at their capture of Jerusalem in 614. BP repeatedly stresses that Ganjak marked the border between the Armenian and the Persian realms in the southeast, but Eremyan suggests that this reference is to the district rather than to the city itself. This is probably the case, since the references give the name only without any precise description, with the exception of V.v, which speaks of the "side" (*koys*) of Ganjak.

See AON, pp. 416–417; Eremyan, *Ašχarh.*, p. 46; *idem, Map* D/6; Markwart, *Catalogue*, p. 108; Christensen, *L'Iran*, pp. 142 n. 1, 165–167, 448; Frye, *Heritage*, pp. 221, 229, 259 n. 23, pls. 4–5; Osten and Naumann, *Takht-i Suleiman*; Russell, *Zor. Arm.*, p. 263, 483.
III.vii; IV.xxi; V.i, iv–vi, xxxiv
pp. 74, 154, 186, 193–194, 196, 215
Maps, J/9–10.
See also "Atrpatakan."

Gardman/Gardmanajor ‹ Gardman + Arm. *jor*, "valley/gorge"
Sixth district of Utik', according to the *Ašχarhac'oyc'* (33/44). It lay in the upper valley of the Šamχor River between the district of Šakašēn and Lake Sewan and should not be confused with the Iberian duchy of Gardabani, as is done by Eremyan. The homonymous princes, whom BP leaves anonymous instead of recording their proper names, as is its common practice, are given a fanciful Haykid ancestry by MX, II.viii (= MK, pp. 139–140). They are also known to the late *Gahnamak*, "Rank List," and are attributed 1,000 retainers by the *Zōrnamak*, "Military List." They seceded from King Aršak II in favor of Ałuank' after the Roman–Persian peace of 363 (IV.l), were briefly reconquered when the *sparapet* Mušeł Mamikonean brought the northern border of the Armenian kingdom to the Kur River ca. 370 (V.xiii), and lost again after the partition of Greater Armenia ca. 387. The first dynasty of Gardman was replaced soon thereafter by the Mihranids of Iran, who were also to rule Ałuank' after 628.

See AON, p. 352; Eremyan, *Ašχarh.*, pp. 46, 118; *idem, Map* B/6; Hewsen, "Armenia," p. 341; *idem*, "Vitaxates"; T'. X. Hakobyan, *Ašχarhagrut'yun*, p. 236 and map; Adontz, *Armenia*, pp. 175–176, 192, 194, 204–205, 207, 325, 67*, 69*, 121*, 124*–125*, 158*; Toumanoff, *Studies*, pp. 187–188, 216, 223, 230 n. 280, 231 n. 284, 240, 245, 252, 475, 482–484 and n. 499.
III.xvii; IV.l; V.xiii
pp. 92, 167, 200
Maps, I–J/4–5.
See also "Ałuank'"; "Kur"; "Šakašēn"; "Utik'"; and Appendix I, "Aršak II"; "Mušeł."

Gardmanajor, see "Gardman."

Garni; Lat. Gornea(s)
Residence of the Aršakuni kings situated above the Azat River in their innermost *ostan*. This fortress, which may go back to Urartian times, is first attested as Gornea(s) by Tacitus (*Ann.*, XII.xlv), and the building of a residence for princess Xosroviduχt by Trdat the Great recorded by MX, II.xc (= MK, p. 247), is seemingly confirmed by the inscription found at the site. The remains of a classical structure found within the walls of the fortress and now reconstructed as a temple are the only example of a classical building extant in Greater Armenia, but its date and purpose have been the subjects of some disagreement among scholars.

See AON, p. 365; Eremyan, *Ašχarh.*, p. 46; *idem, Map* B/6; T^c. X. Hakobyan, *Ašχarhagrut^cyun*, pp. 141–142 and map. On the inscription and the temple, see Trever, *Armenia*; pp. 174–211; Aṙak^celyan, "Gaṙni," pp. 15–198; Der Nersessian, *Armenian Art*, p. 19 and fig. 8; Yovhannēsean, HB, pp. 853–867; Krkyašaryan, *Gaṙni*; Bart^cikyan, "Gaṙni"; Feydit, "Gaṙni"; Wilkinson, "A Fresh Look"; Jahukyan, "Stugabanut^cyunner," p. 96, has proposed a hypothetical etymology: Gaṙni ‹ ?Urart. *garini*, "fortress."
III.viii
p. 75
Maps, H/5.
See also Appendix I, "Aršakuni"; and Appendix III, *ostan.*

Gaweč, see "Baṙaēj."

Gawt^can, see "Gołt^cn."

Gogarēnē, see "Gugark^c."

Gogovit, see "Kogovit."

Gołt^cn/Gawt^can; Gk. Κολθηνή(?); Lat. Colthene(?)
Thirty-third district of Vaspurakan, according to the *Ašχarhac^coyc^c* (33/44), though it lay north of the Araxes River in the region of modern Ordubad and was consequently a portion of southern Siwnik^c, from which ruling house its dynasts were descended, according to MX, II.viii (= MK, p. 143). Toumanoff, however, considers them a branch of the Bagratuni. They are recorded in all the Lists of Armenian *naχarar*s, and the *Zōrnamak*, "Military List," attributes 500 retainers to them. Bishops from the district are also recorded in the Armenian conciliar lists (GT^c, pp. 73, 149, 151; Michael the Syrian, II, p. 497). Gołt^cn was renowned for its wine, and pagan traditions were long preserved there, as attested by the activity of St. Maštoc^c (Koriwn, v, xiii, pp. 40, 60 = trans., pp. 28, 36) and by the pagan songs and tales alluded to by MX, II.xxx, xlix, lxi; III.xlvii, lx (=MK, pp. 121, 190, 203, 310, 333). Gołt^cn may perhaps be identified with the Kolθēnē of Ptolemy (V.xii.4), but the district of Kołt^c is more likely.
See Ałayan, "Gołt^can"; AON, p. 346; Eremyan, *Ašχarh.*, pp. 48, 117; *idem, Map* G/6–7; T^c. X. Hakobyan, *Ašχarhagrut^cyun*, pp. 174–175 and map; Adontz, *Armenia*, pp. 190, 192, 195, 201, 205, 207, 228, 256, 263, 462–463 n. 65, 67*, 69*–70*, 93*, 97*–99*, 102*, 125*, 136*, 160*; Toumanoff, *Studies*, pp. 110 n. 173, 203–204 and n. 230, 226, 228, 240, 245, 251–252, 323 and n. 78.
III.xii
p. 82
Maps, I–J/7.
See also "Kołt"; "Siwnik^c"; and Appendix I, "Atom."

Gomkunk^c ‹ Arm. *gom*, "stable" + diminutive suffix; "little stable"
Village in the district of Tarōn granted by the Queen P^caṙanjem to the priest Mrjiwnik. It is not otherwise attested.
See AON, p. 420.
IV.xv
p. 145
See also "Tarōn"; and Appendix I, "Mrjiwnik."

Gordyēnē, see "Korčēk^c."

Gornea, see "Gaṙni."

Great Copʿkʿ, see "Copʿkʿ Mec."

Greater Armenia, see "Mec Haykʿ."

Gugarkʿ; Gk. Γωγαρηνή Lat. Gogarena; Iberian or Mazkʿutʿkʿ March
   One of the main border regions of Greater Armenia in the north, forming the Armeno-Iberian marchlands northeast of Taykʿ and west of Utikʿ, according to the *Ašχarhacʿoycʿ* (34–35/46). The region presumably took its name from the local tribe of the Gugarkʿ and was known as Gogarēnē to Strabo (*Geogr.*, XI.xiv.2, 4–5), but as Obarēnē to Ptolemy (V.xii.4). It was partially subdivided in the fourth century, with some of its districts belonging to Iberia/Virkʿ rather than to Armenia. BP mentions only two of its Armenian districts: Joropʿor and Kołbopʿor.
   Gugarkʿ was one of the semi-autonomous border principalities of the Armenian kingdom, forming its Iberian or Mazkʿutʿkʿ March, and was governed by a *bdeašχ*, usually styled "the other *bdeašχ*," see Aa, dccxcv; Ag, cxxxv; Vg, xcviii = Va, lxxxvi, or "the keeper of the Mazkʿutʿkʿ March" (*sahmanakaln . . . i Maskʿetʿacʿ kołmanēn*), Aa, dccclxxiii. These *bdeašχ*s are also known to MX, II. viii, xi (*Vracʿ bdeašχ ̇ɷ mecɷ̇*); III.vi, lx (= MK, pp. 140, 147, 258, 333), who traces their appointment to King Vałaršak and gives them an Iranian ancestry, though this descent was probably true of only one dynasty, according to Toumanoff. The princes of Gugarkʿ are not known to the late Lists of *naχarar*s except for the *Zōrnamak*, "Military List," which makes them commanders of the "Northern Gate," with the disproportionately large contingent of 4,500 retainers.
   Like most of the marchlands, Gugarkʿ wavered in its allegiance to the Armenian crown, and the territory was disputed between Armenia and Virkʿ. According to BP, the *bdeašχ* of Gugarkʿ abandoned King Aršak II after the Roman–Persian peace of 363 and went over to Iran (IV.l). The principality was temporarily reconquered by the Armenian *sparapet* Mušeł Mamikonean ca. 370 and the native Gušarid dynasty annihilated (V.xv), when the northern border of the Armenian kingdom was temporarily pushed back to the Kur River. Gugarkʿ was again lost after the partition of the Armenian kingdom ca. 387. It survived under the local Iranian dynasty of the Mihranids as one of the two *bdeašχ*s recorded in post Aršakuni times (see, e.g., ŁPʿ, xxv, xxvii–xxviii, xxxi, lix, pp. 47, 52, 55, 59, 107 = *Ełišē*, pp. 261, 265, 269, 273, 324, etc. who calls him the *bdeašχ* of Virkʿ). Gugarkʿ was reclaimed for Armenia only in the eighth and ninth centuries under the Bagratuni dynasty.
   See AON, pp. 275–276; Eremyan, *Ašχarh.*, pp. 48, 118; *idem, Map* B/5–6; Tʿ. X. Hakobyan, *Ašχarhagrutʿyun*, pp. 237–238 and map; Hewsen, "Armenia," pp. 334, 339; *idem,* "Ptolemy," pp. 114, 148; *idem,* "Vitaxates"; Marquart, *Ērānšahr*, pp. 165–170; Adontz, *Armenia*, pp. 23, 33–34, 173, 175–176, 179, 194, 197–198, 205–206, 222–225, 230, 232, 321, 370, 452 n. 91, 497–498 n. 76, 524 n. 87, 69*, 73*, 75*, 118*, 121*, 124*–125*, 159*–160*; Toumanoff, *Studies*, pp. 128–129, 131–133, 143, 165, 183–192, 223, 227, 240, 245, 260–264, 467–473, 474, 499; Garitte, *Documents*, pp. 72–73; Kiessling, "Gogarene"; Edwards, "Artvin."
   IV.l; V.xv
   pp. 167, 201
   Maps, G/3.
   See also "Jor/Joropʿor"; "Kołb"; "Kur"; "Miǰnašχarh Hayocʿ"; "Taykʿ"; "Utikʿ"; "Virkʿ"; Appendix I, "Aršak II"; "Gugarkʿ"; "Mazkʿutʿkʿ"; "Mušeł"; and Appendix III, *bdeašχ*.

Gurzan, see "Virk^c."

Haband, Miws "The Other" Haband/Sisakan i Kotak/P^cok^cr Siwnik^c

Two districts are known under the name of Haband to the *Ašχarhac^coyc^c* (33/44). The first, belonging to the province of Siwnik^c, lay between the Orotan and the Araxes rivers. The other, which is the one referred to by BP, was known as *Miws Haband*, "The Other Haband." It belonged to the region of Arjaχ further east on the border of Ałuank^c, to which it passed after the partition of the Armenian kingdom, ca. 387. It was also known subsequently under the name of "Lesser Siwnik" (*Sisakan-i Kotak* or *P^cok^cr Siwnik^c*), which is the form used by MX, III.iii (= MK, p. 256). No dynasts are recorded from this district, until the ninth century.

> See AON, pp. 348, 350; Eremyan, *Ašχarh.*, pp. 34, 70, 117; *idem, Map* G/7; Hewsen, "Armenia," pp. 332, 341; Marquart, *Ērānšahr*, p. 120; Adontz, *Armenia*, pp. 174, 120*, 125*, 169*.
> III.vi
> p. 73
> Maps, J–K/6.
> See also "Ałuank^c"; "Amaraz"; "Arjaχ."

Hac^ceac^c Draχt, Arm. "Ash Grove/Garden"

Site of the hermitage of St. Daniēl below the temple of Vahagn/Heraklēs near Aštišat of Tarōn. It is also known to MX, III.xiv (= MK, 267), who gives no indication of its locality. According to BP, the spring at which St. Gregory had baptized a great host (cf. Aa, dcccxiv) was also located there.

> See AON, p. 444.
> III.xiv
> pp. 87, 90
> See also "Aštišat"; and Appendix I, "Daniēl"; "Vahagn."

Hac^cekeac^c/Hac^cekac^c gewł (attested in the genitive); "Ash Village"

Village in the district of Tarōn to which BP (III.xix) refers as a *karčazat gewł*. It was otherwise known as the birthplace of Mesrop Maštoc^c, according to Koriwn (iii, p. 36 = trans. p. 37), who also gives the form Hac^cekac^c, and to MX, III.xlvii (= MK, p. 309). Eremyan locates it southeast of Aštišat and north of the Meł River. The Russian translation of Koriwn (p. 133 n. 57) asserts that this village survived under the name of *Xas geł* until 1915.

> See AON, p. 444, *Hacik^c*; Eremyan, *Map* G/4, *Hac^cek*; T^c. X. Hakobyan, *Ašχar-hagrut^cyun*, p. 154 and map; Manandyan, *Feodalizm*, pp. 118–119
> III.xix
> p. 94
> Maps, E/7.
> See also "Aštišat"; "Tarōn"; Appendix I, "Vrik"; and Appendix III, *karčazat*.

Hanjit, see "Anjit."

Hašteank^c; Gk. Ἀσθιανηνή/Ἀσταυνίτις; Lat. Asthianena

Second district of Cop^ck^c at the source of the Tigris, according to the *Ašχarc^coyc^c* (30/40). It lay south of Xorjean between Tarōn in the East and Balahovit in the West. The usual form of the name found in later classical authors, such as Procopius (*De aed.*, III.iii.7) or George of Cyprus (no. 964, p. 49), is Asthianenēs or Astianikēs, but Ptolemy gives it as Astaunitis (V.xii.7).

Hašteank^c passed to the Roman sphere of influence, probably still as part of the larger Cop^ck^c/Sophēnē, under the terms of the peace of Nisibis of 298 (Petr. Patric., *Ad*

467

gen., iii), but it is distinguished as a separate Satrapy in the Justinianic legislation (CJ, I.29.5; *Novella* xxxi). The princes of the district belonged to the Kaminakan family, which may have been a junior Aršakuni line, according to MX, II.viii, xxii, xxxv, lxii; III.xxii, xxxi (= MK, pp. 144, 159, 176, 205, 278, 288). They are not listed in either the later *Gahnamak*, "Rank List," or in the *Zōrnamak*, "Military List," but they are to be found under the name of Hašteank‛ in the listing of Armenian *naxarar*s given in the *Vita* of St. Nersēs, v, p. 34 (= CHAMA, II, p. 26), and bishops are said to have been sent to the district by St. Gregory the Illuminator (Vg, clxxi = Va, clix). Hašteank‛ seems to have remained in the Roman sphere of influence, for it is not mentioned by BP, who calls it a mere *gawaṙ* (III.xii), after the reign of King Tiran. Like almost all the other Satrapies, its autonomy was apparently limited by the emperor Zeno at the end of the fifth century (Procopius, *De aed.*, III.i.17–29), and it was abolished by Justinian, who incorporated it into the new Byzantine province of Armenia IV in 536 (*Novella* xxxi).

    See AON, pp. 225, 227, 228, 230, 248, 291–292; Eremyan, *Ašχarh.*, pp. 62, 116; *idem, Map* G/4; T‛. X. Hakobyan, *Ašχarhagrut‛yun*, p. 217 and map; Hewsen, "Armenia," p. 327; *idem*, "Ptolemy," p. 115; Baumgartner, "Asthianēnē"; Adontz, *Armenia*, pp. 16–18, 27, 202, 257, 358 n. 22, 379 nn. 23–24, 380 nn. 27–29, 149*, 161*; Toumanoff, *Studies*, pp. 172, 192, 216, 223, 226, 245; Garitte, *Documents*, pp. 101–102, 205.

    III.ix, xii

    pp. 77, 82

    Maps, C/7

    See also "Cop‛k‛"; "Tarōn"; Appendix I, "Grigor/Gregorids"; "Kaminakan, house"; "Tiran"; and Appendix III, *gawaṙ*.

Hēr/Xēr/Xoy

    Ninth district of Parskahayk‛, according to the *Ašχarhac‛oyc‛* (32/43). It formed the area surrounding the modern town of Xoy in Iranian Azerbaijan. Most scholars place it north of the adjacent district of Zarawand, but Eremyan reverses the order on his map to the *Ašχarhac‛oyc‛*. The two districts are usually treated as a single unit in Armenian medieval sources (e.g., Aa, dccxcv) and the dynasts are usually known as princes of Zarawand and Hēr, as is also the case in BP where both are linked into a single *gawaṙ*.

    See AON, pp. 259–261, 338; Eremyan, *Ašχarh.*, pp. 63, 117 and map G/6, but not on the fourth-century *Map*; T‛. X. Hakobyan, *Ašχarhagrut‛yun*, pp. 231–232 and map; Hewsen, "Armenia," p. 330; Marquart, *Ērānšahr*, pp. 109–110; *idem*, "Parskahayk‛," p. 253; Adontz, *Armenia*, pp. 248–249, 162*.

    III.viii

    p. 75

    Maps, H–I/7–8

    See also "Hrsijor"; "Zarawand"; and Appendix III, *gawaṙ*.

Hiberia, see "Virk‛."

Hiwsisakan Cov, see Northern Sea.

Hrsijor

    This name is otherwise unattested as either a toponym or that of a *naxarar* house. Toumanoff identifies it with "the valley" (*jor*) of Hēr.

    See Toumanoff, *Studies*, p. 219 and n. 256.

    IV.xi

    p. 133

    See also "Hēr"; and Appendix I, "Surik."

Iberia, see "Virk^c."

Iberian March, see "Gugark^c."

Ingilēnē, see "Angełtun."

Janǰanak
Locality granted to Vač^cē I Mamikonean in reward for his victory over the Mazk^cut^ck^c. Not otherwise attested or identified.
III.viii
p. 75
See also "C^clu Gluχ"; "Jr̈bašχk^c"; and Appendix I, "Mazk^cut^ck^c"; "Vač^cē I."

John the Precursor, St., shrines of
The transfer of the relics of the saints John the Precursor (*Karapet*) and At^cana-
ginēs/Athenogenes to Aštišat of Tarōn is part of the Armenian received tradition set out
in Aa, dcccx–dcccxvi; cf. MX, III.ii (= MK, p. 255), who gives it only a brief mention,
and in the late and garbled version of the *History of Tarōn*, pp. 96–100 intended to
bolster the claims of Aštišat and especially of the monastery of Surb Karapet at Muš
in Tarōn. See also III.iii, n. 4. The martyrium of St. John at Aštišat seems to have been
the main shrine dedicated to St. John's cult, but his other shrine at Bagawan (IV.xv;
V.xliii) was also familiar to Armenian sources, e.g. Aa, dcccxxxvi; MX, II.lxvi (= Mk,
p. 213).
See Ōrmanean, *Azgapatum*, I, cols. 88–96; Garitte, *Documents*, pp. 217, 316–320;
Avdoyan, *Ps. Yovhannēs Mamikonean*; and III.iii nn. 4, 6, 7.
III.iii, xiv, xvi; IV.[xiv], xv xvi; V.xliii
pp. 68, 86, 91–92 [139], 141, 226
See also "Aštišat"; "Bagawan."

Jor/Joray ‹ Arm. *jor*, "valley"
Pass in southern Armenia between Tarōn and Asorestan that marked the border of
the Aršakuni kingdom but lay within it, according to Anasyan (IV.l n. 5). It is also
mentioned by Sebēos, xlii, p. 138 (= trans. p. 100, "Dzor"), Łewond, iii, p. 9 (= trans.
p. 51), and Asołik, I.v; II.iv, pp. 35, 120 (= trans. pp. 35, 152, "Tzor"). It should probably
be identified with the Bitlis pass.
See AON, p. 447, *Jor*²; Eremyan, *Ašχarh.*, p. 63 and map G/4–5, *Jorapahak*; T^c. X.
Hakobyan, *Ašχarhagrut^cyun*, map opp. p. 52, who places it N. of Bitlis.
IV.l
p. 167
Maps, E/8
See also "Asorestan"; "Mec Hayk^c"; "Tarōn"; and the next entry.

Jor/Jorop^cor ‹ Arm. *jor*, "valley" + *p^cor*, "gorge"
First district of Gugark^c, according to the *Ašχarhac^coyc^c* (34/46). Toumanoff gives
it on his map as the southeasternmost district lying along the southern tributaries of the
Kur in the borderland between Virk^c and Ałuank^c and encompassing the valley of the
Jora/Akstafa River. Its precise location is still debated because of contradictions in the
sources. Eremyan omits it altogether from his fourth-century *Map*, and Hakobyan
places it south of Kołbop^cor.
The territory of Jorop^cor formed a part of the Iberian March ruled by the *bdeašχ* of
Gugark^c, and its ruling house was probably a cadet line of the Gušarid dynasts of
Gugark^c. Jor had presumably become a separate principality before 339, since its
princes are recorded by BP in the reign of King Tiran (III.xii), and Jor is described as

a "realm" (*ašχarh*) though it is called a *gawaŕ* in IV.l. It defected from Aršak II after the Roman–Perisan peace of 363 (IV.l), was presumably briefly reconquered ca. 370 when the Armenian *sparapet* Mušēl Mamikonean carried the border of the Aršakuni kingdom back to the Kur River (V.xiii, xv), and was lost once again after the partition of Greater Armenia (ca. 387), as it is listed among the Iberian lands taken from Armenia in the *Ašχarhac*oyc* (28/39). The absence of the princes of Joropᶜor from all of the later Lists of *naχarar*s is probably also indicative of their separate status outside Armenia after 387.

> See AON, pp. 353–354, and esp. 490; Eremyan, *Ašχarh.*, pp. 63–64, 118 and map B/6, but not the fourth-century *Map*; Hewsen, "Armenia," pp. 334, 338; *idem*, "Vitaxates"; Tᶜ. X. Hakobyan, *Ašχarhagrut*yun*, pp. 238–239; Toumanoff, *Studies*, pp. 186–187 and n. 175, 190 and n. 198, 216, 223, 226, 237 n. 306, 245, 259, 467, 468 n. 134, 469, 470, 472 n. 155, 474, 482–483 n. 203, 483–484 n. 205, 487, maps.
>
> III.xii; IV.l
>
> pp. 82, 167
>
> Maps, H–I/4
>
> See also "Aluankᶜ"; "Gugarkᶜ"; "Jor/Joray"; "Kur"; "Virkᶜ"; Appendix I, "Aršak II"; "Gorutᶜ"; "Mušēl"; "Tiran"; Appendix III, *ašχarh*; *gawaŕ*; and the preceding entry.

Joropᶜor, see "Jor/Joropᶜor."

Jrabašχkᶜ, Arm. "ponds/pools."

District granted as a reward to Vačᶜē I Mamikonean for his victory over the Mazkᶜutᶜkᶜ by King Xosrov Kotak, it is identified with the Sukawet Mountains, marking the northern border of the district of Bagrewand in the *Vita of the Oskean Saints* (p. 65), but may perhaps have been the district of Gabelean north of these mountains.

> See AON, p. 465, *Jur*; Eremyan, *Ašχarh.*, p. 108, *Sukawet*; *idem*, *Map* G/5, where he places it rather to the south of the mountains.
>
> III.viii
>
> p. 75
>
> Maps, F/5–6
>
> See also "Bagrewand"; "Cᶜlu Gluχ"; "Janjanak"; and Appendix I, "Mazkᶜutᶜkᶜ"; "Vačᶜē I"; "Xosrov II/III."

Kainē Polis, see "Valaršapat."

Karenitis, see "Karin."

Karin; Gk. Καρηνῖτις; Lat. Carenitis

Ninth district of Upper Armenia (*Barjr Haykᶜ*), according to the *Ašχarhac*oyc* (29/40), also known to Strabo (*Geogr.*, XI.xiv.5) and Pliny the Elder (NH, V.xx, 83). It lay at the sources of the northern Euphrates River and formed the district of the city to which it gave its Armenian name, Karin/Karnoy kᶜalakᶜ. The city is not mentioned in BP which speaks exclusively of the *gawaŕ*, and probably became an important strategic center only after its fortification by the Byzantine Empire, which gave it the name Theodosioupolis (mod. Erzurum); see Procopius (*Bell. Pers.*, I.x.18; *De aed.*, III.v.2–12). The district of Karin probably formed part of the royal domain of the Aršakuni (V.xliv), and no princes are recorded from this district, but bishops are said to have been sent to it by St. Gregory the Illuminator himself (Vg, clxxii = Va, clx), although they passed to the jurisdiction of the imperial church after the partition of Armenia (ca. 387) which transferred Armenia Interior to Byzantium .

See AON, pp. 213, 287–288; Eremyan, *Ašχarh.*, pp. 58, 116; *idem, Map* B–G/4; Hewsen, "Armenia," p. 326; *idem,* "Orontid," pp. 351, 354; Tᶜ. X. Hakobyan, *Ašχarhagrutᶜyun,* pp. 209–211 and map; Weissbach, "Karenitis"; Adontz, *Armenia,* pp. 21, 39, 43–44, 98–100, 115, 257, 267, 284, 307, 332, 395 nn. 12a–b, 14, 118*–119*, 124*, 163*; Toumanoff, *Studies,* p. 193 nn. 207, 209; Manandyan, *Trade and Cities,* pp. 87–90; Garitte, *Documents,* p. 102–104; Garsoïan, "Mediaeval Armenian City," pp. 70, 74, 82; *idem.,* "Separation."
IV.xii; V.xxxvii, xliv
pp. 134, 219, 228
Maps, D–E/4
See also "Marag"; Appendix I, "Aršakuni"; "Grigor/Gregorids"; and Appendix III, *gawaṙ; kᶜaɫakᶜ.*

Kaspē, see "Kazbkᶜ."

Kaspianē, see "Kazbkᶜ."

Kazbkᶜ/Kaspē; Gk. Κασπιανή Lat. Caspiane
District on the eastern border of Greater Armenia south of the Kur, presumably named after the homonymous tribe, which had disappeared by the time of Strabo (*Geogr.,* XI.iv.5, xiv.5), who attributes the district to both Aɫuankᶜ/Albania and Armenia. They are also known to Aa, xix, dcccxlii, and the district should be identified with the one named Pᶜaytakaran in the *Ašχarhacᶜoycᶜ* (33/44), according to Eremyan (cf. V.xiv n. 2). Princes from this district are included in all the late Lists of *naχarars,* and the *Zōrnamak,* "Military List," attributes 3,000 retainers to them, although Toumanoff refuses to acknowledge their existence and treats the name exclusively as a toponym, as is the case in BP (IV.l), which refers to Kazbkᶜ as both an *ašχarh* and an *erkir* (see IV.xiv n. 2). The region fell away from Aršak II after the Roman–Persian peace of 363, was temporarily reconquered by the *sparapet* Mušeɫ Mamikonean ca. 370, and was lost again to Atrpatakan after the partition of the Armenian kingdom ca. 387.
See AON, pp. 210, 268–270; Eremyan, *Ašχarh.*, pp. 57, 67, 89, Pᶜaytakaran; *idem, Map* B/8, Pᶜaytakaran; Hewsen, "Armenia," p. 333, Pᶜaytakaran; *idem,* "Ptolemy," pp. 118–119, *Kaspianē; idem,* "Orontid," p. 352; *idem,* "Caspiane"; Adontz, *Armenia,* pp. 175–176, 191, 194, 201, 203, 206–207, 221–222, 257, 307, 67*, 69*–70*, 87*–88*, 164*; Toumanoff, *Studies,* pp. 129, 132, 230 n. 277, 232 n. 287.
IV.l; V.xiv
pp. 167, 200
Maps, L/6–7
See also "Aɫuankᶜ"; "Atrpatakan"; "Kur"; "Pᶜaytakaran"; Appendix I, "Aršak II"; "Mušeɫ"; and Appendix III, *ašχarh; erkir.*

Kesaria, see "Caesarea."

Khaldia, see "Xaɫtekᶜ."

Kog, see "Kogovit."

Kogovit/Kog/Kovg/Gogovit ‹ *Kogay* + Arm. *hovit,* "valley"
Thirteenth district of the region of Ayrarat on the Maku River, south of the Araxes River, and of Mt. Ararat, according to the *Ašχarhacᶜoycᶜ* (34/45). Kogovit contained the royal fortress of Darewnkᶜ as well as the royal foundation of Aršakawan and MX, III.xxiii (= MK, p. 278), calls it Aršak II's "own beloved province." Kogovit may consequently have formed part of the royal domain, though Toumanoff suggests the possibility that it was already held by the Bagratuni family in the period of the

Aršakuni. There is no evidence in the sources for this hypothesis, but Kogovit had indeed become a Bagratuni domain at the time of its transfer to the Byzantine Empire under the terms of the peace concluded in 591 between the Emperor Maurice and Xusrō II Parwīz. No princes from the district are mentioned in either the *Gahnamak*, "Rank List" or the *Zōrnamak*, "Military List," but the late listing of the *Vita* of St. Nersēs, p. 34 (= CHAMA, II, p. 26), includes the Kogovteankʿ. BP invariably treats this name as a toponym, to which it refers sometimes as a "district" (*gawaṙ*) (IV.xii), but more commonly as a "land" (*erkir*) (III.vii; V.i), and even by the awkward locution, "the land of the district of Kog" ([*y*] *erkirn Kog gawaṙi*). Like its qualifications, the forms of the name vary widely. Gogovit is also attested.

> See AON, pp. 342, 364–365, 441; Eremyan, *Ašχarh.*, pp. 59, 118; *idem, Map* G/5–6; Hewsen, "Armenia," p. 335; Tʿ. X. Hakobyan, *Ašχarhagrutʿyun*, pp. 134–136 and map; Adontz, *Armenia*, pp. 180, 202, 231, 236, 240–242, 247–248, 438 n. 37, 455 n. 14, 456 n. 25, 120*, 121*, 126*, 165*; Toumanoff, *Studies*, pp. 202, 321–323 and n. 77, 342–344 and n. 16.
> III.vii; IV.xii; V.i, xliii
> pp. 74, 134, 186, 225
> Maps, G/6–7
> See also "Aršakawan"; "Ayrarat"; "Darewnkʿ"; Appendix I, "Arsăkuni"; and Appendix III, *erkir*; *gawaṙ*.

Kolb/Kolbopʿor, ‹ Arm. Kolb + *pʿor*, "gorge"

Second (or possibly third) district of Gugarkʿ, according to the *Ašχarhacʿoycʿ* (34/46). Toumanoff gives it on his map as the middle one of the districts lying along the Inja River (a southern tributary of the Kur) between Cobapʿor and Joropʿor in the borderland between Virkʿ and Aluankʿ. Nevertheless, its precise location has long been debated because of contradictions in the sources. Like neighboring Joropʿor, Kolbopʿor formed one of the *gawaṙs* of the Iberian March ruled by the *bdeašχ* of Gugarkʿ, and its ruling house was probably a cadet line of the Gušarid dynasts of Gugarkʿ. It had apparently become a separate principality before 339, because its prince is recorded by BP in the reign of King Tiran (III.xii). Kolb, together with Jor, defected from Aršak II after the Roman–Persian peace of 363 (IV.l), it was presumably briefly reconquered ca. 370, when the *sparapet* Mušel Mamikonean carried the border of the Aršakuni kingdom back to the Kur River (V.xiii, xv), and was presumably lost again after the partition of Greater Armenia ca. 387, for it is listed among the Iberian lands taken from Armenia in the *Ašχarhacʿoycʿ* (28/39). The absence of the princes of Kolb from all of the later Lists of *naχarars* is probably also indicative of their separate status outside Armenia after 387.

> See AON, pp. 354–355 and especially 490; Eremyan, *Ašχarh.*, pp. 60, 118; *idem, Map* B/6; Tʿ. X. Hakobyan, *Ašχarhagrutʿyun*, map, who places it north of Joropʿor; Hewsen, "Armenia," p. 338; *idem*, "Vitaxates"; Toumanoff, *Studies*, pp. 186–187 and n. 175, 190 and n. 198, 218, 223, 227, 237 n. 306, 245, 259, 467 n. 131, 468–470, 472 n. 155, 482–483 and n. 203, 499; and maps I, II.
> III.xii; IV.l
> pp. 82, 167
> Maps, H/3–4
> See also "Gugarkʿ"; "Joropʿor"; "Kur"; "Mec Haykʿ"; "Virkʿ"; Appendix I, "Aršak II"; "Manawaz"; "Mušel"; "Tiran"; and Appendix III, *gawaṙ*.

Kolbopʿor, see "Kolb."

Kolthēnē, see "Goltʿn" and "Koltʿ."

Koltʿn/Koχtʿ; Gk. Κολθηνή (?); Lat. Colthene (?)

Twelfth district of Arjaχ, according to the *Ašχarhacʿoycʿ* (33/44). It lay on the Koltʿ (Šamkʿor) River next to Šakašēn and may have been the Kolθēnē of Ptolemy (V.xii.4).

BP refers to it only in connection with the reconquest of the Armeno–Ałuankᶜ marchlands by the *sparapet* Mušeł Mamikonean ca. 370. It must, however, have been lost again after the partition of Greater Armenia ca. 387, since the *Ašχarhacᶜoycᶜ* (33/44) lists it among the Armenian lands lost to Ałuankᶜ. The princes of Kołtᶜn, who are not named by BP, were still known to MK/D, II.xxxii; III.x (= MD, pp. 137, 197) up to the eighth century, and a bishop of Šamkᶜor and Kołt is likewise recorded.

See AON, pp. 350–351; Eremyan, *Ašχarh.*, pp. 60, 117; *idem, Map* B/7; Hewsen, "Armenia," p. 332; *idem,* "Ptolemy," pp. 114, 148; Weissbach, "Kolthene"; Adontz, *Armenia*, pp. 176, 325, 120, 124*–125*, 165*; Toumanoff, *Studies*, pp. 259.

V.xiii

p. 200

Maps, I–J/4–5

See also "Ałuankᶜ"; "Arjaχ"; "Gołtᶜn"; "Šakašēn"; and Appendix I, "Aršak II"; "Mušeł."

Korčaykᶜ, see "Korčēkᶜ."

Korčekᶜ/Korčaykᶜ; Gk. Γορδυηνή

Sixth region of Greater Armenia, containing eleven districts of which Kordukᶜ was the first, according to the *Ašχarhacᶜoycᶜ* (29/40, 32/43), which gives this region a very broad extent, perhaps corresponding to that of the ancient kingdom of Gordyēnē (Strabo, *Geogr.*, XI.xii, 4; xiv, 8; XVI.i, 1, 24; Ptolemy, V.xii.9; cf. Kōtaia), along the northern bank of the Tigris east of Mokkᶜ. In the fourth century, however, the toponym Korčēkᶜ appears to have referred to a smaller area placed by both Hewsen and Eremyan east of Kordukᶜ on the upper course of the Great Zab. This smaller Korčēkᶜ seems to have been part of the royal domain and lay north of the Adiabenian or the Median March known to BP as Noširakan. The region directly west of this smaller Korčēkᶜ, which would form the western portion of Greater Korčēkᶜ in the later *Ašχarhacᶜoycᶜ* (i.e., the district named Tmorikᶜ by BP, but not by the *Ašχarhacᶜoycᶜ*), entered in the fourth century into the Assyrian march of the Armenian kingdom ruled by the *bdeašχ* of Kordukᶜ (q.v.). BP refers to Korčēkᶜ as a district (*gawaṙ*), and uses the term exclusively as a toponym, mentioning no princes there. Nor are any mentioned in the later Lists of *naχarars*, though MX, II.lxiv (= MK, p. 209), claims that some lesser (unnamed) families were to be found there. The absence of any local princes would also support the argument that in the fourth century this smaller Korčēkᶜ was part of the Aršakuni royal domain.

See AON, pp. 255–259, 333–335; for the most recent scholarship on this subject, Hewsen, "Vitaxates"; also *idem,* "Armenia," p. 329, where he was still following the earlier indications of Eremyan; *idem,* "Ptolemy," pp. 115, 150; Eremyan, *Ašχarh.*, pp. 60, 117; *idem, Map* D/5–6, where he includes not only the smaller Korčēkᶜ, but the entire area formed by the eleven districts of the greater Korčēkᶜ of the *Ašχarhacᶜoycᶜ* into a greater Kordukᶜ; Tᶜ. X. Hakobyan, *Ašχarhagrutᶜyun*, pp. 228–230 and map; Baumgartner, "Gordyene"; Adontz, *Armenia*, pp. 175, 177, 179, 209–210, 493 n. 59, 118*, 124*–125*, 165*; Toumanoff, *Studies*, pp. 128–133, 179–182; Markwart, *Südarmenien*, pp. 53*, 353, 357, 363, 373, 422, 513; Garitte, *Documents*, pp. 219–220.

IV.xlviii; V.xliii; VI.iii.

pp. 166, 225, 228, 234

Maps I, G–H/8–9; II, D–G/8–9

See also "Kordikᶜ"; "Kordukᶜ"; "Noširakan"; "Tmorikᶜ"; "Sałmas"; Appendix I, "Aršakuni"; "Šahak II"; and Appendix III, *gawaṙ*.

473

Kordikʿ/Kord(r)ikʿ

Second, third, and fourth districts of Greater Korčēkʿ, according to the *Ašχarhacʿoycʿ* (32/43), which lists three separate districts: *Verin*, "Upper," *Miǰin*, "Middle," and *Nerkʿin*, "Lower," under that name. These three districts are relegated to a narrow band running north and south along the eastern border of the small district of Kordukʿ. All four districts formed part of the Greater Korčēkʿ, which the *Ašχarhacʿoycʿ*, in opposition to BP, treats as one of the major regions of Greater Armenia.

In the fourth century, however, the toponym Kord(r)ikʿ does not seem to have been subdivided. It referred to a single extensive and "rugged" area (*amur ašχarh*; BP, IV.l) stretching eastward from the small district (*gawaṙ*) of Kordukʿ and was included together with it in the larger Assyrian March or Greater Kordukʿ. The scant and often obscure Armenian sources on this subject are fortunately clarified by the cycle of the *Vitae* of St. Gregory, specifically by Vg and the parallel Va. According to Vg (xcviii = Va, lxxxvi), the lands of the toparch of Kordukʿ lay next to those of the Andriokorditoi, and those of the satrap of Zarawand and Hēr adjoined the latter (ἕκτος δὲ ὁ τοπάρχης τῶν Κοδρουανῶν χώρας ... πλησίον ὑπαρχούσης τῶν ᾽Ανδριοκοδρίτων ... ὁ σατράπης Ζαυραβανδῶν καὶ Χειρῶν χώρας ... πλησίων τῶν Κοδριτῶν). Garitte was troubled by the prefix *Andrio-* of the Kodritoñ in the first part, and by the fact that these people adjoined both Kordukʿ and Zarawand/Hēr. A solution has, however, been proposed by Hewsen. The Greek *Andrio-* corresponds clearly to BP's qualification of Kordikʿ/Kordrikʿ as *amur*, especially since the parallel Va reads *fortes qrḍytn*. Far from presenting difficulties, the double adjacence of Kordikʿ clarifies its position in the fourth century. It seems to have been a large and mountainous principality adjoining the *gawaṙ* of Lesser Kordukʿ in the west, probably in the area later called *Miǰin* Kodrikʿ in the *Ašχarhacʿoycʿ* (because relatively low *Nerkʿin* could not be called "rugged" [*amur*], while *Verin* coincided at least in part with the district called Tmorikʿ in the fourth century). From the border of Lesser Kordukʿ, this greater Kordikʿ may then have stretched eastward along the mountains north of the March of Noširakan; it perhaps included the royal lands called Korčēkʿ in BP (see preceding entry), and thence reached as far as the border of the principality of Zarawand and Hēr, which lay along the western shore of Lake Urmiah. The precise area covered by forth-century Kordikʿ cannot, of course be estimated, but its position in the mountainous districts between Kordukʿ and Zarawand seems reasonably clear.

See Hewsen, "Vitaxates"; Eremyan, *Ašχarh.*, pp. 60, 86, 108, 117; *idem, Map* D/5; Garitte, *Documents*, pp. 219–220.

IV.l; V.x

pp. 167, 200

Maps, F–G/7–9

See also "Korčēkʿ"; "Kordukʿ"; "Noširakan"; "Tmorikʿ"; "Zarawand"; and Appendix III, *amur; ašχarh; gawaṙ.*

Kord(r)ikʿ, see "Kordikʿ."

Korduēnē, see "Kordukʿ."

Kordukʿ; Gk. Κορδυηνή; Lat. Corduena; Syr. Bēθ Qardū: Assyrian March

First district of Korčēkʿ, according to the *Ašχarhacʿoycʿ* (32/43), and probably equivalent to the fifth-century eparchy of Bēθ Qardū, dependent on the metropolitan of Hedayab (Arbela). In the fourth century, however, the toponym Kordukʿ seems to have been taken in two senses: (1) Lesser Kordukʿ, the smaller "district" (*gawaṙ*) of Kordukʿ proper, also known to the *Ašχarhacʿoycʿ*, lying southeast of Aḷjnikʿ and perhaps including at least a part of the later Nerkʿin Kordikʿ; (2) Greater Kordukʿ (identified as a *koḷmn*), a much larger area that included the above mentioned Lesser

Korduk^c together with Tmorik^c and the larger Kordik^c of BP, to form the middle or Assyrian March of southern Armenia, facing Asorestan or the western portion of Adiabēnē. This Greater Korduk^c was known to classical authors as Korduēnē/ Corduena (AM, XXV.vii.9; XXVII.iii, v; Petr. Patric., *Ad gen.*, iii). The importance of its ruler, merely styled "lord" (*tēr*) by BP but referred to by Aa, dccclxxiii, as "the-warden-of-the-Marches of the region of Asorestan (*sahmanakaln yAsorestaneayc^c kołmanēn*)," is confirmed by Vg, xcviii (= Va, lxxxvi), which refers to him as a toparch (= *bdeašχ*) and superior to his eastern neighbors ruling in Kordik^c, who were merely hyparchs, as well as by AM (XVIII.vi.20), who knows him as the "*satrapa Corduenae.*" From these titles it seems altogether probable that in the fourth century the ruler of Greater Korduk^c was indeed the *bdeašχ* of the Assyrian March whose name is not given by BP, but who seems to correspond to the "prince of Korduk^{c}" in Aa, dccxcv (cf. dccclxxiii, where the reference is to the "warden-of-the-March of Asorestan").

According to Petr. Patric. (*loc. cit*), Korduk^c passed to the Roman sphere of influence under the terms of the Peace of Nisibis of 298 and was retroceded to Persia by the emperor Jovian in 363 (AM, XXV.vii.4), an action presented by BP (IV.l) as a defection of the prince of Korduk^c from his lord Aršak II. The whole of greater Korduk^c, including Kordik^c and Tmorik^c, was briefly reconquered by the Armenian *sparapet* Mušeł Mamikonean ca. 370 (V.x), and was finally lost after the partition of Greater Armenia ca. 387. Even before 363, the prince of Korduk^c seems to have held a semi-autonomous position vis-à-vis the Armenian crown. BP (III.ix) lists him among the "good servants" of King Xosrov Kotak, leading the Armenian army against the rebellious *bdeašχ* of Ałjnik^c, but Toumanoff argues on the basis of Va, lxxxvi (= Vg, xcviii with a lacuna at this point), that the ruler of Korduk^c was not subject to the authority of the Armenian *sparapet*, as were the other magnates of the realm. AM (XVIII.vi.20–22) has him negotiate directly with the Romans; the later *Zōrnamak*, "Military List," attributes 1,000 retainers to him as the commander of the "West [sic] gate," though he is not included in the other late Lists of Armenian *naχarar*s, probably because of his separation from Armenia ca. 387.

The bishop of Korduk^c, who dated from the days of St. Gregory the Illuminator according to Aa, dcccxlii, dcccxlv (cf. Vg, clxxii = Va, clx), likewise seems to have been distinguished from the rest of the "bishops of the realm of Armenia," together with his colleague from Ałjnik^c (IV.xv, at the end of the chapter). Bishops of Qardu are still listed as present at Syrian councils in Persia as late as the beginning of the seventh century.

See AON, pp. 218–220, 333–334. For the most recent research on the subject, see Hewsen, "Vitaxates"; cf. *idem, Armenia*, p. 329; Eremyan, *Ašχarh.*, pp. 60, 117; idem, *Map* D/5 (for the district of Lesser Korduk^c proper) and D/5–6 (for his greatly extended Greater Korduk^c); T^c. X. Hakobyan, *Ašχarhagrut^{c}yun*, p. 230 and map; Baumgartner, "Gordyene"; Marquart, *Ērānšahr*, pp. 167, 169–171; *idem, Südarmenien*, pp. 116, 118, 130, 215, 219, 346, 350, 372, 378, 386, 409, 513, 515, neither of which is up to date by now; Adontz, *Armenia*, pp. 175, 177, 195, 197–198, 202, 205–206, 230, 257, 267, 285, 323, 87*–88*, 90*, 120*, 125*, 160*; Toumanoff, *Studies*, pp. 131, 160–161, 166 n. 63, 180–181 and nn. 141–142, 182 nn. 144, 146, 197 n. 222, 211 n. 238, 216, 223, 240, 244–245; Garitte, *Documents*, pp. 219–220; *Syn. Or.*, pp. 272, 285, 618, 618.

III.ix–x, xiv; IV.xv, l; V.x, xxvi

pp. 77, 90, 146, 167, 200, 206

Maps I, E–G/8–9 ("Greater" Korduk^c = The Assyrian March); I–II, E–F/8–9 ("Lesser" Korduk^c)

See also "Ałjnik^c"; "Asorestan"; "Korček^c"; "Kordik^c"; "Miǰnašχarh Hayoc^c"; "Sararad"; "Tmorik^c"; Appendix I, "Aršak II"; "Jon"; "Mušeł"; "Xosrov II/III"; and Appendix III, *bdeašχ; gawaṙ; kołmn.*

Kovg, see "Kogovit."

Koχtʿ, see "Kołtʿn."

Ktesiphon, see "Tispon."

Kur; Gk. Κῦρος; Lat. Cyrus; Georg. Mtkvari; modern Kur
    Major river of northeastern Anatolia, flowing generally southeastward from the district of Taykʿ/Tao in the Armeno–Iberian marchlands to the Caspian Sea. It now receives the Araxes in its lower course as its major southern tributary, but in antiquity the two rivers may perhaps have had separate estuaries, according to Muraviev (cf. Strabo, *Geogr.*, XI,i, 5; iii, 2; iv, 2; viii, 6; xiv, 3, 7, 13; Pliny, NH, VI.x, 26; xv, 3, 9; xvii, 44–45). BP gives the Kur as the proper boundary between the kingdom of Greater Armenia and Virkʿ/Iberia, as well as Ałuankʿ. In fact, however, the marchlands south of the river were disputed, lost as a result of the defections following the Roman–Persian peace of 363 (IV.l), briefly reconquered by the Armenian *sparapet* Mušeł Mamikonean ca. 370, and finally lost to Armenia after the partition of the Aršakuni kingdom ca. 387. See *Ašχarhacʿoycʿ* (28–29/38–39, 33, 35/44, 46).
    See AON, pp. 357–358, 370; Eremyan, *Ašχarh.*, pp. 61, 119–120; *idem, Map* B/5–G/8; Hewsen, "Armenia," pp. 338–341; Muraviev, "Ptolemeeva Karta."
    III.vii; V.xiii,xv
    pp. 73, 200–201
    Maps, E–M/3–6.
    See also "Ałuank"; "Taykʿ"; "Virkʿ"; and Appendix I, "Mušeł."

Kura, see "Kur."

Kyros, see "Kur."

Lsin
    Locality presumably in the neighborhood of the royal encampment at Šahapivan, but not otherwise attested.
    Epʿrikean, *Baṙaran*, II, p. 115 gives the reference to BP, but no further identification.
    IV.xv
    p. 143
    See also "Šahapivan."

Mahkertun ⟨ Arm. Mahkert + *tun* "house"; Gk. οἶκος Μαχούρτων; Syr. Bēθ Māhqert
    Southeasternmost district of Greater Armenia, reaching to the Persian border. It encompassed the uppermost course of the Lesser Zab and lay in the region of modern Revanduz. Before its shift to the Sasanians as a result of the Roman–Persian peace of 363, Mahkertun formed one of the component districts of the southern Armenian March of Media or Adiabēnē ruled by the *bdeašχ* of Noširakan, who may indeed have been none other than the prince of Mahkertun (see Aa, dcccxlii, who seems to single him out as *the* lord of the southeast; Ag, clii; cf. BP, V.l). This prince is known to both Aa and BP, but not to MX or to any of the later Lists of *naχarars*, presumably because the territory had long since passed to the Sasanian Empire, although it was probably briefly reconquered ca. 370 as part of Noširakan. The eparchy of Bēθ Māhqert belonging to the metropolitan see of Ḥedayab/Arbela is recorded in the Syriac conciliar acts of 410.
    See AON, p. 320; Hewsen, "Vitaxates"; Eremyan, *Ašχarh.*, pp. 64–65, 69, 72, 118; *idem, Map* D/6; Marquart, *Ērānšahr*, pp. 23–24, 109, 169–170, 176; *idem, Süd-armenien*, pp. 378–379; Adontz, *Armenia*, pp. 175, 177–178, 87*, 88*, 167*; Tou-

manoff, *Studies*, pp. 165–166, 198, 223, 226, 228, 237 n. 306; *Syn. Or.*, pp. 272, 285, 617, 669; Manandyan, "Mahkertun," pp. 34–37; Fiey, *Assyrie*, I, pp. 48–49, 225–303, who suggests the equation with Marga.
IV.1
p. 167
Maps, H–I/10
See also "Noširakan."

Małχazan/Maχazean
Town in eastern Armenia identified with modern Mahla in the vicinity of Xoy. A link with the domain of the *małχaz* may be indicated by the name.
See Eremyan, *Ašχarh.*, p. 64; *idem*, *Map* G/6; Inčičean, *Storagrutʿiwn*, p. 527.
IV.xxx, xlvii
pp. 160, 166
Maps, H–I/7–8
See also Appendix I, "Xoṙχoṙuni, house"; and Appendix III, *małχaz*.

Mambrē
Locality in Copʿkʿ Mec on the Mamušeł. Its site cannot be identified because it depends on the location of the river (see next entry). Hübschmann suggested a possible link with the Byzantine fortress of Mambri in Commagene built by Diocletian and refortified by Justinian (Procopius, *De aed.*, II.viii.7), but the name may well be derived in the given context from the Biblical plain in which Abraham received the visit of the three angels (Gen. 13:18; 18:1, etc.), since its name is given as "Mambrē" in the Armenian Bible as well as in the Septuagint, as against the "Mamrē" of the Hebrew original.
See AON, pp. 310, 448; Markwart, *Südarmenien*, pp. 121, 132, 162.
V.xxvii–xxviii
pp. 206–207
See also "Copʿkʿ Mec" and the next entry.

Mamušeł, river
River that may have marked the border between Copʿkʿ Mec and Ałjnikʿ, though this location is hardly reconcilable with the association between it and the village of Mamuš, west of Muš and south of the Euphrates–Arsanias (mod. Murad-su), proposed by Tomaschek. Markwart suggests an identification with the Farqin-su. It is otherwise unattested.
See AON, pp. 310 and n. 3, 369; Tomaschek, "Sasun," p. 12; Markwart, *Südarmenien*, pp. 121, 123, 132, 162; also Kalhōkecʿi, ACH, pp. 54–55. I am indebted to Dr. J.-M. Thierry for this reference.
V.xxvii
pp. 206–207
See also "Ałjnikʿ"; "Copʿkʿ Mec."

Manawazakert, see "Manazkert."

Manazkert/Manawazakert ‹ Manawaz + Arm. *kert*, "built/building"; Gk. Μανζικίερτ; modern Malasgird
Locality north of Lake Van standing on the border of the medieval districts of Harkʿ and Apahunikʿ to which it is usually attributed. By the seventh century it was identified with Vaspurakan in the *Ašχarhacʿoycʿ* (32/43), which refers to it as a *cʿamakʿakłzi*, "land-island." BP first identified it as the "seat" (*bun gahoykʿ*) of the Manawazean family (III.iv), calling it simultaneously a "town" (*awan*) and a "village" (*gewł*). It also records its transfer to the family of Bishop Ałbianos, in whose family it remained during

the fourth and fifth centuries. This information is missing in Aa, MX, and Koriwn, who are curiously silent on the subject; but Manazkert is known as a bishopric to both ŁP^c, II.xxiii, III.lxii, pp. 44, 110 (= *Ełishē*, p. 258; CHAMA, II, p. 320), and Ełišē, ii, p. 27 (= *Ełishē*, p. 81).

Later in the Middle Ages the town was famous for the council of union between the Armenian and the Syrian churches in 725/6, for an important fortress, the seat of the Kaysite emirate in Armenia (DAI, xliv), and for the defeat of the Byzantine army by the Seljuq Alp Arslan in 1071.

See AON, pp. 449–450; Eremyan, *Ašχarh.*, p. 65; *idem, Map* G/5; T^c. X. Hakobyan, *Ašχarhagrut^cyun*, pp. 155–156 and map; Adontz, *Armenia*, pp. 32, 245–246, 258–259, 261–265, 271, 375 n. 9, 458 n. 45, 459 nn. 47, 51–52, 468 n. 26, 469 n. 31b, 472 n. 53, 94*–95*, 100*–102*, 120*, 210*; also, for the later period, Honigmann, *Ostgrenze*, pp. 94, 120 n. 1, 122, 142, 147, 149, 151, 152 n. 2, 154, 157, 162, 167; Ter Ghewondyan, *Arab Emirates*, pp. 7, 17, 32, 36, 44, 51–52, 59, 65–66, 71, 80, 84–85, 87–88, 90, 105–106, 109, 111–112, 115–116, 123, 127–129, 132–135, 139–141, 144–145, etc.
III.iv; V.xxix; VI.ii
pp. 70, 210, 234
Maps, F/6–7
See also "Apahunik^c"; and Appendix I, "Ałbianos"; "Manzwazean, house."

Mantzikiert, see "Manazkert."

Marac^c amur erkir, "the inaccessible/impregnable land of the Mark^c ["Medes"]
Because the Armeno–Iranian frontier in the fourth century lay in the region of Atrpatakan, a portion of Media with its native population lay within the Armenian Aršakuni realm, though the *Ašχarhac^coyc^c* understandably treats Media as a separate entity on the basis of Ptolemy and its own seventh-century date (40–41/53–54, cf. 32/43). In the opinion of Eremyan, this region included the southeastern border districts forming the Median or Adiabenian March, ruled by the *bdeašχ* of Noširakan. Parspatunik^c, however, which the *Ašχarhac^coyc^c* (33/44) gives as the twenty-sixth or twenty-seventh district of Vaspurakan lying northeast of Lake Urmiah, seems equally suitable. This is the *Marac^c kołmank^c*, the "regions of the Medes" of Eremyan's fourth-century map. The land of the Medes seceded from Aršak II after the Roman–Persian peace of 363 (IV.l). It was briefly reconquered by the *sparapet* Mušeł Mamikonean ca. 370 (V.xi) and was returned to Persia after the partition of Armenia ca. 387.

See Eremyan, *Ašχarh.*, pp. 65, 77, 115, 117–118; *idem, Map* D/5–6; Hewsen, "Armenia," p. 336; Manadyan, "Mahkertun," pp. 40–45.
IV.xxiv, l; V.xi
pp. 158, 167, 200
Maps, I–K/7–8?
See also "Atrpatakan"; "Noširakan"; Appendix I, "Aršak II"; Mušeł"; and Appendix III, *amur; erkir.*

Marag/Marg
Village in the district of Karin and birthplace of St. Xad, according to BP. MX III.xx (= MK, p. 274) takes this name as a common rather than a proper noun and consequently identifies Xad as being *i maragac^c Karnoy*, "from the meadows of Karin." It has not been identified.

See AON, p. 451; Thomson, MK, p. 274 n. 6.
IV.xii
p. 134
See "Karin"; and Appendix I, "Xad."

Marg, see "Marag."

Masis/Neχ Masis, Mt.; mod. Süphan daği
Mountain in the district of Apahunikᶜ, directly north of Lake Van. It is called Neχ Masis by the *Ašχarhacᶜoycᶜ* (31/42) and is to be identified with the modern Süphan daği and not with the Azat Masis/Ararat (mod. Agri daği).
> See AON, pp. 347, 370, 489 note; Eremyan, *Ašχarh.*, p. 72; *idem, Map* G/5; Markwart, *Südarmenien*, pp. 10*–11*, 15*; Adontz, *Armenia*, p. 245.
> III.xx
> p. 96
> Maps, F/7.
> See also "Aliorskᶜ"; "Apahunikᶜ."

Maχazean, see "Malχazan."

Mazkᶜutᶜkᶜ March, See "Gugarkᶜ."

Mcbin ‹ Syr. Nṣīwīn; Gk. Νίσιβις/Antioch of Mygdonia
City forming the center of the region known as Aruastan or Mygdonia in northern Mesopotamia and attested in Assyrian records as Nasabina. It was refounded as a Greek *polis* by Seleukos Nikator under the name of Antioch in Mygdonia (Strabo, *Geogr.*, XI.xii, 4; xiv, 2; XVI.i, 23; Pliny, NH, VI.xvi, 42), but soon reverted to its original name of Nisibis. It became a Roman city from the days of the emperor Septimius Severus, or perhaps earlier, under Lucius Verus. MX, II.xxxvi (= MK, p. 177) and the *Primary History*, Sebēos, pp. 47, 53 (= MK, pp. 357, 365), associate it with King Sanatruk, but this is probably due to a confusion with Mcurn (see next entry). In the Aršakuni period, Mcbin stood at the border between the Roman and Sasanian empires. The peace whereby the kingdom of Greater Armenia and the Autonomous Satrapies of the south passed to the Roman sphere of influence was signed there in 298 (Petr. Patric., *Ad gent.*, iii). The Persians besieged it unsuccessfully in 337, 346, and 350, but it was surrendered to them by the emperor Jovian in 363 (IV.xxi = AM, XXV.vii.9). In the fifth century it was designated along with Artašat/Artaxata in northern Armenia as one of the three official customs posts for trade between the Byzantine Empire and Iran (CJ, IV.lxiii.4). It was one of the major sees of the Church of Persia and from the sixth century it became the seat of the famous Nestorian School of the Persians, which moved there from Edessa. In keeping with its practice when referring to Greek "cities," BP qualifies Mcbin a *kᶜalakᶜ*, and sources show that it had a considerable Armenian population in the Middle Ages.
> See AG, p. 295 no. 30; Jones, *Cities*, pp. 214–215, 218, 220–221; Manadyan, *Trade and Cities*, pp. 31, 56–57, 60–61, 82–83, 85, 112–113, 116; van Esbroeck, "Le Roi Sanatrouk," pp. 265, 277; Vööbus, *School of Nisibis*; Eremyan, *Map* D/4; Tᶜ. X. Hakobyan, *Ašχarhagrutᶜyun*, map, where he places the city within the confines of Armenia; Fiey, *Nisibe*; Ter Petrosyan, "Hayerə."
> III.x; IV.xx–xxi
> pp. 77, 80, 150, 154
> Maps, D/9
> See also "Artašat"; "Aruastan"; "Mcurn"; Appendix I, "Šapuh"; "Yakob"; and Appendix III, *kᶜalakᶜ*.

Mcurn, see "Mcurkᶜ."

Mcurkᶜ/Mcurn
City on the Euphrates, the precise location of which is unknown. It stood at the confluence of the Euphrates–Arsanias (mod. Murad-su) and the Kara-su, according to

Markwart, but Hübschmann put it in Tarōn not far from Aštišat, as does Eremyan, who places it northeast of that locality. The tradition of the city's foundation by King Sanatruk given by BP is also recorded by the *Primary History*, Sebēos, p. 47 (= MK, p. 357), which mentions Sanatruk's royal palace located there and gives it as the home of the philosopher Mar Aba. Both in the *Primary History* and in MX, II.xxxvi (= MK, p. 177), however, the city is incorrectly identified with Mcbin/Nisibis (see preceding entry). Manandyan dates the foundation of the city to the first century A.D., on the basis of the association with King Sanatruk, whose chronology is, however, still disputed, and he assumed that the city had disappeared by the fifth century, because BP refers to it in the past tense.

> See AON, p. 401; Eremyan, map (A.D. 298–385) in HŽP, II, G/3; Markwart, "Untersuchungen," p. 237; Manandyan, *Trade and Cities*, pp. 82–83; Abgaryan, *Sebēosi patmutʿiwn*, pp. 147–153; van Esbroeck, "Le Roi Sanatrouk," pp. 265, 277.
> IV.xiv
> p. 140
> See also "Aštišat"; "Mcbin"; "Tarōn"; Appendix I, "Sanatruk"; and Appendix III, kʿałakʿ.

Mec Haykʿ; Gk. Ἀρμενία ἡ μεγάλη; Lat. Armenia Maior; "Greater Armenia," "Armenia."

Armenia is still listed as part of the Sasanian Empire in the third century, ŠKZ, Parth. 1, 4; RGDS, nos. 3, 10, pp. 48–51; Tansar; *Paikuli*, p. 11. Nevertheless, KKZ, 12 includes it in *Anērān*.

In the fourth century, the toponym Mec Haykʿ designated the Aršakuni kingdom east of the Euphrates, by contrast to the imperial province (subsequently divided in two) of Armenia Minor west of the river (cf. Pliny, NH VI.ix, 25). According to the *Ašχarhacʿoycʿ* (29/39) but not BP, it was composed of fifteen provinces. BP gives its borders as Satala in Armenia Minor to the northwest and Ganjak of Atrpatakan in the southeast. Moreover, it claims that the Kur River was the normal boundary in the north separating the Armenian realm, including the March of Gugarkʿ, from Virkʿ and Ałuankʿ (V.xiii, xv). These boundaries agree generally with those known to Aa, dcccxlii, but they are somewhat more detailed. In the south, Mec Haykʿ bordered successively, from west to east, on Aruastan/Mygdonia through the March of Ałjnikʿ; on Asorestan through the March of Kordukʿ; and on Adiabēnē through the March of Noširakan. BP uses the terms Haykʿ, "Armenia," and Mec Haykʿ as synonyms and contains no reference to Armenia Minor.

The relationship of the kingdom of Greater Armenia to the southern Satrapies during the fourth century is ambiguous, since BP never mentions their autonomous existence, yet classical sources state that they maintained a considerable degree of autonomy until the reign of Justinian, or at least Zeno (Procopius, *De aed.*, III.i.17–29). The information given by BP is especially valuable for the sharp reduction of the territory of Greater Armenia through the loss of its border territories resulting from the Roman–Persian peace of 363 (IV.l); for their brief reconquest in the reign of King Pap (ca. 370); and for their ultimate loss at the partition of the Aršakuni kingdom between Rome and Persia, ca. 387 (VI.i); along a line running north and south from Karin/Theodosioupolis to Dara west of Nisibis in Mesopotamia.

> See Eremyan, *Ašχarh.*, pp. 66–70, 116–118; Hewsen, "Armenia," pp. 326–337; Adontz, *Armenia*, pp. 7–53; Garsoïan, *Armenia*, pp. 341–346; *idem*, "Locus," pp. 29–35; Gignoux, *Glossaire*, pp. 15, 46; *idem*, "La liste," pp. 84, 90–91; Sprengling, *Third-Century Iran*, pp. 7, 14, 47, 52; Honigmann and Maricq, RGDS, pp. 11–12, 39; Herzfeld, *Paikuli*, pp. 98–99, 102–103; Tansar, p. 63.

P.S., III.iii–xiv, xvi–xxi; IV.i–v, xi–xvi, xviii–xl, xlii, xlv–lv, lviii–lix; V.i–ii, iv–vii, ix–xi, xiv–xvi, xix–xxi, xxiii–xxiv, xxix–xxxii, xxxiv–xxxv, xxxvii–xliv; VI.i, vii, x, xiv–xvi

pp. 63, 68–71, 73–82, 84, 86, 90–100, 107–109, 111–114, 116, 122–124, 132–134, 136–139, 146–154, 156–176, 178–179, 185–191, 193–204, 210–213, 215–218, 220–225, 228–230, 233–235, 237–239

Maps, I, A–M/3–9; II, D–J/4–8

See also "Ałjnik^c"; "Ałuank^c"; "Ganjak"; "Gugark^c"; "Korduk^c"; "Kur"; "Miǰnašχarh Hayoc^c"; "Noširakan"; "Satał"; "Virk^c"; and Appendix I, "Aršak II"; "Aršakuni"; "Hayk^c"; "Mušeł."

Mecamōr, river

Northern tributary of the Araxes, flowing down from Aragacotn past the city of Vałaršapat. According to MX, II.xlix (= MK, p. 190), the site of the city of Artašat was at the junction of the two rivers. However, the course of the Mecamōr had already shifted by the seventh century, and the former bed of the river formed a swamp, since this alteration is recorded in the *Ašχarhac^coyc^c* (34/45).

See AON, pp. 362, 408, 452; Eremyan, *Ašχarh.*, p. 66 and map B/6 (the river is indicated but not named in his fourth-century *Map*; Manandyan, *Trade and Cities*, p. 45.

III.viii

p. 75

Maps, G/5

See also "Artašat"; "Vałaršapat."

Median March, see "Noširakan."

Məzur, see "Mzur."

Miǰagetk^c Asoroc^c, "Syrian Mesopotamia"

See "Asorestan," and Eremyan, *Ašχarh.*, pp. 70, 113–114 and map D/3–4.

IV.xxi

p. 154

Mēǰnašχarh Hayoc^c, see "Miǰnašχarh Hayoc^c."

Midlands, see "Miǰnašχarh Hayoc^c."

Miǰnašχarh Hayoc^c/Mēǰnašχarh Hayoc^c, "Armenian Midlands"

Central region of Greater Armenia/Mec Hayk^c. BP uses the term to distinguish the core of the Aršakuni kingdom, as opposed to the border districts of Ałjnik^c, Arjaχ, Gugark^c, Korduk^c, Noširakan, P^caytakaran, Šakašēn, and Utik^c, which were lost to Armenia after the partition of the realm ca. 387.

See AON, p. 280; Eremyan, *Ašχarh.*, pp. 66, 68, 69, 71, 118; Hewsen, "Armenia," p. 336; *idem*, "Vitaxates"; Adontz, *Armenia*, pp. 169–182.

IV.xxi, xxiii–xxiv, l; V.i, iv; [VI.i]

pp. 154, 156, 158, 167, 186, 189, [234]

Maps, D–J/4–8

See also "Ałjnik^c"; "Arjaχ"; "Gugark^c"; "Korduk^c"; "Mec Hayk^c"; "Noširakan"; "P^caytakaran"; "Šakašēn"; "Utik^c."

Miws Haband, see "Haband."

Mtkvari, see "Kur."

Muzur, see "Mzur."

Mygdonia, see "Aruestan."

Mzur/Məzur/Muzur; Gk. κλίμα Μουζουρῶν
    Third district of "Upper Armenia" (*Barjr Haykᶜ*), according to the *Ašxarhacᶜoycᶜ* (29/40), but originally part of Ekełeacᶜ. It lay along the Munzur River and Mountains in western Greater Armenia between Daranałikᶜ and Ekełeacᶜ in the north and Copᶜkᶜ Šahēi in the south. No princes are recorded from this district, which Eremyan gives as a patriarchal domain, though it is not listed among those given by BP (IV.xiv), which refers to it as a *gawaṙ*. It was still known to George of Cyprus (p. 49) as *klima Muzurōn*.
    See AON, pp. 285–286; Eremyan, *Ašxarh.*, pp. 71, 116; *idem, Map* G/3; Hewsen, "Armenia," p. 326; *idem*, "Orontid," p. 350–351; Adontz, *Armenia*, pp. 39–40, 43, 45, 182, 395 n. 13, 53*, 118*, 124*, 170*.
    IV.xxiv
    p. 157
    Map I, B/6.
    See also "Copᶜkᶜ Šahei"; "Daranałikᶜ"; "Ekełeacᶜ" and Appendix III, *gawaṙ*.

Naxčawan; Gk. Ναξουάνα; Ar. Nashawā; mod. Naxiǰewan
    City north of the Araxes but belonging to Vaspurakan, according to the *Ašxarhacᶜoycᶜ* (33/44), though it was temporarily attributed to Siwnikᶜ in the tenth century and BP does not identify its district. The city was founded in antiquity and was already known to Ptolemy under the name of Naxouana (V.xii.5), and MX, I.xxx, II.vii (= MK, pp. 119–120, 139), suggests that King Tigran settled it with captive Medes, but neither he nor BP indicate the district to which it belonged in the fourth century. The position of Naxcăwan on the east–west trade route along the valley of the Araxes insured its prosperity, and it survived its sack by Šāhpuhr II p. 363, with the deportation of its Armenian and much larger Jewish population to Persia (IV.lv). By the beginning of the eighth century, it was held by an Arab garrison, was disputed between Siwnikᶜ and Vaspurakan and subsequently became one of the autonomous Arab emirates in Armenia. It is also familiar to TᶜA who makes it the seat of the bishop of Mardpetakan and notes his move in the ninth century to an otherwise unknown locality, III.ii, xxv, pp. 128, 240 (= *Thom. Arts*, pp. 195, 303).
    See AON, 346, 455; Eremyan, *Ašxarh.*, p. 72 and map G/6; the city is given an administrative district in the fourth-century *Map*, but there is no mention of this in the sources; Hewsen, "Ptolemy," pp. 126, 149; Tᶜ. X. Hakobyan, *Ašxarhagrutᶜyun*, p. 175 and map; Manandyan, *Trade and Cities*, pp. 86–87; also, for the later period, Ter Ghewondyan, *Arab Emirates*, pp. 72–73, 75–76, 99–103, 120–121, 140, 141.
    IV.lv
    p. 176
    Maps, H–I/6–7
    See also Appendix I, "Hreaykᶜ"; and Appendix III, *kᶜałakᶜ*.

Nicaea, see "Nikia."

Nihorakan/Nixorakan
    District of southeastern Greater Armenia lying west of the Kohi Nihorakan mountains (mod. Zagros) and attributed by the *Ašxarhacᶜoycᶜ* (32/43) to Parskahaykᶜ. BP is the only other source to mention this district and its princes. The district most probably lay north of Dassəntrē and Mahkertun, as indicated by Eremyan and Hewsen,

and formed a component part of the Median or Adiabenian March, ruled by the *bdeašχ* of Noširakan, as implied by BP (IV.l). Consequently, it cannot be associated with the region known to Arab writers as *dāχerrakān* east of Lake Urmiah and south of Tabriz, as was suggested by Adontz and Nyberg.

See AON, p. 320, who questioned the association with *dāχerrakān*; Eremyan, *Ašχarh.*, p. 72; *idem, Map* D/5–6; Hewsen, "Vitaxates"; Adontz, *Armenia*, pp. 177–178, 120*, 171*; Manandyan, "Mahkertun," pp. 37–39; Nyberg, "Mishkīn," pp. 150–151.
IV.l
p. 167
Maps, H/9
See also "Dassəntrē"; "Mahkertun"; "Noširakan."

Nikaia, see "Nikia."

Nikia; Gk. Νικάια; Lat Nicaea
City in Bithynia referred to in BP only as the site of the first oecumenical council held in 325, which it surprisingly describes as a mere synod (*siwnhodos*), though it has always been recognized as oecumenical by the Armenian church. Aa, dccclxxxiv, referred to it correctly as "*mec žołovn Nikiay.*"
See Jones, *Cities*, pp. 150, 154, 159–161, 164–166; Ruge "Nikaia."
III.x
p. 79

Niphates, see "Npat."

Nisibis, see "Mcbin."

Niχorakan, see "Nihorakan."

Nor Kʿałakʿ, see "Vałaršapat."

Nor Širakan, see "Noširakan."

Northern sea/Hewsisakan Cov
BP gives no further identification of this toponym associated with the martyrdom of St. Grigoris (III.vi). Most scholars have consequently followed the indication of MX, III.iii (= MK, p. 256), and identified it with the Caspian Sea. Peeters, however, has argued persuasively on the basis of the context in BP for an identification with Lake Çildir, northwest of the Armenian plateau.
See Peeters, "Les débuts," pp. 23–24.
III.vi
p. 73
Maps, F–G/4?
See also "Vatneay, plain"; and Appendix I, "Grigoris."

Noširakan/Nor Širakan ‹ Parth. *ntwšrkn*; Gk. ᾿Αδιαβηνή "Adiabenian or Median March"
Listed as part of the Sasanian Empire in ŠKZ, Parth. 24; Phl. 30 = RGDS nos. 20, 60, pp. 46–47, 68–69, ᾿Αδιαβηνή.
Easternmost Median or Adiabenian March of southern Armenia, ruled by the homonymous *bdeašχ* (IV.l) who is also known to Aa, dccclxxiii, "*bdeašχkʿn . . . zaṙaǰin sahmanakaln i Nor Širakan kołmanēn.*" This toponym, first attested in ŠKZ (the trilingual victory inscription of Šāhpuhr I, 240–272?), is also found in the Armenian *Primary History*, ii, p. 54 (= MK, p. 365), as well as in Sebeōs, xi, p. 78. Noširakan clearly must have faced some of eastern Adiabene directly south of it, but the precise

extent of the March (to which BP, V.ix, refers as an *ašχarh*) has long been disputed because of the confusion between the village of Širakan west of Lake Urmiah in the *Ašχarhacᶜoycᶜ* (40/53) and the northwestern Armenian district of Širak. Eremyan has posited a vast area encompassing the territories south-southeast of the Assyrian March of Kordukᶜ, reaching to Lake Urmiah and including its entire western shore up to Zarawand, which he places farther north. Nonetheless, the presence of the major mountain chain of the Zagros dividing this large area into an eastern and a western portion makes the unity of the two unlikely. Recently, Hewsen has suggested that Širakan on the western shore of Lake Urmiah and Noširakan or Nor Širakan to the west of the mountains were more likely to have been separate districts. The Adiabenian or Median March ruled by the *bdeašχ* of Noširakan, the easternmost of the three Marches of southern Armenia, would consequently have been composed of only three districts, Dassəntrē and Mahkertun along the border, and Nihorakan farther to the north.

The *bdeašχ*s of Noširakan are known to BP, even though he does not give their names, as well as to Aa, dcccxlii–dccclxxiii—who claims that the district was evangelized in the days of St. Gregory—but to no other Armenian source. They are not included in the later Lists of *naχarar*s, probably because this area was no longer part of Armenia. They may have been none other than the princes of Mahkertun, ruling the entire area of which their own district was a part, but this is not attested in the sources. The Arcrunis are also mentioned as lords of this district. Noširakan fell away from Aršak II after the Roman–Persian peace of 363 (IV.l), was briefly reconquered by the *sparapet* Mušeł Mamikonean ca. 370 (I.ix), and was finally lost after the partition of Armenia ca. 387.

See Gignoux, *Glossaire*, pp. 30, 59; *idem*, NPS, nos. 692, 695, p. 136; Sprengling, *Third-Century Iran*, pp. 9, 12, 14, 19; Honigmann and Maricq, RGDS, pp. 11, 17, 39; AON, pp. 319–320; for the most recent studies, Hewsen, "Vitaxates"; Eremyan, *Ašχarh.*, pp. 25, 33–34, 49, 52, 59, 64, 67, 72, 74, 77; *idem, Map* G–D/6; Marquart, *Ērānšahr*, pp. 23–24, 109, 165–166, 169–171, 176, 178; *idem, Südarmenien*, pp. 59*, 120, 378–379; *idem, Catalogue*, pp. 81–82, 105; Manandyan, "Nor-Širakan," pp. 19–34; Adontz, *Armenia*, pp. 175–178; Henning, "Notes," pp. 49–50; Maricq, RGDS, p. 46 n. 4. But cf. Dilleman, *Haute-Mésopotamie*, pp. 112–113, 120, 124, 260, 269–271, 305–307.

IV, l; V, ix

pp. 167, 200

Maps, F–H/9–10

See also "Dassəntrē"; "Korčēkᶜ"; "Kordukᶜ"; "Mahkertun"; "Miĵnašχarh Hayocᶜ"; "Nihorakan"; "Zarawand"; Appendix I, "Arcruni, house"; "Aršak II"; "Mušeł"; and Appendix III, *ašχarh; bdeašχ.*

Npat; Gk. Νιφάτης, Mt.

Mountain on the border of Bagrewand and Całkotn near the source of the Euphrates–Arsanias (mod. Murad-su). The town of Bagawan stood at the foot of its northeastern, slope according to the *Ašχarhacᶜoycᶜ* (34/45). This mountain was familiar to classical authors in the form Niphatēs (Ptolemy, V.xii.l; Strabo, *Geogr.*, XI.xii.4; xiv.2) as well as to Armenian sources (Aa, dcccxviii; MX, III.xxxvii = MK, p. 297; ŁPᶜ, lxxvi, p. 141), last of which is patently not the only known reference, *pace* Sanspeur.

See AON, pp. 361–363, 370, 457; Eremyan, *Ašχarh.*, p. 72; *idem, Map* G/5; Markwart, "Parskahaykᶜ," pp. 278–281; Sanspeur, "Arménie," pp. 120, 160.

V.iv

p. 189–191

Maps, F/6–7

See also "Bagawan"; "Bagrewand."

Ołakan/Ołkan; Gk. Ὀλανή Lat. Volandum

Main fortress of the Mamikonean family in the district of Tarōn, on the bank of the Euphrates-Arsanias (mod. Murad-su) east of Aštišat. It was known to Strabo (*Geogr.*, XI.xiv.6), who calls it Olanē (*pro* Olakanē), and was probably the *castellum Volandum* mentioned by Tacitus (*Ann.*, XIII.xxxix). MX, II.lxxxiv (= MK, 235–236), claims that it had originally been the possession of the Słkuni house but was wrested from it by the Mamikoneans in the reign of Trdat the Great. There is, however, no reference to this transfer in BP. The destruction of the fortress by the Persians is recorded by Ełišē, iii, p. 69 (= *Ełishē*, p. 119).

See AON, pp. 326, 459–460; Eremyan *Ašχarh.*, p. 74; *idem, Map* G/4; T꜀. X. Hakobyan, *Ašχarhagrut꜀yun*, pp. 153–154 and map; Adontz, *Armenia*, pp. 243–244, 381 n. 30, 457 n. 37, 213*; Toumanoff, *Studies*, p. 209; Yovhannēsean, HB, pp. 176–179.

V.iii
pp. 188–189
Maps, D/7
See also "Tarōn"; and Appendix I, "Mamikonean, house."

Olanē, see "Ołakan."

Ołkan, see "Ołakan."

Ordoru/Ordru/Orduru

"Home village" (*bun gewł*) of the Orduni house, granted to the bishop of Basean by King Xosrov Kotak after the annihilation of the family. BP underscores that the village was in the district of Basean without further precisions; Eremyan places it directly north of the city of Karin; but its exact location has been disputed.

See Adontz, *Armenia*, p. 383 n. 38c, 214*; Eremyan, *Map* G/4; T꜀. X. Hakobyan, *Ašχarhagrut꜀yun*, p. 116; Honigmann, *Ostgrenze*, p. 214 and n. 7; Honigmann and Maricq, RGDS, pp. 54 n. 2, 177.

III.iv
p. 70
Maps, D–E/5?
See also "Basean"; and Appendix I, "Orduni, house"; "Xosrov II/III."

Ordru, see "Ordoru."

Orduru, see "Ordoru."

Ōšakan/Awšakan

Locality in the district of Aragacotn directly north of the city of Vałaršapat, and renowned in the Armenian tradition as the resting place of St. Maštoc꜀ (Koriwn, xxvi, p. 94 = trans. p. 50). It has tentatively been identified with the Astakana of Ptolemy (V.xii.7), though Hewsen disagrees. According to MX, III.ix (= MK, p. 262), Ōšakan was granted to Vahan Amatuni by King Xosrov Kotak in reward for his services in the Mazk꜀ut꜀k꜀ war. There is no mention of this gift in BP, who merely records the defeat of the Mazk꜀ut꜀k꜀ near the fortress, but Ōšakan is known as a possession of the Amatuni to ŁP꜀ as well, I.xix, p. 38 (= CHAMA, II, p. 278), cf. MX, III.lxvii (= MK, p. 349).

See AON, p. 364; Eremyan, *Map* B/6; Hewsen, "Ptolemy," p. 132; T꜀. X. Hakobyan, *Ašχarhagrut꜀yun*, p. 133 and map; Toumanoff, *Studies*, p. 197; Yovhannēsean, HB, pp. 787–791.

III.vii

p. 74

Maps, G–H/5

See also "Vałaršapat"; and Appendix I, "Amatuni, house"; "Mazkʿutʿkʿ"; "Xosrov II/III."

Oskikʿ

Village in the district of Całkotn near the sources of the Euphrates–Arsanias (mod. Murad-su) to which St. Gind retired. It is associated by BP with the site of the retirement of St. Gregory the Illuminator; but see VI.xvi n. 9.

> See AON, p. 361, 460; Eremyan, *Ašχarh.*, p. 74 and map G/5; but it is not given on the fourth-century *Map*.
>
> VI.xvi
>
> p. 240
>
> Maps, G/6.
>
> See also Appendix I, "Gind"; "Grigor/Gregorids."

Osχay/Oχsa/Toχay

Presumed village in the district of Basean, said to have been twice the site of a major Persian defeat by the Armenians from which the king of kings escaped alone. It is unattested outside the text of BP, and in one of the mss the name appears in the form Toχay. Peeters noted the parallel between the two battles and identified Osχay with the *castellum Auaxa* of the *Notitia dignitatum*, xxxviii, pp. 83–84, but Adontz identifies the latter with Awaza. Melikʿ-Ōhanǰanyan argued for a purely symbolic name reflecting the Armenians' "rancor" (*oχ*) against the Persians, as being in keeping with the epic character of the context (see III.xxi n. 12).

> See Inčičean, *Storagrutʿiwn*, p. 387, *Oχsay*; Peeters, "Intervention," pp. 230–249 and n. 4; Adontz, *Armenia*, pp. 81–82; Melikʿ-Ōhanǰanyan, "Tiran-Trdati vepə," II, pp. 70–71, 76.
>
> III.xxi; IV.xxii
>
> pp. 98, 155
>
> Maps, E/5–6?
>
> See also "Basean."

Oχsa, see "Osχay."

Palestine/Palestinacʿuocʿ erkir

The toponym "Palestine" in BP unquestionably denotes the general geographical area, rather than the Roman provinces of the same name. The only reference to the region is related to the presumed transportation of large Jewish colonies from it into Armenian cities in the reign of Tigran the Great.

> See Avi-Yonah, "Palaestina."
>
> IV.lv
>
> pp. 175–176
>
> See also Appendix I, "Hreaykʿ"; "Tigran."

Palestinacʿuocʿ erkir, see "Palestine."

Pʿaytakaran/Balasakan ‹ Parth. *blʿskn*

Attested as one of the provinces of the Sasanian Empire in ŠKZ, Parth. 2; KKZ, 12. City placed by BP in the district of Kazbkʿ (V.xiv and n. 2). The *Ašχarhacʿoycʿ* is acquainted with the district of Pʿaytakaran (29/40, 33/44) but not with the city of the same name. The city of Pʿaytakaran (*Pʿaytakaran kʿałakʿ*) recorded in BP should not be confused with Baylakan, as has sometimes been done, and its exact location is disputed between Eremyan, who places it north of the lower Araxes, and Hakobyan, who locates it south of the same river. According to Aa, dcccxlii, Pᶜaytakaran marked the border of Greater Armenia on the side of the Kazbkᶜ and was an Armenian city, "*Pᶜaytakaran kᶜałakᶜ arkᶜayutᶜeann Hayocᶜ,*" but cf. ŁPᶜ, II.xxxiii, p. 63 (= CHAMA, II, p. 292) and Ełišē iii–iv, pp. 86, 96–97 (= *Ełishē*, pp. 140, 147, 277), both of whom seem to place the city beyond the Armenian border in Atrpatakan. The entire region is said to have been evangelized by St. Maštocᶜ (Koriwn, xvii, p. 72 = trans. p. 41, "Baghas"), who refers to it as Balasakan and where the city is first associated with Ałuankᶜ, though it subsequently was separated from it. MX, III.iii–iv, vi (= MK, pp. 256–257, 259) makes it the center of the realm of the Mazkᶜutᶜkᶜ. Like the rest of the northeastern march-lands, Pᶜaytakaran must have defected from the Armenian kingdom along with the district of Kazbkᶜ after the Roman–Persian peace of 363 (IV.l, where it is not mentioned by name), since it is explicitly mentioned in the brief reconquest of the region by the Armenian *sparapet* Mušeł Mamikonean, ca. 370 (V.xiv). It was finally lost to Atrpa-takan at the partition of the Armenian kingdom ca. 387, since the *Ašχarhacᶜoycᶜ* (*loc. cit*) lists the entire province of Pᶜaytakaran among the lands lost to Atrpatakan (see also above, ŁPᶜ and Ełišē). Sebēos, i, p. 26 (= trans. p. 5) records the shift to Pᶜaytakaran of the *diwan* of Siwnikᶜ in 591 so that it should no longer be in Armenia. The district is probably to be identified with the Persian province of Balasakan in the Kusti Kapkoh (*Ašχarhacᶜoycᶜ*, 40/53).

   See Gignoux, *Glossaire*, pp. 20, 49; Sprengling, *Third-Century Iran*, pp. 7, 14, 47, 52; Honigmann and Maricq, RGDS, pp. 40, 80–87; AON, pp. 267–270; Eremyan, *Ašχarh.*, pp. 77, 88; *idem, Map* G/7; Tᶜ. X. Hakobyan, *Ašχarhagrutᶜyun*, pp. 232–233 and map; Hewsen, "Armenia," p. 333; *idem*, "Caspiane"; Marquart, *Ērānšahr*, pp. 119–120; Adontz, *Armenia*, pp. 171–172, 176, 466 n. 13, 87*–88*, 118*, 215*; Petrosyan, "Pᶜaytakaran"; Perikhanian, "Zametki," I.i.
   V.xiv
   p. 200
   Maps, M/6
   See also "Ałuankᶜ"; "Atrpatakan"; "Kazbkᶜ"; "Mec Haykᶜ"; "Siwnikᶜ"; Appendix I, "Mazkᶜutᶜkᶜ"; "Mušeł"; and Appendix III *kᶜałakᶜ*.

Persia, see Appendix I, "Parskᶜ."

Phasianē, see "Basean."

Pᶜokᶜr Siwnikᶜ, see "Haband."

Ṙan, see "Ałuankᶜ."

Ṙštunikᶜ
   First district in Vaspurakan, according to the *Ašχarhacᶜoycᶜ* (32/43). It lay along the southern shore of Lake Van and included the island of Ałtᶜamar as well as the localities of Van-Tosp and Ostan, the latter of which was the seat of the Ṙštuni house. The district (to which BP refers as both an *ašχarh*, III.x, and a *gawaṙ*, IV.lix; V.xxxvii) was incor-porated into the domain of the Arcruni early in the Arab period.
   See AON, pp. 333, 339; Eremyan, *Ašχarh.*, pp. 79, 117; *idem, Map* F/5; Hewsen, "Armenia," p. 331; Tᶜ. X. Hakobyan, *Ašχarhagrutᶜyun*, pp. 165–167 and map; Adontz, *Armenia*, p. 516 n. 53, 120*, 125*, 175*; Toumanoff, *Studies*, p. 213.
   III.viii, x, xviii; IV.iv, xi, lix; V.xxxvii
   pp. 76, 79, 179, 220
   Maps, F/8

See also "Ałt⁽amar"; "Van"; Appendix I, "Arcruni, house"; "Řštuni, house"; and Appendix III, *gawaṙ*.

Sagistan, see "Sakastan."

Šahapivan

Locality in the district of Całkotn southwest of the city of Zarehawan according to Eremyan, though its precise location is not known. In the fourth century, it was the site of one of the Aršakuni game preserves and of the royal "home camp" (*bun banak*), according to BP, see IV.xv n. 8, (whose Iranian counterpart was located at T⁽awrēš), though MX, III.xxiii (= MK, p. 278), calls it Gnel's "own mountain which had come to him from his maternal grandfather Gnel Gnuni." This seems unlikely since the domain of the Gnuni family was in Ałiovit and not in contiguous Całkotn, which lay further north. In the mid-fifth century, Šahapivan was the site of an important church council (443/4), but it does not seem to have been an extensive center of population as it is known as a monastery rather than a town.

See AON, p. 457; Eremyan *Ašχarh.*, p. 56, *Całkotn* and 85, *Tatēon awan*; *idem*, "Razvitie," pp. 41–42; T⁽. X. Hakobyan, *Ašχarhagrut⁽yun*, p. 122 and map; Garsoïan, "Banak ark⁽uni."

IV.xv

p. 141

Maps, G/6?

See also "Ałiovit"; "T⁽awrēš"; "Zarehawan"; Appendix I, "Aršakuni"; "Gnel Aršakuni"; "Gnuni, house"; and Appendix III, *bun banak*.

Šakašēn ‹ Ir. *Saka*, "Scythian" + Arm. *šēn*, "dwelling/edifice"; Gk. Σακασηνή

Seventh district of the region of Utik⁽ lying south of the Kur River between Gardman and Utik⁽ proper, according to the *Ašχarhac⁽oyc⁽* (33/44–45). The district took its name from the Saka or Scythians who had settled there and it was known as Sakasēnē to Greek geographers (Ptolemy, V.xii.4; Strabo, *Geogr.*, XI.viii.4; xiv.4). Šakašēn formed a part of the disputed Armeno–Albanian marchlands south of the Kur and was probably lost as a result of the Roman–Persian peace of 363, although BP does not state this explicitly, and notes only the brief reconquest of the district by the Armenian *sparapet* Mušeł Mamikonean, ca. 370. The district must have passed back to Albania at the partition of the Armenian kingdom ca. 387, since it is listed along with Utik⁽ among the lands lost to Ałuank⁽ in the *Ašχarhac⁽oyc⁽* (*loc. cit.*), and MK/D, III.xii p. 312 (= MD, p. 203), knows it as part of Ałuank⁽. The local rulers from the Daštakaran house are attested until the seventh century (Sebēos, xlviii, p. 166 and n. 624 = trans. p. 135 and the late *Vita* of St. Nersēs, v, p. 35 = CHAMA, II, p. 26, as well as MK/D), but they are unknown to BP and other Armenian sources.

See AON, pp. 352–353, 457; Eremyan, *Ašχarh.*, pp. 73, 118; *idem*, *Map* B/6–7; Hewsen, "Armenia," pp. 333; *idem*, "Ptolemy," pp. 114, 149; T⁽. X. Hakobyan, *Ašχarhagrut⁽yun*, p. 237 and map; Marquart, *Ērānšahr*, pp. 118, 170; Adontz, *Armenia*, pp. 324, 121*, 124*–125*, 175*; Toumanoff, *Studies*, pp. 220, 451 n. 53, 467 and n. 128, 482 n. 199.

V.xiii

p. 200

Maps, H–J/4.

See also "Ałuank⁽"; "Gardman"; "Kur"; "Miǰnašχarh Hayoc⁽"; "Utik⁽"; and Appendix I, "Mušeł."

Sakasēnē, see "Šakašēn."

Sakstan/Sagistan/Sistan ‹ Ir. *Saka*, "Scythian" + Arm./Ir. suffix of place -*stan*; Gk.Σεγιστανή, Σακαστανή

Attested in ŠKZ, Parth. 2, 19; Phl. 24; RGDS, nos. 4, 42, pp. 48–49, 58–59, Σεγισ-τανή.

Twelfth region of the *K^custi Nmŕoǰ* (Ir. *Kust-i Nēmrōz*) in southern Iran, according to the *Ašχarhac^coyc^c* (40/53). Sakstan lay on the eastern border of Iran south of Khorasan and formed a separate principality conquered in the third century A.D. by Ardašīr I and governed thereafter for the Sasanian state by a *marzpan*.

See AG, pp. 71–72 no. 161; JIN, p. 279, *Sakastan*; Marquart, *Ērānšahr*, pp. 16, 26, 35–39; Herzfeld, "Sakastan"; Sprengling, *Third-Century Iran*, pp. 7–8, 14, 18; Honigmann and Maricq, RGDS, pp. 40, 94–98; Gignoux, *Glossaire*, pp. 33, 63.

IV.xlv

p. 165

See also Appendix III, *marzpan*.

Sałamas/Sałmas

Locality that BP places in the southeastern district of Korčēk^c. Nevertheless, both Eremyan and Hakobyan disregard BP's indication and locate it in the district of Zarawand northeast of Lake Urmiah in the vicinity of modern Salmas/Kuneh Šahr-i Šāhpuhr(?).

See AON, pp. 256, 338 and n. 3; Eremyan, *Map* G/6; T^c. X. Hakobyan, *Ašχarhagrut^cyun*, p. 232 and map.

IV.xlviii

p. 166

Maps, H/8?

See also "Korčēk^c."

Sałmas, see "Sałamas."

Sararad/Ararad, Mt.

Mountain in the southern district of Korduk^c on which Noah's ark had come to rest, according to BP. It should not be confused with the mod. Mt. Ararat to the north, which was known as Azat Masis at the time. The tradition of the landing of the ark in southern Armenia was also known to a number of ancient and Armenian sources (see III.x n.3). Eremyan places it in the southeastern part of Korduk^c almost due north of T^clman. There is no evidence as to its precise location but it is probably the Mt. Ğūdi associated with the ark in the Syriac, Talmudic and Koranic traditions.

See AON, p. 333; Markwart, *Südarmenien*, pp. 214–223, 250; Fiey, *Nisibe*, pp. 179, 221–223, 227; Peeters, "Jacques de Nisibe," pp. 318–337; El², Djudi.

III.x

pp. 77, 79

Maps, F/9

See also "Korduk^c"; and Appendix I, "Yakob."

Satał; Gk Σάταλα; Lat. Satala; mod. Sadak

Attested in ŠKZ, Parth. 8; RGDS, no. 18, pp. 52–53, 81.

City in Armenia Minor south of the upper course of the Gayl/Lykos River (mod. Kelkit çayi). Both BP and Aa, dcccxlii, use it as a reference point to indicate the northwest frontier of Greater Armenia. Satala is recorded in the *Not. dig.* (Or. xxxviii.13) as the headquarters of the XV Legion Apollinaris, which was stationed there from the time of the emperor Trajan. It is also known as a garrison point to BP (III.xxi) and was refortified by Justinian in the sixth century (Procopius, *De aed.*, III.ix.2–5). In addition to its military importance, Satala in the fourth century was also a bishopric and a *polis* on the main circuit road connecting the main centers of Armenia Minor— Sebastē, Nikopolis, Satala, and Melitēnē—with Caesarea of Cappadocia.

See Eremyan, *Ašχarh.*, p. 80; *idem, Map* B–G/3; Ruge, "Satala"; Jones, *Cities*, p. 171; Honigmann, *Ostgrenze*, pp. 7, 19; Cumont and Cumont, *Studia Pontica II*, pp. 342–351; Adontz, *Armenia*, pp. 49–51, 61–65, 73, 79–80, 82, 113, 117, 133, 137, 395 n. 25, 43*, 46*, 54*, 57*, 62*–63*, 87*–88*, 90*–91*, 106*, 127*, 129*–133*, 218*; Manandyan, *Trade and Cities*, pp. 79, 91–95, etc; Bryer, *Topography of Pontus*, pp. 11–14; Gignoux, *Glossaire*, p. 63; Sprengling, *Third-Century Iran*, pp. 7, 16; Honigmann and Maricq, RGDS, pp. 13, 147.
III.vii, xxi
pp. 74, 98
Maps, C/4–5.
See also Appendix III, *k* *ałak* *.

Satala, see "Satał."

Širak; Gk. Σιρακηνή

Ninth district of the region of Ayrarat lying along the upper and middle course of the Aχurean/Arpa-çayi river, according to the *Ašχarhac* *oyc* * (34/45). It was known to Greek geographers as Sirakēnē (Ptolemy, V.xii.4) and was presumably evangelized in the days of St. Gregory (Vg, clxxii = Va, clx). In the fourth century Širak formed part of the domain of the Kamsarakan, as is explicitly stated by BP (IV.xix), which refers to it as a *gawaŕ*, and confirmed in the seventh century by the inscription of Nerseh Kamsarakan on the church of the Theotokos at T* *alin. Other houses were, however, also to be found in the district, such as the cadet branch of the Dimak* *sean, listed as Dimak* *sean of Širak in the *Gahnamak*, "Rank List," and possibly the Gnuni, according to an inscription found at Mastara on the border of the district. Another inscription from Mren also places the Sahaŕuni house on the border of the district. In the ninth century, Širak, together with adjacent Aršarunik* *, was sold by the Kamsarakan to the Bagratuni and its centers, Širakawan and the fortress of Ani, became successive Bagratuni capitals.

See AON, p. 364; Eremyan, *Ašχarh.*, pp. 73–74, 118; *idem, Map* B/5; Hewsen, "Armenia," p. 335; *idem*, "Ptolemy," pp. 114, 119; T* *. X. Hakobyan, *Ašχarhagrut* *yun*, pp. 124–129; Adontz, *Armenia*, 46, 193, 236–238, 240–241, 257, 324, 455 n. 12, 497–498 n. 76, 83*, 121*, 126*, 176*; Garitte, *Documents*, pp. 102–104, 233–234. Ališan, *Ayrarat*, p. 138; *idem, Širak*; Toumanoff, *Studies*, pp. 202, 206, 214; Kretschmer-Honigmann, "Sirakene."
III.xi; IV.iv, xix
pp. 81, 111, 149
Maps, G/4–5
See also "Aršarunik* *"; "Ayrarat"; Appendix I, "Dimak* *sean, house"; "Gnuni, house"; "Grigor/Gregorids"; "Kamsarakan, house"; and Appendix III, *gawaŕ*.

Sirakēnē, see "Širak."

Sisakan, see "Siwnik* *."

Sisakan-i Kotak, see "Haband."

Siwnik* */Sisakan (after the sixth century); Gk. Φαυηνή/Σαυηνή?

Ninth region of Greater Armenia (*Mec Hayk* *), comprising twelve districts and lying east of Ayrarat between the Araxes River and Arjaχ, according to the *Ašχarhac* *oyc* * (33/44). In the fourth century it included most of the area south-southeast of Lake

Sewan down to the Araxes. The name of the region may be attested in Strabo (*Geogr.*, XI.xiv.4) in the form Phauēnē (*pro* Sauēnē, cf. XI.xiv.5, Phaunitis), but the form Sunitai (in the plural as in Armenian), referring to a people rather than a place, is given by Procopius (*Bell. Pers.*, I.xv.1). MX, I.xii (= MK, p. 91), gives the legendary derivation from an eponymous Sisak for the later name of the region, Sisakan, first attested in the sixth-century *Chronicle* of Ps. Zach. Rhet. (XII.vii). Although Siwnikᶜ is familiar to all Armenian sources, had been evangelized in the days of St. Gregory (Vg, clxxi = Va, clix), and formed part of the Armenian Midlands, as opposed to the border districts, it always stayed a little apart from the Armenian kingdom despite BP's reference to it as a mere *gawaṙ* (IV.xx; V.xliii). Sebēos, i, p. 26 (= trans. p. 5) also records the shift of its *diwan* to Pᶜaytakaran. Hence it remained a separate entity, the homonymous princes of which always tended to be suspect to the Armenians. It did not defect from Aršak II, however, and its sack by the Persians in their campaign following the Persian-Armenian peace of 363 was particularly brutal, according to BP (IV.lviii).

See AON, pp. 210, 237–238, 263–275; Eremyan, *Ašχarh.*, pp. 81, 117; *idem, Map* G/6–7; Hewsen, "Armenia," pp. 332, 336–337; *idem,* "Arcᶜaχ"; Tᶜ. X. Hakobyan, *Ašχarhagrutᶜyun*, pp. 175–201 and map; *idem,* "*Ašχarhagrutᶜyun Syuniki*"; *idem,* "Syunikᶜi teritoria"; Marquart, *Ērānšahr*, pp. 120–122; Ališan, *Sisakan*; Adontz, *Armenia*, pp. 171–172, 174, 179, 226, 235–236, 324–325, 435 n. 15, 495–497 n. 72, 118*, 120*, 124*–125*, 177*; Toumanoff, *Studies*, pp. 131–132, 137, 332; Henning, "Farewell," p. 512, identifies Siwnikᶜ in the Paikuli inscription and equates ŠKZ, Parth. 2, *sykn* with Siwnikᶜ, though Maricq, RGDS, no. 3, pp. 48–49 gives Μαχελονία for the Greek equivalent; see Honigmann and Maricq, RGDS, pp. 172–174. Cf. Humbach and Skjærvø, *Paikuli*, 3.1 §92, pp. 71 and 124, *šykᶜ[n]*.
III.ix; IV.iv, xx; V.xliii
pp. 77, 152, 227
Maps, H–J/5–7
See also "Arjaχ"; "Ayrarat"; "Mec Haykᶜ"; "Miǰnašχarh Hayocᶜ"; "Pᶜaytakaran"; Appendix I, "Grigor/Gregorids"; "Siwni"; and Appendix III, *gawaṙ*.

Sophanēnē, see "Copᶜkᶜ Mec."

Sophēnē, see "Copᶜkᶜ" and "Copᶜkᶜ Šahēi."

Sper; Gk. Συσπίριτις; modern Ispir.
Seventh district of Upper Armenia (*Barjr Haykᶜ*) lying along the upper course of the Çoruh River, according to the *Ašχarhacᶜoycᶜ* (29/40). Its center was at Smbataberd/Smbatawan (mod. Baiburt). The name of the district was derived from the tribe of the Saspeires, known to Herodotus (I.104, 111; III.94; IV.37, 40, etc.), and it was usually known to Greek geographers as Suspiritis (Strabo, *Geogr.*, XI.xiv.9, 12). It is probably to be identified with the later locality of Pharangion of Procopius (*Bell.Pers.*, II.xxix.14; *Bell. Goth.*, IV.ii.6). The district was apparently evangelized in the days of St. Gregory (Vg, clxxii = Va, clx) and Mesrop Maštocᶜ sent disciples there, according to MX, III.lx (= MK, p. 333), although this is not recorded by Koriwn.

The princes of Sper were the Bagratuni, as is unanimously stated by the Armenian sources (V.xliv), cf. MX, II.xxxvii, lxiii; III.xliii (= MK, pp. 179, 207, 306), and they are occasionally referred to as Speracᶜikᶜ, Sebēos, xlviii, p. 165 (= trans. p. 134). The district was also famous in antiquity for its gold and silver mines, which helped support the rise of the Bagratuni house, but BP identifies it merely as a *gawaṙ.*.

See AON, p. 287; Eremyan, *Ašχarh.*, pp. 81, 116; *idem, Map* B/4; Hewsen, "Armenia," p. 326; Tᶜ. X. Hakobyan, *Ašχarhagrutᶜyun*, p. 209 and map; Weissbach, "Suspiritis"; Adontz, *Armenia*, pp. 22, 39, 43, 98, 241–242, 257, 307, 313, 486 n.

19, 90*, 118*, 121*, 124*, 170*; Toumanoff, *Studies*, pp. 132, 137, 138 n. 240, 193, 202, 321–322 n. 76, 323–324 nn. 77, 81, 326.

V.xliv

p. 228

Maps, C–D/4–5

See also Appendix I, "Bagratuni"; "Grigor/Gregorids"; and Appendix III, *gawaṙ*.

Susianē, see "Xužastan."

Suspiritis, see "Sper."

Syrian Mesopotamia, see "Miǰagetkʿ Asorocʿ."

Tačar mayri, see "Tiknuni."

Tamoritis, see "Tmorikʿ."

Tao, see "Taykʿ."

Tapʿer

Bridge at Artašat leading over the Araxes River to the plain beyond (III.xii). It is also known to Aa, xxxiii, but not to Ag. Malχasyancʿ (p. 317 n. 36) suggests a derivation of the name from the plural of *tapʿ* "land/earth," hence "plain" from the direction of the bridge, but this seems unlikely in this period.

See HArmB, IV, pp. 390–391.

III.xii; IV.lv

pp. 82, 175

Maps, H/5–6.

See also "Artašat."

Tarawn, see "Tarōn."

Tarōn/Tarawn; Gk. Ταρωνῖτις

Third district of Turuberan, according to the *Ašχarhacʿoycʿ* (29/40), which lay due west of Lake Van. The area of Tarōn was vast but does not seem to have been too clearly defined at first, for BP refers to it as a "district" (*gawaṙ*; III.xvi, xix; IV.xiv, xv; V.iii; VI.xvi), but also as a "province" (*nahang*; III.xiv; IV.xv) and a "land" (*erkir*; III.iii, xiv, xv). Similarly, Aa, dcccix, refers to it as an *erkir*, while MX, I.vi; II.lxxxiv; III.xxxi, lxvii (= MK, pp. 80, 236, 288, 348), speaks of both a *gawaṙ* and a "region" (*koɫmn*). Some of this confusion may stem from the fact that Tarōn appears to have been divided into two portions from ancient times, according to MX, II.viii, lxxxiv (= MK, pp. 144, 235–236). The eastern portion, with the fortress of Oɫakan, belonged to the Sɫkuni family, and the western, to the Vahuni priestly clan supervising the shrine of Vahagn/ Heraklēs at Aštišat. In the fourth century, this division seems to have been perpetuated, with the Mamikonean supplanting the Sɫkuni at Oɫakan (V.viii; III.xviii n. 5), cf. MX, II.lxxxiv (= MK, p. 235–236), while Aštišat, along with former temple estates, passed to the patriarchal house of St. Gregory (III.iii; IV.xiv, cf. Aa, dcccix–dcccxv) as the area was Christianized (Vg, clxxii = Va, clx). In the fifth century, the patriarchal lands also passed to the Mamikonean with the marriage of Sahakanoyš, the only child of the last Gregorid patriarch St. Sahak I, to Hamazasp Mamikonean. Tarōn was the center of Syrian influence on early Armenian Christianity in the fourth century.

See AON, pp. 325–327; Eremyan, *Ašχarh.*, pp. 85, 116; *idem*, *Map* G/4; Hewsen, "Armenia," p. 326 and n. 26; Tʿ. X. Hakobyan, *Ašχarhagrutʿyun*; pp. 151–154 and map; Markwart, *Südarmenien*, pp. 294–298, 305–310, 318–328, *et passim*;

Adontz, *Armenia*, pp. 242–245, 179*; Toumanoff, *Studies*, pp. 132, 138, 172 n. 94, 202, 209, 210; Garitte, *Documents*, pp. 103, 236.

III.iii, xiv, xvi, xix; IV.iv, xiv–xv; V.iii; VI.xvi

pp. 68, 86, 90–91, 93–94, 113, 139, 145, 188, 239

Maps, D–F/7

See also "Aštišat"; "Gomkunkᶜ"; "Hacᶜeacᶜ Draχt"; "Hacᶜekacᶜ"; "Mcurkᶜ"; "Ołakan"; Appendix I, "Danielᵉ"; "Gind"; "Grigor/Gregorids"; "Mamikonean, house"; "Vahagn"; and Appendix III, *erkir*; *gawaṙ*; *kołmn*; *nahang*.

Taronitis, see "Tarōn."

Tᶜawrēš/Tᶜawrēž; mod. Tabriz

Locality in Atrpatakan east of Lake Urmiah and presumed site of the Sasanian "home-camp" (IV.xxv; V.ii). It may be identified with the Gabris of Ptolemy (VI.ii.8), but BP is the first Armenian source to refer to the site, and it is not known to MX. The Iranian institution of the royal camp with its Armenian counterpart is an example of the parallels between the two societies.

See Eremyan, *Ašχarh.*, p. 53; *idem*, *Map* G/7; Minorsky, "Tabriz"; Garsoïan, "Banak arkᶜuni."

IV.xxv, xxxix; V.ii

pp. 159, 163, 187

Maps, J/8.

See also "Atrpatakan"; "Šahapivan."

Tᶜawrēž, see "Tᶜawrēš."

Taykᶜ; Georg. *Tao*

Fourteenth region of Greater Armenia (*Mec Haykᶜ*) comprising eight districts and lying to the northwest at the sources of the Kur River, according to the *Ašχarhacᶜoycᶜ* (35/46), which first joins all of its territories under a single name, perhaps reflecting the situation following the Roman–Persian peace of 591. The name of the region was derived from that of the tribe of the Taochoi known to Xenophon (*Anab.*, IV.iv.8; vi.5; xi.1, 17; V.v.17), and was known as Tao to the Georgians, though this term may refer only to its northwestern part. Taykᶜ formed part of the Armeno–Iberian marchlands southwest of Gugarkᶜ and seems to have remained entirely Armenian during the fourth century. This extensive region, to which BP refers invariably as a "realm" (*ašχarh*), was divided into three portions. (1) The principality of Taykᶜ proper in the northwest; it was the intrinsic domain of the Mamikonean to which they returned as a refuge abandoning their other possessions, according to BP (III.xviii, IV.ii), which stresses its impregnable and inaccessible character (*amur ašχarh*). In keeping with his policy of ignoring the Mamikonean family (see Intro., pp. 44–45), MX, II.vi, III.xliv (= MK, pp. 135, 307), does not mention the presence of the family in the district, but the Tayecᶜi are attributed 1,000 retainers in the late *Zōrnamak*, "Military List," and are included in the List of *naχarar*s in the *Vita* of St. Nersēs, v, p. 35 (= CHAMA, II, p. 26). (2) The principality of Bołχa/Bułχa to the southeast of the first, ruled by a secondary line of the Dimakᶜsean family, still remembered in the late listing of the *Gahnamak*, "Rank List." (3) The principality of Koł/Kola northeast of Bołχa, ruled by native homonymous princes. The region of Taykᶜ was presumably evangelized in the days of St. Gregory (Vg, clxxii = Va, clx), and the principality remained a domain of the Mamikonean until the eighth century when it passed to the Bagratuni and became the possession of the Iberian branch of the family.

See AON, pp. 276–278; Eremyan, *Ašχarh.*, pp. 84, 118; *idem*, *Map* B/4–5; Hewsen, "Armenia," pp. 334–335, 336–337; Tᶜ. X. Hakobyan, *Ašχarhagrutᶜyun*, pp. 241–243 and map; Tašean, "Taykᶜ"; Adontz, *Armenia*, pp. 23, 173, 179, 194, 236,

243–244, 246, 306–307, 344, 180*; Toumanoff, *Studies*, pp. 209–210, 230 n. 278, 231, 247 and n. 330, 252, 254, 499; Garitte, *Documents*, pp. 103, 235–236. Edwards, "Artvin"; Bryer, *Topography of Pontus*, pp. 57–60; Thierry, "Tayk."
III.xviii; IV.ii, xviii; VI.xi
pp. 93, 107, 148, 238
Maps, D–E/4–5
See also "Eraχani"; "Gugark^c"; "Kur"; "Mec Hayk^c"; "Virk^c" Appendix I, "Bagratuni, house"; "Dimak^csean, house"; "Grigor/Gregorids"; "Kiwrakos"; "Mamikonean, house"; and Appendix III, *amur*; *ašχarh*.

Thospitis, see "Tozb."

Throne of Anahit, see "Atoṙ Anahtay."

Tigranakert ‹ Tigran + Arm. *kert*, "built/building"; Gk. Τιγρανόκερτα; Lat. Tigranocerta

City in Aljnik^c founded as the new capital of Armenia by Tigran the Great soon after 80 B.C. and largely populated with the deported inhabitants of Mazaka (later Caesarea) in Cappadocia. From its eponymous name, following the model of the multiple Alexandrias, and the descriptions in classical sources (Strabo, *Geogr.*, XI.xii, 4; xiv.15; XII.ii.9; XVI.i.23; Appian, *Mithr.*, X.67; Plutarch, "Lucullus," xxi–xxii, xxvi, xxix) it was an extensive urban center of Hellenistic type, although a game preserve of Iranian type was laid out beyond the city walls; cf. III.viii n. 5. The city was taken and sacked by Lucullus in 69 B.C., but even after it had ceased to be the capital of the Armenian kingdom it remained a city of importance, still listed in the *Tabula Peutingeriana* until its sack by Šāhpuhr II. The precise location of the city is still disputed. Most scholars had accepted the hypothesis of Lehmann-Haupt that it stood at the site of the medieval Martyropolis (Arm. Nprkert, Ar. Miyāfarīqīn, mod. Silvan), but doubts have recently been raised as to this identification, and a return to the suggestion that it be identified with Arzn, where extensive ruins are still visible, has been suggested by Syme, Sinclair and other scholars, while Dilleman still makes a case for Tell Armen, southwest of Mardin.

See AON, pp. 473–475; Eremyan *Ašχarh.*, pp. 73, 86; *idem*, *Map* G/4, who not only identifies it with Nprkert but gives it a considerable administrative district; *Tabula Peutingeriana*, pp. 745–748; T^c. X. Hakobyan, *Ašχarhagrut'yun*, pp. 221–224; Mommsen, "Tigranocerte"; Lehmann-Haupt, *Armenien*, I, pp. 381–429, 501–523; *idem*, "Tigranocerta"; Marquart, "Mīpherqēt"; Manandyan, *Trade and Cities*, pp. 58–63, 86, 91–93, 101–102, 103–106; Sarkisian, *Tigranakert*. Also for the most recent review of the evidence, Chaumont, "Tigranocerte"; Nogaret, "Quelques problèmes"; Sinclair, *Eastern Turkey*; Dilleman, *Haute-Mésopotamie*, pp. 247–163.
IV.xxiv; V.xxvii
pp. 157, 207
Maps, D–8?
See also "Aljnik^c"; Appendix I, "Šapuh"; "Tigran"; and Appendix III, *k^calak^c*.

Tigranocerta, see "Tigranakert."

Tigranokerta, see "Tigranakert."

Tiknuni/Tačar mayri, "Forest palace"
Rural residence erected by King Xosrov Kotak in connection with the hunting preserve or "paradise" created by him in the plain of the Mecamōr River inside the royal domain of Ayrarat. BP is the only source to record both the planting of this preserve

and the name of the "Forest palace," though MX, III.viii (= MK, p. 261) and ŁPᶜ, lxviii, p. 144 (= CHAMA, II, p. 343) mention the king's other preserve, Xosrovakert.

> See AON, pp. 472, 475; Dandamayev, "Paradeisioi"; Seyrig, "Jardins"; Garsoïan, "Mediaeval Armenian City," pp. 77–79; *idem*, "Banak arkᶜuni" and III.viii n. 5.
> III.viii
> p. 75
> See also "Ayrarat"; "Mecamōr"; "Xosrovakert"; Appendix I, "Xosrov II/III"; and Appendix III, *tačar*.

Tᶜil

Locality in northwestern Ekełeacᶜ to the north of the Euphrates River (mod. Kara su) and still extant under the same name due west of mod. Erzincan. According to Aa, dcclxxxvi, Tᶜil had been the site of a temple to the goddess Nanē, called Athena by MX, II.xiv (= MK, p. 152), and had been given to the church after the destruction of the shrine by St. Gregory the Illuminator. In the fourth century, it was the burial place of the Gregorid patriarchs, St. Aristakēs (see III.xiv n. 9) and St. Nersēs the Great, though other patriarchs of the family were buried at Tᶜordan. BP (III.xiv; V.xxiv), supported by MX, II.xci (= MK, p. 249), stresses that Tᶜil was an ecclesiastical domain belonging to the Gregorid family. The precise size and status of the locality is difficult to determine since BP refers to it alternately as a "town" (*awan*) and a "village" (*gewł*) and even links the two in a single phrase: "in the town of Tᶜil his own village" (*i Tᶜiln yawann yiwr gewłn*; V.xxiv).

> See AON, pp. 286; Eremyan, *Map* G/3; Tᶜ. X. Hakobyan, *Ašχarhagrutᶜyun*, p. 206–207 and map; Honigmann, *Ostgrenze*, pp. 79ff.; Adontz, *Armenia*, pp. 39, 222*; Garitte, *Documents*, p. 214; Carrière, *Huit sanctuaires*; Boudoyan and Thierry, "Thil."
> III.ii, xiv; V.xxiv–xxv
> pp. 67, 88, 205
> Maps, B/5–6
> See also "Ekełeacᶜ"; "Tᶜordan"; Appendix I, "Aristakēs"; "Grigor/Gregorids"; "Nersēs I"; and Appendix III, *awan*; *gewł*.

Tispon/Tizbon ‹ Phl. Tesbon; Gk. Κτησιφῶν; Lat. Ctesiphon

Sasanian capital in the district of Asorestan, on the left bank of the Tigris River (cf. Strabo, *Geogr.*, XVI.i.16), and, together with Seleucia on the opposite bank, seat of the Persian patriarchate known as the Great Church of Kokē. BP refers to it as a *kᶜałakᶜ*, as he does for the Greek cities, but mentions it explicitly only in connection with the martyrdom of Mari (IV.xvi) and the proposed reward of King Aršak II (IV.xx), but Malχasyancᶜ (pp. 319 n. 49, 326 n. 108) also takes the mentions of Asorestan in III.xẍ and IV.xx as references to Ctesiphon.

> See Christensen, *L'Iran*, pp. 95, 127, 383–390; Pigulevskaya, *Villes*, pp. 34, 66, 121, 171; Macomber, "Authority"; *Syn. Or.*, pp. 670, 675, 683.
> IV.xvi, xx, liv
> pp. 147, 151, 170
> See also "Asorestan"; Appendix I, "Aršak II"; "Mari"; "Sasanians"; and Appendix III, *kᶜałakᶜ*.

Tizbon, see "Tispon."

Tmorikᶜ ‹ Syr. *Tmōrāyē*; Gk. Ταμωνῖτις?

Region in the southern borderland of Greater Armenia apparently equated with the three districts of Upper, Middle, and Lower Kordikᶜ by the *Ašχarhacᶜoycᶜ* (32/43), which does not mention the name Tmorikᶜ. Kordikᶜ/Kordrikᶜ eventually gave its name to Tmorikᶜ, according to MX, II.liii (= MK, p. 196). Tmorikᶜ is attested from Assyrian times in the form Tumurru, but it may have been confused with Tarōn by Strabo (*Geogr.*, XI.xiv.5), if the editorial emendation of the text is correct. In the fourth century, Tmorik' seems to have coincided with only the *Verin*, "Upper" Kordik' of the *Ašxarhac'oyc'*, the terrain of which warranted BP's qualification of *amur gawaṙ* (IV.l), and to have been one of the component parts of the Assyrian March governed by the *bdeašx* of Korduk'. Together with the rest of the Assyrian March, the homonymous prince of Tmorik' defected from Aršak II after the Persian–Roman peace of 363 (IV.l). The district was briefly reconquered by the *sparapet* Mušeł Mamikonean, ca. 370 (V.x), and presumably lost again with all of Korduk' after the partition of Armenia (ca. 387). A bishop of Tmorik' is, however, attested in the Armenian conciliar list of 505 (GT', p. 42). In the later Middle Ages the district belonged to the Bagratuni and later to the Arcruni.

> See AON, pp. 213, 334–337; Eremyan, *Ašxarh.*, pp. 53, 86; *idem, Map* D/5; Hewsen, "Vitaxates"; T'. X. Hakobyan, *Ašxarhagrut'yun*, pp. 86, 230 and map; Markwart, *Südarmenien*, pp. 350, 352–354, 383–386; Adontz, *Armenia*, pp. 175, 177, 258, 260, 264, 484 n. 11, 120*, 125*, 180*; Toumanoff, *Studies*, pp. 200, 202, 204 n. 230, 321–323 and n. 78; Garitte, *Documents*, pp. 219–220.
>
> IV.l; V.x
> pp. 167, 200
> Maps, E–F/9
> See also "Kordik'"; "Korduk'"; "Mec Hayk'"; Appendix I, "Arcruni, house"; "Aršak II"; "Bagratuni, house"; "Mušeł"; and Appendix III, *amur; gawaṙ.*

T'ordan; mod. Doğan köy

Locality in northwestern Daranałik' between Til' and Ani, though the Karšuni version of the *Vita* of St. Gregory mistakenly places it in Ekełeac' (Vk, ccxcviii–ccxcix). According to both Aa, dcclxxxiv, and MX, II.xiv (= MK, p. 152), T'ordan had been the site of a temple of the god Baršamin/Ba'al Šamīn and had been given to the church after the destruction of this shrine by St. Gregory the Illuminator. BP knows nothing of this past or of the subsequent transfer of the relics of St. Gregory from the Cave of Manē to T'ordan (Vk, ccxciii–ccc), cf. MX, II.xci (= MK, pp. 249–250 and n. 14), but, as in the case of T'il, it stresses that T'ordan was part of the patriarchal domain and the burial place of the Gregorid patriarchs, St. Gregory himself, St. Vrt'anēs, and St. Yusik, though probably not St. Aristakēs (see III.xiv n. 9). Despite its importance, T'ordan does not seem to have been a large center in this period, for BP, in agreement with Aa, dcclxxxiv, invariably refers to it as a "village" (*gewł*), even though MX, II.xiv (= MK, p. 152) describes it as a "town" (*awan*).

> See AON, p. 284; Eremyan, *Ašxarh.*, pp. 49, 53; *idem, Map* G/3; T'. X. Hakobyan, *Ašxarhagrut'yun*, p. 205; Adontz, *Armenia*, pp. 39, 222*; Garitte, *Documents*, pp. 214; van Esbroeck, "Nouveau témoin," pp. 93–94, 161–162; *idem*, "Témoignages littéraires," pp. 387–418; Carrière, *Huit sanctuaires.*
>
> III.ii, xi, xii, xiv
> pp. 67, 82, 84, 86
> Maps, B/5–6
> See also "Ani"; "Daranałik'"; "T'il"; Appendix I, "Grigor/Gregorids"; "Vrt'anēs"; "Yusik I"; and Appendix III, *awan; gewł.*

Tosb, see "Tosp."

Tosp/Tosb/Tozb ‹ Urart. Tušpa; Gk. Θωσπῖτις(?)

Second district of Vaspurakan on the eastern shore of Lake Van, according to the *Ašxarhac'oyc'* (32/43). Tosp lay around the stronghold of Van and took its name from the Urartian name of the city, Tušpa. Classical sources (e.g. Ptolemy, V.xii.3, 8) consequently called it Thōspitis and extended this name to the adjoining lake, though Markwart and Minorsky have objected to this identification. Tosp appears to have been a *gawaṙ* and part of the domain of the Ṙštuni (IV.lix), from whom it passed later to the Arcruni.

> See AON, pp. 340, 371, 476; Eremyan, *Ašχarh.*, pp. 86, 117; *idem, map* G/5; Hewsen, "Armenia," p. 330 and nn. 43–44; *idem*, "Ptolemy," pp. 115, 136, 150; Tᶜ. X. Hakobyan, *Ašχarhagrutᶜyun*, pp. 167–171 and map; Adontz, *Armenia*, pp. 250, 464 n. 73, 120*, 125*, 181*; Toumanoff, *Studies*, p. 213; Markwart, *Südarmenien*, p. 28; Minorsky, "L'ouvrage," pp. 146–147.
>
> IV.lv, lix; V.xxxvii
>
> pp. 176, 179, 220
>
> Maps, F–G/7–8
>
> See also "Van"; Appendix I, "Arcruni, house"; "Ṙštuni, house"; and Appendix III, *gawaṙ*.

Toχay, see "Osχay."

Tozb, see "Tosp."

Uṙhay ‹ Syr. Urhai; Gk. ῎Εδεσσα; Lat. Edessa

> Attested in ŠKZ, Parth., 9, 11; Phl. 14, *Urhā*; RGDS, nos. 19, 24, pp. 52–55, ῎Εδεσσα.

Major center in northwestern Mesopotamia existing from antiquity and refounded as a Greek *polis* in 304 B.C. by Seleukos Nikator, who probably gave it the name of Edessa. The city was ruled by the native Abgarid dynasty until the mid-third century A.D., then disputed between Rome and the Sasanians, though it ultimately remained on the Roman side. Edessa was a great commercial and intellectual center where Maštocᶜ first sought an alphabet for the Armenians (see Koriwn, vii, p. 46, who calls it "Edesia" = trans. p. 30). It was the home of the "School of the Persians" until it was closed as heretical by the emperor Zeno in 489, when its scholars moved across the Persian border to recreate it at Nisibis. As in the case of Greek cities, BP refers to it as a *kᶜałakᶜ*.

Tradition long linked Edessa with Armenia through the legend of the conversion of King Abgar, translated into Armenian (Labubna, *Tᶜułtᶜ*), and of the mission of St. Thaddeus to Armenia. MX, who claims to have seen the Edessan Armenian archives (II.xxvii, xxxviii = MK, pp. 165, 181, cf. 13), turns Abgar into an Armenian king to whom he attributes the founding of Edessa, II.xxvi–xxvii (= MK, pp. 163–165), and links the tradition of St. Thaddeus to the Bagratuni house, II.xxxiii (= MK, p. 170). Nevertheless, despite the presence of a large Armenian population in Edessa in the medieval period, there is no evidence to support the claim attributed by BP to King Pap (V.xxxii) that the city had been built by, or had ever belonged to the Armenians.

> See Segal, *Edessa*; Jones, *Cities*, pp. 215–216, 220–222; Thomson, MK, pp. 39–40; Eremyan, *Map* D/3. Dilleman, *Haute-Mésopotamie*; Gignoux, *Glossaire*, pp. 18, 48; Sprengling, *Third-Century Iran*, pp. 7–8, 10, 16; Honigmann and Maricq, RGDS, pp. 13, 14, 143–145, 148, 151.
>
> V.xxxii
>
> p. 213
>
> Maps, A/4–5
>
> See also "Mcbin"; Appendix I, "Bagratuni, house"; "Pap"; "Tᶜadēos"; and Appendix III, *kᶜałakᶜ*.

497

Uti, see "Utik^c."

Utik^c/Uti; Gk. Οὐιτια/'Οτηνή; Lat. Otene

Twelfth region of Greater Armenia (*Mec Hayk^c*), lying between the Kur River and the district of Arjaχ to the south, according to the *Ašχarhac^coyc^c* (33/44–45). Utik^c was composed of eight or nine districts with its center at Partaw (Ar. Bardha^ca). It was familiar to classical sources: Ptolemy (V.xii.4), who also places it along the Kur River; Strabo (*Geogr.*, XI.vii.1; viii.8; xiv.14), who associates it with the tribe of the Ouitioi and places it next to Sakasēnē; Pliny the Elder (NH, VI.xvi, 42); as well as to Armenian sources. Aa, xxviii, calls its city Xałχał, the "winter quarters of the Armenian kings," and lists its princes in the train of St. Gregory on his journey to Caesarea of Cappadocia, dccxcv. MX, II.viii, cf. II.xliv–xlv (= MK, pp. 140, 184–185), and ŁP^c xxxv, p. 35 (= *Ełishē*, p. 279) however, associate Utik^c with Ałuank^c rather than with Armenia, and MK/D, II.ii, p. 114 (= MD, p. 67) as well as Ełišē, iii, p. 75 (= *Ełishē*, p. 127), calls Xałχał the residence of the Albanian and not the Armenian kings.

Like all the northeastern marchlands south of the Kur River, Utik^c was disputed between Armenia and Ałuank^c, and in the first part of the fourth century it formed part of the Aršakuni kingdom. The loss of Utik^c as a result of the Roman–Persian peace of 363 is not mentioned by BP (IV.l), but its reconquest by Mušeł Mamikonean ca. 370 is explicitly recorded (V.xiii). It was lost once again at the partition of the Armenian kingdom ca. 387, as it is listed among the lands lost by Armenia to Ałuank^c in the *Ašχarhac^coyc^c* (33/44). The homonymous princes of Utik^c are not mentioned in BP; are listed in Aa, dccxcv. MX, II.viii (= MK, p. 140) gives them a Haykid descent, and they are included in the late *Zōrnamak*, "Military List," which attributes 1,000 retainers to them, but not in the other Lists of *naχarars*, presumably because they were no longer part of the Armenian kingdom. Utik^c was reannexed by the Armenian Bagratids in 922.

See AON, pp. 270–275; Eremyan, *Ašχarh.*, pp. 75–76, 118; *idem, Map* B/7, where only the district of Utik^c proper and not the larger region is given; Hewsen, "Armenia," pp. 333, 341; *idem,* "Ptolemy," pp. 114, 148; T^c. X. Hakobyan, *Ašχarhagrut^cyun*, pp. 235–237 and map; Marquart, *Ērānšahr*, pp. 117–119, 170; Adontz, *Armenia*, pp. 174–176, 179, 230, 324–325, 118*, 120*–121*, 124*–125*, 182*; Toumanoff, *Studies*, pp. 110 n. 173, 129, 132, 160, 219, 224, 227, 244, 259.

V.xiii

p. 200

Maps, J/5.

See "Ałuank^c"; "Arjaχ"; "Caesarea"; "Kur"; "Miĵnašχarh Hayoc^c"; "Šakašēn"; and Appendix I, "Aršakuni"; "Mušeł."

Vałaršapat ‹ Arm. Vałarš + *pat*, "fortify/wall" = *Nor Kałak^c*, "New City" ‹ Gk. Καινὴ πόλις, "New City"

City in the district of Ayrarat, probably founded in the early second century A.D. by the Aršakuni King Vałarš as its name indicates, but a legendary account of its foundation is given by MX, II.lxv (= MK, pp. 210–211). Ca. A.D. 163 the Romans designated it as the capital of Armenia with the name *Kainē polis*, "New City," and an inscription records the stationing there of a *vexillatio* of the XV Legion Apollinaris (CIL no. 6052). Vałaršapat was the residence of the Armenian Aršakuni kings at the time of the Christianization of the country, according to Aa, xxxi, cxxii, cl, clxvii, dcccxli, and the *martyria* of the Hřip^csimean saints were built there by St. Gregory the Illuminator, Aa, dcclvii–dcclxi, dcclxv–dcclxx, dcccclxxxi, cf. MX, III.xxvii, lxvii (= MK, pp. 283, 349). The status of Vałaršapat as the "mother church" (*mayr ekełeac^c kat^cołikē*) of Armenia and the resting place of the martyrs is also underscored by the *Ašχarhac^coyc^c* (34/45). Very little notice is taken of the city in BP, however, which focuses on the mother church of Aštišat and mentions Vałaršapat only twice, in connection with, (1) the Mazkᶜutᶜkᶜ war (III.vii); and (2) its sack by the Persians with the deportation of its population (IV.lv), an event also recorded by MX, III.xxxv (= MK, p. 293). Vałaršapat obviously maintained its religious importance and prestige but did not recover as an urban center after the Persian destruction, except possibly in the reign of Vramšapuh described by Koriwn, ix, xvi, xxvi, pp. 50, 70, 92 (= trans. pp. 32, 40, 49). BP qualifies it as a "city" (kᶜałakᶜ), a term rarely used in the text for an Armenian center by contrast to Greek ones, but this may well be by association with the Armenian translation of the city's Greek name, Nor Kᶜałakᶜ = Kainē Polis, which was also current (see, e.g., Koriwn, *loc. cit.*).

> See AON, pp. 279, 456, 469; KWCO, p. 106, *Edschmiatzin*; Eremyan, *Ašχarh.*, p. 82; *idem, Map* B/6; Tᶜ. X. Hakobyan, *Ašχarhagrutᶜyun*, pp. 130–133 and map; Gelzer, "Die Anfänge," p. 131; Manandyan, *Trade and Cities*, pp. 83–86; Solodukho, "Sviazi"; Kᶜałantᶜar, *Vałaršapat*; Sardaryan, "Hin Vałaršapat"; Tiratsian, "Vałaršapat"; Khatchatrian, "Données"; *idem*, "Monuments"; Gignoux, *Glossaire*, p. 36; *idem*, NPS, no. 934, p. 173.
>
> III.vii; IV.lv
> pp. 74, 175
> Maps, H/5
> See also "Aštišat"; "Ayrarat"; Appendix I, "Aršakuni"; "Hřipᶜsimē"; "Mazkᶜutᶜkᶜ"; "Vałarš," for additional bibliography on that name; Appendix III, kᶜałakᶜ; katołikē; mayr ekełecᶜeacᶜ.

Valley-of-Gardman, see "Gardman."

Van, lake, see "Bznuneacᶜ cov."

Van/Van-Tosp ‹ Urart. Biaina/Biainili ‹ Urart. Tušpa; Gk. Θωσπῖτις(?)
  Major city and stronghold on the eastern shore of Lake Van. The name of the city is derived from the native name for the Urartian kingdom, Biaina or Biainili, of which it was the capital under the name of Tušpa. This name subsequently spread to the surrounding district of Tosp. The city was known to Ptolemy, who calls it Buana (V.xii.10) and perhaps Thōspia (V.xii.8) by contamination with Tosp, while Diod. Sic. (II.xiii.3) calls it the city of the Χαυῶν (genitive plural). Armenian sources also commonly referred to it as the "city of Semiramis" (see, e.g., MX, II.xix = MK, p. 157), but this name does not occur in BP. In the fourth century, Van was a stronghold of the Řštuni house (IV.lix) and BP refers to it as an *amur kᶜałakᶜ* (IV.lv), but it was taken by Šāhpuhr II (post 363) and its Armenian and much larger Jewish populations deported to Persia. The strategic position of the city on the cliff dominating the shore plain, however, insured its survival as a fortress, and it passed with all of Vaspurakan to the Arcruni house.

> See AON, pp. 340, 469; Eremyan, *Ašχarh.*, p. 52; *idem, Map* G/5; Hewsen, "Ptolemy," pp. 136, 138; Tᶜ. X. Hakobyan, *Ašχarhagrutᶜyun*, pp.168–170; Manandyan, *Trade and Cities*, pp. 64, 87, 148; Toumanoff, *Studies*, pp. 50, 213.
>
> IV.lv, lix; V.xxxvii
> pp. 176, 179, 220
> Maps, F–G/7–8
> See also "Tosp"; and Appendix I, "Hreaykᶜ" "Řštuni, house"; "Šapuh"; and Appendix III, *amur; kᶜałakᶜ*.

Van-Tosp, see "Van."

Vanand
  Eighth district of Ayrarat, according to the *Ašχarhacᶜoycᶜ* (34/45). Vanand lay west of Širak between the Aχurean and Upper Kur Rivers around the central fortress of

Kars. It was originally known as Upper Basean, a toponym still recorded by MX, II.v (= MK, pp. 135–136), but had evolved into a separate principality (invariably identified as a *gawaṙ* in BP), in the fourth century. The homonymous princes of the district, Vanandean or Vanandacᶜi, are recorded in Armenian sources until the seventh century when Vanand passed to the Bagratuni, but BP does not mention them after the reign of King Tiran (III.xiv). The *Zōrnamak*, "Military List," attributes 1,000 retainers to them, and a cadet line is also included in the *Gahnamak*, "Rank List." Vanand was presumably evangelized as part of Basean in the days of St. Gregory (Aa, dcccxlv; Vg, clxxii = Va. clx), but separate bishops of Vanand are found in later conciliar lists (ŁPᶜ, xxiii, p. 44; Ełišē, ii. p. 28 = *Ełishē*, pp. 82, 258; GTᶜ, p. 73; Duin, *Canons*, p. 214).

See AON, pp. 361, 363–364; Eremyan, *Ašχarh.*, pp. 82, 118; *idem, Map* B/5; Hewsen, "Armenia," p. 335; Tᶜ. X. Hakobyan, *Ašχarhagrutⁱyun*, p. 123–124 and map; Adontz, *Armenia*, pp. 188, 192–194, 200, 202, 205, 207–208, 228, 236–237, 256, 263, 269, 442 n. 20, 443–444 n. 24; 67*–69*, 71*, 77*, 90*, 93*–97*, 99*–100*, 102*, 121*, 126*, 182*; Toumanoff, *Studies*, pp. 215, 224, 227–228, 231, 240, 245, 247–248, 250, 252; Thierry and Thierry, "Kars."

III.xii, xiv; IV.xxii; VI.xii

pp. 82, 87, 155, 238

Maps, F/4–5

See also "Ayrarat"; "Basean"; "Ereweal"; "Kur"; "Širak"; Appendix I, "Artawan"; "Bagratuni, house"; "Grigor/Gregorids"; "Vorot"; and Appendix III, *gawaṙ.*

Varaz ‹ Phl. *warāz*, "wild boar"

Mountain on which the Aršakuni court sought refuge during the last battle with Meružan Arcruni. It is not otherwise attested or identified.

See AON, p. 470.

V.xliii

p. 226

See also Appendix I, "Aršakuni"; "Meružan"; "Varaz," for additional bibliography on that name.

Vatneay, plain

Site of the martyrdom of St. Grigoris. Its location is disputed. Eremyan identifies it with the "plain of Vardan" (*Vardaneay dašt*), and most other scholars locate it along the western shore of the Caspian Sea, either north or south of the lower Araxes, but Peeters, interpreting BP's reference to the "Northern Sea" as referring to Lake Çildir, places this plain on this lake's shore northwest of the Armenian plateau. Despite the mountainous location of the lake, a considerable plain is to be found directly to the northeast.

See Eremyan, *Ašχarh.*, p. 83, *Vardaneay dašt*, and map G/7, but it is not indicated on the fourth-century *Map*; Peeters, "Les débuts," p. 23.

III.vi

p. 73

Maps, G/4? or L/5–6?

See also "Northern Sea"; and Appendix I, "Grigoris."

Virkᶜ ‹ Parth. Viržān; Phl. Virzān; Georg. Kartⁱli; Gk. Ἰβηρία; Lat. Hiberia; modern western and central Georgia

Attested as part of the third-century Sasanian Empire in ŠKZ, Parth. 2,25; Phl. 30; RGDS nos. 3, 60, pp. 48–49, 68–69, Ἰβηρία; KKZ, 12.

Kingdom lying north of Greater Armenia (*Mec Haykᶜ*) from the Kur River to the Caucasian chain, between Eger/Colchis to the west and Ałuankᶜ to the east, according to the *Ašχarhacᶜoycᶜ* (28/38–39). Its capital was at Mcᶜχeta, just north of the river, near mod. Tbilisi, which became the capital only in the fifth century but is the only one known to the seventh-century *Ašχarhac̣oyc̣*. Virk̇ᶜ/Iberia was familiar to classical authors: Ptolemy (V.x), Strabo (*Geogr.*, XI.i.5, ii.15, 18–iii.6), who gives an extensive description of the country and its social structure, and Pliny the Elder (NH, VI,iv, 12; xi, 29; xii, 30; xv, 39–40); as well as to the Sasanian inscriptions (ŠKZ, line 2, p. 7 = trans. p. 14; KKZ, line 12, p. 47 = trans. p. 52). At the turn of the fourth century, the local Pᶜaṙnabazid and Aršakuni dynasties of Iberia were replaced by the Iranian Mihranids, known locally as Chosroids. The Iberian kingdom was briefly split by the Roman conquest under Valens ca. 371 (AM, XXVII.xii.16–17, cf. BP, V.xv), but it was soon reunited under the Persian candidate (AM, XXX.ii.2). Its suzerainty was conceded to the Sasanians by the Byzantine–Persian peace of 532 and the monarchy abolished by the Persians in 580. Both the kingship of Iberia and its status as an *ašχarh* are attested in BP.

All early Armenian sources stress the close relations of Virk̇ᶜ and Armenia, particularly its Christianization in the fourth century, and the creation of its alphabet by Mesrop Maštocᶜ in the fifth (see, e.g., Koriwn, xv, xviii, xxi, pp. 62, 72, 78 = trans. pp. 37, 42, 44; MX, II.lxxxvi, III.liv = MK, pp. 238–240, 322). BP (III.v–vi) makes St. Gregory the Illuminator's grandson St. Grigoris bishop of Virk̇ᶜ and Aḷuankᶜ, though Virk̇ᶜ is omitted by MX, III.iii (= MK, pp. 255–256). Armenian sources also mention Virk̇ᶜ frequently as the ally of Greater Armenia (Aa, xix; MX, I.xxix; II.xxii, xliv, xlvi, lxxxv; III.xxvii, xxix = MK, pp. 119, 159, 184, 186, 237, 282, 285; ŁPᶜ, xxi, xxv, xxvii–xxviii, pp. 43, 47–48, 50–54; Eḷiše, i, iii, iv, pp. 10, 19, 93 = Eḷishē, pp. 64, 72, 145, 256, 260–261, 263–266, etc.; cf. GTᶜ, pp. 43, 46), but, as in the case of Aḷuankᶜ, the two kingdoms contended over the control of the marchlands south of the Kur River, and especially for the allegiance of the *bdeašχ* of Gugarkᶜ. BP (V.xv) even claims that the *sparapet* Mušeḷ Mamikonean conquered the whole of Virk̇ᶜ and executed its Pᶜaṙnabazid king ca. 370, but this is a patent exaggeration in the light of the division of the kingdom recorded by AM (*loc. cit.*) and BP's own admission that the border between Armenia and Virk̇ᶜ was then set at the Kur.

See Eremyan, *Ašχarh.*, pp. 83–84, 119; *idem*, Map A–B/5–6, where the southern border is, however, questionable; Hewsen, "Vitaxates,"; *idem*, "Armenia," pp. 337–340; Treidler, "Iberia"; Boltunova, "Iberia"; Adontz, *Armenia*, pp. 7–8, 167, 170–176, 179, 187, 229–230, 257, 307, 315–318, 327, 488 n. 38, 506 n. 13, 73*–74*, 76*, 91*, 109*–111*, 162*; Toumanoff, *Studies*, pp. 56–57, 59, 67, 75, 77–78 n. 86, 80–84 esp. n. 105, 86–103, 141–143, 150, 185–192, 253–256, 264–266, 317–318, 437–499; *idem*, *Manuel*, p. 80; Gignoux, *Glossaire*, pp. 36, 67; Sprengling, *Third-Century Iran*, pp. 7, 9, 12, 14, 19, 47, 52; Honigmann and Maricq, RGDS, pp. 11, 17, 39.
III.v–vi; V.xv
pp. 70, 72, 201
Maps, F–H/1–3
See also "Aḷuankᶜ"; "Gugarkᶜ"; "Jor/Joropᶜor"; "Koḷb"; "Kur"; "Mec Haykᶜ"; Appendix I, "Aršakuni"; "Grigoris"; "Mušeḷ"; "Pᶜaṙnawazean"; "Vaḷēs"; and Appendix III, *ašχarh*; *bdeašχ*; *sparapet*.

Xaḷtekᶜ; Gk. Χαλδία
Border region of northwestern Armenia and the Byzantine Empire reaching up toward the northeastern shore of the Black Sea. The name is derived from the Khaldioi already known to Xenophon (*Cyrop*, III.ii), and the region is also known to MX, III.xliv (= MK, p. 307); Aa,dcccxlii.

See AON, pp. 200 n. 2, 277 and n. 3; Tašean, *Hay bnak'c'ut'iwnə*; idem, "Xaltik'";
T'. X. Hakobyan, *Ašχarhagrut'yun*, p. 60; Bryer, *Topography of Pontus*, I, pp.
299–318; II, pls. 238–261.
IV.lix
p. 180
Maps C/4
See also Appendix I, "Samuēl."

Xartizan

Region of Persia, not otherwise attested or identified.
See (?)Marquart, *Ērānšahr*, p. 161, the *gaza* of Xarzan; (?)Eremyan, *Map* D/8,
"Patižahar."
IV.xxii
p. 155

Xaχ; mod. Hah

Village or town in the district of Ekeleac' slightly northwest of T'il and north of the
Gayl/Lykos River (mod. Kelkit çayi). It can be identified with the modern village of
Hah. BP locates there a presumed palace of King Pap where St. Nersēs was murdered,
but the importance of the locality cannot be defined with precision. Both MX, III.xxx-
viii (= MK, p. 299) and the *Vita* of St. Nersēs, xii, p. 84 (= CHAMA, II, p. 36) call it
a "village" (*gewl*), but BP alternates between *gewl* and "town" (*awan*) on one occasion.
See Adontz, *Armenia*, pp. 39–40, 224*; Eremyan, *Map* G/3; USAF Map 340 AI for
Hah.
V.xxiv
pp. 204–205
Maps, B/5–6.
See also "Ekeleac'"; "T'il"; Appendix I, "Nersēs I"; "Pap"; and Appendix III, *awan*;
gewl.

Xer, see "Hēr."

[Xoṙχoṙunik']

Not attested as a toponym in BP,
See Appendix I, "Xoṙχoṙuni."

Xosrovakert ‹ Arm. Xosrov + *kert*, "built"

Hunting preserve created by the *sparapet* Vač'ē I Mamikonean for King Xosrov
Kotak in the distric of Ayrarat, south of the other royal preserve, which was around the
palace of Tiknuni. The creation of Xosrovakert is also known to MX, III.viii (= MK,
p. 261), though his description is far terser, and it is mentioned by LP', lxviii, p. 144
(= CHAMA, II, p. 343).
See AON, p. 434; Dandamayev, "Paradeisioi"; Seyrig, "Jardins"; Garsoïan, "Banak
ark'uni"; and III.viii n. 5.
III.viii
p. 75
See also "Ayrarat"; "Tiknuni"; and Appendix I, "Vač'ē"; "Xosrov II/III."

Xu

Plain in the district of Bagrewand, where King Pap was encamped at the time of his
murder. It is not otherwise attested or identified.
See Ep'rikean, *Baṙaran*, II, p. 209, who lists but does not identify it.
V.xxxii
p. 213

Maps, F/5–6?
See also "Bagrewand"; and Appendix I, "Pap."

Xužastan ‹ Parth. Hūzistān; Syr. Bēθ Hūzājē; Gk. Οὐζηνή, Σουσίς; Ar. Al-Ahwāz
Attested in ŠKZ, Parth. 1, 16; RGDS, nos. 2, 35, pp. 46–47, 56–57, Οὐζηνή.
Second district of southern Iran or Kusti-Nmroǰ, according to the *Ašχarhacᶜoycᶜ*
(40–41/53–54). It bordered on the Persian gulf and was separated from Babylonia to
the west by the Tigris River (cf. Strabo, *Geogr.* XV.iii.2–4). The Achaemenid capital of
Susa was located there, and it was known to the Greeks as Susis or Susiana. In Sasanian
times it was ruled by a *vitaxa* or *bdeašχ*, according to AM (XXIII.vi.14). Its main center
was the city of Gundēšāhpuhr, and the "Castle of Oblivion" was also located in this
district. During the fifth and sixth centuries Xužastan had considerable religious and
commercial contacts with Armenia. Cf. e.g. Ełišē, vii, pp. 160, 179, 181–182; ŁPᶜ, li,
liv–lv, pp. 89, 94–95, 102–104 (= *Ełishē*, pp. 209–210, 226, 228–229, 305, 311–313, 318—
321); GTᶜ, pp. 41, 47, 70, 72, 79, etc.).
> See Marquart, *Ērānšahr*, p. 27; Christensen, *L'Iran*, pp. 198–199, 307; Gignoux,
> *Glossaire*, p. 54; Sprengling, *Third-Century Iran*, pp. 7, 8, 14, 16; Honigmann and
> Maricq, RGDS, pp. 11, 15, 39.
> IV.lv; V.v, vii
> pp. 176, 196–197
> See also "Anyuš"; and Appendix III, *bdeašχ*.

Zarawand/Zarewand
Eighth district of the region of Parskahaykᶜ northwest of Lake Urmiah according to
the *Ašχarhacᶜoycᶜ* (32/43). It should not be confused with the district of Zarehawan,
also found in Parskahaykᶜ, and a number of scholars place it south of Hēr, with which
it is invariably linked; but Eremyan and Hakobyan reverse the order. A fanciful etymology from Zruan is given by MX, I.vi (= MK, p. 80). The homonymous princes,
known to MX, I.xxxi; II.viii (= MK, pp. 123, 142–143) as Zarehawanikᶜ or Zareha-
wanean, are not mentioned by BP. Nevertheless the local princes must have been of
considerable importance since Aa, dccxcv, lists them along with the *bdeašχ*s among the
major Armenian magnates, referring to them as "prince prefect" (*išχann šahap*), and
they may well have been the rulers of the entire province of Parskahaykᶜ/Širakan,
including the whole of the western shore of Lake Urmiah. Their domain would consequently adjoin Kordikᶜ in the west. Zarawand and Hēr are treated in BP as a single
gawaṙ and in the tenth century, they were joined in the single district of Ṙotakkᶜ.
> See AON, pp. 259–261, 338; Eremyan, *Ašχarh.*, pp. 51–52, 117; *idem, Map* G/6;
> Hewsen, "Armenia," p. 330; *idem*, "Vitaxates"; Tᶜ. X. Hakobyan, *Ašχarha-
> grutᶜyun*, pp. 231–232 and map; Marquart, *Ērānšahr*, pp. 109–110; *idem*, "Parska-
> haykᶜ," pp. 253, 262, 267, 275.
> III.viii
> p. 75
> Maps, H–I/7–9
> See also "Hēr"; "Kordikᶜ"; "Noširakan"; and Appendix III, *gawaṙ*; *išχan*; *satrap*.

Zarehawan ‹ Zareh + Arm. *awan*, "town"
City in the district of Bagrewand or adjoining Całkotn, not to be confused with its
namesake in Parskahaykᶜ (*Ašχarhacᶜoycᶜ*, 32/43). The city was evidently founded by
the Erwandid/Artašēsid dynasty, for it records the name of its founder Zareh/Zariadris
in the early second century B.C. (see Strabo, *Geogr.*, XI.xiv.5 and the Aramaic inscription of Artašēs I). It was presumably a foundation of Hellenistic type since its name

follows the eponymous model of the multiple Alexandrias and it had a mixed Armenian and Jewish population. The city was presumably an important urban and commercial center (identified as a *kᶜałakᶜ* in BP, IV.lv) until its sack by the Persians and the deportation of its population to Iran p. 363 (IV.lv). After this destruction, Zarehawan is mentioned only as a ruined site (V.xliii) or an unimportant village (ŁPᶜ, II.xxviii, p. 63 = CHAMA, II, p. 292).

> See AON, pp. 427–428; Eremyan, *Ašχarh.*, p. 52; *idem, Map* G/5; Tᶜ. X. Hakobyan, *Ašχarhagrutᶜyun*, pp. 64, 80, 122 and map; Manandyan, *Trade and Cities*, pp. 64, 86–87, 96, 155; Toumanoff, *Studies*, pp. 73–74, 282, 286, 290–297, 299, 305, 309, 310 n. 32, by contrast to Markwart, *Genealogie*, p. 20; Perikhanian, "Inscription," pp. 18–20, on the name Zareh; Garsoïan, "Mediaeval Armenian City," pp. 69, 73.
> IV.lv, lviii; V.xliii
> pp. 175, 178, 225
> Map
> See also "Bagrewand"; Appendix I, "Hreaykᶜ"; and Appendix III, *kᶜałakᶜ*.

Zarewand, see "Zarawand."

Zarišat ‹ Zareh + MIr. *šād*, "joyous, joyful"

City northeast of Lake Van in the district of Ałiovit, which should not be confused with its namesake in Vanand. BP locates the city in Ałiovit, but it probably belonged to the eastern portion of the district, which formed part of the Aršakuni domain, for MX, III.xxiii (= MK, p. 279), refers to it as a "royal city." Zarišat was probably founded by King Artašēs I (ca. 188–160 B.C.) in honor of his father, Zareh, whose name is recorded in his inscription. It was presumably a foundation of Hellenistic type since its name follows the eponymous model of the multiple Alexandrias, and it had a mixed Armenian and Jewish population. The city was presumably an important center, as BP calls it a "great city" (*mec kᶜałakᶜ*), until its sack by the Persians and the deportation of its population to Iran (post 363).

> See AON, p. 428; Eremyan, *Ašχarh.*, p. 52; *idem, Map* G/5; Tᶜ. X. Hakobyan, *Ašχarhagrutᶜyun*, pp. 80, 156 and map; Manandyan, *Trade and Cities*, pp. 64, 86–87; Perikhanian, "Inscription," pp. 18–20; *Boyce*, "Zariadris"; Garsoïan, "Mediaeval Armenian City," pp. 69, 73; CPD, p. 78, *šād*.
> IV.lv
> p. 176
> Maps, F–G/6–7
> See also "Ałiovit"; "Vanand"; Appendix I, "Aršakuni"; "Hreaykᶜ"; and Appendix III, *kᶜałakᶜ*.

Appendix III: Technical Terms

The main purpose of this Appendix is to note the usages of the technical terms in the text of BP that have been identified by an asterisk within the body of the translation, and to serve simultaneously as one of the indices of foreign influences on Aršakuni Armenian society. For this latter goal, etymologies have been provided wherever possible for the terms discussed, though some remain as yet unidentified, while others, marked by a question mark, are still debatable hypotheses. Even at this stage, however, the clear preponderance of Iranian derivations for BP's titles and technical terms, as, indeed, for the prosopography of Appendix I, forms part of the evidence for the profoundly Iranized character of the text. As such, it bears out the conclusions of A. Meillet, E. Benveniste, G. Bolognesi, H. W. Bailey, A. Perikhanian, R. Schmitt, M. Leroy, and others as to the paramount influence of Middle Iranian (primarily Parthian) on the Classical Armenian vocabulary, and the underlying similarity of the two societies. Of particular interest in this connection is the ubiquitous presence of the Iranian suffix *-pat/bad* in Armenian titles, not only those of clearly Iranian derivation, such as *sparapet*, but even in Greek or Syriac hybrids, such as *episkoposapet* and *kʿahanayapet* (see Benveniste, "Remarques"; Leroy, "Composés en -pet"; and Belardi, "Origine").

The theological vocabulary found in the homiletic passages of BP has been omitted here, since the problems of its translation have already been extensively discussed by R. W. Thomson in his Introduction to *The Teaching of Saint Gregory* (AaT) and the article on "Philosophical Terms," as well as by Dom Louis Leloir in the Introduction to his *Paterica armeniaca*, and their pattern has been followed in this translation.

For the sake of convenience, variant grammatical forms of the same term have normally been subsumed under the main entry (*aṙaǰnord/aṙaǰnordem*, *vankʿ/vanakan*, etc.) unless they form a specific title (e.g., *ašχarhakal*, *gawaṙatēr*) or contain some additional semantic material (e.g., *išχan*, "prince, ruler, official"/*išχanutʿiwn*, "principality" but also "dominion, authority, jurisdiction").

Despite the resulting length, it has seemed preferable for the sake of clarity to collect together into one entry the components of such groups as *martyria*; *zēn*, "weapons"; *zōrkʿ*, "army, forces, troops" (The English forms carry an asterisk in the text only when they render the Arm. *banak* rather than the ubiquitous *zōrkʿ*); as well as the main types of solitaries—*anapataworkʿ*, *mianjn*, *vanakan*, etc., instead of scattering them according to alphabetical position.

As in the case of the first two Appendices, BP's spelling has been preferred and no pretense at an exhaustive analysis or bibliography has been attempted.

505

abelay see *mianjn.*

agarak ‹ ?Sk. *ágra*; cf. Gk. ἀγρός; Lat. *ager*; Georg. loanword *agarak-i*
"farm, villa, holding, estate"
Normally an agricultural holding devoid of dwellings, as opposed to an inhabited village (see VI.x).
See NBHL, I, p. 3; HArmB, I, p. 77; HBB, I, p. 3, which gives the definitions: *"mšakvac kam mšakeli hoł; ařhasarak hołayin kaluac"*; Sargsyan, "Dastakertnerə."
III.xvi, xix; VI.x
pp. 92, 94, 238
See also *dastakert; kaluac;* and Appendix II, "Agarak."

aleln, see *zen,* j.

alelnaworkʿ, see *zōrkʿ*, II.f.

altar, pagan, see *bagin.*

ambarakapet, see *hambarakapet.*

amrocʿ ‹ *amur*
"stronghold, fortress, fortification"
See NBHL, I, p. 76; HArmB, I, p. 161, *amur*; HBB, I, p. 72.
III.viii; IV.lv; V.v, xxxi
pp. 76, 174, 195, 211
See also *berd;* and the next entry.

amur
"strong, fortified, inaccessible, impregnable"
This term is used in BP both for fortified sites and for naturally inaccessible regions, such as Arjaχ, Kordikʿ, Tmorikʿ (IV.l), Taykʿ (III.xviii, IV.ii) or the "Land of the Medes" (IV.xxiv, l). It is often found in conjunction with the noun *berd,* "fortress," though the latter is also found alone (see, e.g., III.viii).
See NBHL, I, p. 73; HArmB, I, p. 161; HBB, I, p. 69.
III.vii, viii, xviii; IV.ii, xviii, xix, xxiv, xl, xlviii, l, lv, lviii; V.i, iv, v, xxxiv, xliii
pp. 74–75, 93, 107, 148–149, 157–158, 163, 166–167, 174, 176, 178, 186, 190, 195, 215, 226
See also *berd;* and Appendix II, "Arjaχ"; "Kordikʿ"; "Maracʿ amur erkir; "Taykʿ"; "Tmorikʿ."

anapatakan, see *anapatawor*

anapatawor/anapatakan ‹ Arm. *anapat*, "desert" ‹ Phl. *an-ābādān*, "uncultivated" + suffix of attribution -*awor*, -*akan*
"anchorite, desert dweller"
As indicated by the etymology of the term and by the context in BP, this was the most extreme group among the solitaries. The term *čgnawor,* "ascetic, athlete, mortifier, champion" was also associated with them (V.xxviii), as was that of *abelay* (‹ Syr. *ābila*, "mourner") VI.xvi.
The *anapataworkʿ* were invariably wanderers without any fixed locus or possessions, though some of them took shelter in caves, while the *leařnakan* (who were evidently the social as well as the semantic equivalent of the Syrian *tūrayē*) "dwelled-on-mountains" (VI.vi, xvi). All of these characteristics associate the *anapataworkʿ* of fourth-century Armenia with the Syrian anchoretic tradition rather than with any type of sedentary

solitaries. BP is the best witness for their presence in Armenia, but see also Aa, dcccxlviii, dcccliii, dcccclv, and Koriwn, xxii, p. 80 (= trans. p. 45).

> See NBHL, I, p. 110; HBB, I, p. 89; CPD, p. 8, *an-ābādān*; Leroy, "Emprunts," p. 57, *anapatakan*; Leloir, *Paterica armeniaca*, p. ix, who translates, "*anachoreta, eremita*"; *idem*, "Ephrem," pp. 108, 126; Vööbus, *Asceticism*, I, pp. 220–229, II, pp. 1–11, 14–35, 353–360, etc. See also III.xiv n. 15; IV.iv n. 19; V.xxvii n. 4; VI.xvi n. 4.
>
> III.xiv; V.xxv–xxvii; VI.vi, xvi
>
> pp. [87], 205–207, 235 (*anapatakankᶜ*), 239–240
>
> See also *mianjn*; *van(kᶜ)*; and Appendix I, "Daniēl"; "Epipᶜan"; "Gind"; "Šaḷitay."

anchorite, see *anapatawor.*

anderjapet, see *(h)anderjapet.*

aparan (pl. *tantum*) ‹ OP *apadāna-*
"palace"
In BP this term is used interchangeably with *tačar* for eastern palaces but not for the Roman imperial palaces, for which the transliteration *paḷat* ‹ Lat. *palatium* is invariably preferred (see III.xxi, IV.v, etc.).

> See NBHL, I, p. 274; HArmB, I, pp. 230–231; HBB, I, p. 207, *aparankᶜ*; AG, p. 104 no. 47; Schmitt, "Iranisches Lehngut," p. 88; Leroy, "Emprunts," pp. 62, 68 no. 28; Gignoux, *Glossaire*, pp. 45, *'bdny*, 46, *'pdn, 'pdnk*, etc.
>
> III.viii; IV.xii, xiv, xxxix; V.iv, xxiv
>
> pp. 75, 135, 139–140, 163, 190, 204
>
> See also *tačar.*

apizak ‹ ?
Hapax. A breast ornament that Toumanoff equates with the *ploumia* or gold embroidery that formed part of the regalia of the autonomous Armenian satraps according to Procopius (*De aed.*, III.i.22); but the brooch or cloak fastener that formed part of the same regalia (*idem*) may also be intended. Cf. the regalia described in MX, II.xlvii (=MK, pp. 187–188); also Eḷišē, vi, pp. 136–137 (=*Eḷishē*, pp. 187–188); Malalas, p. 413; Agathias, III.xv.2 (= trans. p. 84); etc.

> See NBHL, I, p. 276; HArmB, I, p. 234; HBB, I, p. 208; Malχasyancᶜ, p. 399 n. 191; Toumanoff, *Studies*, p. 134 n. 235; Hacᶜuni, *Tarazin*, p. 100.
>
> V.xxxviii
>
> p. 222

apostoleion, see *martyrium.*

appanage, see *sephakan.*

aṙaǰnord/aṙaǰnordem ‹ Arm. *aṙ*, "on, to" + *aǰn*, "right"; i.e., "first"
"guide, spiritual guide, leader"/"to guide, lead spiritually"
Both the noun and the verb are normally used in BP in their spiritual sense to designate the ecclesiastical hierarchs, especially the Armenian patriarchs and their spiritual guidance. Aa, dccci, spells out in detail the qualities and functions of the *aṙaǰnord* in his portrayal of St. Gregory: "*zmec zGrigor tesuč* [overseer] *ew vardapet* [spiritual-teacher] *aṙaǰnordutᶜean astuacagnacᶜ čanaparhacᶜn* [leader in divine paths], *ew hoviw* [shepherd] *ew bžišk* [physician] *kacᶜusǰikᶜ*." In all references to the traitor Meružan Arcruni, however, and once or twice in the case of the *sparapet* Manuēl Mamikonean, (V.xxxvii), the terms are used in the basic secular sense of "guide, leader/guidance, leadership."

> See NBHL, I, pp. 290–291; HArmB, I, p. 246, *aǰ*; HBB, I, p. 221.

507

III.iii, xiii–xv, xvii, xx; IV.iii–v, xi, xii, xxiii, xxiv, xxxi–xxxvi, xl, xlii, lviii; V.i, ii, xxiii, xxxvii, xlii, xliii; VI.iii, iv, xi–xiv, xvi

pp. 68, 84–87, 89–92, 95, 108, 110, 113, 116–117, 119, 123, 133–134, 156–157, 161–164, 178, 185–187, 203, 221, 224–225, 235, 238–239

aṙak῾elaran, see *martyrium*.

aṙalezk῾ , see Appendix I, "Aṙlezk῾."

aranc῾ k῾aǰ, see *k῾aǰ aranc῾*.

archbishop, see *ark῾episkopos*.

archdeacon, see *ark῾idiakon*.

archer, see *zōrk῾*, II.f.

ark῾episkopos ‹ Gk. ἀρχιεπίσκοπος

"archbishop"

This Greek title is used for the bishop of Caesarea in Cappadocia, as is the case in Aa, dcccxx, but not for Armenian hierarchs, for whom the Armenian hybrid semi-translation *episkoposapet* is invariably used.

See NBHL, I, p. 385; HArmB, I, p. 347; HBB, I, p. 288.

IV.iv, ix, x

pp. 112, 130, 132

See also, *episkoposapet*; and the next entry.

ark῾episkoposapet ‹ Gk. ἀρχιεπίσκορος + Arm. *pet* ‹ Ir. *pati*, "chief"

"chief-archbishop"

This remarkable tautological hybrid occurs only in the confused titulature of Eusebios of Caesarea, as part of the legendary aspects of the consecration of St. Nersēs as patriarch of Armenia, and on two occasions in reference to St. Nersēs himself (IV.xv; V.iv). It is not part of the normal titulature of Armenian primates.

See NBHL I, p. 385; HArmB, I, p. 347, *ark῾episkopos*;

HBB, I, p. 288; Leroy, "Composés en -pet," nos. 22, 26, pp. 123, 126.

IV.iv, xv; V.iv

pp. 111, 142, 190

See also *episkoposapet*; *pet*; and Appendix I, "Eusebios"; "Nersēs I"; and the preceding entry.

ark῾idiakon ‹ Gk. ἀρχιδιάκονος

"archdeacon"

Hapax, according to Ačaryan. The Greek form is used only once in BP, to distinguish St. Nersēs's archdeacon Murik, while the Armenian term, *sarkawagapet* is used in VI.xvi for Nersēs's other archdeacon, Trdat.

See NBHL, I, p. 385; HArmB, I, p. 348; HBB, I, p. 288 and IV, p. 193, *sarkawagapet*.

IV.xv

p. 142

See also *sarkawagapet*; and Appendix I, "Trdat/Trdac."

armor, see *zēn*.

arms, see *zēn*.

army, see *banak*, *zōrk῾*.

arrow, see *zēn*, j.

ascetic, see *anapatawor*.

aspar, see *zēn*, g.

asparēs, see *asparēz*.

asparēz/asparēs ‹ Phl. *asprēs*, "racecourse" = Gk. στάδιον, 'ιπποδρόμος "racecourse, hippodrome"

Measure of distance equivalent to the length of a racecourse or stadium. It was traditionally set at 1/8 of a Roman mile or 600 Greek feet = 606.75 English feet. The term was also used for the racecourse itself, and both meanings are found in BP.

See NBHL, II, p. 316; HArmB, I, pp. 273–274; HBB, I, 237, *asparēs*; Malχasyanc^c, p. 338 n. 187; CPD, p. 12, *asprēs*; Liddell and Scott, *Lexicon*, στάδιον; Schmitt, "Iranisches Lehngut," p. 90; Leroy, "Emprunts," p. 58.

IV.xv, lviii; V.xxxvii

pp. 141, 178, 219

aspet ‹ MIr. **asp(a)pet* ‹ *asp*, "horse" + *bad*, "master, lord,"

Attested in ŠKZ, Parth. 25; Phl 31; RGDS no. 60, pp. 68–69, ἀσπιπίδ; *Paikuli*, Parth. 17; Phl. 7, 15; Nisa documents; etc.

"master-of-the horse, commander-of the-cavalry"

This title, which was hereditary in the Bagratuni house, as is also attested by Aa, dccxcv, dccclxxiii, is clearly derived from the Iranian "master of the horse," despite Adontz's attempted derivation from *viθapaitiš*. Toumanoff agreed with Adontz's analysis that no separate "master- of-the-horse or -cavalry" could have existed in the early medieval Armenian army next to the *sparapet* or "commander-of-the-army;" since "the Armenian army . . . to all intents and purposes was exclusively cavalry." Consequently, he concluded that "whatever the etymological significance of the term it must have been merely a family title of the Bagratuni and not an office." This hypothesis seemed supported by references to the Bagratuni as "Aspetianoi" by Procopius (*Bell. Pers.*, II.iii.12–18)—cf. Theoph. Sim., III.vii—and by Gignoux's attestation of a possible *Asp-(arbād)* on a seal from Tehran. Nevertheless, the evidence of BP unquestionably shows the presence of some infantry detachments next to the dominant cavalry in the Armenian Arsacid forces, both the *aspet* and the *sparapet* are listed in the victory inscription of Šāhpuhr I (ŠKZ) and the *aspet* appears even earlier on an ostrakon from Nisa.

See NBHL, I, p. 316; HArmB, I, 274–275; HBB, I, p. 237; AG, p. 109, no. 67; Gignoux, *Glossaire*, pp. 17, 47; *idem*, NPS, no. 142, p. 48, *Asp-(arbād)*); Sprengling, *Third-Century Iran*, pp. 9, 12, 19; Maricq, RGDS, p. 66 n. 4; Honigmann and Maricq, RGDS, p. 17; Schmitt, "Iranisches Lehngut," p. 90; *idem*, IN, pp. 329, 330; Leroy, "Emprunts," p. 58; *idem*, "Composés en *-pet*," no. 7, 114; Adontz, *Armenia*, pp. 311–312; Christensen, *L'Iran*, pp. 103–104; Toumanoff, *Studies*, pp. 324–326; Lukonin, "Institutions," pp. 703–704, who does not differentiate sufficiently between the *aspet* and the *sparapet*; see also IV.iv n. 5; Chaumont, "Ostraca," pp. 21–22.

IV.iv (?); V.xliv

pp. [111], 228

See also *pet*; *sparapet*; *zōrk^c*, II; and Appendix I, "Bagratuni, house."

assembly, see *žołov*.

ašχarawand/ašχarhawand ‹ ?OP **awi-sara-banda-*, "crown tie"

Hapax. Presumably the knot tying the royal diadem over the crown and from which flowed the undulating ribbons denoting the "royal glory" of the Iranian monarchs.

See HArmb, I, p. 217; HBB, I, p. 193; Malχasyanc^c , p. 339 n. 191; AG, p. 101, no. 35; and for the representations in Sasanian art, Ghirshman, *Persian Art*, pls 145, 147, 148, 164; Garsoïan, "Substratum," figs., 5, 7, 9, especially the coin of Bahrām II in the Hermitage Museum, etc.

V.xxxviii

p. 222

ašχarh ‹ MIr. cf.. Phl. *šahr*; Av. *χšaθra-*, "realm, kingdom, state"
Term attested in ŠKZ, Parth. 2–5, 9–12, 15–17, 20, 29; Phl. 2, 12–16, 20, 25; KKZ, 1, 7–14; etc.
"realm, country, world"
This term is occasionally used to designate the world (e.g., III.xi). Throughout the text, however, it is normally used in a political and administrative sense to denote the "realm" of Armenia and occasionally of other regions, by contrast to the geographical connotation of "land," for which the term *erkir* is invariably used. This distinction is especially evident in such locutions as (III.vi) *ašχarhin Hayastan erkrin*, "of the realm of the land of Armenia"; (III.vii) *zerkirn Hayoc῾ ašχarhin*, "the land of the realm of Armenia"; etc. (see also III.xi, xxi; IV.xxxi; V.i)

> See Gignoux, *Glossaire*, pp. 34–35, 53; Sprengling, *Third Century Iran*, pp. 7–9, 10–11, 14–19, 46–48, 49–59; NBHL, I, pp. 259–260; HArmB, I, pp.. 217–218; HBB, II, pp. 193–194; AG, p. 101, no. 36; Schmitt, "Iranisches Lehngut," p. 88; and Intro., p. 48.

> P.S.; III.iii–xviii, xx, xxi; IV.i–v, vii, xi–xiii, xv–xvi, xviii–xx, xxii–xxv, xxx, xxxi, xxxvii, xlvi, l–lii, liv–lv, lvii–lix; V.i–ii, iv–vii, ix, xv, xx, xxiii, xxiv, xxvii–xxviii, xxxi, xxxiv, xxxvii, xxxviii, xliv; VI.i, iii, xiv, xvi

> pp. 63, 69–71, 73–86, 90–94, 96–100, 107, 109, 111–114, 116–117, 119–120, 122–123, 126, 132–139, 141, 146, 148–150, 154–162, 166–169, 171, 173–179, 185, 187–189, 191, 194–196, 199–204, 207–208, 211–212, 215, 218–219, 221–223, 228–229, 233–235, 238–239

> See also *erkir*; *erkir haykakan lezuin*; and Appendix II, "Ałuank῾"; "Atrpatakan"; "Ayrarat"; "Cop῾k῾"; "Jor/Jorop῾or"; "Kordik῾"; "Tayk῾"; "Virk῾"; etc.

ašχarh Hayoc῾ lezuin, see *erkir haykakan lezui*.

ašχarhakal ‹ Arm. *ašχarh + kal* (aor. stem of *unim*), "have, hold"
"holder/keeper/ruler-of-a-realm"
Term used to designate the senior magnates. Adontz equates them with the *hazarawor* and *biwrawor* of III.viii, and the NBHL gives the Greek version as κοσμοκράτωρ. The *ašχarhakal* was probably the administrator of an area, as opposed to its "native-lord," *ašχarhatēr*; but both might be the same person.

> See NBHL, I, p. 261–262; HBB, p. 195; Manandyan, *Feodalizm*, pp. 38–40.

> III.viii, xxi; IV.xii

> pp. 76, 97, 134

> See also *gawaṙakal*, and the next entry, as well as the additional bibliography under *ašχarh*.

ašχarhatēr ‹ Arm. *ašχarh + tēr*, "lord"
"lord-of-a-realm"
Term used interchangeably with *ašχarhakal* for senior magnates. They are, however, distinguished by BP. The *ašχarhatēr* was probably the "native-lord" of the area as opposed to its governor.

> See NBHL, II, p. 264; HBB, I, pp. 196–197.

> III.iv, viii, x

> pp. 69, 76, 78

> See *gawaratēr*; and the two preceding entries, as well as the additional bibliography under *ašχarh*.

ašχarhawand, see *ašχarawand*.

ašχarhažołov, see *žołov*.

atᶜoṙ ‹ ? probably related to Gk. θρόνος
"chair, seat, throne, see"
With one exception (IV.xiii) this term is used in its ecclesiastical sense, normally to designate the patriarchal see.
See NBHL, I, p. 12; HArmB, I, p. 89; HBB, I, p. 14; AG, p. 300, no. 5; Garitte, *Narratio*, pp. 50–51.
III.iii, v, x, xii, xiv (also *atᶜoṙakal*), xv–xvi, xix; IV.iii–v (also *atᶜoṙakicᶜ*), ix, x, xii, xiii, xv (*atᶜoṙakicᶜ*);V.xxv
pp. 68, 70, 80, 82, 86–87, 89, 91, 94, 108–112, 117, 119, 130–132, 136–137, 141, 205
See also *gah*.

atᶜoṙakal, see *atᶜoṙ*.

atᶜoṙakicᶜ, see *atᶜoṙ*.

atrušan ‹ MIr. **ātarōšan-*, "(place) of burning fire"
"fire altar/temple"
Term used exclusively of the Iranian fire temples, as opposed to other non-Christian shrines such as *bagin*s and *mehean*s, though *atrušan*s could be found in conjunction with them. The context in both IV.xxiii and lix suggests that the Armenian *atrušan*s were either separate buildings or interior shrines, as in the case of the fire altar found under the high altar of the cathedral of Ejmiacin. Like the Iranian *atrušan*s, however, they could be either interior or outdoor shrines.
See NBHL, I, p. 336 HArmB, I, pp. 290–291; HBB, I, p. 251; AG, pp. 110–111, no. 72; MHD, pp. 442–443, *ātur-rōk*; cf., however, Boyce, "Sacred Fires," p. 64, who proposes ‹ *ādurōg*, "little fire." Benveniste, "Terminologie," pp. 56–58; Bailey, *Dictionary*, p. 309, *byuvāre* ‹ *auš*, "burn"; Erdman, *Feuerheiligtum*; Schiffmann, *Feuerheiligtümer*; Russell, *Zor. Arm.*, pp. 481–514; Gignoux, *Glossaire*, p. 30; *idem*, NPS, no. 22, p. 28; *idem*, "Noms propres," pp. 76–78; Perikhanian, *Iran*, pp. 161, 335; Christensen, *L'Iran*, p. 161 fig. 5; and for an illustration of the Ejmiacin fire altar, *Ejmiacin*.
IV.xxiii, lix; V.i
pp. 156, 180, 187
See also *bagin*; *mehean*.

authority, see *išχanutᶜiwn*.

awag/awagkᶜ ‹ ?
"senior, elder, first, nobles"
The term is used either as an adjective or in the plural as a collective noun for the nobility.
See NBHL, I, p. 387; HArmB, I, pp. 350–351; HBB, I, p. 289.
III.xvii, xviii, xx; IV.v, xxii; V.xxix, xxxv, xxxviii
pp. 92–93, 96–97, 122, 152–153, 168, 210, 216, 222
See also *awagani*.

awag episkopos, see *senior-bishop*.

awagani ‹ Arm. *awag*, "senior"
"nobles, nobility"
Collective noun used for the nobility interchangeably with *awagkᶜ* as well as *naχarar*, the latter being by far the most common in the text.

See NBHL, I, p. 387; HArmB, I, p. 350, *awag*; HBB, I, p. 289.

III.viii, xi, xii, xiv, xxi; IV.xx, l; V.i, ii, xxxv, xxxviii, xliv

pp. 76, 80, 83, 90, 98, 167, 185, 187–188, 216, 222, 229

See also *awag*; *gorcakal*; *naχarar*.

awan ‹ Phl. *āvahan*; OP *āvahana-*; Av. *vah-*, present stem of *vaŋh-* "to dwell," despite Hovannisyan's inconvincing attempt at an Urartian derivation

"town, village, dwelling place."

Population center normally larger than a *gewł*, "village," as is evidenced in the description of the growth of Aršakawan (IV.xii). The difference between the two terms is, however, by no means clear, as the same locality is often referred to by both terms simultaneously; see, e.g. Tʿil (V.xxiv).

See NBHL, I, p. 389; HArmB, I, pp. 353–354, who defines it as *giwłakʿałakʿ*, *mec giwł*; HBB, I, p. 291; AG, p. 112, no. 78; CPD, p. 113, *āwahan*; Schmitt, "Iranisches Lehngut," p. 88; and for the rejection of A. Š. Hovhannisyan's proposed Urartian derivation of this term, "Iranakan"; Asatryan, "Hayerenum," pp. 191–192.

III.ii, iv, viii, xiv, xix; IV.xii xv, li; V.xxiv, xxvii, xxxi, xliii

pp. 67, 70, 76, 88, 93, 135 (*awananayr*), 141, 168, 204–205, 207, 211, 225–226

See also *gewł*, and Appendix II, "Aršakawan"; "Tʿil."

axe, see *zēn*, i.

axe-bearers, see *zōrkʿ*, II.c.

aχořapet ‹ Phl. *āχwarr*, Arm. *aχoř*, "stable, manger" + *pet*, "chief"

Title attested in ŠKZ, Phl. 24, as "stable-lord."

"chief-stabler, head-of-the-stables"

See NBHL, I, p. 15; HArmB, I, p. 99, *aχoř*; HBB, I, p. 20; Gignoux, *Glossaire*, p. 45; Leroy, "Composés en *-pet*," no. 17, p. 123; Schmitt, "Iranisches Lehngut," p. 90, *aχoř*; Sprengling, *Third-Century Iran*, pp. 9, 18; CPD, p. 14, *āχwarr*; Harmatta-Pékáry, "Pārsīk Ostracon," p. 470, no. 5.

IV.xvi

p. 146

See also *pet*.

azat-/azatutʿ iwn ‹ Parth *āzāt*; Phl. *āzād*, "free, noble"

"free, noble/freedom, nobility"

Lowest stratum of the Iranian and Armenian nobility in the early medieval period, distinct from the *sepuh*s of the great *naχarar* clans, but in no case merely "free" as opposed to "servile." The term is also used as a general one for the nobility as a whole. As such it appears as a component in a number of Sasanian personal names. The *azat*s in Armenia were the retainers of the magnates and formed the contingents of the noble cavalry (*azatagund*). In later sources they are said to have held domains (*χostak*s) granted by their lords, but this term is not attested in BP, nor is there any reference to the status of the lower clergy as part of the *azat* class, though this privilege is mentioned in ecclesiastical canons.

See NBHL, I, p. 4; HArmB, I, p. 83; HBB, I, p. 6; AG, pp. 91–92, no. 2; Gignoux, *Glossaire*, pp 19, 48; *idem*, NPS, nos. 160–165 pp. 51–52; Schmitt, "Iranisches Lehngut," p. 88; Leroy, "Emprunts," p. 56; CPD, p. 15; Bailey, "Iranian Studies," I, pp. 953—955. On the character and rights of the *azat* class, see Christensen, *L'Iran*, pp. 111–113; Adontz, *Armenia*, pp. 213, 342–343; Manandyan, *Feoda-lizm*, pp. 44, 90–94, 103–118, 122–147, 160; Toumanoff, *Studies*, pp. 123–127;

Perikhanian, *Iran*, pp. 14–17, 59, 211-213, 223—225, 302 n. 32; *idem*, MDH,
p. 455; *idem*, "Le Lexique," pp. 11–16; Lukonin, "Institutions," p. 700.
III.xx, xxi; IV.iii, iv, v (*azatutᶜiwn*), xv, lv, lviii; V.ii (also *azatutᶜiwn*), v (*azatanoyn*),
xv, xxiii, xxx, xxxiv, xliv
pp. 96-97, 108, 114, 116, 118, 141, 173, 178, 187–188, 195, 201, 203, 210-211, 215,
230
See also *sepuh*; and the next entry.

azatagund ‹ Ir., Arm. *azat*, "noble" + *gund*, "contingent"/**azataχumb, azatazōrk**
"noble-contingent"
Special contingents of cavalry for which the Armenian army was particularly re-
nowned, in contrast to the non-noble detachments (*ṙamikspas*, see III.xx and n. 15).
The term is also used of the Iranian *puštipan* (IV.liii).
See Christensen, *L'Iran*, pp. 111-112, *āzdhān*, and the bibliography under *azat*.
III.xi (*azataχumb*), xxi (*azatazōrkᶜ*); IV.xv, liii, lv; V.i, xxiv
pp. 80, 98, 145, 170, 174, 185, 205
See also *puštipan*; *ṙamikspas*; *zōrkᶜ*, I; and the preceding entry.

azataχumb, see *azatagund.*

azatutᶜiwn, see *azat.*

azg/azgakanutᶜiwn ‹ ?Phl. *azg*, "branch"
"race, clan, tribe, nation, line, generation"
General term for lineage ("race or clan") as against the smaller units, *tohm* and *tun*,
"house, family." It is occasionally used for entire "tribes" such as the Alans or the Mazkᶜutᶜkᶜ (e.g., III.vii), but appears a few lines later in the same context to designate the
royal clan of the Aršakuni.
See NBHL, I, pp. 6–7; HArmB, I, pp. 84–85; HBB, I, pp. 8–9; CPD, p. 16; Bailey,
Dictionary, p. 466, *haysgā*-; Adontz, *Armenia*, pp. 333, 370. Perikhanian, *Iran*,
pp. 309–310.
P.S.; III.iii, iv, vi–xiv, xviii, xx; IV.ii, iii–vi, xii, xiv, xv, xix, xxxii, xxxvii, li, liv, lv,
lvii, lviii; V.i, iv, xv, xvii, xxv, xxviii, xxx, xxxiv, xxxv, xxxvii, xliv; VI.vi
pp. 63, 69–70, 72, 74, 76–78, 81–82, 84–86, 88, 90, 93–96, 107–108, 114, 120, 125, 134
(*mecazgikᶜ*), 139–141, 143, 145, 149, 161, 163, 168, 173–174, 176–178, 186, 194,
201, 205, 208, 210, 215, 217–218, 235
See also *tohm*; *tun* and Appendix I, "Alankᶜ"; "Aršakuni"; "Mazkᶜutᶜkᶜ."

azgakankᶜ, see *azgakicᶜ.*

azgakanutᶜiwn, see *azg.*

azgakicᶜ ‹ Arm. *azg;* **azgakankᶜ/azgayin**
"kinsman"
Normal term for kinsmen, though *ełbayr*, "brother" is used on a number of occasions
in the same sense; see III.vii and n. 6.
See bibliography under *azg.*
III.vii, xiii; IV.v, xxxii (*azgayin*), xxxiii, xxxvii ((*azgakan*), lix (*azgayin*); V.ii
pp. 73, 85, 122, 161, 163, 180, 187
See also *azg*; *ełbayr.*

azgayin, see *azgakicᶜ.*

bagin ‹ Ir. *bag*, "god" ‹ OP **bagina*-, "place or altar of a god"
"pagan-altar, shrine"

Pagan altar or shrine bearing a cult image, as opposed to a fire altar or *atrušan* or the Christian altar, for which the term *sełan*, "table" is invariably used. BP links the term with a *mehean* or "temple"; see, e.g., III.iii, *baginkʿ mehenicʿn*, "altars of the temples." Cf. Aa, dcccix, who seems to use *bagin* as a synonym for *mehean*.

> See NBHL, I, p. 400; HArmB, I, p. 373, *bag²*; HBB, I, p. 301; Boyce, "Temple Cult"; Russell, *Zor. Arm.* pp. 481, 486–488.
>
> III.iii, xiv
>
> pp. 68, 87
>
> See also *atrušan*; *krapaštutʿiwn*; *mehean*.

bambišn ‹ Ir. *bāmbišn*, "queen"

"queen"

The term, which is attested in ŠKZ with the ideograms Parth. 18, 20, 21, 23, 27, MLKTH; Phl. 25, 26, 29–30, MLKT', and as *b'nbyšn* in Turfan MP, is distinguished by Benveniste and Mackenzie from *bānūg*, "lady," which is found in the form *b'nykn* in MP inscriptions. The Iranian sense of the word was known in Armenia (see e.g., Sebēos, vi, p. 63 and 221 n. 208), but it was also mistaken for a proper name, as is the case in BP, III.xv, xix; IV.iii. The normal term for "queen" in BP is the Armenian *tikin*, "lady," though on one occasion (III.xxi) it uses *bambišn* correctly for the Sasanian queen, together with the more common *tiknacʿ tikin*.

> See NBHL, I, p. 430; HArmB, I, pp. 401–402; HBB, I, 322; AG, pp. 116–117 no. 98; CPD, p. 17; Gignoux, *Glossaire*, pp. 28, 57; *idem*, NPS, no. 185, p. 55 *Bānūg*; Tedesco, "Bānbišn"; Benveniste, *Titres et noms propres*, pp. 27–29; Back, SSI, p. 220; Sprengling, *Third-Century Iran*, pp. 8–9, 11–12, 17–19; Lukonin, "Institutions," pp. 712–713; *idem*, "Ametist," pp. 383–385 and fig. 2, for the representation of the queen of queens, Denak.
>
> III.xxi
>
> p. 99
>
> See also *tikin*; and Appendix I, "Bambišn."

banak/banakim ‹ MIr. *bunag*, "camp"; cf. Georg. loanword *banake*.

"camp, army, host/encamp"

The term is found in BP in both its meanings, though *zōrkʿ* is far more common for "army," and the meaning of "camp" for *banak* is preponderant. The normal residence of the peripatetic Armenian Aršakuni court seems to have been in such encampments provided with a variety of tents (see III.xviii, *banak arkʿuni* and IV.xv), rather than in the capital of Artašat or other urban centers. According to BP, both the Armenian Aršakuni and the Sasanians had main or "home" camps (*bun banak*). Of these, the first was located at Šahapivan (IV.xv) and the second at Tabriz in Atrpatakan (V.ii). Although the ordinary camps must of necessity have been protected from attack, BP usually seems to differentiate between ordinary *banak*s and the more elaborate "fortified-camp," *łakiš*, though the two terms are occasionally interchangeable (see IV.xliii, xlviii), l, lv, lviii). See also V.iv, for the fortification of a *banak*, which presumably turned it into a *łakiš*.

> See NBHL, I, p. 433; HArmB, I, p. 405, which gives "army" as the first sense of *banak*; HBB, I, p. 326; CPD, p. 20, *bunag*; Cf. Abełyan, Koriwn, pp. 112–113 n. 93; Garsoïan, "Banak arkʿuni"; *idem*, "Mediaeval Armenian City," p. 78.
>
> III.vi, vii (with both meanings), viii, xi, xii, xiv, xvi, xviii, xx, xxi; IV.xii, xv, xix, xx, xxii, xxiv, xxv, xl, xliii, xlviii, l, lv, lviii; V.i, ii (with both meanings), iv, xxiv, xxxii, xxxvii, xxxviii, xli, xliii, xliv.
>
> pp. 72–76, 80, 82, 87, 90–91, 93, 97–99, 135, 141–143, 145, 149–150, 152–153, 155, 158–159, 163–164, 166–167, 174, 178, 186–189, 205, 213, 219, 223–225, 227–228
>
> See also *bun banak*, *łakiš*; and Appendix II, "Artašat"; "Šahapivan"; "Tʿawrēš."

banner, see *drōšm.*

barj ‹ NWIr. **barz*; cf. Phl. *bāliš*; Av. *baraziš-*, "pillow"
"cushion, position"
Like *gah*, "throne," the *barj*, "cushion" occupied by a magnate in the presence of the ruler at court indicated his social position or rank in the hierarchy of the nobility, both in Aršakuni Armenia and in Iran. The number of pillows heaped on the feasting couch of an individual likewise denoted his importance.

> See NBHL, I, p. 461; HArmB, I, pp. 425–426; HBB, I, pp. 345–346; AG, p. 428, no. 70; CPD, p. 17; AirWb, p. 950; and on the importance of piled cushions as an indication of status, Sperber, "Adventures," pp. 91–93; Dentzer, "Iconographie"; *idem*, "Banquet"; Garsoïan, "Locus," pp. 59–61 and figs. 3–4.
> III.xi; IV.ii, 1, liv; V.vii
> pp. 81, 108, 168, 172, 198
> See also *bazmakan; gah; patiw.*

barjerēc^c ‹ Arm. *barj*, "cushion" + *erēc^c, elder, senior"*
"senior-in-rank, most-distinguished"
Term used interchangeably with *gaherēc^c* to indicate the seniority and consequently the superiority of a magnate among his peers.

> See the bibliography under *barj.*
> III.ix
> pp. 76–77
> See also *gaherec^c*; and the preceding entry.

baχt ‹ MIr. *baχt*, "fate, destiny, luck"; cf. Av. *baγō.baχta-*, "allotted by the gods"
"[good] fortune, destiny, fate"
Term used together with *p^caṙk^c*, "glory" in Iranian royal formulae to denote the supernatural qualities granted by the gods to the legitimate king. The same concept was evidently still understood in fifth-century Armenia, as indicated by BP (see IV.xxiv n. 12).

> See NBHL, I, p. 425; HArmB, I, pp. 389–390; HBB, I, p. 317; Gignoux, *Glossaire*, p. 20, *bḫt*; AG, pp. 115–116, no. 94; CPD, pp. 16, *bagōbaχt*, 17, *baχt*; and Garsoïan, "Prolegomena," cols. 185–186, 225–228 nn. 65, 67, for the supernatural implications of the term.
> IV.xxiv
> p. 158
> See also *p^caṙk^c.*

bazmakan/bazmoc^ck^c ‹ Arm. *bazmim*, "recline, take one's ease" ‹ Phl. *bazm*, "feast" + *-akan*, derivative suffix
"banqueting-couch, feasting-couch, feast"
This term seems to refer to the ceremonial couch or throne used for the king and the magnates during feasts and banquets in Armenia and Iran. It was characterized by a pile of cushions (*barj*) at one end against which the individual reclined, the number of which corresponded to his rank. On occasion it appears to have been long enough to accommodate more than one person (III.xix, *bazmakanakic^c*). This type of couch is sometimes referred to as *taχt* ((IV.xvi) or *gah* (V.xxiv). The form *bazmoc^c*, defined as "a place to take one's ease" (*teḷi bazmeloy*) by Ačaryan, seems to refer to some sort of royal feasting hall (IV.xv and n. 29).

> See NBHL, I, pp. 407 (*bazmakan*), 418–419 (*bazmem*), 419 (*bazmoc^c*); HArmB, I, p. 376; HBB, I, pp. 306 (*bazmakan*) 312 (*bazmel, bazmoc^c*); AG, p. 144, no. 88; CPD, p. 18 (*bazm, bazmāwurd*); Dentzer, 'Iconographie; *idem*, "Banquet" Harper, "Thrones"; Russell, "Review"; Sperber, "Adventure"; Gignoux, *Glossaire*,

p. 21, *bzmy*; Ghirshman, "Notes iraniennes, V"; Garsoïan, "Locus," pp. 54–62, esp. 57–59 and nn. 96–99; Azarpay, "Bowls."
III.xix (also *bazmel, bazmakanakic῾*), xx; IV.ii, iv, vi, xiv, xv (*bazmoc῾k῾*), xvi (*bazmim*), liv (also *bazmim*), lv; V.vii, xxiv (*bazmel . . . yark῾unakan gahoysn*) xxxii (*bazmim*), xxxv, xxxvii
pp. 94, 96, 108, 115, 126, 139, 143, 146, 172, 174, 198–199, 204, 213–214, 216, 218
See also *barj*; *gah*.

bazmim, see *bazmakan*.

bazmoc῾, see *bazmakan*.

bdeašχ ‹ MIr loanword; cf. Phl *bitaχš*, from the base OIr. *aχš*, "observe" and *paiti*, "chief"; cf. Av. *aiwiāχšaya-*, "superintendent" = Gk. βιτάξης, πιτιάξης; Lat. *vitaxa*
The title is attested in ŠKZ, Parth. 23, 25, 27; Phl. 29, 31, 33; RGDS nos. 56, 61, 64, pp. 64–65, 68–71.
"Toparch, marcher-lord."
Title of the marcher-lords of Aršakuni Armenia who had precedence over all the magnates and may originally have been independent hereditary rulers (III.ix) subsequently compelled to acknowledge the sovereignty of the Armenian king. The title is widely attested in Greek, Latin, Aramaic, Georgian, and Armenian sources, as well as on the inscriptions and gems found at Aramazis-Khevi near Mc῾χeta in Georgia.
The origin of the *bdeašχ*s has often been linked to the four kingly attendants attributed to Tigran II by Plutarch ("Lucullus," 21.6), but this thesis remains unproven, as does A. M. Danielyan's suggestion of a military reform carried out by Trdat III in imitation of that of Diocletian. The similarity of the *bdeašχ*s to Iranian *marzpans* likewise seems doubtful, for the latter seem to have been appointed officials in this period. As "marcher-lords" the *bdeašχ*s are also referred to as "keepers" (*sahmanakal*) or "guardians" (*sahmanapah*) of the borders by both BP and Aa, dccclxxiii, *pace* Lukonin, who posited them as members of the central administration.
Both Aa (*loc.cit*) and BP make it clear that there were altogether four *bdeašχ*s in Aršakuni Armenia: (1) the *bdeašχ* of Ałjnik῾ or "great *bdeašχ*," who was the "keeper-of-the Arabian March" (*sahmanakaln . . . yAruestan kołmanēn*, III.ix; Aa, dccxcv) and had precedence over the other three; (2) the *bdeašχ* of Gugark῾ (IV.l), also called "the other *bdeašχ῾*" (*miws bdeašχn*), who was the "keeper-of-the Mazk῾ut῾k῾ or Iberian March (*sahmanakal . . . Mask῾t῾ac῾ kołmanēn*, Aa, dccxcv, dccclxxiii); or *yašχarhēn Vrac῾ bdešxn*, ŁP῾, xxv, p. 47 (= Ełishē, p. 261), etc.; cf. MX, II.viii, xi; III.vi, lx (= MK, pp. 140, 147, 258, 333); (3) the *bdeašχ/sahmanakal* of Noširakan (*bdeašχk῾n . . . sahmanakaln i Nor Širakan kołmanēn*, IV.l; Aa, dccclxxiii), who was probably the keeper-of-the Adiabenian or Median March, although this is not specified; and (4) the "keeper-of-the Asorestan/Assyrian March (*sahmanakaln yAsorestaneayc῾ kołmanēn*, Aa, dccclxxiii), who may have been the *bdeašχ* or "lord" of Korduk῾ (IV.l; V.x), though his office is not mentioned. The title is also known to AM, XXIII.vi.14.
The importance of the Aršakuni *bdeašχ*s was still remembered in later times with contingents of knights assigned to them in the *Zōrnamak*, "Military List"; nevertheless the title, and presumably the institution, disappeared soon after the end of the dynasty in Armenia. There is one mention of the *bdeašχ* of Ałjnik῾ in the mid-fifth century given in ŁP῾, II.xxxiii, p. 63, but he is not recorded in the parallel passage of Ełishē. Only the *bdeašχ* of Gugark῾, keeper of the Iberian March, is still familiar to ŁP῾ (II.xxv, p. 47 = Ełishē, p. 261) in this period.
See NBHL, I, pp. 478–479; HArmB, I, p. 434; HBB, I, p. 357; AG, pp. 119–120 no. 109; *Paikuli*, I, p. 78, no. 3, also pp. 51 and 229–230; Gignoux, *Glossaire*, pp. 20, 50; Bailey, "Kharoṣṭī Inscription," p. 27 n. 2 to line 9 Maricq, RDGS, pp.

17–18, 51; Pagliaro, "Bitaχs"; Bolognesi, "Tradizione culturale," p. 576; Sprengling, *Third-Century Iran*, pp. 9, 11–12, 18–19; Benveniste, *Titres et noms propres*, p. 65 n. 2; Łapancʿyan, *"Pitiaḥs"*; Greppin, *"Išχan,"* pp. 57–58; Krkyašaryan, "Bdešχutʿyunner," who suggests an Urartian origin; Danielyan, "Trdat III-i řeformə." See also, for the nature and distribution of the office Marquart, "Markgrafen"; Adontz, *Armenia*, pp. 172–173, 175–178, 193–194, 197, 205, 222–225, 232, 318, 321, 344, 360, 445 n. 29, 446 n. 35b, 452 n. 91, 489 n. 39, 524 n. 87, 68*–69*, 72*–76*, 83*; Manandyan, *Feodalizm*, pp. 34–38; Toumanoff, *Studies*, pp. 131–132, 154–192, 244–245, 264–266, 468–469; Christensen, *L'Iran*, pp. 22–23, 101–102; Lukonin, "Institutions," pp. 735–736; Henning, "Silver Bowl," on the *bdeašχ* of Iberia. For an analysis of the territories governed by the *bdeašχ*s, see Hewsen, *"Vitaxates"*; for the archaeological and epigraphic material from Aramazis-Khevi, Apakidze, *et al.*, *Mtskheta*, I, pp. 69–73, pls. LIX/3, LX–LXI; and Amiranashvili, "Serebrianaia chasha," pls. 1–2, for the representation of a *bdeašχ* on a Sasanian silver cup; Eilers, "Bidiahš," pp. 209–210; for the use of the term by AM.
III.ix; IV.xxiv, l; V.xv, xvi
pp. 76–77, 157, 167, 201
See also *marzpan*; *sahmanapah*; and Appendix II, "Ałjnikʿ"; "Gugarkʿ"; "Kordukʿ"; "Noširakan."

berd ‹ ?Aram. BYRT', "fortress," used as the ideogram for Phl. *drubušt*, "fortress"
"fortress, castle"
This term is usually used for a man-made stronghold, by contrast to *amur*, which can also refer to a naturally impregnable or inaccessible site, though the two terms are occasionally found interchangeably or together (e.g., III.viii).
See NBHL, I, p. 483; HArmB, I, pp. 442-443; HBB, I, p. 364; AG, p. 301 no. 14.
III.vii, viii, xii; IV.xviii, xix, xxiv, xl, liv, lv, lviii, lix; V.i, iii, v, vii
pp. 74–75, 84, 148–149, 157, 163, 173–175, 178–179, 186–189, 195–199
See also *amur*; *amrocʿ*; *miǰnaberd*; and next entry.

berdakal ‹ Arm. *berd*, "fortress" + *kal* (aor. stem of *unim*), "have, hold"
"keeper-of-a-fortress, garrison"
Term usually used in its first sense.
See NBHL, I, p. 483; HArmB, I, p. 442, *berd*; HBB, I, p. 364.
IV.lv, lviii, lix; V.i
pp. 175, 178–179, 186–187
See also *ostikan*, and the preceding entry.

bnak tēr ‹ Arm. *bun*, "root, base" ‹ MIr. *bun*, "beginning"; "natural, true, authentic" + *tēr*, "lord"
"true, native-lord(s)"
Formula consistently used in BP to characterize the Aršakuni dynasty and thus to underscore the fact that the kingship of Armenia was the hereditary office of this family (see Intro., pp. 43–44, 48, 50).
See NBHL, I, pp. 511–512, *bun*; Garsoïan, "Prolegomena," cols. 180, 196–197 nn. 22–25; MHD, p. 451, *bun*; CPD, p. 20, *bun*.
III.xi, xx, xxi; IV.xxiv, li; V.iv, v, vii, xx, xliv
pp. 81–82, 95, 97–98, 158, 169, 194, 196, 198–199, 202, 228–229
See also *tēr*; and Appendix I, "Aršakuni."

bodyguard, see *pʿuštipan.*

bondage, see *struk/caṙay.*

border, see *sahman.*

border-guard, see *sahmanapah.*

boundary, see *sahman.*

bow, see *zēn*, j.

brave, see *kʿaǰ.*

brother, see *ełbayr.*

bun

> **-banak** ‹ Arm. *bun* + *banak* (see above *banak* and *bnak tēr*)
> "home camp"
> Main residence of the peripatetic Aršakuni or Iranian court
> See Garsoïan, "Mediaeval Armenian City," p. 78
> IV.xv; V.ii
> pp. 141, 143, 187
> See also Appendix II, "Šahapivan"; "Tʿawrēš."

> **-gahoykʿ/gewł** ‹ Arm. *bun* + *gah* (see above *bnak tēr* and below *gah*)
> "seat, home village"
> Main village or fortress of a *naχarar* family
> III.iv
> p. 70
> See also *gah*; *naχarar*; and Appendix II, "Manazert."

camp, see *banak.*

canopy, see *χoran.*

caravan, see *karawan.*

caṙay/caṙayutʿiwn ‹ ?

> "servant, vassal/servitude, bondage, submission "
> Term indicating the entire range of service to a superior, including noble vassalage to an overlord or king, but usually distinguished in BP, except for some Biblical passages, from actual slavery, *struk* (see IV.xv n. 44).
> See NBHL, I, p. 1011; HArmB, II, pp. 447–448; HBB, II, pp. 330–331; AG, p. 305, no. 42; S. E. Hakobyan, *Caṙa*; *idem*, *Šinakanutʿyun*, pp. 188–194; Adontz, *Armenia*, p. 349; *idem*, "L'aspect"; Manandyan, *Feodalizm*, pp. 45, 59–60, 117–118, 153–159, 165–166, etc.
> III.v, ix, x, xi, xiv, xx, xxi; IV.iv–vi, ix, xii, xv, xxi, xxiii, li–lv, lvii, lviii; V.iv, vi, xv, xxiv, xxviii, xxxi, xxxiii, xxxvii, xxxviii; VI.i
> pp. 71, 76–78, 80, 89, 96, 98, 114, 118, 125, 130, 135, 142, 154, 156, 168–172, 176–178, 191–192, 196, 201, 204, 208, 213–214, 218, 221–222, 234
> See also *struk.*

caṙayut^ciwn, see *caṙay.*

castle, see *berd.*

cathedral/catholic, see *katolikē.*

cavalry, see *zōrk^c*, I.

ceremonial robe, see *patmučan* .

cgnawor, see *anapatawor.*

chair, see *at^cor.*

chamberlain, see *senekapet.*

chief, see *pet.*

   -archbishop, see *ark^cepiskoposapet.*

   -bishop, see *episkoposapet*; also *senior bishop.*

   -executioner, see *dahčapet.*

   -stabler, see *aχorapet.*

chorepiskopos, see *k^corepiskopos.*

citadel, see *miǰnaberd.*

city, see *k^calak^c.*

clan, see *azg.*

club, see *zēn*, k.

club-bearer, see *zōrk^c*, II, g.

commander, see *zōravar.*

commander-in-chief, see *sparapet, zōravar.*

community/congregation, see *uχt; van(k^c).*

confines, see *sahman.*

contingent, see *gund.*

coronant, see *t^cagakap.*

council, see *žolov.*

counsellor, see *handarjapet.*

count, see *koms.*

country, see *ašχarh.*

covenant, see *uχt.*

cushion, see *barj.*

dagger, see *zēn*, f.

dahčapet ‹ **Arm.** *dahič* ‹ *M.Ir. *dahīč*; Phl. *dḥyc*, "soldier, executioner" + *pet*, "chief" "chief-executioner"

519

See NBHL, I, p. 592; HArmB, I, p. 615, *dahič*; HBB, I, p. 483; AG, p. 133, no. 159; Harmatta-Pékáry, "Pārsīk Ostracon" pp. 469–470, no. 4; Gignoux, *Glossaire*, p. 21.

IV.xv; but probably not III.x (see III.x n. 12).

p. 143

See also *pet.*

dasapet ‹ ?Parth. **dasapet*; cf. Phl. *dahibed*, "village ruler," "ruler of a country" "headman-of-a-village-community"

This title seems to have ranked among the minor nobility as head or representative of the peasants (IV.li, *dasapet šinakanac‘*). As such it would presumably be the equivalent of a Gk. κωμάρχης, but its distinction from *dehkan/dehkanut‘iwn* is not clear.

See NBHL, I, p. 598, which gives the Gk. equivalent as Ταξίαρχος and consequently equates it with a more important dignity; HBB, I, p. 491; CPD, p. 23, *dahibed;* and for the rank of this office, Adontz, *Armenia*, p. 355, who keeps it at village level; Manandyan, *Feodalizm*, pp. 82 n. 1, 187; Perikhanian, *Iran*, pp. 19, 301 n. 17.

IV.li

p. 168

See also *dehkanut‘iwn; pet*

dastakert ‹ Parth. **dast-kirt*; Phl. *dast(a)gird*, "settlement, estate" ‹ OP *dastakarta-*, "made by hand, property"

Term attested in ŠKZ, Parth. 16, 17, 25, 29, 30; Phl. 30; RGDS nos. 37, 60, 70, pp. 56–57, 68–69, 72–73, where it is used both as "possession, property" and as an honorific to designate the "creature, possession of the gods or the king," pp. 14, 250. "estate, domain"

The term is apparently used in BP in its sense of "estate"; rather than in the alternate sense of "grant, foundation," though this sense is possible in IV.xii and li. In Iran, the term designated a "royal estate," as in the case in IV.xii, but in Armenia it could also be used of *naxarar* "holdings" (IV.li), and thus emphasized the autonomy of the magnates' possessions, even when they were granted by the crown. Sargsyan does not differentiate between *dastakert* and *agarak* where these terms refer to rural estates.

See NBHL, I, p. 559; HArmB, I, p. 627; HBB, I, p. 492; Gignoux, *Glossaire*, pp. 20, 49–50; idem, NPS, no. 309, p. 75 for the use in personal names; Sprengling, *Third-Centry Iran*, pp. 8–9, 12, 16–17, 19; Maricq, RGDS, pp. 56–57 n. 3; Honigmann and Maricq, RGDS, pp. 15, 17, 18; AG, p. 135 no. 169; Schmitt "Iranisches Lehngut," p. 89; Pigulevskaia, *Villes*, pp. 151–153; Sargsyan, "O dvukh znacheniiakh," pp. 97–101 (= French trans. pp. 43–50); idem, "Dastakertnerə," pp. 77–94; Perikhanian, MHD, pp. 458–460, *dastkart*; Henning, "Silver Bowl," p. 355.

IV.xii, li

pp. 134–135, 168

See also *agarak; kaluac; naxarar; ostan; sephakan;* and Appendix II, "Aršakawan."

datawor/dataworut‘iwn ‹ Phl. *dādwar*; OP *dātabara*, "judge"

Title attested in ŠKZ. Parth. 24, 29, Phl. 30(?), 35; RGDS nos. 58, 67, pp. 68–69, 72–73, δικαστής.

"judge, arbiter, office-of-judge"

Terms used in BP as in Iran in association with ecclesiastical office.

See NBHL, I, p. 601–602; HArmB, I, pp. 630–631; HBB, I, p. 495; AG, p. 136, no. 173; Sprengling, *Third-Century Iran*, pp. 9, 12, 18, 19; CPD, p. 23, *dādwar*; Gignoux, *Glossaire* pp. 21, 50; Manandyan, *Feodalizm*, pp. 76–79; Honigmann

and Maricq, RGDS, pp. 17–18; Perikhanian, MHD, pp. 461–462, *dātaβar*; Garsoïan, "Protecteur des pauvres," p. 21 nn. 1–4, for the bibliography on the seals
bearing this title.
III.xiv, xxi; IV.xiii, liii; V.iv, xliii
pp. 86, 97, 137, 192, 226
See also Appendix II, "Basean."

dataworut'iwn, see *datawor.*

dayeak ‹ Ir **dāy* "care, nurture"; cf. Phl. *dāyag*, "nurse, foster-mother, servant"; Av.
daēnu-, "that which gives milk"
"foster-father, tutor"
The institution of *dayeak*s whereby *naxarar* youths were raised by foster-fathers of
their own social class was widely prevalent in Aršakuni Armenia and is also attested for
Sasanian princes (ŠKZ, Parth. 25, Phl. 31; RGDS nos. 60, 61) according to Maricq,
Gignoux, and Lukonin, though the term itself does not occur in these lines. The *topos*
of the only surviving child of a massacred clan saved by his *dayeak* is familiar to Aa,
xxxiv, xxxvi, MX, II.xxxvii, III.xv (= MK, pp. 179, 269), and is repeatedly found in BP.
Once established in youth, this special relationship seems to have been perpetuated
thereafter. The privilege of being *dayeak*s to the royal Aršakuni heir seems to have been
a prerogative of the Mamikonean house, though this privilege is obscured by MX's
alteration of Trdat the Great's foster-brother (*dayeakordi*) from Artawazd Mamikonean
to Artawazd Mandakuni (MX, II.lxxxii = MK, p. 232). Other members of the Aršakuni
family could have *dayeak*s from other *naxarar* houses, e.g. Bat Sahaṙuni, the *dayeak* of
the appointed King Varazdat, who attempted unsuccessfully to substitute him for the
Mamikoneans in their hereditary office of *sparapet* (V.xxxv, xxxvii). MX, II.lxxvii
(= MK, p. 224) seems to suggest a similar relationship between Awtay Amatuni and the
royal princess Xosroviduχt, although he uses the term *snuc'oł*, "nurturer, nurse" rather
than *dayeak*, and BP mentions the female *dayeak* of Princess Hamazaspuhi Mamikonean (IV.lix). Cf. Aa, clvi, clxviii, for Gayianē and Hrip'simē.
See NBHL, I, p. 593; HArmB, I, pp. 618–619; HBB, I, p. 485; Gignoux, NPS,
no. 754, p. 146, *Parikān*; Maricq, RGDS, p. 68 n. 6; but cf. Sprengling, *Third-
Century Iran*, p. 19 "Sasan who manages Parikan. . . ."; Malχasyanc', p. 320,
n. 58; CPD, p. 25, *dāyag*; AirWb, p. 662; Nyberg, *Manual*, II, p. 61, *dāyak*,
"mother"; Perikhanian, *Iran*, pp. 125, 327 n. 192; Bedrosian, *"Dayeakut'iwn,"*
pp. 23–47; Widengren, *Feudalismus*, pp. 69–80; Lukonin, "Institutions,"
pp. 702–705; *idem, Kul'tura*, p. 43 n. 17.
III.xviii; IV.ii, xi, xlvii, liii, lix (nurse); V.xxxv, xxxvii
pp. 93, 107–108, 133, 166, 170, 179, 215, 217–218
See also *naxarar*; *snuc'ič'*; and Appendix I, "Aršakuni"; "Artawazd I"; "Bat"; "Hamazaspuhi"; "Mamikonean, house."

defender, see *ʃatagov.*

dehkan/dehkanut'iwn ‹ Phl. *dehgān, dahigān*, "countryman, farmer"
"supervisor/supervision-of-peasants"
BP uses this term only once, in connection with the Gnuni's hereditary office of
hazarapet. NBHL defines it as the "first degree of officialdom" (*skizbn gorcakalut'ean*),
but this seems unlikely, considering the high rank of the Gnuni house who held this
office as *hazarapet*s, and Ačaryan raises the *dehkan*s to the rank of "heads of districts"
(*gawaṙatēr*). The distinction between the *dehkan*s and *dasapet*s cannot be made on the
basis of BP, but the *dehkan*s may well have been higher in rank.
See NBHL, I, p. 608, which also defines *dehkanut'iwn* as *kusakalut'iwn*,
"governorship-of-a-region," as do the other Armenian dictionaries; HArmB, I,

p. 647, *dehkan*; HBB, I, p. 502; CPD, p. 24, *dahigān*; Perikhanian, MHD, p. 464, *dehkān*, which she defines as "servant of the king"; Christensen, *L'Iran*, pp. 112, 259.

IV.ii

p. 108

See also *dasapet*; *hazarapet*; and Appendix I, "Dehkan"; "Gnuni, house."

dehkanutʿiwn, see *dehkan*.

demon/devil, see *dew*.

deputy/vicar, see *etełapah*.

desert dweller, see *anapatawor*.

dew/diwapaštutʿiwn ‹ Parth., Phl. *dēw*, "demon, devil"

"demon, evil spirit, forces of evil"

The original sense of this term, "divinity," survives only in archaic compounds and in EIr., especially Sogdian. In BP, *dew* is invariably used in its secondary meaning of "evil spirits, powers of evil."

See NBHL, I, p. 611; HArmB, I, pp. 657–658; HBB, I, p. 508; AG, p. 140, no. 193; CPD, p. 26; Schmitt, "Iranishes Lehngut," p. 95; Christensen, *Démonologie*; Macler, *Les dew*; Nyberg, *Religionen*, pp. 96, 106, 112, 186, 338, 365ff., 397; Hambröer, *Dämonenglaube*, pp. 55ff; Russell, *Zor. Arm.*, pp. 437–442.

III.xx; IV.xliv; V.xxii, xxxi; VI.viii

pp. 94, 164–165, 202–203, 212 (*diwapaštutʿiwn*), 236

See also Appendix I, "Pap."

diadem/dignity/distinguished, see *patiw*; *patuakan*.

district, see *gawaṙ*.

diwapaštutʿiwn, see *dew*.

domain, see *dastakert*; *kaluac*; *tun*.

dominion, see *išχanutʿiwn*; *tērutʿiwn*.

drōšm ‹ Parth. *drafš*, "banner"; cf. Phl. *drōšom*, "mark, brand"; Av. *drafša-*, "flag, banner"

"banner, standard"

In Armenia as well as in Iran, the great magnates were entitles to display coats of arms and carry their own standards, as would be the case in later feudal Europe. BP refers specifically to the *gndicʿ ew drōšucʿ tearkʿ*, "the lords with contingents and banners" (IV.iii), and these coats of arms are visible on the victory relief of Ardašīr I at Firūzābād.

See NBHL, I, pp. 643, *drōšm* and 645, *drōš*; HArmB, I, p. 694; HBB, I, p. 545; AG, pp. 146–147, no. 211; Schmitt, "Iranisches Lehngut," p. 90; CPD, p. 28, and Perikhanian, MHD, p. 467, both of whom give the Pahlavi meaning of "mark, seal, brand" for *drōš*; Christensen, *L'Iran*, pp. 210–212; Cardona, "Études étymologiques"; Garsoïan, "Prolegomena," cols. 224 n. 62, for the prerogative of the Armenian *naχarars* to display coats of arms; and Ghirshman, *Persian Art*, figs. 163–166, for the Firūzābād relief.

III.vii; IV.ii, iii, xx; V.i, xliii

pp. 73, 108, 150, 186, 226

dweller

-in-the-desert, see *anapatawor.*

-in-the-mountains, see *leaṙnakan.*

dwelling, see *van(kʿ).*

-for-virgins, see *kusastan.*

earth, see *erkir.*

ełbayr
"brother, kinsman"
Although it is normally found in its basic sense of sibling born of the same parents, this term also occurs in the looser sense of member of the same family or clan, without indication of the precise degree of relationship. On several occasions, it is also used in its general Christian or its ecclesiastical sense, though there is no indication from the context that the "brothers" referred to lived in a coenobium, as is suggested by the usual translation, "monk." On the contrary, the community at Mambrē (*ełbayranocʿ*) founded by Epipʿ an (V.xxvii–xxviii), which even included hermits living in the mountains, was a highly decentralized one, so that the translation "brother" or at most "religious" seems preferable in this case as well. Cf. Aa, dccvi on the "brothers" brought by St. Gregory from Sebastē, who could hardly have been monks in the early fourth century.
> See NBHL, I, p. 652; HArmB, II, pp. 15–16; HBB, I, pp. 586–587; Garsoïan, "Nersēs le Grand," p. 167 and nn. 107–108, for the "brothers" from Sebastē.
> III.iii, v–vii, ix, xi, xiii, xix; IV.ii, vi, xi, xv, xvi, xviii, xxii, l; V.xx, xxvii, xxviii, xxxi, xxxvii, xxxviii, xliii, xliv; VI.vi, xvi
> pp. 68, 71, 72, 74, 77, 81, 85, 93–94, 108, 126, 133, 141–142, 144, 146–150, 155, 167, 202, 207–209, 213, 217–219, 222, 228, 235, 240
> See also *azgakicʿ; mianjn; van(kʿ).*

ełbayranocʿ, see *mianjn/mianjnanocʿ.*

elite troops, see *matenik gund.*

encampment, see *banak.*

episkoposapet ‹ Gk. ἐπίσκοπος; cf. Lat. *episcopus* + Arm. *-pet*, "chief"
"chief-bishop"
Term usually used interchangeably with *hayrapet* and *kʿahanayapet* to distinguish the Armenian primates of the Gregorid house, to whom it is exclusively reserved, from the patriarchs of other families, whom BP does not treat as equally legitimate, and for whom it prefers the various terms for "senior bishop" (*awag* or *gluχ episkoposacʿ*). See Intro., p. 15, and P.S. nn. 6, 9.
> See NBHL, I, p. 660; HArmB, II, p. 29; HBB, I, p. 564; Leroy, "Composés en *-pet*," nos. 22, 26, pp. 123, 126.
> III.iii, iv, vii, xi; IV.iv, v, ix, xi–xv, xix, li; V.i, iv, v, xxi, xxiii, xxix; VI.v
> pp. 68–70, 74, 80–81, 111, 113, 116, 122, 130, 133–134, 138–142, 149, 168, 185–186, 190–191, 194, 202–203, 210, 235
> See also *senior-bishop; hayrapet; kʿahanayapet; pet;* and Appendix I, "Grigor/Gregorids."

erkir ‹ ?

"land, earth, ground"

This term is occasionally used to denote the "earth" in general, especially in Biblical citation, as well as for foreign territories. With regard to Armenia, its most common use, it denotes the geographical aspect of the country, as opposed to the political connotation of *ašχarh* or *išχanutʿiwn* (see, e.g., III.xi, *ašχarh hayastan erkrin*, "the realm-of-the-land of Armenia," or III.ix, *yerkrēn yišχanutʿenēn Hayocʿ*, "from the land-of-the-Armenian-dominion"). On occasion it can also be used to designate a larger region such as Tarōn (III.iii), by contrast to a smaller "district" (*gawaṙ*).

See NBHL, I, pp. 693–693; HArmB, II, pp. 63–64; HBB, I, p. 593.

III.iii, iv, vi–xv, xvii–xxi; IV.i–vii, x, xii–xv, xx–xxv, xxvii–xxxii, xxxiv, xxxv, xxx-viii–xl, xlii, xlvii, l, liii–lix; V.i, iii–v, vii–ix, xii–xvii, xx, xxi, xxvii–xxxii, xxxiv, xxxv, xxxvii–xliv; VI.i, xvi

pp. 68–71, 73–80, 83–84, 90–94, 96–100, 107–109, 112–113, 116–124, 126–127, 131, 134–135, 137, 140, 143, 145, 150, 153–156, 158–164, 166–167, 170–171, 173–180, 185–188, 191–194, 196–202, 206–213, 215–216, 218–225, 227–228, 230, 234, 239

See also *ašχarh*; *išχanutʿiwn*; Appendix II, "Aljnikʿ"; "Apahunikʿ"; "Copʿkʿ"; "Kogovit"; "Tarōn"; and the next entry.

erkir haykakan lezui/erkir lezuin Tʿogormakan ašχarhin/ašχarh amenayn Hayocʿ lezuin

"land-of-Armenian-speech/tongue"

This locution is the broadest definition of Armenia in cultural rather than political or geographical terms. It presumably included the regions of Armenia Minor west of the Euphrates, which were still demographically if not administratively Armenian in the mid-fifth century. See, e.g., the *Answers* of the Lesser Armenian bishops to the emperor Leo I, ca. 451. This terminology is also used by MX, I.xiv, *zχōss ew lezus haykakan*; I.xiv; II.iii, viii (= MK, pp. 95, 133, 139). The locution was also used for lands lost by Armenia after the partition of ca. 387, as distinguished from the Armenian Midlands (e.g. GTʿ, p. 130).

See Adontz, *Armenia*, pp. 58*–59*, 179 for the *Answer* of the bishops from Armenia II and the lost Armenian lands.

III.xiii; IV.xii; V.xxx

pp. 84, 134, 211

See also *ašχarh*; Appendix II, "Miǰnašχarh Hayocʿ"; and the preceding entry.

estate, see *agarak*; *dastakert*; *kaluac*.

etełapah/tełapah ‹ Arm. *teł*, "place" + *pah/pahel*, "guardian, protector"

"vicar, deputy"

Although the form *tełapah* is given as preferable by the dictionaries, BP uses *etełapah* in its ecclesiastical rather than its secular connotation.

See NBHL, I, p. 664, *etełapah* and IV, p. 863, *tełapah*; Ačaryan, IV, p. 392, *teł*; HBB, IV, p. 389, *tełapah*.

IV.xii–xiii

pp. 134–136

See also Appendix I, "Xad."

family/house, see *tohm*; *tun*.

foot soldiers, see *zōrk^c* II.

forces, see *zork^c*.

fort/fortress, see *amroc^c*; *berd.*

fortified, see *amur.*

fortified-camp, see *łakiš.*

fortune, see *baχt.*

foster-father, see *dayeak*; *snuc^cič^c.*

free, see *azat.*

frontier, see *sahman.*

gah/gahoyk^c ‹ Parth. MP *gāh,* "place, throne"; OP *gāθu-,* "place, position"
The term occurs in KKZ, 4, 5, 7, 10, with the sense of both "throne " and "rank"
"throne (secular), rank, position"
The "throne" (*gah*) or "cushion" (*barj*) occupied by a *naχarar* at court functions
indicated his rank in the hierarchy of the nobility and was probably related to the
number of his retainers. The so-called "Rank List" or *Gahnamak* that has come down
to us is probably later and partially fictitious, as has been demonstrated by Adontz;
nevertheless, it preserves the memory of an authentic structure that existed in Iran as
well as Armenia. The form *gahoyk^c* is also found in the sense of the "seat" of a clan
(III.iii) or a royal "banqueting couch" (IV.xvi = V.xxiv).
See NHBL, I, p. 522; HArmB, I, p. 502; HBB, I, p. 406; Gignoux, *Glossaire,* p. 22;
AG, p. 125, no. 125; Schmitt, "Iranisches Lehngut," p. 89; Sprengling, *Third-
Century Iran,* pp. 46–47, 49–51; CPD, p. 34; also for the hierarchy of the nobility
and the authenticity of the *Gahnamak,* Adontz, *Armenia,* pp. 185–186, 191–193,
203–204, 208, 214–215, 218, 234, 67*–68*, 70*–72*; Toumanoff, *Studies,*
pp. 239–231; B. H. Harut^cyunyan, "Gahnamak"; Christensen, *L'Iran,* pp. 62–63;
Chaumont, "L'ordre des préséances"; Garsoïan, "Prolegomena," cols. 182,
207–208 nn. 42–43; *idem,* "Social Structure"; and IV.ii nn. 8–9.
III.xi; IV.ii, xvi, xviii, xx, xliv, liv, lix (height); V.iv, xxiv
pp. 81, 108, 146, 149, 153, 165, 172, 179, 194, 204
See also *at^coṙ*; *barj*; *bazmakan*; *bun gahoyk^c*; *patiw*; and the next entry.

gaherēc^c ‹ Arm. *gah,* "throne" + *erēc^c,* "senior, elder"
"senior/superior in rank"
Title used interchangeably with *barjerēc^c* to indicate the seniority and hence the
superiority of an individual to his peers within the *naχarar* hierarchy.
See NBHL, I, p. 525; Adontz, *Armenia,* pp. 214, 223–224; Toumanoff, *Studies,*
p. 163, n. 41, though his translation of BP III.ix is incorrect at this point, according to Anasyan, "Review," p. 21; also the remaining bibliography under *gah.*
III.ix
pp. 76–77
See also *barjerec^c*; *naχarar*; and the preceding entry.

gahoyk^c see *gah.*

gargmanak ‹ ?Phl. *warrag,* "ram" + *mānāg,* "like, resembling"; **garg-mānāg,* "ram-like"
Hapax of uncertain origin and meaning. It was either a helmet ornament or preferably the helmet or headdress itself, as suggested by the context. It was usually sur-

mounted by a crest. See, e.g., the crown on the Sasanian silver plate from the Walters Gallery, and cf. the honorific crown described by MX, II.xlvii (= MK, p. 187).

See NBHL, I, p. 530; HArmB, I, p. 521; HBB, I, p. 4414; CPD, pp. 53, *mānāg*, 87, *warrag*; Toumanoff, *Studies*, p. 134 nn. 234–235; Ghirshman, *Persian Art*, p. 218 fig. 259 for the Walters Gallery plate.

V.xxxviii

p. 221

garrison, see *berdakal.*

gawaṙ ‹ ?

"district, canton"

This is the most common term used to distinguish a district geographically and admistratively. The size and importance of such a district is not altogether clear, however, nor is its relations to the presumably larger *nahang*, "province," a term that BP uses rarely and only for Tarōn within Armenia (III.xiv; IV.xv), or to *ašχarh*. The seventh-century *Ašχarhac^coyc^c* (p. 29ff.) describes Greater Armenia as having fifteen *gawaṙ*s, then goes on to call each of them an *ašχarh* containing a number of lesser *gawaṙ*s. In BP, a single region such as Tarōn is indiscriminately called a *gawaṙ*, *nahang*, *koɫmn*, "region" and *erkir*, "land." Nevertheless, the most common usage in BP seems to refer to the smallest administrative or geographical unit.

See NBHL, I, p. 533; HArmB, I, pp. 527–528, which defines the term imprecisely as "*nahang kam nahangi mi bažinə*"; HBB, I, p. 417; Bailey, *Dictionary*, p. 15, **āgū*, "village."

III.ii, iv, vi–viii, x–xii, xiv, xvi, xix, xxi; IV.iv, xii–xv, xviii–xx, xxii–xxiv, xlviii, l, lv, lviii, lix; V.i, iii, vi–viii, x, xiii, xv, xvii–xix, xxi, xxiv–xxix, xxxi, xxxii, xxxiv, xlii–xliv; VI.i, v, vi, xii, xiii, xvi

pp. 67, 70, 72–75, 77–79, 81–82, 84, 86–88, 90–91, 94, 98, 113–115, 134, 136, 138–139, 141, 145, 148–149, 152, 155–158, 166–167, 174, 176, 178–179, 186, 188, 196, 198–202, 204–207, 210–213, 215, 224–225, 228, 233–235, 238–240

See also *ašχarh*; *erkir*; *koɫmn*; *nahang*; and the next two entries.

gawaṙakal ‹ Arm. *gawaṙ*, "district" + *kal* (aor. stem of *unim*), "hold, have"

"keeper/governor-of-a-district"

This term, which seems clearly differentiated from *gawaṙatēr*, had an administrative rather than a hereditary character (see V.i).

See NBHL, I, p. 533 and the bibliography under *gawaṙ*.

III.iv; IV.xiii; V.i

pp. 69, 136, 185

See also *ašχarhakal*; *gawaṙ*; *gawaṙatēr*.

gawaratēr/tēr gawarin ‹ Arm. *gawaṙ*, "district," + *tēr*, "lord"

"lord-of-a-district"

On the basis of its composing elements and of its use to characterize Garegin Ṙštuni (IV.lix; V.xxxvii), this term seems to refer to the hereditary lord of a district, as distinguished from the "district-governor" (*gawaṙakal*).

See NBHL, I, p. 533, and the bibliography under *gawaṙ.*

IV.xii, li, lix; V.i, vi, xxxii, xxxvii, xlii, xliii

pp. 134, 168, 179, 185, 196, 201, 214, 220, 224, 227

See also *ašχarhatēr*; Appendix I, "Garegin II"; and the preceding two entries.

gawit^c ‹ ?MIr. *gāw*, "cow" + Arm. *it^c* = ? "cow pen," cf. *gawazan*, "cow staff," but not Av. *gaoyaoiti-*, "pasture land"

"forecourt, narthex"

The addition of an exo–narthex or *gawit*^c also called *žamatun*, "house-of-prayer" on the facade of most Armenian churches is a late architectural development usually considered to postdate the eleventh century. These additions, or occasionally separate buildings, were used for purposes deemed unsuitable for the church itself, such as ecclesiastical assemblies, or the burial of distinguished personages. The appearance of this term in BP is an interesting *hapax* for the late fifth century and appears to refer to the open forecourt of a shrine rather than to an enclosed building.

    See NBHL, I, p. 533; HArmB, I, p. 528; HBB, I, pp. 417–418; Ag, pp. 126–127, no. 132; also Der Nersessian, *Armenian Art*, pp. 167–181; Maffei, *Architectura*, p. 26; S. X. Mnatsakanian, *Arkhitektura*.

    III.iii

    p. 69

generation, see *azg*.

geoł, see *gewł*.

gewł/giwł/geoł ‹ ?
    "village"
    Basic term for a village, presumably smaller than an *awan*, which Ačaryan defines as *mec giwł*. Nevertheless, the terms seem to have been interchangeable at times; both are occasionally applied to the same locality (see, e.g., V.xxiv, "*i T^ciln yawann yiwr gewłn*").

    See NBHL, I, p. 549; HArmB, I, p. 563, cf. 353–354, *awan*; HBB, I, p. 441, *giwł/gewł*.

    III.ii, iv, vi, xi, xii, xiv, xix–xxi; IV.iv, xii, xiv, xv, xxiv, li; V.iv, vi, xxiv, xxv, xxxi, xxxv, xliii; VI.ii, vi, viii, x.

    pp. 67, 70, 73, 82, 84, 88, 94, 97–98, 113, 134, 139, 141, 145, 168, 194, 196, 205, 212–213, 217, 226, 234–236, 238

    See also *awan*; and next entry.

gewłak^całak^c/k^całak^cagewł ‹ Arm. *gewł*, "village" + *k^całak^c*, "walled enclosure, city"; equivalent to Gk. κωμόπολις
    "*kōmopolis*, fortified village"
    Center of population of intermediate size between a "village" (*gewł*) and a "walled unit or city" (*k^całak^c*). As such, it presumably would be approximately equivalent to an *awan*; but the term may also refer to a fortified village surrounded by walls, and Małχasyanc^c hesitates between the two definitions. This compound, which occurs with either component in initial position, is rare in the fifth century but is a favorite of the tenth-century historian John the Kat^cołikos.

    See NBHL, II, p. 969, *k^całak^cagiwł*, which is the form preferred by the other dictionaries; HArmB, IV, p. 542; HBB, IV, p. 536.

    IV.xiii

    p. 138

    See also *awan*; *k^całak^c*; Appendix II, "Ařest"; "Aršakawan"; "Artašat"; and the preceding entry.

giwł, see *gewł*.

glory, see *p^cařk^c*.

gluχ episkoposac^c, see *senior-bishop*.

glχawor episkopos, see *senior-bishop*.

gorcakal/gorcakalut^ciwn ‹ Arm. *gorc*, "work" + *kal* (aor. stem of *unim*), "have, hold" ‹ Gk. ϝέργον, "work"
    "official, office"

The Armenian nobility of the Aršakuni period presented the double aspect of hereditary dynasts and royal officials. These two aspects often overlapped, for the great offices, at least—except for the *mardpet*—were hereditary in certain *naχarar* clans (e.g., the office of *sparapet* in the Mamikonean house). The two groups cannot, however, be equated, since by no means all *gorcakal*s, especially inferior ones, were *nahapet*s of noble clans, and one individual might accumulate several offices. BP clearly marks the distinction between the two groups, especially in IV.ii and n. 9, "*mecameckʿn yiwrakʿančʿiwr gahu, ew gorcakalkʿn yiwrakʿančʿiwr čʿapʿu.*"

> See NBHL, I, p. 575; HArmB, I, p. 583, *gorc*; HBB, I, p. 463; AG, p. 436, no. 101, *gorc*; Adontz, *Armenia*, pp. 185–186, 339, 354, 440 nn. 1a, 2, 519 n. 63, 527 n. 103, though some of his western parallels are now out of date in view of the evidence of closer Iranian ones; Manandyan, *Feodalizm*, pp. 60–65, 67–69, 71–79, 81–83, 121–123; Toumanoff, *Studies*, pp. 112–127, for the double aspect of the Armenian aristocracy, though he does not specifically discuss the term *gorcakal*.
>
> III.xiv (*gorcakalutʿiwn*), xx; IV.ii, iii (*gorcakalutʿiwn*), ix, li; V.vi (*gorc*), vii (*gorcakalutʿiwn*), xxxv (*gorc*) in the sense of "office", xxxvii (*gorc*) in the same sense
>
> pp. 86, 97, 108–109, 130, 168–169, 196, 198, 217
>
> See also *aspet*; *awgani*; *hazarapet*; *išχan*; *mardpet*; *mecamec*; *nahapet*; *naχarar*; *senekapet*; *sparapet*; *tēr*.

gorcakalutʿiwn, see *gorcakal*.

grand chamberlain, see *mardpet*.

great sepuh, see *mec sepuh*.

greatest, see *mecamec*.

guardian/warden-of-the-marches/borders, see *sahmanapah*.

guardsman, see *pʿuštipan*.

gugaz ‹ ?

> "irregular levies" ?
>
> *Hapax* of uncertain origin. The meaning, "irregular troops" or "levies," is derived from the context of the two chapters in which the term occurs.
>
> See NBHL, I, p. 578; HArmB, I, p. 587, which defines it as "*ankanon zōrki amboχ*"; HBB, I, p. 466; Malχasyancʿ, p. 313 n. 16.
>
> III.vii–viii
>
> pp. 74–75
>
> See also *matenik*; *zōrkʿ*.

guide, see *aṙajnord/aṙajnordem*.

gumapet/gamapet ‹ ? + Arm. *-pet*, "chief"

> "leader of a detachment"?
>
> *Hapax* of uncertain origin and meaning, and Leroy rejects the reading *gumapet* of the text. The NBHL equates *gamapet* with *gundapet*, "leader of a contingent," in V.xxxvii; these would be the shield-bearers of Manuēl Mamikonean's forces. The spelling of this term varies in the mss. of BP (see Venice ed., p. 246 n. 1).
>
> See NBHL, I, p. 526, *gamapet*; HArmB, I, p. 509, *gamapet*; HBB, I, p. 468; Malχasyancʿ, p. 338 n. 189; AG, p. 126, no. 128, who suggests a tentative Persian etymology; Leroy, "Composés en *-pet*," no. 5, pp. 110–111.
>
> V.xxxvii
>
> p. 220

See also *pet.*

gund ‹ Parth., Phl. *gund*, "gathering, detachment, troop"; cf. Arab. loanword from Persian, *jund*

"contingent, detachment, host"; originally, "gathering, ball, globe, sphere"

The original sense of the term is found only once in BP, in reference to the "clots" of blood that flowed from the mouth of St. Nersēs (V.xxiv). Elsewhere it is used consistently in its military sense. *Gund* usually refers to the "contingent" formed of the retainers of a particular commander or magnate, who led it in battle and to whom it was primarily loyal—see, e.g., III.vii for Sanēsan "with his own contingent" (*Sanēsan tʿagaworn Mazkʿtʿacʿ bun gndawn*); V.xxxvii, for the respective contingents of the king and the *sparapet* Manuēl Mamikonean (*gundn arkʿunakan aṙaǰi manuēlean gndin*); or even V.xliii, for the "gang" (*iwrow sepʿhakanawn gndawn hrociwn*) of the archtraitor Meružan Arcruni—rather than to the entire mass of an army, for which the term *zōrkʿ* is usually reserved. On a few occasions, however, the distinction between the two terms is blurred, or *gund* is used in a general sense, whether it be the miraculously immobilized "mob" of pagan priests at Aštišat (III.iii) or the "hosts" of angels leading the soul of St. Nersēs (V.xxv).

By the sixth century, the appearance of the signature of a bishop of the *Sepʿhakan gund* in Armenian conciliar acts (GTʿ, p. 73) suggests that this term was evolving from its military toward a territorial sense, as was the case with the Greek θέμα and the Arabian *jund*. There is no indication of this development in BP, nor is a separate *Sepʿhakan gund* recorded in the text.

 See NBHL, I, pp. 581–582; HArmB, I, pp. 593–595; HBB, I, p. 469; AG, pp. 130–131, nos. 147, 148; Schmitt, "Iranisches Lehngut," p. 90; CPD, p. 38, *gund*[l]; Adontz, *Armenia*, pp. 181, 249, 463 n. 70; Garsoïan, "*Gund.*"

 III.iii, vii, viii, xx, xxi; IV.iii, iv, xi, xviii, xx, xxii, xxiv, xxv, xxvii, xxxiii, xxxvii, xxxix, xli, xlvi–xlviii, liii; V.i, ii, iv, v, xxiv, xxv, xxxvii–xl, xliii

 pp. 68, 73–76, 96–98, 108, 116, 133, 148–151, 155, 158–159, 161, 163–164, 166, 170, 186–187, 189–191, 193–196, 204–205, 217, 219–220, 223–228

 See also *banak; gugaz; matenik gund; zōrkʿ.*

gusan ‹ Phl. *gōsān*, "minstrel, bard"; cf. Georg. *mgosani*

"bard, minstrel"

In both Armenia and Iran, the *gusan*s were not mere entertainers, but were also the transmitters of the oral epic traditions, "[one] who proclaims the worthiness of kings and heroes of old" (Boyce, "*Gōsān*," p. 11). Consequently, the *gusan*s were not invariably drawn from the lower classes, and training in the minstrel tradition was part of the education of a gentleman, even though the twelfth canon of the Fourth Council of Duin (*Kanonagirkʿ* II, p. 212) condemns *azat*s living in monasteries and polluting them with *gusan*s. They are familiar to both BP and MX, I.xxxi (= MK, p. 123), though the latter does not use the term, with the exception of I.xiv (= MK, p. 96). See Intro., pp. 30–35 for the presence of the oral "Gestes" in BP.

 See NBHL, I, p. 582; HArmB, I, pp. 597–598; HBB, I, p. 470; AG, p. 131, no. 149; Boyce, "Parthian Literature," pp. 1155–1160; *idem*, "*Gōsān*"; Grigoryan, *Gusanakan ergerə*; Christensen, *L'Iran*, pp. 373, 413; Ačaryan, "Armeniaca II," pp. 3–4.

 III.xix; V.vii, xxxii

 pp. 94, 199, 214

hall, see *tačar.*

hambarakapet/ambarakapet ‹ Phl. *hambār*, "store, warehouse" + Arm. *-pet*, "chief" "overseer-of-stores, quartermaster"
Important Iranian official. This office does not seem to have existed in contemporary Aršakuni Armenia, though the title was familiar to ŁP^c and Ełišē as well, and the word *hambar* was common.
See NBHL, II, p. 25, *hambar*; HArmB, III, pp. 23–24; HBB, I, p. 57 *ambarakapet*; Malχasyanc^c, p. 329 n. 124; AG, p. 178, 336; Harmatta-Pékáry, "Pārsīk Ostrakon," p. 470, no. 6; Schmitt, "Iranishes Lehngut," p. 91, *ambar*; CPD, p. 40, *hambār*; Christensen, *L'Iran*, pp. 215, "*Ērān ambāraghbadh*," 228 fig. 34.
IV.xlviii
p. 166
See also *pet*.

(h)anderjapet/anderjapet ‹ Parth., Phl. *handarz*, "advice, injunction, testament" + Arm. *-pet*, "chief"
Attested in ŠKZ, Parth. 27; Phl. 33; RGDS no. 64, pp. 70–71, βασιλισσῶν ἀνδαρζαβίδ.
"counselor, adviser, governor"
In Sasanian Iran, counselors were found in various estates of society, e.g. *andarzapat i wāspuhragān*, *moghān andarzpat*, and Perikhanian consideres them to have been administrators as well. The mistaken derivation from Arm. *handerj*, "clothes, clothing" has led a number of scholars (e.g. Lauer, pp. 123–124; CHAMA, I, pp. 265–266, and even Leroy) to interpret this title as "master-of-the-wardrobe", while Markwart suggested," *Meuteschalk*.
See NBHL, II, p. 41, which also suggests a mistaken *dispensator, oeconomus*; HArmB, I, pp. 188–189, *anderj*; Sprengling, *Third-Century Iran*, pp. 9,12,19; HBB, I, p. 105, *anderjapet*; Malχasyanc^c, pp. 328–329 n. 122; followed by Gevorgian's, p. 218 n. 68, with bibliography; AG, p. 72 sub no. 161, Sakastan, 98–99 no. 28, 510; CPD, p. 41, *handarz*; Gignoux, *Glossaire*, pp. 23, 52; *idem*, "Pour une Évaluation," pp. 4–6; Nyberg, *Manual*, II, p. 94; Leroy, "Composés en -*pet*," no. 13, pp. 119–121; Markwart, *Untersuchungen*, p. 216 n. 10; Perikhanian, MHD, p. 487, *(h)andarz*¹; *idem*, "*Le Lexique*," pp. 20–21; *idem, Iran*, p. 222; Christensen, *L'Iran*, pp. 99, 114, 120, 135, 411.
IV.xlv, xlvii
pp. 165–166
See also *pet*.

hark ‹ Phl. *harg*, "duty, tribute"; cf. Arab. *kharādj*
"tribute, tax"
General term for tribute or taxes, by contrast to the more specific *has, sak, baž, kōšik*, etc. BP uses the term invariably in the sense of "subject to tribute" and not of "necessity" or "office."
See NBHL, II, p. 62¹; HArmB, III, p. 60; HBB, III, 69; Schmitt, "Iranisches Lehngut," p. 91; CPD p. 43, *harg*; Perikhanian, MHD, p. 488, *hark ut bās*; Adontz, *Armenia*, pp. 363–365, 524–526 nn. 91–93, 97–101a; Manandyan, *Feodalizm*, pp. 85–89, 154–159, 166, 173, 234; *idem*, "Harkerə."
IV.iv, viii, xvii; V.viii–xix, xxxvii
pp. 108, 114, 129, 148, 200–201, 222
See also *has*; *kōšik*; *ptuł*; and Appendix V *f*.

has ‹ ?
"tax"

Form of land tax similar to the Arab. *kharādj*, according to Manandyan, but a general rather than merely a land tax, according to Avdalbegyan. *Has* is also mentioned by Ełišē among the extortionate taxes laid by the Sasanians on Armenia (ii, p. 23 = *Ełishē*, p. 77 and n. 9), where Thomson gives the translation "levies."

    See NBHL, II, p. 49; HArmB, III, pp. 46–47; HBB, III, p. 56²; Adontz, *Armenia*, pp. 363–364, 525 n. 93; Manandyan, *Feodalizm*, pp. 131–132, 140, 181, 205, 207–208, with references to his earlier articles; Avdalbegean, "Has."

    V.xxxviii

    p. 222

    See also the preceding entry.

hayr, see *mardpet.*

hayrapet/hayrapetut⁽ᶜ⁾iwn ‹ Arm. *hayr*, "father" + -*pet*, "chief"

"patriarch/patriarchal office"

    Title used for the primates of the Armenian church from the Gregorid house, but not for primates of other families, though P⁽ᶜ⁾ařēn is given this title in the dubious Book VI. He is, however, said to occupy the patriarchal throne, "*nstaw . . . yat⁽ᶜ⁾or hayrapetakan*" (III.xvi), while Šahak of Manazkert is merely said to have "succeeded to the position of the patriarchs" (*yajordeac⁽ᶜ⁾ zteł̇i hayrapetac⁽ᶜ⁾n*). In the case of Gregorid primates, the title of *hayrapet* alternates interchangeably and possibly anachronistically with those of *episkoposapet* and *k⁽ᶜ⁾ahanayapet.*

    See NBHL, II, p. 33; HArmB, III, p. 31, *hayr*; HBB, III, p. 40; Leroy, "Composés en -*pet*," nos. 19, 26, pp. 124, 126; also Intro., p. 15; P.S., nn. 6, 9.

    III.x–xii, xiv, xvi, xvii, xix; IV.iii, iv, xiii, xiv; V.i, xxii, xxv, xxix–xxxi, xliv; VI.v, vi, viii

    pp. 78, 82–83, 86–87, 89, 91–92, 94, 108, 110–112, 136–139, 185, 187, 203, 205, 210–212, 229, 235–236

    See also *episkoposapet*; *k⁽ᶜ⁾ahanayapet*; *pet*; *senior-bishop*; and Appendix I, "Grigor/Gregorids"; "P⁽ᶜ⁾ařēn"; "Šahak I."

hazarapet/hazarapetut⁽ᶜ⁾iwn ‹ Parth. *ḥzrwpt/hazāruft*; Phl. *ḥz'lwpt/hazārbad*; OP *ḥazārajpati-* = Gk. χιλίαρχος, "thousander, chiliarch"

    Title attested in ŠKZ, Parth 23, 25; Phl. 29, 31; RGDS nos. 56, 61, pp. 64–65, 68–69, ἅζαροπτ, ἀζάριπτιος(?)

"chancellor/office of chancellor" ?

    Despite the military etymology of the name and its Iranian derivation, the office of *hazarapet*, lengthily described in BP (IV.ii) but seemingly unknown to MX, seems to have differed from its Iranian functions and to have been purely civilian in its Armenian aspect. In most Scriptural passages (Luke 8:3; Mark 11:1, but not Matt. 20:8; I Cor. 4:1) it is used to translate the Greek ἐπίτροπος or οἰκονόμος, "administrator, guardian, manager." As described in BP, the *hazarapet* was entrusted with the overall supervision of the peasantry (*šinakan*), namely, with economic productivity, buildings, and perhaps the collection of taxes, as opposed to the military command of the *sparapet*; though the late *Vita* of St. Nersēs indiscriminately entitles all the Mamikonean brothers both *zōravark⁽ᶜ⁾*, "commanders" and *hazarapet*s i, p. 17 (= CHAMA, II, pp. 22–23). In Sasanian Iran, however, though the title is attested without any specification in ŠKZ, lines 23, 25, p. 9 (= trans. pp. 18–19, IV.6.b–c, "thousand-lord"), it is not associated with that of *w'slwš'n sld'*, "chief of the cultivators" found on a late Sasanian seal. In Adontz's opinion, the shift from a military to a civilian office had already taken place in early Achaemenid times, but this hypothesis is not supported by the evidence, and both Toumanoff and Lukonin still view the *hazarapetut⁽ᶜ⁾iwn* as a military command in the later period, at least in Iran.

In Aršakuni Armenia, the position of *hazarapet* first belonged to the house of Anjit (III.xii), but it passed to the Gnuni in the middle of the fourth century (IV.ii), and Koriwn, xxvi, p. 92 (= trans., p. 50) attributes it to Vahan Amatuni. In the period following the disappearance of the Armenian Aršakuni, the prestige of the title escalated, following the Sasanian pattern, so that both ŁPᶜ, xx, p. 39 and Ełišē, ii, pp. 23, 28 (= *Ełišē*, pp. 76, 82, 252) use it to translate the Iranian title of *wuzurg framādār*, "grand-vizir, prime minister." No trace of this development can, however, be observed in BP.

See NBHL, II, p. 2; HArmB, III, pp. 6–7; HBB, III, p. 9; AG, p. 174 no. 328; Gignoux, *Glossaire*, pp. 24, 54; Honigmann and Maricq, RGDS, p. 17; Schmitt, "Iranisches Lehngut," p. 89; Benveniste, *Titres et noms propres*, pp. 61–71; Leroy, "Composés en -*pet*," nos. 17, 26, pp. 123, 126; Markwart, *Untersuchungen*, pp. 227–234; also Adontz, *Armenia*, pp. 339–340, 362; Manandyan, *Feodalizm*, pp. 69–73; Sprengling, *Third-Century Iran*, pp. 9, 11–12, 18–19, "thousand lord"; Toumanoff, *Studies*, pp. 171 n. 88, 205–206 n. 234; Christensen, *L'Iran*, pp. 113–114; Widengren, *Feudalismus*, Chaumont, "*Chiliarque*"; Lukonin, "Institutions," pp. 737–738; Russell, *Hazarabād*.

III.xii; IV.ii

pp. 82, 108

See also *dehkan*; *pet*; *šinakan*; *sparapet*; *zōrawar*, Appendix I, "Amatuni, house"; "Gnuni, house"; and Appendix II, "Anjit."

hazarapetut'iwn, see *hazarapet.*

hecealk', see *zōrk'*, I.

helmet, see *zēn*, h.

hereditary, see *sephakan.*

hermit, see *mianjn.*

hermitage, see *mianjnanoc'.*

hetewak, see *zōrk'*, II.

hetiotk', see *zōrk'*, II.

high priest, see *k'ahanayapet.*

hippodrome, see *asparēz.*

holding, see *agarak*; *dastakert*; *kaluac.*

home camp, see *bun banak.*

> **village,** see *bun gahoyk'*.

honor/honorable, see *patiw.*

host, see *zōrk'*; *gund.*

house/household, see *tohm, tun.*

hramanatar/hramatar ‹ Parth., MP *framādār*, "commander, ruler, chief"
Title attested in ŠKZ, Parth 26, 28, Phl. 32, 34; RGDS nos. 62, 66, pp. 68–69, 72–73, ἐπίτροπος.
"lawgiver, director"

One who issues orders or decrees. In one ms. BP gives the earlier form *hramatar* (see Venice ed., p. 47 n. 1). See also III.xiii and n. 24 for the unusual use of this title in a religious context.

> See NBHL, II, pp. 132–133; HArmB, III, p. 131; Honigmann and Maricq, RGDS, pp. 17–18; HBB, III, p. 145; Gignoux, *Glossaire*, pp. 32, 60; AG, pp. 183–184, no. 354; Sprengling, *Third-Century Iran*, pp. 9, 12, 19; Schmitt, "Iranisches Lehngut," p. 89; CPD, p. 32, *framādār*; Perikhanian, MHD, p. 475, *framān*[1].
> III.xiii, xiv
> p. 86

hramatar, see *hramanatar.*

hraparak ‹ Parth. **frapādak*, "public square, front yard"
"public, public square, open space before a palace"
The term is normally used in BP to designate a public square, royal or other, but it also appears in its original sense of "open/openly, publicly" in IV.xvi.
> See NBHL, II, p. 136; HArmB, III, p. 132–133; HBB, III, p. 147; Leroy, "Emprunts," p. 56 no. 6; Adontz, *Armenia*, pp. 296–298.
> III.xxi; IV.xii, xiv–xvi, lv, lvi; V.vi, xxiv
> pp. 99, 134, 139, 142 (royal-square), 146, 176–177, 197, 204

hrovartak ‹ Parth., MP *frawardag*, "letter, document"
"official letter, letter-patent"
Official document used to accredit an envoy or to send official orders. Cf. ŁP[c], xcix, p. 178 (= CHAMA, II, p. 365), where the term is translated *decret.*
> See NBHL, ii, p. 143; HArmB, III, p. 137, which defines the term as *ark[c]uni hramanagir*, "royal decree"; HBB, III, p. 153; AG, p. 184, no. 359; Schmitt, "Iranisches Lehngut," p. 89; CPD, p. 33, *frawardag*; Perikhanian, MHD, p. 476, *fravartak.*
> III.xvi, xx, xxi; IV.iv, xi, xviii, lii; V.iii, vii, xxxviii, xliv
> pp. 91, 95, 98–99, 111, 133, 148, 169, 188, 199, 221, 229

idol worship, see *k̇rapaštut[c]iwn.*

imperial, see *kaysr.*

inaccessible/impregnable, see *amur.*

infantry, see *zōrk[c]*, II.

irregular levies, see *gugaz.*

išχan ‹ Ir. **χšāna-*; cf. Sogd. *'yšwn/aχšāwan*, "king"
"prince, ruler, official"
This title is normally used interchangeably with *tēr*, "lord" or *naχarar* in BP. In the case of Persians (III.xx) or Romans (V.xxxii, xxxiv) it also takes on the sense of "official."
> See NBHL, I, p. 864; HArmB, II, p. 246; HBB, II, p. 167; Schmitt, "Iranisches Lehngut," p. 89; Benveniste, "Titres," pp. 7–9; Greppin, "*Išχan*"; A. Š. Hovhannisyan, "Iranakan," who proposes a dubious Urartian etymology.
> III.iv, vi, viii–xvii, xx, xxi; IV.iii–v, ix, xi, xii, xx, l. lv, lviii; V.iv, vii, xxx, xxxii–xxxiv, xxxvii
> pp. 69, 72, 75–78, 81–83, 85, 87, 90, 92, 95–97, 99, 108, 111, 123, 130, 132, 135, 151, 153, 167, 173, 178, 189, 198, 210, 213–215, 218
> See also *gorcakal*; *naχarar*; *tēr.*

išχanutʿiwn/išχanakan (see etymology of the preceding entry)
"principality, princely, authority, dominion, jurisdiction"
Term used more commonly in BP to denote authority or, interchangeably with *tērutʿiwn*, "dominion," than in its basic sense of "principality."
See NBHL, I, pp. 865–866; HBB, II, p. 168; Adontz, *Armenia*, p. 339; and the bibliography of the preceding entry.
III.ix, xii, xiv, xv, xxi; IV.ii, iv–vi, viii, ix, xii, xiv, xvii, xx, xxiv, l. li, lvii, lviii; V.iii, v, vii, xxi, xxix, xxxi, xxxiii, xxxvii, xxxviii, xliv
pp. 77, 82–83, 86–87, 91, 99, 108, 114, 117, 119, 123–124, 127–130, 134–135, 139, 148, 150, 167–169, 177–178, 188, 195, 197–198, 202, 210–211, 214, 218, 221–222, 229
See also *tērutʿiwn*; and the preceding entry.

jatagov ⟨ Phl. *jādag-go(w)*, "advocate, intercessor"
"defender, advocate, protector, accuser"
Term usually appearing in a religious context, e.g., "defender of of the faith, defender of the truth." Its rarer opposing sense of "accuser" is not found in BP. The combined title of "defender of the destitute" (*jatagov . . . zrkelocʿ*; IV.iii), a precise calque of the Iranian title, *driyōšan jadag-go(w)*, is a *hapax* in Armenian literature. See also IV.iii n. 12.
See NBHL, II, pp. 670–671; HArmB, IV, p. 124; HBB, IV, p. 136; Leroy, "Emprunts," p. 55; CPD, pp. 46, *jadag-go(w)*, 27, *driyōs*; cf. Bailey, "Indo-Iranian," pp. 16–17; Perikhanian, MHD, pp. 466–467, *driyōšan yātakagōβīh*, 550, *yātakgoβ*; Garsoïan, "Protecteur des pauvres," with additional bibliography.
IV.iii, viii
pp. 109, 128

javelin, see *zēn*, l.

judge, see *datawor*.

kʿahanayapet ⟨ Syr. *kāhnā*; Aram. *kāhanā*; Hebr. *kōhēn*, "priest + Arm. *-pet*, "chief"
"chief-priest"
Hybrid title commonly used for the primates of Armenia from the Gregorid house interchangeably with *hayrapet* and *episkoposapet*, as well as for the high priest of the Jews (IV.lv). It is, however, not used for non-Gregorid primates, with the possible exception of V.xliv, where the reference is ambiguous.
See NBHL, II, p. 968; HArmB, IV, pp. 539–540, *kʿahanay* HBB, IV, p. 535; Leroy, "Composés en *-pet*," nos. 23, 26, pp. 125–126; AG, pp. 229–230, no. 538, p. 318 no. 120. See also, Intro., p. 15 and P.S., nn. 6, 9.
P.S.; III.iii, v, vi, viii, x–xiii, xv, xx (*mec kʿahanaykʿ*); IV.iii, vii, xi, xv, lv, lvii; V.i, iv, xxiv, xxvii, xxxi, xliv; VI.xvi
pp. 63, 68, 70, 73, 76, 79, 81, 84–86, 91, 95, 109, 126, 133, 142–143, 176–177, 186, 190–191, 203–204, 206, 212, 229, 239
See also *episkoposapet*; *hayrapet*; *katʿołikos*; *pet*; *senior-bishop*; and Appendix I, "Grigor/Gregorids."

kʿaj/kʿajutʿiwn ⟨ ?
"brave, valiant, valorous, valor, very"
This term is occasionally used merely for intensification with the sense of "very, mighty, powerful," as in III.xx; V.xxxv, *kʿaj arbeal*; IV.xli, *kʿaj mtaw acēkʿ*; etc., or for Christ (V.xx, *howiv kʿaj*), or the saints (III.iii, xii) who are God's champions. The most common usage in BP, however, is to denote the supernatural valor that is one of the

main characteristics distinguishing the legitimate ruler of Iran in the Zoroastrian tradition. This quality was bestowed on them by the god Vərəθraγna (Arm. Vahagn), who was himself "created victorious" (*pērōzgar*), as is explicitly stated by Aa, cxxvii "*kʿaǰutʿiwn hascʿē jez i kʿaǰēn Vahagnē* (may valor come to you from valorous Vahagn)." This heroic epithet also became part of the Sasanian royal title, according to MX.xvii, xxvi, li (= MK, pp. 271, 282, 317), "*Mazdecʿacʿn kʿaǰ Šapuh arkʿayic ʿarkay* (most valorous of the Mazdeans, Šapuh king of kings)." BP normally reserves this title for the hereditary ruling dynasty of the Aršakuni in Greater Armenia (e.g. V.v, "*aṙ Aršak kʿaǰ*"), thus showing that he was still acquainted with its transcendental implications, as does his transfer of the epithet to the Mamikonean family (IV.ii, *kʿaǰasirtkʿ, kʿaǰanunkʿ*) and especially to his hero Mušeł (V.ii, iv, etc.), as part of his apotheosis of the Mamikonean and possibly because of their traditional claim of royal descent (V.iv, xxxvii). Aside from these two families, this epithet is attributed to only two nobles, Vahan Amatuni (III.viii) and especially Aršak II's faithful retainer Drastamat (V.vii); as well as on occasion to the nobles in general, presumably because their loyalty made them share in the valor of their king (III.vii, viii, "*arancʿ kʿaǰacʿn or vastakecʿin nma* (to the valiant men who had toiled for him [King Xosrov]," IV.xxiii); and on one occasion (III.xx) to King Tiran's favorite horse, in order to underscore his supernatural qualities.

See NBHL, II, p. 981; HArmB, IV, pp. 554–555; HBB, IV, pp. 550, *kʿaǰ*, 554, *kʿaǰutʿiwn*; Bailey, *Problems*, p. xvii; Szemerényi, "Iranica, V"; Garsoïan, "Locus," pp. 41–45, 50–53, 64; *idem*, "Substratum," pp. 156–160 *et passim*; Intro. p. 54, and III.iii n. 8.

P.S.; III.iii, vi–viii, x–xii, xx; IV.ii, vi, x, xii, xv, xvi, xx, xxii–xxiv, xxvii, li; V.ii, iv–vii, xx, xxviii, xxxiv–xxxvii, xliv; VI.xiv

pp. 63, 68, 73–76, 78, 81, 83, 94, 96, 107–108, 126, 131, 136, 145, 147, 151, 155–156, 158, 160, 168, 188, 190–191, 194–195, 197–198, 201–202, 209, 215–218, 228–230, 238

See also Appendix I, "Aršakuni"; "Drastamat"; "Mamikonean, house"; "Mušeł"; "Vahagn"; "Vahan Amatuni"; and the next entry.

kʿaǰ arancʿ/arancʿ kʿaǰ ‹ Arm. *kʿaǰ* + *ayr*, "man"

"most-valiant-of-men"

Transcendental epithet normally reserved for the legitimate ruler of Iran (V.iv; cf. MX, III.xlii = MK, p. 305, *Diwcʿazancʿ kʿaǰ*, "most-valiant-of-heroes") and the royal Aršakuni house of Armenia (III.xi, IV.xxiv, etc.; cf. Aa, xvii, dcccxcii). This epithet may also have been transferred to the Mamikonean as part of their apotheosis, though the precise formula is never used (V.xxxvii, *ayr kʿaǰ*; IV.ii, *azgin kʿaǰacʿn Mamikonenicʿ*).

See the bibliography of the preceding entry.

III.xi; IV.xxiv; V.iv

pp. 81, 157, 189

See also the preceding entry; and Appendix I, "Aršakuni."

kʿałakʿ ‹ ?Syr. *karkha*, "city"; cf. Georg. *kʿalakʿi*

"walled enclosure, city"

In its developed sense of "city," this term is used by BP almost exclusively for urban centers outside the borders of Armenia, such as Caesarea of Cappadocia (III.xvii; IV.iii, etc.), Athens (III.xiii), Nisibis and Amida (III.x; IV.xx), Edessa (V.xxxii), Ctesiphon (IV.xvi, liv), etc. In Armenia it is reserved for the two capitals—Artašat (III.xii; IV.lv) and Tigranakert (IV.xxiv; V,xxvii)—as well as for Aršak II's ill-fated foundation of Aršakawan (IV.xii–xiiii); for the holy city of Vałaršapat (III.viii; IV.lv), though in this case the use of the term may have been influenced by the city's classical name, Καινὴ πόλις, "new city," and for Armenia's Hellenistic foundations destroyed by the Persians ca. 364 (IV.lv). In its basic sense, the term is found applied to Ałiorsk‛ (III.xx, *tełwoyn orum anun koč‛i k‛ałak‛ Ałiorsk‛*, "at the place called the enclosure of Ałiorsk‛"), which was clearly a walled hunting preserve and not a "city." This sparing use of the term within the confines of Greater Armenia and its broad distribution outside the borders suggest the scarcity of urban foundations within the Aršakuni realm after the Hellenistic period.

See NBHL, II, p. 969; HArmB, IV, pp. 542–544; HBB, IV, pp. 535–536; AG, p. 318, no. 121; B. N. Aŕakelyan, "K‛ałak‛neri bnakč‛ut‛yunǝ"; *idem,* "K‛ałak‛neri varč‛ut‛yunǝ"; V. M.,Haroutiounian, "Urbanisme"; Eremian, "Razvitie"; Pigulevskaia, "Gorod"; *idem, Villes*; Sarkisian, "Iz istorii"; Garsoïan, "Mediaeval Armenian City."

III.vii, viii, x, xii, xiii, xvii, xx, xxi; IV.iii, v–xiv, xvi, xx, xxi, xxiv, liv–lvi, lviii, lix; V.iv, v, vii, xiv, xxvii, xxix, xxxii, xxxiv, xxxv, xxxvii, xliii

pp. 74–75, 77–78, 80, 82, 84, 92, 96, 98, 109, 123–124, 127–133, 135–137, 140, 147, 150, 154, 157, 170, 175–176, 178–179, 190, 195, 197, 200, 207, 210, 213, 215–217, 220, 225

See also *gewłak‛ałak‛*; and Appendix II, "Ałiorsk‛"; (a) "Amid"; "Ankyra"; "Athens"; "Bałχ"; "Caesarea"; "Mcbin"; "P‛aytakaran?"; "Satał"; "Tispon"; "Uŕhay," for foreign cities; (b) "Artašat"; "Eruandašat"; "Mcurk‛"; "Naχčawan"; "Vałaršapat"; "Van"; "Zarehawan"; "Zarišat," for Armenia's destroyed Hellenistic foundations.

k‛ałak‛agewł, see *gewłak‛ałak‛.*

kaluac

"possession, holding, domain"

General term for the possession, presumably hereditary, of a domain or holding.

See NBHL, I, p. 1033[1]; HBB, II, pp. 365–366; Adontz, *Armenia,* p. 362; Manandyan, *Feodalizm,* pp. 27, 198–201, 204.

III.ii

p. 67

See also *agarak; dastakert; ostan; sephakan.*

kaparčk‛, see *zēn,* j.

karawan/karewan ‹ Phl. *kārāwan,* "caravan, military column"

"military column, army, crowd, people"

This term always carries the military connotation of an army drawn up or on the march, rather than the economic one of traveling merchants in BP. It is used in the same fashion by Ełišē, ii, p. 18 (=*Ełishē,* p. 72 and n. 1, etc.) and by MX, III.1 (= MK, p. 315).

See NBHL, I, pp. 1065, *karawan,* 1068, *karewan*; HArmB, II, p. 547; HBB, II, p. 492[3]; Malχasyanc‛, p. 328 n. 116; AG, p. 167, no. 307; CPD, p. 49; OP, p. 179; Gignoux, *Glossaire,* pp. 25, 55.

III.xxi; IV.xxv; V.ii

pp. 98, 159, 187

karčazat, perhaps the same as *harčazat* ‹ ?*harč,* "concubine + MIr. *zād,* "born"

"born of a concubine"(?)

Hapax omitted from most major dictionaries. Malχasyanc‛, the only one to attempt an explanation, proposes its equation with the inferior stratum of the nobility (*storin kargi aznuakan*), who were still endowed with minor property such as villages. But it might equally be possible that *karčazat,* considering the context and the similarity of *k* and *h* in Armenian script, should be taken as *harčazat,* and translated as "son of a concubine, of concubine class." This interpretation seems more likely since the sources do not indicate stratifications within the *azat* class. No conclusion is possible at this point, however.

Neither NBHL nor HArmB lists this term. See HBB, II, p. 409; Malχasyanc^c, p. 318 n. 45; CPD, p. 97, *zādag, zādan, zāy*; Manandyan, *Feodalizm*, p. 17, 118–119; *Knnakan tesut^ciwn* II/1, p. 248.

III.xix

p. 94

See also *azat*.

karewan, see *karawan*.

kat^colikē ‹ Gk. καθολική

"catholic, main or cathedral church"

Either meaning is possible in context, especially in IV.iv.

See NBHL, I, p. 1032; HArmB, II, pp. 481–482; HBB, II, p. 363; AG, p. 353, no. 165.

III.xiv; IV.iv

pp. 87, 114

kat^colikos/kat^colikosut^ciwn ‹ Gk. καθολικός

Title anachronistically used on occasion to designate the primates of the Armenian church, as well as those of Iberia and Caspian Albania (III.vi) and St. Basil of Caesarea (IV.ix). This anachronism likewise occurs in the version of Aa, dccciv, dccclxii that has come down to us, but as in the case of BP, its appearance in the text reflects a usage postdating the middle of the fifth century, as was noted by Garitte. The traditional titles of the primates in the fourth century normally used by BP were *episkoposapet*, perhaps *hayrapet*, and *k^cahanayapet*.

See NBHL, I, p. 1032; HArmB, II, p. 482; HBB, II, p. 363; AG, p. 353, no. 166; Garitte, *Narratio*, pp. 56–57, 155, 207; KWCO, pp. 162–164.

III.vi, x, xii, xvi, xvii; IV.iv, v, vii, ix, xiii–xv; V.i, xxix

pp. 72, 79, 82, 91–92, 111, 116, 126, 130, 136–137, 139, 142, 145–146, 210

See also *episkoposapet*; *hayrapet*; *k^cahanayapet*; Appendix I, "Barseł"; "Grigor Lusaworič^c"; "Grigoris"; "Nersēs I"; "P^caṙēn"; "Šahak I"; "Yusik I"; and Appendix II, "Ałuank^c"; "Virk^c."

kat^colikosac^c kat^colikos ‹ Gk. καθολικός

"*kat^colikos* of *kat^colikoi*"

Title anachronistically and incorrectly attributed by BP to the bishop of Caesarea in the mid-fourth century.

See bibliography of the preceding entry.

IV.iv

p. 111

See also Appendix I, "Eusebios"; and the preceding entry.

kat^colikosut^ciwn, see *kat^colikos*.

kaysr/kayserakan ‹ Gk. καῖσαρ; Lat. *caesar*

"emperor, imperial"

Title also attested in ŠKZ, Parth 3, 4, 9, 11; Phl. 14; RGDS no. 6, 7, 9, 10, 20, pp. 48–53.

Correct title for the emperor of the Romans in the fourth century, but BP constantly alternates it with the unofficial "king of the Greeks" (*t^cagaworn Yunac^c*; e.g. III.xxi;

IV.i, vi, *et passim*), which would have run counter to Byzantine usage and been altogether unacceptable to the imperial chancellery.

See NBHL, I, p. 1046; HArmB, II, p. 509; Sprengling, *Third-Century Iran*, pp. 7, 8, 10, 15, 16; HBB, II, p. 379; AG, p. 354, no. 171; GLRB, II, pp. 616–617; Gignoux, *Glossaire*, pp. 26, 56; Honigmann and Maricq, RGDS, pp. 12, 14.

III.xx, xxi; IV.i, v, vii, viii, x, xi, xiii, xv, xvi, xx, lv; V.i, xxxiv

pp. 95, 98–99, 107, 116, 121–122, 127–129, 132–133, 136, 145, 147, 149, 174, 185, 215

kayserakan, see *kaysr.*

keeper/warden

-of-the-border, see *sahmanakal.*

-of-a-district, see *gawaṙakal.*

-of-a-fortress, see *berdakal.*

-of-a-realm/country, see *ašχarhakal.*

-of-a-region, see *koḷmakal; kusakal.*

kinsman, see *azgakicʿ; eḷbayr.*

koḷmakal ‹ Arm. *koḷmn*, "region, side" + *kal* (aor. stem of *unim*), "have, hold"
"keeper- or governor-of-a-region"

Thomson (MK, pp. 139–140 = MX, II.viii) translates this title as "governor" or "military governor," but it is evident from the context that the area of authority entrusted to these officials lay along the border of the Armenian kingdom, as is also suggested by the word itself. The distinction between the *koḷmakal* and the *kusakal* is not altogether clear, but both BP and Aa, dccxcvi, list them separately.

See NBHL, I, p. 1112; HArmB, II, p. 622, *koḷmn*; HBB, II, p. 461.

IV.li

p. 168

See also *kusakal*; and the next entry.

koḷmn
"region, portion, side"

Term used either in a general sense, or to designate a major area lying on the border of the Armenian kingdom, e.g. Tarōn (IV.iv), Basean (IV.xxiv), Aḷjnikʿ (IV.l), etc., even Cappadocia (IV.xi), Aḷuankʿ and Virkʿ (III.vi). It is clearly superior to a simple "district" (*gawaṙ*; see, e.g., IV.iv; V.xxiii). Aa, dccclxxiii, uses this term for the Marches of Armenia governed by the *bdeašχs*.

See NBHL, I, p. 1112; HArmB, II, pp. 621–622; HBB, II, p. 461, *koḷm.*

III.v–vii, xiv, xix, xx, xxi; IV.iv–vi, viii, xi–xiii, xxii–xxiv, xxvi, xxviii, xlv, l, liv, lv, lix; V.iv, v, vii, viii, xi, xv, xxix, xxxi, xli; VI.i

pp. 70, 72, 74, 86, 97–98, 113, 120, 124, 127, 129 (party), 133–134, 136, 155–157, 159, 165–167, 172, 176, 179, 191, 194, 197–201, 210–212, 224, 234

See also *bdeašχ; gawaṙ*; and Appendix II, "Aḷjnikʿ"; "Aḷuankʿ"; "Basean"; "Copʿkʿ"; "Gamirkʿ"; "Tarōn"; "Virkʿ."

kōmopolis, see *gewḷakʿaḷakʿ.*

koms ‹ Gk. κόμης ‹ Lat. *comes*, "count"
"count"

Late Roman title for various high officials. It was also given to the governor of imperial Armenia after the end of the Aršakuni dynasty in the western portion of the

538

country, a title still remembered by Procopius (*De aed.*, III.i.14–15), and maintained for Armenia III after the reform of Justinian (*Novella*, XXXI.i, iii). These developments obviously postdate the span of BP's narrative, in which the title of "count" is used exclusively for Adē (V.i) and not for Terentius (V.i, iv–vi, xxxii; also MX, III.xxxvi–xxxvii, xxxix = MK, pp. 295-296, 300-301), although St. Basil invariably uses the title in his *Letters* to the latter (*Ep.*, xcix, cv, ccxix), and not to the former (*Ep.*, cxlviii–cxlix to Trajan).

> See NBHL, I, p. 1114; HArmB, II, p. 628; HBB, II, p. 406; AG, p. 359, no. 215; GLRB, II, p. 677. On the imperial counts in Armenia, see Adontz, *Armenia*, pp. 93–101, 106–108, 133, 139, 35*–37*; Toumanoff, *Studies*, pp. 133–134, cf. 152, 193–195 nn. 208, 213; Jones, LRE, I, pp. 229 and n. 26, 271. On Terentius and Trajan/Adē, see Garsoïan, "Politique," pp. 313–320.
>
> V.i
> p. 185
> See also Appendix I, "Adē"; "Terēnt."

kᶜorepiskopos ‹ Gk. χορεπίσκοπος
"*chorepiskopos*, rural bishop"
The entire system of Armenian bishops, who were clan rather than urban representatives, effectively blurs the traditional early Christian hierarchical distinction between the "bishop" of a *polis* or *civitas* and the rural *chorepiskopoi* (cf., however, Vg, clxxii, but not Va, clx), although the distinction of titles was always maintained (cf. *Kanonagirkᶜ*, index, s.v.v.). BP uses this title even for a great hierarch such as St. Daniēl.

> See NBHL, II, p. 1011; HArmB, IV, p. 589; HBB, IV, p. 585; AG, p. 338, no. 506. On the office of the *chorepiskopoi* in general and in Armenia, see Lampe, *Lexicon*, s.v.; Jedin, *Church History*, I, p. 353; II, p. 233; Garitte, *Documents*, p. 104; *Kanonagirkᶜ*, I, pp. 105, 111–112, 187, 210–212, 369–370, 372, 403; II, pp. 7, 16, 91; KWCO, p. 88.
>
> III,xiv
> pp. 86–88, 90
> See also Appendix I, "Daniēl."

kōšik ‹ ?
"salary, reward? stipend?"
Neither the origin of this term nor its precise meaning is known. As observed by Malχasyancᶜ, its sense in VI.viii is clearly "reward, salary," but in V.xxxviii, where this meaning is unsuitable, he suggests the equivalence with *roċik*, "stipend" (V.xxxviii n. 6).

> The term is not found in NBHL. See HArmB, II, p. 687, *kōšik²*; HBB, II, p. 511, *košik²*.
>
> V.xxxviii; VI.viii
> pp. 222, 236
> See also *roċik*.

kṙapaštutᶜiwn ‹ Arm. *kṙem*, "make an image" + *paštem* ‹ Phl. *parist*, "serve, worship"
"idolatry, idol-worship"
General term for pagan practices in pre-Christian Armenia, but the etymology implies that the precise reference should be to idolatry.

> See NBHL, I, p. 1127; HBB, II, p. 490; CPD, p. 65, *paristīdan*.
>
> III.iii, xiv; IV.v
> pp. 68, 88, 119
> See also *bagin*; *kᶜurm*.

kᶜurm ‹ Syr. *kumrā*, "priest"
"pagan priest"

Term reserved exclusively for the pagan, as opposed to the Christian, priesthood in sources dealing with early Armenia (see, e.g., Aa, dcclxxxi, dcccxiii, dcccxl, etc.; MX, II.viii = MK, p. 142; the *History of Tarōn*, pp. 79–80, 87–90, 94, 105–106, etc). As in the case of *kṛaspaštutʻiwn*, however, the etymology of the term and particularly the specific link between the *kʻurm* and the *mehean* in MX imply that these were priests connected with idolatrous cults. They seem to have formed a separate hereditary caste like the Magians.

    See NBHL, II, p. 1013; HArmB, IV, p. 596; HBB, IV, p. 588; AG, p. 320, no. 130; Perikhanian, *Khramovye obedieniia*; Chaumont, "Conquêtes sassanides," p. 700, who distinguishes them from fire priests.

    III.iii

    p. 69

    See also *bagin*; *mehean*; and the preceding entry.

kusakal ‹ Arm. *koys* ‹ Phl. *kust*, "region" + *kal* (aor. stem of *unim*), "have, hold"; cf. Phl. *kustag bed*, "district commander"

    "keeper-, governor-, or prefect-of-a-region, *topokrator*"

    Term seemingly interchangeable with *kołmakal*, but the two are listed separately in IV.li and Aa, dccxcv–dccxcvi. Possibly the *kusakal*s were governors of interior regions while the *kołmnakal*s had authority along the borders, but this would run counter to the derivation from Arm. *koys*, "side" and Phl. *kustak*, "border, province," according to Perikhanian. No distinction is explicitly made in the text.

    See NBHL, I, p. 1123; HArmB, II, p. 630, *kóys*; HBB, II, 484; CPD, p. 52, *kust¹*, *kustag bed*; Perikhanian, MHD, p. 496, *kustak*.

    III.xxi; IV.li

    pp. 97, 168

    See also *kołmakal*.

kusastan ‹ Arm. *koys*, "virgin, maiden" + the suffix of place, *-(a)stan*

    "female-monastery/convent(?), dwelling-place-of-consecrated-virgins"

    This term, which occurs only on one occasion in BP (V.xxxl), has invariably been interpreted as referring to female monasteries or convents. Nevertheless, both the context in BP and the absence of any hard evidence for the existence of truly coenobial communities in Armenia during the fourth century suggest that this interpretation is anachronistically derived from the later development of all "monastic" terminology in Armenian. Consequently, the *kusastan*s may well have been dwelling places for consecrated virgins, rather than any form of organized female monasticism, which cannot be securely dated before the sixth century even in Syria, according to Fiey. See V.xxxi nn. 2–5, and cf. IV.iv, n. 19; V.xxvii n. 4; and VI.xvi n. 3; Aa, cxxxviii.

    See Murray, *Symbols*, pp. 14–16; Vööbus, *Asceticism*, I, pp. 197–208; Fiey, "Céno-bitisme;" Jargy, "Pacte"; Nedungatt, "Covenanters"; Garsoïan, "Nersēs le Grand," pp. 160–161, where I was, however, still unduly influenced by the "monastic" interpretation.

    V.xxxi

    p. 211

    See also *anapatawor*; *mianjn*; *van(kʻ)*.

lady, see *tikin*.

łakiš/lakiš ‹ ?Phl. *laškar*, "army" with metastasis

    "fortified-camp"

    Army post or fortified camp protected by ditches, earthworks, etc. (See Ełišē, iv, p. 96 = *Elishē*, p. 149; Sebēos, xlii, p. 136 = trans. p. 97) for the description of the fortification of one such camp, though Sebēos uses the term *banak* throughout.) In BP also, the term *łakiš* is interchangeable with *banak*, "camp" on several occasions (e.g. IV.xliii, xlviii).

> See NBHL, I, p. 877, *lakiš* and II, p. 162, *łakiš*, the preferred spelling; HArmB, II, p. 261; HBB, III, p. 183; Malχasyancᶜ, p. 328 n. 118; AG, p. 157, no. 264, *laškᶜar*; CPD, p. 52, *laškar*.
> IV.xxxvi, xliii, xlviii, lv; V.xli
> pp. 162, 164, 166, 174, 224
> See also *banak*.

lance, see *zēn*, a.

lancer, see *zōrk*, I.d, II.a.

land, see *erkir*.

lawgiver, see *hramanatar*.

leader/leadership, see *aṙajnord*.

leaṙnakan, see *anapatawor*.

legēon/legēovn ‹ Gk. λεγεών; Lat. *legio*
"legion"
Basic Roman army unit composed of ten cohorts of heavily armed infantry and some 300 cavalry auxiliaries, thus totaling between 4,200 and 6,000 men. According to Bolognesi, the Armenian form shows that the Latin term came into Armenian by way of Greek. This would be the expected pattern, but the essentially infantry character of the formation is still clear (V.v).

> See NHBL, I, pp. 881–882; HArmB, II, p. 271, *legēovn*; HBB, II, p. 190; Bolognesi, "Tradizione culturale," p. 603; OCD, pp. 492–493.
> V.v, xxxii
> pp. 195, 213–214

legēovn, see *legēon*.

letter-patent, see *hrovartak*.

lodging, see *van(kᶜ)*.

lord, see *tēr*.

  -of-a-district, see *gawaṙatēr*.

  -of-a-realm, see *ašχarhatēr*.

lordship, see *tērutᶜiwn*.

magistrianos Gk. μαγιστριανός, μάγιστρος
"senior official, courier, escort"
Title used for a number of officials of the Roman empire in this period, but its use in Syriac to designate "couriers" or "escort" is the one most suitable for the context in BP.

> See NHBL, II, p. 188; HArmB, III, p. 220, *magistros*; HBB, III, p. 230; AG, p. 362, no. 246; Payne Smith, *Dictionary*, I, p. v; DuCange, *Glossarium*, I, p. v; Peeters, "SS Serge et Théodore," p. 70 n. 5.
> IV.x

pp. 131–132

magnate, see *mecamec*.

mail-clad, see *zēn*.

maintenance, see *ročik*.

małχaz ‹ ?Assyr. *malχazu*; cf. ?Arab. *malik*, "king"
"king, prince, lord"
Hereditary title of the Xoṙχoṙuni house and presumably of tribal origin, according to Adontz. The precise character of the office, beyond general "leadership," is not known or specified in BP, though MX, II,vii (= MK, p. 137) identifies it as that of the "commander of the royal bodyguard," a definition accepted by Ačaryan. Neither this specific office nor the existence of such a guard in Armenia is attested in other sources, though the house of the Małaχaz-uni, presumably the Xoṙχoṙuni, is generally familiar, e.g. Aa, dccxcv, dccclxxiii. Nevertheless, ŁPᶜ, xxii (= *Ełishē*, p. 258), turns Vriv Małχaz into a Mamikonean and the *sparapet* of Armenia.
> See NHBL, II, p. 199, *małχazutʿiwn*; HArmB, III, p. 239, *tʿagawori pahapanneri głχawor*; HBB, III, p. 244; and on the office itself, Adontz, *Armenia*, pp. 311–312, 318, 321–322, 70*, 72*–76*; Manandyan, *Feodalizm*, pp. 67–69; Toumanoff, *Studies*, pp. 208–209; Perikhanian, *Iran*, pp. 68–69.
> III.xii; IV.xi; V.xxxviii, xliii
> pp. 82, 133, 221, 227–228
> See also *sparapet*; and Appendix I, "Garǰoyl"; "Xoṙχoṙuni, house."

mardpet/hayr-mardpet/mardpetutʿiwn ‹ Arm. *Mard.* + *-pet*, "chief" ‹ SW Ir. *mardpet* ‹ NWIr. *marzpet* ‹ "*keeping, wardening*"; ‹ Arm. *hayr*, "father"; the etymology of this title and its possible link to that of *marzpan* are still debated
"grand chamberlain"?
Seemingly a double title held by one of the chief officials of the Aršakuni court in the fourth century. The two parts were originally separate, according to Toumanoff:
(a) *Hayr* or *hayr tʿagawori*, "father of the king" (V.vi) was the title of the grand chamberlain, who had been a eunuch and had the supervision of the royal household, treasures, and wardrobe, as is stated in the epilogue of the *Zornamak*, "Military List." The title "eunuch" is attested in ŠKZ, Parth. 28–29; Phl. 34; RGDS no. 66–67, pp. 72–73, εὐνοῦχος.
(b) *mardpet* was originally a tribal title like *małχaz*, meaning "commander, chief of the Mards" (cf. Pliny the Elder, NH, VI.v.2), though Lukonin suggests a derivation from MIr. *mart*, "battle, war." The dynasty holding this title (obviously not eunuchs, as Toumanoff pointed out) was known to Aa, dccxcv, "*išχann mardpetutʿean išχanutʿeann*," and ruled over the homonymous district of Mardastan or Mardpetakan, later Vaspurakan, east of Lake Van, which is recorded in the *Ašχ.* (32/43). This principality presumably became the appanage of the *hayr* or grand chamberlain, who thereby gained the second title (cf., however, IV.xiv n. 6).
In the fourth century, the *hayr-mardpet* was not a dynast or invariably a eunuch (IV.xiv n. 5) but a royal official who supervised and controlled all the royal fortresses, and the treasure they contained, so that Harutʿyunyan even suggests an equivalence with the Greek office of γαζοφύλαξ, "treasurer," though Gignoux has recently re-identified it as a military title. In the fifth century, the title and appanage of the *mardpet*, but not the title of *hayr*, seem to have passed to the Arcruni house and were subsumed under their name. The title of *mardpet* is still used by ŁPᶜ in conjunction with the name Arcruni, xxxiv, xxxix, pp. 64, 71 (= *Ełishē*, pp. 278, 286), though Thomson separated

the two in his translation; but Ełišē, v, p. 116 (= *Ełishē*, p. 168) merely speaks of "prince Arcruni" in the parallel passage.

See NHBL, II, p. 224; HArmB, III, pp. 280–281; HBB, III, p. 227; Sprengling, *Third-Century Iran*, pp. 9, 12, 19; Bailey, "Armeno-Indoiranica," pp. 108–117; Gignoux, *Glossaire*, pp. 34, 64; *idem*, "Pour une évaluation," pp. 8–9; Honigmann and Maricq, RGDS, p. 18. The analysis of Toumanoff, *Studies*, pp. 131, 168–170 and nn. 71, 81–86, 176–179 and nn. 115–121, 200, 220, 237 n. 305, 248, 314, has now replaced most earlier studies; but see also Harmatta-Pékáry, "Pārsīk Ostracon," p. 473, no. 23; Ē. L. Danielyan, "Marderi cʿełə"; Vardanyan, "*Marderə*"; Manandyan, *Feodalizm*, pp. 63–671 Perikhanian, *Iran*, p. 313 nn. 49, 51; B. H. Harutʿyunyan, "Mardpetakan"; Adontz, *Armenia*, pp. 195, 315, 322–323, 341, 492 nn. 54–57, 513–514 n. 43, 69*, 135*, etc., on the tribal basis of the *mardpetutʿiwn* and the "Military List"; AON, pp. 343–344, 351 and Eremyan, *Ašχarh.*, p. 65 and map G/6, on Mardastan; Garitte, *Documents*, p. 224, on the bishops sent by St. Gregory to the region, who are not mentioned in Aa but are listed in Vg and Va. See Borisov and Lukonin, *Gemmy*, pp. 48 no. 1, 74 no. 1, fig. 1, for the representation of a Sasanian *mardpet*; Lukonin, "Ametist," pp. 382–383; also Chaumont, "Institutions," II; and Intro., pp. 15, 47 and n. 66 for BP's antagonism to the *mardpets*.

III.xvii, xviii; IV.iv, xiv, lv; V.iii, vi, vii, xxiv, xxxiii

pp. 92–93, 111, 139–140, 174, 188–189, 196–198, 204–205, 214

See also *gorcakal*; *pet*; *senekapet*; and Appendix I, "Arcruni"; "Głak"; "Drastamat."

magnate, see *mecamec*.

margarēanocʿ, see *martyrium*.

martyrium/aṙakelaran/margarearan/margarēanocʿ/vkayanocʿ
"shrine" (1) "of the Apostles/*apostoleion*" (*aṙakelaran*); (2) "of the prophets/*propheteion*" (*margarēanocʿ*); (3) "of the martyrs and saints/*martyrium*" (*vkayanocʿ, vkayaran*)

The closest term to *martyrium* in Armenian is the phrase *vkayaran srbocʿ* (lit. "testimonial place of the saints" IV.xiv), or simply *vkayaran/vkayanocʿ*, "testimonial place" (IV.x; V.i, xx, xxvii, xxviii, xliv). Two other distinguishing terms, however, are also found in BP in reference to the shrines erected over the relics of the respective holy men: *aṙakalaran*, "*apostoleion*, place of the Apostles or Disciples of Christ" (III.iii), and *margarēanocʿ*, "*propheteion*, place of the prophet [John the Precursor]" (III.iii, xiv, xvi). The term *hangist*, "resting place" of the Apostles or saints is also used (III.xiv, xvi). In this early period, these *martyria* or "shrines" were *maturn*, "chapels" rather than churches, and several of them could be clustered in a single sacred locality such as Aštišat of Tarōn, or Vałaršapat, ın the case of the Hṙipʿsimean saints (see Aa, dccxxxvi-dccxxxviii, dcclxv–dcclxx).

See NHBL, I, p. 299 (*aṙakʿelaran*), II, p. 218 (*margarēanocʿ*), p. 826 (*vkayaran*); HArmB, I, pp. 256–257 (*aṙakel*), III, pp. 276–277 (*margarē* ‹ Phl. **margar*; Sogd. *mārkrāy/mārkarāk*, "sorcerer"), IV, p. 344 (*vkay* ‹ Parth. **vikāy*?; Av. *vīkaya-*, "witness"); HBB, I, p. 226 (*aṙakelaran*), III, p. 272 (*margarēaran*), IV, p. 347 (*vkayaran*); AG, p. 248, no. 625 (*vkay*); Schmitt, "Iranisches Lehngut," p. 89 (*vkay*); Gignoux, "Pour une évaluation," p. 12 n. 68; CPD, p. 38, *gugāy*; Bailey, "Armeno-Indoiranica," p. 90; Grabar, *Martyrium*; S. S. Mnatsakanian, "Usipal'nitsy"; Arcruni, "Pamiatniki."

aṙakelaran: III.iii, xiv (*hangist aṙakelocʿn*). *margarēaran*: III.iii, xiv, xvi (cf. V.xliii). *vkayaran/vkayanocʿ*: III.iii, xvi (*hangist srbocʿ*); IV.x, xiv; V.i, xx, xxvii, xxviii, xliv

pp. 68, 86, 91–92, 131, 139, 187, 202, 207–208, 229
See also Appendix II, "Aštišat"; "Bagawan"; "Vałaršapat."

marzpan ‹ Phl. Parth. *marzbān* ‹ *marz/mard*, "border district, march" + *bān*; Av. *panā-*, "protector"
"keeper/warden-of-the-marches, marquess"
The title is first attested at present on ostracon 1899 from Nisa, dated 72 B.C.
Persian high official of quasi-royal rank (Toumanoff translates the title as "viceroy") who governed one of the provices of the Iranian empire in the name of the king of kings. Leroy maintains the link between *marzbān* and *marz*, "border," but in Gignoux's opinion, these officials no longer had any relation with border districts in Sasanian times.
The term *marzpan* is commonly found in early Armenian sources or replaced by the equivalents *sahmanakal* or *sahmanapah*. In BP it occurs only with relation to Atrpatakan (III.xx) and Armenia itself (V.xxxviii), both of which clearly lay on the frontiers of the Sasanian realm. Moreover, *marzpan* is a term used exclusively for Persian officials, while their Armenian counterparts entrusted with the protection of the Armenian borders are identified with the hereditary *bdeašχs* or as *sahmanapah*s. After the end of the Aršakuni dynasty early in the fifth century, Persarmenia, east of the line of demarcation between the Romans and the Sasanians, was ruled until the Arab invasions of the mid-seventh century by *marzpan*s appointed by the Iranian king of kings as his officials, but a number of them were native dynasts.
See NHBL, II, p. 224; HArmB, III, pp. 282–283; HBB, III, p. 278¹; AG, p. 193, no. 402; Schmitt, "Iranisches Lehngut," p. 89 *marz*; Leroy, "Emprunts," no. 31, pp. 69–70, -*pan*; Bailey, "Armeno-Indoiranica," pp. 108–117; CPD, p. 54, *marz(o)-bān*; Gignoux, *Glossaire*, pp. 28, 58; *idem*, "Pour une évaluation," pp. 7–9; *idem*, "Marzbān"; *idem*, NPS, no. 591, p. 120, for the use of Marzbān as a personal name; Chaumont, "Ostraca," p. 19. For the office, see also Christensen, *L'Iran*, pp. 102, 131–139, 266, 373; Adontz, *Armenia*, pp. 94, 96, 165–182, 212, 218–219, 226; Toumanoff, *Studies*, pp. 133, 153, 197; Perikhanian, *Iran*, p. 16.
III.xx; V.xxxviii
pp. 95, 222–223
See also *bdeašχ*; *sahmanapah*; *satrap*; and Appendix I, "Surēn Parsik"; "Varazšapuh."

maškapačēn/maškaparčēn/maškapatčean/maškaperčan ‹ Phl. *maškawarzān*, "royal pavilion"
"royal pavilion"
This term is found in a number of variants and even in the direct transcription of thc Phl. *maškawarzān* (V.ii). There seems to be no reason to restrict its use exclusively to the royal harem, as suggested by Malχasyancᶜ. It seems to have been the royal pavilion used by the Iranian king of kings and consequently more elaborate than a mere "tent" (*χoran*). Cf. IV.xv, *χoran arkᶜuni*, for the royal tent of Aršak II.
This term is found in neither NHBL nor HArmB. See HBB, III, p. 259; Malχasyancᶜ, p. 319 n. 50; AG, p. 192, no. 394; CPD, p. 55, *maškabarzēn*.
III.xxi; V.ii
pp. 98, 188
See also *χoran*.

maškaparčēn, see *maškapačēn*.

maškapatčean, see *maškapačēn*.

maškaperčan, see *maškapačēn*.

master, see *tēr*.

matenik gund ‹ Phl. *mādayān*, "essence, basis, core, essential, chief"
Cf. the compound *maygān-pat/m'dknpt* in ŠKZ, Parth. 24; Phl. 30; RGDS no. 58, pp. 66–67, μαιγανπεδ

"elite/choice troops"

Term used to distinguish the specially selected contingents of the regular army, as opposed to the "irregulars" (*gugaz*). It is also known to Ełišē, v, p. 115 (= *Ełishē*, p. 167) who uses the form *gund matean*. Most scholars have likened them to the Persian "immortals," though Danielyan has argued inconvincingly for a "palace guard" appearing after the putative reform of Trdat III, and Nyberg as well as Thomson take it to mean the center or core of the army.

See NHBL, II, p. 214; HArmB, III, pp. 268–269²; HBB, III, p. 267, cf. p. 266, *matean*; Malχasyanc⟨ p. 313 n. 20; Gignoux, *Glossaire*, pp. 27, 56, who suggests "*archiviste*?" for *m'dknpet*; Nyberg, *Manual*, II, *Mātiyān*; Sprengling, *Third-Century Iran*, pp. 9, 12, 19; Maricq, RGDS, p. 66 n. 10; Honigmann and Maricq, RGDS, p. 17; AG, p. 192, no. 396; CPD, p. 53, *mādayān²*; Arzumanyan, "*Matean gund*," suggested the unacceptable ⟨ *matak*, "mares"; Lukonin, "Institution," p. 711; Chaumont, "Chiliarque," p. 153; Danielyan, "Trdat III-i reformə," pp. 217–218.; Thomson, *Ełishē*, p. 67 n. 6.

III.viii

p. 75

See also *banak*; *gugaz*; *gund*; *zōrk⟨*, I.c.

mayr ekełec⟨eac⟨ ⟩ Arm. *mayr*, "mother" + *ekełec⟨i* ⟨ Gk. via Syr. ἐκκλησία, "church"
"mother church"

This term is reserved exclusively in BP for the church of Aštišat of Tarōn. Aa, dcccxiv, is also acquainted with Aštišat as the "first church" (*skizbn šineloy ekełec⟨eac⟨*), but he never uses the term *mayr ekełec⟨eac⟨*, which would challenge the primacy of Vałaršapat (see III.xiv n. 11).

See NHBL, II, p. 201; HBB, III, p. 247, col. 3, *mayr*; AG, p. 472, no. 275, *mayr*.

III.iii, xiv; IV.iv

pp. 68, 86, 90, 113

See also Appendix II, "Aštišat"; "Vałaršapat."

mayrak⟨ałak ⟨ Arm. *mayr*, "mother" + *k⟨ałak⟨*, "city"; calque of the Gk. μητρόπολις
"metropolis"

Term also found in the form *mayr k⟨ałak⟨ac⟨n* (III.xii; IV.iv). BP uses it exclusively for Caesarea of Cappadocia, perhaps in its ecclesiastical sense, because the city was the metropolitan see of Cappadocia I by the fifth century. The term is never applied by BP to the secular capital of Armenia, Artašat, which is almost invariably referred to as *mec k⟨ałak⟨* (III.viii, xii; IV.lv, but not lvi), though the term is used elsewhere for the new capital of Duin (GT⟨, p. 146).

See NHBL, II, p. 201; HArmB, III, p. 246, *mayr*; HBB, III, p. 249.

III.xii, xvi; IV.iv

pp. 82, 91, 111

See also Appendix II, "Artašat"; "Caesarea."

mazdezn, see Appendix I, "Mazdezn."

mec sepuh ⟨ "large, great" + *sepuh* ⟨ Phl. *wāspuhr*, "member of a *naχarar* house"
"great *sepuh*"

Term used on one occasion in BP for Gnel Aršakuni, the nephew of Aršak II. This is the only indication in BP of a hierarchy among the *sepuh*s of a noble house in the fourth century and may be a mere distinction of Gnel's outstanding qualities. In the fifth century, however, ŁP⟨ (xxiii, xxv, xxxii, pp. 45, 47, 62 = *Ełishē*, pp. 258, 260, 276, etc.) mentions *awag sepuh*s (senior *sepuh*s) as well as ordinary *sepuh*s, though the distinction is not always maintained in the translation. Malχasyanc⟨ takes the term as applicable to the brother or son of a *tanutēr* of a clan but gives no supporting evidence.

See HBB, IV, p. 202; Henning, "Survival," pp. 95–97; Adontz, *Armenia*, p. 357; Manandyan, *Feodalizm*, pp. 51–52; and the bibliography under *sepuh*.

IV.xv

p. 143

See also *sepuh*; *tanutēr*; and Appendix I, "Gnel Aršakuni."

mecameck' ‹ Arm. *mec*, "large, great"

"greatest, highest, mighty, mightiest, very great, magnates"

Term normally reserved in BP for the most senior and powerful *naχarars*. The Armenian *mecameck'* corresponded to the Sasanian *wuzurgān* and were most likely the *megistanes* of Tacitus (*Ann.*, II.lvi).

> See NHBL, II, p. 238; HArmB, III, p. 295, *mec*; HBB, III, pp. 292–293; CPD, p. 93, *wuzurg*, "big, great"; Leroy, "Redoublement," p. 71, for redoubling as a superlative; Christensen, *L'Iran*, pp. 110–111; Adontz, *Armenia*, pp. 339, 344; Manandyan, *Feodalizm*, pp. 41ff.; Perikhanian, *Iran*, p. 68.
>
> III.iii, viii, xi, xii, xiv, xvii, xx, xxi; IV.ii–vi, xii, xiii, xv, xx, xxiii, xlv, l, li, lv; V.i, ii, iv, vi, xxi, xxiii–xxv, xxvii, xxviii, xxxii–xxxv, xxxvii, xxxviii, xliii, xliv; VI.vii, xvi
>
> pp. 68, 76, 80, 82–83, 87, 90, 92, 96–97, 106 (enormous), 108, 111–112, 114, 116, 124, 134–135 (very great), 138 (very large), 141, 151–153, 156, 165, 167–168, 172–173, 176, 185–186, 188, 191, 193, 196, 202–206, 208–209, 213–216, 221–222, 225, 228–229, 235, 239

See also *naχarar*; *satrap*; and the next entry.

mecazgi ‹ Arm. *mec*, "large, great" + *azg*, "clan, race"

"member of a great house"

Synonym of *mecamec*, used in BP on only one occasion.

> See NHBL, II, pp. 234–235; HBB, III, p. 291; and the bibliography of the preceding entry.
>
> IV.xii
>
> p. 134

See also the preceding entry.

mehean OP **Maiθryāna-*, "temple or place of Mithra," though Meillet denies the connection with Mithra, an opinion now superseded

"pagan temple"

Term normally used by classical Armenian sources to designate a temple in a general sense and not one specifically dedicated to Mithra (see, e.g., Aa xlviii dccix, dccxxix, dcclxxxiv, dcclxxvi, dcccix; MX, I.ii; II.xiv, xxvii, xl = MK, pp. 67, 151–152, 165, 182, etc.). The *mehean* was distinct from either a *bagin*, "altar of a cult," or an *atrušan*, "fire-altar," though it could contain either one of them. See e.g., III.iii, *bagink' mehenic'n*, "altars of the temples"; also MX, I.ii, xiv; II.xxvii, xl (= MK, pp. 67, 151–152, 165, 182).

> See NHBL, II, p. 254; HArmB, III, p. 296; HBB, III, p. 298; AG, p. 194, no. 406; Meillet, "Termes religieux," pp. 233–234; Widengren, *Religionen*, p. 214; Gerschevitch, "Sonne," pp. 87–88; Russell, *Zor. Arm.*, pp. 263–265, 297, 489–490, 495; Frye, "Mithra," p. 60; Chaumont, "Conquêtes sassanides," pp. 696–697 and nn. 191, 192, who still shares Meillet's opinion; Lelekov, "K semantike."
>
> III.iii, xiv; IV.v (*mehenasēr*)
>
> pp. 68, 87, 123

See also *atrušan*; *bagin*; *k'urm*.

menak, see *mianjnunk⁽*.

metropolis, see *mayrak⁽ałak⁽*.

miaban/miabanut⁽iwn, see *van(k⁽)*.

mianjn/mianjnanoc⁽ ‹ Arm. *mi*, "one" + *anjn*, "person"
"hermit"/"hermitage, community-of-hermits, lavra"
On the basis of later developments, these terms, as well as *abełay, ełbayr, menak, miaban, vanakan*, and indeed the Greek μοναχός are usually translated indiscriminately as "monk" and their communities as "monasteries." Most of the terms themselves, and their contexts in BP particularly, point to solitaries in this period and not to organized monasticism. Consequently, the translation "monk/monastery" seems both anachronistic and insufficiently precise for the groups referred to in BP.
The more general terms—*abełay* (‹ Syr. *'abīlā*, "mourner") *ełbayr*, "brother" (in its ecclesiastical sense), *menak, miaban* (linked with *vanakan*, however, in IV.iv)—may have been used of both the wandering "anchorites" (*anapatawork⁽*) and the more sedentary groups. In the case of *mianjn/mianjnanaoc⁽k⁽*, which seem to be use interchangeable with the terms *vanakan/van(k⁽)* and *ełbayr/ełbayranoc⁽*, more settled communities may be intended, although, even in this case, it is evident from the context that Koriwn, iv, p. 38 (= trans. pp. 27–28), uses the phrase *miaynakec⁽akan karg* in the sense of wandering anchorites; cf. also xxii, pp. 80–84 (= trans. pp. 45, 47), for Maštoc⁽ and his disciples. None of the evidence found in BP points to the presence of coenobia of Basilian type in fourth-century Armenia, and they are indeed unlikely at such an early date. The contexts suggests invariably, at most, communities of solitaries, either hermits or communities of the lavra type, grouped together under the guidance of a leader or *protos*, as is clearly indicated in the case of Gind (VI.xvi) or in the case of the community founded by Epip⁽an at Mambrē, which he left to return to a peripatetic life (V.xxvii–xxviii) and of which at least one "brother" isolated himself from the rest of the community (cf. also the encomia on St. Gregory in Aa, dcccxlviii, dcccliii, dcccclv, etc). Such communities would be in keeping with those generally found in the Christian East, and more particularly in Syria, during this period.
See NHBL, I, p. 2; II, pp. 250, 262, 270; HArmB, II, pp. 15–16; III, pp. 316–318, *mi*; HBB, I, pp. 2, 586–587; III, pp. 304, 320, 326; Leloir, *Paterica armeniaca*, I, p. ix, who translates *miabanakeac⁽k⁽* as "*coenobium*" but indicates his doubt on the rendition of *abełay* as "*monachus*" by giving the Armenian term in parentheses as well, and who renders both *miaynakeac⁽* and *menakeac⁽* as "*solitarius*"; see also his charcterization of contemporary Syrian practices, "Ephrem," p. 108 (IV.iv n. 19); Vööbus, *Asceticism*, I, pp. 222–234; II, pp. 61–69, 111–123, 355–356, where he, however, seems to admit the presence of some coenobial types by accepting the translation of *vank⁽* as "monastery"; Canivet, *Théodoret*, pp. 207–215; III.xiv n. 15; IV.iv n. 19; V.xxvii n. 4, xxviii n. 2; VI.xvi, nn. 3, 4, 12.
abełay: VI.xvi; *menak*: VI.vi, xvi; *mianjn/mianjnanoc⁽*: V.xxvii, xxviii; VI.xvi pp. 207, 235, 239
See also *anapatawork⁽; ełbayr; kusastan; van(k⁽)*; and Appendix I, "Daniēl"; "Epip⁽an"; "Gind"; "Šałitay."

mightiest, see *mecamec*.

mijnaberd ‹ Arm. *mēǰ*, "middle, inside" + *berd*, "fortress, castle"
"citadel, akropolis"
Early sources now supported by some archaeological explorations, indicate that the Armenian cities surviving into the fourth century were of Hellenistic type with an

interior "citadel" or "akropolis," but the only one mentioned in BP is that of Van. Cf., e.g., MX, II.xxxix (= MK, p. 182) on Eruandašat, etc.

See NHBL, II, p. 279; HArmB, III, p. 313, *mēǰ*; HBB, III, p. 336; AG, p. 474, no. 289, *mēǰ*; Aṙakʿelyan, *Artašat I*, for Artašat and also Duin, p. 17.
IV.lix
p. 179
See also *berd*; *kʿałakʿ*; Appendix II, "Van."

mother church, see *mayr ekełecʿeacʿ*.

-city, see *mayrakʿałakʿ*.

mountain-dweller, see *anapatawor*.

nahang ‹ Phl. *nahang*, "province"
Term attested in KKZ, line 12, etc.
"province"
Term used to designate a unit presumably larger than a "district" (*gawaṙ*), though their relationship is not altogether clear. It is used only once with reference to an Armenian territory in BP (IV.xv), which much prefers the term *gawaṙ*.

See NHBL, II, p. 402; HArmB, III, pp. 422–423; HBB, III, p. 438; CPD, p. 57; Perikhanian, MHD, p. 500; Gignoux, *Glossaire*, p. 30.
III.x; IV.xiv, xv; V.xxix (probably in the ecclesiastical sense of eparchy)
pp. 79, 86, 145, 210
See also *ašxarh*; *gawaṙ*; and Appendix II, "Tarōn."

nahapet ‹ MP **nāfapet*; OIr. **nāfa-pati*, "head of a family"
"head of a *naxarar* family or clan"
Senior member and consequently head of a *naxarar* family. This term is normally equivalent and interchangeable with *tanutēr*, and occasionally with the more general *naxarar*, though BP usually distinguishes them (see, e.g., IV.iii and especially xv). In the fourth century, the title came with seniority within the particular house and not by royal appointment. BP uses it once in an ecclesiastical context; see Intro., p. 50, and IV.iii and n. 4.

See NHBL, II, p. 402; HArmB, III, p. 423; HBB, III, p. 439; AG, p. 200, no. 428, who derives it from *nax*; Meillet, "Quelques mots parthes," pp. 1–3; Leroy, "Emprunts," p. 61; *idem*, "Composés en *-pet*," pp. 111–112; cf. Gignoux, *Glossaire*, pp. 30, *nhwpty*, 59; CPD, p. 57, *nāf*. On the dignity itself, Adontz, *Armenia*, pp. 185, 343, 351, 369, 371; Manandyan, *Feodalizm*, pp. 43, 47–54, 57, 288, 299; Toumanoff, *Studies*, pp. 114–117 and n. 185, 131 n. 229, where he claims that the term *nahapet* is used only with family names, though this is not borne out by BP; Perikhanian, *Iran*, pp. 58, 64, 68, 69, 77.
III.iv, vii, viii, xii, xvi, xxi; IV.ii, iii, xi, xii, xv, xvi, xviii, xx, xxxii; V.xxxv, xxxvii, xlii
pp. 69–70, 74–75, 82, 91, 98, 108, 133–134, 140–141, 147–148, 152, 161, 215, 217–218, 224
See also *naxarar*; *pet*; *sepuh*; *tanutēr*; and Appendix I, "Manuēl."

nation, see *azg*.

nawasard ‹ Parth. **navasārd*; cf. OP **nava-sārda*; Av. nava- + saraδ- "new year"; cf. Syr. loanword, *nausard-ēl*, "new year of God"
"new year, new year's festival"

First day of the new year celebrated with a festival, and first month of the year in both the Armenian and the Iranian calendar. The transformation of the term to *nōg-rōz* in Pahlavi suggests an earlier borrowing into Armenian. The term is familiar to Aa, dcccxxxvi and n. 1, as well as MX, II.lxvi (= MK, p. 213) and Koriwn, xxiv, p. 86 (= trans. p. 48).

See NHBL, II, p. 408; HArmB, III, pp. 435–436; HBB, III, p. 446; AG, p. 202, no. 435; CPD, p. 61, *nōgrōz*; Leroy, "Emprunts," p. 57; Marquart, "Nauroz"; Taqizadeh, "Festivals"; Ōdabašyan, "Navasard"; Pōłosean, *Tōnə*.

IV.xv
p. 141

naχarar ‹ Parth. **naχvadar* (attested as a proper name in Gk. "Nohodares"); Armenian loanword *naχa-* ‹ MIr. *naχva*; Phl. *naχust* + MIr. *-dār*, "keeper, holder"
"noble"

The etymology of this term has long been disputed but is now generally accepted. *Naχarar* seems to have been the general term designating the first estate of Aršakuni society superior to the *azat* and referring to the nobility rather than to a particular rank or office. It is commonly used to translate Gk. σατράπης (eg. III Kgs. 20–21; Dan. 6:1, etc.). It included all the members of an Armenian noble family, the *tanutēr* or *nahapet* and the *sepuh*s, though it is occasionally used interchangeably with *nahapet*. As members of the hereditary nobility, the *naχarar*s were autonomous dynasts and equal *de jure*, though their hierarchy was rigorously fixed according to their *gah* at court functions. This position, which was probably related to the number of their retainers, was recorded in a "Throne List" (*Gahnamak*), of which only later and probably fictionalized examples have survived (but see also MX, III.li = MK, p. 316; MK/D II.i, pp. 106–107 = MD, pp. 61–62), though these may refer to a later period. *De facto*, the *naχarar*s were clearly divided into "magnates" (*barjerecʽkʽ; gaherēcʽkʽ, mecameckʽ*) and "juniors" (*krtser*), as is repeatedly recorded in BP. Despite the efforts of the crown to curb the autonomy and turbulence of the magnates (III.viii) and to turn them into royal officials (IV.ii), the *naχarar*s continued to exercise their ancestral prerogatives and to claim their hereditary offices without the kings' sanction (V.xxxvii), and the account of their unabated centrifugal tendencies forms one of the main themes in BP.

See NHBL, II, p. 599; HArmB, III, pp. 420–421; HBB III, p. 435; AG, pp. 514–515; Marr, "Ētimologiia," pp. 170–173; Benveniste, "Titres," pp. 5–7; Leroy, "Emprunts," pp. 60–61; no. 14; cf. *idem*, "Composés en -*pet*," no. 15, p. 122, *naχarar-a-pet*; CPD, pp. 58, *naχust*, 24, -*dār*; Bailey, *Dictionary*, p. 190; Perikhanian, *Iran, idem*, "Ostaniki," pp. 50–51. On the social significance of the term, see Adontz, *Armenia*, pp. 191–218, 227–233, 67*–72*, 262* *et passim*; Manandyan, *Feodalizm*, pp. 32–89 *et passim*; Toumanoff, *Studies*, pp. 34–40, 110ff., 115–116 n. 188, 130–131 n. 229 for the tension between "dynasticism" and "feudalism" in Aršakuni Armenia; Kostanyan, "*Naχarar*"; Chaumont, "L'ordre de préséances"; Garsoïan, "Prolegomena," cols. 182–183, 187–189, 207–213 nn. 42–44, 231–234 nn. 75–83.

P.S.; III.iii, iv, vii, viii, xi–xiv, xvii, xviii, xx, xxi; IV.iii, iv, xiii–xv, xix, xx, xxiii, xxxvi, xxxviii–xlii, xlv, l, li, lviii, lix; V.iv, vi, vii, xv, xxiv, xxx, xxxiv, xxxv, xxxvii, xxxviii, xliv; VI.i

pp. 63, 68–69, 74–76, 80, 82–84, 87, 90, 92–93, 96–98, 108, 112, 136, 139–141, 149–152, 156, 162–165, 167–168, 178, 193, 196, 198, 201, 204, 210, 215, 220–221, 228–229, 233

See also, *azat*; *barjerecⁱ*; *gah*; *gaherecⁱ*; *gorcakal*; *išχan*; *mecamec*; *nahapet*; *sepuh*.

net, see *zēn*, j.

nizak, see *zēn*, a.

nizakakicⁱ ‹ Phl. *nēzag*, "spear" = Arm. -*kicⁱ* "united, joined, partners"
   "companions-in-arms"; lit. fellow-spearmen"
   Normal term for companions-in-arms in BP, presumably indicating a particular part-
   nership uniting two *naχarars*.
   See NHBL, II, p. 425; HArmB, III, p. 451, *nizak*; HBB, III, p. 462; AG, p. 204,
      no. 442; Schmitt, "Iranisches Lehngut," p. 90; CPD, p. 59, *nēzag*.
   III.vii; V.xlii, xliii
   pp. 74, 224, 226–227
   See *naχarar*; and Appendix I, "Babik Siwni"; "Bagrat Bagratuni"; "Garegin I
      R̊štuni"; "Mehandak I R̊štuni"; "Vahan Amatuni"; "Manuēl Mamikonean";
      "Varaz Kaminakan."

nizakaworkⁱ, see *zōrkⁱ*, I.d, II.a.

noble, see *azat*; *naχarar*.

   -contingent, see *azatagund*.

nobility, see *awag*; *awagani*; *naχarar*.

notar/nōtar ‹ Gk. νοτάριος
   "scribe, recorder, secretary"
   This term is used for imperial clerks instead of the normal Armenian *dpir* ‹ Phl. *dibīr*,
   "scribe."
   See NHBL, II, p. 456; HArmB, III, p. 478; HBB, III, p. 489; AG, p. 368, no. 295;
      GLRB, II, p. 786; Gelzer, "Die Anfänge," p. 111 n.; Peeters, "SS Serge et Théo-
      dore," p. 67 and n. 4.
   IV.v
   p. 122
   See also *semiar*.

nran, see *zen*, f.

nuirakapet ‹ Parth. **nivēdag*; cf.Phl. *niwistan* ‹ OIr. *ni-vaēd-*, "announce, proclaim" +
   Arm. -*pet*, "chief"
   "master of ceremonies"
   High Sasanian office attested for Kartir in KKZ, 8.
   The *nuirakapet* appears to have been the head of the royal bodyguard who intro-
   duced visitors into the royal presence, according to Ačaryan. In Iran, this office seems
   to have been hereditary in the family of the Zik, despite KKZ.
   See NHBL, II, p. 451; HArmB III, pp. 470–471, *nuirak*; HBB III, p. 484; AG, p. 41
      no. 72, *Zik*, who calls him "capo dei sbirri"; CPD, p. 60, *niwistan*; Sprengling,
      Third-Century Iran, pp. 47, 51; JIN, p. 385, no. 2, *Zik*, who qualifies the office as
      that of *kanzler*; Perikhanian, *Iran*, p. 69; Leroy, "Composés en -*pet*," p. 124.
   IV.xxxv
   p. 162
   See also *pet*; and Appendix I, "Zik."

nurse/nurture, see *dayeak*; *snuc ⁱčᶜ*.

oath, see *uχt*.

office/official, see *gorcakal*; *išχan*.

official-letter, see *hrovartak*.

official-robe, see *patmučan*.

ostan ‹ Phl. *awestām*, "province, district"
"royal domain"
Despite considerable controversy over the meaning of this term, the most recent study by Perikhanian indicates that it referred primarily to the royal domain of the Aršakuni kings of Armenia, as had been argued by Hübschmann, Manandyan, and Malχasyancᶜ, rather than to the "royal court or palace" (*curtis dominicalis*), according to Adontz's hypothesis. At first the *ostan* referred to the "royal domain" (*ostan arkᶜuni*) as was the case in Iran under the Sasanians, according to Shaki, but the term was subsequently used for the nuclear domain of all the great *naχarar* houses, such as the Arcruni, Bagratuni, or Kamsarakan.
See NHBL, II, pp. 522–523; HArmB III, p. 570, which defines the term as "*ereweli tᶜagaworakan kᶜałakᶜ*"; HBB, III, p. 572, which identifies it exclusively with the royal domain, "*Aršakuneacᶜ tᶜagaworutᶜean žamanak arkᶜunikin patkanoł gawaṙ kaluac (hakagrutᶜeamb naχararakan kaluacneri)*" Malχasyancᶜ, p. 326 n. 104; AG, p. 215, no. 490; AON, pp. 460–461; Shaki, "Terms," pp. 96–100; CPD, p. 14, *awestām*; Perikhanian, "Ostaniki"; *idem, Iran,* p. 222; *idem,* MHS, p. 505, *ōstān*; Adontz, *Armenia,* pp. 35, 99, 195, 238, 240–241, 250, 351–352, 359–361, 391 n. 25, 463 n. 71, 516 n. 53, 523 n. 86, 69*; Manandyan, *Feodalizm,* pp. 56–59, 95–100, 104, 116–117, 123–124; Toumanoff, *Studies,* pp. 114, 125–126 n. 215, 127 n. 222.
IV.xix; V.xviii
pp. 149, 201
See also *dastakert*; *kaluacᶜ*; *sephakan*; *tun*.

ostikan ‹ Phl. *ōstīgān*, "firm, strong, sure, reliable"
"overseer, guardian, governor"
This title is used in BP both for governors of provinces, Persian as well as Armenian, and for the supervision of the royal fortresses entrusted to the *mardpet* Drastamat (V.vii), though the normal term in this case seems to be *berdakal*.
See NHBL, II, 523; HArmB, III, p. 570; HBB, III, p. 572; AG, pp. 215–216, no. 492; CPD, p. 61, *ōstīgān*; Perikhanian, MHD, p. 306, *ōstīkānīh*; Bailey, "Armeno-Indoiranica," p. 112; Adontz, *Armenia,* pp. 35, 391 n. 25; Toumanoff, *Studies,* pp. 168, 176–177, 178 n. 119, 119 n. 121.
IV.lv, lvi; V.vii, xiv, xvi
pp. 176–177, 198, 200–201
See also *berdakal*; *mardpet*; *marzpan*; and Appendix I "Drastamat."

pagan

-**priests**, see *kᶜurm*.

-**temple**, see *atrušan, bagin, mehan*.

palat, see *aparan*.

p'andiṙ/p'anduṙ ‹ ?Lyd. *pandoira*
"stringed instrument, lute"
Originally a three-stringed instrument from Asia Minor but subsequently modified.
See NHBL, II, p. 932; HArmB, IV, pp. 479–480; HBB, IV, p. 486; Malxasyanc',
p. 337 n. 178; AG, p. 395, no. 11.
V.xxxi
p. 212
See also *vin*.

p'aṙawor, see *p'aṙk'*.

p'aṙk'/paṙawor ‹ NW MIr., median *farnah-; cf. MIr. *xwarrah*; Av. *x'varanah*-
"glory/glorified"
Term commonly used in BP not merely in its general sense, but much more specifically to designate the "transcendental glory" accompanying and protecting the legitimate king of Iran in the Zoroastrian tradition (see, e.g., IV.xxiv; cf. Aa, cxxvii and
Karnāmag, xii.4, p. 28), and as such incorporated into the royal Iranian formula *baxt
ud xwarrah*, "fortune and glory" (cf. CD, LXII.v.2). With the Christianization of Armenia this royal supernatural quality was transferred to God and His saints (see, e.g.,
Yusik, III.v; Daniēl, III.xiv; Nersēs, IV,iv, etc.). Its usage in its original sense by BP and
Aa indicates, however, that its Zoroastrian implications were still understood in late
fifth-century Armenia.
See NHBL, II, p. 933; HArmB, IV, pp. 482–483; HBB, IV, pp. 488–489; AG, p. 254,
no. 659; Gignoux, *Glossaire*, pp. 22, 51; *idem*, NPS, p. 9, who prefers the translation *lumière*; Schmitt, "Iranisches Lehngut," p. 94; Bolognesi, *Fonti*; Skjærvø,
"Farnah-"; Bailey, "Armeno-Indoiranica, pp. 100–101; Ajello, *P'aṙk'*; CPD, p. 96,
xwarrah; Garsoïan, "Prolegomena," cols. 184–187, 226–229 nn. 65–72; *idem*,
"Locus," pp. 42–45, with further bibliography; Shahbazi, "Symbol."
III.v, xiv; IV.i, iv, v, x, xiii, xiv–xvi, xx, xxiv, lvii; V.iv, xxviii, xxx, xxxvii, xxxviii
pp. 71, 89, 107, 112, 114, 116–118, 120, 131, 136, 140, 143, 146, 151 (*mecap'aṙ*), 158,
177, 192, 208, 210, 218, 222
See also *baxt*.

patiw; Ir. loanword; cf. Sogd. *ptβy*, *ptβy'*, *ptβyw*
"diadem," thence, "honor"
The diadem which, together with the *gah* or *barj*, indicated the rank and office of a
naxarar (see, e.g., III.xi, Artawazd II; V.xxxvii, Manuēl; also IV.ii). The secondary
meaning deriving from the first was "honor," "dignity," and the term is commonly used
in that sense.
See NHBL, II, p. 610; HArmB, IV, p. 43; HBB, IV, pp. 63–64; Malxasyanc', p. 339
n. 191; Manandyan, *Feodalizm*, pp. 83–84; Lukonin, "Institutions," pp. 706–707.
III.v, x–xiii, xv, xvii, xviii, xx, xxi; IV.ii, iv, viii, xii, xvi, xxi, l, li; V.i, iii, iv, vii, xxviii,
xxix, xxxi, xxxii, xxxv, xxxvii
pp. 71, 80 (*mecapatiw*)–81, 83, 86, 91–93, 95–96, 99 (*mecapatiw*)–100, 108, 128, 135,
146–147, 168–169, 189, 194, 198, 208, 210, 212–213, 216, 218
See also *patuakan*; and cf. *barj*; *gah*.

patmočan, see *patmučan*.

patmučan/patmōčan ‹ Parth. *padmōžan*; Phl. *paymōg*, *paymōzan*, "garment, robe"
"robe, honorific-robe, ceremonial robe, official robe"

Robe bestowed by the king on an official or magnate to honor him. It was stripped off as a sign of disgrace (see III.xxi n. 19). The term can also refer to any ample outer garment, robe or mantle.

See NHBL, II, p. 616; HArmB, IV, p. 46, who renders it *"erkar ew pᶜaɫawor verarku kam zgest"*; HBB, IV, p. 69; AG, pp. 224–225, no. 519; Schmitt, "Iranisches Lehngut," p. 92; Leroy, "Emprunts," p. 64.

III.x, xxi; IV.iii; V.vi, vii, xxxviii

pp. 79, 99, 109–110, 197–198, 221

patriarch, see *hayrapet.*

patuakan/patuem ‹ Arm. *patiw,* "honor"

"honorable, distinguished, dignitaries, precious/to honor"

Term deriving its meaning from the secondary sense of *patiw,* "honor" rather than from the basic sense of "diadem."

See NHBL, II, p. 618; HBB, IV, p. 70; and bibliography under *patiw.*

III.iii, iv, xi, xii, xiv, xvi, xx, xxi; IV.iv, vii, viii, xi, xvi, xx; V.i, iv, xxiii, xxiv, xxxv, xxxvii, xliv; VI.vii

pp. 68–69, 81, 83, 86, 90–91, 96, 99, 112, 116, 121 (precious), 124, 126, 128, 133, 147, 151, 187, 191, 194, 203, 205, 216, 221–222, 229,235

See also *patiw.*

pavilion, see *maskapačen.*

peasant, see *šinakan.*

pet/petutᶜiwn ‹ MIR. *-bed*; cf. OIr. *-pati-*, Av. *paitiš,* "master, lord"

"chief, chieftain"

Term only occasionally found alone in BP as a synonym for *tēr* or *naχarar,* but very common as the suffix in compound titles derived primarily from Iranian, e.g. *aχorapet, hazarapet, mardpet, sparapet,* etc., as well as in hybrids such as *episkoposapet.* See also the preface to the Šahapivan, *Canons.*

See NHBL, II, p. 645; HArmB, IV, pp. 73–74; HBB, IV, pp. 93–94; AG, p. 229, no. 538; Schmitt, "Iranisches Lehngut," pp. 89, 102; CPD, p. 18, *-bed.* Also Benveniste, "Remarques"; Leroy, "Composés en *-pet*; *idem*, "Emprunts," p. 66; Belardi, "Origine"; *Kanonagirkᶜ,* I. p. 428.

III.xiv, xx, xxi; IV.ii, iii, v

pp. 90, 97, 108, 119

See also *naχarar; tēr;* and all compound titles in *-pet.*

pikesmen, see *zōrkᶜ,* i.

portion, see *koɫmn.*

priest, pagan, see *kᶜurm.*

prince, see *išχan.*

principal bishop, see *senior bishop.*

principality, see *išχanutᶜiwn.*

propheteion, see *martyrium.*

province, see *nahang.*

ptuɫ, "fruit"

"type of tax"

Term presumable used for an ecclesiastical tax in kind, perhaps "first fruits," though Adontz equates it with the Arabian *bahrak*.

See NHBL, II, p. 665; HArmB, IV, pp. 112–113; Malχasyancʿ, p. 336 n. 177; Adontz, *Armenia*, pp. 364–365 and n. 95.

V.xxxi

p. 211

See also *hark*.

public/public square, see *hraparak*.

publicly, see *hraparak*.

pʿuštipan ‹ Phl. *puštīban, puštēpan*, "supporter, bodyguard"

"guardsman, bodyguard"

Seemingly the royal guard of Iran, also sent out on special occasions (V.vii). They were noble (*azatagund*) and consequently must have served primarily on horseback, though presumably not at court. BP is familiar with them, but does not mention them in Armenia.

See NHBL, II, p. 959; HArmB, IV, p. 525; HBB, IV, p. 522; AG, p. 221, no. 507, *paštpan*, p. 255, no. 665, *puštipan*; CPD, p. 70, *puštībān*; Nyberg, *Manual, II*, p. 163, s.v.; Bolognesi, "Tradizione culturale," p. 575; Christensen, *L'Iran*, pp. 390, 395; Chaumont, "Chiliarque," pp. 153–154.

IV.liii; V.vii

pp. 170, 199

See also *azatgund*; *zōrkʿ*, I.a.

queen, see *bambišn*; *tikin*.

quiver, see *zēn*, j.

race, see *azg*.

racecourse, see *asparēz*.

ṙamik ‹ Phl. **ramīg, ram(ag)*, "herd, flock"

"non-noble, people, folk"

Term that included all of the "non-noble" (*an-azat*) third estate of society in the towns and the countryside (see ŁPᶜ III.xcix, p. 178 = CHAMA, II, p. 365). It included the "peasants" (*šinakan*), from whom the *ṙamik* are specifically distinguished (III.xxi) but whose taxable status they shared. Despite their non-noble rank, the presence of *ṙamik*s was accepted in the councils of the realm, according to BP (III.xxi).

See NHBL, II, p. 680; HArmB, IV, p. 140; HBB, IV, p. 157; AG, p. 233, no. 557; CPD, p. 70, *ram(ag)*; Schmitt, "Iranisches Lehngut," p. 89, *rām*; Adontz, *Armenia*, pp. 223, cf. 299–300, 333, 361–362, 520 n. 71, 524 n. 89; *idem*, "L'Aspect," pp. 155–156; *idem*, "Šinakanutʿiwn," esp. pp. 181–188; Manandyan, *Feodalizm*, pp. 148–153, 188–189, 215; Toumanoff, *Studies*, p. 127 n. 122; Widengren, *Feudalismus*, pp. 123–124; *idem*, "Recherches," pp. 99–100, 148–170.

III.xxi

p. 97

See also *azat*; *šinakan*; *žoɫov*; and the next entry.

ṙamikspas ‹ Arm. *ṙamik* + *spas*, "service, office, function"

"non-noble service, cavalry"

Term referring to "non-noble" service in general, usually on foot, and BP (III.xx) states explicitly that Tiran was seized by the Persians because the cavalry was absent and only a few guards and *ṙamik* detachments remained to protect the king and his household: "*očꞌ okꞌ ēr or mnaceal ēr aṙ tꞌagaworin, ew očꞌ gund ew ayrewji; baycꞌ miayn sakaw . . . ṙamikspas.*" It is, however, evident from both BP and other Armenian sources that the *ṙamikspas* also served on horseback in the Arsacid army as well as in the period of the Marzpanutꞌiwn (see *zōrkꞌ*, I.b).

See the bibliography under the preceding entry and under *zōrkꞌ*, I.b.

III.xx

p. 96

See also *azatagund*; *zōrkꞌ*, I.b; and the preceding entry.

realm, see *ašχarh*; see also *erkir haykakan lezui*.

region, see *koḷmn*.

regular contingent, see *matenik gund*.

resting-place-of-the-saints, see *martyrium*.

reward, see *kōšik*.

robe, see *patmučan*.

ṙočik ‹ Phl. *rōzīg*; "daily bread, sustenance"; cf. OP *rauča*-, "day"
"maintenance, stipend, nourishment, livelihood, allowance"
Term referring to maintenance not only in money but also in kind; see also MX, II.viii (= MK, p. 144); Eḷišē, iii, p. 64 (= *Eḷishē*, p. 114 and n. 1, etc.), also MHD, 34.3, 97.16, pp. 99, 282.

  See NHBL, II, p. 681; HArmB, IV, pp. 145–146; HBB IV, p. 163[2]; AG, p. 234, no. 559; Schmitt, "Iranisches Lehngut," p. 93; CPD, p. 72, *rōzīg*; Nyberg, *Manual*, p. 170, *rōc*, "day"; Perikhanian, MHD, p. 518; *idem, Iran*, p. 163; Adontz, *Armenia*, pp. 219, 450 nn. 57, 60; Manandyan, *Feodalizm*, pp. 181–182, 229–230.

  IV.iv, v; V.xxxi, xxxviii

  pp. 113, 120, 211, 222

  See also *kōšik*.

ruler, see *išχan*.

sahman ‹ Phl. *sāmān*, "limit, boundary"
"boundary, borderland, confines, frontier; (pl.) territory"
The term normally refers to the frontier or boundary of a country, but in the plural it takes the sense of the area within the borders, and consequently the territory of the unit under discussion (e.g. III.xxi).

  See NHBL, II, pp. 687–688; HArmB, IV, p. 162; HBB, IV, p. 174; AG, p. 235, no. 564; CPD, p. 73, *sāmān*.

  III.iv, v–viii, x, xi, xiv, xvii, xxi; IV.iv, xvii, xxi, xxiii–xxvi, xxviii–xxxi, xxxviii, xliii, liv; V.i, ii, iv–vi, xiii, xv, xx, xxi, xxix–xxxi, xxxiv, xxxvii, xxxix, xlii, xliii; VI.i

  pp. 70, 73–74, 76–77, 81, 89, 92, 98, 112–113, 148, 154, 156–161, 163–164, 171, 185–187, 193–194, 196, 200–202, 210–212, 215, 218, 220, 223–224, 233–234

  See also *koḷm*; Appendix II, "Atrpatakan"; and the next entry.

sahmanapah ‹ Arm. *sahman*, "border" + *pah*, "guard, guardian"
"warden-of-the-marches, border-guard"

This term usually refers to a high official or magnate (e.g. V.vi, the *hayr-mardpet*), but on occasion it may have been used in BP to designate the troops guarding the borders of Armenia (IV.xxi, xxxi). The form *sahmanakal*, with the sense of "marcherlord, keeper-of-the-marches," is also attested as a synonym for *bdeašχ* in Aa, dccclxxiii, but it is not found in BP.

See NHBL, II, p. 688; HBB, IV, p. 175; and the bibliography of the preceding entry.
III.xx; IV.ii, iii, xxi, xxxi; V.v, vi
pp. 94, 108, 154, 161, 195–196
See also *bdeašχ*; *mardpet*; *marzpan*; and the preceding entry.

sakraworkᶜ, see *zōrk*ᶜ, IIc.

sakur, see *zēn*, i.

sałwart, see *zēn*, h.

šapstan takaṙapet ⟨ Phl. *šabestān*, "gynecaeum, private apartments" + Arm. *takaṙ*, "cup"; cf. Phl. *takōk*, NP *tagār*, "cup, jar" + Arm. *-pet*, "chief"
"chief cupbearer, butler of the royal apartments, eunuch cupbearer"
The term refers to the chief cupbearer of the royal apartments, as is obvious from its etymology, and there is no evidence for the tentative identification "council, secret council" suggested by Hübschmann for *šapstan*. Christensen identifies the Iranian *takār-bagh* as the "master of the court," and Lukonin, lists the Parthian *špystn*, Phl. *š'pstn* (attested in ŠKZ, Parth. 28–29; Phl. 34; RGDS nos. 66–67, εὐνῦχος) among the great officials; cf. *mardpet*.

See NHBL, II, p. 839, *takaṙapet*; HArmB, III, p. 495; IV, p. 361, who considers it to be a Persian military title, *"parsik mi zōravari titłosə"*; HBB, III, p. 500; Malχasyancᶜ, p. 329 n. 123; AG, pp. 211, no. 472, 251, no. 639; CPD, pp. 78, *"šabstan*, 81, *takōk*, "drinking vessel"; Gignoux, *Glossaire*, pp. 34, 64; Sprengling, *Third-Century Iran*, pp. 9, 12, 19; Honigmann and Maricq, RGDS, p. 18; Leroy, "Composés en *-pet*," no. 8, p. 123. Christensen, *L'Iran*, p. 394; Lukonin, "Ametist," pp. 383–384; *idem*, "Institutions," pp. 712–713; JIN, p. 287.
IV.xlvi
p. 166
See also *mardpet*.

satrap ⟨ Gk. σατράπης OIr. *χšaθra-pāran*, "protector of the realm"; cf. Phl. *šasab*, "satrap"; transmitted to Armenian by way of Greek
Title attested in ŠKZ, Parth. 26–28; Phl. 32–35; RGDS nos. 62–64, 66–67, pp. 68–73.
"satrap, prince, magnate"
This rarely used Armenian form (derived by way of Greek) of the Iranian title occurs several times in BP, rather than the more common Armenian derivation, *šahap*, which is found only once in the text as a proper name (VI.xi). In Malχasyancᶜ's opinion, the title *satrap* is used in BP to designate the greatest magnates, *mecameck*ᶜ, or even the *bdeašχ*s, rather than mere provincial governors. This usage would be in keeping with contemporary practices. In a number of cases the Iranian satraps were native, semi-independent rulers who had recognized the ultimate overlordship of the king of kings or, in the case of the southern Armenian Satrapies after the peace of 298, that of the Roman emperor. See, e.g., the listing in the *Gahnamak*, "Rank List," of "the satrap lord of Cop ᶜkᶜ/ Sophanenē" (*šahapn Cop*ᶜac*ᶜ tēr*). Adontz mistook the first term for a proper name, but the identification of the lords of Sophanenē as "satraps" is confirmed by the decree of Theodosius II addressed to *Gaddanae Satrapae Sophanenae* (CTh, XII.xiii.6;

cf. Justinian's *Novella*, XXXI.i.3–4). There is no trace in BP of the evolution of the *šahap/satraps* into financial officers and Persian urban officials postulated by Eremyan and Kostanyan.

See NHBL, II, p. 699; HArmB, III, pp. 482–483, *šahap*; HBB, IV, p. 190; Malχasyanc͑, p. 321 n. 63; AG, pp. 208–209, no. 461; CPD, p. 79, *šasab*; Schmitt, "Iranisches Lehngut," p. 89, *šahap*; *idem*; "Satrap"; *idem*, IN, p. 7, *Šahrab*; Gignoux, *Glossaire*, pp. 34, 53; Adontz, *Armenia*, pp. 88–89, 134, 191, 334–337, 507–508 n. 22, 2*, 35*, 67*; Toumanoff, *Studies*, pp. 40 n. 14, 287; Sprengling, *Third-Century Iran*, pp. 9, 12, 19; Christensen, *L'Iran* pp. 100, 101–103, 136–137 and n. 1, 140 n. 2; Honigmann and Maricq, RGDS, pp. 17–18; Widengren, "Recherches," pp. 136–137; Lehmann-Haupt, "Satrap"; Perikhanian, *Iran*, pp. 16, 68–69, where she defines the *šahap* as a military governor; Eremyan, "Osnovnye cherty," pp. 41–42; *idem*, "Razvitie," p. 25; Kostanyan, "*Naχarar*"; *idem*, "Termin ShAhAP."

IV.iii–v

pp. 108, 112, 116, 124

See also *bdeašχ*; *mecamec*; Appendix I, "Kiwrakos"; and Appendix II, "Cop͑k͑."

seat, see *at͑or*; *bun gahoyk͑*.

semiar ‹ Gk. *σημειάριος, σημειογράφος

"tachygrapher, stenographer"

As in the case of the *notar*, this term is used for Roman imperial secretaries, but not for their Armenian counterparts. In the form σημειογράφος this is the technical term for Roman shorthand court recorders, but Aa, xcix, prefers the Armenian form *atenakal dpirk͑n*.

See NHBL, II, p. 706; HArmB, IV, p. 200; HBB, IV, p. 200; AG, p. 378, no. 391; Gelzer, "Die Anfänge," p. 111 note; Peeters, "SS Serge et Théodore," IV, 67 n. 4

IV.v

p. 122

See also *notar*.

senekapet ‹ Arm. *seneak*, "room, chamber" + *-pet*, "chief"

"chamberlain"

The precise duties of this palatine office and their differentiation from those of the *hayr-mardpet* as "grand-chamberlain" have been disputed. BP (IV.iii) describes St. Nersēs. Before his consecration as patriarch, as having pursued a military career (*zinuorut͑ean gorcakalut͑ean*) in that he served as royal *senekapet* holding the royal sword on state occasions, but he then goes on to exaggerate the all-inclusiveness of his duties (see IV.iii n. 7). The *Vita* of St. Nersēs, ii, p. 15 (but *not* the translation, CHAMA, II, p. 23), attributes to the *senekapet* the guard of the royal treasure. Such a duty might perhaps have been possible at court but not in the case of the royal fortresses where part of the royal treasure was kept, since this would have been a direct usurpation of the explicit prerogatives of the *mardpet* (V.vii). As this office was clearly military in nature (see also III.xx), it may perhaps have been equivalent to that of "royal swordbearer," *špšyl'ty/ spsyrdr* (attested in ŠKZ, Parth. 27, Phl. 33, RGDS no. 64, σπαφόρος) rather than to a civilian chamberlain, though the presumably lesser *senekapet* of the crown prince Pap (IV.xliv) does not seem to have had other than aulic duties. As in the case of the *mardpet*, the office of royal *senekapet* does not seem to have been hereditary, for it is found both in the patriarchal Gregorid house (IV.iii) and in that of the princes of Siwni (III.xx).

See NHBL, II, p. 706; HArmB, IV, p. 201; HBB, IV, p. 201; Gignoux, *Glossaire*, pp. 34, 64; Sprengling, *Third-Century Iran*, pp. 9, 12, 19; Leroy, "Composés en

-*pet*," no. 20, p. 125; Adontz, *Armenia*, pp. 341, 512 n. 41; Manandyan, *Feoda-lizm*, p. 79; Lukonin, "Institutions," pp. 710–711.

III.xx; IV.iii, xliv

pp. 94–95, 109–110, 165

See also *gorcakal*; *mardpet*; *pet*; *zōrkʿ*; and Appendix I "Nersēs I"; "Pʿisak."

senior, see *awag*; also *barjerecʿ*; *gaherecʿ*; and *senior-bishop*.

senior-bishop = *awag episkoposacʿ*, *gluχ episkoposacʿ*, *glχawor episkopos*

"senior bishop, head bishop, principal bishop"

Title seemingly used to distinguish the presiding non-Gregorid bishop/primate of Armenia after the death of St. Nersēs, by contrast to the titles of *episkoposapet*, *hay-rapet*, and *kʿahanayapet* invariably used for the "legitimate" Gregorid primates in whose family the title was hereditary, and who are never referred to as merely "senior" among other bishops (see P.S. nn. 6, 9). It is not used for the earlier non-Gregorid primates, Pʿaŕēn and Šahak, who were ordained anachronistically and ambiguously *to* the *katʿołik*ate of Armenia, but who were duly consecrated at Caesarea (III.xvi, xvii), or, curiously, for the uncanonically appointed Čʿunak (IV.xv).

See bibliographies under *awag*, *episkoposapet*, *katʿołikos*, also Bolognesi, "Armé-niaca,", pp. 11–12, for the fundamental meaning of *gluχ*, "tête, *chef*"; and Vailhé, "Eglise."

P.S. (*glχawor*); V.xxix (*awag*); VI.iii–iv (*gluχ*), xv (*glχawor*)

pp. 63, 210, 234–235, 238

See also *awag*; *episkoposapet*; *hayrapet*; *kʿahanayapet*; *katʿołikos*; and Appendix I, "Aspurak"; "Šahak II."

sephakan/sepʿakan ‹ Arm. *sepuh*

"hereditary, possession"

Personal domain or appanage of a *sepuh* or a member of a *naχarar* house. The term is usually taken to reflect a post-Aršakuni development, but Manandyan demonstrated its earlier use on the basis of BP. In the fourth century, however, it seems to have referred to a family, as well as to an individual holding (IV.xiv; cf. MX, II.xii = MK, p. 148, "*yiwreancʿ sepʿakan gewłn yAštišat [Vahuneacʿ]*"). Manandyan argues that *sephakan* holdings were alienable as against the unalienable *tanutirakan kaluac*, but this hy-pothesis is not supported in BP, which insists on the hereditary aspect of the *sepha-kanutʿiwn*.

See NHBL, II, p. 706; HArmB IV, p. 202, *sepuh*; HBB, IV, p. 202; Marr, "Ētimolo-giia," pp. 286–289; Perikhanian, "Le Lexique," pp. 16–23; *idem, Iran*, pp. 135, 221–223, 347 n. 83, 348–350 nn. 103, 111; Adontz, *Armenia*, pp. 357–359, 522–523 n. 82; Manandyan, *Feodalizm*, pp. 77, 192–195; Toumanoff, *Studies*, pp. 124, 191 n. 199; Widengren, "Recherches," pp. 116–119; and bibliography under *sepuh*.

IV.xiv, xxiii, lix; V.xliii

pp. 139, 156, 180, 225

See also *kaluac*; *naχarar*; *sepuh*; and the next entry.

sepuh ‹ NWIr. *vispuhr*; cf. Av. *visō. puθra-*, "son of a noble house; Sogd. *višpuš*, "heir"; and the parallel Arm. forms *Vaspur-akan*, *sephakan*

Attested in ŠKZ under the ideogram BRBYTʾ, Parth. 21; Phl.26, 31; RGDS nos. 49, 60–61, pp. 62–63, 68–69.

"member of a noble house"

Any member of a *naχarar* house other than its *nahapet* or *tanutēr*. The *sepuh*s were not minor nobility, such as the *azat*s, because such great magnates as the *sparapet* of

Armenia could be included among them (IV.ii). Cf. ŁP^c, xxxvi, p. 67 (= *Ełishē*, p. 281, "*sepuhk^c omank^c yiwrak^canč^ciwr tohmē*").

See NHBL, II, p. 707; HArmB IV, p. 202; HBB IV, p. 202; Benveniste, "Titres," pp. 9–10; *idem, Titres et noms propres*, pp. 22–26; Gignoux, *Glossaire*, pp. 20, 49; Perikhanian, *Iran*, p. 221; *idem,* "Le Lexique," p. 19; Bailey, *Dictionary*, pp. 292–293, *bäsivärai*; Marr, "Ētimologiia"; Adontz, *Armenia*, pp. p. 305, 311–312, 315, 333, 342–343, where he equates *sepuh* and *azat*, 357–361, 371, 521 n. 77, 522 n. 80, 523 nn. 83–86, 78*–79*; Manandyan, *Feodalizm*, pp. 41–42, 50–52, 79, 120; Toumanoff, *Studies*, pp. 114–115 and n. 186, 124, 126, 130, etc.; Sprengling, *Third-Century Iran*, pp. 9, 12, 18–19; Honigmann and Maricq, RGDS, pp. 16–17.

V.xxxvii
p. 220
See also *azat*; *mec sepuh*; *nahapet*; *naχarar*; *sparapet*; *tanutēr*; and the preceding entry.

sepuh, mec, see *mec sepuh.*

šert, see *zēn*, k.

šertawork^c, see *zōrk^c*, II.g.

servant/service/servitude, see *caṙay.*

shield, see *zēn*, g.

shieldbearer, see *zōrk^c*, I.e, II.b.

shrine, see *martyrium.*

side, see *kołmn.*

šinakan ‹ Arm. *šēn*, "village, locality" ‹ ?MIr. **šēnakān*; cf. Av. *šayana-*, "village" "peasant"

This group formed the overwhelming majority of the population in general during the Aršakuni period and of the non-noble "third estate" in particular, though they are clearly distinguished from the *ṙamik* in BP (III.xxi). We know very little of the exact status of this group. Personally free, and under the supervision of the *hazarapet*, they seem to have been bound to the land and subject to both taxes and corvées, as were the Roman *coloni* and the western medieval serfs. Despite their inferior status, however, some of the *šinakan* seem to have been admitted to participate in the council of the realm (III.xxi); cf. GT^c, pp. 41, 73–74; Šahapivan, *Canons*, iii, v, vii, ix, xi.

See NHBL, II, p. 477; HArmB, III, p. 513, *šēn*; HBB, III, p. 516; AG, pp. 213–214, no. 480; Bailey, *Dictionary*, p. 68, *kṣīra-*, "country, kingdom"; Widengren, *Feudalismus*, pp. 113–114, 123, 126; *idem,* "Recherches," pp. 69–70; Adontz, *Armenia*, pp. 333, 361–362; *idem,* "L'aspect," pp. 150–151; *idem,* "Šinakanut^ciwn"; Manandyan, *Feodalizm*, pp. 123–125, 152–156, 159–163, 165–171, 174–179, 182–189, 204–205, 208, 210–211, 214–215, 221–222, 239, 304–319; *idem,* "Problema," pp. 21–23, 27; Manandyan, "Ditołut^cyunner"; Avdalbegyan, "Hay šinakani ašχatavarjə"; Toumanoff, *Studies*, p. 127 and n. 222; *Kanonagirk^c*, I, pp. 433, 437, 439, 441, 443.

III.xiii, xxi; IV.ii, iv, li; V.xxiii, xxx, xliv
pp. 84, 97–98, 108, 116, 168, 203, 210–211, 230
See also *hazarapet*; *ṙamik*; *žołov.*

siwnhodos ‹ Gk. σύνοδος, by way of Syr. *sunhodos*
"synod, provincial ecclesiastical council"

This term is correctly used by BP, but in III.x it is curiously applied to the oecumenical council of Nicaea I (325), which has always been recognized as such by the Armenian church (cf. Aa, dccclxxxiv). As observed by Ačaryan and Malχasyancᶜ, but not by Hübschmann, this word did not come from Greek directly into Armenian but rather from Syriac because of the intercalated *h*. The usage in III.x may consequently have been taken over from the Syriac original of the *Vita* of James of Nisibis (see III.x nn. 1, 19).

> See NHBL, II, p. 717; HArmB IV, p. 222; HBB, IV, p. 223; Malχasyancᶜ, p. 336 n. 173; AG, p. 380, no. 410; Lampé, *Lexicon*, pp. 1334–1335; GLRB, II, p. 1051.
> III.x; IV.iv; V.xxix
> pp. 79–80, 113, 210
> See also *žołov*.

slak, see *zēn*, j.

slave, see *struk*.

snucᶜičᶜ/snucᶜanem ‹ Arm. *snucᶜanem*, "I nourish"
> "nurturer, nurse, foster-father/to nurture"
> Term used together with or as a synonym for *dayeak*. Cf. V.xxxvii, *ibrew zsan snucᶜanēr*, "nurtured them as his nurslings"
> See NHBL, II, p. 726; HArmB, IV, pp. 170–171, *san*, "foster-son, nursling"; HBB, IV, p. 237.
> III.v, xviii; IV.ii, iv, v, xi, xv; V.xxxv, xxxvii
> pp. 70, 93, 107, 112, 113, 119, 134, 145, 215, 221
> See also *dayeak*.

solitary, see *anapatawor*; *mianjn*; *van(kᶜ)/vanakan*.

solitary-community, see *van(kᶜ)*.

sopᶜestēs ‹ Gk. σοφιστής; cf. Phl. *sōfistā*
> "sophist, teacher"
> Term used by BP to refer to an imperial personage only, and not to Armenians.
> See NHBL, II, p. 734; HArmB, IV, p. 257; HBB, IV, pp. 251–252; AG, p. 380, no. 417; CPD, p. 75, *sōfistā*; GLRB, II, p. 1001.
> IV.x
> pp. 131–132

sophist, see *sopᶜestēs*.

sovereignty, see *terutᶜiwn*.

spar, see *zēn*, g.

sparakir, see *zōrkᶜ*, I.e, II.b

sparapet/sparapetutᶜiwn ‹ Parth. *spa-pat*, Phl. *spāhbed*; OP **spadapati-*, "general, commander"
> Title attested in ŠKZ, Parth. 24; Phl. 29; RGDS no. 57, pp. 65–66.
> "marshal of Greater Armenia, commander-in-chief of the army": Toumanoff prefers "high constable"
> The title of *sparapet* is frequently, though not invariably, used together with that of *zōravar* or *mec zōravar*, "commander-in-chief," despite the tautology. Eremyan traces the title back to the second century A.D., but, together with Aa, dccxcv, dccclxxiii and

ŁP⁺, *passim*, BP is the main source for the study of this office in Aršakuni Armenia and the period immediately following, Cf. Theoph. Sim., II.viii; Intro., pp. 49–50 and n. 208; also III.iv n. 2.

During the fourth century, the office of the *sparapet* was clearly the most important one after that of the king, and he could even act as ruler in the absence of an effective king (V.xxxvii–xliv). Throughout this period, the *sparapetutʿiwn*⁺ was hereditary in the Mamikonean house, which held it "by nature, fundamentally, originally" (*i bnēn*; V.xxxvii). Like the other contemporary offices of this type it belonged to the family as whole and did not necessarily pass in direct line from father to son. On one occasion, the *sparapetutʿiwn* even appears to have been split between two members of the Mamikonean house, Artawazd II and Vasak (III.xviii). Even so, the hereditary character of the office was such that it was not affected by the inability of the holder of the title to perform the duties of his office because of his extreme youth (III.xi). The royal attempt to interfere in the normal succession and to bestow this office on the member of another family was viewed as a flagrant abuse naturally ending in tragedy (V.xxxv, xxxvii). The evidence of ŁP⁺ makes it amply clear that the power of the Mamikonean *sparapet*s did not depend on the favor of the Aršakuni kings whom they outlived, and the same is obvious from the career of Manuēl in BP (V.xxxvii).

See NHBL, II, pp. 738–739; HArmB, IV, p. 263; HBB, IV, p. 255; AG, p. 240, no. 588; Schmitt, "Iranisches Lehngut," Leroy, "Composés en *-pet*," no. 26, p. 126; CPD, p. 75. *spāhbed*; Gignoux, *Glossaire*, pp. 33, 63; Christensen, *L'Iran*, pp. 107 n. 3, 108, 130–132, 370–371, 518–522, etc.; Sprengling, *Third-Century Iran*, pp. 9, 11, 18; Honigmann and Maricq, RGDS, p. 17; for the contemporary Sasanian office, Widengren, "Recherches," pp. 101–104; *idem, Feudalismus*, p. 73; Adontz, *Armenia*, pp. 185, 188, 222, 230, 339, 362, 510 n. 29a, 517–518 n. 54, 72*–73*, 74*, 79*–80*, 90*, 94*, 97*; Manandyan, *Feodalizm*, pp. 73–75; Toumanoff, *Studies*, pp. 97 n. 144, 112 n. 176, 132, 141 n. 253, 160, 162, 201, n. 228, 209, 210–211 n. 238, 325–326 and n. 89; Eremyan in HŽP, I, p. 829; Lukonin, "Institutions," pp. 703–705, who does not clarify the distinction of this office from that of *aspet; idem*, "Ametist," pp. 381–382 and fig. 1; Bedrosian, "*Sparapetutʿiwn*"; Garsoïan, "Prolegomena," cols. 182, 211–212 n. 44b.

III.iv, viii, xi; IV.ii, iv, xi, xv, xvi, xix–xxv, xxvii, xxxiv, xxxvi, xxxviii, xlvii, l, liii–lv; V.i–v, viii, x, xiv, xv, xx, xxiv, xxx, xxxiii–xxxviii, xl, xlii–xliv

pp. 69, 76, 80–81, 108, 133, 141, 146–147, 150–152, 154–155, 158–159, 162–163, 166–167, 170, 173–174, 185–190, 193, 195, 199–201, 204–205, 210, 214–226, 228, 230

See also *aspet; gorcakal; pet; stratelat; zōravar;* and Appendix I, "Mamikonean, house."

spear, see *zēn*, a.

spearbearer, see *zōrkʿ*, I.d, II.a.

spiritual-leader/leadership, see *arajnord*.

spiritual-teacher/teaching, see *vardapet*.

standard, see *drōšm*.

stratelat ‹ Gk. στρατελάτης
    "*stratēlatēs*, commander"

Byzantine title used in BP either as a synonym for *sparapet-zōravar* (IV.ii, xi; cf. Vg, cxxxv; GT⁺, p. 90, "*Stratelat‹ē› ew Hayocʿ zawravar‹ē›*"), or in its early Byzantine usage to designate the *magister militum* (V.i, though in this case it confuses the true *magister*,

Trajan/Adē, with Count Terentius). This term is also used in its Byzantine sense by MX, III.xxxvi (= MK, p. 295), who likewise misapplies the term to Terentius, who was a *dux* and *comes rei militari*.

> See NHBL, II, p. 755; HArmB, IV, p. 280; HBB, IV, p. 272; AG, p. 382, no. 434; GLRB, II, p. 1014; Guilland, *Institutions*, I, pp. 385-392.
> IV.ii, xi; V.i, ii, v
> pp. 108, 133, 185, 187, 194-195
> See also *sparapet*; *zōravar*; and Appendix I, "Adē"; "Terent."

strong/stronghold, see *amur*; *amroc^c*.

struk/strkut^ciwn ‹ ?
"slave/bondage"
Term used instead of *caray* (from which it is explicitly distinguished: Duin, *Canons*, ix, "*i carayut^ciwn i strkut^ciwn arkanel*") only to underscore the unworthiness of the patriarch appointed by Aršak II (IV.xv, "*struk i strkac^c ark^cuni*"). The only other use is in the locution (III.xiv) "*luc č^car strkut^cean carayutean.*" with its Scriptural allusion.

> See NHBL, II, p. 755; HArmB, IV, p. 281; HBB, IV, p. 272; Manandyan, *Feodalizm*, pp. 117-118, 236-240; *idem, Problema*, pp. 3, 12, 19; Adontz, "Sinakanut^ciwn," pp. 188-194; Eremian, "O rabstve"; Toumanoff, *Studies*, pp. 96 n. 142, 127 and n. 222; Perikhanian, "Rabovladenie"; *Kanonagirk^c*, II, p. 209; Hakobyan, "Cara"; *idem*, "Strukt^cyun."
> III.xiv; IV.xv
> pp. 89, 146
> See also *caray*; and Appendix I, "Č^cunak."

submission, see *caray*.

suin, see *zēn*, l.

sunak, see *zēn*, l.

sunawork^c, see *zōrk^c*, i.

sur, see *zēn*, c.

suser, see *zēn*, b.

suserawork^c, see *zōrk^c*, II.d.

sword, see *zēn*, b-e.

swordbearer, see *zōrk^c*, II.d.

synod, see *siwnhodos*.

tačar ‹ Parth. *tažar*; OP *tačara-*, "*palace*"
"palace, temple, hall"
BP commonly uses this term in the sense of "hall" or "palace" interchangeably with *aparan* (e.g. V.xxiv), though the *tačars* may not have been as elaborate buildings as *aparank^c* (cf. III.viii, *tačar mayri*, though it is also referred to as an *aparan*). Occasionally, the term is also used in its ecclesiastical sense (III.xix), or quite often as a "banqueting hall" (V.xxxii).

> See NHBL, II, p. 841; HArmB, IV, p. 365; HBB, IV, p. 368; AG, pp. 251, no. 640, 515; Schmitt, "Iranisches Lehngut," p. 95.
> III.viii, ix, xix; IV.ii, iv, v, lv; V.vi, xxiv, xxxii, xxxviii

pp. 75, 77, 93–94, 108, 115, 120, 174, 197, 204, 214, 222
See also *aparan.*

tᶜagakap ‹ Arm. *tᶜag* ‹ MP *tāg*, "crown" + *kap*, "tie, bond, knot"
"royal coronant"
Title first attested in an Aramaic inscription of King Artašēs I at the beginning of the second century B.C. and granted to the Bagratuni according to MX, I.xxii; II.iii, xlvii (= MK, pp. 111, 132–133, 187–188). In the fourth century this office was undoubtedly hereditary in the Bagratuni house, as is repeatedly noted by the Armenian sources (see e.g., Aa, dccxcv, dccclxxiii; the *Primary History*, Sebēos, ii, p. 54 = MK, p. 365; and reiterated throughout MX). Even BP, which normally denigrates the role of the Bagratuni in the affairs of Armenia, is forced to recognize this fact. Cf. Theoph. Sim., III.viii, second Iranian dignity which was hereditary in the Sūrēn house.

> See NHBL, I, p. 788; HArmB, II, pp. 134–135, *tᶜag*; HBB, II, p. 72; AG, p. 153, no. 243; Schmitt, "Iranisches Lehngut," p. 89, *tᶜag*; Nyberg, *Manual*, II, p. 189, *tāg*; Perikhanian, "Inscription," pp. 18, 22; Christensen, *L'Iran*, p. 107; Adontz, *Armenia*, pp. 339, 369; Manandyan, *Feodalizm*, pp. 61–62; Toumanoff, *Studies*, pp. 112 n. 176, 132, 160, 162, 202, 325 n. 88, 326, 342; Garsoïan, "Prolegomena," cols. 182, 210 n. 44a; Widengren, "Recherches," p. 104, *tᶜagadir.*

V.xliv
p. 228
See also Appendix I, "Bagratuni"; "Sūrēn Pahlaw."

takarapet, see *šapstan takarapet.*

tanutēr ‹ Arm. *tun* (gen. *tan*), "house, family" + *tēr*, "lord, master"
"master/lord of the house or family"
Senior member of a *naχarar* family; the term is used in BP interchangeably with *nahapet* or even *tēr*, "lord." Manandyan notes that although the Aršakuni kings occasionally appointed *tanutēr*s (e.g. IV.ii), they were at best ratifying or acknowledging a dynastic *fait accompli* (cf. V.xxxvii). During his tenure the *tanutēr* had absolute dominion (*terutᶜiwn*) over the *sepuh*s of his family, whom he led into battle, and over the administration of the common clan property, though he could neither alienate it nor will it to his heirs until the sixth-century reforms of Justinian in the imperial portion of Armenia.

> See NHBL, II, p. 843; HArmB, IV, p. 427, *tun*; HBB, IV, p. 371; AG, p. 498, no. 405; Benveniste, *Vocabulaire*, I, pp. 294–296, 305; Adontz, *Armenia*, pp. 141–146, for the deleterious results of the Justinianic reforms, 185, 213, 343–344, 348, 351–353, 357–359, 371, 516 n. 52, though some of his western equivalents have been superseded by the closer Iranian parallels; Manandyan, *Feodalizm*, pp. 43, 47–54, 57, etc.; Toumanoff, *Studies*, pp. 114 and n.185, 116–117, 130–131 n. 229, 143 n. 261, 433 n. 30; Widengren, "Recherches," pp. 100, 116.

III.xx; IV.ii, xvi, xviii, l; V.xxxvii, xxxviii, xliv
pp. 96, 108, 147–148, 168, 217–218, 222, 228
See also *nahapet; naχarar; sepuh; tēr; tun.*

tasanord ‹ Arm. *tasn*, "ten" + *-ord*, ordinal suffix
"tenth, tithe"
The context in BP suggests an ecclesiastical tax, but Malχasyancᶜ argues rather for a secular one paid by the peasants to their overlord.

> See NHBL, II, p. 848; HArmB, IV, p. 378, *tasn*; HBB, IV, p. 377; Malχasyancᶜ, p. 336 n. 177; AG, p. 496 no. 394, *tasn.*

V.xxxi
p. 211

tax, see *hark*.

teaching, spiritual, see *vardapetut'iwn*.

telapah, see *etelapah*.

temple

> **Christian**, see *tačar*.

> **pagan**, see *atrušan; bagin; mehean*.

tent, see *χoran*.

tent guards, see *zōrk'*, II.h.

tēr ‹ ?

> "lord, master"
> Term used throughout BP, both in its Scriptural sense and to designate the hereditary "lord" of a family or district. In the latter sense it is used interchangeably with *išχan, nahapet, tanutēr*, as well as in numerous other compounds.
>> See NHBL, II, p. 872; HArmB, IV, pp. 401–403; HBB, IV, p. 409; Manandyan, *Feodalizm*, pp. 45, 46–50, 57–59, etc.; Adontz, *Armenia*, pp. 286, 311, 313–315, 317, 321, 342–344, 347–348, 351, 371; Dowsett, "*Tēr*," for the critique of Adontz' etymology; Toumanoff, *Studies*, p. 114 and n. 85, where he still accepted Adontz's derivation.
>> P.S.; III.iii, v–viii, x–xiv, xvii–xx; IV.iii–vi, viii–x, xii–xvi, xix, l–lii, liv, lv, lvii, lix; V.i, iv, v, xix, xxiv, xxviii, xxxvii, xxxviii, xlii–xliv; VI.ix, xvi
>> pp. 63, 68–72, 74–81, 83, 85–90, 92–97, 108–112, 114–126, 128–132, 134–138, 140, 142–143, 145–147, 149, 167–169, 172, 174, 177, 179, 187, 190–196, 204, 208–209, 219–220, 222, 224, 227–229, 237, 239
>> See also *išχan; nahapet; pet; tanutēr; terut'iwn; tikin*.

territory, see *sahman*.

terut'iwn ‹ Arm. *tēr*

> "lorship, dominion, sovereignty"
> Term used in BP as the equivalent of the more common *išχanut'iwn*.
> See bibliography under *tēr*.
> III.x, xviii, xx; IV.ii, v, xv, xvi, V.xxxvii, xlii, xliv
> pp. 77, 93, 95, 108, 119, 141, 147, 218, 224, 228
> See also *išχanut'iwn; tēr*.

throne

> **episcopal**, see *at'oṙ*.

> **naχarar**, see *gah*.

tikin ‹ ?

> "lady, queen"
> This title, which is the feminine of *tēr*, "lord" is almost invariably used in BP in the sense of "queen," both in the case of the "queen" of Armenia and of the "queen-of-queens" of Persia (III.xxi; V.ii, "*tiknac' tikin*"), though the Iranian term *bambišn* is also used in III.xxi. This title was also an attribute of the goddess Anahit where it translated the MP *bānūg*.

See NHBL, II, p. 875; HArmB, IV, 406 and 401, *tēr*; HBB, IV, pp. 412–413; Benveniste, *Titres et noms propres*, pp. 27, 46; Dowsett, "*Tēr*," refuting the hypothesis of Adontz, *Armenia*, pp. 313–314.

III.iii, xx, xxi; IV.x, xv, lv, lix ("lady"); V.ii, iii, xxxvii, xxxviii, xliii, xliv

pp. 69, 96, 98 (*tiknac^c tikin*), 131, 145, 173–176, 179, 187 (*tiknac^c tikin*), 188, 221–223, 226–228

See also *bambišn*; *tēr*; and Appendix I, "Anahit"; "Aršakuni, anonymous queens I–II,"; "P^caranjem"; "Zarmanduχt."

tohm ‹ Parth, Phl. *tōhm/tōhmag*, "seed, stock, family"
"house, family, lineage"
Term designating the family unit of a *naχarar* house, In this sense it is used in BP interchageably with *tun* in reference to the *naχarar* families of the fourth century.

See NHBL, II, p. 887; HArmB, IV, pp. 417–418; HBB, IV, p. 430; AG, p. 253, no. 652; Schmitt, "Iranisches Lehngut," p. 93; CPD, p. 83, *tōmag*; Perikhanian, MHD, pp. 126–127, 528, *tōχmak*; idem, *Iran*, pp. 309–310 n. 19; Adontz, *Armenia*, pp. 305, 333, 507–509 n. 22.

III.iii, iv, vi–viii, xi–xiv, xvi–xviii; IV.ii, iii, iv, xi, xiv–xvi, xviii, xix, xxix, xxxi, xxxii, xxxviii, l, lviii, lix; V.xx, xxxiv, xxxv, xxxvii; VI.i

pp. 69–70, 72, 74, 76 (*azgatohm*), 81–82, 86 (*tohmakanut^ciwn*)-87, 91–93, 107–108, 114, 133, 139, 141, 145–149, 160–161, 163, 167, 178–179, 202, 215, 217, 220, 233

See also *naχarar*; *tūn*.

tohmakanut^ciwn, see *tohm*.

town, see *awan*.

tribe, see *azg*.

true-lord, see *bnak tēr*.

tun
"house, household, domain"
Term used interchangeably with *tohm* in the sense of a "noble house, family." It is also used in the sense of "domain" in BP and even in its original sense of an actual "house, building" (V.vi). It is also occasionally used together with *tohm* (e.g. V.vi, xi, xvii, "*tun tohmin*").

See NHBL, II, p. 891; HArmB, IV, pp. 427–429; HBB, IV, pp. 436–437; Adontz, *Armenia*, pp. 315, 333, 343–344, 347–348, 351; Toumanoff, *Studies*, pp. 114, and 114–115 n. 185, 116–117; Widengren, "Recherches," pp. 100–101, 149.

III.iv, v, viii, ix, xi, xiii–xviii, xx; IV.iii, xiii, xvi, xviii–xx, xxiii, xliv, l, li, lv; V.v–viii, xxx, xxxvi, xlii; VI.v, viii

pp. 69, 71, 76–77, 81–82, 84, 86, 90–92, 95–96, 108, 110–111, 137, 146, 148–149, 151–152, 156, 165, 167, 169, 175, 194, 197, 199, 217, 224, 235–236

See also *ostan*; *tohm*.

t^cur, see *zēn*, d.

tutor, see *dayeak*.

uχt ‹ Parth. **uχt*; Av. *uχti-*
"covenant, pact, congregation, oath, pledge"
The term is used in BP in the full range of its meanings from the basic "oath" to the "covenant" between God and man, and including the "congregation" of the clergy, where it appears as a synonym for the clergy, cf. Syr. *qeyāmā*. In its sense of "oath" it

is used interchageably with *erdumn*, but with the possible exception of IV.xxiii it is not found in BP with the connotation of "oath of fealty" or of "vassalage."

See NHBL, II, pp. 541–542; HArmB, III, pp. 593–594; HBB, III, pp. 593–594; AG, p. 216, no. 293; Schmitt, "Iranisches Lehngut," p. 89; Benveniste, "Éléments parthes," p. 30; Bolognesi, "Tradizione culturale," p. 578; Adontz, *Armenia*, pp. 349–350, 355, 520 n. 27; Toumanoff, *Studies*, p. 117 n. 192; Jargy, "Pacte"; Nedungatt, "Covenanters"; Thomson, *Eḷishē*, pp. 9–10.

III.iii, v, xi, xiv, xxi; IV.v, ix, x, xii, xiii, xv, xvi, xviii, xxi, xxiii, xxiv, li, liii, liv, lix; V.iv, xx, xxxii, xxxvii, xliii, xliv

pp. 68, 72, 80–81, 87, 98, 116, 123, 130, 132, 134, 136, 139, 141, 147–148, 153–154, 156, 158, 169–171, 179, 191, 193, 202, 213, 226, 228–229

vahan, see *zēn*, g.

vahanaworkꜥ, see *zōrkꜥ*, I.e, II.b.

vaławorkꜥ, see *zōrkꜥ*, II.e.

valiant, see *kꜥaǰ*.

valor/valorous, see *kaǰ*.

vałr, see *zēn*, e.

vanakan, see *van(kꜥ)*.

van(kꜥ)/vanakan/vaneraykꜥ ‹ Ir. *vahana; OP *āvahana-*
"dwelling, residence, lodging, community-of-solitaries"/dweller-in-a-community-of-solitaries"

As in the case of *mianjn/mianjnanocꜥ*, *miabanakan*, with which they are often used interchangeably, these two terms *van(kꜥ)/vanakan* have usually been taken in their later sense of "monastery/monk." It is, however, quite evident from the context of the term that *van/vankꜥ* occurs quite frequently in BP in its basic sense of "dwelling/residence," since neither the "lodging" of the sophist and the imperial officials (IV.x), nor the "house" of the wardrobe (V.vi), nor even the residences of the patriarch Nersēs (IV.xxiv) or of the dubious bishop Yohan (VI.ix) could have been "monasteries." In the cases in which these terms are clearly used in BP in their ecclesiastical sense, there is no indication in the context that they were to be taken in the later centralized sense, and consequently that coenobia existed in fourth century Armenia. The contexts suggest rather groups of hermits, or at most a lavra. The references to village *vankꜥ* in the *Canons* of St. Sahak (ca. 397–438) must at best reflect a fifth-century pattern and Akinean has even suggested that this document should be dated in the seventh century. The pattern in Armenia consequently follows the one observed by Fiey in Mesopotamia.

See NHBL, II, pp. 781–782, where the secular meanings of the term are given in first place, and the religious "monastery" in second; HArmB, IV, pp. 302–303, *van*²; HBB, IV, pp. 298, *vanakan*, 300, *vankꜥ*, where *bnakaran* and *ōtꜥewan* are given as the first meanings; Leloir, *Paterica armeniaca*, I, p. ix, who gives both *laura* and *monasterium* as the translations of *vankꜥ* and has evident misgivings over the rendition of *vanakan* as *monachus*, since he adds the Armenian term in every case. Akinean, *Sahak*, I. See also Fiey's conclusion, *Assyrie*, II, pp. 822–823, "rien ne permet de rattacher ces 'avoués' [fils ou filles du pacte] à des couvents établis.... Aucune trace ne subsiste de fondations antérieures à la seconde moitié du IVᵉ siècle."

IV.iv, x (lodging), xii; V.vi (house), xxiv (residence), xxvii, xxxi; VI.ix, xvi
pp. 113, 131, 134, 197, 204, 206–207, 212, 237
See also *kusastan*; *mianjn*.

vanerayk^c, see *van(k^c)*.

vardapet/vardapetut^ciwn ‹ SOIr. *varda-; Parth. *wrdpty*; cf. ?Av. *varǝz*-, "perform, do";
?*vard*-, "increase" + Arm. *pet*, "chief"; the folk-etymology ‹ *vard*, "rose" cannot be
taken seriously despite its prevalence
Attested as a personal name in ŠKZ, Parth. 27–28; Phl. 33, *wrdpt*; RGDS no. 64,
pp. 70–71, Γουλβαδ
"spiritual-teacher/teaching, instructor/instruction"
This term is regularly used to translate διδάσκαλος, διδαχή/διδασκαλία in the
Gospels, and Benveniste has proposed the widely accepted derivation "maître de pratique," though Gignoux still expresses reservations over this definition
In fourth-century Armenia, these terms connoted Christian instruction in general,
such as Aa or the *Teaching* of St. Gregory (AaT), and *vardapet* does not seem to have
carried its subsequent restricted meaning of "doctor of divinity." Gignoux even suggests
the possibility of some religious administrator/administration.
See NHBL, II, p. 792; HArmB, IV, pp. 318–320; HBB, IV, p. 309; Sprengling, *Third-
Century Iran*, pp. 9, 12, 19; Honigmann and Maricq, RGDS, p. 18; Back, SSI,
pp. 269–270; Benveniste, "Titres," p. 10; *idem*, "Études," p. 69; Modi, "Alexander," p. 111, who cites Ys.9.24 to link the term to the Av. verb *varǝd*-, "increase,"
and the teaching of the Aθravan (priest); Gignoux, *Glossaire*, pp. 34, 53; *idem*,
NPS, no. 398, p. 90, *Gulbed*; *idem*, "Pour une évaluation," pp. 9–10; Maricq,
RGDS, p. 70 n. 13; Schmitt, "Iranisches Lehngut," p. 102; Leroy, "Emprunts,"
pp. 59–60; *idem*, "Composés en *-pet*," no. 6, pp. 113–114; Bailey, "Armeno-
Indoiranica," pp. 114–115; Thomson, "Vardapet"; Alphandéry, "*Vardapet*"; Christensen, *L'Iran*, p. 120.
III.i–iii, xi, xiii–xv, xx; IV.iii–v, vii, xi–xiii, xv, lvii; VI.xvi
pp. 67, 69, 82, 84, 88–91, 97, 109, 112–113, 116, 123, 127, 133, 136, 142, 177, 239
See also *pet*.

vardapetut^ciwn, see *vardapet*.

vassal, see *caray*.

very, see *k^caǰ*; *mecamec*.

vicar, see *etełapah*.

village, see *gewł*.

vin ‹ Phl. *win*
"a form of guitar/lute"
Stemmed instrument similar to the *pandir*, but seemingly originating in the East. The
particularities distinguishing the two instruments are not known.
See NHBL, II, p. 823; HArmB, IV, p. 340; HBB, IV, p. 343; Malχasyanc^c, p. 337
n. 178; AG, p. 247, no. 622; CPD, p. 91, *win*.
V.xxxi
p. 212
See also *p^candir*.

vkayanocʿ, see *martyrium*.

vow, see *uχt*.

vsemakan ‹ Arm. *vsem*, "eminent, elevated, august, noble"
"high official" (?)
This title, often mistaken for a personal name, is frequently given a religious meaning (e.g. NHBL, ἱερός, *sacer*), but in the context of BP, a high military official seems more suitable and is in no way precluded by the derivation of the term.
    See NHBL, II, p. 831; HArmB, IV, pp. 348–349, which defines the term as "*geragoyn, veh, barjr*"; HBB, IV, p. 353.
    IV.xxix, xxxiv
    pp. 160, 162
    See also Appendix 1, "Apakan"; "Dmawund."

warden-of-the-marches, see *bdeašχ*; *marzpan*; *sahmanapah*.

weapon, see *zēn*.

world, see *ašχarh*.

χoran ‹ ?Phl. *χwaran*, "banquet"
"tent, baldachin, canopy, pavilion, tabernacle"
In Biblical passages, this term can refer to the canopy of heaven or the tabernacle of the sanctuary (IV.v), but its normal meaning in BP is "tent," both royal and ordinary, presumably slightly less elaborate than the *maškapačēn* of the Sasanian king of kings, though the *χoran arkʿuni* (IV.xv) may well have matched it. In the fourth century, the peripatetic courts of Iran (IV.liv) and of Armenia spent much of their time in encampments filled with tent that served not only for royal residences, *χoran arkʿuni*, but even for religious purposes, *ekełecʿaχoran* (IV.xv).
    See NHBL, I, p. 972; HArmB, II, p. 406; HBB, II, p. 290; CPD, p. 95, *χwaran*; Ghilain, *Essai*, p. 57; Benveniste, "Éléments parthes," pp. 28–30, who questions the derivation χoran ‹ χwaran; Garsoïan, "Banak arkʿuni."
    III.xx (*χoranapah*); IV.v, xv, xviii, xx, liv, lviii; V.xxxii, xxxviii
    pp. 96, 117, 142–143, 149, 152–153, 171, 178, 213, 222
    See also *maškapačēn*; *zōrkʿ*, II.h, for the *χoranapahkʿ*.

χoranapahkʿ, see *zōrkʿ*, II.h.

χrasaχ/frasaχ ‹ Phl. *frasang*
"parasang"
Measure of distance equivalent to four Roman miles, ca. 5,250 meters.
    See NHBL, I, p. 992; HArmB, IV, p. 491, *pʿarsaχ*; HBB, IV, p. 492, *pʿarsaχ*; Malχasyancʿ, p. 338 n. 184; AG, pp. 183–184, no. 357; CPD, p. 32, *frasang*; Nyberg, *Manual*, II, p. 76; Benveniste, "Emprunts," p. 764.
    V.xxxvii
    p. 218

zēn ‹ Phl. *zēn*, "weapon, armor, arms"
"weapon, armor" (in compounds) "armor-clad"
This term is usually given in BP in its more common sense of "weapon," but it also occurs with the sense of "armor" (e.g. V.vii) and in a series of compounds (*aspazēn* ‹ *asp*, "horse" + *zēn*; *patezēn/patenazēn* ‹ *pat*, "encompass, surround" + *zēn*; *spaṙazēn* ‹ *spaṙ*,

"totally, completely" + *zēn*) with the sense of "armor-clad." For this chain-mail armor, essentially similar to that of the contemporary Iranian heavy cavalry, see also *zōrk^c*, I.a.

The main weapons recorded in text are as follows:

(a) *nizak* ‹ Phl. *nēzag*, "long lance, spear." The *nizak* is also attested in MX, I.xxiv (= MK, p. 113) and ŁP^c, III, xix–xxi, lxxiv, lxxxi, pp. 124–125, 127, 134, 149 (= CHAMA II, pp. 331–332, 334, 337, 346), etc. It was the main weapon of the armored cavalry used to charge the foe and seems identical with the one depicted on Parthian and Sasanian monuments at Dura-Europos, Naqš-i Rustam, Firuzabad, etc. The *nizak*, together with the *suser*, was the main battle weapon of the nobility and the one most commonly mentioned in BP. Its prevalence is also evident from the compound *nizakakic^c*, "fellow-spearman," normally used in the text to designate a close "companion in arms" (III.vii; V.xlii, xliii). As indicated, the *nizak* was the characteristic weapon of the heavy cavalry, but a separate corps of *nizakawork^c* is also referred to; see *zork^c*, II.a.

(b) *suser* ‹ Phl. *šamšer/šafšer*, "long sword," also attested in MX, I.xxiv (= MK, p. 113). This was the heavy sword normally carried into battle and on the hunt, as indicated by the prevalence of this term in BP and of its representation on Iranian monuments. The *suser* was worn by the king and the nobles, and on state occasions, the "royal sword" (*suser ark^{c}uni*) is said to have been carried by the royal "chamberlain" (*senekapet*; IV.iii); cf. the title of "sword-bearer" in ŠKZ, Parth. 27; Phl. 33, RGDS no. 64, pp. 70–71 and the numerous representations on Sasanian hunting plates. The *suser* seems to have been worn hanging from a loose secondary belt and enclosed in a scabbard. Parthian and Sasanian monuments show it clearly worn on the left in battle and hunting scenes, though the king holds it directly in front of himself on state occasions. Like the *nizak*, the *suser* was primarily the weapon of the noble *azat*-cavalry, but a separate group of *suserawork^c* may also have existed (see *zōrk^c*, II.d). The term *suser* is also used together with *sur* in stereotype formulae, e.g., "*harkanēin i sur suser*" (see next entry).

(c) *sur*, "sword" in general. As opposed to *suser*, *t^{c}ur*, and even *vaɫr*, this term is not found in BP outside of stereotype formulae of which the most common is "*ənd sur haneł*" (III.vii; IV.xvii, xx, etc.) and Appendix V, b.

(d) *t^{c}ur* ‹ ? "short sword." According to Tirac^{c}yan, this was a shorter sword with a double prong on the pommel hanging directly from the belt and was of the *akinak/acinaces* type known among the Scythians and Achaemenids. According to BP, it was worn together with the *suser* (V.vi) and could be carried into battle by *sparakir* officers (V.xxxvii), though its presence there is attested on only that occasion. The presence of the *t^{c}ur* worn simultaneously with the *suser* is attested by the statue of Kaniška and silver plates of the hunting Šāhpuhr II and Yazdgard I in the Hermitage Museum.

(e) *vaɫr* ‹ ? "short sword, dagger." This term is also attested in BP (IV.xv, xx), but in both cases in the compound *vaɫrawork^c* (see *zōrk^c*, II.e). This term is also attested in MX, III.lv (= MK, p. 325) in the form *vaɫakan* where it is translated "dagger" by Thomson, while the Armenian lexicographers prefer "small sword," e.g. NBHL, "*parvus gladius, culter*," s.v. *vaɫakawor*. Neither the etymology of the term nor its aspect and use can be determined.

(f) *nran* ‹ ? "dagger." Although Armenian lexicographers hesitate over this term, which they identify with both *suser* and *t^{c}ur^c*, Tirac^{c}yan and Seyrig have shown that it was a short dagger apparently worn by noblemen strapped to the right thigh and unconnected to any belt. This hypothesis is clearly confirmed by BP (V.vi, xxxii, xxxv), Palmyrene funerary monuments and Sasanian Hermitage plates, where the *nran*, or a clear tie on the right thigh, is shown. There is no evidence in BP for the *nran* being carried in battle, since it is always mentioned in the context of the royal court; but the Hermitage plates also show it worn in hunting scenes.

569

(g) *spar/aspar* ‹ Phl. *spar*; *vahan* ‹ ? "shield." Both terms refer to shields, though the first is attested in BP only in the compound *sparakir*. No difference between the two can be distinguished in the text, but the *vahan*s used by guards on state occasions are said to have been embossed with gold (V.xxxii). No shields are mentioned in the equipment of the *azat*-cavalry (see *zōrkʿ*, I.a), nor are they normally represented in Sasanian scenes except on the knight on the lower register at Taq-i Bostān. They were, however, unquestionably carried into battle by the *sparakir* and *vahanaworkʿ*, as is obvious from their names (see *zōrkʿ*, II.b) as well as by the *sakraworkʿ* and *šertawork* on occasion (see *zōrkʿ*, II.c., f).

(h) *salawart* ‹ ? Ir. "helmet." Helmets are mentioned in BP on only two occasions (IV.xx, xlii), both referring to the armor-clad cavalry, but they are not specifically singled out in the detailing of the armor worn by Manuēl Mamikonean (V.xxxvii). In the absence of a precise description it seems reasonable to suppose that the helmet did not cover the face—King Varazdat aimed his lance at Manuēl's mouth (*loc. cit*)—and consequently did not seem to have had the additional mail attachments visible on the representation at Taq-i Bostan, which covered all but the eyes of the knight.

(i) *sakur* ‹ ? Syr. *səqūrā*, "axe, battle-axe." The *sakur* appears to have been the double-edged battle-axe, as it is distinguished from the ordinary hatchet (*kacʿin*) of III.x, but BP gives no precisions, using the term only once (V.xxxii) outside of the compound *sakraworkʿ*. These axes were obviously carried by the *sakraworkʿ*, but also on occasion by the *sparakir* and the *šertaworkʿ* (see *zōrkʿ*, II.b, c, f). Because the *sakur* does not seem to have been a noble weapon, the only representation of an axe known to me is found on the "Klimova" plate representing a royal apotheosis or the Moon god himself, but even that is a hatchet rather than a true battle-axe.

(j) i) *aleln* ‹ ? "bow," found only in the compounds *alelnaworkʿ* (IV.xx), *alelnakaparč* except for a Scriptural citation (IV.xv) cf. MX, I.xxiv (= MK, p. 113); *dipalelunkʿ*, "slingers"; ii) *kaparčkʿ* ‹ Phl. *kantigr*, cf. Syr. *qəṭerq(a)*, "quiver," found in BP only in the compound *alelnakaparč* (VI.viii). *net* ‹ ? Phl. *nad, nay*, "arrow"; and *slak* ‹ ? "arrow."

The entire equipment of archers is rarely mentioned in BP, and in the case of *aleln* and *kaparčkʿ* it is only attested in compounds. The terms *net* and *slak* are seemingly used interchangeably and, as indicated in VI.vii and n. 4, the heavy *alelnakaparč*, or quiver containing both the bow and arrows, was not carried on the back, but worn slung around the hips, low on the right side of the rider, a position confirmed by Sasanian silver plates, although it may have been fastened directly to the back of the saddle in earlier Parthian times. Archery must have been used in combat, as is evidenced by the exploit of Artawazd III Mamikonean (V.xliii) and by the inclusion of a bow and quiver among the weapons of the young bandit returning from a raid (VI.viii). A group of *alelnaworkʿ* is likewise mentioned (IV.xx). The use of the hunting bow favored by Parthian and Sasanian courts, as is repeatedly attested in Iranian art, is not mentioned in BP.

(k) *šert* ‹ ? lit. block or splinter of wood, "club, cudgeon." This weapon is given as the characteristic on of Mazkʿutʿkʿ barbarians (III.vii), although it is also mentioned in the Persian army (III.xx). A group of *šertaworkʿ* may also have existed in Armenia (see *zōrkʿ*, II.g).

(l) *suin.sunak* ‹ Syr. *sūwīnā*, "short lance, javelin, pike." This term is attested only once in BP in the compound *sunakaworkʿ* (see *zōrkʿ*, III.h). The weapon is also attested in MX, II.v (= MK, p. 134), where the context clearly suggests that it was hurled at the enemy, but BP gives no indication of its form or use.

See, for weapons in general, Tiracʿyan, "Utochnenie," for the *suser*, *tʿur*, and *nran*; Kʿalantʿaryan, "Sparazinutʿyunə," on armor; *idem*, "Zenkerə"; Bivar, "Cavalry Equipment;" Seyrig, "Armes"; Gabba, "Influenze"; Garsoïan, "Armement"; Malandra, "Glossary," though BP's vocabulary is rarely found there.

For the etymologies of the various terms, their meaning, and their figurative representations, see for *zēn*: NHBL, I, p. 7531 HArmB, II, pp. 93–94; HBB, II, pp. 22–23; AG, p. 151, no. 233; CPD, p. 99; *aspazēn*, NBHL, I, p. 315; HArmB, I, p. 217; HBB, I, p. 237; AG, p. 108, no. 61; *patenazēn*, NHBL, II, p. 608; HBB, IV, p. 61; *spaṙazēn*, NBHL, II, p. 735; HArmB, IV, p. 260, *spaṙ*; HBB, IV, p. 253. (a) *nizak*: NBHL, II, p. 425; HArmB, III, p. 451; HBB, III, p. 462; CPD, p. 59; Ghirshman, *Persian Art*, figs. 63c, 67, 69, 122, 156, 166, 219, 220, 235 (bottom); Harper, *Silver*, pls. xi a–b, p. 16, etc. (b) *suser*: NBHL, II, p. 732; HArmB, IV, p. 252; HBB, IV, p. 249; CPD, pp. 78–79; Trousdale, "Long Sword"; Ghirshman, *Persian Art*, figs. 98, 100, 110, 195, 205, 248, 250, 253, etc.; Harper, *Hunter*, pp. 83–84, figs. 28–28a; for the use of the ceremonial royal-sword, see Ghirshman, *Persian Art*, figs. 212–213, 235 (upper register), 242, 244–246; Harper, "Thrones," pls. i–iva, v–vi; Harper and Meyer, *Sasanian Silver*, pls. xvi, 33–36. (c) *sur*: NBHL, I, p. 733; HArmB, IV, pp. 254–255; HBB, IV, pp. 250–251. (d) *t⁽ur⁾*: NBHL, I, p. 822; HArmB, II, pp. 254–255; HBB, II, p. 126; Harper, *Hunter*, p. 84, fig. 28a; and for the representations of the *t⁽ur⁾* worn simultaneously with the *suser*, Ghirshman, *Persian Art*, fig. 350; Harper and Meyer, *Sasanian Silver*, pls. xv = 16, 24, 29. (e) *vaḷr*: NBHL, II, pp. 772 (*vaḷakawan*), 774 (*vaḷr*); HArmB, IV, pp. 247–248 (*vaḷakawor*), 248 (*vaḷr*); HBB, IV, p. 291, "short sword"; Thomson, MK, p. 325, "dagger." (f) *nran*: NHBL, II, p. 455; HArmB, III, p. 477; HBB, III, p. 487, no. 1; Harper and Meyer, *Sasanian Silver*, pls. 12 and 38, fig. 17b, for the clasps on the right thigh; Lukonin, *Iran*, pl. xix; Tirac⁽yan⁾, "Utochnenie," fig. 6; Seyrig, "Armes," p. 58[16], fig. 12; Colledge, *Palmyra*, fig. 61. (g) *spar/ aspar*: NBHL, I, p. 315 (*aspar*); HArmB, I, p. 273 (*aspar*); HBB, I, p. 237 (*aspar*); AG, pp. 108–109, no. 65 (*aspar*); CPD, p. 75 (*spar*); also *vahan*; NBHL, II, p. 771; HArmB, IV, p. 165; HBB, IV, p. 177; AG, pp. 235–236, no. 566; Harper, *Hunter*, pp. 89–90, figs. 31–31a. (i) *sakur*: NHBL, II, p. 687; HArmB, IV, p. 160; HBB, IV, p. 173; Harper, "Thrones," pl. I (?). (j) *aḷeḷn*: NBHL, I, p. 57; HArmB, I, p. 126; HBB, I, p. 42; also *kaparčk⁽⁾*: NBHL, I, p. 1054; HArmB, II, p. 523; HBB, II, p. 390; CPD, p. 49, *kantigr*; also *net*: NBHL, II. p. 413; HArmB, IV, p. 224; HBB, IV, p. 224; for representations of the various attributes of archery, Ghirshman, *Persian Art*, figs. 62, 63a, 125a, 232, 247–248, 250, 252–253, 295d, 314, 340; Harper, *Hunter*, p. 37, pl. 12; Harper and Meyer, *Sasanian Silver*, pls. x, xii, xiii, xvi. See also, *ibid.*, pls., x, xii, 8, 9, 13, 15, 17, 20 23, 25, 28, 31–32; Colledge, *Palmyra*, fig. 33; Perkins, *Dura-Europos*, pl. 38, for the wearing of the quiver hung on the right side of the rider, but cf. *ibid.*, pls. 16, 26, for the fastening to the saddle. (k) *šert*: NBHL, II, p. 476; HArmb, III, p. 511; HBB, III, p. 513. (l) *suin/ sunakan*: NBHL, II, pp. 731–732; HBB, IV, pp. 747 (*suin*), 748 (*sunak*).

zēn: III.xviii, xx (*spaṙazēn*); IV.xx (also *patenazēn sparazēn*), xxi (*spaṙazēn*), xxii, xxiii, li, lv; V.ii, iv, vi (*patezēn*), xxxvi–xxxviii, with the sense of "armor" (also *aspazēn*, *spaṙazēn*), xl (also *spaṙazēn*), xliii (*spaṙazēn*). (a) *nizak*: III.vii (*nizakakic⁽⁾*); IV.ii, xxxii, li; V.iv (also *nizakabnaw*), v, xxx, xxxvii, xlii (*nizakakic⁽⁾*), xliii (also *nizakakic⁽⁾*). (b) *suser*: III.xii; IV.iii (*suser ark⁽unakan⁾*) xvi, xviii, xxi (with *sur*), xxii, xxiv, xxxvi, li, lvii; V.i (with *sur*), vi, xxxii; VI.viii. (c) *sur*: III.vii–ix, xviii, xxi; IV.xvii, xx, xxi (with *suser*), xxii, xxiv–xxvi, xliii, xlviii, li, liv; V.i (with *suser*), ii, xv, xvii–xix, xxxix, xli, xliii. (d) *t⁽ur⁾*: V.vi, xxxvii; VI.viii. (e) *vaḷr* (only in compounds), see *zōrk⁽⁾*, II.e. (f) *nran*: V.vi, xxxii, xxxv. (g) *spar* (only in compounds), see *zōrk⁽⁾*, II.b; also *vahan*: V.v, xxxii, xxxvii. (h) *saḷawart*: IV.xx; V.xliii. (i) *sakur*: (for compounds, see *zōrk⁽⁾*) V.xxxii. (j) *aḷeḷn*; IV.xv; VI.viii (*aḷeḷnakarpač*); also *net*: IV.xiv, xxxix; V.xxxv–xxxvi, xliii; also *slak⁽⁾*: IV.li;

V.xxxv. (k) *šert* (only in compounds) see *zōrkʿ*, II.g. (l) *suin* (only in compounds) see *zōrkʿ*, II.i. For complete references to warriors carrying particular weapons, see *zōrkʿ*, II

pp. *zēn*: 93, 96 (*sparazēn*, 150 (*patezēn*), 153–156, 168, 173 (*sparazēn*), 187, 190, 191, 193, 196 (*patezēn*), 197, 217, 219 (*aspazēn, sparazēn*), 221, (*sparazēn*), 224, 226–227 (*sparazēn*); (a) *nizak*: 74, 108, 161, 168, 191, 193–194, 197, 210, 219, 224, 227; (b) *suser*: 83, 109–110 (*arkʿunakan*), 146, 149, 154–155, 157–158, 162, 168, 177, 186, 197, 214, 236; (c) *sur*: 74–75, 77, 93, 99, 148, 151, 154–155, 157–159, 164, 166, 168, 171, 186–187, 201, 223–224, 227; (d) *tʿur*: 197, 220, 236; (f) *nran*: 197, 214, 217; (g) *spar/vahan*: 195, 213, 214, 220; (h) *saławart*: 150, 226; (i) *sakur*: 213–214; (j) *ałełn/ałełnakaparč*: 150, 236; *net/slak*: 140, 163, 168, 217, 227–228
See also *nizakakicʿ*; *zōrkʿ*.

zindakapet/zndakapet/zndkapet ‹ ?Phl. *zēn*, "weapon"; ‹ ?Phl. *zīndag*, "alive, living" + Arm. *pet*, "chief"
Cf. ŠKZ, *zynd'nyk*, Parth. 28; Phl. 34; RGDS no. 65, pp. 70–71 ἐπὶ τῆς φυλακῆς. Persian military dignity: "jailer"?
The precise nature of this Persian office remains uncertain despite the evidence of ŠKZ. Various explanations based on proposed etymologies have been suggested: "commander-of-the-elephants," "commander of a group or company," and most improbably, "commander of the Zindīk or Zandīk/Manichaean heretics," though "jailer" is now prevailing.
See HArmB, II, p. 96; HBB, II, p. 24; Malχasyancʿ, p. 328 n. 120; AG, p. 41, no. 73; CPD, p. 99; JIN, p. 368; Gignoux, *Glossaire*, pp. 38, 68; Sprengling, *Third-Century Iran*, pp. 9, 12, 19; Honigmann and Maricq, RGDS, p. 18.
IV.xliii
p. 164
See also *pet*.

zndakapet, see *zindakapet*.

zndkapet, see *zindakapet*.

žołov/žołovem ‹ ?
"council, assembly/assemble, gather together, collect"
Although this term is used both in its general sense and in that of an ecclesiastical council, BP also uses the term with reference to the "council of the realm or general council" (*ašχarhažołov*), an institution that brought together the nobility—including both magnates and lesser nobles—and the clergy, as in Iran, but at which the third estate—*ramik* and *šinakan*—was also represented and on occasion allowed to participate in the deliberations. This council advised the king and helped to designate a patriarch (IV.iii). It could also meet in the absence of the king (III.xxi; V.xxxiii) and even in opposition to him (IV.li). The institution of the council was known in Iran from early times. It is recorded for the Parthian period by Strabo (*Geogr.*, XI.ix.3) and Justinus (*Epitome*, XLI.iv.2; XLII.iv.l), and under the Sasanians, by Aa, xxix, dcxci, and Tansar (pp. 61–63), etc. Instead of declining, as was the case in Sasanian Iran, the Armenian council maintained itself vis-à-vis the king and went on to survive him (ŁPʿ, xxii, xxvii, pp. 44–45, 50, 52–53 (= Ełishē, pp. 257–258, 263–266, etc.).
See NHBL, I, p. 836; HArmB, II, pp. 232–233; HBB, II, p. 144; Manandyan, *Feodalizm*, pp. 79–83; Lukonin, "Institutions," pp. 689–690, 698–708; Garsoïan, "Prolegomena," cols. 183–187 and nn. 46, 78.
III.x, xx, xxi; IV.iii–v, ix, x, li; V.xxix, xxxi, xxxiii, xliv
pp. 79, 97, 108–109, 111, 113, 123, 129–132, 168–169, 210, 212, 214, 228
See also *siwnhodos*.

zōravar/zōravarutʻiwn/zōragluχ ‹ Phl. *zōr*, "power, strength"; cf. NP *zōravar*, "general"

"commander, general"

Military title generally though not invariably reserved for Armenians as opposed to foreigners (cf., however, IV.lv; V.i, ii). Either alone, or especially in conjunction with *mec*, "great" or *Hayocʻ*, *zōravar* takes on the connotation of "commander-in-chief" and is used either interchangeably with or jointly with the title of *sparapet*.

See NHBL, I, p. 756; HArmB, II, pp. 114–115, *zōr*; HBB, II, p. 43; AG, p. 152, no. 239; Schmitt, "Iranisches Lehngut," p. 90; CPD, p. 99, *zōr*.

P.S.; III.iv, vii–ix, xi, xvi, xviii, xx, xxi; IV.ii, iii, ix, xi, xvi, xviii–xx, xxii, xxiv, xxvii (*zōragluχ*), xxix–xxxv, xxxvii, xl, xli, xliii (*zōragluχ*), xlv (*zōragluχ*), xlvi–xlix (*zōragluχ*), liii, liv, lv (both forms); V.i (both forms), ii–iv, vi, xiv, xvi, xx, xxxii, xxxv, xxxvii–xl, xlii–xliv; VI.i .

pp. 63, 69–70, 74–77, 80–81, 91, 93, 96–97, 107–108, 130, 133, 146–152, 154–156, 158–167, 170, 173, 175–176, 185–191, 193–194, 196, 200–202, 213, 215–219, 221–226, 228, 230, 233

See also *sparapet*; *stratelat*; *zōrkʻ*.

zōrkʻ/zōr ‹ Phl. *zōr*, "power, strength"

"army, forces, host"

The Arsacid Armenian army depicted in BP was conceived to be a royal one (e.g. IV.xx, xxii, etc.), but it was in fact controlled and commanded by the hereditary Mamikonean *sparapet*. Internally, it was subdivided into a collection of *gund*s or "contingents" (see, e.g., III.xxi, *bazmagund banakn* even though the reference here is to the Romans), each of which was loyal to its "lord," who led it in battle (e.g. V.iv, v, xliii, etc.). Even the king, as lord of Ayrarat, had his own contingent, *gundn arkʻunakan* (e.g. V.xxxvii). Other army commanders or junior *zōrawar*s are also mentioned (e.g. IV.ii, the younger Mamikonean brother, IV.xx, Bagos, etc.). Judging from BP's description of St. Nersēs's career before his consecration, the office of *senekapet* also had military aspects, but these are not specified beyond hyperbole (IV.iii and n. 7; also above, *senekapet*). Finally, in spite of Adontz's and Toumanoff's rejection of the presumed hereditary title of the Bagratuni, *aspet*, "master-of-the-horse," as equivalent to that of *sparapet*, the *aspet* (cf. V.xliv) may in fact have been the separate commander of the *azat*-cavalry, as infantry detachments are also mentioned in BP. For the best listing of army units, see IV.xx and possibly xv, though the second passage perhaps refers to haphazard groups armed with the weapons that came hand to hand, rather than to profesionally trained detachments. Recently, Danielyan has argued for a major reform under Trdat III, modeled on Diocletian's system of four prefectures. This thesis, however, which relies on the four divisions of the late and semi-fictious *Zōrnamak*, "Military List," remains unconvincing.

(I) *ayrewji* ‹ Arm. *ayr*, "man" + *ji*, "horse," or more commonly, *hecealkʻ/hecelazōr* ‹ Arm. part. of *hecanim*, "mount, ride + *zōr*, "force." This branch unquestionably formed the bulk of the Armenian army and was renowned beyond its borders; see, e.g., Sebēos, xlviii, p. 164 (= trans. pp. 132–133). Its aspect and function provide additional links between Armenian and Iranian societies.

(I.a) *azatagund/hecealkʻ* [*sparazēn* (III.xii; V.xl), *zrahaworkʻ* (V.vi), *patenazēn* IV.xx; V.vi)]. These terms (for which see also *zēn*) refer to the noble cavalry, with both the rider and his steed armor-clad. In battle, the knight was covered from head to foot like the contemporary Persian nobles in an iron, probably mail, body armor (*zrah*) and wore a helmet (*saławart*) as well. The horse was likewise caparisoned in metal (*aspazēn* ‹ Phl. *asp* "horse" + *zēn*, "armor," V.xxxvii, or *sparazēn*). The basic weapons carried by the armor-clad cavalry were the *nizak* and *suser*, and perhaps occasionally a bow with arrows; but no additional shield is mentioned in their armament (see *zēn*, a, b, g, j). The description in BP matches the numerous representations of Parthian and Sasanian knights at Dura-Europos, Firuzabad, Naqš-i Rustam, Ṭaq-i Bostan, etc. This heavy cavalry was also known to classical authors, who refer to them as *cataphracti* or *clibanarii* (AM, XXIII.vi.83; XXIV.vi.8; *Not. Dig.*, pp. 13, 17, 21; Justinius, *Epitome*, XL.ii, 10: "*Munimentum ipsis equisque loricae plumatae sunt, quae utrumque toto corpore tegunt*"; etc.) See also Strabo, *Geogr.*, XI.xiv, 9, and Nöldeke, *Tabari*, p. 479 n. 1.

(I.b) *ṙamikspas.* In addition to the noble cavalry, a servile cavalry seems also to have existed. To be sure, BP (II.xx and n. 14) specifically distinguishes the cavalry from the *ṙamikspas*, but this is not the case in other Armenian sources of the period: ȽPʿ, xlviii, lxxviii, pp. 84, 144 (= CHAMA, II, p. 343, mistranslated), speaks of the *ṙamik ayrujioyn*, and the twelfth canon of the Council of Duin in 640 still distinguishes clearly between the two cavalries: "*Omankʿ yazatacʿ ew yṙamik hecelocᵐ*" (Whoever, from the noble and servile cavalry). Consequently, Widengren, followed by Perikhanian, has identified the *ṙamikspas* as lightly armed mounted archers similar to the *equites sagittarii* of the *Not. Dig.*, pp. 17 line 31, 83 lines 11–12 (among the troops assigned to the *dux Armeniae*), and elsewhere; cf. also Ełišē, iv, p. 96 (= *Ełishē*, p. 148). Nevertheless, we have no information about the arms carried by the *ṙamikspas*, and a separate corps of archers, *alełnaworkʿ*, is mentioned in BP (see below, II.f).

(I.c) *matenik gund.* If, as has been postulated, this was a noble elite corps, it must have been mounted. But BP (III.viii) merely distinguishes it from the "irregular" *gugaz*, and the "army" *banak*, *zōrkʿ*, without any specification of rank or armament (see *matenik gund*).

(I.d) *nizakaworkʿ* ‹ Arm. *nizak*, "lance, spear" + suff. of attribute *-awor*, "lancer, spearmen." As indicated in I.a, most of the *nizakaworkʿ* belonged to the armored cavalry, of which the lance was the characteristic weapon. Nevertheless, some of them may have been on foot (see below, II.a).

(I.e) *sparakir* ‹ Phl. *spar*, "shield + root of Arm. *krem*, "bear"; *vahanaworkʿ* ‹ Arm. *vahan*, "shield" + suff. of attribute *-awor*, "shield-bearers." Most of the shield-bearers served as guardsmen on foot (see below, II.b). Nevertheless, some of them must have been mounted, for they are explicitly said to have dismounted to guard Garegin Ṙštuni (V.xxxvii).

(II) *hetewak/hetiotkʿ* ‹ Arm. *otkʿ*, "foot," cf. Phl. *payādag/paydag*, "on foot"; "footsoldiers, footmen, infantry." This term is rarely used in BP (III.vii; IV.xv; V.xxxii), which prefers to record detachments by their distinguishing weapon, and it is used exclusively in conjunction with the name of such a detachment. Nevertheless, the evidence in BP does not support the usual contention that the Aršakuni army was composed exclusively of cavalry, and suggests that the footsoldiers may also have been cuirassed or "armor-clad" (*kuṙ varealkʿ*) on occasion (V.xxxii). See also Ełišē, p. 100 (= *Ełishē*, p. 152). The Latin loanword *legio* is always used with the connotation of infantry (see V.v n. 9).

(II.a) *nizakaworkʿ* ‹ Arm. *nizak*, "lance, spear" + suff. of attribute *-awor*, "lancers, spearmen." As indicated above (I.a, d), the bulk of the *nizakaworkʿ* should be equated with the noble armor-clad cavalry. Nevertheless, they are distinguished from the cavalry in IV.xv, xx, so that some non-noble detachments of spearmen may also have existed.

(II.b) *sparakir* ‹ Arm. *spar*, "shield" + *kir/krem*, "bear": "shield-bearers"; *vahanaworkʿ* ‹ Arm. *vahan*, "shield" + suff. of attribute *-awor*, "shield-bearers." Together with the *nizakaworkʿ*, these detachments are the ones most commonly mentioned among the field troops in both the Armenian and the contemporary Roman army (see e.g., V.v). As mentioned above (see I.e), some of them must have served in the cavalry. Nonetheless, they are explicitly distinguished from the cavalry in IV.xx, and must also have served on foot when doing guard duty in royal residences (V.vi, xxxii). The *sparakir* and

vahanawork^c are always distinguished by name (e.g. V.v, xxxii), but there is no indication of difference in their armament or functions, as the two terms are often used
interchangeably in the same chapter. Their armament is not indicated beyond the
obvious shield, which also seems to have been carried by *sakrawork*^c and *šertawork*^c
(see below, II.c, g).

(II.c) *sakrawork*^c ‹ Arm. *sakur*, "axe" + suff. of attribute *-awor*, "axemen." In addition to their axe, the *sakrawork*^c seem to have carried a shield (V.vi, xxxii). Although
there is no special mention in the text to that effect, the context suggests that these
axemen probably served on foot as guardsmen rather than as soldiers in the field. Cf.
IV.xxix n. 1 for the *taprik zōrk*^c as axe-men.

(II.d) *suserawork*^c ‹ Arm. *suser*, "long sword" + suff. of attribute *-awor*, "swordsmen." As in the case of the *nizakawork*^c (see above, I.a; II.a), the *suserawork*^c should
primarily be identified with the armored cavalry. Nevertheless, they are specifically
distinguished from the cavalry in IV.xx and referred to as "servants" (*spasawork*^c) in
IV.xv, so that non-noble infantry detachments of swordsmen may also have existed.

(II.e) *vałrawork*^c ‹ Arm. *vałr/vałrakan*, "short sword, dagger?" + suff. of attribute
-awor, "swordsmen?" Nothing is known of this detachment beyond its name.

(II.f) *ałełnawork*^c ‹ Arm. *ałełn*, "bow" + suff. of attribute *-awor*, "bowmen, archers."
As indicated above (I.a; cf. *zēn*, j), bows must occasionally have been carried by the
armor-clad cavalry, and they have been postulated for the *ṙamikspas* (I.b), but the
ałełnawork^c are distinguished from the cavalry in IV.xx, so that some of them must have
served on foot.

(II.g) *šertawork*^c ‹ Arm. *šert*, "piece of wood, club, cudgel" + suff. of attribute *-awor*,
"club-bearers." The *šertawork*^c are explicitly identified as "infantry" (*hetework*^c) in
III.vii. They seem to have served as Persian guards for prisoners in Armenia (III.xx),
though they were a regular part of the Mazk^cut^ck^c army (III.vii), and they apparently
carried shields (III.xx).

(II.h) *χoranapahk*^c ‹ Arm. *χoran*, "tent" + *pah/pahem*, "guard": "tent-guards." Nothing specific is known of these guards, who are mentioned only once (III.xx), or of their
armament. The term may have merely a general meaning and the *χoranapah* should
perhaps be identified with the *šertawork*^c (see above, II.g) or other groups who also did
guard duty, such as the *sparakir/vahanawork*^c or the *sakrawork*^c (see above, II.b, c), but
this is not specified and a special corps of guards for the royal tent is entirely possible.

(II.i) *sunawork*^c ‹ Arm. *suin*, "javelin, pike" + suff. of attribute *-awor*, "pikesmen."
This group is mentioned only once in BP (IV.xv) among servants (*spasawork*^c), and may
consequently not have formed a separate detachment, though their weapon was also
known to MX (see *zēn*, l).

In addition to these more or less regular troops, irregular *gugaz* levies are also
mentioned by BP (see *gugaz*). On the other hand, neither the Persian *puštipan* (IV.liii,
V.vii; see *puštipan*) nor the elephants III.viii; IV.xxii, xxiv, xxxiii, xl, etc.), with which
the author of the text was clearly family, are recorded by BP in the Armenian army. The
figures reaching into hundreds of thousands, and even millions, given for the various
armies are obviously fantastic for the period and are probably to be taken as equivalent
to the "innumerable" hosts as great as "the sands of the seashore," or as "the stars in
the heavens" of epic and Scriptural formulae (see Appendix V.*i*).

For the term *zōrk*^c/*zōr* in general, see NBHL, I, p. 755 (*zōr*); HArmB, II, pp.
114–115 (*zōr*); HBB, II, p. 44; AG, p. 152, no. 239; CPD, p. 99 (zōr). For the
etymologies of the various units, see the listing below as well as separate entries
such as *gund*, etc. For the etymologies of the detachments identified by their
weapons, see the corresponding entry under *zēn*; and for Trdat III's putative army
reform, see Danielyan, "Trdat III.i ṙeformə." (I) *ayrewji*: NHBL I, p. 99, HArmB,
I, p. 173, *ayr*; HBB, I, p. 84, *ayruji*. (I.a) *heceal(k*^c*)*: NHBL II, p. 81; HArmB, III,

p. 75, *hec*; HBB, III, p. 89. For the cavalry in general both *azat* and *ŕamik*, see MHD, A16; 11-14, 14-16; A19; 2-6; pp. 359-360, 365-366; Bivar, "Cavalry Equipment"; Gabba, "Influenze"; Christensen, *L'Iran*, pp. 111-112; 206, 306; Adontz, *Armenia*, pp. 311-312; Toumanoff, *Studies*, pp. 324-326; Manandyan, *Feodalizm*, pp. 103-119; *idem*, "Voĭsko"; Widengren, "Recherches," pp. 99-100; 163-164 (*ŕamikspas*); Perikhanian, *Iran*, pp. 17, 300 n. 14, 324 n. 163 (*ŕamikspas*); Sulimirski, "Archers"; also, for armored cavalry see Khavanov, "Katafractarii"; Diethart and Dintsis, "Leontoklibanarier"; and for the representations of armor-clad Iranian cavalry, Ghirshman, *Persian Art*, figs. 63c, 163, 166, 220, 235, etc. (II) *hetewak*: NHBL, II, p. 91; HArmB, III, pp. 83-84, *het*; HBB, III, p. 98. For the compounds of *zēn* having the meaning of armor—*aspazēn, patenazēn, spaŕazēn*— and detachments identified by their weapon, see *zēn*, svv.

Zōrk': *passim*. (I) *ayrewji/hecealk'*, III.vii, xx; IV.xx, xxi, xxiii; V.vii, xxxviii, xl; VI.viii (?) (Ib) *ŕamikspas*, III.xx; (I.d)*nizakawork'*: IV.xx, xxi; V.v, vi [xxxvii, xliii] and (IIa) below; (Ie) *sparakir/vahanawork'*: V.xxxvii and (IIb) below; (II) *hetewak/hetiotk'*, : III.xx; IV.xv, xxxvi (*hetiotk'*); V.xxxii, xxxvii; (IIa) *nizakawork'*, IV.xv; (IIb) *sparakir/vahanawork'*, III.xx; IV.xv; V.v (both terms), vi, xxxii; (IIc) *sakrawork'*, IV.xv, xx; V.vi, xxxii; (IId) *suserawork'*, IV.xv, xx; (IIe) *vaŕrawork'*, IV.xv, xx; (IIf) *aŕeŕnawork'*, IV.xx; (IIg) *šertawork'*, III.vii; IV.lv; (IIh) *χoranapahk'*, III.xx; (IIi) *sunawork'*, IV.xv

pp. *Zōrk'*, *passim*; (I) *ayrewji/hecealk'*, 73, 96, 150, 154, 156, 198, 221, 224, [236]; (Ib) *ŕamikspas*, 96; (Id) *nizakawork'*, 150, 154, 194-196 [219, 227] and (IIa) below; (Ie) *sparakir/vahanawork'*, 220 (both terms) and (IIb) below; (II) *hetewakk'/hetiotk'*, 73, 142, 162, 213, 218; (IIa) *nizakawork'*, 142; (IIb) *sparakir/vahanawork'*, 97 (*vahanap'ak*), 142, 194-195 (both terms), 197, 213-214; (IIc) *sakrawork'*, 142, 150, 197, 214; (IId) *suserawork'*, 142, 150; (IIe) *vaŕrawork'*, 142, 150; (IIf) *aŕeŕnawork'*, 150; (IIg) *šertawork'*, 73, 96-97, 175 (*šertap'ak*); (IIh) *χoranap'ahk'*, 96; (IIi) *sunawork'*, 142.

See also *aspet; azatagund; banak; gugaz; gund; matenik gund; puštipan; ŕamikspas; senekapet; sparapet; zēn; zōravar.*

Appendix IV: Scriptural Quotations and Allusions

All citations are given separately, even when some refer to the same passage. The relevant notes in the Commentary are included throughout to identify similar references, group citations or allusions, and assist in the location of these references in the text, especially in the case of allusions that are not set off in quotations marks.

No attempt has been made to list such ubiquitous formulae as "put to the sword" or "deliver [someone] into [someone else's] hands," because they are far too numerous and no definite link with any particular Scriptural passage is possible. Some of the more common ones in BP are listed in Appendix V, which should also be consulted in this connection.

All references and numberings are given according to the Armenian Bible (Zōrapean/Zōrab edition).

Possible, but distant, allusions are indicated by an asterisk(*).

Genesis:

1:26	IV.v (n. 20); V.xxviii (n. 19)
1:28	IV.v (n. 27)
2:7	IV.v (n. 13); IV.lvii (n. 2); V.xxviii (n. 9)
3:3	V.xxviii (n. 10)
4:11–12	IV.xv (n. 24)
4:23–24	V.xxviii (n. 7)
*8:4	III.x (n. 3)
*11:8–9	III.xiv (n. 32)
13:10	IV.xiii (n. 10)
13:13	IV.xiii (n. 10)
*14:10	IV.xiii (n. 12)
*15:15	III.xvi (n. 6)
18:20–19:29	IV.xiii (n. 10)
22:1–13	IV.vi (n. 4)
22:11–12	III.x (n. 6)
*24:49	IV.xiii (n. 3)
*25:8	III.xvi (n. 6)
35:9–15	IV.vi (n. 4)
41:14	IV.vi (n. 4)
41:39–45	IV.vi (n. 4)
49:29	III.xvi (n. 6)
49:33	III.xvi (n. 6)

Exodus:
3:2–4	IV.vi (n. 4)
*9:9–11	IV.xiii (n. 19)
16:4–22	IV.vi (n. 4)
17:5–6	III.x (n.5); IV.vi (n. 4)
17:8–13	V.iv (n. 15)
20:5	IV.iii (n. 14)

Leviticus:
*19:28	IV.iv (n. 24)
*26:33	III.xiv (n. 32)

Numbers:
*16:30	IV.liv (n. 18)
*16:33	IV.liv (n. 18)
20:2–11	III.x (n. 5)
27:17	III.xiv (n. 32)

Deuteronomy:
4:27	III.xiv (n. 32)
5:32	IV.xiii (n. 3)
*14:1	IV.iv (n. 24)
17:11	IV.xiii (n. 3)
28:14	IV.xiii (n. 3)
*28:27	IV.xiii (n. 19)
*28:29	III.xiii (n. 2)
28:48	III.xiv (n. 34); IV.li (n. 14)
*28:64	III.xiv (n. 32)
*30:3	III.xiv (n. 32)
*32:26	III.xiv (n. 32)

Joshua:
*1:7	IV.xiii (n. 3)
*4:3–9	III.vii (n. 4)
*7:26	III.vii (n. 2)
*8:29	III.vii (n. 2)

I Kings:
3:19	IV.xiv (n. 8)
22:17	III.xiv (n. 32)

III Kings:
4:20	V.xlii (n. 4)
*12:4	III.xiv (n. 34); IV.li (n. 14)
*12:9–11, 14	III.xiv (n. 34); IV.li (n. 14)
*14:15	III.xiv (n. 32)
17:8–16	IV.xii (n. 12)
22:17	III.xiv (n. 30)

IV Kings:
*4:1–7	IV.xii (n. 12)
*10:10	IV.xiv (n. 8)
*19:37	III.x (n. 3)

Scriptural Quotations and Allusions

II Paralipomena:
*10:4	III.xiv (n. 34); IV.li (n. 14)
*10:9–11:4	III.xiv (n. 34); IV.li (n. 14)
*18:16	III.xiv (n. 32)

Nehemiah:
1:8	III.xiv (n. 32)

Esther:
1:19	IV.xv (n. 36); IV.xx (n. 14); V.iv (n. 4)
3:9	IV.xv (n. 36); IV.xx (n. 14); V.iv (n. 4)
*5:4	IV.xv (n. 36); IV.xx (n. 14); V.iv (n. 4)
8:5, 8	IV.xv (n. 36); IV.xx (n. 14); V.iv (n. 4)

I Maccabees:
2:22	IV.xiii (n. 3)
2:49	V.iv (n. 24)
*2:69	III.xvi (n. 6)
6:43–46	IV.xxii (n. 7)

II Maccabees:
*3:19	V.xxxi (n. 2)
*3:35	III.x (n. 21); III.xxi (n. 18)
*4:35	V.xliv (n. 16)
7:28	III.xiv (n. 22); IV.xiii (n. 6); IV.lvii (n. 2); V.iv (nn. 21, 30); V.xxviii (n. 8)
*9:15	III.xiii (n. 8)
15:17	IV.vi (n. 14)

III Maccabees:
*1:10	V.xxxi (n. 2)

Psalms:
7:10	V.xxviii (n. 21)
7.12	IV.xiii (n. 8)
7:16	IV.xiii (n. 12)
15:6	V.xxiv (n. 9)
15:8	IV.v (n. 36)
18:4–5	IV.v (n. 43)
18:8–11	IV.v (n. 42)
*20:7	IV.v (n. 36)
26:8	IV.v (n. 36)
*26:12	V.iv (n. 20)
35:2	III.xix (n. 2)
40:2	V.iv (n. 20)
41:11	V.iv (n. 17)
*43:22	V.xxviii (n. 21)
*54:16	IV.liv (n. 18)
57:5–6	IV.xv (n. 19)
57:7	IV.xv (n. 20)
57:8	IV.xv (n. 21)
*57:9	IV.xv (n. 23)
57:10	IV.xv (n. 25)

63:6	III.xiv (n. 38)
67:6	IV.xiii (n. 6)
78:10	V.iv (n. 17)
94:4	V.iv (n. 21)
103:2	IV.v (n. 12)
113:5–6	III.xiii (n. 3)
115:13–14	IV.lvii (n. 5); V.xxiv (n. 4); V.xxviii (n. 5)
115:18	IV.lvii (n. 5); V.xxiv (n. 4); V.xxviii (n. 5)
118:39	V.iv (n. 28)
*118:176	III.xiv (n. 32)
140:8	III.xix (n. 7)

Proverbs:

*28:10	IV.liv (n. 18)
*28:17–18	IV.liv (n. 18)

Ecclesiastes:

7:21	V.iv (n. 29)

Job:

*37:8	IV.xiii (n. 17)

Isaiah:

*3:5	III.xiii (n. 12)
*3:9	IV.xiii (n. 10)
*5:5–7	IV.viii (n. 4)
5:9	IV.xiii (n. 16)
6:9–10	III.xiii (n. 3)
*13:20–22	IV.xiii (n. 17)
*16:10	IV.viii (n. 4)
*19:2	III.xiii (n. 12)
*29:15	III.xiv (n. 38)
32:13–14	IV.xiii (n. 17)
*34:38	III.x (n. 3)
37:7	III.xviii (n. 2)
40:12–13	V.iv (n. 23)
40:21	IV.v (n. 12)
40:22	V.iv (n. 22)
*53:6	III.xiii (n. 7); III.xiv (n. 30); IV.v (n. 52)
*55:10–11	IV.iv (n. 14)
*61:1	IV.iv (n. 9)

Amos:

5:10	III.xiii (n. 14)

Joel:

2:17	V.iv (n. 17)

Habakkuk:

2:9	IV.xiii (n. 15)

Zecharia:

*10:2	III.xiv (n. 32)
*13:7	III.xiii (n. 7); III.xiv (n. 32); IV.v (n. 52)

Malachi:
  4:2   IV.v (n. 28)

Jeremiah:
  *3:13   III.xiv (n. 32)
  3:17   III.xiii (n. 21)
  4.22   III.xiii (nn. 3, 16)
  5:21   III.xiii (n. 3)
  *10:22   IV.xiii (n. 17)
  *10:25   IV. xiii (n. 17)
  *11:8   III.xiii (nn. 5, 21)
  11:10   III.xiv (n. 21)
  *12:8–14   IV.xiii (n. 17)
  13:10   III.xiii (nn. 5, 21); III.xiv (n. 21)
  16:12   III.xiii (n. 21)
  22:13   IV.xiii (n. 14)
  25:15   IV.xv (n. 22)
  27:10   IV.xiii (n. 17)
  *28:10–14   III.xiv (n. 34); IV.li (n. 14)
  *48:44   IV.liv (n. 18)
  *49:16   VI.xvi (n. 11)
  50:6   III.xiv (n. 32)
  *50:17   III.xiii (n. 7); III.xiv (n. 32); IV.v (n. 52)

Lamentations:
  1:14   III.xiv (n. 34); IV.li (n. 14)
  2:1   III.xiv (n. 33)
  5:18   IV.xiii (n. 17)

Daniel:
  3:27–45   V.xiv (n. 27)
  4:24   IV.iv (n. 31)

Ezekiel:
  2:3–4   III.xiii (n. 17)
  6:8   III.xiv (n. 32)
  12:2   III.xiii (n. 3)
  29:12   III.xiv (n. 32)
  30:23, 26   III.xiv (n. 32)
  34:5–6, 8   III.xiii (n. 7); III.xiv (n. 32); IV.v (n. 52)

Matthew:
  1:20   III.v (n. 13)
  3:16   IV.iv (n. 9)
  *5:3–11   IV.v (n. 33)
  6:9   V.xxviii (n. 25)
  6:19–20   IV.ix (n. 6)
  6:33   IV.vi (n. 13)
  7:6   V.iv (n. 31)
  7:13   III.xiii (nn. 4–5)
  9:29   IV.v (n. 40)
  9:36   III.xiii (n. 7); III.xiv (n. 32); IV.v (n. 52)
  10:14   III.x (n. 13)

10:40	IV.xv (n. 16)
12:39	IV.vi (n. 10)
13:13–15	III.xiii (n. 3)
13:18–30	IV.xiii (n. 23)
*13:37–42	III.v (n. 18); IV.xiii (n. 23)
14:15–21	IV.vi (n. 5)
15:14	III.xiii (n. 4)
*18:23–35	IV.li (n. 9)
19:21–24	IV.iv (n. 35)
22:39	IV.iii (n. 9)
23:31–32	III.xiv (n. 30)
*25:14–28	IV.li (n. 9)
26:26–28	IV.vi (n. 7)
26:31	III.xiii (n. 7); III.xiv (n. 32); IV.v (n. 52)
27:25	IV.iii (n. 14)
27:50	V.xxiv (n. 13)

Mark:

1:10	IV.iv (n. 9)
4:12	III.xiii (n. 3)
6:11	III.x (n. 13)
6:34	III.xiii (n. 7); III.xiv (n. 32); IV.v (n. 52)
6:35–44	IV.vi (n. 5)
8:12	IV.vi (n. 10)
*10:24	IV.iv (n. 35)
11:29–30	III.v (n. 11)
12:31	IV.iii (n. 9)
14:22–24	IV.vi (n. 7)
14:27	III.xiii (n. 7); III.xiv (n. 32); IV.v (n. 52)

Luke:

*1:45	IV.v (n. 33)
3:22	IV.iv (n. 9)
*4:18	IV.iv (n. 9)
6:39	III.xiii (n.4)
8:10	III.xiii (n. 3)
9:5	III.x (n. 13)
9:10–17	IV.vi (n. 5)
10:16	IV.xv (n. 16)
*10:19	V.xxvii (n. 8)
11:29	IV.vi (n. 10)
*12:33	IV.iv (n. 35); IV.ix (n. 6)
16:9	IV.iv (n. 36)
17:6	V.xxviii (n. 23)
18:22	IV.ix (n. 6)
22:19–20	IV.vi (n. 7)

John:

1:9	IV.iii (n. 19)
1:32	IV.iv (n. 9)
4.24	IV.v (n. 31)
4:36	IV.iv (n. 14)
6:5–13	IV.vi (n. 5)

6:26	IV.vi (n. 5)
*7:35	VI.xvi (n. 10)
10:11	IV.lv (n. 14); V.xxviii (n. 24)
10:14–15	IV.lv (n. 14); V.xxviii (n. 24)
12:40	III.xiii (n. 3)
*12:44–45	IV.v (n. 34)
*14:2	III.ii (n. 4)
14:9	IV.v (n. 34)
*16:25	IV.v (n. 38)
19:34	IV.vi (n. 6)
*20:29	IV.v (n. 34)

Acts:

1:1	III.xii (n. 15); IV.iv (nn. 15, 21, 30, 45); IV.v (n. 29); V.xliv (n. 11)
1:24	V.xxviii (n. 22)
7:55	IV.iv (n. 32)
7:58	V.xxiv (n. 12)
9:36–41	IV.iv (n. 33)
*13:51	III.x (n. 13)
15:20	IV.iv (n. 26)
*17:16	III.xiii (n. 8)
18:25	IV.iii (n. 11)
20:28	V.iv (n. 16)
23:6	IV.iii (n. 17)
*28:3–6	V.xxvii (n. 8)
28:26–27	III.xiii (n. 3)

James:

1:6	IV.vi (n. 9)
4:3	III.xiv (n. 35)
5:10–11	IV.iv (n. 46)
5:20	III.xiv (n. 6)

I Peter:

| 1:20 | IV.iv (n. 16) |
| *3:15 | III.vi (n. 3) |

Romans:

1:20	III.xiii (n. 18)
3:18	III.xix (n. 2)
6:2–5	IV.iii (n. 17)
6:10	IV.iii (n. 17)
7:22	IV.iii (n. 16)
8:21	IV.v (n. 25)
10:2	IV.iii (n. 10)
11:8	III.xiii (n. 3)
11:36	V.iv (n. 26)
12:11	IV.iii (n. 11)
*15:19	III.x (n. 4)

I Corinthians:

| 2:16 | V.iv (n. 25) |

*3:6–9	IV.iv (n. 14)
6:19	IV.v (n. 32)
11:2	IV.iii (n. 10)
13:12	IV.v (n. 37)
14:1	IV.iv (nn. 20, 38)

II Corinthians:

4:3–4	III.xiii (n. 2)
*4:6	III.v (n. 15)
5:17	IV.v (n. 22)
*6:4	III.v (n. 19)
8:9	IV.xiii (n. 7)
*9:2	IV.iv (n. 39)

Galatians:

2:7	IV.iv (n. 34)
2:9–10	III.v (n. 17); IV.iv (n. 34)
2:20	IV.iii (n. 17)
3:27	IV.iii (n. 17)
4:18	IV.iv (nn. 20, 40)
4:19	III.xiv (n. 28)

Ephesians:

2:3	III.xiii (n. 5)
5:18	VI.xii (n. 2)
6:5	IV.iv (n. 27); IV.li (n. 7)
6:9	IV.iv (n. 27)
6:17	III.xii (n. 11)

Philippians:

2:5	IV.iv (n. 44)
2:7 (1st passage)	IV.v (n. 14)
2:7 (2nd passage)	IV.v (n. 18); V.xxviii (n. 17)
2:7 (3rd passage)	IV.v (n. 23)

Colossians:

1:12	V.xxiv (n. 5)
1:16	IV.v (n. 26)
1:18	IV.v (n. 24)
1:18–20	IV.v (n. 26)
2:12	IV.iii (n. 17)
3:22	IV.iv (n. 27); IV.li (n. 7)

I Thessalonians:

4:16	V.xxv (n. 5)
5:12	IV.iv (n. 42)

Hebrews:

1:3 (1st passage)	IV.v (n. 9); V.xxviii (n. 13)
1:3 (2nd passage)	IV.v (n. 11); V.xxviii (n. 14)
*4:12	V.xxviii (n. 21)
*6:7–8	III.v (n. 18)
10:34	IV.ix (n. 6)

11:3	III.xiii (n. 18)
11:26	III.v (n. 10)
11:37–38	VI.xvi (n. 4)
11:39–40	IV.v (n. 39)
12:2	IV.iv (n. 41)
13:7	IV.iv (n. 43)
13:17	III.xiv (n. 27)

I Timothy:
*6:1–2	III.vi (n. 3); IV.iv (n. 27); IV.li (n. 7)

II Timothy:
3:17	IV.iii (n. 11)

Titus:
2:7	IV.v (n. 29)
2:14	IV.iv (nn. 20, 37)
3:8	IV.iv (nn. 20, 37)

Apocalypse:
1:5	IV.v (n. 24)
3:12	III.v (n. 17); IV.iv (n. 34)

Appendix V: Epic and Scriptural Formulae

A listing of the main formulae that run through the text like refrains and provide supporting evidence for its close connection to the oral literary tradition has been given in the present Appendix. Some of them are clearly Scriptural in origin, as in the case of (b) "put to the sword," (g) "as numerous as the sands of the seashore," (h) "as numerous as the stars in the heavens." Others, partially the introductory formula, (a) "he began to speak . . . and said," (c) "not a single one of them survived, not a one," and especially (d) "the king alone fled on a single horse," are more epic in character and are often grouped together.

† In all cases, the beginning of a formulaic repetition has been identified by a dagger in the body of the translation. In the present Appendix, the Arabic numbers given in parentheses indicate the page in the Venice (1933) edition on which it occurs.

586

(a)

"he began to speak . . . and said"

This introductory formula is by far the most common in BP, and it reproduces a familiar practice of oral literature (see Introduction, n. 138). Its form remains remarkably constant, but it also occurs in a number of variants, all of which maintain the binary form of the model.

III

xiv	(49)	*Skseal χōsel* [Daniēl], yaŕaǰ matuc^ceal, *asēr·*
xx	(63)	*χōsel sksaw* Tiran, *ew asē.*
xxi	(64)	*χōsel sksan* ayr ǝnd ǝngeri, *ew asen.*

IV

v	(90)	Isk na [Nersēs] *χōsel sksaw ew asē.*
vi	(102)	*ibrew χōsec^caw* [Nersēs], *ard· asē·.*
viii	(107)	[Vałēs] *sksanēr χōsel ew asēr.*
x	(110)	*sksanēin* surbk^cn *χōsel, ew asēin.*
xiii	(119)	Nersēs mtanēr aŕ t^cagaworn, *χōsēr* ǝnd nma *ew asēr·.*
xiii	(121)	*χōsel sksanēr* episkoposapetn Nersēs . . . , *ew asēr·.*
xv	(128)	Nersēs matuc^ceal . . . *χōsēr* ǝnd nma, *ew asēr.*
xv	(128)	*χōsel sksanēr* surb Nersēs, *ew asēr.*
xv	(130)	*χōsel sksanēr* t^cagaworn, . . . *asē.*
xv	(140)	*χōsel sksanēr* t^cagaworn Parsic^c Šapuh . . (incomplete).
xx	(142)	*χorhrdakic^c* ark^cayn Parsic^c . . . *χōsel sksanēr* . . . *ew asēr·*
li	(168)	*χōsel sksan* ǝnd Nersisi *ew asen.*
liv	(171)	t^cagaworn Parsic^c Šapuh . . . *χōser* ǝnd nosa *ew asēr·*
liv	(174)	[Aršak] *sksanēr χōsel ew asel.*
lvi	(181)	[Šapuh] *χōsel sksaw, asē.*

V

iv	(198)	*χōsēr* t^cagaworn Ałuanic^c . . . , *asēr.*
vi	(209)	*χōsel sksaw* Dłakn *ew asē.*
xxiv	(221)	[Nersēs] *χōsel sksaw ew asē.*
xxx	(231)	amenayn mard erkirn Hayoc^c hawanēin *χōsein ew asēin.*
xxx	(231)	*χōsēin* išχank^cn ew naχarark^cn, *ew asēin.*
xxx	(231)	*χōsēr* Mušeł sparapetn Hayoc^c *ew asēr.*
xliii	(254)	aynpisi bans *χōsēr* . . . , *ew asēr·.*
xliii	(256)	*χōsel sksaner* sparapetn Manuēl . . . , *ew asēr.*

Variant (i) The parallel formula for answers:

IV

iii	(79)	oč^c egit [Nersēs] *tal* noc^ca banic^cn *patasχani* . . . , *ew asēr.*
v	(97)	[Nersēs] *et patasχani ew asē.*
viii	(108)	*Et patasχani* Basilios t^cagaworin *ew asēr.*
x	(112)	[Sargis ew T^ceodoros] *Patasχani tueal asēin.*
x	(112)	Nora [sop^cestn] *patasχani tueal, asē.*
xx	(141)	*tayin patasχani* naχarark^cn iwr Šaphoy . . . , *ew asen* c^cna·
xx	(141)	*tayr patasχani* Šapuh t^cagawor Parsic^c . . . , *ew asē.*
li	(168)	Nersēs *χōsēr* ǝnd nosa . . . (incomplete)
liv	(172)	Isk k^cawdeayk^cn etun nma *patasχani ew asen.*
liv	(175)	Vasak *tueal patasχani asē.*
lvi	(181)	Isk [Zuit^c] *tueal patasχanî asē.*

V

iv	(198)	Bayc῾ Meružanay Arcrunwoy *patasχani tueal* Uṙnayri, *asac῾*.
iv	(204)	Isk zōrawarn Mušeł *tayr patasχani* t῾agaworin Papay, *ew asēr*ʼ
xxii	(219)	Isk na [Pap] *patasχani tayr* mardkann *aselov*ʼ
xxxv	(241)	ew t῾agaworin *patasχani tueal, asē.*
xxxvii	(244)	Isk Varazdat t῾agaworn *patgam yłēr patasχani* . . . , *ew asēr.*
xliii	(254)	Ew ułeworac῾n *tueal patasχani, asac῾in.*

Variant (ii) More distant, but still recognizable variants of the model:

III

iii	(20)	zardarn *skseal χōsel, χostovan linēin*ʼ
vi	(26)	*sksaw k῾arozel ew aweraranel* noc῾a K῾ristoss: *asē* c῾nosaʼ
x	(36)	Isk na [Yakob] *pndeal vičēr ew asēr.*
xi	(37)	Zors matuc῾eal *sp῾op῾ēr* znosa mecn Vrt῾anēs, *ew asēr.*
xii	(42)	na [Yusik] *ənddēm barbaṙeal asēr.*

IV

iii	(79)	*ałałkēin* aṙaǰi t῾agaworin. *asēin,*
iii	(79)	Apa *zbołok῾ barnayin* bazmut῾iwnk῾ zōrac῾n, *ew asēin*ʼ
v	(92)	acē *t῾ap῾ē* Aṙak῾ealn miangamayn *ew asē*ʼ
vi	(101)	Apa *mχit῾arel ew k῾aǰalerel* sksaw zamenayn Nersēs, *ew asē.*
vi	(103)	ew hanapaz *mχit῾arēr* znosa surbn Nersēs, *ew asēr.*
viii	(106)	Apa *załałak hareal goč῾ēin* aṙ Barsilios, *ew asēin.*
viii	(107)	Ew mtanēr Ewsebios aṙ kaysrn *χndrēr* i nmanē, *ew asēr.*
x	(111)	*dnēin žam* [surbk῾n] *ew asēin.*
xii	(116)	amenayn mard *haṙač῾elov vayēin, ew asēin* i havanel banic῾n *iwreanc῾* . . . aṙ hasarak amenec῾un *aselov*ʼ
xiv	(123)	Ew zsurb tełeōk῾n k῾amaheal *arhamarēr* [mardpet], *ew asēr.*
xiv	(124)	Šawaspn, *skseal patmel* martpetin *sut* . . . , *ew asē.*
xv	(128)	*sksanēr patmel* . . . *asē.*
xv	(130)	*patgam yłēr* aṙ kin meṙeloyn, *asē*ʼ
xliv	(163)	Apa *skseal čč῾el vayel* pataneakn [Pap], *ew asē* c῾mayr iwr.
li	(169)	*załałak harkanēin. k῾aroz kardac῾eal* ʼ *mimeanc῾ jayn aṙnēin* . . . ew *asēin.*
liii	(170)	*darjeal aṙakeac῾* aṙ Aršak . . . , *ew asē.*
liv	(174)	*yotn ekac῾, asē* . . .
liv	(175)	Apa *harc῾anēr* t῾agaworn Parsic῾ Šapuh *ew asē.*
lv	(178)	*Ew oč῾ aṙnoyr zays yanjn* . . . , *ayl asēr.*
lvi	(181)	*ed cunr ew asē.*

V

i	(193)	episkoposapetn Nersēs *ōrhnēr* zzōravarn Mušeł, *ew asēr.*
iv	(198)	*χndrēr pargews* Uṙnayr . . . , *ew asēr.*ʼ
iv	(198)	Apa *č῾aṙnoyr zayn nma yanjn* Terēnt . . . *ayl asē.*
iv	(199)	*yišeac῾* . . . *zhin zroyc῾sn* . . . , *ew asē.*
iv	(199)	ʼi t῾agaworin Papay jeṙn arkanēr, *erdnoyr ew asēr*ʼ
iv	(200)	*ałałakel sksaw* t῾agaworn Pap aṙ Nersēs *ew asē.*
iv	(203)	Bayc῾ apa *ambastan linēin k῾sut῾eamb* aṙ mec t῾agaworin Papay . . . , *ew asēin.*
iv	(204)	*layr e veray* . . . Mušełi, *ew asē.*
v	(205)	[Uṙnayr] *tayr nma tełekut῾iwn. asēr.*

v	(206)	Šapuh tᶜagaworn . . . *zarmacᶜeal . . . ew asēr*
vi	(209)	*kočᶜecᶜin* zDłakn, *ew asen.*
xxvii	(226)	*ew ibrew gitacᶜ* surbn Epipᶜan, *asē.*
xxvii	(226)	*sksaw pᶜorjel znosa* Epipᶜan, *asē.*
xxxiii	(237)	ew apa *hastatecᶜaw ays ban* i χorhrdeann *ew asen.*
xxxv	(239)	*sksaw kᶜsis matucᶜanel* znmanēn ał tᶜagaworin Varazdatay . . . , *ew aseł*
xxxvii	(243)	*patgam ylēr* sparapetn Hayocᶜ Manuēl . . . *ew asēr*
xxxvii	(245)	isk Manuēl *ałałakēr* zkni orduocᶜ iwrocᶜ, *ew asēr.*
xxxvii	(246)	Ałałakeacᶜ Gareginn *ew asē.*
xxxvii	(246)	Ew *et hraman* Hamazaspean . . . , *asē.*
xliii	(254)	*harcᶜanēr* Merużann *ew asēr,*
xliii	(256)	Apa *jayn tueal yałaĵ kočᶜeacᶜ* zMerużann Manuēl, *ew asē* cᶜnaˋ
xliv	(259)	*sksaw lal, ew aseł*
xliv	(260)	ew *ałačᶜeacᶜ* ews ztᶜagaworn Aršak, *ew asē.*

VI		
viii	(270)	Ew ałnn χonarhil *hramayēr ew asēr.*
ix	(271)	*Ałałakēr* ał na ayr mi yaygwoyn, *ew asē.*
ix	(272)	yałnēr aygordn *kayr yałōtᶜs ew asēr.*
x	(272)	*mi mi ban χałnelov . . . aselovˋ*

A number of other binary introductory formulae are found in the text, but they have been omitted because some suggestion of a verb of saying was not present in both halves.

(*b*)

"put to the sword"

This formula is unquestionably derived from Scriptures, but it is far too common there to permit a direct reference to any passage.

III		
vii	(28)	*ənd sur hanin* zamenesean,
viii	(30)	*sur et dnel* i veray iwrocᶜ zōracᶜn:
ix	(32)	*ənd sur hanin* zamenayn.
xviii	(57)	*hancl ənd sur,*
xxi	(66)	*ənd sur* zamenayn banakn *hanēin,*

IV		
xvii	(135)	zamenayn mard miangamayn *hancᶜen ənd sur* . . .
xx	(140)	Ał hasarak *ənd sur haneal* . . .
xxi	(145)	*harkanēin i sur suseri iwreancᶜ.*
xxii	(147)	*ənd sur hanēr* zamenesean.
xxiv	(149)	*arkanēin i sur suseri* iwreancᶜ.
xxiv	(151)	*ənd sur hanēin* zzōrsn amenayn Parsicᶜ.
xxiv	(151)	*arkanēin* znosa *i sur suseri* iwreancᶜ.
xxv	(152)	Ew zamenayn zayr erkrin *hanēin ənd sur.*
xxvi	(153)	*ənd sur hanēr* zamenayn zōrsn Parsicᶜ,
xliii	(162)	*hanēr ənd sur* ał hasarak zamenesean,
xlviii	(165)	Ew zamenesean *ənd sur hanēin* ał hasarak,
liv	(172)	ew zusumnakicᶜs nocᶜa *hanel ənd sur:*

V

i	(193)	ew zamenayn zzōrsn *arkanēr i sur suseri* iwroy,
ii	(195)	ew zamenayn karewan banakin aṙ hasaṙak *ənd sur hanēr* . . .
xv	(215)	ew *hanēr ənd sur* zamenayn azats ew zazgs naχararac‘n'
xvii	(216)	ew zazgsn *hanēr ənd sur.*
xviii	(216)	ew *hanēr ənd sur:*
xix	(217)	*Hanēr ənd sur* ztears gawaṙin.
xxxix	(251)	*arkanēr i sur* zzōrsn Parsic‘.
xli	(252)	*ənd sur hanēr* zamenesean i łakišn,
xliii	(257)	*ənd sur haneal* zzōrsn Meružanay,

(c)
"not a single one . . . not a one"

This formula, which also occurs in Scriptures (e.g., Exod. 14:28), is often, but not invariably, found together with the preceding as well as the following ones. Occasional variations of the basic model occur, but it is usually identifiable.

III

iv	(21)	ew *oč t‘ołoyr* zerkoc‘unc‘ tohmac‘n zorj koriwn ew *oč‘ zmi.*
vii	(28)	ew *oč‘ mi ok‘ oč aprec‘uc‘anēr.*
vii	(29)	*oč‘ mnac‘* i noc‘anē ew *oč‘ mi.*
viii	(31)	ew *oč‘ tołin* i noc‘anē ew *oč‘ mi:*
ix	(32)	*ayl ok‘ oč‘ ēr mnac‘eal* yazgēn,
xiii	(43)	zi *oč‘ mi ok‘ goyr* . . .
xiii	(44)	*oč‘ ok‘* i noc‘anēn ew *oč‘, mi oč‘,* ew *oč‘ mi* ban, ew *oč‘* kēs bani . . .
xiii	(45)	*oč‘ ok‘ ayn ok‘ goyr,*
xiii	(46)	*Ew oč‘ ayl ok‘ i* nmin tanē . . . *goyr ok‘.*
xiii	(46)	*Ew ayl oč‘ ok‘* ēr,
xv	(54)	Bayc‘ . . . *oč‘ ok‘ goyr,*
xvii	(56)	Apa ibrew *oč‘ ok‘ goyr* i tanēn Grigori . . .
xvii	(57)	ew *oč‘ mi ok‘* i t‘agaworac‘n Hayoc‘ *oč ok‘* gtanēr . . .
xix	(59)	ew *oč‘ ok‘ i noc‘anē* . . .
xix	(59)	ew *oč‘ ok‘* išχeac‘ . . . mtanel . . . ewoč‘ i dursn ert‘al . . . ew *oč‘.* . . . *ok‘.* . . . anc‘anel:
xx	(62)	*Ew oč‘ ok‘ ēṙ or mnac‘eal* ēr aṙ t‘agaworin, ew *oč‘* gund . . .
xxi	(66)	ew *oč‘ zmi oč‘ aprec‘uc‘anēin:*

IV

x	(112)	ew *oč‘ ok‘* i kesarac‘woc‘ . . . ew *oč‘ mi ok‘.*
xiii	(121)	*oč‘ mnac‘* i noc‘anē ew *oč‘ mi.*
xv	(132)	*Ew oč‘ mi ok‘ oč‘* hawaneac‘ gal.
xx	(140)	aynpēs zi *oč‘ aprec‘uc‘anēin* i noc‘anē ew *oč‘ zmi:*
xxii	(146)	*oč‘ aprec‘uc‘anēin* ew *oč‘ zmi,*
xxii	(146)	*oč‘ aprec‘uc‘anēin* yaync‘anē ew *oč‘ mi.*
xxii	(147)	ew *oč‘ mi* i noc‘anēn *oč‘ caχein.*
xxvii	(153)	ew *oč‘ aprec‘uc‘anēr mi* i noc‘anē ew *oč‘ mi.*
xxix	(154)	zi ew *mi oč‘ aprec‘uc‘anēr:*
xxx	(155)	ew *oč‘ t‘ołoyr* i noc‘anē ew *oč‘ mi.*

xxxiv	(157)	*ew zmin i noc͟ʿanē oč͟ʿ aprecʿucʿanēr:*
xli	(161)	*ew oč͟ʿ mi i nocʿanēn oč͟ʿ aprecʿucʿanēr.*
xlvii	(164)	*ew zōrsn anmi arareal.*
xlviii	(165)	*ew oč͟ʿ mi oč͟ʿ aprecʿucʿanēin.*
l	(167)	*oč͟ʿ mi inč͟ʿ irsˋ*
li	(168)	*ew oč͟ʿ mi ayr oč͟ʿ okʿ ē ertʿalocʿ . . .*
liv	(172)	*ew oč͟ʿ mi am oč͟ʿ karacʿakʿ.*
lv	(178)	*ew oč͟ʿ tʿoɫin mi, ew oč͟ʿ toɫin bnaw kʿar i kʿari veray.*
lix	(184)	*ibrew oč͟ʿ mi okʿ yanjn aṙnuin . . .*

V		
i	(193)	*ew oč͟ʿ mi zok͟ʿ aprecʿucʿanēr:*
iv	(202)	*zi oč͟ʿ icʿē ardar . . . , ew oč͟ʿ okʿ ē minč͟ʿew i mi.* (this phrase may be an allusion to Ecclesiastes 7:21, but the reiterated negative has been added).
vi	(209)	*oč͟ʿ zmi zēn oč͟ʿ karacʿ gtanel.*
xxxii	(237)	*Ew ayl inč͟ʿ okʿ oč͟ʿ karacʿ yandgnel asel inč͟ʿ ənd nosa ew oč͟ʿ inč:*
xxxv	(241)	*ew ayl oč͟ʿ inč oč͟ʿ:*
xxxvii	(242)	*zi oč͟ʿ mi i nocʿanēn oč͟ʿ aprecʿucʿanēin . . .*
xli	(252)	*ew oč͟ʿ zmi oč͟ʿ aprecʿucʿanēr i nocʿanēn:*
xliii	(257)	*ew zmi i nocʿanēn oč͟ʿ aprecʿucʿanēin:*

(*d*)

"the king alone fled on a single horse"

This formula, which is part of the standard setting of the total rout of the enemy, often appears in conjunction with the preceding two. It is normally applied to the king of Persia, but a variant, which is often no more than an echo, is also used for the traitor Meružan Arcruni.

III		
xxi	(66)	*Baycʿ miayn tʿagaworn prceal mazapur, pēšapik mi surhandak aṙaǰi, prceal elanēr pʿaχstakan.*

IV		
xxi	(145)	*ew miaji čoɫopreal arkʿayn Parsicʿ Šapuh pʿaχč͟ʿēr:*
xxii	(147)	*baycʿ miayn miaji mazapur čoɫoprēr tʿagaworn Šapuh pʿaχuč͟ʿeal . . .*
xxiv	(151)	*miayn tʿagaworn miaji čoɫopreal mazapur paχč͟ʿēr.*
xxv	(152)	*Miaji čoɫopreal tʿagaworn pʿaχčēr, . . .*

V		
ii	(195)	*Apa miaji mazapur tʿagaworn Parsicʿ Šapuh čoɫopreal pʿaχčēr.*
v	(206)	*Ew sakawukʿ paχč͟ʿēr Šapuh tʿagaworn Parsicʿ i paterazmē anti.*

Variant (i) This variant closes a series of successive chapters.

IV		
xxiv	(151)	*Baycʿ yaynm nuagi ews aprēr* Meružann . . . , *pʿaχucʿeal . . .*
xxxi	(156)	*Baycʿ miayn č͟ʿaragorc Meružann miaji čoɫopreal, pʿaχč͟ʿēr . . .*
xxxii	(156)	*Baycʿ Meruzann* Arcruni *pʿaχucʿeal aprēr . . .*
xxxiii	(157)	*baycʿ Meružan pʿaχčēr*

591

xxxiv	(157)	*Bayc' miayn p'axč'ēr č'aragorcn Meružan:*
xxxv	(158)	Ayl angram ews *oč' karēin bur̄n arkanel zMeružann.*
xxxvi	(158)	*Bayc' Meružann* aprēr *p'axsteay:*
xxxvii	(159)	Hrewšołumn *ew Meružann p'axč'ēin:*
xxxix	(160)	*Bayc' miayn p'axč'ēr Meružann* ənd nosa ekeal:
xl	(160)	*Bayc' miayn* aprēr sakawuk' *p'axuc'eal Meružann,*
xli	(161)	*ew Meružann p'axč'ēr:*
xlii	(161)	*Bayc' miayn p'axč'ēr Meružann:*
xliii	(162)	*Bayc' miayn čołopreal* aprēr *Meružann* vatanšan.
xlv	(164)	*bayc' miayn* aprēr *Meružann* Arcruni *p'axuc'eal.*
xlvi	(164)	*Bayc' miayn p'axč'ēr Meružann, apreal* linēr:
xlvii	(164)	*bayc' miayn Meružann i* tačik *ji* nsteal *p'axč'ēr:*
xlviii	(165)	*bayc' miayn Meružann* artak'oy gndin dipeal, *p'axč'ēr:*
xlix	(169)	*Bayc' Meružann ew ayn angam p'axč'ēr:*

V

| i | (193) | *bayc' miayn Meružann* č'aragorc *p'axčēr miaji:* |

Variant (ii): Though still more distant from the model, these variants are still identifiable.

V

| iv | (203) | *bayc' sakawk' i bazmac' k'ajajik' p'axsteayk'* linēin: |
| xxxviii | (250) | *Bayc'* zmarzpan *Surēnn miaji arjakēr,* |

(e)

"fell upon the camp by night"

The unexpected attack on the enemy camp, usually by night or at dawn, was unquestionably part of contemporary military tactics. Nevertheless, its repetition takes on a formulaic character, especially when linked with the preceding formulae *(b-d)*.

III

vii	(28)	*ankanēr i veray banakin, yar̄awōtun žamun ayganaloys paštamann.*
viii	(31)	Ew sok'a ... *ankan i veray banakin,*
xxi	(66)	*zbanakn* ark'ayin Parsic' ... *banakeal* ... yankaskac χałałut'ean ... *i tuənǰēn žamun, ankanēin i veray* t'agaworin Parsic',

IV

xx	(140)	[Vasak] elanēr *ankanēr i veray banakin:*
xxii	(147)	[Aršak] *ankanēr gišeri ... i veray banakin* Parsic'
xxiv	(151)	[Vasak] *ankanēr i veray banakin* t'agaworin Parsic' *i gišeri yełakarcumn žamanaki:*
xxxvi	(158)	[Vasak] elanēr *i gišeri ankanēr i nerk's i łakišn* ...
xliii	(162)	*ankanēr i gišeri i veray łakišn* Paskac' ...
xlviii	(165)	ew daranamut linēr ənd kołmans banakin, ew *i gišerin ankanēr i łakišn:*

V

ii	(195)	Mušeł *ankanēr i veray banakin* ...
xxxviii	(250)	zōravar Hayoc' Manuēl ... *ankanēr i veray banakin* Surenay:
xli	(252)	*Ankanēr i veray banakin* Manuēln *i gišeri* ...

(*f*)
"took hostages from the survivors . . . and imposed tribute on them"

This formula closes the series of chapters describing Mušeł Mamikonean's reconquest of the rebellious border districts of Armenia (ca. 370). It is not found elsewhere in the text.

V
viii (213) *ew i harki kac͑uc͑anēr, ew ařnoyr* zbazums *pandands* i noc͑anē:
ix (213) *ew i mnac͑ordac͑n ařnoyr pandands. ew* zbnakič͑s erkin *i harki* caṫayut͑ean *kac͑uc͑anēr*:
x (214) dnēr *hark mnac͑ordac͑n, ew ařnoyr pandands*:
xi (214) *ew mnac͑ordac͑n* dnēr *harks, ew ařnoyr pandands*:
xii (214) *ew zmnac͑ordac͑n ařnoyr pandands, ew zmnac͑ealsn i harki kac͑uc͑anēr*:
xiii (215) *ew zmnac͑ordsn i harki kac͑uc͑anēin, ew pandands* i noc͑anē *ařnuin*:
xiv (215) *ew zmnac͑ordsn i harki kac͑uc͑anēr, ew ařnoyr pandands* i noc͑anēn,
xv (215) *ařnoyr pandands, ew mnac͑ealsn i harki kacucanēr*:
xvi (216) *ew mnac͑ealsn i harki kac͑uc͑anēr*, . . . (incomplete).
xvii (216) *ew ařnoyr pandands, ew* zazgn *i harki kac͑uc͑anēr*:
xviii (216) ew ink͑eank͑ kayin *i harki* caṫayut͑ean:
xix (217) *ařnoyr pantands . . . i harki* caṫayut͑ean . . . *kac͑uc͑anēr*:

(*g*)
"kept watch over the borders"

This formula occurs primarily in Book IV as the closing in lists of victories, especially those of Vasak Mamikonean.

IV
xxi (145) [Vasak's army] *zsahmans Parsic͑ pahēin*.
xxiv (151) [Vasak's army] *sahmanac͑n zgušanayin* minč͑ew zamenayn awurs kendanut͑ean iwreanc͑:
xxv (152) *ink͑eank͑ zgušac͑ealk͑ sahmanōk͑ erkrin iwreanc͑*, pah arkeal *pahēin mecaw zgušut͑eamb*:
xxvi (153) *ew ink͑eank͑* darjeal *unēin zčakatun tełi*:
xxvii (153) *ew ink͑n* kayr *k͑ajut͑eamb unelov zčakatun tełi*:
xxx (155) *ew zgušanayr zsahmanōk͑ erkrin iwroy*:
xxxviii (159) *ew ink͑eank͑ zgušanayin sahmanac͑n iwreanc͑*:

V
i (194) *zgušac͑eal zsahmanōk͑n erkrin iwroy· pahel ziwr ašχarhn* . . .
xxxiv (238) [Mušeł] *ew zgušanayr zsahmanōk͑n Hayoc͑*, orpēs sovor ēr . . .

(*h*)
"all the days of his/their life/lives"

This chronological formula is primarily found in an ecclesiastical context, but it is occasionally found with reference to secular figures.

III

ii	(18)	*zamenayn awurs kenacʿ iwrocʿ* [Aristakēs]
v	(25)	*zamenayn awurs kenacʿ iwrocʿ* [Yusik]
viii	(31)	*zamenayn awurs kenacʿ nocʿa* [Vačʿē and Vahan]
xi	(39)	*zamenayn awurs kenacʿ iwrocʿ* [Artawazd]
xii	(42)	*zamenayn awurs kenacʿ iwrocʿ* [Yusik]
xix	(58)	*zamenayn awurs kenacʿ iwreancʿ* [Pap and Atʿánaginēs]

IV

iv	(89)	*ǝst amenayn awurcʿ iwrocʿ žamanakacʿn amacʿ kenacʿ iwrocʿ* [Nersēs]
xxiv	(151)	*zamenayn awurs kendanutʿean iwreancʿ* [Vasak's army]
xliv	(163)	*zamenayn awurs kenacʿ iwrocʿ* [Pap]

V

i	(193)	*zamenayn awurs kenacʿ kʿocʿ* [Mušeł]
xx	(217)	*zamenayn awurs kenacʿ iwrocʿ* [Mušeł]
xx	(217)	*zamenayn awurs kenacʿ iwrocʿ* [Mušeł]
xxii	(219)	*zamenayn awurs kenacʿ iwrocʿ* [Pap]
xxvi	(224)	*zamenayn awurs kenacʿ iwrocʿ* [Šałitay]
xxviii	(229)	*zamenayn awurs kenacʿ iwrocʿ* [the brother at Mambrē]
xxix	(231)	*zamenayn awurs kenacʿ iwrocʿ* [Yusik II]
xxxviii	(251)	*zamenayn awurs kenacʿ iwrocʿ* [Manuēl]
xlii	(253)	*zamenayn awurs kenacʿ nora* [Manuēl]
xlii	(253)	*zamenayn awurs kenacʿ nora* [Manuēl] (repeat)

VI

ii	(267)	*zamenayn awurs kenacʿ iwrocʿ* [Zawēn]
ii	(267)	*zamenayn awurs kenacʿ iwrocʿ* [Zawēn] (immediate repeat).
vi	(269)	*zamenayn awurs kenacʿ iwrocʿ* [Ałostom]
x	(272)	*zamenayn awurs kenacʿ iwrocʿ* [Yohan]
xi	(273)	*zamenayn awurs kenacʿ iwrocʿ* [Kiwrakos]
xiii	(273)	*zamenayn awurs kenacʿ iwreancʿ* [Tirik and Movēs]
xiv	(274)	*zamenayn awurs kenacʿ iwrocʿ* [Aharon]
xv	(274)	*zamenayn awurs kenacʿ iwrocʿ* [Aspurak]
xvi	(275)	*zamenayn awurs kenacʿ iwreancʿ* [the solitaries]

(i)

These two formulae are unquestionably derived from the Scripture, but they are far too common there to permit a direct reference to any passage.

Formula (i) "like the sands of the seashore"

III

viii	(31)	*ibrew zawaz ař apʿn covu.*

IV

xx	(139)	*ibrew zawaz ař apʿn covu* bazmutʿeambkʿ:
xxii	(145)	antʿiw ew anhamar *ibew zawaz ař apʿn covu,*.
xxiv	(151)	bazmutʿeamb *ibrew zawaz ař apʿn covu,*
xxv	(152)	*ibrew zawaz* bazmutʿeamb,

xxxii (156)   *ibrew zawaz* [Venice ed., p. 156 n. 1, one ms *aṙ ezer*] *covu*;
xxxv (158)   *ibrew zawaz covu bazmut^ceamb*

Formula (ii) "like the stars in the Heavens"

III
viii   (31)   *ibrew zasteṅn erknic^c,*

IV
xxv   (152)   zgerut^ciwn erkrin *k^can zasteṅs* bazmut^ceamb:

(*j*)

Although they are not found in anything like the frequency of the preceding examples, the following formulaic expressions have been included for the sake of completeness. The last group, despite the variation in wording, appears to be an echo of a Persian formula also found in the Book of Esther, e.g., 3:9, "*et^cē kamk^c ic^cen ark^cayi*," etc.

(*i*) "in the same month, in the same week, on the same day"

IV.xxi   (146)   *I nmin amsean i nmin šabatu i nmin awur* . . .
IV.xxi   (146)   *Isk i noin ami i nmin šabati i nmin isk awur,*

(*ii*) "had the men trampled by elephants and the women impaled on pointed carriage-poles"

IV.xxiii   (148)   *zars tayin i koχumn p^clac^c, ew zkanays ənd c^cic^c saylic^c hanēin.*
IV.xxiv   (149)   *zkanays ew zmankti hanēin ənd c^cic saylic^c,*
IV.xxiv   (149)   *Ew zaranc^c . . . tayin i koχumn płac^c.*
IV.xlviii   (182–183) *zamenayn ayr i č^cap^c haseal koχan arareal p^clac^c, ew zamenayn zkin ew zmanuk hanel ənd c^cic^c saylic^c:*

(*iii*) "may it be your (royal) will . . . "

IV.xv   (131)   *Kam lic^ci . . . k^cez ark^cayi,*
IV.xx   (138)   *et^cē kam lic^ci ełbōrd . . .*
IV.xx   (141)   *zinc^c ew kamis, iw kamis*ʼ
IV.liv   (173)   *zinč^c ew pētk^c ē k^cez, ara zis, zinč^c ew kam ic^cē.*
IV.liv   (176)   *zinč^c ew kamis*ʼ *ara.*
IV.lvi   (181)   *T^cē pēt ic^cē, ayl zinč^c kamis χōsel ew aṙnel*ʼ
V.iv   (198)   *Kam lic^ci k^cez, aṙanc^c k^caj,*
V.iv   (199)   *Kamk^c k^co kataresc^cin.*

(*k*)

Alliteration is a common pattern in BP, as in oral literature in general. Some of the alliterative clusters recur on a number of occasions around a single subject, even if they contain some variations, as is the case with the first group of examples cited. Others occur only once, but the cumulative intent is evident in all cases.

(*i*) These clusters, with one exception, refer to the Armenian troops:

"with one heart, one accord, and one mind/will/faith"

IV
xxi (145)   *miasirtk^c miaban miamitk^c*

xxiv   (150)   *miamitk῾* ew *miasirtk῾* ēin *miabanut῾ean*

V
ii (194)   *miamits . . . miabans miakams*
v (207)   *mtermut῾iwn miamtut῾eann*
v (207)   *miaban miamit*
xxviii (227)   *miabans miahawans* (in this case, the solitaries as "athletes" and "champions" of Christ)

(ii)

III
vii (28)   *ant῾iw anhamar*
x (36)   *mecapatiw mecapargew mecareac῾* zna
xi (37)   *zanōrēn zankrōn zanastuac῾*
xii (41)   *amenewin zamenayn yamenayni*
xii (42)   *patiwn patuakal patuakanut῾eann*
xviii (57)   *č῾arasirt č῾araχorhurd č῾aragorc*
xx (62)   *mecapēs mecarec῾aw*
xx (62)   *tiranenkn* ew *tiradružn tiraspanun tiramatnič῾n* P῾isakay . . .
xx (63)   *mecaw pataragōk῾* ew *patuakan əncayiwk῾* ew *mecašuk῾ mecaranōk῾*
xxi (65)   *aṙnul ayrel ew awerel*
xxi (66)   *yanhogut῾ean yankaskac῾* χalalut῾ean:
xxi (66)   *mecapargew, mecapatiw mecarēr*

IV
ii (77)   *alanazgik῾ alanadrōšk῾ arcuēnšank῾*
ii (77)   *barenšans barehambawk῾ baregorck῾*
v (89)   *mecapaycaṙ* p῾aṙōk῾ *mecaw* šk῾ov *mecareac῾* noc῾a
vi (103)   *zant῾iw zanč῾ap῾ zankšiṙ zanhamemat* bareac῾n . . .
xv (132)   *Zanaržans zankatar zanǰnǰeli . . . zanaržans zantes zanlur* . . .
xx (140)   *amenayn ant῾iw* ew *anč῾ap῾* zōrōk῾n
xxii (145)   *ant῾iw* ew *anhamar*
xxii (147)   *miayn miaǰi mazapur* . . .
xxiii (148)   *anč῾ap῾* ew *ant῾iw zamenayn*
xxxii (156)   *anč῾ap῾s* ew *ant῾iw* ew *anhamar*
lv (179)   *k῾akeal k῾andēin*

V
vi (208)   *yankarcorēn yanpatrastic῾* arkanel
vi (209)   *Mecapēs mecarec῾aw* i nmanēn
xx (217)   *barekac῾ barekir barekamac῾*
xxxv (240)   *yankarcōrēn yanpatrastic῾ yelakarcumn* žamu
xxxviii (248)   *mecapēs mecaranōk῾* patueac῾ znosa
xxxviii (249)   *mecapēs zmtermut῾iwn miamtut῾eann*
xxxviii (250)   banakeal ēr *yanhogs yankarc* ew *anneng* χalalut῾eamb . . . *yankarcorēn yelakarcumn* . . .

VI
xvi (275)   *nelealk῾, taṙapealk῾* ew *tarakusealk῾*
xvi (275)   *aninč῾k῾ anstac῾uack῾ anχnamk῾, aṙanč darmanoc῾ amenewin*

Bibliography
Maps

Bibliography

This Bibliography has been subdivided into three sections:
  (I) Manuscripts, Editions, and Translations of the text.
  (II) Original Sources:
      A) Armenian
      B) Classical: Greek and Latin
      C) Oriental: Iranian, Syriac, etc.
  (III) Literature.

All the works included under Section II have been listed according to language rather than according to content: thus, the Armenian text of the "Agatᶜangełos Cycle" (Aa) will be found in II.A, but its Greek version (Ag) will be listed in II.B, etc. Cross-references are included in all cases.

All anonymous *Acts* or *Lives* of saints are listed under the saint's name.

In all cases, the modern translation of an original source has been listed immediately after the main entry in the original language, or its ancient version, as has been the case throughout this work. Thus, MK (the English translation of MX) is to be found under MX. Any Introductions, commentaries or notes have been given under the name of the editor and/or translator and are consequently included under the editor's name in Section III.

Only a sampling of the works relating to the multiple aspects of the *Epic Histories* could be included in Section III, as any attempt at an exhaustive survey of the relevant scholarship would be manifestly impossible. Some theses unacceptable to the present writer have been included for the sake of balance, but the pertinent reservations have been noted in the apposite notes or entries of the Commentary and Appendices.

As indicated in the Translator's Preface, the various forms of the same author's name have been grouped together under the modern Armenian transliteration of his name (i.e., Łafadaryan/Kafadarian, Čᶜukaszyan/Tchoukassizian), with all variants indicated and cross listed. In the case of Armenian names beginning with Ter/Der, this initial component has been treated an integral part of the name, but the particules de, van, von have been disregarded for alphabetical purposes.

All Festschrifts and similar collections are listed under the name of the person to whom they are dedicated.

All entries are listed alphabetically according to the abbreviated form used throughout this work and the presence of any definite article has been disregarded in this listing.

In the case of references to Sources the usual practice has been followed, i.e., Roman capitals = Book, Roman minuscules = chapter, Arabic numbers = subsection (e.g., II.vi.12).

All Abbreviations not included in the Bibliography are to be found in the front of this volume under Abbreviations.

I: Manuscripts, Editions, and Translations of the text

Manuscripts

*Manuscript numbers marked with an asterisk contain only fragments.

Jerusalem

341	1599 (earliest ms known except for the fragmentary Venice *673)
307	1624
303	1649
1553	1649
230	1678–1679
436	1707

Matenadaran

1867	1622
2748	1624
*6321	1624
1862	1641
3071	1651–1661
*7029	1654
4584	1668
*8813	1668
1482	1678
3965	1624? 1684–1702
*8344	XVIIth century
1785	1700
*6096	1701
3079	1720
*6554	XVIII century

Venice

*673	1224
875	1426? (date added later)
1706	1637

721	1681 (= A.E. 1129)
1176	? (not available)
1188	a. 1761 (when ms brought to St. Louis)
1646	? (not available)
2460	a. 1743 (printed text from lost ms with corrections dating from 1743)

Vienna

967	XVIII–XIX century
819	Copied in 1852 from an undated ms.
762	1910–1911

Editions

Buzandaran patmutʿiwn, šaradreal Buzanday meci patmagri . . . (Constantinople, 1730), *editio princeps*.

Pʿawstosi Buzandacʿwoy Patmutʿiwn Hayocʿ i čʿors dprutʿiwns (Venice, 1832; 2d ed., 1889; 3d ed., 1914; 4th ed., 1933).

Kʿ.[erovbē] P.[atkanean], *Pʿawstosi Buzandacʿwoy Patmutʿiwn Hayocʿ* (St. Petersburg, 1883).

Pʿawstosi Biwzandacʿwoy Patmutʿiwn Hayocʿ (Tiflis, 1912), a reprint of the 1883 St. Petersburg edition.

Ps. Pʿawstos, *Buzandaran Patmutʿiwnkʿ* [*The Epic Histories*]. Classical Armenian Text Reprint Series, gen. ed. John A. C. Greppin (Delmar, N.Y., 1984), with an Introduction by N. G. Garsoïan, a reprint of the 1883 St. Petersburg edition.

As indicated in the Introduction, there is as yet no critical edition of the text.

Translations

French

Jean-Baptiste Emin, "Bibliothèque historique en quatre livres, traduite pour la première fois de l'Arménien," in Victor Langlois, ed., *Collection des historiens anciens et modernes de l'Arménie* (Paris, 1867), vol. I, pp. 201–310.

This translation was made from the 1832 Venice edition; it omits some passages of a religious character, namely, prayers and homilies. The version is not always sufficiently precise and its scholarship is often out of date.

German

M. Lauer, *Des Faustus von Byzanz Geschichte Armeniens aus dem Armenischen übersetzt mit einer Abhandlung über die Geographie Armeniens* (Cologne, 1879).

This translation was also made from the 1832 Venice edition, and omits some of the religious passages. It is, however, more accurate than the French version.

Modern Armenian

Stepᶜannos Malχasyancᶜ, *Pᶜawstos Buzand Patmutᶜyun Hayocᶜ* (Erevan, 1947; repr. Cairo, 1954; 2d rev. [posthumous] ed., Erevan, 1968).

This translation was made from the 1912 Tiflis edition by one of the leading specialists of "Pᶜawstos's" work. It is the most complete, except for most of the long homily of St. Nersēs (IV.v) and a few small fragments. All of these passages were, however, included by the editors of the 1968 edition, which is therefore complete. The notes of the 1968 edition do not, however, coincide invariably with those of the 1947 edition, which are fuller.

Russian

M. A. Gevorgian, *Istoriia Armenii Favstosa Buzanda* (Erevan, 1953).

As has been long pointed out, this translation was made on the whole from Malχasyancᶜ's 1947 translation into Modern Armenian, rather than from the original text.*

---

*It has come to my attention, after the completion of the present translation, that a privately published and distributed English translation of the text has recently appeared. As this translation had not gone through the normal scholarly due process, I have not felt constrained to consult it.

II: Sources

A: Armenian Texts

Aa   BHO 328–331
Agat'angełay Patmut'iwn Hayoc', ed. G. Tēr Mkrtč'ean
and St. Kanayeanc' (Tiflis, 1909); repr. CATRS (1980),
with an Introduction by R. W. Thomson.
TRANSLATION:
Agathangelos. History of the Armenians, trans.
R. W. Thomson (Albany, N.Y., 1976).
See also II.B, Ag; III, Thomson, Aa.

AaT   "Vardapetut'iwn srboyn Grigori," Aa, cclix–dccxl,
pp. 134–372.
TRANSLATION:
*The Teaching of Saint Gregory: An Early Armenian
Catechism*, trans. R. W. Thomson (Cambridge, Mass.,
1970).
See also III, Thomson, AaT.

Abraham Xostovanoł *Abrahamu Xostovanołi Vkayk' arewelic'*, ed. G. Tēr
Mkrtč'ean, (posthumous edition by M. Tēr Movsēsean,
Ējmiacin, 1921).
See also III, Tēr Petrosyan, *Abraham Xostovanoł.*

Acta   See under the name of the saint.

Acta apocrypha (Arm.) See Abraham Xostovanoł; see also AGA.

Addē, St., *Acta*   "Vkayabanut'iwn srboyn Addēi hayrapetin," LVVS, X
(1814), pp. 141–144.
TEXT AND TRANSLATION:
*"Yišatak ē Addē hayrapetin Edesioy k'ałak'in, ašakerti
T'adēosi/Commémoration d'Addai, évêque de la ville
d'Edesse, disciple de Thaddée (16 K'aloc' = 24
Décembre)*, ed. and trans. G. Babayan, PO XVIII/1
(1924), pp. 97-101.
See also Labubna, *T'ułt'*; T'adēos, *Acta*; II.C, Addai,
Doctrina.

AGA   *Ankanon girk' ařak'elakank'* in *T'angaran haykakan
hin ew nor dprut'eanc'*, ed. K'. Č'rkean, vol. III (Venice, 1904).
See also Abraham Xostovanoł.

Anania Širakac⁻i [Ps.]	See *Ašχ.* (short).
Anaphora of St. Gregory	See Basil, St., *Anaphora.*
Aphraat (Arm.)	*La version arménienne des oeuvres d'Aphraate le Syrien*, ed. and trans. G. Lafontaine, CSCO 382 (text), 383 (translation) (Louvain, 1977).
	See also II.C, Aphraat (Syr.); III, Lafontaine, *Aphraat.*
Apothegmata (Arm.)	See *Varkᶜ harancᶜ/Apothegmata.*
Aristakēs, St., etc., *Vitae* (long)	BHO 108–109:
	"Vkayabanutᶜiwn surb hayrapetacᶜn Hayocᶜ Aristakisi, Vrtᶜanisi, Yuskay, Grigorisi, Daniēli," in Abuladze, *Sviazi*, pp. 62–68.
(short) *Vitae*	"Patmutᶜiwn varucᶜ ew nahatakutᶜeancᶜ erǰanik hayrapetacᶜn Aristakisi, Vrtᶜanisi, Yuskann, Grigorisi, ordwocᶜ ew tᶜoṙancᶜ srboyn Grigori," *Sopᶜerkᶜ* X (1854), pp. 47–56.
Asołik	See Stepᶜannos Tarōnacᶜi.
Astuacašunčᶜ	*Astuacašunčᶜ matean Hin ew Nor Ktakarancᶜ*, ed. Y. Zōhrapean/Zōhrab (Venice, 1805); repr. CATRS (1984), with an Introduction by C. Cox.
Ašχ. (long)	*Ašχarhacᶜoycᶜ Movsēsi Xorenacᶜwoy* ed. A. Soukry (Venice, 1881).
	TRANSLATION:
	Géographie de Moïse de Corène, trans. A. Soukry, *Idem.*
(short)	"*Ašχarhacᶜoycᶜ*," in Anania Širakacᶜi, *Matenagrutᶜyunə*, ed. A. G. Abrahamyan (Erevan, 1944).
	TRANSLATION:
	"Géographie attribuée à Moyse de Khoren," in J. Saint-Martin, *Mémoires*, II, pp. 318–377.
Augēn Mār, *Vita* (Arm.)	Matenadaran ms 1552 (XIIIᵗʰC.)
	See also II.C; III, Melkonyan *Armianskiǐ perevod.*
Basil, St., *Anaphora*	*Srbazan pataragamatoycᶜkᶜ Hayocᶜ*, eds. Y. Gatᶜṙčᶜean and Y. Tašean (Vienna, 1897), pp. 120–159.
	TRANSLATION (corrected):
	"L'anaphore" ed. and trans. A. Renoux, "L'anaphore," pp. 83–108.
	See also III Renoux, "L'anaphore."
Liturgy (Arm.)	*Ibid.*
Vita (Arm.)	BHO 164.
	LVVS I, pp. 220–233.
	See also II.B, Amphilochus [Ps.]; II.C Basil, St., *Vita* (Syr.).
Book of Hours	See *Žamagirkᶜ.*
Book of Letters	See GTᶜ
Daniēl, St., *Vita*	See Aristakēs, St., etc., *Vitae* (long).
David of Sasun	See *Sasna crer.*
Dawitᶜ Anyałtᶜ	*Dawtᶜi Anyałtᶜi verlucutᶜiwn neracutᶜean Porpᶜiwri*, ed. and trans. S. S. Arewšatyan (Erevan, 1976).
Duin (A.D. 640), *Canons*	"Kanonkᶜ Dəwnay Surb Žołovoyn," *Kanonagirkᶜ*, II, pp. 200–215.
	TRANSLATION:
	"Kanony chetvertogo Dvinskogo sobora," trans. S. K. Arewshatian, BM, VI (1962), pp. 450–455.

Ełišē	*Ełišēi vasn Vardanay ew Hayocʿ paterazmin*, ed. E. Tēr Minasean (Erevan, 1957).
	TRANSLATION:
	Ełishē = Ełishē. History of Vardan and the Armenian War, trans. R. W. Thomson (Cambridge, Mass., 1982). See also III, Thomson, *Ełishē*.
Ełishē	See Ełišē.
Erasimos, St., *Vita*	*Codex Constantinopolitanus arm.* 705 (A.D. 1403). See also II.B, Gerasimos, St., *Vita* (Gk.); II.C, Gerasimos, St., *Vita* (Syr.); III, Akinean, "Pʿawstos."
Eusebius of Caesarea, Chron.	*Ewsebios Kesaracʿi žamanakakankʿ erkmasneay*, ed., M. Awgerean, 2 vols. (Venice, 1818).
HE (Arm.)	*Ewsebiou patmutʿiwn ekełecʿwoy*, ed. E. V. Čʿarean (Venice, 1977). See also II.B, Eusebius of Caesarea, EH.
Eznik Kołbacʿi	*Eznik De Deo*, eds. and trans. L. Mariès and C. Mercier, PO XXVIII/3–4 (1959).
Gahnamak ("Rank List")	"*Gahnamak*/Throne List," in Adontz, *Armenia*, pp. 67*–68*.
	TRANSLATION:
	Ibid., pp. 191–193.
Gahnamak [Ps.]	"*Pseudo Gahnamak*," in Adontz, *Armenia*, 70*–72*
	TRANSLATION:
	Ibid., pp. 200–203.
Gregory, St., *Teaching*	See AaT.
Vitae	BHO 328–347. See also Aa; II.B, Ag; Vg; II.C, Va, Vk, George, bishop of the Arabs. *Ep.*
Greg. Naz., *Panegyric* (Arm.)	Gregorius Nazianzenus, "Drevnearmianskiĭ perevod 'Epitafii' Grigoriia Nazianzina," KV 3 (1980), pp. 161–217. See also II.B, Greg. Naz., *Oratio XLIII*.
Grigoris, St., *Vita*	See Aristakēs, St., etc., *Vitae*.
GTʿ	*Girkʿ Tʿłtʿocʿ*, ed. Y. Izmireancʿ (Tiflis, 1901).
History of Tarōn	Scc Yovhannēs Mamikonean [Ps.].
James of Nisibis	See Yakob Mcbnecʿi, St., *Vita* (Arm.).
John the Katʿołikos	See Yovhannēs Drasχanakertcʿi.
John Mamikonean [Ps.]	See Yovhannēs Mamikonean [Ps.].
Kanonagirkʿ	*Kanonagirkʿ Hayocʿ*, ed. V. Hakobyan, 2 vols. (Erevan, 1964–1971).
KG	Kirakos Ganjakecʿi, *Patmutʿiwn Hayocʿ*, ed. K. A. Melikʿ-Ōhanǰanyan (Erevan, 1961).
	TRANSLATION:
	"*Histoire d'Arménie* par le vartabied Kirakos de Gantzak," in *Deux historiens arméniens*, trans. M.-F. Brosset (St. Petersburg, 1870).
Koriwn	*Varkʿ Maštocʿi*, ed. M. Abełean (Erevan, 1941; repr. 1962; Cairo, 1954); repr. CATRS (1985), with an Introduction by K. H. Maksoudian.
	TRANSLATIONS:
	a) *The Life of Mashtots*, trans. B. Norehad (New York, 1964); repr. CATRS (1985).

b) Koriwn. *Zhitie Mashtotsa*, trans. Sh. V. Smbatian and K. Melik-Ohandzhanian (Erevan, 1962).
See also Akinean. "Koriwn."

Labubna, *Tʿultʿ* — *Tʿultʿ Abgaru* (Venice, 1868).
TRANSLATION:
Léroubna d'Edesse, *"Histoire d'Abgar et de la prédication de Thadée,"* trans. J.-R. Emine, CHAMA I (1867), pp. 317–331.
See also Addē; I.C, Addai, *Doctrina.*

Łewond — Łewond. *Aršawankʿ Arabacʿ i Hayastanum* (St. Petersburg, 1887)
TRANSLATION:
Ghewond, *Histoire des guerres et des conquêtes arabes en Arménie*, trans. V. Chahnazarian (Paris, 1856)

List of Katʿołikoi — *Codex Parisinus arm.* 121, in Sanspeur, "Nouvelle liste," cols. 186–187.
TRANSLATION:
Ibid., cols. 187–188.
See also I.B, *Greek List.*

Listing of Historians — Anasyan, *Matenagitutʿyun*, I, pp. xlix–liv.

Liturgy (Arm.) — See Basil, St., *Liturgy* (Arm.)

ŁPʿ — Łazar Pʿarpecʿi, *Patmutʿiwn Hayocʿ*, eds., G. Tēr Mkrtčʿean and St. Malxaseancʿ (Tiflis, 1913); repr. CATRS (1985), with an Introduction by D. Kouymjian.
TRANSLATIONS:
a) *Ełishē*, appendix, pp. 251–327, partial, but preferable.
b) "Lazare de Pharbe: *Histoire d'Arménie*," trans. S. Ghésarian, CHAMA, II (1869), pp. 259–367.

LVVS — *Liakatar varkʿ ew vkayabanutʿiwn srbocʿ orkʿ kan i hin tōnacʿoycʿi ekełecʿwoy Hayastaneaycʿ*, ed., M. Awgerean, 12 vols. (Venice, 1810–1814).
See also *Varkʿ srbocʿ.*

Maštocʿ, *Vita* — See Koriwn.

MD — See MK/D.

Michael the Syrian — See Mixaēl Asori.

"Military List" — See *Zōrnamak* ("Military List").

Mixaēl Asori/"the Syrian," Chron. (Arm.) — *Tearn Mixaēli patriarkʿi asorwocʿ žamanakagrutʿiwn* (Jerusalem, 1870 and 1871).
See also II.C, Michael the Syrian.

YKʿ — "Yałags kʿahanayutʿean," in Mixaēl Asori, *Chron.* (Arm.) (Jerusalem, 1871), Appendix.

MK — See MX.

MK/D — Movsēs Kałankatuacʿi, *Patmutʿiwn Ałuanicʿ ašxarhi*, ed. V. Aṙakʿelean (Erevan, 1983).
TRANSLATIONS:
a) MD = *The History of the Caucasian Albanians by Movsēs Dasxurançi*, trans. C. J. F. Dowsett (London and New York, 1961);
b) Movsēs Kalankatuatsi, *Istoriia strany Aluank*, trans. Sh. V. Smbatian (Erevan, 1984).

MU — Mattʿēos Uṙhayecʿi, *Patmutʿiwn Mattēosi Uṙhayecʿwoy* (Jerusalem, 1869).

TRANSLATION:
Bibliothèque historique arménienne. Chronique de Matthieu d'Edesse continuée par Grégoire le prêtre, trans. E. Dulaurier (Paris, 1858).

MX   Movsēs Xorenac'i, *Patmut'iwn Hayoc'*, eds. M. Abełean and S. Yarut'iwnean (Tiflis, 1913).
TRANSLATION:
MK = Moses Khorenats'i, *History of the Armenians*, trans. R. W. Thomson (Cambridge, Mass., 1978). See also III, Thomson, MK.

MX [Ps.]   See *Ašχ.* (long).

Nersēs, St., *Vita*   BHO 795ff.; "Patmut'iwn srboyn Nersisi Part'ewi Hayoc' hayrapeti," *Sop'erk'* VI (1853), pp. 9–115.
TRANSLATION:
"Généalogie de la famille de saint Grégoire et vie de saint Nersès patriarche des Arméniens," trans. J. -R. Emine, CHAMA, II (1869), pp. 21–41.

Oskeank', Sts., *Acta*   "Ban ew asut'iwn čšmarit Srboc' Oskeanc' kahayanic'," *Sop'erk'* XIX (1854), pp. 59–66.

Paul, hermit, *Vita*   BHO 912–912; *Vark' haranc'/Apothegmata*, I, pp. 82–88. See also II.B, Jerome, St.; II.C, *Apothegmata* (Syr.).

Paul and Thekla, *Acta*   BHO 1155; *Vark'srboc'* (1874), I, pp. 513–531.
TRANSLATION:
The Apology and Acts of Apollonius and Other Monuments of Early Christianity, trans. F. C. Conybeare (London, 1894), pp. 61–88.

Primary History   "Xostabanut'iwn yaṙaǰkay patmut'eanc'," Sebēos, i, pp. 47–55.
TRANSLATION:
MK, Appendix, pp. 357–367.

"Rank List"   See *Gahnamak* ("Rank List").

Rituale armenorum   *Rituale armenorum*, ed. F. C. Conybeare (Oxford, 1905).

Sahak, St., *Canons*   "Kanonk' srboyn Sahakay Hayoc' hayrapeti," *Kanonagirk'*, I, pp. 363–421.

Šahapivan, *Canons*   "Hayoc' kanonis gluχk' I [XX], Kanonk' Šahapivani," *Kanonagirk'*, I, pp. 422–466. See also III, Akinean, ed.

Sargis, St., *Vita*   BHO 1053; *Vark' srboc'*, II, pp. 272–279. See also II.B, Sergios, St., *Vita* (Gk.); II.C, Sergios, St., *Vita* (Syr.).

Sasna Crer   Sasunc'i Dawit', *Haykakan žołovrdakan ēpos*, 2d ed. (Erevan, 1961).
TRANSLATION:
David of Sasoun, *The Armenian Folk Epic in Four Cycles*, trans. A. K. Shalian (Athens, Ohio, 1964).

Sebēos   *Patmut'iwn Sebēosi*, ed. V. G. Abgarean (Erevan, 1979).
TRANSLATION:
Histoire d'Héraclius par l'évêque Sebêos, trans. F. Macler (Paris, 1904).

Sergios   See Sargis, St., *Vita*.

Soc. Schol., EH (Arm.)	*Sokratay Sk⁽c⁾olastikosi "ekełec⁽c⁾akan patmut⁽c⁾iwn ew patmut⁽c⁾iwn varuc⁽c⁾ Sitbestriosi episkoposi Hŕovmay*, ed. M. Tēr Movsēsean (Vałaršapat, 1894). See also II.B, Soc. Schol., EH (Gk.).
Sop⁽c⁾erk⁽c⁾	*Sop⁽c⁾erk⁽c⁾ Haykakan*, 24 vols., (Venice, 1853–1854)
Step⁽c⁾annos Orbelean	Step⁽c⁾annos Orbelean, *Patmut⁽c⁾iwn nahangin Sisakan*, ed. K. Chahnazarian, 2 vols. (Paris, 1859).
	TRANSLATION:
	Histoire de la Siounie, trans. M.-F. Brosset, 2 vols. (St. Petersburg, 1866).
Step⁽c⁾annos Tarōnac⁽c⁾i/ Asołik	*Step⁽c⁾anosi Tarōnec⁽c⁾woy Asołkan, Patmut⁽c⁾iwn tiezera-kan* ed. St. Małχaseanc⁽c⁾ (St. Petersburg, 1885).
	TRANSLATION:
	Histoire universelle par Etienne Açogh⁽c⁾ik de Daron, trans. E. Dulaurier (Paris, 1883).
Synaxarion	See *Yaysmawurk⁽c⁾*.
T⁽c⁾A/T⁽c⁾A Cont.	T⁽c⁾ovma Arcruni, *Patmut⁽c⁾iwn tann Arcruneac⁽c⁾*, ed. K. Patkanean (St. Petersburg, 1887).
	TEXT AND TRANSLATION:
	T⁽c⁾ovma Arcruni ev Ananun patmut⁽c⁾iwn tann Arcruneac⁽c⁾, ed. and trans. V. M. Vardanyan (Erevan, 1985).
	TRANSLATION:
	Thom. Arts. = *Thomas Artsruni, History of the House of the Artsrunik⁽c⁾*, trans. R. W. Thomson (Detroit, 1985).
	See also III, Thomson, *Thom. Arts.*
T⁽c⁾adēos, *Acta* (Arm.)	BHO 1145;
	"Vkayabanut⁽c⁾iwn ew giwt nšarac⁽c⁾ S. T⁽c⁾adēi aŕakeloy ew Sandχoy," *Sop⁽c⁾erk⁽c⁾* VIII (1853), pp. 9–58.
	See also Addē, *Acta*; Labubna, *T⁽c⁾ułt⁽c⁾*; II. B, Thaddeus, St.; II. C, Addai.
T⁽c⁾ekł *et al.*, *Vitae*	Abraham Xostovanoł, pp. 189–196.
	See also II.B, Thekla, St.; II.C, Thekla *et al.*, *Vitae.*
T⁽c⁾ēodoros, St., *Vita*	BHO 1171–1173;
	"Patmut⁽c⁾iwn Amasia k⁽r⁾ałak⁽c⁾i ew yałags snndean srboyn T⁽c⁾ēodorosi zōravari," *Sop⁽c⁾erk⁽c⁾* XVI (1854), pp. 55–80.
	See also II.B, Theodore, St., *Vita.*
Tēr Israēl	See *Yaysmawurk⁽c⁾*.
Thaddeus	See T⁽c⁾adēos, *Vita.*
Thekla	See T⁽c⁾ekł *et al.*, *Vitae.*
Theodore	See T⁽c⁾ēodoros, St., *Vita.*
Thom. Arts.	See T⁽c⁾A.
Vardan Arewelci⁽c⁾	Vardan vardapet, *Ašχarhac⁽c⁾oyc⁽c⁾*, ed. H. Pērpērean (Paris, 1960).
Vardapetut⁽c⁾iwn S. Grigori	See AaT.
Vark⁽c⁾ haranc⁽c⁾/ Apothegemata (Arm.)	BHO 861–862;
	Vark⁽c⁾ srboc⁽c⁾ haranc⁽c⁾ ew k⁽r⁾ałak⁽c⁾awarut⁽c⁾iwnk⁽c⁾ noc⁽c⁾in əst krkin t⁽c⁾argmanut⁽c⁾eann naχneac⁽c⁾, ed. N. Sargsean, 2 vols. (Venice, 1855).
	TRANSLATION:
	Paterica armeniaca a PP Mechitaristi edita (1855) nunc latine reddita, trans. Dom. L. Leloir, CSCO, Subsidia, 42, 43, 47, 51 (Louvain, 1974–1976).

	See also, II.B, *Apothegmata* (Gk.); and II.C, *Apotheg-mata* (Syr.); III, Leloir, *Paterica armeniaca.*
Varkᶜ srbocᶜ	*Varkᶜ ew vkayabanutᶜiwn srbocᶜ*, 2 vols. (Venice 1874). See also LVVA.
Vitae	See under the name of the saint.
Vkaykᶜ arewelicᶜ	See Abraham Xostovanoł.
Vrtᶜanēs, St., *Vita*	See Aristakēs, St., etc., *Vitae.*
Yakob Mcbnecᶜi, St., *Vita*	BHO 407–409; "Patmutᶜiwn srboyn Yakovbay Mcbnay hayrapetin," *Sopᶜerkᶜ* XXII (1861), pp. 5–63; *Varkᶜ srbocᶜ*, II, pp. 83–107. See also II.B, James of Nisibis, St., *Vita* (Gk.); and II.C, James of Nisibis, St., *Vita* (Syr.).
Yaysmawurkᶜ	*Le Synaxaire arménien de Ter Israel*, G. Babayan, ed. and trans. PO V/3 (1909, repr. 1980), VI/2 (1910, repr. 1980), XV/3 (1920), XVI/1 (1922), XVIII/1 (1924), XIX/1 (1925), XXI (1927–1930).
Yovhannēs Drasχanakertcᶜi	*Yovhannou katᶜołikosi Drasχanakertcᶜoy, Patmutᶜiwn Hayocᶜ*, ed. M. Emin (Moscow, 1853, repr. Tiflis, 1912); repr. CATRS (1980), with an Introduction by K. H. Maksoudian. TRANSLATION: Yovhannēs Drasχanakertcᶜi, *History of Armenia*, trans. K. H. Maksoudian (Atlanta, 1987). See also III, Maksoudian, *Yovhannēs Drasχanakertcᶜi.*
Yovhannēs Mamikonean [Ps.]	Yovhan Mamikonean, *Patmutᶜiwn Tarōnoy*, ed. A. Abrahamyan (Erevan, 1941). TRANSLATION: *Ps. Yovhannēs Mamikonean. The History of Tarōn*, trans. L. Avdoyan (Atlanta, forthcoming).
Yusik, St., *Vita*	See Aristakēs, St., etc.
Žamagirkᶜ	*Žamagirkᶜ Hayastaneaycᶜ S. Ekełecᶜwoy* (Jerusalem, 1915).
ZG	See Yovhannēs Mamikonean [Ps.].
Zōrnamak ("Military List")	"*Zōrnamak*/Military List," in Adontz, *Armenia*, pp. 68*–69*, TRANSLATION *Ibid.*, pp. 193–195.

B: Classical Texts

Acta	See under the name of the saint.
Acta Apocrypha	*Acta apostolorum apocrypha*, ed. R. A. Lipsius and M. Bonnet, 2 vols. (Leipzig, 1891–1903; repr. Darmstadt, 1959). See also II.A, Abraham Xostovanoł.
Aelianus	Aelianus, *De natura animalium*, ed. R. Hercher (Leipzig, 1864).
Aesop	*Caxton's Aesop*, ed. R. T. Lenaghan (Cambridge, Mass. 1967).

Ag	BHG 713. *La version grecque ancienne du livre arménien d'Agathange*, ed. G. Lafontaine (Louvain, 1973). See also II.A, Aa; III, Lafontaine, Ag.
Agathias	*Agathiae Myrinaei historiarum libri quinque*, ed. R. Keydell, CFHB II (Berlin, 1967). TRANSLATION: *Agathias. The Histories*, trans. J. D. Frendo, CFHB IIA (Berlin, 1975).
AM	*Ammiani Marcellini rerum gestarum libri qui supersunt*, ed. and trans. J. C. Rolfe, 3 vols., Loeb.
Amphilochus [Ps.]	*SS Patrum Amphilochi Iconensis Methodii Patarensis et Andreae Cretensis opera omnia*, ed. F. Combefisius (Paris, 1644). See also II.A, Basil, St., *Vita* (Arm.); and II.C, Basil, St., *Vita* (Syr.).
Apothegmata (Gk.)	*Sanctorum Senum Apothegmata*, PG LXV (1858), cols. 76–440. TRANSLATIONS: a)*Les Sentences des Pères*, collection alphabétique, trans. L. Regnault (Solesmes, 1981). b)*Les Sentences des Pères du Désert*, série des anonymes, trans. L. Regnault (Solesmes-Bellefontaine, 1985). See also II.A, *Vark^c haranc^c*; II.C, *Apothegmata* (Syr.).
Appian, *Mithr.*	"The Mithridatic War," in *Appian's Roman History*, ed. and trans. H. White, Loeb, vol.II.
Syr.	"The Syrian War," in *Appian's Roman History*, ed. and trans. H. White, Loeb, vol.II.
Athanasius, St., *Vita Antonii*	S. P. N. Athanasius, *Vita Antonii*, PG XXVI, pp. 835–877.
Aulus Gellius	The Attic Nights of Aulus Gellius, ed. and trans. J. C. Rolfe, 3 vols., Loeb.
Aur. Vict.	*Aurelius Victor Liber de caesaribus*, P. Dufreigne (Paris, 1975).
Basil, St., *Letters*	*Collected Letters of Saint Basil*, ed. and trans. R. J. Deferari, 4 vols., Loeb.
Panegyric	See Greg. Naz., *Oratio XLIII*.
Vita	See Amphilochus [Ps.].
Cassian	See John Cassian.
CD	*Cassius Dio's Roman History*, ed. and trans. E. Cary, 9 vols., Loeb.
CJ	*Codex Justinianus*, ed. P. Krüger, CJC II.
CJC	*Corpus Juris Civilis*, eds. T. Mommsen, P. Krüger, *et al.*, 3 vols. 8th ed. (Berlin, 1906).
Climachus	See John Climachus, St.
Constantine Porphyrogenitus	See DAI
CTh	*Codex Theodosianus*, ed. T. Mommsen (Berlin 1905). TRANSLATION: *The Theodosian Code*, trans. C. Pharr (Princeton, 1952).

Cyril of Skythopolis	*Kyrillos von Skythopolis*, ed. E. Schwartz, TU XLIX/2 (Leipzig, 1939).
DAI	Constantine Porphyrogenitus, *De administrando imperio*, ed. and trans. G. Moravcsik and R. J. H. Jenkins, 2 vols. (Budapest and London, 1949–1962; repr. Washington, D.C., 1968).
Diod. Sic.	*Diodorus Siculus, The Library of History*, ed. and trans. F. R. Walton, 12 vols., Loeb.
Egeria	See Etheria.
Etheria	Ethérie, *Journal de voyage*, ed. and trans. H. Pétré, SC 21 (Paris, 1957).
Eusebius of Caesarea, HE (Gk.)	*The Ecclesiastical History*, ed. and trans. K. Lake and J. Oulton, 2 vols., Loeb.
MP	"De martyribus Palestinae," ed. E. Schwartz, in *Historia ecclesiastica* (Leipzig, 1908), Paralipomena, pp. 907ff.
Eutropius, *Breviarium*	*Eutropii breviarium ab urbe condita*, ed. C. Santini (Leipzig, 1979).
Festus, *Breviarium*	*The Breviarium of Festus*, ed. J. W. Eadie (London, 1967).
Georg. Cypr.	*Georgii Cyprii descriptio orbis Romani*, ed. H. Gelzer (Leipzig, 1890).
Gerasimos, St., *Vita*	John Moschus, cvii, cols. 2965ff.
"Greek List"	"La liste grecque des catholicos arméniens et sa version géorgienne," in Garitte, *Narratio*, Appendix, pp. 402–415.
Greg. Naz., *Oratio XLIII*	Gregorius Nazianzenus, *Oratio XLIII in laudem Basilii Magni*, PG XXXVI, cols. 493–606. See also II.A, Greg. Naz., *Panegyric*.
Poemata	*Poemata historica*, I, *De seipso*, PG XXXVII, cols. 970–1452.
Gregory, St., *Vitae* (Gk.)	See Ag, Vg; also II.A, Aa; II.C, George, bishop of the Arabs, *Ep.*; Va; Vk.
Herodotus	*Herodotus, The Histories*, ed. and trans. A. D. Godfrey, 4 vols. Loeb.
Hilarius of Arles	Hilaire d'Arles, *Vie de saint Honorat*, ed. and trans. M. D. Valentin, SC 235 (Paris, 1977).
Hippolytus, *Chronicle*	Hippolytus, *Chronik*, GCS, 46, eds. A. Bauer and R. Helm (Berlin, 1955).
Honoratus, St., *Vita*	See Hilarius of Arles.
James of Nisibis, *Vita* (Gk.)	BHG 769; "Iakobos," Theodoret of Cyr, *Hist. Phil.*, I, pp. 160–193. See also II.A, Yakob Mcbnec°i, St. *Vita* (Arm.); and II.C, James of Nisibis, St. *Vita* (Syr.).
Jerome, St.	*Vita S. Pauli primi eremitae*, PL XXIII, cols. 17–30. See also II.A, Paul, hermit.
John Cassian	Jean Cassien, *Conférences*, ed. and trans. E. Pichéry, 3 vols., SC 42, 54,64 (Paris, 1955–1959).
John Climachus, St.	*S.P.N. Johannis Climachi scala paradisi*, PG LXXXVIII, cols. 596–1209.
John Moschus	*Johannis Moschi pratum spirituale*, PG LXXXVII.3, cols. 2851–3112.

Josephus, *Ant. Jud.*	Fl. Josephus, *Jewish Antiquities*, ed. and trans. R. Marcus and L. H. Feldman, Loeb, vols. IV-IX.
Bell. Jud.	Fl. Josephus, *The Jewish War*, ed. and trans. H. St. John Thackeray, Loeb, vols. II-III.
Julian, *Letters*	"Letters," in *The Works of the Emperor Julian*, ed. and trans. W. C. Wright, Loeb, vols. II-III.
Panegyric	"Oration I, Panegyric in Honor of the Emperor Constantius," in *The Works of the Emperor Julian*, ed. and trans. W. C. Wright, Loeb, vol. I.
Justinus, *Epitome*	Justin, *Abbrégé des histoires philippiques de Trogue Pompée*, eds. and trans. E. Chambry and L. Thély-Chambry, 2 vols. (Paris, s.d.).
Libanius	"Oratio LIX," in *Opera*, ed. R. Förster, vol. IV (Leipzig, 1910–1923; repr. Hildesheim, 1963).
Malalas	*Johannis Malalae chronographia*, ed. L. Dindorf, CSHB (1831).
	TRANSLATION:
	Johannes Malalas, *The Chronicle*, trans. E. Jeffreys (Melbourne, 1987).
Men. Prot.	*Ex historia Menandri Protectoris excerpta de legationibus barbarorum ad Romanos*, ed. I. Bekker and B. G. Niehbuhr, CSHB (1929), pp. 281–425.
	TRANSLATION:
	The History of Menander the Guardsman, ed. R. C. Blockley (Liverpool, 1985).
Moschus	See John Moschus.
Narratio	*Narratio de rebus Armeniae*, ed. G. Garitte (Louvain, 1952), pp. 26–47.
	See also III, Garitte, *Narratio*
Nomina	*Patrum Nicaenorum nomina*, eds. H. Gelzer *et al.* (Leipzig, 1898).
Not. dig.	*Notitia dignitatum accedunt Notitia urbis Constantinopolitanae et Laterculi prouinciarum*, ed. O. Seeck (Berlin, 1876; repr. Frankfurt a/Main, 1962).
Novellae	*Novellae*, ed. R. Schoell, CJC, 10th ed. (Zürich, 1972).
Palladius	Palladius, *The Lausiac History*, ed. Dom C. Butler, (Cambridge, 1904).
	TRANSLATION:
	Palladius, *The Lausiac History*, trans. R. T. Meyer (London, 1965).
Paul, hermit, *Vita*	See Jerome, St.
Paul and Thekla, *Acta*	BHG 1710–1716;
	Acta Pauli et Theclae, in *Acta apocrypha*, I, pp. 235–272.
	TRANSLATION:
	"Acts of Paul and Thecla," in *The Ante-Nicene Fathers*, eds. A. Roberts *et al.* (New York, 1926), VIII, pp. 487–492.
	See also Thekla, St., *Vita*; II.A, Paul and Thekla, *Acta*; II.C, Thekla, St., *Acta*.
Petr. Patric., *Ad gen.*	*Ex historia Petri Patricii et Magistri excerpta de legationibus romanorum ad gentes*, ed. I. Bekker and B. G. Niehbuhr, CSHB (1829), pp. 133–136.

Ad rom.	*Ex historia Petri Patricii et Magistri excerpta de legationibus gentium ad romanos*, eds. I. Bekker and B. G. Niehbuhr, CSHB (1829), pp. 121–132.
Pliny the Elder, NH	Pliny the Elder, *The Natural History*, ed. and trans. H. Rackam, 10 vols., Loeb.
Plutarch, "Alexander"	Plutarch, "Alexander," *Lives*, ed. and trans. B. Perrin, Loeb, vol. VII.
"Artaxerxes"	Plutarch, "Artaxerxes," *Lives*, ed. and trans. B. Perrin, Loeb, vol. XI.
"Crassus"	Plutarch, "Crassus," *Lives*, ed. and trans. B. Perrin, Loeb, vol. III.
"Lucullus"	Plutarch, "Lucullus," *Lives*, ed. and trans. B. Perrin, Loeb, vol. II.
"Pompey"	Plutarch, "Pompey," *Lives*, ed. and trans. B. Perrin, Loeb, vol. V.
Pratum spirituale	See John Moschus.
Procopius, *Bell. goth.*	Procopius, "The Gothic War," *Works*, ed. and trans. H. B. Dewing, Loeb, vols. III–IV.
Bell. pers.	Procopius, "The Persian War," *Works*, trans. H. B. Dewing, Loeb, vol. I.
Bell. vand.	Procopius, "The Vandalic War," *Works*, ed. and trans. H. B. Dewing, Loeb, vol. II.
De aed.	Procopius, "Buildings," *Works*, ed. and trans. H. B. Dewing and G. Downey, Loeb, vol. VII.
Ptolemy	*Claudii Ptolemaei Geographia*, ed. C. Müller (Paris, 1901).
RGDS (Gk. version)	*"Res gestae divi Saporis,"* in Maricq, *Classica et orientalia*, pp. 46–73. See also II.C, ŠKZ; III, Honigmann and Maricq, RGDS.
Rufinus	*Rufini Historia monachorum*, PL XXI, cols. 389–412.
Sabas, St., *Vita* (Gk.)	*"Bios tou hosiou patros hēmōn Saba,"* in Cyril of Skythopolis, pp. 85–200. See also II.C, Sabas, St., *Vita* (Syr).
Septuagint	*Septuaginta*, ed. A. Rahlfs, 2 vols., 7th ed. (Stuttgart, n.d.).
Sergios, St., *Vita*	BHG 1624–1629; "S. Sergius," AASS, Oct. III, pp. 833–883. See also II.A, Sargis, St., *Vita*; and II.C, Sergios, St., *Vita* (Syr.).
Soc. Schol., EH	*Sōkratou Scholastikou ekklēsiastikēs historia*, ed. W. Bright (Oxford, 1878). See also II.A, Soc. Schol., EH (Arm.).
Soz., EH	Hermias Sozomenos, *Kirchengeschichte*, ed. J. Bidez, GCS 50 (Berlin, 1960).
Strabo, *Geogr.*	*The Geography of Strabo*, ed. and trans. H. L. Jones, 8 vols., Loeb.
Tabula Peutingeriana	*Itineraria Romana. Römische Reisewege an der Hand the Tabula Peutingeriana*, ed. C. Miller (Stuttgart, 1916).
Tacitus, *Ann.*	Tacitus, *Annales*, ed. and trans. J. Jackson, 3 vols., Loeb.

Thaddeus, St., *Acta*	*Acta apocrypha*, I, pp. 273–378.
	See also II.A, Tᶜadēos, *Vita*; II.C, Addai.
Thekla, St., *Mir.*	BHG 1717;
	Miracula, in Dagron, *Ste. Thècle*, pp. 284–412.
Vita	*Vita* in Dagron, *Ste. Thècle*, pp. 168–283.
	See also Paul and Thekla, *Acta*; II.A, Paul and Thekla;
	II.C, Thekla, St., *Acta*; III, Dagron, *Ste. Thècle*.
Theodore, St., *Vita*	BHG 277ff., 281ff.
	a) "*Theodorus Tiro*," AASS, Feb. III, pp. 30ff.
	b) Nikephoros Ouranos, "*Martyrion tou hagiou Theodōrou*," in Halkin; "Théodore le Conscrit," pp. 313–324.
	c) *Theodoros Theron. Textkritische Ausgabe der vormetaphrastischen Legende* ed. H. Starck (Freizing, 1912).
Theodoret of Cyr, HE	Theodoret of Cyr, *Historia Ecclesiastica*, ed. F. Scheidweiler, GCS, 2 ed. (Leipzig, 1954).
Hist. Phil.	Theodoret de Cyr, *Histoire philothée, Histoire des moines de Syrie*, ed. and trans. P. Canivet and A. Leroy-Molighen, SC 234, 257 (Paris, 1977–1979).
Theoph. Sim.	*Theophylacti Simocattae Historiae*, ed. C. de Boor (Leipzig, 1887; rev. ed. by P. Wirth, 1972).
	TRANSLATION:
	Theophylaktos Simokattes, *The History of Theophylact Simocatta*, eds. M. and M. Whitby (Oxford, 1986).
Velleius Paterculus	*Velleius Paterculus and Res Gestae Divi Augusti*, trans. F. W. Shipley, Loeb.
Versions	*Les versions grecques des actes des martyrs persans sous Sapor II*, ed. and trans. H. Delehaye, PO II/4 (1906), pp. 401–560
Vg	*Codex Scorialensis gr.* X.III.6 (A.D. 1107), in Garitte, *Documents*, pp. 23–116.
	See also II.C, Va, Vk.
Xenophon, *Anab.*	Xenophon, *The Anabasis*, ed. and trans. W. Miller, 2 vols., Loeb.
Cyrop.	Xenophon, *The Cyropaedia*, ed. and trans. W. Miller, 2 vols., Loeb.
Zosimus	*Zosimi comitis et exadvocati fisci historia nova*, ed. L. Mendelssohn (Leipzig, 1887; repr. Hildesheim, 1963).
	TRANSLATION:
	Zosimos, *New History*, trans. R. T. Ridley (Canberra, 1982).

C: Oriental Texts

Acta	See under the name of the saint.
Addaï, *Doctrina*	BHO 24.
	The Doctrine of Addaï the Apostle, ed. G. Phillips (London, 1876), pp. 1–53;
	Extracts in AMS I, pp. 51–52.
	TRANSLATION:
	"The Teaching of Addaeus the Apostle," in *The Ante-Nicene Fathers*, ed. A. Roberts *et al.*, VIII (New York, 1926), pp. 657–665.

	See also II.A, Addē, St., *Acta*; II.B, Thaddeus, St.
Liturgia	*Liturgia sanctorum apostolorum Adaei et Mari*, ed. I. Abeloos (Urmi, 1890–1892).
	TRANSLATION:
	"The Liturgy of Addai and Mari," in Brightman *Liturgies*, pp. 245–305.
AMS	See Abbreviations.
Aphraat (Syr.)	"Aphraatis demonstrationes," ed. I. Parisot, *Patrologia Syriaca* I–II (Paris, 1894–1907).
	TRANSLATIONS:
	a) Latin, *Idem*
	b) "Selections from the Demonstrations of Aphrahat the Persian Sage," in *A Select Library of Nicene and Post-Nicene Fathers*, ed. P. Schaff and H. Wace, 2d ser. XIII/2, pp. 345–412.
Apothegmata (Syr.)	BHO 843, 846–853, 865–866;
	AMS VII.
	The Wit and Wisdom of the Christian Fathers of Egypt: The Syrian Version of the Apothegmata patrum, ed. F. A. W. Budge (Oxford, 1934).
	TRANSLATION:
	Les pères du désert. Textes choisis et présentés, trans. R. Draguet (Paris, 1949).
	See also II.A, *Vark⁽ haranc⁽/Apothegmata*; and II.B, *Apothegmata* (Gk.).
ASMO	See Abbreviations.
Augēn Mār, *Vita* (Syr.)	BHO 120–121; AMS, III, pp. 376–479.
	See also II.A, Augēn Mār, *Vita* (Arm.).
Ayādgan ī Zarērān	*Ayādgan ī Zarērān*, ed. and trans. D. Monchi-Zadeh, (Uppsala, 1981).
Bahrām Yašt	"*Bahrām Yašt*," in *The Sacred Books of the East*, ed. F. M. Müller, XXIII (Oxford, 1880), pp. 231–248.
Basil, St., *Vita* (Syr.)	BHO 170;
	AMS VI, pp. 297–335.
	See also II.A, Basil, St., *Vita* (Arm.); and II.B Amphilochus [Ps.].
Chron. Séert	*Histoire nestorienne (Chronique de Séert)* ed. and trans. Mgr. Addaï Scher, PO, IV/3; V/2; VII/2; XIII/4 (1907–1918).
Dionysius of Tell-Mahrē (Ps.)	*Chronique de Denys de Tell-Mahré*, ed. and trans. J.-B. Chabot (Paris, 1895).
George, bishop of the Arabs, *Ep.*	BHO 334;
	"Epistula ad presbyterum Iesum," in *P. Lagardii Analecta Syriaca* (Leipzig, 1858).
	Garitte, *Documents*, x, pp. 408–419.
	TRANSLATION:
	"Eine Brief Georgs Bischofs der Araber an den Presbyter Iesus," *Theologische Studien und Kritiken* 56 (1883), pp. 278–371; repr. with corr., *Georg des Araberbischofs Gedichte und Briefe* (Leipzig, 1891), pp. 44–60.
	See also II.A, Aa; II.B, Ag, Vg; II.C, Va, Vk.

Gerasimos, St., *Vita* (Syr.)	BHO 324. See also II.A, Erasimos, St., *Vita*; II.B, Gerasimos, St., *Vita*.
Gregory, St. *Vitae*	See George, bishop of the Arabs, *Ep.*; Va, Vk; II.A, Aa; II.B, Ag, Vg.
Jāmasp Nāmag	"To the Žamasp-Nāmak," ed. and trans. H. W. Bailey, BSOS VI (1930–1932), pp. 55–85, 581–600.
James of Nisibis, St., *Vita* (Syr.)	BHO 405–406. AMS IV, pp. 262–273. See also II.A, Yakob Mcbnec‘i, St., *Vita* (Arm.); and II.B, James of Nisibis, St., *Vita* (Gk.).
Kārnāmag-i Ardašīr	*The Kârnâmak-i Artaskhshîr Pâpākân*, trans. E. R. Antia (Bombay, 1900).
KKZ	"Kartīr KZ," in Sprengling, *Third-Century Iran*, pp. 46–53.
"Littérature sassanide"	See III, Griniaschi, ed.
Mares *et al.*, *Vitae*	"*Mares discipulus et LXX ap. Orientis*," BHO 610; AMS I, pp. 45–94.
Mari, *Acta*	"*Acta Maris*" in Abeloos, "Acta Maris."
MHD	*Mātakdān ī Hazār Dātastān. Sasanidskiĭ Sudebnik.* *Kniga tysiachi sudebnykh resheniĭ*, ed. and trans. A. G. Perikhanian (Erevan, 1973). See also III, Perikhanian, MHD.
Michael the Syrian	*Chronique de Michel le Syrien patriarche jacobite d'An- tioche* (1166–1199), ed. and trans. J.-B. Chabot, 4 vols. (Paris, 1900–1905). See also II.A, Miχaēl Asori
Mihir Yašt	*The Avestan Hymn to Mithra*, ed. and trans. I. Gershe- vitch (Cambridge 1967).
OP	R. G. Kent, *Old Persian*, 2d ed. (New Haven, 1953), "The Texts," pp. 116–157.
Pahlavi Texts	See III, West, P.T.
Paikuli	a) Paikuli, *Monuments and Inscriptions of the Early History of the Sassanian Empire*, ed. and trans. E. Herzfeld, 2 vols. (Berlin, 1924). b) *The Sasanian Inscriptions of Paikuli*, ed. and trans. H. Humbach and P. O. Skjærvø (Wiesbaden, 1978–1983).
Sabas, St., *Vita*	BHO 553; AMS VI, pp. 380–404. See also II.B, Sabas, St., *Vita* (Gk.).
Šāhnāmag	*Le Shah Nameh, ou Le Livre des Rois par Abu'l Kasim Firdousi*, ed. and trans. J. Mohl, 7 vols. (Paris, 1838– 1878; repr. 1976).
Šahr. ī Ērān.	*Šahristānīha ī Ērānšahr: A Catalogue of the Provincial Capitals of Ērañšāhr*, ed. and trans. J. Markwart (Rome, 1931).
Šallita, St., *Vita* (Syr.)	BHO 1034. AMS I, pp. 424–465.
Sergios, St., *Vita* (Syr.)	BHO 1052; AMS III, pp. 283–322.See also II.A, Sargis, St., *Vita*; and II.B, Sergios, St., *Vita*.

ŠKZ (Parth. and Pahl. versions)	a) In Sprengling, *Third-Century Iran*, pp. 7–9, 10–12.
	b) "Res Gestae divi Saporis," in A. Maricq, *Classica et Orientalia*, pp. 46–73.
	TRANSLATION:
	Sprengling, *Ibid.*, pp. 14–20.
	Cf. II.B, RGDS (Greek version).
SSI	*Die Sasanidischen Staatsinschriften*, ed. M. Back, AI XVIII (1978).
Syn. Or.	*Synodicon orientale*, ed. and trans. J.-B. Chabot (Paris, 1902).
Tabari	*Geschichte der Perser und Araber zur Zeit der Sasaniden aus der arabischen Chronik des Tabari*, trans. T. Nöldeke (Leiden, 1879; repr. Graz, 1973).
	See also III, Nöldeke, *Tabari*.
Tansar	*The Letter of Tansar*, trans. M. Boyce (Rome, 1968).
Thekla, St., *Acta* (Syr.)	BHO 1152–1154.
	Apocryphal Acts of the Apostles, ed. W. Wright (London, 1871), I, pp. 128–169.
	See also II.A, Paul and Thekla, *Acta*; II.B Paul and Thekla, *Acta*, Thekla, St.
Thekla *et al.*, *Vita* (Syr.)	BHO 1157.
	AMS, II, pp. 308–313;
	ASMO, pp. 123–127.
	See also II.A, Tᶜekł *et al.*, *Vitae*.
Va	*Codex Sinaiticus ar.* 460 (IXth C.)
	BHO 332.
	a) Marr, *Kreshchenie*, pp. 66–148.
	b) Garitte, *Documents*, pp. 27–116.
	See also Vk; II.B, Vg.
Vk	*Codex Hierosolymitanus (S. Marcus) karshuni* 38; van Esbroeck, "Nouveau témoin," pp. 22–95.
	See also Va; and II.B, Vg.
Zach. Rhet. [Ps.]	Zacharias Rhetor, *Historia ecclesiastica*, ed. E. W. Brooks, CSCO (1919–1924).
	TRANSLATION:
	The Syriac Chronicle known as that of Zacharias of Mytilene, trans. F. C. Hamilton and E. W. Brooks (London, 1899).

III: Literature

Abeghian   See Abełyan.
Abełean   See Abełyan.
Abeloos, "Acta Maris"   J. B. Abeloos, "Acta S. Maris, Assyriae, Babyloniae ac Persidis sæculo I apostoli," AB IV (1885), pp. 43–138.
Abełyan/ Abeghian/   M. Abełyan, "Hay žołovrdakan aṙaspelnerə M. Xo-
Abełean, "Aṙaspelnerə"   renac῾u Hayoc῾ patmut῾ean meǰ," *Ararat* (1899–1901); also published separately (Vałaršapat, 1900).
Erker   *Manuk Abełyan Erker*, 7 vols. (Erevan, 1966–1975).
Grakanut῾yun   M. Abełyan, *Hayoc῾ hin grakanut῾yan patmut῾yunə*, I (Erevan, 1944); reprinted in *Erker* III (1968), *passim*. Russian version (partly condensed): M. Abegian, *Istoriia drevnearmianskoĭ literatury*, I, trans. K. Melik῾-Ōhanǰanyan (Erevan, 1948, rev. ed. 1975).
"*Šahnama*"   M. Abełyan, "'*Šahnama*'-i otanavori č῾ap῾ə hay banastełcut῾yan meǰ," in *Erker* V (1971), pp. 446–452.
"Tałač῾ap῾ut῾yun"   M. Abełyan, "Hayoc῾ lezvi tałač῾ap῾ut῾yun. Metrik," in *Erker* V (1971), pp. 9–381.
"Vēpə"   M. Abełean, "Hay žołovrdakan vēpə," *Azgagrakan Handēs* (1906–1908); repr. separately (Tiflis, 1908).
"Vipakan bana-   M. Abełyan, "Hay vipakan banahyusut῾yun," in *Erker* I
hyusut῾yun"   (1966), pp. 5–23.
"Volksepos"   M. Abeghian, "Das armenische Volksepos," *Mitteilungen der Ausland-Hochschule an der Universität Berlin* XLII (1940), pp. 225–238.
Volksglaube   M. Abeghian, *Der armenische Volksglaube* (Leipzig, 1899); repr. in *Erker* VII (1975), pp. 449–579.
"Xndirə"   M. Abełyan, "P. Buzandi Hayoc῾ patmut῾yan aṙaǰin ew erkrord dprut῾yunneri χndirə," *Grakanut῾yun*, I, appendix ii; repr. in *Erker* III (1968), pp. 644–647.
"Yerger"   M. Abełyan, "Hin gusanakan žołovrdakan yerger," *HSXH Petakan Hamalsarani Gitakan Tełekagir* (1927–1930); repr. in *Erker* II (1967), pp. 11–280.
Abełyan, M., ed.   See II.A, Koriwn.
Abgaryan, "Mamikonyan-   G. V. Abgaryan, "Mamikonyanneri zruyc῾i hnaguyn
neri zruyc῾i ałbyurə"   ałbyurə hay matenagrut῾yan meǰ (Buzandarani korac dprut῾yunneri kapakc῾ut῾yamb)," BM VII (1964), pp. 237–269.
Sebēosi patmut῾yuwnə   G. V. Abgaryan, *Sebeosi patmut῾yunə ew ananuni aṙełcvacə* (Erevan, 1965).

Abgaryan, V. G., ed.	See II.A, Sebēos.
Abrahamyan, ed.	Anania Širakacʿi, *Matenagrutʿyunə*, ed. A. G. Abra-hamyan (Erevan, 1944).
	See also II.A, *Ašχarhacʿoycʿ* (short).
Abuladze, *Sviazi*	I. V. Abuladze, *Gruzino-Armianskie literaturnye sviazi v IX–XI vv.* (Tbilisi, 1944).
	See also II.A, Aristakēs, St., etc., *Vita* (long).
Ačaṙyan, "Armeniaca II"	H. Ačaṙyan, "Haykakankʿ / Armeniaca II," *Telekagir* (1945/1–2), pp. 3–7.
"Armeniaca V"	H. Ačaṙyan, "Haykakankʿ / Armeniaca V," *Telekagir* (1946/6), pp. 21ff.
Patmutʿyun	H. Ačaryan, *Hayocʿ lezvi patmutʿyun*, 2 vols. (Erevan, 1951).
Ačaryan, H., ed.	See Abbreviations, HAnjB; HArmB.
Accademia dei Lincei, *Oriente cristiano*	Accademia dei Lincei, *Atti del Convegno Internazionale sul Tema: L'Oriente cristiano nella storia della civiltà*, Quaderno 62 (Rome, 1964).
La Persia	Accademia dei Lincei, *Atti del Convegno Internazionale sul Tema: La Persia e il mondo Greco-Romano*, Quaderno 76 (Rome, 1966).
La Persia nel Medioevo	Accademia dei Lincei, *Atti del Convegno Internazionale sul Tema: La Persia nel Medioevo*, Quaderno 160 (Rome, 1971).
Ačemean, "Čanaparh"	H. Ačemean, "'Čanaparh ənd Eljers ē'," HA XLI (1927), cols. 194–196.
Adoncʿ	See Adontz.
Adonts	See Adontz.
Adontz/Adoncʿ/Adonts, *Armenia*	N. Adontz, *Armenia in the Period of Justinian: The Political Conditions Based on the Naχarar System*, ed. and trans. N. G. Garsoïan (Louvain, 1970).
"L'aspect"	N. Adontz, "L'aspect iranien du servage," RSJB II (Paris, 1937), pp. 141—158.
"Favst"	N. Adonts, "Favst Vizantiĭkiĭ kak istorik," KhV VI (1922), pp. 235–272 (all published).
"Fêtes"	N. Adontz, "Les fêtes et les saints de l'église arménien-ne," ROC VI/XXVI (1927–1928), pp. 74–104, 225–278 (all published.)
	See also Renoux, "Fêtes."
"Hosankʿner"	N. Adoncʿ, "Kʿalakʿakan hosankʿner hin Hayastanum," in *Usumnasirutʿiwnner*, pp. 17–48.
"Nachalʿnaia istoriia"	N. Adonts, "Nachalʿnaia istoriia Armenii u Sebeosa v" ee otnosheniakh kʿ trudam" Moiseia Khorenskogo i Favsta Vizantiĭskogo," VV VIII (1901/1–2), pp. 64–105
"Šinakanutʿiwn"	N. Adoncʿ, "Hay hin šinakanutʿiwnə," in *Usumnasirutʿiwnner*, pp. 157–205.
Usumnasirutʿiwnner	N. Adoncʿ, *Patmakan usumnasirutʿiwnner*, ed. A Xondkarean (Paris, 1948).
"Vestiges"	N. Adontz, "Les vestiges d'un ancien culte en Arménie," AIPhO, IV/2 (1936) = *Mélanges Franz Cumont*, pp. 501–516.
AG	See Abbreviations.
Ajello, "Aṙlez"	R. Ajello, "Sulle divinità armene chiamate Aṙlez," *Oriente moderno* XVIII/7–8 (1978), pp. 303–316.

620

"Pᶜaṙkᶜ" R. Ajello, "Armeno 'pᶜaṙkᶜ,' avestico 'χvarᵊnah'," *Studi iranici* (1977), pp. 25–33.

Akinean/Akinian, "Artašir" N. Akinean, "Artašir Papakani vepᵊ yunarēn Agatᶜange-łosi mēǰ" HA LXI (1947), cols. 457–581.

"Aždahak" N. Akinean, "Biwraspi Aždahak ew hamaynavarn Maz-dak hay awandavēpi mēǰ ᵊst Movsēs Xorenacᶜwoy," HA L (1936), cols. 1–21.

Dasakan hayerēn N. Akinean, *Dasakan hayerēn ew Viennayi Mχitᶜarean dprocˤᵊ* (Vienna, 1932).

"Grigor" N. Akinean, "Grigor Lusaworčᶜi tōnerᵊ Nēapolisi marmareacᶜ tōnacᶜoycᶜin vray," HA LXI (1947), cols. 600–614.

Karmir Vardan N. Akinean, *Karmir Vardan ew Awarayri čakatamartᵊ ᵊst Łazar Pᶜarpecᶜi. Matenagrakan-patmakan usumna-sirutᶜiwn* (Vienna, 1951); repr. from HA LXV (1951).

Koriwn N. Akinean, "Koriwn, patmutᶜiwn varucᶜ S. Maštocᶜi vardapeti," HA LXIII (1949), cols. 171–320.

Maštocᶜ N. Akinean, *S. Maštocᶜ vardapet; keankˤn ew gorcunēutᶜiwnᵊ handerj kenagrutᶜeamb S. Sahakay* (Vienna, 1949); repr. from HA XLIX (1935), LI (1938), and LXII (1948).

"Nkaragir" N. Akinean, "Nkaragir kargacᶜ i banicᶜ Eznkan ericᶜu," HA LI (1937), cols. 517–532.

"Pᶜawstos" N. Akinean, "Pᶜawstos Biwzandi ałbiwrnerēn," HA XXXVIII (1924), cols. 97–102.

"Reihenfolge" N. Akinian, "Die Reihenfolge der Bischöfe Armeniens des 3. und 4. Jahrhunderts (219–439)," AB LXVII (1949) = *Mélanges Paul Peeters*, I, pp. 74–86.

Sahak N. Akinean, *Kˤnnutᶜiwn S. Sahaki veragruac kanon-neru ew Hayocᶜ ekełecᶜakan tarin Ē [VII] daru skizbᵊ*, I (Vienna, 1950); repr. from HA LX (1946) and LXI (1947).

"Sebēos" N. Akinean, "'Sebēosi Žamanakagirn'ew Pᶜ. Biwzan-deay A. [I] Patmutᶜiwnᵊ," HA LII (1938), cols. 9–56.

Tesil N. Akinean, *Tesil S. Sahakay. Matenagrakan-patmakan kˤnnutᶜiwnᵊ* (Vienna, 1948); repr. of "Kᶜnnutᶜiwn tes-lean S. Sahakay," HA L (1936) and LI (1937).

"Tiritᶜ" N. Akinean, "Erg tr̄pᶜanacᶜ Tiritᶜay, antesuac ełerergutᶜiwn mᵊ D [IV] daru hay angir dprutᶜenēn," HA XXXVIII (1924), cols. 1–19.

Akinean, ed. N. Akinean, ed., "Šahapivan žołovin kanonnerᵊ. Mate-nagrakan usumnasirutᶜiwn," HA LXIII (1949), Mχitᶜar Tōnagirkᶜ, cols. 79–170.
See also II.A, Šahapivan, *Canons*.

Akinean and Tēr Połosean, N. Akinean and P. Tēr Połosean, "Matenagrakan
"Łazar Pᶜarpecᶜi" hetazōtutᶜiwnner. Łazar Pᶜarpecᶜi," HA LXXXVI (1972); LXXXVII (1973).

"Tᶜadēi vkayabanutᶜiwn" N. Akinean and P. Tēr Połosean, "Matenagrakan hetazōtutᶜiwnner. Tᶜadēi ew Sandχtoy vkayabanutᶜiwn," HA LXXXIII (1969), cols. 399–426; LXXXIV (1970), cols. 1–34, 129–148.

Akinian See Akinean.

Akopian, A. A. See Hakobyan, A. H.

Ałayan, "Gołt͑an" "Gołt͑an ‹ Gołt͑n tełanunə," *Tełekagir* (1957/12), pp. 51–52.

Aliev, "Albania" K. Aliev, "K voprosu o plemenakh Kavkazskoĭ Albanii," in *Orbeli Sbornik*, pp. 15–19.

Ališan/Alishan, *Ayrarat* Ł. Ališan, *Ayrarat* (Venice, 1888).
Hayapatum Ł. Ališan, *Hayapatum* (Venice, 1901).
Širak Ł. Ališan, *Širak* (Venice, 1881).
Sisakan Ł Ališan, *Sisakan* (Venice, 1893).

Allen, "March-Lands" W. E. D. Allen, "The March-Lands of Georgia," *The Geographical Journal* 74 (1929), pp. 150–156.

Alphandéry, "*Vardapet*" P. Alphandéry, "Note sur une étymologie du mot *vardapet*," REArm, IX/1 (1929), pp. 1–3.

Altheim and Stiehl, F. Altheim and R. Stiehl, *Ein asiatischer Staat. Feudalis-*
Asiatische Staat *mus unter den Sassaniden und ihre Nachbaren* (Wiesbaden, 1954).

Amaduni See Amatuni.
Amatuni/Amaduni, K. Amaduni, *Disciplina armena II, Monachismo. Stu-*
Disciplina armena *dio storico-canonico e fonti canoniche* (Venice, 1940).
Testi K. Amaduni, ed., *Testi vari di diritto canonico armeno (secoli IV–XVIII)* (Vatican, 1952).

Amiranashvili, "Serebria- Sh. Ia. Amiranashvili, "Serebrianaia chasha
naia chasha" rannesasanidskoĭ ēpokhi iz raskopok v Aramaziskhevi," in Orbeli, *Sbornik*, pp. 283–293.
First Published as:
"Une coupe en argent du début de l'époque sassanide provenant des fouilles d'Armazis-Khevi (Géorgie)," RSO 34 (1959), pp. 149–162.

Ananean/Ananian, P. Ananian, "La data e le circostanze della consecra-
"La data" zione di S. Gregorio Illuminatore," LeM LXXIV (1961), pp. 43–73, 319–360; trans. from *Pazmaveb* 117–118 (1959–1960).

"Sebēos" P. Ananean, "Sebēosi patmut͑ean ařaǰin č͑ors gluχnerə," *Pazmaveb* (1971), pp. 9–24, 181–194.

Ananian See Ananean.
Anassian See Anasyan.
Anasyan/Anassian, H. S. Anassian, "Une mise au point relative à l'Al-
"Ałuank͑" banie Caucasienne (Ałuank͑)," REArm n.s. VI (1969), pp. 299–330.

Matenagitut͑yun H. S. Anasyan, *Haykakan Matenagitut͑yun E–ŽE [V–XVIII] dd.*, 2 vols. (Erevan, 1959–1976).

Review H. S. Anasyan, "Buzandarani řuseren t͑argmanut͑yunə (graχosut͑yun)," typescript (1975).

Ant͑abyan, "Vardan" P͑. Ant͑abyan, "Vařdan arewelc͑u patmut͑ean ałbyurnerə," BM 14 (1984), pp. 78–103.

AON See Abbreviations
Apakidze *et al., Mtskheta* A. M. Apakidze *et al., Mtskheta*, I (Tbilisi, 1958).
Arakelian See Arak͑elyan.
Arak͑elyan/Arakelian, B. N.
Artašat I B. N. Arak͑elyan, *Artašat I* (Erevan, 1982).
"Ervandašat" B. N. Arak͑elyan, "Ortel en gtnvel Ervandašat ew Ervandakert k͑ałak͑nerə," PBH (1965/3), pp. 83–94.

"Gaŕni" B. N. Arakelyan, "Excavations at Gaŕni 1949–1950, 1951–1955: Contributions to the Archaeology of Armenia," *Russian Translation Series of the Peabody Museum* III/3 (Cambridge, Mass, 1968), pp. 13–198.

"Haykakan mšakuytᶜə" B. N. Aŕakᶜelyan, "Erku himnakan ułłutᶜyunneri jewavorumə hin haykakan mšakuytᶜi meǰ," PBH (1979/2), pp. 45–53.

"Kałakᶜayin varčᶜutᶜyunə" B. N. Aŕakᶜelyan, "Kᶜałakᶜayin varčᶜutᶜyunə ew inkᶜnavarčᶜutᶜyunə miǰnadaryan Hayastanum," PBH (1961/3–4), pp. 58–81.

"Kᶜałakᶜneri bnakčᶜutᶜyunǰ" B. N. Aŕakᶜelyan, "Hayastani miǰnadaryan kᶜałakᶜneri bnakčᶜutᶜyan socᶜialakan kazmə," PBH (1958/2), pp. 39–66.

Patkerakᶜandaknerə B. N. Aŕakᶜelyan, *Haykakan patkerakᶜandaknerə IV–VII darerum* (Erevan, 1949).

"Zametki" B. N. Arakelian, "Zametki o khoziaĭstve i byte gorodov drevneĭ Armenii," PBH (1982/3), pp. 46–55.

Aŕakᶜelyan, V. D., *Grakanutᶜyun* V. D. Aŕakᶜelyan, *Grakanutᶜyun ew matenagrutyun. Lezvi Institut gitakan ašxatutᶜyan žołovacu* 3 (Erevan, 1948).

Armen, "Aršakunikᶜ" H. Kᶜ. Armen, "Aršakunikᶜ ew Lusaworčᶜyanner," PBH (1967/1), pp. 54–64.

Artsruni, *Pamiatniki* S. S. Artsruni, *Kul'tovo-memorial'nye pamiatniki v sisteme armianskoĭ srednevekovoĭ kul'tury* (Erevan, 1986).

Arutiunian, "Delenie" V. A. Arutiunian, "Administrativnoe delenie zakavkazskikh vladeniĭ sasanidskogo Irana soglasno trudu Elishē," KV I (1979), pp. 19–35 and map.

Arzumanyan, "*Matean gund*" N. A. Arzumanyan, "Haykakan skznałbyurnerum hišadakoł 'matean gund' zoramacə," PBH (1973/2), pp. 154–161.

Asatrian See Asatryan, also Hasatryan.

Asatryan, "Hayerenum" G. S. Asatryan, "Hayerenum iranakan mi kᶜani pᶜoχaŕutᶜyunneri harcᶜi šurǰ," PBH (1982/2), pp. 191–193.

Asdourian/Asturean, *Armenien und Rom* P. Asdourian, *Die politischen Beziehungen zwischen Armenien und Rom von 190 v. Chr. bis 428 n. Chr.* (Venice, 1911).

Asmussen, "Bemerkungen" J. Asmussen, "Einige Bemerkungen zur sasanidischen Handarz-Literatur," in Accademia dei Lincei, *Persia nel Medioevo*, pp. 269–276.

"Christentum" J. Asmussen, "Das Christentum in Iran und sein Verhältnis zum Zoroastrismus," *Studia Theologica* 16 (1962), pp. 1–22.

Xᵘāstvānīst J. P. Asmussen, *Xᵘāstvānīst, Studies in Manicheism* (Copenhagen, 1965).

Astuacaturean, *Hamabarbaŕ* Tᶜ. Astuacaturean, *Hamabarbaŕ Hin ew Nor Ktakarancᶜ* (Jerusalem, 1895).

Aubert, "Eusèbe de Césarée" R. Aubert, "Eusèbe de Césarée en Cappadoce, 362–370," DHGE X (1963), cols. 1436–1437, no. 16.

Aubineau, "Le panégyrique de Thècle" M. Aubineau, "Le panégyrique de Thècle attribué à Jean Chrysostome: La fin retrouvée d'un texte mutilé," AB XCIII (1975), pp. 349–362.

Aucher, J.-B. See Awgerean.

Avdalbegyan, M. M. Avdalbegyan, *Hay gełarvestakan arjaki*

Skzbnavorum	*skzbnavorumə (V dar)* (Erevan, 1971).
Avdalbegyan/Awtalbēkean "Has"	Tʻ. Avdalbegyan, "Has sak u baž," *HSXH Gitutʻyan ew Arwesti Instituti Telekagir* (1926/1). Repr. in *idem, Hetazotutʻyunner*, pp. 363–413.
"Hay šinakani ašχatavarjə,"	Tʻ. Avdalbegyan, "Hay šinakani u geljkuhu ašχatavarjə hingerord darum," *HSXH Gitutʻyan ew Arwest Instituti Telekagir* III (1928), pp. 51–81; repr. in *idem, Hetazotutʻyunner*, pp. 275–304.
Hetazotutʻyunner	Tʻ. Avdalbegyan, *Hayagitakan hetazotutʻyunner* (Erevan, 1969).
"Meružan"	Tʻ. Awtalbēkean, "Meružan Arcrunu zayroytʻə," HA XL (1926), cols. 384–387; repr. in *idem, Hetazotutʻyunner*, pp. 132–134.
"Mihr"	Tʻ. Awtalbēkean, "Mihr Hayocʻ mēj," HA XLI–XLII (1927–1928); repr. in *idem, Hetazotutʻyunner*, pp. 13–101.
Avdoyan, L., ed. and trans., *Pseudo-Yovhannēs Mamikonean*	L. Avdoyan, ed. and trans. "Introduction and Commentaries on *Pseudo-Yohvannēs Mamikonean's History of Tarōn* (in press). See also, II.A, Yovhannēs Mamikonean [Ps.].
Avi-Yonah, "Palaestina"	M. Avi-Yonah, "Palaestina," PW, Supp. XIII (1973), cols. 322–454.
Awgerean, M./Aucher, J.-B., ed.	See II.A, Eusebius of Caesarea, *Chron.*; Abbreviations LVVS; and NHBL.
Awtalbēkean	See Avdalbegyan.
Aytənean, *Kʻnnakan kʻerakanutʻiwn*	A. Aytənean, *Kʻnnakan kʻerakanutʻiwn ardi hayerēn lezui* (Vienna, 1866).
Azarpay, "Bowls"	G. Azarpay, "Nine Inscribed Khoresmian Bowls," *Artibus Asiae* XXXI (1969), pp. 185–203.
"Crowns"	G. Azarpay, "Crowns and some Royal Insignia in Early Iran," IA 9 (1922), pp. 108–115
Azarpay and Henning, "Hunting Scene"	G. Azarpay and H. W. Henning, "A Hunting Scene on an Inscribed Sasanian Silver Vessel," IA 7 (1967), pp. 145–152.
Babayan, G., ed.	See II.A, *Yaysmawurkʻ*.
Bachrach, *Alans*	B. S. Bachrach, *A History of the Alans in the West* (Minneapolis, 1973).
Back, SSI	M. Back, "Die sassanidischen Staatsinschriften," AI XVIII (1978/9).
Bailey, "Armeno-Indoiranica"	H. W. Bailey, "Armeno-Indoiranica," TPS (1956), pp. 88–126.
Dictionary	H. W. Bailey, *Dictionary of Khotan Saka* (Cambridge, 1979).
"Indo-Iranian"	H. W. Bailey, "Indo-Iranian Problems," in *Studies in Indo-Asian Art and Culture, II, Acharya Raghu Vira Commemoration Volume* (New Delhi, 1973), pp. 15–19.
"Iranian"	H. W. Bailey, "Iranian in Armenian," REArm n.s. II (1965), pp. 1–3.
"Iranian Studies"	H. W. Bailey, "Iranian Studies I," BSOAS VI (1930–1932), pp. 942–955.
"Kharoṣṭi Inscription"	H. W. Bailey, "A Kharoṣṭi Inscription of Seṇavarma King of Oḍi," JRAS (1980), pp. 21–29.

"Kusanica" H. W. Bailey, "Kusanica," BSOAS XIV/3 (1952), pp. 420–434.

Problems H. W. Bailey, *Zoroastrian Problems in the Ninth-Century Books*, rev. ed. (Oxford, 1971).

"Review" H. W. Bailey, "Review" of A. Christensen, *L'Iran sous les Sassanides*, BSOAS IX (1937–1939), p. 232.

Baker, "Syriac" A. Baker, "Syriac and the Origins of Monasticism," *Downside Review* LXXXVI (1968), pp. 342–353.

Bardy, "Basile" G. Bardy, "Basile, St.," DS I (1937), cols. 1273–1283.

Barkhudarian, "Urartskoe proiskhozhdenie" S. Barkhudarian, "Urartskoe proiskhozhdenie armianskogo roda Artsruni," in Orbeli *Sbornik*, pp. 29–38.

Barthold See Bartold.

Bart'ikyan, "Garni" H. Bart'ikyan, "Garnii hunaren arjanagrut'yunə ew Movses Xorenac'in," PBH (1965/3), pp. 238–244.

Bartold/Barthold, "Allān" V. V. Barthold, "Allān," EI² I, pp. 327–328; repr. in *idem, Socheneniia*, II/1, pp. 327–330.

"Arrān" V. V. Barthold, "Arrān," EI² I, pp. 478–479; repr. in *idem, Socheneniia* III, pp. 334–335.

"Ēpos" V. V. Bartold, "K istorii persidskogo ēposa," ZVO XXII (1915), pp. 257–282; repr. in *idem, Socheneniia* VII, pp. 383–408.

"Feodalizm" V. V. Bartold, "K voprosu o feodalizme v Irane," *Novyĭ Vostok* XXVIII (1930), pp. 108–116; repr. in *idem, Socheneniia* VII, pp. 459–468.

Iran V. V. Bartold, "*Istoriko geograficheskiĭ obzor*" *Irana* (St. Petersburg, 1903) repr. in *idem., Socheneniia* VII, pp. 31–225.

Socheneniia V. V. Bartold, *Socheneniia*, 9 vols. (Moscow, 1963–1977).

Baumgartner, "Akilisene" A. Baumgartner, "Akilisene," PW, I (1893), col. 1168.

"Artaxata" A. Baumgartner, "Artaxata," PW, II (1896), col. 1311.

"Asthianene" A. Baumgartner, "Asthianene," PW, II (1896), col. 1789.

"Gordyene" A. Baumgartner, "Gordyene," PW, VII (1910), cols. 1594–1595.

Baumgartner and Streck, "Arzanene" A. Baumgartner, "Arzanene," PW, II (1896), col. 1498; rev. by M. Streck, "Arzanene," PW, Supp. I (1903), col. 147.

Baus, ed., *Imperial Church* K. Baus, ed., *The Imperial Church from Constantine to the Early Middle Ages*, vol. II of *History of the Church*, ed. H. Jedin and J. Dolan (New York, s.d. [1980]).

Baynes, "Rome and Armenia" N. H. Baynes, "Rome and Armenia in the Fourth Century," *English Historical Review*, XXV (1910), pp. 625–643; repr. in *idem, Byzantine Studies and Other Essays* (London, 1955), pp. 186–208.

Beck, "Terminologie" E. Beck, "Zur Terminologie des ältesten syrischen Mönchstum," *Studia Anselmiana* 38 (1956), pp. 254–267.

Bedrosian, "*Dayeakut'iwn*" R. Bedrosian, "*Dayeakut'iwn* in Ancient Armenia," *Armenian Review* 37/2 (1984), pp. 23–47.

"*Sparapetut'iwn*" R. Bedrosian, "The *Sparapetut'iwn* in Armenia in the Fourth and Fifth Centuries," *Armenian Review* 36/2 (1983), pp. 6–46.

625

Belardi, "Origine"	W. Belardi, "Sulle origine delle voci armene antiche composte con *pat*," RL 5 (1962), pp. 149–169.
Belck, "Majafarkin"	W. Belck, "Majafarkin und Tigranokerta," *Zeitschrift für Ethnologie* XXXI (1899), pp. 600–608.
Benveniste, "Éléments parthes"	E. Benveniste, "Éléments parthes en arménien," REArm n.s. I (1964), pp. 1–39.
"Emprunts"	E. Benveniste, "Sur quelques emprunts iraniens en arménien," HA XLI (1927), cols. 761–764.
"Études"	E. Benveniste, "Études iraniennes," TPS (1945), pp. 39–78.
Mélanges	*Mélanges linguistiques offerts à Emile Benveniste* (Paris, 1975).
"Mots d'emprunt"	E. Benveniste, "Mots d'emprunt iraniens en arménien," BSL LIII (1957–1958), pp. 55–71.
"Notes"	E. Benveniste, "Deux notes iraniennes," BSL XXXII/1 (1930), pp. 86–91.
"Remarques"	E. Benveniste, "Remarques sur les composés arméniens en -*pet*," HA LXXV (1961), cols. 631–640.
"Le terme"	E. Benveniste, "Le terme iranien *mazdayasna*," BSOAS XXXIII (1970), pp. 5–9.
"Terminologie"	E. Benveniste, "Sur la terminologie iranienne du sacrifice," JA 252 (1964), pp. 45–58.
"Titres"	E. Benveniste, "Titres iraniens en arménien," REArm IX (1929), pp. 5–10.
Titres et noms propres	E. Benveniste, *Titres et noms propres en iranien ancien* (Paris, 1966).
"Traditions"	E. Benveniste, "Traditions indo-iraniennes sur les classes sociales," JA 230 (1938), pp. 529–550.
Vocabulaire	E. Benveniste, *Le vocabulaire des institutions indo-européennes*, 2 vols. (Paris, 1973).
Berbérian, *Memorial*	H. Berbérian, *Armenian Studies in Memoriam Haïg Berbérian*, ed. D. Kouymjian (Lisbon, 1986).
Bickerman, *Memorial Volume*	*Ancient Studies in Memory of Elias J. Bickerman* JANES XVI–XVII (1984–1985 [1987]).
Bidez, *Mélanges*	See AIPhO II.
Bivar, "Arsacids"	A. D. H. Bivar, "The Political History of Iran Under the Arsacids," CHI III/1 (1983), pp. 21–99.
"Cavalry Equipment"	A. D. H. Bivar, "Cavalry Equipment and Tactics on the Euphrates Frontier," DOP 26 (1972), pp. 271–291.
"Eastern Iran"	A. D. H. Bivar, "The History of Eastern Iran," CHI III/1 (1983), pp. 181–231.
Bivar and Shaked, Inscription"	A. D. H. Bivar and S. Shaked, "The Inscription at Shīmbār," BSOAS XXVII (1964), pp. 265–290.
Biwzandac͑i	See Norayr Biwzandac͑i.
Bogharian	See Połarean.
Bolognesi, "L'Armenia"	G. Bolognesi, "L'Armenia tra Oriente e Occidente: Incontro di tradizione linguistiche nei secoli che precedono e seguono la prima documentazione scritta," *Quaderni del seminario di iranistica . . . e caucasiologia dell'Università degli Studi di Venezia 7, Transcaucasica II* (Venice, 1980), pp. 26–42.

"Armeniaca" G. Bolognesi, "Armeniaca: Emprunts iraniens et calques grecs en arménien," in Leroy and Mawet, eds., *L'Arménien*, pp. 3–15.

Fonti G. Bolognesi, *Le fonti dialettali degli imprestiti iranici in armeno* (Milan, 1960).

"Nuovi aspetti" G. Bolognesi, "Nuovi aspetti dell'influsso iranico in armeno," HA LXXV (1961), cols. 657–684.

"Rapporti" G. Bolognesi, "Rapporti lessicali tra l'armeno e l'iranico," RL 96 (1962), pp. 235–258.

"Studi" G. Bolognesi, "Studi armeni," RL 5 (1962), pp. 105–147.

"Tradizione culturale" G. Bolognesi, "La tradizione culturale armena nelle sue relazione col mondo persiano e col mondo greco-romano," Accademia dei Lincei, *La Persia*, pp. 569–603.

Boltunova, "Iberia" A. Boltunova, "Opisanie Iberii v Geografii Strabona," VDI (1947/4), pp. 142–160.

Borisov, "Nadpisi" A. Ia. Borisov, "Nadpisi Artaksia (Artashesa) tsaria Armenii," VDI (1946/2), pp. 97–104.

Borisov, and Lukonin, *Gemmy* A. Ia. Borisov and V. G. Lukonin, *Sasanidskie gemmy* (Leningrad, 1963).

Botte, "Anaphore syrienne" B. Botte, "Problèmes de l'anaphore syrienne des apôtres Addai et Mari," OS 10 (1965), pp. 89–106.

Boudoyan and Thierry, "Thil" G. Boudoyan and J. M. Thierry, "Les églises de Thil (Korluca)," REArm n.s. IX (1972), pp. 179–191.

Boulenger, *Grégoire* F. Boulenger, *Grégoire de Nazianze. Discours funèbres en l'honneur de son frère Césaire et de Basile de Césarée* (Paris, 1908). See also II.B *Greg. Naz.*

Bowman, "Iran" J. Bowman, "The Influence of Iran upon Christianity," *Milla wa-Milla* V (1965), pp. 32–40.

Boyce, "Festivals" M. Boyce, "Iranian Festivals," CHI III/2 (1983), pp. 792–813.

"Festschrift" *Homages and Opera Minora: Papers in Honour of Professor Mary Boyce* (Leiden, 1985).

"Gōsān" M. Boyce, "The Parthian Gōsān and Iranian Minstrel Tradition," JRAS (1957), pp. 10–45.

History M. Boyce, *A History of Zoroastrianism*, I–II (Leiden, 1975–1982).

"Mithra" M. Boyce, "On Mithra's Part in Zoroastrianism," BSOAS XXXII (1969), pp. 10–34.

"Mysteries of the Dog" M. Boyce, "Death and the Mysteries of the Dog," in *idem, Persian Stronghold*, pp. 139–163.

"On the Calendar" M. Boyce, "On the Calendar of Zoroastrian Feasts," BSOAS XXXIII (1970), pp. 513–539.

"Parthian Literature" M. Boyce, "Parthian Writings and Literature," CHI III/2 (1983), pp. 1151–1165.

"Persian Literature" M. Boyce, "Middle Persian Literature," *Handbuch der Orientalistik*, I, *Iranistik* (Leiden, 1968), pp. 31–66.

Persian Stronghold M. Boyce, *A Persian Stronghold of Zoroastrianism* (Oxford, 1977).

"Pious Foundations" M. Boyce, "The Pious Foundations of the Zoroastrians," BSOAS XXXI (1968), pp. 270–289.

"Sacred Fires" — M. Boyce, "On the Sacred Fires of the Zoroastrians," BSOAS XXXI (1968), pp. 52–68.

"Some Remarks" — M. Boyce, "Some Remarks on the Transmission of the Kayanian Heroic Cycle," *Serta Cantabrigiensia* (Mainz, 1954), pp. 45–52.

"Temple Cult" — M. Boyce, "On the Zoroastrian Temple Cult of Fire," JAOS XC/3 (1975), pp. 454–465.

"Zariadris" — M. Boyce, "Zariadris and Zarēr," BSOAS XVII (1955), pp. 463–477.

Braun, *Akten* — O. Braun, *Ausgewählte Akten persischer Märtyrer* (Munich, 1915).

Brightman, *Liturgies* — F. Brightman *et al.*, eds. and trans. *Liturgies Eastern and Western* (Oxford; 1896; 2d ed., 1965).

Brock, "Christians" — S. Brock, "Christians in the Sasanian Empire: A Case of Divided Loyalties," *Studies in Church History* 18 (1982), pp. 1–19.

Brow, "Azerbaijan" — T. Burton Brow, "Azerbaijan Ancient and Modern," JRCAS XXVI (1949), pp. 168–177.

Brown, "Holy Man" — P. Brown, "The Rise and Function of the Holy Man," JRS 61 (1971), pp. 80–101.

Brunner, "Kušānšāhs" — C. J. Brunner, "The Chronology of the Kušānšāhs," ANS 19 (1974), pp. 145–164.

Bryer, *Topography of Pontus* — A. Bryer, *Byzantine Monuments and the Topography of Pontus*, 2 vols. (Washington, D.C., 1985).

Bürchner, "Kaisareia" — L. Bürchner, "Kaisareia," PW, X/2 (1919), col. 1523.

Bury, "Singara" — J. B. Bury, "The Date of the Battle of Singara," BZ V (1896), pp. 302–305.

Byzantine Saint, The — See Hacker, ed., *Byzantine Saint*.

Caetani di Teano, "Populi cristiani" — L. Caetani di Teano, "I populi cristiani sottomessi ai Sassanidi," *Bessarione* XX–XXI (1906–1907), pp. 232–254.

Čʿamčʿean, *Patmutʿiwn Hayocʿ* — M. Čamčʿean, *Patmutʿiwn Hayocʿ i skzbanē minčʿew cʿam Teaṙn 1784*, 3 vols. (Venice, 1784–1786).

Canivet, "Contributions" — P. Canivet, "Contributions archéologiques à l'histoire des moines de Syrie," *Studia patristica* 13, TU 116 (1975), pp. 444–460.

Théodoret — P. Canivet, *Le monachisme syrien selon Théodoret de Cyr* (Paris, 1977). See also II.B, Theodoret of Cyr, *Hist. Phil.*

Cardona, "Études étymologiques" — G. R. Cardona, "Études étymologiques domaine arménien: Arménien *drōšm, drōšmel* et syriaque, *rušma*," *Orbis* XV (1966), pp. 489–492.

Carrière, *Abgar* — A. Carrière, *La légende d'Abgar dans l'Histoire de Moïse de Khoren* (Paris, 1895).

Huit sanctuaires — A Carrière, *Les huit sanctuaires de l'Arménie payenne* (Paris, 1899).

Chabot, *Frontière* — V. Chabot, *La frontière de l'Euphrate de Pompée à la conquête arabe* (Paris, 1897).

Chaumont, "Anahita" — M.-L. Chaumont, "Le culte de la déesse Anahita dans la religion des monarques d'Iran et de l'Arménie au 1ᵉʳ siècle de notre ère," JA 253 (1965), pp. 167–181.

L'Arménie	M.-L. Chaumont, *L'Arménie entre Rome et l'Iran. Aufstieg und Niedergang der römischen Welt*, II (Berlin-New York, 1976).
"Chiliarque"	M.-L. Chaumont, "Chiliarque et curopalate à la cour des Sassanides," IA X (1973), pp. 139–165.
"Conquêtes sassanides"	M.-L. Chaumont, "Conquêtes sassanides et propagande mazdéenne," *Historia* XXII (1973), pp. 664–710.
"Le culte"	M.-L. Chaumont, "Le culte d'Anāhitā à Stakhr," RHR CLIII (1958), pp. 154–175.
"Ere"	M.-L. Chaumont, "A propos d'une ère d'Artaxata capitale de la Grande Arménie," REArm n.s. XVIII (1984), pp. 397–409.
"Etats"	M.-L. Chaumont, "Etats vassaux dans l'empire des premiers sassanides," AI 2d ser. I/4 (1975), pp. 89–156.
"Institutions"	M.-L. Chaumont, "Recherches sur les institutions de l'Iran ancien et de l'Arménie, I: Les fonctions de l'intronisateur royal et du chef de la cavalerie chez les Arsacides et les Sassanides," JA 249 (1961), pp. 297–320; "II: Argapat et dizpat," JA 250 (1962), pp. 11–22.
"Kartir"	M.-L. Chaumont, "L'inscription de Kartir à la Kaᶜbah de Zoroastre," JA 248 (1960), pp. 339–380.
"L'ordre des préséances"	M.-L. Chaumont, "L'ordre des préséances à la cour des Arsacides d'Arménie," JA 254 (1966), pp. 473–497.
"Ostraca"	M.-L. Chaumont, "Les ostraca de Nisa: Nouvelle contribution à l'histoire des Arsacides," JA 256 (1968), pp. 11–31.
Recherches	M.-L. Chaumont, *Recherches sur l'histoire d'Arménie de l'avènement des Sassanides à la conversion du royaume* (Paris, 1969).
"Rois"	M.-L. Chaumont, "Les grands rois sassanides d'Arménie," IA VIII (1968), pp. 81–93.
"Sassanides"	M.-L. Chaumont, "Les Sassanides et la christianisation de l'Empire iranien au IIIᵉ siècle de notre ère," RHR CLXV (1964), pp. 165–202.
"Tigranocerte"	M.-L. Chaumont, "Tigranocerte: données du problème et état des recherches," REArm n.s. XVI (1982), pp. 89–110.
Chitty, *Desert*	D. Chitty, *The Desert a City* (Oxford, 1960).
Christensen, *Démonologie*	A. Christensen, *Essai sur la démonologie iranienne* (Copenhagen, 1941).
Gestes	A Christensen, *Les gestes des rois dans la tradition de l'Iran antique* (Paris, 1936).
L'Iran	A. Christensen, *L'Iran sous les Sassanides*, 2d ed. (Paris, 1944).
Chrysos, *Legal Relations*	E. Chrysos, *Some Aspects of Roman-Persian Legal Relations* (Thessaloniki, 1976).
Colledge, *Palmyra*	M. A. R. Colledge, *The Art of Palmyra* (London, 1976).
Parthians	M. A. R. Colledge, *The Parthians* (New York-Washington, D.C., s.d. [1967]).
Connolly, "Aphraates"	R. H. Connolly, "Aphraates and Monasticism," JTS VI (1905), pp. 522–539.

Considine, "Semantic Approach" — P. Considine, "A Semantic Approach to the Identification of Iranian Loanwords in Armenian," in *Szemerényi Festschrift*, pp. 213–228.

Conybeare, *Apology* — F. C. Conybeare, *The Apology and Acts of Apollonius and Other Monuments of Early Christianity* (London, 1894).

"Canons" — F. C. Conybeare, "The Armenian Canons of St. Sahak Catholicos of Armenia (390–439 A.D.)," AJT II (1898), pp. 828–848.

Rituale — F. C. Conybeare, *Rituale Armenorum* (Oxford, 1905).

Conybeare, F. C., ed. — See II.A, Paul and Thekla, *Acta* (Arm.)

Covakan — See Połarean.

Cowe, *Daniel* — S. P. Cowe *The Armenian Version of Daniel: Diplomatic Text and Investigation of Textual Affinities* (in press).

CPD — See Abbreviations.

Čʿugaszyan/Tchoukassizian, "Byuraspi Aždahaki ałaspeł" — B. L. Čʿugaszyan, "Byuraspi Aždahaki ałaspeł əst Movsēs Xorenacʿu," *Tełekagir* (1958/1), pp. 67–84; repr. in *idem, Hay-Iranakan ařnčʿutʿyunner*, pp. 62–90.

"Echos" — B. L. Tchoukassizian, "Echos de légendes épiques iraniennes dans les ʿLettresʾ de Grigor Magistros," REArm n.s. I (1964), pp. 321–329.

Hay-Iranakan ařnčʿutʿyunner — B. L. Čʿukaszyan, *Hay-Iranakan grakan ařnčʿutʿyunner* (V–XVII dd.) (Erevan, 1963).

Cumont, F., *Mélanges Franz Cumont* — See AlPhO IV/2 (1936).

Cumont and Cumont, *Studia Pontica II* — F. Cumont and E. Cumont, *Voyages d'exploration archéologique dans le Pont et la Petite Arménie: Studia Pontica* II (Brussels, 1906).

Dagbashean, *Favstos Buzand* — O. Dagbashean, *Favstosʾ Buzandʾ i falʾsifikatorʾ ego istorii. Issledovanie obʾ istochnikakhʾ Moïseia Khorenskogo* (Vienna, 1889).

Dagron, *Ste. Thècle* — G. Dagron, *Vie et miracles de sainte Thècle* (Brussels, 1978).

Dandamayev, "Paradeisoi" — M. A. Dandamayev, "Royal Paradeisoi in Babylonia," AI XVII = *Orientalia J. Duchesne-Guillemin Oblata* (1984), pp. 113–117.

Danielyan, A. M., "Trdat III-i ŕeformə" — A. M. Danielyan, "Trdat III-i zinvorakan ŕeformə," PBH (1974/4), pp. 207–218.

Danielyan, Ē. L., "Haykakan bažanman taretʿivə" — Ē. L. Danielyan, "Haykakan bažanman taretʿivə 387 tʿe 385?" PBH (1980/1), pp. 203–214.

"Marderi cʿełə" — Ē. L. Danielyan, "Marderi cʿełə hin Hayastanum (m.tʿ.a. V-m.tʿ. I dd.)," PBH (1976/1), pp. 203–208.

Dashian — See Tašean.

Debevoise, *Parthia* — N. Debevoise, *A Political History of Parthia* (Chicago, 1938).

Delehaye, "Euchaïta" — H. Delehaye, "Euchaïta et la légende de S. Théodore," in *Ramsay Festschrift*, pp. 129–134.

Légendes — H. Delehaye, *Les légendes grecques des saints militaires* (Paris, 1909).

Légendes hagiographiques — H. Delehaye, *Les légendes hagiographiques* (Brussels, 1927).

Origine — H. Delehaye, *L'origine du culte des martyrs*, 2d ed. (Brussels, 1933).

Passions	H. Delehaye, *Les passions des martyrs et les genres littéraires*, 2d rev. ed. (Brussels, 1966).
"Recueils"	H. Delehaye, "Les recueils antiques des miracles des saints," AB LXIX (1951), pp. 119–130.
Delehaye, ed.	See also II.A, *Versions*.
Dentzer, "Banquet"	J.-M. Dentzer, "L'iconographie iranienne du souverain couché et le motif du banquet," *IXe Congrès International d'Archéologie classique* (Damascus, 1969), pp. 10–21.
"Iconographie"	J.-M. Dentzer, "Aux origines de l'iconographie du banquet couché," *Revue archéologique* n.s. (1971), pp. 215–238.
Der Nersessian, *Aght^camar*	S. Der Nersessian, *Aght^camar Church of the Holy Cross* (Cambridge, Mass. 1965).
Armenian Art	S. Der Nersessian, *Armenian Art* (London, s.d.).
Devos, "Martyrs persans"	P. Devos, "Les martyrs persans à travers leurs actes syriaques," Accademia dei Lincei, *La Persia*, pp. 213–225.
D'iakonov, "Mar Evgen"	A. P. D'iakonov, "K istorii siriĭskogo skazaniia o sv. mar Evgene," KhV VI/2 (1918), pp. 107–174.
D'iakonov and Livshits, "Nisa"	I. M. D'iakonov and V. A. Livshits, "Iz materialov parfianskoĭ kantseliarii 'Staroĭ Nisy'," in Orbeli, *Sbornik*, pp. 321–333.
Diethart and Dintsis, "Leontoklibanarier"	J. M. Diethart and P. Dintsis, "Die Leontoklibanarier," **BYZANTIOΣ** *Festschrift für Herbert Hunger* (Vienna, 1984, pp. 66–84).
Dilleman, "Ammien Marcellin"	L. Dilleman, "Ammien Marcellin et les pays de l'Euphrate et du Tigre," *Syria* XXXVIII (1961), pp. 87–158.
Haute-Mésopotamie	L. Dilleman, *La Haute-Mésopotamie orientale et les pays adjacents* (Paris, 1961).
Dirr, "Kaukasische Jagdgott"	A. Dirr, "Der Kaukasische Wild- und Jagdgott," *Anthropos* XX (1925), pp. 139–147.
Doise, "Le partage"	J. Doise, "Le partage de *l'Arménie sous Théodose I*," REA XLVII (1947), pp. 274–277.
Dölger, *Sonne der Gerechtigkeit*	F. J. Dölger, *Die Sonne der Gerechtigkeit und der Schwartze: Eine religions-geschichtliche Studie zum Taufgelöbnis*, 2d ed. (Münster, 1971).
Dowsett, "Eznik"	C. J. F. Dowsett, "On Eznik's Refutation of the Chaldaean Astrologers," REArm n. s. VI (1969), pp. 45–65.
MD	C. J. F. Dowsett, trans. "Introduction and notes to MD. See also II.A, MK/D.
"Tēr"	C. J. F. Dowsett, "*Armenian tēr, tikin, tiezerk^c*," ICMC (s.d. [1964]), pp. 135–145.
Drijvers, "Origins"	H. J. W. Drijvers, "Hellenistic and Oriental Origins," in Hacker, ed. The *Byzantine Saint*, pp. 25–33.
DuCange, *Glossarium*	D. DuCange, *Glossarium mediae et infimae latinitatis*, ed. L. Favre, 10 vols. (Paris, 1937–1938).
Duchesne–Guillemin, "Art"	J. Duchesne-Guillemin, "Art and Religion under the Sasanians, "*Mémorial Jean de Menasce*, pp. 147–167.
Dōšīzä	J. Duchesne-Guillemin, "Pers. *dōšīzä* 'jeune fille, vierge' et ses parallèles," LeM 59 (1946), pp. 571–575.
"Fire"	J. Duchesne-Guillemin, "Fire in Iran and Greece," *East and West*, XIII/2-3 (1962), pp. 198ff (repr. in *Opera Minora* III [Tehran, 1987], pp. 9–17).

631

Mélanges	See AI XVII (1984).
Dumézil, "Les Albaniens"	G. Dumézil, "Une chrétienté disparue: Les Albaniens du Caucase," JA 232.1 (1940/1), pp. 125–132.
Heur	G. Dumézil, *Heur et malheur du guerrier* (Paris, 1969).
"Nom"	G. Dumézil, "Le nom des 'Arya,'" RHR CXXIV (1941) pp. 36–59.
"Riþsula	G. Dumézil, "La riþsula et la structure sociale Indo-européenne," RHR CLIV (1958), pp. 1–9.
"Tripertita"	G. Dumézil, "'Tripertita' fonctionnels chez divers peuples Indo-européens," RHR CXXXI (1946), pp. 53–72.
"Vahagn"	G. Dumézil, "Vahagn," RHR CXVII (1938), pp. 152–170.
"Vərəθraγna"	G. Dumézil, "À propos de Vərəθraγna," AIPhO, IX = *Mélanges Henri Grégoire*, I (1949), pp. 223–226.
Duneau, "Aspects"	J. F. Duneau, "Quelques aspects de la pénétration de l'hellénisme dans l'empire perse sassanide," *Mélanges offerts à R. Crozet*, I (Poitiers, 1966), pp. 13–22.
Dussaud, *Syrie*	R. Dussaud, *Topographie historique de la Syrie antique et médiévale* (Paris, 1927).
Dzhafarov, "Albania"	Iu. R. and M. I. Dzhafarov, "O lokalizatsii khramovoĭ oblasti v Kavkazskoĭ Albanii," VDI (1985/2), pp. 29–44.
Edwards, "Artvin"	R. W. Edwards, "The Fortifications of Artvin: A Second Preliminary Report on the Marchlands of Northeast Turkey," DOP 40 (1986), pp. 165–182.
"Doğubeyazit"	R. W. Edwards, "The Fortress of Doğubeyazit," RE-Arm n.s. XVIII (1984), pp. 435–459.
"Kola"	R. W. Edwards, "The Vale of Kola: A Final Preliminary Report on the Marchlands of Northeast Turkey," DOP 42 (1988), pp. 119–141.
"Oltu-Penek Valley"	R. W. Edwards, "Medieval Architecture in the Oltu-Penek Valley: A Preliminary Report on the Marchlands of Northeast Turkey," DOP 39 (1985), pp. 15–37.
Eganyan *et al.*, eds., *Cʿucʿak jeragracʿ*	O. Eganyan, A. Zeytʿunyan, and Pʿ. Artʿabyan, eds., *Cʿucʿak jeragracʿ Maštocʿi anvan Matenadarani*, 2 vols. (Erevan, 1965, 1970).
Eilers, "Bidiahš,"	W. Eilers, "Bidiahš," IIJ 5 (1961–1962), pp. 203–232.
Festschrift	W. Eilers, *Festschrift für Wilhelm Eilers* (Wiesbaden, 1967).
Ějmiacin	*Treasures of Ějmiacin* (Ejmiacin, s.d.).
Ělčʿibekyan, "Kʿušanneri masin"	Ž. Ělčʿibekyan, "Hay miǰnadaryan skzbnaḷbyurnerə Kʿušanneri masin," *Lraber* (1974/8), pp. 85–97.
Elnitskiĭ, "Armenia"	L. Elnitskiĭ, "Iz istorii antitserkovnykh i anti-khristianskikh tendentsiĭ v Armenii v IV^{om} v. n.ē.," VDI (1965/2), pp. 122–131.
E.M.	See M[atatʿean], E.
Ēmin, "Faustus de Byzance"	N. O. Ēmin, "Faustus de Byzance," in *Issledovaniia i statʾi N.O. Ēmina po armianskoĭ mifologii istorii i istorii literatury za 1858–1884 gg.* (Moscow, 1896), pp. 266–274.
Enoki, "Ephthalites"	K. Enoki, "On the Nationality of the Ephthalites," *Memoirs of the Research Department of the Toyo Bunko (The Oriental Library)* 18 (1959), pp. 1–57.
Ensslin, "Hannibalianus"	W. Ensslin, "Zu dem vermuteten Perserfeldzug des rex Hannibalianus, *Klio* XXIX (1936), pp. 102–110.

"Trdat"	W. Ensslin, "Trdat," PW, VIA/2, cols. 246–249.
Ep^crikean, *Baṙaran*	S. Ep^crikean, *Patkerazard bnašχarhik baṙaran*, 2 vols. (Venice, 1903), all published.
Erdmann, *Feuerheiligtum*	K. Erdmann, *Das iranische Feuerheiligtum* (Leipzig, 1941; repr. Osnabrück, 1969).
"Jagdschalen"	K. Erdmann, "Die sassanidischen Jagdschalen," JPKS 57 (1936), pp. 193–231.
Kunst	K. Erdmann, *Die Kunst Irans zur Zeit der Sasaniden* (Berlin, 1943).
"Unbekannte"	K. Erdmann, "Eine unbekannte sassanidische Jagdschale," JPKS 59 (1938), pp. 209–217.
Eremian	See Eremyan.
Eremyan/Eremian, *Ašχarh.*	S. T. Eremyan, *Hayastanə əst 'Ašχarhac^coyc^c-i* (Erevan,1963), with map.
"KZ"	S. T. Eremyan, "Naχš-i Ṙustemi 'Kaba-i Zardušt' hušarjani arjanagrut^cyan vkayut^cyunnerə Hayastani masin," PBH (1966/2), pp. 59–69.
Map	S. T. Eremyan, *Mec Hayk^ci t^cagavorut^cyunə IV darum (298–385 t^ct^c)* (Erevan, 1979). Separate map.
"Narody"	S. T. Eremian, "Narody Kavkaza po Ptolemeiu i Armeniia," *Etnograficheskiĭ Kongress, VIII* (Moscow, 1964).
"O rabstve"	S. T. Eremian, "O rabstve i rabovladenii v drevneĭ Armenii," VDI (1950/1), pp. 12–26.
"Osnovnye cherty"	S. T. Eremian, "Osnovnye cherty obshchestvennogo stroia v ēllinisticheskiĭ period," *Tełekagir* (1948/11), pp. 33–73.
"Razvitie"	S. T. Eremian, "Razvitie gorodov i gorodskoĭ zhizni v drevneĭ Armenii" VDI (1953/5), pp. 11–31.
"Strana"	S. T. Eremian, "Strana 'Makheloniia' nadpisi Kaba-i-Zardušt," VDI (1967/1), pp. 47–58.
"Torgovye puti"	S. T. Eremian, "Torgovye puti Zakavkaz'ia v ēpokhu Sasanidov," VDI (1939/1), pp. 79–97.
Esaian, "Zashchitnoe vooruzhenie"	S. Esaian, "Zashchitnoe vooruzhenie v drevneĭ Armenii" PBH (1962/1), pp. 192–209.
Esbroeck, "Abraham le Confesseur"	M. van Esbroeck, "Abraham le Confesseur (Ve s.) traducteur des passions des martyrs perses," AB 95 (1977), pp. 169–179.
"Chronique"	M. van Esbroeck, "Chronique arménienne," AB 80 (1962), pp. 423–445.
"Commentaire"	M. van Esbroeck, "Commentaire philologique: Origine arménienne de Vk," REArm n.s. VIII (1971), pp. 96–167.
"Nouveau témoin"	M. van Esbroeck, "Un nouveau témoin du livre d'Agathange," REArm n.s. VIII (1971), pp. 13–167. See also II.C, Vk.
"Le roi Sanatrouk"	M. van Esbroeck, "Le roi Sanatrouk et l'apôtre Thaddée," REArm n.s. IX (1972), pp. 241–283.
"Témoignages littéraires"	M. van Esbroeck, "Témoignages littéraires sur les sépultures de S. Grégoire l'Illuminateur," AB 89 (1971), pp. 387–418.
"Thaddée"	M. van Esbroeck, "L'apôtre Thaddée et le roi Sanatrouk," *Communicazione per il II convegno Armenia-Assiria* (Rome, 30 May 1984), typescript.

Ettinghausen, "Bahram Gur" — R. Ettinghausen, "Bahram Gur's Hunting Feats or the Problem of Identification," *Iran* 17 (1979), pp. 25–31 and pls.

Fedwick, *Basil* — P. J. Fedwick, *The Church and the Charisma of Leadership of Basil of Caesarea* (Toronto, 1979).

Feld, "Bericht" — O. Feld, "Bericht über eine Reise durch Kilikien," *Istanbuler Mitteilungen* 13–14 (1963–1964), pp. 88–107.

Fernandez–Marcos, *Thaumata* — N. Fernandez–Marcos, *Los thaumata de Sofronio: Contribución al estudio de la incubatio cristiana* (Madrid, 1975).

Festugière, "Lieux-communs" — A.-J. Festugière, "Lieux-communs littéraires et thèmes de folklore dans l'hagiographie primitive," *Wiener Studien* 73 (1960), pp. 133–152.

Moines — A.-J. Festugière, *Les moines d'Orient*, 4 vols. (Paris, 1961–1965).

Feydit, "Énigme" — F. Feydit, "Serait-ce la solution de l'énigme du Livre VI de Fauste de Byzance?" *Pazmaveb* (1966), pp. 95–97.

"Gaṙni" — F. Feydit, "A propos de Gaṙni," *Armeniaca* (Venice, 1969), pp. 184–189.

"Histoire" — F. Feydit, "L'Histoire de Fauste de Byzance comprenait-elle deux livres aujourd'hui perdus?" *Pazmaveb* (1958), pp. 140–143

Passage" — F. Feydit, "Un passage énigmatique de Fauste de Byzance," *Pazmaveb* (1957), pp. 282–284.

Fiey, "Āḏarbāygan" — J.-M. Fiey, "Āḏarbāygan chrétien," LeM 86 (1973), pp. 397–435.

Assyrie — J.-M. Fiey, *L'Assyrie chrétienne*, 3 vols. (Beirut, s.d.).

"Awgen" — J.-M. Fiey, "Aones, Awun et Awgin (Eugène): Aux origines du monachisme mésopotamien," AB 80 (1962), pp. 52–81.

"Cénobitisme" — J.-M. Fiey, "Le cénobitisme féminin dans les églises syriennes orientales et occidentales," OS 10 (1965), pp. 281–306.

"Ichodenah" — J.-M. Fiey, "Ichodenah de Basra," OS 11/4 (1966), pp. 443–450.

Nisibe — J.-M. Fiey, *Nisibe métropole syriaque orientale et ses sufragants des origines à nos jours*, CSCO 388, subs. 54 (Louvain, 1977).

Forsyth, "Cilicia" — G. H. Forsyth, "Architectural Notes on a Trip Through Cilicia," DOP 11 (1957), pp. 223–236.

Foss, "Caesarea" — C. Foss, "Caesarea," DMA III (1983), p. 9.

Frend, "Monks" — W. H. C. Frend, "The Monks and the Survival of the Roman Empire in the Fifth Century," *Past and Present* 54 (1972), pp. 3–24.

Frye, "Arrān" — R. Frye, "Arrān," EI² I, pp. 660–661.

Heritage — R. Frye, *The Heritage of Persia* (Cleveland–New York, 1963).

"Mithra" — R. Frye, "Mithra in Iranian History," in *Mithraic Studies*, ed. J. R. Hinnells, I (Manchester, 1975), pp. 62–67.

"Sasanians" — R. N. Frye, "The Political History of Iran Under the Sasanians," CHI III/1 (1983), pp. 116–180.

Fussman, "Chronique" — G. Fussman, "Chronique des études kouchanes (1975–1977)," JA (1978), pp. 319–336.

Gabba, "Influenze"   E. Gabba, "Sulle influenze reciproche degli ordinamenti militari dei Parti e dei Romani," Accademia dei Lincei, *La Persia*, pp. 51–73.

Galvin, "Addai"   R. J. Galvin, "Addai and Mari Revisited: The State of the Question," *Dunwoodie Review* 10 (1970), pp. 3–31.

Gandolfo, "Martyrium"   F. Gandolfo, "Un martyrium sepolcrale armeno: la capella degli apostoli a Karenis," *Istituto di Storia dell'Arte Roma, Annuario*, I (1973–1974).

Garagašean, *Patmut⁽iwn*   A. Garagašean, *K⁽nnakan patmut⁽iwn Hayoc⁽* (Tiflis, 1895).

"P⁽awstos"   A. Garagašean, "P⁽awstos Buzandi masin," HA X (1896), cols. 200–201.

Garitte, *Documents*   G. Garitte, *Documents pour l'étude du livre d'Agathange* (Vatican, 1946).
See also II.A, Aa; II.B, Ag, Vg; II.C, Va.

"Georges"   G. Garitte, "La notice de Georges évêque des Arabes sur S. Grégoire l'Illuminateur," in *idem, Documents*, X, pp. 408–419.
See also II.C, George, bishop of the Arabs, *Ep.*

Narratio   G. Garitte, *La Narratio de rebus Armeniae*, CSCO, Subs. 4 (Louvain, 1952).
See also II.A, *Narratio*; II.B, "Greek List."

Garsoïan, "Armement"   N. Garsoïan, "L'art iranien comme témoin de l'armement arménien sous les Arsacides," *Atti del V simposio internazionale di arte armena* (Venice, in press).

Armenia   N. G. Garsoïan, *Between Byzantium and the Sasanians* (London, 1985).

"Artašat"   N. G. Garsoïan, "Artašat (Artaxata)," DMA, I (1982), pp. 588–584.

"Banak ark⁽uni"   N. G. Garsoïan, "Banak ark⁽uni əst Buzandaran Patmut⁽iwnk⁽-i," in *Acts of the IVth International Symposium on Armenian Medieval Art* (Erevan, 1985).

"Buzandaran Patmut⁽iwnk⁽"   N. G. Garsoïan, "K voprosu o pervoï glave Buzandaran Patmut⁽iwnk⁽-a," in *Acts of the International Symposium on Medieval Armenian Literature* (Erevan, 1986).

"Gund"   N. G. Garsoïan, "*Gund*-θέμα dans les sources Arméniennes," in *Actes du XVᵉ Congrès International d'Études Byzantines* (Athens, 1980), IV, p. 121.

"Hiérarchie"   N. G. Garsoïan, "Le rôle de l'hiérarchie chrétienne dans les rapports diplomatiques entre Byzance et les Sassanides," REArm n.s. X (1973), pp. 119–138; repr. in *idem, Armenia*, viii.

"Introduction"   N. G. Garsoïan, "Introduction" to *The Epic Histories Attributed to P⁽awstos Buzand*, CATRS (1984), pp. v–xvii.

"Locus"   N. G. Garsoïan, "The Locus of the Death of Kings: Iranian Armenia the Inverted Image," in *The Armenian Image in History and Literature*, ed. R. Hovannisian, ed. (UCLA, 1980), pp. 27–64; repr. in *idem, Armenia*, xi.

"Mediaeval Armenian City"   N. G. Garsoïan, "The Early Mediaeval Armenian City: An Alien Element?" *Bickerman Memorial Volume*, pp. 67–83.

"Nersēs le Grand"	N. G. Garsoïan, "Nersēs le Grand, Basile de Césarée et Eustathe de Sébaste," REArm n.s. XVII (1983), pp.145–169; repr. in *idem, Armenia,* vii.
Paulician Heresy	N. G. Garsoïan, *The Paulician Heresy* (Paris-the Hague, 1967).
"Politique"	N. G. Garsoïan, "Politique ou orthodoxie? L'Arménie au quatrième siècle," REArm n.s. IV (1967), pp. 297–320; repr. in *idem, Armenia,* iv.
"Prolegomena"	N. G. Garsoïan, "Prolegomena to a Study of the Iranian Elements in Arsacid Armenia," HA XC (1976), cols. 177–234; repr. in *idem, Armenia,* x.
"Protecteur des pauvres"	N. G. Garsoïan, "Sur le titre de Protecteur des pauvres," REArm n.s. XV (1981), pp. 21–32; repr. in *idem, Armenia,* vi.
"Quidam Narseus"	N. G. Garsoïan, *"Quidam Narseus*: A Note on the Mission of St. Nersēs the Great," in *Armeniaca* (Venice, 1969), pp. 148–164; repr. in *idem, Armenia,* v.
"Šahak of Manazkert"	N. G. Garsoïan, "The Enigmatic Figure of Bishop Šahak of Manazkert," HA CI (1987), pp. 883–895.
"Secular Jurisdiction"	N. G. Garsoïan, "Secular Jurisdiction over the Armenian Church (IV–VIIth centuries)," in *Ševčenko Festschrift,* pp. 220–250; repr. in *idem, Armenia,* ix.
"Separation"	N. G. Garsoïan, "Some Preliminary Precisions on the Separation of the Armenian and Imperial Churches. I: The Presence of 'Armenian' Bishops at the First Five Œcumenical Councils," *Hussey Festschrift* (pp. 249–285).
"Social Structure"	N. G. Garsoïan, "Armenia: Social Structure," DMA, I (1982), pp. 488–491.
"Substratum"	N. G. Garsoïan, "The Iranian Substratum of the ᶜAgatᶜangełos' Cycle," in Garsoïan *et al.,* eds., *East of Byzantium,* pp. 151–174; repr. in *idem, Armenia,* xi, pp. 151–189.
Garsoïan *et al.,* eds., *East of Byzantium*	N. G. Garsoïan, T. F. Matthews, and R. W. Thomson, eds., *East of Byzantium: Syria and Armenia in the Formative Period* (Washington, D.C., 1982).
Gatᶜrčean, "Pᶜawstos"	Y. Gatᶜrčean, "Pᶜawstos Biwzandacᶜi," HA III (1889), pp. 40–43.
Gatᶜrčean and Tašean, eds., *Srbazan patarag*	Y. Gatᶜrčean and Y. Tašean, eds., *Srbazan pataragamatoycᶜkᶜ Hayocᶜ* (Vienna, 1897). See also II.A, Basil, St., *Liturgy* (Arm.).
Gaudemet, *L'église*	J. Gaudemet, *L'église dans l'empire romain* (Paris, s.d. [1958]).
Gauthiot, "Mots parthes"	R. Gauthiot, "A propos de mots parthes empruntés par l'arménien," MSL 19 (1916), pp. 125–129.
Gelzer, "Die Anfänge"	H. Gelzer, "Die Anfänge der armenischen Kirche," BSGW XLVII (1895), pp. 109–174.
Gelzer *et al.,* eds., *Nomina*	H. Gelzer, H. Hilhenfeld, and O. Cuntz, eds., *Patrum Nicaenorum nomina* (Leipzig, 1898). See also II.B, *Nomina.*
Gershevitch, *Mithra*	I. Gershevitch, *The Avestan Hymn to Mithra* (Cambridge, 1959; repr. 1967).
"Sonne"	I. Gershevitch, "Die Sonne das Beste," *Mithraic Studies,* ed. J. R. Hinnels, I (Manchester, 1975), pp. 68–89.

Gevorgyan, *P^cavstos Byuzand* — V. Gevorgyan, *P^cavstos Byuzandi "Hayoc^c Patmut^cyan" bnagri harc^ci šurǰ* (Erevan, 1963).

Gharibian — See Łaribyan.

Ghilain, *Essai* — A. Ghilain, *Essai sur la langue parthe* (Louvain, 1939).

Ghirshman, *Chionites* — R. Ghirshman, *Les Chionites-Hephthalites, Mémoires de la délégation archéologique française en Afghanistan*, XIII (Cairo, 1948).

"Notes iraniennes, V" — R. Ghirshman, "Notes iraniennes, V: Scènes de banquet sur l'argenterie sassanide," *Artibus Asiae* 16 (1953), pp. 51–71.

"Notes iraniennes, VI" — R. Ghirshman, "Notes iraniennes VI: Une coupe sassanide a scènes de chasse," *Artibus Asiae* 18 (1955), pp. 5–19.

"Notes iraniennes, XIII" — R. Ghirshman, "Trois épées sassanides," *Artibus Asiae* 26 (1963), pp. 293–311.

Persian Art — R. Ghirshman, *Persian Art* (London, 1962).

Gignoux, "La Chasse" — P. Gignoux, "La chasse dans l'Iran sassanide," in *Orientalia Romana: Essays and Lectures*, ed. G. Gnoli, 5 (Rome, 1983), pp. 101–118.

Glossaire — *Glossaire des inscriptions pehlevies et Parthes*, CII, supp. ser. I (London, 1972).

"La liste" — P. Gignoux, "La liste des provinces de l'Ērān dans les inscriptions de Šābuhr et de Kirdīr," AAASH XIX (1971), pp. 83–93.

"Marzbān" — P. Gignoux, "L'organisation administrative sassanide: le cas du Marzbān," *Jerusalem Studies in Arabic and Islam* 4 (1984), pp. 1–29.

"Noms propres" — P. Gignoux, "Les noms propres en moyen-perse épigraphique," in *Pad nām i Yazadān* (Paris, 1979), pp. 35–100.

Notes d'épigraphie" — P. Gignoux, "Notes d'épigraphie et d'histoire sassanide," in Benveniste, *Mélanges*, pp. 213–223.

NPS — P. Gignoux, "Noms propres sassanides en moyen-perse épigraphique," in *Iranisches Namenbuch* II/2, eds. M. Mayhofer and R. Schmitt (Vienna, 1986).

"Pour une évaluation" — P. Gignoux, "Pour une évaluation de la contribution des sources arméniennes à l'histoire sassanide," in *Colloque de Budapest* (1984), typescript.

"Problèmes" — P. Gignoux, "Problèmes d'interprétation historique et philologique des titres et noms propres sassanides," AAASH XXIV/1–4 (1976), pp. 103–108.

"Sceaux" — P. Gignoux, "Sceaux chrétiens d'époque sassanide," IA XV (1980), pp. 299–314.

"Toponymes" — P. Gignoux, "Nouveaux toponymes sassanides," JA 262 (1974), pp. 299–304.

Goddard, *Art* — A. Godard, *L'art de l'Iran* (Paris, 1962).

Gough, "Cilician Churches" — M. Gough, "The Emperor Zeno and some Cilician Churches," *Anatolian Studies* 22 (1972), pp. 199–212.

Grabar, *Martyrium* — A. Grabar, *Martyrium: Recherches sur le culte des reliques et l'art chrétien ancien*, 3 vols. (Paris, 1943–1946).

Graffin, "Jacques de Nisibe" — R. Graffin, "Jacques de Nisibe," DS, VIII (1974), p. 50.

Grégoire, *Mélanges* — *Mélanges Henri Grégoire*, see AIPhO IX.

Greppin, "*Išχan*" J. Greppin, "A Note on Arm. *išχan* ʿruler'," *Annual of Armenian Linguistics* 3 (1982), pp. 57–59.

"Nominal Suffixes" J. Greppin, "The Middle Persian Nominal Suffixes in Classical Armenian," REArm n.s. X (1973–1974), pp. 1–9.

Gribomont, "Monachisme en Asie Mineure" J. Gribomont, "Le monachisme au IVᵉ siècle en Asie Mineure de Gangres au Messalianisme," *Studia Patristica* II (1957), pp. 400–415.

"Monachisme en Syrie" J. Gribomont, "Le monachisme au sein de l'Église en Syrie et en Cappadoce," *Studia Monastica* 7 (1965), pp. 7–24.

Grigoryan, *Gusanakan ergerə* Š. S. Grigoryan, *Hayoc' hin gusanakan ergerə* (Erevan, 1971).

Griniaschi, ed., "Littérature sassanide" M. Griniaschi, ed., "Quelques specimens de la littérature sassanide préservés dans les bibliothèques d'Istanbul," JA (1966), pp. 1–142.

Guilland, *Institutions* R. Guilland, *Recherches sur les institutions byzantines*, 2 vols. (Berlin–Amsterdam, 1967).

Guillaumont, "Le dépaysement" A. Guillaumont, "Le dépaysement comme forme d'ascèse dans le monachisme ancien," *Annuaire de l'École pratique des Haute Etudes, Section de sciences religieuses* LXXVI (1968–1969), pp. 31–58.

"Perspectives" A. Guillaumont, "Perspectives actuelles sur les origines du monachisme," *The Frontiers of Human Knowledge. Lectures Held at the Quincentenary Celebrations of Uppsala University, 1977*, ed. T. T. Segerstedt (Uppsala, 1978), pp. 111–123.

Güterbock, "Römisch-Armenien" K. Güterbock, "Römisch-Armenien und die römische Satrapien im 4. bis 6. Jahrhundert," *Schirmer Festschrift*, pp. 1–58.

Gutschmid, "Glaubwürdigkeit" A. von Gutschmidt, "Über die Glaubwürdigkeit der armenischen Geschichte des Moses von Khoren," BSGW XXVIII (1876).

Guyer See Herzfeld and Guyer, *Meriamlik*; also Spanner and Guyer, *Rusafa*.

Hacker, ed. *Byzantine Saint* S. Hacker, ed., *The Byzantine Saint, XIVth University of Birmingham Symposium, Studies Supplementary to Sobornost* V (London, 1981).

Hacʿuni, *Drōšnerə* V. Hacʿuni, *Hay drōšnerə*, 2d ed. (Venice, 1930).

Tarazin V. Hacʿuni, *Patmutʿiwn hin Hay tarazin* (Venice, 1924).

Hakobyan, A. H./ Akopian, A. A., "Favst" A. A. Akopian, "ʿIstoriia Armenii' Favsta Buzanda kak istochnik *Povesti o Vachagane*," KV V (1987); pp. 72–81.

"Gargaracʿinerə" A. H. Hakobyan, "Gargaracʿinerə əst antik ew haykakan skizbnałbyurneri," PBH (1982/4), pp. 116–130.

Hakobyan, S. E., "Caṙa" S. E. Hakobyan, "Caṙa-ałaχin-struknerə ew nrankʿ socʿialakan drutʿyunə miǰnadaryan Hayastanum," PBH (1962/1), pp. 124–138.

"Gyułakan hamaynkʿə" S. E. Hakobyan, "Gyułakan hamaynkʿə Hayastanum vał ew zargacʿac feōdalizmi žamanakašrǰannerum," PBH (1965/1), pp. 201–218.

"Hay gyułacʿiutʿyun" S. E. Hakobyan, "Hay gyułacʿiutʿyan hołin amracʿman ew čortacʿman harcʿi šurǰ," PBH (1963/1), pp. 173–194.

Patmut῾yun	S. E. Hakobyan, *Hay gyułac῾iut῾yan patmut῾yun*, I (Erevan, 1957).
"Soc῾ialakan haraberut῾yunner"	S. E. Hakobyan, "Soc῾ialakan haraberut῾yunneri artac῾alumə 'Kanonagirk῾ Hayoc῾'-um," PBH (1966/4), pp. 67–82.
"Strukt῾yun"	S. E. Hakobyan, "Strukt῾yun ew strkakan hasarakakan formac῾in hin Hayastanum," *Telekagir* (1948).
Hakobyan, T῾. X., *Ašχarhagrut῾yun*	T῾. X. Hakobyan, *Hayastani patmakan ašχarhagrut῾yun*, 4th ed. (Erevan, 1984).
Ašχarhagrut῾yun Syunik῾i	T῾. X. Hakobyan, *Patmakan ašχarhagrut῾yunə Syunik῾i t῾agaworut῾yan* (Erevan, 1966).
Syunik῾i t῾agaworut῾yunə	T῾. X. Hakobyan, *Syunik῾i t῾agaworut῾yunə* (Erevan, 1966).
"Syunik῾i teritoria"	T῾. X. Hakobyan, "Syunik῾i t῾agavorut῾yan teritoria," in Erewani Pethamalsaran, *Gitašχatut῾yunner* 43 (1955).
Halkin, "Théodore le conscrit"	F. Halkin, "Un opuscule inconnu du magistre Nicéphore Ouranos: La Vie de saint Théodore le Conscrit," AB 80 (1962), pp. 308–324. See also II.B, Theodore, St., *Vita*.
Hamabarbaṙ	See Astuacaturean; Łaribyan.
Hambarean, "Gargarac῾ik῾"	H. Hambarean, "Gargarac῾ik῾ t῾ē Gugarac῾ik῾?" HA XXIV (1910), cols. 241–242.
Hambröer, *Dämonenglaube*	J. Hambröer, *Armenischer Dämonenglaube in religionswissenschaftlicher Sicht* (Vienna, 1962); repr. from HA LXXV (1961).
HAnjB	See Abbreviations.
Hannaway, "Hunt"	W. Hannaway, "The Concept of the Hunt in Persian Literature," BMFB 69 (1971), pp. 21–34.
Hannestad, "Relations"	K. Hannestad, "Les relations de Byzance avec la Transcaucasie et l'Asie Centrale aux 5ᵉ et 6ᵉ siècles," *Byz.*, XXV–XXVII (1955–1957), pp. 421–456.
Hanson, *St. Patrick*	R. P. C. Hanson, *The Life and Writings of the Historical Saint Patrick* (New York, 1983).
Harmatta, "Cusanica"	J. Harmatta, "Cusanica," AOASH XI, pp. 191–220.
Harmatta-Pékáry, "Parsīk ostracon"	M. Harmatta-Pékáry, "The Decipherment of the Pārsīk Ostracon from Dura-Europos and the Problem of Sāsānian City Organization," in Accademia dei Lincei, *La Persia nel Medioevo*, pp. 467–475.
HArm B	See Abbreviations
Harnack, *Dogma*	A. Harnack, *History of Dogma*, IV (New York, 1961).
Haroutiounian, V. M.	See Harut῾yunyan, V. M.
Harper, *Hunter*	P. O. Harper, *The Royal Hunter* (New York, 1978).
"Sasanian Silver"	P. O. Harper, "Sasanian Silver," CHI III/2 (1983), pp. 1113–1129.
"Thrones"	P. O. Harper, "Thrones and Enthronement Scenes in Sasanian Art," *Iran* XVII (1979), pp. 49–64 and plates.
Harper and Meyers, *Silver*	P. O. Harper and P. Meyers, *Silver Vessels of the Sasanian Period*, I, *Royal Imagery* (New York, 1981).
Harut῾yunyan, B. H., "Gahnamak"	B. H. Harut῾yunyan, "'Gahnamaki' t῾vagrman harc῾i šurjə," PBH (1976/2), pp. 56–74.
"Mardpetakan"	B. H. Harut῾yunyan, "Mardpetakan ew Angełtan gorcakalut῾yunnerə Aršakuneac῾ Hayastanum," *Lraber* (1984/4), pp. 41–49.

Harut*ᶜ*yunyan/Haroutiou-nian, V. M., "K*ᶜ*ałak*ᶜ*a-šinakan kulturan" "Urbanisme"

V. M. Harut*ᶜ*yunyan, "Miǰnadaryan Hayastani k*ᶜ*ałak*ᶜ*ašinakan kulturan," PBH (1963/2), pp. 85–99.

V. M. Haroutiounian, "L'urbanisme en Arménie au moyen-âge," REArm n.s. V (1968), pp. 51–64.

Hasratyan/Hasratian, "Amaras"

M. Hasratian, "L'ensemble architectural d'Amaras," REArm n.s. XII (1977), pp. 243–259; trans. from *Lraber* (1975/5), pp. 35–52.

HBB

See Abbreviations

Heffele-Leclercq, *Conciles*

K. J. Hefele and H. Leclerq, *Histoire des conciles*, 11 vols. (Paris, 1907–1938; repr. Hildesheim, 1973).

Hendricks, "Vie"

O. Hendricks, "La vie quotidienne du moine syrien oriental," OS V (1960), pp. 293–330.

Henning, "Farewell"

W. B. Henning, "A Farewell to the Khagan of the Aq-Aqatärän," BSOAS XIV (1952), pp. 501–522; repr. in AI XV (1977), pp. 337–408.

"Fragments"

W. B. Henning, "Three Iranian Fragments," in C. B. Welles *et al.*, *The Excavations of Dura-Europos*, Final Report V, part 1, *The Parchments and Papyri* (New Haven, 1959), pp. 414–417.

Memorial

W. B. Henning Memorial Volume, eds. M. Boyce and I. Gershevitch (London, 1970).

"Notes"

W. B. Henning, "Notes on the Great Inscription of Šāpūr I," in *Jackson Memorial*, pp. 40–54; repr. in AI XV (1977), pp. 415–430.

"Parthian Inscription"

W. B. Henning, "A New Parthian Inscription," JRAS (1953), pp. 132–136; repr. in AI XV (1977), pp. 409–413.

"Silver Bowl"

H. W. Henning, "A Sasanian Silver Bowl from Georgia," BSOAS 24 (1961), pp. 353–356; repr. in AI XV (1977), pp. 555–558.

ŠKZ

W. B. Henning, "The Great Inscription of Šāpur," BSOAS IX (1937–1939), pp. 823–849; repr. in AI XIV (1977), pp. 601–628.

"Survival"

W. B. Henning, "The Survival of an Ancient Term," *Indo Iranica* (Wiesbaden, 1964), pp. 95–97.
See also Azarpay and Henning, "Hunting Scene."

Herzfeld, "Sakastan"

E. Herzfeld, "Sakastan," *Archäologische Mitteilung aus Iran* IV (1932), pp. 1–116.

Herzfeld, E., ed.

See II.C, *Paikuli*.

Herzfeld and Guyer, *Meriamlik*

E. Herzfeld and S. Guyer, *Monumenta Asiae Minoris Antiqua*, II, *Meriamlik und Korykos zwei christliche Ruinenstätten des Rauhen Kilikiens* (Manchester, 1930).

Hewsen, "Albania"

R. H. Hewsen, "Ethno-History and the Armenian Influence upon the Caucasian Albanians," in *Classical Armenian Culture*, ed. T. Samuelian (Philadelphia, 1982), pp. 27–40.

"Arc*ᶜ*aχ"

R. H. Hewsen, "The Kingdom of Arc*ᶜ*aχ," *Medieval Armenian Culture*, ed. M. Stone and T. Samuelian (Chico, Cal., 1983), pp. 42–68.

"Armenia"

R. H. Hewsen, "Armenia According to the Ašχarhac*ᶜ*oyc*ᶜ*," REArm n.s. II (1965), pp. 319–342.

"Artaxiad" R. W. Hewsen, "Introduction to Armenian Historical Geography: The Boundaries of Artaxiad Armenia," RE-Arm n.s. XIX (1985), pp. 55–84.

"Caspiane" R. H. Hewsen, "Caspiane: An Historical and Geographical Survey," HA LXXXVII (1973), cols. 87–106.

"Orontid" R. H. Hewsen, "Introduction to Armenian Historical Geography, III: The Boundaries of Orontid Armenia," REArm n.s. XVIII (1984), pp. 347–365.

"Primary History" R. H. Hewsen, "The Primary History of Armenia: An Examination of the Validity of an Immemorially Transmitted Historical Tradition," *History in Africa* II (1975), pp. 91–100.

"Ptolemy" R. H. Hewsen, "Ptolemy's Chapter on Armenia: An Investigation of His Toponyms," REArm n.s. XVI (1982), pp. 111–150.

"Successors" R. H. Hewsen, "The Successors of Tiridates the Great: A Contribution to the History of Armenia in the Fourth Century," REArm n.s. XIII (1978–1979), pp. 99–126.

"Tiridates" R. H. Hewsen, "In Search of Tiridates," JSAS 2 (1985–1986), pp. 11–49.

"Vitaxates" R. H. Hewsen, "Introduction to Armenian Historical Geography: The Vitaxates of Arsacid Armenia," RE-Arm n.s. XXI (1988).

Hild, *Kappadokien* F. Hild, *Das byzantinischen Strassensystem in Kappadokien* (Vienna, 1977).

Hoffman, *Auszüge* G. Hoffman, *Auszüge aus syrischen Akten persischer Märtyrer* (Leipzig, 1880).

Holzey, *Thekla-Akten* C. Holzey, *Die Thekla-Akten, ihre Verbreitung und Beurteilung in der Kirche* (Munich, 1905).

Honigmann, "Klöster" E. Honigmann, "Nordsyrische Klöster in Vorarabischerzeit," *Zeitschrift für Semitistik* I (1922), pp. 15–33.

"Liste" E. Honigmann, "La liste originale des Pères de Nicée," *Byz.* XIV (1939), pp. 17–76.

"Nordsyrien" E. Honigmann, "Historische Topographie von Nordsyrien im Altertums," *Zeitschrift des deutschen Palästina-Vereins* XLVI (1923), pp. 149–193; XLVII (1924), pp. 1–64.

"Original Lists" E. Honigmann, "The Original Lists of the Members of the Council of Nicaea, the Robber-Synod and the Council of Chalcedon," *Byz.* XVI (1944), pp. 20–80.

Ostgrenze E. Honigmann, *Die Ostgrenze des byzantinischen Reiches von 363 bis 1071* (Brussels, 1935).

Honigmann and Maricq, RGDS E. Honigmann and A. Maricq, *Recherches sur les Res Gestae divi Saporis*, Mémoires de l'Académie royale de Belgique, Classe des Lettres, XLVII/4 (Brussels, 1953). See also II.B, RGDS.

Hovhannisyan See also Johanisyan, Yovhannēsyan.
Hovhannisyan, A. See Johanisyan.
Hovhannisyan, A. Š., "Iranakan" A. Š. Hovhannisyan, "Iranakan pʿoχaɫutʿyunner hamarvoɫ mi kʿani baɫeri šurǰ," PBH (1981/3), pp. 253–259.

Hovhannisyan, M. *See* Yovhannēsean.

Hovhannisyan, S. H., "Psakadrutᶜyun"

S. H. Hovhannisyan, "Psakadrutᶜyan iravakan kargavorumə vał feodalakan Hayastanum," PBH (1972/1), pp. 193–205.

Hübschmann, "Namen"

H. Hübschmann, "Iranisch-armenische Namen auf *karta, kert, gird*," ZDMG 30 (1876), pp. 138–141. See also Abbreviations, AG; AON.

Hülser, "Athenai"

Hülser, "Athenai," PW, II (1896), col. 2022.

Humbach, "Ātur Gušnasp"

H. Humbach, "Ātur Gušnasp und Takht i Suleiman," in *Eilers Festschrift*, pp. 189–191.

Humbach and Skjærvø, *Paikuli*

H. Humbach and P. O. Skjærvø, *The Sassanian Inscription of Paikuli*, vol. 3/2, *Commentary* (Wiesbaden, 1983). See also II.C, *Paikuli*.

Hussey, *Festschrift*

ΚΑΘΗΓΗΤΡΙΑ. *Essays Presented to Joan Hussey on her Eightieth Birthday*, ed. J. Chrysostomides (Camberley, 1988).

Inčičean, *Hnaχōsutᶜiwn*

Ł. Inčičean, *Hnaχōsutᶜiwn ašχarhagrakan Hayastaneaycᶜ ašχarhi*, 3 vols. (Venice, 1835).

Storagrutᶜiwn

Ł. Inčičean, *Storagrutᶜiwn hin Hayastaneaycᶜ ašχarhi* (Venice, 1822).

Inglisian, "Literatur"

V. Inglisian, "Die armenische Literatur," in *Handbuch der Orientalistik*, I/vii, *Armenisch und Kaukasische Sprachen* (Leiden and Cologne, 1963), pp. 156–250.

International Conference on the History, Archaeology and Culture of Central Asia in the Kushan Period (Dushambe, 1968): An Annotated Bibliography (Moscow, 1968)

Irmscher, "Theodore"

J. Irmscher, "Theodore[3] von Euchaïta," RGG VI (1962), cols. 747–748.

Iskandaryan, "Aršak II"

S. Iskandaryan, "Erb ew orter ē grvel ᶜAršak II' ōperan?" *Lraber* (1986/4), pp. 38–41.

Iushkov, "Albania"

S. V. Iushkov, "K voprosu o granitsakh drevneǐ Albanii," IZ I (1937).

Jackson, *Memorial*

A. V. W. Jackson, *Prof. Jackson Memorial Volume* (Bombay, 1954).

Jahukyan, "Anjnanunnerə"

G. B. Jahukyan, "Bnik hayeren armatnerov kazmvac haykakan anjnanunnerə," PBH (1984/4), pp. 32–43.

"Stugabanutᶜyunner"

G. B. Jahukyan, "Stugabanutᶜyunner," PBH (1963/4), pp. 85–98.

Janin, "Euchaïtes"

R. Janin, "Euchaïtes," DHGE XV (1963), cols. 1311–1313.

Jargy, "Instituts monastiques"

S. Jargy, "Les premiers instituts monastiques et principaux représentants du monachisme syrien," *Proche Orient Chrétien* IV (1954), pp. 109–117.

"Pacte"

S. Jargy "Les 'Fils et Filles du Pacte' dans la littérature monastique syriaque," OCP (1951), pp. 304–320.

Jedin, *Church History*

H. Jedin and J. Dolan eds., *Handbook of Church History*, 4 vols. (New York, 1965–1980).

JIN

See Abbreviations

Johanisyan

See also Hovhannisyan, Yovhannēsean.

Johanisyan, *Israel Ory*

A. Johanisyan, *Israel Ory und die armenische Befreiungsidee* (Munich, s.d. 1913).

Jones, *Cities*

A. H. M. Jones, *The Cities of the Eastern Roman Provinces* (Oxford, 1937).

LRE — A. H. M. Jones, *The Later Roman Empire*, 3 vols. (Oxford, 1964); American ed., 2 vols. (Norman, Okla., 1964).

Jones *et al.*, *Prosopography* — A. H. M. Jones, and J. R. Martindale, and J. Morris, *The Prosopography of the Later Roman Empire*, 2 vols. to date (Cambridge, 1971, 1980).

Kafadarian — See Łafadaryan.

K⁽ᶜ⁾alant⁽ᶜ⁾ar, *Vałaršapat* — A. K⁽ᶜ⁾alant⁽ᶜ⁾ar, *Hin Vałaršapati pełumnerə* (Erevan, 1935).

Kalantarian — See K⁽ᶜ⁾alant⁽ᶜ⁾aryan.

K⁽ᶜ⁾alant⁽ᶜ⁾aryan/Kalantarian, "Dvin kałakə" — A. A. K⁽ᶜ⁾alant⁽ᶜ⁾aryan, "Dvin k⁽ᶜ⁾ałak⁽ᶜ⁾i šertagrut⁽ᶜ⁾yan harc⁽ᶜ⁾i šurĵ," *Lraber* (1969/5), pp. 57–67.

Dvini mšakuyt⁽ᶜ⁾ə — A. A. K⁽ᶜ⁾alant⁽ᶜ⁾aryan, *Dvini nyut⁽ᶜ⁾akan mšakuyt⁽ᶜ⁾ə 4–8dd.* (Erevan, 1970).

"Glinianye plitki" — A. A. Kalantarian, "Glinianye plitki s izobrazheniiami iz Akhtsa," PBH (1985/4), pp. 227–231.

"Knk⁽ᶜ⁾adrōšmner" — A. A. K⁽ᶜ⁾alant⁽ᶜ⁾aryan, "Sasanyan knk⁽ᶜ⁾adrōšmneri ew dranc⁽ᶜ⁾ kiřakan oroš kołmeri masin," PBH (1977/3), pp. 195–205.

"Novye materialy" — A. A. Kalantaryan, "Novye materialy o dvortsakh rannesrednevekovoĭ Armenii," in *The Second International Symposium on Armenian Art, Collection of Reports*, II (Erevan, 1978, [1981]), pp. 111–118.

"Sparazinut⁽ᶜ⁾yunə" — A. A. K⁽ᶜ⁾alant⁽ᶜ⁾aryan, "Paštpanakan sparazinut⁽ᶜ⁾yunə vał miĵnadaryan Hayastanum," *Lraber* (1965/10), pp. 68–74.

"Zenkerə" — A. A. K⁽ᶜ⁾alant⁽ᶜ⁾aryan, "Zenkerə V–VIII darerum əst Dvini hnagitakan pełumneri," PBH (1965/4), pp. 241–248.

Kalhōkec⁽ᶜ⁾i, ACH — P. Kalhōkec⁽ᶜ⁾i, *Asiakan čanaparhordut⁽ᶜ⁾iwn i Hayrenis* (Constantinople, 1881).

Kanayeanc⁽ᶜ⁾, "K⁽ᶜ⁾aĵanc⁽ᶜ⁾ tun" — S. Kanayanc⁽ᶜ⁾, "K⁽ᶜ⁾aĵanc⁽ᶜ⁾ tan ē žołovrdakan vepə," *Ararat* (1917), pp. 522–524.

Kapantsian — See Łapanc⁽ᶜ⁾yan.

Karlgren, *Festschrift* — B. Karlgren, *Studia Bernardo Karlgren dedicata* (Stockholm, 1959).

Kasser, "Acta Pauli" — R. Kasser, "Acta Pauli," *Revue d'histoire et de philosophie religieuse* 40 (1960), pp. 45–57.

Kent, R. G. — See II.C, OP.

Khachatrian, Z. D. — See Xač⁽ᶜ⁾atryan, Ĵ. D.

Khalatiants, *Arshakidy* — G. Khalatiants, *Armianskie Arshakidy v" Istorii Armenii Moĭseia Khorenskago* (Moscow, 1903).

Ēpos — G. Khalatiants, *Armianskiĭ Ēpos" v" Istorii Armenii Moĭseia Khorenskago* (Moscow, 1896).

Khatchatrian, *Architecture* — A. Khatchatrian, *L'Architecture arménienne du IVe au VIe siècle*, Bibliothèque des cahiers archéologiques 7 (Paris, 1971).

"Données" — A. Khatchatrian, "Données historiques sur la fondation d'Edjmiatsin à la lumière des fouilles récentes," HA LXXVI (1962), cols. 100–109.

"Monuments" — A. Khatchatrian, "Les monuments funéraires arméniens des IV–VIIe siècles," BF I (1966), pp. 179–192.

Khavanov, "Katafraktarii" — A. M. Khavanov, "Katafraktarii i ikh rol' v istorii voennogo iskusstva," VDI (1968/1), pp. 180–191.

643

Kherumian, "Féodalité"   R. Kherumian, "Esquisse d'une féodalité oubliée," *Vostan* I (1948–1949), pp. 7–56.

Kiessling, "Gogarene"   M. Kiessling, "Gogarene," PW, VII/2 (1912), cols. 1553–1555.

Knobloch, "*Erkin*"   J. Knobloch, "Zu armenische *erkin*, ᶜHimmel' und *erkir*, ᶜErde'," HA LXXV (1961), cols. 541–544.

Kogean, *Hayocᶜ ekełecᶜin*   S. Kogean, *Hayocᶜ ekełecᶜin* (Beirut, 1961).

Kamsarakannerə   S. Kogean, *Kamsarakannerə "tearkᶜ Širakay ew Aršaruneacᶜ" patmakan usumnasurutᶜiwn* (Vienna, 1926); repr. from HA XXXVIII–XL (1922–1924).

Köllwitz, *Ausgrabungen*   J. Köllwitz, *Neue deutsche Ausgrabungen* (Berlin, 1965).

Kostanian   See Kostanyan.

Kostanyan/Kostanian, "Naχarar"   S. S. Kostanyan, "'Naχarar' termini masin," PBH (1973/3), pp. 151–160.

"Termin ShAhAP"   S. S. Kostanian, "Termin ShAhAP v rannesrednevekovykh armianskikh istochnikakh," KV I (1979), pp. 120–131.

Kovalevskaia, *Alany*   V. B. Kovalevskaia, *Kavkaz i Alany* (Moscow, 1984).

Kretschmer-Honigmann, "Sirakene"   K. Kretschmer-Honigmann, "Sirakene²," PW IIIA/1 (1927), cols. 282–283.

Krkyašaryan, "Bdešχutᶜyunner"   S. M. Krkyašaryan, "Bdešχutᶜyunneri aṙaJacᶜumə Hayastanum," PBH (1966/4), pp. 257–262.

"Gaṙni"   S. M. Krkyašaryan, "Ews mi angam Gaṙnii arjanagrutᶜyan masin," PBH (1965/3), pp. 235–238.

"Išχanutᶜyunə"   S. M. Krkyašaryan, "Tᶜagavorakan išχanutᶜyunə Aršakunyacᶜ Hayastanum," PBH (1971/1), pp. 196–206.

Krüger, "Jakob von Nisibis"   P. Krüger, "Jakob von Nisibis in syrischer und armenischer Überlieferung," LeM 81 (1968), pp. 161–179.

Labourt, *Christianisme*   J. Labourt, *Le Christianisme dans l'empire perse sous la dynastie des sassanides, 224–632* (Paris, 1904).

Łafadaryan/Kafadarian, "Dvin"   K. Łafadaryan, *Dvin kᶜałakᶜə ew nra pełumnerə*, 2 vols. (Erevan, 1952, 1982).

"Fouilles"   K. Kafadarian, "Les fouilles de la ville de Dvin (Duin)," REArm n.s. II (1965), pp. 283–301.

"Mehyan"   K. Łafadaryan, "Dvin kᶜałakᶜi himnadrman žamanaki ew miJnaberdi hetᶜanosakan mehyani masin," PBH (1966/2), pp. 41–58.

"Petakan divan"   K. Łafadaryan, "Petakan divani mnacᶜordnerə Dvinum," PBH (1974/2), pp. 101–112.

Lafontaine, Ag   G. Lafontaine, "Introduction and Commentary" on Ag See also II.B, Ag.

Aphraat   G. Lafontaine, "Commentary on *Aphraat*" See also II.A, Aphraat, Arm.

Grégoire de Nazianze   G. Lafontaine, *La version arménienne des "Discours" de Grégoire de Nazianze: Tradition manuscrite et histoire du texte*, CSCO 446, subs. 67 (Louvain, 1983).

Lamberterie, "Armeniaca"   C. de Lamberterie, "Armeniaca, I–VIII: études lexicales," BSL 73 (1978), pp. 243–285.

Langlois, V., ed.   See Abbreviations, CHAMA.

Łapancᶜyan/Kapantsian, "*Pitiahs*"   G. Kapantsian, "O dvukh sotsial'no politicheskikh terminakh drevnego blizhnego vostoka: *evri*—ᶜvladyko, tsar' i *pitiahs (bitiahš)*,—'vladetil' ili pravitel' oblasti," VDI (1949), pp. 10–13.

Łaribyan, *Hamabarbaṙ* A. S. Łaribyan gen. ed., *Haykakan Hamabarbaṙ* 7, *Movsēs Xorenacʿi*, 3 vols. (Erevan, 1975–1976).

Lassus, *Monuments* J. Lassus, *Les monuments chrétiens de la Syrie septentrionale* (Paris, 1934).

LeBachelet, "Arianisme" X. LeBachelet, "Arianisme," DTC, I (1863), cols. 1779–1863.

Lebon, "Concile" J. Lebon, "Sur un concile de Césarée," LeM 51 (1938), pp. 89–132.

Leclerq, "Thècle" H. Leclerq, "Thècle," DACL XV/2 (1953), cols. 2225–2236.

Lehmann, "Some Questions" H. J. Lehmann, "Some Questions Concerning the Armenian Version of the Epistle of James," *Aarhus Armeniaca. Acta Jutlandica* 56 (Aarhus, 1982). pp, 57-82.

Lehmann-Haupt, *Armenien* K. Lehmann-Haupt, *Armenien einst und jetzt*, 3 vols. (Berlin, 1910–1931).

"Satrap" C. F. Lehmann-Haupt, "Satrap," PW, IIA/1, col. 82–188, esp. 176–180.

"Tigranocerta" C. F. Lehmann-Haupt, "Tigranocerta," PW, 30/1 (1936), cols. 982–1007.

Lelekov, "K semantike" L. A. Lelekov, "K semantike i tipologii khramovykh sooruzheniĭ armianskogo iazychestva," PBH (1983/1), pp. 58–64.

Leloir, "Ephrem" Dom L. Leloir, "La pensée monastique d'Ephrem et Martyrius," in *Symposium Syriacum (1972)*, OCA 197 (Rome, 1974), pp. 105–131.

"Essai" L. Leloir, "Essai sur la silhouette spirituelle du moine d'après la collection arménienne des apothegmes," RE-Arm n.s. V (1968), pp. 199–230.

"Le moine" L. Leloir, "Le moine selon la tradition arménienne," *Armeniaca* (1969), pp. 16–32.

"Orientations" L. Leloir, "Les orientations essentielles de la spiritualité des Pères du désert d'après les '*Paterica* arméniens'," *Revue de Théologie et de Philosophie* I (1974), pp. 30–47.

Paterica armeniaca L. Leloir, ed. and trans., "Introduction" to the *Paterica armeniaca* I (Louvain, 1974), pp. v-xii. See also II.A, *Varkʿ harancʿ/Apothegmata*.

"Solitude" L. Leloir, "Solitude et sollicitude: Le moine loin et près du monde selon les *Paterica* arméniens," *Irénikon* XLVII (1974), pp. 307–324.

Lenormant, *Divination* F. Lenormant, *La divination et la science des présages chez les chaldéens* (Paris, 1875).

Leo (Babaχanean, A.) Leo, *Hayocʿ patmutʿiwn*, I (Tiflis, 1917); repr. in *Leo erkeri žołovacu*, I (Erevan, 1966).

Le Quien, *Oriens* M. Le Quien, *Oriens Christianus*, 3 vols. (Paris, 1740; repr. Graz, 1958).

Leroy, J. *Monks* J. Leroy, *Monks and Monasteries in the Near East* (London, 1963).

Leroy, M. "Composés *apa-*" M. Leroy, "Les composés arméniens à premier terme *apa-*," *Mélanges Benveniste*, pp. 367–373.

"Composés en *-pet*" M. Leroy, "Les composés arméniens en *-pet*," AIPhO 15 (1958–1960), pp. 109–128.

645

"Emprunts"

M. Leroy, "Emprunts iraniens dans la composition nominale en arménien classique," REArm n.s. XVII (1983), pp. 51–72.

"Les mots"

M. Leroy, "Les mots arméniens en -*arēn*," ICMC (1964), pp. 131–133.

"Redoublement"

M. Leroy, "Le redoublement comme procédé de formation nominal en arménien classique," in Leroy and Mawet, eds., *L'Arménien*, pp. 62–75.

"Suffixes"

M. Leroy, "Suffixes d'origine iranienne dans la toponymie arménienne," SOnoM 4 (1961), pp. 517–521.

Leroy and Mawet, eds., *L'Arménien*

M. Leroy and Fr. Mawet, eds., *La place de l'arménien dans les langues indo-européennes* (Louvain, 1986).

Lipsius, *Apokryphen Apostolgeschichte*

R. A. Lipsius, *Die apokryphen Apostelgeschichte und Apostellegenden*, 2 vols. (Braunschweig, 1897).

Lipsius and Bonnet, eds.

See II.B, *Acta apocrypha*.

Livshits, "Cusano-Indica"

V. A. Livshits, "Cusano-Indica," in Pigulevskaia *Sbornik*, pp. 161–171.
See also D'iakonov and Livshits, "*Nisa*."

Löffler, "Sergius"

K. Löffler, "Sergius and Bacchus," CE XIII (1912), p. 728.

Lozinski, "Parthian Dynasty"

P. Lozinsi, "The Parthian Dynasty," IA XV (1984), pp. 119–139.

Lucius, *Heiligenkult*

E. Lucius, *Die Anfänge des Heiligenkult in der christlichen Kirche* (Tübingen, 1904).

Lukonin, "Ametist"

V. G. Lukonin, "Reznoï ametist s izobrazheniem tsaritsy tsarits Denak," Orbeli, *Sbornik*, pp. 379–385.

"Institutions"

V. G. Lukonin, "Political, Social and Administrative Institutions, Taxes and Trade," CHI III/2 (1983), pp. 681–746.

Iran

V. G. Lukonin, *Iran v ēpokhu pervykh Sasanidov* (Leningrad, 1961).

Kul'tura

V. G. Lukonin, *Kul'tura sasanidskogo Irana* (Moscow, 1969).

"Zavocvaniia"

V. G. Lukonin, "Zavoevaniia sasanidov na vostoke i problema kushanskoï absolutnoï khronologii," VDI (1972/3), pp. 20–44.
See also Borisov and Lukonin, *Gemmy*

Lynch, *Armenia*

H. F. B. Lynch, *Armenia: Travels and Studies*, 2 vols. (London, 1901; repr. Beirut, 1965).

MacDermott, *Conversion*

B. MacDermott, "The Conversion of Armenia in 294 A.D.," REArm n.s. VII (1970), pp. 281–360.

MacKenzie, D. "Master of Ceremonies"

D. MacKenzie "A Zoroastrian Master of Ceremonies," Henning, *Memorial*, pp. 264–271.
See also Abbreviations, CPD.

MacKenzie, M., *Resafa*

M. MacKenzie, *Eine befestigte spätantike Anlage vor den Stadtmauer von Resafa* (Mainz, 1984).

Macler, *Les dew*

F. Macler, *Les dew arméniens* (Paris, 1929).

Macomber, "Authority"

W. F. Macomber, "The Authority of the Catholicos-Patriarch of Seleucia-Ctesiphon," OCA CLXXXI (1968), pp. 179–200.

Maenschen-Helfen, *Huns*

O. Maenschen-Helfen, *The World of the Huns* (Berkeley, 1973).

Maffei, *Architectura*   F. de Maffei, "Introduction" to *Architectura medievale armena* (Rome, 1968).

Maksoudian, *Yovhannēs Drasχanakertcʿi*   K. H. Maksoudian, trans. "Introduction and Commentary" on Yovhannēs Drasχanakertcʿi.
See also II.A, *Yovhannēs Drasχanakertcʿi.*

Malandra, "Glossary"   W. W. Malandra, "A Glossary of Terms for Weapons and Armor in OIr," IIJ XV/4 (1973), pp. 264–289.

Malχaseancʿ   See Malχasyancʿ.

Malχasyancʿ/Malχaseancʿ, "Introduction"   S. Malχasyancʿ, "Introduction" to *Pʿawstos Buzand Patmutʿyun Hayocʿ* (Erevan, 1947; posth. ed. 1968); a virtual reprint of *Usumnasirutʿiwn.*

"Neršapuh Ṙmbosean"   S. Malχasyancʿ, "Neršapuh Ṙmbosean ew 'Buzandaran patmutʿiwnkʿ' baṙeri meknutʿiwnə," *Tełekagir* (1947/4), pp. 91–93.

"Nkatołutʿiwn"   S. Malχaseancʿ, "Mi nkatołutʿiwn Pʿawstosi patmutʿean masin," *Zeitschrift für armenische Philologie*, I/1 (1901), pp. 64–66.

Usumnasirutʿiwn   S. Malχaseancʿ, *Usumnasirutʿiwn Pawstos Biwzandi patmutʿean* (Vienna, 1896); repr. from HA X (1896); virtually reprinted in *idem*, "Introduction."

"Xndirner"   S. Malχasyancʿ, "Žamanakagrakan χndirner Hayocʿ hin matenagrutʿyan mej," *Tełekagir* (1944/6–7), pp. 7–24.
See also, Abbreviations HBB.

Manandian, A.   See Manandyan, H.

Manandyan, H./ Manandian, A., "Ditołutʿyunner"   H. Manandyan, "Ditołutʿyunner hin Hayastani šinakanneri drutʿyan masin marzpanutʿyan šrǰanum," *HSXH Petakan Hamalsarani gitakan Tełekagir* (1925), pp. 3–45; repr. in *idem*, *Erker*, IV (1981), pp. 11–62.

Erker   *Hakob Manandyan Erker*, 6 vols. (Erevan, 1977–1985).

Feodalizm   H. Manandyan, *Feodalizm hin Hayastanum* (Erevan, 1934); repr. in *idem*, *Erker*, IV (1981), pp. 187–436.

"Harkerə"   H. Manandyan, "Hayastani arkʿuni harkerə marzpanutʿyan šrǰanum," *Gitutʿyan ew Arvesti Instituti Tełekagir* (1926/1), pp. 3–44; repr. in *idem*, *Erker*, IV (1981), pp. 63–115.

Hetazotutʿyunner   H. Manandyan, *Patmakan-ašχarhagrakan manr hetazotutʿyunner* (Erevan, 1945); repr. in *idem*, *Erker*, V (1945), 288–323.

Kʿnnakan tesutʿyun   H. Manandyan, *Kʿnnakan tesutʿyun hay žołovrdi patmutʿan*, II/1 (Erevan, 1945); repr. in *idem*, *Erker*, II (1978).

"Mahkertun"   H. Manandyan, "*Mahkertun, Nihorakan, Dasn ew 'Amur ašχarhn Maracʿ*,'" in *idem*, *Hetazotutʿyunner*, pp. 34–45; repr. in *Erker*, V (1984), pp. 313–323.

"*Nachal'naia istoriia*"   A. Manandian, "'Nachal'naia istoriia Armenii' Mar Abasa (k voprosu ob istochnikakh Sebeosa, Moïseia Khorenskogo i Prokopiia Tsezariĭskogo," PSb II (1956), pp. 69–86 (posthumous publication).

"Nor-Širakan"   H. Manandyan, "Nor-Širakan erkirə ew 'Noširakani bdeašχ'ə," in *idem*, *Hetazotutʿyunner*, pp. 19–34; repr. in *idem*, *Erker*, V (1984), pp. 301–313.

647

"Poids"	H. Manandian, "Les poids et les mesures dans les plus anciennes sources arméniennes," REArm n.s. III (1966), pp. 315–345.
"Problema"	A. Manandian, "Problema obshchestvennogo stroïa doarshakidskoĭ Armenii," IZ, XV (1945), pp. 3–28.
Problemner	H. Manandyan, *Hin Hayastani ew Andrkovkasi mi k῾ani problemneri masin* (Erevan, 1944); repr. in *idem, Erker,* V (1984), pp. 256–287.
Tigrane II	H. Manandian, *Tigrane II & Rome,* trans. H. Thorossian (Lisbon, 1963).
"Tntesakan kyank῾ə"	H. Manandyan, "Nyuter hin Hayastani tntesakan kyank῾i patmut῾yan," *Tełekagir* I (1927/2), pp. 29–42; II (1928/4), pp. 43–82; repr. in *idem, Erker,* IV (1981), pp. 116–170.
Trade and Cities	H. Manandian, *The Trade and Cities of Armenia in Relation to Ancient World Trade,* trans. N. G. Garsoïan (Lisbon, 1965).
"Voĭsko"	A. Manandian, "Zametke o feode i feodal'nom voĭske Parfii i Arshakidskoĭ Armenii (Tiflis, 1932); repr. in *idem, Erker,* IV (1981), pp. 171–186.
"Zarasp leṙə"	H. Manandyan, "Zarasp leṙə ibrew Hayastani haravarevelyan sahman," in *idem, Hetazotut῾yunner,* pp. 9–15; repr. in *idem, Erker,* V (1984), pp. 293–297.
Manuč῾aryan, *K῾nnut῾yun*	A. A. Manuč῾aryan, *K῾nnut῾yun Hayastani IV–XI dareri šinararakan vkayagreri* (Erevan, 1977).
Maricq, *Classica et Orientalia*	A. Maricq, *Classica et Orientalia* (Paris, 1965).
"Hatra"	A. Maricq, "Hatra de Sanatrouq," in *idem, Classica et Orientalia,* pp. 1–16.
RGDS	A. Maricq, ed. and trans., "Notes" to RGDS. See also, Honigman, E. and Maricq, A., RGDS; II.B, RGDS.
Mariès, L. ed. and trans.	See II.A, Eznik.
Markwart/Marquart, "Beiträge"	J. Marquart, "Beiträge zur Geschichte und Sage von Ērān," ZDMG XLIX (1895), pp. 628–672.
"Catalogue"	J. Markwart, "A Catalogue of the Provincial Capitals of Ērānšahr," ed. J. Messina, *Analecta orientalia,* 3 (Rome, 1931).
Entstehung	J. Markwart, *Die Entstehung der armenischen Bistümer,* ed. J. Messina (Rome, s.d. [1932]); repr. from OCP XXVIII/2 (1932), pp. 141–236.
Ērānšahr	J. Marquart, *Ērānšahr nach der Geographie des Ps. Moses Xorenac῾i* (Berlin, 1901).
"Genealogie"	J. Markwart, "Die Genealogie der Bagratiden und das Zeitalter des Mar Abas und Ps. Mosēs Xorenac῾i," *Caucasica,* VI/2 (1930), pp. 10–77.
"Markgrafen"	J. Marquart, "Die Markgrafen," in *idem, Ērānšahr,* Excursus 1, pp. 165–179.
"Mīpherqēt"	J. Marquart, "Mīpherqēt und Tigranokerta," HA XXX (1916), cols. 68–135.
"Nauroz"	J. Markwart, "Das Nauroz seine Geschichte und seine Bedeutung," in *Modi Memorial,* pp. 709–765.

"Parskahayk^c" J. Markwart, "La province de Parskahayk^c", REArm n.s. III (1966), pp. 252–314; trans. from PBH (1961).

Streifzüge J. Marquart, *Osteuropäische und ostasiatische Streifzüge* (Leipzig, 1901; repr. Hildesheim, 1961).

Südarmenien J. Markwart, *Südarmenien und die Tigrisquellen* (Vienna, 1930); repr. from HA XXVII–XXIX, XXXIV (1913–1915, 1920).

"Untersuchungen" J. Marquart, "Untersuchungen zur Geschichte von Eran, 5: Zur Kritik des Faustus von Byzanz," *Philologus* LV (1896), Supplementband X, Heft 1, pp. 217–229; Armenian trans. in HA III (1898), cols. 316–320.

Marquart See Markwart.

Marr, "Ētimologiia" N. Ia. Marr, "Ētimologiia armianskago *sepuh* ʿsepuh' i gruzinskago *sep^ce*," ZVO XI (1899).

Kreshchenie N. Ia. Marr, *Kreshchenie armian", gruzin", abkhazov" sv. Grigoriem"* (St. Petersburg, 1905).

"O nachal'noĭ istorii" N. Ia. Marr, "O nachal'noĭ istorii Armenii Anonima. K" voprosu ob" istochnikakh" istorii Moĭseia Khorenskago," VV I (1894), pp. 264–306.

Martindale, J. See Jones and Martindale, *Prosopography*.

M[atat^cean], E., *P^cawstos* E. M., *P^cawstos Biwzand* (Vienna, 1890).

Mathews, ed. See Garsoïan *et al.*, eds., *East of Byzantium*.

Matikean, *Ananunə* A. Matikean, *Ananunə kam kełc Sebēos* (Vienna, 1913).

"Aralēznerə" A. Matikean, "Aralēznerə hay grakanut^cean mēj," HA XXXVII (1923), cols. 481–495.

Mayerhofer, IPNB M. Mayerhofer, *Iranisches Personal Namenbuch*, I, 3 fasc. (Vienna, 1977–1979).

Meillet, "Ekełeçi" A. Meillet, "Le mot ekełeçi," REArm IX (1929), pp. 131–136.

"Elisée" A. Meillet, "Sur un passage d'Elisée," REArm VI/1 (1926), pp. 1–3.

Etudes A. Meillet, *Etudes de linguistique et de philologie arméniennes*, 2 vols. (Lisbon, 1962, Louvain, 1977).

"Etymologies" A. Meillet, "Etymologies arméniennes," MSL 11 (1900), pp. 390–401.

"Influence" A. Meillet, "De l'influence parthe sur la langue arménienne," REArm I/1 (1920), pp. 9–14.

"Mots iraniens" A. Meillet, "Sur les mots iraniens empruntés par l'arménien," MSL 17 (1911), pp. 242–250.

"Quelques mots parthes" A. Meillet, "Sur quelques mots parthes en arménien," REArm II (1922), pp. 1–6.

"Termes religieux" A. Meillet, "Sur les termes religieux iraniens en arménien," REArm I (1921), pp. 233–236.

Melik^c-Ōhanǰanyan, "Firdusi" K. Melik^c-Ōhanǰanyan, "Firdusi yew Irani vipakan motivner 'Šah-name'-um u hay matenagrut^cyan mēj," in *Firdusi žołovacu* (Erevan, 1934), pp. 1–116.

"Tiran-Trdati vepə" K. Melik^c-Ōhanǰanyan, "Tiran-Trdati vepə əst P^cawstos Buzand," *Tełekagir* (1947/6), pp. 59–74; (1947/7), pp. 59–77.

"Vep" K. Melik^c-Ōhanǰanyan, "Hay-iranakan žołovrdakan vep," in *Firdusi žołovacu* (Erevan, 1934), pp. 157–230.

Melik^c-Ōhanǰanyan, ed. See II.A, KG.

Melik^c-P^cašayan, *Anahit*

K. V. Melik^c-P^cašayan, *Anahit dic^cuhu paštamunkə* (Erevan, 1963).

Melikset-Bek/Melikset-Bekov, "K istorii"

L. Melikset-Bek, "K istorii gunnov v vostochnom Zakavkaz'e," *Doklady AN Azerb. SSR* (1957/6).

"Sledy"

L. Melikset-Bekov, "Sledy 'Istorii Armenii' Fausta Vizantiĭskogo v drevnegruzinskoĭ literature," *Soobshchenia A.N. Gruz. SSR* III (1942), pp. 359–362.

Melikset-Bekov

See Melikset-Bek.

Melk^conyan, "Abgar"

H. H. Melk^conyan, "Armianskiĭ perevod siriĭskoĭ legende ob Abgare," KSINA 86 (1965), pp. 45–50.

"Armianskiĭ perevod"

H. H. Melk^conyan, "Armianskiĭ perevod 'Zhitiia Mar-Avgena' (iz istochnikov Favsta Buzanda)," PSb 17(80) (1967), pp. 121–124.

Haraberut^cyunner

H. H. Melk^conyan, *Hay-asorakan haraberut^cyunneri patmut^cyunic^c* (Erevan, 1970).

"Mšakut^cayin haraberut^cyunnerə"

H. H. Melk^conyan, "Hay-asorakan mšakut^cayin haraberut^cyunnerə IV–V darerum," PBH (1963/2), pp. 127–138.

Menasce, *Fondations pieuses*

J. de Menasce, *Feux et fondations pieuses dans le droit sassanide* (Paris, 1964).

Mémorial

Mémorial Jean de Menasce, eds. Ph. Gignoux and A. Tafazzoli (Louvain, 1974).

"Protecteur des pauvres"

J. de Menasce, "Le protecteur des pauvres dans l'Iran sassanide," in *Mélanges Henri Massé* (Tehran, 1963), pp. 282–287.

Menewišean, "Abgar"

H. G. Menewišean, "Abgaru zroyc^c Movsēs Xorenac^cwoy patmut^cean mēǰ," HA X (1896), col. 281, 347.

Mercier, C., ed.

See II.A, Eznik Kołbac^ci.

Meshcherskaia, "Apotrpeichiskie teksty"

E. N. Meshcherskaia, "Legenda ob Abgare i apotropeichiskie teksty na grecheskom iazyke," PSb 26(89) (1978), pp. 102–106.

"Legenda"

E. N. Meshcherskaia, "Legenda ob Abgare v literaturakh vizantiĭskogo kul^cturnogo kruga," KV III (1982), pp. 97–107.

Meyers

See Harper and Meyers, *Silver*.

Michel, "Idolatrie"

A. Michel, "Idolatrie," DTC, VII (1930), cols. 602–669.

Miller, *Tabula Peutingeriana*

K. Miller, *Itineraria romana. Römische Reisewege an der Hand der Tabula Peutingeriana* (Stuttgart, 1916).

Miner, *Festschrift*

Gatherings in Honor of Dorothy E. Miner (Baltimore, 1974).

Minorsky, "Ādharbaydjān"

V. V. Minorsky, "Ādharbaydjān," EI² I, pp. 188–191.

"Dvin"

V. V. Minorsky, "Le nom de Dvin," REArm X (1930), pp. 117–120; first published in JA (1930).

"L'ouvrage"

V. V. Minorsky, "L'ouvrage de J. Markwart sur l'Arménie méridionale," REArm n.s. II (1965), pp. 143–164.

"Roman Campaigns"

V. V. Minorsky, "Roman and Byzantine Campaigns in Atropatene," BSOAS XI/2 (1944), pp. 243–265.

"Tabriz"

V. V. Minorsky, "Tabriz," EI¹, IV, pp. 631–642.

Mlaker, "Die Herkunft"

K. Mlaker, "Die Herkunft der Mamikonier und der Titel Cenbakur," WZKM XXXIX (1932), pp. 133–145.

Mnac^cakanyan, A. Š., *Ałvank^c*

A. Š. Mnac^cakanyan, *Ałvanic^c ašχarhi grakanut^cean harc^ceri šurǰə* (Erevan, 1966).

Mnacᶜakanyan/Mnatsakanian, S. S., "Usipal'nitsy"
S. S. Mnatsakanian/Mnatsakanian "Problemy genezisa rodovykh usipal'nits Armenii," *Haykakan Arvest*, II (1984), pp. 19–35.

Mnacᶜakanyan/Mnatsakanian, S. X., *Arkhitektura*
S. X. Mnatsakanian, *Arkhitektura armianskikh pritvorov* (Erevan, 1952).

"Dvin"
S. X. Mnacᶜakanyan, "Dvin palati kaṙucᶜman žamanaki masin," PBH (1974/2), pp. 212–232.

"Ob odnom"
S. X. Mnatsakanian, "Ob odnom neizvestnom tipe sooruzheniĭ drevnearmianskoĭ arkhitektury," *Teḷekagir* (1952/7), pp. 95–105.

Mnatsakanian
See Mnacᶜakanyan.

Modi, "Alexander"
J. J. Modi, "Alexander the Great and the Destruction of the Ancient Literature of the Parsees at his Hands," *Oriental Conference Papers* (Bombay, 1932), pp. 58–116.

Memorial
Dr. Modi Memorial Volume (Bombay, 1930).

Mommsen, "Tigranokerte"
T. Mommsen, "Lage von Tigranokerte," *Hermes* IX (1875); pp. 129ff.

Morris
See Jones *et al.*, *Prosopography.*

Muradian
See Muradyan.

Muradyan, K. M., *Barseḷ*
K. M. Muradyan, *Barseḷ Kesaracᶜin ew nra "Vecᶜōrean" hay matenagrutᶜyan meǰ* (Erevan, 1976).

"*Ēpitafia*"
K. M. Muradyan, "Drevnearmianskiĭ perevod 'Ēpitafii' Grigoriia Nazianzina," KV II (1980), pp. 155–217. See also II.A, Greg. Naz., *Panegyric.*

Grigor
K. M. Muradyan, *Grigor Nazianzin hay matenagrutᶜyan meǰ* (Erevan, 1983).

Muradyan, P. M., "Kul't "Grigoriia"
P. M. Muradian, "Kavkazskiĭ kul'turny mir i kul't Grigoriia Prosvetitelia," KV 3 (1982), pp. 5–20.

"Vinitel'nye formy"
P. M. Muradian, "Vinitel'nye formy v iminitel'nom po danym toponimiki Armenii," *Lraber* (1971/4), pp. 21–38.

Muraviev, "Ptolemeeva Karta"
S. N. Muraviev, "Ptolemeeva karta Kavkazskoĭ Albanii i uroven' Kaspii," VDI (1983/1), pp. 117–147.

Murray, "Ascetical Vows"
R. Murray, "The Exhortation to Candidates for Ascetical Vows at Baptism in the Ancient Syrian Church," NTS 21 (1974–1975), pp. 58–79.

Symbols
R. Murray, *Symbols of Church and Kingdom: A Study in Early Syriac Tradition* (Cambridge, 1975).

Muyldermans, "Costume"
J. Muyldermans, "Le costume liturgique arménien. Etude historique," LeM XXXIX (1926), pp. 253–324.

"Fragment"
J. Muyldermans, "Un fragment arménien de l'oraison funèbre de Basile de Césarée par Grégoire de Nazianze," HA XLI (1927), cols. 13–16.

Mžik, *Erdmessung*
H. Mžik, *Erdmessung Grad, Meile, Stadion nach den altarmenischen Quellen* (Vienna, 1933); repr. from HA XLVII (1933), cols. 432–458.

Nalbandian
See Nalbandyan.

Nalbandyan/Nalbandian, G. M., "Armianskie imena"
G. M. Nalbandian, "Armianskie lichnye imena iranskogo proiskhozhdeniia," Avtoreferat dissertatsii (Tbilisi, 1971), not available to me.

"Baṙeri verakangnumə"
G. M. Nalbandian, "Parskereni mtᶜagnvac korac baṙeri verakangnumə hayereni ōgnutᶜyamb," *Teḷekagir* (1962/1), pp. 79–86.

Nalbandyan, V. S., "Gnel"	V. S. Nalbandyan, "Gnel-Tiritʿyan vipakan avandutʿyan patmakan himkʿi harcʿi šurjə," PBH (1964/4), pp. 83–100.
"K voprosu"	V. S. Nalbandian, "K voprosu ob istoricheskoĭ osnove odnogo iz predaniĭ v 'Istorii Armenii' Pavstosa Buzanda," *Uroki armianskoĭ drevnosti* (Erevan, 1985), pp. 102–126.
"Novoye prochtenie"	V. S. Nalbandian, "Novoe khudozhestvennoe prochtenie stranits drevneĭ armianskoĭ istorii (Po povodu istoricheskogo romana 'Arshak Vtoroĭ' Percha Zeĭtuntsiana)," *Uroki armianskoĭ drevnosti* (Erevan, 1985), pp. 127–153.
Naumann, "Takht-i Suleiman"	R. Neumann, "Takht-i Suleiman und Zendan-i Suleiman," *Archäologische Anzeiger* (1965), pp. 643–650. See also Osten and Naumann, *Takht-i Suleiman.*
Nedungatt, "Covenanters"	G. Nedungatt, "The Covenanters of the Early Syriac-Speaking Church," OCP XXXIX (1973), pp. 191–215.
Neuman, "Die Fahrt"	K. J. Neuman, "Die Fahrt des Patrokles auf dem Kaspischen Meere und der alte Lauf des Oxus," *Hermes* XIX (1884), pp. 165–300.
Neusner, "Adiabene"	J. Neusner, "The Conversion of Adiabene to Christianity," *Numen* XIII (1966), pp. 144–150.
"Armenia"	J. Neusner, "Jews in Pagan Armenia," JAOS, LXXXIV/3 (1964), pp. 230–240.
Babylonia	J. Neusner, *A History of the Jews in Babylonia,* I, *The Parthian Period* (Leiden, 1969).
Nogaret, "Quelques problèmes"	M. Nogaret, "Quelques problèmes archéologiques et topographiques dans la région de Maiyāfāriḵīn," REArm n.s. XVIII (1984), pp. 411–433.
Nöldeke, *Iranische Nationalepos*	T. Nöldeke, *Das iranische Nationalepos,* 2d ed. (Berlin-Leipzig, 1920).
"Ortsnamen"	T. Nöldeke, "Über îrânische Ortsnamen auf *kert* und andere Endung," ZDMG XXXIII (1879), pp. 143–156.
Tabari	T. Nöldeke, *Geschichte der Perser und Araber zur Zeit der Sasaniden* (Leiden, 1879; repr. Graz, 1973); See also II.C, Tabari.
Norayr Biwzandacʿi, *Koriwn*	Norayr Biwzandacʿi, *Koriwn vardapet ew norin tʿargmanutʿiwnkʿ* (Tiflis, 1900), not available to me.
"Pʿawstos"	Norayr Biwzandacʿi, "Pʿawstos Biwzand ew iwr Patmutʿiwn Hayocʿ," *Kʿnnasēr* I (1887); not available to me.
Novoselʾtsev, "Politicheskaia granitsa"	A. P. Novoselʾtsev, "K voprosu o politicheskoĭ granitse Armenii i Kavkazskoĭ Albanii v antichnyĭ period," KV I (1979), pp. 10–18.
"Sasanidskie pamiatniki"	A. P. Novoselʾtsev, "K voprosu ob otrazhenii istorii Armenii v sasanidskikh pamiatnikakh," KV III (1982), pp. 21–28.
Nyberg, *Manual*	H. S. Nyberg, *A Manual of Pahlavi,* vol. II, *Glossary* (Wiesbaden, 1974).
"Mishkīn"	H. S. Nyberg, "The Pahlavi Inscription at Mishkīn," BSOAS XXXIII (1970), pp. 144–153.
Religionen	H. S. Nyberg, *Die Religionen des alten Iran* (Osnabrück, 1938).

"Westgrenze" H. S. Nyberg, "Die sassanidische Westgrenze und ihre-Verteidigung," in *Karlgren,* Festschrift, pp. 316–321.

Oates, *Studies* D. Oates, *Studies in the Ancient History of Northern Iraq* (London, 1968).

Ōdabašyan, "Navasard" A. A. Ōdabašyan, "Navasardyan tonaχmbut^cyunneri verapruknerǝ," PBH (1974/3), pp. 113–125.

Onofrio, *Dvin* M. d'Onofrio, *Le chiese di Dvin* (Rome, 1973).

"Palais" M. d'Onofrio, "Certains Palais résidentiels de l'Arménie du Ve au VIIe siècle après J.-C.," in *Reports of the Second International Symposium on Armenian Art*, II (Erevan, 1978 [1981]), pp. 90–110.

Orbeli, "Bytovye rel'efy" J. A. Orbeli, "Bytovye rel'efy na khachenskikh" krestnykh" kamniakh" XII i XIII vekov"," ZVO XXII.3–4 (1915); repr. in *idem, Izbrannye Trudy*, pp. 196–204.

"Gorod bliznitzov" J. A. Orbeli, "'Gorod bliznitzov' Διοσκουρίας i plemia 'Voznits' ^cΗνίοχοι" ZMNP n.s. XXXIII (1911), pp. 195–215.

Sbornik *Issledovaniia po istorii kul'tury narodov vostoka. Sbornik v chest' Akademika I. A. Orbeli* (Moscow-Leningrad, 1960).

Trudy J. A. Orbeli, *Izbrannye trudy* (Erevan, 1963).

Orbeli and Trever, *Metall* *Sasanidskiĭ metall/Orféverie sassanide* (Moscow, Leningrad, 1935).

Oriente cristiano See Accademia dei Lincei, *Oriente cristiano*.

Ōrmanean, *Azgapatum* M. Ōrmanean, *Azgapatum*, I (Constantinople, 1912).

"Ditołut^ciwnner" M. Ōrmanean, "Trdatē Artašēs žamanakagrakan ditołut^ciwnner, HA XXIII (1909), cols. 197–201, 241–246.

Oskean, "Arc^caχ" H. Oskean, "Arc^caχi vank^cerǝ," HA LXV–LXVII (1951–1953).

Barjr Hayk^c H. Oskean, *Barjr Hayk*^c (Vienna, 1951); repr. from HA LXII–LXIV (1948–1950).

"Bznuneac^c cov" H. Oskean, "Bznuneac^c covi kłzineru anapatnern u vank^cerǝ," HA LIII (1939) cols. 25–77; LIV (1940), cols. 156–196.

"Gnunik^c" H. Oskean, "Gnuneac^c ew Ařberani vankerǝ," HA LIV (1940), cols. 192–213.

Gnunik^c *ew Řštunik*^c H. Oskean, *Gnuneac*^c *ew Řštuneac*^c *naχararut*^c*iwnnerǝ* (Vienna, 1952); repr. from HA LXV–LXVI (1951–1952).

"Gugark^c" H. Oskean, "Gugark^ci vank^cerǝ," HA LXXI (1957), cols. 13–25, 185–191, 292–307.

"Řštunik^c" H. Oskean, "Řštuneac^c gawaři vank^cerǝ," HA LIII (1939), cols. 159–195; LIV (1940) cols. 21–38.

"Tigranakert" H. Oskean, "Tiarpēk^ciri kam Tigranakerti nahangin vank^cerǝ," HA LXXV (1961), cols. 39–71.

Usumnasirut^c*iwnner* H. Oskean, *Usumnasirut*^c*iwnner hay naχararut*^c*iwnneru masin* (Vienna, 1955); repr. from HA LXVIII (1954).

"Van-Tosp" H. Oskean, "Van-Tosp vank^cerǝ," HA LIII (1939), cols. 38–75, 164–192.

"Xarberd" H. Oskean, "Xarberd gawaři vankerǝ," HA LXXIV (1960), cols. 177–204.

Osten and Naumann, *Takht-i Suleiman*	H. van der Osten and R. Naumann, *Takht-i Suleiman. Verläufiger Bericht über die Ausgrabungen* (Berlin, 1961).
Outtier, *"Vitae Patrum"*	B. Outtier, "Un patéricon arménien (*Vitae Patrum*), II, pp. 505–635," LeM 84 (1971), pp. 299–351.
Pagliaro, "Bitaχs"	A. Pagliaro, "Mediopersiano bitaχs armeno bdeašχ: ὁ ὀφθαλμός τοῦ βασιλέως," RSO 12 (1929–1930), pp. 160–168.
"Riflessi"	A. Pagliaro, "Riflessi di etimologie iraniche nella tradizione storiografica greca," *Rendiconti dell'Academia Nazionale dei Lincei.* Classe di Scienze morale, storiche e filologiche, Series VIII/9 (1954), pp. 33–146.
Païkova, "K voprosu"	A. V. Païkova, "K voprosu ob ēvolutsii agiograficheskogo zhanra v siriĭskoĭ literature," KV III (1982), pp. 89–96.
Palmer, *Festschrift*	*Studies in Greek, Italic and Indo-European Offered to Leonard L. Palmer* (Innsbruck, 1976).
Patkanian/Patkanov, *Bibliographicheskiĭ ocherk*	K. N. Patkanian, *Bibliographicheskiĭ ocherk armianskoĭ istoricheskoĭ literatury* (St. Petersburg, 1879).
"Essai"	K. N. Patkanian, "Essai d'une histoire de la dynastie des Sassanides d'après les renseignements fournis par les historiens arméniens," trans. J. Prud'homme, JA 6ᵉ sér. 7 (1866), pp. 101–236.
Vanskie nadpisi	K. N. Patkanov, *Vanskie nadpisi i znachenie ikh" dlia istorii Peredneĭ Azii* (St. Petersburg, 1881).
Patrubany, "Faustos Buzandaçi"	L. von Patrubany, "Die Geschichte Armeniens des Faustos Buzandaçi," *Sprachwissenschaftliche Abhandlungen*, II (1900), pp. 1–5, 17–23.
Peeters, "Adiabène"	P. Peeters, "Le passionnaire d'Adiabène," AB XLIII (1925), pp. 261–326.
"Calendrier"	P. Peeters, "S. Grégoire l'Illuminateur dans le calendrier lapidaire de Naples," AB LX (1942), pp. 91–130.
"Les débuts"	P. Peeters, "Les débuts du christianisme en Géorgie d'après les sources hagiographiques," AB L (1932), pp. 5–58.
"Intervention"	P. Peeters, "L'intervention politique de Constance II dans la grande Arménie en 338," BARB XVII (1931), pp. 10–47; repr. in *idem, Recherches*, I, pp. 222–250.
"Jacques de Nisibe"	P. Peeters, "La légende de S. Jacques de Nisibe," AB XXXVIII (1920), pp. 285–373.
Mélanges	See AB LXII (1949).
"Persécution"	P. Peeters, "Le début de la persécution de Sapor d'après Fauste de Byzance," REArm I (1920–1921), pp. 15–33; repr. in *idem, Recherches*, I, pp. 59–77.
Recherches	P. Peeters, *Recherches d'histoire et de philologie orientales*, 2 vols. (Brussels, 1951).
"Socrate"	P. Peeters, "A propos de la version arménienne de l'historien Socrate," AIPhO II = *Mélanges Bidez* (1934), pp. 649–675; repr. in *idem, Recherches*, I, pp. 310–336.
"S. Serge"	P. Peeters, "La passion arménienne de S. Serge le stratélate," *Hušarjan* (Vienna, 1911), pp. 186–192; repr. in *idem, Recherches*, I, pp. 25–36.

"SS Serge et Théodore" P. Peeters, "Un miracle de SS Serge et Théodore et la Vie de S. Basile dans Fauste de Byzance," AB XXXIX (1921), pp. 65–88.

Tréfond P. Peeters, *Le Tréfond oriental de l'hagiographie byzantine* (Brussels, 1950).

Peña *et al.*, *Les reclus* I. Peña, P. Castellana, and R. Fernandez, *Les reclus syriens* (Milan, 1980).

Perikhanian, "Agnaticheskie gruppy" A. G. Perikhanian, "Agnaticheskie gruppy v drevnem Irane," VDI (1968/3), pp. 28–52.

"Buzand" A. G. Perikhanian, "Sur arm. *buzand*," in Berbérian, *Memorial*, pp. 653–658.

"Inscription" A. G. Perikhanian, "L'inscription arméenne du roi Artašēs," REArm n.s. III (1966), pp. 17–29.

Iran A. G. Perikhanian, *Obshchestvo i pravo Irana v parfianskiĭ i sasanidskiĭ periody* (Erevan, 1983).

"Iranian Society" A. G. Perikhanian, "Iranian Society and Law," CHI III (1983), pp. 627–680.

Khramovye ob'edineniia A. G. Perikhanian, *Khramovye ob'edineniia Maloĭ Azii i Armenii IV v. do n.ē.–III v. n.ē.* (Moscow, 1959).

"Le lexique" A. G. Perikhanian, "Notes sur le lexique iranien en arménien," REArm n.s. V (1968), pp. 9–30.

MHD A. G. Perikhanian, ed. and trans., "Introduction, notes and Appendix" to MHD.
See also II.C, MHD.

"Ostaniki" A. G. Perikhanian, "Drevnearmianskie vostaniki," VDI (1956/2), pp. 44–58.

"Papirusy" A. G. Perikhanian, "Pekhleviĭskie papirusy sobraniia GMII im. A. S. Pushkina," VDI (1961/3), pp. 78–93.

"Rabovladenie" A. G. Perikhanian, "K voprosu o rabovladenii i zemlevladenii v Irane parfianskogo vremeni," VDI (1952/4), pp. 13–27.

"Zametki" A. G. Perikhanian, "Ētimologicheskie zametki, I," PBH (1982/1), pp. 55–62.

Perkins, *Dura-Europos* A. Perkins, *The Art of Dura-Europos* (Oxford, 1973).

La Persia See Accademia dei Lincei, *La Persia*.

La Persia nel Medioevo See Accademia dei Lincei, *La Persia nel Medioevo*.

Petrosyan, "Pᶜaytakaran" S. G. Petrosyan, "Pᶜaytakaranə ew Parspatunikᶜə m. tᶜ. I dari errord kᶜaŕordum," PBH (1975/2), pp. 167–182.

Pietschmann, "Aigyptos" R. Pietschmann, "Aigyptos," PW, I (1894), cols. 978–1005.

Pigagnol, *Empire* A. Pigagnol, *L'empire chrétien* (Paris, 1947; repr. 1972).
Mélanges *Mélanges Pigagnol* (Paris, 1966).

Pigulevskaia, "Gorod" N. V. Pigulevskaia, "Gorod blizhnego vostoka v ranniem srednevekov'e," VDI (1969/1), pp. 65–69.

Sbornik *Ēllinisticheskiĭ Blizhniĭ Vostok, Vizantiia i Iran. Istoriia i filologiia. Sbornik v chest' semidesitiletiia chlena-korrespondenta Akademii Nauk SSSR N. V. Pigulevskoĭ* (Moscow, 1967).

Villes N. V. Pigulevskaia, *Les Villes de l'état iranien aux époques parthes et sassanides* (Paris–The Hague, 1963); trans. of *Goroda irana v rannem srednevekov'e* (Moscow–Leningrad, 1956).

Poidebard and Mouterde, "St. Serge"	A. Poidebard and V. Mouterde, "À propos de saint Serge: Aviation et épigraphie," AB 67 (1949) = *Mélanges Paul Peeters*, I, pp. 109–116.
Połarean/Bogharian, N./Co-vakan, *Hay grołner*	Norayr ark^cep. Połarean, *Hay grołner E [V]-ŽĒ [XVII]* dar. (Jerusalem, 1971).
"Koriwn"	N. Covakan, "Koriwn vardapeti erkerə IV: P^cawstos," *Sion* (1983), cols. 152–155.
Mayr c^cuc^cak	Norayr ark^cep. Połarean, *Mayr c^cuc^cak jeṙagrac^c srboc^c Yakobeanc^c*, 9 vols. to date (Jerusalem, 1966-).
Pōłosean, *Tōnə*	E. Pōłosean, *Nor tarvay tōnə hin ew nor Hayoc^c k^cōv* (Vienna, 1952).
Radermacher, "Hippolytus und Thekla"	L. Radermacher, "'Hippolytus und Thekla' Studien zur Geschichte von Legende and Kultus," Kaiserl. Akad. d. Wiss. in Wien, philos.-hist. Kl., *Sitzungsberichte* (Vienna, 1916).
Raffi, *Samuēl*	Raffi, *Samuēl*, 1st ed. (Tiflis, 1885).
Ramsay, *Festschrift*	*Anatolian Studies Presented to Sir William Ramsay*, eds. W. H. Butler and W. M. Calder (Manchester, 1923).
Renoux, A./C., "Anaphore"	A. Renoux, "L'anaphore arménienne de saint Grégoire l'Illuminateur," in *Eucharisties d'Orient et d'Occident*, II, (*Lex Orandi* 47), (Paris, 1970), pp. 83–108.
"A propos"	C. Renoux, "A propos de G. Winkler, 'The Armenian Night-Office, II'," REArm n.s. XVIII (1984), pp. 593–598.
"Fêtes"	C. Renoux, "'Les fêtes et les saints de l'église arménienne' de N. Adontz," REArm n.s. XIV (1980), pp. 287–305; XV (1981), pp. 103–114.
Restle, *Architektur*	M. Restle, *Studien zur frühbyzantinischen Architektur Kappadokiens*, 2 vols., (Vienna, 1979).
Rice, *Jerome*	E. F. Rice, Jr., *Saint Jerome in the Renaissance* (Baltimore–London, s.d. [1985]).
Riess, "Astrologie"	E. Riess, "Astrologie," PW, II/2 (1896), cols. 1802–1828.
Rostovtzeff, *Iranians and Greeks*	M. Rostovtzeff, *Iranians and Greeks in South Russia* (1922, repr. New York, 1969).
Ruge, "Kaisareia"	W. Ruge, "Kaisareia," PW, III (1897), col. 1289.
"Kappadokia"	W. Ruge, "Kappadokia," PW, X/2 (1919), cols. 1910–1917.
"Nikaia"	W. Ruge, "Nikaia," PW, XVII/1 (1936), cols. 226–243.
"Satala"	W. Ruge, "Satala," PW, 2d ser., III (1927), col. 59.
Russell, "Armeno-Iranica"	J. R. Russell, "Armeno-Iranica," in Boyce *Festschrift*, pp. 447–458.
"Hazarabād"	J. R. Russell, "Hazārabad," DMA, VI (1985), pp. 116–117.
"Name"	J. R. Russell, "The Name of Zoroaster in Armenia," JSAS 2 (1985-1986), pp. 3–10.
"Review"	J. R. Russell, "Review" of Davoud Monchi-Zadeh, *Die Geschichte Zarērs*, JAOS 106/4 (1986), pp. 807–808.
Zor. Arm.	J. R. Russell, *Zoroastrianism in Armenia* (Cambridge, Mass., 1987).
"Zoroastrian Problems"	J. R. Russell, "Zoroastrian Problems in Armenia Mihr and Vahagn," *Classical Armenian Culture*, ed., T. Samuelian (Philadelphia, 1982), pp. 1–7.

Sachau, "Verhältnissen" E. Sachau, "Von den rechtlichen Verhältnissen der Christen im Sassanidenreich," MSOS X (1907), pp. 69–75.

Sahakyan, "Syunikᶜ" T. M. Sahakyan, "Syuneacᶜ naχararutᶜyan derə Aršakunineri tᶜagavorutᶜyan žamanakašrǰanum," PBH (1975/2), pp. 159–166.

Sahinian See Sahinyan.

Sahinyan/Sahinian, A. Sahinyan, "Ējmiajni mayr tačari skzbnakan
Ējmiajin" teskᶜə," PBH (1966/3), pp. 71–93.

"Nouveaux Matériaux" A. Sahinian, "Nouveaux Matériaux concernant l'architecture arménienne du haut moyen-âge," REArm n.s. IV (1967), pp. 193–202.

Šahnazaryan, A., Bagratuni A. Šahnazaryan, Bagratunyacᶜ naχararakan tohmi cagumə (Erevan, 1948).

Šahnazaryan, N.A. See Shahnazarian.

Saint-Martin, Mémoires J. Saint-Martin, Mémoires historiques et géographiques sur l'Arménie, 2 vols. (Paris, 1818–1819).

Sanspeur, "Arménie" C. Sanspeur, "L'Arménie au temps de Peroz," REArm n.s. XI (1975–1976), pp. 83–172.

"Nouvelle liste" C. Sanspeur, "Une nouvelle liste de Catholicos dans le ms. arménien 121 de Paris," HA LXXXVII (1973), cols. 185–202.

Sardaryan, "Hin Vałaršapat" S. Sardaryan, "Hin Vałaršapati tełagrutᶜyunə əst hnagitakan ew matenagrakan tvyalneri," Lraber (1975/7), pp. 52–69.

Sargisean See also Sargsyan.

Sargisean, B., Agatᶜangełos B. Sargisean, Agatᶜangełos ew iwr bazmadarean gałtᶜnikᶜə (Venice, 1890).
See also II.A, Varkᶜ harancᶜ/Apothegmata.

Sargsyan/Sarkisian, G. X./ G. X. Sargsyan, "Dastakertnerə ew agaraknerə V
Kh., "Dastakertnerə" dari haykakan ałbyurnerum," PBH (1962/3), pp. 77–94.

Hēllenistakan Hayastanə G. X. Sargsyan, Hēllenistakan darašrǰani Hayastanə ew Movsēs Xorenacᶜi (Erevan, 1966).

"Iz istorii" G. Sarkisian, "Iz istorii gorodskoĭ obshchiny v Armenii (IV v. n.ē)," VDI (1955/3), pp. 48–62.

"O dvukh G. Sarkisian, "O dvukh znacheniiakh termina dastakert
znacheniiakh" v rannekh armianskikh istochnikakh," in Pigulevskaia, Sbornik, pp. 97–101; trans. as "Les deux significations du terme dastakert dans les anciennes sources arméniennes," REArm n.s. V (1968), pp. 43–50.

"Obozhestvlenie" G. Kh. Sarkisian, "Obozhestvlenie i kulʹt tsareĭ i tsarskikh predkov v drevneĭ Armenii," VDI (1966/2), pp. 3–26.

Tigranakert G. Kh. Sarkisian, Tigranakert (Moscow, 1960).

Sarkisian See Sargsyan.

Sauvaget, "Sergiopolis" J. Sauvaget, "Les Ghassanides et Sergiopolis," Byz. XIV (1939), pp. 126–130.

Scarcia, "Eracle iranico" G. Scarcia, "Ricognizione a Shimbār note sull' Eracle iranico," OA XVIII (1979), pp. 255–275.

"Herakles" G. Scarcia, "Herakles-Verethragna and the Miᶜrāj of Rustam," AOASH XXXVII/1–3 (1983), pp. 85–109.

Schiller, Iconography G. Schiller, The Iconography of Christian Art, 2 vols. (Greenwich, Conn., 1972).

Schippmann, *Feur-heiligtümer*	K. Schippmann, *Die iranischen Feuerheiligtümer* (Berlin, 1971).
Grundzüge	K. Schippmann, *Grundzüge der parthischen Geschichte* (Darmstadt, 1980).
Schirmer *Festschrift*	*Festgabe der juristischen Fakultät zu Königsberg für ihren Senior Johann Theodor Schirmer* (Königsberg, 1900).
Schiwietz, *Mönchtum*	S. Schiwietz, *Das morgenländische Mönchtum*, III, *Das Mönchtum in Syrien, Mesopotamien und das Aszetentum in Persien* (Mödling, 1938).
Schmitt, "Artaxerxes"	R. Schmitt, "Artaxerxes, Ardašīr und Verwandte," InL 5 (1979 [1980]), pp. 61–72.
IN	R. Schmitt, "Iranische Namenschichten und Namentypen bei altarmenischen Historikern," BzN n.f. 19/3 (1984), pp. 317–331.
"Iranisches Lehngut"	R. Schmitt, "Iranisches Lehngut im Armenischen," RE-Arm n.s. XVIII (1983), pp. 73–112.
"Ostgrenze"	R. Schmitt, "Die Ostgrenze von Armenien über Mesopotamien, Syrien bis Arabien," in *Die Sprachen im römischen Reich der Kaiserzeit*, ed. G. von Neuman and J. Untermann (Cologne, 1980), pp. 187–214.
"Satrap"	R. Schmitt, "Der Titel 'Satrap'," in Palmer, *Festschrift*, pp. 373–390.
"Sūrēn"	R. Schmitt, "Sūrēn aber Kārin. Zu den Namen zweier Parthergeschlechter," *München Studien zur Sprachwissenschaft* 42 (1983), pp. 197–203.
Scöld, "L'origine"	H. Scöld, "L'origine des Mamiconiens," REArm V/1 (1925), pp. 131–136.
Seeck, "Traianus"	O. Seeck, "Traianus," PW, 30/2 (1937), col. 2089.
Untergang	O. Seeck, *Geschichte der Untergang der Classischen Welt*, 2 vols. (Berlin, 1895, 1901). See also II.B, *Not. Dig.*
Segal, *Edessa*	J. B. Segal, *Edessa "The Blessed City"* (Oxford, 1970).
"Mesopotamian Communities"	J. B. Segal, "Mesopotamian Communities from Julian to the Rise of Islam," PBA 41 (1955), pp. 109–139.
Sellwood, "Adiabene"	D. Sellwood, "Adiabene," EIr I.5, pp. 456–458.
Ševčenko, *Festschrift*	*Okeanos: A Tribute to Ihor Ševčenko*, eds. C. Mango and O. Pritsak, *Harvard Ukrainian Studies* 7 (1984).
Seyrig, Antiquités	H. Seyrig, *Antiquités syriennes* II (Paris, 1938) repr. from *Syria* (1936–1938).
"Armes"	H. Seyrig, "Armes et costumes iraniens de Palmyre" in *idem, Antiquités*, pp. 45[3]–73[31].
"Jardins"	H. Seyrig, "Retour aux jardins de Kasr el-Hisr" in *idem Antiquités*, pp. 1[24]–8[31].
Shahbazi, "Symbol"	S. Shahbazi, "An Achæmenid Symbol II: Farnah '(God-given) Fortune' Symbolized," AMI n.f. 13 (1980), pp. 119–143.
Shahnazarian, A.	See Šahnazaryan.
Shahnazarian, N. A., "Otnosheniia"	N. A. Shahnazarian, "Persidsko-Rimskie otnosheniia v IV v. v 'Istorii Armenii' Favsta Buzanda," Εἰρήνη (1978), pp. 494–495.
Shaki, "Terms"	M. Shaki, "A Few Unrecognized Middle Persian Terms and Phrases," *Orientalia Lovaniensia Analecta* XVI- (Leiden, 1984), pp. 96–100.

Shanidze, "Novootkrytyĭ alfavit"	A. Shanidze, "Novootkrytyĭ alfavit kavkazskikh Albantsev i ego znachenie dlia nauki," *Enis istoriisa da mater kulturis instituti N. Marisa saχ.* IV/1 (Tbilisi, 1938).
Shepherd, "Banquet and Hunt"	D. G. Shepherd, "Banquet and Hunt in Medieval Islamic Iconography," in Miner, *Festschrift*, pp. 79–92.
"Sasanian Art"	D. G. Shepherd, "Sasanian Art," CHI III/2 (1983), pp. 1055–1112.
Shirinian, "Sokrat"	M. S. Shirinian, "Kratkaia redaktsiia drevnearmianskogo perevoda 'tserkovnoĭ istorii' Sokrata Skholastika," VV 43 (1982), pp. 231–241.
"Tekstologicheskoe zanachenie"	M. S. Shirinian, "Tekstologicheskoe znachenie drevnearmianskogo perevoda 'Tserkovnoĭ istorii' Sokrata Skholastika," KV IV (1984), pp. 172–186.
Sinclair, *Eastern Turkey*	T. A. Sinclair, *Eastern Turkey, an Architectural and Archaeological Guide*, 3 vols. (London, 1987-).
Skjærvø, *Farnah-*	P. O. Skjærvø, "Farnah-: mot mède ou vieux-perse?" BSL LXXVII/1 (1983), pp. 241–259. See also Humbach and Skjærvø, *Paikuli.*
Socin, "Tūr ʿAbdīn"	A. Socin, "Zur Geographie des Ṭūr ʿAbdīn," ZDMG XXXV (1881), pp. 237–269.
Solodukho, "Sviazi"	Iu. A. Solodukho, "K voprosu ob Armiano Irakskikh torgovykh sviaziakh v IV v.," in Orbeli, *Sbornik*, pp. 128–132.
Sophocles	See Abbreviations, GLRB.
Spanner and Guyer, *Rusafa*	H. Spanner and S. Guyer, *Rusafa. Die Wallfahrstadt des Heiligen Sergios* (Berlin, 1926).
Sperber, "Adventures"	D. Sperber, "The Adventures of Rav Kahana," in *Irano-Judaica*, ed. S. Shaked (Jerusalem, 1982), pp. 83–100.
Sprengling, *Third-Century Iran*	M. Sprengling, ed. and trans., *Third-Century Iran: Sapor and Kartir* (Chicago, 1953). See also II.C, KKZ and ŠKZ.
Stein, *Bas Empire*	E. Stein, *Histoire du Bas Empire*, trans. J. R. Palanque, 2 vols. (Paris-Brussels, 1949, 1959).
"Fauste de Buzanta"	E. Stein, "Fauste de Buzanta a-t-il écrit en grec?" in *Bas-Empire*, II, Excursus U, pp. 835–836.
Stengel, "Alexandreia"	Stengel, "Alexandreia," PW, I/1 (1893), cols. 1375–1398.
Streck, "Arzanene"	See Baumgartner and Streck.
Struve, "Review"	V. V. Struve, "Review" of K. Trever, *Albania*, VDI (1960/3), pp. 174–183.
Sukiasian, *Armenia*	A. G. Sukiasian, *Obshchestvenno-politicheskiĭ stroĭ i pravo Armenii v ēpokhu rannego feodalizma* (Erevan, 1963).
Sulimirski, "Archers"	T. Sulimirski, "Les archers à cheval, cavalerie legère des anciens," *Revue internationale d'histoire militaire* 12 (1952), pp. 447–461.
Svazyan, "Čenerə"	H. S. Svazyan, "Čenerə ew ʿCenacʿ ašχarhəʾ əst haykakan ałbyurneri," PBH (1976/4), pp. 203–212.
Szemerényi, *Festschrift*	*Studies in Diachronic, Synchronic and Typological Linguistics: Festschrift for Oswald Szemerényi* (Amsterdam, 1979).
"Iranica V"	O. Szemerényi, "Iranica, V," AI 2d ser. 2 (1975), #59–70.

Taqizadeh, "Festivals" S. H. Taqizadeh, "The Iranian Festivals Adopted by the Christians and Condemned by the Jews," BSOAS X (1939–1942), pp. 632–653.

Tašean, Y./Dashian, J., Y. Tašean, *Agatᶜangełos ař Georgay Asori episkoposin*
Agatᶜangełos *ew usumnasirutᶜiwn Agatᶜangełeacᶜ grocᶜ* (Vienna, 1891).

Hay bnakčᶜutᶜiwnə Y. Tašean, *Hay bnakčᶜutᶜiwnə Sew Covēn minčᶜew Karin: patmakan tełagrakan usumnasirutᶜiwn* (Vienna, 1973); repr. from HA XXXVII (1923).

"Sahmanə" Y. Tašean, "Hin Hayastani arewmtean sahmanə. Pᶜokᶜr Haykᶜ ew Kołopenē (Sebastia)," HA LI–LIX (1937–1945).

"Taykᶜ" Y. Tašean, "Taykᶜ, Dracᶜikᶜ ew Xotorǰur: patmakan tełagrakan usumnasirutᶜiwn," HA, LXXXIV–LXXXVII (1970–1973).

Vardapetutᶜiwn Y. Tašean, *Vardapetutᶜiwn aṙakelocᶜ anvawerakan kanunocᶜ matean* (Vienna, 1898).

"Xałtikᶜ" Y. Tašean, "Xałtikᶜ, Sew Get u Hamšēn: patmakan tełagrakan usumnasirutᶜiwn," HA, LXXXVIII–LXXXIX (1974–1975).

Tchoukassizian See Čᶜukaszyan.

Tedesco, "Bānbišn" P. Tedesco, "Persian bānbišn," BSL 26 (1926), pp. 64–66.

Ter Ghewondyan, A. Ter Ghewondyan, *The Arab Emirates in Bagratid*
Arab Emirates *Armenia*, trans. N. Garsoïan (Lisbon, 1976).

Ter Martirosov, "Terrakoty" F. S. Ter Martirosov, "Terrakoty iz Artašata," *Lraber* (1973/3), pp. 82–91.

Ter Mikelian, *Armenische* A. Ter Mikelian, *Die armenische Kirche in ihren Beziehungen zur byzantinischen (vom IV. bis zum XIII. Jahrhundert)* (Leipzig, 1892).
Kirche

Ter Minassiantz See Ter Minasyan.

Ter Minasyan/Ter Minas- E. Ter Minasyan, "Abraham Xostovanołi 'Vkaykᶜ
siantz, "Abraham Arewelicᶜ'-ə ew nra asorakan skzbnatipə," *Banber*
Xostovanoł" *Hayastani Gitakan Instituti.Žołovacu* I–II (1921–1922), pp. 114–126; repr. in *idem, Hetazotutᶜyunner*, pp. 65–87.

Armenische Kirche E. Ter Minassiantz, *Die Armenische Kirche in ihren Beziehungen zu den syrischen Kirchen bis zum Ende des 13. Jahrhunderts*, TU XI/4 (Leipzig, 1904).

Hetazotutᶜyunner E. Ter Minasyan, *Patma-banasirakan hetazotutᶜyunner* (Erevan, 1971).

"Zgon" E. Ter Minasyan, "'Zgon' kočᶜvac grkᶜi hełinaki harcᶜə,"PBH (1964/1), pp. 257–264; repr. in *idem, Hetazotutᶜyunner*, pp. 411–424.

Tēr Mkrtčᶜean See Ter Mkrtčᶜyan.

Ter Mkrtčᶜyan/Tēr Mkrtcᶜ- G. Ter Mkrtčᶜyan, *Hayagitakan usumnasirutᶜyunner*
ean, *Hayagitakan usum-* (Erevan, 1979).
nasirutᶜyumner
"Pᶜawstos" G. Tēr Mkrtčᶜean, "Pᶜawstosi jeṙagrerə," ZAP II (1904), pp. 267–286; repr. in *idem, Hayagitakan usumnasirutᶜyunnerə*, I, pp. 352–374.

Ter Mkrčᶜyan, ed. See II.A, Abraham Xostovanoł.

Ter Petrossian See Ter Petrosyan.

Ter Petrosyan/Ter Petros-
sian, *Abraham
Xostovanoł*
    L. H. Ter Petrosyan, *Abrahamu Xostovanołi "Vkayk^c
Arewelicə"* (Erevan, 1976).
See also II.A, Abraham Xostovanoł.

"L'attribution"
    L. Ter Petrossian, "L'attribution du recueil des Passions
des martyrs perses à Maroutha de Maypherqat," AB 97
(1979), pp. 129–130.

"Hayerə"
    L. H. Ter Petrosyan, "Hayerə miǰnadaryan Mcbinum ew
Mec Hayk^ci haravayin nahangnerum," PBH (1979/1),
pp. 80–92.

"Traduction"
    L. P. Ter Petrosyan, "La plus ancienne traduction des
Chroniques: études préliminaire," REArm n.s. XVIII
(1984), pp. 215–225.

Tēr Połosean, G., "Pawstos"
    G. Tēr Połosean, "Nkatołut^ciwnner P^cawstosi
patmut^cean verabereal," HA XXVIII, XXX (1901,
1916); repr. (Vienna, 1901, 1919).

Tēr Pōłosean, P., "Barseł"
    S. Barseł Kesarac^ci ew ir grut^ciwnnerə Hayerēn
targmanut^ceamb," HA LXXXII, cols. 386–418; LXX-
XIII, cols. 129–158, 257–292, 385–398 (1968–1969).
See also Akinean and Tēr Połosean, "Łazar P^carpec^ci."

Thierry, "Eglises"
    J.-M. Thierry, "Les églises à double abside," REArm
n.s. XVII (1984), pp. 515–549.

"Tayk"
    J.-M. Thierry, "Les monuments du Tayk, de Tao-
Klardjéti et des districts avoisinants," *Byz.* 44(1984),
pp. 421–428.
See also Boudoyan and Thierry; Thierry and Thierry.

Thierry and Thierry, "Kars"
    N. Thierry and M. Thierry, "A propos de quelques mon-
uments chrétiens du vilayet de Kars (Turquie)," REArm
n.s. VIII (1971), pp. 189–213.

"Monuments"
    N. Thierry and M. Thierry, "Notes sur des monuments
arméniens de Turquie," REArm n.s. II (1965), pp. 165–
184.

Thomson, Aa
    R. W. Thomson, trans. "Introduction and notes" to Aa
(see II.A).

AaT
    R. W. Thomson, trans., "Introduction and commentary"
to AaT (see II.A).

Ełishē
    R. W. Thomson, trans., "Introduction and notes to
Ełishē (see II.A, Ełišē).

"Instruction"
    R. W. Thomson, "Early Armenian Catechetical Instruc-
tion," *Armeniaca* (1969), pp. 98–108.

"Introduction"
    R. W. Thomson, *An Introduction to Classical Armenian*
(Delmar, N.Y., 1975).

MK
    R. W. Thomson trans. "Introduction and notes" to MK
(see II.A, MX).

"Philosophical Terms"
    R. W. Thomson, "Some Philosophical Terms in the
Teaching of Gregory," REArm. n.s. I (1964), pp. 41–46.

Thom. Arts.
    R. W. Thomson trans., "Introduction and notes" to T^cA
(see II.A, T^cA).

"Vardapet"
    R. W. Thomson, "Vardapet in the Early Armenian
Church," LeM LXXV (1962), pp. 367–384.

Thomson, ed.
    See Garsoïan *et al.*, eds., *East of Byzantium.*

Tirac^cyan/Tiratsian,
"Armavir"
    G. A. Tirac^cyan, "Armaviri ɫełumnerə," *Lraber*
(1972/2), pp. 36–42; (1973/5), pp. 95–103; (1974/12),
pp. 54–67.

"K antichnym istokam" G. A Tiratsian, "K antichnym istokam armianskoĭ rannesrednevekovoĭ kulʿtury (po arkheologicheskim dannym)," PBH (1983/2–3), pp. 55–64.

Kul'tura G. A. Tiratsian, *Kul'tura rannefeodal'noĭ Armenii (IV–VII vv)* (Erevan, 1980).

"Utochnenie" G. Tiratsian, "Utochnenie nekotorykh detaliĭ sasanidskogo vooruzheniia po dannym armianskogo istorika IV v. n.ē. Favsta Buzanda," in Orbeli, *Sbornik*, pp. 474–486.

"Vałaršapat" G. A Tiratsian, "K voprosu o gradostroitel'noĭ strukture i topografii drevnego Valarshapata," PBH (1977/2), pp. 81–97.

Tisserant, "Jacques de Nisibe" E. Tisserant, "Jacques de Nisibe," DTC, VIII (1923), cols. 292–295.

Tomaschek, "Albania" W. Tomaschek, "Albania," PW, I/1 (1894), cols. 1303–1304.

"Ankyra" W. Tomaschek, "Ankyra," PW, I/2, cols. 2222.

"Daranalis" W. Tomaschek, "Daranalis," PW, IV (1901), cols. 2151.

"Sasun" W. Tomaschek, "Sasun und das Quellengebiet des Tigris," Kaiserl. Akad. d. Wiss. in Wien, philos.-hist. Kl., *Sitzungsberichte* CXXXIII (Vienna, 1896).

Toumanoff, "Mamikonids" C. Toumanoff, "The Mamikonids and the Liparitids," *Armeniaca* (1969), pp. 125–137.

Manuel C. Toumanoff, *Manuel de généalogie et de chronologie pour l'histoire de la Caucasie chrétienne* (Rome, 1976).

Studies C. Toumanoff, *Studies in Christian Caucasian History* (Georgetown, 1963).

"Third-Century Arsacids" C. Toumanoff, "The Third-Century Arsacids: A Chronological and Genealogical Commentary," REArm n.s. VI (1969), pp. 233–281.

Tournebize, "Amatouniq" F. Tournebize, "Amatouniq," DHGE, II, cols. 990–993.

"Ardzrouniq" F. Tournebize, "Ardzrouniq," DHGH III, cols. 1627–1630.

Histoire F. Tournebize, *Histoire politique et religieuse de l'Arménie* (Paris, 1910).

Treidler, "Iberia" H. Treidler, "Iberia," PW, supp. IX (1962), cols. 1899–1911.

Trever, K./C. V., *Albania* K. V. Trever, *Ocherki po istorii i kul'ture Kavkazskoĭ Albanii* (Moscow–Leningrad, 1959).

"Anahita" C. Trever, "A propos des temples de la déesse Anahita en Iran sassanide," IA VII (1967), pp. 121–132.

Armenia K. V. Trever, *Ocherki po istorii kul'tury drevneĭ Armenii* (Moscow–Leningrad, 1953).

"Kushany" K. V. Trever, "Kushany," *Sovetskaia Arkheologiia* 21 (1954), pp. 131–147.

"Sasanidskoe bliudtse" K. V. Trever, "Novoe 'Sasanidskoe' bliudtse Ērmitazha," in Orbeli *Sbornik*, pp. 256–270.

Trousdale, "Long Sword" W. Trousdale, "The Long Sword and Scabbard Slide in Asia," *Smithsonian Contribution to Anthropology* XVII (Washington, D.C., 1975).

Trümpelmann, "Sasanian Graves" L. Trümpelmann, "Sasanian Graves and Burial Customs," in *Arabie orientale, Mésopotamie et Iran méridional de l'Âge du Fer àu début de la période islamique* (Paris, 1984), pp. 317–329.

Turcan, "Nisibe" R. Turcan, "L'abandon de Nisibe et l'opinion publique," in *Mélanges Pigagnol*, pp. 875–890.

Ulbert, *et al.*, *Resafa* T. Ulbert, *et al.*, *Die Basilka des Heiligen Kreuzes in Resafa-Sergiopolis* (Mainz, 1986).

Ulubabyan, "Albania" B. A. Ulubabyan, "ʿAlbania', ʿAłuankʿ' ew ʿAṙan' tełanunnerə," PBH (1971/3), pp. 115–125.

Dravgner B. A. Ulubabyan, *Drvagner hayocʿ arevelicʿ kołmancʿ patmutʿyan (V–VII dd)* (Erevan, 1981).

University of Michigan, *Sasanian Silver* University of Michigan Museum of Art, *Sasanian Silver: Late Antique and Early Mediaeval Arts of Luxury from Iran* (Ann Arbor, 1967).

USAF See Abbreviations.

Vailhé, "Eglise" S. Vailhé, "Formation de l'Eglise arménienne," EO XVI (1913), pp. 109–122.

Vardanyan, "Marderə" V. M. Vardanyan, "Marderə Vaspurakanum," PBH (1971/3), pp. 49–60.

Vööbus, *Asceticism* A. Vööbus, *History of Asceticism in the Syrian Orient*, CSCO 184, 197, 2 vols. (Louvain, 1958, 1960).

"Celibacy" A. Vööbus, "Celibacy, a Requirement for Admission to Baptism in the Early Syrian Church," in *Papers of the Esthonian Theological Society in Exile*, I (Stockholm, 1951).

"Origins" A. Vööbus, "The Origins of Monasticism in Syria," *Church History* XX/4 (1951), pp. 27–37.

School of Nisibis A. Vööbus, *History of the School of Nisibis*, CSCO 266 (Louvain, 1965).

Weber, D., "Papyri" D. Weber, "Pahlavi Papyri und Ostraca," *Middle Iranian Studies,= Orientalia Lovaniensia Analecta* XVI (Louvain, 1984), pp. 25–43.

Weber, S., *Katholische Kirche* S. Weber, *Die katholische Kirche in Armenien. Ihre Begründung und Entwicklung vor der Trennung* (Freiburg i/B., 1903).

Weissbach, "Atropatene" F. H. Weissbach, "Atropatene," PW, II (1896), cols. 2149–2150.

"Karenitis" F. H. Weissbach, "Karenitis," PW, X (1919), cols. 1939–1940.

"Kolthene" F. H. Weissbach, "Kolthene," PW, XI/1 (1921), col. 1124.

"Sophene" F. H. Weissbach, "Sophene," PW, 2d ser. V (1927), cols. 1015–19019.

"Suspiritis" F. H. Weissbach, "Suspiritis," PW, 2d ser. VI (1932), cols. 1831–1832.

West, P.T. E.W. West, *Pahlavi Texts* = F. Müller, *Sacred Books of the East* V (Oxford, 1880). See also II.C *Pahlavi Texts*.

Widengren, *Feudalismus* G. Widengren, *Der Feudalismus im alten Iran* (Cologne–Opladen, 1969).

"Recherches" G. Widengren, "Recherches sur le féodalisme iranien," OSu V (1956), pp. 79–170.

Religionen G. Wiedengren, *Die Religionen Irans* (Stuttgart, 1965).

Wiessener, "Auseinandersetzung" G. Wiessener, "Zur Auseinandersetzung zwischen Christentum und Zoroastrismus in Iran," in *XVII Deutscher Orientalistentag*, II (Wiesbaden, 1969), pp. 411–417.

Märtyrerüberlieferung	G. Wiesner, *Untersuchungen zur syrischen Literaturgeschichte*, I, *Zur Märtyrerüberlieferung aus der Christenverfolgung Schapurs II* (Göttingen, 1967).
Wikander, *Feuerpriester*	S. Wikander, *Feuerpriester in Kleinasien und Iran* (Lund, 1946).
"Problèmes"	S. Wikander, "Problèmes Irano-arméniens," *Studia Linguistica* 2 (1948), pp. 48–53.
Wilkinson, "A Fresh Look"	R. D. Wilkinson, "A Fresh Look at the Ionic Building at Gaṙni," REArm n.s. XVI (1982), pp. 221–244.
Windischmann, *Anahitā*	F. Windischmann, *Die persische Anahitā oder Anaitis* (Munich, 1858).
Winkler, "Agatᶜangełos"	G. Winkler, "Our Present Knowledge of the History of Agatᶜangełos and its Oriental Versions," REArm n.s. XIV (1980), pp. 125–141.
"Gottesdienst"	G. Winkler, "Zur Geschichte des armenischen Gottesdienstes im Hinblick auf den mehreren Wellen erfolgten griechischen Einfluss," OC 58 (1974), pp. 154–172.
Initiationrituals	G. Winkler, *Das armenische Initiationrituale*, OCA 217 (Rome, 1982).
"Night Office I"	G. Winkler, "The Armenian Night Office I: The Historical Background of the Introductory Part of *Gišerayin žam*," JSAS I (1984), pp. 93–114.
"Night Office II"	G. Winkler, "The Armenian Night Office II," REArm n.s. XVII (1983), pp. 471–551.
"Teaching"	G. Winkler, "Some Extraordinary Features in the Teaching of St. Gregory (Agathangeli Historia)," in *Aarhus Armeniaca* (Aarhus, 1982), pp. 125–140.
Wolski, "Aristocratie"	J. Wolski, "L'aristocratie parthe et les commencements du féodalisme en Iran," IA VII (1967), pp. 133–144.
"Remarques"	J. Wolski, "Remarques sur les institutions des Arsacides," *Eos* XLVI (1954), pp. 59–82.
Wüst, "Mithras"	E. Wüst, "Mithras," PW XV/2 (1932), cols. 2131–2155.
Xačᶜatryan, Ž. D./ Khachatrian, Zh. D.,	
Artašat	Ž. D. Xačᶜatryan, *Artašat II* (Erevan, 1981).
"Iranakan-haykakan ałersner"	Ž. D. Xačᶜatryan, "Iranakan-haykakan dicᶜabanakan ałersneri harcᶜi šurǰ," *Lraber* (1981/1), pp. 54–72.
"Koroplastika"	Zh. D. Khachatrian, "Ob antichnoĭ koraplastiki Armenii," VDI (1979), pp. 87–104.
Xalateancᶜ	See Khalatiants.
Yovhannēsean	See also Hovhannisyan, Johannisian.
Yovhannēsean, M., HB	M. Yovhannēsean, *Hayastani berderə* (Venice, 1970).
Zarpᶜanalean, *Matenadaran*	G. Zarpᶜanalean, *Matenadaran haykakan tᶜargmanutᶜeancᶜ naχneacᶜ (Dar D [IV]–ŽG [XIII])* (Venice, 1889).
Patmutⁱwn	G. Zarpᶜanalean, *Patmutⁱwn hay hin dprutᶜean (D [IV]–ŽG [XIII] dar)*, 4th ed. (Venice, 1932).
Zeimal, "Transoxiana"	E. V. Zeimal, "The Political History of Transoxiana," CHI III/1 (1983), pp. 232–262.
Zōhrapean/Zōhrab, Y., ed.	See II.A, *Astuacašunčᶜ*.

Maps

The two maps appended to this volume are intended to present as closely as possible the extent of the Arsacid Armenian kingdom at the beginning and the end of BP's text. Of necessity, however, the boundaries must remain approximate at best.

The toponyms included in the maps are normally restricted to those found in the text of BP. Consequently, later territorial units, such as Turuberan and Vaspurakan have been omitted despite their importance.

In the case of centers of population, the size of the type used corresponds to their relative size and importance at a given time. Thus, the capital of ARTAŠAT and such cities as ZARĒHAWAN and ZARIŠAT (on Map I), have been reduced to Artašat, Zarēhawan and Zarišat (on Map II) to indicate their diminution in size or their ruined state after their destruction by the Sasanians following the Peace of Jovian of 363. Conversely, Amid (on Map I) corresponds to AMID (on Map II) in accordance with the growing importance of this city. All disputed sites have been distinguished by a question mark. Those which cannot be identified at present have been omitted altogether even though they are discussed in Appendix II.

As in the case of all the other portions of this text, the spelling of BP has been retained.

Some differentiation has been made between

■ = fortress, where a toponym is explicitly identified in the text of BP as a fortress and nothing more; and

• ● = Village, town, etc., even though many of these centers of population were fortified points as well.